# LET'S GO:
# Israel
# & Egypt

"Its yearly revision by a new crop of Harvard students makes it as valuable as ever."
**—The New York Times**

"Value-packed, unbeatable, accurate, and comprehensive."
**—The Los Angeles Times**

"A world-wise traveling companion—always ready with friendly advice and helpful hints, all sprinkled with a bit of wit." **—The Philadelphia Inquirer**

"Lighthearted and sophisticated, informative and fun to read. [Let's Go] helps the novice traveler navigate like a knowledgeable old hand."
**—Atlanta Journal-Constitution**

"All the essential information you need, from making a phone call to exchanging money to contacting your embassy. [Let's Go] provides maps to help you find your way from every train station to a full range of youth hostels and hotels." **—Minneapolis Star Tribune**

"Unbeatable: good sight-seeing advice; up-to-date info on restaurants, hotels, and inns; a commitment to money-saving travel; and a wry style that brightens nearly every page." **—The Washington Post**

## ▪ Let's Go researchers have to make it on their own.

"The writers seem to have experienced every rooster-packed bus and lunar-surfaced mattress about which they write." **—The New York Times**

"Retains the spirit of the student-written publication it is: candid, opinionated, resourceful, amusing info for the traveler of limited means but broad curiosity." **—Mademoiselle**

## ▪ No other guidebook is as comprehensive.

"Whether you're touring the United States, Europe, Southeast Asia, or Central America, a Let's Go guide will clue you in to the cheapest, yet safe, hotels and hostels, food and transportation. Going beyond the call of duty, the guides reveal a country's latest news, cultural hints, and off-beat information that any tourist is likely to miss." **—Tulsa World**

## ▪ Let's Go is completely revised each year.

"Up-to-date travel tips for touring four continents on skimpy budgets."
**—Time**

"Inimitable.... Let's Go's 24 guides are updated yearly (as opposed to the general guidebook standard of every two to three years), and in a marvelously spunky way." **—The New York Times**

# Let's Go Publications

Let's Go: Alaska & The Pacific Northwest
Let's Go: Britain & Ireland
Let's Go: California
Let's Go: Central America
Let's Go: Eastern Europe
Let's Go: Ecuador & The Galápagos Islands
Let's Go: Europe
Let's Go: France
Let's Go: Germany
Let's Go: Greece & Turkey
Let's Go: India & Nepal
Let's Go: Ireland
Let's Go: Israel & Egypt
Let's Go: Italy
Let's Go: London
Let's Go: Mexico
Let's Go: New York City
Let's Go: Paris
Let's Go: Rome
Let's Go: Southeast Asia
Let's Go: Spain & Portugal
Let's Go: Switzerland & Austria
Let's Go: USA
Let's Go: Washington, D.C.

Let's Go **Map Guide:** Boston
Let's Go **Map Guide:** London
Let's Go **Map Guide:** New York City
Let's Go **Map Guide:** Paris
Let's Go **Map Guide:** San Francisco
Let's Go **Map Guide:** Washington, D.C.

# LET'S GO

## The Budget Guide to
# Israel
# & Egypt
# 1997

**Joshua D. Fine**
Editor

**David L. Miller**
Associate Editor

**Rachel Lebejko**
Assistant Editor

**Macmillan**

# HELPING LET'S GO

If you want to share your discoveries, suggestions, or corrections, please drop us a line. We read every piece of correspondence, whether a postcard, a 10-page e-mail, or a coconut. All suggestions are passed along to our researcher-writers. Please note that mail received after May 1997 may be too late for the 1998 book, but will be retained for the following edition. **Address mail to:**

> **Let's Go: Israel & Egypt**
> **67 Mt. Auburn Street**
> **Cambridge, MA 02138**
> **USA**

Visit Let's Go at **http://www.letsgo.com,** or send e-mail to:

> **Fanmail@letsgo.com**
> **Subject: "Let's Go: Israel & Egypt"**

In addition to the invaluable travel advice our readers share with us, many are kind enough to offer their services as researchers or editors. Unfortunately, the charter of Let's Go, Inc. enables us to employ only currently enrolled Harvard-Radcliffe students.

Published in Great Britain 1997 by Macmillan, an imprint of Macmillan General Books, 25 Eccleston Place, London SW1W 9NF and Basingstoke.

Maps by David Lindroth copyright © 1997, 1996, 1995, 1994, 1993, 1992, 1991, 1990, 1989, 1988 by St. Martin's Press, Inc.

Map revisions pp. 69, 84-85, 89, 129, 145, 175, 179, 201, 239, 245, 267, 281, 297, 323, 339, 355, 379, 449, 463, 473, 497, 519, 528-529 by Let's Go, Inc.

Published in the United States of America by St. Martin's Press, Inc.

ISBN: 0 333 68671 3

First edition
10 9 8 7 6 5 4 3 2 1

**Let's Go: Israel & Egypt** is written by Let's Go Publications, 67 Mt. Auburn Street, Cambridge, MA 02138, USA.

# About Let's Go

## THIRTY-SIX YEARS OF WISDOM

Back in 1960, a few students at Harvard University banded together to produce a 20-page pamphlet offering a collection of tips on budget travel in Europe. This modest, mimeographed packet, offered as an extra to passengers on student charter flights to Europe, met with instant popularity. The following year, students traveling to Europe researched the first, full-fledged edition of *Let's Go: Europe*, a pocket-sized book featuring honest, irreverent writing and a decidedly youthful outlook on the world. Throughout the 60s, our guides reflected the times; the 1969 guide to America led off by inviting travelers to "dig the scene" at San Francisco's Haight-Ashbury. During the 70s and 80s, we gradually added regional guides and expanded coverage into the Middle East and Central America. With the addition of our in-depth city guides, handy map guides, and extensive coverage of Asia, the 90s are also proving to be a time of explosive growth for Let's Go, and there's certainly no end in sight. The first editions of *Let's Go: India & Nepal* and *Let's Go: Ecuador & The Galapágos Islands* hit the shelves this year, and research for next year's series has already begun.

We've seen a lot in 37 years. *Let's Go: Europe* is now the world's bestselling international guide, translated into seven languages. And our new guides bring Let's Go's total number of titles, with their spirit of adventure and their reputation for honesty, accuracy, and editorial integrity, to 30. But some things never change: our guides are still researched, written, and produced entirely by students who know first-hand how to see the world on the cheap.

## HOW WE DO IT

Each guide is completely revised and thoroughly updated every year by a well-traveled set of 200 students. Every winter, we recruit over 120 researchers and 60 editors to write the books anew. After several months of training, Researcher-Writers hit the road for seven weeks of exploration, from Anchorage to Ankara, Estonia to El Salvador, Iceland to Indonesia. Hired for their rare combination of budget travel sense, writing ability, stamina, and courage, these adventurous travelers know that train strikes, stolen luggage, food poisoning, and marriage proposals are all part of a day's work. Back at our offices, editors work from spring to fall, massaging copy written on Himalayan bus rides into witty yet informative prose. A student staff of typesetters, cartographers, publicists, and managers keeps our lively team together. In September, the collected efforts of the summer are delivered to our printer, who turns them into books in record time, so that you have the most up-to-date information available for *your* vacation. And even as you read this, work on next year's editions is well underway.

## WHY WE DO IT

At Let's Go, our goal is to give you a great vacation. We don't think of budget travel as the last recourse of the destitute; we believe that it's the only way to travel. Living cheaply and simply brings you closer to the people and places you've been saving up to visit. Our books will ease your anxieties and answer your questions about the basics—so you can get off the beaten track and explore. Once you learn the ropes, we encourage you to put Let's Go away now and then to strike out on your own. As any seasoned traveler will tell you, the best discoveries are often those you make yourself. When you find something worth sharing, drop us a line. We're Let's Go Publications, 67 Mt. Auburn St., Cambridge, MA 02138, USA (e-mail: fanmail@letsgo.com).

## HAPPY TRAVELS!

*On a trip to Israel, you try the local food.*

*Tap your foot to the local tunes.*

*Chat with the local folk.*

*Then the plane lands.*

The Airline of Israel

# Contents

# JORDAN 461

# SYRIA 518

# APPENDIX 555
# INDEX 563

# Acknowledgements

This is a damn good book, and we have a lot of people to thank for it. Liz shepherded us through the wilderness of deadlines and led us to the Promised Land. Elissa and Alex gave immeasurable help. Kevin kept our spirits and our stomachs well fed. DanO and Mike tamed the computer demons. Yori lent 24-hour support. Amara provided neighborly warmth. Gene made men out of us. And the rest of Story St. helped and cheered. Bela Karolyi told us we could do it. And we did.—**I&E**

This book is unbeatable thanks to its team. Dave has boundless energy, constant cheer, and unswerving dedication. Rachel is as knowledgeable as she is tireless; a limitless source of smiles and reassurance. Daveena, Emily, Ray, Jason, and Yori made sure I had fun. Thanks and love to the Ben Davids, G-ma & G-pa. To my parents, who introduced me to this wonderful region and cultivated my love for it. To Yoni, for being my silly brother. And to my brother David and my new sister Tziona, who will spend their first married year in the Holy Land, this book is for you.—**JDF**

Sincere thanks to Josh—a tireless editor, late-night buddy, and true leader, and to Rachel—a miracle of humor, diligence, and sanity. To Jay and Chris for friendships that continue despite our separation, and to the boys for always being there when I get home. A heartfelt thanks to my family for slowly letting go while never holding me tighter, and to my brother—the newest and brightest light in the City of Lights. My eternal love to Sybil, the sweet angel who keeps me going. This book is for my mother, in the hope that you'll take me with you when you return.—**DLM**

Josh (☺), thank you for your guidance, humor, and dedication. Dave, your goofy shirts and zany wit constantly delighted me. I couldn't imagine a more (be)perfect (be)team. *Shokran jazilan*. Liz, Allison, and Michelle, thanks for your invaluable help. DanO, I *am* technologically cursed. Eti and Özge (my other half), thanks for everything. Team E&G: the hammock rocks. Thanks to my family, my dogs, Grant, Neda, and Joanie. BJ, you are my light and my joy. I love you. —**RL**

| | |
|---|---|
| **Editor** | Joshua D. Fine |
| **Associate Editor** | David L. Miller |
| **Assistant Editor** | Rachel Lebejko |
| **Managing Editor** | Elisabeth Mayer |
| | |
| **Publishing Director** | Michelle C. Sullivan |
| **Production Manager** | Daniel O. Williams |
| **Associate Production Manager** | Michael S. Campbell |
| **Cartography Manager** | Amanda K. Bean |
| **Editorial Manager** | John R. Brooks |
| **Editorial Manager** | Allison Crapo |
| **Financial Manager** | Stephen P. Janiak |
| **Personnel Manager** | Alexander H. Travelli |
| **Publicity Manager** | SoRelle B. Braun |
| **Associate Publicity Manager** | David Fagundes |
| **Associate Publicity Manager** | Elisabeth Mayer |
| **Assistant Cartographer** | Jonathan D. Kibera |
| **Assistant Cartographer** | Mark C. Staloff |
| **Office Coordinator** | Jennifer L. Schuberth |
| | |
| **Director of Advertising and Sales** | Amit Tiwari |
| **Senior Sales Executives** | Andrew T. Rourke |
| | Nicholas A. Valtz, Charles E. Varner |
| | |
| **General Manager** | Richard Olken |
| **Assistant General Manager** | Anne E. Chisholm |

# Maps

# Researcher-Writers

**Rachel Averbuck**                                    *Cairo, Mediterranean Coast, Oases*
Rachel combined boundless energy, copious writing (and writing, and writing…), cultural sensitivity, and gumshoe investigating to create the most fabulous Cairo chapter in *Let's Go* history. In her sojourn in the Egyptian capital, Rachel managed to become a local celebrity, hobnobbing with ambassadors and Austrian chefs, and scooping the competition with the newest restaurants and cheapest hotels. When not in the urban jungle, Rachel covered endless desert treks, finding her spiritual home in Siwa, and instantly became the star of every town she passed through.

**Alexander de la Fuente**                                    *Nile Valley, Alexandria*
We needed a pinch-hitter, and in a bat of the eye, Alex left the *Let's Go* office and jumped in to the *felucca* and *fuul* world of the Nile Valley. While we sorely missed him in Cambridge, Alex delighted us with hilarious anecdotes and impressed us with frameable prose. Braving petty theft and searing heat ("It's nothing like Tallahassee"), he sorted out the diamonds from the dumps in the Valley Towns. The second great Alex to visit Alexandria, he made the maze of tramways and buses lucid. Alex would stop at nothing to get the most accurate copy possible—even if it meant riding a nameless horse through the desert for 10 hours.

**Ofer Malamud**                                    *Northern Israel*
Ofer scoured his beloved North to find every worthwhile museum and ruin the region has to offer. Enlightening us on everything from proper falafel consumption to art appreciation, Ofer used his eclectic background to provide a unique insight into Israeli culture. His exhaustive research left no Galilean stone or Mediterranean pebble unturned. Trudging through the Golan's brutal heat with an injured foot, Ofer captured the pulse of the North with stellar write-ups of far-flung hikes, spectacular castles, quirky museums, and unbeatable hostels.

**Katherine Model**                                    *Nile Delta, Suez Canal, Sinai, Eilat, Aqaba*
Katie wrote the book on budget travel. Her itinerary took her through three countries and her penchant for adventure brought her face to face with a bevy of Middle Eastern cultures. From the fast-paced action of Cairo's glitzy neighborhoods to the slothful movements of Dahabitants, Katie captured what it means to live in the region in her vivid copy. A veteran traveler, Katie knows more about border crossing bureaucracies than Bibi, Hosni, or the King himself, and could teach Cousteau a thing or two about the underwater world.

**Taya Weiss**                                    *Jordan, Syria*
Our fearless researcher, Taya searched the bowels of Aleppo's *souq* and Amman's tangled traffic to put the cheapest, cleanest, coolest hotels and restaurants in print. Charming the region with her heart-melting smile and a vicious right hook, Taya would let nothing stand in the way of crafting sparkling prose. She laughed at trouble, whether it came in the form of overeager Jordanian adolescents or nosy British tourists interrupting a soothing *hammam*. We thank Taya for finding the best of the Levant ("The best *fuul!* The best fig trees!"). You will, too.

**Stephanie Wexler**                                    *Jerusalem, Tel Aviv, Negev, West Bank*
Israel's two great cities needed someone like Steph. Super-efficient and culturally adept, Steph was able to find pagefuls of excellent new hostels and still have enough time for extra-curricular jaunts up north. Equally at home in Tel Aviv's *midraḥov* and Jerusalem's ebullient *souq*, Steph unearthed bargain shops, mouth-watering restaurants, and lesser-known sights. Steph's up-to-the-minute insights on Israeli pop culture brightened her copy (and the book) with spunk and spirit.

# How to Use This Book

You hold in your hands the definitive guide to travel in the Middle East—a labor of love, lunacy, and laughs packed with so many hints, helpers, travel secrets, and bits of advice that it may seem like a trip to the region couldn't possibly add anything more. While the idea may have some merit, don't return your ticket just yet. This guide is only the beginning.

Israel, Egypt, Jordan, Syria, and the Palestinian Authority together make up one of the most fascinating regions of the world. A visit to all five will provide you with a deep understanding of the area's peoples, histories, cultures, and conflicts. We've included information to help you cross borders and given you all you need to get your bearings and find your way once you're there.

The **Essentials** section is chock full of information you'll find useful before you go. Look here for information on visas and vaccines. We'll tell you how to get money and where to go for help when you run out. There are suggestions for when to go, what to bring, how to find a job, and where to study.

The second part of the Essentials section is the **Introduction to the Region.** After a brief read-through of the highlights of 10,000 years of history and culture, you'll be able to impress your hostel-mates as you casually mention the effects of Oslo II, the attack of the Hyksos, or the teachings of Baha'u'llah. You'll know what to look for in synagogues and why the ancient Egyptians built all those pyramids.

The countries are organized roughly from southwest to northeast. Within each country, we start with the capital and then list regions emanating from there. We begin each country with a **Once There** section, loaded with hints on using the buses, staying in hotels, and keeping in touch with the folks back home. The **Life and Times** section tells you about the music scene, the food, and the politics.

A typical city starts with an **introduction,** designed to give a feel for the place and to help you decide if it's worth the trip. Next we list **practical information:** tourist offices, transportation, and other useful stuff. Within the **accommodations** and **food** sections, establishments are listed in order of value. The cheapest isn't necessarily first; we tell you who'll give you the most for your pound, shekel or dinar. Finally, we list **sights** and **entertainment.** In the larger cities, entertainment also includes cultural events, shopping, and sports.

The last part of the book is the **appendix.** Look here for dates of holidays in 1997, average climate, and a useful language glossary.

---

## A NOTE TO OUR READERS

The information for this book is gathered by *Let's Go*'s researchers during the late spring and summer months. Each listing is derived from the assigned researcher's opinion based upon his or her visit at a particular time. The opinions are expressed in a candid and forthright manner. Other travelers might disagree. Those traveling at a different time may have different experiences since prices, dates, hours, and conditions are always subject to change. You are urged to check beforehand to avoid inconvenience and surprises. Travel always involves a certain degree of risk, especially in low-cost areas. When traveling, especially on a budget, always take particular care to ensure your safety.

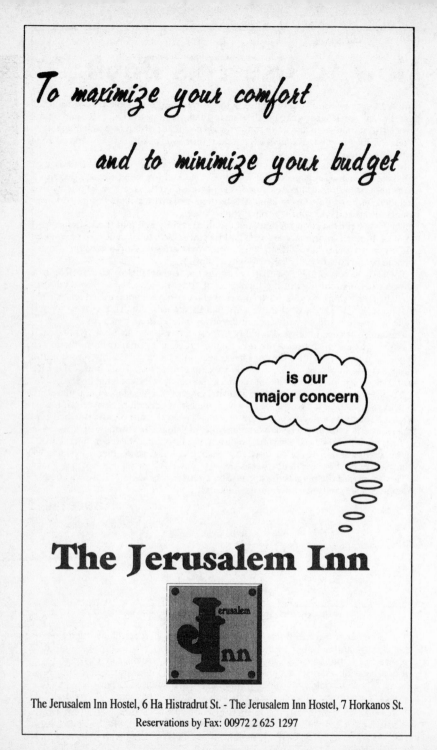

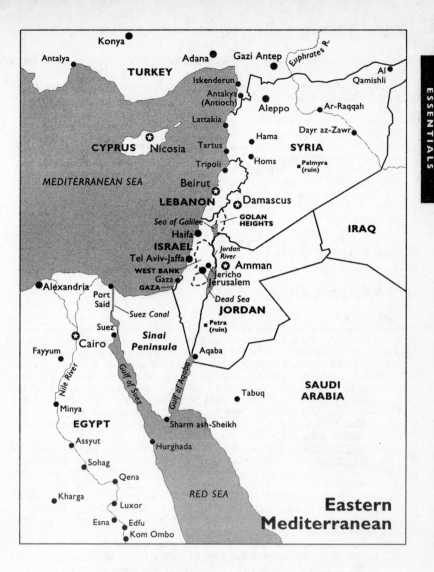

# ESSENTIALS

The five countries covered in this guide comprise one of the world's most fascinating regions. This is where the written alphabets began, where monotheism developed into three dynamic faiths, and where people constructed massive tributes that continue to astound and mystify visitors 3000 years later. Within sweeps of millennia, ancient civilizations came, conquered, and were conquered, leaving behind records of human achievement that still remain undiscovered. The natural backdrop for this immense history is no less remarkable: eerie deserts dotted with lush oases, flourishing groves of olive and citrus trees, mountains and hills carpeted with pine trees and

I

traversed by streams, moonscaped caves and canyons, and psychedelic underwater worlds.

In this land known for its near infinite past and at times impossibly convulsive present, the single most impressive feature is the extent to which these two are inextricably tied. The region is dotted with *tels,* a word used in both Arabic and Hebrew to denote a hill formed by level after level of habitation. These physical reminders of the passage of time often contain more than a dozen different strata of civilization. Far from sterile museum displays, the build-up of history literally supports the present. All over the region, 20th-century apartments mingle with 12th-century monasteries, and stones taken from thousand-year-old ruins pave the streets of modern cities.

The citizens of Egypt, Israel, Jordan, Syria, and the West Bank are no less tied to history than the buildings around them. It's this bond with the past which fuels the region's deep conflicts, but it also accounts for the intense love of land and country that characterizes the people of Middle East.

# PLANNING YOUR TRIP

## ■ When to Go

### HOLIDAYS

Arrange your itinerary with an awareness of **holidays** (for a comprehensive listing of religious and national holidays for Israel, Egypt, Jordan, and Syria see the **appendix,** p. 555). In Muslim countries, many businesses are closed on Friday, the day of prayer. On holidays, they may close during the afternoon, but are generally open in the morning. The dates of these holidays are difficult to pin down ahead of time, as Islamic holidays are based on a lunar calendar. Approximate dates for 1997 follow: **Ras as-Sana** (May 8) is the Islamic New Year's Day, and **Mawlid an-Nabi** (Jul. 17) celebrates Muhammad's birthday. The most important event and the one most likely to inconvenience self-indulgent travelers is **Ramadan** (Dec. 31-Jan. 16), the annual month-long fast during which Muslims abstain from food and drink from dawn to sunset. During this time, most restaurants close up shop until sundown. Shops may open for a few hours in the morning and a short time after *iftar,* the breaking of the fast; government services are either closed entirely or open only in the morning. It would be rude to eat in public at this time. The celebratory, three-day **Eid al-Fitr** feast marks the end of Ramadan. **Eid al-Adhah** (Apr. 8), commemorates Abraham's intended sacrifice of his son Ishmael and coincides with the *hajj* to Mecca, the fifth pillar of Islam.

In Israel, most businesses close Friday afternoon for **Shabbat,** the Jewish sabbath, and reopen at sundown on Saturday. They also close for Jewish holy days, which begin at sunset on the previous day. 1997 dates follow: **Pesah,** or Passover (Apr. 22-28), celebrates the exodus of the Jews from Egypt. Observant Jews refrain from eating bread and pastries; products made with regular flour and leavening agents may be hard to come by in Jewish areas. **Shavu'ot** (June 11) celebrates the giving of the Torah. **Rosh Ha-Shana** (the Jewish New Year; Oct. 2-3) is only slightly less holy than **Yom Kippur** (Oct. 11), the holiest day of the Jewish calendar; observant Jews fast in atonement for their sins and Israel shuts down entirely. **Sukkot** (Oct. 16-22), the festival of the harvest, commemorates the Israelites' wilderness wanderings and culminates with **Simḥat Torah** on Oct. 23.

Secular Israeli holidays include **Yom Ha-Sho'ah** (Holocaust Day, May 4) and **Yom Ha-Zikaron** (Memorial Day, May 11), and **Yom Ha'Atzma'ut** (Independence Day, May 12). On both *Yom Ha-Sho'ah* and *Yom Ha-Zikaron,* sirens signal moments of silence. Israel also has a plethora of cultural festivals. The **Israel Festival** takes place in Jerusalem (May-June), followed by the **Jerusalem Film Festival** (later in June). Other noteworthy events include the rocking **Hebrew Music Celebrations** in Arad (mid-

July), attracting mostly young crowds and the internationally acclaimed **Jazz in the Red Sea** festival in Eilat (late August).

In addition to holidays, it would be wise to think about when everyone else in the region is vacationing and whether you want to share your precious air and space with them. **Egypt's** high and low seasons depend partly on the region: Cairo is a year-round mob scene, while summertime is partytime in Alexandria and on the Mediterranean and Red Sea Beaches. In the Sinai, Oases, and Upper Egypt, reasonable temperatures make winter the high season, especially for wealthier tourist; the flip-side is that students revel in summertime bargains. North Americans and students favor summer for visiting **Israel** and the **West Bank;** Europeans prefer winter. **Jordan's** peak season are spring and autumn, while Syria receives many visitors in the summer. If you can stand the climate, off-season travel means smaller crowds, lower prices, and greater local hospitality, not to mention more falafel.

## CLIMATE

In southern **Egypt,** summer temperatures often reach 49°C (120°F) and can push 54°C (129°F). Fortunately, it's dry; your body's cooling system should know what to do. Winter here is perfect. In arid Cairo, pollution makes summer afternoons hellish. Alexandria is temperate year-round, but the humidity might wilt your new papyrus. The Red Sea Coast is comfortably warm in winter and hot but dry in summer; higher elevations in the Sinai can be freezing in winter and on summer nights.

In **Israel,** the coastal plain is a sweaty steambath in summer. Cacti love Eilat and the Jordan Valley, where it's hot and dry (except on the humid Dead Sea) in summer and mild in winter. The Negev Desert is not as hot; it has cool summer nights perfect for camel cuddling, and winter nights that actually qualify as "cold." Summer in **Jerusalem** is hot and dry with mild evenings, winter is crisp and cool, but occasionally rainy and even snowy. The landlocked, hilly **West Bank** is spared the summer humidity of the Mediterranean coast, but not the heat. Summer afternoons blister; mild nights invite long walks. Winters can be cold, rainy, and sometimes snowy.

Most attractions in **Jordan** are in the mountain region, where summer days could melt a cheap wig but evenings are deliciously cool. Winters are cold, and frequent rain mangles traffic even further. Aqaba enjoys balmy winter weather. **Syria** has a widely varying Mediterranean climate: semi-arid, with sunny days and cool nights. There are four distinct seasons.

Refer to the **appendix** for a chart of average temperatures and rainfall for major Middle Eastern cities (p. 555).

# ■ Useful Information

## TOURIST AND INFORMATION OFFICES

Contact these agencies well in advance of your departure, just in case.

**Egyptian Tourist Authority: Canada:** 1253 McGill College Ave. #250, Montreal, Que. H3B 2Y5 (tel. (514) 861-4606; fax 861-8071). **U.K.:** 170 Piccadilly, London W1V 9DD (tel. (0171) 493 52 82 or 83; fax 408 02 95). **U.S.:** 630 Fifth Ave. #1706, New York, NY 10111 (tel. (212) 332-2570; fax 956-6439); Wilshire San Vicente Plaza, 83-83 Wilshire Blvd. #215, Beverly Hills, CA 90211 (tel. (213) 653-8815; fax 653-8961); 645 N. Michigan Ave. #829, Chicago, IL 60611 (tel. (312) 280-4666; fax 280-4788).

**Israel Government Tourist Office (IGTO): Canada:** 180 Bloor St. W #700, Toronto, Ont. M5S 2V6 (tel. (416) 964-3784; fax 964-2420). **South Africa:** Nedbank Gardens 5th floor, 33 Bath Ave., Rosebank, P.O. Box 52560, Saxonwold 2132, Johannesburg (tel. (11) 788 1703/4/5; fax 447 3104). **U.K.:** 18 Great Marlborough St., London W1V 1AF (tel. (0171) 434 36 51; fax 437 05 27). **U.S.:** 800 Second Ave., New York, NY 10117 (tel. (212) 499-5600 or (800) 596-1199; fax 499-5645); 6380 Wilshire Blvd. #1718, Los Angeles, CA 90048 (tel. (213) 852-5500; fax 852-

5555); other offices in Chicago and Dallas. For information on travel to Israel, call (800) 596-1199.

**Jordan Information Bureau: U.K.:** 11/12 Buckingham Gate, London SW1E 6LB (tel. (0171) 630 92 77; fax 233 75 20). **U.S.:** 2319 Wyoming Ave. NW, Washington, D.C. 20008 (tel. (202) 265-1606; fax 667-0777).

**Palestinian Embassies and Information Offices: Australia:** P.O. Box 97, 109 Drummond St. 2nd floor, Carlton, Victoria 3053 (tel. (06) 295 0222). **U.K.:** 4 Clareville Grove, London SW7 5AR (tel. (0171) 370 32 44; fax 370 00 49). **U.S.:** 1730 K St. NW #1004, Washington, D.C. 20006 (tel. (202) 785-8394; fax 887-5337).

## TRAVEL ORGANIZATIONS

**Council on International Educational Exchange (Council),** 205 East 42nd St., New York, NY 10017-5706 (tel. (888) COUNCIL (268-6245); fax (212) 822-2699; e-mail info@ciee.org; http://www.ciee.org). A private, nonprofit organization, Council administers work, volunteer, and academic programs around the world. They also offer identity cards, including the ISIC and the GO25, and a range of publications, including the magazine *Student Travels* (free). Call or write for more information.

**Federation of International Youth Travel Organizations (FIYTO),** Bredgade 25H, DK-1260 Copenhagen K, Denmark (tel. (45) 33 33 96 00; fax 33 93 96 76; e-mail mailbox@fiyto.org), is an international organization promoting educational, cultural and social travel for young people. Member organizations include language schools, educational travel companies, national tourist boards, accommodation centers and other suppliers of travel services to youth and students. FIYTO sponsors the GO25 Card.

**International Student Travel Confederation,** Herengracht 479, 1017 BS Amsterdam, The Netherlands (tel. (31) 20 421 2800; fax 20 421 2810; http://www.istc.org; e-mail istcinfo@istc.org) The ISTC is a nonprofit confederation of student travel organizations whose focus is to develop, promote, and facilitate travel among young people and students. Member organizations include International Student Rail Association (ISRA), Student Air Travel Association (SATA), ISIS Travel Insurance, and the International Association for Educational and Work Exchange Programs (IAEWEP).

## USEFUL PUBLICATIONS

The U.S. General Services Administration publishes the quarterly *Consumer Information Catalogue.* The catalogue lists more than 200 free or low cost booklets, including travel information. For a free copy, write to Consumer Information Catalogue, Pueblo, CO 81009 (tel (719) 948-4000). For more travel information, the U.S. Department of State publishes two helpful booklets: *Passports: Applying For Them the Easy Way* (Item 362C, 50¢) and *Foreign Entry Requirements* (Item 361C, 50¢). When you write for one or both, send a check for 50¢ per booklet to: R. Woods, Consumer Information Center, Pueblo, CO 81009.

Pamphlets available for all info-hungry *Let's Go* travelers from the Government Printing Office (GPO) include: *Your Trip Abroad* which contains tips on obtaining a passport and customs information ($1.25); and *Tips for Travelers to the Middle East and North Africa* which has info on currency regulations, customs, dual nationality and other travel tips for the countries in this part of the world ($1.50). To receive one of the above pamphlets, send a check for the appropriate amount to: Superintendent of Documents, P.O Box 371954 Pittsburgh, PA, 15250-7954 (tel. (202) 512 1800); fax 512-2250). If you have a fax, dial the **Bureau of Consular Affairs** at (202) 647-3000 and follow the voice instructions for up-to-date information on Middle East countries. By phone call (202) 647-5225.

**Bon Voyage!,** 2069 W. Bullard Ave., Fresno, CA 93711-1200 (tel. (800) 995-9716, from abroad (209) 447-8441; mail 70754.3511@compuserve.com). Annual mail order catalog offers a range of products for everyone from the luxury traveler to the diehard trekker. All merchandise may be returned for exchange or refund within 30 days of purchase, and prices are guaranteed (Lower advertised prices will be matched and merchandise shipped free).

**Hippocrene Books, Inc.,** 171 Madison Ave., New York, NY 10016 (tel. (212) 685-4371; orders (718) 454-2366; fax 454-1391). Free catalog. Publishes travel reference books, travel guides, foreign language dictionaries, and language learning guides which cover over 100 languages.

**Specialty Travel Index,** 305 San Anselmo Avenue, Suite 313, San Anselmo, CA 94960 (tel. (415) 459-4900; fax 459-4974; e-mail spectrav@ix.netcom.com; http://www.spectrav.com). Published twice yearly, this is an extensive listing of "off the beaten track" and specialty travel opportunities. One copy $6, one-year subscription (2 copies) $10.

**Transitions Abroad,** 18 Hulst Rd., P.O. Box 1300, Amherst, MA 01004-1300 (tel. (413) 256-3414; fax 256-0375; email trabroad@aol.com). Invaluable magazine lists publications and resources for overseas study, work, and volunteering. Also publishes *The Alternative Travel Directory,* a comprehensive guide to living, learning, and working overseas ($20; postage $4).

## INTERNET RESOURCES

Along with everything else in the '90s, budget travel is moving rapidly into the information age. And with the growing user-friendliness of personal computers and internet technology, much of this information can be yours with the click of a mouse.

There are a number of ways to access the **Internet.** Most popular are commercial internet providers, such as **America Online** (tel. (800) 827-6394) and **Compuserve** (tel. (800) 433-0389). Many employers and schools also offer gateways to the Internet, often at no cost (unlike the corporate gateways above). The following web sites can be wonderful resources for researching and planning your travel dreams. Just make sure you don't forgo your travels for virtual visitations.

**The CIA World Factbook** (http://www.odci.gov/cia/publications/95fact) has tons of vital statistics on the country you want to visit. Check it out for an overview of a country's economy, or an explanation of their system of government.

**The Student and Budget Travel Guide** (http://asa.ugl.lib.umich.edu/chdocs/travel/travel-guide.html) is just what it sounds like.

**The Interactive Travel Guide** (http://www.developnet.com/travel) began as The Cheap Travel Page and has expanded its scope some, but is still useful for the budget traveler.

**Foreign Language for Travelers** (http://www.travlang.com) can help you brush up on your Hebrew.

**A Comprehensive Travel Guide to Egypt** (http://www.hway.net/egyptour) has tons of information on hotels and recreation, from budget to luxury travel.

**Egypt has it All!** (http://its-idsc.gov.eg/tourism), run by the Egyptian tourist authority, is a glossy travel mag on Egypt. Information on all the major tourist sites and cities.

**Lines in the Sand** (http://tiger.ab.ca/mideast/DIX-00.HTM) can fill you in on what's been happening in the Middle East. Their extensive news archive documents regional developments, especially issues relating to the peace process.

# ▧ Documents and Formalities

File applications for all documents several weeks in advance of your planned departure date. Some offices suggest applying in the winter off-season (August-December) for speedier service. Before leaving, make a few photocopies of all important documents and credit cards; leave one copy with someone you can easily contact and strap a few to your skin. Your passport number is especially important. Consulates also recommend that you carry an expired passport or a notarized copy of your birth certificate in a separate part of your baggage.

When you travel, always carry two or more forms of identification, including at least one photo ID. Many places (especially banks) require several IDs for cashing

ESSENTIALS

traveler's checks. Also carry a few extra passport-size photos that you can attach to the various IDs and visas you may eventually acquire.

## EMBASSIES AND CONSULATES

**Egyptian Embassies: U.S.:** 3521 International Court NW, Washington, D.C. 20008 (tel. (202) 895-5400; fax 244-4319). **Canada:** 454 Laurier Ave. E, Ottawa, Ont. K1U 6R3 (tel. (613) 234-4931 or 35 or 58; fax 234-9347). **U.K.:** 26 South St., London W1Y 6DD (tel. (0171) 499 2401; fax 355 3568). **Australia:** 1 Darwin Avenue, Yarralumla, Canberra ACT 2600 (tel. (06) 273 44 37 or 38; fax 273 42 79).

**Egyptian Consulates: U.S.:** 1110 Second Ave., Suite 201, New York, NY 10022 (tel. (212) 759-7120 or 2; fax 308-7643); 3001 Pacific Ave., San Francisco, CA 94115 (tel. (415) 346-9700; fax 346-9480); and offices in Chicago and Houston. **Canada:** 3754 Côte-des-Neiges, Montreal, Que. H3H 1V6 (tel. (514) 866-8445; fax 937-0588). **U.K.:** 2 Lowndes St., London SW1 XQET (tel. (0171) 235 9719 or 77). **Australia:** 335 New South Head Rd., Double Bay, Sydney NSW 2028 (tel. (02) 362 34 83; fax 327 10 96); 124 Exhibition St., 9th floor, Melbourne, Victoria 3000 (tel. (03) 654 86 34; fax 650 83 62).

**Israeli Embassies: U.S.:** 3514 International Drive NW, Washington, D.C. 20008 (tel. (202) 364-5500 or 5527; fax 364-5423). **Canada:** 50 O'Connor St., Suite 1005, Ottawa, Ont. K1P 6L2 (tel. (613) 567-6450, 6453, or 6455; fax 237-8865). **U.K.:** 2 Palace Green, London W8 4QB (tel. (0171) 957 95 00 or 95 47; fax 957 95 55). **Australia:** 6 Turrana St., Yarralumla, Canberra ACT 2600 (tel. (06) 273 20 45, 13 09, or 13 00; fax 273 42 73). **New Zealand:** D.B. Tower 111, Terrace, P.O. Box 2171, Wellington (tel. (4) 472 23 62 or 68; fax 499 06 32; e-mail israel-ask@israel.org.nz). **South Africa:** Trade Center, Nedbank Gardens, 5th floor, 33 Bath Ave., Rosbank, Johannesburg (tel. (11) 788 17 00; fax 447 31 04).

**Israeli Consulates: Australia:** 37 York St., 6th flr., Sydney NSW 2000 (tel. (02) 264 79 33; fax 290 22 59). **Canada:** 180 Bloor St., Toronto, Ont. M5S 2V6 (tel. (416) 961-1126; fax 961-7737). **South Africa:** Church Square House 3rd floor, Corner Spien and Plein St., P.O. Box 180, Cape-Town (tel. (021) 45 72 05 or 15; fax 461 00 75). **U.S.:** 800 Second Ave., New York, NY 10017 (tel. (212) 499-5400; fax 490-9186); 6380 Wilshire Blvd. #1700, Los Angeles, CA 90048 (tel. (213) 852-5500; fax 852–5555; e-mail israelinfo@primenet.com). Other offices in San Francisco, Miami, Atlanta, Chicago, New Orleans, Boston, Philadelphia, and Houston.

**Jordanian Embassies: U.S.:** 3504 International Dr. NW, Washington, D.C. 20008 (tel. (202) 966-2664; fax 966-3110). **Canada:** 100 Bronson Ave. #701, Ottawa, Ont. K1R 6G8 (tel. (613) 238-8090; fax 232-3341). **U.K.:** 6 Upper Philimore Gardens, London W8 714B (tel. (0171) 937 36 85; fax 937 87 95). **Australia:** 20 Roebuck St., Red Hill ACT 2603, Canberra (tel. (06) 295 99 51; fax 239 72 36).

**Jordanian Consulates: U.S.:** 866 United Nations Plaza #554, New York, NY 10017 (tel. (212) 752-0135; fax 826-0830); P.O. Box 3727, Houston, TX 77253 (tel. (713) 224-2911).

**Syrian Embassies: U.S.:** 2215 Wyoming Ave. NW, Washington, D.C. 20008 (tel. (202) 232-6313; fax 232-4357). **U.K.:** 8 Belgrave Square, London, SW1 (tel. (0171) 245 90 12).

**Syrian Consulate: U.S.:** 820 Second Ave., New York, NY 10017 (tel. (212) 661-1553).

## PASSPORTS

Before you leave, photocopy the page of your passport that contains your photograph and identifying information, especially your passport number. Carry this photocopy in a safe place apart from your passport, and leave another copy at home. Consulates also recommend that you carry an expired passport or an official copy of your birth certificate in a part of your baggage separate from other documents. You can request a duplicate birth certificate from the Bureau of Vital Records and Statistics in your state or province of birth.

If you do lose your passport, it may take weeks to process a replacement, and your new one may be valid only for a limited time. In addition, any visas stamped in your old passport will be irretrievably lost. If this happens, immediately notify the local police and the nearest embassy or consulate of your home government. To expedite its replacement, you will need to know all information previously recorded and show identification and proof of citizenship. Some consulates can issue new passports within two days if you give them proof of citizenship. In an emergency, ask for immediate temporary traveling papers that will permit you to re-enter your home country.

Your passport is a public document belonging to your nation's government. You may have to surrender it to a foreign government official; but, if you don't get it back in a reasonable amount of time, inform the nearest mission of your home country.

**United States** Citizens may apply for a passport, valid for 10 years (five years if under 18) at any federal or state **courthouse** or **post office** authorized to accept passport applications, or at a **U.S. Passport Agency,** located in Boston, Chicago, Honolulu, Houston, Los Angeles, Miami, New Orleans, New York, Philadelphia, San Francisco, Seattle, Stamford, or Washington DC. Refer to the "U.S. Government, State Department" section of the telephone directory, or call your local post office for addresses. You must submit the following: 1) proof of U.S. citizenship (a certified birth certificate, certification of naturalization or of citizenship, or a previous passport); 2) identification bearing your signature and either your photograph or physical description (e.g. an unexpired driver's license or passport, student ID card, or government ID card); and 3) two identical, passport-size (2in. by 2in.) photographs with a white or off-white background taken within the last six months. It will cost $65 (under 18 $40). You can **renew** your passport by mail or in person for $55. Processing takes two to four weeks. Passport agencies offer **rush service** for a surcharge of $30 if you have proof that you're departing within 10 working days (e.g., an airplane ticket or itinerary). Abroad, a U.S. embassy or consulate can usually issue a new passport, given proof of citizenship. For more info, contact the U.S. Passport Information's **24-hour recorded message** (tel. (202) 647-0518).

**Canada** Application forms in English and French are available at all **passport offices, post offices,** and most **travel agencies.** Citizens may apply in person at any one of 28 regional Passport Offices across Canada. Travel agents can direct the applicant to the nearest location. Canadian citizens residing abroad should contact the nearest Canadian embassy or consulate. Along with the application form, a citizen must provide: 1) citizenship documentation (an original Canadian birth certificate, or a certificate of Canadian citizenship); 2) two identical passport photos taken within the last year; 3) any previous Canadian passport; and 4) a CDN$60 fee (paid in cash, money order, or certified check) to Passport Office, Ottawa, Ont. K1A OG3. The application and one of the photographs must be signed by an eligible guarantor (someone who has known the applicant for two years and whose profession falls into one of the categories listed on the application). Processing takes approximately five business days for in-person applications and three weeks for mailed ones. A passport is valid for five years and is not renewable. If a passport is lost abroad, Canadians must be able to prove citizenship with another document. For additional info, call (800) 567-6868 (24hr.; from Canada only) or call the Quebec Passport Office at (819) 994-3500. In Metro Toronto, call (416) 973-3251. Montréalers should dial (514) 283-2152. Refer to the booklet *Bon Voyage, But...* for further help and a list of Canadian embassies and consulates abroad. It is available free of charge from any passport office.

**Britain** British citizens, British Dependent Territories citizens, British Nationals (overseas), and British Overseas citizens may apply for a **full passport,** valid for 10 years (five years if under 16). Apply in person or by mail to a passport office, located in London, Liverpool, Newport, Peterborough, Glasgow, or Belfast. The fee is UK£18. Children under 16 may be included on a parent's passport. Processing by mail usually takes four to six weeks. The London office offers same-day, walk-in rush service; arrive early.

**Ireland** Citizens can apply for a passport by mail to either the Department of Foreign Affairs, Passport Office, Setanta Centre, Molesworth St., Dublin 2 (tel. (01) 671 16 33), or the Passport Office, 1A South Mall, Cork (tel. (021) 627 25 25). Obtain an application at a local Garda station or request one from a passport office. The new Passport Express Service offers a two-week turn-around and is available through post offices for an extra IR£3. Passports cost IR£45 and are valid for 10 years. Citizens under 18 or over 65 can request a three-year passport that costs IR£10.

**Australia** Citizens must apply for a passport in person at a post office, a passport office, or an Australian diplomatic mission overseas. An appointment may be necessary. Passport offices are located in Adelaide, Brisbane, Canberra City, Darwin, Hobart, Melbourne, Newcastle, Perth, and Sydney. Application fees are adjusted frequently. For more info, call toll-free (in Australia) 13 12 32.

**New Zealand** Application forms for passports are available in New Zealand from travel agents and Department of Internal Affairs Link Centres, and overseas from New Zealand embassies, high commissions, and consulates. Completed applications may be lodged at Link Centres and at overseas posts, or forwarded to the Passport Office, P.O. Box 10-526, Wellington, New Zealand. Processing time is 10 working days from receipt of a correctly completed application. An urgent passport service is also available. The application fee for an adult passport is NZ$80 in New Zealand, and NZ$130 overseas for applications lodged under the standard service.

**South Africa** Citizens can apply for a passport at any Home Affairs Office. Two photos, either a birth certificate or an identity book, and a $12 fee must accompany a completed application. South African passports remain valid for 10 years. For further information, contact the nearest Department of Home Affairs Office.

## VISAS AND VISA EXTENSIONS

A **visa** is an endorsement that a foreign government stamps into a passport; it allows the bearer to stay in that country for a specified purpose and period of time. Most visas cost US$10-70 and entitle you to spend about a month in a country, within six months to a year from the date of issue. For more information, send for *Foreign Visa Requirements* (50¢) from Consumer Information Center, Pueblo, CO 81009 (tel. (719) 948-3334), or contact **Center for International Business and Travel (CIBT)**, 25 West 43rd St. #1420, New York, NY 10036 (tel. (800) 925-2428 or (212) 575-2811 from NYC). The CIBT secures visas for travel to and from all countries. The service charge varies. If you lose your visa overseas (via a stolen passport, for example), you must get a new one immediately to prove that you are allowed to be there; in Egypt, you will not be permitted to leave the country without a valid Egyptian visa. For a new Egyptian visa, go to the nearest passport office. In Israel, Jordan, and Syria, go to your embassy or consulate.

> Until Syria and Israel formalize a peace treaty (which could be a while), you will not be allowed to enter Syria if you have an Israeli stamp on your passport. See **Border Crossings**, p. 38.

**Egypt** Visas can be easily obtained in advance, apply by mail or in person at the nearest Egyptian embassy or consulate. Provide the application and 1) your passport, which must be valid at least six months from the date of issue of your visa; 2) a passport-sized photo; and 3) the fees in cash or a certified check (US$15 for U.S. citizens, more for others). If applying by mail, include a stamped, self-addressed, certified envelope and allow at least 10 days for delivery. If you apply in person the process takes one day. In case of emergencies, visas can be obtained at the airport in Cairo, and with some restrictions at the borders.

Visas are good for entry within six months of the date of issue, valid for one month, and easily extended (see below). An Egyptian visa does not permit the holder to work. When applying, you can request a **multiple-entry visa** for travel in and out of Egypt, allowing you to reenter any number of times while the visa is valid. Visitors crossing the border from Israel to the **Taba** Hilton Hotel *only* do not require an Egyptian visa and need only present their passports at the border checkpoint. Visits to Sinai from Israel or Jordan can be made on a two-week **Sinai-only visa,** available at borders.

**Israel** Visitors' visas are free for U.S., Canadian, British, Irish, Australian, Kiwi, and South African citizens at the point of entry if your passport is valid at least nine months beyond your time of arrival. These visas are valid for three months but are extendable (see below). **Study visas** can be obtained from an Israeli embassy or consulate prior to departure or from any Office of the Interior once in Israel. Show proof of acceptance at an educational institution, proof of sufficient funds, a medical statement, and two photos; if you are under the age of 18, you also need a letter indicating parental consent. For temporary work in Israel, have your employer in Israel contact the Office of the Interior and arrange a **work visa** before you leave. Cruise ship passengers visiting Israel are issued **landing cards** allowing them to remain in the country as long as the ship is in port. No visa application is required. **Collective visas** are issued by Israeli embassies or consulates for groups of five to 50 people.

**Jordan** Visas may be obtained upon arrival at Queen Alia Airport in Amman, or in person or by mail from any Jordanian embassy or consulate (can take up to five days). Requirements include a valid passport (for at least six months), a completed application form with one photo, and a self-addressed stamped envelope. Visas cost US$20 for U.S. citizens, and at least that for other nationalities. A **group visa** can be issued for tours of 10 persons or more, provided all have valid American passports. These are valid for one month and can be renewed at any police station (see below). If you take the ferry between the Sinai and Aqaba, visa procedures are simplified but the visa itself is limited (see **Sinai: From and To Jordan,** page 246).

**Syria** Visas must be obtained before arrival in the country. Applications are available from any Syrian embassy. Send two completed applications (not photocopied), your passport (without evidence of a trip to Israel), two signed photos, a self-addressed envelope stamped for US$2, and payment (by money order *only*) to the embassy. Six-month single-entry visas and three-month double-entry visas cost US$15; six-month multiple-entry visas cost US$30. They will return the passport with your tourist visa in it. You may also have luck applying at Syrian embassies in Egypt or Jordan (see **Cairo** and **Amman: Practical Information,** page 95 and p. 475).

**Visa extensions** are normally granted for six months to one year in Egypt, Israel, Jordan, and Syria. Egyptian visa extensions are available in Cairo at the Mugamma' Building or at any passport office, Israeli visa extensions at offices of the Ministry of the Interior, Jordanian visa extensions at the Ministry of the Interior in Amman, and Syrian visa extensions at any immigration office. To get an Egyptian visa extension, you must show evidence of having changed at least US$200 into Egyptian pounds.

## CUSTOMS: COMING HOME

Upon returning home, you must declare all articles that you acquired abroad and pay a duty on the value of those articles that exceed the allowance established by your country's customs service. Goods and gifts purchased at duty-free shops abroad are not exempt from duty or sales tax at your point of return; you must declare these items as well. "Duty-free" merely means that you need not pay a tax in the country of purchase. It is wise to make a list, including serial numbers, of valuables that you carry from home. If you register this list with customs before your departure and have an official stamp it, you will avoid import duty charges and ensure an easy passage home.

See Once There: Entry sections for each country for specific declaration and duty information.

**United States** Citizens returning home may bring US$400 worth of accompanying goods duty-free and must pay a 10% tax on the next US$1000. You must declare all purchases; have sales slips ready. Goods are considered duty-free if they are for personal or household use (this includes gifts). You must be over 21 to bring liquor into the U.S. If you mail home personal goods of U.S. origin, you can avoid duty charges by marking the package "American goods returned." For more information, consult the brochure *Know Before You Go,* available from the U.S. Customs Service, Box 7407, Washington, D.C. 20044 (tel. (202) 927-6724).

**Canada** Citizens who remain abroad for at least one week may bring back up to CDN$500 worth of goods duty-free once per calendar year. Canadian citizens or residents who travel for a period lasting between 48 hours and six days can bring back up to CDN$200 with the exception of tobacco and alcohol. You are permitted to ship goods except tobacco and alcohol home under this exemption as long as you declare them when you arrive. For more information, write to Canadian Customs, 2265 St. Laurent Blvd., Ottawa, Ontario K1G 4K3 (tel. (613) 993-0534).

**Britain** Citizens or visitors arriving in the U.K. from outside the EU must declare any goods in excess of the following allowances: 250g tobacco; still table wine (2L); perfume (60 cc/mL); and UK£136 worth of all other goods including gifts and souvenirs. You must be over 17 to import liquor or tobacco. For more information about U.K. customs, contact Her Majesty's Customs and Excise, Custom House, Nettleton Road, Heathrow Airport, Hounslow, Middlesex TW6 2LA (tel. (0181) 910 37 44; fax 910 37 65).

**Ireland** Citizens must declare everything in excess of IR£34 (IR£17 per traveler under 15 years of age) obtained outside the EU or duty- and tax-free in the EU above the following allowances: 250g tobacco; 2L still wine; 50g perfume. Travelers under 17 are not entitled to any allowance for tobacco or alcoholic products. For more information, contact The Revenue Commissioners, Dublin Castle (tel. (01) 679 27 77; fax 671 20 21; e-mail taxes@ior.ie; WWW http:\\www.revenue.ie) or The Collector of Customs and Excise, The Custom House, Dublin 1.

**Australia** Citizens may import AUS$400 (under 18 AUS$200) of goods duty-free, in addition to the allowance of 1.125L alcohol and 250 cigarettes or 250g tobacco. You must be over 18 to import either of these. There is no limit to the amount of Australian and/or foreign cash that may be brought into or taken out of the country. However, amounts of AUS$5000 or more, or the equivalent in foreign currency, must be reported. All foodstuffs and animal products must be declared on arrival. For information, contact the Regional Director, Australian Customs Service, GPO Box 8, Sydney NSW 2001 (tel. (02) 213 20 00; fax 213 40 00).

**New Zealand** Citizens may bring home up to NZ$700 worth of goods duty-free if they are intended for personal use or are unsolicited gifts. Only travelers over 17 may bring tobacco or alcoholic beverages into the country. For more information, consult the *New Zealand Customs Guide for Travelers,* available from customs offices, or contact New Zealand Customs, 50 Anzac Ave., Box 29, Auckland (tel. (09) 377 35 20; fax 309 29 78).

**South Africa** Citizens may import duty-free: 400 cigarettes; 1L of spirits; 250mL toilet water; and 50mL perfume; and other items up to a value of SAR500. Amounts exceeding this limit but not SAR10,000 are dutiable at 20%. Goods acquired abroad and sent to the Republic as unaccompanied baggage do not qualify for any allowances. You may not export or import South African bank notes in excess of SAR500.

# The World At a Discount

Save **20%** to **50%** on Airfare (major carriers)

Save **10%** to **50%** on Museums & Theaters

Save **10%** on AT&T Calls to the U.S.

Save **15%** on Greyhound Travel

Save up to **40%** on Train Passes

Save **10%** to **30%** on Accommodations

Worldwide Discounts in more than **90** countries

## The International Student Identity Card
## Your Passport to Discounts & Benefits

With the ISIC, you'll receive discounts on airfare, hotels, transportation, computer services, foreign currency exchange, phone calls, major attractions, and more. You'll also receive basic accident and sickness insurance coverage when traveling outside the U.S. and access to a 24-hour, toll-free Help Line. Call now to locate the issuing office nearest you (over 555 across the U.S.) at:

Free 40-page handbook with each card!

# 1-888-COUNCIL (toll-free)

For an application and complete discount list, you can also visit us at **http://www.ciee.org/**

Council

**CIEE: Council on International Educational Exchange**

Address inquiries to the Commissioner for Customs and Excise, Private Bag X47, Pretoria 0001. The agency prints *South African Customs Information* for visitors and residents who travel abroad. South Africans residing in the U.S. should contact the Embassy of South Africa, 3051 Massachusetts Ave., NW, Washington DC 20008 (tel. (202) 232-4400; fax 244-9417) or the South African Home Annex, 3201 New Mexico Ave. #380, NW, Washington DC 20016 (tel. (202) 966-1650).

## YOUTH, STUDENT, & TEACHER IDENTIFICATION

The **International Student Identity Card (ISIC)** is the most widely accepted form of student identification, and can procure you discounts for sights, theaters, museums, accommodations, train, ferry, and airplane travel, and other services. Present the card wherever you go, and ask about discounts even when none are advertised. It also provides accident insurance of up to US$3000 with no daily limit. In addition, cardholders have access to a toll-free Traveler's Assistance hotline whose multilingual staff can provide help in medical, legal, and financial emergencies overseas.

Many student travel offices issue ISICs, including Council Travel, Let's Go Travel, and STA Travel in the U.S.; Travel CUTS in Canada; and any of the organizations under the auspices of the International Student Travel Confederation (ISTC) around the world. When you apply for the card, request a copy of the *International Student Identity Card Handbook,* which lists by country some of the available discounts. You can also write to Council for a copy. The card is valid from September to December of the following year. The fee is US$18. Applicants must be at least 12 years old and degree-seeking students of a secondary or post-secondary school. Because of the proliferation of phony ISICs, many airlines and some other services require other proof of student identity: a signed letter from the registrar attesting to your student status and stamped with the school seal and/or your school ID card. The US$19 **International Teacher Identity Card (ITIC)** offers similar but limited discounts, as well as medical insurance coverage. For more info on these cards consult the organization's new web site (WWW http:\\www.istc.org).

Federation of International Youth Travel Organizations (FIYTO) issues a discount card to travelers who are under 26 but not students. Known as the **GO25 Card,** this one-year card offers many of the same benefits as the ISIC, and most organizations that sell the ISIC also sell the GO25 Card. A brochure that lists discounts is free when you purchase the card. To apply, you will need a passport, valid driver's license, or copy of a birth certificate; and a passport-sized photo with your name printed on the back. The fee is US$16, CDN$15, or UK£5. For information, contact Council in the U.S. or FIYTO in Denmark.

## DRIVING PERMITS AND INSURANCE

An **International Driving Permit** is honored for driving in Egypt, Israel, Jordan, and Syria. If you plan to drive a car while abroad, you must have an **International Driving Permit (IDP),** though certain countries allow travelers to drive with a valid American or Canadian license for a limited number of months. Most car rental agencies don't require the permit. A valid driver's license from your home country must always accompany the IDP. It may be a good idea to get one anyway, in case you're in a position (such as an accident or stranded in a smaller town) where the police may not read or speak English.

Your IDP must be issued in your own country before you depart. U.S. license holders can obtain an International Driving Permit (US$10), valid for one year, at any **American Automobile Association (AAA)** office or by writing to the main office, AAA Florida, Travel Agency Services Department, 1000 AAA Drive (mail stop 28), Heathrow, FL 32746-5080 (tel. (407) 444-4245; fax 444-4247). For further information, contact a local AAA office.

Canadian license holders can obtain an IDP (CDN$10) through any **Canadian Automobile Association (CAA)** branch office in Canada, or by writing to CAA Central Ontario, 60 Commerce Valley Drive East, Thornhill, Ontario L3T 7P9 (tel. (416) 221-4300).

Most credit cards cover standard insurance. If you rent, lease, or borrow a car, you will need a **green card,** or **International Insurance Certificate,** to prove that you have liability insurance. All of the countries in this book accept a green card as proof of insurance. Obtain the card through the car rental agency; most of them include coverage in their prices. If you lease a car, you can obtain a green card from the dealer. Some travel agents offer the card, and it may be available at the border. Verify whether your auto insurance applies abroad; even if it does, you will still need a green card to certify this to foreign officials.

# ■ Money

## CURRENCY AND EXCHANGE

You can easily get by in most cities and towns in this book for less than US$40 per day. Ultra-budgeteers can travel through much of the region for less than US$5. No matter how low your budget, if you plan to travel for more than a couple of days, you will need to keep handy a larger amount of cash than usual. Carrying it around with you, even in a money belt, is risky; personal checks from home will probably not be acceptable no matter how many forms of identification you have (even some banks shy away from accepting checks).

It's a good idea to bring enough foreign currency to last for the first 24-72 hours of a trip, depending on the day of the week you will be arriving. Observe commission rates closely and check newspapers to get the standard rate of exchange. Often tourist offices, exchange kiosks, or black-market hole-in-the-walls offer the best rates. A good rule of thumb is to go to offices which only have a 5% margin between their buy and sell prices.

Since you lose money with every transaction, convert in large sums (unless the currency is depreciating rapidly), but don't convert more than you need, because it may be difficult to change it back to your home currency, or to a new one. If you are using traveler's checks or bills, be sure to carry some in small denominations (US$50 or less), especially for times when you are forced to exchange money at disadvantageous rates.

## TRAVELER'S CHECKS

Traveler's checks are one of the safest and least troublesome means of carrying money. Several agencies and many banks sell them, usually for face value plus a 1% commission. American Express and Visa are the most widely recognized, though other major checks are sold, exchanged, cashed, and refunded with almost equal ease. Keep in mind that in rural areas, traveler's checks are less readily accepted than in cities with large tourist industries. If you're ordering your checks, do so well in advance, especially if large sums are being requested.

Each agency provides refunds if your checks are lost or stolen, and many provide additional services. (Note that you may need a police report verifying the loss or theft.) Inquire about toll-free refund hotlines (in the countries you're visiting), emergency message relay services, and stolen credit card assistance when you purchase your checks.

You should expect a fair amount of red tape and delay in the event of theft or loss of traveler's checks. To expedite the refund process, keep your check receipts separate from your checks and store them in a safe place or with a traveling companion; record check numbers when you cash them and leave a list of check numbers with someone at home; and ask for a list of refund centers when you buy your checks. Keep a separate supply of cash or traveler's checks for emergencies. Be sure never to countersign your checks until you're prepared to cash them.

Buying traveler's checks in the currency of the country you're visiting is not the best idea in the Middle East. The most readily accepted checks are in U.S. dollars and British pounds; the German mark will sometimes be taken, as well. Checks in other currencies won't get you very far—if the place will exchange it, you'll probably get a crummy rate. Be sure to keep cash on hand in less touristy regions; smaller establishments may not accept traveler's checks. *Bring your passport whenever you plan to use the checks.* The smallest denomination is usually US$20 or equivalent. Get a few of these so that if you have to exchange money at a poor rate you won't lose too much.

**American Express:** Call (800) 221-7282 in the U.S. and Canada; in the U.K. (0800) 52 13 13; in New Zealand (0800) 44 10 68; in Australia (008) 25 19 02. Elsewhere, call U.S. collect (801) 964-6665. American Express traveler's checks are available in British pounds, German marks, and U.S. dollars, among other currencies. They are the most widely recognized and the easiest to replace if lost or stolen. Checks can be purchased for a small fee at American Express Travel Service Offices, banks, and American Automobile Association offices (AAA members can buy the checks commission-free). Cardmembers can also order them via phone (tel. (800) ORDER-TC (673-3782)). American Express offices cash their checks commission-free (except where prohibited by national governments), although they often offer slightly worse rates than banks. You can also buy Cheques for Two which can be signed by either of two people travelling together. Request the "Traveler's Companion" booklet for a listing of travel office addresses and stolen check hotlines worldwide. Traveler's cheques are also available over America OnLine.

**Citicorp:** Call (800) 645-6556 in the U.S. and Canada; in the U.K. (44) 181 297 4781; from elsewhere call U.S. collect (813) 623-1709. Sells both Citicorp and Citicorp Visa traveler's checks in U.S. dollars, British pounds, and German marks. 1-2% commission on check purchases. Checkholders are automatically enrolled for 45 days in the Travel Assist Program (hotline (800) 250-4377 or collect (202) 296-8728) which provides travelers with English-speaking doctor, lawyer, and interpreter referrals as well as check refund assistance and travel information.

**Visa:** Call (800) 227-6811 in the U.S., (0800) 895 492 in the U.K., or 017 33 318 949 collect from anywhere else in the world. Any kind of Visa traveler's checks can be reported lost at the Visa number.

**Thomas Cook MasterCard:** Call (800) 223-9920 in the U.S. and Canada; elsewhere call U.S. collect (609) 987-7300; from the U.K. call (0800) 622 101 free or (1733) 502 995 collect. Checks in U.S. dollars and British pounds. 1-2% commission on check purchases. Buy the checks at a Thomas Cook office for potentially lower commissions, and cash them for no commission.

## CREDIT CARDS

Credit cards are of limited day-to-day value in the Middle East—usually only places too expensive for the budget traveler will accept them. They are invaluable, however, if you need an instant cash advance. Both **Visa** (800 336-8472) and **MasterCard** (800 999-0454) give cash advances at affiliated banks (only likely to be found in capital cities). Credit card companies get the wholesale exchange rate, generally 5% better than the retail rate used by banks and even better than that used by other currency exchange establishments. **American Express** cards also work in some ATMs, as well as at AmEx offices and major airports. All such machines require a **Personal Identification Number (PIN).** You must ask American Express, MasterCard, or Visa to assign you one before you leave; without this PIN, you will be unable to withdraw cash with your credit card abroad. Contact your company to find out what additional services they provide; possible benefits include emergency assistance and car rental collision insurance.

## CASH CARDS

Cash cards may be the most convenient source for cash in Israel. There are now well over 200 Cirrus (U.S. tel. (800) 4-CIRRUS (424-7787)) **automated teller machines**

**ESSENTIALS**

(ATMs) available at Bank Ha-Poalim branches, with many also on the PLUS network (U.S. tel. (800) 843-7587). ATMs in Egypt, Jordan, and Syria are becoming more common, especially in heavily touristed areas, but are still relatively rare. Cirrus charges US$5 for each withdrawal outside the U.S.

Depending on the system that your bank at home uses, you will probably be able to access your own personal bank account whenever you're in need of funds. ATM machines get the same wholesale exchange rate as credit cards. There is often a limit on the amount of money you can withdraw per day, and computer network failures are not uncommon. Be sure to memorize your PIN code in numeral form since machines abroad often don't have letters on the keys. Also, if your PIN is longer than four digits, be sure to ask your bank whether the first four digits will work, or whether you need a new number.

## GETTING MONEY FROM HOME

Try to avoid this horror. Carry a credit card or a separate stash of traveler's checks. Even a single US$50 bill can sustain you for quite some time in the Middle East.

One possibility is to use an **American Express** card (see p. 15). AmEx allows cardholders to draw cash from their checking accounts at any of its major offices and many of its representatives' offices, up to US$1000 every 21 days (no service charge, no interest). Unless using the AmEx service, avoid cashing checks in foreign currencies; they usually take weeks and a US$30 fee to clear.

Money can be **wired** directly from bank to bank for about US$30 per US$1000, plus the commission charged by your home bank. You may need to arrange in advance for your bank to send money from your account to foreign banks on specific dates. Bring ID when you go to pick up your money.

**Western Union** (tel. (800) 325-6000 in the U.S.) is convenient for cabling cash to more than 40 cities in Israel and major cities in Egypt (including Alexandria, Cairo, Luxor, Port Said, and even Sharm esh-Sheikh). There are also Jordanian branches in

Amman and Irbid; Syria has no Western Union. Rates to send money from the U.S. start at US$29 (for sending US$200-300). **American Express Moneygram Service** (tel. (800) 926-9400) provides "10-minute delivery" in about an hour. Moneygram service is available in Amman, Cairo, Jerusalem, and Tel Aviv.

In emergencies, U.S. citizens can have money sent via the State Department's **Overseas Citizens Service, American Citizens Services,** Consular Affairs, Public Affairs Staff, Room 4831, U.S. Department of States, Washington, D.C. 20520 (202-647-5225; at night and on Sundays and holidays 202- 647-4000, fax 202-647-3000; http://travel.state.gov). For a fee of US$15, the State Department will forward money within hours to the nearest consular office. The office serves only Americans in the direst of straits abroad. The quickest way to have the money sent is to cable the State Department through Western Union depending on the circumstances.

## BARGAINING

As a general rule, the only places where prices are non-negotiable are restaurants, licensed gold shops, and stores that are part of international chains. Even then, hell, give it a try. Prices quoted to tourists (especially blond ones with accents) can be as high as ten times the "real" price (whatever that is), so don't be embarrassed to offer a fraction of the asking price. A good strategy is to offer what you want to pay even before inquiring about the price. Or ask the price in a somewhat blasé fashion, knit your brow, offer about half, and begin the bidding. You'd better be prepared to pay any price you offer; no backing off. If vendors decline your bid but call or chase after you, the haggling may continue in the street. In this case you've got them on the ropes. Staying at a hotel for several nights boosts your bargaining leverage; even starred hotels often strike deals.

# ■ Safety and Security

Politics in the Middle East can easily intrude on travel; keep apprised of events. U.S. citizens can check on the latest government travel advisories by calling the State Department's **Citizens' Emergency Center** (202-647-5225; see above). They can also use the number in emergency situations while traveling.

Travelers are frequently the most obvious targets for crime: they often carry large amounts of cash and they are not as savvy as locals. Do your best to blend in; avoid fumbling about with the tourist map in the middle of the *souq*. Try to always appear confident, even when you lose bodily control. An obviously bewildered bodybuilder is more likely to be harassed than a stern and confident- 98-pound weakling.

A good self-defense course will give you more concrete ways to react to different types of aggression, but it might cost you more money than your trip. **Model Mugging,** a national organization with offices in several major cities, teaches a very effective, comprehensive course on self-defense. Contact Lynn S. Auerbach on the East Coast (617-232-7900), Alice Tibits in the Midwest (612-645-6189), and Cori Couture on the West Coast (415-592-7300). Course prices vary from $400-500. Women's and men's courses are offered. Community colleges frequently offer self-defense courses at more affordable prices.

Common sense and a few precautions should carry you safely through your travels. **Don't put money in a wallet in your back pocket.** If you carry a purse, buy a sturdy one with a secure clasp, and carry it crosswise on the side. Buy some small combination padlocks for a little added security to your backpack or suitcase. A **money belt** or **neck pouch** is the best way to carry cash. The best combination of convenience and invulnerability is the nylon, zippered pouch with belt that should sit inside the waist of your pants or skirt. A **neck pouch,** although less accessible, is also safe. In city crowds and especially on public transportation, pick-pockets are amazingly deft at their craft. Hold your bags tightly. Make **photocopies** of important documents and keep them in a separate place. Also keep a stash of money separate from the rest to use in an emergency or in case of theft. Label each piece of luggage.

Among the more colorful aspects of important tourist nations are the **con artists.** Be aware of certain classics: sob stories that require money, rolls of bills "found" on the street, mustard spilled (or saliva spat) onto your shoulder, distracting you for enough time to snatch your bag. Contact the police if a hustler is particularly insistent or aggressive. In Egypt especially, where a thriving tourist industry has existed for years and where tourism is often the only source of income, hustlers have finetuned the con into an art. Beware of people who have the time and patience to gain your trust over a period of a few days, only to rob you of your valuables the second that you let your guard down. This is especially true on **feluccas.**

In cities, and elsewhere, extra vigilance may be wise, but there is never need for paranoia. Stick to busy, well-lit streets. Tourist information, and hotel and hostel managers can be valuable sources of advice on which areas to avoid. If you're in a dorm-style room or have no lock on your door, sleep with all valuables on your person or under your pillow; laying your pack alongside the bed won't do. The same holds for **overnight trains;** steer clear of empty compartments. **Trains** in general are notoriously easy spots for thieving, as are **buses.** Don't check your luggage on trains, as it is often "lost" this way.

**Travel Assistance International by Worldwide Assistance Services, Inc.** provides its members with a 24-hr. hotline for emergencies and referrals. Their year-long frequent traveler package ($226) includes medical and travel insurance, financial assistance, and help in replacing lost documents. Call (800) 821-2828 or (202) 828-5894, fax (202) 828-5896, or write them at 1133 15th St. NW, Suite 400, Washington, D.C. 20005-2710.

## TERRORISM

Terrorism is a threat in the Middle East as it is everywhere, from Oklahoma City to Manchester. Travelers need not feel like powerless bystanders, however. The chances of becoming a victim of terrorism are low, and can be lowered further by

taking certain precautions. You should be aware of the possibility of danger, without letting it paralyze you.

Militant Islamic groups in **Egypt** have targeted tourists in recent years. In April 1996, 18 Greek tourists were killed in a terrorist attack in Cairo, and several days later fundamentalists vowed to step up attacks against Americans. By dressing modestly, avoiding large organized tours, and respecting local sensibilities, you will be less conspicuous as a tourist, and less prone to attack. Remember, though, that even the guy with the tour group hat, the Hawaiian shirt, and the camcorder is probably safe. **Middle Egypt,** worlds apart from Cairo and Luxor, is also far more dangerous. Tourists should avoid Asyut, the center of the fundamentalist movement. Tourist police hover around visitors in many Nile valley towns. They may seem gruff and intrusive, but they are there to protect you.

Terrorists in **Israel** target public transportation and crowded areas. The best defense is to learn the pattern of previous incidents. Most bus bombings in Israel occur in the early morning rush hour. If your plans are flexible, try to avoid bus travel at this time. As terrorism has sadly become a part of life in the country, Israelis look at abandoned purses and backpacks in a different light. Don't leave anything unattended, or it will be snatched up by the police and possibly blown to bits. Alert authorities if you see an abandoned package, or put it in a *bor bitahon* (security pit). Traveling in the **West Bank** can be dangerous, especially in a car with yellow license plates. Jewish travelers should avoid identifying themselves as such. Simply placing a baseball cap over a *kippah* can prevent stares and hostility.

Terrorism is not much of a threat in **Jordan**, while a string of bombings in **Syria** in May 1996 prompted the American embassy to issue an **advisory.** If planning an extended stay in Syria, register with your embassy and always stay apprised of the current situation. This should include getting news from sources outside of Syria.

## ALCOHOL AND DRUGS

In 1991, 1271 of the 3050 Americans who ended up in foreign jails were brought up on drug charges. Laws vary from country to country, but, needless to say, **illegal drugs** are best avoided altogether. Some countries do not differentiate between "hard" drugs and more mainstream ones such as marijuana. The Islamic law forbidding **alcohol** is like the American law against jaywalking—lots of people do it anyway. Egypt's drinking age is 21, and Israel's, Jordan's, and Syria's are 18. Only Israel's restriction is enforced. The U.S. State Department warns that "U.S. citizens are subject to the laws of the country in which they travel." This is true of all other nationalities as well. Viewers of *Midnight Express* will remember that penalties for possession, use, or trafficking in **illegal drugs** are severe throughout the Middle East. Both Egypt and Syria may impose the death penalty on anyone convicted of smuggling or selling. Consulates can do no more than bring floral arrangements to the prisoner, provide a list of attorneys, and inform family and friends.

# ■ Health

Common sense is the simplest prescription for good health while you travel: eat well, drink and sleep enough, and don't overexert yourself. Travelers complain most often about their feet and their gut, so take precautionary measures. Drinking lots of fluids can often prevent dehydration and constipation, and wearing sturdy shoes and clean socks and using talcum powder can help keep your feet dry. To minimize the effects of jet lag, "reset" your body's clock by adopting the time of your destination immediately upon arrival. Most travelers feel acclimated to a new time zone after two or three days.

## BEFORE YOU GO

It is always a good idea to see a doctor before traveling, especially if you will be abroad for more than a month or two or if you will be hiking or camping.

For minor health problems, bring a compact **first-aid kit,** including bandages, aspirin or other pain killer, antibiotic cream, a thermometer, a Swiss Army knife with tweezers, moleskin, a decongestant for colds, motion sickness remedy (such as Dramamine), anti-diarrheals, sunscreen, insect repellent, calamine lotion, and an antihistamine (the centuries of dust can trigger allergies you never knew you had).

Write the names of any people you wish to be contacted in case of a medical emergency in your passport. Also list any allergies or medical conditions you would want doctors to be aware of. If you wear glasses or contact lenses, carry an extra prescription or pair. Allergy sufferers should find out if their conditions are likely to be aggravated in the Middle East, and should bring enough medication for the duration of the trip. Carry up-to-date, legible prescriptions or a statement from your doctor, especially if you use insulin, a syringe, or a narcotic. While traveling, be sure to keep all medication in carry-on luggage.

Take a look at your **immunization** records before you go; some countries require visitors to carry vaccination certificates. Travelers over the age of two should be sure that the following vaccines are up to date: Measles, Mumps, and Rubella (MMR); Diptheria, Tetanus, and Pertussis (DTP or DTap); Polio (OPV); Haemophilus Influenza B (HbCV); and Hepatitis B (HBV). A booster of Tetanus-diptheria (Td) is recommended once every ten years, and adults travelling to the Middle East should consider an additional dose of Polio vaccine if they have not already had one during their adult years. Hepatitis A vaccine and/or Immune Globulin (IG) is recommended for travelers to all developing regions. If you will be spending more than four weeks in a developing country, you should also consider the typhoid vaccine. Check with a doctor for guidance through this maze of injections. Needles are your friends.

## ON-THE-ROAD AILMENTS

The hot temperatures and low sanitation standards of the Middle East can make even the most careful traveler ill. Drink *lots* of water (as much as 10L per day may be necessary to avoid dehydration), always cover your head with something white when you go out in the sun, and ease into street food slowly. Avoid excessive caffeine and alcohol, both of which can cause dehydration. Remember what Uncle Mort told you about urine: steer for the clear, bellow if it's yellow. It's a good idea to carry high sun protection factor (SPF) sun block and to apply it liberally and often. SPFs of 15 or 20 are strong enough for the fairest skin. This is not the place to work on a tan—even the dark-skinned or pre-tanned are not immune.

**Heatstroke** can occur without direct exposure to the sun. If ignored, it can lead to serious medical problems such as death. Symptoms include cessation of sweating, increased body temperature, flushed skin, and intense headache. Wear a hat, sunglasses, and a lightweight longsleeve shirt to avoid heatstroke. Experts recommend giving heatstroke victims cold fruit juice or salted water, cooling them off with wet towels and shade, and rushing them to the hospital.

You should drink only bottled water or beverages, boiled water (it does no good to simply heat it), or treated water, especially in Egypt and Syria. You can make boiled water taste better by adding a little salt or pouring it into another container. Less reliable and not as tasty is water treated with iodine or other chemicals (such as Potable-Aqua tablets). Even if the locals drink the water, it may not be safe for you until you have been in the area for a while

Anywhere you've been warned not to drink the water, pass up ice cubes, raw vegetables or other raw foods (especially seafood), and peeled fruit. Don't brush your teeth with tap water, and don't even rinse your toothbrush under the faucet. Keep your mouth closed in the shower. Lightly salting your food should suffice to replace the salt carried away by perspiration. Be sure that the cooked food you eat is still hot (breads are safe cold), and that the animal products you eat (meat, dairy, fish, eggs) are completely cooked or pasteurized. Always wash your hands before eating. Your bowels will thank you.

Beware of unwittingly ingesting **parasites,** which skulk about in unsafe water and food. Quaffing untreated stream or lake water could result in a case of **giardia,** a parasitic disease that can stay with you for years. Swim, bathe, or wade in fresh water in Egypt's Nile River delta and valley, and risk the peril of **schistosomiasis.** This infection is mediated by the larvae of a flatworm that can penetrate unbroken skin. Bath water should be heated to 50°C (122°F, uncomfortably hot but far below the boiling point) or treated with chlorine or iodine. If you are exposed to unsafe water, rub the exposed area vigorously with a towel and apply rubbing alcohol. The dread schistosomiasis is treatable with drugs.

Sooner or later, no matter how careful you are, you'll probably get diarrhea, affectionately known among its victims as **"Pharaoh's Revenge."** The Revenge typically strikes 10 to 12 days after arrival, lasts from two to four days if you rest up, and may be accompanied by fever and fatigue. Drink plenty of liquids to keep well-hydrated; an electrolyte solution (like the one used for babies) dissolved in your water tastes disgusting but helps. Commonly recommended medications for diarrhea are Lomotil, Immodium, Pepto-Bismol, and Bactrim. The first three can help relieve the symptoms of diarrhea, but they are *not* cures, and may even delay recovery. Avoid using them at the beginning—they should only be used if you are well on the way to recovery, are feeling healthy enough to continue on your journey, and want something to ease your discomfort. Bactrim is an antibiotic which can only be obtained with a prescription; your doctor can prescribe it to you before you leave, and it is usually taken for five days. Avoid anti-diarrheals if you suspect you have been exposed to contaminated food or water; this unfortunate combination puts you at risk for cholera, typhoid fever, and other diseases. Diarrhea may be the symptom of a parasitic condition which could haunt your gastro-intestinal tract for years. If it does not subside, see a doctor immediately. A local doctor may be more familiar with your new internal friends. Also consult a doctor if children develop traveler's diarrhea, since treatment is different.

In rural areas of the Nile Delta, Fayyum, the oases, and Southern Egypt near the Sudan border, you risk getting **malaria,** which is borne by mosquitoes. If you plan on hiking or staying overnight in high-risk areas, you may want to take weekly anti-malarial drugs before you leave. Contact your doctor for a prescription. **Dengue fever** is an "urban viral infection" also borne by mosquitoes. There is no vaccine and no treatment; the only prevention is to avoid mosquito bites. To treat the symptoms, rest, drink lots of water, and take fever-reducing medication such as acetaminophen (but avoid aspirin). There have been sporadic Dengue outbreaks recently in Egypt, but the Middle East is generally considered a low-risk area for Dengue.

You can thwart mosquitoes and other wee blood-suckers by wearing long pants and sleeves, shoes and socks, and insect repellent. Buy a bednet if you will be camping, and spray it, along with your sleeping bag, backpack, clothes, and shoes, with **permethrin.** Taking **vitamin B-12** pills regularly can eventually make you smelly to insects, as can **garlic** pills (but then *no one* will bite you).

**Typhoid fever** is transmitted through contaminated food and water and by direct contact with an infected person. The CDC recommends vaccinations (70-90% effective) if you will be hiking, camping, or staying in small cities, villages, or rural areas.

**Hepatitis A** is a viral infection of the liver acquired primarily through contaminated water or food, as well as from sexual contact. Symptoms include fatigue, fever, loss of appetite, nausea, dark urine, jaundice, vomiting, aches and pains, and light stools. Ask your doctor about a new vaccine called "Harvix," or ask to get an injection of immune globulin (IG; formerly called Gamma Globulin). Risk is highest in rural areas and the countryside.

## WOMEN'S HEALTH

Women traveling in unsanitary conditions are vulnerable to urinary tract and bladder infections, common and severely uncomfortable bacterial diseases which cause a burning sensation and painful and sometimes frequent urination. Drink tons of vitamin-C-rich juice, plenty of clean water, and urinate frequently, especially right after intercourse. Untreated, these infections can be fatal. If symptoms persist, see a doctor. If you're prone to yeast infections, take along an over-the-counter medicine, as treatments may not be readily available in rural Egypt or Syria. Tampons and pads are sometimes hard to find when traveling; certainly your preferred brands may not be available, so it may be advisable to take supplies along. Some women also use diaphragms or cervical caps to temporarily trap menstrual flow. Refer to the *Handbook for Women Travellers* by Maggie and Gemma Moss (published by Piatkus Books) or to the women's health guide *Our Bodies, Our Selves* (published by the Boston Women's Health Collective) for more extensive information specific to women's health on the road.

If you are overseas and want an **abortion,** contact the **United States abortion hotline** (tel. (800) 772-9100; Mon.-Fri. 9:30am-12:30pm and 1:30-5:30pm), 1436 U St. NW, Washington, D.C. 20009. The hotline can direct you to organizations which provide information on the availability of and techniques for abortion in other countries. Your embassy can also provide a list of doctors who perform abortions.

## AIDS, HIV, AND CONTRACEPTION

All travelers should be concerned about **HIV,** the human immunodeficiency virus that causes **AIDS,** which is transmitted through an exchange of body fluids with a person who is HIV-positive. Transmission may also occur if these fluids come into contact with a noninfected person's mucous membranes (like the mouth). For more information on AIDS, call the **U.S. Center for Disease Control's 24-hr. Hotline** at (800) 342-2437 (TTY (800) 243-7889, Mon.-Fri. 10am-10pm; in Spanish (800) 344-7332, daily 8am-2am).

The **World Health Organization (WHO)** (tel. (202) 861-3200) provides statistical material on AIDS internationally. For country-specific restrictions for HIV-positive travelers, write to the Bureau of Consular Affairs, Room 6831, N.S, U.S. Department of State, Washington, D.C. 20520. In Europe, call 41 22 791 46 73 (Switzerland), or write to the **UNAIDS,** 20 Avenue Appia, 1211 Geneva 27, Switzerland.

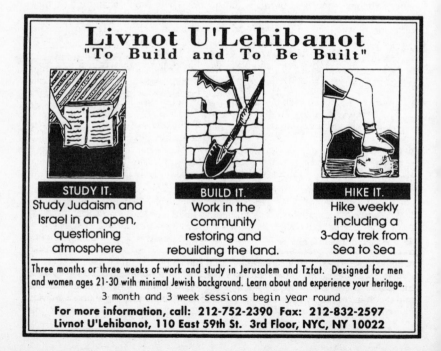

Stock up on **condoms** before leaving (although in Israel your favorite brand is most likely available). **Contraceptives** are not always available, or safe, in the Middle East; women on the pill should bring all they'll ever need.

## HEALTH RESOURCES AND ORGANIZATIONS

**Global Emergency Medical Services (GEMS),** 2001 Westside Drive, Suite 120, Alpharetta, GA 30201, (tel. (800) 860-1111; fax (770) 475-0058), provides 24-hr. international medical assistance and support through registered nurses with on-line access to your medical information, your primary physician, and a worldwide network of screened, credentialed English-speaking doctors and hospitals.

**International Association for Medical Assistance to Travelers (IAMAT)** offers a free membership including an ID card, a directory of English-speaking doctors world-wide, and medical brochures. Contact chapters in the **U.S.,** 417 Center St., Lewiston, NY 14092 (tel. (716) 754-4883; fax (519) 836-3412; e-mail iamat@sentex.net; http://www.sentex.net/iamat), **Canada,** 40 Regal Road, Guelph, Ontario, N1K 1B5 (tel. (519) 836-0102) or 1287 St. Clair Ave. West, Toronto, M6E 1B8 (tel. (416) 652-0137, fax (519) 836-3412), **New Zealand,** P.O. Box 5049, Christchurch 5.

**Medic Alert Foundation,** 2323 Colorado Ave., Turlock, CA 95382. Provides a stainless steel **Medic Alert** identification tag (US$35 the first year, and $15 annually thereafter) for those with existing medical conditions (e.g. diabetes, allergies to antibiotics, epilepsy, heart conditions).

**U.S. Center for Disease Control (CDC),** 1600 Clifton Rd. NE, Atlanta, GA 30333 (tel. (404) 639-3311). Maintains an international travelers' hotline (tel. (404) 332-4559; fax 332-4565; http://www.cdc.gov), providing printed information through fax. Document code for "disease directory" (information on various diseases and on travelers' health) is 000005. Also publishes the booklet *Health Information for International Travelers* (US$14).

# ■ Insurance

Beware of buying unnecessary travel coverage—your regular policies may well extend to many travel-related accidents. **Medical insurance** (especially university policies) often cover costs incurred abroad. Canadians are protected by their home province's health insurance plan for up to 90 days after leaving the country; check with the provincial Ministry of Health or Health Plan Headquarters for details. Australia has Reciprocal Health Care Agreements (RHCAs) with several countries; when traveling in these nations, Australians are entitled to many of the services that they would receive at home. The Commonwealth Department of Human Services and Health can provide more information. Your **homeowners' insurance** (or your family's coverage) often covers theft during travel. Homeowners are generally covered against loss of travel documents (passport, plane ticket, railpass, etc.) up to $500.

**ISIC** and **ITIC** provide US$3000 worth of accident and illness insurance and US$100 per day up to 60 days of hospitalization. They also offer up to US$1000 for accidental death or dismemberment, up to US$25,000 if injured due to an airline, and up to $25,000 for emergency evacuation due to an illness. The cards also give access to a toll-free Traveler's Assistance hotline (call collect to the US (713) 267-2525) whose multilingual staff can provide help in emergencies overseas.To supplement ISIC's insurance, **Council** (see Travel Organizations, above) offers the inexpensive Trip-Safe plan with options covering medical treatment and hospitalization, accidents, baggage loss, and charter flights missed due to illness; they and **STA** also offer more comprehensive and expensive policies. **American Express** cardholders receive automatic car rental and travel accident insurance if flight purchases are made with the card (For customer service call (800) 528-4800).

Always carry policy numbers and proof of insurance. Remember that insurance companies usually require a copy of the police report for thefts or evidence of having paid medical expenses (doctor's statements, receipts) before they will honor a claim and may have time limits on filing for reimbursement. Check with each insurance carrier for specific policies. The carriers listed below have 24-hr. hotlines.

**Travel Guard International,** 1145 Clark St., Stevens Point, WI 54481 (tel. (800) 826-1300 or (715) 345-0505; fax (715) 345-0525). Comprehensive insurance programs starting at US$44. Programs cover trip cancellation and interruption, bankruptcy and financial default, lost luggage, medical coverage abroad, emergency assistance, and accidental death.

**Travel Insured International, Inc.,** 52-S Oakland Ave., P.O. Box 280568, East Hartford, CT 06128-0568 (tel. (800) 243-3174; fax (203) 528-8005). Insurance against accident, baggage loss, sickness, trip cancellation and interruption, travel delay, and default. Covers emergency medical evacuation and flight insurance.

**Wallach and Company, Inc.,** 107 West Federal St., P.O. Box 480, Middleburg, VA 20118-0480 (tel. (800) 237-6615, fax (540) 687–3172) or e-mail wallach.r@mediasoft.net). Comprehensive medical insurance including evacuation and repatriation of remains and direct payment of claims to providers of services. Other optional coverages available.

# ■ Alternatives To Tourism

## STUDY

Foreign study programs vary tremendously in expense, academic quality, living conditions, degree of contact with local students, and exposure to the local culture and language. Local libraries and bookstores are helpful sources for current information on study abroad, and there's also a study abroad website (www.studyabroad.com/liteimage.html). **Council** sponsors over 40 study abroad programs throughout the world. Contact them for more information (see p.4).

**Biblical Archaeology Society,** 4710 41st St. NW, Washington, D.C. 20016 (tel. (202) 364-3300; fax 364-2636). The society provides information on digs and organizes travel/study tours. Also publishes the *Biblical Archaeological Review.*

**College Semester Abroad, School for International Training,** Admissions, Kipling Rd., P.O. Box 676, Brattleboro, VT 05302 (tel. (800) 336-1616 or 258-3279; fax 258-3500). Runs semester- and year-long programs featuring cultural orientation, intensive language study, homestay, and field and independent study in Israel and Jordan (among many others). Programs cost US$8200-10,300, all expenses included. Financial aid is available, and U.S. financial aid is transferable. Most U.S. colleges will transfer credit for semester work done abroad.

**Institute of International Education (IIE),** 809 United Nations Plaza, New York, NY 10017-3580 (tel. (212) 984-5413 for recorded information; fax 984-5358). For book orders: IIE Books, Institute of International Educations, PO Box 371, Annapolis Junction, MD 20701 (tel. (800) 445- 0443; fax (301) 953-2838; e-mail iiebooks@iie.org.). A nonprofit, international cultural exchange agency. Publishes *Academic Year Abroad* (US$43 plus US$4 shipping) and *Vacation Study Abroad* (US$37 plus US$4 shipping), exhaustive tomes on alternatives to tourism.

**International Association for the Exchange of Students for Technical Experience (IAESTE),** 10400 Little Patuxent Pkwy. #250, Columbia, MD 21044-3510 (tel. (410) 997-3068 or 3069; http://www.softaid.net/aipt/aipt/html). 8- to 12-week programs in 50 countries for students with 2 years of technical study. Nonrefundable US$50 application fee; apply by Dec. 10 for summer placement.

**Peterson's Guides,** P. O. Box 2123, Princeton, NJ 08543-2123 (tel. (800) 338-3282; fax (609) 243-9150; http://www.petersons.com). Their comprehensive *Study Abroad* annual guide (US$27) lists programs worldwide and provides essential information on the study abroad experience in general.

## VOLUNTEERING

**The Archaeological Institute of America,** 656 Beacon St., Boston, MA 02215-2010 (tel. (617) 353-9361; fax 353-6550), puts out the *Archaeological Fieldwork*

*Opportunities Bulletin* (US$11), which lists over 250 field sites throughout the world. This can be purchased from Kendall/Hunt Publishing, 4050 Westmark Drive, Dubuque, IA 52002 (tel. (800) 228-0810).

**Council** (see Travel Organizations, above) offers 2- to 4-week environmental or community service projects in over 30 countries around the globe through its Voluntary Services Department (US$250-750 placement fee). 18 and over.

**Peace Corps,** 1990 K St. NW, Washington, D.C. 20526 (tel. (800) 424-8580; fax (202) 606-4469; http://www.peacecorps.gov). Write for their "blue" brochure, which details applicant requirements. Opportunities in a variety of fields (from agriculture to business) in developing nations worldwide. Volunteers must be U.S. citizens willing to make a 2 year commitment.

**Volunteers for Peace,** 43 Tiffany Rd., Belmont, VT 05730 (tel. (802) 259-2759; fax 259-2922; e-mail vfp@vermontel.com; http://www.vfp.org). A non-profit organization that arranges for speedy placement in over 800 work camps around the world. *International Workcamp Directory* (US$12) provides up-to-date listings. Registration fee US$175. Free newsletter.

## WORK

**Office of Overseas Schools,** A/OS Room 245, SA-29, Dept. of State, Washington, D.C. 20522-2902 (tel. (703) 875-7800). Teaching jobs abroad.

**Transitions Abroad Publishing, Inc.,** 18 Hulst Rd., P.O. Box 1300, Amherst, MA 01004-1300 (tel. (800) 293-0373; fax (413) 256-0373; e-mail trabroad@aol.com). Publishes a bimonthly magazine listing opportunities and printed resources for those seeking to study, work, or travel abroad, and *The Alternative Travel Directory,* a mammoth listing of information for the "active international traveler."

**Vacation Work Publications,** 9 Park End St., Oxford OX1 1HJ (tel. (01865) 24 19 78; fax 79 08 85). Publishes a wide variety of guides and directories with job listings and information for the working traveler. Opportunities for summer or full-time work in countries all over the world. Write for a catalogue of publications.

## EGYPT

### Study

The **American University in Cairo (AUC)** offers semester, year, and summer programs for study abroad, intensive Arabic, and graduate degree study. Instruction is in English. Popular topics include Arabic language, Egyptology, and Middle East studies. Tuition and fees for 1996-97 are US$4775 per semester; US$2370 for the summer session. AUC is located in the center of modern Cairo, just off Tahrir Square at 113 Qasr el-Aini St. For more information, write to Office of Student Affairs, American University in Cairo, 866 United Nations Plaza LG517, New York, NY 10017-1889 (tel. (212) 421-6320; fax 688-5341).

Three other Cairene universities have programs for foreign students, transferable for credit at most universities. They are **'Ain Shams University,** El Khalifa El Maamoun St., **Al Azhar University,** El Nasr Rd., Cairo (tel. (02) 262 32 78 or 79), and **Cairo University,** El Gamaa St. Those interested should contact the Department of International Students, **Egyptian Cultural and Educational Bureau,** 1303 New Hampshire Ave. NW, Washington, D.C. 20036 (tel. (202) 296-3888; fax 296-3891), or **AmidEast** in the U.S. (1730 M St. NW Suite 1100, Washington, D.C., 20036; tel (202) 776-9601; fax 822-6563), in Cairo (6 Kamel ash-Shinawy St. 2nd floor, Garden City, P.O. Box 96 Magles el-Shaab; tel (02) 354 13 00 or 355 31 70; fax 355 29 46), or in Alexandria (tel. (03) 482 2117; fax 483 3811).

Several language institutes offer shorter-term studies in Arabic. **Berlitz Language Centers** specialize in colloquial and simplified literary Arabic; contact them at 165 Muhammad Farid St., Cairo (tel. (02) 391 50 96); 28 Sa'ad Zaghloul Blvd., Alexandria (tel. (03) 808 226); 37 Sha'ul Ha-Melekh Ave., Tel Aviv 64298 (tel. (03) 695 21 31; fax (03) 695 21 34); 40 W. 51st St., New York, NY 10020 (tel. (212) 765-1000); or at any of their locations world-wide. They also offer cultural training.

The **Egyptian Center for International Cultural Cooperation,** 11 Shagarat ed-Durr St., Zamalek, Cairo (tel. (02) 341 54 19) teaches classical and colloquial Arabic, and sponsors cultural activities such as art exhibitions, lectures, and tours.

### Work and Volunteer

Some people look for temporary jobs upon arrival in Na'ama Bay or Alexandria. Ask at the **American Chamber of Commerce** in Cairo at the Marriott Hotel (tel. (02) 340 88 88) for lists of member companies. Work permits can be obtained through any Egyptian consulate, or in Egypt from the Ministry of the Interior.

The **Supreme Council for Youth and Sport in Egypt** (Foreign Relations Administration) runs programs in which students of different nationalities spend two to four weeks working together on agricultural or sociological projects. Contact the Council at 26th July St., Oqba Sq., Giza (tel. (02) 346 17 01) or the Egyptian Embassy.

**American Field Service (AFS),** 220 E. 42nd St., 3rd floor, New York, NY 10017 (tel. (800) 237-4636 or 876-2376; fax (212) 949-9379; http://www.afs.org/usa), offers summer-, semester-, and year-long homestay Egypt exchange programs for high school students and graduating high school seniors and short-term service projects for adults. Financial aid is available.

## ISRAEL

The University Student Department of the **American Zionist Youth Foundation (USD/AZYF)** is a clearinghouse for many programs, offering tours and study or work/volunteer/archaeological dig programs. University programs offer classes in English or Hebrew. There are fully accredited programs in Jerusalem, Tel Aviv, Haifa, and Be'er Sheva. Contact the USD/AZYF at University Student Department, Israel Action Center, 110 E. 59th St. 4th floor, New York, NY 10022 (tel. (800) 27-ISRAEL (274-7723) or (212) 339-6940; fax 755-4781).

### Work and Apprenticeships

Unemployment in Israel is high, greatly limiting work opportunities; foreigners must also compete with the new immigrants from the Soviet Union. American or European companies with branches in Israel are a possible source of employment. Another option is volunteer work in exchange for room and board. Some people look for temporary jobs upon arrival in Eilat.

The **Jewish Agency** is a good clearinghouse for work and volunteer opportunities throughout the country. Their representatives will help you find a kibbutz, a place to study Hebrew, or a volunteer organization.The multilingual staff is trained to work with immigrants and long-term visitors. English speakers should ask for Tziki Aud. Write to the Information and Service Center, P.O. Box 31677, Jerusalem 91030 (tel. (02) 623 20 99 or 18 23, or 624 65 22; fax 623 53 28).

### Kibbutzim

Israel's 250 Kibbutzim, communal settlements whose members divide work and profits equally, are often eager for volunteers. Kibbutzim vary greatly in size, number of volunteers, and ideological basis. Volunteers generally work six eight-hour days per week, with several days off per month, and receive a small monthly allowance in addition to various other benefits; the work is generally physical, in agriculture, industry, or service. Prior knowledge of Hebrew is helpful, but non-speakers can learn Hebrew quickly if they desire through the Ulpan program (see **Ulpanim,** p. 29). Accommodations are most often in dormitory settings. Try to get a written promise of placement on a specific kibbutz before arriving in Israel. Kibbutz life can be seductive in its routine, and many volunteers find themselves staying longer than planned.

To apply for any kibbutz program, contact your local Kibbutz Aliya Desk or the main office at 110 E. 59th St., 4th floor, New York, NY 10022 (tel. (800) 247-7852; fax 318-6134; e-mail: projoren@aol.com; http://www.webflex.com/kibbutz.htp). Applicants must be age 18-35 with no children (exception: Kibbutz Hanaton accepts families for periods of one year); there is a two-month minimum commitment and no maximum stay length. After being interviewed and given the appropriate application and medical forms, you will be sent to the **Kibbutz Program Center, Volunteer Office** in Tel Aviv, 18 Frishman St., Center Ben Yehuda, Tel Aviv 61030 (tel. (03) 527 88 74 or 524 61 56; fax 523 99 66), where you will be assigned to a kibbutz. For information and listings, get a copy of the 1996 edition of *Kibbutz Volunteer,* Vacation Work Publications, 9 Park End St., Oxford, OX1 1HJ, U.K. (tel. (01865) 241 978, UK£7.99 plus UK£2.50 shipping). **Project 67,** 10 Hatton Garden, London EC1N 8AH, U.K. (tel. (0171) 831 76 26), places volunteers on Kibbutzim and *moshavim* for two to four months.

### Moshavim

*Moshavim* provide a somewhat different work experience from kibbutzim. *Moshavim* are agricultural communities in which farms and homes are privately owned and operated. You will receive free lodging either with a family or in a house with other workers. In return, you work a six-day week, at least eight hours per day. Workers are paid about US$300 per month and are expected to pay for their own food. Applicants must be aged 18-35 and physically fit. Write the organizations listed above for kibbutzim or contact **Volunteers Moshavim Movement,** 19 Leonardo da Vinci St., Tel Aviv (tel. (03) 695 84 73; fax 691 89 96).

### Archaeological Digs

Work on archaeological digs consists largely of digging pits, shoveling shards, and hauling baskets of dirt for eight to ten hours per day in searing heat—beginning at 5am; don't dream of discovering ancient treasures.

The "Dig for a Day" program by Archaeological Seminars is designed for the curious tourist. The three-hour program at the Beit Guvrin National Park includes a short seminar on the history of the area, excavation, a crawl through an unexcavated cave system and a tour of the park (US$25). Reservations are a good idea. Write to them at P.O. Box 14002, Jaffa Gate, Jerusalem 91140 (tel. (02) 627 35 15; fax (02) 627 26 60).

### Volunteer

**Shatil,** a project of the New Israel Fund, places volunteers with organizations working in areas such as civil and human rights, Jewish-Arab coexistence, the status of women, and religious tolerance. Contact them at the **New Israel Fund,** 1625 K St. NW #500, Washington, D.C. 20006-1604 (tel. (202) 223-3333), or at 9 Yad Ha-Rutzim St., P.O. Box 53410, Jerusalem 91534 (tel. (02) 672 30 95; fax 672 30 99).

The **Volunteers for Israel** program places participants in non-combat support jobs in the Israeli military. The 3-week program involves menial work such as washing dishes or mending equipment. You will wear army fatigues, army boots, and sleep in army barracks, but don't expect to carry an Uzi or keep the uniform afterwards. The program offers reduced airfare on El Al or Tower Air, provided you fulfill your commitment. There may also be a special fare for those under 26. Contact: Volunteers for Israel, 330 W. 42nd St. #1618, New York, NY 10036 (tel. (212) 643-4848; fax 643-4855). Application includes a US$100 registration fee.

### Living Experiences

A blend of work, study, and life in general, **Project Otzma,** the Jewish Service Corps, is a ten-month program for Jews aged 20 to 24 that incorporates kibbutz and *moshav* life, youth villages, immigrant absorption, and Hebrew study (tel. (212) 598-3532; fax 529-5842). Also consider the Peace Corps-style **Sherut La'Am** (contact them through AZYF, above).

**Livnot U'Lehibanot: To Build and To Be Built** offers 3-week or 3-month study and work experiences in Jerusalem and Tzfat. Four hours per day of discussion-oriented classes and seminars exploring one's Jewish heritage and the land of Israel, and four hours per day of building and community service projects, plus hikes throughout the country. Open to ages 21-30. Contact: Livnot U'Lehibanot, 110 E. 59th St. 3rd floor, New York, NY 10022 (tel. (212) 752-2390; fax 832-2597) or at 27 Ben-Zakkai, Katamon, Jerusalem 93585 (tel. (02) 679 34 91; fax 679 34 92; e-mail livnot@jerusaleml.datasrv.co.il).

## Study

### Ulpanim

An *ulpan* is a five-month program providing intensive Hebrew and Jewish culture instruction. Israel has about 100 *ulpanim.* **Kibbutz Ulpanim** offer instruction together with work. Contact the **Kibbutz Aliya Desk** (see Kibbutzim, above).

The **Municipality of Jerusalem Department of Culture** can place in you in any *ulpan* in the city. They're located at 11 Bezalel St. (tel. (02) 563 37 18). Two of the city's better known *ulpanim* are **Beit Ha-Noar Ha'Ivri,** 105 Ha-Rav Herzog, Jerusalem 92622 (tel. (02) 678 94 41; fax 678 86 42) and **Mo'adon Ha'Oleh,** 9 Alkalai St., Jerusalem (tel. (02) 563 37 18).

**Ulpan Akiva,** Netanya, offers a live-in program at its seaside campus for students from around the world—Jews, non-Jews, Israelis, and new immigrants. Daily program includes five hours of Hebrew study, social and cultural activities, tours, trips, and special *Shabbat* activities. Three-, eight-, 12-, and 20-week courses are accredited by several universities. Costs vary. Contact: **Ulpan Akiva Netanya,** P.O. Box 6086, Netanya 42160, Israel (tel. (09) 835 23 12 or 13 or 14; fax 865 29 19), or **World Zionist Organization Ulpan Center,** 136 E. 58th St., New York, NY 10022 (tel. (212) 432-7399).

### Universities

Programs for foreign students range in length from one summer to four years. **Year-abroad** programs usually begin with a four- to nine-week *ulpan* to learn Hebrew before the semester begins in October. Courses are usually in English; those who know Hebrew have the option of taking regular university courses. University programs are usually preceded by a *mekhina* (see *Mekhinot,* below). Admission for undergraduates requires proficiency in Hebrew and often at least one year of college.

For all programs contact: **Israel Student Authority,** 15 Hillel St., Jerusalem (tel. (02) 624 11 21) or the New York consulate's Office of Academic Affairs.

**Ben-Gurion University,** Center for International Student Programs, Office of Student Services/NA, 342 Madison Ave. #1224, New York, NY 10173 (tel. (212) 687-7721; fax 370-0686; e-mail bguosp@haven.ios.com). In Israel, contact: Center for International Student Programs, P.O. Box 653, Beer Sheva 84105 (tel. (07) 646 11 44; fax 647 29 48; e-mail osp@bgumail.bgu.ac.il). Students must be enrolled at an accredited college or university.

**Canadian Friends of Haifa University,** 1110 Finch Ave. W #510, Downsview, Ont. M3J 2T2 (tel. (800) 388-2134, or (416) 665-4462; fax 665-4468), or Mt. Carmel Haifa 31905 (tel. (04) 824 07 66; fax 824 03 91).

**Hebrew University of Jerusalem,** 11 E. 69th St., New York, NY 10021 (tel. (212) 472-2288; fax 517-4548), or Mount Scopus, Jerusalem 91905 (tel. (02) 588 21 11).

**Technion-Israel Institute of Technology,** contact the American Technion Society National Office, 810 Seventh Ave., New York, NY 10019 (tel. (212) 262-6200).

**Tel Aviv University,** Office of Academic Affairs, 360 Lexington Ave., New York, NY 10017 (tel. (212) 687-5651; fax 687-4085), or Ramat Aviv, Tel Aviv 69978 (tel. (03) 640 86 39; fax (03) 640 95 82).

### Mekhinot

Students who are not proficient in Hebrew but wish to enter a full undergraduate degree program usually first enroll in mekhina (preparation) programs, providing a year of intensive Hebrew and a chance to develop study plans. Mekhinot are offered by the universities and other schools of post-secondary education. Note that mekhina participation does not guarantee acceptance to a university; students must still take entrance examinations.

## WEST BANK

During much of the *intifada,* all four West Bank universities—Birzeit, Bethlehem, Hebron, and An-Najah—were closed by the Israeli authorities as security threats. Today, most West Bank schools have resumed classes. Check the programs for foreign students at **Birzeit University** north of Ramallah. The six-week International Summer Program offers courses in Modern Standard Arabic, Colloquial Arabic, and courses in the social sciences and arts. The same courses are offered as the Palestinian and Arabic Studies Program over a period of one semester (Sept.-Feb.and Feb.-June). Programs cost US$500, $600 for language courses. For information, write to International Programs, Birzeit University, P.O. Box 14, Birzeit, Via Israel. Birzeit University also sponsors two-week international work camps with Palestinian students in August and September; contact the Student Affairs Office.

Several organizations aid in planning excursions to the West Bank. The **Palestine Human Rights Information Center** in East Jerusalem (tel. (02) 628 70 77) provides information on the current political situation and human rights issues. Director Jan Abu-Shakra gives free lectures on the *intifada* to small groups. Call ahead (open daily 8am-2pm). The office is off Salah ad-Din St.; turn onto Az-Zahra St. and take the first right after the National Palace Hotel. **Al-Haq,** P.O. Box 1413, Ramallah (tel. (02) 995 64 21; fax 995 49 03), the West Bank affiliate of the International Commission of Jurists, is a Palestinian human rights organization that publishes informative booklets and reports and maintains a small legal library with free public access (open Mon.-Sat. 8am-4pm; office at 31 Main St., near the Latin Convent).

## JORDAN

**Work** It's difficult for foreigners to find jobs in Jordan, although English skills are in demand. A combination of perfect English and business or banking skills is optimal. Positions must be arranged before arrival in order to get a work visa. **Work permits** can be secured from the Ministry of Labor. **Residence permits** are required for stays of more than three months.

Some science-related apprenticeships are available through **IAESTE** (see p. 24). Volunteers for **archaeological digs** are in demand.

**Study** Two Jordanian universities are open to foreign students. The **University of Jordan Language Centre** (Al-Jubaiha, Amman) offers a six-level intensive program in Arabic (classical and spoken) for non-native speakers. All levels are offered regularly and concurrently during the fall (Sep.-Jan.), spring (Feb.-May), and summer (June-Aug.) terms. Tuition fees for the fall and spring are JD340, for the summer JD205. Write to Director, Language Centre, University of Jordan, Amman 11942, Jordan, for application forms (tel. (06) 843 555, ext. 3436 or 3439; fax 832 318). **Yarmouk University** in Irbid (tel. (02) 271 100) has a more conservative atmosphere (although you shouldn't plan on wearing shorts at either). The courses for foreign students at Yarmouk will be offered only if there are enough people interested in enrolling. Both schools guarantee dormitory housing for women. A Jordanian embassy, consulate, or information bureau (see p. 4 and 6) can provide further information on either school.

## SYRIA

As in Jordan, work for foreigners is scarce in Syria. A **residence permit** is required, as visitors on tourist visas are not allowed to work; bureaucratic nightmares abound. Tutoring or teaching English as a second language are your best bets for employment. Archaeological digs offer hard work for no pay; volunteers are generally welcome. Few Westerners study in Syria. Universities are state-run, so the curricula do not vary, but graduate students and lecturers can individualize their course of study to a degree. Contact the Syrian Embassy for assistance and information.

# ■ Specific Concerns

## WOMEN AND TRAVEL

Sense and sensitivity are the best means of avoiding threatening situations in all Middle Eastern countries. Locals are more accustomed to Western codes of dress in major cities and at tourist sites than in other places. Away from metropolitan areas in Egypt, Syria, Jordan, in the West Bank, and in both the Orthodox Jewish and Arab sections of Israel, however, it's advisable to emulate the dress and behavior of local women as much as possible. Modest dress (nothing sleeveless or tight, skirts and pants well below the knees) will allow you to travel more comfortably as a guest in another culture. Only on or very near the beaches of tourist resorts are locals used to seeing women in bathing suits. Don't smoke in public in Arab areas, and avoid sitting alone in cafés. In Islamist-controlled areas, covering your hair in public (with a head scarf) is wise. In general, however, no matter what you do short of dressing like a devout Muslim woman, you will be subjected to looks, comments, and perhaps even touching in crowded areas. Fortunately, it rarely goes further than that; violent attacks on foreign women are uncommon in the Middle East.

Men may not understand that you are irritated or angered by their pursuit. In some cases, the best answer to come-ons is none at all; avoiding eye contact will also reduce the chances of an uncomfortable situation. It may help to wear headphones (but stay aware), as men will be less likely to direct comments toward you if they think you can't hear them.

Passivity goes only so far. Sometimes it seems that the only way to get your point across is with a sharp rebuke. Some women may resort to a quick slap across the face. Most Middle Eastern men will turn into guilty-faced boys after being publicly confronted. Asking an older man for assistance may shame the offending parties into backing down. If a situation becomes genuinely threatening, don't be afraid to yell in any language to call attention to your situation. *Let's Go* lists emergency, police, and consulate phone numbers in most cities. Memorize them or carry them around with you, with change for the phone and enough extra money for a bus or taxi.

Israeli standards of dress are liberal even by Western standards; women will experience far less harassment there than in Arab countries. Egypt has lately grown more conservative than Jordan, Syria, the West Bank, and Arab parts of Israel. Women should not travel alone in Jordan (comments and whistles are common) or Syria.

Strolling arm in arm with another woman, a common Middle Eastern practice, may be helpful. Wearing a wedding ring is also smart, especially if you're traveling with a man, as unmarried intimacy between the sexes may be perceived as immoral.

Consider staying with religious organizations or in hostels with singles which lock from the inside. Forego cheaper places in remote areas of town in favor of youth hostels or more centrally located hotels. Choose train compartments occupied by other women or couples. It's best to bring along a male companion if you go on a *felucca* cruise. On public transportation, cover up when going from urban areas to tourist sights (such as Saqqara or Dendera in Egypt or Petra in Jordan). Once you arrive, you can peel off some portion of your coverings for relief from the heat. *Never* hitchhike—it's especially dangerous in Israel—and beware of cars that may be following you. In cabs, keep your luggage handy and the door unlocked.

Avoid walking alone in unpopulated areas: alleys, dark streets, and even isolated sights are best avoided. If you lose your way, ask other women or couples for directions. If you think you are being followed, walk quickly and confidently to the nearest public area. A whistle or an airhorn on your keychain is always useful. Avoid late-night treks. Consider enrolling in a **Model Mugging** course to learn how to be in tune with your surroundings and not as vulnerable (see **Safety and Security**, p. 17). Don't take unnecessary risks, but in spite of these precautions, don't lose your spirit of adventure. These books can offer more information and advice, and be sure to see individual country introductions.

**Handbook For Women Travelers** by Maggie and Gemma Moss. £8.99 from Piaktus Books, 5 Windmill St., London W1P 1HF (tel. (0171) 631 0710).

**A Journey of One's Own,** by Thalia Zepatos (Eighth Mountain Press US$17). The latest thing on the market, interesting and full of good advice, plus a specific and manageable bibliography of books and resources.

**Women Travel: Adventures, Advice & Experience** by Miranda Davies and Natania Jansz (Penguin, US$13). Info on specific foreign countries plus a decent bibliography and resource index. And the sequel *More Women Travel* is $15.

## OLDER TRAVELERS

**Senior citizens** are eligible for a wide range of discounts on transportation, museums, movies, theaters, concerts, restaurants, and accommodations. If you don't see a senior citizen price listed, ask and you may be delightfully surprised.

**National Council of Senior Citizens,** 1331 F St. NW, Washington, D.C. 20004 (202-347-8800). Memberships are US$12 a year, US$30 for three years, or US$150 for a lifetime. Individual or couple can receive hotel and auto rental discounts, a senior citizen newspaper, use of a discount travel agency, supplemental Medicare insurance (if you're over 65), and a mail-order prescription drug service.

**Pilot Books,** 103 Cooper St., Babylon, NY 11702 (tel. (516) 422-2225). Publishes a large number of helpful guides including *The International Health Guide for Senior Citizens* (US$5, postage US$2). Call or write for a complete list of titles.

## BISEXUAL, GAY, AND LESBIAN TRAVELERS

If open expressions of gay affection in Israel are uncommon, they are nonexistent in the rest of the Middle East. Israel (particularly Tel Aviv) is a world apart from its Arab neighbors in terms of the public and legal status of gays, lesbians, and bisexuals and the availability of gathering places and support organizations. Homosexuality is completely invisible in the Arab world, and they want it to stay that way. Public displays of affection are a bad idea for people of every sexual orientation. Behind closed doors (and everything in Arab countries occurs behind closed doors) is another story. There is *no* gay and lesbian assistance in Egypt, Jordan, or Syria. The only organization for gay and lesbian concerns in Israel is the **Society for the Protection of Personal Rights,** P.O. Box 376 04, Tel Aviv 61375 (tel. (03) 629 36 81; fax 525 23 41), or P.O. Box 3592, Haifa (tel. (04) 867 26 65). A community center, library, and coffee shop are located in the basement at 28 Naḥmani St., Tel Aviv. The society's gay and lesbian hotline is the **White Line** (Ha-Kav Ha-Lavan; tel. (03) 629 27 97; operates Sun.-Thurs. 7:30-11:30pm).

**International Gay Travel Association,** Box 4974, Key West, FL 33041 (tel. (800) 448-8550; fax (305) 296-6633; e-mail IGTA@aol.com; http://www.rainbow-mall.com/igta). An organization of over 1100 companies serving gay and lesbian travelers worldwide. Call for lists of travel agents, accommodations, and events.

**International Lesbian and Gay Association (ILGA),** 81 rue Marché-au-Charbon, B-1000 Bruxelles, Belgium (tel./fax 32-2-502-24 71; e-mail ilgaşilga.org). Provides political information, such as homosexuality laws of individual countries.

**Spartacus International Gay Guides** (US$32.95), published by Bruno Gmunder, Postfach 110729, D-10837 Berlin, Germany (tel. (30) 615 00 30; fax (30) 615-9134). Lists bars, restaurants, hotels, and bookstores around the world catering to gays. Also lists international gay hotlines and homosexuality laws for each country. Includes Egypt, Israel, Jordan, and Syria (US$29.95).

**Women Going Places** (Inland Book Company, US$14) A women's resource and travel guide emphasizing women-owned enterprises; geared toward lesbians.

## DISABLED TRAVELERS

Inform airlines and hotels of disabilities when making reservations; time may be needed to make arrangements. Travelers with seeing-eye dogs should inquire as to the quarantine policies of the destination country. The following services and resources can be invaluable in planning or researching trips with disabled travelers.

**Access Project (PHSP),** 39 Bradlet Gardens, West Ealing, London W13 8HE, England. Researched by persons with disabilities. They cover traveling, accommodations, access to sights and entertainment. Sells *Access in Israel* (£4).

**Flying Wheels Travel Service,** 143 W. Bridge St., Owatonne, MN 55060 (tel. (800) 535-6790; fax (507) 451-1685). Arranges international trips for groups and individuals in wheelchairs or with other sorts of limited mobility.

**Society for the Advancement of Travel for the Handicapped (SATH),** 347 Fifth Ave., #610, New York, NY 10016 (tel. (212) 447-7284; fax (212) 725-8253). Publishes quarterly travel newsletter *SATH News* and information booklets (free for members, US$13 each for nonmembers) with advice on trip planning for people with disabilities. Annual membership US$45, students and seniors US$25.

**Yad Sarah,** 43 Haneviim St., Jerusalem 95141 (tel. (02) 624 44 44; fax 624 44 93). With 76 branches throughout Israel, it is the country's largest volunteer organization. Free loan of medical and rehabilitative equipment, oxygen service and transport service for persons in wheelchairs. Call the English speaking P.R. director at least 2 weeks in advance to book airport pick-up and for help with special needs.

## TRAVELERS WITH CHILDREN

Family vacations are recipes for disaster—unless you slow your pace and plan ahead a bit. When deciding where to stay, remember the special needs of young children; if you pick a hostel, call to make sure it's child friendly. If you rent a car, make sure the rental company provides a car seat. Consider using a papoose-style device to carry your baby on walking trips.

Restaurants often have children's menus and discounts. Virtually all museums and tourist attractions also have a children's rate. Be sure that your child carries some sort of ID in case of an emergency, and arrange a reunion spot in case of separation.

Children under two generally fly for 10% of the adult airfare on international flights (this does not necessarily include a seat). International fares are usually discounted 25% for children from two to eleven.

## DIETARY CONCERNS

The Middle East is a vegetarian's delight, with widely available meatless dishes (including many street foods). See Life and Times: Food sections for each country.

Kosher restaurants abound in Israel, and many are listed in this book. Levels of *kashrut* are often visibly posted. The rules applied in Israeli kosher restaurants satisfy *halal* requirements, though travellers keeping kosher in Arab countries are generally restricted to vegivore fare.

# ■ Travel Etiquette

Standards of dress and behavior are much more conservative in the Arab world than in the West. Egypt, Jordan, Syria, and the West Bank all mix Western and traditional Arab dress. In Egypt, there are some liberal enclaves, though the rise of Islamic fundamentalism is moving less touristy areas in a conservative direction; Jordan and Syria are less liberal. Public behavior in all these areas should be reserved. Israel, except in some Arab and Jewish-Orthodox regions, is more liberal in its dress code than many Western countries. Consult the introductions to individual countries and cities for specific information about proper etiquette.

In holy places, modest dress is the norm. Do not visit sanctuaries during services unless you are worshipping, in which case you are always welcome. Remove your shoes before entering a mosque. Women should completely cover their hair in a mosque; men should cover their heads in a synagogue.

Photography is often forbidden in holy places, archaeological sites, and museums. It is absolutely forbidden at some military installations, border crossings, railroad stations, ports, airfields, and the Aswan High Dam.

# ■ Packing

Fashion is the least of your worries when trekking through the Sinai or uncovering the hidden treasures of Palmyra. The key is to dress modestly without irrigating the Holy Land with sweat. A general rule is to pack only what you absolutely need, then remove half the clothes and take twice the money.

Decide whether a backpack, light suitcase, or shoulder bag is most suitable for your travels. If you're planning to move around a lot, a sturdy **backpack** is hard to beat. A small **daypack** is indispensable for flights, sight-seeing, and holding your valuables. "Fanny-packs" look silly and are easily stolen.

**Natural fibers** clobber synthetics in the heat. Dark colors hide dirt, but light colors deflect sun. After a day in an oasis, a little dirt won't be a big deal. In Arab areas and any holy site, both men and women should cover their knees and upper arms to avoid offending local rules of **modesty** (see Travel Etiquette, above). Jeans are heavy and difficult to wash; take khakis or light cotton **trousers** instead. **Shorts** are okay in touristy areas. Bring one wool sweater (or something with Polartec) for cooler nights; wool is warmer and more lightweight than any jacket. Ba-aa-aa-aa-aa!

Appropriate shoes are vital: well-cushioned **sneakers** are good for walking. Lace-up leather shoes with firm grips provide better support and social acceptibilty than athletic shoes. For forays into the Sinai, a good pair of **hiking boots,** with good ventilation, is a must. A double pair of socks—light absorbent cotton inside and thick wool outside—will cushion feet, keep them dry, and help prevent blisters. If you only want to bring one pair, the best all-around footwear are **sneakers-cum-hiking boots**. Talcum powder in your shoes and on your feet can prevent sores, and moleskin is great for blisters. Break in your shoes before you leave home. You should also bring a comfortable pair of **sandals** for urban trekking in sweltering climes.

Laundromats are often hard to find, so washing clothes in your hotel sink is often a better option. Bring a small bar or tube of **laundry soap** (Dr. Bronner's castile soap, available in camping stores, serves as detergent, shampoo, toothpaste, and more!), a **rubber squash ball** to stop up the sink, and a travel clothes line. Also pack deodorant, razors, condoms, tampons (often impossible to find), re-hydration and constipation pills, and ibuprofen. **Contact lens** supplies are rare and expensive. Either bring enough saline, etc. for the entire trip or wear your glasses.

**Electric current** in Israel, Egypt, Jordan, and Syria is 220V. Travelers with appliances designed for 110V (North America) should bring a **converter.** Most outlets are made for round prongs, so even if your machine has a built-in converter you'll also need an **adapter** to change the plug shape. Get them both before you leave.

**Film** is generally more expensive abroad. Some foreign airport X-ray machines are film-safe and some are not—better to play it safe and protect your film with a special lead-lined bag available from any photo shop. (Or ask the sometimes unwilling security people to check it by hand.) It is always a good idea to bring along a **first-aid kit.** And finally, bring a small **towel;** hostels and inexpensive hotels don't provide them.

# GETTING THERE

## ■ Budget Travel Services

Common services include student rates on tickets, tours, maps and guides, travel gear, and ID cards (see **Youth, Student, & Teacher Identification,** p. 13)

**Council Travel** (http://www.ciee.org/cts/ctshome.htm), the travel division of Council, a full-service travel agency specializing in youth and budget travel. Railpasses, discount airfares, hosteling cards, guidebooks, budget tours, travel gear, and student (ISIC), youth (GO25), and teacher (ITIC) identity cards. Offices in Emory Village, 1561 N. Decatur Rd., **Atlanta,** GA 30307 (tel. (404) 377-9997); 2000 Guadalupe, **Austin,** TX 78705 (tel. (512) 472-4931); 273 Newbury St., **Boston,** MA 02116 (tel. (617) 266-1926); 1153 N. Dearborn, **Chicago,** IL 60610 (tel. (312) 951-0585); 10904 Lindbrook Dr., **Los Angeles,** CA 90024 (tel. (310) 208-3551); 205 E. 42nd St., **New York,** NY 10017 (tel. (212) 822-2700); 530 Bush St., **San Francisco,** CA 94108 (tel. (415) 421-3473); 4311½ University Way, **Seattle,** WA 98105 (tel. (206) 632-2448); 3300 M St. NW, **Washington, D.C.** 20007 (tel. (202) 337-6464). For other U.S. cities, call (800) 2-COUNCIL (226-8624). In the U.K., 28A Poland St. (Oxford Circus), **London,** W1V 3DB (tel. (0171) 437 7767).

**STA Travel,** 6560 Scottsdale Rd. #F100, Scottsdale, AZ 85253 (tel. (800) 777-0112 nationwide; fax (602) 922-0793). A student and youth travel organization with over 100 offices worldwide offering discount airfares for young travelers, railpasses, accommodations, tours, insurance, and ISICs. 16 offices in the U.S.; call for the nearest one. In the U.K., 6 Wrights Ln., **London** W8 6TA. In New Zealand, 10 High St., **Auckland** (tel. (09) 309 97 23). In Australia, 222 Faraday St., **Melbourne** VIC 3050 (tel. (03) 349 69 11).

**Let's Go Travel,** Harvard Student Agencies, 67 Mt. Auburn St., Cambridge, MA 02138 (800-5-LETS GO (553-8746) or 617-495-9649). HI-AYH memberships, ISICs, ITICs, FIYTO cards, guidebooks (including every *Let's Go*), maps, bargain flights, and a complete line of budget travel gear. All items available by mail; call or write for a catalog (or see the catalog in the center of this publication).

**Campus Travel,** 52 Grosvenor Gardens, London SW1W 0AG (http://www.campus-travel.co.uk.) 41 branches in the U.K. Student and youth fares on plane, train, boat, and bus travel. Flexible airline tickets. Discount and ID cards for youths, travel insurance for students and those under 35, and maps and guides. Puts out travel suggestion booklets. Telephone booking service: in North America call (0171) 730 2101; in Europe call (0171) 730 3402; worldwide call (0171) 730 8111; in Manchester call (0161) 273 1721; in Scotland (0131) 668 3303.

**Red Bear Tours,** Suite 11A, 401 St. Kilda R, Melbourne, Victoria 3004, Australia ((03) 98 67 38 88; fax 98 67 10 55; e-mail bmccunn@werple.mira.net.au). Specializes in independent arrangements for travel to Israel, Egypt, and Turkey.

**Travel CUTS (Canadian Universities Travel Services Limited):** 187 College St., Toronto, Ont. M5T 1P7 (tel. (416) 979-2406; fax 979-8167; e-mail mail@travelcuts).

Canada's national student travel bureau and equivalent of Council, with 40 offices across Canada. Also in the U.K., 295-A Regent St., **London** W1R 7YA (tel. (0171) 637 3161). Discounted international airfares open to all; special student fares to all destinations with valid ISIC. Issues ISIC, FIYTO, GO25, and HI hostel cards. Offers free *Student Traveller* magazine, as well as information on the Student Work Abroad Program (SWAP).

**WST Charters,** 65 Wigmore St., London W1H OJU (tel. (0171) 224 0504; fax 224 6142). Offers student and youth fares to destinations worldwide; sells ISIC. Specializes in charter flights to Israel and Egypt.

# ■ By Plane

Off-season travelers enjoy lower fares and a greater availability of inexpensive seats. Peak season rates begin around May and run until September. Peak season rates to Israel also apply around religious holidays. If you plan carefully, you can travel in summer and still save with shoulder- or low-season fares. An indirect flight via Brussels or Athens could cost considerably less than a direct flight.

Find a travel agent who specializes in the Middle East. Commissions are smaller on budget flights, so some agents may not have the initiative to search for the cheapest fare. The Sunday *New York Times* lists bargain fares, and student travel organizations (see above) often offer discounts. *The Airline Passenger's Guerrilla Handbook* (US$15; last published in 1990) is a more renegade resource. On the web, try the **Air Traveler's Handbook** (http://www.cis.ohio-state.edu/hypertext/faq/usenet/travel/air/handbook/top.html) for very complete information on air travel.

## COMMERCIAL AIRLINES

If you choose to fly with a commercial airline, you'll be paying for reliability and flexibility. You can't fly standby to Israel, Egypt, Jordan, or Syria. **Advanced Purchase Excursion (APEX) Fares,** commercial airlines' lowest regular rates, provide confirmed reservations and permit you to arrive in and depart from different cities. Reservations usually must be made seven to 21 days in advance with 7- to 14-day minimum and 30- to 90-day maximum stay. Beware hefty penalties for canceling or altering reservations. Also, be sure to ask for student, youth, or senior fares. You may have to wait until three days before departure to get these fares. Fares shown were compiled June to August 1996, from the airlines themselves, and are for mid-range round trips. Prices often vary within the peak three months; keep your eyes open.

**British Airways** (tel. (800) 247-9297). Round-trip London to Amman or Damascus US$569, to Tel Aviv US$1418, to Cairo US$765.

**Delta Airlines** (tel. (800) 241-4141). Round-trip NYC to Tel Aviv US$1130.

**EgyptAir** (tel. (800) 334-6787). Egypt's national airline. Round-trip New York City to Cairo US$1600 (student fare available). London to Cairo US$1100.

**El Al** (tel. (800) 223-6700). Israel's national airline. Round-trip New York City to Tel Aviv US$1019. Round-trip London to Tel Aviv US$540.

**KLM Royal Dutch Airlines** (tel. (800) 374-7747). Round-trip NYC-Amsterdam to Tel Aviv US$1130, to Amman US$1534, to Damascus US$1682, to Cairo US$1682.

**Middle East Air** (tel. (212) 664-7310). Round-trip London to Beirut US$550.

**Olympic Airways** (tel. (800) 223-1226). Round-trip Athens to Tel Aviv US$371.

**Royal Jordanian Airlines** (tel. (800) 223-0470). Jordan's national airline. Round-trip New York City to Amman US$1369. London to Amman US$888.

## AIRLINE TICKET CONSOLIDATORS

Ticket consolidators, also known as "bucket shops," resell unsold tickets on commercial and charter airlines. Look for their tiny ads in weekend papers (in the U.S., the Sunday *New York Times* is best), and start around. The benefits are many: cheap tickets, few maximum age or stay limits, extra flexibility, and no advance purchase requirements. But you won't be able to use your tickets on another flight if you miss yours, and you'll have to go back to the consolidator to get a refund, rather than the airline. Pay with a credit card so you can stop payment if you never receive your tickets. Insist on a **receipt** that gives full details about the tickets, refunds, and restrictions. If they don't want to give you one or just generally seem clueless or shady, use a different company. Kelly Monaghan's *Consolidators: Air Travel's Bargain Basement* (US$7 plus US$2 shipping) from the Intrepid Traveler, P.O. Box 438, New York, NY 10034 (e-mail intreptrav@aol.com), is an invaluable source for more information and lists of consolidators by location and destination. Cyber-resources include **World Wide** (http://www.tmn.com/wwwanderer/WWWa) and Edward Hasbrouck's incredibly informative **Airline ticket consolidators and bucket shops** (http://www.gnn.com/gnn/wic/wics/trav.97.html).

**Dollarwise Travel,** 7221 NW 12th St., Miami, FL 33126 (tel. (305) 592-3343), specializes in flights from the U.S. to the Middle East, and **Tourlite International,** 551 Fifth Ave., New York, NY 10176 (tel. (800) 272-7600), specializes in budget flights, and tours to the Mediterranean region. For a processing fee, depending on the number of travelers and the itinerary, **Travel Avenue**, Chicago, IL (tel. (800) 333-3335) will search for the lowest international airfare available and even give you a rebate on fares over US$300.

## CHARTER FLIGHTS

Charter flights offer consistently economical airfares. You may book them until the last minute, though summer flights fill up several months in advance. Later in the season, companies have empty seats and either offer special prices or cancel flights. Charters are more of a bargain in high season, because APEX fares (see Commercial Airlines, above) on commercial carriers are competitively priced in winter. Fares advertised in newspapers are usually the lowest possible, but you should always read the fine print. Charter flights allow you to stay abroad up to one year, and often let you "mix-and-match" arrivals and departures from different cities. Once you have made your plans, however, flexibility wanes. You must choose your departure and return dates when you book your flight, and if you cancel your ticket within two or three weeks of departure, you will lose some or all of your money. Travel insurance usually does not cover cancellations for reasons other than serious illness, natural disaster, or death.

Expect to be crowded and to spend at least part of your vacation exploring the majestic airports of the world. Companies reserve the right to cancel flights up to 48 hours before departure. Though they will do their best to find you another flight, the delay could be days, not just hours. The companies also reserve the right to add fuel surcharges even after you have made final payment. Charter companies often have messy reservations systems—pick up your ticket well before the departure date and arrive at the airport several hours early.

Charter coverage of the Middle East varies from year to year, so consult a travel agent for companies offering flights. Try **Interworld** (tel. (305) 443-4929); **Travac** (tel. (800) 872-8800) or **Rebel**, Valencia, CA (tel. (800) 227-3235).

# ■ By Bus, Train, or Ferry

**Buses** and **trains** can bring you from Northern Europe to ports along the Mediterranean where you can board ferries to Israel or Egypt. You can also go by bus from Europe to Syria and Jordan via Turkey. Buses from **Antakya** (Antioch) head to Aleppo, Damascus, and Amman.

Several **ferry lines** sail from Europe to Israel. Fares vary considerably, depending mainly on your tolerance for discomfort. Outdoor deck seats may cost as little as US$60-70 for a three-day trip, but clean bathrooms are hard to come by. More comfortable are the three- or four-berth inside cabins that companies offer at reduced student fares. The following sail between Greece and Haifa.

**Louis Cruise Lines, Ltd.: Greece:** 11 Mavrokordatou St., Piraeus 18538 (tel. (01) 429 14 23 or 14 24; fax 429 14 45). Operates the *Princesa Cypria* between Piraeus and Haifa, via Limassol, Cyprus, once per week. Prices start at around $100.
**Mano Passenger Lines, Ltd.: Israel:** 97 Ben-Yehuda St., Tel Aviv (tel. (03) 522 46 11; fax 522 45 99); 2 Sha'ar Palmer St., Haifa (tel. (04) 866 77 22; fax 866 76 66).
**Stability Line Caspi Ltd.: Israel:** 76 Ha'Atzma'ut Rd., P.O. Box 27, Haifa (tel. (04) 867 44 44; fax 867 44 56); 3 Yanai St., Jerusalem (tel. (02) 244 266); 1 Ben-Yehuda St., Tel Aviv (tel. (03) 510 6834; fax 660 989). **Greece:** 11 Sachtouri St., Piraeus (tel. (01) 413 2392 or 2395). Operates the *Vergina* between Piraeus and Haifa once per week April 2-Oct. 30.

# ONCE THERE

## ■ Border Crossings

Overland border crossing policies in the Middle East seem to change with the weather; check with government tourist offices for the latest information. As late as September 1996, Syria would not admit travelers with evidence of a visit to Israel in their passports. Israeli officials can give you a detachable visa stamp upon request. Egyptian and Jordanian entry stamps from borders with Israel may also keep you out of Syria.

In 1992, the U.S. State Department stopped issuing second passports valid only for travel to Israel. You can still obtain limited-duration (2-yr.) second passports: pick up the standard passport-by-mail form at your nearest federal building and send it in along with a detailed written statement explaining why you require a second pass-

port, your present passport, and $55. For more information, contact the Washington Passport Agency (see **Passports,** p. 6).

For all border crossings, we recommend that you have at least US$20 worth of the currency of each country involved, plus the same in U.S. currency. There are exchange facilities at most borders, but they could be closed or out of cash. For more information on border crossings, please see specific crossing sites: **Egypt to Israel and Jordan,** p. 263; **Israel to Egypt and Jordan,** p. 439 or p. 390; **Jordan to Egypt and Israel,** p. 507.

# ■ Accommodations

## HOSTEL ASSOCIATIONS

For millions of people worldwide, nothing spells budget travel like h-o-s-t-e-l. Some wouldn't spend a night in a hostel if their life depended on it, and some wouldn't stay anywhere else. Hostels are generally dorm-style rooms with bunk beds; some allow families and couples to have private rooms. Some offer kitchens, storage areas, laundry facilities, and bike or moped rentals. They may also close during daytime "lockout" hours, have curfews, require you to do chores (although this is less and less common), or impose a maximum stay. Prices range, on the whole, from US$5 to US$25 per night; affiliated hostels often have lower rates for members.

**Hostelling International (HI),** the universal trademark adopted by the International Youth Hostel Federation (IYHF), is the largest hostelling organization; look for the triangle. HI membership is almost never required in Middle Eastern hostels, but will get you a small discount. You need not be a youth. Travelers over 25 may pay a slight surcharge for a bed, while children under 12 may receive a discounted rate.

Most people get a membership card before they leave, since some hostels don't sell them on the spot. They are available from Council Travel and STA and from the hostelling organization of your own country. HI encourages visitors to make reservations ahead of time. If you have Internet access, check out the **Internet Guide to Hostelling** (http://hostels.com). Reservations for HI hostels can be made via the International Booking Network (IBN), a computerized system which allows you to book to and from HI hostels (more than 300 centers worldwide) months in advance for a nominal fee. Most countries have their own HI branch.

### Hostelling Membership

**An Óige (Irish Youth Hostel Association),** 61 Mountjoy St., Dublin 7 (tel. (01) 830 4555; fax 830 5808; http://www.touchtel.ie). One-year membership is IR£7.50, under 18 IR£4, family IR£7.50 for each adult, with children under 16 free.

**Australian Youth Hostels Association (AYHA),** Level 3, 10 Mallett St., Camperdown NSW 2050 (tel. (02) 565 1699; fax 565 1325; e-mail YHA@zeta.org.au). AUS$42, renewal AUS$26; under 18 AUS$12.

**Egyptian Youth Hostel Association,** 1 El-Ibrahimy St., Garden City, Cairo (tel. (02) 354 05 27 or 356 14 48; fax 355 03 29).

**Israel Youth Hostels Association (ANA),** 1 Shazar St., P.O. Box 6001, Jerusalem 91060 (tel. (02) 655 84 00; fax 655 84 30). Youth Travel Bureau organizes tours to Israel, Egypt, and Jordan. Write for *Israel on the Youth Hostel Trail.*

**Hostel Association of South Africa,** P.O. Box 4402, Cape Town 8000 (tel. (21) 419 1853; fax 216 937). Membership SAR45; Students SAR 30; Group SAR120; Family SAR90; Lifetime SAR225.

**Hostelling International-American Youth Hostels (HI-AYH),** 733 15th St. NW, Suite 840, Washington, D.C. 20005 (202-783-6161; fax 783-6171; http://www.taponline.com/tap/travel/hostels/pages/hosthp.html). Maintains 34 offices in the U.S. 1-yr. HI memberships: adults US$25; under 18 US$10; over 54 US$15; and US$35 for family cards. Available at many travel agencies, local Council offices, and the national office in DC.

**Hostelling International-Canada (HI-C),** 400-205 Catherine St., Ottawa, Ontario K2P 1C3, Canada (tel. (613) 237-7884; fax 237-7868). Canada-wide membership/

customer service line (800) 663-5777. Membership fees: 1-yr., under 18 CDN$12; 1-yr., over 18 CDN$25; 2-yr., over 18 CDN$35; lifetime CDN$175.

**Scottish Youth Hostels Association (SYHA),** 7 Glebe Crescent, Stirling FK8 2JA (tel. (01786) 45 11 81; fax 45 01 98). Membership UK£6, under 18 UK£2.50.

**Youth Hostels Association of England and Wales (YHA),** Trevelyan House, 8 St. Stephen's Hill, St. Albans, Hertfordshire AL1 2DY, England (tel. (01727) 855215; fax 844 126). Enrollment fees are: UK£9.30; under 18 UK£3.20; UK£9.30 per parent with children under 18 enrolled free; UK£125.00 for lifetime membership.

**Youth Hostels Association of New Zealand (YHANZ),** P.O. Box 436, 173 Gloucester St., Christchurch 1 (tel. (643) 379 99 70; fax 365 44 76; e-mail hostel.operations@yha.org.nz; http://yha.org.nz/yha). Annual membership fee NZ$24.

**Youth Hostels Association of Northern Ireland (YHANI),** 22 Donegall Rd., Belfast BT12 5JN, Northern Ireland (tel. (01232) 315 435; fax 439 699). Annual memberships UK£7, under 18 UK£3, family UK£14 for up to 6 children.

## ALTERNATIVE ACCOMMODATIONS

Many **colleges and universities** open their residence halls when school is not in session—some do so even during term-time. These are popular with many travelers, especially those looking for long-term lodging, so reserve ahead. The following programs can help you find other budget accommodations for longer stays.

**Barclay International Group,** 150 West 52nd Street, New York, NY 10022 (tel. (800) 845-6636 or (212) 832-3777; fax (212) 753-1139), arranges hotel alternative accommodations (apartment, condo, cottage, b&b or villa rentals) in Israel. Most are equipped with kitchens, telephones, TV, concierge and maid service. Rentals are pricey (at least $500/week off-season), but cheaper than comparably-serviced hotels. Good for families, businesspeople, or Kosher or vegetarian travelers.

**Hometours International, Inc.**, P.O. Box 11503, Knoxville, TN 37939 (tel. (800) 367-4668; e-mail hometours̨aol.com), offers lodging in apartments, houses, villas, and castles in Israel. Brochures are US$5.

**Intervac U.S., International & USA Home Exchange**, PO Box 590504, San Francisco, CA 94159 (tel. (415) 435-3497; fax 435-7440; e-mail IntervacUS@aol.com). Part of a worldwide home-exchange network. Publishes 4 catalogs per year, containing more than 9000 homes in 34 countries on 6 continents. Members contact each other directly. US$70 gets you three of the company's catalogs and inclusion of your own listing in one.

## CAMPING

Camping in the Middle East can be an incredibly rich, rewarding experience. It can also be prohibitively difficult and dangerous. Sleeping under the wide-open desert sky, on top of a temple mount, or amid a lush oasis could be the most memorable parts of your travels. To make sure that they're memorable for the right reasons, plan ahead. The right **equipment** and up-to-date information from rangers or other travelers are imperative.

The three most important things to remember when hiking or camping: stay warm, stay dry, and stay hydrated. The vast majority of life-threatening wilderness problems stem from a failure to follow this advice. If you are going on any hike, overnight or just a day hike, that will take you more than one mile from civilization, you should pack enough equipment to keep you alive should disaster befall. This includes rain gear, warm layers (wool or synthetic, not cotton!) especially a hat and mittens, a first-aid kit, high energy food, and water.

Your camping list will depend heavily on the duration and destination of your trip, but some essentials should be toted by everybody: a **frame backpack** for any trip longer than an overnight; a Swiss Army knife; a **hat; matches;** a **sleeping bag** rated to the temperature of the coldest night you might encounter; calamine lotion, snake bite medicine, and lotion for sunburns; a sturdy pair of **hiking boots;** and a camel's worth of **water** *and* **water-purification tablets.** Some other items to consider include a tent, a stove, a plastic groundcloth, a flashlight, and insect repellent.

# ▓ Keeping in Touch

## MAIL

Mail can be sent internationally through **poste restante** (the international phrase for General Delivery) to most cities and towns; it's well worth using and more reliable than you might think. Mark the envelope "HOLD" and address it, for example, "Sybil WATKINS, *Poste Restante*, City, Country." The last name should be capitalized and underlined. The mail will go to a special desk in the central post office, unless you specify a post office by street address or postal code. As a rule, it is best to use the largest post office in the area; sometimes, mail will be sent there regardless of what you write on the envelope.

It helps (though is not imperative) to use the appropriate translation of *Poste Restante*. When picking up your mail, bring your passport or other ID. If the clerks insist that there is nothing for you, have them check under your first name as well. *Let's Go* lists post offices in the Practical Information section for each city and denotes which offices will hold mail.

**American Express** offices throughout the world will hold mail for members (and often non-members) if you contact them in advance. Under this free **"Client Letter Service,"** they will hold mail for 30 days, forward upon request, and accept telegrams. The last name of the person to whom the mail is addressed should be capitalized and underlined (see **Traveler's Checks,** p. 14).

If regular airmail is too slow, there are a few alternatives. **International Express Mail Service (EMS)** is operated by national postal services, providing relatively quick deliveries at reasonable rates. It is available throughout the Middle East. For faster (and more expensive) delivery, you can use one of the private companies. Try **DHL** (tel. (2) 317 83 00 in Australia, (800) 225-5345 in Canada and the U.S., (1) 844 41 11 in Ireland, (9) 636 50 00 in New Zealand, (11) 921 36 00 in South Africa, and (181) 818 80 00 in the U.K.) or **Federal Express** (800) 463-3339 in the US and Canada. FedEx will get a letter from Cairo to New York in three days for a whopping US$43.88, or from New York to Cairo in four days for $32.50.

**Aerogrammes,** printed sheets that fold into envelopes and travel via airmail, are available at post offices. They should be marked *par avion*. Airmail between the Middle East and the U.S. or Europe usually takes about two weeks. Allow *at least* two weeks for Australia and New Zealand.

**Surface mail** is by far the cheapest and slowest way to send mail. It takes one to three months to cross the Atlantic, appropriate for sending large quantities of items you won't need to see for a while. When ordering books and materials from abroad, always include a few **International Reply Coupons (IRCs)**—a way of providing the postage to cover delivery. They're available from your post office (US$1.05).

## TELEPHONES

You can usually make direct international calls from **pay phones,** but you may need to drop your coins as quickly as your words. In some countries, pay phones are card-operated, and some even accept major credit cards. Be wary of more expensive, private pay phones and insidious in-room hotel phones.

Operators in most countries will place **collect calls** for you. It's cheaper to find a pay phone and deposit just enough money to be able to say "Call me" and give your number (though some pay phones can't receive calls).

Some companies, seizing upon this "call-me-back" concept, have created callback phone services. Under these plans, you call a specified number, ring once, and hang up. The company's computer calls back and gives you a dial tone. You can then make as many calls as you want, at rates about 20-60% lower than you'd pay using credit cards or pay phones. This option is most economical for loquacious travelers, as services may include a US$10-25 per month minimum. Call **America Tele-Fone** (tel. (800) 321-5817), **Globaltel** (tel. (770) 449-1295), **International Telephone** (tel. (800) 638-5558), and **Telegroup** (tel. (800) 338-0225).

A **calling card** is another, cheaper alternative; your local long-distance phone company provides you an access number (either toll-free or charged as a local call) to connect instantly to an operator in your home country. The calls (plus a small surcharge) are then billed either collect or to a calling card. For more information, call **AT&T** about its **USADirect** and **World Connect** services (tel. (800) 331-1140, from abroad (412) 553-7458), **Sprint** (tel. (800) 877-4646), or **MCI WorldPhone** and **World Reach** (tel. (800) 996-7535). MCI's WorldPhone also provides access to MCI's Traveler's Assist, which gives legal and medical advice, exchange rate information, and translation services. For similar services for countries outside the U.S., contact your local phone company. In Canada, contact Bell Canada **Canada Direct** (tel. (800) 565 4708); in the U.K., British Telecom **BT Direct** (tel. (800) 34 51 44); in Ireland, Telecom Éireann **Ireland Direct** (tel. (800) 250 250); in Australia, Telstra **Australia Direct** (tel. 13 22 00); in New Zealand, **Telecom New Zealand** (tel. 123); and in South Africa, **Telkom South Africa** (tel. 09 03).

## OTHER COMMUNICATION

Domestic and international **telegrams,** are slower than phone but faster than post, arriving in one to two days. **Faxes** are cheaper and more immediate. You can pay to send or receive faxes in most cities across the Middle East.

Daily newspapers including the *London Times,* the *Wall Street Journal* (International Edition), the *New York Times* and the *International Herald Tribune* are available at train stations and kiosks in major cities in the Middle East. *The Economist* and international versions of *Time* and *Newsweek* are also easy to find.

If you're spending a year abroad and want to keep in touch with friends or colleagues in a college or research institution, or simply are addicted to the blinking cursor of the cyber-world, **electronic mail (e-mail)** is an attractive option. Befriend college students as you go and ask if you can use their e-mail accounts, or search through http://www.easynet.co.uk/pages/cafe/ccafe.htm to find a list of cybercafes around the world from which you can drink a cup of joe and e-mail him, too. Another possibility is **America Online,** 8615 Westwood Center Drive, Vienna, VA 22070 (tel. (800) 827-6364). The interactive computer service now offers "GLOBALnet," making it possible for American net-junkies to access the internet, sexy chat rooms, and of course e-mail through their home accounts while travelling in 70 countries (though not Syria or Jordan), for a US$6-12 per hour surcharge. GLOBALnet only works on computers with AOL software already installed, so to use the service you must travel with your own portable computer or install the software on computers as you go and log on as a guest.

# INTRODUCTION TO THE REGION

## ■ History

### ANCIENT EGYPT

Around 7000 BCE, hunter-gatherers from the increasingly arid Sahara began to settle in the Nile valley. Divided into regional nomes (separate autonomous chiefdoms), the earliest Egyptians developed a variety of relatively advanced cultures and religions. Ancient Egyptian legend tells of King Menes, who conquered Lower (northern) Egypt, uniting it with Upper (southern) Egypt, founding one of the most powerful and lasting civilizations of history. The actual task was probably accomplished by Narmer, who conquered the Delta region from Upper Egypt around 3000 BCE before being eaten by a hippo.

The first two dynasties of pharaohs (the Early Dynastic Period) ruled from Abydos. Their successors, the pharaohs of the Old Kingdom (c. 2650-2150 BCE) built a new capital, Memphis, around 2600 BCE. Successive pharaohs oversaw the construction of complicated irrigation systems and grandiose monuments using only the manual skills of conscripted peasants. Many, including the ancient Egyptians themselves, have viewed this era as the apex of ancient Egyptian civilization. The Old Kingdom elite exploited the faith and labor of the peasantry to live lives of unrestrained hedonism. The all-powerful pharaohs (who were seen as embodiments of the god Horus) feared only death; their most magnificent monuments represent attempts to defeat this all-powerful enemy. Two generations after the first step pyramid was built at Saqqara, the pharaohs were organizing skilled builders and tens of thousands of laborers to build the classic, smooth-sided pyramids. At a time when even China had scarcely emerged from the Stone Age, Egyptians had invented writing and papyrus, formed a national economy, traded with Canaan and Lebanon, recorded the regnal years of eight dynasties of pharaohs, and were crafting extraordinarily creative ivory and metal art along with a few of humanity's most impressive monumental structures.

The absolute authority of the pharaoh began to wane by the 20th century BCE and the Old Kingdom drew to an end as local governors regained power. The increasing fragmentation was aggravated by drought, bankruptcy, and the long-lived Pepi II, whose death ended pharaonic rule. After a century of feuding, famine, and disorder (the First Intermediate Period), the princes of Thebes conquered and centralized the whole kingdom. Mentuhotep II of Thebes became the first pharaoh of the 11th dynasty, establishing the Middle Kingdom (approx. 2040-1786 BCE).

During the Middle Kingdom, contact with the southern kingdoms of Nubia and Kush spawned subsidiary pharaonic cultures. In Egypt itself, conservatism and order reigned supreme; the Old Kingdom was considered to have been a Golden Age destroyed by innovation, while the First Intermediate Period was seen as an awful, chaotic disruption of an "eternal" order of totalitarian rule by the god-pharaoh (see ma'at, p. 58). Internal political rivalries weakened the Egyptian dynasties in the 18th century. Around 1650 BCE, the Hyksos rode in from Asia on their chariots, conquered Egypt, and established the 15th and 16th dynasties. Upon the expulsion of the Hyksos by the ever-plotting Theban princes almost a century later, Egypt was resuscitated as the New Kingdom (approx. 1550-1075 BCE).

The capital at Thebes became the center of a theocratic police state. The high priests of the sun (now embodied in the god Amun) wielded exorbitant power, often controlling the pharaoh himself. Egypt "modernized" its formerly primitive army, adapting the bronze weapons and chariots of the Hyksos, and invaded Africa, Palestine, and Syria. Now an empire ruled by warrior kings, Egypt established control over the eastern Mediterranean. Trade in wood, olive oil, and slaves brought stability and prosperity to Egypt, though the rivalry between the pharaoh and the priests of Amun often brought disruption.

Despite the achievements of aggressive pharaohs like Thutmosis III and Ramses II, the New Kingdom slowly crumbled. The competition between temple and state was won by the priests of Amun, and the state collapsed around 1075 BCE. Lower Egypt was ruled by dynasties centered in the Delta, while Thebes became the theocratic center of Upper Egypt. After a last-ditch attempt by the conservative Kushites (Ethiopians in Sudan) to re-establish centralized Egyptian authority, the Assyrians (670 BCE), followed by the Persians (525 BCE), pounced "like wolves on the fold."

The Persian dynasty interrupted pharaonic rule and was, despite a policy of social non-interference, deeply loathed. For the next 200 years the Egyptians struggled to overthrow the Persians; periodically succeeding, only to be subjugated again. When Alexander the Great arrived in 332 BCE, he was received as a liberator. After ousting the Persians, he set off for the oracle of Amun in the distant Siwa Oasis. There, he was promptly declared the Son of Amun and the legitimate pharaoh of Egypt. But after dutifully founding another Alexandria, the new pharaoh went on his way and never returned. Upon Alexander's death the empire broke up and his general Ptolemy took control of Egypt, becoming the pharaoh Ptolemy, Son of God (see p. 58). Alexandria swelled into a cosmopolitan center of trade and learning; its 500,000-volume library contained all of the Greeks' knowledge under one roof.

In 48 BCE, more than a century after Rome made its first, tentative overtures to the ever-feuding Ptolemies, Julius Caesar came to Egypt and fell captive to the allure of Cleopatra VII, Queen of Egypt. Cleopatra, facing challenges from other claimants to the throne, accepted an alliance with Caesar that left her secure—until his assassination four years later. Sensing danger as well as opportunity, Cleopatra conspired with Marc Antony, one of three successors vying to succeed Caesar. Although these events sparked one of history's most celebrated love affairs, Roman third wheel Octavian grabbed the empire for himself, ruthlessly crushing the affair and the Ptolemaic dynasty in 30 BCE.

Political stability and an increasingly entrenched bureaucracy characterized the Egypt of Imperial Rome and then Byzantium. During this period, Egypt was the breadbasket of the Mediterranean, supplying most of the grain needed to support the empire's growing urban population. In 451 CE, not quite two centuries after the Byzantine emperors adopted and promoted Christianity, the Coptic Church split from the church of Constantinople due to doctrinal differences.

## THE ANCIENT LEVANT

An important trade route between Egypt and Mesopotamia, the Levant was periodically conquered by both, as well as by the charioteering Hyksos and Hittites. The Bible begins the recorded history of the area with the story of Abraham, the first of the Patriarchs. The semi-nomadic Amorite tribes' migration to Palestine almost four thousand years ago has been linked with the biblical tradition of Abraham's (Avraham in Hebrew, Ibrahim in Arabic) journey from Chaldea (Genesis 12). These Semitic-speaking people were the ancestors of the people of Palestine. Meticulous Egyptian records (a rarity today) attest to the existence of a troublesome people known as the 'Apiru, who were possibly the ancestors of the Hebrews. These semi-nomads frequently troubled Canaan's Egyptian-controlled kings, who pleaded to their overlords for help in the 14th century.

Whether or not the 'Apiru became the Israelites remains a mystery. Some theorize that the Israelites were highlanders who united in opposition to the urban, valley-dwelling Canaanite traders. Others believe that the Israelites were forced from the coastal area by the invading "sea peoples" in the 13th-century BCE. The invaders, now believed to be the descendants of the Myceneans of Greece, became known as the Philistines. Their cities included the ports of Gaza, Ashkelon, and Jaffa.

Whatever their origins, evidence shows that the scattered tribes of the Judean and Galilean hills began interacting around 1200 BCE. The next two centuries are known as the Period of Judges. Local leaders, Gideon and Samuel among them, united the Israelite tribes under a new god, Yahweh, to fight off the encroaching Egyptians, Canaanites, and Philistines. Possibly inspired by the arrival of Semitic brethren from Egypt (the Exodus), the Israelites managed to establish their own kingdom under Saul at the end of the 11th century BCE.

The Israelite kingdom reached its peak during the reign of Saul's successor, David, and that of David's son, Solomon. The construction of the Temple of Jerusalem is considered Solomon's most formidable feat, but the cost of the Temple and other civil projects proved a heavy burden for his subjects. After Solomon's death in 922 BCE, social and political unrest split the empire into the Kingdom of Israel in the north, which was never particularly happy to be ruled by Jerusalem-centric southerners, and the Kingdom of Judah in the south. Philistia had been reduced to a small coastal strip around Gaza, though the Phoenicians, a sea-faring people from the area between Akko and Tartus, prospered from the decline of the Egyptian Empire.

The Assyrians conquered Phoenicia and Israel in the late 8th century BCE. The ten tribes of northern Israel were taken into captivity and never returned. Judah was made a vassal state of the Assyrian empire until the Assyrians themselves were crushed by the Babylonians. The Babylonian king Nebuchadnezzar conquered Judah, razed the Temple, burned Jerusalem, and deported many Jews to Mesopotamia (the Babylonian Captivity or Exile) in 587 BCE. When the Persians defeated Nebuchadnezzar's successor some 50 years later, King Cyrus permitted the Jews to return to Jerusalem and to build the Second Temple. The Israelites prospered intellectually and economically under the Persians, although an increasing Greek presence, especially in Philistia, encouraged Alexander the Great to conquer the region in 333 BCE. His heirs, the Ptolemies, succeeded in 323 BCE.

The Syrian-based Seleucids displaced the Ptolemies in 198 BCE and attempted to Hellenize the Jews. Judas Maccabeus, responding to the persecutions of Antiochus IV, led a revolt of the Jewish lower-classes. Victorious, the Maccabees resanctified the Temple in 164 BCE and founded the Hasmonean Dynasty. In spite of potent internal conflict, the Hasmonean Dynasty ruled Palestine for over a century.

The Nabateans, originally a nomadic Arab tribe, made their way into the area south of the Dead Sea around the 2nd century BCE, taking advantage of the enmity between the Ptolemies and the Seleucids to establish their hold on those lands and emerging as an independent kingdom by about 169 BCE. The Nabateans also interacted with the Hasmoneans, sometimes as allies, sometimes as enemies, and took control of at least a part of the Red Sea trade route, which proved to be an important source of income. With Petra (in modern Jordan) as its capital, the Nabatean kingdom continued to flourish, even when it became a Roman client state in the first century CE. In 106 CE, the Roman emperor Trajan was finally able to conquer Petra. He abolished the kingdom and reorganized its territories into a Roman province.

In 63 BCE, the Roman general Pompey swept in, secured much of modern-day Israel, and ruled via Herod the Great. The territory was made into a Roman province (Judea) in 44 CE. Jerusalem rebelled in 65-6 CE. In 70 CE the Roman general Titus, faced with the choice of sparing the Temple at great military cost or burning Jerusalem, chose to save his men and burned the Temple with the rest of Jerusalem. Three years later the Romans captured the last Jewish stronghold at Masada (see page 416). The Romans exiled the majority of the population, dispersing them throughout the empire. The reconquered province was dubbed Palestine (after the Philistines).

The Decapolis, a loose association of trading cities, thrived as allies of Rome in what is now north Jordan and south Syria. These Hellenistic cities, which included Gerasa (Jerash) and Philadelphia (Amman), shared a common culture and heritage as well as commercial and security interests.

With the division of the empire into Latin West and Byzantine East in 330 CE, Palestine came under the supervision of Constantinople. Although little changed administratively, the adoption of Christianity by the Emperor Constantine in 331 created increased interest in what to many was the "Holy Land." Led by proto-pilgrim St. Eleni (Constantine's mother), pilgrims and devout financiers built churches and endowed monasteries and schools. The Ghassanids, a Christian Arab client state in northern Syria, acted as a buffer between Palestine and Persia. Behind the frontier, political stability, disrupted only during the Samaritans' revolt in 529 and a brief Persian invasion a few decades later, fostered a new sense of prosperity in the region.

## THE RULE OF THE CALIPHS

After the death of the Prophet Muhammad in 632 CE, Bedouin armies, inspired by Islam and the prospect of substantial booty, ventured outside their traditional strongholds in central Arabia and, by 642, had conquered Mesopotamia, Palestine, Syria, Persia, and Egypt. The Egyptians, tired of Byzantine taxation and religious rigidity, appreciated the Arabs' relative tolerance, if not Islam itself.

Muhammad's death had given rise to political confusion, as he had designated no successor. Amid vigorous debate as to whether the successor had to be a blood relative, Abu Bakr, confidante and father-in-law of Muhammad, was chosen as the first successor (*khalifa*, or caliph). Ruling from 632-34, he was followed by Omar (634-44), Uthman (644-56), and finally Ali (656-61), all based in Medina. The election of Ali, the Prophet's nephew and son-in-law, incited a civil war and produced a lasting schism in Islam between the Sunni (the "orthodox," who believe that the caliph should be chosen by the community of believers), and the Shi'i (those who supported Ali's claim and who believe that the caliph should be a direct descendant of the prophet). This division notwithstanding, the first four caliphs are known to most Muslims as the Rashidun (the Rightly Guided Caliphs). With the advent of the Umayyad Dynasty, founded by the Caliph Mu'awiya in Damascus in 661, Shi'i opposition was crushed and a Sunni hereditary caliphate (unrelated to the Prophet) was installed. Eighty years later, the Islamic world stretched from Narbonne to Samarkand. By 750, when the 'Abbasids overthrew the Umayyads on charges of decadence and impiety, the majority of the peasantry had converted to Islam. A mammoth bureaucracy, operating out of Baghdad and composed of everything from tax officials to scribes to Islamic jurists *(ulama)*, helped run the empire.

Successive 'Abbasid caliphs, usually based in Baghdad, were never without challenges; the rival Umayyad family had established a potentially troublesome dynasty in Spain, while various Shi'a dynasties flourished on the borders of the 'Abbasid empire. The Shi'a Fatimids, attacking eastward from their domain in Tunisia, expelled the 'Abbasids from Egypt in 969. They established Cairo as their new capital to replace the old 'Abbasid center, Fustat. By 977, the Fatimids had captured most of Palestine, controlled Jerusalem, and were prospering through trade. It was the Fatimid Caliph Al Hakim who broke the long-established trend of Muslim toleration of other faiths and destroyed the Church of the Holy Sepulchre.

Europe's internal violence and economic prosperity, and rumors of Seljuk policies regarding the treatment of Christian pilgrims prompted western Europeans to launch a series of Crusades aimed at the recapture of the Holy Land. Impelled by desires for land, power, and heavenly reward, Crusaders wrought havoc. Massacring the Muslim and Jewish inhabitants of Jerusalem in 1099, the Crusaders established a feudal kingdom under Godfrey I and then Baldwin I. Consistently out-numbered and out-classed, the second and third Crusades were choked at the hands of the Zengids of Damascus and Salah ad-Din (a Kurd), founder of the short-lived Ayyubid Dynasty (1171-1250). Salah ad-Din dethroned the Fatimids in 1192 with a vast army of Turkish slaves *(mamluks)*. The fourth through seventh Crusades did little good to anyone but the Venetians, who thrived on trade with the Middle East. The Crusader States fell one by one, Edessa in 1144, Jerusalem in 1187, Acre in 1291. The Crusaders did, however, manage to capture Christian Byzantium in 1204.

Although Salah ad-Din's victories over the Crusaders made him a hero among his people, his finely disciplined slave armies became a scourge for his successors. Chosen as youths, then trained and equipped by the palace, the Mamluks were technically property of the Sultan (secular leader) but their collective strength threatened the Sultan's authority, which was often tenuous at best. In 1250, 'Izz al-Din, a Mamluk of the Bahri clan, resolved to dispense with formality as well as the Ayyubids and rule the sultanate directly. Chronic instability and infighting followed. Lifestyles for those at the top were still lavish; life expectancies, however, decreased dramatically. By 1291, Mamluks controlled all of the former Crusader outposts, including Acre, Shobak, and Montfort. They even managed to stop the Mongols at 'Ayn Jalut (1260), though the Horde had already sacked Baghdad and destroyed the 'Abbasid Caliphate (1258), as well as taken Aleppo and Damascus (both in 1260).

## THE OTTOMAN CENTURIES

When the Ottoman Empire, expanding out from Anatolia, gained formal sovereignty over Egypt and Palestine in the early part of the 16th century, Mamluks still retained most of their political power. But via appointments, bribery, and assassination, the Ottoman sultans maintained real and effective control. Manipulating their local "representatives" and playing them against one another, the Ottoman rulers enjoyed seemingly indelible authority.

When the gates of Vienna stood against Ottoman armies in 1683, the Ottomans began worrying about the fate of their increasingly decrepit empire. While European nation states had grown more and more powerful, the Ottoman Empire had languished. The animated ports of Syria, Palestine, and Egypt had once provided the sole access to the East; now, they were relegated to insignificance as Portuguese sailors finagled their way around the Horn of Africa. Egypt's economy—for two centuries buttressed by the Arabian and Yemeni coffee trade—collapsed when European investors cultivated their own, cheaper coffee in the Java islands and, turning the tables, sold it to Cairene merchants. At the same time, the Spanish discovery of the New World created opportunities for seemingly limitless economic expansion. The once-formidable Ottoman Empire became "the sick man of Europe."

Napoleon's successful 1798 invasion of Egypt surprised even the grumpiest European pessimist. The French occupation of Egypt, although a failure, marked the first intrusion of modern European colonialism into the Middle East. Upon the withdrawal of the French army in 1801, resurgent Mamluks sought to regain former prerogative. An Ottoman general, Muhammad Ali (who ruled 1805-1848), stepped in to prevent this. Born in Greece to an Albanian couple in 1769, Muhammad Ali had served in the Turkish campaign against the French occupation of Egypt and had fought Napoleon's forces in the battle of Abu Kir. In 1805, he took over after the Egyptian revolt against the Turkish *Wali*, crushing his rivals in a bloody, invitation-only dinner party at the Citadel in Cairo. Building upon the administrative apparatus left by the French, Muhammad Ali modernized the civil service, created a regular tax system, and appropriated the vast feudal estates of his Mamluk enemies. He also laid the foundations of the modern Egyptian state, sparked the Europeanization of the country, introduced education in the arts and sciences, and paved the way for an independent dynasty. In lieu of buying more potentially rebellious slaves, Muhammad Ali conscripted peasants to stock his army. Those who managed to avoid the army labored under watch to build a new, massive irrigation network indispensable to the modernization of Egyptian agriculture.

Naturally, a resurgent Egypt led by a nominally faithful "servant" disturbed the Ottoman sultan. Avoiding direct confrontation, the sultan ordered Muhammad Ali to send Egypt's armies to face a Wahhabi revolt in central Arabia and, shortly thereafter, a Greek revolt. The dramatic Greek victory enraged Muhammad Ali far more than it weakened him. By the late 1830s, his violent forays into Palestine, Syria, Lebanon, and Arabia left him with more of the Ottoman Empire than the sultan himself controlled. But when Muhammad Ali began to march on Istanbul—his armies reached central Turkey—France and Britain threatened to intervene to preserve the balance of power. Muhammad Ali was forced to withdraw to Egypt. The Ottoman sultan responded by granting the Europeans unrestricted access to Egypt's markets but at the same time recognized Muhammad Ali and his descendants as Khedives (hereditary rulers) of Egypt.

Egypt's situation did not improve much under Muhammad Ali's successors, despite the Ottoman Empire's attempts at reforms (the *tanzimat*). Economic and political crises went unabated. Modernization of the economy (and financing the Egyptian rulers' trips to foreign spas) left Egypt indebted to British and French bankers. At the same time, the developing strategic interest in the newly completed Suez Canal made it a focus for British, French, and German foreign ministers.

The Egyptian government's declaration of bankruptcy and stirrings in the Egyptian army prompted the British to send an expeditionary force, which captured Egypt in 1882, defeating the out-gunned Khedieval forces in Alexandria. Although the Egyptian Khedive remained on the throne, all decisions were made by the British Consul General Lord Cromer (alias Evelyn Baring, or "Lord Over-Bearing") who dominated Egypt for almost three decades. Lord Cromer monitored Egyptian finances with a tight fist, salaried the Khedive and the royal family, and made it his task to ensure full payment to British investors. To learn more about Egyptian and Arabic history, read Albert Hourani's masterpiece *A History of the Arab Peoples.*

## THE RISE OF ZIONISM AND THE BRITISH MANDATE

Although small Jewish communities were present in Palestine over the 18 centuries following the Roman exile, the vast majority of the world's Jews existed in diaspora communities in Europe, the Middle East, North Africa, and, more recently, the Americas. Throughout this period, Jews maintained the hope of someday returning to and rebuilding the ancient homeland. This hoped-for future was termed "the ingathering of the exiles" (*Kibbutz Gluyot* in Hebrew) and became the focus of the modern political movement of Zionism among European Jews in the late nineteenth and early twentieth centuries.

After centuries of persecution, Jews in many European countries were eventually emancipated in the 19th century. Exposed to various contemporary European political movements, some Jews flocked to the banner of revolutionary socialism while others preached complete assimilation. A third group was inspired by nationalism and, unconvinced that European nations would accept Jews as full citizens, preached a Jewish return to Zion (a biblical synonym for Israel).

In 1882, a group of Jews made *aliya* (or "going up," the term for Jewish immigration to Israel) to the Holy Land, forming agricultural settlements based on private land ownership (*moshavim*). Many were sponsored by Parisian Baron Edmund de Rothschild. In 1896, Austrian journalist Theodore Herzl, who had witnessed the Dreyfus trial, published a pamphlet entitled *The Jewish State,* prophesying the establishment of a Jewish homeland as the answer to Jewish persecution. This had been proposed in such earlier works as Leo Pinsker's *Auto-Emancipation,* but never before had a secular, pro-Enlightenment Jew like Herzl articulated such ideas. Herzl initially considered Uganda and South America as sites for the Jewish state. Only the Holy Land, however, had the emotional lure necessary to bring the Diaspora Jews.

The second *aliya* (1904-1914) witnessed the development of cooperative agricultural settlements (kibbutzim), led by Jews who shared the socialist principles, sense of urgency, and nationalism needed to sustain the Zionist movement. Zionists acted in two directions: "Political Zionism" sought to gain international support for the establishment of a Jewish state while "Practical Zionism" sought to build up the Jewish community in Palestine and to develop its economic infrastructure.

During World War I, the British government, at war with the German-allied Ottomans, conducted secret and separate negotiations with both the Arabs and the Zionists to enlist their help. To obtain Arab support, Britain pledged, in 1915-16 correspondence between Sharif Hussein of Mecca (of the Hashemite family) and British High Commissioner in Egypt, Sir Henry McMahon, to back "the independence of the Arabs" in exchange for an Arab declaration of war against Turkey. The Arab revolt started in June 1916, assisted by the dynamic Lawrence of Arabia, who led attacks on Ottoman forces throughout what is now Jordan. At the same time, Britain sought political support from Jews worldwide by offering sympathy to the Zionist movement. The November 1917 Balfour Declaration stated that Britain viewed "with favour the establishment in Palestine of a national home for the Jewish people, it being clearly understood that nothing shall be done which may prejudice the civil and religious rights of existing non-Jewish communities in Palestine." Many Arabs were outraged, and Hussein's suspicions grew. The vague wording of the Balfour Declaration and the ambiguity of the boundaries agreed upon in the McMahon-Hussein correspondence only complicated the situation.

Meanwhile, the British and French had made a separate deal. The 1916 Sykes-Picot Agreement divided the region into zones of permanent British and French influence, giving control neither to Arabs nor to Jews. At the war's end, the various promises made by Britain to the Arabs, the Jews, and the French resulted in a muddled system of mandates: the newly created League of Nations awarded the two Western European powers control over the various territories from which the Ottomans had been expelled with the stated purpose of preparing these countries for independence. Great Britain was thus given a mandate over Palestine (which included modern-day Israel, Jordan, the West Bank, and Gaza) and Iraq, while France was accorded Syria and Lebanon.

France, for its part, drove Sharif Hussein's son Faisal out of Syria, where he had seized control. In 1921, Britain made good on one of its promises: Faisal's younger brother Abdallah was established as *emir* (prince) of Palestine east of the Jordan River, dubbed the Emirate of Transjordan and granted independence in 1946.

Throughout the inter-war years, British and French colonial rule was constantly tested by rising Arab and Jewish nationalism. In Egypt, Sa'ad Zaghloul founded the Wafd party, which forcefully criticized English rule and the Egyptian monarchy. After a skirmish between British soldiers and Egyptian peasants, Britain granted King Fouad nominal independence, taking care to sign treaties that protected British military bases, economic interests, and the Suez Canal.

In Palestine, the intervening 30 years of British rule saw institutional and economic development under the leadership of David Ben Gurion's Labor Movement. Land was extensively purchased from Arab owners, many of whom resided in neighboring countries, and Jewish immigration to Palestine increased. The Arab population of Palestine grew more and more anxious that they were in danger of losing their clear majority, and Palestinian Arab nationalist organizations such as the Higher Arab Council were established in an effort to combat Zionist activities and influence British policy. Leaders such as the Grand Mufti of Jerusalem, Haj Amin al-Husseini, sought support abroad for the termination of the British mandate and the cessation of all Zionist activity.

The British tried various unsuccessful tactics to appease one side or the other. Several commissions of inquiry were sent to Palestine to calm Arab fears of the growing Jewish presence. Various policy directives, known as "White Papers," restricted Jewish immigration and distinguished the Jewish "national home" pledged by the Balfour Declaration from the sovereign state sought by the Zionists. The clash between Arab and Jewish nationalism, however, was not averted. With the rise of Nazism in Germany, tens of thousands of European Jews sought to enter Palestine by legal or illegal means. Underground Jewish efforts to assist illegal immigration led to greater friction between the *yishuv* and the Mandatory Government. Meanwhile, growing Arab discontent with the developing situation culminated in the Arab Revolt of 1936-39, which the British were only able to put down with considerable military force. With the outbreak of the Second World War, Zionist leaders patched up their relationship with the British to support the war effort against Germany.

## THE 1948 (INDEPENDENCE) WAR

Shortly after the conclusion of World War II, an exhausted Great Britain submitted the question of Palestine to the newly formed United Nations. The U.N. General Assembly voted in 1947 to partition Palestine into two states, Jewish and Arab. The Jewish leadership accepted the resolution with some reluctance, while Palestinian Arab leaders and the governments of neighboring Arab states rejected the plan completely, denying the U.N.'s authority to divide and distribute territories they considered to be Arab patrimony. As the British prepared to evacuate Palestine in accordance with the partition resolution, Jews and Arabs clashed in sporadic skirmishes, purchased arms overseas, and planned for imminent, full-scale war.

On May 14, 1948, the British mandate over Palestine ended and David Ben-Gurion declared the independence of the State of Israel. The next day, a combined army of Syrian, Iraqi, Lebanese, Saudi, Egyptian, and Jordanian troops marched in from the north, west, and south. Few observers gave the new state much chance for survival, but the war's results became clear with the signing of armistices in the spring of 1949. Israel had secured not only its U.N.-allotted territory but also some Palestinian Arab-designated land in the north and in the West Bank. Other land intended for the Arab state was secured during the war by Egypt (the Gaza Strip) and Jordan (the West Bank and half of Jerusalem). Thousands of Palestinian refugees crowded into camps in the West Bank, Gaza, and bordering Arab states. The dispossessed Palestinians came to bitterly remember the 1948 War as *An-Naqba*, the catastrophe.

On April 9, 1948, the Palestinian village of Dayr Yasin, which had entered into a nonaggression pact with the Hagana (one of the Jewish underground fighting organizations), was attacked by the more aggressive and extreme LEHI and Irgun forces. These groups killed about 250 men, women, and children. The massacre was advertised via loudspeakers in Haifa and Jaffa, spurring Arabs to leave the country, figuring that they would return to their homes when the Arab armies won the war.

Abdallah annexed the West Bank in 1950 and declared a unified Hashemite Kingdom of Jordan; this move met an icy reception from Palestinians and other Arab governments. Some felt that Jordan was becoming too accommodating of Israel. To the Palestinians, Jordanian rule was not much different from any other foreign occupation. In 1951, Abdallah, praying in Al Aqsa Mosque in Jerusalem, was assassinated by a Palestinian youth. After a six month tenure by Abdallah's eldest son, Talal, who resigned due to schizophrenia, the crown passed to King Hussein. Not quite 18 when he assumed the throne—which he holds to this day—Hussein embarked on a bold agenda aimed at raising Jordan's status in the Arab world.

## THE SUEZ CRISIS

Egypt, weakened by struggles between Wafdist nationalists and the monarchy, was in a shambles after its 1948 loss to Israel. In 1952, following a bloody confrontation between British soldiers and Egyptian police officers, a group of young army officers led by charismatic heartthrob Colonel Gamal Abd an-Nasser bloodlessly seized power from the late King Fouad's corrupt son, Farouk. Calling themselves the "Free Officers," Nasser's cabinet instituted major economic reforms and foreign policy changes, while avoiding the bilateral alignments of the Cold War. Drawing from the writings of countless Arab nationalists, Nasser espoused a highly emotional brand of pan-Arabism, hoping to unify the Arabic-speaking masses into one state powerful enough to resist imperial encroachments and to take control of Palestine. When Nasser forced Britain to withdraw from Egypt in 1954, many puppet Arab leaders dependent on foreign assistance became alarmed by his growing popularity.

The United States and other foreign powers, which had undertaken extensive development of the oil fields of Arabia, feared their arrangements with local monarchs would collapse if Nasserism spread. Nasser, alarmed by a British-led alignment of conservative Middle East states (the Baghdad Pact), had begun buying Soviet arms from Czechoslovakia in defiance of a 1950 West-imposed arms control deal. In 1956, the United States clumsily attempted to curtail Nasser's power by withdrawing its offer to finance the Aswan High Dam. Rather than yield to the snub, Nasser nationalized the previously international Suez Canal to use its revenues for the dam.

Israel, Britain, and France devised a scheme to take the canal. Israel would attack Egypt with French logistical support; a Franco-British "peace-keeping" force would follow. Initially, the conspiracy worked well: Israel took the Sinai and dealt Nasser's military a major blow. The Anglo-French force entered Egypt and began the seizure of the canal under the pretext of separating Egyptian and Israeli combatants. The military victors, however, had not considered world reaction to their adventure. The United States and the Soviet Union, both furious, applied intense diplomatic pressure. When Israel, Britain, and France withdrew their troops to placate the U.S., Nasser was heralded as the savior of the Arab world without having won a battle.

After gaining independence from the British and French in April 1946, Syria experienced civilian government for three years. A military coup banished this oddity once and for all in March 1949; and by 1954, the pan-Arabist Ba'th party had crept into power. Racked with internal feuding, Syria joined Egypt in 1958 in forming the United Arab Republic (UAR). Nasser trumpeted the UAR as a triumph of pan-Arabism, but the Syrians were irritated by its unwieldy and Egypt-dominated government. Nonetheless, even after the 1961 secession of Syria from the UAR, Nasser remained at the forefront of Arab politics. In 1964, he hosted two Arab summits and helped create the Egypt-based Palestine Liberation Organization (PLO), keeping the Palestinian movement under Cairo's suspicious eye. One PLO faction was led by a fiery young Palestinian nationalist, Yassir Arafat. His FATAH party (the Arabic acronym for PLO written backwards) would eventually lead the PLO.

## THE 1967 SIX-DAY WAR

In 1963, the Syrian coup which interrupted the Egypto-Syrian joy ride gave way to the Syrian Ba'th party (led by Hafez Al Asad), which in February 1966 split off from the larger Ba'th party and began focusing its efforts on developing Syrian nationalism (rather than pan-Arabism) and maintaining power.

Meanwhile, from bases sanctioned by the governments of Jordan, Syria, and Lebanon, the PLO raided Israel; Israel hit Palestinian refugee camps. The cycle of raids and reprisals created tension on Israel's northern border, and a Syrian-Israeli air battle took place in April 1967. When Syria's hard-line government turned up the rhetoric, Nasser stepped in, concentrating the Egyptian army in the Sinai and successfully demanding the withdrawal of the U.N. buffer-zone troops stationed there since 1956. Israeli Prime Minister Levi Eshkol nervously warned that a blockade of the Straits of Tiran would be taken as an act of aggression. Nasser, under pressure from Syria and Saudi Arabia, initiated a blockade on May 22, 1967.

Jordan, Iraq, and Syria deployed troops along Israel's borders. On June 5, 1967, Israel launched a preemptive strike against air fields in the Sinai, obliterating the Egyptian air force before it ever got off the ground. The U.S., eager to embarrass Soviet-backed Egypt and having received assurances that the attack would eventually bring peace, had condoned the attack. Eshkol appealed to King Hussein not to get involved; but when it became clear that Jordanian shelling would continue, Israel saw an opportunity: it delayed acceptance of a U.N.-sponsored cease-fire (initially rejected by the Arab nations) until it could take East Jerusalem.

East Jerusalem fell to Israel on June 7, and by June 9 all parties had accepted the cease-fire. Shortly afterwards, Israel annexed East Jerusalem, much to the United State's chagrin. From Egypt, Israel had won the Sinai Peninsula (all the way to the Suez Canal) and the Gaza Strip, from Syria the Golan Heights, and from Jordan the West Bank. Nasser resigned, but a swell of public sympathy prompted him to reclaim his post. Staggered by yet another defeat, the Palestinians decided it was up to them to carry on the struggle. In 1969, Arafat's FATAH took over the PLO from its pro-Nasser leadership and undertook the liberation of Palestine through propaganda and guerilla warfare.

With the U.S. behind Israel and the USSR behind Nasser, any local conflict now raised the threat of superpower confrontation. U.N. Security Council Resolution 242, passed in November 1967 and accepted by all parties, stipulated "withdrawal of Israeli armed forces from territories occupied in the recent conflict" and "acknowledgment of the sovereignty, territorial integrity, and political independence of every State in the area." Bickering over the intentional ambiguity of the document began almost immediately, while the situation on the Israeli-Egyptian border (the Suez Canal) degenerated into what was known as the War of Attrition.

## THE PLO AND JORDAN

Among the PLO groups vying for control at the time were the Popular Front for the Liberation of Palestine, begun in 1967 by pan-Arabist Dr. George Habash and backed by Iraq; Ahmad Jibril's Syria-backed FATAH; and Marxist-Leninist Nayif Hawatmeh's Popular Democratic Front for the Liberation of Palestine (PDFLP), also backed by Syria. Among their differences was the fact that FATAH was composed mostly of Sunni Muslims, while Habash, Hawatmeh, and many of their adherents were Christian. In addition, Arafat stressed that Palestinians should not get involved in rivalries among Arab states, while Habash and Hawatmeh sought to radicalize the Arab governments into fighting the West and helping to liberate Palestine. Factionalism became a constant feature of Palestinian politics. The rivalries between factions were manipulated by the various by Arab states supporting them, though FATAH consistently sought to maintain contact with all Arab regimes.

The 1967 War created 400,000 more Palestinian refugees, most of whom went to Jordan. With this influx of Palestinians, the Jordanian government and the PLO were thrown together in a tense relationship: Hussein wanted to hold secret peace negotiations with the Israelis, while the PLO hoped to use Jordan as a base for attacks on Israeli-held territory. Responding to PLO raids, the Israeli army attacked the Jordanian town of Karameh. Though the towns resident Palestinians were defeated, the image of FATAH members standing together (with Jordanian support) against Israeli forces became a tremendously successful propaganda image for FATAH. Young recruits flocked, allowing the PLO increased control over the refugee camps, and threatening Hussein's sovereignty.

In September 1970, Hussein and Arafat's conflicting ambitions exploded. Infuriated by a hard-line PLO faction's hijacking of a number of commercial airliners (to protest the exclusion of Palestinians from negotiations between Israel, Egypt, and Jordan), Hussein declared war on the PLO. Martial law was imposed, and fighting between Jordanian and PLO troops took over three thousand lives. September 1970 became known among Palestinians as Black September. After Arab League mediation and Nasser's personal intervention, an agreement was forged, requiring the PLO to reluctantly move its headquarters to Lebanon.

## WAR AND PEACE: 1970-1981

Nasser died suddenly of a heart attack that same September. Vice President Anwar es-Sadat assumed control of Egypt and promptly began dismantling Nasser's legacy of state socialism. He also announced the *infitah* (opening), a plan to promote foreign investment and revive the economy. Anxious for his own security, Sadat exposed Nasser's extensive secret police network and released political prisoners, including members of the formerly suppressed religious opposition.

President Asad of Syria reassumed his country's reins in February 1971 and was sworn in as President for seven years. Asad, an Alawite Muslim of penurious heritage, had held power for a short time at the beginning of Ba'th monopoly, but had lost his position in 1966. After reassuming office, Asad called for the popular election of a

173-member People's Assembly that would draft a new constitution. Completed in March 1973, the constitution contained a clause requiring the President of Syria to be a follower of Islam. Sunni Muslims used this clause to object to Asad's presidency, holding that Alawites are not true Muslims. It was not until a high-ranking religious authority deemed Alawites devout followers of Islam that the road to domination was cleared for Asad.

Meanwhile, the war of attrition along the Suez Canal was an increasingly heavy burden for Egypt to bear. In order to alleviate his country's financial crisis, Sadat sought to reopen the lucrative canal and reclaim the desperately needed Sinai oil fields. In 1972 Sadat expelled the numerous Soviet military advisors in Egypt and, seeing little hope in negotiations, began making preparations to attack Israel.

On October 6, 1973, when many Israelis were in synagogues for Yom Kippur (the Day of Atonement), Egypt and Syria, eager to regain their lost territories, launched a surprise assault. In the war's first three days, Egypt overwhelmed Israeli defenses in the Sinai and Syrian forces thrust deep into the Golan, threatening Galilee. Because Egypt and Syria's preparatory moves had been perceived by the Israeli government to be bluffs, Israel's reserves had not been activated and it appeared that Israel was on the verge of defeat. Sadat, who had planned only to cross into the Sinai and hold the position, decided to press on with the battle, refusing a U.S.-brokered cease-fire. Accepting America's terms, Israel received formerly withheld U.S arms and, over a number of weeks, pushed the Egyptians and Syrians back.

All parties finally agreed to disengage forces in January 1974, in an agreement negotiated by then U.S. Secretary of State Henry Kissinger. The subsequent Sinai I and II agreements returned much of the Sinai to Egypt. Both sides, though, had suffered tremendous losses. Israeli public uproar over the government's unpreparedness prompted Prime Minister Golda Meir to resign in April. Israel had won, but the aura of invincibility it had earned over the years had dissipated.

In October 1974, the Arab League declared in Rabat, Morocco that the PLO, not Jordan, was "the sole legitimate representative of the Palestinian people." This incensed King Hussein; but when the other 20 Arab nations assented to PLO representation in the League, he was forced to agree. In November 1974, the United Nations General Assembly voted to give the PLO observer status in the U.N. as representatives of the Palestinian people.

Throughout the 1970s, an increasing number of Israelis began to settle in the occupied territories. On November 11, 1976, the U.N. Security Council condemned this West Bank policy and demanded that Israel follow the Geneva Convention's rules regarding occupied territory. Although Prime Minister Yitzhak Rabin (of the left-leaning Labor party) discouraged permanent West Bank settlement, the next government (after 1977), under Prime Minister Menahem Begin of the right-wing Likud bloc, invested money and effort in new settlements.

Eager to regain the Sinai, Sadat decided to seek a unilateral peace with Israel. In October 1977, he declared that he would even go to Jerusalem to make peace. The next month, Sadat made a historic visit to Jerusalem and was officially welcomed.

By September 1978, Begin and Sadat had forged an agreement with the help of U.S. President Jimmy Carter at Camp David, the presidential retreat in Virginia. The most successful and lasting stipulation was Israel's agreement to relinquish the Sinai in exchange for peace and full diplomatic relations with Egypt. More muddled were the stipulations concerning Israel's control of the West Bank and Gaza. By the time of the signing of the Accords, there was still confusion as to what Israel was expected to do: Sadat returned to Cairo content that Palestinians in the occupied territories would be granted full personal and territorial sovereignty within the next five years, while Begin maintained that nothing regarding the occupied territories had been agreed upon.

After the Camp David Accords, early hopes that other Arab states would negotiate with Israel evaporated. The PLO, Syria, and Jordan were adamant about guarantees for the Palestinians; more distant Arab states issued statements of disapproval, but felt no need to interfere. Egypt, viewed as a traitor to Palestine by many, was left isolated and turned to the U.S for financial support. Islamists, whom Sadat had courted in his battles against the Nasserist left, objected to this open alliance with the West. In October 1981, in response to cracking down on Fundamentalists, Sadat was assassinated. The Egyptian government acted swiftly to crush an Islamist riot in Assyut, and Hosni Mubarak, Sadat's Vice President, was sworn in.

Though sticking to the terms of the 1979 Camp David peace treaty, Mubarak held Egypt at arm's length from Israel, keeping the diplomatic air cool for most of the 1980s in an attempt to reintegrate Egypt with the rest of the Arab world. In 1984, Egypt restored relations with the Soviet Union and was readmitted to the Islamic Conference, and by 1988, the Arab League had invited Egypt to rejoin and dropped demands that Egypt sever ties with Israel.

## THE ISRAELI INVASION OF LEBANON

It had long been apparent that the June 6, 1982 Israeli invasion of Lebanon, dubbed Operation Peace for Galilee by Defense Minister Ariel Sharon, was intended not simply to create a protective buffer zone, but to wipe out PLO forces operating from Palestinian refugee camps that had been attacking northern Israel. When the Israeli army, after surrounding the PLO in Beirut, began shelling the city at an enormous civilian cost, Israeli citizens joined in the world-wide chorus of condemnation. With the massacre of civilians at the Sabra and Shatila refugee camps by Lebanese Christian Phalangists operating in Israeli-controlled territory, the Israeli government's position eroded even further. Under an agreement negotiated by the U.S., most fighting ended in 1983. Israel, worried about the continued Syrian presence and active Shi'i militia in Lebanon, did not fully withdraw until 1985 and continues to maintain a strip of southern Lebanese territory as a security zone.

## THE INTIFADA

On December 8, 1987, an Israeli armored transport and several Arab cars collided in Gaza; four Palestinians were killed and several injured in the crash. The Palestinians' despair after 20 years of Israeli military occupation and frustration with Israel's unwillingness to negotiate over Palestinian autonomy turned demonstrations at the victims' funerals into an upheaval that spread to the West Bank. The Palestinian *intifada*, or uprising, was a tremendous shock to everyone, the PLO (at this point relocated to Tunis) included. At first, Israeli authorities viewed the *intifada* ("throwing off" or "shaking off" in Arabic) as a short-lived affair which would peter out much as earlier agitations had. But after Palestinians in the territories began establishing networks to coordinate their hitherto sporadic civil disobedience and strikes, the *intifada* came alive, and gained a shadowy leadership all its own.

By mid-1988 it became apparent that the *intifada* was not abating. The constant appearance of the Israeli Defense Force violently suppressing demonstrators on television screens throughout the world inspired increasing criticism of Israel's Palestinian policies. U.S. Secretary of State George Schultz proposed an international peace conference to be attended by the permanent members of the UN Security council. The Americans and the Israelis, however, refused to allow the PLO to attend until the organization renounced terrorism and accepted Israel's right to exist.

In the summer of 1988, King Hussein suddenly dropped his claims to the West Bank and ceased assisting in the administration of the territories, which Jordan had been doing since 1967. Hussein's move left Israel and the United States without a negotiating partner, since they refused to negotiate with the PLO. Arafat seized the opportunity to secure a PLO role in negotiations by renouncing terrorism, recognizing Israel's right to exist, and proposing an independent Palestinian state. Israeli Prime Minister Yitzhak Shamir (Likud) presented his own proposal (actually formulated by then-Defense Minister Rabin), promising elections in the territories but insisting that neither the PLO nor PLO-sponsored candidates take part. This seemed ridiculous to those who considered all Palestinians members of the PLO. Nonetheless, the United States and Egypt began trying to draw up a list of acceptable candidates. Shamir then qualified his proposal by insisting that Arab residents of East Jerusalem be barred from participation. The PLO, local Palestinians, and Egypt could not stomach any recognition of the decades-old Israeli claim that Jerusalem, whole and undivided, was Israel's eternal capital, nor that Palestinian refugees living outside the occupied territories should not be allowed to return.

Many Palestinians became convinced, by late 1989, that Yassir Arafat had weakened the position the Palestinians had gained as a result of the *intifada*. They were also worried by the increasing numbers of Soviet Jews immigrating to Israel and the growing number of Israeli settlements in the West Bank. A PLO faction launched an attack against Israeli hotels on the coast near Tel Aviv. The raid was foiled before it inflicted any damage, and Israel, backed by the United States, pressured Arafat to denounce the incident. His refusal to do so attested to FATAH's waning power relative to more militant factions. The United States and the PLO terminated their discussions that summer.

## THE GULF WAR AND THE PEACE PROCESS

The Gulf Crisis began when Iraqi troops marched into Kuwait on August 2, 1990. Early on, Iraqi President Saddam Hussein had slyly suggested "linkage" as a way of solving the Gulf crisis—that is, he would withdraw from Kuwait when Israel withdrew from the West Bank, Gaza, and Golan, and when Syria withdrew from Lebanon. This gesture, along with promises to liberate Palestine, won Saddam the support of Palestinians. In fighting that lasted from January 16 to February 28, 1991, a coalition formed by the United States, various European countries, Egypt, Syria, Saudi Arabia, and the other Gulf states disabled Baghdad and forced Iraq to withdraw from Kuwait. During the conflict, 39 Iraqi SCUD missiles fell on Tel Aviv and Haifa. Israel, under pressure from the U.S. and fearful of an Arab-Israeli conflagration and of chaos in Jordan, did not retaliate.

The war damaged the Jordanian economy, burdening it with approximately 300,000 Palestinians no longer welcome in the Gulf countries. Across the river, Israel's demographics were also in flux, as the collapse of regimes brought in 450,000 Jewish immigrants from the former Soviet Union and Ethiopia.

The Gulf Crisis demonstrated dramatically the need for a comprehensive peace in the region. When the cease-fire was announced, hope was high that parties such as Israel and Syria—for the first time on the same side of a regional conflict—could be brought to the bargaining table. In July 1991, Syria surprised the world with the announcement that it would attend a regional peace conference. At a summit meeting in Moscow, U.S. President George Bush and Russian President Mikhail Gorbachev decided to host the conference jointly, and even issued invitations. A hesitant Israeli cabinet, uneasy about losing some $10 billion in additional U.S. aid, voted to attend the proposed conference provided that the PLO and residents of East Jerusalem not take part.

On October 30, 1991, the Madrid peace conference was convened, with Israel carrying on separate negotiations with Syria, Lebanon, Egypt, and a joint Jordanian-Palestinian delegation. This unprecedented gathering quickly bogged down in discussions of UN Resolution 242, Palestinian autonomy and rights, Jerusalem, Israeli settlements, and the PLO's role. Subsequent sessions held in Washington, D.C. did not get much further. The Palestinian representatives, including Faisal al-Husseini and Hanan Ashrawi, were in constant contact with the PLO; the charade of PLO non-involvement was wearing thin.

On June 23, 1992, an Israeli election ousted Shamir's Likud, whose West Bank settlements had attracted U.S. ire, and brought in a pragmatic Labor-led government under Yitzhak Rabin. Rabin curtailed settlement and promised Palestinian autonomy. Optimism accompanying the first round of talks under the new Israeli government, held in November 1992, was soon undermined. Hamas, a rejectionist-Islamist Palestinian faction which had been growing in popularity (especially in Gaza) as Palestinians became frustrated with negotiations, carried out several terrorist attacks on Israelis. In response, the Israeli government deported 415 Palestinians, some of whom were Hamas activists and some of whom claimed no connection to the organization, in December 1992. The Palestinian representatives at the negotiations refused to resume talks until the deportees, trapped in the freezing no-man's-land between Israel and Lebanon, were allowed to return.

Then, almost a year later, Israel and the PLO surprised the world by announcing that representatives meeting secretly in Oslo had successfully negotiated an agreement on a framework for solving the Israeli-Palestinian conflict peacefully. The Declaration of Principles on Interim Self-Government Arrangements (the D.O.P—also known as the Oslo Accord) was signed on the White House lawn on September 13, 1993, with President Bill Clinton presiding over the ceremony. The DOP provided for mutual recognition between Israel and the PLO as well as a plan for the implementation of Palestinian autonomy in the Gaza Strip and the Jericho Area with the autonomous areas to be expanded in stages over a five-year transitional period. The transitional period, according to the DOP, is to be followed by an agreement on final status arrangements such as: refugees, settlements, security arrangements, borders, foreign relations, and Jerusalem.

The DOP was followed by the negotiation and signing of several other Israeli-Palestinian agreements. The first was the Gaza/Jericho Agreement which provided the details for Israeli withdrawal from these two areas and the creation of a Palestinian Authority (PA) headed by Yassir Arafat and a 24-member council. Following the implementation of the Gaza/Jericho Agreement, the two sides signed the Early Empowerment Agreement which transferred several spheres of government in the West Bank to the Palestinian Authority (PA).

In 1991, having led part of the Arab world against Iraq in the Gulf War, Egypt was invited to head the Arab League, marking the country's re-emergence at the helm of the Arab world. The Arab League is now headed by former Egyptian foreign minister Esmat Abd el-Meguid. In June 1992, Mubarak met with new Israeli Prime Minister Yitzhak Rabin, the first meeting of leaders of the two countries in six years. Egypt is also beginning to recapture its former position of power within the world arena; in 1992, Boutros Boutros-Ghali, a respected Egyptian diplomat involved in the Camp David negotiations, became the new U.N. Secretary-General. Cairo proudly hosted, on a stage outfitted with massive Egyptian flags, the signing of the 1994 agreement between the Palestine Liberation Organization and the Israeli government.

Israeli agreements with other Arab countries followed soon after; and throughout the second half of 1994 the world saw history being made daily. In September, Morocco and Israel established diplomatic relations. In October, Jordan and Israel ended the state of war that had existed between them since 1948. The border between Eilat and Aqaba was opened, and Israelis were allowed into Jordan for the first time. Finally, negotiations with Syria were begun, concentrating on peace between the two countries in exchange for the withdrawal of Israeli troops from the Golan Heights. Such a withdrawal is highly controversial within Israel and the Israeli Government has stated that it will place any agreement negotiated with Syria on a national referendum to be decided upon by the Israeli public.

## THIS YEAR'S NEWS

With the passage of the sweeping Interim Agreement (also called "Oslo II"), Israel agreed to withdraw from most West Bank towns and the Palestinian Authority agreed to hold its first ever election (see **West Bank: Political History**, p. 445). In summer 1996, the future of Hebron, the last major West Bank town under Israeli occupation, was still a sticking point. Support for the peace process in both societies has been plagued by frustration, anxiety, and persistent mistrust. Many on both sides feel that they are getting the raw end of the deal—some Israelis argue that they are giving up their defensive territorial depth in exchange for pieces of paper that can be torn up in a moment. Some Palestinians fear that Israel will never grant them total independence and interpret the current process as a "sell-out" on the part of their leadership.

Opposition to the peace process took a tragic turn in the past year, as extremists from both sides resorted to violence. On November 4, 1995, 25-year-old Yigal Amir, a

Jewish right-wing university student, shot and killed Israel's Prime Minister Yitzhak Rabin. Rabin had just finished delivering a rousing speech in front of 100,000 Israelis at one of the largest rallies Tel Aviv had ever seen. After his oration, the crowd sang *Shir La-Shalom* (A Song for Peace). Rabin folded a paper with the lyrics and placed it in his chest pocket. The bullet, meant to derail the peace talks, pierced the lyrics; the blood-stained song sheet was read at the Prime Minister's funeral. The psychological shock waves of Rabin's death are still reverberating throughout Israel. Never before in the history of the Jewish people has a leader been killed by a fellow Jew. The square where the assassination took place, renamed in Rabin's memory, has been transformed into a makeshift shrine and a spot for reflection and healing (see **Goodbye Friend**, p. 334). Over one million Israelis, Arabs and Jews alike, filed by the slain leader's coffin in the days following the murder. Rabin's funeral drew over 50 world leaders to Jerusalem, including Jordan's King Hussein, Egypt's President Mubarak, and representatives from four other Arab states.

After the assassination, Acting Prime Minister Shimon Peres called for early elections. The slaying boosted the Labor party's popularity, as many moderates turned away from Likud disgusted to see where opposition to the peace could lead. That trend shifted four months later, when a string of four Hamas-sponsored terrorist attacks prompted Israelis to demand stricter security and caused many to reconsider the value of the peace process. Arafat finally cracked down on militant rejectionist factions, and outlawed all Hamas activities, but his actions came too late for many Israelis. Four bombs and 58 deaths severely damaged a precarious sense of trust, and set the stage for the conservative victory in the Israeli elections.

In April, *Hizballah* guerillas stepped up Katyusha rocket attacks on Israel's northern settlements. The Lebanon-based movement draws support from Iran and Syria, and has been periodically attacking northern settlements like Kiryat Shmona over the past few years. Determined to demonstrate force, Peres ordered a retaliation. Northern Israelis slept in bomb shelters, while many residents of southern Lebanon were forced to flee their homes and seek refuge in northern cities. On April 19, *Hizballah* fighters launched a missile from outside a U.N. refugee camp. The Israeli retaliation hit the camp, killing over 100 Lebanese civilians and provoking outrage within the international community. American Secretary of State Warren Christopher shuttled between Damascus and Jerusalem hoping to broker a cease-fire. An agreement was eventually reached, but Syrian-Israeli peace negotiations were immeasurably set back.

Benjamin Netanyahu, leader of the conservative Likud party, defeated Shimon Peres in a hairline victory (50.4% to 49.6%) in the May 1996 Israeli elections. Implications for the peace process have yet to be determined. Netanyahu vowed to continue the peace talks, but also assures his people that he will proceed slowly, emphasizing that Israeli security will never be compromised.

# ■ Religion

## RELIGION IN ANCIENT EGYPT

The people of pre-Dynastic Egypt were ruled by a bewildering array of local gods representing the cosmos, the natural elements, animals, and the life-cycle. Each independent district had its own local deity, pair of deities, or trinity, and in the early days, these gods were represented by animals. The Greeks and Romans considered these representations to be evidence of barbarism in otherwise advanced Egypt. The Greek influence certainly played no small part in the shift from animal deities to deities with human form and costume. As Egypt was united, the pharaohs found that they needed one syncretic pantheon to link these disparate cults. The Heliopolian Theogony, centered near the first capital, Memphis, was a complex faith explaining the emergence of an ordered world out of chaos. The leading god, Rē-Atum, was represented by the sun. His descendants were known as the Ennead. They included Geb (earth) and Nūt (Sky), who were worshipped as the parents of the moon, stars, humans, and younger gods, Osiris, Isis, Seth, and Nephthys. These youthful deities were adapted from southern cults, and they were held dear by the majority of Egyptians.

The most enduring cult was the Osiris cycle. Centered at Abydos on the Upper Nile, this popular faith helped Egyptians understand the most important things in life: sex, death, the seasons, and royal succession. According to the religion, Seth murdered his brother Osiris, a king from time immemorial, and scattered the pieces of his body throughout Egypt. His faithful sister-wife Isis found his remains all over the kingdom and erected monuments over each of the body parts; this is why there were so many temples to Osiris. Subsequently, Isis conceived and gave birth to Horus, who became Osiris' son and heir. Young Horus avenged Osiris and took back the crown from his usurping uncle. The pharaohs saw Horus as the ideal of the rightful and strong ruler, and identified themselves with him while on earth. Upon death they were identified with Osiris, who was seen as the king of the dead. The pharaoh was thus literally a god and worshipped as such, and the religious fervor he engendered united the country. Seth was viewed as the god of foreigners, and represented the invasions that infrequently troubled Egypt.

The first pharaohs imposed the Memphite Theogony over the earlier cults, adapting a new god, Ptah, who represented the boundary between order and chaos and was the father of the Ennead. At the same time, Horus was provided with a wife, Hathor. This pair, originally worshipped at Hierakonpolis (near modern Edfu), provided the Egyptians with a young, attractive couple to worship. Middle and New Kingdom pharaohs installed the sun-god Amun (similar to the older, more low key Rē-Atum), his wife, Mut, and their sun, Khonsu over the older gods, thus concentrating Egyptian state-religion around Thebes. All these centralizing efforts had little effect on the faith of the Egyptian masses, who neither understood nor cared much for the aristocratic gods imposed by the high-priests. They only saw the eternal order of a world ruled by the god-pharaoh and characterized by constants as the daily rising of the sun and the annual flooding of the Nile. Any change was viewed as evil, a disruption of the divinely-ordained order, which, in its most complex and complete form, was venerated as *Ma'at*.

Some historians believe that in the Old Kingdom only the pharaoh could enter the afterworld. Minor royalty took to grouping their tombs around the king's, hoping that the proximity would also draw them into the next life. By the time of the Middle Kingdom, the netherworld was open to all of the righteous, and Egyptians' central concern became life after death. By the New Kingdom, priests were selling funerary services to anyone who could pay. Through all of these periods, earthly existence was seen as a short interlude to be endured until the afterlife brought eternal happiness and reward to those who passed divine judgement. The divine and secular worlds, however, were not strongly demarcated; the preservation of the earthly body through mummification was considered essential for the afterlife of the *Ka*, or soul, and the tomb had to be supplied with all the comforts of life.

The Pyramid Texts were spells inscribed on the walls of the royal pyramids to ensure the success of the king or queen's journey to their afterlife. As the underworld democratization took hold, these texts were adopted by more plebeian folk and inscribed on the sides of their coffins. The New Kingdom's Book of the Dead, a collection of spells written on papyrus and put in sarcophagi, described not only how to get to the afterworld but also how to enjoy oneself once there.

The Macedonian Ptolemies, who ruled Egypt in the wake of Alexander, sought to become pharaonic god-kings to their subjects. By merging Greek and Egyptian elements in the Serapis cult and building temples to the ancient gods, they achieved what Assyrian and Persian invaders before them never could—they became spiritual successors of the pharaohs. Many of the great temples of Upper Egypt date to Ptolemaic times. The conquerors, however, may have been more influenced than influencing; the mystery cults of Osiris, Isis, and Horus spread throughout the Hellenistic world and were pervasive in the later Roman Empire.

## JUDAISM

Because Judaism does not have a founding figure, neither theologians nor historians can pinpoint a date when Judaism began. The Israelite religion has been evolving, however, for perhaps the past four millennia. According to the Bible, Abraham was the first to establish a covenant with God with his self-circumcision at the ripe age of 99. This act is symbolically repeated with each generation of Jewish males. Luckily, the ritual is gotten over with on the eighth day of life and a *moyel* (circumciser), not the baby, performs the honors. Abraham's grandson, Jacob (a.k.a. Israel) fathered twelve sons from whom descended twelve tribes, the nation of Israel. Abraham, together with his son Isaac and grandson Jacob, are believed to be buried with their wives, Sarah, Rebecca, and Leah in the Cave of the Makhpela in Hebron. Because, Ishmael, Abraham's other son, is believed to be the ancestor of Islam, the resting place of the patriarchs and matriarchs are holy to both faiths.

The Bible says that the founding period of the Israelite nation was the generation spent wandering in the Sinai desert en route from Egypt to the Holy Land, under the leadership of Moses. It was this generation that received the Torah, the central text of Judaism, at Mt. Sinai. Historians theorize that the disparate tribes later known as the Israelites periodically united under a national god by the third millennium BCE. This god, Yahweh, is thought to have been a young, warlike version of the older Canaanite deity, El (or Elyon, see Exodus 3:15). Some scholars believe Yahweh (God) was introduced to the highland Canaanites by Semitic tribes escaping from Egypt (see **The Ancient Levant,** p. 44), and that He was worshipped as an alternative to the lowland storm-god, Baal. When the Israelites formed a kingdom, worship of God was centralized in the capital, Jerusalem.

Historians estimate the present form of the Torah to be 2500 years old, although the Torah has been continuously interpreted and re-interpreted over the centuries in an effort to maintain its vitality and applicability. The Written Torah, (also known as the Pentateuch, or the Books of Moses), which consists of the first five books of the Bible, formed the template for the Oral Torah, a series of interpretations and teachings eventually codified in final form around 200 CE as the *Mishnah*. The *Mishnah,* along with the *Gemara,* are the basis of the Babylonian and Jerusalem *Talmuds,* finalized sometime in the 5th century CE. The Talmud was the springboard for a new series of interpretations and teachings that continue to build upon each other. "Torah," which has come to refer to all Jewish thought and teachings, has been at the core of Jewish life through most of history.

### The Synagogue and Jewish Life

Among Jews, faith in God is assumed, and the energy of Jewish life is concentrated on observing the commandments. The Torah contains 613 *mitzvot* (commandments) including directives for ritual observances and instructions concerning moral behavior. Over the ages, rabbis have interpreted these *mitzvot* and expanded them to include countless more. This entire set of laws is called *halakha* (literally "the way"). Much of modern Jewish life revolves around the synagogue (*beit knesset* in Hebrew, *shul* in Yiddish). The Hebrew word means "house of assembly" whereas the Yiddish word means "school," demonstrating the multi-faceted role the synagogue plays in Jewish life. The *aron ha-kodesh* (holy ark) houses the Torah scrolls and determines the orientation of the synagogue. Synagogues normally face toward Jerusalem, and within Jerusalem, they face the Temple Mount. Above the *aron ha-kodesh,* a flickering *ner tamid* (eternal flame) usually hangs. The raised platform from which prayers are led is called the *bima.* Most orthodox synagogues are in Israel and contain a *mehitza* or divider between men's and women's sections. Usually, the two sections have separate entrances. Men should cover their heads when entering a synagogue. Often there is a box of *kippot* (skullcaps, sing. *kippah*) by the entrance. Head coverings symbolize a reverence for God. Worshippers wear other items as reminders of their devotion. The *talit,* or prayer shawl, has four *tzitzit,* a set of strings twisted and knotted to symbolize the commandments. On weekdays, worshippers wear *tefillin,* boxed scrolls wrapped around the arm and head with leather straps. Visitors are welcome at most synagogues during prayer services. There are three prescribed prayer times every day: in the morning (the *shaharit* service), in the afternoon (the *minha* service), and in the evening (the *ma'ariv* service). Smaller synagogues, however, do not meet for every service. On *Shabbat* and holidays there is an additional service during the day. The *Kabbalat Shabbat* service, on Friday nights, welcomes in the Sabbath. Visitors to a synagogue should dress modestly and on Shabbat or holidays, dressy attire is in order. Interesting times to visit are when the Torah scroll is brought out and read: Shabbat, holidays and each Monday and Thursday. It is at these times when you might catch a *Bar Mitzvah* ceremony (*Bat Mitzvah* for girls), a coming of age ritual signifying the point at which a Jew becomes legally eligible to fulfill the *mitzvot*. Remember that photographs on *Shabbat* and holidays are highly inappropriate.

*Judaism,* by Michael Fishbane, provides an excellent, concise introduction to the religion. Other good sources include Bernard Bamberger's *The Story of Judaism*, Isadore Epstein's *Judaism*, and Milton Steinberg's *Basic Judaism*.

## CHRISTIANITY

Christianity began in Judea among the Jewish followers of Jesus. The most significant sources on the life of Jesus are the Gospels. Scholars agree that the "synoptic gospels" of Mark, Matthew, and Luke were written in that order some time after 70 CE, drawing on an oral tradition which recorded the words of Jesus. The Gospel of John was written about 100CE, but has roots as old as the others. These sources provide a history influenced by the experiences of the church fathers and the belief that Jesus was the Messiah ("anointed one;" Christ).

Various datings of historical events date the birth of Jesus, the man regarded by millions as their savior, between 4 BCE and 6 CE. According to Matthew, Bethlehem is the birthplace of Jesus, and Mary and Joseph moved to Nazareth to protect him; in Luke, Jesus' parents are only temporarily in Bethlehem; and in Mark and John, the birth is not even mentioned. The Bible states Jesus was conceived and brought forth by Mary, a virgin, making him a product of God's creative power and free from humanity's original sin. Catholics additionally hold that Mary herself was conceived without sin: the Immaculate Conception.

Jesus was baptized (ritually washed) in the Jordan River by John the Baptist, a popular evangelist later hailed as the reincarnation of the 9th-century prophet Elijah, herald of the Messiah. Afterwards, Jesus preached in the Galilee, speaking passionately for the poor and the righteous, most notably in the Sermon on the Mount.

After about three years of preaching, Jesus went to Jerusalem, where the Passion, the events of his death, took place. The Gospels give slightly differing accounts, but key events in the story include Jesus throwing the money-changers out of the Temple, eating the Last Supper, being betrayed by Judas, being arrested in the Garden of Gethsemane, and being condemned to death by Pontius Pilate and the Romans at the urging of the Pharisees. On Good Friday, he carried his cross down the Via Dolorosa, stopping at what became known as the Stations of the Cross, until he reached the hill of Golgotha (or Calvary; now marked by the Church of the Holy Sepulchre), where he was crucified.

### History of Christianity

According to the Gospels, three days after Jesus' crucifixion, on what is now celebrated as Easter, three women went to Jesus' tomb to anoint his body and discovered the tomb empty. An angel announced that Jesus had been resurrected; Jesus subsequently appeared to the Apostles and performed miracles. Later, on Pentecost, the Apostles were given "tongues of fire" and were directed to spread the Gospel. The Resurrection is the point of departure for the Christian faith, the beginning of a new age in which the faithful wait for Christ's *parousia*, or second coming.

At first, Christianity was a sect of Judaism, accepting the Hebrew Bible. But Christianity's defining tenet that Jesus was the Messiah severed it from mainstream Judaism. St. Paul (originally Saul of Tarsus), successfully adapted the faith of Christianity to meet the spiritual needs of the largest body of converts: former pagans. Paul abandoned standard Jewish practices like required circumcision, further separating Christianity from Judaism. The Book of Acts documents the early Christians, and the Letters of Paul, which comprise most of the rest of the New Testament, gives advice to the early Christian communities and explains the delay of the second coming. As Christianity developed further, it absorbed earlier practices. The adaptation of ancient festivals such as the winter solstice helped draw the common people to the new religion, while the incorporation of Platonic doctrines brought many intellectuals into the fold.

The Christian faith was officially legitimized by the Edict of Milan, issued by Emperor Licinius in 313 CE, which proclaimed the toleration of Christianity. In 325 CE, the Emperor Constantine made Christianity the official religion of the struggling Empire. Constantine also summoned the first of seven Ecumenical Councils, held in Nicaea, to elaborate and unify the content of the faith. The Council of Nicaea came up with an explicit creed, declaring that Jesus Christ was of the same essence as the Father, and that there were three equal parts to God. This crucial doctrine of the Trinity, which is only implicitly supported in the Gospels, maintains that the Father, Son, and Holy Spirit are distinct persons yet all one God.

The Church was called "the body of Christ" and believed to be integral and indivisible. Nonetheless, the Christian community suffered many schisms. The Egyptian (Coptic) Church broke off in the 3rd century (see below), when other eastern branches (the Nestorians and Maronites are examples) began to drift apart from western Christianity. In 1054, the Great Schism, caused primarily by the inflexible Cardinal Humbert, split Christendom into the western Roman Catholic Church and the Eastern Orthodox Church. Whereas Rome upheld the universal jurisdiction and infallibility of the Pope, Orthodoxy stressed the infallibility of the church as a whole. The Spirit, according to the Orthodox, proceeds through the Father, while Roman theology dictates that the Spirit proceeds from the Father and the Son. Orthodox Christians believe that God is highly personal, that each man can find God by looking within himself. In 1517, the German monk Martin Luther sparked the Reformation, which quickly split northern Europe from Roman Catholicism, and led to the development of Protestantism. Protestantism is itself composed of many sects, which generally believe in salvation through faith rather than good works. Eastern Orthodoxy, too, is divided into multiple nationalist traditions (Greek, Russian, Armenian). Only in the 18th century did these diverse churches come to speaking terms, and only in the 20th has the ecumenical movement brought extensive cooperation.

The central part of the church service for Catholics is the mass, basically a reenactment of the last supper: the priest blesses bread and wine and they are changed to Jesus' body and blood by the Holy Spirit. The congregation receives the host just as the apostles did. When visiting churches, it is inappropriate to partake in communion if not a Catholic.

Williston Walker's *History of the Christian Church* and Steven Reynolds's *Christian Religious Tradition* are good introductory books on Christianity.

### The Coptic Church

"Copt" derives from the Greek word for Egyptian, *Aiguptious,* shortened in Egyptian pronunciation to *qibt,* the Arabic word for Copt. Copts in Egypt usually have tattoos of either a domed cathedral or a tiny cross on their wrists. Of 58 million Egyptians, five to seven million are Copts, most of whom live in Cairo or Middle Egypt. Today, portions of the liturgy are still conducted in Coptic, though most of the service is in Arabic. The Copts recognize their own patriarch—spiritual authority resides in Cairo and Alexandria.

According to Coptic tradition, St. Mark introduced Christianity to Egypt in 62 CE. Mass conversions transformed Alexandria into a Christian spiritual center, but Roman persecution increased proportionately. The bloodiest days passed under Diocletian, who murdered so many Christians that the Copts date their Martyr's Calendar from 284 CE, the beginning of his reign.

In 451 CE, the Alexandrian branch of the Church declared theological and political independence from Constantinople, forming the Coptic Orthodox Church. The split derived from a dispute over the interpretation of the Trinity. While the Ecumenical Council at Chalcedon defended the definition of Christ's nature as diphysite, with the human and the divine aspects clearly differentiated, the doctrine of the new Coptic Church centered around monophysitism, which holds that Christ's nature is of such unity that the human and divine elements are fused and indivisible.

The Byzantine Emperor Justinian sought to restore unity by exiling Coptic clergy to isolated desert monasteries. Rebellious Copts thus welcomed the Persians as liberators when they captured Egypt in 619. Since the 7th century, the Egyptian Christian community has lived as a religious minority in an Islamic state. Relations between the Copts and the Muslims have vacillated throughout history, as the Islamic government has used Qur'anic verses and extracts from the Hadith to justify either lenient or oppressive treatment. Recently, the Copts have felt besieged by Egypt's increasingly vocal Islamists, and acts of violence are often concentrated in Coptic population centers.

Coptic Christianity served as a link between the Roman-pharaonic and Islamic eras, leaving its own mark on modern Egypt. Coptic art incorporates the influences of pharaonic and Hellenistic cultures. The Coptic cross borrows from the *ankh*, the hieroglyphic sign for "life," as well as from the crucifix on Golgotha. Embroidered tapestries and curtains displaying nymphs and centaurs descend from Greco-Roman mythology. Islamic art often borrows from the Coptic style; many of Cairo's mosques were engineered by Coptic architects, and some are converted Coptic churches. Unlike the monumental art of the pharaohs, the art of the Copts tends to preserve ancient folk media.

Coptic churches usually have one of three shapes: cruciform, circular (to represent the globe, the spread of Christianity, and the eternal nature of the Word), or ark-shaped (the Ark of the Covenant and Noah's Ark are symbols of salvation). The churches are divided into three chambers. The eastward sanctuary (*haikal*) containing the alter lies behind a curtain or *iconostasis,* a wooden screen of icons. The next chamber, the choir, is the section reserved for Copts. Behind the choir is the nave, which consists of two parts, the first of which is reserved for the *catechumens* (those who are preparing to convert). The back of the nave is for the so-called weepers, or sinners. These Christians, having willfully transgressed, were formerly made to stand at the very back of the church. Above Coptic altars hang ostrich eggs, symbolizing the Resurrection (life out of what seems lifeless). The ostrich egg, of religious importance in pre-Christian times, was preserved as a symbol of God's eternal love and care for the Church. Jill Kamil's *Coptic Egypt: History and Guide,* Barbara Watterson's *Coptic Egypt,* and Iris H. Elmasry's *Introduction to the Coptic Church* are all good introductions to the religion.

## ISLAM

The Arabic word *islam* means, in its general sense "submission," and Islam the religion is the faithful submission to God's will. Islam has its roots in revelations received from 610 to 622 CE by Muhammad, who was informed by the Angel Gabriel of his prophetic calling. These revelations form the core of Islam, the Qur'an (recitation). Muslims believe the Arabic text to be perfect, immutable, and untranslatable—the words of God embodied in human language. Consequently, the Qur'an appears throughout the Muslim world—the majority of which is non-Arabic speaking—in Arabic. Muhammad is seen as the "seal of the prophets," the last of a chain of God's messengers which includes Jewish and Christian figures such as Abraham, Moses, and Jesus. The Qur'an incorporates many of the biblical traditions associated with these prophets.

Muhammad rapidly gathered followers to his evolving faith. Staunchly monotheistic, Islam was met with ample opposition in polytheist Arabia, leading to persecution in Muhammad's native city of Mecca. In 622, he and his followers fled to the nearby city of Medina, where he was welcomed as mediator of a long-standing blood feud. This *Hijra* (flight, or emigration) marks the beginning of the Muslim community and of the Islamic calendar. For the next eight years, Muhammad and his community defended themselves against raids and later battled the Meccans and neighboring nomadic tribes. In 630 Mecca surrendered to the Muslims, making Muhammad the most powerful man in Arabia. After the surrender, numerous Meccans converted to the new faith voluntarily. This established the pattern for *jihad* (struggle), referring first and foremost to the spiritual struggle against one's own desires, then to the struggle to make one's own Muslim community as righteous as possible, and lastly to the struggle against outsiders wishing to harm the Muslim community. Sadly, only the last aspect is commonly known to the West.

Islam continued to grow after the Prophet's death, flourishing in the "Age of Conquest." The four Rightly Guided Caliphs *(Rashidun)* who succeeded Muhammad led wars against apostate nomadic tribes. Faith in Islam was the strength of the Arab armies, which defeated the once-mighty Persian empire by the year 640. The fourth Caliph, Muhammad's nephew and son-in-law Ali, was the catalyst for the major split in the Muslim world. Ali slowly lost power, and was murdered in 661. The *Shi'at Ali* (Partisans of Ali or Shi'a) believe Ali, as a blood relative of the Prophet, to be the only legitimate successor to Muhammad, thus separating themselves from Sunni Muslims. Contrary to popular Western perception, Shi'ism is not a creed of fanaticism or fundamentalism, but is Islam with a sharp focus on divinely chosen leaders (or *Imams*) who are blood descendants of the Prophet through Ali and his wife, the Prophet's daughter Fatima.

The prophet Muhammad is not believed to be divine, but rather a human messenger of God's word. His actions, however, are sanctified because God chose him to be the recipient of revelation; several verses of the Qur'an demand obedience to the Prophet. The stories and traditions surrounding the Prophet's life have been passed on as *sunna,* and those who follow the *sunna* in addition to the teachings of the Qur'an are considered to be especially devout Muslims. The term Sunni is derived from *sunna.* The primary source for *sunna* is the *Hadith,* a written collection of sayings attributed to Muhammad. A *hadith* had to go through a rigorous verification process before it was accepted as true; the tale had to be verified by several sources, preferably those who saw the action with their own eyes, and the greatest weight was given to testimony by Muhammad's close followers and relatives.

In the 10th century, under the weight of tradition and consensus, Sunni Muslim scholars *(ulama)* proclaimed "the gates of *ijtihad* (individual judgment)" closed; new concepts and interpretations could no longer stand on their own but had to be legitimized by tradition. This proscription notwithstanding, *ijtihad* continues today, though not on the scale of the first centuries of Islam. There have been numerous reform movements throughout the Islamic world, including the Wahhabbi movement in the Arabian peninsula, the movement of the thinker Jamal ad-Din al-Afghani in the Middle East, and Muhammad Iqbal in South Asia. There are four main schools of thought in the Islamic legal system, and the applicability of *sharia,* or Islamic law, is a subject of much strife in a number of Muslim countries, which have seen challenges to entrenched governments by movements carrying the banner of Islam (or their interpretation of it).

Any place where Muslims pray is a mosque or *masjid,* best translated as "place of prostration." The *imam* (leader of prayer, not to be confused with the Shi'a leaders) gives a sermon *(khutba)* on Friday. In many areas of the Islamic world, men and women still pray in different sections of the mosque. Women must cover their hair and everyone must remove their shoes.

The Sufis are a mystical movement within Islam, stressing the goal of unity with God. They are organized in orders, with a clear hierarchy from master to disciple. Different orders prescribe different ways of life in order to reach Allah; some preach total asceticism, others seem almost hedonistic in their pursuit of pleasure. Sufi *sheikhs* (masters) and saints are reputed to perform miracles, and their tombs are popular pilgrimage destinations. Jalal ad-Din Rumi, the great medieval intellectual, founded the famous order of the whirling dervishes. The term "whirling dervish" derives from the joyous spinning and dancing, meant to produce a state of mind conducive to unity with Allah, at Sufi festivals. Marijuana has also been used by some of the Sufis for this purpose.

## Pillars of Islam

*Allahu akbar. Ash-hadu an la ilaha illa Allah. Ashadu anna Muhammadan rasul Allah.* (God is great. I swear that there is no god but God. I swear that Muhammad is God's messenger.) These words compose the first lines of the Islamic call to prayer *(adhan),* which emanates hauntingly five times a day from the live or recorded *muezzins* perched atop their minarets. The first line glorifies God *(Allah).* The next two lines form the *shahadah* (the testimony of faith), which is the first of the five pillars of Islam. It reflects the unity of God *(tawhid),* an important doctrine in Islam, and the special place of Muhammad as God's final Messenger. Any person who wishes to convert to Islam may do so by repeating these lines three times, thereby completing the first pillar of Islam and becoming a Muslim. Enemies of Islam often memorized the lines before going into battle, thus providing themselves with an emergency survival tactic.

The second pillar is prayer *(salat),* performed five times per day, preferably directly following the call of the muezzin. However, if someone is unable to pray at that exact moment, the prayer may be made up and performed whenever possible before the next prayer time. Prayers, preceded by ablutions, begin with a declaration of intent and consist of a set cycle of prostrations. No group or leader is necessary for prayers—they constitute a personal communication with God. The person praying must face Mecca as he or she does so. The word for Friday in Arabic means "the day of gathering;" on that day, communal prayer is particularly encouraged.

The third pillar is alms *(zakat,* or purification). Every Muslim who can afford to is required to give one third of his or her income to the poor.

It is believed that Muhammad received the Qur'an during the month of Ramadan. Fasting during this holy month is the fourth pillar of Islam. Between dawn and sunset, Muslims are not permitted to smoke, have sexual intercourse, or let any food or water pass their lips; exceptions are made for women who are pregnant or menstruating, people who are sick, and people who are traveling—they must make up the fast at a later date. Fasting is meant to teach Muslims to resist temptation and thereby control all their unchaste urges. In addition, by experiencing hunger they are meant to better understand the plight of the poor; and also to be more thankful for the food which Allah has provided them. Finally, Ramadan inspires a sense of community among Muslims. Ideally, Muslims read the Qur'an during the daylight hours. As soon as the evening *adhan* is heard, they break the fast and begin a night of feasting, visits to friends and relatives, and revelry. In places like Cairo, the city stays up until just before dawn. In quieter areas, a neighbor may circulate to houses, banging a drum and waking people for *suhur,* a small meal eaten just before dawn in an attempt to avoid extreme hunger upon waking. During the month, offices and businesses not catering to tourists may be closed or keep shorter hours.

The last pillar, required only once in a lifetime, is pilgrimage *(hajj).* Only Muslims who are financially and physically able to are required to fulfil this pillar by journeying to Mecca and Medina during the last month of the Muslim calendar, and those who are able to make the trip talk about it for the rest of their lives. While *hajj* is essentially a re-creation of the actions of the Prophet Muhammad, its effects are to unite Muslims and to stress the equal status of all people who submit to the will of *Allah,* regardless of gender, degree of wealth, race, or nationality. All pilgrims, from Gulf Princes to Cairo street-sweepers, must wrap themselves in white cloth and remove all accessories, which might indicate wealth, and all perform the same rituals. If you are traveling during *hajj,* you may experience delays and general pandemonium in airports.

As with any religion, degrees of interpretation and observance produce a wide range of practices. For more, try *An Introduction to Islam* by Frederick Denny,

*Islam: The Straight Path* by John Esposito, or *Ideals and Realities of Islam* by Seyyed H. Nasr. A sampling of Islamic texts can be found in Kenneth Cragg and Marston Speight's *Islam from Within*. If you feel inspired enough to study the Qur'an, read Muhammad Pickthall's *Meaning of the Glorious Koran*.

## Mosque Architecture

Several architectural features deserve special attention in mosques. There are two basic designs. The Arab style, based on Muhammad's house, has a pillared cloister around a courtyard, while the Persian style has a vaulted arch on each side. Most prominent are the towering minarets from which the chants of the *muezzin* summon the faithful to prayer five times daily. Mosques are generally rectangular with cool arcaded porches *(riwaqs)* surrounding a central open courtyard *(saha)*. These usually contain a central covered fountain *(sabil)* for ablutions before prayer. The focus of each mosque is the *qibla* wall, which holds the prayer niche *(mihrab)* and indicates the direction of Mecca. Particularly in Mamluk mosques, the *mihrab* and *qibla* are elaborately decorated with marble inlay and Kufic inscriptions. Because some religious teachers consider representations of nature (animals, people) to be blasphemous imitations of God, abstract artwork dominates the mosques' decorations. In the Fatimid period, interlaced foliate patterns in carved stucco and plaster were popular ornamentation. Geometric patterns and elegant calligraphy appeared later, in Mamluk times. Particularly beautiful examples of work from this period are found on the pulpits *(minbars)* that usually stand beside the *mihrab*. Under the seat of the *minbar,* on the side, there is often an archway, allowing you to cross to the other side as you make a wish, called a "wishing door."

# OTHER FAITHS

### The Druze

The faith of the Druze, a staunchly independent sect of Shi'i Muslims, centers around a hierarchy of individuals who are the sole custodians of a religious doctrine hidden from the rest of the world. Many Druze consider themselves a separate ethnicity as well as a religious group, while others consider themselves Arabs. The Druze believe that the word of God is revealed only to a divinely chosen few, and that these blessed few must be followed to the ends of the earth. Wherever the Druze settle, however, they generally remain loyal to their host country. Israel has a Druze population of about 85,000; Syria 500,000; and Lebanon 300,000.

The religion was founded in 1017 by an Egyptian chieftain, Ad-Darazi, who drew upon various beliefs in the Muslim world at the time, especially Shi'ism. The Druze believe that God was incarnated in human forms, the final incarnation being the Fatimid Caliph Al Hakim (996-1021, see p. 46). The Druze have suffered a history of persecution and repression for their beliefs, which may partially explain the group's refusal to discuss its religion. The late 1600s was a period of prosperity, however, and under Emir Fakhir ad-Din the Druze kingdom extended from Lebanon to Gaza to the Golan Heights. Sixteen villages were built from the Mediterranean Sea to the Jezreel Valley to guard the two major roads on which goods and armies were transported. In 1830, a Druze revolt against the Egyptian pasha was crushed, along with all but two of the 14 Druze villages in the Carmel (see Isfiya and Daliyat Al Karmel, p. 366). In the 1860s, Ottoman rulers encouraged the Druze to return to the Carmel.

Because the Druze will not discuss their religion, most of what Westerners know about them comes from British "explorers" who fought their way into villages and stole holy books. Many of the Druze themselves are not completely informed. As far as outsiders know, Jethro, father-in-law of Moses, is their most revered prophet. The most important holiday falls in late April. In Israel, Druze gather in the holy village of Ḥittim, near Tiberias. Devout Druze are forbidden to smoke, drink alcohol, or eat pork, but many young Druze do not adhere strictly to these prohibitions. Some Druze believe in reincarnation, and may tell you about their past lives. Gabriel Ben-Dor's *The*

*Druze in Israel: A Political Study,* details the ideology, lifestyle, and political situation of the Druze.

### The Baha'i

This movement began in Teheran in 1863, when Mirza Hussein Ali (a son of Persian nobility) turned 46, renamed himself Baha'u'llah ("Glory of God"), and began preaching non-violence and the unity of all religions. Baha'u'llah's arrival had been foretold in 1844 by the Persian Siyyid Ali Muhammad (also known as Al Bab, or "Gateway to God"), the first prophet of the Baha'i religion, who heralded the coming of a new religious teacher and divine messenger. Baha'u'llah was imprisoned and then exiled to Palestine, where he continued his teachings in the city of Acre (Akko). Baha'u'llah is buried near Acre. Al Bab is buried in Haifa, which is now home to a large Baha'i population.

Baha'u'llah's teachings fill over 100 volumes; his religion incorporates elements of major Eastern and Western religions. Baha'i believe in a Supreme Being, accepting Jesus, Buddha, Muhammad, and Baha'u'llah as divine prophets. Baha'i Scripture includes the Bible, the Qur'an, and the Bhagavad-Gita. A central doctrine of the faith regards the Baha'i vision of the future. Instead of warning of a final Judgement Day or an end of the world (like many other religions), Baha'u'llah prophesied a "flowering of humanity," an era of peace and enlightenment to come. Before this new age can arrive, however, the world must undergo dreadful events to give civilization the impetus to reform itself. The Baha'i espouse trans-racial unity, sexual equality, global disarmament, and the creation of a world community. The rapidly-growing Baha'i faith currently boasts nearly six million adherents, with 2 million converts worldwide in the last decade.

### The Karaites

The small sect of Jews known as the Karaites dwell principally in Ashdod, Be'er Sheva, and the Tel Aviv suburb of Ramla. The community, whose existence dates to the 9th century CE, counts about 15,000 adherents today. Formed out of the political and religious turmoil following the Muslim invasion, Karaites adhere strictly to the five books of the Torah, though they reject all later Jewish traditions. They are generally cohesive, and have their own religious courts. To an outsider, however, their practices appear similar to those dictated by traditional Jewish observance.

### The Samaritans

Currently, the Samaritan community is a tiny one, with roughly 550 adherents divided between Nablus on the West Bank and Holon, a suburb of Tel Aviv. Originally the residents of Samaria, Samaritans consider themselves the original Israelites, descended from the tribes of Joseph (Manasseh and Ephraim) from whom other Israelites learned monotheism. The religion is seen by non-members as an offshoot of Judaism marked by literal interpretation of the Samaritan version of the Old Testament and the exclusion of later Jewish interpretation (i.e. the *Mishnah*, the Talmud, and all books of the Hebrew Bible after Joshua) from its canon. A gradual, centuries-long separation between the two religions culminated with the destruction of the Samaritan temple on Mt. Gerizim by the Hasmonean king John Hyrcanus in 128 BCE. The mountain is still the most holy site of the Samaritan religion. Centuries of persecution by the various rulers of Palestine shrunk the community further and included thousands of deaths in a 529 CE uprising against Byzantine rule. While the Rabbinate does not recognize Samaritans as Jews, the Israeli government applies the Law of Return (granting settlement rights) to them.

# ■ Let's Go Picks

You've seen the Pyramids, walked the Via Dolorosa, gone to Petra, and climbed Mt. Sinai—without this handy guide, your vacation might be over. In our tireless search for the best the Middle East has to offer, we think we may have finally found it.

## THE ULTIMATE CAIRENE NIGHT

The glass and steel towers of downtown mirror the pinkish glaze of the silent Nile, and the corniche swells with evening strollers. Nights in Cairo, even if all you do is have tea on the riverbank, are magnificent. The **sufi dancers** at **El Ghourri** (p. 126) seem to float in the air as they spin to get closer to God—and the free performances are unforgettable. Afterwards, rest your legs and lull your mind at **Fishawi's** (p. 122), the coolest place in Islamic Cairo to smoke a **sheesha.** The apple tobacco will tickle your lungs and warm your body.

## THE GREATEST OF THE GREAT OUTDOORS

The splendor of the **Ein Avdat Nature Reserve** (p. 427) in Israel's Negev captured the heart of David Ben-Gurion. Trails slink through wadis and past hermit caves, waterfalls, and the remains of a Byzantine fortress. The **Wadi el-Ruwayan** lake and waterfalls (p. 143) near Fayyum, Egypt, come pretty close to paradise. Cool, cobalt waters ripple beside sand dunes, separated by only a few meters of lush greenery.

## THEY DON'T MAKE RUINS LIKE THEY USED TO

Sometimes a pile of rubble is just that, but occasionally the ancients managed to put together a pretty fine stack of rocks. Our favorites include **Beit Guvrin National Park** in Israel (p. 345), with a spectacular underground network of rooms and caves, and a breathtaking above ground setting. **Kalabsha Temple** (p. 211) is magnificently perched above Lake Nasser in Upper Egypt, and while the ruins themselves are not as impressive as Luxor's more famous sites, the isolation of Kalabsha allows visitors to explore the pylons and obelisks as if discovering them for the first time. The imposing **Nimrod's Fortress** in northern Israel (p. 409) has great surrounding hikes and was supposedly built high enough to be within arrow-shooting distance of God.

## FAVORITE POINTS OF VIEW

There's only one place to be during sunsets in Palmyra, Syria—the **Qal'at ibn Maan,** 150m above the ancient city (p. 542). As the colonnades and countryside blush, the view from the castle terrace seems to extend through time and space. The most idyllic spot in Siwa, Egypt, is the **Fatnas Pool** (p. 170). Accessible via a small causeway, bathers are treated to a view across a salt lake to an endless sea of sands. The perspectives change with every step from atop the **ramparts** around the Old City of Jerusalem (p. 297), providing unsurpassed views of the City of Gold's domes and spires. The world's best views from a toilet seat are in the **Petra's bathrooms** (p. 495). Windows from the stalls overlook the rose-red ruins at the greatest and most picturesque "throne" you'll ever find.

## BEST LAST LICKS

You can cool off on hot Jerusalem days with a sweet and dreamy frozen yogurt (pronounced *frrrozen*) at **Katzefet** (p. 297). Look for glass mix-in cases of flaked chocolate, chopped nuts, *halva*, and fruits. In Egypt, cold treat cravings are best satisfied at **Mandarin Koedar,** with locations across the country (Cairo, p. 123; El Agami, p. 160). It's like licking silk. Exposed tongue sightings in Jordan cluster around **Ata Ali** ice cream parlors (Aqaba, p. 505).

# EGYPT مصر

| | |
|---|---|
| US£1=3.45 Egyptian pounds (E£) | E£1=US$0.29 |
| CDN$1=E£2.50 | E£1=CDN$0.40 |
| UK£1=E£5.24 | E£1=UK£0.19 |
| IR£1=E£5.56 | E£1=IR£0.18 |
| AUS$1=E£2.63 | E£1=AUS$0.38 |
| NZ$1=E£2.33 | E£1=NZ$0.43 |
| SAR1=E£0.75 | E£1=SAR1.33 |

> For important information on travel in general and some specifics on Egypt, see the Essentials section of this book. Egypt's **International Phone Code** is 20.

The Arab Republic of Egypt (Goumhouriyyat Misr El Arabiyya, or simply Misr) is the child of the Nile Valley. By a trick of northeastern African geography, the world's most fertile valley blooms right smack in the middle of the planet's greatest desert. The river's bounty and the hostility of the surrounding wasteland encouraged the formation of a settled society with a strong cultural and political identity that endured numerous foreign invaders over the past 5000 years.

Ancient Egyptian agriculture relied upon the Nile's annual flood. The Pharaoh's control over the yearly inundation was one of the bases for his claim to divinity; today modern technology has taken over that role. The Aswan High Dam is perhaps the most obvious example of the melding of the ancient and modern evident throughout Egypt. Completed in 1970, the dam ended the flooding; prayers and sacrifices to the Nile have been replaced by irrigation pumps and hydroelectric power.

Egypt is a budget traveler's paradise. The sights are stunning, the culture fascinating, and you'll almost never get caught in the rain. Best of all, you can live like a pharaoh on pennies a day (almost). But independent travel in Egypt can be a challenge; it requires plenty of time, stamina, and a relaxed, patient attitude.

The tourist's Egypt has five regions. The first is the **Mediterranean Coast.** Highlights include Alexandria, Egypt's summer capital, Marsa Matrouh, home to incredible beaches, and the beautiful Siwa Oasis, a pilgrimage to the West. The **Nile Valley** is the most popular region and, in terms of distance and sights, the most tremendous. It is divided into Upper Egypt in the South, Middle Egypt (in the middle), and Lower Egypt in the North (designated with respect to the direction of the river's flow—upstream and downstream). Lower Egypt includes the Nile Delta and Cairo, while Upper Egypt includes Luxor and Aswan. Nubia (currently underwater), where African and Egyptian culture merge, begins at the First Cataract of the Nile at Aswan and extends south into the Sudan.

The least explored region is the **Western Desert,** where palms shade the paradisiacal waterholes of Bahariyya, Farafra, Dakhla, Kharga, and Baris. Finally, on Egypt's **Red Sea Coast** and the **Sinai Peninsula,** snorkeling, scuba-diving, hiking, windsurfing, and spectacular scenery will revitalize museum-mutilated or temple-tired minds.

# ONCE THERE

## ■ Entry

A **visa** is required to enter Egypt (see Essentials: "Visas and Visa Extensions" on page 9). Generally, all personal items brought into the country to be taken out upon departure are exempt from taxes. There is no formal declaration for personal items.

Upon arrival at **Cairo International Airport** (often reminiscent of Rodin's *The Gates of Hell*), purchase a visa stamp at any currency exchange booth, if you have

not done so already. Visas cost around US$15. Visas can be purchased at any point of entry to Egypt; two-week Sinai-only visas can be purchased at the Israeli border. Visas purchased at the airport are good for one month but can be renewed at police stations or at passport offices in major towns if you provide one photograph, E£12, and receipts showing that at least US$200 has been changed into Egyptian currency. You must register your passport at a passport office within seven days of your arrival or risk a large fine and complications in getting out of the country. There are passport offices in most cities and towns. Or ask your hotel manager to handle the paperwork for you. If for some reason you are unable to register, the U.S. consulate issues an affidavit for U.S. citizens, with which you may register late at the Mugamma' in Tahrir Square in Cairo.

As you exit customs, you will likely be approached by individuals who claim to be "tourist agents" or employees of the Ministry of Tourism. They wait for unescorted travelers and, pretending to help you, set you up in their employers' hotels, which are not always a credit to the industry. Do not let anyone direct you to a hotel or even a cab; take **cabs** from the official stand, which is monitored 24 hours a day by tourist police officers wearing black berets and arm bands. Don't pay more than E£25-30 for a ride to downtown Cairo.

Bus #422 runs from the airport to Tahrir Sq. (35pt), leaving from in front of the parking lot at the terminal. Bus #400 and minibus #27 (25pt and 50pt) leave from the lot in front of the old terminal. Bus #400 goes to the airport from Tahrir Sq., and minibus #27 from the Mugamma' stop. Gem Travel runs a 24-hour **shuttle bus** to downtown ($4). The counter will be on the right as you exit customs.

All **trains** into Cairo stop at **Ramses Station.** Bus #59 runs from there to Tahrir Sq. Black and white **taxis** to Tahrir Sq. cost about E£2. The **metro,** just opposite the station, will whisk you to Tahrir Sq. for 50pt. To walk (½hr.), climb the pedestrian overpass and walk south on Ramses St., away from the statue of Ramses II.

**Buses** from the Sinai, Israel, and Jordan usually drop passengers off at Abbasiyya Station. Buses from Jordan usually drop you off at Abd el-Moneim Riyadh Station. To reach Tahrir Sq., hop into a southbound black and white cab (E£3.50-4.50) or walk left down Ramses St. as you leave the station, beyond the overpass, and to the first bus stop on the right. From here many buses travel to Tahrir Sq.

It used to be that the first sight to visit in Cairo was the voluminous gray building in Tahrir Sq. **(El Mugamma'),** home to **Passport Registration.** As of August 1996, however, visitors of all nationalities need only get their passport stamped upon entry—no further hassle required. For more information, see Cairo: Practical Information, p. 95.

# ■ Getting Around

Transport to obscure sights may not be as plentiful in summer (the off-season for tourism). Before that camel, Peugeot, or minibus spirits you off to a distant praying baboon statue or Nilometer, make sure it's up for the ride back as well. See **Cairo Transportation,** p. 90, and **Alexandria Transportation,** p. 148, for more information on getting around these zoos.

> Road travel in Egypt is extremely hazardous. Egypt has one of the highest road casualty rates in the world. To lower your risk, avoid overcrowded buses and minivans, and avoid night travel whenever possible. If the bus driver is operating the vehicle in a reckless manner, demand to be let off immediately, and report the incident to the American Embassy. In Egypt, 43.2 people are killed in traffic accidents for every 100 million km of vehicle travel; in the U.S., the comparable rate is 1.1 persons. (Source: *Association for Safe International Road Travel*)

**Travel Restrictions** It is prudent to check with the local tourism authorities or the Ministry of the Interior before venturing in private transport off the main roads in the Western Desert (especially near the Libyan and Sudanese borders), along the Suez Canal and Red Sea Coast, and in the Sinai. If you need a permit, apply at the Ministry of the Interior in Cairo at 110 Qasr el-Aini St. (tel. 354 83 00). In restricted zones, the police are entitled to confiscate your passport and hold you for questioning. If you find yourself in such a pickle, sincere apologies and professions of ignorance may put the matter to rest.

The law (seldom enforced) forbids Egyptians from traveling or even walking with foreigners without special permission. A travel agent's license, a marriage certificate proving the Egyptian and the foreigner are married, and wads of bribe money have all been used as ways to get around this restriction, but it is meant to protect you.

**Trains** Egypt's railway system was the first established in both the Arab world and in Africa. The first short lines were built in 1834, linking quarries in Moqattam with the Nile. Trains now serve even the smallest of towns. Schedules and signs in the anarchic train stations are never in English, but schedules can be obtained from the tourist office or, as a last resort, from ticket windows; a fellow passenger or the man-on-the-platform can also help you out. It is not at all unusual for a train to come three hours late, and schedules and prices are in constant flux.

A good thing about trains is that they offer **student discounts** of up to 50%. **Air-conditioned second-class** cars have comfy reclining seats and are a great value; shelling out more for first-class gets you slightly larger seats and loud, annoying Egyptian videos. Third class cars are sorely overcrowded and not entirely safe, so tourists are often not allowed to use them for long trips. **Second-class sleeper cars,** available on some regular trains, might be more comfortable for trips of ten hours or more, but, at a cost several times that of regular second-class, they are overpriced. They are also difficult to book; plan well in advance. Discounts on sleepers are less than on regular seats, and you might not get a discount at all on the luxurious **wagon-lits.** You can reserve space in a sleeper at the *wagon-lit* offices in Cairo, Luxor, Aswan, and Alexandria. Purchase other tickets at the station of departure; allow plenty of time to stand in line. For a fee, a travel agent or your hotel will send someone to buy a ticket for you. Seats for Cairo-Alexandria (especially in summer) and Cairo-Upper Egypt (especially in winter) should be reserved one or two days in advance.

Round-trip reservations cannot be arranged at the point of departure. If you intend to take a sleeper, take care of return reservations as soon as you reach your destination. During the last week of Ramadan and the following week, as well as before Eid el-Adha, trains are completely booked. If you plan to travel during these periods, book your tickets at least one week in advance.

If lines are long and you're in a hurry, try boarding the train without a ticket. The conductor will usually sell you one on board for a small fine, even if the train is full. The real problem will be finding a seat or an empty space on the floor. If you miss your train and you're lucky, you may be issued a ticket on the next train out—even if there are officially no seats available. Just act helpless and foreign. If you want to return reserved tickets, go to the stationmaster's office before the scheduled departure and your money (minus a little) will be refunded.

**Buses** Only large cities have intracity bus systems. The public buses are inexpensive but often slow, crowded, and brain-meltingly hot. In some places they are your only option.

Private companies include the **West Delta Bus Company, East Delta Bus Company,** and **Superjet.** Regular West Delta buses are on par with public buses, but they have a deluxe branch called **Golden Arrow.** Golden Arrow and Superjet are air-conditioned and have bathrooms and refreshments available on board. Unfortunately, they often show Egyptian melodramas replete with women in head scarves shrieking at unsustainable volumes. They serve routes from Cairo-Alexandria and Cairo-Luxor. The East Delta Bus Company runs generally comfortable, air-conditioned buses throughout the Sinai. When you buy a ticket for one of these luxury buses, you will be assigned to a particular seat.

**Taxis** Another way to get from one town to another or between towns and sights is the **service taxi** (pronounced ser-VEES). We refer to them throughout the book as *service;* they are also known as *taxi bin-nafar* (particularly in Middle and Upper Egypt) and *taxi ugra.* Keep all three names in mind. They can take the form of Peugeot station-wagons and other cars, covered pick-up trucks, or minibuses, and depart from stands in the various cities and towns. In smaller towns the "stand" may be nothing more than a stretch of road. Simply board the vehicle and wait for it to fill up, which usually takes 15 to 30 minutes. When tourism is slow, it will take longer to collect companions. Drivers depart when their cars are full or when everyone is tired of waiting and the passengers have agreed to split the price of a full carload. The best thing about *service* is flexibility—no schedules or incorrect timetables. You're also unlikely to be cheated because all passengers pay the same amount. Finally, the ride can be a bonding experience, with Cleopatras circulating freely and Egyptian pop blasting on the radio. One disadvantage is that *service* drivers are all insane, though there are fewer crashes than you'd expect.

The intracity version of *service* is the **minibus,** prowling the same streets day in, day out. Flag one down and pay the bargain-basement fare once aboard. **Private taxis** are cheap and convenient in Cairo (where they are black and white) and Alexandria (black and yellow or orange). Understanding and skillfully using them will make you feel like a stud on wheels. (See **Cairo Transportation,** p. 90, and **Alexandria Transportation,** p. 148.)

**"Special"** is Egyptian code for **rip-off.** If this word is mentioned in your presence, calmly repeat *"La"* (No) and the words you have learned for *service. Bin-nafar* and *ugra* are particularly helpful in this situation. Within cities, avoid being ripped off by hailing a private taxi on the street instead of in front of a tourist trap. If a cabbie approaches you first, be especially wary. Either don't talk about the price before you get in and pay what is appropriate when you get out (our city and sights listings give estimates) or settle on a suitable price before you climb in.

**Hitchhiking** Hitching is not common in the highly populated parts of Egypt. In recent years, the newspapers have been full of crimes perpetrated by hitchhikers along the roads between Cairo and Alexandria. Because of this, drivers may be reluctant to pick people up. Rides are reportedly easy to obtain in isolated areas, such as along the Great Desert Road, or for short jaunts in remote parts of the Nile Valley, where public transportation is difficult to find. Many drivers who pick up hitchhikers will expect money anyway, so public transportation should be used where it is available, which is almost everywhere. **Women, whether in a group or alone, should not hitchhike.** Nobody traveling alone should accept a ride in a private car. Egypt is mostly sparsely traveled desert; never count on getting a ride before you **die of dehydration.** *Let's Go* does not recommend hitchhiking. Don't hitchhike.

**Car Rental** Renting a car is a useful option only in the Sinai and Oases. If you plan to drive, remember to obtain the necessary permits (see the specific area you plan to drive in). There are few places to drop off rental cars. An **International Driver's License** is theoretically required to drive in Egypt. Any insurance you have will not cover you here, and rental companies don't always provide insurance; plan to invest in proper coverage. Age requirements are not always strictly enforced by rental agencies. The cheapest rentals run around US$35 per day. It is often cheaper and easier to make reservations with a car rental agency before you leave your home country. Realize your life is forfeit once you enter the melee of Egyptian motoring.

**Planes** **EgyptAir** serves major cities in Egypt out of Cairo International Airport. All prices listed are out of Cairo, one-way, economy class: to Luxor (1hr., US$105); Aswan (1½hr., US$145); Alexandria (45-50min., US$62); Abu Simbel (1¾hr., US$207); and Hurghada (1hr., US$114). EgyptAir's main office in the U.S. is at 720 Fifth Ave., New York, NY 10019 (tel. (800) 334-6787). See Practical Information listings for offices in specific cities. **Air Sinai,** in the courtyard of the Nile Hilton, is a charter created to serve the Sinai and Israel. Call (62) 44 28 31 for information. Below are one-way fares; the round-trip is probably not discounted. Foreigners may have to pay in U.S. dollars. Air Sinai flies from Cairo to Sharm esh-Sheikh (50min., US$120), from Hurghada to Sharm esh-Sheikh (50min., US$83), and between Cairo and Tel Aviv (40min., US$183). For more information, contact the office at 12 Qasr en-Nil St., Cairo (tel. (02) 75 06 00 or 75 07 29) or another EgyptAir office.

# ■ Useful Addresses

**Tourist Services** The **Egyptian Tourist Authority (ETA)** has offices in most major cities. The **Tourist Police** are actually meant to assist visitors. Go to them in case of theft or if you feel you have been taken advantage of in any way. Most offices employ at least one person who speaks some English. The officers' uniforms are black in winter, white in summer, with green "Tourist Police" arm bands.

**Medical Emergencies and Health** Luxury hotels may have resident doctors, and other hotels can usually get someone dependable in an emergency. You can also ask your embassy for a list of recommended physicians and pharmacists, or see individual city listings. Several major hospitals in Cairo provide 24-hr. service, including the **Misr International** (12 Sataya St., Finney Sq., Dokki; tel. 360 82 61 through 82 69), the **Anglo-American Hospital** (Botanical Garden St., Gezira-Zamalek; tel. 340 61 65), and the **As-Salaam International Hospital** (Corniche en-Nil, Ma'adi; tel. 363 80 50, emergency 362 33 00).

Even big-city **pharmacies** (identifiable by the snake-on-a-staff symbol or by a red crescent) do not carry American or European brand-name drugs; the Egyptian brands are, however, equally effective and reliable. They are also much, much cheaper. Before you do any major traveling, stock up on headache, diarrhea, and constipation pills. Also take along some of the electrolyte and nutrient rehydrating solution used for babies; if you get dehydrated or experience a minor sunstroke, this will help your recovery process. Egypt is a bit more relaxed about prescriptions than the U.S. Condoms are available over the counter at city pharmacies. Ask for *kabout, tops,* or *'azil.* "Tops" is the Egyptian-made condom brand. Condoms are not available in small towns or in conservative Middle Egypt. Other things you will have trouble finding are anti-perspirant, deodorant, and tampons. Pads are usually uncomfortable wads of cotton, though Always brand has begun to appear in many towns. Pharmacists in Egypt are authorized to write prescriptions and give injections. There should be at least one pharmacy in each town, although finding a 24-hr. store may prove difficult in small towns. **Dial 123 for emergencies.** (Also see Essentials: **Health** on p. 19 and Practical Information listings for various cities.)

# ■ Money Matters

**Currency and Exchange** Egypt's array of coins and banknotes is gradually becoming simplified as the old bills and coins pass out of circulation and into the hands of numismatists. The **Egyptian pound (E£)** (gin-EEH) is divided into 100 **piasters (pt)** (*irsh,* plural u-ROOSH). Technically, piasters are divided into 10 *millims,* but the only vestige of this minuscule denomination is an extra zero to the right of the decimal point on some posted prices. **Banknotes** are color coded and printed with Arabic on one side and English on the other; the notes come in the following denominations: E£100 (green), E£50 (red), E£20 (green), E£10 (red), E£5 (blue), E£1 (brown), 50pt (red and brown), and 25pt (blue). Bills do not vary much in size. It's best to break your large bills into smaller denominations of E£1 and below, as most people are reluctant to make change. **Coins** come in denominations of 5pt (copper-colored) and 10pt and 20pt (both silver-colored—check the Arabic numbering). Hoard them; they are useful for various piddling expenses. Shopkeepers may not bother with change below 25pt; fight for your right to coinage or accept the oft-proffered candy or gum instead.

The **currency exchange system** was completely revised, to the great advantage of the tourist, in 1986. The government tried to destroy the black market by co-opting its business—of course, the black market adjusted (currently about E£4 per US$). Be sure to **save all exchange receipts.**

To buy a plane or boat ticket out of Egypt, find out the price in pounds, exchange exactly that amount at the official rate, and then present your receipt as you purchase the ticket. You are not allowed to carry more than E£20 into or out of Egypt, nor would you want to, so exchange what you think you'll use, or visit the 24-hr. bank at the airport on your way out to change back what you haven't used.

**Prices** A brief lesson in Egyptian Arabic: After *min fadlak* (please) and *shukran* (thank you), the most important word to know is *khawaga* (kha-WA-ga), because you are one. *Khawaga* means "tourist," but is understood locally as "clueless and rich." No matter how destitute you consider yourself, you are probably wealthy by Egyptian standards. Egyptians know this. Aside from those in hotels and restaurants, most prices are not posted, which means that *khawagas* may be charged more than Egyptians. Avoid salesfolk and shops near tourist hubs and look upon unsolicited offers of goods or services with grave suspicion, even if (especially if) you are told there is no charge. Agree on a price before you accept anything, and do not pay until you receive the goods. At official sites, entrance fees are set and **students get discounts of up to 50%** with proper student ID, making the purchase of an ISIC worthwhile. Shutterbugs are slapped with a photography/video fee, usually E£5-10. The people who work at ticket kiosks will charge you the correct fee (bring exact change), but guides who solicit your business at sights and museums should be ignored. Report serious hustlers and rip-off artists to the Tourist Police.

Shopping in Egypt can be an adventure. For basics, you should go where the Egyptians go and pay what the Egyptians pay; rare is the department store clerk or pharmacy that thrives on ripping off *khawagas*. For souvenirs and native sundries, stoke your cynicism. Valuable craftwork is out there, but it's rare. Avoid souvenir shops and kiosks flanking tourist attractions. The bazaars in the cities are chaotic, but they are the best places to find great leather, woodwork, glassware, textiles, or jewelry. There are great deals everywhere on beautifully crafted silver. The key word is: **bargain.** (See Essentials: "Bargaining" on page 17.)

**Tipping and Bakhsheesh** Another crucial Arabic word for *khawagas* to know is *bakhsheesh,* the art of tipping. It is an ancient tradition in Arab societies and was going on long before *khawagas* trampled onto the scene. Although *bakhsheesh* is different from straightforward charity, it stems from the belief that those who have should give to those who have not, particularly in return for a favor or service. There are three kinds of *bakhsheesh.* The most common is similar to **tipping**—a small reward for a small service. Baggage handlers, guards, and bathroom and parking attendants expect to receive a tip of 25pt-E£1. Do not let yourself be railroaded into forking over huge sums—if a smiling worker demands E£5, smile back and give 25pt-E£1. *Bakhsheesh* becomes most useful when used to procure special favors; almost any minor rule can be broken for *bakhsheesh.* If a custodian gives you a private tour of a mosque or lets you in long after hours, a pound or two is in order. Never expect recipients of *bakhsheesh* to make change—one more reason to carry small bills. Ignore demands for more if you feel you've been fair and only tip in exchange for a service—i.e. don't tip smiles.

The second kind of *bakhsheesh* is the giving of **alms.** Everywhere in Egypt you will encounter beggars who are willing to bestow rhetorical blessings upon you in return for a little charity. There are also those who insist on opening a door before you can get to it or snatch your baggage from your hands and then demand *bakhsheesh.* The final form of *bakhsheesh* is simply a **bribe,** generally a bad idea. Don't try to tip government officials. Offering *bakhsheesh* to people of rank is quite insulting.

**Business Hours** On Friday, the Muslim day of communal prayer, most government offices, banks, and post offices are closed. Bank hours are ordinarily Sunday to Thursday 8:30am-noon (although some banks in big cities are open daily), with money exchange available daily 8:30am-noon and 4-8pm. Foreign banks keep longer business hours, usually Sunday to Thursday 8am-3pm. Other establishments, such as restaurants, remain open seven days a week. Store hours are ordinarily Saturday to Thursday 9am-2pm and 5-8pm (9pm in winter), with many stores also open Friday. Government office hours are usually 9am-2pm. Do your government business in the morning, as workers often leave before official closing times. Archaeological sites and other points of interest are typically open 8am-5pm, though in summer the most important ones are open 6am-early afternoon.

During the month-long holiday of **Ramadan** (Dec. 31-Jan. 16 in 1997), some restaurants close entirely, while some others open only after sundown when the fast is broken. The streets empty at dusk as everyone sits down to *iftar* (the breaking of the fast), after which business resumes. Shops close at 3:30pm during Ramadan and reopen from 8-11pm. In the middle of the night, about 2-3am, Egyptians sit down for the second daily meal of Ramadan (*suhur,* pronounced su-HOOR) before going to sleep. Although traveling during Ramadan can be inconvenient, the excitement of nighttime celebrations offsets daytime hassles.

# ■ Accommodations

**Hostels** Egypt's HI youth hostels vary in quality. Most are grungy, crowded, and tucked away in obscure corners that are difficult to find and far away from any interesting activity. Most destinations offer much nicer accommodations for only slightly more money. Keep a careful eye on your valuables and take your passport and money to bed with you. Advance reservations are usually unnecessary. A valid **HI** card is seldom required, but at some hostels it will save you some money. You can get an International Guest Card at Egyptian hostels for E£24. For hostel expenses, don't count on being able to use your credit card or traveler's checks. Most hostels have kitchen facilities. Write to the **Egyptian Youth Hostel Association,** 1 El Ibrahimy St., Garden City, Cairo (tel. (02) 354 0527). The Youth Travel Department also answers questions, helps plan tours, has maps, and sells International Guest Cards.

**Hotels** Egypt's hotels run the gamut from opulent new resort complexes to ramshackle dives in dingy alleys; somewhere in between is an array of clean, comfortable, inexpensive hotels. Prices depend almost solely upon competition. In towns with heavier tourist traffic, you may spend as little as E£6 per night for clean, comfortable surroundings. Lower-quality accommodations in a town with very few hotels and even fewer visitors might cost E£15-25. Prices vary considerably between high and low season. The high season in Alexandria is June-August, in the Nile Valley October-April. There is a hotel tax which varies by location, averaging around 21%. Unless otherwise noted, the tax is already included in the price. Breakfast is not included in prices unless listed. Cash is the way to go; outside Cairo, credit cards and traveler's checks won't do you much good.

Many budget hotels have private bedrooms but shared bathrooms. In most places, E£5-10 extra will secure the luxury of a private bath. Air-conditioning also increases the price. Fans are usually included in the room price, especially in the hotter regions of the country. Do not expect to find towels, cute little bars of soap, or bottles of shampoo and conditioner. Don't count on toilet paper, either. (Guess what that little squirting pipe in the toilet is for.) Any place can send your laundry out for 50pt-E£1 per piece. Many hotels will allow you to use their washing machines and kitchens, but bring your own soap.

Be careful: in places where competition is fierce, competition is fierce. In the savage jungle of the tourism industry, consider yourself a lion cub amongst hyenas. You will start off defenseless and lost, but can grow into a fearsome budget travel machine. The most important thing to remember is that everyone who approaches you is trying to get your money, despite what they may say. Hotel owners and their agents will lie and scheme to get you in their clutches. Beware of impostors. Locals know which hotels have a good reputation and will do almost anything to get your business. Don't be afraid of being rude and nasty should the situation demand it. There have been many cases of male hotel employees harassing female visitors. These range from Peeping Tom incidents to unwanted sexual advances. In general, if you keep your distance you will increase your chances of passing through unbothered. Make it clear early on what your reaction to such attention will be.

---

### Ah, to be a khawaga

An Arabic sign at popular tourist sights reads "Keep Heliopolis clean. Cleanliness is very important to tourists and Heliopolis is often one of the first places they see." Many Egyptians wonder why they aren't encouraged to keep the city clean for themselves. Egypt's reliance on the tourist industry has led it to apply a different set of rules to foreigners than to natives. Most foreign couples, married or not, can take a room together in a hotel. For Egyptian couples, it's not so simple. In all but the cheapest hotels, only a married couple can share a room. Borrowing your friend's wedding rings won't do, either—a marriage license is required. Tourists can also gamble, a sport forbidden to citizens. While your foreign status might subject you to unwanted hassles and scams, it also grants you a degree of freedom withheld from most Egyptians.

# ▓ Keeping in Touch

**Mail** Airmail letters and postcards from Egypt to any destination outside the Middle East cost 80pt. Most hotels sell stamps, though a 5pt surcharge may be added. The most dependable place to receive mail is at **American Express offices; Poste restante** is also available in major cities. Confusion over first and last names can be avoided by printing the last name in capital letters. As a general rule, mail to Egypt is much faster than mail from Egypt. In either case, don't hold your breath—two or three weeks' delivery time is normal. In theory, all mail leaving Egypt is opened and inspected.

For faster service that won't break the bank, seek international **Express Mail Service (EMS),** available almost everywhere. It costs E£28 per kg and usually takes 3-20 days to the U.S. and 3-15 days to Europe. To send packages by **Federal Express,** contact the office at 1079 Corniche en-Nil St., Garden City, Cairo (tel. (02) 357 1304; fax 357 1318). **DHL International Courier** delivers stuff door-to-door all around the world. The main office is at El Mona Towers, 16 Lebanon St., Mohandiseen, Cairo (tel. (02) 302 9801; fax (02) 302 9810).

**Telephone** **Long-distance** and **international calls** can be made from most government telephone offices (*maktab et-telephonat, centrale* in Alexandria), usually open 24 hours and packed to capacity in the evenings. In very small towns the process is less than a joy—your hair may turn gray before you hear mom's voice on the line. In most cities you can make calls using brand-new, life-saving **phone cards** emblazoned with the Sphinx's stern visage (E£20 or E£40). The cards are sold at some telephone offices for use at bright orange phones either in the offices themselves or in train stations and other public places. Alternatively, go up to the desk and provide the number you are calling and the amount of time for which you would like to speak. You will be called to a booth when your call comes through and asked to hang up when your time is up. Rates are lower at night. Refuse to pay for incorrect connections. You can also call from private phones with international lines, definitely a luxury. Major hotels have good connections but can be expensive.

For AT&T **collect calls,** USADirect, or World Connect, call (02) 510 02 00 (AT&T) from anywhere in Egypt. Some ritzy hotels have USADirect phones in their lobbies; some also have UK, Canada, and JapanDirect. Call (02) 355 5770 for MCI WorldPhone or collect calls. Call (02) 365 3643 for CanadaDirect calls using a Bell Canada calling card. Kiwis should call (02) 365 3764 to reach their island home direct, while Brits should call (02) 365 3644 to reach theirs. These telephone numbers are in Cairo, and you will pay as if you had been talking to someone in Cairo for the duration of your call overseas. Don't try to explain the process to telephone office employees. Tell them you are calling Cairo and pay for that call. You can also call from the gray, coin-operated pay phones in most telephone offices, but you risk being unceremoniously cut off if you neglect to pump it with coins every two seconds or so. The orange phones are more convenient. The Cairo operator can place a collect call for you or connect you to any number in the U.S. if you have that party's calling card. The **international phone code** for calling to Egypt is **20.**

**Local calls** can be dialed direct anywhere in Egypt (10pt for 3min.), but attempting to call BFE may be more pain than pleasure. Use the gray coin-operated payphones. Be wary of using phones in hotel rooms; it could cost an arm and an ear.

**Telegraph and Fax** Telephone offices and hotels have **telex** and **cable** services (see individual town listings). **Fax** is becoming widely available. While telephone offices are the least expensive, hotels and private companies like American Express are the most reliable.

# ■ Women Travelers

Foreign women unescorted by men will undoubtedly be harassed by Egyptian men. Harassment can take many forms, from a mildly sinister "hello," to frightening and potentially harmful physical contact. Western women have the reputation, transferred through movies, television, etc., of being "free" in their dealings and their behavior. Watch especially for the vipers in Luxor. Some common-sense precautions will limit uncomfortable moments; dress conservatively and do not visit isolated areas alone. Nightclubs, along with crowded public transportation, especially third-class train cars and intracity buses, are best avoided. ("Nightclubs" in the West are equivalent to "discos" in the Middle East; Middle Eastern "nightclubs" are something completely different. See Alexandria Entertainment, p. 159.)

Other "precautions" do not necessarily mesh with common sense. For example, a 50-year-old man will have no qualms about harassing ten women; but if there is even one man in your group, the dynamic changes considerably. Also, the concept of friendship between men and women has not quite reached these shores. Many Egyptian men still think that if a woman even speaks to them, this implies a sexual advance of some sort. They will believe the same about any non-Egyptian male friends you make. Use this to your advantage by travelling with groups of tourists in possibly dangerous areas. The best way to deal with harassment from strangers in the street is to ignore it, but repeated advances or harassment should be quelled with a loud, indignant response in front of many people. Alert the tourist police—that's why they're there. For more information, see Essentials: Safety & Security, p. 17, and Women and Travel, p. 31.

# LIFE AND TIMES

The burgeoning population of Egypt, 63 million strong, is composed of a broad spectrum of cultures and classes, including Christian Copts (many of whom reside in Cairo and Middle Egypt), Bedouin, and southern Egyptians claiming to be the pure and direct descendants of the Pharaohs. The majority claim Arab ancestry or mixed Arab and Egyptian blood, while the upper classes boast of Turkish heritage. Dark-skinned Nubians from southern Egypt began migrating north when their villages were flooded out of existence by the creation of Lake Nasser. The Nubians fill mostly menial jobs in today's urban centers and suffer through racism to which most Egyptians will not admit. Finally, people with Greek, Armenian, Jewish, Kurdish, and Albanian origins add spice to the mix, especially in Alexandria. But there is one important commonality that unites these ethnicities: most people consider themselves wholly Egyptian. The great majority of the lower class lives in appalling poverty, some relying on family and relatives abroad (usually in the Gulf) for support. The cheapest commodity in resource-poor Egypt is labor. Along the banks of the Nile, *fellaheen* farm the rich land as their ancestors did 5000 years ago, but Egypt must supplement these products with imported food.

Egyptians are known throughout the Arab world for their sense of humor and love of fun. Although tourism and poverty here have made hospitality less common than in other Arab countries, you won't be in Egypt long before you are invited to tea, a meal, or a wedding. Directions and advice are freely offered, but some Egyptians so fear looking foolish that they will give incorrect directions rather than fail to offer assistance. Most hosts or helpers will expect something in return.

Egypt is a conservative, patriarchal society with a strong Islamic tradition. Western mores do not apply, especially in matters of family and sex. The visibility and freedom of most Egyptian women is limited. Do not challenge traditions or mores by trying to force yourself into arguments or places in which you do not belong. Violent crime is uncommon in Egypt, and it is usually safe to wander in large cities.

From the Western tourist's point of view, a disconcerting characteristic is Egyptians' apparent lack of concern for time. You must simply accept this, slow down, and mellow out. Your temper is most likely to howl in encounters with Egypt's mind-occluding bureaucracy; don't spend more time buying train tickets and placing phone calls than exploring ancient temples. Bring every book ever written by Naguib Mahfouz (or better yet, *Let's Go*) to read as you wait in line, and relax.

# ■ Government & Politics

According to its 1971 constitution, Egypt is a "democratic, socialist state," but in reality it's neither democratic nor socialist. It is more of an election-legitimated authoritarian regime, in which the president serves a six-year term and is almost inevitably reelected for additional terms. He appoints the vice-president and ministers. Since the 1952 revolution, successions to the presidency have happened only when Gamal Abd en-Nasser died in 1970, and then when his successor Anwar es-Sadat was assassinated in 1981. The legislative branch consists of the 444-member People's Assembly, half of whom must be workers or peasants, and 30 of whom must be women. This popularly elected assembly ratifies all laws as well as the national budget. Despite the regime's ultimate authority (the assembly is very much a rubber-stamp body), and the (relatively small) internal secret police force, Egypt's government is relatively liberal for an Arab nation.

The most significant political threat to current President Hosni Mubarak's regime comes from the Islamist parties. Mubarak's inauguration followed the assassination of Sadat by militants whose aim was to overthrow the Egyptian government and establish an Islamic republic in its place. Islamists gained parliamentary strength in the May 1984 elections for the People's Assembly. A fundamentalist group, the Muslim Brotherhood, joined with the Wafd Party, and the alliance achieved the necessary 8% minimum for parliamentary representation. Islamists were also elected to university student councils, often gaining majorities and faculty support; they have now gained control over most professional syndicates. In attempts to quell the Islamic militants, the government acquiesced to several fundamentalist demands. Mubarak has consistently appeased Islamic moderates (the majority) in order to isolate militants, who have been targets of brutal repression. Alcohol was banned on EgyptAir flights. *Dallas* was taken off TV (to the chagrin of many), and an Islamic newspaper, *Al-Liwa'al-Islami,* was initiated. Divorce laws were also changed, allowing the state to force annulments on intellectuals declared apostate.

The past several years have seen a rise in Islamist-generated violence, with militants based in Middle Egypt striking at the status quo via attacks on government figures and assassinations of secularist intellectuals. Civilian and tourist deaths shook Egyptian society in 1993, and massive jailings and several executions failed to stop the Islamists. The focus of their violence has recently shifted to governmental and security forces. The country as a whole remains stable but tense and under tight security controls. For more information, see the warning for traveling in Middle Egypt (p. 173). An attempt on Mubarak's life by Sudanese Islamists in July of 1995 raised tensions on Egypt's southern border, and waves of anti-Sudanese propaganda may lead to greater crises in the near future.

# ■ Economy

At the beginning of this century, Egypt was the richest of the Arab nations. However, Egypt's mushrooming population and shortage of arable land have greatly inhibited its economic development. All but 4% of Egypt is desert, and the land that is fertile is overcrowded. Nonetheless, Nasser's land reform greatly altered the economy's complexion; in 1952, 3% of the population owned more than half of the land, while today, no private citizen may own more than 50 acres.

About half of the Egyptian labor force works in the agricultural sector, growing primarily cotton, corn, rice, and grain. A growing proportion of workers is involved in manufacturing, which now accounts for as much income as agriculture. The government employs almost all the rest of the work force in its colossal bureaucracy. As the population grows at nearly 2.4% per year (in 1993, down from a high of 3% in 1985), many educated Egyptians leave to find work in wealthy, neighboring oil states (there may be as many as 3 million expatriated workers). Illiteracy remains high (over 50% of the population over 10 years old), poverty is widespread, and the typical diet is inadequate.

To help combat these problems, Egypt's government follows whatever political wind is carrying the most money and, as a result, receives vast amounts of foreign aid. Through the 1970s, Saudi Arabia, Qatar, Kuwait, and the United Arab Emirates supplied Egypt with tens of billions of dollars in aid, and in 1977 formed the Gulf Organization for the Development of Egypt (GODE). After the Camp David Accords in 1979, Egypt received grants from the United States as well. Under the Carter Plan, the U.S., Western Europe, and Japan agreed to provide Egypt with US$12.25 billion over five years. For its support in the Gulf War, Egypt received further assistance from the West (including the forgiving of US$6.7 billion of military debt to the U.S.) and renewed aid from the Gulf states. Revenue from the Suez Canal has consistently been about US$1.5 billion per year during the last decade. The US$3.5 billion per year tourism industry doesn't hurt, either. That's a lot of *kabab*.

## ■ Religion and Holidays

About 94% of Egypt's population is Sunni Muslim. Most other Egyptians are Christian Orthodox of the Coptic (Egyptian) Church. Smaller religious minorities include Shi'a Muslims, Protestants, Roman Catholics, Greek Orthodox, and Jews. Government offices and banks close for Islamic holidays (see When to Go, p. 2), but tourist facilities remain open. Though sometimes inconvenient, Ramadan can be a wonderful time to visit, especially in festive Cairo or Alexandria.

Along with the Islamic festivals, watch for the two Sufi rituals of **Zikr** and **Zar**. In the former, a rhythmic group dance builds in fervor, and the group members become whirling dervishes, mesmerized into a communal trance. The latter is a group dance performed by women, primarily as an exorcism rite. Both rituals are practiced on Fridays in some populous areas. The Coptic celebrations of Easter and Christmas are tranquil affairs marked by special church services.

**Sham en-Nissim** falls on the first Monday after Coptic Easter (approximately April 24). Though its origins are a hodgepodge of Coptic and pharaonic influences, it has developed into a secular holiday. Egyptians traditionally spend the day at a picnic eating *fasikh*, a dried, salted fish difficult for most Western palates to appreciate.

The major national holidays, observed officially by banks and government offices but without public celebration are **New Year's Day** (Jan. 1), **Union Day** (Feb. 28), **Sinai Liberation Day** (April 25), **Labor Day** (May 1), **Evacuation Day** (June 18), **Revolution Day** (July 23 in Cairo, July 26 in Alexandria), **National Day** (Oct. 6), **Suez City and National Liberation Day** (Oct. 24), and **Victory Day** (Dec. 23).

## ■ Language

One of the earliest forms of writing was Egyptian **hieroglyphs** (sacred carvings). Alongside this pictorial system developed the **heiratic,** an abbreviated cursive script, which retained only the vital characteristics of the pictures. After the 22nd Dynasty, scribes changed the hieratic writing to a form known as **Enchorial** or **Demotic,** used primarily in secular contexts. *The Book of the Dead* was translated into this script. Well before the end of the Roman period in Egypt, hieroglyphs had been fully replaced by Demotic, Greek, and Latin. Egyptian no longer served as the spoken language. **Coptic,** today used only in liturgy, is a derivation of ancient Egyptian that uses Greek letters plus six letters of Demotic.

Since the Islamic conquest, the primary language of Egypt has been Arabic. Modern **Egyptian Arabic** differs greatly from classical Arabic, and the Egyptian dialect varies significantly from that used in Jordan, Syria and other Arab nations. Even within Egypt the vernacular varies; Cairo, Lower Egypt, and Upper Egypt each have their own dialects. For more information, see the **Language Glossary, p. 557.**

The most comprehensive English-to-Arabic dictionary of Egypt's spoken dialect is the *Pocket Dictionary of the Spoken Arabic of Cairo,* compiled by Virginia Stevens and Maurice Salib, available at the American University of Cairo Bookstore. The *Cairo Practical Guide* includes a useful list of words; *Berlitz Arabic for Travelers* is helpful if you can master their cryptic transliteration system.

Most educated Egyptians speak at least a bit of English, and some are fluent. French is also commonly spoken among the Egyptian upper classes.

## ■ The Arts

Throughout most of the second half of the 20th century, Egypt has had a near monopoly on the Arabic entertainment industry. Egyptian films, widely distributed and appreciated throughout the Arab world, range from emotionally wrenching, skillfully done modern dramas to hilarious comedies pitting down-and-out students against evil capitalists and bumbling police officers, with a smattering of southern Egyptians (stereotypically portrayed as idiots) thrown in for comic relief. The musicals of the 50s and 60s, still very popular, featured well-dressed young hipsters singing their hearts out and knitting their brows in consternation over the cruelty of love, the generation gap, and the difficulty of college examinations.

Mini-dramas or short-term soap operas are also popular. In these, women swimming in oceans of green and blue eye shadow and wearing head scarves hung with golden coins battle insults to their reputations, pine quietly for the hard-working medical student upstairs, and thank Allah profusely when chastity and morality win out in the end. The country also boasts many theatrical successes; summertime brings brightly-painted billboards advertising plays patronized by Egyptians and Gulf vacationers.

### LITERATURE

Most of the writings of the **ancient Egyptians,** such as the *Book of the Dead,* deal with magic and religion. The ancients dabbled in poetic love songs as well. The *Song of the Harper* advises immediate gratification in the face of transitory life. Folklore was not as often preserved in stone, but *The Tale of the Eloquent Peasant* has survived to tell of a slippery peasant and his travails.

**Modern literature** offers insights into the nation's culture. In 1988, Cairene novelist Naguib Mahfouz became the first Arab to win the Nobel Prize for literature. His *Midaq Alley* describes the life of a stifled young girl in the streets of 1960s Islamic Cairo, and his classic allegory *Children of Gebelawi,* banned in Egypt, retells the stories of the Qur'an in a modern Cairo setting. *Miramar, Fountain and Tomb, Palace Walk,* and other works by Mahfouz are also readily available in translation. Yusuf Idris, a leading short-story writer, offers a witty account of modern Egyptian middle-class life in his *Cheapest Nights.* Sunallah Ibrahim's *The Smell of It,* a semi-autobiographical account of his life after release from prison, was censored in all Egyptian editions, but unabridged copies are available in the West. Master writer Taha Hussein's best-known work is his autobiography *Al Ayyam;* also worth reading is Tawfik el-Hakim's *Bird from the East.* For a range of Egyptian fiction, pick up *Arabic Short Stories,* edited by Mahmoud Manzalaoui. The Egyptian theater of the absurd is mostly composed of el-Hakim's *Fate of the Cockroach and Other Plays.* Egyptian feminist Nawal es-Saadawi, whose novels include *The Circling Song,* is controversial within Egypt and widely known among women of developing countries.

Many **non-Egyptians** have written accounts of their travels and experiences within the country. In *The Innocents Abroad,* Mark Twain describes his misadventures in Egypt and other countries. *Flaubert in Egypt* (edited by Francis Steegmuller) also tells tales of the stranger-in-a-strange-land variety. In *Maalesh: A Theatrical Tour of* *the Middle East,* French playwright Jean Cocteau makes insightful and humorous observations about Egypt. For an eye-opening account of early Western explorers exploring the Nile, read Alan Moorehead's *The White Nile.* The companion volume, *The Blue Nile,* includes hair-raising chapters on the French invasion of Egypt and the rise of Muhammad Ali. Michael Ondaatje's award-winning *The English Patient* contains wonderful descriptions of early desert expeditions. Another classic for travelers is Olivia Manning's *Levant Trilogy,* about the wartime marriage of two British citizens who meet in Cairo during the 1940s.

Plenty of **histories** of Egypt have been written, as have cultural, theological, and archaeological studies. For an exhaustive eye-witness account of 1850s Egypt and Arabia, dig into Sir Richard Francis Burton's *Narrative of a Pilgrimage to Mecca and Medina.* In *The Riddle of the Pyramids,* the English physicist Kurt Mendelssohn proposes bizarre solutions to archaeological puzzles. John Wilson's *Culture of Ancient Egypt* provides an excellent overview for pharaonic-era enthusiasts. E.M. Forster's *Alexandria: A History and a Guide* is a comprehensive guide to the city (for greater amusement read Forster's *Pharos and Pharillon*). A superb source of inspiration for adventures in Islamic Cairo is Richard Parker and Robin Sabin's *A Practical Guide to Islamic Monuments in Cairo.* Anwar Sadat's autobiography *In Search of Identity* is engrossing, as is his wife Jehan's *A Woman of Egypt.*

## MUSIC

With a musical tradition probably more rich and diverse than that of any other Middle Eastern country, Egypt is the capital of the Arab music industry and a magnet for aspiring artists from all over the Arab world. Some Egyptian music falls into the larger category of Arabic music that, between the 7th and 10th centuries, was so highly esteemed by Middle Easterners that hyperprotective measures were taken against the infiltration of Western musical trends. While Western classical music is characterized by mellifluous harmonies, Arabic classical music favors simple, extended melodic lines. Usually a single instrument speaks the melody while percussion instruments chant in the background.

The type of music you will hear most often in Egypt, blaring from taxis, *qahwas,* and homes, is a slightly updated brand of traditional classical music. Sayyid Darwish and the legendary Muhammad Abd el-Wahhab began as early as the 1910s and 20s to integrate Western instrumentation and techniques into Arabic song. What resulted was a mesmerizing music with Arab melodies and repetition backed by traditional percussion instruments, with violins, other stringed instruments, and sometimes full orchestras accompanying. This type of music had its heyday in the 40s, 50s, and 60s; its popularity shows no signs of waning today.

In the 40s, 50s, and 60s, emphasis fell on strong, beautiful voices to unite the music's sometimes disparate elements. Several "greats" of Egyptian music emerged, and every Egyptian has his or her favorite singer/composer/performer. The hands-down winner, however, is Umm Kulthum, whose incredible, versatile voice enraptures. This woman began by singing religious music for festivals in the provinces with her brother and father, and went on to tour Europe, sing Egyptian anthems, and generally dominate the airwaves throughout the Arab World for fifty years. Her diction and mastery of the Arabic language are widely noted and respected. You will probably not leave Egypt without hearing Umm Kulthum or seeing her sunglasses-clad face on a television screen or wall mural. Others with a loyal following include Abd el-Halim Hafez and Farid Atrash; more recent favorites are Warda and Fairouz.

The 80s and 90s saw a wholesale incorporation of Western influences into Egyptian pop music. This music features danceable, often synthesized drumbeats and comes with music videos and posters of teen heartthrobs. Many of its purveyors are one-hit wonders; every summer three or four tapes will be the undeniable hits. Teen dream Amr Diab, however, has endured. His upbeat songs, best taken in small doses, provide sing-along and dance material at weddings, parties, and in discos.

Another important part of one's introduction to Egyptian music scene is traditional folk music. Consisting mainly of drums and nasal horns, the mesmerizing music nearly compels you to sway back and forth as though in a religious trance. You can catch inexpensive performances in the Abd el-Wahhab theater in Alexandria. Nubian music is equally entrancing. In general, it eliminates the horns and focuses on slow, almost physical drumbeats and chant-like choruses. In Aswan, ask for *musiqa nubiyya.*

Your experience of Egypt will not be complete without the music; try to sample the many wares. Stores selling tapes are plentiful and more than willing to play a tape for you before you decide whether or not to purchase it. Just mention any of the artists described above and watch the shopkeeper's face light up in recognition. Tapes cost between E£5 and E£7.

# ■ Food

French, Greek, Persian, and Turkish cuisine flavors Egyptian fare. Since food in Egypt often wreaks havoc upon unhabituated digestive systems, it is mistakenly reputed to be strongly spiced; the truth is that it can sometimes be rather bland. Intestines new to the scene should avoid green salads in all but the expensive restaurants and eat fruit only after it has been washed well and, preferably, peeled.

The Egyptian breakfast of choice, which also serves as a snack or cheap meal throughout the day, is *fuul* (pronounced fool), cooked fava beans slightly mushed, blended with garlic, lemon, olive oil, and salt, and eaten with bread and vegetables. What's known as falafel in Israel—chick peas and/or fava beans mashed, shaped into balls, and fried—is called *ta'miyya* in Egypt. This, too, is eaten all day, often in sandwiches. Try the larger *ta'miyya* made with peppers. *Lu'met el-qadi,* a distant cousin of pancake batter fried into golden balls and served with syrup and/or powdered sugar, is available fresh in the early mornings.

Egyptian families generally eat large lunches and lighter dinners. A meal extremely popular with children is *mulukhiyya,* a green leaf (Jew's Mallow, little-known in the West) finely chopped and cooked with chicken broth and garlic into a thick soup. It is either served over rice or with bread. Vegetable stews including okra *(bamya),* green beans *(fasulia),* and peas *(bazella)* are also common, cooked in tomato sauce with lamb and ladled over rice. *Biftek,* sometimes represented on restaurant menus as veal panné, is thinly sliced veal, breaded and fried.

Egyptian restaurants do not even come close to representing the variety of Arabic cuisine; it is rare for meals cooked at home to make their way onto restaurant menus. On a certain long strip of the Nile Valley, you might feel that all you will ever get to eat will be *kofta, kabab,* and chicken. These carnivorous joys are almost always served with tomato-less salads, bread or rice, and *tahina,* a sesame-based sauce which adds invaluable TANG! to any meal. *Kofta* is spiced ground beef wrapped around skewers and grilled; *kabab* is chunks of lamb cooked the same way. Chicken is either fried (without batter), roasted on a rotisserie, or skewered, grilled, and called *shish tawouq.* Most expensive restaurants go the European route. All manner of badly-done quiches and even *paella* have been spotted. A couple of Egyptian specialties, however, should not be missed. Stuffed pigeon *(hamam)* is a source of national pride. Fish *(samak),* shrimp *(gambari),* and squid are great in sea-skimming towns.

In addition to *fuul* and *ta'miyya,* several street foods offer instant gratification for rumbling bellies. *Kibdeh* (liver) sandwiches smell disgusting until you try them; ask around in Luxor and Aswan to see which stands make the best. Corn cooked over coals in the big cities taxes both your stomach and your teeth. *Shawerma* made its way from the Levant to Egypt only a few years ago; it is supposed to be sinfully fatty lamb rolled into a pita with vegetables and *tahina,* but Egyptians will slap any sort of meat into bogus French bread and call it *shawerma.* The ever-popular *kushari,* a cheap, carbo-filled, tasty meal consisting of various shapes of pasta plus rice, lentils, and fried onions in a bit of tomato sauce. Slather on the hot sauce to give your taste-buds a ride. *Fitar* are flaky, chewy, doughy delights, filled with anything and everything and eaten either as a meal or for dessert.

Other desserts include *ba'laweh* (ubiquitous all over the Mediterranean), rice pudding flavored with rose-water (*roz bel laban*), and various Frenchified pastries and chocolates. The best dessert option is fruit. Steel-coat your stomach and indulge; it would be a shame to miss Egypt's ruby-red watermelon *(butteekh)* and unbelievable figs *(teen)*. Late summer produces the papaya-like *teen shoki* (cactus fruit), sold from wooden donkey carts by old men or young boys with leather hands. Unless you like splinters, allow them to peel it for you on the spot.

Shopping in the *souq* (market) is the cheapest alternative to restaurants, but you must select your food carefully. Bread, subsidized by the government, is available in three types: *aish baladi* (round unleavened loaves made with coarse flour), *aish shami* (similar to baladi but made with refined white flour), and *aish fino* (leavened French-style loaves). Cheese comes in two locally produced varieties: *gibna beida* (white feta cheese) and *gibna rumi* (a hard, yellow cheese with a sharp flavor). You can also get Danish-supervised feta (in year-long shelf life, no-refrigeration-needed packs—the stuff is great for long road trips or cheap breakfasts in your room) or imported cheeses at reasonable prices. *La Vache Qui Rit* (The Laughing Cow) is so popular that it has been adopted as a disparaging nick-name for President Hosni Mubarak. *Zabaadi* (yogurt) comes unflavored and makes a filling side dish.

Fruit juices are a great value and a crucial re-hydrator for travelers. Small stands all over serve juice in season (sweet orange and mango juice abound in summer) along with perennial favorites like *'asab* (sugar cane juice, said to increase sexual prowess), *tamr hindi* (tamarind), *farawla* (strawberry), and *'er 'asous* (carob).

Egyptians are coffee and tea fiends. Egyptian tea, similar to the Western variety, is normally taken without milk and with enough sugar to make it syrupy. Though you can get Western-style coffee, Egyptians prefer *ahwa* (Arabic coffee), which comes in three degrees of sweetness: *ahwa saada* (no sugar), *ahwa mazbuta* (just right), and *sukkar ziyaada* (with a full year's harvest of sugar cane). Especially when you are in Upper Egypt, try *karkadeh,* a red drink unlike anything you've ever tasted, made by brewing hibiscus flowers and served hot or cold. Egypt brews its own beer, Stella, which costs between E£2.50 and E£6 in restaurants and bars (Stella brewed for domestic consumption comes in green bottles; export Stella comes in brown bottles, tastes no better, but costs more. You figure it out.) Egypt also produces a selection of justifiably obscure red and white wines, sold for E£2-5 per bottle. Non-alcoholic beer (Birell and Brew) is also available.

# Cairo القاهرة

> I arrived at length at Cairo, mother of cities and seat of Pharaoh the tyrant, boundless in multitude of buildings, peerless in beauty and splendor, the meeting-place of comer and goer, the halting-place of feeble and mighty, whose throngs surge as waves of the sea.
> —Ibn Battuta

Like Athens or Rome, Cairo transcends the modern country over which it now presides. The glory of this one-time capital of Cheops and Muhammad Ali has been the ultimate goal of world leaders since the beginning of recorded history. The Crusaders, Napoleon, and Hitler all tried to achieve the pharaonic immortality that only a conquest of *El Qahira*—"the Victorious"—could have assured.

Modern Cairo takes after the grand monuments that have become its symbol. Just as the sheer magnitude of the Pyramids can only be appreciated from a distance, Cairo itself becomes incomprehensible when viewed too close. As the largest city in Africa, this mass of 16 million people is pure chaos at first glance—an urban explosion offering no apparent reason or order. Thoroughfares are clogged, horns screech, and pedestrians follow a throbbing, never-ending push to nowhere.

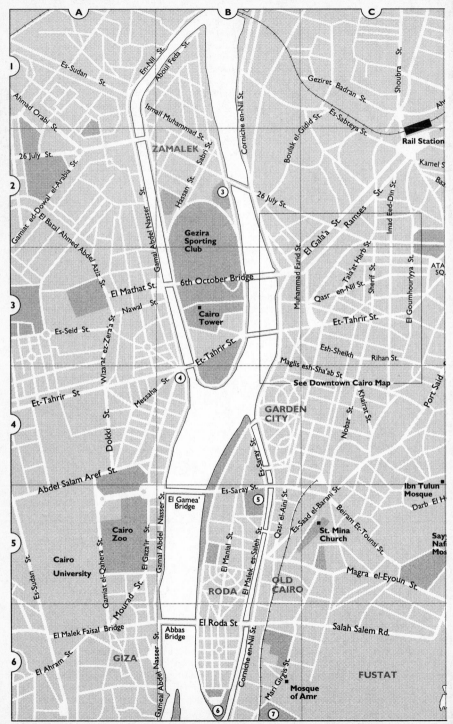

Es-Sudan St.

En-Nil St.

Aboul Feda St.

Ahmad Orabi St.

Ismail Muhammad St.

Geziret Badran St.

Es-Sabreya St.

Shoubra St.

**Rail Station**

Kamel S

26 July St.

ZAMALEK

Sabri St.

Corniche en-Nil St.

Boulak el-Gidid St.

Ba

Gamiat ed-Dowal el-Arabia St.

El Batal Ahmed Abdel Aziz St.

Hassan St.

26 July St.

El Gala'a St.

Ramses

Imad Eed-Din St.

ATA
SQ.

El Mathat St.

Gamal Abdel Nasser St.

**Gezira
Sporting
Club**

Muhammad Farid St.

Tala'at Harb St.

Sherif St.

El Goumhourhyya St.

Nawal St.

6th October Bridge

Qasr en-Nil St.

Es-Seid St.

**Cairo
Tower**

Et-Tahrir St.

Esh-Sheikh

Rihan St.

Port Said

Et-Tahrir St.

Wizarat ez-Zera'a St.

Et-Tahrir St.

Messaha St.

Maglis-esh-Sha'ab St.

**See Downtown Cairo Map**

**GARDEN
CITY**

Khairat St.

Nobar St.

Abdel Salam Aref St.

Dokki St.

Es-Saray St.

Es-Saray St.

Qasr el-Aini St.

**Ibn Tulun
Mosque**

Darb El H

**El Gamea'
Bridge**

Gamal Abdel Nasser St.

**St. Mina
Church**

Es-Saad el-Barani St.

Beiram Et-Tounsi St.

Say
Naf
Mos

**Cairo
Zoo**

Gamiat el-Qahera St.

El Gaza'ir St.

El Manial St.

El Malek es-Saleh St.

Magra el-Eyoun St.

**Cairo
University**

Es-Sudan St.

Mourad St.

**RODA**

**OLD
CAIRO**

El Malek Faisal Bridge

**GIZA**

Gamal Abdel Nasser St.

**Abbas
Bridge**

El Roda St.

Salah Salem Rd.

El Ahram St.

Corniche en-Nil St.

**FUSTAT**

Mari Girgis St.

**Mosque
of Amr**

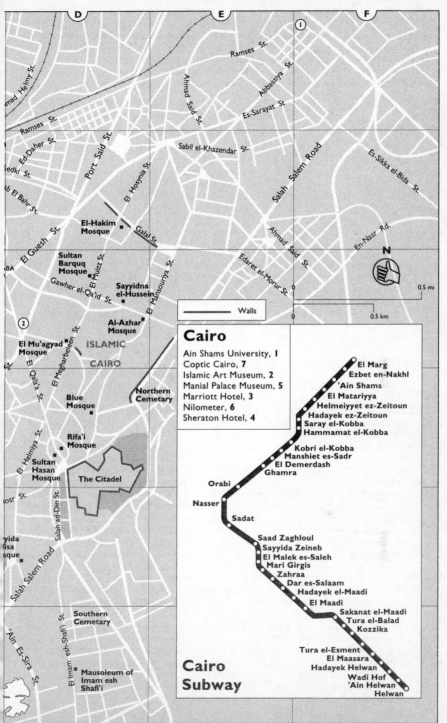

## Cairo

Ain Shams University, **1**
Coptic Cairo, **7**
Islamic Art Museum, **2**
Manial Palace Museum, **5**
Marriott Hotel, **3**
Nilometer, **6**
Sheraton Hotel, **4**

## Cairo Subway

Only after weeks in the metropolis can one begin to understand any of this. Slowly, a living, infinitely complex organism unfolds. Somehow, amid tangled webs of unlabled streets and hordes of merchants and hawkers who elsewhere could form a city unto themselves, Cairenes find their way to favorite *sheesha* halls and navigate perfectly the infinite bazaars. And, as the muezzin makes his call, millions of Cairo's faithful descend on the hundreds of ornate places of worship: mosques, churches, and even a synagogue.

This city is a rare work of art which offers beauty and dirt at every level. Some of Cairo's monuments awe with their sheer magnitude: the Pyramids, the Citadel, the sprawling cityscape, and Africa's largest cathedral. Others entice with their miniscule intricacy: the latticework of a *mihrab,* the icons of Coptic churches, and the ancient gold and turquoise treasures of the Egyptian Museum.

Slashing the city in half is the silently flowing Nile, the life artery to Cairo and its country. As the sun sets on the banks of this eternal river, the city's breakneck pulse finally slows down and an unlikely serenity takes over. Framed by forests of minarets glowing in the late afternoon sun, Cairenes stroll by the riverside, relaxing after another day in one of the most difficult and fascinating cities in the world.

# ■ History

The strategic significance of the sandy plateau just above the Nile Delta did not escape the Pharaohs of the Old Kingdom. In the vicinity of contemporary Cairo on the western bank, the ancient capital of Memphis flourished as one of the world's earliest urban settlements. On the eastern bank, pharaonic remains suggest the presence of slightly older, similarly important cities—Heliopolis and Khery-Aha, later known as Babylon. When the upper and lower kingdoms of Egypt united around 3000 BCE, Memphis was the natural choice for a capital. Heliopolis became an important religious center around 3100 BCE. Even though the royal capital moved to Thebes and elsewhere after 2250, Memphis and Heliopolis remained important political and religious centers until the Ptolemaic period, when Heliopolis faded along with the cult of the sun (see "Religion in Ancient Egypt" on page 57). Memphis endured until the beginning of the Christian era, when massive population shifts left only two settlements: Giza on the western bank, and Babylon, an economic base for the Romans protected by its Byzantine fort, on the eastern bank.

During the first century CE, St. Mark introduced Christianity to Egypt. Romans, intent on maintaining control, resisted, and bloody wars ensued. For 600 years, the Coptic Church marked the wrists of its faithful with tattoos, and left even more enduring marks on the Cairene landscape by building the churches of Old Cairo.

The early decades of the 7th century CE found Cairo in the throes of power struggles with the Persian and Byzantine empires—Memphis and Alexandria changed hands continuously. Warfare near Babylon drove many urban dwellers to the villages, leaving the city bereft and deserted by the time of the Arab conquest in 641. General Amr Ibn el-As, head of the invading Arab forces, came to Egypt with specific instructions from Caliph Omar to center the new state at Babylon, not Alexandria. Babylon had a strategically superior location, and the desert-dwelling invaders found the Mediterranean culture of Alexandria suspicious. Amr founded the outpost of Fustat (the Latin and Byzantine roots of which mean "entrenchment"), the seed of modern Cairo, on part of the plain due east of the ruins of Babylon. On the western edge of Fustat, Amr built Egypt's first mosque. Political expansion and upheavals caused the settlement to expand to the north and northeast.

In 868 the 'Abbasid governor Ibn Tulun, appointed from Baghdad, declared Egypt an independent state. He built a palatial new city around his Grand Mosque, modeling it after the elaborate metropoli of Iraq where he had been educated. When the Fatimids swept in from Tunisia in 969, they occupied the empty northern sector of the plain and built a magnificent walled city for the new caliph and his court. Today, three of the gates survive (Baab el-Futuh, Baab en-Nasr, and Baab Zuweila). Legend has it that Gawhar Al-Sikelli, the Fatimid leader, set up a primitive telegraph system of bells connected by strings with which his astrologers could alert all of the workmen to begin construction at the most auspicious moment. A crow landed on the line just as Mars, the planet of war, was ascendant, and the workers began to build. Peeved but resigned, Gawhar dubbed the city El Qahira, "The Victorious."

Fustat continued to swell in size and grandeur and became known by the Semitic name for Egypt, Misr. This was Cairo's Golden Age, when, along with Damascus and Baghdad, it was a center of the most advanced culture west of China. During the 11th century, the twin cities of El Qahira and Fustat enjoyed a symbiotic relationship, and both thrived. But these two would stand triumphant for less than a century: Fustat suffered from plague, famine, and political unrest.

The Ayyubid Kurd Salah ad-Din overthrew the Fatimids in 1171. He opened the walled enclosure of El Qahira to the populace and built another fortress, the Citadel, on the hills to the south, above the rubble of Fustat. During the short reign of the Ayyubids and the longer, but more violent period of the Mamluk Sultans, the city continued to expand. Throughout the Middle Ages, it was far more populous than any city in Europe. Almost every sultan and prominent *amir* graced the place with a mosque, school, or hospital, usually raiding pharaonic ruins for building materials. The casing stones of the Giza Pyramids and Memphis are now strewn throughout Islamic Cairo.

Mamluk, meaning "one who is owned," was used to describe non-Muslim Turkish children who were captured and brought to Egypt as slaves. They received intense training in military arts and eventually ruthlessly overthrew their masters. There were basically two Mamluk periods: Bahri and Burgi. The Bahri Mamluks (1250-1382 CE) received their name (*bahr* means river) because their original barracks were on Roda Island in the Nile. The still-standing complexes of Sultan Qalaoun, Sultan Hasan, and the Mosque of Sultan Baybars date from this period. The second group of Mamluks, the Burgi (so named because *burg* means "tower," signifying the towers of the Citadel in which they lived), reigned from 1382-1517 CE. During this period, each Mamluk tried to outdo his competitors by building bigger, better mosques and complexes. Nearly every Mamluk was murdered by a rival; Qaytbay was the lone Sultan who died a natural death. The Mosque of Barquq, the buildings of El Ghouri, and the Tomb of Qaytbay stand as reminders of the Mamluk period.

The Ottoman conquest of 1516 reduced Cairo to a provincial center. Power was given to incompetent viceroys, and disorder and mutinies reigned, yet the Turks held onto Cairo for centuries. Although Napoleon successfully invaded Egypt in 1798, the Ottomans, allied with British sea forces, drove him out and proclaimed the Albanian Muhammad Ali ruler. The extravagant royal family built with little respect for Egyptian architecture, erecting Turkish-style mosques and palaces, including the enormous Mosque of Muhammad Ali in the Citadel, a lavish imitation of the grand mosques of Istanbul. The European-educated *khedives* (hereditary rulers) who succeeded Muhammad Ali, designed the broad, straight avenues of the New City, new land created by the Nile's westward shift.

After the Suez Canal opened in 1869, the British thought Egypt too strategic to trust to "foreign" hands, and took Cairo for themselves in 1882. Many of the budget hotels downtown are in the run-down remains of colonial buildings. The early 20th century witnessed the creation of a new Heliopolis, planned by aristocrat Baron Empain as a haven for Europeans. Two years after the 1952 revolution under Gamal abd en-Nasr (Nasser), the British agreed to pull out.

During the late 1960s, Cairo's population fluttered around 4 million. By 1980, it had ballooned into 14 million, and today it races toward 17 million. Population pressure has necessitated the continuous construction of new suburbs. The latest, Medinet Nasser, was built on the edges of the Eastern Desert in an attempt to preserve the precious arable land in the Nile Valley itself.

# ■ Orientation

## METROPOLITAN CAIRO

Metropolitan Cairo consists of two distinct administrative districts: **Cairo,** on the eastern bank of the Nile, and **Giza,** on the western bank. Under the auspices of the British and French colonialists, the city rulers planned a system of *midans* (squares) from which straight avenues radiate. **Tahrir Square** (Midan et-Tahrir, Liberation Square) is the center of the Downtown area. The three most important streets that radiate out from the square are Qasr El 'Aini Street, Tala'at Harb Street, and Ramses Street. **Qasr El 'Aini Street** runs south from Tahrir Sq. and ends at **Old Cairo,** the historical and spiritual center of the Copts (Egyptian Eastern Orthodox Christians), also known as Coptic Cairo. Just south of Tahrir Sq., sandwiched between Qasr El 'Aini St. and the Nile, is the serene **Garden City** residential area. Foreign embassies and banks cluster in this neighborhood, where you can also see many of the city's best-preserved 19th-century colonial mansions. The American University of Cairo (AUC) and various government buildings (Parliament, the Ministry of Social Affairs, and the Ministry of the Interior, among others) line Qasr El 'Aini St. On **Tala'at Harb St.**, running east from Tahrir Sq., you'll find most of the budget hotels. Running all the way to the airport, **Ramses Street** heads northeast away from the Nile. It passes through **Ramses Square,** next to which is the Cairo train station, also called **Ramses Station.** Farther out on Ramses St. are the Cairo Stadium, home to intense soccer rivalries, and **Heliopolis,** a fashionable suburb where you will find architectural extravagances and the residence of President Mubarak.

The main bridge crossing the Nile from the Downtown area is **Tahrir Bridge,** connecting Tahrir Sq. to the southern tip of **Gezira Island.** On this more verdant end of the island are a large public garden, two private sporting clubs and the Cairo Tower. The northern half is Cairo's ritziest residential area, **Zamalek;** this is the name by which the entire island often goes. South of Zamalek is its fellow Nile isle, **Roda Island,** the site of the 19th-century Manial Palace Museum and the Nilometer, the pharaonic device for measuring the flood.

Past Tahrir Bridge on the western bank of the Nile, the Cairo Sheraton Hotel presides over the residential neighborhood of **Dokki,** home to a handful of important embassies. North of Dokki lies **Mohandiseen** (Engineer's City), built in the late 1950s by President Nasser as a neighborhood for engineers. It is now a middle-class residential area. South of Dokki, past the Cairo Zoo and across the Giza Bridge, is **Giza**

---

### The Pros of Cons in Cairo

Although you may miss out on a wonderful personal encounter, it's safest to assume that anyone approaching you in Cairo wants something. Scams begin the moment you step off the plane and get your passport stamped. The guy with the photo-ID card on his lapel asking you if you have anything to declare probably isn't one of the customs officials—the true ones hang out at the customs office. This guy wants to get you in his buddy's cab to Cairo for E£25, to have you check in at his uncle's E£100 a night hotel because the one you want is "full," and to show you the Pyramids and sell you perfume at inflated prices. Instead, take the shuttle or the public bus to town. Be firm and strong in your conviction to go to the hotel you have selected.

Travel agents in the downtown area have been known to add airport taxes (there is no departure tax from Cairo) and other fees to tickets. Sometimes they charge massive cancellation fees if you get fed up and decide not to book a ticket through their office. You should demand receipts for every pound you hand over and have them give you written estimates, including all taxes, for every flight you purchase, even if you're just going across the street.

The scams we've listed are just the tip of the iceberg. Innovative scammers think up new methods daily. Help take a bite out of scams.

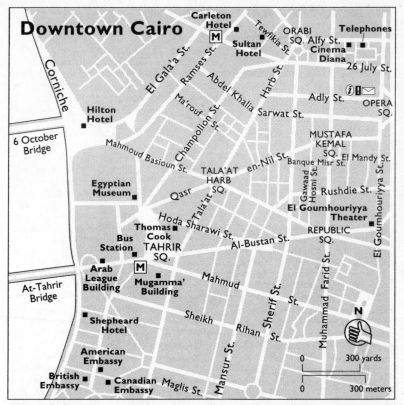

**Downtown Cairo**

Carleton Hotel
Sultan Hotel
ORABI SQ. Alfy St.
Telephones
Tewfikia St.
Cinema Diana
26 July St.
Corniche
El Gala'a St.
Ramses St.
Abdel Khalig Sarwat St.
Harb St.
Adly St.
OPERA SQ.
Hilton Hotel
Ma'rouf St.
Champollion St.
MUSTAFA KEMAL SQ. El Mandy St.
6 October Bridge
Mahmoud Basioun St.
en-Nil St.
Banque Misr St.
El Gawaad Hosni St.
Rushdie St.
Egyptian Museum
Qasr
TALA'AT HARB SQ.
Tala'at St.
El Goumhouriyya Theater
El Goumhouriyya St.
Hoda Sharawi St.
Thomas Cook
REPUBLIC SQ.
Bus Station
TAHRIR SQ.
Al-Bustan St.
Arab League Building
Mugamma' Building
Mahmud
Sherif St.
Muhammad Farid St.
Shepheard Hotel
Sheikh
Rihan St.
St.
N
American Embassy
Mansur St.
0      300 yards
British Embassy
Canadian Embassy
Maglis St.
0      300 meters

At-Tahrir Bridge

**Square.** Pyramids Road, whose overpriced bars provide nightly sleazefests, begins at the square and runs to the **Pyramids of Giza.**

The major streets in Cairo are often labelled in both English and Arabic. *Your Handy Map of Cairo* (E£15), comprehensive although a bit cumbersome, is available in most major bookstores. *Egypt Today* (E£9) publishes updated street listings each year. Look for their *Dining Guide,* their *Travel & Recreation Guide,* and their *Business Review* (E£15 each). *Egypt Today* itself is published monthly. Most maps and guides are available at the AUC or Shorouk bookstores (see Practical Information, p. 95).

## DOWNTOWN CAIRO

**Tahrir Square** is the heart of Cairo. Buses depart from here for every metropolitan destination. At the north end of Tahrir St. facing the square is the sandstone **Egyptian Museum;** adjacent to it on the west side of the square is the Nile Hilton. At the southern end of the square is the massive, concave **Mugamma' Building,** headquarters of the Egyptian bureaucracy, where you must register your passport within seven days of arrival. The **American University in Cairo (AUC),** directly to the east of the Mugamma' Building across Qasr El 'Aini St., has gardens filled with English-speaking Egyptians and Arabic-speaking Americans, plus an excellent bookstore.

**Tala'at Harb Street** runs from the northeast side of Tahrir through Tala'at Harb Sq. **Ramses Square** to the north and **'Ataba Square** to the east (both major transportation hubs) form a rough triangle with Tala'at Harb Sq. enclosing the main business and shopping district, which is crammed with travel agents, banks, restaurants, juice stands, clothing stores, language schools, and budget hotels.

# ■ Cairo Transportation

A little aggravation is good for the soul.

## WALK LIKE AN EGYPTIAN

One positive aspect of Cairo's layout is that almost everything in the city is within easy walking distance of Tahrir Sq. Though it may take more time, you can see most of the sights of the downtown areas and Roda and Zamalek Islands without using mechanized transport (an attractive proposition, considering Cairo traffic and driving habits). Islamic Cairo might be a little too far for a walk, however. Many argue that walking is the only way to see the city; on foot, you will indubitably catch many fascinating glimpses of Cairo life which would go unseen from a bus or car.

Cars reign supreme in Cairo; drivers expect pedestrians to look after themselves. If you realize that crossing the street is basically a real-life game of *Frogger,* you might increase your fun ratio. It is wise to face oncoming traffic and heed the horns. A long, uninterrupted honk usually indicates that the driver is either unwilling or unable to swerve. Don't be alarmed if you are pushed or tugged by Egyptians attempting to avoid cars. Ignore traffic lights; everyone else does. Cairenes warn against being too careful when you cross a street—if you stop short or break into a run you'll upset the rhythm of the drivers speeding toward you.

## METRO

The Cairo Metro system, completed in 1987, is a world apart from the rest of Cairo public transport. A joint project with the French and the Japanese, the Metro is the coolest, cleanest, and fastest ticket in town. Trains run along a single 40km route linking the southern industrial district of Helwan to El Marj in Heliopolis, with a number of stops downtown (look for the enormous, red "M" signs). Two more lines, connecting Shubra and Giza, are scheduled for completion in 1997. Downtown stations feature TV screens with random programs, including *America's Funniest Home Videos,* cartoons, and Egyptian ads. Trains run about every six minutes (5:30am-1am, winter 5:30am-midnight; 30-80pt). Keep track of your ticket; you'll need it to exit. The stations downtown are Mubarak (Ramses Sq. and Railway Station), Orabi (Orabi St. and Ramses St.), Nasser (26 July St. and Ramses St.), Sadat (Tahrir Sq.), Sa'ad Zaghloul (Mansur St. and Ismail Abaza St.), Sayyida Zeinab (Mansur St. and Ali Ibrahim St.), El Malik es-Saleh (Salah Salem Road), and Mar Girgis (Old Cairo). Trains are often packed and sweaty during rush hour (before 9am and between 2 and 5pm). Men take heed: the first and second compartments are always **reserved for women.**

## TAXI

Never take the large, unmetered, colorful Peugeot taxis within the city—they charge E£2-3 for a ride around the corner, and the only advantage is their luggage rack. Avoid as well taxis that lurk in front of major hotels. Instead, flag the metered **black-and-white taxis** that often carry passengers collectively.

To hail a taxi, pick a thoroughfare headed in the general direction you wish to travel, stand on the side of the street, stretch out your arm as a taxi approaches, and scream out your destination as it goes by. If the drivers are interested in your business, they'll stop and wait for you to run over to their cars. Jump in and repeat your destination. Don't be alarmed if the taxi seems to be going in the wrong direction; drivers sometimes take circuitous routes to avoid traffic-clogged main arteries.

Meters have been installed in all Cairo taxis, but drivers rarely use them, since passengers jump in and out—haggling only implies that you don't know what you owe. Cairenes simply hail a cab, hop in, and pay what they think is adequate upon arrival. *Never* ask the driver for the fare. Usually, the most comfortable way to handle the situation is to open the door as you are paying with folded bills and leave the taxi without looking to the driver for approval. Also, try to have the exact change—the last thing you want is the driver taking an "adequate" share of your E£20 bill.

Rides in the downtown area (from Ramses Sq. to Garden City or Zamalek to Islamic Cairo) should cost about E£3-4. From downtown, Mohandiseen and the Northern or Southern Cemeteries cost E£4, the Pyramids or Imbaba E£5-7, and Ma'adi and Heliopolis E£6-8. You will be expected to pay extra for additional passengers, suitcases, and waiting. A taxi to or from the airport should cost no more than E£20 all told, but they have you at their mercy.

Do not expect a taxi driver to speak English, or to know the location of every address or street. Try to identify a major landmark or thoroughfare near your destination and learn to pronounce it in Arabic. Better yet, have someone at the tourist office or your hotel write out the address and directions in Arabic.

**River taxis** provide a more relaxing means of transportation to Old Cairo. Boats depart every 30-40 minutes to the Nile barrages and Old Cairo (via Giza) from the corniche in front of the television building, about 750m north of Tahrir Sq. (50pt).

## MICROBUS

If you manage to get on the right microbus, these 14-seaters are the best way to get to areas of Cairo not reached by metro. They function more like buses than taxis, but differ from minibuses. Generally, they follow fixed routes to certain destinations but tend to be flexible as long as all passengers are going to the same area. Microbus stops are sometimes marked by a wooden shelter. Listen to the drivers as they yell out destinations. It's a good idea to know the Arabic pronunciation, as drivers won't be yelling in English. From **'Ataba Sq.** microbuses go to Ramses Sq., Tahrir Sq., Northern Cemetery, Zamalek, Islamic Cairo, and Heliopolis. From **Tahrir Sq.** microbuses leave for Heliopolis, Giza Sq., Dokki, Mohandiseen, and the Pyramids. Fares range from 50pt to E£1 for the luxury of not having to stand.

## MINIBUS

Red-and-white or orange-and-white Mercedes minibuses operate along many of the same routes served by the far less tourist-friendly city buses. Don't confuse these with the older, privately operated multi-colored taxi-vans. Although more expensive than the regular buses (25-75pt), the minibuses are also far more comfortable. Finding the right one may be confusing, but most Egyptians will be glad to help. The following are important minibus routes. Minibus numbers appear in Arabic only:

### From the Nile Hilton Station
**#16** (١٦): Gala'a Bridge—Agouza.
**#24** (٢٤): Ahmed Hilmi Sq.—Shubra.
**#25** (٢٥): Airport.
**#35** (٣٥): 'Abbasiyya.
**#54** (٥٤): Citadel—Cemetery—Baab al-Louq—Sayyida Zeinab.
**#76** (٧٦): 'Ataba Sq.—Tahrir Sq.—Bulaq ad-Dakrur.
**#77** (٧٧): Bulaq ad-Dakrur—Khan el-Khalili.
**#84** (٨٤): 'Ataba Sq.—Tahrir Sq.—Dokki, Giza.

### From 'Ataba Square
**#26** (٢٦): Roxy, Tahrir Sq.—Dokki—Giza.
**#48** (٤٨): Zamalek.
**#57** (٥٧): Citadel.

### From the Mugamma' Station
**#24** (٢٤): Abbasiyya Sq.—Roxy.
**#27** (٢٧): Masr el-Gadida—Airport (old terminal).
**#30** (٣٠): Nasr City—'Abbasiyya Sq.—Ramses Sq.
**#32** (٣٢): Mugamma'—Ramses Sq.—'Abbasiyya.
**#49** (٤٩): Tahrir Sq.—Zamalek.
**#50** (٥٠): 'Ataba Sq.—Citadel.
**#52** (٥٢), **56** (٥٦): Ma'adi—Old Cairo.

**#54** (٥٤): Tahrir Sq.—Rifa'i Mosque—Ibn Tulun Mosque—Citadel—Southern Cemetery.
**#55** (٥٥): Ma'adi via Dar es-Salaam.
**#58** (٥٨): Ramses Sq.—Manial (no stop at Tahrir Sq.).
**#59** (٥٩): Ramses Sq.—Tahrir Sq.
**#82** (٨٢): Nadi el-Rimaya Sq.
**#83** (٨٣): Pyramids (*haram*).

## BUS

This should be your last resort. Few foreigners actually brave the bus system; those who are so inclined, however, should pass up overcrowded vehicles so as to avoid unabashed stares, wandering hands, and unbearable heat. Sometimes the buses get so full that all you see is a tangle of mangled limbs and the sparks that fly when the bottom of the overburdened bus scrapes the road. The red-and-white and blue-and-white public buses run often and everywhere, and they're the cheapest available means of transportation (10-25pt), but have a high breakdown potential. Numbers and destinations are usually written in Arabic. Most buses run 5:30am-12:30am (during Ramadan 6:30am-6:30pm and 7:30pm-2am). Ask someone at the station to point out the correct bus. Cairo's central local bus depot is **Abd el-Moneim Riyadh Station** to the north of the Egyptian Museum, just below the towering triangular Ramses Hilton. Several buses depart from in front of the old **Arab League Building,** to the west of the Mugamma' along Tahrir St., adjacent to the bridge. Other bus stations are at **Midan El 'Ataba ('Ataba Square),** east of the Azbekiyya Gardens (to the Citadel, the Manial Palace, Giza, and Tahrir Square), and at **Giza** (to the Pyramids, airport, and Citadel).

Outside the main stations, catching a bus is merely a matter of chasing one down and properly timing your leap, as they seldom come to a full stop. Except at a terminus, enter through the rear doors which have been torn off most buses to facilitate this practice. To disembark, pick a moment when the bus is not moving too rapidly and face the front as you jump off. If you want the bus to come to a full halt at an official bus stop, you must exit through the front door. The front of a bus is generally less crowded than the rear, so it's worth the effort to push your way forward. When traveling by bus, keep wallets and valuables securely embedded in your person. Although violent crime is rare in Cairo, a *khawaga* on a crowded bus is an irresistible opportunity for the occasional pickpocket.

### From the Arab League Building

**#13** (١٣): Zamalek.
**#19** (١٩), **102** (١٠٢), **110** (١١٠), **166** (١٦٦), **203** (٢٠٣): Dokki.

### From 'Ataba Square

**#404** (٤٠٤): Citadel—Tahrir Sq.
**#801** (٨٠١), **951** (٩٥١): Citadel.
**#904** (٩٠٤): Mugamma' Station—Pyramids.
**#930** (٩٣٠): Qanatir.

### From Giza Square

**#3** (٣): Pyramids.
**#30** (٣٠): Ramses Station.
**#907** (٩٠٧): Tahrir Sq.—Airport.
**#949** (٩٤٩): Airport.

### From the Abd el-Moniem Riyadh Station

**#8** (٨): Tahrir Sq.—Qasr el-'Aini—Manyal—Giza—Mena House Hotel (Pyramids).
**#63** (٦٣), **66** (٦٦): Al Azhar—Khan el-Khalili.
**#72** (٧٢): Sayyida Zeinab—Citadel—Mausoleum of Imam Esh-Shafi'i.
**#75** (٧٥): Islamic Museum—Baab Zuweila.
**#82** (٨٢), **182** (١٨٢): Imam Esh-Shafi'i Mausoleum—Southern Cemetery—Citadel.

**#99** (٩٩): Agouza—Sudan St.—Lebanon Sq. (Midan Libnan).
**#128** (١٢٨): 'Abbasiyya Sq.—'Ain Shams.
**#173** (١٧٣), **194** (١٩٤), **609** (٦٠٩): Tahrir Sq.—Citadel.
**#173** (١٧٣), **403** (٤٠٣): Citadel—Sultan Hasan.
**#174** (١٧٤): Sayyida Zeinab—Ibn Tulun—Sultan Hasan—Citadel.
**#400** (٤٠٠): Old Cairo Airport via Heliopolis (Midan Roxy).
**#422** (٤٢٢): New Cairo Airport.
**#666** (٦٦٦): El Gaili Museum.
**#900** (٩٠٠): Tahrir Sq.—Qasr el-'Aini—Manial (Youth Hostel)—Cairo University—
   Giza—Pyramids—Holiday Inn Hotel (very crowded except early in the morning).
**#923** (٩٢٣): Giza Sq.

### From Ramses Station
**#30** (٣٠): Giza Sq.
**#160** (١٦٠): Citadel—Tahrir Sq.

## ■ Intercity Transit

For more information see Getting Around, p. 70.

### SERVICE TAXI

These are best for short trips. From Ramses station, catch them to Alexandria (E£11), Suez (E£6), Ismailiyya (E£6), Port Said (E£9), or El Arish (E£13). You can also hire *service* to Fayyum (E£5) at Giza Square by the train station; to Alexandria (E£11) from in front of the Nile Hilton; and to Wadi Natrun from Kolali Sq (about E£10). The Ahmed Hilmi Square bus station covers Mansura (E£9), Tanta (E£6), Zagazig (E£5), and the rest of the Delta. You'll have to hunt for taxis to the Sinai. Ask the driver for the price before starting the trip so that you don't face a nasty surprise upon arrival. *Service* are slightly cheaper than buses, and you'll get there faster.

### BUS

Unfortunately, Cairo has no single bus depot. You'll have to sniff out the various points of departure. Augmenting the **public bus system,** which can be crowded, chaotic, and not quite sanitary, private operators run similar routes, sometimes at slightly higher prices. These buses are clean, air-conditioned, and often serve food and show Egyptian films. One drawback is that reservations, especially for popular destinations, must be made ahead of time, in person. Public buses running to Upper Egypt tend to be in poorer condition.

   **To Sinai and Israel:** The **East Delta Bus Company** (tel. 83 95 83) and its subsidiary, the South Sinai Company (tel. 82 47 53), run buses from **Abd el-Moneim Riyadh Station,** beneath the Ramses Hilton **to Sharm esh-Sheikh** (6:30am and 4:30pm, E£31; 7 and 9am, 1 and 3pm, E£41; 10 and 11pm, E£46; and 10:50pm E£51; 7hr.), to Dahab (7am, E£46; 4pm, E£36; and 10pm, E£56; 8hr.); to Nuweiba (7:30am, E£41; and 10pm, E£51; 8hr.); and to Taba (7:30am, E£46; and 10pm, E£66; 9hr.). Buses to El Arish and Israel leave from **Abassiyya Station,** 5km northeast of Ramses Station at the end of Ramses St. From Tahrir or Ramses Sq. you can catch local bus #54, 710, or 728 or minibus #24 or 32. Buses leave for Tel Aviv (Mon., Wed. 8am, 10hr., E£100) and Jerusalem (Mon., Wed. 10am, 8hr., E£120). Reserve these long hauls in advance. **Misr Travel** also sends buses from the **Cairo Sheraton** in Dokki to Tel Aviv and Jerusalem (daily 5am, 10hr., E£102, round-trip E£153; Sun., Tues. and Thurs. 3:30pm, E£119, round-trip E£170). You can buy your ticket from Misr Travel at 7 Tala'at Harb St. (tel. 393 02 01 or 59; open Sat.-Thurs. 9am-8pm) or at the Sheraton (tel. 335 54 70).
   **To Alexandria and North Coast:** Buses leave from **Abd el-Moneim Riyadh Station,** north of the Cairo Museum and next to the Ramses Hilton, and they pass by **Giza Station,** Giza Sq. The best is the comfy and air-conditioned **Superjet** to Alexandria (every hr., 5:30am-11pm, 3hr., E£19, at night E£21, VIP express E£28), and

Marsa Matrouh (7am, 5hr., E£36). The almost-as-good **Golden Arrow** also runs buses to Alexandria (every hr., 5:30am-12:30am, E£16, E£18 at night) and Marsa Matrouh (7:15, 7:45, and 8:30am (no A/C), and 5:45pm, 5hr., E£30, E£22 without A/C). The **West Delta Bus Company** sends its mediocre buses along the same schedule but for less, as well as to Wadi Natrun (about every hr., 6am-10pm, 2hr., E£24, money collected on board).

**To Upper Egypt and Hurghada:** The ancient green public buses are best avoided; they are dirty, crowded, and unsafe. A better choice would be **Upper Egypt Bus Co.** to Hurghada (9am, noon, 11 and 11:30pm, midnight, and 12:30am, 7hr., E£35, E£5 more at night); to Aswan (3pm, 13hr., E£50) or to Luxor (9:15pm, 9hr., E£45). Buses leave from **Abd el-Moneim Riyadh Station** at the base of the triangular Ramses Hilton. If these coaches are booked up, try both Golden Arrow and Superjet at the same station.

**To the Western Oases:** Buses leave from **Al Azhar Station,** 45 Al Azhar St. (tel. 390 86 35), 25m from intersection with Port Said St. through a driveway on the south side of the street. Private companies run daily buses (some with A/C) to: Bahariyya (10am, 5hr., E£10); Farafra (Sat., Mon., and Thurs., 8am, E£25); Dakhla (7am, 5pm, and 5pm, 12hr., E£30-37); and to Kharga (10am and 8pm, E£25 and E£32, 12hr.). You can also catch a **service** or **minibus** to Bahariyya (5hr., E£11) or Kharga through Asyut (E£23) from Ramses Station or Sayyida Zeinab Station.

**To the Eastern Delta and Canal Zone:** Buses leave from **Kolali Square** (Midan El Kolali; tel. 574 28 14), a 5-min. walk from Ramses Sq. (follow the elevated road to your right for 2 blocks; turn right and the station office is located 50m up on the right). **East Delta Bus Company** runs every hr. 6:30am-6:30pm to Port Said (E£10-12), Suez (E£4.50-5) and Ismailiyya (E£5.25-6.25). Frequent service to Mansura (7:30am-8:30pm, E£6.30) and Ras el-Bar (7:30am-4:30pm, E£13). **Superjet** goes to Port Said (every 30min., 5:45am-5pm, E£15) from **Abd el-Moneim Riyadh Station.**

**To Arab countries and Turkey:** Buses depart from Abd el-Moneim Riyadh Station. Add US$32 to all fares for ferry. East Delta Bus Co. runs buses to **Jordan** (9pm, 1 day, E£63), **Syria** (9pm, 1 day, E£113), and **Turkey** (9pm, 2 days, E£318).

## TRAIN

Ticket windows at Ramses Station (Metro: Mubarak) are open 8am-10pm. The **tourist office** (open daily 8am-9pm), on the left as you enter the station, can write out your destination and other details in Arabic to avoid confusion. Which line you stand in depends upon whether you are reserving a seat in advance or trying to buy a ticket for the same day (often impossible). Women (and men traveling with women) can take advantage of the special women's line that may form at crowded times, which is much shorter and faster than the corresponding men's line. In addition, women are permitted (and expected) to push to the front of the line, head held high. Third class travelers (not safe for unescorted women) can buy tickets on board the train. Students get 30% discounts on fares with an ISIC or student ID.

The trains enter their berths at least half an hour before departure time. None of the train numbers or destinations are in English, but fellow travelers and the tourist police may lend a hand. Nonetheless, be prepared for yet another confusion infusion (also see specific town listings).

Tourists are expected (though not required) to ride first or second class due to security concerns. For long trips, such as to Luxor and Aswan, only two express trains are reserved for tourists. These trains depart at 7:30am and 10pm to **Luxor** (9-12hr., first class E£53, students E£37.10, second class with A/C E£33, students E£23.10) and **Aswan** (13-16hr., 1st class E£63, students E£44.10, 2nd class with A/C E£39, students E£27.30). **Sleepers** to Luxor and Aswan cost the same whacko price for both destinations (E£293 one way, no student discount available) and depart at 7:45pm. The express train makes stops in Minya, Sohag, Asyut, and Qena. Trains to **Alexandria** are comfortable, frequent, and tourist-restriction free (6am-9:30pm, E£8-14). Trains to **Port Said** leave at 6:20, 8:40, and 11:30am, and 2:35 and 6:35pm (3hr., 2nd class A/C E£14, no A/C E£6.30).

In between waiting in lines and declining offers for taxis, take a moment to admire the towering **Statue of Ramses II** in front of the train station. The statue was excavated in 1888 near the remains of the ancient city of Memphis.

## PLANE

Tourists pay triple what Egyptians pay for airfare within Egypt. EgyptAir flies to Luxor, Sharm esh-Sheikh, Aswan, and Hurghada, while Air Sinai flies to the Sinai and Israel. **EgyptAir** has offices at 6 Adly St. (tel. 391 12 56) and in the Nile Hilton (tel. 76 52 00 or 77 24 10; reservations and information 392 74 44 or 72 05). **Air Sinai** is at the Nile Hilton (tel. 76 09 48; open daily 9am-5pm).

# ■ Practical Information

A reliable directory for goods and services is the *Cairo Telephone List*, published by the Ma'adi Women's Guild and available for E£20 at the American Chamber of Commerce, Marriott Hotel #1541, Zamalek (tel. 340 88 88).

**Tourist Office:** Sprinkled throughout the city, the offices provide free maps and info. **Cairo International Airport** (tel. 66 74 75), at the entrance as well as next to the duty-free shops. In theory, open 24hr. **Giza** (tel. 385 02 59), in front of Mena House Hotel. Open Sat.-Thurs. 8am-5pm. **Railway Station** (tel. 76 42 14), on the left if you enter the station's main entrance. Open daily 8am-9pm. **5 Adly St.** (tel. 391 34 54), a 20-min. walk from Tahrir Sq. Follow Tala'at Harb St. and turn right on Adly St. The office is 3 blocks down on your left, marked "Tourist Police." Open daily 8am-8pm.

**Tourist Police: 5 Adly St.** (tel. 126, 39 19 44, or 390 60 28), in the same building as the Tourist Office. Other locations at **Cairo International Airport** (tel. 247 25 84), **Giza** (tel. 385 02 59), the **Manial Palace Hotel**, and **Ramses Station.**

**Student Cards: Medical Scientific Center:** 103 Mathaf el-Manial St., El Manial (tel. 363 88 15). South of the Manial Palace across the street from Kentucky Fried Chicken (look for the ISIC sign). Much more comprehensive and helpful than the name implies. Provides ISIC and Go25 cards (E£20; bring a photo). Great source of information for travelers. Student volunteer staff speaks excellent English and will quote prices for sights and entertainment. The center gives out free maps and pamphlets, and organizes excursions to the Pyramids and Sufi dancing.

**Thomas Cook:** 17 Mahmoud Bassiouny St. (tel. 574 37 76 or 39 55 or 39 67; fax 76 27 50), ½ block west of Tala'at Harb Sq. Travel agency, money transfers, currency exchange, and cash advances on MC/Visa. Cashes traveler's checks. Come here to replace a lost MC/Visa. Open daily 8am-5pm. Other offices throughout city.

**Passport Office:** 2nd floor of the **Mugamma Building,** the massive concave gray edifice at the southern side of Tahrir Sq. Registration open Sat.-Thurs. 8am-8pm. Open for visa extensions, Sat.-Thurs. 8am-1pm. Prior to Aug. 1996, a mandatory stop on all travelers' itineraries. Now, passport registration is not required; you just need to get it stamped at the border. Not as jam-packed is the second floor of the **Ministry of Economy and Foreign Trade Building,** 8 Adly St. (tel. 390 43 63), next to the EgyptAir office. Open Sat.-Thurs. 8am-1:30pm. Bring a passport photo for visa extensions (2-6 mo. E£14, 1 yr. E£50).

**Embassies: U.S.:** 5 Latin America St., Garden City (tel. 354 82 11), 2 blocks south of Tahrir Sq. For the consulate, enter on Lazaughli St. around the block. Lost or stolen passports replaced overnight for US$65 or E£ equivalent (US$55 for a renewal). Open Sun.-Thurs. 8am-4:30pm, consulate 8am-noon. **Canada:** 5 Midan es-Saraya el Kobra, Garden City (tel. 354 31 10 or 19), 3rd floor of Arab-African Bank Bldg. Passports replaced within 2 working days for E£145. Embassy open Sun.-Thurs. 8:30am-4:30pm, visas 8-11am. **U.K.:** 7 Ahmed Ragheb St., Garden City (tel. 354 08 50), south of U.S. Embassy. Handles **New Zealanders'** affairs, too. Will replace both nationals' passports within five days (E£99 for 32-page passports, E£148 for 48-page passports, payable only in E£). Open Sun.-Wed. 8am-1:30pm., Thurs. 8am-1pm. **Australia:** World Trade Center, 11-12th floors, 1191 Corniche en-Nil, Bulaq, past the 26th July Bridge (tel. 575 04 44). Passports generally replaced in 3-7 working days (AUS$106 for 32-page passports, AUS$159 for 64-page passports, payable in E£ equivalent only). Immediate replacement in case of emergency. Open Sun.-Wed. 8am-4pm, Thurs. 8am-1:30pm, visas 9:30am-noon. **Ireland:** 3 Abu el-Feda St., Zamalek, in the Abu el-Feda building (tel. 340 82 64 or 85 47; fax 341 28 63). Passports replaced for E£78, new passports E£234. Consular services open Sun.-Thurs. 9am-noon. Embassy open Sun.-Thurs. 8am-3pm. **South Africa:** 21/23 Giza St., 18th Floor, Giza (tel. 571 72 38 or 39). File applications for new passports here; they're then sent to South Africa for processing. The entire process takes 8 weeks. In the meantime, you are issued a 1-pg. Emergency Passport good for 3 months (E£50). Consular services open Sun.-Thurs. 9am-noon. Embassy open Sun.-Thurs. 8am-4:30pm. **Israel:** 6 Ibn el-Malik St., Dokki (tel. 361 03 80 or 04 58). Cross over to Dokki from Roda Island on University Bridge (El Gama'a). The street to the right of and parallel to the bridge is Ibn el-Malik. Look up at the top floors for the Israeli flag or for the security guards by the entrance who will ask to see your passport. Visas E£45 for all nationalities. Open Sun.-Thurs. 10am-12:30pm. **Jordan:** 6 El Goheina St., Dokki (tel. 348 55 66, 61 69, or 75 43, or 349 99 12), 2 blocks west of the Cairo Sheraton. Visas (photograph and letter of introduction required) free for Aussies, E£28 for New Zealanders, E£63 for Britons, E£70 for Americans, E£91 for Canadians. Same day service (pick up visas noon-2pm). Open Sat.-Thurs. 9am-noon; it's wise to arrive early to avoid the crowd. **Syria:** 18 Abd er-Rahim Sabri St., Dokki (tel. 337 70 20). Bring 2 photos for a visa (valid for one entry only; free for Canadians and Australians, E£116 for Americans). You are advised to apply for visas in your home country. Open 9am-2:30pm, visas 9am-1pm. Any evidence of having been to Israel prohibits obtaining a Syrian visa, but you can get a new passport at your country's embassy.

**Currency Exchange:** Banks and exchange services litter downtown. **Bank Misr** has branches at the Ramses and Nile Hiltons, Marriott, Shepherd, and other major hotels, with a main office at 151 Muhammad Farid St., downtown (tel. 391 75 71). All branches open Sat.-Thurs. 8:30am-2pm and 6-9pm. **Cairo Barclays International Bank,** 12 Sheikh Yousef Sq., Garden City (tel. 354 94 15 or 22), 3 blocks south of Tahrir Sq. along Qasr El 'Aini St., accepts traveler's checks and has worldwide money transfer services. Open Sun.-Thurs. 8:30am-2pm; during Ramadan, 10am-1pm. Foreign banks are closed Fri.-Sat., but most Egyptian banks are open Sat. Money can be wired to Egypt through **Citibank,** 4 Ahmed Pasha St., Garden City (tel. 355 18 73 or 74; open Sun.-Thurs. 8:30am-2pm). Also see American Express and Thomas Cook listings.

**American Express:** 15 Qasr en-Nil (tel. 574 79 91-96), off **Tala'at Harb Sq.,** opposite EgyptAir, toward Ramses St. Cashes traveler's checks. Members can have money sent and use **Client Letter Service.** Non-clients may use letter service for $3. Open daily 8:30am-5pm. Letter service open Sun.-Thurs. 8:30am-4:30pm. Other locations: **Nile Hilton** (tel. 578 50 01-03), **Marriott Hotel** (tel. 341 01 36), **Pullman Ma'adi** (tel. 350 78 51), **Mohandiseen,** 4 Syria St. (tel. 70 79 08 or 14).

**Western Union:** 1079 Corniche en-Nil, Garden City, in the FedEx office (tel. 357 13 00, 74-5, or 84-5). Worldwide money transfer. Open Sun.-Thurs. 8:30am-9pm.

**ATM:** The **Egyptian British Bank** has machines that accept **Visa, Plus, Global Access,** and **Express Net** cards. Locations in Semiramis Intercontinental, Nile Hilton and Ramses Hiltons, Zamalek Marriott, and Cairo Sheraton.

**Federal Express** (tel. 357 13 04) at 1079 Corniche en-Nil, Garden City, opposite the Meridien on the east bank of the Nile. Open 24hr.

**Telephone Office: Main Office,** Ramses St., 1 block north of 26th July St. Other offices in Zamalek, Airport, Ma'adi, Tahrir Sq, Adly St., and Alfy St., under the Windsor Hotel. Look for the handset sign. All open 24hr. Collect and credit card calls available at the USADirect, U.K. Direct, Canada Direct, and Japan Direct phones in the lobbies of the Ramses Hilton, Marriott, and SemiRamis hotels. For a 25% surcharge, you can make international calls easily at the business service offices in the Meridien, Sheraton, and Nile Hilton hotels (24hr.). All major hotels have local pay phones, operated with expensive tokens (25-50pt.). **Directory Assistance:** Tel. 140.

**Telegraph and Telex Office:** 'Ataba Sq., opposite the main post office. Open 24hr. Most of the telephone offices have these services and can send **faxes.**

**Faxes:** You may send and receive faxes at the business office of the Ramses Hilton (fax 575 71 52 or 578 22 21). They charge according to destination for sending and E£4 per page to receive.

**Flights, Trains, Buses, Metro, Taxis:** See Transportation, p. 89.

**Car Rental:** For maniacs willing to risk life and limb to achieve relative freedom of mobility: **Avis** (tel. 354 86 98 or 74 00), open daily 8am-3:30pm. Branch at Cairo International Airport (tel. 291 42 66, 77, 88) is open 24hr. Join millions of middle-class Egyptians driving in a Fiat 128 (known in Cairo as "the 28") for US$36. Charge for each additional km over 100km.

**Lockers:** On the ground floor of Ramses Station, 30pt per day (14-day max.). Ask anyone in uniform, *"Feen al-makhzan?"* (Where are the lockers?) Open 24hr. Dubious security. Most hotels have safe deposit boxes, and many will store luggage. Be sure to get **written proof** of having stored anything.

**English Bookstores: AUC Bookstore,** Hill House, American University in Cairo, 113 Qasr El 'Aini St. (tel. 357 53 77), has classic novels, guidebooks, and maps. Bring your passport, you'll need it to enter the high security campus. Open Sun.-Thurs. 8:30am-4pm, Sat. 10am-3pm. AUC Press also has a bookstore at 16 Muhammad Ibn Thakeb St., Zamalek (tel. 339 70 45). **Lehnert and Landrock,** 44 Sharif St., between Adly St. and 26th July St. (tel. 393 53 24), also has a wide selection of guidebooks and maps. Open Mon.-Fri. 9:30am-2pm and 4-7:30pm, Sat. 9:30am-1:30pm. **Madbuli** in Tala'at Harb Sq. (tel. 575 64 21; open daily 10am-10pm) offers books on Egypt and by Naguib Mahfouz. Also at 45 El Batal Ahmed Abd el-Aziz St. (tel. 347 74 10; open 24hr). **Shorouk Bookshop,** Tala'at Harb Sq. (tel. 391 24 80), is packed with schlock romance and whodunits. Look harder to find guidebooks, Arabic phrase books, and maps. Open daily 9am-10pm, Ramadan 10am-4pm and 8pm-12am. **Anglo-Egyptian,** 165 Muhammad Farid St. (tel. 391 43 37), has new and used books at reasonable prices. Open Mon.-Sat. 9am-1:30pm and 4:30-7:30pm.

**Newspapers and Magazines:** The *Egyptian Gazette* and the *Al-Ahram Weekly* (both 75pt), Egypt's two English newspapers, come out every Thursday. *Egypt Today*, a monthly magazine (E£7), is handy for current restaurant and entertainment listings. All publications are sold at **The Reader's Corner,** 33 Abd el-Khaleq Sarwat St., downtown (open Mon.-Sat. 9:30am-7pm). Kiosks along Tala'at Harb Sq., near AUC, or at the intersection of 26th July and Hasan Sabri St., Zamalek, sell American and European periodicals.

**American Cultural Center:** 5 Latin America St., Garden City (tel. 354 96 01 or 76 27 04; library 355 05 32 or 357 34 12), across from the British Embassy. If you'll be in Egypt for at least 12 months you are eligible to join. To do so, take along your passport (any nationality) and two photos. Members can borrow books and watch videos in the library. Occasional free films and lectures; call 357 33 66 for a schedule. Open Sun.-Fri. 10am-4pm; winter Mon. and Wed. 10am-7pm, Tues. and Thurs.-Fri. 10am-4pm.

**Film Developing: Kodak,** 20 Adly St., opposite the synagogue (tel. 394 22 63). Camera batteries and film. Open Mon.-Sat. 9am-9pm. If you can't find it, Kodak signs swarm around Tala'at Harb, Adly, and Alfy St. Developing prices are about E£2-3 for processing and 50pt per print.

**Supermarkets: Sunny Supermarket,** 11 El Aziz Osman St., Zamalek (tel. 342 11 21 or 341 20 32), next door to the Mayfair Hotel, south of 26 July St. Gargantuan range of Egyptian and Western products offered, for not-quite-budget prices. Will deliver. Open daily 8am-10pm. **Seoudi Market,** 25 Midan El Missaha St., Dokki (tel. 348 84 40 or 41), also at 50 El Quds esh-Sharif St. (Jerusalem St.), Mohandiseen (tel. 344 00 37 or 346 03 91), and 15 Ahmad Hishmat St., Zamalek (tel. 341 35 86 or 340 95 96), all open 10am-11pm. A fully-stocked supermarket with fair prices.

**Laundry: Circle Cleaning,** 24 26th July St. (tel. 76 08 55), near the Supreme Court and the intersection with Tala'at Harb St. Open daily 9am-9pm. You're probably better off either doing it yourself or paying one of the maids in your hotel to do your load (50pt per piece is reasonable).

**Toilets:** Most squares have public toilets; ask for *el-hammam*. These are often crowded and will offend your nostrils. If you are in the downtown area, you can always go about it the Rachel way and walk confidently into one of the five-star hotels, which are sure to have plenty of toilet paper in their stalls.

**Swimming Pools:** The **Fontana Hotel,** Ramses Sq. (tel. 92 21 45 or 23 21), has a teal-tiled pool on its 7th-floor patio (E£10 per day). Cairo's many sporting clubs sell day passes for E£20. The best are the **Gezira Sporting Club,** in front of the Marriott Hotel in Zamalek (tel. 340 22 72), the **Ma'adi Sporting Club,** 8 En-Nadi Sq. (tel. 350 55 04), and the **Heliopolis Sporting Club,** 17 El Merghany St. (tel. 291 48 00). Sometimes the guards insist that you enter with a club member, sometimes they don't.

**Pharmacy:** 24-hr. **Victoria Pharmacy,** 90 Qasr El 'Aini St., Garden City (tel. 354 86 04). **Pharmacy Mondial,** 2 Ahmed Hishmat St., Zamalek (tel. 341 11 80). Ask for Dr. Mamdouh. Open daily 9:30am-10pm. **Zarif Pharmacy,** Tala'at Harb St., next to Shorouk Bookshop.

**Hospitals:** The best-equipped is **As-Salaam International Hospital,** Corniche en-Nil, Ma'adi (tel. 363 80 50, emergency 362 33 00). **Anglo-American Hospital,** Botanical Garden St., Gezira-Zamalek (tel. 340 61 62-65) below the Cairo Tower. **Cairo Medical Center,** Roxy Sq., Heliopolis (tel. 258 05 66, 02 17, or 10 03).

**Emergency: Fire:** Tel. 125, or 391 01 15. **Ambulance:** Tel. 123.

**Police:** Tel. 122, 126, or 303 41 22 or 51 22; central station: tel. 13.

**Main Post Office:** 55 Sarwat St., the corner of 'Ataba Sq., under the dome (tel. 391 26 14). Often crowded, but blissfully empty just before the office closes. Packages require an export license from the airport; major hotels and tourist shops also provide this service. Open Sat.-Thurs. 8:30am-7pm; Ramadan 9am-3pm. **Poste restante** located around the corner on Bidek St. Open Sat.-Thurs. 8am-6pm. **Express Mail (EMS)** on Bidek St. across from *poste restante* (open daily 24hr.). Most branches in Cairo sell stamps and have EMS. One conveniently located branch is in Tahrir Sq. (tel. 575 43 13) at 13 Metitte Bash St., a small alley opposite the eastern wall of the Egyptian Museum (open Sat.-Thurs. 9am-5pm).

**Telephone Code:** 02.

# ■ Accommodations

Don't believe the guy at the airport who tells you all the *Let's Go* listings have either gone out of business or spontaneously combusted (we thoroughly check hotels for explosive potential). Downtown Cairo, on and around **Tala'at Harb Street,** is littered with dozens of budget hotels and dorms occupying the upper floors of colonial buildings. If you want to splurge on one of the swankier listings, you'll be rewarded with the chilling effects of high-powered air conditioning.

When selecting your room, keep in mind that the higher up you go, the farther away you are from the noise. Moreover, breezes at higher elevations keep mosquitoes away (they get altitude sickness) and help travelers endure the hot summer months. All of the prices listed below include continental breakfast and all places have fans and 24-hr. hot water unless otherwise noted. Check-out time is usually noon, although you can often negotiate an extra hour or two. Maids at each establishment will be psyched to earn a little extra cash if you have them do your laundry (usually about 50pt per article). If you are planning on being in Cairo for a while or are here during the low season, try to bargain for a reduced rate. Single-sex groups should have no problem renting a **flat** (E£500-800 per month), but building owners often frown upon renting to mixed sex groups. The billboard at Sunny Market in Zamalek lists available apartments.

**Youth Hostel (HI),** 135 Malek Abd el-Aziz es-Saud St., Manial Roda Island (tel. 364 07 29; fax 98 41 07). Take metro to Sayyida Zeinab. Exit to the right and walk straight to the Nile. Cross the Sayala Bridge and continue straight across Roda Island to the main channel of the Nile. Turn left just before the University (El Gama'a) bridge (with Salah ad-Din mosque to your right); the hostel is 10m away on the left. A quieter, cleaner alternative to other "traveler" hostels, the HI houses a mixture of foreign backpackers and young Egyptians. Bunk beds are crammed into spartan but clean single-sex rooms. The men's section tends to fill faster than the women's; call ahead. The hotel features clean, new bathrooms, a large kitchen for guests, a reasonably-priced restaurant, and a comfortable lounge area. Non-members pay E£4 extra per night. No lockout. Curfew 11pm. Dorm beds (6 per room) E£8.10. Triples E£12.10.

## BUDGET HOTELS

**Sultan Hotel,** 4 Souq et-Tewfikia St., 1st and 5th floors (tel. 77 22 58), off Tala'at Harb St. on the market street running parallel to 26 July St. The bedrooms could use a bit of a makeover and mice make occasional cameos, but the helpful staff, perfect location, and unbeatable price compensate. Ask the staff anything about Cairo; they honestly want you to love their city. Try to get the room with the fruit market view. The 5th floor rooms are less crowded, cheaper, and breezier. Dorm beds E£6. Doubles E£15. 1st-floor dorm beds E£7. Expressive paintings by talented travelers adorn the bedroom walls. Breakfast is not included, but guests may use the kitchen. Free luggage storage.

**Venice Hotel,** 4 Souq et-Tewfikia, 4th floor (tel. 574 32 69), in the same building as the Sultan Hotel. Cool breezes waft into the spacious rooms of this brand-new hotel (opened July 1996). All rooms have either balconies or windows, making up for a lack of fans. Redone hardwood floors and spotless bathrooms confound budgeteers who only pay E£8 for a dorm bed. Singles E£12. Doubles E£20. Less English is spoken here than at the Sultan.

**Safary Hotel,** 4 Souq et-Tewfikia St., 5th floor (tel. 575 07 52), in the same building as the Sultan Hotel. Japanese tourists, the faithful frequenters of this longtime hostel, cook up communal meals in the palatial kitchen and kick back in the sitting room. Dorm rooms have anywhere from 2-5 beds (E£6 each).

**Anglo-Swiss Hotel,** 14 Champollion St., 6th floor (tel. 575 14 97), 2 blocks west of Tala'at Harb Sq. From Tahrir Sq., turn right on Champollion in the northeastern end of the square next to the museum. The hotel will be to your left at the intersection with Mahmoud Bassinni St. You can play a prelude on the piano in the sunny dining hall before retiring to quiet, clean rooms with hardwood floors and balconies. Clean bathrooms. Flexible check-out times. Free luggage storage. Singles E£25. Doubles E£45, with bath E£50. Triples E£45, with bath E£60. 15-25% discounts depending on duration of stay. Renovations planned to be finished in January 1997 will add a satellite TV to the lobby and snazz up the rooms a bit. Helpful staff can fetch train and bus tickets for you (E£4 charge per ticket) or secure you an ISIC card (E£25).

**Pension Select Hotel,** 19 Adly St., 8th floor (tel. 393 37 07), next to the synagogue. High above the street noise, Select offers spacious three-per-room dorm style set-ups. Rahim, the gracious, elderly proprietor, is a relief from the young whipper-snappers who hassle you in the street. All dorm beds E£12. Solo travelers should resist being fooled into paying a surcharge.

**Pensione Roma,** 169 Muhammad Farid St. (tel. 391 10 88 or 13 40), 1 block south of 26 July St. and 2 blocks east of Tala'at Harb St., turn right on Adly St. then left after the synagogue; look for the hotel's green sign above the Gattegno department store. High ceilings and refurbished hardwood floors transport you to Italy. Toilet paper, towels, and soap make Roma seem like more than a budget hotel. Nothing is perfect, however. Some travelers have complained of a bed-bug problem here. The dining room serves E£10 plates of steak, potato, and veggies, along with many other menu items, and the salon area is grand. Free lockers. Singles E£22.75. Doubles E£41.50, with bath E£46. French, Italian, and English spoken.

**Hotel Beau Site,** 27 Tala'at Harb St. 5th floor (tel. 392 99 16). Large double beds, balconies, spacious rooms, and well-kept hardwood floors compensate for the peeling walls. The hotel is rarely crowded, making for a calm atmosphere. White-tiled communal W.C.s are as large as the bedrooms in other hotels. Dorm beds E£12, singles E£15, doubles with queen size bed E£25.

**Hotel Minerva,** 39 Tala'at Harb St. (tel. 392 06 00 or 01 or 02), one block toward Tala'at Harb Sq. from 26 July St. Reception is 4doors past Bamboo Clothing Store on your right. Uniformed maids keep this joint spotless. Each room has an armoire, coffee table, and newly finished hardwood floors. Crisp white sheets are folded down for you. No private baths, but the communal ones are military-academy clean. Singles E£22, doubles with large user-friendly beds E£28.

**Gresham Hotel,** 20 Tala'at Harb St. just off Tala'at Harb Sq. (tel. 575 90 43). Renovations have made the hardwood floors and common baths gleam. Rooms are blessed with good quality mattresses and bureaus, but no fans. Be sure to ask for a room with a balcony. Single E£25, with A/C and bath E£50, doubles E£35, with bath E£45, with A/C E£55.

**Hotel Petit Palais,** 45 Abd el-Khalek Sarwat St. (tel. 391 18 63), ½ block west of Opera Sq. and El Goumhouriyya St. Run by the same people as the Ismailia, with the same facilities at a less frenetic pace. Carpeted rooms (rare in Cairo), and spotless, shared bathrooms. Media-starved Europeans watch MTV and 56 other channels in the lobby. Dorm beds (4 per room) E£15. Spacious singles E£25. Doubles E£40. Triples E£45.

**Hotel Viennoise,** 11 Mahmoud Bassiouny St. (tel. 574 31 53; fax 575 31 36), at Champollion St., 1 block from Tahrir Sq. Look for the big yellow sign. Vast corridors and a grand lobby decorated with 19th-century European furniture do little to ameliorate fanless rooms. The manager speaks French, German, and Spanish. Singles E£20, with bath E£30. Doubles E£27, with bath E£30. Triples E£39.

**Hotel Nefertiti,** 39 Tala'at Harb St. (tel. 392 51 53), 2 floors above Bamboo clothing store, 100m from Cinema Metro. Enter through the alleyway to the right, next to the entrance for Hotel Minerva. Ideal for groups of 2 or 3 who want a private, clean room. Rooms are a little dark and drab, but the price is right. Doubles with shower E£15. Triples with shower E£21. Breakfast not included.

**Sun Hotel,** 2 Tala'at Harb St., 9th floor (tel. 578 17 86), look for the sign on your right just as you leave Tahrir Sq. Brand new hotel has carpets and MTV, and is smack dab in the middle of downtown Cairo. Staying on the 9th floor eliminates street noise, and the massive beds and spacious dorm rooms help you get a good night's sleep. Each bed has a personal nightstand. Breakfast included. Sheets are changed daily. Dorm rooms E£15, singles E£25, doubles E£40.

## A BIT SWANKIER

**Windsor Hotel,** 19 Alfy Bey St. (tel. 591 58 10 or 52 77; fax 92 16 21), behind Cinema Diana. Very clean, with an atmosphere of old-time grandeur. The Barrel Bar, so named because all the furniture is made from retired barrels, was once the British Officers' Club. Monty Python's Michael Palin hung out at the Windsor while filming *Around the World in Eighty Days*. Excellent service. All rooms have A/C, towels, crisp sheets, and comfy beds. Singles with shower E£59, with shower and toilet E£76. Doubles with shower E£81, with toilet E£102. These prices include breakfast, tax, and are dependent on you flashing your *Let's Go* to get the 25% discount. 5% credit card service charge.

**Carlton Hotel,** 21 26 July St. (tel. 575 50 22; fax 575 53 23), beside Cinema Rivoli, near Tala'at Harb St. and 26 July St. intersection. Metro stop: Nasser. Colonial lobby and hardwood floors are just the beginning. Each room has satellite TV, A/C, and a balcony with patio furniture. Large breakfast included. Singles E£65, doubles E£85.

**El Malky Hotel,** 4 El Hussein St., next to El Hussein Mosque and Khan el-Khalili market (tel. 92 88 04). Situated in the heart of Islamic Cairo, El Malky gets you away from downtown. You'll need to get used to the *muezzin* call to prayer five times a day, as Cairo's most famous mosque is next door. Singles with TV, fridge, and balcony E£35, with A/C E£45, doubles E£45, with A/C E£55.

**Mayfair Hotel,** 9 Aziz Osman St. (tel. 340 73 15), parallel to Hassan Sabri St., on the corner of Ibn Zinky St. 2 blocks south of 26 July St., Zamalek. Tidy rooms (most with balconies) conveniently located in the heart of Zamalek, but noise from the school across the street could rob you of the peace you paid for (not a concern in the summer). Sip tea on the homey veranda or take advantage of the great restaurants, pastry shops, and bars of Zamalek while you escape from the madness of downtown Cairo. Rooms with or without private bath and A/C. Singles E£20-35. Doubles E£34-60. E£2 discount for *Let's Go* users.

**Horris Hotel,** 5 July 26 St. (Tel. 591 04 78 or 05 47, or 08 55), or enter from Alfy St. behind Cinema Diana. Try to get a room on the upper floors to enjoy a spectacular view of the city from the flowerific balconies. Three reasonably-priced restaurants

(E£15 per meal) along with a barren bar and a disco on the roof. All rooms have A/C and are clean and spacious. Not to be confused with the Horrus Hotel. Singles E£43, doubles E£74, triples E£88. International telephone service.

# ■ Food

Cairo is one of the world's great cities, and has the diverse restaurant line-up to prove it. If you choose to stick with the same old *fuul* and falafel (more often called *ta'miyya* in Egypt), you'll only need 60pt to fill your stomach. *Kushari*, an Egyptian speciality (with lentils, macaroni, rice, grilled onions, and tomato sauce) will only set you back about E£1.50. Wash it all down with exhilarating fruit juices, on sale anywhere you see bags of fruit hanging around a storefront. At places without waiters, pay first and then exchange your receipt for food. Hygiene might not be a priority at most food and juice stands (especially those without signs), but if you stick with the crowds you should be all right.

A clean sit-down meal is often worth the investment, and will be relatively cheap by Western standards. Even at more expensive restaurants, you can create a handsome meal out of hummus, *tahina, baba ghannoush,* and salad for under E£7. *Fatir,* a *fillo* dough-like flat bread with vegetables, meats, jam, or sweets piled on top and stuffed inside, is far tastier than the imitations of Italian pizza in town and, at E£5-10, usually cheaper. There are a 5% sales tax on food and a 10-12% service charge at sit-down restaurants included on the bill; a small **tip** (E£1) is still in order.

While eating local food is an essential component of the Egyptian experience, the (cleaner, faster, air-conditioned) Western alternative is always there. Fast food chains have invaded Cairo in the past few years. In the downtown area, they're lined up across from the AUC on Mahmoud St. **Pizza Hut** offers slices for E£1.90 each (home delivery 356 26 28 or 27 55). Next door, **KFC** is a bit cheaper and more crowded, but serves buns instead of the flaky biscuits so treasured by the Colonel and his cohorts. Opposite the AUC gate is **McDonald's** (tel. 355 81 31), where a combo meal sizzles for E£8.50 (all 3 open 11am-midnight and have delivery service).

## DOWNTOWN

**Felfela,** 15 Hoda Sharawi St. (tel. 392 27 51 or 28 33), off Tala'at Harb St., 1 block south of Tala'at Harb Sq. Consistently excellent. A favorite among Egyptians and tourists alike, this award-winning restaurant, started by an Egyptian model in 1958, is the first of a chain that now extends to Alexandria. Bursting with bamboo, aquariums, and mosaics, the ambience cannot be beat. Spiced *fuul* (E£2-4.50) and falafel dishes (E£1.60-5). Full meal of *wara 'einab* (stuffed grape leaves) E£10, spaghetti E£4.25. Also delicious is *om ali,* a pastry baked with milk, honey, and raisins (E£5). Another entrance on Tala'at Harb St. leads to a self-service counter with cold drinks and sandwiches (40-80pt). Open daily 7am-12:30am.

**El Tahrir,** 169 Tahrir St. (tel. 355 84 18), 1 block east of Tahrir Sq. on the right; the English sign is *inside* the shop; if you get to the American University or the green pedestrian overpass, you've gone too far. Clean and crowded with Egyptians. The best *kushari* in town (huge bowl for E£2). Beware: that's hot sauce in the wine bottles. The off-white liquid is a lemon concoction. Open daily 6:30am-11pm.

**Estoril Restaurant,** 12 Tala'at Harb St. (tel. 574 31 02), across the street from Felfela's take-away counter. Madame Lena and her son and daughter run this Greek/Italian restaurant which also serves Egyptian specialties. Stop in for a beer (E£6) and receive an assortment of four salads and sauces to nibble on with bread—a great midday snack. An extra E£2.50 gets you a plate of scrumptious *dolmas*. Plenty of vegetarian options (ravioli E£8.40). The *prix fixe* dinner includes soup, salad, entree of chicken or fish, and dessert (E£19). Open daily noon-4pm and 7:30-11pm.

**Le Pacha,** 15 Mahmoud Bassiouni St., one block west of Tala'at Harb Sq. (tel. 574 61 69). Chomp on *spaghetti bolognaise* (E£3.75) or breaded or grilled chicken fillet (E£15) in this small air-conditioned restaurant. Open daily 8am-midnight.

**Brazilian Coffee Shop,** 38 Tala'at Harb St.; at the intersection with Adly St., look for the Miami Cinema. Air-conditioned restaurant upstairs serves up real cappuccino (E£2) and espresso (E£1.75). A great place to read the morning paper. Sausage and potato dinner E£10, mixed grill dinner E£15. Open daily 6am-midnight.

**Ali Hassan al-Hati,** 3 Halim St. (tel. 591 60 55), between Alfy St. and July 26th St., 1 block south of the Windsor Hotel. High ceilings, crystal chandeliers, soaring mirrors, and forlorn waiters. Flavorful *kabab* (E£9), *kofta* (E£9), and fish (E£11). Try the *fatteh* (garlic, meat or vegetables poured over crunchy baked bread and covered with a yogurt sauce, E£2-3.50). Open daily noon-11pm.

**El Haty,** 8A July 26th St. (tel. 391 88 29), in an alleyway to the south of the street. Not to be confused with the restaurant upstairs, where the average meal costs more than E£30. Unimpeachably hygienic. Salads E£1.40, sandwiches E£2-4, entrees E£7-16.50. The lunch special (*kofta, kabab,* oriental rice or macaroni, salad, bread, and dessert) is E£14.50. Credit cards. Open daily noon-midnight.

**New Kursaal,** 5 Imad ed-Din St. (tel. 591 85 78), at the intersection with Alfy Bey St.; look for the green awning. Professional service and good food, including *tagen* (meats and vegetables baked in a clay pot) and *kobeba* (ko-BAY-ba, beef with crushed wheat). Salads E£1.50, meals E£5-18, sandwiches E£1.50-5, alcoholic drinks E£5-11, desserts E£2-4. Open daily 10am-1am.

## ZAMALEK

If you want a break from downtown Cairo, search out the tree-lined boulevards of Zamalek. All restaurants listed here are north of 26 July St. Consider visiting a pastry shop or bar for dessert and drinks after your meal.

**Al Dente,** 26 Bahgat Ali St. (tel. 340 91 17), from the Western Corniche, take a right onto Anis Pasha St. Al Dente is two blocks ahead on your left. This new Italian eatery has built a good reputation in a remarkably short time. The secret lies with chef Sa'ad, who has 15 years of experience in Italy. A wide selection of pastas with 18 different sauces. AUC professors rave about the *alla crema di noci* (E£13), and the *al salmone* (E£19). If that's too much for your pocketbook, try the tasty *aglio e olio* (garlic and olive oil) at E£4; two orders of this provides a carbo-load for the weary traveler. Open daily noon-2am.

**Harry's Pub,** Cairo Marriott Hotel, Zamalek. Wide selection of drinks; you name it, they've got it, but be prepared to pay dearly. The all-you-can-eat buffets on Fri. (chicken), Sat. (Chinese), and Sun. (roast beef) are a surprisingly inexpensive E£10 and are sure to please the famished foreigner. (Served 1-6pm). A/C and satellite TV. Open daily noon-1:30am.

**Maison Thomas,** 157 26 July St. (tel. 340 70 57), on your right near the base of the bridge as you come into Cairo from Zamalek. Italian deli replete with hanging salami, olives, and rounds of cheese. Salad niçoise is a refreshing E£10. Don't miss the calzone: the regular size easily feeds two people (E£16), and the large is a bit absurd (E£23). Take away, eat in, or home delivery. Open 24hr.

**Bon Appetit,** 2 Ismail Muhammad St. (tel. 340 43 82 or 91 08), 1 block from the Flamenco Hotel on the western side of Zamalek. The big sandwiches are highly praised by Zamalek residents, particularly AUC students living in the hostel a few minutes from here. This is perhaps the cleanest place to try a brain or a tongue sandwich (E£6.75). If you are not that adventurous, the mammoth chicken fillet (E£7) will keep you clucking for days. Open 10:30am-midnight. Visa, MC, AmEx.

**Hana Korean Restaurant,** 21 Ma'had as-Swissry St. (tel. 340 18 46), in the En-Nil Zamalek Hotel. Take a right off of 26 July St. onto Hassan Sabri St. (which is also called Brazil St.). You will see the sign about 100m on your right proclaiming "Korean, Chinese, Japanese." Decorated with Chinese lanterns, this air-conditioned haven is popular with in-the-know locals and expats. Don't miss the Korean BBQ (*Bulgogi*), with its tender slices of beef you barbecue right at the table (E£19). The *kimchi* (pickled cabbage) fried rice (E£13) is scrumptious, and an order of egg rolls made (for once) with real egg instead of pastry is a bargain at E£6. Open daily noon-10:30pm.

## MOHANDISEEN

**Al-Omda,** 6 El Gazeir St. (tel. 346 22 47), a few doors from the Atlas Hotel on Gam'at ed-Duwal St., down an unmarked staircase. This popular, clean, air-conditioned joint serves tasty pizza and stuffed grape leaves (E£8-E£15). Excellent *fuul* and falafel (E£1) and *kushari* (E£3), but make sure you ask for it specifically, as you may be given a menu which includes only the pricier dishes. Open 24hr.

**My Queen,** Gam'at ed-Duwal el-Arabiyya St. (Arab League St.), across from the overpass at the end of the street; the Atlas is at the other end of the same street. Don't be fooled by My Queen's appearance. Yes, she's a moving van (customers are served either in their cars or on their feet); no, she doesn't look appetizing, but how can you argue with delicious *kofta, shawerma, kibda* (liver), *sish tawouq*, and other sandwiches for only E£3-5? Come here on a Thurs. night (or Fri. morning) around 2am and find half of Cairo's teeny-boppers chowing down after a long night at one of Cairo's discotheques. No vegetarian dishes. Reasonable prices and prompt service.

**Prestige Pizza,** 43 Geziret al-Arab (tel. 347 0383), just east of Wadi en-Nil St. If you're coming from Gam'at ed-Duwal St., turn right before Al Ahli Bank. A favorite pizza place among wealthier Cairenes. Look around you in the outdoor section to see Egypt's top actors and film producers scarfing down slices. Generous "small" pizzas E£5-8, large E£12-15. Good Egyptian lentil soup, too. Open daily noon-2am. E£2.25 cover charge. AmEx, Visa, MC.

## KHAN EL-KHALILI

**Al Gamhorya,** on Al Azhar St. one block east of the green pedestrian overpass at El Ghouri Mosque and Mausoleum. Look for the white marble façade with red trimmed windows. A break from the madness of Khan el-Khalili and a perfect *kushari* (E£1) stop-off. Open daily 9am-11pm.

**Coffee Shop Naguib Mahfouz,** 5 El Badistante Lane (tel. 90 37 88 or 93 22 62), 2 blocks west of El Hussein Mosque. This pricey restaurant is an oasis of delectable food in the maddening bustle of the *Khan*. A hangout of Nobel laureate Naguib Mahfouz. Every night, live music accompanies a Lebanese meal: *ema* (dumplings, E£6.50), *kabab* or *kufta* (E£26), *tabbouleh* or other salad (E£4). Exotic fruit drinks E£3.50-5.50. Minimum charge E£3.50 per person, E£1.10 music charge. Open daily 11:30am-1:30am; Ramadan 8am-4am. Visa, MC, AmEx.

**Egyptian Pancakes,** 7 Al Azhar Sq. (tel. 90 86 23), 1 block from the intersection of Al Azhar St. and Gohar el-Qa'it St. Meat or sweet *fatir* E£8-11. These have nothing to do with Western pancakes; they're much better. Open 24hr.

## SPLURGES

It's easy to fill your stomach for mere piasters in Cairo, but if you're in the mood to spend a bit more, you can feast like a pharaoh for the money it would take to get an appetizer elsewhere in the world.

**Maroush,** 64 Lebanon St., Mohandiseen (tel. 645 09 72), a E£4-5 taxi ride from downtown. The best Lebanese restaurant in Egypt fills its tables with students, expats, and upper-class Cairenes. Fluffy, pearl-white pita bread is served piping hot with your *sambousek* appetizer (E£1.75) or salad (E£4.50). The Maroush Chicken, especially mouthwatering (E£22), is the most expensive of the entrees (E£10-22). Upstairs is an A/C room which takes AmEx. Downstairs and outside, the *sheesha*-smoking crowd is more laid back. Open daily 8am-2am.

**Tabasco,** 8 Amman Sq., Mohandiseen (tel. 336 55 83—you must call for a reservation). This is *the* new restaurant for 1997, and Cairenes in the know can't stop gabbing about it. Dim candlelight and soft jazz soothe the weary budgeteer, and the food makes even the most critical of gourmet mouths smile. Every week the menu changes but the prices stay in the same range: Appetizers E£10-24, pasta E£12-17, main dishes E£21-34. The filet mignon with blue cheese is grilled to perfection (E£34). Open daily 8pm-2:30am. Visa, MC, AmEx.

**Peking,** 14 Saraya el-Azbakia St. (tel. 591 23 81), behind Cinema Diana, between Alfy and 26 July St. This romantic, lantern-lit, air-conditioned restaurant is one of Cairo's most popular Chinese restaurants. Spicy calamari and spring rolls are particularly good. Don't miss the honey-walnut Tarte Lee for dessert (E£6.50). A full meal with a starter, three dishes, and dessert will set you and a friend back E£30 each. Open noon-midnight. Alcohol served. Other branches in Mohandiseen (tel. 349 90 86), New Ma'adi (tel. 352 34 50), and Heliopolis (tel. 418 56 12). Free delivery (tel. 591 23 81). AmEx, Visa, MC.

# ■ Sights

## ISLAMIC CAIRO

Cairo's medieval district is home to resplendent mosques and monuments which are touted as some of the finest Islamic architecture in the world. Unlike Damascus and Baghdad, the two other Middle Eastern capitals of the medieval Islamic world, Cairo was spared the devastation of Mongol invasions. Attacks today come not from roving warriors, but from the ever-encroaching modern world. Packed with mosques, lumbershops, metal factories, and homes, Islamic Cairo has a wrinkled, withered exterior. Beneath the Muslim city's dingy façade lies a wealth of ornate friezes, Arabesque stucco, finely-carved wooden grillwork, and vaulted and domed ceilings. Countless minarets serve as observation decks from which you can get your bearings as well as a magnificent view of the city. To get the most out of your visit, you might want to brush up on Islam before you go (see **Islam,** p. 62).

Many of the important monuments charge admission (E£.50-1.50; ½ off with ISIC). In sights that don't charge, and mosques in particular, you will be expected to give *bakhsheesh.* If you've purchased a ticket, you should not have to pay extra to climb the minaret. When visiting smaller monuments or when trying to see the interiors of tombs, don't be bashful about hunting down the custodian. Opening hours are estimates at best, so declare your interest to whomever is around and usually the caretaker will magically swish into being. If you confine your tour of Islamic Cairo to unlocked doors, you'll miss many of the city's treasures.

Most mosques are open from 8am-5pm, but visitors are not welcome during prayer times. Wait a few minutes after the congregation has finished before entering. Night visits are not permitted, although some travelers rave about watching the sunset paint Cairo dusty pink and yellow from atop a minaret. Avoid visiting mosques on Friday afternoons when the Muslim community gathers for afternoon prayer. Certain highly venerated mosques—Sayyidna Hussein, Sayyidna Zeinab, and Sayyidna Nafisa—are believed to contain the remains of descendants of Muhammad and are officially closed to non-Muslims, although some tourists adept in subtlety and modesty have been known to enter.

Visitors must dress modestly in Islamic Cairo; revealing clothing will attract a great deal of unsolicited and unfriendly attention and will prevent admission to many mosques. Residents consider shorts, miniskirts, and exposed shoulders disrespectful. In some cases head coverings are required (these can usually be rented for a few piasters). In some mosques (such as Muhammad Ali) an entire toga is provided for free (modish, modest, and mint-colored). Sensible shoes are also a must and, since you will be asked to remove your shoes altogether, socks are a good idea. Bring a plastic bag for your shoes to avoid the 50pt charged by custodians to "take care" of your shoes while you are touring or simply carry them with the soles facing one another. Never place the soles of your shoes on the floor of a mosque.

It takes at least two days to explore Islamic Cairo. We suggest spending your first day in southern Islamic Cairo at Ibn Tulun Mosque and working your way to central Islamic Cairo and the Citadel. El Muizz St., Khan el-Khalili, and the northern walls can fill a second day. However, even a two-day itinerary is rushed. A set of two detailed maps of Islamic Cairo is published by SPARE (Society for the Preservation of Architectural Resources in Egypt). The *City Map of Cairo* (E£7) has an indexed map of

Islamic Cairo. For in-depth descriptions and history, we recommend *Islamic Monu-ments in Cairo: A Practical Guide* by Caroline Williams. The book and most maps are available at the AUC bookstore.

If you are planning to follow *Let's Go's* **suggested tour** starting from the southern monuments, take minibus #54 or bus #72 from Tahrir Sq. or take the metro to Sayy-idna Zeinab and then bus #501 (25pt) to Kadri St. which leads straight up to Ibn Tulun. If coming from Giza, take bus #923; from the Pyramids, take bus #905, but it might be more convenient for a group to share a taxi (E£5) to Masjid Ibn Tulun.

## Ibn Tulun Mosque

The **Mosque of Ibn Tulun** is the largest, 3rd oldest (879 CE), and most sublime of Cairo's Islamic monuments. Facing Ibn Tulun from Kadri St., the entrance is around the left side. Once in the gate, Gayer-Anderson Museum is to your left and the mosque's courtyard is straight ahead. The serene courtyard covers almost seven acres and has six *mihrabs* indicating the direction to Mecca. In the center of the courtyard, an ablution fountain, or *mayda'a*, added in 1296 by a Mamluk sultan, is still used for washing before prayer.

Ahmed Ibn Tulun, son of a Turkish slave, was sent to Egypt as governor of El Fustat in 868 and became governor of the entire province in 879. He declared independ-ence from Baghdad and built a new royal city, *Qataii*, north of the original capital of El Fustat. This grand mosque is all that remains. The minaret, with its unusual exter-nal staircase, was probably built in the 13th century to resemble Ibn Tulun's original tower, which in turn was modeled after the minaret at the Great Mosque of Samarra in Iraq. A less substantiated theory explaining the unique external staircase attributes the design to the architectural period, built before it became clear that the *muezzin*, or prayer caller, could see impure things during his ascent to the top of the minaret. His glimpses of unveiled women relaxing in their homes or of people doing less than ascetic things in the streets led architects to build inner stairwells with hopes that the *muezzin* would have an easier time staying focused on the prayer he was about to deliver. Both the minaret and roof are accessible without having to lay out *bakhs-heesh*. (Open daily in the summer 8am-6pm, until 5pm in the winter, until 4pm in Ramadan. Admission E£6, students E£3.)

On the right, as you step out of the main courtyard of Ibn Tulun Mosque is the spectacular **Gayer-Anderson Museum** (see **Museums,** p. 119). Exit from the main entrance of Ibn Tulun and head left. Take a right at the intersection with Khodairi St., which eventually will turn into Saliba St.

## Sabil Umm Abbas

On the left side of Saliba St., this mosque became the home of the **Life and Culture Center** in 1990 when the ministry of culture moved artists here from their well-known center on Roda Island. Now, tucked away in Islamic Cairo, the artists rarely get visitors and are anxious to share their passion with interested travelers. Contem-porary Egyptian artists employ the techniques of their ancient predecessors. Artists specialize in textile production, batik, printing, glass blowing, and silk screening. Be sure to speak with Muhammad Reda Nasr, whose unique art combines calligraphy and nature (canvases are often made from egg shells and leaves). His subjects are meant to portray the many sides of Egypt (open Sat.-Thurs. 9am-2pm; free).

Continue north on Saliba St. between the double **Mosques of Shaykhon.** The one on the right has well-kept stained glass and a super painting of Mecca on the far southwestern wall (look for the guard if it's locked; free).

Exit the mosque and continue north on Saliba St. which becomes Shaykhon St. At the fork, stay left and you'll eventually see Sultan Hasan and Rifa'i Mosque on your left and the Citadel to your right through Salah ad-Din Sq.

## Sultan Hasan and Rifa'i

The 19th Mamluk Sultan of Egypt, Sultan en-Nasser Hasan, busted the bank in build-ing this *madrasa* and mausoleum in 1356 C.E. When he died, no one wanted to deal with the unfinished project, so they let it stand until it became a tourist attraction. To

EGYPT

reach these massive edifices and the Citadel, you can either approach from the south by following *Let's Go*'s suggested tour starting at Ibn Tulun or you can take bus #173 or #194 from Tahrir or minibus #72. From 'Ataba Sq., take Muhammad Ali St. which becomes El Al'a (Citadel) St. from the southern edge of the square.

Spurned by devotees of pharaonic art because much of it was built with exterior casing stones pilfered from the Pyramids at Giza, **Sultan Hasan** is not a mosque but a combination *madrasa* and mausoleum with an added prayer niche. The commodious interior courtyard—32m on each side—belongs to the Madrasa of Sultan Hasan and is surrounded by four enormous vaulted *iwans,* arcades off the courtyard, each of which once housed one of the four schools of judicial thought in Sunni Islam. Hundreds of *qanadeel* (decorated oil lamps) hang just above head level, to bring the mammoth building to a more human scale. Inside the southeastern *iwan,* the *mihrab* is flanked by a pair of Crusader columns. On either side of the eastern-most *mihrab,* bronze doors open into the Mausoleum. (Open Sat.-Thurs. 8am-5pm in summer, 8am-6pm in winter, 8am-4pm in Ramadan, Fri. 9-11am and 2-5pm. Admission E£6, students E£3.)

Directly across from the Sultan Hasan Mosque stands the enormous **Rifa'i Mosque.** Rifa'i's stupendous size and polished interior will make your neck sore as you marvel at the awe-inspiring ceiling and marble tombs. Named after Imam Ahmed ai-Rifa'i, an Egyptian spiritual leader, the mosque was completed in 1912 by Khedive Isma'il's mother, Princess Koshair Hanem. She is buried here with her son Isma'il and grandsons King Fouad and King Farouk, Egypt's last monarch. In the room next to Farouk lies the tomb of Muhammad Reza Pahlavi, the last Shah of Iran. On the other side of the mosque, look for the mosaic-decorated *mihrab* and the elegant *maballigba,* a wooden stand where the *muezzin* echoes the *imam's* prayers. The stand is depicted on the E£10 note. Both the Rifa'i and Sultan Hasan Mosques are illuminated at night. (Open Sat.-Fri. 8-11am and 2-6pm. Admission E£6, students E£3.)

Between these two mosques is a pleasant garden filled with children playing *futbol* and adults reading the paper. It's a good spot to rest tired feet before you hit more mosques and the Citadel.

## The Citadel (El Al'a)

Dominating Islamic Cairo, the lofty **Citadel** (*El Al'a*) was begun by Salah ad-Din in 1176 and has been continually expanded and modified since then, most notably by the Mamluks and Muhammad Ali. To reach the Citadel, take bus #82, 83, or 609 from Tahrir Sq. From 'Ataba Sq., you can take bus #401 or minibus #50 or 55. You can enter from either the northern or the southern gate. From Hasan and Rifa'i head left along the wall past the post office on your right. The road, Baab el-Gded St., dead-ends at the gate to the Citadel. (Open daily 8am-6pm, in winter 8am-5pm, Ramadan 8am-4pm. Entrance locked one hour before closing time. Admission E£10, students E£5, including all the museums and mosques.) The complex contains three large mosques and four operating museums.

As you enter from the northern gate, the **Police National Museum** is to your right. Enter to examine mounds of confiscated narcotics or just say no and walk past the uninspiring exhibit. Much more interesting than the museum is the spectacular view of Cairo and the Pyramids from the garden. The **Military National Museum,** a joint venture spearheaded by President Hosni Mubarak and North Korea's Kim Il Sung in 1990, has fighter jets, tanks, and missiles on display in the garden. Inside, you'll find a detailed reconstruction of the citadel complex and well-documented accounts of Egypt's war ventures.

Between these museums and the mosque of Muhammad Ali is the **Mosque of Sultan En-Nasir,** built from 1318 to 1335 by one of the great Bahri Mamluk builders. En-Nasir made many additions to the Citadel, but this mosque was the only one to survive the renovations of Muhammad Ali. Unfortunately, the interior of the mosque was largely gutted by Ottoman Sultan Selim the Grim, who made off with its marble panels. Nonetheless, the mosque still has some impressive features: pharaonic and Coptic columns, a high wooden ceiling from India, and an olive oil-operated chandelier.

Just south of the mosque lies **Yousef's Well,** built by Crusader prisoners. A water wheel, or *saqya,* worked by oxen was used to raise water during wartime.

Near the far eastern end of the northern enclosure is a lovely, small-domed mosque known as the **Mosque of Suleiman Pasha,** the first Ottoman mosque in Cairo, built in 1527. The mosque, also known as Sariat el-Gabal (the mountain palace), has a small prayer hall decorated with different calligraphic styles and a courtyard consisting of 4 *iwans.*

To reach the massive **Mosque of Muhammad Ali,** head for the thin, unadorned Turkish minarets (the ones that look like pencils). Muhammad Ali leveled the western surface of the Citadel, filled in the famous 13th-century Mamluk palace Qasr el-Ablaq, and built his mosque on the ruins in 1830 as a reminder of Turkish dominion. Modeled after the Hagia Sophia mosque in Istanbul, the edifice is more attractive from a distance. The mosque was refurbished by the Department of Antiquities during the 1980s—its silver domes and marble-and-alabaster decorations now twinkle on the Cairo skyline. While popular with tourists and postcard makers, it is hated by art historians, who consider it a third-rate copy of the great Ottoman mosques in Istanbul and an obnoxious reminder of Muhammad Ali's ego.

The mosque consists of two parts: the courtyard and the Prayer Hall. The courtyard's main attraction is not the elaborate ablution fountain in the center, but rather a nameless, 17m-deep well whose underground cavity is as big as the courtyard itself. Call down something polite, and the well-dwellers will echo mystical, magical music right back at you. A charming and unexpected French gingerbread clock overlooks the courtyard; King Louis Philippe of France presented the clock in 1845 in appreciation of Muhammad Ali's gift of the obelisk from Luxor Temple that now stands in the Place de la Concorde in Paris. The interior is quite impressive, especially just after prayers when the large chandelier and tiny lanterns are lit. The edifice is also known as the Alabaster Mosque because it is covered inside and out with the clearest alabaster, hauled over from Beni Suef. (One outer face remains bare; when Muhammad Ali died, so did the funding.) The Prayer Hall is lit by a huge chandelier, and 365 lanterns (symbolizing the days in a year) provide additional lighting. A die-hard francophile, Muhammad Ali put splashes of Parisian decor across the five large domes and 15 smaller ones that tower overhead. His tomb is to the right as you enter the prayer hall.

**Qasr el-Gowhara** (the Diamond Palace), built in 1811 by Muhammad Ali and named after one of his wives, lies to the southwest of the Muhammad Ali Mosque. In 1974, a burglary attempt resulted in a fire that destroyed half of the palace. The surviving half consists of a large reception room where Muhammad Ali received 500 of his closest Mamluk allies and cordially slaughtered them. The elaborate wooden benches next to the wall concealed the murder weapons in hidden compartments below the seats. Also on display are a few of the gold- and silver-adorned tapestries from the Ka'ba in Mecca. Mecca presented Egypt with one of these tapestries every year until 1961. Only die-hard Muhammad Ali fans should walk over to the **Carriage (Hatour) Museum,** housing carriages of the great one's family.

## Blue Mosque and Mosque of Qijmas el-Ishaqi

Coming after some of the other mosques of Islamic Cairo, the **Blue Mosque,** or Mosque of Aqsunqur, can be a bit anticlimactic. If you have the energy, however, it's worth a peek. The first street after the Hasan and Rifa'i mosques, if you proceed around the Salah ad-Din rotary in a clockwise fashion, is Baab el-Wazir St. This street hugs the northwestern wall of the Citadel. Follow it until it breaks free of the wall at the post office on your right. The mosque is a few blocks to the north. The 14th-century edifice owes its name to the colored Syrian tiles that line the interior. The flowery tiles were added in 1652 by a Turkish governor homesick for Istanbul's grand tiled mosques. The prayer hall, to the right, has one of the oldest marble *minbars* (pulpits) in the Islamic world. The top of the minaret is a great vantage point for viewing the Citadel to the south, Khan el-Khalili to the north, and the southern end of the pastel-colored City of the Dead to the east. (Open daily 8am-6pm in summer, 8am-5pm in winter, 8am-4pm in Ramadan. Admission E£3, students E£1.50.)

To reach the simple and unobtrusive **Mosque of Qijmas el-Ishaqi,** turn right as you leave the Blue Mosque and continue up the same street; its name changes to Darb el-Ahmar (Red Way) in memory of Muhammad Ali's massacre of the Mamluk generals here. The mosque's unremarkable façade gives no inkling of the serene, colorful interior light from the stained-glass windows. Under the prayer mats in the east *iwan* lies an ornate marble mosaic floor. Tip the custodian to uncover it for you. El Ishaqi was Chief of the Royal Stable and Chargé d'Affairs for the annual pilgrimage to Mecca. As you step out, notice the grillwork of the *sabil* on your right and the carved stonework of the columns. Head back to Salah ad-Din Sq. to catch a ride home. Bus #194 goes to Tahrir and a cab should run you E£2.

## Fatimid Cairo: El Muizz Street and Al Azhar

You can take bus #922 or minibus #77 to Al Azhar Mosque and the Khan el-Khalili area. A taxi to this area from downtown should run you E£2-3, though it's only a 20-minute walk. Head west on Al Azhar St. for about 200m and turn left on El Muizz lid-Din Allah, which runs north-south through the medieval city, connecting its northern and southern gates and providing a good place to begin a tour of the district. If you stand on the corner of El Muizz lid-Din Allah and Al Azhar, Baab el-Futuh will be to the north, Baab Zuweila to the south, and Al Azhar Mosque one block east.

### Southern El Muizz Street

Today El Muizz St. is a minor thoroughfare bisected by the much larger Al Azhar St., but during the Fatimid period, it was the main avenue of the city. At the southern corners of the intersection of Al Azhar and El Muizz St. stand some impressive Mamluk structures. The **Madrasa of Sultan El Ghouri** (1503) occupies the southwest corner. El Ghouri, the last powerful Mamluk sultan, invested so heavily in construction that the area is often called *El Ghouriyya*. In addition to the school and *wakala*, he restored the citadel and reconstructed the pilgrimage road to Mecca. His *madrasa's* minaret was the first four-crowned minaret in Egypt. The *madrasa* was under renovation during the summer of 1996, with no estimated opening date.

Across El Muizz St. from the *madrasa* is the **Mausoleum of El Ghouri,** where sufi dancers enchant travelers Wednesday and Saturday nights at 8pm (see Performing Arts, p. 126). The **Wakala of El Ghouri** is easier to miss. From the mausoleum and mosque, head east on Al Azhar St. then right onto Sheikh Muhammad Abduh St. At #3 (on your right) you'll see the magnificently-preserved *wakala* (built in 1505), now transformed into a center for handicrafts and folkloric arts. The structure originally served as a commercial hotel. (Mausoleum and *wakala* open Sat.-Thurs. 8am-5pm. Admission to all three is E£6, students E£3.)

Head back to El Muizz St., walk two blocks south of Madrasa el-Ghouri past textile stores, then turn left onto Khushqadam St. just before El Fakahani Mosque (look for the signs). On the left is the 16th-century **House of Gamal ed-Din,** the most splendid surviving Ottoman mansion in Cairo, with beautiful wooden ceilings, Turkish tiles, and *mashrabiyyahs* (open daily 9am-5pm; admission E£3, students E£1.50).

Farther south along El Muizz St. on the right at the corner of Ahmed Maher St. is the entrance to the **Mosque of El Mu'ayyad,** built between 1415 and 1420. Look for the two minarets towering above the Fatimid gate, a stone-carved dome, and an imposing *muqarnas* portal. The huge door may remind you of the ones at Sultan Hasan Mosque—it was stolen from there. The interior has a pleasant garden, and the *qibla riwaq* is covered by an extensively restored ceiling. At the northern end of the *qibla* wall is the mausoleum of the alcoholic Mamluk sultan, El Mu'ayyad. The second mausoleum, at the other end of the wall, is an Ottoman addition. (Open 9am-8pm. Admission E£6, students E£3.)

**Baab Zuweila** is the most impressive of the three remaining gates of Fatimid Cairo. The gate, named after the Berber tribe which helped build it, had two cylindrical towers, now replaced by the minarets of El Mu'ayyad Mosque. Egyptians also call it *Baw-wabet el-Metwali* (the Gate of the Tax Collector), after the civil servant who used to wait for victims at the gate.

Across the street from Baab Zuweila and to the right stands the **Zawiya of Sultan Faraj** (built in 1408), a small rectangular structure. During the 19th century, execution by strangulation was carried out beside the railings outside. Access is difficult for non-Muslims. Opposite this structure, across the street from Baab Zuweila, stands the elegant **Mosque of Salih Talai,** built in 1160. When the mosque was erected, the street was at the level of the series of shops standing behind the iron railing. The five keel arches form a remarkable projecting portal, unique in Cairo. The courtyard opens into a small *riwaq*. The custodian (who will expect E£1 *bakhsheesh*) will show you to the roof (open 9am-5pm). Continuing south on El Muizz St., you'll enter a covered bazaar known as the **Street of Tentmakers,** followed a few blocks down by a similar covered alley called the **Street of Saddlemakers.** Turning left as you step out of Baab Zuweila, you'll find yourself on Darb el-Ahmar St. heading toward the Citadel. A right turn leads to Ahmed Maher St., lined with the shops of carpenters, tombstone-carvers, and metalworkers. The street leads out to Baab el-Khalq Sq. on Port Said St., across from the Museum of Islamic Art.

If you want to backtrack, head back up El Muizz St. to explore the northern sights. Al Azhar and Khan el-Khalili are essential stops before you proceed north of the intersection of El Muizz and Al Azhar Streets.

### Al Azhar and Khan el-Khalili

The oldest continuously operating university in the world and the foremost Islamic theological center, the **University and Mosque of Al Azhar** stands just a few steps from the midpoint of Al Muizz St. at the end of Al Azhar St., facing the large square. Al Azhar University was established in 972 CE by the Shi'a Fatimids and rose to preeminence in the 15th century as a center for the study of Qur'anic law and doctrine, a position it still holds. Ever since the Ayyubids came, the emphasis has been on Sunni learning. Students are often found sitting on the plush red carpets of the *riwaq*, or arcaded aisle around the courtyard, cramming for exams. Don't be afraid to approach these learned souls and ask them to share their knowledge of Islam with you. To reach the central court, enter through the double arched gate and pass under the minaret of Qaytbay (built in 1469). Although the stucco decoration of the courtyard's façade is a reconstruction, the *mihrab* (the niche indicating the direction to Mecca) in the central aisle is original. The library, just left of the main entrance, holds over 80,000 manuscripts. For about E£1 the caretaker will allow you to climb one of the locked minarets for a fantastic view of Cairo and Khan el-Khalili below you. Check the first wooden door on your left after you enter the courtyard to see if it is unlocked before you hand over the money to the doorman.

Around the corner from the mosque is the institute where Al Azhar's 8000 students take classes between October and May. The theological curriculum has remained virtually unchanged since the Mamluk era; physics and medicine are more recent arrivals. Women, although allowed in the mosque, may not study at Al Azhar. They attend a "sister school" near Abbasiyya Sq. You can still observe the traditional form of instruction: Socratic questioning with a professor seated in the center of a circle of students. (Open Sat.-Thurs. 9am-7pm, Fri. 9am-noon and 2-7pm. Admission E£6, students E£3.) Women without head coverings must don a long wrap provided free at the entrance.

Across El Hussein Sq., 100m north of Al Azhar Mosque, stands **Sayyidna el-Hussein Mosque,** highly revered throughout the Islamic world as the resting place of the skull of Hussein, grandson of the prophet Muhammad. The head is rumored to have been transported to Cairo in a green silk bag in 1153, almost 500 years after the death of its owner in the battle of Karbala in Iraq. The present edifice was built in the 1870s by Khedive Isma'il and is distinctly Turkish in style (note the pencil-like minarets). Recent renovations did away with the mosque's unique exterior and left it looking like any other modern mosque. If you choose to enter this mosque, realize that you are in a very sacred place. Women enter around the corner into a room from which they approach the elaborate glowing trunk containing the remains of Hussein. Shorts or tank tops are entirely out of the question.

On Mawlid an-Nabi (the Birthday of the Prophet), the president of Egypt traditionally comes to pray at Sayyidna el-Hussein while boisterous festivities take place in the square. During Ramadan, this square is the best place to witness the breaking of the fast after evening prayers (about 8pm). Restaurants display their fare half an hour before prayers begin, and famished patrons stampede to the tables afterwards. After blood sugar levels return to normal, the square erupts in celebration.

**Khan el-Khalili,** the largest tourist bazaar in Egypt, lies to the west of El Hussein Sq. Mamluk prince Garkas el-Khalili established the market in the 1380s. Today, the market thrives on tourists bringing back that perfect little gift for Aunt Rhodie in Tallahassee. As you meander through the *souq* you will undoubtedly be asked if you'd like to "see my perfume store" or if you would like to buy "real papyrus, no banana leaf." It can be annoying, but it can also be fun. Revel in the free-market frenzy as you pass through copperware, perfume, spice, gold and silver, or *sheesha* sections of this massive bazaar. Though the tacky souvenirs are often overpriced, the time-honored institution of bargaining still thrives. Be ferocious if you intend to strike a good deal (often a third of the starting price, if not less). **Fishawi's** offers respite from the market bustle with flavored *sheesha* and exotic juices (see ahwas and Casinos, p. 122). The farther you go from the heart of the market, the more authentic the wares become. A word of **warning,** though: Khan el-Khalili is a thief's paradise; wallets can easily disappear in a crowded alley or while you are haggling.

Slightly less tourist-ridden is **El Muski,** the long bazaar where Egyptians shop for men's cologne, shoes, cloth, furniture, pillowcases, and food. El Muski stretches from El Muizz St. all the way to Port Said St., running parallel to and one block north of Al Azhar St. If you're walking between Islamic and downtown Cairo, El Muski is a convenient route.

### Northern El Muizz Street

Between Al Azhar Mosque and Baab el-Futuh, El Muizz St. is lined with Fatimid and early Mamluk architectural attractions. This area is dubbed **Bayn el-Qasrayn,** Arabic for "between the two palaces," after the two Fatimid palaces that once stood here, and gives its name to one of Naguib Mahfouz's novels. El Gammaliya St. runs roughly parallel to El Muizz St. from Baab en-Nasr past the Mosque of el-Hussein to the square in front of Al Azhar. To minimize mileage, you can walk from Al Azhar up El Muizz St., through both Baab el-Futuh and Baab en-Nasr, and then return by way of El Gammaliya St. Expect to shell out a total of about E£15 if you plan to enter each of the sites listed below. If you're short on funding, this is still a wonderful way to see ancient Islamic architecture from the outside, if not from within.

A good tour starts by proceeding north on El Muizz St. from the intersection with Gohar el Qa'id St. After passing four little side streets you can see the **Tomb and Madrasa of Malik es-Salih Ayyub** on your right, its nearly square minaret gracing the heavens. The entrance is off a small alley on the right. The *madrasa* has ornate keel-arched windows and the minaret crowns a passageway. El Malik es-Salih Ayyub, the last ruler of Salah ad-Din's Ayyubid Dynasty, was the husband of Shagarat ad-Durr, an indomitable Turkish slave who became ruler of Egypt (see the Tomb of Shagarat ad-Durr, p. 114). The custodian has keys to the adjacent domed mosque which was recently restored by a German team.

The **Mausoleum, Madrasa,** and **Hospital of Qalawun** lie further along on El Muizz St. Mamluk sultan Qalawun sponsored the construction of these impressive edifices in 1284 before his death en route to attack the Crusader fortress in Akko (see Akko, p. 368). Qalawun's architects were influenced by the Crusader architecture of the Levant, hence the Romanesque windows. The three high *iwans* of the original *muristan* (mental hospital) remain. The ornate stucco work inside is original, though the undersides of the arches have been restored. To gain access to the mausoleum, hunt down the guard, purchase a ticket, and unlock the door. The exquisite wood screen separating the tomb from the rectangular forecourt dates from the original construction. (Complex open daily 10am-6pm. Admission E£3, students E£1.50.)

Video cameras are not allowed without written permission from a tourist office; the nearest one is on Ed-darb al-Asfar St., next to Beit es-Suheimi.

Before the 14th century, Egypt was the world's center for glasswork, and stained-glass windows adorn many of Cairo's mosques. The Qalawun mausoleum offers especially dazzling glass and mosaic work. The intricately embellished tomb caused quite a controversy at the time of its construction, as Islamic doctrine (as opposed to pharaonic procedure) forbids displaying wealth at the time of burial. By the 11th century, however, the practice of building ornate tombs, especially for rulers, was not unusual, and by the 13th century, lavish burial sites had become commonplace.

Just north of Qalawun's mausoleum and tomb stands his son's, the **Mausoleum-Madrasa of En-Nasr Muhammad,** completed in 1304. En-Nasr Muhammad's 40-year reign marked the height of prosperity and stability in Mamluk Egypt. The square minaret exhibits an exceptional, intricately carved stucco surface, but almost nothing of the interior remains. The authorities like to blame the 1992 earthquake, but the custodian says it was simple neglect. You can still see the four iwans, but they are in bad shape (open daily 10am-6pm; free).

Next door, to the north along El Muizz St., is the **Mosque of Sultan Barquq.** Barquq, the first Circassian Mamluk sultan, seized power through a series of heinous assassinations. His mosque was erected in 1386, a century after Qalawun's complex, and the difference in styles is striking. The inner courtyard has four *iwans,* the largest and most elaborate of which doubles as a prayer hall. Its beautiful timber roof has been restored and painted in rich hues of blue and gold. Four porphyry columns, quarried in pharaonic times from the mountains near the Red Sea, support the ceiling. The round disks of marble floor are slices of Greek and Roman columns, used because Egypt has no indigenous marble. (Open daily 9am-6pm. Admission E£3, students E£1.50.)

El Muizz St. comes to a fork north of the Mosque of Barquq. Walk 25m down Darb Kermez St., the small side street to the right of the fork, and you'll find all that remains of **Qasr Bishtak,** a lavish palace from the 14th century that originally stood five stories high. All floors of the palace had running water, a technological achievement unmatched in Europe for another 300 years. In the center of the fork is the slim 18th-century **Sabil Kuttab of Abd er-Rahman Kathuda,** an active Qur'anic school. You should pay less than E£5 (students E£3) to see both together (open daily 8am-6pm).

Bear left at the fork and continue north along El Muizz St. to the next right-hand side street. On the corner stands the small but architecturally important Fatimid **Mosque of El Aqmar.** Built in 1125, this was the first Cairene mosque to have a stone-façade-and-shell motif within the keel-arched niche. *El Aqmar* means "the moons" and refers to the way the stone façade sparkles in the moonlight. The northern corner is typical of later Cairene architecture: the height of the cut is just about equal to that of a loaded camel, and the chink was intended to make the turn onto the side street easier for the hump-equipped creatures to negotiate.

Proceeding north from El Aqmar Mosque, turn right on Ed-Darb el-Asfar (the next sidestreet on the right) and follow the winding alley about 50m. The doorway on the left marked with a small, green plaque is the entrance to Cairo's finest old house, the 16th-century **Beit es-Suheimi.** The *sheikh* of Al Azhar Mosque, Suheimi, built this elaborate residence for himself and his various wives. The house sports carved wooden ceilings, stained-glass windows, tile mosaics, marble floors, and fountained salons. Both the mosque and the house are under renovation, but will reopen in 1997. Walk along the same alley, away from El Muizz St., and you'll eventually come to El Gammaliya St. Across the street is the façade of the 14th-century *khanqah* (Sufi establishment) of **Baybars el-Gashankir.** Erected in 1310, this building is the oldest surviving example of a *khanqah* in Cairo. From here, continue north on El Gammaliya St. until you pass through Baab en-Nasr; Baab el-Futuh is to the left.

### Northern Walls

Islamic Cairo is bordered on the north by the extensive remains of the Fatimid walls. Built in 1087, these colossal fortifications are the best surviving examples of pre-Crusader Islamic military architecture. The original walls built by Gawhar as-Sikelli in 969 had eight gates, two on each side. Three of the rampart's original gates still stand. **Baab en-Nasr** (Victory Gate), at the top of El Gammaliya St., and **Baab el-Futuh** (Conquest Gate), at the northern end of El Muizz St., in front of the El Hakim Mosque, are connected by a stretch of wall so thick it easily accommodates a tunnel; these walls once wrapped all the way around the Fatimid city to **Baab Zuweila.**

The Fatimid **Al Hakim Mosque,** just inside the walls between the two gates (entrance off El Muizz St.), was built between 990 and 1010 and remains the second largest mosque in Cairo. Al Hakim, the grandson of El Muizz, was known to some contemporaries as the "Mad Caliph." His unpredictable rages meant death to Christians, Jews, his enemies, his friends, and, on one occasion, all the dogs in Cairo. He enforced the confinement of women by forbidding cobblers to make shoes for them. He even banned the cooking of *mulukhiga*, a green vegetable eaten throughout Egypt, and renamed it *mulukiyya*, meaning royal, restricting its consumption to his family. He was assassinated soon after he announced that he was an incarnation of the Divinity. His chief theologian, Ad-Darazi, fled to Syria where he founded the Druze sect. The structure was recently restored (amid great controversy) by the Aga Khan foundation. Rather than restoring the mosque to its original appearance, they chose to curry it up with chandeliers and a day-glo *mihrab*, outraging many art historians and Islamic experts. (Open daily 8am-8pm. Admission E£3, students E£1.50.)

## CITIES OF THE DEAD

The Cities of the Dead teem with life, if you know where to look. The areas to the northeast and south of the Citadel contain hundreds of tombs and mausolea erected since the Mamluk era. These Cities of the Dead double as a shanty town, home to hundreds of thousands of Cairenes. Unlike most graveyards, the Cities of the Dead have streets, house numbers (unlike in the city center), and even a regular postal service. The modern residents of the medieval necropoli dwell amidst the funerary architecture, and many households have even incorporated the grave markers into their houses and yards. Tombs serve as clotheslines and soccer goals. On Fridays, the grave sites swarm with visitors arriving to pay their respects to the deceased. Many of the grave plots are enclosed by walls, encompassing an adjoining chamber and small house where families pray for their dead relatives on holy days. The Egyptian custom of picnicking at the family tomb on feast days may be an ancient holdover from pharaonic times, when the corpse was believed to require nourishment to ensure good health in the afterlife. Visitors are not permitted in the mosques on Fridays or during prayers. Many areas of the necropoli are uninhabited: don't be surprised if you turn a corner and find yourself alone with ancient apparitions.

Mamluk sultans, unlike their more pious Islamic predecessors, spared no expense in the construction of their final resting places—perhaps because they knew that their dynasties would not survive. Elaborate tomb complexes with domed mausolea, mosques, and adjoining *madrasas* were erected for Cairo's rulers. Gravestones built for the families of Mamluk nobles vary widely; cenotaphs of all shapes and sizes dot the crowded thoroughfares of the royal necropoli.

The **Northern Cemetery,** northeast of the Citadel, is characterized by wide avenues and courtyards. It contains the finest monuments of the Cities of the Dead, with beautiful modern mausolea alongside structures dating from the later Mamluk period (14th-16th centuries). A visit to the Northern Cemetery can be tacked onto a tour of Islamic Cairo. Follow Al Azhar St. due east, around the north side of Al Azhar Mosque, over a slight hill to the six-lane Salah Salem St. Cross this deathtrap and enter the cemetery 250m beyond the green overpass (covered with Coca-Cola ads). Bus #176 from 'Ataba Sq. terminates just in front of the Mausoleum of Barquq. Also, bus #77 or 904 from Tahrir Sq. will take you to the vicinity. The far more crowded **Southern Cemetery** houses Ayyubid mausolea and the oldest Mamluk tombs (12th-14th centuries). It's accessible by foot from Ibn Tulun, the Sultan Hasan Mosque, or the Citadel. Take bus #82 or 182 or minibus #54 from Tahrir Sq. From Ibn Tulun or Sultan Hasan, proceed east to Salah ad-Din Sq., just southeast of the Citadel, then head directly south following the southern slope of the Citadel. When you reach the traffic circle, walk under the overpass and take the right-hand fork, El Qdiriyya St., which becomes Imam esh-Shafi'i St., the main thoroughfare in the cemetery. Although most of the people here are dead and therefore harmless, the isolated areas should be avoided at night, especially by women.

## Northern Cemetery

At the northern end of the cemetery, the imposing **Mausoleum of Barquq** (*Khanka Faraq Ibn Barquq*), easily identified by its matching pair of ornately sculpted minarets, is a good place to start your tour. Built in 1400 for Sultan Barquq by his son, this enormous family plot encompasses 5329 square meters. The *minbar* beneath the western arcade was donated by the Mamluk ruler Qaytbay. Two matching domes—the earliest stone domes in Cairo—shelter the family mausolea located in either corner. Sultan Barquq is interred below the northeast corner of the complex, and his two daughters occupy the chamber beneath the southeast dome. In the northeast corner of the complex, the second story holds the remains of a large *kuttab* (Islamic school) and numerous monastic cells that once housed Sufi mystics. The admission fee should get you around the mausolea and let you climb the minaret. (Open daily 8am-6pm, 8am-5pm in winter. Admission E£6, students E£3.)

Just around the corner to the southwest in front of the Mausoleum of Barquq stands the **Tomb of Barsbay el-Bagasi.** Built in 1456, the tomb is decorated with an intricate geometrical design resembling a tulip, a variation on the Moroccan motif of *dari w ktaf* (cheek and shoulder). The nearby **Tomb of Amir Suleiman** was built about 90 years later; its dome is decorated with a series of zig-zag stripes. Admission to these two tombs is free but the caretaker will expect *bakhsheesh* (E£1).

The **Mosque and Mausoleum of Sultan Ashraf Barsbay** are 50m south of the Mausoleum of Barquq, along the cemetery's main thoroughfare. Originally intended as a *khanqah* (Sufi establishment), the 15th-century mosque has meticulously fashioned marble mosaic floors; lift the protective prayer mats to see the colorful tilework. Adjoining the mosque to the north is the Barsaby's Mausoleum, a domed chamber containing his and his slaves' remains, an elaborately decorated *mihrab,* and gleaming mother-of-pearl and marble mosaics. (Open daily 9am-sunset. Free.)

Follow the same road south to reach the 15th-century **Mausoleum and Mosque of Qaytbay,** the cemetery's most celebrated structure. Approach through the open square for the best view of the façade's polychrome-striped brickwork, recognizable from the Egyptian one-pound note. Qaytbay was a Mamluk slave who rose through the ranks of the army to become leader of Egypt near the end of the 15th century. Reigning for 28 years, he became a powerful sultan who imposed order after years of anarchy. Qaytbay was not without enemies, and he watched his back. He designed the mosque with three secret doors for quick escapes. Apparently his efforts paid off—Qaytbay was the only Mamluk ruler not to be assassinated. Looking out for himself even in death, Qaytbay situated the prayer niche so that it would require the devotee to pray over the ruler's remains before reaching Allah. Enter the complex through the marble northern doorway, passing through a rectangular sanctuary. In the office to your left is a hole leading to a massive well beneath the mosque. The domed mausoleum, to the right, houses the marble tombs of Qaytbay and his two younger sisters. Also in the chamber are two black stones bearing footprints said to be those of the Prophet Muhammad. The 40m minaret is adored by architects for its elaborately decorated tiers. (Open daily 9am-9:30pm. Admission E£6, students E£3.)

Follow the main road south of the mausoleum through the **Gate of Qaytbay,** a stone archway that once guarded the entrance to the tomb complex to reach two more monuments. When this thoroughfare intersects with a paved road, turn right and head west toward Salah Salem St. Just beyond the next main street (Sultan Ahmed St.) are the remains of the **Tomb of Umm Anuk** (1348), a ribbed dome adjoining a sweeping pointed archway. Umm Anuk was the favorite wife of Sultan En-Nasir Muhammad, and her devoted husband presented her with an appropriately lavish tomb. He also constructed the **Tomb of Princess Tolbay** across the way for his principal wife. Muslim law required him to treat the two women equally, but the sultan apparently obeyed only the word and not the spirit of Qur'anic law.

Sultan Ahmed St. goes north to the Mausoleum of Barquq (where you can pick up the #167 bus). Heading west to the overpass leads you to Al Azhar St.; south brings you to the Citadel.

## Southern Cemetery

The Southern Cemetery's most impressive edifice is the celebrated **Mausoleum of Imam esh-Shafi'i.** The largest Islamic mortuary chamber in Egypt, the mausoleum was erected in 1211 by Salah ad-Din's brother and successor in honor of the great Imam esh-Shafi'i, founder of one of the four schools of judicial thought of Sunni Islam. Shafi'i Islam is still the dominant judicial school in Egypt and much of East Africa. In 1178, Salah ad-Din built a large monument over the grave of Imam esh-Shafi'i, currently housed within the 13th-century mausoleum and often crowded with Muslims offering prayers. The teak memorial shows the Imam himself, and is one of the finest surviving pieces of Ayyubid wood carving. There are two mosques adjoining the tomb chamber, one dating from 1190, the other from 1763. The older mosque is closed to non-Muslims. The other, open to all, remains a vital center of worship. (Open daily 6am-7pm. Free, but E£1 *bakhsheesh* is appropriate.)

The **Mosque of Sayyida Nafisa,** Egypt's third-holiest Islamic shrine, stands on the western edge of the Southern Cemetery not far from Es-Sultaniyya, and honors the great-great-great-granddaughter of the Prophet. One of Cairo's three congregational mosques, Sayyida Nafisa is closed to non-Muslims. To reach the mosque from the main intersection southeast of the Citadel, walk southwest on Salah Salem St. alongside the 12th-century **Wall of Salah ad-Din.** Sayyida Nafisa's tall single minaret and ornate dome rise to the right as you reach the cemetery. After Sayyida Nafisa's death in 824, her tomb attracted droves of pilgrims. So many mausolea were erected in the immediate vicinity of her tomb that historians suspect that it was the construction of this sacred shrine that sparked the development of the Southern Cemetery.

Adjoining the Mosque of Sayyida Nafisa on the eastern side are the less-than-impressive **Tombs of Abbassid Caliphs.** At the peak of their authority, the Abbassid caliphs ruled the entire Muslim world (except Spain) from Baghdad. The last reigning caliph fled Baghdad in 1258 after invading Mongols toppled the regime. The Mamluk sultan welcomed him upon his arrival in Egypt and went so far as to exalt the deposed caliph in an effort to legitimize his own sinecure. Subsequent Mamluk rulers continued to harbor a succession of caliphs, all the while preventing them from gaining any real power. Finally, the sultan in Istanbul declared himself caliph in 1517, thereby consolidating the authority of the Ottoman Sultanate. With Egypt under Ottoman rule, it was impossible for the regional government to protest the abolition of their local charade of religious authority. Though the Abbassid caliphs have been deposed, their succession continues to the present day; members of the family are still buried within the walls of the 13th-century mausoleum. Inside are wooden memorials marking the graves of the caliphs. The caretaker will need to unlock the gates (E£1 *bakhsheesh*).

From the square in front of Sayyida Nafisa, turn right along El Khalipha St. to find the **Tomb of Shagarat ad-Durr,** the last Ayyubid building to be built in Cairo (1250) and the burial place of a politically prominent Muslim woman. Shagarat ad-Durr (Tree of Pearls) was a slave who rose to power after marrying Es-Salih Ayyub, the final ruling member of Salah ad-Din's Ayyubid Dynasty. She concealed the Sultan's death in 1249 for three months until her son returned from Mesopotamia to claim the throne. Realizing that her frail son would never muster the authority to command a following among Mamluk slave troops, the wily queen promptly engineered his murder. Proclaiming herself Queen, Shagarat ad-Durr governed Egypt alone for 80 days before marrying the leader of the Mamluk forces, engineering the succession of the Mamluk Dynasty. The renegade couple managed to consolidate power over the next several years, but their happy rule ended when the queen discovered that her new husband was considering a second marriage and had him murdered. Not to be outdone, the prospective second wife avenged the death of her lover by beating Shagarat ad-Durr to death with a pair of wooden clogs and then hurling her body from the top of the Citadel, leaving it to the jackals and dogs. The remains were put together in this small tomb which fails to reflect the significance of its owner. Even so, the wall mosaics are worth the E£1 *bakhsheesh*.

If you turn left at the small market square beyond the tomb, you will reach the Mosque of Ibn Tulun. If you go straight, a right turn at the next big street will return you to the Citadel and the Mosque of Sultan Hassan.

## OLD CAIRO

A day's exploration through Coptic Cairo and Fustat will confirm the image of Cairo as a meeting place of the minds: Coptic, Jewish, and Islamic monuments sit side by side here. Nine hundred years before victorious Fatimids founded the city of El Qahira, the Roman fortress town of Babylon occupied the strategic apex of the Nile Delta just 5km south of the later city site. This outpost became a thriving metropolis during the 4th century CE, and a number of churches were built within the walls of the fortress. In addition to a handful of beautiful Coptic churches, Old Cairo possesses the excellent Coptic Museum, the Mosque of Amr, and the Fustat area.

Located outside the walls of the Islamic city, Old Cairo has also once been the center of Cairo's Jewish community. Although most of the Jewish population of the city left in 1949 and 1956, approximately 30 Jewish families still inhabit this quarter and worship at the ancient Ben-Ezra synagogue. The fact that Old Cairo is outside the "Islamic City" is somewhat misleading, for it also contains the remains of the first Islamic capital of Egypt, El Fustat.

The easiest way to reach Old Cairo is to take the Metro from Tahrir Sq. towards Helwan to Mari Girgis station (30pt). Buses #92, 94, 134, or 140 also run from Tahrir Sq., stopping beside the Mosque of Amr. If you take a taxi to the outskirts of Old Cairo (E£2-3), tell the driver you want to go to *Masr el-Qadima* or *Gami 'Amr*. Once in Old Cairo, all of the sights listed below are within easy walking distance. Most of Cairo's Coptic churches are tucked away from the street, and the older structures possess simple entrances. Though none of the churches in Coptic Cairo charge admission, all contain donation boxes. Those seeking the quiet serenity common to European churches should avoid these sights on Sunday or the churches' Saint's day when hundreds of Coptic Cairenes and their children migrate from church to church receiving blessings and pronouncing their faith. (Churches open daily, roughly 9:30am-5pm, with masses held each morning from 7-9am. Photography prohibited).

### Coptic Cairo

Ancient Egypt invariably inspires images of towering pyramids, hieroglyphics, mummy cases slathered in jewels, and Cleopatra. Many assume that the pharaonic era shifted directly into the Islamic age of mosques, medieval fortifications, and integration into the Arab world. But for a period beginning in 30 BCE, Hellenistic culture and, later, Christianity were the dominant forces in Egypt. In the first century CE, Christianity stood as a symbol of resistance against Rome, and continued to be so even after the Roman Empire adopted Christianity in the 4th century CE. Egyptian Christianity was spread by the agency of the Coptic Orthodox Church, which split off from the main body of the Christian Church in 451. Currently, some five to seven million Egyptians are Copts. Most live in Cairo or in Middle Egypt (see **The Coptic Church**, p. 61).

In front of the Mari Girgis Metro Station is the **Coptic Museum** (tel. 363 97 42 or 362 87 66), home to the world's largest and finest collection of Coptic art, texts, textiles, metalwork, and iconographic materials (see **Museums,** p. 119). If you don't have expendable pounds for the museum, you can get a pretty good idea of the Coptic tradition by visiting the area's churches for free.

In front of the museum stands Cairo's only substantial classical ruin: the imposing **Roman battlement** that originally flanked the main entrance to the **Fortress of Babylon,** built by Emperor Trajan in the first century CE. This particular bastion (the only remaining one of ten) extended over a full acre, but it only comprised a fraction of the mammoth fortress, which encompassed 60 acres. It took invading Muslims more than seven months to overpower the fortifications in the 640-641 siege. Babylon surrendered only when ordered by Patriarch Cyrus. This section of the fortress was originally part of a massive harbor quay (the fortress overlooked the Nile before the river shifted west). A flight of stairs leads down to the slime-flooded foundation. Visitors are not permitted to use the stairs at all, much less swim.

With your back to the Coptic Museum, the 3rd-century **Church of El Mu'allaqa** (also known as the Church of St. Mary and St. Dimiana), is on your left. The name translates as "the hanging" because it was once suspended 13m above the ground between two bastions of the Fortress of Babylon. Repeatedly restored, it is almost impossible to discern what is new and old about this place of worship. Pointed arches and colorful geometric patterns enliven the main nave; in the center, an elegant pulpit used only on Palm Sunday rests on 13 slender columns—one for Christ and each of his disciples. The conspicuous black marble symbolizes Judas. El Mu'allaqa is ark-shaped, its roof is held up by eight pillars on each side of the church, one for every member of Noah's family. Because an altar can only administer the liturgy once per day, this church contains seven. Ostrich eggs symbolizing the Resurrection hang over head. Some of these altars are set off by a cedar altar screen. The screen is inlaid with pentagons and crosses of ebony and ivory—all of which are fit together without nails, like a jigsaw puzzle. In the chapel to the right you can sometimes see a carpenter making the intricate lattice.

Among El Mu'allaqa's 110 icons is the thousand-year-old image of St. Mark made with impressively bright natural pigments. The careful observer of the icon of St. Boktor will notice that the tormentor standing above him is striking him with the left hand, traditionally thought of as the weaker hand. Boktor is being tortured, not mercifully killed. The most mesmerizing of the icons is that of the Virgin with her baby son—the 8th-century eyes seem to follow you. This church holds a special place in the annals of Coptic belief due to its congregation's involvement in the miracle of Mokattam Mountain. A troublesome caliph, so the story goes, picking on the biblical claim that those of faith can move mountains, proposed an ultimatum to Pope Ibrahim Ibn ez-Zar'a and the Coptic population: prove it or die. The congregation stayed to pray in this church three days and three nights. On the third day, each *Kyrie eleison* (Lord have mercy), accompanied by a bow en masse, shook the earth and moved Mokattam a few inches. Coptic Orthodox masses are held at El Mu'allaqa on Friday 7:30-11am and Sunday 6:30-8:30am and 8:40-11:15am.

On the opposite side of the Coptic Museum is the 6th-century Greek Orthodox **Church of Mari Girgis** (Church of St. George). Erected over one of the towers of the Fortress of Babylon, this church worships the Roman soldier and saint, George. You can't miss him depicted atop his stallion slaying a reckless dragon. The common circular layout of this church teems with worshippers intent on touching the chains which were supposedly used to torture St. George. These same chains, interestingly enough, are also around the corner at the nunnery—go figure. If you're in town, visit on April 11th, Saint George's special day. (Open daily 8am-12:45pm and 2:30-5:15pm. Free.)

To the left of St. George's Church (when you are facing it), a staircase on Mari Girgis St. (labelled by a yellow sign proclaiming "free entrance") descends into Old Cairo proper. The first main doorway on the left is marked with a tin plaque indicating the 14th-century **Nunnery of St. George.** Get thee there. You might witness a chain-wrapping ceremony in the chapel. Worshippers symbolically reenact the Saint's persecution and recite a prayer. With your back to the nunnery, head to the left about 50m, until you see the entrance to the **Church of Abu Serga** (St. Sergius) on your right. This 10th-century church has sunken several feet below street level. The Holy Family is believed to have rested in the church's crypt.

Leaving the Church of Abu Serga, turn right and head to the end of the alley. Just to the left lie the cavernous 5th-century **Church of St. Barbara** (pronounced bar-BAR-a) and the Fatimid-era Church of St. Cyrus and St. John. Legend holds that when the caliph discovered both Christian churches being restored, he ordered the architect to destroy one of them. Unable to choose, the architect paced back and forth between the two buildings until he died of exhaustion. Moved by this tragedy, the caliph allowed both churches to stand. The Church of St. Barbara was rebuilt in the 10th century, when the decorated aisles were added. St. Barbara was killed by her father when she attempted to convert him. Her bones rest in the tiny chapel accessible through a door to the right as you enter the church. St. Catherine's bones reputedly lie here as well (see **St. Catherine's,** p. 251). An inlaid wooden *iconostasis* from the 13th century graces the church's ornate interior. Most of the furniture is now in the Coptic Museum.

With your back to St. Barbara's, the **Ben-Ezra Synagogue** is approximately 25m to the left. The synagogue that occupied the site in pre-Christian times was demolished in the first century CE to make room for construction of the Roman fortress. Later, a Christian church was built on the site; the building was transformed into the present synagogue in the 12th century. Distinctive Sephardic ornaments and a collection of manuscripts, including 6th-century Torah scrolls are kept here. Although most of the Jewish population emigrated, about 120 Jews still live in Cairo.

## Fustat

Adjoining Coptic Cairo to the north are the partially excavated remains of Fustat, one of the oldest Islamic settlements and the capital of Egypt during its first 250 years as a Muslim province. The architectural remains of Fustat are insubstantial, and a stroll through the site reveals little more than traces of cisterns, drains, cesspits, and rubbish. In the northwest corner of the site, the **Mosque of Amr,** Egypt's first mosque, has been restored for use. In addition to architectural fragments, thousands of pieces of fine Islamic pottery and imported Chinese porcelain have been discovered here; they are currently displayed at the Islamic Museum and in the new Islamic Ceramics Museum. Also behind the Mosque of Amr is the **pottery district,** where you can watch modern-day artisans at work. Kilns heave black smoke from fires fed by leather scraps and garbage. Hold your valuables close as you trudge through what could have easily been the set for *Mad Max Beyond Thunderdome*. Ask before you snap a Kodak moment; some of these guys have been known to ask for E£5.

To reach Fustat, take the Metro to the Mari Girgis station. With your back to the station, head north along Mari Girgis St. for about five minutes until you see the Mosque of Amr minarets on your right. Fustat sprawls over the large area behind the mosque. If you venture out to this district in the heat of summer, bring plenty of water. Also beware that the ground near the site is unstable in places. This area is best avoided at night.

Fustat was the name of a garrison town that some historians maintain comes from the Latin word for entrenchment, *fossatum.* A different account of the founding of Fustat holds that the conquering general Amr sent word to the caliph in Medina that the magnificent Roman port of Alexandria would be the perfect place for the capital of Egypt. To Amr's dismay, the caliph preferred to establish his outposts along desert trade routes, invulnerable to the naval attacks of seafaring Christians. The disappointed general returned to Babylon to find that a white dove had nested in his tent during his absence. Interpreting this as a divine omen, Amr founded the new capital of Egypt on the site of his tent, and dubbed it *El Fustat* (City of the Tent).

Fustat remained the capital of Egypt until the Fatimids established the neighboring city of El Qahira in 969 CE. By the middle of the 12th century the Fatimid Dynasty was flailing; in 1168, Crusader King Amalric of Jerusalem invaded and fought the Fatimids near Cairo. During the battle, Fustat was burned to the ground to prevent it from falling into the hands of the Crusaders. Except for the great mosque, little survived of the city; by the end of the 14th century Fustat was virtually abandoned.

Credit for the construction of Egypt's first mosque goes to Amr himself, who made many lasting contributions to the nation. During his rule, the mosque served as the seat of government, the post office, *caravanserai,* and the city's religious center. The huge, open square could accommodate nearly 12,000 worshipers (the size of Amr's army). Fustat later acquired a large treasury, numerous mansions, and elaborate plumbing and sewage systems, the likes of which were not seen in Europe until the 17th century.

The present-day Mosque of Amr occupies the site of the original building of 642, and is four times the size of its predecessor. The oldest portion of the current mosque is its crumbling southeast minaret, added during the Ottoman period. The mosque's 18th-century design includes a single, spacious courtyard lined on four sides by stately white marble columns, pilfered from local Roman and Byzantine buildings during medieval times. The mosque was renovated so extensively in the mid-1980s that many tourists find it hard to believe that this is Cairo's oldest mosque. (Admission E£3, students E£1.50. Open daily 9am-5pm.)

Near the Mosque of Amr is **Deir Abu Saffein,** a complex of three 8th-century Coptic churches. Walk straight down the street directly opposite the entrance to the mosque; the wooden entrance to the churches will be about 500m ahead on your right. (Complex open 8am-5pm.)

The main attraction is the **Church of St. Mercurius Felopatir** (or the Church of Abu Seiffein), dating from the 4th century but extensively restored during the Middle Ages. St. Mercurius Felopatir, a Roman Christian soldier, assured his frazzled king that divine assistance would dispose of the annoying Berbers who were troubling the Empire. After a Roman victory, the king beheaded the no-longer-useful Mercurius. He is called Abu Seiffein (which means "two swords") because an angel gave him a heavenly sword to go with his military saber. The cathedral contains 14 altars, various relics of saints venerated in the Orthodox Church, several early icons, and the original, delicate ebony/ivory/cedar wood *hegab* or *iconostasis,* which separates the nave of the church from its front vestibule. The elaborate gabled roof is itself an impressive feat of Coptic carpentry, as every piece is fitted with the next without the help of screws or nails.

On the northern wall of the main chamber, an icon picturing St. Barsoum marks the entrance to a tiny vaulted crypt where the saint supposedly lived with a cobra for 25 years. For 50pt the caretaker will let you descend into the dusty burial chamber. Mass is celebrated in this crypt on St. Barsoum's feast day, September 10. If the *bawwab* (caretaker) is in a good mood (the E£5 it takes to lift his spirits may not be worth it), he'll take you upstairs to see the ancient, tiny Churches of St. George of Rome, St. John the Baptist, and the 144,000 Martyrs, all of which were rediscovered when the plaster was accidentally chipped away from multiple layers of icons.

Down the street is the late 4th-century **Church of St. Shenouda,** dedicated to one of the most famous Coptic saints. This chapel contains two fine *iconostases*—one of red cedar and the other of ebony—and seven altars. The smallest of the three main structures at Deir Abu Saffein is the early 8th-century **Church of the Holy Virgin,** a one-room chapel crammed with rare icons, paintings, and three altars. The *odass* (liturgy) is read in these churches Sun. 6-10am, Wed. 8am-noon, and Fri. 7-11am.

Crossing the Nile from Old Cairo towards Giza, you may want to stop at the **Nilometer,** at the southern tip of Roda Island. Designed to measure the height of the river and thereby predict the yield of the annual harvest, the structure dates from the 9th century BCE. Under Muhammad Ali's reign, it was restored and the conical dome was added. Narrow steps descend into a paved pit well below the level of the Nile, culminating at the graduated column that marks the height of the river. The entrance to the Nilometer is often locked, but if you express interest, one of the local children will pester the nearby custodian (admission E£3, students E£1.5; open Sat.-Thurs., 9am-4pm). The eastern entrance is always locked—wait at the western side for assistance.

## MODERN CAIRO

Cairo's sidewalks teem with thousands of people who seem to be intent on going nowhere. Vendors bellow the virtues of their wares while overhead laundry flutters from the remnants of colonial architecture. In the evenings, particularly on weekends, the latest cinematic gem lets out every two hours and hundreds of film connoisseurs flood the streets, pastry shops, and *ahwas*. To avoid summer heat and yearlong bustle, evenings are ideal times to meander through the city. An evening stroll along the **Nile** is a Cairene tradition not to be missed.

Cairo's two main islands merit short visits. Dominating **Zamalek** (also called Gezira or "the island") is the 187m **Cairo Tower (Burg El Qahira).** Early or late in the day, the view from the breezy top of the tower is film-frying—you can see the Pyramids, the medieval citadel, and the Delta. For E£14 you can take the elevator to the observation deck, and for another E£10 you will be allowed to use your camcorder. For E£46, you can have soup, salad, entree, dessert, and the view at the rotating restaurant "Panorama" on the 14th floor. (Open daily 8am-1am.)

Settled only in the last century, Zamalek was once symbolic of Cairo's colonial society; today its quiet streets house diplomats and the expatriate community. The southern third of the island is occupied by the Gezira Sporting Club, the ultimate symbol of British privilege until the 1952 Revolution. The club has become a focal point for upper class Cairene life. The one-block stretch around and along Hassan Sabri St. north of 26th July St. is lively; colorful shops, cafés, hip bars, and grocery stores specializing in imported foods predominate. On the eastern shore of the island, near the 26th July Bridge, towers the palatial **Cairo Marriott Hotel.** Built by Khedive Isma'il to house foreign dignitaries and heads of state attending the Suez Canal opening ceremonies in 1869, the palace became a hotel in 1952 and is today considered one of the best luxury hotels in the Middle East.

On the southern tip of Roda Island stands one to Central Cairo's most noteworthy ancient monuments: the Nilometer, best visited when you tour Old Cairo (see **Old Cairo,** p. 115). At the northern end of the island, near the Meridien Hotel, stands the wacky Manial Palace Museum (see **Museums,** p. 119).

Walking west across the island from the palace and over the University (El Gama'a) Bridge, you'll reach a lush section of the neighborhood of **Giza.** Straight ahead, at the end of the broad boulevard, lies the handsome, crowded campus of **Cairo University.** Along the boulevard to the north stretches the neglected **El Urman Garden** (Botanical Gardens), the best place in town to toss a frisbee or vegetate under a shady tree. (Open daily 8:30am-5pm in summer, 8am-4pm in winter. Admission 50pt. Camera privileges 50pt.) Along the full length of the boulevard to the south and facing the botanical gardens is the **Cairo Zoo,** one of the oldest in the world. If zoos have a tendency to make you blue, this one will horrify you with downtrodden animals in dreary conditions. On the other hand, it's a great place to mingle with Egyptian families. The lax security allows you unusually close contact with the animals. Tip a zookeeper and he'll let a giraffe eat off your head. If you time the photo well, it looks like a kiss. Watch Makaka the monkey smoke a cigarette (hopefully he won't croak before your eyes). Open daily 8am-5pm, but avoid Fridays, when there are more people than animals. (Admission is 10pt, 20pt extra for the reptile house and "special collections").

## MUSEUMS

### Egyptian Museum

The **Egyptian Museum,** the world's unrivaled warehouse of pharaonic treasures, stands in Tahrir Sq. The most conspicuous displays in the museum are not always the most interesting; try not to overlook smaller rooms tucked away around the museum. You will spend several days, however, if you try to examine every single piece; your ticket is good for the entire day, so consider a lunch break to help clear your mental palate. Unless you choose to buy the E£100 catalog, the first exhibit to examine should be the wall map to the left of the entrance or the CD-ROM presented by the Cultural Preservation Foundation to the right of the entrance.

In the small glass case opposite the entrance, behind the 3000-year-old monkey, is the **Narmer Palette,** which commemorates the unification of Upper and Lower Egypt in about 3100 BCE by King Narmer. Some believe that King Narmer was the incarnation of Menes, the mythical founder of united Egypt. (See **Ancient Egypt,** p.

43.) From here, the corridors and rooms leading around the central domed court present a chronological sampling of pharaonic art from the Old Kingdom to the Greco-Roman period.

The unusually well-preserved paint on the statues of Prince Rahotep and his wife Nofret (room #32) expresses the extraordinary realism of funerary statues sculpted 47 centuries ago. Nearby stands the world's oldest colossal metal statue, depicting the warlike King Pepi I of the 4th Dynasty. The statue was fashioned by beating heated metal sheets around a wooden core.

Walking down the west corridor, the four rooms on your right each merit a few minutes. The first two feature the best of the Old Kingdom, including a diorite statue of Chephron and a wooden statue named "Sheikh el-Balad" by workers who discovered it resembled their boss. The third room displays limestones from the Middle Kingdom. The fourth room's claim to fame is the "Egyptian Mona Lisa," an eerie painting in the left corner next to a sandstone mini-chapel from the New Kingdom. Like those of her Italian cousin, the eyes seem to follow you.

In the **Akhenaton room** at the rear of the first floor stands statues of the heretical pharaoh who introduced a form of monotheism. He worshiped Aton as the sun god and source of life, representing him as a disk with rays that ended in hands, sometimes holding *ankhs,* the Egyptian symbol for life (see **Ancient Egypt,** p. 43). Akhenaton-period artwork is recognizable by its distinctly realistic portraits.

Of all the collections in the museum, the cornucopia from **Tutankhamun's tomb** is surely the best-displayed and most popular. Originally squeezed into less than 100 cubic meters, the treasures now occupy an entire quarter of the **second floor.** The eastern corridor contains decorated furniture, golden statues, delicate alabaster lamps, weapons, amulets, fossilized undergarments, and other bare necessities for a King of the Underground. Room #4, the most magnificent of all, flaunts the famous coffins and funeral masks, as well as an astounding collection of amulets, scarabs, and jewelry. The elegant mask is made with more than 4kg of solid gold inlaid with quartz and lapis lazuli. In the hallway sit the King's internal organs, each with its own gilded coffin.

When your eyes become gold-plated, head to the rooms off the corridor toward the center of the building. Room #43, off the eastern hall, holds a collection of toys, tools, weapons, and household items that reveal how people lived and artisans worked thousands of years ago. Animal rights activists would be proud to see Room #53, where mummified cats, dogs, birds, and excited monkeys repose in honor.

Last, and probably least, the controversial mummy room is in the southeastern corner of the second floor. President Sadat closed the famed room in 1981 because the display offended some Islamist groups, and the re-opening of the room was delayed by the mummies' continued decomposition, which had left them offensive to just about everyone. Now restored and lodged in an isolated, air-conditioned, dimly lit room, the mummies might offend your budget and will not enhance your understanding of the mummification process since there are absolutely no descriptions. Consider, however, that this may be your only opportunity to stare a 5000 year old man in the eye. Admission to see the carcasses costs E£30, E£15 for students. You might not get your mummy's worth; the monkey near room #53 will give you an idea of what its human uncles look like. (Museum open daily 9am-4:45pm. Admission E£10, students E£5. Camera privileges E£10.)

### The Coptic Museum

Located in the 19th-century Qasr ash-Shama on Mari Girgis St., the **Coptic Museum** (tel. 363 97 42 or 362 87 66) houses the world's finest collection of Coptic art, with 14,000 pieces. Halls are paved with spotless white marble and a host of elegantly carved wooden *mashrabiyya* screens cover the windows. An added attraction is the museum's location on the site of the ancient Roman fortress of Babylon. The museum, founded in 1908, is home to Coptic metalworks, frescoes, textiles, psalm books, and icons. Compare an icon of the Virgin Mary suckling the Baaby Jesus and a carving of the goddess Isis suckling her son, the sun-god Horus. The museum displays a variety of architectural fragments (niches, columns, pulpits, etc.) brought from the sanctuary of St. Menas at Maryut and the monastery of St. Jeremiah at Saqqara, as well as illuminated manuscripts and numerous paintings, icons, and ivories. Don't miss the Coptic textiles (located on the second floor), which were once exported to many quarters of the world. The Library of Gnostics, next to the textiles, contains 7000 volumes of non-standard gospels (e.g., Thomas' gospel) from the 13th and 14th centuries, along with other Coptic texts from various periods. Some of these shine with intricate gold foil, while others barely remain in one piece. The ticket office sells somewhat useful guides for E£4.50 or you can diligently read the English introductions on the walls of each of the sections of the museum. Respite for the museum-weary awaits in the building's tranquil courtyard. The museum is directly across from the Mari Girgis stop on the Metro. (Open daily. Admission E£8, students E£4. Camera privileges E£10, video E£100.)

## Museum of Islamic Art

Easily combined into your walk through Fatimid Cairo, the **Museum of Islamic Art** is housed in a massive pink building in Baab el-Khalq Sq. at the intersections of Port Said St., Muhammad Ali St., and Ahmed Maher St. (tel. 390 99 30). The museum is the hiding place of many of the artifacts that seem to be missing from the mosques, mausoleums, and *madrasas* of Cairo. Carpets, wood carvings, metalwork, glassware, ceramics, and pottery are masterfully presented in this generally quiet and uncrowded museum. Be sure not to miss the gold leaf Qur'ans in the calligraphy room. (Open Sat.-Thurs. 9am-4pm, Fri. 9am-11:30am and 1:30-4pm in winter, 9am-12:30pm and 2-4pm in summer. Admission E£8, students E£4.)

## Other Museums

**Gayer-Anderson Museum** Originally two separate buildings, these 16th- and 18th-century mansions were merged when Major Gayer-Anderson, an English art collector, arrived here in the 1930s. You may recognize some of the rooms from the James Bond flick *The Spy Who Loved Me.* Anderson filled his home with eclectic artifacts and furniture. When he left Egypt in the 1940s, he gave the mansion and its contents to the Egyptian government. Plan on spending at least an hour enjoying the fourfold wonder of this museum: it is an example of a Mamluk Mansion with secret rooms and wooden *mashrabiyya* screens which allowed women to see out from inside without being visible from the streets; it is also a well-organized museum of Egyptian artifacts; it boasts beautiful Turkish, Persian, and Syrian decorations; and it is a window into the life of Gayer-Anderson and his collection of really cool stuff. Check out the portrait of the Major himself posing as a sphinx in the English Reading Room. A guard will lead you through the maze-like mansion to ensure protection of the priceless pieces. Along the way, he might point out secret passageways and facts about the art. Open daily 8am-3:30pm. Admission E£8, students E£4. Camera E£10, camcorder E£25.

**The Manial Palace Museum** (tel. 98 74 95), at the northern edge of Roda Island; the entrance is near the Cairo Youth Hostel on Sayala St., which leads to Cairo University Bridge. In a complex built by Muhammad Ali in the last century, visitors have access to the "reception palace," a private mosque, a residential palace, a throne room, and a fascinating collection of Islamic art. The most intriguing artifact in King Farouk's hunting museum is right by the entrance: a beautiful table made from an elephant's ear. Also has an enthralling collection of Muhammad Ali's royal furnishings. Open Sat.-Thurs. 9am-4pm, Fri. 9am-1pm and 2-4pm. Admission E£5, students E£2.50. Camera E£10, video E£175.

**The Museum of Egyptian Modern Art** (tel. 341 66 65), within the Opera Complex, Zamalek. Simply walk over the bridge from Tahrir Sq. Tastefully exhibited Egyptian paintings and sculptures from 1922-present. A welcome reminder that in a city known for its ancient offerings art is not confined to coffins. Open Tues.-Sun. 10am-1pm and 5-9pm. Admission E£10, students E£5. If you don't want to fork over the fee, head to the Opera House's free art gallery, open daily 10am-1:30pm and 4:30-8:30pm.

**The Mukhtar Museum** (tel. 340 25 19), after Tahrir Bridge and just before El Galaa Bridge on Tahrir St. in Zamalek. Built by architect Ramses Wissa Wassef, this museum is devoted to the works of sculptor Mahmoud Mukhtar (1891-1934). The museum's most well-known piece is the *Awakening of Egypt*. You might recognize Mukhtar's sculpture from his piece in front of the Cairo Zoo or the statue of the man with a massive raised hand at the base of the Tahrir Bridge. Open Tues.-Sun. 10am-1pm and 5-9pm. Admission E£1, students 50pt.

**The Mahmoud Khalil Museum,** 1 Kafour St., Giza, 200m from the Giza Sheraton (tel. 336 23 76). Contains a fantastic collection of European and Islamic art, including works by Monet, Renoir, Van Gogh, Toulouse-Lautrec, Degas, and Rubens, as well as Chinese jade carvings and Islamic pottery and tiling. Open Sat.-Thurs. 10am-6pm. Admission E£10, students E£5. Passport or other ID required.

**Mugamma' el-Funun** (Center of Arts, tel. 340 82 11), on the corner of Ma'had es-Swissry St. and 26th July Bridge, Zamalek. Formerly the residence of Aisha Fahmy, today the center has rotating exhibits by Egyptian and foreign artists. It also houses a cinema, theater, and library. Open mid-Sept. through mid-July Sat.-Thurs. 10am-1:30pm and occasionally 6-9:30pm (only for important exhibitions). Free.

**Museum of Islamic Ceramics,** El Gezira Arts Center, 1 Sheikh Marsafy St., Zamalek, across from the Marriott Hotel. Houses a rare collection from the Ayyubid, Fatimid, and Mamluk eras. Expected to open early in 1997.

**The Agricultural Museum** (tel. 360 86 82), at the western end of the 6th October Bridge, Dokki, behind a large, attractive garden. A run-down building exhibits more than you ever wanted to know about Egyptian agriculture. Also on display is the only remaining mummified Apis bull from the Serapium at Saqqara. Open Sat.-Thurs. 10am-2pm, Fri. 10am-noon. Admission E£1, students 50pt.

**October War Panorama,** Urubu St., Heliopolis (tel. 60 23 17). Demonstrations of the Suez crossing and the Bar-Lev line's destruction tell the Egyptian version of the 1973 war with Israel. Commentary is in Arabic, but it's easy to figure out. Open Wed.-Mon. 9:30am-9pm. Demos at 9:30, 11am, 12:30, 6, and 7:30pm. Admission E£8. Probably isn't worth the haul out to Heliopolis.

# ■ Entertainment

As the sun sets on The Egyptian capital, *sheesha* smoke fills the air, the corniche fills up with strollers, and the upper-crust gets decked-out for *discothèques* and chi-chi bars. *Cairo by Night,* a free weekly periodical available in hotels, describes happenings around town, and *Egypt Today,* a monthly magazine sold at newsstands, runs articles on attractions in the metropolitan area and lists foreign films, musical performances, and art exhibits. Butt-grabbing is free at Cairo's cheaper bars; the sleaze-free zones are confined to expensive hotels.

During **Ramadan,** nightlife assumes an entirely new dimension. Cairenes take to the streets around Al-Azhar and Hussein Sq. and along the corniche and the bridges across the Nile. Starting at around 10pm, there are street theater performances, magic shows, and general shenanigans. Most cinemas have midnight screenings.

## AHWAS AND CASINOS

Although you'll never guess it from looking at Cairo's drivers, city folk love to relax, contemplate their navels, and twiddle thumbs in the *ahwahs* (or *qahwahs*) that dot many street corners and alleyways east of the Nile. A typical *ahwah* will have gossipers in one corner, backgammon players in another, and *sheesha* smoke and steam from Turkish coffee everywhere. In headier days, revolutionaries used to plot around café tables. *Sheesha* smoke is much stronger than cigarettes, but infinitely more delicious. *Sheesha tilfah* (apple flavored) is sweet and smooth. Foreign men and women are welcomed at all *ahwas* listed below, but not all *ahwas* in the city.

**Fishawi's Khan el-Khalili** (tel. 90 67 55), 4 doors down from El Hussein Hotel, in the same alley, just off El Hussein Sq. Since 1752, this traditional teahouse in the heart of the old bazaar has served the most famous and gooey *sheesha* in Egypt. Nicknamed "Café des Miroirs," Fishawi's is furnished in 19th-century European style with hammered brass tables that can barely hold two cups. Enjoy the atmosphere with a pot of mint tea (E£1), or, even better, a cold *karkadeh* (E£1) in the summer heat. Let the aroma of the *sheesha* (E£1.50) lull you. Open daily 24hr.

**Maroush,** see Splurges, p. 103. In addition to serving great food, Maroush is a cool, quiet *sheesha* spot with a mixed clientele.

**Bint es-Sultan,** As-Sawra Sq., Mohandiseen, behind the Shooting Club (Nadi es-Sayd). This ritzy *ahwa* has breezy, outdoor tables for pleasurable idleness. Min. charge E£7 in the evening. Open daily 10am-1am.

In the evenings, middle-class Egyptian couples swarm to the cafés, called **casinos,** lining the Nile on Gezira Island. Some of these are boats permanently anchored at the edge of the water. The **Casino an-Nil,** on the west side of Tahrir Bridge, is one of the best (minimum charge E£6). Dozens of others range from simple to swank. Most are jammed on Thursday nights, partially because of post-nuptial *haflahs* (parties). For real **gambling,** head for the Nile Hilton, Marriott, or Sheraton hotel. You must show your passport to enter and are not permitted to game with Egyptian currency. Don't worry—they can change E£ to US$ faster than you can lose them (minimum bet US$5). Drinks are free as long as you gamble.

## PASTRIES, ICE CREAM, AND COFFEE

Cairo has a pyramid-sized sweet tooth. Egyptian creations are honey-soaked, sticky, and delicious. Western cafés sell the familiar flaky croissant-like stuff. Ice cream flavors range from exotic mango to basic but bold chocolate.

**El 'Abd,** 25 Tala'at Harb St. (tel. 392 44 07), opposite the Arab Bank building—look for the surging mass of customers. Known for its cakes and ice cream (a whopping 3-scoop cone is E£1.50, 2-scoopers E£1), the croissants here are the best in Cairo (E£1). Pay first, then take the token to the scooper. You can ask to try any of the pastries. Open daily 9am-11pm. Another branch is on 26 July St. one block east of the intersection with Tala'at Harb St.

**La Poire,** 18 Latin America St. (tel. 355 15 09), across the street from the British Embassy in Garden City. Oozing éclairs and honeysuckle *ba'laweh* titillate the tongue. All pastries made on the premises (E£1.65). One of the best selections of ice cream flavors in Cairo (E£1.50 per scoop). Chocolate truffles will make you dizzy (3 for E£2). Cappuccino or espresso E£1.70. Open daily 7am-11:30pm.

**The Roastery,** 3 Makka St., Mohandiseen (tel. 361 10 95). Coming from As-Sawra square with Bint es-Sultan on your right, Makka is the first street on the right and the Roastery will be on your right. 1-min. walk from Bint es-Sultan. The frothing of the cappuccino machine replaces the sound of slapping dominoes, and freshly ground espresso supplants the scent of *sheesha*. For those homesick for a Seattle-style coffee shop, this brand new, spotless branch of the San Francisco-born Roastery serves all your favorite espresso drinks (another Roastery is in the Shooting Club). Open Sat.-Thurs. 8am-midnight, Fri. 10am-midnight.

**Mandarin Koedar,** 17 Shagaret ed-Durr St., Zamalek (tel. 340 50 10), take a right off 26 July St. at the Misr Gas Station onto Shagaret ed-Durr St. This ice cream parlor will be 200m on your right. The best ice cream in Cairo is served by uniformed scoopers in this air-conditioned oasis. The chocolate and hazelnut-chocolate are to die for. Each E£1 scoop is well worth it. Open daily 9am-11pm

**Simonds Coffee Shop,** July 26th St., Zamalek (tel. 340 94 36), just east of the intersection with Hasan Sabri St. Terrific cappuccino, espresso, hot chocolate (E£1), and lemonade (75pt). Ideal for breakfast and chocolate binges. All cakes E£1. Open daily 8am-9pm.

**Flamenco Postres,** 11 Corniche Abul Feda (tel. 340 08 15, ext. 422), next to the Flamenco Hotel on the western side of Zamalek. Foreigners living in Zamalek covet the loaves of Bavarian bread packed with nuts and other delights (E£8). Open daily 7am-11pm.

**Samadi,** 47 El Batal Ahmed Abd el-Aziz St., Mohandiseen, off Gam'at ed-Duwal St. Most Egyptians recognize Samadi as the best pastry shop in Egypt. Crunchy, toasty, and super sweet treats. Try their *burma,* a distant cousin of baklava. Open daily 9am-3am.

## CLUBS

Cairo is oceans away from Rio, Barcelona, or Montréal. Dance clubs are fewer, tamer, and less crowded. The clubs on **Pyramids Road** in Giza can overflow with sweaty shimmiers, and evenings often degenerate into pick-up fests. Major hotels spin disco balls above more behaved crowds.

**Atlas,** or **Tamango,** Atlas Zamalek Hotel, 9th floor. In summer 1996, *the* place to shake your booty to the latest European and Arabic dance music. Filled with Drakkar-Noir/Armani-clad Egyptians, young expats, and students. Dress doesn't have to be formal. Men unaccompanied by women are not welcome. Admission E£40. Open daily 10:30pm-3:30am.

**Atlantis,** Shepherd Hotel, Corniche en-Nil, Garden City (tel. 355 34 00). Expensive, but the DJ is possibly the best in Cairo. Russian strip show (almost) on Thursday and Friday nights. Couples only, E£45.

**Jackie's,** Nile Hilton, Tahrir Sq. (tel. 578 04 44). There aren't any posers here; the "aristocrat of discos" is a club for Cairo's true elite. Music is often as stuffy as the clientele. Couples only. Minimum charge E£25. Open daily 10pm-3am.

**Casanova Disco** (tel. 341 47 46), in the El Burg Hotel, Zamalek; over the Tahrir Bridge, by the Opera House. Solo men are not admitted to this new, popular hotspot. Cover charge of E£30 includes a drink. Open daily 11:30pm-4:30am.

## BARS

Cairenes aren't known for beer-guzzling, but they do support a good number of bars, considering the Islamic prohibition against alcohol. The liveliest bars are filled with non-Muslim expats. For great eats with your pint, try **Harry's Pub** (see p. 102).

**Deals,** 2 Sayyid el-Bakri St., Zamalek (tel. 341 05 02), a right off 26 July St. at the base of the bridge to downtown. Appetizers (a.k.a. "No Big Deals") run E£4-8. English-style fish and chips grease the palate at E£18. Posters from Bogart flicks and the soothing voice of Al Green add to the sleek ambience of this popular A/C bar and snack pad. Open daily 4:30pm-late.

**Pub 28,** 28 Shagaret ed-Durr St., Zamalek (tel. 340 92 00), kitty-corner to the Mandarin ice cream store. Take a right off 26 July St. at the Misr Gas Station and head down Shagaret ed-Durr until you see the pub's brick facade on your left. The dimly lit restaurant/bar is a top choice of foreign residents of Cairo, upper class Egyptian businessmen, and the occasional flight attendant. Steaks are juicy and big (E£24), and the club sandwich won't break your bank (E£10). Visa and AmEx.

**Odeon Palace,** off Tala'at Harb St., 1 block east of Tala'at Harb Sq. A relaxing spot for insomniacs. Cheap beer, food, and *sheesha* on the roof. Open 24hr.

**Cellar,** 22 Taha Hussein St., Zamalek (tel. 341 67 51). Head north on Shagaret ed-Durr St. off of 26 July St., until it zigzags and becomes Taha Hussein St. Near the President Hotel on the left. Louis Armstrong, Miles Davis, and Aretha Franklin grace your ears as entrees (E£9-35) and beer (E£8) satiate your tummy. Not as hip or accessible as Pub 28 or Deals. Visa, MC, AmEx. Open daily noon-2am.

**Garden Bar,** El Goumhouriyya St., in the Atlas Hotel, draws gay men and an expatriate crowd with rock music on Thurs. and Fri. nights 11pm-1am. Drinks are expensive, but there's no cover charge.

## SHOPPING

Selling and buying in the Egyptian capital transcends mundane business—it's an ancient art form. As in most of the Middle East, bargaining is required. Successful merchants enjoy the haggle as much as customers do. Think of bargaining as a game to be savored, not a battle to be won. If you play hardball, the merchant will not lower the price—chatting will bring you more success. Be dramatic. Walk away in disbelief several times. Your starting price should be half the asking price at most. Never get too enthusiastic about the beauty of the object in question. Instead, point out flaws in workmanship and design. Having a friend discourage you from your purchase also helps.

The biggest **market** is Cairo's famous **Khan el-Khalili** (see p. 110). Other markets, though smaller, are more accurate examples of Cairene life. In the market south of **Sayyida Zeinab,** each alley offers different wares (take the Metro to Sayyida Zeinab and walk 5min. towards the high minarets of the Sayyida Mosque). Other major markets are located northeast of **'Ataba Square** and in **Bulaq** (from Tahrir Sq., walk eastward along Tahrir St., then up Abd el-Aziz St. for 'Ataba Sq.; take bus #46 for Bulaq). The lively **Souq el-Tewfikia** runs between Ramses and Tala'at Harb St., one block north of 26th July St. Produce stalls stand beside kitchen-equipment vendors, all laid out in brilliant displays. On hot summer days, watch out for hose-holding shopkeepers who water the entrance to their shops to reduce heat and settle the dust.

If bargaining doesn't appeal to you, head to one of Cairo's **department stores,** monstrous consumer meccas peddling anything from refrigerators to bikini waxings. The **World Trade Center** on the corniche, north of the Ramses Hilton, is the biggest. A bit less expensive is the **El Yamama Center** (affectionately called the Yo Mama Center by expats), 3 Dr. Taha Hussein St. in Zamalek, where you can watch music videos or sporting events on the large-screen TV in the ground floor café.

## Papyrus

The papyrus sold throughout Cairo is usually banana leaf. To see the real stuff, head to **Dr. Ragab's Papyrus Factory,** a right turn off the Gala'a Bridge heading west from Tahrir Sq. These papers are much more expensive than stuff you find in the *Khan*. Real papyrus can be scrunched up and will not retain any wrinkles, while banana leaf crackles and stays crunched. Few paintings in the *Khan* are hand done; most are stamped on the leaf. **Wafik Ismail Ali,** near the Khan el-Khalili Naguib Mahfouz Coffeeshop, has vivid banana leaf (disguised as papyrus) pieces (medium-sized pieces about E£8-10). Instead of searching the bowels of the bazaar for true papyrus, look at artwork and design quality (back home, no one will know the difference between pharaonic paper and banana leaf).

## Backgammon

*Et-tawileh* boards range from E£80-120, depending on quality and bargaining skills. Make sure the board is absolutely flat when opened and laid on a table, as occasionally they are warped or wobbly. Pieces are often made separately from the board. Check to see that they fit on the triangles, and that there are 15 of each color. You should pay less if the pieces are plastic. If you don't want to buy your board in the *Khan,* try **Maka el-Mokarama** (tel. 393 89 80), 7 Adly St., next to the tourist office. They have good-quality boards without the hassles and fun of Khan el-Khalili.

## Spices and perfume

Thousands of perfume and spice stores give sections of Cairo a fragrant smell. Egyptian spices like *za'tar* are excellent and hard to come by in the West. The quality of perfumes range dramatically. Rub some perfume on the back of your hand—if it's oily or shiny, they've added oil to the perfume to stretch the liquid weight. An ounce can go for as low as E£8. **Harraz Agricultural Seeds, Medicinal, and Medical Plants Co.,** 1 Baab el-Khalq St. sells every imaginable spice at reasonable prices (open Sat.-Thurs. 9am-9pm). If the self-proclaimed "sheikh of spice" won't cut you a good deal, **Khodr,** next door, has similar wares.

## Textiles and clothing

At the **tent-makers bazaar,** south of Baab Zuweila in Islamic Cairo, you can commission the making of a Bedouin tent (far out of a budget traveler's price range) or buy **appliqué pillowcases** (E£12-50) and **bed covers** (prices start at E£300). The **Nomad Gallery,** at 14 Saraya el-Gezira, 1st floor, Zamalek (tel. 341 19 17), near the Marriott, is known for its top-quality jewelry, textiles, and crafts. They're not big bargainers here, but their prices are as low as you could get them at the tent-makers bazaar (open Mon.-Sat. 10am-3pm; credit cards accepted).

There's a daily **second-hand clothing market** at the east end of 26th July Bridge. The stands hawk modern Western clothing, 1960s Western clothing, and even some traditional Egyptian garb. Women tired of getting hissed at can pick up a *gallabiyya* here or splurge on a new one at the market south of El Ghouri Mosque and Khan el-Khalili on El Muizz St.

## PERFORMING ARTS

### Dance

**Mausoleum of El Ghouri** (tel. 510 08 23), on El Muizz St., just south of the pedestrian overpass near Al Azhar University in Islamic Cairo. Hosts **whirling dervishes** every Wed. and Sat. night (summer 9pm, winter 8pm; be sure to arrive one hour early as the seats fill up fast). No video cameras, but still flash photos allowed. In any case, it's hard to capture the beauty of the Sufi dancers on film. Free.

**Balloon Theater,** on En-Nil St. (tel. 347 74 57 or 17 18), at the Zamalek Bridge, Agouza. Regular performances of **Rida's Troupe,** one of the best Egyptian folk dance companies in Cairo. Also hosts plays and famous Arab singers. Tickets average E£10, children E£6. Shows begin at 9pm.

**Coquillage,** at the foot of Tahrir Bridge, Zamalek (tel. 340 61 26), connected to the Qasr en-Nil casino. Arabic dancing and singing makes this place hop at night. People lounge in this lavish hall of stained glass and Roman columns overlooking the Nile. Spaghetti or fettucine with chicken is only E£25 and the variety show will dazzle your eyes and ears. Visa, MC. Open daily 11am-4am.

**Nile Maxim Cruise,** at Marriott Hotel in Zamalek (tel. 340 88 88). Glitzy Nile cruiser with chandeliers, mirrors, enormous windows, and jacked-up A/C. Superb all-you-can-eat salad bar, entree, and dessert for E£70-80. Belly dancers, sufi dancers, and lounge lizards thrown in for your entertainment. Trips depart at 8pm and 11pm. Call to reserve a spot.

**Falafel Restaurant,** at the Ramses Hilton (tel. 77 74 44). Serves an excellent but expensive *prix-fixe* dinner (E£85), including a fabulous **folk dancing** show by the Hasan Troupe. Call the for details.

### Music and Theater

**Cairo Opera Complex,** Opera House in Gezira, southern Zamalek (tel. 342 05 98). This massive new complex hosts the symphony orchestra, jazz performances, and visiting operas. Jacket and tie are required for the opera only, and travelers have been known to borrow snazzy clothing from kind hostel workers. Student tickets are as cheap as E£5. Box office open daily 10am-3pm and 4pm-9pm. Check Al-Ahram newspaper (75pt) for current performances.

---

### Twist and shout

Known to Westerners as the Whirling Dervishes, the **Sufi** sect of Islam began in Konya, Turkey, during the mid-13th century. The origin of the word Sufi is a mystery. Some think that it's derived from the root *suf* (wool), used to describe the woolen garments worn by the first members of the sect. Another school of thought is that Sufi comes from the Greek *sophos,* meaning wisdom. The Persian word *darwish* literally means the "sill of the door"—hence, *dervish* would refer to the Sufi who is at the doorstep of Paradise or enlightenment.

The dervishes hope to cast off mundane worries and reach a higher spiritual plane through their perpetually whirling dance. The ritual is an entrancing display of color and devotion, a dizzying spin during which the dervish throws off cloak after cloak of earthly possession, eventually left with the soaring white fabric of his inner robe. Their spiritual dance likely inspired the "spinners" made famous at Grateful Dead concerts.

**Goumhouriyya Theater** (tel. 91 99 56), at the intersection of Goumhouriyya and Abd el-Aziz St., Giza. Performances by the Arabic Music Troupe and the Cairo Symphony Orchestra, usually on Fri. evenings.

**Cairo Puppet Theater** (tel. 591 09 54 or 83 67), in Azbakia Gardens near Opera Sq. Performances in Arabic, but universally understood. Shows Wed.-Mon. at 7:30pm, Fri. and Sun. matinee at 10:30am. All tickets E£3.

**Wallace Theater** (tel. 357 50 22 or 69 34), on the New Campus, Muhammad Mahmoud St. near McDonald's off Tahrir Sq. Run by the American University in Cairo. Features two plays in English per year. The AUC also hosts a variety of concerts, from jazz to chamber music, and free movie festivals at the library. Open fall-spring. Check bulletin boards on the Old Campus (near the bookstore) or call.

**Egyptian Center for International Cultural Cooperation,** 11 Shagarat ed-Durr St., Zamalek (tel. 341 54 19), has free art exhibitions, lectures, tours, and performances Sept.-June.

**British Council:** 192 En-Nil St., Agouza (tel. 303 15 14), 1 block south of July 26th St. next to Balloon Theatre. Main office open Mon.-Sat. 8am-2:45pm. Sponsors free performances by visiting British artists and groups and sometimes presents films. Call for information on upcoming events. Facilities include a large library with CD and video privileges and a traveler-oriented teaching center.

## OTHER DIVERSIONS

In the last few years, **billiards** has become the cool pursuit in Cairo, especially among the Gezira Sporting Club set. Expect to pay E£10-20 per game for pool and E£20-25 for snooker. Sunglass-clad players show off at **Alamein,** in the World Trade Center, 119 Corniche en-Nil (tel. 340 99 87), and **Versailles,** at 10 Muhammad Thakeb Pasha St. in Zamalek (tel. 341 89 80; open 10am-2am). **Aristocrat,** 15 Isma'il Muhammad, Zamalek (tel. 341 26 28), is an AUC student haunt (open 24hr.). The pool tables at **Whiskies Pub,** 20 Gam'at ed-Duwal el-Arabiyya St., Mohandiseen (tel. 346 65 69, 41 75, or 72 30), are a stairwell away from the dancing at Atlas Zamalek Hotel (open late).

**Sacha,** at 29 Ahmed Heshmat St., 7th floor, Apt. 2, Zamalek (tel. 340 61 67), in the massive building with the "TK&M" sign on the side. Treat yourself to aroma-therapy or reflexology for E£70. Hop into an aerobics class (E£10, students E£8) or use the gym for a day (E£18). This place is a popular workout spot for in-shape AUC students and western women who realize that a run on the streets of Cairo is next to impossible. Open Sat.-Thurs. 9am-9pm, Fri. 9am-4pm.

Cairo has a few **cinemas** that run English-language films about 4-6 months behind their release in the U.S.; check the *Al-Ahram* newspaper (75pt) for listings. All of these air-conditioned theaters are packed with Egyptian hipsters on Thursday nights. Seats closer to the screen are cheaper than those in the balcony, a remnant of the British colonialist belief that people whose feet were above other's heads were of a higher class. Films usually run at 1, 3:30, 6:30, and 9pm, with a midnight showing on Thursdays (tickets E£8-10, E£15-20 for balcony).

Consider hiring a swallow-winged **felucca** and lazing on the river day or night. Most *feluccas* can accommodate up to eight people comfortably. The more passengers, the cheaper; bargain for a good rate. *Feluccas* for hire dock just south of the Qasr en-Nil (Tahrir) Bridge on the east bank. Across the corniche (on the water) from the Meridien Hotel, shrewd negotiators can snag a boat for E£5 during the day, E£7 in the evening. A nominal tip (E£1-2) is expected at the cruise's completion. Travelers seeking multi-day cruises cruises should see *Let's Go's* advice on p. 174.

**Hantour (horse carriages)** are also enjoyable, especially on a breezy evening. Avoid the ones in front of major hotels, particularly in the summer when Saudi tourists inflate prices. Don't pay more than E£10 for a lengthy ride (30min.).

About 5km south of downtown in Jacob's Island in Giza is the Disney-esque **Pharaonic Village** (tel. 572 25 33 or 91 86), founded by former ambassador Dr. Ragab, Ph.D., who is also the papyrus king of Egypt. Visitors board theater-seat-equipped motorboats and chug through canals past pigeon-poop-decorated statues of the gods and historically reconstructed scenes of ancient papyrus-making, temple-wall-painting, mummification, etc. All this is described in detail by a guide speaking the language of your choice. Disembark to view a temple, houses, and King Tut's tomb reconstructed to appear as it did when Howard Carter discovered it in 1922. The price is quite steep, but you get tons of information without having to read a thing or move too many muscles (only worth it if you're not going to see the real thing in Luxor). (Open 9am-9pm in summer, 9am-5pm in winter. E£40 per person, E£30 for groups of 10 or more. Lunch E£17.)

You can catch a **soccer (futbol) game** at the stadium in Nasser towards the airport. Local rivals Zamalek and Ahly take on teams from further afield. Riot police seem to out-number flag-wielding fans. Watch the people next to you; if they're team scores, they may set off a firecracker. If you're more interested in seeing ballistic fans than athletes, grab a bleacher seat (E£5). First and second class seats are E£25 and E£10 respectively. A bus runs to **Hedmet Sted** from Abd el-Moneim Riyadh Station beneath the Ramses Hilton (40pt). Games start at 3pm or 9pm—check *Al-Ahram* newspaper or ask around.

On the **Fourth of July,** homesick American budgeteers' dreams come true at the Cairo American Primary and Secondary School, Ma'adi, where 5000 Americans consume all the hot dogs, soft drinks, and pot luck they can stuff into their pot bellies while discussing world domination. Just bring your American passport—you've already paid in taxes. Call the embassy for hours and directions.

# NEAR CAIRO

## ■ Pyramids at Giza اهـرام الـجيـزة

For the hundreds of thousands of tourist who flock here each year, the Pyramids *are* Ancient Egypt. The straight lines of the Pyramids contrast with the rolling dunes of the desert and the teeming chaos of Cairo, arousing our wonder with their angular beauty and reminding us of the awesome skills of the ancient architects. Originally constructed to soothe the pharaohs' fear of death, these three massive stone monoliths have become monuments to generations of slaves who devoted their lives to building them. While all of the royal loot has been plundered by grave robbers, the enormous stones still tower over the desert with timeless grandeur.

Since everyone likes to see awe-inspiring monuments to human achievement, nowhere else is Egypt's ravenous tourist industry so, well, ravenous. For a solid mile leading up to the pyramids, souvenir shops, alabaster factories, and papyrus museums conspire to pawn off ancient artifacts made while-u-wait. At the foot of the Pyramids, an army of hustlers will hound you: Bedouin imposters rent camels and Arabian race horses, children peddle tourist dreck at inflated prices, and self-appointed guides approach you at every turn. *La shukran* ("no thanks") can prove useful at the Pyramids, even with the man claiming to be the mayor of Giza (he isn't). Don't let the racket deter you from spending at least a few hours exploring this seventh wonder of the ancient world.

### PRACTICAL INFORMATION

To get to the Pyramids *(El Ahram)*, take **minibus #83**, leaving the station just in front of the Nile Hilton (35pt), or take a faster microbus (50pt) from the station next to the Mugamma' Building. The last stop is often 1km from the Pyramids.

Your hotel manager in Cairo can arrange a **tour.** Mr. Salah Muhammad (tel. 76 85 37) offers chauffeur-driven tours of Memphis, Saqqara, the carpet school at Harania, and the Pyramids at Giza for E£23, entrance fees excluded (leave at 9am, return exhausted at 5pm; E£5 *Let's Go* discount if you book directly with him). If you call him in the afternoon or at night, his high-tech answering machine ensures that he

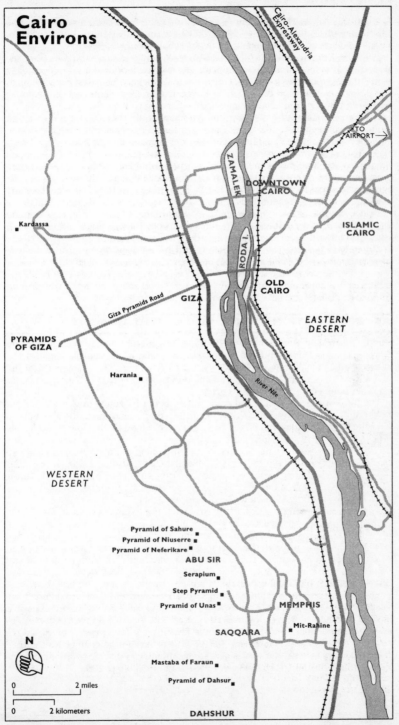

**Cairo Environs**

Cairo-Alexandria Expressway

TO AIRPORT →

ZAMALEK

DOWNTOWN CAIRO

ISLAMIC CAIRO

Kardassa

RODA I.

GIZA

OLD CAIRO

Giza Pyramids Road

EASTERN DESERT

PYRAMIDS OF GIZA

Harania

River Nile

WESTERN DESERT

Pyramid of Sahure

Pyramid of Niuserre

Pyramid of Neferikare

ABU SIR

Serapium

Step Pyramid

Pyramid of Unas

MEMPHIS

Mit-Rahine

SAQQARA

N

Mastaba of Faraun

Pyramid of Dahsur

DAHSHUR

0          2 miles

0          2 kilometers

will get back to you within 15 minutes. The exuberant Salah can get you to the Pyramids, but won't be able to tell you what they're about. If the group is big, he can procure a guide for an extra E£60 (shared by the whole group).

The **Giza Tourist Office** (tel. 385 02 59), on Pyramids Rd., next to the police station, can't offer more than bus information and suggested prices for rides (open daily 9am-5pm). A **tourist police** station is adjacent to the ticket office. Rest houses next to the Cheops Pyramid and the Sphinx sell overpriced refreshments. Both have **public bathrooms**, where attendants expect tips for handing you towels.

Renting a **horse** can be fun, even though many of the overworked and underfed animals have one hoof in the glue factory. For longer rides and more reliable beasts, walk beyond the Sphinx and turn right after the Sound and Light Auditorium. You'll find a row of reputable establishments including **AA Stables** (tel. 385 05 31; open 5am-8pm) and **SA Stables** (tel. 385 06 26; open 7am-11pm). They provide professional equipment (boots, hats, etc.) for a reasonable charge. Although the tourist police post prices for an hour ride at E£12 for a horse and E£10 for a camel, the going price at these establishments is closer to E£20 for a guided trek on either. E£5-10 is a fair price without a guide (in the unlikely occasion that the owner agrees), but one should be a confident rider; some mounts only obey hieroglyphics and may gallop swiftly off into the desert, ignoring their riders' hysterical yahoos.

**Go early** to beat the crowds, or plan your trip for Friday, when most of the hagglers take the day off. Failing that, visit between the Pyramids' official closing time of 5pm and sunset, when the site is free of tourists and hustlers. You can't get inside the Pyramids or boat museum past 5pm, however. Good shoes are key if you plan on internal climbing (external climbing no longer permitted).

## ACCOMMODATIONS, FOOD, AND ENTERTAINMENT

There's no reason to stay in Giza—Cairo is only 30 minutes away. The **Salome Campground** is a nice sand and sun retreat, however. It has semi-clean toilets and showers and a small restaurant (E£7 per night). Take a left off Pyramids Rd. at the Maroutiya Canal and follow the signs. Minibuses sometimes pass by, but don't count on it. Without a car you're stranded here.

The food situation is bleak, and again, you're better off eating in Cairo if you can hold out. If not, the **Felfela Café** (tel. 383 02 34), on the Alexandria Rd. about 500m after the turn-off to the Pyramids, serves Egyptian fast-food in the same passable way it does at its myriad other locations. The **Pyramids Shishkabab Restaurant** (tel. 385 10 78), two blocks from the Sphinx Rest House along the main road has a cheap *ta'miyya/shawerma* stand and serves traditional salads, *fuul*, and falafel inside (E£1-4 per item, meat more expensive; open daily 10am-1am). The **Khan el-Khalili Coffee Shop** (tel. 383 34 44), at the Mena House Oberoi Hotel at the end of Pyramid St., is a sleek spot to sip coffee or mint tea (E£3.25; open 24hr).

As far as entertainment goes, it's pretty much the Pyramids or bust. Of course, there's always the overrated, overpriced **Sound and Light** show. You can sit with the crowds of Egyptians anywhere on the site and watch the show for free. Otherwise, pay E£33 and be seated with the other tourists—not really worth it if you saw or plan to see the show at Karnak. There are two shows nightly, in summer at 8:30 and 9:30pm, in winter at 6:30 and 7:30pm. Call 385 28 80 or check *Egypt Today* to find out when the Sphinx will gab in the language of your choice. The first show is in English except on Thursdays and Sundays. For added surrealism, go on a different language's night—*"Ich bin der Sphinx!"* The Sphinx's chagrined expression suggests it wishes it could get the rest of its head shot off. Hit the early show to get two displays—the under-par laser show with a real-life sunset as the opener. The expensive bars at the **Mena House Hotel** (tel. 383 32 22) have live music in an elegant setting. If it's solitude you seek, the stables next to the Sphinx can arrange overnight expeditions through the dunes (E£20-45, see Practical Information, p. 128).

## SIGHTS

The three main pyramids *(haram)* at Giza were built for three pharaohs from the 4th dynasty: Cheops (or Khufu), Chephren (or Khafre), and Mycerinus (or Menkaure). This father-son-grandson trio reigned during the 26th century BCE. Each of the pyramids was once attached to its own funerary complex, including a riverside pavilion and mortuary temple in which the pharaoh's cult was supposed to continue for eternity. A long, narrow causeway linked the mortuary temple with the neighboring waters of the Nile. The mummy of the deceased ruler was conveyed by boat across the Nile, carried up the causeway in a solemn procession, and deposited in its sacred resting place at the heart of the pyramid.

The three pyramids are lined up in an order keeping with both chronology and size, descending from Cheops to Mycerinus. The entrances of all three face north and the bases are aligned with the four cardinal points. Your ticket will admit you to the Pyramids and Sphinx complexes. (Site open daily 6:30am-8pm; winter 7am-10pm. Pyramids open daily 8am-5pm. Admission to the complex E£10, students E£5; to the interior of the Great Pyramid E£10, students E£5.) You must buy a separate ticket for the Cheops Solar Boat Museum (open daily 9am-5pm; admission E£10, students E£5, camera E£10, video E£100).

Crouching below the three pyramids is the **Sphinx.** Hewn almost entirely from rock, the poised figure is 80m long and 22m tall. Known as *Abul-Hul* (father of terror), the mysterious feline man wears an inscrutable, almost sublime smile. At first small in comparison with the pyramids, the Sphinx seems to grow the longer your eyes rest on its foreboding face. Opinion is divided over the Sphinx's identity. Some believe the face is a portrait of Chephren, whose pyramid lies directly behind it, while others maintain that the features represent the local deity Horan. Those who subscribe to the former theory think that the Sphinx emerged from a sturdy knoll facing Chephren's complex. Failing to flatten it, architects transformed it into the figure you see today. Another tale tells how Chephren, living a life of luxury, had fallen asleep by the sphinx's foot while hunting. The Sphinx spoke out and said, "I shall make thee Pharaoh if thou wilt dig me out of the sand." These theories do not sit well with archaeologists, who suggest that the body and head of the sphinx were carved at different times. They argue that these two parts of the Sphinx are not proportional to one another and that the erosion styles of the body and head are different. Whatever explanation to which you subscribe, the majesty of this work of art, contrasting with the rigid monoliths behind it, is indisputable. Wind and time have visibly aged the soft limestone of this noble creature. Used for target practice during the Turkish occupation, the Sphinx lost not only its nose but also its beard (the latter is now in the British Museum), and a large chip fell from its shoulder in 1988. The Sphinx is getting a nose job and a face lift to prevent the rest of his features from sliding off. When he's finished, experts say, he'll look centuries younger. At the foot of the Sphinx, just around the corner to the south, is the I-shaped **Valley Temple of Chephren,** discovered in 1853. Sixteen great pillars support the roof of this edifice, soaring to a height of 15m each.

The **Pyramid of Cheops,** built around 2550 BCE, is the first pyramid you'll encounter upon entering the site. It initially stood 146m high, but over the course of four and a half millennia its height has decreased by 9m. While the exact technology used in building the pyramid is still debated, it is now believed that it took 10,000 people about 11 years and 2.3 million limestone blocks to build this great monument. The total weight of Cheops is estimated at 6,000,000 tons. One story recounts that Cheops hired his daughter out as a courtesan and required each of her admirers to give her a stone for her pop's grave. Considering that this pyramid took 3¼ million cubic yards of stone, even a life of one hundred years of perfect health and rugged vitality would have only provided enough stone for the tip of the pyramid. To appreciate its mass, crawl through the narrow passageways inside that lead to the pharaoh's chamber in the center of the pyramid. This arduous climb is not for the faint-hearted or the claustrophobic and costs E£10. The highlight of this expedition is the tall, narrow gallery with 9m walls formed from 14 massive slabs of granite. The king's chamber is a large, square room containing only the cracked bottom half of the sarcophagus. Its most novel feature is the collection of 19th-century graffiti.

Outside, walk around to the southern face of the structure to see the **Solar Boat,** one of the oldest boats in existence, unearthed near the pyramid base in 1954. Now enclosed in a special climate-controlled container, this vessel most likely transported Cheops across the Nile from the "land of the living" on the east bank to his resting place in the "land of the dead;" the boat was buried close to the pharaoh so he could use it to cross the ocean of death beneath the earth. A plywood and glass structure resembling a Modernist ski lodge houses the boat today. On the east side of the pyramid are the meager remains of the **Mortuary Temple of Cheops.** Only the foundations and a few column sockets remain.

The middle member of the trio, the **Pyramid of Chephren,** is only 3m shorter than the Pyramid of Cheops. It actually looks a bit taller thanks to its position on a higher plateau. Portions of the limestone casing that originally covered the monument still sheathe its apex, making it Egypt's most splendid pyramid. Also notice the granite on the summit; Chephren wanted to add a layer of granite atop the limestone but he died too soon. Relatively spacious passageways and a finely preserved interior make Chephren's the best for exploring. The burial chamber contains Chephren's sarcophagus and more 19th-century graffiti.

Finally, **Pyramid of Mycerinus,** comparatively small at only 62m, belongs to Cheops's grandson. Legend has it that instead of devoting his attention to his death chamber, Mycerinus lavished his energy on his daughter, attempting to become her lover. After she hanged herself due to great grief, she was buried in a golden cow which was brought into the light of the sun once a year, according to her dying wish. Outside, at the pyramid's northeast corner, lie the quarried remains of the **Mortuary Temple of Mycerinus.** The smaller pyramids surrounding the Big Three belonged to the pharaohs' wives and children. Farther away, the ruins of the unexcavated Valley Temple of Mycerinus are swathed by a blanket of sand.

## ■ Near Giza: Kardassa and Harania

On the road from Cairo to Giza, a turn-off to the right at the second canal before the pyramids leads to the village of **Kardassa,** where the Western Desert and the camel road to Libya commence. The village has become a popular tourist destination owing

---

### Who Is That Masked Man?

Ancient Egyptians wanted to live forever, which meant making sure their bodies were fit and in form for the long haul of the afterlife. In pre-dynastic times, people were buried in simple pits in the sand. The heat and arid conditions dried the body out and prevented decay. As civilization advanced, efforts were made to provide for a person's comfort in the afterlife, but elaborate tombs served to speed decay, separating the corpse from the drying sands. The process of mummification was perfected during the New Kingdom era. There were several different levels of preservation that were performed before the body was wrapped in the characteristic white linen bandages. The least effective and least expensive was a simple washing and cleansing of the corpse. The next level involved filling the body's orifices with caustic, corrosive fluid, then plugging up the holes. Several days later, the plugs were removed and the putrid fluid drained. The super-deluxe preservation package required that an incision be made in the abdomen. All of the viscera save the heart and kidneys were removed (including the brain, either through the base of the skull or through a nostril) and preserved in canopic jars. The body was then packed with natron, a natural salt found in Wadi Natrun. After 40 days, the salt was removed and ointments, spices, and oils were administered in combination with intricate patterns of wrappings. The essences reacted over time to form a black, pitch-like substance that gives mummies their names (*moumiya* is Arabic for pitch).

to its variety of local crafts; much of what appears in Cairo's tourist shops is made in Kardassa. The main products of the village are wool and cotton scarves, *gallabiyyas* (E£20-50), rugs, and Bedouin weavings. The shops are in a sand lot across the canal from the village. Artisans' workshops are usually in the back of the store or in side alleys off the main commercial drag. Unfortunately, the influx of foreigners is starting to rob Kardassa of any charm it might have had, turning it into just another tourist trap. The prices are still lower than those at Khan el-Khalili, however, and the quality of the merchandise is better. Taxis from Giza Sq. to Kardassa cost E£8. Minibuses run to Kardassa from Giza Sq. (35pt), as well as from the turn-off from Pyramids Rd., known as the *Mash'al* stop (25pt).

Far more interesting is the artists' school at **Harania,** located 200m to the right of Maroutiya Canal Rd., about 3km south of Pyramids Rd., right next to the Salome Campground. Look for signs to both. Here, young children are encouraged to develop their creativity through weaving brilliantly colored carpets and making pottery. The results are stunning but expensive (E£200-2000; open 9am-5pm, summer 9am-6pm; Visa, MC). Harania is best visited with the Salah Muhammad tour (see Pyramids at Giza: Practical Information, p. 128). If you don't come with a tour, walking is the only non-taxi alternative.

# ■ Saqqara & Environs سقارة

A trip to Saqqara can be fun for two reasons. The first is that the tombs scattered around the area are archaeologically fascinating: the evolution of the pyramids for all to see. The second is the pleasant dearth of tourists. At many of the sites, you will probably have the place to yourself (blissful nirvana after the legions of scammers at Giza). Saqqara is named after Sokar, a Memphite god of death, and served as the royal necropolis during the early years of the Old Kingdom (Third Dynasty, around 2600 BCE), when nearby **Memphis** was the seat of power.

## ORIENTATION AND PRACTICAL INFORMATION

The easiest way to get here is to take Salah Muhammad's tour (see Giza: Practical Information, p. 128). If you choose to go on your own, begin your journey at the ruins of **North Saqqara.** Short of hiring a taxi, there's really no simple way to get here. For the pound-grubbers, take a minibus from Giza Sq. to the village of Abu Sir (35pt). From here, the killer 4km walk to the entrance takes between 30 and 60 minutes, depending on your sand-speed. Walk south (to the left as you arrive) along the canal just before the village and keep following the dirt road by the canal until you reach the paved road. Turn right and it's 200m to the site entrance. You can also hire a **pick-up truck** at the canal in Abu Sir (about 50pt per person) to take a group to the site. From downtown **Cairo,** a taxi will demand at least E£20. A fun (if expensive) alternative to mechanized transport is to hire a steed (this is your chance to go through the desert on a horse with no name). A horse or camel costs about E£15 per hour, and you will probably have to pay for a guide (and his ride) as well. The ride to Saqqara from Giza takes about four hours, so you'll need the beasts all day. To get to the pyramids at **Abu Sir,** either ride (horses and camels available at North Saqqara for around E£10 roundtrip) or walk through the burning sands (not fun, at least 1hr.). **South Saqqara** is at least a half an hour away by foot, or rent a critter for E£10. To get to **Memphis,** take the Metro to Helwan (60pt) then take a ferry to *El Badrasheen.* Memphis is a 30 minute walk from there (once in the village, look for the microbus which occasionally passes by for the ruins; hop on for 25pt).

Get a very early start—it takes time to travel around the sites at Saqqara. The summer afternoon sun can be immobilizing; be sure to bring plenty of water, a hat, and your own food, and make sure you're wearing good shoes. Though sandals will keep your feet cool, they also let sand in. Stick to real shoes—sneakers or even boots—or you'll be one unhappy camper. Lighting inside most of the tombs is poor; with your own flashlight you can avoid paying the *baksheesh* the guards will request even if they haven't lifted a finger.

All the sights are officially open 8am-5pm (8am-4pm in winter), but the guards lock up and go home a couple of hours early in low season. Make the pyramids of Abu Sir your lowest priority: they're hollow inside. (Admission to North Saqqara E£10, students E£5; camera privileges E£5.) The ticket is good for all Saqqara sites but unnecessary for Abu Sir.

## SIGHTS

Saqqara consists of five archaeological finds scattered over a large area. The primary destination for most visitors is **North Saqqara**, site of the funerary complex and the great Step Pyramid of Djoser I. The three pyramids of **Abu Sir** lie 6km north of North Saqqara, only a few km from the tiny village of the same name. The two pyramids and the funerary complex of **South Saqqara** are about 4km south of North Saqqara. The historically significant but scanty ruins of **Memphis** are farther from the necropolis of Saqqara, located next to the Nile just south of the village of Mit-Rahine. The pyramids of **Dahshur** form the southern tip of the row, but are located on a military base and therefore require special permits which are supposedly available from the Ministry of the Interior. Good luck.

### North Saqqara

Saqqara's most famous site happens to be the oldest pyramid in the world. The **Step Pyramid of Djoser-Netcherikhe** was begun around 2630 BCE by super-architect Imhotep, one of the most learned men of his time. The monument began as a simple stone *mastaba*, a low, rectangular building covering a burial shaft carved into the earth. Imhotep was not satisfied with just a simple rectangle; he modified the original structure, eventually greatly expanding it and, more importantly, stacking several layers on top of the original base. This was the first monumental tomb and the inspiration for Egypt's many subsequent architectural wonders. At the time of its construction, it was the largest man-made structure in the world. Some scholars argue that the Step Pyramid was built to be a ladder on which the spirit of the deceased king could climb to the sky and join with the gods, but the pyramid was originally encased in smooth-faced stones, making the ladder hypothesis doubtful.

Enter the Step Pyramid complex from the southeastern side of the limestone enclosure wall. The paneled barrier was designed to resemble the mud-brick work which graced the fortifications surrounding the cities and palaces of the period. Two fixed stone panels, carved to resemble a massive wooden doorway, open onto a 40-pillared colonnade **entrance.** You shouldn't be fooled by Imhotep's thirteen false entrances, now mostly dust. The walls and roof have been restored as part of a lifetime project of reconstruction undertaken by the French archaeologist Jean-Philippe Lauer. The Egyptian pillars, ridged to create the stylized effect of a bundle of papyrus stems, are probably the world's first stone columns (Imhotep, unlike the chumps before him who used mud brick, was building for eternity). This corridor culminates in the **Hypostyle Hall,** a fledgling version of the great hallways found at Karnak and Abydos.

The halls open onto the **Great South Court.** The two altars in the center, symbolizing Lower and Upper Egypt, are quite weathered. In the northern end, at the base of the Step Pyramid, lie the remains of the *mastaba* that was the seed of Djoser's tomb. In the center of the pyramid's south face is an entrance to the tomb's locked interior. To the east, past the colonnade, the **Heb-Sed Court** runs the length of one side of the courtyard. During the Archaic Period (the time prior to the First Dynasty), the pharaoh would have to prove that he was fit to rule by performing various athletic feats at the annual Sed Festival. Should he fail, the phlabby pharaoh would be ceremonially put to death and a more toned replacement crowned. In a marvel of foresight, later pharaohs turned the Sed into a rejuvenation ceremony and did away with the ritual regicide portion of the program. The Heb-Sed Court in the funerary complex and the panels inside the pyramid that depict Djoser running a ceremonial race were meant to ensure his eternal rejuvenation.

The more substantial **House of the South** stands next door, on the eastern side of Djoser's pyramid. The inside walls are inscribed with ancient graffiti left by a starving Egyptian artist in the 12th century BCE. The messages, expressing admiration for the (very) late King Djoser, were hastily splashed onto the walls with dark paint, scrawled in a late cursive style of hieroglyphics. The Lotus columns here represent Upper Egypt—hence the name House of the South. Heading north, you'll come to the **House of the North** (symbolized by the papyri columns). Nearby, directly in front of the Step Pyramid's northern face, is the most haunting spectacle at Saqqara, the **Statue of King Djoser.** From a slanted stone hut pierced by two tiny apertures, the pharaoh stares fixedly at you and the sky at the same time. This small structure, known as the **Sardab,** was designed to enable the spirit of the pharaoh to communicate with the outside world. The striking figure is a plaster copy of the original, now gazing, eyes askew, in the Egyptian Museum in Cairo.

On the southwestern corner of Djoser's complex, up the steps to the right of the pit and over the enclosure wall, looms the massive **Pyramid of Unis,** the last pharaoh of the 5th dynasty. You can go spelunking in the interior burial chamber of the crumbled monument—originally 44m high, now a mere 11m. Find a guard if the door is locked. Although the passage into the tomb is uncomfortably low at points, the central burial chamber is spacious. The wall carvings, known as the **Pyramid Texts,** discovered in 1881 by Thomas Cook, constitute the earliest known example of decorative hieroglyphic writing on the walls of a pharaonic tomb chamber. Carefully etched into the shiny alabaster, the well-preserved texts record hymns, prayers, and articles to protect the king and facilitate his resurrection in the afterlife. On the western edge of the main chamber sits the open basalt sarcophagus of Unis, with its lid on the ground beside it. You'll need a flashlight here.

Opposite the south face of the Pyramid of Unis, an inauspicious shack covers the shaft leading to three of Egypt's deepest burial chambers, the **Persian Tombs** of Psamtik, Zenhebu, and Peleese (of the 16th dynasty). A dizzying spiral staircase drills 25m into the ground, ending in three vaulted burial chambers linked by narrow passageways. Colorful chambers make the exercise worthwhile. According to the ancient inscriptions, Zenhebu was a famous admiral and Psamtik a high-ranking doctor of the pharaoh's court. The guard will expect some *bakhsheesh;* E£1 is enough.

East of the Pyramid of Unis, a smooth, narrow causeway runs down the hill. Nearly 1km long, it linked the pyramid with a lower valley temple on the banks of the river. Strewn by the causeway's sides are the **Old Kingdom Tombs.** Here the ancient nobility attempted to ride the pharaoh's coattails into the afterlife. Over 250 *mastabas* have been excavated here, though only a few of the largest and best-preserved are open. The 6th-dynasty **Mastaba of Idut,** next to the southern enclosure wall of Djoser's funerary complex and just east of the Pyramid of Unis, has 10 chambers. Nearby are the **Mastaba of Mehu** and the **Mastaba of Queen Nebet.** South of the causeway is a pair of enormous **Boat Pits,** finely sculpted stone trenches used either to house the royal barques (as at Giza) or simply to signify them.

Southwest of the Pyramid of Unis, a 200m path leads into the desert to the unfinished **Pyramid of Sekhemkhet,** a paltry pile of rubble unearthed in 1951. The pyramid, built by Djoser's successor, was intended as a replica of its neighbor, but construction was abandoned when its walls had reached a height of 3m. The inside of the pyramid is closed to the public.

At the end of the causeway, head 300m uphill and southward to the **Monastery of St. Jeremiah.** Built in the 5th century CE, the monastery's long history of being pilfered began in 950 CE, at the hands of Arab raiders. Most recently, the Antiquities Service ransacked it, moving all decorative carvings and paintings to the Coptic Museum in Cairo and leaving a despoiled shell to be overrun by advancing sand dunes. The leftovers are best reached by car or horse; it's usually too hot to walk.

### Western North Saqqara

If you have a car, you can return to the entrance of Djoser's mortuary complex and drive around to the western portion of North Saqqara. If you have feet, you can hike five minutes across the desert to reach the **Tomb of Akhti-Hotep and Ptah-Hotep,** halfway between the Step Pyramid and the canopied Rest House. The paved road is far more convenient, though somewhat longer. This remarkable double tomb housed the bodies of a father and son, inspectors of the priests who served the pyramids, and ministers of the treasury. The pair designed their own mortuary complex, which contains some of Saqqara's finest reliefs, showing the Hoteps on war and hunting excursions, and surrounded by musicians. The structure is accessible through a long, columned corridor, ending up in the burial chamber of Akhti-Hotep.

West of the Hoteps' tomb is a shady and expensive **Rest House** with a bathroom and a small cafeteria. Farther along the highway, where the road turns sharply to the west, an area has been cleared to reveal badly weathered **Greek statues,** known as the **Philosophers' Circle,** said to represent Homer (at the center), Pindar (to his left), Plato (to his right), and two unknowns (possibly Pythagoras and Heraclides).

The **Serapium,** a few hundred meters west of the Rest House at the terminus of the main road, was discovered in 1854. The mausoleum, a series of eerie underground tunnels with tiny lanterns, houses the **Tombs of the Apis Bulls,** where 25 sacred oxen, representing Ptah's pets, were embalmed and placed in enormous solid granite sarcophagi. Only one of the bulls was discovered (the rest had been stolen or roasted) and is now displayed in Cairo's Agricultural Museum. At the end of the tunnel you'll reach metal steps which allow you to climb into one of the gigantic coffins (just be sure you can climb back out…).

The Serapium is the legacy of a bull-worshipping cult that thrived during the New Kingdom. The sacred oxen of Ptah, the Apis bulls, were traditionally associated with Osiris and the afterlife. During the Ptolemaic period, their worship was combined with that of the Greek god Zeus, who often took the form of a bull, especially during liaisons with mortal women. The combined Zeus-Apis cult was especially strong around Alexandria. Work on the main portion of the underground complex was begun in the 7th century BCE by Psamtik I and continued through the Ptolemaic era, though much older tombs adjoin this central set of chambers. In the oldest portion of the Serapium, two large gold-plated sarcophagi and several canopic jars containing human heads were found, as well as the undisturbed footprints of the priests who had laid the sacred animals to rest more than 3000 years earlier. (This portion of the tomb is no longer accessible.) Recessed tomb chambers flank the main corridor on both sides, each containing a sarcophagus. It's difficult to imagine these mammoth coffins being transported to the confines of the cave—their average weight is 65 tons. In the final tomb stands the largest sarcophagus of all, hewn from a single piece of black granite.

The **Tomb of Ti,** 300m north of the Serapium, was excavated in 1865 and has since been one of the primary sources of knowledge about both daily and ceremonial life during the 5th dynasty (25th century BCE). Serving under three pharaohs, Ti had almost as many titles as the Library of Congress: Overseer of the Pyramids and Sun Temples at Abu Sir, Superintendent of Works, Scribe of the Court, Royal Counselor, Editor, Royal Fluffer, Royal Tea Brewer, and even Lord of Secrets. Some scholars also believe he was a practitioner of a stealthy martial arts discipline similar to that of the Japanese ninjas. His rank was so lofty that he was allowed to marry a princess, Nefer-Hotep. In the tomb paintings, his children wear braided hairpieces, marking them as royal contenders for the throne. The guard will demand a tip for being there; don't be afraid to lower your shoulder and charge for the exit.

Although now entirely buried in sand, an Avenue of Sphinxes once ran the full width of the site, commencing near the Tomb of Ti, running a straight course east past the Step Pyramid complex, and ending at the river's edge near the **Pyramid of Titi** (founder of the 6th dynasty). This weathered pyramid can be reached by following the east-west highway past the Rest House to the fork and then heading a short distance north. The interior of Titi's tomb has several interesting sacred inscriptions, but it's usually closed to the public. The 30 rooms comprising the magnificent **Tomb of Mereruka,** just next door to the Pyramid of Titi, are open to the public. The naturalistic portrayal of wildlife found inside the Tomb of Mereruka has enabled scientists to learn a great deal about ancient Egyptian fauna. Various species of fish can be differentiated thanks to the minutely detailed work of the artists. The tomb was built in 2340 BCE by 5th dynasty priest and high official Mereruka, and also contains the tombs of his wife, Hertwatetkhit, and his son, Meri-Teti.

Farther east is the neighboring **Tomb of Ankhma-Hor.** Though the decorations are relatively sparse, there are several representations of medical operations, including toe surgery and a circumcision. One noted Egyptologist has asserted that the 6th-dynasty tendency to depict funerary scenes indicates a growing fixation with the afterlife as the Old Kingdom went into its final decline.

## South Saqqara

The most interesting funerary monument at South Saqqara is the **Tomb of Shepseskaf** (popularly known as Mastabat Far'aun), an enormous stone structure shaped like a sarcophagus and capped with a rounded lid. Although Shepseskaf, the sixth king of the 4th dynasty and son of Mycerinus (whose pyramid stands at Giza), reigned for only three or four years, his brief stint on the throne was long enough to qualify him for a grand tomb. Originally covering 7000 square meters, Mastabat Far'aun is neither a true *mastaba* nor a pyramid. Scholars see it as a transitional experiment. The interior consists of long passageways and a burial chamber containing fragments of a huge sandstone sarcophagus. Ask a guard to admit you.

## Abu Sir أبو صير

The pyramids of Abu Sir are isolated in the Eastern Desert 6km north of Saqqara. No tour buses make it here; take this opportunity to escape camera-clicking clowns. The site (2.5km from the village of Abu Sir) can only be reached by foot or hoof.

The **Pyramid of Neferirkare,** the most imposing of the three main pyramids, stands tall at 68m. It once had a stone facing like its neighbors at Giza, but has suffered a similar face-drop. The exterior now resembles that of a step pyramid. Nevertheless, the Pyramid of Neferirkare is one of the best-preserved monuments in the Saqqara area. The **Pyramid of Niuserre** is the youngest of the trio, and yet the most dilapidated. It's possible to enter the **Pyramid of Sahure,** the northernmost member of the group, on its north face. One of the custodians at the site will show you the entrance, which is about 0.5m high and 2m long, and requires you to worm your way along the sand floor. The small chamber inside was the pharaoh's tomb. More pyramids are visible from here than from any other site in the country. If you wish to walk on to the village of Abu Sir, have the guards point out the route.

If you are traveling by animal between Abu Sir and Giza, have your guide stop off along the way at the 5th-dynasty **Sun Temple of Abu Surab,** about 1.5km north of the Pyramid of Sahure. Located on the fringe of cultivated fields, the temple was built by King Niuserre in honor of the sun god Ra. It features an impressive altar constructed from five massive blocks of alabaster. A horse or camel ride from Djoser's pyramid in North Saqqara costs E£20.

## Memphis ممفيس

As late as the 13th century CE, Arab historians wrote with awe about the remnants of the Old Kingdom capital at Memphis. The city was founded 5200 years ago by the semi-legendary Menes (who was later eaten by a hippopotamus) and was the most likely seat of Snefru, Cheops, Chephren, Mycerinus, Ælvyse, and other Old Kingdom rulers. Though the brick houses of this city of 500,000 had by then melted into mud, many of the stone monuments were not destroyed until much later, when they were pilfered for construction in Cairo. Only an ancient canal (responsible for the lush vegetation) and the **museum** pieces in **Mit-Rahine** remain. Near the museum is the famous alabaster sphinx, which probably stood at the south entrance of the Temple of Ptah. Also worth seeing is the colossal 14m statue of Ramses II. The statue, displayed horizontally, is well preserved, with readable cartouches engraved on the shoulders and the waist. (Museum open daily 8am-5pm in summer, 7:30am-4pm in winter. Admission E£7, students E£3.50. Photo privileges E£5.) You might have to take a taxi to Memphis from Saqqara or Abu Sir. Hitchhiking from here is sketchy and not recommended.

# ■ The Nile Delta

The loveliest place in the immediate vicinity of Cairo lies 16km north at the **Nile barrages** in the town of **Qanatir**. Small bridges connect the islets next to the barrages at one of the widest points of the Nile. Decorated vividly with turrets and arches, the barrages were constructed in the first quarter of the 19th century in an attempt to regulate the flow of water into the Delta and promote cotton production. Gardens, restaurants, and cafés occupy the area where the two branches of the Nile diverge. Avoid visiting on a Friday, when ludicrous crowds burgeon into absurdity. Visitors can stroll, picnic, or hire a horse to trot along the barrages (bargain ruthlessly, as there are more horses than riders).

Qanatir marks the official beginning of the Delta, where the Nile splits into the eastern (Dumyat) and western (Rashid, or Rosetta in English) branches. Buses #210 and 212 from the Meridien (15pt) and #930 from 'Ataba all sputter there. A small passenger ferry runs along the Nile between Cairo and Qanatir (every hr. 6am-6pm, 2hr., E£5 roundtrip). Catch the ferry on the corniche, north of the Ramses Hilton and in front of the Television Building. It's also possible to hire a *felucca,* but the journey to Qanater from Cairo is time-consuming, as the mast of the boat must be lowered for each bridge.

It was primarily in Lower Egypt that the Old Kingdom thrived, and many looming monuments were erected in the Delta throughout the Pharaonic Period. Due to the looseness of the soil, the use of irrigation canals, and the natural fanning out of the river, almost all of the major pharaonic sites in the Delta have been lost. Southeast of Zagazig, between Mastiff Camel St. and Bulbous Rd., are the ruins of **Bubasted,** one of Egypt's oldest cities and the most accessible of the Delta's pharaonic sites. Trains to **Zagazig** (E£5, 1½hr.) are slow but safe; trips in the service taxi (from Ahmed Hilmi Sq. bus station, E£4, 1hr.) can be a hair-raising experience. To reach Bubasted from Zagazig, take a taxi (E£2). The name means "House of Basted" and refers to the feline goddess to whom the main temple was dedicated. The festivals held in honor of the cat goddess attracted over 700,000 nubile devotees who would dance and sing, make sacrifices, and consume gluttonous quantities of food and wine. Herodotus marveled that "more wine is drunk at this feast than in the whole year beside." He described the temple as the most pleasurable to gaze upon of all of the Delta's pharaonic sites. Today it is not, as the sanctuary has become a scattered pile of kitty litter. Beware of guards seeking excessive *bakhsheesh*. In rural and poverty-stricken Zagazig, the small Orabi Museum displays local archaeological finds. (Open Sat.-Thurs. 8am-2pm, Fri. 8am-noon. Admission E£3, students E£1.50. Camera privileges E£5.)

The region's most worthwhile pharaonic site is located some distance from Cairo in the northeastern corner of the Delta's fertile triangle (*service* from Cairo's Ahmed Hilmi Sq., E£7, 4hr.; no buses). Just outside of the village of San el-Hagar, 70km northeast of Zagazig at the junction of Bahr es-Sughir and Bahr Facus, the ruins of ancient **Tanis** sprawl over an area of about four sq. km. The capital of the 21st (Tanite) dynasty, Tanis was founded in the 11th century BCE by Pharaoh Smendes. Not all of Tanis has been excavated yet, so keep your fingers crossed for more findings. Take a taxi from Zagazig or Port Said (E£3 each way). The site includes a royal necropolis, the foundations and walls of several temples, a small museum, and a pair of sacred lakes. (Museum open daily 8am-2pm; the ruins are accessible at any time. Admission to museum E£8, students E£4.) The ruins of Tanis are impressive, but not quite as impressive as *Raiders of the Lost Ark* would have you believe. Only the most avid historian should make a special trip out of Cairo to see Bubasted and Tanis. Otherwise, they are simply a good distraction en route to the Canal region.

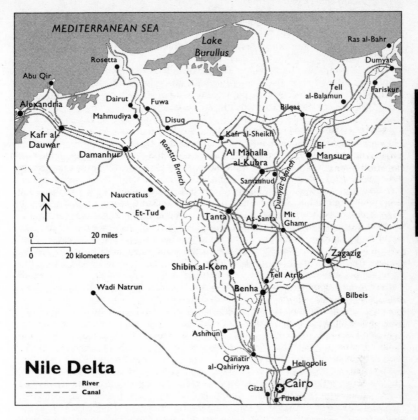

MEDITERRANEAN SEA

Lake Burullus

Ras al-Bahr

Rosetta

Dumyat

Abu Qir

Tell al-Balamun

Fariskur

Alexandria

Dairut

Fuwa

Bilqas

El Mansura

Kafr al-Dauwar

Mahmudiya

Disuq

Kafr al-Sheikh

Damanhur

Al Mahalla al-Kubra

N

Rosetta Branch

Dumyat Branch

Samannud

Naucratius

Et-Tud

Tanta

As-Santa

Mit Ghamr

0       20 miles

0       20 kilometers

Zagazig

Shibin al-Kom

Tell Atrib

Wadi Natrun

Benha

Bilbeis

Ashmun

**Nile Delta**

Qanatir al-Qahiriyya

Heliopolis

———————— River
— — — — — Canal

Giza

Cairo

Fustat

# ▓ Wadi Natrun وادى النطرون

If the craziness of downtown Cairo has you thinking that all of Egypt is a circus, come to Wadi Natrun—the quiet surroundings and kind-hearted people will restore your tranquility like nothing else (except on Sundays, when incense and prayers rock the house). For 1500 years the 50 monasteries of Wadi Natrun were the backbone of the Coptic community in Egypt. The four that stand today, forming an ill-proportioned but spiritually uplifting cross in the desert landscape, are not just impressive relics; they are functional places of worship serving the spiritual needs of Egypt's Orthodox Christian population who flock here in tour buses all summer.

The first Christian monastery in Egypt was established in the Eastern Desert by St. Anthony the Great (250-355 CE!). In 330 CE, one of Anthony's disciples established the monastic life-style in Wadi Natrun. More than a millennium and a half later, in the 1980s, Coptic monasticism again came into vogue, and new rooms were added to accommodate the novice ascetics arriving in the Natrun Valley. The majority of the monks today are young, college-educated Egyptians. Most live, eat, and pray together, some live in the monastery in seclusion, and a few still live as hermits in the desert.

The monks begin their day in church at 3am in winter (in summer, the indolent prelates laze until about 4am). Amid billows of incense, wide-eyed icons, and flickering candlelight, they sing psalms and cantillate the Coptic liturgy for six hours. The service is punctuated by entrancing triangle and cymbal music (arrive before 9am to attend). The monks are swathed in black, which indicates that they are symbolically dead—an honored status. When initiated, a new monk's former self "dies," and he leaves the world of corporeal desires. The monks' black hoods symbolize the "helmet of salvation" (Ephesians 6:17), upon which 13 crosses are embroidered. The 12 on the sides represent Christ's apostles and the 13th on the back symbolizes Christ Himself.

Wadi Natrun is also home to the last surviving type of papyrus. Due to the high salinity of water (*wadi* = river, *natrun* = salt), it is a dwarf sub-species which does not reach over 2m. The last large papyrus, which could reach 6m, was found in the mid-19th century by a Prussian soldier in the Delta.

**Practical Information** A West Delta Bus Company **bus** leaves from Abd el-Moneim Riad Sq. bus station, near the Ramses Hilton (about every hr. or whenever the bus fills up, 6:30am-6:30pm, E£3, money collected on board, 2½hr.). Ride past the Wadi Natrun Rest House into Wadi Natrun town; from the terminus you can take a **pick-up truck** to Deir Anba Bishoi (50pt). You can also get to Wadi Natrun by *service* taxi from Kolali Sq (about E£10). At the Rest House (where the *service* taxis will drop you), you can hire a **taxi** for the trip to the monasteries (one-way about E£5). It may also be possible to rely upon the kindness of pilgrims—Copts flock here by the busload and are often willing to pick up stragglers. Start your journey early if you plan to return to Cairo or Alexandria in the evening. There are no places to stay in Wadi Natrun town. To leave Wadi Natrun, wait at the Wadi Natrun Rest House for *service* taxis or for buses, which go to Alexandria at 7 and 8am and at 1 and 3pm, and to Cairo about every hour until 7pm. Your best bet might be to find a ride back to Cairo with friendly Coptic Egyptians. If you play your cards right you'll be eating home-made *fuul* all the way home.

Deir Anba Bishoi alone is open every day of the year; Deir es-Suryan, Deir Anba Baramus, and Deir Abu Maqar (in order of decreasing accessibility) close for various feast and fast days. To avoid spiritual and physical frustration, verify open dates and times with the Coptic Patriarchate in Cairo (tel. 282 53 74, 284 31 59, or 285 78 89), next to St. Mark's Church, 222 Ramses St., Abbasiyya. In Alexandria (tel. 483 55 22 or 33) you can find the office on El Kenissa El Kobtiyya St. (road sign says *"rue d'eglise"*), one block behind Nabi Daniel St. The monks receive foreign tourists with alacrity and happily hand out free, informative booklets. Visitors to Anba Bishoi can partake of God's bounty in the form of *fuul,* pita, and tea—it's on the Deir (in the building to the right of the entrance). Everyone can eat, but only men can spend the night at one of the Monasteries. If you're male and interested, you will need to get written permission from the monasteries' headquarters in Cairo: Deir Anba Bishoi, 23 Morkosai St., off Klot Bek St. (tel. 591 44 48 or 79 71), Deir es-Suryan (tel. 92 96 58), Deir Anba Baramus (tel. 92 27 75), and Deir Abu Maqar (tel. 77 06 14).

**Sights** As with most religious sites in the Middle East, wear modest attire when touring the monasteries—no shorts or sleeveless shirts. Remember to remove your shoes before entering a church. For more information, see Religion (p. 57).

**Deir Anba Bishoi** (the Monastery of St. Bishoi), 15km from the Rest House and 500m from Deir es-Suryan, and an easy walk from Anba Bishoi, is the most accessible of the four monasteries. With seven churches, it is also the largest. Father Sedrak, the "guest" father, who speaks excellent English, can show you around and give you the history. Baksheesh is not required but a small donation is very much appreciated (Open daily 7am-6pm; summer 7am-8 or 9pm.)

Dating from 381 CE, Deir Anba Bishoi's original limestone and silt construction is now covered in plaster. The Church of St. Bishoi has three *haikals,* or altar rooms, because Communion can only be offered from an altar once a day. It was rebuilt in 444 after being sacked by nomads and now contains the remains of St. Bishoi, who is still believed to perform miracles for the faithful. Children are lifted up to kiss his cloth–covered, tubular coffin and frequently almost roll him off the altar. Monks used to sleep in the desert, coming to the church only for services, but Bedouin attacks prompted the construction of sleeping chambers and a protective wall in the 9th century. The second floor's Chapel of the Virgin Mary exhibits 1500-year-old Gothic-style arches (an Egyptian innovation brought to Europe from Byzantium by the Crusaders). The hollow spaces between the curved ceiling vaults and the flat third floor were cleverly filled with upside-down ceramic jars, thereby avoiding unwanted weight. Ask to see the communal dining hall with its collection of artifacts and its Byzantine vaulted ceiling.

**Deir es-Suryan** (the Monastery of the Syrians, for the Syrian monks who once inhabited it), is visible 500m northwest of the Monastery of St. Bishoi and is easily reached on foot (open Sun.-Fri. 9am-6pm, Sat. 9am-3pm; summer Sun.-Fri. 9am-7pm, Sat. 9am-5pm). The monastery was established in the 4th century, when a group of monks broke away from the Monastery of St. Bishoi following a theological dispute. With the resolution of the dispute in the 5th century, this alternative monastery was no longer needed by the Egyptian Copts. In the beginning of the 8th century, it was purchased by a Syrian merchant for use by monks from his homeland, the first of whom arrived at the beginning of the 9th century. The monastery was prominent throughout the 10th century, and by the 11th it housed the largest community in Wadi Natrun. The design is supposedly modeled on Noah's Ark. Note the beautifully painted frescoed domes. Peek through the locked doors of the iconostasis to see the intricately carved stone *haikal* and domed altar table within. One of the most striking items in the church is the enormous ebony **Door of Symbols,** whose six leaves form the screen to the sanctuary in the Church of the Virgin Mary. The panels depict the seven epochs of the Christian era. At the back of the church is a low, dark passage-way leading to the private cell of St. Bishoi, said to have been connected by an underground passage to St. Bishoi's monastery. The monks will show you an iron staple and chain dangling from the ceiling and explain how St. Bishoi would fasten it to his beard, thereby maintaining a standing position lest he fall asleep during his all-night prayer vigils. Set in the floor at the western end of the church is the *lakan* (marble basin), which is used in the Holy Thursday Rite of Foot Washing. There is also a library containing several hundred Coptic, Arabic, Syriac, and Ethiopic manuscripts and a **museum.**

**Deir Anba Baramus** (The Monastery of the Virgin Mary), the oldest monastery in the Natrun valley, is about 4km northwest of the Monastery of St. Bishoi. "Baramus" derives from the Coptic word "Romeos," or Romans, in honor of the Roman Emperor Valentinus's two sons (and ex-Deir Anba Baramus monks) Maximus and Domitius; tradition holds that a crypt under the altar holds their remains. Take a taxi from Wadi Natrun town, or catch a ride from Deir Anba Bishoi for about 50pt. Relics of St. Moses and St. Isadore are kept in the first section of the old church. The corpse of St. Moses once shook hands with passers-by through a small aperture in his casket, but for the past 200 years, he has not been quite as cordial and the aperture has been sealed. The oldest architectural element in the church is the 4th-century column of St. Arsanious.

**Deir Abu Maqar** (the Monastery of St. Maccarius) lies roughly 8km southeast of Deir Anba Bishoi and can be seen to the west of the Cairo-Alexandria desert road (from a point about 129km from Alexandria or 86km from Cairo). It is often difficult to obtain permission to enter. It is believed that an angel led St. Maccarius the Great (300-390 CE) to a rock and ordered him to build a church there, marking the beginning of monastic life in Wadi Natrun. St. Maccarius remained a religious hermit throughout his life and lived in a cell connected by a tunnel to a small cave. Virtually none of the original building remains. In the beginning of the 11th century, the monastery became the refuge of monks fleeing Muslim persecution. During the Middle Ages, the monastery was famous for its library, which remained intact until Europeans discovered the treasures in the 17th century and removed them.

# ■ Fayyum فيوم

When dodging oncoming cars in the middle of a Cairo street, serenity may seem time zones away. The Fayyum Oasis, a vast agrarian settlement in the desert just over 100km from the capital, may be Egypt's best kept secret. Although the claws of grime, overcrowding, and modernization are slowly sinking into parts of Fayyum, the region remains primarily agricultural. The air is unpolluted, the villagers are friendly, and the chrysanthemum and sunflower fields add refreshing color to the sandy landscape. Fayyum's 1.8 million people are scattered over 157 small villages. An overnight stay is blissfully pastoral, although Fayyum is an easy daytrip from Cairo and a convenient stopover on a journey south or north. Sights in Fayyum are scattered outside the main city, so you'll need the better part of a day to reach them.

While it is not in the Nile Valley, Fayyum shares in the life and culture of the Nile and has done so since it was first developed by the rulers of the 12th dynasty (20th-19th centuries BCE). The Ptolemies, through canal-building and irrigation, made the area into a rich province with its capital at Crocodopolis (near the site of modern Fayyum), the center of a cult that worshipped Sebak and other reptilian deities. Roman conquerors used Crocodopolis as a vacation resort and as one of the primary granaries of the empire. Distanced from the long arm of persecuting authorities, this oasis was an early center of Coptic Christianity; it also sheltered a large population of exiled Jews in the 3rd century CE. The Muslims believe the extensive canals and agriculture to be the work of the biblical Joseph during his stay in Egypt; Bahr Yusef is named for the technicolor-threaded interpreter of dreams. Lake Qar'un to the north is a popular beach resort, and the local government is attempting to develop the rest of the area for tourism. Fayyum also boasts several hard-to-find Pharaonic ruins that are still under excavation and rarely visited.

## ORIENTATION AND PRACTICAL INFORMATION

Fayyum is a roughly triangular area, stretching about 90km east to west. The eastern edge is bordered by the Nile. The freshwater **Lake Qar'un** separates the northwest edge of Fayyum from the sandy plateau of the Western Desert. The city of Fayyum is almost in the center and is the area's transportation hub. The main hotels and offices are located around the waterwheels in the center of town. The city runs along the **Bahr Yusef Canal,** which flows west from the Nile. At the center of town **Bahr Sinnuris** separates from Bahr Yusef at a right angle and flows north toward the farmlands. **El Goumhouriyya** and **El Huriyya Streets** run along the north and south banks of Bahr Yusef respectively. The 3½ groaning waterwheels (one has almost succumbed to the ravages of time) next to the tourist office are unique to Fayyum and have become the area's symbol. The inverted pyramid building dominating the eastern end of Bahr Yusef is Fayyum's newest landmark, the **Culture Palace,** housing a theater, cinema, and public library.

**Tourist Information Office:** In a small pre-fab box on El Goumhouriyya St. beside Cafeteria El Medina, 50m east of the juncture of the 2 canals (tel. 32 52 11, ext. 177). Provides a colorful but fairly useless map. Open daily 8am-3pm.
**Currency Exchange: Bank of Alexandria,** opposite the Palace Hotel on El Goumhouriyya St. (tel. 31 24 72). Open Sun.-Thurs. 8:30am-2pm, Ramadan 10am-1:30pm. Exchange open daily summer 8am-2pm and 6-9pm; winter 5-8pm.
**Telephone Office:** On southern bank of Bahr Yusef, 2 bridges west of the tourist office. International calls available. Open 24hr.
**Buses and Service:** The bus station behind the youth hostel, 1km east of the tourist office, serves **Cairo** (every 15min., 6am-8pm, 2hr., E£3.50). *Service* leave from here to Giza Sq. in Cairo (E£5; faster but more dangerous). Another bus/*service* station serves Beni Suef and **points south.** Walk to the 3rd bridge over the canal west of the tourist office, turn left, and walk 1km. Don't be misled by the local bus depot past the main crossroads: the station is 200m farther down on the right.
**Local Transportation: Service** travel around town and to nearby locales (50pt-E£1), but the town is easily walkable. You can also hire a **hantour** (horse-drawn carriage) for about E£1 anywhere in town.
**Police:** Dial 123 in an emergency.
**Post Office:** 100m south of the first bridge east of the tourist office. Open Sat.-Thurs. 8am-3pm. **EMS** and **poste restante** available.
**Telephone Code:** 048.

## ACCOMMODATIONS

Fayyum City has a few cheap beds, but the 40-km long Lake Qar'un and heavenly Wadi el-Ruwayan are much more peaceful roosting options. The **Fayyum Youth Hostel** (ask for *"shabab"*) at Hadaka, Block 7, Flat #7 (tel. 32 36 82) is clean, budget-friendly, and has a common kitchen for guest use. With your back to the hustlers at the Cairo bus stop, turn left and walk 250m to the intersection with a five-story red brick building. Take a sharp left, then another left at the green "FYH" sign 50m ahead. The hostel is the second building on the right (dorm beds E£3). The **Palace Hotel** (tel. 32 12 22), on El Huriyya St. one block west of the tourist office under a blue English sign, has clean, breezy rooms overlooking the canal, with folded-down sheets, towel, and soap. Owner Ashraf Arafa speaks flawless English and is more helpful than the tourist office. (Singles E£20, with shower E£30, with A/C E£45. Doubles E£35, with shower E£45, with A/C E£60. Tax and continental breakfast included. Lunch and dinner E£13-15.)

## FOOD

*Kushari* and falafel shops cluster around the railroad tracks. **Cafeteria El Medina** (tel. 32 20 28), in the town center, has a pleasant view of the waterwheels, outdoor seating, attentive service, and tasty spiced pigeon. Meals with rice are E£20-25. The **Governorate Club,** on Governorate St., has the best *kabab* in town but watery *tahina*. Ask your *hantour* driver for *Nadi el-Muhafzah*. You can get full meals here for under E£10 (open until 1am). For a sugar shot, head over to **Lebanon Pastry** (tel. 32 29 36) on El Goumhouriyya St. (3 bridges from the tourist office), which offers ice cream and Egyptian sweets for 25pt-E£1 (open daily 10am-1am).

## SIGHTS

The main attractions within Fayyum city are Egyptians living tourist-free lives. Visitors who weren't ossified by the Islamic architecture in Cairo should visit the Mamluk **Mosque of Qaytbay,** about 1km west of the town center, along the canal, at the very end of El Huriyya St. The mosque is named for the Mamluk Sultan El Ashraf Seif ed-Din Qaytbay, who ruled Egypt from 1468 to 1496. It was built by a river that once flowed here, allowing worshippers to wash before prayers. The ivory on the *mihrab* was brought all the way from Somalia. For a quick introduction to the rural life of Fayyum, head north out of town along Bahr Sinnuris. After 2km of boundless green fields, you'll reach the first of seven **waterwheels,** still used in the irrigation system. Unlike Western versions, these great wooden tires are not used to power pumps, but are pumps themselves, ingeniously using the flow of the stream to lift the water to a higher level.

## ■ Near Fayyum

**Ain Sileen Springs,** 18km northwest of town, is the most easily reached but least rewarding of the area's attractions. The road to the springs winds through fields bristling with corn, palms, fruits, and vegetables, split into perfect sections by canals. The most convenient way to get there is to take a *service* or bus from the station (35-50pt). Several restaurant-cafés provide a place to sit and imbibe as the murky streams babble by. The water, high in titanium, is supposedly good for hypertension. Drink from the springs at your own risk. The springs feed a small swimming pool crammed with Egyptian children. Foreigners bathing here will create a stir; foreign women will cause widespread apoplexy. A visit to the "Exhibition of Productive Families," which displays local carpet and clothing articles, will arouse less controversy. There's a tourist office 50m from the springs road and several small farm stands selling the sweetest mangos you'll ever taste. A restaurant with gorgeous views of the greenery serves *kabab* (E£10), pigeon (E£7), and salads (E£1).

Fifteen km farther north past sunflower patches is the salt-water **Lake Qar'un**, lined with expensive hotels and day-use picnic areas on its southern shore. The beaches have a tropical feel, with toasty sand, warm, inviting, blue-green water, and palm frond *palapas* offering shade. The beaches are within daytripping range from Cairo and a quick jaunt from cheap rooms in Fayyum. The closest you can get to budget lakeside accommodations is the air-conditioned **Waha Hotel** (singles E£40, doubles E£60; tax and breakfast included). In winter, the hotel rents jet skis, wind surfers, and other water toys. **Tourist police** are located near the Auberge Hotel.

To reach Ain Sileen, Lake Qar'un, or any point north of Fayyum, walk north from the information stand to the railroad tracks running parallel to Bahr Yusef Canal. Turn left and walk to the fourth crossing; you'll find a "taxi" stand 300m down on your left. Pickup trucks shuttle between Fayyum and Ain Sileen (50pt) and Lake Qar'un (E£1). It will probably be necessary to change trucks at the village of **Sanhur** to reach the lake; the total price should be the same.

Wonderful **Wadi er-Ruwayan** lake and waterfalls are an hour's drive from Lake Qar'un, along what becomes a pure desert passage. You can hire a taxi from Fayyum or Lake Qar'un to bring you here (no more than E£40 per carload), and hitching is reportedly easy (although always risky) in the winter. Sand dunes and cool cobalt waters ripple side by side, separated by no more than a few meters of lush greenery. If you find it hard to tear yourself away, lounge amidst camel herds at the aptly named **Paradise Safari Camp,** owned by English-speaking Muhammad Marzuk (E£17.50 per person; breakfast included). The camp, on the lake's shore, is surrounded by golden dunes ripe for exploration. Each large tent has two crisp-sheeted beds and a nightstand with a candle (there is no electricity here besides the generator, which is used solely for the refrigerator in the kitchen). The three waterfalls, a two-minute walk from the camp, plunge 3m over the mossy rocks into a clear lake (admission to park E£5, car E£5). Be sure to bring plenty of sunblock and insect repellent. A restaurant serves meals for E£15.

Far less spectacular is **Hawara Pyramid,** 9km southeast of Fayyum City, built by Amenemhat III's daughter to honor her father (19th century BCE). In order to confuse grave robbers, she had the entrance constructed at the southern side of the pyramid. This little device, however, did not prevent looters from snagging Amenemhat's body and booty. Climb to the top for an excellent view of the region. The best way to reach Hawara is to take a private (E£10) or collective (E£2) taxi 6km toward Hawara and then walk 3km into the desert.

# Mediterranean Coast

## ■ Alexandria الا سكندر ية

Cleopatra doesn't live here anymore. Nor would she want to, after seeing the changes the city has undergone since her rendezvous with the asp. The wonders that made Alexandria *the* place to be in the first century CE—the world's greatest library, the monumental lighthouse, the tomb of Alexander the Great—are all gone. The famed Hellenistic city is literally buried under the new metropolis. But don't fret; the library would be musty by now and the lighthouse malfunctioning. Modern Alexandria has been called the Pearl of the Mediterranean, a wonderful blend of Middle Eastern and European culture. The few ancient sites that have been excavated are complemented by European architecture: stony façades, colorful mosaics, and red brick tiles characterize the buildings along the encircling curve of the bay.

Cairenes by the thousands are attracted to Alexandria during the summer, and with good reason. Although Alexandria shares the dirt, crowding, noise, and poverty associated with Cairo, a different spirit pervades this city. Whereas summer in Cairo sears streets and patience alike, in Alexandria it gently warms vacationing Gulf Arabs, Afri-

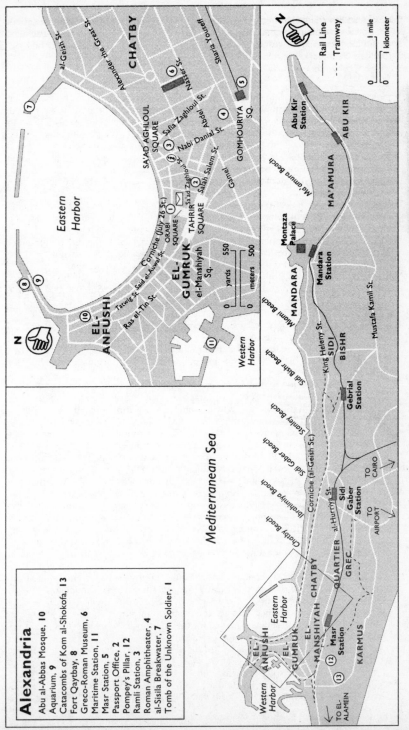

EGYPT

**Alexandria**

Abu al-Abbas Mosque, 10
Aquarium, 9
Catacombs of Kom al-Shokofa, 13
Fort Qaytbay, 8
Greco-Roman Museum, 6
Maritime Station, 11
Masr Station, 5
Passport Office, 2
Pompey's Pillar, 12
Ramli Station, 3
Roman Amphitheater, 4
al-Sisila Breakwater, 7
Tomb of the Unknown Soldier, 1

Rail Line
Tramway

1 mile
1 kilometer

*Mediterranean Sea*

*Eastern Harbor*

*Western Harbor*

CHATBY

EL-ANFUSHI

EL-GUMRUK

GOMHOURIYA SQ.

SA'AD AGHLOUL SQUARE

TAHRIR SQUARE

ORABI SQUARE

el-Manshiyah Sq.

al-Geish St.

Alexander the Great St.

Shaha Youseff

Nasser St.

Safia Zaghloul St.

Nabi Danial St.

Said Zaghloul St.

Salah Salem St.

Gamel Abdel

Corniche (July 26 St.)

Corniche (al-Auwal St.)

Tatwig St.

Ras el-Tin St.

Said el-Auwal St.

ABU KIR

Abu Kir Station

MA'AMURA

Montaza Palace

Mandara Station

MANDARA

Miami Beach

Ma'amura Beach

SIDI BISHR

Gebrial Station

Sidi Bishr Beach

King Helmy St.

Stanley Beach

Sidi Gaber Beach

Sidi Gaber Station

Corniche (al-Geish) St.

al-Hurriya St.

Ibrahimiya Beach

QUARTIER GREC

Chatby Beach

EL-MANSHIYAH

EL-GUMRUK

EL-ANFUSHI

Masr Station

KARMUS

TO CAIRO

TO AIRPORT

TO EL-ALAMEIN

Mustafa Kamil St.

550 yards

500 meters

cans, and Egyptians. During the day hundreds of thousands splash in the Mediterranean, while at night they stroll along the corniche or fritter their time in theaters, nightclubs, cafés, and restaurants until the wee hours. If El Qahira is "The Conqueror," then El Iskandariyya is surely the spoils.

## HISTORY

Alexander the Great was in good spirits in 331 BCE, for that year the over-achieving young emperor had wrested Egypt from the Persians. After a triumphant but tasteful reception at Memphis, he set off for the Oracle of Amun in the distant Siwa Oasis to discover whether or not he was actually the offspring of divinity—he was. On the way down the seacoast he happened upon Rhakotis, a small fishing village blessed with a fine natural harbor. Instantly enamored by the spot, he ordered a city to be built there. Exhibiting a charming Ramsesian modesty, he dedicated it to himself. Then, leaving his architect Dinocrates behind to figure out the details, he left for Siwa and never came back.

Upon Alexander's death nine years later, Egypt fell into the hands of his general, Ptolemy Soter. Ptolemy glorified his former employer with attention to the new city. He even got carried away and hijacked Alexander's corpse—which was on its way to Siwa according to the emperor's last wishes—and interred it with great pomp under Alexandria's main square. The body, its tomb, and the whole of the Ptolemaic city are now supposedly buried somewhere underneath the downtown jungle.

Ptolemy and his descendants dedicated themselves to bringing the best of Greek civilization to Egyptian soil. The Museion, including the famous 500,000-volume Library, was the greatest center of learning in the ancient world. Euclid invented his geometry here, while Erastosthenes estimated the circumference of the earth. To satisfy the spiritual needs of his subjects, Ptolemy gathered a committee of Egyptian and Greek theologians who together devised a tremendously popular syncretic faith in which aspects of the Hellenic god Zeus and the Pharaonic god Apis (in the form of a bull) were fused into the new deity, Serapis. Pompey's Pillar is from a temple built for the new god by Diocletian.

With the construction of the Lighthouse of Pharos Island under Ptolemy II, the city became the site of one of the seven wonders of the ancient world. The immense 400-ft. tower featured multiple mirrors and a flaming beacon. Ships packed the previously unused harbor with increasing frequency and Alexandria traded its way to become the richest commercial center of its day. The city's bountiful culture inevitably solicited the attention of those pesky Romans. When Roman general Pompey's 48 BCE power grab went sour at Pharsalus, he fled to Egypt with his rival Julius Caesar in hot pursuit. There they found a 15-year-old king, Ptolemy XIV, fighting a civil war with a 20-year-old queen—his sister and wife—the enchanting Cleopatra VII. Whether you prefer Shakespeare's version or Hollywood's, the story is all too familiar. Ptolemy tried to charm Caesar by assassinating Pompey, but Cleopatra tried more subtle tactics: she won his favor and bore his child. After Caesar's death she and Marc Antony hooked up, pragmatically dreaming of ruling the known world. But it was not to be: defeated by Octavian (soon to be the Emperor Augustus Caesar) at the Battle of Actium, the lovers committed suicide rather than be paraded through Rome in chains.

Alexandria lost superpower status under Roman control as its fortunes waxed and waned with those of the Empire. Scholarly interests shifted from science to theology. The first Greek translation of the Hebrew Bible, the Septuagint, was written here for the expatriate Jewish population after the destruction of the Temple in Jerusalem. Many think that the translation is named for the 70 scholars who each labored in isolation and yet reputedly produced the exact same text.

Legend also teaches that St. Mark introduced Christianity here in 62 CE, founding what would become the Coptic Church. Mass 3rd-century conversions transformed Alexandria into a Christian spiritual center, but Roman persecutions increased accordingly. The oppression reached a bloody height under Diocletian, who murdered so many Christians that the Copts date their calendar from the beginning of his reign, calling it the Martyr's Calendar. The basilica of the **Church of St. Mark** is visible today on Coptic Church St.

Once Emperor Constantine converted, the influence of the Christians grew and they turned on their pagan neighbors with vengeful fury. The last remnant of the Great Library was burned during anti-Roman riots in 309. The Egyptian Church differed from the Byzantine and challenged the authority of the latter by establishing a Patriarchate of its own in Alexandria. The Byzantines persecuted the schismatic Copts to such a degree that when Amr Ibn el-Ass conquered Egypt (with an army of recently Islamicized Arabs) in 640, he was received as a liberator. Alexandria fell on hard times under Arab Rule. The new capital in Cairo eclipsed Alexandria's glory, and a series of earthquakes in the 13th century finally reduced the immense lighthouse to rubble. Pharos Island itself gradually silted in and became a peninsula, attached by an hourglass-shaped isthmus. The Mamluks exiled political opponents to Alexandria, and by the time the canal from the Nile dried up, the city found itself a neglected backwater has-been.

Napoleon Bonaparte arrived to try his luck in Egypt in 1798. After fortifying the city walls and building some forts, the French forces got spanked by Admiral Nelson in the naval battle at Abu Qir, and took to their heels in 1801.

The modern city burst forth, rejuvenated, when Muhammad Ali made it a port for his navy and redug the canal to the Nile. During the 19th century Alexandria became a favorite holiday spot for expatriate Europeans, wealthy Turks, and Egyptians. The entire colonial government migrated here from Cairo for the summer. After the Revolution of 1952, Alexandria endured extensive building and heavy crowding. Today, with over five million inhabitants, it is Egypt's biggest port, second-largest city, and summer capital. Perhaps the most famous history of the city, the fabulous *Alexandria: A History and Guide,* was written by one-time resident E.M. Forster.

## ORIENTATION

The governorate of Alexandria stretches from Abu Qir Bay to the western harbor. The entire 28km of coastline is crowded with glistening skyscrapers and deteriorating hotels jockeying for position near the Mediterranean. Ancient Alexandria was built around Pharos Island (now a peninsula separating the Eastern and Western harbors), and the area still serves as the heart of the city. This downtown commercial district, called **El Manshiyya, Mahattat er-Raml** (Raml Station), or simply **El Balad** (the city), is the hub of Alexandria's transportation network, nightlife, and tourist trade. Along the gentle curve of the eastern harbor, just west of downtown, lies **El Goumrouk,** a colorful, grandiose, residential neighborhood that is home to many old mosques. Immediately southeast of El Manshiyya lies **El Attarien,** which encompasses **Misr Railway Station,** the city's main depot. South of El Manshiyya and El Attarien, the streets of **Karmouz** overflow with students, workers, and the rest of the proletariat. Here you will find Pompey's Pillar and the Catacombs of Kom esh-Shoqafa. El Anfoushi occupies the furthest tip of Pharos Island, and is home to the majestic Fort Qaytbay.

When downtown, the best way to orient yourself is **Sa'ad Zaghloul Square,** on the waterfront with a massive statue of the man himself. Four streets border the square: on the north side is the **corniche;** on the west side in front of the Cecil Hotel is **Nabi Daniel Street,** running south through downtown to the **service taxi station;** on the east side is **Safia Zaghloul Street,** the city center's principal north-south boulevard, running through downtown and ending at Misr Station; on the south side of the square heading east is **Alexander the Great Street;** and on the south side heading west to Orabi Sq. is **El Ghorfa et-Tigariyya Street.** Both Safia Zaghloul and Nabi Daniel run south up a slight hill at the top of which they are intersected by **Sultan Hussein Street,** and then descend to their intersections with **Al Huriyya St.**

Bordering the southeast corner of Sa'ad Zaghloul Sq. is **Raml Station Square,** the main depot for the intracity tramway and a hub for intercity buses. Many municipal buses and minibuses service the busy stop in front of the square on the corniche or on the south side across from Trianon Café. To add to the confusion, this municipal bus stop on the south side of Sa'ad Zaghloul Sq. is sign-posted "Raml Station."

Heading west on Raml Station Sq.'s south side is **Sa'ad Zaghloul Street** (which does *not* border Sa'ad Zaghloul Sq.), a main shopping artery which runs to **Orabi Square.** The two squares serve as transportation nuclei. All yellow trams out of Raml Station pass through here and this is where a number of minibuses begin their journeys. The southern end is also called Tahrir Sq., and the larger general area El Manshiyya Sq.

The **corniche** starts at the northern tip of El Anfoushi and winds the length of the city to reach **Montaza Palace** and **Ma'mura Beach** (a swell hangout for the kids), which demarcate the city's far eastern borders. Note that the corniche is also called **26th July Road** along the Eastern Harbor and **El Geish Road** between Es-Silsilah breakwater (the western promontory of the Eastern Harbor) and Montaza.

In addition to the corniche, the stretch from downtown to Ma'mura is traversed by two main arteries. The first one inland is **Alexander the Great (El Iskandar al-Akbar) Street** which changes its name to Omar Lotfy Street in Chatby, Sidi Gaber Street as it heads past the sporting club, Ahmed Shawki Street in Roushdi, President Abdel Salam 'Aret Street from Gleem to the Victoria tram station (the end of the line), and finally Khaled Ibn al-Walid Street through Sidi Bishr until it ends at Miami (yes, Miami) Beach. The second is **Abu Qir,** also called Fouad Street or Al Huriyya Street, though officially named Gamal Abd en-Nasser Street. Lined with banks, businesses, and travel agencies, Abu Qir runs all the way to Montaza.

Needless to say, Alexandria is confusing—a map is critical to success. *Archaeological Sites of Alexandria* (E£25) is an excellent all-purpose map available at **Al-Ma'aref Bookstore,** or for more money and less hassle at the Cecil Hotel giftshop. The Schutz American School's *Guide Book to Alexandria* (E£25), with its fold-out neighborhood maps, is great for navigating the city's tangled streets.

Alexandria is a big city and has its share of hustlers. Two scams have become popular recently: taking tourists to the duty-free store to buy alcohol (then who knows where), and impersonating police officers. While the first is relatively harmless, the second should be brought to the attention of the tourist police. Nevertheless, pedestrians should feel pretty safe both day and night. Foreign women, as always, will have to deal with comments and stares.

## GETTING AROUND

Your feet will serve you well in downtown Alexandria. The main squares, transportation centers, and the corniche all lie within walking distance along clogged and crowded streets. A brisk half-hour walk will take you from old Pharos Island to the Shooting Club along the corniche (especially enjoyable at night).

To visit the rest of the city, take a municipal tram, bus or minibus, or a private microbus or taxi. **Trams** all start from Raml Station and come in two colors. Blue trams head east and pass by the Sporting Club before ending at En-Nasr Station. Yellow trams head west and pass Orabi Sq. before turning north or south. They run every few minutes until midnight (sometimes until 1am; Ramadan until 2am) for only 10pt per ride. The middle car of every three-car tram is for women only; on two-car trams, one is marked "ladies" and the other "gentlemen." Hop on at any stop and pay on board. Find out which one to take by looking at maps in the stations or talking to Alexandria's finest. The tram is comfortable and convenient, though slow for longer runs.

### City Buses

There are four main terminals—two in Sa'ad Zaghloul Sq. (on the northern corniche side and on the southern intercity bus stop side), one in Orabi Sq., and one in Misr Station. Buses run from approximately 5:30am to midnight or 1am (2am during Ramadan) and cost 10-25pt, 50pt to outside beaches like El Agami or Montaza. Buses are only marked in Arabic numerals.

**#220** (٢٢٠): From Orabi Sq. to Sidi Bishr.
**#221** (٢٢١): From Orabi Sq. to Ma'mura.
**#238** (٢٣٨): From Orabi Sq. along the corniche to Montaza.
**#250** (٢٥٠): From Misr Station to Montaza and Abu Qir.
**#260** (٢٦٠): From Orabi Sq. to Montaza Palace and Abu Qir.
**#302** (٣٠٢) and **310** (٣١٠): From Orabi Sq. to the airport.
**#309** (٣٠٩): From the south side of Sa'ad Zaghloul Sq. to Pompey's Pillar.
**#460** (٤٦٠): From the south side of Sa'ad Zaghloul Sq. to El Agami (Hannoville, through Bitash).

## Minibuses

A more appetizing alternative to the crowded city buses, these run from 5:30am to 1am (2am in Ramadan) and cost 25-50pt. Stand somewhere on the side of the street and hold up the number of fingers equal to the number of passengers in your group. If there's room inside, the driver will nod and pull over.

**From Orabi Square: #703** (٧٠٣), **710** (٧١٠) to the zoo and airport; **#724** (٧٢٤) to Sa'ad Zaghloul Sq., the zoo, Smouha, and Sidi Gaber; **#736** (٧٣٦) to Ma'mura.
**From Sa'ad Zaghloul Sq.: #707** (٧٠٧) to Kom esh-Shoqafa; **#724** (٧٢٤) to the zoo, Smouha, and Sidi Gaber train station; **#750** (٧٥٠), **760** (٧٦٠) to El Agami.
**From Misr Station: #728** (٧٢٨) to Montaza and Abu Qir; **#729** (٧٢٩) to Abu Qir, **#755** (٧٥٥), **765** (٧٦٥) to El Agami; **#770** (٧٧٠) to Ma'mura.
**From Montaza: #719** (٧١٩) to Sa'ad Zaghloul Sq. and Qaytbay.
**From Ras et-Tin: #735** (٧٣٥) to Montaza (along the corniche).

## Taxis

A local taxi ride in Alexandria is marginally less death-defying than in Cairo, and a comparatively inexpensive way to avoid the slow grind of the tram and the sardine-can squalor of the city buses. Don't wait for an empty taxi: hail one going in your direction containing one or two passengers and shout your destination into the window. The meters never run, so pay as you please. No matter how big your group (3 is the maximum), you can get away with E£2 to almost anywhere, E£3 if you're feeling generous. Longer trips (Montaza or Abu Qir) enter the E£4-5 range, and past midnight E£5-7 is expected. Long trips past midnight (the length of the city to Montaza) will be E£10. There is a E£1 minimum (even for a block or two) and as a tourist you will be haggled for more than the fair price.

## INTERCITY TRANSIT

Alexandria lies at the junction of lush Delta farmlands, the barren Western Desert, and the Mediterranean coast. Cairo is a three-hour drive to the southeast on either of two roads. The scenic Delta road (231km) crosses both branches of the Nile and passes through the industrial city of Tanta, while the desert road (225km) nudges Wadi Natrun and passes through Giza.

### Buses

**Superjet Buses** (tel. 482 43 91) offer A/C, snacks, drinks, bathrooms, and annoyingly loud Egyptian movies. Buses depart from ticket booth on south side of Sa'ad Zaghloul Sq. Buses to Cairo every 30min. around the clock. To downtown E£17, to the airport E£22 (3hr.). From 5pm to 12:30am, E£28 to either destination. Daily buses to: Marsa Matrouh (7:45am and 4pm in summer only, 6hr., E£20); Hurghada (1:45 and 8pm, 12hr., E£65); and Port Said (6:45am, 4½hr., E£20).
**West Delta Bus Company** (tel. 80 96 85) has 2 types of buses. Regular buses run to destinations within Egypt and are not A/C, while **Golden Arrow** buses are reserved for longer distances, and offer the same luxuries as Superjet. Daily buses go to: Cairo, stopping at Giza Sq., Tahrir Sq., and usually the airport (every 30min.-1hr., 5:30am-10:30pm and 12:30am, 3hr., E£13-20 depending on destination and time of departure); Marsa Matrouh (7, 8, 11am, 1, and 5pm, 6hr., E£10-15); Port Said (A/C at 6am and 4:30pm, E£15; non-A/C at 8am and noon, E£12; 4½hr.);

Ismailiyya (7am and 2:30pm, both with A/C, 5hr., E£10); Suez (9 and 11am, 4½hr., E£12); Siwa (noon, A/C, 8hr., E£20); Hurghada (6pm, A/C, 12hr., E£37); Tanta (10am, noon, 4, and 6pm, no A/C, 1½hr., E£8, ); Mansura (7am, noon, 1, and 3pm, no A/C, 3hr., E£6); Zagazig (8 and 10am, 2 and 4pm, 3hr., E£7); Dumyat (Damietta) (6:30 and 7:30am, 2 and 3:30pm, 3hr., E£10); and Mataria (2:30pm, 3hr., E£10).

## Trains

In addition to the regular, slow, non-air-conditioned trains to Cairo that run constantly (inquire at the tourist office in Misr Station), there are two varieties of express trains. The turbo **Turbini** trains leave at 7am, 2, 3, 6, 7:30, and 10pm for E£22 first class, E£20 second class; the 8am and 7pm departures are E£2-3 cheaper (2hr., 30% student discount). The slightly slower French line departs at 6, 8:15, 10, 11am, 1, 3:30, 5, 7:30, 8, 9, and 9:30pm (2½hr.; E£17 first class, E£12 second class, 30% student discount). Trains to Marsa Matrouh leave at 6:40am (with A/C, E£17) or 1:30pm (without A/C, E£8) and take six hours. A train direct to Luxor and points south leaves at midnight (12hr., E£18, no A/C), and to Luxor only at 10:10pm (11hr.; E£60 1st-class, E£36 2nd-class, student discounts available).

## Service Taxis

*Service* are cheap and generally comfortable alternative to bus or train transport. Because of all the competition from other means of transportation, however, they depart less frequently than in other cities. Shared vans or station wagons (mainly Peugeots) depart from Misr Station, in front of the main gates. *Service* go to Cairo (3hr. by the desert road, E£10), Marsa Matrouh (3hr., E£10), Tanta (2hr., E£4), Mansura (3hr., E£4), Abu Qir (30min., 60pt), Zagazig (2hr., E£10), Rashid (1hr., E£3), and Port Said (4hr., E£10).

## Planes

**EgyptAir** is at 19 Sa'ad Zaghloul St., just east of Raml Station Sq. (tel. 482 59 38, open daily 8am-8pm). Alexandria's small airport lies several km southeast of downtown. Local buses #302 and 310 and minibuses #703 and 710 run between Orabi Sq. and the airport. **Lufthansa,** 6 Tala'at Harb St. (tel. 483 59 83 or 70 31), flies nonstop from Alexandria to Frankfurt Wed. and Sun. at 8am. **Olympic Airlines,** on Sa'ad Zaghloul St. one block east of EgyptAir (tel. 482 10 14 or 72 95; fax 482 89 01; open Mon.-Fri. 8:30am-4:30pm, Sat. 8:30am-12:30pm), flies from Alexandria to Athens (one way E£920, E£610 for youth).

# PRACTICAL INFORMATION

**Tourist Office:** Main office on Nabi Daniel St., at the southwest corner of **Sa'ad Zaghloul Sq.** English spoken fluently. Open in summer daily 8:30am-6pm, winter 8:30am-5pm, Ramadan 9am-4pm, holidays 8am-2pm. Branch offices at **Misr Station** (tel. 492 59 85; same hours) and the **Maritime Station** (tel. 480 34 94; open 8am-5pm and additional hours for boat arrivals), and at the **airport** (tel. 420 10 36). Pick up a free copy of *Alexandria by Night and Day,* which lists restaurants, hotels, travel agents, and a train schedule to Cairo, and *Alexandria and the Beaches,* which includes a map and descriptions of the sights along the coast.

**Tourist Police: Montaza Palace** (tel. 547 33 95). Branch office upstairs from the tourist office in **Sa'ad Zaghloul Sq.** (tel. 483 33 78). Both open 24hr. Also branches in the **amphitheater** (tel. 490 62 73), **Citadel** (tel. 80 91 44), and the **Greco-Roman Museum** (tel. 482 89 12). **Emergency Phone Number:** 126.

**Passport Office:** 28 Tala'at Harb St. (tel. 483 71 72). Walk west on Sa'ad Zaghloul St. from Raml Station Sq. and bear left on Falaky St. when Sa'ad Zaghloul curves toward the sea. Tala'at Harb St. is your first left. Open Sat.-Wed. 8:30am-2pm and 7-9pm, Thurs. 8:30am-1:30pm and 7-9pm (evening hours for passport registration only). The passport office is a hassle; conduct your business in Cairo if possible.

**Consulates: U.K.,** 3 Mena St., Rushdi (tel. 546 70 01), off Kafr Abdou St. About 6km east of downtown, several blocks south of the corniche. Open Sun.-Thurs. 8am-1pm. **Ireland,** 36 Khafra Abd Street, Roushdi (tel. 546 46 86). Open Sun.-Thurs.

9am-3pm. **Israel,** 207 Abd es-Salem Aref St., Loran (tel. 586 38 74). Open Sun.-Thurs. 9:30am-12:30pm. For **U.S.** consular questions, contact the American Center (see Cultural Centers, below) or the U.S. Embassy in Cairo.

**Currency Exchange:** Many exchange places offer better rates than banks but will only take cash. Egyptian banks are on every other downtown corner; most are open Sat.-Thurs. 8:30am-noon or 2pm and 5-7 or 8pm. For the fastest service, hit the **National Bank of Egypt** in the **Cecil Hotel** in Sa'ad Zaghloul Sq. (open Sun.-Thurs. 9am-9pm, Fri.-Sat. 9am-1pm and 6-8pm) or in the **Sheraton Montaza** on the corniche (tel. 548 05 50; open daily 9am-10pm). The **Bank of Alexandria,** centrally located at 59 Sa'ad Zaghloul St. (tel. 483 85 88 or 89), is open daily 8:30am-2pm and 6-10pm. **Bank Misr,** Safia Zaghloul St. between the Metro Cinema and Al Huriyya St. won't redeem traveler's checks, but gives Visa and MC advances. Open Sun.-Thurs. 8:30am-2pm.

**American Express:** Main office at 34 El Mou'asker er-Roumani St., 50m south of the Pizza Hut on the corniche in Rushdi (tel. 85 73 43 or 17 08; fax 545 73 63). Open Sat.-Thurs. 8:30am-5pm. Full service office, but it doesn't hold mail. Friendly, smaller branch office that will hold mail is **Eyres Travel,** 26 Al Huriyya St. (tel. 483 00 84 or 12 75), 5 blocks south of Sa'ad Zaghloul Sq. (via Safia Zaghloul St.). Open Mon.-Sat. 9am-1pm.

**Thomas Cook:** 15 Sa'ad Zaghloul Sq., P.O. Box 6 (tel. 482 78 30; fax 483 40 73). Full range of Thomas Cook services. Open daily 8am-5pm. Another office in the **airport** (tel. 420 87 64) exchanges currency and traveler's checks.

**Telephone Office:** The 24-hr. **Raml Station Sq.** office charges E£24 for 3min. to the U.S.; minimal phone card discount. Also at **Misr Station** (24hr.; phones require cards, but they don't sell them), at the west end of **Sa'ad Zaghloul St.** on the corner of Sultan Hussein St. (open daily 7am-midnight), and in the post office on Safia Zaghloul St. **Luxury hotels** (try the Cecil in Sa'ad Zaghloul Sq.) will let you call overseas but charge more. **Information:** tel. 125.

**Car Rental: Avis,** in the Cecil Hotel, Sa'ad Zaghloul Sq. (tel. 480 72 24; fax 483 64 01; open daily 8am-10pm) rents a Fiat (E£127, 50pt. every km over 100). Insurance and emergency assistance are extra—but if you really want to drive in this vehicular slaughterhouse they're probably worth it.

**Cotton Candy Machine Rental:** The roving dealership is usually stationed in Orabi Sq. Ask for the "Fluffy Ahmed" week-long special (E£32).

**English Bookstores:** The best is **Al-Ma'aref,** 44 Sa'ad Zaghloul St. (tel. 483 33 03), which also has an entrance on the south side of Sa'ad Zaghloul Sq. Strange selection of textbooks, translations of Arabic works, and trashy paperbacks. Open Mon.-Sat. 10am-9:30pm. Others are located along Safia Zaghloul St., but have very limited selections among stacks of Arabic books.

**Cultural Centers: U.S.,** 3 Phara'ana St. (tel. 481 43 05). Take a left on Al Huriyya St. from Safia Zaghloul St., walk 1 block past the sign for the Greco-Roman Museum, turn left and then the first right. Fine book/video library. Inquire about teaching **jobs** at the English Teaching Program. Cultural events calendar posted outside. Open Sun.-Thurs. 8am-4pm; closed Aug. for inventory. **British Council,** 9 Ptolemies St. (tel. 482 98 90 or 481 01 99). Open Sun.-Thurs. 10am-2pm. Library open Sun.-Thurs. 10am-7:30pm, Sat. 10am-3pm.

**Photography and Film Developing: Kodak,** 45 Safia Zaghloul St. (tel. 483 08 39). Wide selection of film, E£9-30 per roll. Developing E£2.50, plus 75pt per print. Open Mon.-Sat. 9am-10pm.

**Pharmacy:** Many are scattered throughout downtown. **Sadr Pharmacy,** 22 El Ghorfa et-Tigariyya St. (tel. 80 57 80), is open daily 9am-11pm. **Pharmacie Suisse,** 23 Sa'ad Zaghloul St., across from the tram station (tel. 483 36 36), is filled with antique woodwork (not to be missed). Open Sat.-Thurs. 10am-11pm.

**Hospital: El Mowasah,** on Al Huriyya St. in Al Haddara (tel. 421 28 85).

**Ambulance:** Tel. 123.

**Police:** Tel. 122. If possible, contact the Tourist Police (above).

**Post Office:** All open Sat.-Thurs. 8am-3pm and do **EMS** (until 2pm) unless otherwise noted. A branch at the tram stop at **Raml Station Sq.** (tel. 482 07 46) and 2 on **El Ghorfa et-Tigariyya St.** (3 blocks west of Sa'ad Zaghloul Sq. and 2 blocks

west of Orabi Sq.) with no EMS, but **Poste Restante** until 1pm (packages held at **Misr Station,** 10m south of Al Huriyya).
**Telephone Code:** 03.

## ACCOMMODATIONS

E.M. Forster liked Alexandria so much he wrote a book about it and even named a character in *A Room with a View* after the Cecil Hotel. Unfortunately, affordable rooms with views (along the streets running south from the corniche near Raml Station Sq.) come with a menagerie of critters ranging from tiny, bloodthirsty ticks to giant, armor-plated assault roaches (rooms about E£10 per night). It's better to stay in one of the hotels listed below: all are clean, cheap, and within walking distance of the two main squares. None have fans, unless noted; most Alexandrians depend on sea breezes for their air conditioning. In summer, look for corner rooms with cross ventilation.

Streets in **El Manshiyya Sq.** bristle with budget hotels. For a beachside retreat, head out to Sidi Bishr (14km) or Montaza (18km), where the amenities balance the inconvenience of staying so far from the center of town. For serious piaster-pinchers there's **camping** by the beach at Abu Qir for 50pt (see page 159).

**Hotel Marhaba,** 10 Ahmed Orabi Sq. (tel. 480 09 57 or 95 10), on the northwest side of Orabi Sq. The former summer residence of the King of Libya. May not be palatial any more, but the rooms are large and breezy, and there are 3 pool tables (E£10 per hour), an international phone, and a neat coffee shop with a neon-green lit fountain. Louis XV sitting room on each floor, and all rooms have color satellite TV. Shared baths aren't as nice as the rest of the place. Singles E£33, with bath E£53. Doubles E£60, with bath E£65. Tax and breakfast buffet included.

**Hotel Union,** 164 26th July St. (the corniche; tel. 80 73 12 or 77 71); enter on the side street. Modern rooms in an incredible location overlooking the Eastern Harbor. Sea breezes gust through the lobby. Clean shared or private bath, tiled, with bathtub. 5th-floor rooms not as nice as the others. Singles E£23, with bath E£29. Doubles E£28, with bath E£37. Mandatory breakfast E£5.50. TV for rooms with private bath E£3. Extra beds E£10. And let's not forget the 20% tax.

**New Capri Hotel,** 23 El Mina esh-Sharaya (tel. 480 93 10 or 97 03), same building as tourist office in Sa'ad Zaghloul Sq. Recently painted walls and powerful cooling winds give this 8th-floor hotel a clean, fresh feeling. Huge blue-tiled baths, wood floors, and a bright, clean dining room with a lifeboat, just in case. Singles E£28, E£33 with bath. Doubles E£42, with bath E£46. Prices include tax and breakfast.

**Hotel Acropole,** 27 Rue de Chambre de Commerce, 4th floor (tel. 80 59 80). Breezy, lacy TV lounge. Teeny, tiny toilet smells like mothballs. Beds are lumpy and dusty, but oh-so-comfy. Amazing views dictate the price. Singles E£15-25, doubles E£25-30. Breakfast included.

**Hotel Ailema,** 21 Amin Fakri St., 7th floor (tel. 482 70 11). The elaborate entrance with an elevator and revolving door may be the best thing about this place. Aged wood floors, small, spotless bathrooms. Some rooms have miniature breakfast nooks overlooking the sea. Singles E£36, with bath E£39. Doubles E£39, with bath E£54. Breakfast included.

**Sea Star Hotel,** 24 Amin Fakri St. (tel. 483 17 87 or 23 88; fax 483 23 88). With the aquarium and 3-D mosaic extravaganza in the lobby, this place actually looks like a hotel. Spacious carpeted rooms are slightly worn, with excellent baths. A professional operation. International phone and fax and a funk-oozing TV lounge. Singles E£40, doubles E£45.

**Hotel Normandy,** 8 Gamal ed-Din Yassin St., 4th floor (tel. 480 68 30). Mentioned in Australian phenom Ted Simon's landmark travel narrative *Jupiter's Travels.* All rooms have 3 beds, high ceilings, and shared baths. Some have a decent view of the water. The baths are old but clean. Summer rooms E£30 with view, E£25 without. Winter rooms: E£25, E£20. No breakfast served. Ask about discounts for students, groups, or longer stays.

**Hotel Gamil,** 8 Gamal ed-Din Yassin St., 4th floor (tel. 81 54 58). Dedicated to students and youth. Warm, polished wood in the lobby and throughout the rooms.

Small doubles dominated by big beds. Summer E£22, with no view E£16.50. Winter: E£12/E£8. Breakfast E£1.50, but free use of the kitchen.

**Hotel Dar Mekka,** 8 Gamal ed-Din Yassin St., 4th floor (tel. 480 89 40 or 78 72). Light blue molding and pseudo-antique flair make for a quaint lobby. Steamy pink tiled bathrooms manage to stay sanitary. Some rooms have balconies with ocean views. Singles E£25, doubles E£30, triples E£50. No breakfast.

## FOOD

It's no surprise that the cheapest, most abundant food in Alexandria is at *fuul* and *ta'miyya* stands. You shouldn't have to pay more than 50pt for a sandwich. The best are found around Misr Station. **El Anfushi,** also known as Old Alexandria, on the western side of the bay, is full of restaurants that have been patronized by generations of happy Alexandrians (its old buildings provide a feast for the eyes as well as for the palate). Take tram #15 from Raml Station and walk inland a few blocks. **Bakkash** is known for its *kufta* and *kabab,* **Kaddura** for its grilled fish and shrimp (E£5-30). Alexandria is renowned across the Middle East for its seafood; several good marine restaurants are listed below. Raml Station Sq. now boasts three **fast food** joints: Baskin Robbins, McDonald's (tel. 483 28 79 or 02), and KFC (tel. 482 96 58). For homesick sloths, the latter two, as well as Domino's (tel. 546 57 78), will deliver their greasy goods straight to your temporary door.

Excellent meat, fruits, seafood, and vegetables can be found in the *souq* in El Moasker (take any blue tram six or seven stops east and walk south). The fishmongers will cook your purchase on the spot for a modest fee (E£5). Standard supermarkets dot the area around Sa'ad Zaghloul Sq. Gastronomic voyeurs should sneak a peak into **Atelier Trianon,** where a jovial international staff makes all those wonderful pastries (Rue Sharm esh-Sheikh, between Istamboul and Nazmi Boutros St.), and Muhammad Ahmed's **Falafel Workshop** (go up the street from the restaurant and turn right down the first alley, in the brick building on the left), where green industrial-revolution-era falafel churners spin the chickpeas into a heavenly mash.

There are several **spirited** options. The **Asteria** liquor store sells beer, wine, and liquor seven days a week, even during Ramadan (located behind the Elite on the left). The **Venobles** has a similar selection with slightly higher prices (adjacent to the post office near the Spitfire, closed Sun.). If the Egyptian heat has made you *really* thirsty, head to the **Stella depot** behind the Cecil Hotel, where Egypt's finest brew can be bought by the case (E£20 deposit for the bottles and cans, E£2.75 per beer). Look for the Stella label-colored door.

**Muhammad Ahmed Fuul,** 17 Abd el-Fattah el-Hadari St. (tel. 483 35 76), 1 block south of Sa'ad Zaghloul Sq. and 1 block west of Safia Zaghloul St. 10m up on the left; no English sign. They say if you haven't been to Muhammad Ahmed you haven't been to Alexandria. Amazing *fuul,* falafel, and more, and nothing on the menu costs more than E£1.70. Open daily 6am-midnight, later in summer. A/C.

**Restaurant Denis,** 1 Ibn Bassam St. (tel. 483 04 57), 4 blocks east of Sa'ad Zaghloul Sq., adjacent to the corniche. Great budget seafood. Select your prey in the kitchen (fish E£35 per kg, calamari E£30, shrimp E£80) and the friendly proprietor will cook it up and serve it with a variety of breads, dips, and salads. Popular with vacationing families. Beer and wine. Open daily 9am-1am.

**Elite,** 43 Safia Zaghloul St. (tel. 482 35 92), one block north of Al Huriyya St. Breezy, stylin' artists' café and restaurant (since 1900), run by a friendly Greek matriarch. Filled with gallery posters and cynical, world-weary expats. The haze of smoke wavers with a bizarre mix of music: 50s jazz and high-energy techno. Good food, slow service. Rice with meat E£3.50, omelette E£6.50, Stella E£4.50.

**Pagoda Chinese Restaurant** (tel. 482 96 20), 5 blocks east of Sa'ad Zaghloul Sq., adjacent to the Ramses Hotel and the corniche; look for the yellow sign. A wonderful change of pace from Egyptian food, the Pagoda serves honest Americanized Chinese food at honest prices. Beef, chicken, or pork dishes around E£16, seafood around E£20. Alcohol served. Open daily 4pm-midnight.

**EGYPT**

**Taverna** (tel. 482 81 89), on the southern side of Raml Station Sq., across from the trams, next to KFC. Almost-Italian Egyptian food. Excellent pizzas and pastas E£5-9. The highly-touted *shawerma* platter (E£10) tastes like greasy corned beef; try the salad bar (E£5) instead. Good bargains at the ground-level take-away. Open daily 7am-2am. Also at Montaza Gardens (tel. 547 54 38), Manshiyya (tel. 80 49 07), Ekbal (tel. 586 48 02), and Ma'mura (tel. 547 18 63). Visa, AmEx.

**Trianon** (tel. 482 09 86), on the corner of Sa'ad Zaghloul and Raml Station Sq. An institution. Alexandrian lovebirds coo across coffee and cake in the salon while the upper crust dine in the art deco restaurant to piano accompaniment (entrees E£20-30). You can watch the world go by from white armchairs under parasols. Moussaka Trianon E£11, Beef Burguer Le Salon E£15.

**Restaurant Bleck,** 18 Sa'ad Zaghloul St. Walk west on Sa'ad Zaghloul until you're 2 blocks from Orabi Sq. Vegetable soups and salads E£1-4, Lebanese specialties E£4-14, fish and meat E£11-16, *osso bucco*, quail, and brain. Open daily 7am-11pm, limited menu after 7pm (mainly *kobebu*, a hearty meat and grain dish, and stuffed grape leaves).

**Cafeteria Asteria,** 40 Safia Zaghloul St. (tel. 482 22 93), across from the Metro Cinema. Basic, light meals in a breezy setting. The OJ rivals Florida's. Pizza E£7-9, omelettes E£3-5. Open daily 8am-midnight.

**Tikka Grill** (tel. 80 51 14 or 98 42), jutting into the Eastern Harbor near Abu el-Abbas Mosque, 1.5km west of Sa'ad Zaghloul Sq. An Alexandrian favorite with good service, an excellent salad bar, and a sweeping view of the corniche. The entrees are not as good as the supporting cast. Full meals cost around E£30. Alcohol served. Open daily 1pm-2am. AmEx, Visa, MC.

**Gad Restaurant,** on the south side of Raml Station Sq., across from the trams. Gad is a staple in Alexandria, with locations all over town. Large, zesty *ta'miyya* and *fuul* for 35pt. Greaseball *shawerma* for a few E£ more. Open daily 24hr.

**Kadoura Restaurant,** on the corniche about a block before the Tikka Grill sign. More good seafood. Pick your poison downstairs (several varieties of fish, crab, calamari, and sometimes even lobster) then head up the slippery spiral stairs for a great view of the ocean and the corniche crowd below. A gut-busting meal of seafood, salad, bread, and drink (enough for two) E£25. Open noon-midnight.

## SIGHTS

Very little remains of ancient Alexandria, as the modern city was built directly atop the old. The excellent **Greco-Roman Museum,** 5 El Mathaf er-Roumani St. (tel. 482 58 20), displays the best relics of ancient Alexandria and its Hellenistic civilization. The cult of Serapis is well represented; look for handsome sculptures of Zeus, Apis, and the Greek youth Harpocrates with his finger in his ear. The museum's courtyard contains an intriguing crocodile temple attributed to the cult of Phepheros, as well as a mummified crocodile and other assorted delights from Egypt's Greco-Roman past. There's also a large collection of brightly-painted *tanaga* statuettes, a sort of Ptolemaic action figure. To reach the museum walk south from the corniche along Safia Zaghloul St., turn left on Al Huriyya St., then again at the museum sign. (Open Sat.-Thurs. 9am-4pm, Fri. 9-11:30am and 2-4pm, Ramadan and holidays 10am-3pm. Admission E£8, students E£4; camera privileges (no flash) E£10, video E£150.)

From the museum it's an easy meander to the three major ancient sites, all of which lie within a few km of downtown. Just northwest of Misr Station and south of Cinema Amir is the beautifully preserved white marble **Roman Amphitheater,** the only one of its kind in Egypt. Behind the 13-tiered theater struggle the ruins of a Roman bath, villa, and cistern. "Guides" may offer to sneak you in for a fee, but don't bother—almost everything of interest is visible from the theater. From Sa'ad Zaghloul Sq., walk up Nabi Daniel St. past Al Huriyya St. to the next big intersection. Turn left across from a gas station and go 200m; the entrance will be on your left (open daily 9am-4pm, Ramadan 10am-3pm; admission E£3, students E£1.50).

Named by ignorant Crusaders in the Middle Ages, **Pompey's Pillar** actually dates from Diocletian's time (several centuries after Pompey), and was part of the

Serapium, a religious center where the rites of the bull god were conducted. Responding to a revolt in Alexandria, Emperor Diocletian swore that he would massacre the rebellious people until blood stained the knees of his horse. As he entered the defeated and cowering town, his mount stumbled into a pool of blood, prematurely fulfilling his oath. The emperor spared the city and its inhabitants, and the lone 25m pillar remains as a symbol of the people's gratitude to him and his klutzy horse. The ruins of the Serapium (leveled once the Roman Empire turned Christian) were excavated and the best finds were moved to the Greco-Roman museum (site open daily 9am-5pm, Ramadan 9am-3pm; admission E£3, students E£1.50).

To get to the site, take bus #309 from Raml Station Sq. and get off on Karmouz St. when you see the pillar. Enter on the southern side of the complex. You can also take tram #16 or minibus #709.

Just after the entrance to the pillar complex, take a right and climb the hill to reach the **Catacombs of Kom esh-Shoqafa** (Hill of Potsherds), three-leveled Roman tombs descending about 35m. Most noteworthy are the sculptures and reliefs of Egyptian gods with unmistakably virile Roman bodies, a blend of Pharaonic and Roman Art. A statue of jackal-headed Anubis stands near the entrance to the innermost burial chamber. To the left (as you enter the central rotunda) is the Triclinium, a set of three benches upon which mourners could recline and dine during funerary rites. (Open daily 9am-4pm, during Ramadan 9am-3pm. Admission E£6, students E£3; camera privileges E£10.)

For more graves, visit the **Tombs of Chatby,** Port Said St., across from St. Mark's College. Dating from the 4th century BCE, these tombs are believed to be the oldest surviving in Alexandria. The post-mortem trinkets that once filled the two separate chambers have been taken to the Greco-Roman museum (open daily 9am-4pm; admission E£3, students E£1.50; camera privileges E£5).

The **Anfushi tombs,** just east of the Ras et-Tin Palace on Ras et-Tin St., were built for Greek occupants who had adopted Egyptian customs in the first half of the 3rd century BCE. Cut into the limestone of what was once Pharos Island, they are placed in two groups around a staircase leading into an open court and may well extend farther under the palace gardens (open 9am-4pm; admission E£6, students E£3; camera privileges E£5). Take tram #16 or minibus #735. The **Mustafa Kamal Necropolis,** located on Moaskar el-Romani in Rushdi, consists of four tombs from the 2nd century BCE decorated in a more Hellenic style (open daily 9am-4pm; admission E£6, students E£3; camera privileges E£5). To reach the Mustafa Kamal Necropolis, take tram #1, 2, or 5.

The Islamic **Fort Qaytbay** (tel. 80 91 44) was built on the ancient island of Pharos on the foundations of the lighthouse. Silt connected the island to the mainland, leaving the fort at the tip of a peninsula that separates the eastern and western harbors. Built in 1480 CE by the Mamluk Sultan Ashraf Qaytbay, the citadel now houses the remains of the French fleet sunk by Admiral Nelson in the battle of Abu Qir. Notice the small mosque in the center of the tower; the entire fortress is aligned so that its *mihrab* faces Mecca. The fort is still classified as a military installation—try not to photograph anything too secret. (Open daily 9am-4pm and 5-11pm. Admission E£6 during the day, E£10 at night; students ½-price. Camera privileges E£5.)

To reach the fort, take yellow tram #15 west from Raml Station and get off when it makes a sharp left turn, or take any of the buses going to Ras et-Tin. You'll find yourself in the middle of an open-air **fish market.** At the point where the tram turned left, you should make a right on the road between the Kuwait Airlines sign and the mosque; the fort is at the end of this road. Minibus #707 or 719 from Raml Station Sq. will take you to the beginning of the street.

The **Mosque of Morsi Abu el-Abbas** is Alexandria's most prominent and elaborate example of Islamic architecture. Located 1km south of the fort along the corniche, it is the city's largest mosque and a destination for worshipers throughout Egypt. The holy Sidi Shehab ed-Din Abu el-Abbas ibn el-Khazragi came from Andalusia just before the expulsion of the Moors to spread the teachings of the Qur'an throughout Egypt. His tomb rests in the back of the mosque. Legend professes that he rose from his tomb to catch falling bombs during World War II raids. The coffin, like the exterior of the mosque, is often bathed in a green neon glow. Women are only allowed in the back room. (Open daily 5am-10pm, except prayer times; dress modestly.)

The **Eliahou Hannabi Synagogue** on Rue Dr. Hussein Faladi, an alley one block south of Safia Zaghloul St. between Nabi Daniel and Rue Abd el-Fattah el-Hadari, is the modern-day center of Alexandria's ancient Jewish community (open Sun.-Fri. 8am-1pm). The gracious Joe Harari (in the *Communauté Israelite Grand Rabbinate* office to the right as you enter the courtyard) will show you around, let you look at old photographs, and tell you all about Alexandrian Jewry. Built in 1885 by Baron Jacques L. de Menasce for the then-thriving community (there was a synagogue in each neighborhood), the synagogue is a towering edifice with five aisles, stained glass clerestory windows, 28 pink Italian marble columns, dangling chandeliers, and wooden pews (check out the international assemblage of names on the brass seat markers). Most other Jewish buildings in Alexandria have been destroyed. The 1860 **Temple Menasce** in Orabi Sq. still stands but is locked and guarded; the **Temple Chaaré Tefila** on Rue Eleusis in Camp Caesar was reincarnated as a mosque and then a medical clinic, and the **Hospital Israelite Foundation de Menasce** in Sporting is now the Et-Talaba Hospital. Three Jewish cemeteries, one in Mesarita and two in Chatby remain (the guards may let you in).

The **Coptic Orthodox Patriarchate** houses a beautiful church (founded in 67 CE and rebuilt in 1950) at 19 Elah Abad St., adorned with mosaics, stained glass, hanging ostrich eggs, and a finely painted iconostasis. The first 47 patriarchs of the Alexandrian See (beginning with St. Mark) now lie within; their names are listed in a nook on the right side of the church. Mark's relics are in a chapel to the left of the *haikal*. Take off your shoes before you enter. (Open daily with services Wed. at noon and Sun. and Fri. at 8am; foreigners are welcome to attend.)

The 17th-century church in the **Greek Orthodox Monastery of St. Saba** is another impressive testament to the historical importance of Christianity in Alexandria. Inside is a marble columnar table on which St. Catherine was beheaded, as well as beautiful paintings, a spectacular collection of amulets, and a gigantic bronze bell. From Sa'ad Zaghloul Sq. walk up Safia Zaghloul St. to Sultan Hussein St., make a right, then take your second left (open daily 7:30am-12:30pm and 3:30-6pm. Sun. service 8am; foreigners welcome).

Behind the Governor's residence sits the architecturally intriguing **Royal Jewelry Museum,** 27 Ahmed Yehia St., Gleem, originally the Palace of Fatima ez-Zahraa. The museum contains the gleaming baubles of the Muhammad Ali era. Most memorable are the pieces once belonging to the royal family, all of which were nationalized after the reign of King Farouk. Take tram #2 (look for the red sign) to get there. (Open Sat.-Thurs. 9am-4pm, Fri. 9-11:30am and 1:30-4pm. Admission E£10, students E£5; camera privileges E£10.) The **Fine Arts Museum** on 18 Menasha St. (tel. 493 66 16) contains a small but interesting collection of modern Egyptian art as well the city's public library. Exhibitions by contemporary foreign and Egyptian artists are often held here; call for details (open Sat.-Thurs. 9am-1pm and 5-8pm; free). From Misr Station walk east on Mahmoud Bey Salama St., along the southern side of the railroad tracks. The museum is on the right at the first major intersection, about 1km down. You can also take tram #2, 6, or 8.

---

### Show some skin—or else

Ten years ago, spotting a woman on the beach fully covered was unusual. Today, in most public beaches, it's rare to see Egyptian women baring hair, shoulders, or legs, not to mention navels. A few private clubs have reacted by creating a rule stating that women and men *must* wear bathing suits. Anyone fully clothed is not allowed to swim or lie on the beach.

## ENTERTAINMENT

### Beaches

Alexandria's most popular attraction is the waterfront. Rather than sand, the majority of the coastline in Alexandria is lined with a mixture of trash and humans busy depositing it. Environmentalists will be disheartened by both the condition of the beaches and the attitude and behavior of the beachgoers. Nevertheless, the beaches are alarmingly popular—Cairenes come here by the thousands during the blazing summer months. If the hordes and filth haven't scared you away to the Sinai, you'll be pleased to know that some sand strips are nicer than others.

The highlight of Alexandria's eastern beaches is the **Montaza Palace and Gardens** (tel. 547 30 79). Originally built in 1892, this former summer retreat of King Farouk includes 400 acres of gardens. The palace and its museum have been closed to the public, but the gardens and groves are still a favorite picnic spot for Alexandrians. The Gardens can get quite crowded on weekends, especially on Fridays. Ice cream stores, Pizza Hut, Chicken Tikka, a juice place, and a supermarket lie within the garden gates. Along the beach, you can rent pedal boats (E£15), regular boats (E£40), or jetskis (E£180) by the hour. (Admission to the gardens E£2; to a nicer beach in front of the Palestine Hotel E£15. On holidays, admission goes up to E£4 and there's only one grain of sand per person.)

Just east of Montaza you'll find **Ma'mura,** a favorite among Alexandria's youth (admission E£1.25). Both Montaza and Ma'mura can be reached by bus #221, 250, or 260, or by minibus #728, 736, or 770. Closer to the city center lies **San Stefano,** about halfway between Montaza and Sa'ad Zaghloul Sq. Chairs and umbrellas go for E£2-4, small changing rooms on the beach cost E£5 per day, and larger cabanas start at E£20. Take tram #1, 2, or 5 from Raml Station Sq. West of Alexandria, the beaches are much nicer (see p. 160).

### Bars, Clubs, and Discos

The days of Hellenistic hedonism are long gone. Despite its former cosmopolitan glory, nightlife in the city is a do-it-yourself affair. If you yearn for the mystery and exoticism that only quivering, sequin-clad flesh can capture, head to a **nightclub,** found in most luxury hotels. Try the Cecil (open 11:30pm-4am, E£65) or Lourantos (tel. 482 22 00; E£45; call for hours) for something closer to downtown. Many **discos** don't allow men to enter without women and vice versa, and some relegate unescorted males to the bar and forbid them from dancing. These rules change constantly, but are usually relaxed for foreigners (especially wealthy foreigners). Don't get too upset if you are negged—you aren't missing much. There are no cover charges, but **minimum charges** can be steep (often a good indication of drink prices). All of the discos are located in the major hotels and play a mix of Western and Arabic music. The **Ramada** is the youngest and most happening place to shake your groove (entrance on the corniche side; open nightly 10pm-4am; E£25). The beautiful people head to the **Sheraton** to display their Rolexes as they grind (open nightly 10pm-4am, E£26). The small disco at the **Cecil Hotel** is full of day-glo Oriental decor and music to match (open nightly 8pm-1am, sometimes later; E£18).

Once your tapping toes tire, make them heavier in one of several often empty **bars.** The coolest option around is the **Spitfire,** 7 Rue Bourse el-Hadema, two blocks up from the corniche between Sa'ad Zaghloul and Orabi Sq. (Stella E£6). Every inch of this expat favorite is covered in some decal or poster, and mellow western music soothes rattled nerves (they even play Jimmy Buffet's decidedly non-Egyptian classic "Why Don't We Get Drunk and Screw?"). The **Athineos** also has a bar with a view of the corniche, although it's a bit cramped (Stella E£6). To relive WWII memories, head to **Monty's Bar** on the second floor of the Cecil Hotel. Prints of classic paintings and occasional synthesizer music now occupy General Montgomery's former headquarters. If Monty's dim lights have got you down, head up to the **roof garden** for a fantastic view of the square and the water, but be careful where you mack—the sharp, green seats are actually cacti (Stella E£8 at both). The simple, breezy **Greek Club** attracts an older clientele and is popular with TOEFL teachers (Stella E£4.25). Take the blue trams east to El Moaskar, go south two blocks, then take a left; look for the "Micapaciatikoc" sign.

## Coffee, Sweets, and Smokes

Sa'ad Zaghloul Sq. is packed to the gills with coffee and pastry shops, while ice cream parlors melt all over Raml Station Sq. Along the corniche you'll find ritzy cafés and *sheesha* joints; cheaper, more traditional *ahwas* are found further inland.

**Sultana** (tel. 482 27 69), on the south side of Raml Station Sq., across from the trams. Fantastic ice cream, fruit salad, and toppings. Rotating seasonal flavors and made-while-you-watch waffle cones. A madhouse in the evenings. Open daily 8:30am-3am and they deliver.

**Brazilian Coffee Store,** two locations: a sit-down at 20 Salah Salem St. (open daily 7am-10pm) or a stand-up at 44 Sa'ad Zaghloul St. (tel. 482 50 59; open daily 7am-midnight). Home-roasted and ground beans for hot or iced coffee (E£1.50).

**Cafe Baudrot,** 23 Sa'ad Zaghloul St. A fine retreat from the busy street. Great vine-tressled garden in back for beer, tea, and pastry.

**Sofianopoulo Coffee Shop** (tel. 483 15 17), on Sa'ad Zaghloul as it curves seaward. Classic coffee shop with huge roasters and grinders. Cappuccino (E£1.25) is the cheapest around. Tang (the astronaut's drink) on tap. Open 8am-10:30pm.

**Samadi Patisserie,** adjacent to Tikka Grill, doles out generous helpings of *ba'laweh, bashouseh, kinafeh,* and other goodies. Fresh strawberry ice cream E£1.50. Open daily 10:30am-2am. Accepts Visa, MC, AmEx.

**Pastroudis** (tel. 595 43 78), Al Huriyya St., one block west of Safia Zaghloul. Art nouveau atmosphere. Cakes in a classy setting. E£5 minimum charge. Open daily 8am-9pm.

**Delices** (tel. 482 14 32), opposite the corniche in Sa'ad Zaghloul Sq. Cosmopolitan French and Middle Eastern pastry. Pricier and posher than the competition. Open daily 7am-10pm.

## Other Diversions

Alexandrian nightlife buzzes on the corniche. In summer you'll see wedding parties wherever you go, and foreigners are often invited to share in the fun. One of the liveliest areas for an **evening stroll,** people-watching, or *sheesha* is **Ma'mura,** a teenage beachfront hang-out with cafés and restaurants, usually busy past midnight (entrance E£1.25). Across from the mosque you'll find three hangouts: **Antazza Café** (no English sign) serves great *sheesha, fatir,* and pizza; **Minouche** has fine Italian food (E£5-20); and **Cafino** is a music video-equipped bar above the Antazza Café (E£15, open until 3am). Other lively hot-spots are **Sidi Bishr,** along Khalid Ibn al-Walid St. (full of shoppers and snacking strollers until 2am), and **Camp Caesar** on the corniche (with *sheesha* and drink shops blooming until 4am). For a less hectic stroll, amble through the back streets of Anfushi or El Goumrouk, both packed with interesting architecture of varying periods and styles.

**Billiards** tables, charged by the hour, are sprinkled throughout the city. You'll find the hippest table in town at **Cafino** (see above). The **Windsor Palace Hotel,** on the corniche three blocks west of Sa'ad Zaghloul Sq. (café drinks E£25, open until 4am), and **Black and White,** on the left up a side street from the lively Camp Caesar *sheesha* cafés (E£15, 24hr.), both have three tables. You'll also find tables at **Marhaba Hotel** (E£10, alcohol served), **Corail Hotel** (E£12, and you might be able to bring a drink up from the bar in their Chinese restaurant), and **Mercure Hotel** (E£25). For French (3-ball) billiards, head one block up from Raml Station Sq. on Safia Zaghloul St. (E£3). For a wetter version of **pool,** head to the ritzy, air-conditioned, 24-hour **Panorama Pool** (tel. 597 55 25), in Camp Caesar opposite the Panorama wedding hall. The upstairs *sheesha* café will give you a smoke when you're wet and panting.

Every summer the breezy, outdoor **Muhammad Abd el-Wahab Theater,** on the corniche at Raml Station Sq., features **traditional dancing.** Fir'et Rida (Rida's troupe) and El Fir'a el-Qawmiyya (the National Troupe), both featuring legendary belly dancers, perform high-energy dances representative of various areas in Egypt—including the exuberant men's cane dance from Upper Egypt. (Performances nightly 10:30pm; reserve tickets 1 or 2 days in advance. Front-row E£10.50, cheap seats E£5. Avoid the uncomfortable box seats.) You may think you left the **circus** behind when you left Cairo, but the Ringling Brothers' Egyptian cousins are in Alexandria every summer. (Ask at the tourist office for the location of the 2 daily shows; tickets E£2-7.) Every September, the **Alexandria World Festival** brings theater, dancing, and other performing arts to the city. Ask at the tourist office for details.

English-language **movies** are shown at the **Amir** (tel. 492 76 93; admission E£6-15) and the **Metro** (tel. 483 04 32; admission E£6-15), subtitled in Arabic and usually French. The American Cultural Center shows free movies, often around a theme (see **Practical Information,** p. 150).

If the sound of thundering hooves makes your pulse race, head to the **Antoniadis Palace and Gardens** in Smouha on the wide road bordering the zoo. For over 50 years, Alexandria's working classes have gathered here on summer Sundays to watch working horses, with carriages of all kinds, race each other along this road at breakneck speed (arrive by 6pm; free). Ask at the tourist office for info on the various **sporting events** in the Alexandria Municipal Stadium.

Especially in summer, Alexandria's upper crust lives at the **Alexandria Sporting Club** (tel. 85 36 28 or 29), a huge country club that puts your local pool and tennis courts to shame. It's hard to miss—every tram out of Raml Station stops here. The club has a great pool and golf and polo matches. At night, members relax, play billiards, watch movies, stroll, and flirt. Non-members pay E£10 per day and must be accompanied by a member, so find someone at the gates or the tram station. All activities inside cost extra. A cheaper option with less social clout but just as much to do is the **Smouha Sporting Club** (tel. 420 71 41). Admission policy is the same as at Alexandria Sporting Club, but the fee is only E£5. Take minibus #710 or 724.

# ■ Near Alexandria

## ABU QIR أبو قير

The fishing village of **Abu Qir** (pronounced abu EER) lies on a peninsula 5km past Montaza and has yet to be absorbed by Alexandria's relentless expansion. The site of Nelson's 1798 naval victory over that little Frenchman with visions of Egyptian conquest is now a great place to sample Mediterranean seafood. You'll avoid the crowds by visiting on a weekday, but people-watching on the weekends can be as good as the food. There's no shortage of ways to steer to Abu Qir. From Misr Station you can take **local bus** #250, 251, or 260 or **minibus** #729 (every 30min., 7am-10pm, 20min., 50pt). There are also 3rd-class **trains** from Misr or Sidi Gaber Station (every 30min., 6am-10pm, 30min., 45pt), **local taxis** from downtown (15min., E£5-10), or **service taxis** from in front of Misr Station (15min., E£1). Within Abu Qir, horse-drawn carriages (*hantour*) start their trots from El Bahr el-Mayyit St. (E£1).

To get seafood fresher than at Abu Qir's waterfront tables, you'd need to be a shark. Anglers right off the boat will cook the sea creature of your choice right before your eyes. The less adventurous can head to **Zephyrion,** 14 Khalid Ibn al-Walid St. (tel. 560 13 19), an Abu Qir landmark since 1929. A full dinner at the beach pavilion, with lapping waves and lapped beer, costs about E£40. The E£10 octopus (*kaborya*) plate is especially satisfying (open daily noon-midnight). Next door to Zephyrion is the similarly-priced **Bella Vista** (tel. 560 06 28; open daily noon-1am). To reach either restaurant head north to the waterfront from the main mosque; they're both right on the beach.

**Abu Qir Camp** (tel. 560 14 24), located on El Bahr el-Mayyit St. about 500m south of the Zephyrion, supplies the only consistently available **camping** possibilities in the greater Alexandrian area (E£3, with your own tent or one of theirs).

## RASHID (ROSETTA) رشید

Rashid (Rosetta) lies on the northern edge of the Nile Delta, about 45 minutes east of Abu Qir and one hour east of Alexandria. The city serves as the western meeting point of the Nile and the Mediterranean (Dumyat is the eastern meeting point), but has received most of its notoriety from the 1799 discovery of the Rosetta Stone by Napoleon's soldiers. Doted with provincial Ottoman mosques and houses from the 17th and 18th centuries, the port is steeped in Islamic architecture.

The **Rosetta Museum** features nothing of interest, but gives you something to do while in Rosetta (open daily 8am-4pm. Admission E£5, students E£2.50; camera privileges E£10). The badly damaged 17th-century **Zaghloul Mosque** is at the end of the main street running south from the train station. For a more scenic approach, walk inland from the corniche, past the museum, and swing south through the souq. If you look past the rancid water and trash, you'll see some Arabic inscriptions, archways, and columns.

About 5km from Rosetta, the recently restored **Fort of Qaytbay** (not to be confused with the one in Alexandria) guards the strategic entrance to the Nile (open daily 9am-4pm, Ramadan 9am-3pm; admission E£6, students E£3). Built in 1479 by Sultan Ashraf Abu Nasr Qaytbay to serve as a first line of defense against the Ottoman Turks and the Crusaders coming from the Delta, this structure used to overlook the surrounding land; clay and silt deposits have built up around it so that the ground has risen to the level of the fort. Further fortification of the fortress by the French in 1799 required the importation of stone from Upper Egypt. A soldier noticed carvings on one of the stones, and this **Rosetta Stone** enabled Jean-François Champollion to unlock the mystery of the hieroglyphic alphabet. The stone (or a cast of it—the original resides in London) describes the coronation and numerous titles of Pharaoh Ptolemy V in three tongues: Demotic (the common language), ancient Greek (the royal language), and hieroglyphs (the holy language). Recent excavations have revealed Rashid (pharaonically named "Bulubatin") to be a site rich in ancient Egyptian history. The cheapest way to get to the fort is by green-and-white local taxi (E£3-4 one-way, E£5 round-trip). When tourism is down it is risky to take transport out and expect to find something coming back. The romantic way to get there is to find a willing fisherman and go by boat (20min., E£5 per person round-trip). You'll see some beautiful scenery on the way.

To visit the peaceful **Mosque of Abu Mandur,** perched on the bank of the river, catch one of the southbound taxi boats at the main dock just across from the cannon in El Huriyya Sq. (round-trip E£4 per person). A nearby sandy hill offers a nice view of the countryside and an idyllic picnic spot.

**West Delta Bus Co.** buses run from Misr Station in Alexandria (every hr. 8am-10pm, E£1.50). The last return bus leaves at 5pm. You can catch **microbuses** from the Tikka Grill in Alexandria, one block inland from the corniche (E£2.50). The **train** (3rd-class only) runs from Misr Station (9 per day, 6:45am-10pm, 75pt). Trains return to Alexandria (9 per day, 5:50am-7:45pm, 60pt to Ma'mura, 70pt to downtown). **Service taxis** to Alexandria depart somewhat infrequently (E£4).

# WEST OF ALEXANDRIA

Heading west along Egypt's 400km of Mediterranean shore, you will encounter striking white sand beaches, tempting turquoise sea, and many vacationing Egyptian families, especially during the high season (mid-May to mid-Sept.). Bikinis are usually out of the question (leering men with their jaws on the ground sums it up), but at the few spots where a one-piece is acceptable, the beauty of the sea and the peacefulness of the townsfolk makes you quickly forget the overcrowded sand of Alexandria.

**El Agami** (20km from Alexandria) is popular with the Egyptian middle- and upper-classes and makes a convenient daytrip. Continuing west, you will notice that practically every inch of sand has been bought by one "vacation village" or another. Many of these cater to certain segments of Egyptian society: engineers, the police force, and doctors hole up in their private concrete complexes near the beach. Most require a car and membership card. The plush **Aida Beach Hotel** (tel. 410 28 02), 72km from Alexandria, gives a choice of beach-use fees which fluctuate by season. The lower rate (E£8-12) includes snacks; the higher one (E£27-35, 2 person minimum) includes lunch and use of a beach cabin. Both include pool use. If you want to stay the night, be prepared to pay US$30-52 per person in a six-bed villa or US$37-60 in a double room (breakfast and dinner included). Day use at the **Atic Hotel** (tel. 906 07 17), 89km west of Alexandria (you'll see a domed gatehouse with red letters above it), runs you E£45, but you get a beautiful beach, two pools, a playground, and lunch (other amenities extra).

The war cemeteries of **El Alamein**, 99km from Alexandria, mark the site of Africa's fiercest and most significant World War II battles. The cheapest sandy spot in the area is the **Marina Beach Club**, 94km west of Alexandria. The E£15 day charge gets you to their beautiful beach with wealthy Alexandrians zipping around on jet skis, but not into their pools. Closest to Libya is **Marsa Matrouh,** a colorful resort town on a bay, offering one of the world's most beautiful beaches. Though many coastline segments between Alexandria and Matrouh are tantalizingly inaccessible to budget travelers in need of hotels, opportunities for free, secluded camping are virtually unlimited (simply check in with the nearest police or military office).

If you time your day right you could bask and feast at the beach, stop to visit the El Alamein memorials, and make it to Marsa Matrouh by sunset. Microbuses and *service* taxis cruise the Alexandria-Marsa Matrouh road all day; just flag one down (E£3.50 from Alexandria to the Atic, another E£5-8 to get to Marsa Matrouh).

# ■ El Agami العجمى

People don't come to El Agami to swim—the sand further west is less crowded and the surf is more inviting. The sport of choice in this town is people-watching. Middle-class Alexandrian 20-somethings promenade along the shore en masse, but by sunset, the rush back to the city is in full swing. In the peak summer months, the beaches are choked with sun worshippers. Vuarnet sunglasses and cellular phones abound, but exposed female skin is a rarity. Women will feel most comfortable in a long skirt and long-sleeved shirt. During winter months, hours shorten, prices drop, and the town becomes rather quiet.

**Orientation and Practical Information** El Agami is actually two towns in one—Bitash and Hannoville. When Egyptians say "El Agami" they're generally referring only to the former. **Bitash** houses villas and more expensive hotels, while **Hannoville**, 2km further west, has apartment buildings and a few budget hotels. The entrances to the towns are right turns off of the highway. In both cases, you will turn onto the town's main road (Bitash St. or Hannoville St.), each lined with 2km of supermarkets, pharmacies, furniture stores, *sheesha* joints, and restaurants before you hit the end of the road and the Mediterranean.

At the top of Bitash St., across from Cinema Summer Moon and the gas station, is the **bus stop,** where you can catch a summer bus to Cairo (daily 6pm, E£22). The white façade of the **El Wah-Afaa Hospital** (tel. 433 83 18 or 85 06) is further down Bitash St. at #54. At #62, the **Farouk Hospital** (tel. 433 29 25) has a 24-hour English-speaking receptionist (tel. 433 89 25 to reach the hospital's English-speaking doctor at home). Most **pharmacies** on Bitash St. are open 8am-1am in the summer and 8am-9pm in the winter. The **National Bank of Egypt**, at #84, exchanges traveler's checks and cash (open Sun.-Thurs. 8:30am-2pm). The **telephone office,** on the corner of Bitash's intersection with Hanafiyya St., sells cards for its orange phonecard phones (open daily 8am-midnight).

Minibus #760 and bus #460 (both from the south side of Sa'ad Zaghloul Sq. in Alexandria) will drop you off in front of Minas Hotel in **Hannoville**. Minibus #765 and bus #465 (both from Misr Station) depart daily and stop right across the street in front of the Gad Restaurant (all routes run 6am-midnight, 50pt). Halfway between the beach and the road to Alexandria, **Banque Misr** (tel. 430 26 97) changes cash and does Visa and MC cash advances (open Sun.-Thurs. 8:30am-2pm and 6-9pm, Fri. 9am-noon and 6-9pm, Sat. 10am-1:30pm and 6-9pm).

**Transportation** between Bitash and Hannoville is cheap, but requires three bus transfers. From Hannoville, catch any bus heading to the T at the south end of town (25pt), and then catch another bus heading toward Alexandria, which will let you off at Bitash 2km further down (25pt). From here, it's a 2km walk to the heart of Bitash or another 25pt bus ride. Buses shuttle people around until midnight or so during the summer months. A **taxi** between Bitash and Hannoville runs E£3-5 depending on your bargaining skills.

**Accommodations, Food, and Entertainment** To make the most of El Agami, sleep in Hannoville's cheaper beds and wine and dine in Bitash's more interesting restaurants. The **Minas Hotel** in **Hannoville** (no English sign, but 200m from the beach and next door to the Costa Blanca sign) offers solace to the weary traveler with turned-down sheets and rounded balconies (tel. 430 01 50). Don't be put off by the perpetual construction in the lobby—the rooms are the best in town (singles E£25, doubles E£35, all with private shower). Across the street is the **Gad Restaurant** (tel. 430 61 79), part of a chain you might have encountered in Alexandria. Sandwiches range from E£1.50-5 (open daily 10am-midnight).

The culinary epicenter of **Bitash** is where the main road forks into Bitash St. and El Asal St., about 150m before the beach. Since Bitash is growing and changing rapidly, new restaurants spring up all the time. **La Poire** on El Asal St. has excellent *shawerma*, chicken, or roast beef sandwiches (E£4) and is usually packed with Egyptians in the know. The ubiquitous **Kentucky Fried Chicken, Pizza Hut,** and **Baskin Robbins** lurk 100m further down El Asal St., while **McDonald's** spreads its golden arches on Bitash St. about 50m from the fork. For dessert, **Mandarin Koedar** serves excellent ice cream (E£1.50 per scoop) on Hanafiyya St. (take a left at the telecom office, then another left onto Bianky St.). With scoop shops throughout Egypt, this ice creamery is a country-wide favorite (open daily 10am-1am).

There are no budget accommodations in Bitash, but if you can't bear to be away from the excitement, the **Agami Palace Hotel** (tel. 433 03 86; fax 430 93 64) on the beach has singles (E£100) and doubles (E£130), includes breakfast, and offers a variety of activities (billiards, swimming, dancing, etc.).

The cleanest and hippest **beach** (and the most liberal on the Med coast) is the **Fardous (Paradise) Beach** in Bitash. Belly buttons and biceps abound. Turn left onto Hanafiyya St. from Bitash St. at the telephone office and go straight until you reach the private beach. It's hard to get in, but worth a good hour of begging, especially when it's packed and hopping on Fridays. At the end of El Asal St. on the beach, **Fireball** is a new air-conditioned **disco** that opened in summer 1996 and promises to become *the* hip place to be. Two other dance spots are **Felfela,** which serves Egyptian food and has a billiard room and a pool (at night women must be 16 and men 21; open 1pm-4am), and **Michael's,** a pricey, open-air, beachside French restaurant. If you can get the bouncer to select you, **Andrea,** on Armed Forces St., is a cool bar for cocktail-sipping. Yet another in place to be seen is **Hollywood Cues,** a 24-hour billiard room, down the street from the telephone office. For tamer entertainment, **Cinema Summer Moon** (at Bitash St.'s intersection with the road to Alexandria) shows movies in English (11am, 3:30, 6:30, 9:30pm, and midnight; E£2-4).

# ■ El Alamein العلمين

El Alamein is a little too distant from the water to attract many tourists, but there was a time when El Alamein was infinitely less quiet, less out-of-the-way, and certainly less empty. In November 1942, the Allied forces, under the command of the British Field Marshal Sir Bernard Montgomery, halted the advance of the Nazi Afrika Korps here. El Alamein had been pinpointed by the Nazis as the gateway to Alexandria and the key to control of the continent. The Allied victory here marked the beginning of the end for the Axis Powers in North Africa and simultaneously crushed the mystique surrounding the "Desert Fox," German Field Marshal Erwin Rommel, whose force of Panzer tanks had previously seemed invincible. Nearly 10,000 soldiers lost their lives at El Alamein, and 70,000 were wounded.

On the east side of town lies the **British War Cemetery,** the burial place of 7367 men, 815 of whose headstones bear only the somber inscription "Known Unto God." Ringed by purple flowers and set against the seemingly interminable desert, the excruciatingly tidy rows are a dramatic memorial. Maintained by the British War Graves Commission, the cemetery is free and almost always open.

The **War Museum** at the west side of the village is near the bus stop and main square. It contains displays of weaponry and military garb and descriptions of Rommel, Montgomery, and other participants in the battle. A map bedecked with hundreds of tiny red and green bulbs retells the changing fortunes of the North African campaign. (Open daily 8:30am-6pm; winter and Ramadan 9am-4pm; closed Fri. 1-2pm. Admission E£5, camera E£5, video E£20; 50% student discount on entry and photography rates.) The less-frequently visited, citadel-like **German** and **Italian Cemeteries** (8km and 12km west of town, respectively) are perched on a petite peninsula overlooking the sea. Without a private car or hired taxi, it is difficult to get directly to these two monuments. A microbus along the Alexandria-Matrouh road can let you off when you see the monuments 2km in the distance or, if you're lucky, your *service* will deliver you to the site. Whichever way you travel, make sure you're armed with lots of water.

Non-air-conditioned West Delta buses traveling between Matrouh and Alexandria or Cairo can drop you off at El Alamein. During the summer you can usually flag down a **service taxi** or **minibus** heading to Alexandria (E£5, 1hr.) or Marsa Matrouh (E£5-8, 2hr.). During the winter, prospects are bleak and more expensive. A hired taxi is E£90, whether doing a round-trip from Alexandria or a cross-desert run.

# ■ Marsa Matrouh مـرسى مطروح

Fanning out from a bay of purest cobalt blue, this resort city is too often neglected by travelers using it as a springboard to Siwa. During the summer months, Egyptian families pack the mold-and-pour concrete villas and bathe along the 5km crescent of white, sandy, near-perfect beaches. Marsa Matrouh's natural harbor has served travelers, merchants, and soldiers from Alexander the Great to Rommel. Now the majority of sea vessels in Matrouh are rented by the hour, and officers on holiday are the only major military presence in town.

## ORIENTATION AND PRACTICAL INFORMATION

You need to know only two streets to find your way around Marsa Matrouh: the lively **corniche,** which stretches the length of the bay, and busy **Alexandria Street,** which runs perpendicular to the corniche, beginning at the Marsa Matrouh Governorate and heading inland to the train station and hill 1km south of town. Most of the hotels and government offices are clustered along the corniche and the streets running parallel to it. From the corniche inland, the most important of these are **Galaa, Tahrir** (sometimes referred to as Gamal Abd en-Nasser), **Goul Gamal,** and **Allam Er-Rum Streets.** Parallel to Alexandria St. to the east are **Port Said Street** and **Zaher Galal Street.** Parallel to Alexandria St. and three blocks to the west lies **Shokri el-Kowatiy Street,** where you catch buses, minibuses, and *service.*

**Tourist Office:** On the corniche 1 block west of Alexandria St., in front of the Governorate building (tel. 93 18 41). Open Sat.-Thurs. 8am-2pm. For better information and the map-booklet *Alexandria and Marsa Matrouh* head next door to the **Egyptian Tourist Authority.** Open daily 9am-8pm in summer, 9am-6pm in winter; year-round Fri. 10am-1pm and 3-6pm.

**Tourist Police:** Next door to the Tourist Office (tel. 93 55 75). Open 24hr. Nary a word of English spoken.

**Passport Office:** 1 block north and ½ block east of the train station, just off Alexandria St. (tel. 93 53 51). Open Sat.-Thurs. 9am-2pm for passport registration and visas, sometimes open from 6-9pm for passport registration only.

**Currency Exchange: The National Bank of Egypt,** 3 blocks west of Alexandria St. on Galla St., is open daily 8:30am-12:30pm and 6-9pm. **Cairo Bank,** Port Said St., 1 block east of Alexandria St. (tel. 93 49 08) is open daily 9am-2pm and 6-9pm. Both change cash and traveler's checks.

**Telephone Office:** Opposite the post office, it's crowded and unreliable for international calls. Open 24hr. **Hotel Riviera Palace** on Alexandria St. has a more expensive but infinitely more dependable telephone and fax service. Open daily 7am-9pm. **Information:** Tel. 16.

**Flights: EgyptAir,** Galaa St. (tel. 93 43 98), 3½ blocks west of Alexandria St. Flies to and from Cairo (Thurs., Fri., and Sun.; leaves Cairo at 9am, leaves Matrouh at 10:30am; 1hr.; E£340). Office open daily June-Sept. 9am-2pm and 6-9pm. There are no flights during the off-season months.

**Trains:** 1 block east of the southern end of Alexandria St., about 750m from the corniche (tel. 93 30 36). To Alexandria (7am; 6hr.; 3rd class E£7, 2nd class with A/C E£17; 50% student discount).

**Buses: West Delta's** non A/C buses depart from the depot 3 blocks west of the southern end of Alexandria St. To: Alexandria (every 2hr. 7am-7pm; 5hr.; E£11); Cairo (daily 7:30am, 7hr., E£18); and Siwa (daily 7:30am and 3pm; 5hr.; E£7). **Golden Arrow** runs A/C buses to Alexandria (9am, 2, and 3pm; 3hr.; E£20), Cairo (8am, 2:30, 3:30, and 4:30pm; 5hr.; E£30), and Siwa, if a seat opens up on the Alexandria-Siwa bus which passes through Marsa Matrouh (Mon., Wed., Sat., 4pm; 5hr.; E£12). A/C **Superjet** buses (tel. 93 47 87) also go to Alexandria (2:30pm, 3hr., E£23) and Cairo (11am, 3, and 4pm; 5hr.; E£36). Book ahead for Cairo buses, especially during the summer. Both Golden Arrow and Superjet buses depart from their respective ticket booths in front of the tourist office one block west of Alexandria St. A/C bus services are either drastically or totally cut back in the off season (Nov.-May). Check at the ticket booths for departure times.

**Service taxis:** Opposite the West Delta bus station. *Service* to Alexandria (E£10) and Cairo (E£20). Infrequent service to Siwa (E£10).

**Local taxis:** Pick-up truck taxis to 'Agiba and Cleopatra beaches run E£2 one way. The same service to Rommel Beach is approximately 50pt.

**Photo supplies:** Film and batteries can be purchased at the Kodak booth around the corner from the West Delta and Superjet ticket booths. Open daily 9am-1am.

**Pharmacy: El Farghaly Pharmacy,** at the corner of Alexandria St. and Allam er-Rum St., 3 blocks south of the corniche. Open Sat.-Thurs. 8am-1am and Fri. 10am-1am. During winter expect them to close at 9 or 10pm.

**Hospital: Military Hospital,** Galaa St. (tel. 93 52 86), 3 blocks west of Alexandria St. Facilities aren't impeccable—if possible seek treatment in Alexandria or Cairo.

**Police:** on the first street south of the corniche, 2 blocks east of Alexandria St. (tel. 93 33 76; emergency 122). Open 24hr.

**Ambulance:** Dial 123 or 93 43 70.

**Post Office:** 2 blocks east of Alexandria St. and 1 block south of the corniche (tel. 93 43 24). No *poste restante.* Open Sat.-Thurs. 8:30am-3pm.

**Telephone Code:** 03 (even if dialing from Alexandria).

**Getting around** Marsa Matrouh is easy. Most places are only a 10-minute walk. **Bicycles** can be rented from the stands all along the corniche (E£1 per hr., E£5 per day; bargain for long-term rental). Because Marsa Matrouh is so close to Libya, there is a noticeable military presence in the surrounding areas. While unnecessary within the city limits (unless you want to rent a bike), it's wise to carry your **passport** with you outside of town and on the more obscure beaches. There may be a passport check on the road into town.

## ACCOMMODATIONS

Marsa Matrouh's most hoppin' months are July and August, although the tourist season technically lasts from mid-May to mid-September. Although Ramadan brings a quick spurt of Egyptian vacationers, the non-summer months are pretty slow for Matrouh. Mid- to late-September is the ideal time to visit because the crowds have headed back to Cairo and the weather is still idyllic. During the off season, you might find a bargain at one of the upscale hotels on the corniche.

Small, cheap hotels can be found along and near Alexandria St., three or four blocks inland. Few foreigners frequent these places, so many of them have no English signs; some foreigners, especially women, might find a stay here unpleasant. Ask around and talk to the tourist office. Men with small budgets and open minds can rent a bed in a crowded room for E£2-3, but should guard their belongings.

**Hotel Hamada,** corner of Tahrir and Alexandria St. (tel. 93 33 00). Queen-sized beds with fresh sheets await you. Each floor has a living room, shared refrigerator, stove, and clean common bath. Try to get a room with a balcony facing north so you can catch the sea breeze. Singles, doubles, and triples E£10 per bed.

**Ghazala Hotel,** Allam er-Rum St. (tel. 93 35 19), in a 3-story, white building four storefronts east of Alexandria St., 6 blocks from the corniche (around the corner from El Farghaly pharmacy). When this hotel opened 24 years ago, Suleiman Morsi charged backpackers 50pt a room. Although the price has changed with time, the care put into maintaining the spacious rooms and common bathrooms here has not. The hot water is shut off during the summer, but you can warm your heart with journal entries of travelers dating from Augusts past. Singles E£7.50, doubles E£15.

**Hotel Ageba,** Alexandria St. (tel. 93 23 34), about 2 blocks before the hill rises out of town. Big apartment-block building with 200 clean, cheap rooms, some with balconies. Try to get a room facing north on the inside of the building—that way, you'll get the ocean breeze but not the truckers' honking at 6:30am. No hot water in summer. Singles, doubles, and triples with shower are E£10 per person.

**Arafat Hotel** (tel. 93 36 06), east of Alexandria St. on Tahrir St., right next to the Qahwa Auberge. Spotless rooms, sheets, and baths. With hot water year-round, it's the most luxurious budget hotel in town, but costs a bit more. Singles E£20. Doubles E£35. Triples E£60. Quads E£72.

**Rio Hotel,** corner of Galla and Alexandria St. (tel. 93 28 11). The mattresses here are not quite posturepedic, but the common bathrooms are eat-an-egg-off-the-floor clean. Singles E£10. Doubles E£20. Triples E£30. Quads E£40.

Groups of two or more might consider taking one of the many flats in town. **Hotel Awam** (93 23 63) to the west of Alexandria St., on the corniche near the mosque of Awam, has two bedroom flats for up to six people with living room, bathroom, and kitchen for E£50. If you've got a crowd of 9, take a 3-bedroom flat with the same amenities overlooking the sea for E£80 a night. Another option for a couple would be to relax at **Marine Fouad** on Rommel's Peninsula where a wonderful new room with bath, porch overlooking the sea, and three meals a day is E£120 for two (open June-Sept.). Reserve by calling Mr. and Mrs. Boray in Cairo at (02) 241 02 94 or check when you're here to see if space is available.

**Campers** should tell the Egyptian Tourist Authority office (who will pass on the information to the tourist police) where they'll be camping (for free) on the beach. Some tent-pitchers enjoy Rommel's peninsula while most others prefer to head out to the beaches a few km west of Marsa Matrouh.

## FOOD

The cheapest way for a group to eat in Marsa Matrouh is to shop at the local market. Alexandria St. runneth over with grocery stores, bakeries, and fruit and vegetable markets. Falafel, *shawerma*, ice cream, and pastry stands line the corniche.

**Pizza King,** 20m up the first alley to your left past the New Ledo Hotel at the far west end of the corniche. This is possibly the best pizza in Egypt and makes for a perfect sunset picnic overlooking the sea (E£7-10). Open daily 6pm-3am.

**Kushari,** 4 blocks west of Alexandria St. (look for the picture of the waiter holding a bowl of pipin' hot yellow stuff). The only *kushari* joint in town, these guys serve up a massive bowl piled high with grilled onions and chickpeas (E£2). Open daily 6am-midnight.

**Samara Fish Restaurant,** 2 storefronts east of Alexandria St. on Goul Gamal St., 2 blocks south of the corniche. Fabulous meals with bread, rice, salad, and grilled fish of your choice. Lunches and dinners range from E£13-20. Open daily 8am-1am in summer, 8am-9pm in winter.

**Alexandria Tourist Restaurant** (tel. 93 23 15), on Alexandria St., 2 blocks south of the corniche. One of the best budget meals in town. A full fish platter will set you back only E£12. Open daily 9am-midnight.

**Panayatis Greek Restaurant** (tel. 93 24 74), on the west side of Alexandria St., 2 blocks south of the corniche. Nothing particularly Greek about the food, but Panayatis, around since 1922, is the oldest restaurant in Matrouh. Great fish (E£15) and calamari (E£12); the salads (E£1) are worth a try. Stella E£5.25. Open daily 8am-midnight.

**Hani el-Omda** (tel. 93 33 00), 2 doors east of Alexandria St. on Tahrir St. next to Qahwa Auberge. Another fine contender for your stomach space. Dimly lit but cool and clean. ¼kg meat or *kufta* E£7, salads and bread included. Although they claim to be open daily 24hr., this seems to depend on the crowd.

**Restaurant Sharisard,** on the corner of Alexandria and Galla St. across the street from Panayatis (tel. 93 31 61), has good *fuul*, falafel, *shawerma*, and other Egyptian favorites for E£1-2. Open daily 6am-2am.

## SIGHTS, SAND, AND ENTERTAINMENT

The **beaches** surrounding Marsa Matrouh will enchant you. All close after sunset, and as part of a government effort to control drug trafficking, soldiers patrol the coast throughout the night. Five km of soft sand rim Matrouh's crescent-shaped bay, from the town's small port on the east to Lido Beach on the west. As in Alexandria, some women here swim fully clothed. As in all of Egypt (except the Sinai), bikinis and revealing one-piece suits could cause an earthquake. Those itching for the sun should head for **Rommel Beach,** where one-piecers are acceptable, or search out a secluded spot at 'Agiba. The **Beau Site Hotel** (on the far west end of the corniche) has a private beach which is cleaner, less crowded, and more liberal than the public beaches (some belly button sightings reported). There is no charge for non-guests, but they encourage you to rent an umbrella (E£5 per day), a chair (E£4 per day), a pedalboat (E£20 per hr.), a surf kayak (E£5 per hr.), and even particles of sand.

East of the port, the shoreline arches into a peninsula that faces the town from across the bay. This stretch of land, called **Rommel's Isle,** can be reached by donkey cart (E£1), bike (E£5 per day), boat (E£7), or pick-up truck taxi (50pt). The **Rommel Museum,** 3km east of town on the peninsula, contains a mediocre exhibit built into the caves which Rommel used as his headquarters during the North African campaign of World War II. (Open daily 10am-4pm in summer, closed during the winter. Admission 50pt.) On the ocean side of the isle, the rusting wreck of an old U-boat juts out of the water. You can rent a surf kayak to paddle out to the wreck: head toward the red buoy on your left. The sub lies parallel to the beach 20m toward the mosque from the buoy, but you'll need a diving mask to be able to discern it.

To the west of the main town beach, the **Beach of Love** (Shatii el-Gharaam) fondles the western horn of the bay, easily reachable by foot or kayak. Inconsiderate visitors have recently begun to desecrate the sand while worshiping the sun, and heaps of litter float out daily. Fourteen km farther west you'll encounter more wind, less trash, and the beautiful **Cleopatra's Beach,** on the far right-hand side of a small cove called **Cleopatra's Bath.** Legend has it that the queen and Marc Antony would come here to bathe—as the waves crashed into the cove, the water would shoot towards the heavens and cascade back down on the lovers' entangled bodies. **Obaiyid Beach,** calm and shallow, is 18km from Marsa Matrouh, and it fills up with frolicking families who stay at their corporation's tents along the shore. The farthest and most spectacular spot of all is **'Agiba,** about 24km from Marsa Matrouh. Meaning "miracle," 'Agiba is an inlet in a series of rocky cliffs interrupted with caves. Bring your own food, as there is only a soft-drink stand. Along the way, hidden in the sand near Umm Araham village, are the ruins of the tiny **Temple to Ramses II**. 'Agiba's beach can be crowded, but it is possible and to find a private spot below the cliffs and spend the day swimming off the rocks.

To reach these beaches take a shared **taxi** or **minibus** from the bus station (E£2-3 per person to 'Agiba), a shared **pick-up truck** from the stand on the corner 300m north of the main bus station (E£1.50 to 'Agiba), or catch the open-sided *tuf-tuf* bus (E£1.25 to Cleopatra or 'Agiba). The bus shuttles to and from the bus station when there are enough passengers (usually every hr. 9am-4:30pm; summer only).

In Marsa Matrouh, *qahwas* and strolls along the corniche replace bars and discos at night, though bars in the Rady and Beau Site Hotels do serve over-priced drinks. One hundred meters west of the end of the corniche (across from the armed services hotel compound) stands a raised outdoor patio which, during summer, often has energetic live music in a breezy, friendly setting. Both the corniche and Alexandria St. offer fine café and *sheesha* opportunities.

# ■ Siwa Oasis واحة سيوة

In the immortal words of Dorothy after the tornado, "Toto, I don't think we're in Kansas anymore." As enchanting as Oz, Siwa is a world of its own, with language, dress, and customs separate from the rest of Egypt. Here, every Siwan's smile is an affectionate reminder of the oasis's unique charm.

In 331 BCE Alexander the Great made a pilgrimage to Siwa to visit the Oracle of Amun. Today's paved road follows the same path, but buses zoom across the sand dunes in a mere four hours. Siwa's isolation has made it legendary in Egypt's annals. The ancients told tales of strange cities and mysterious kingdoms in the desert. The fickle twists of weather, however, defeated most attempts to find the truth—in 525 BCE a desert sandstorm blew the entire Persian army into smithereens.

In 1984, the Egyptian government completed the road connecting Siwa to Marsa Matrouh, and the town experienced drastic changes. Cairo sought to integrate the oasis into the national economy, leading to better-stocked stores, universal education,

---

### Siwi Made Simple

Most Siwan children's first language is Siwi, a Berber dialect incomprehensible to the rest of Egypt. As the children grow up, parents and schools make sure they speak perfect Arabic so that they can get along when not in Siwa. Siwi is unwritten and at times sounds almost Scandinavian. The possible permutations of the following words should keep you occupied until the donkeys come home:

| | | | |
|---|---|---|---|
| **meshi** | *yes* | **gaf lahk** | *I go* |
| **oula** | *no* | **fill** | *go* |
| **aman** | *water* | **ehk sehk** | *I want* |
| **aksoom** | *meat* | **oushi** | *give me* |
| **azumur** | *olives* | **tene** | *dates* |
| **ihkseik teswi aman** | | *I want to drink water.* | |
| **tanta elhal ineik** | | *How are you?* | |
| **lmany gahat** | | *Where are you going?* | |
| **betin lsmetinik** | | *What is your name?* | |
| **sewil dede** | | *Speak with me.* | |

two new quarries, and more diversified agricultural production. Arabic replaced Siwi, the local Berber dialect, as the language of instruction. Today, younger Siwan women don Egyptian fashions, and *The Bold and the Beautiful* is gradually replacing stories of Siwan folklore from Grandma. Nonetheless, the 300km of barren desert separating Siwa from the rest of civilization preserves many elements of the oasis's unique culture. Siwi, not Arabic, is spoken at home and on the street, and the few married women who venture into town cover themselves from head to toe in their blue *tarfudit* veil. Inside the home, the matron wears an *agabir* (a loose dress, often bright yellow or red) which was part of her dowry. Older women still sport the traditional Siwan costume, with heavy silver jewelry around the neck, arms, and head, and intricately braided hairdos.

The 1990s have seen a steadily increasing flow of tourists into Siwa, and the recent discovery of what might be Alexander's tomb has brought investors from Cairo. With all of the changes Siwans have faced in the past few decades, they steadfastly retain an extremely conservative culture: women travelers should not bare their arms or legs, and no one should consume alcohol.

Ahmed Fakhry's *Siwa Oasis* (E£36), available at the AUC Bookstore in Cairo and several shops in Siwa itself, is a richly detailed 200-page tome. Local tourist guru Mr. Mahdi keeps a copy on hand in the tourist office and will let you borrow it.

## ORIENTATION

Siwa Oasis lies in a desert depression about 300km southwest of Marsa Matrouh. Its western edge comes within 50km of the closed Libyan border. The depression stretches for 82km west to east, and between three and 30km north to south, but most visitors concern themselves only with the **town of Siwa** and the nearby villages and ancient sites.

Siwa's **climate** is similar to that of other oases and Aswan. Winter is pleasantly warm, with cool nights which necessitate sweaters. Summer is brutally hot, and air-conditioning is but a diaphanous mirage. The mild weather and the many local festivals associated with the harvest make fall and winter the best times to visit. You can see Siwa's major "sights" in a day or two, but most tourists linger longer to enjoy the peaceful atmosphere. Five days to a week are needed to really get a feel for Siwa and the Siwans. Eleven thousand people live in the town; 4000 more Siwans plus a few hundred Bedouin live in villages scattered elsewhere in the oasis.

The most practical way to reach Siwa is by bus from Marsa Matrouh or Alexandria, but groups with a car full of courage can travel the 420km stretch of the rough road from Bahariyya. For more information, see the **Siwa-Bahariyya Road**, p. 172.

The paved road from Marsa Matrouh passes the **Arous el-Waha Hotel** and the bright white **tourist office** at the northern edge of town and continues 200m into the center of town, ending at the **King Fouad (Sidi Suleiman) Mosque** and the **town market**. The ruined houses of **ancient Siwa** rise in eerie geometric form just south of the market on a rock acropolis. The town is graced by palm trees on all but the southern side, which rolls gently into the desert. Streets in Siwa have unmarked Siwi names, but most establishments hand out maps like lawyers hand out business cards. The best one can be picked up free at the tourist office.

## PRACTICAL INFORMATION

**Tourist Information Office:** In the new white building across the street from the Arous el-Waha Government Hotel (tel. 613 01). The domain of knowledgeable Mahdi Muhammad Ali Hweity, a sociologist, fluent English-speaker, and native Siwan, who arranges sight-seeing expeditions and provides maps and invaluable information on events. His office is well worth a visit. Open Sat.-Thurs. 8am-2pm and possibly in the late evenings during winter.

**Telephone Office:** Behind the Arous el-Waha Hotel. Open 24hr.

**Buses: West Delta Bus Co.** buses leave Marsa Matrouh daily at 7am and 3pm (4hr., E£7). From Alexandria's Misr Station there's one non-A/C bus daily at 10am (8hr., E£13.50) and one A/C bus at noon (8hr., E£20, winter service unpredictable). You can hop on the A/C bus in Marsa Matrouh if there is an open seat (4pm, 4hr., E£12). From Siwa to Matrouh: 7am and 2pm, 4hr., E£7. The 7am bus continues on to Alexandria (total 8hr., E£13.50). An A/C bus makes the trip as well (noon daily, 4hr., E£10 to Matrouh; 8hr., E£20 to Alexandria).

**Local Bus:** Crawls west from Siwa town near the big mosque to the village of El Maraqi, making a 60km loop and breaking down often along the way (round-trip E£2). There are usually 2 per day (7am and 3pm), but check with the tourist office.

**Bike Rental:** Several establishments in the market square (E£1 per hr., E£5 per day). Hotels will also rent.

**English Bookstore: Hassan's Handicrafts and English Bookshop,** next to the telephone office. Sells a few English AUC books on Egyptian history and culture (including Fakhry's *Siwa Oasis*). Open in the evenings after Mr. Hweity finishes up at the tourist office. The store is named for his son, Hassan.

**Pharmacy: Yousef's Pharmacy,** on the road leading south from the town center towards the Cleopatra Hotel. Wide selection, good English, and A/C. Open summer daily 9am-noon and 7pm-midnight; winter 9am-midnight.

**Hospital:** Go south 1km from the town square and take a right at the first four-story building on your left. Open daily 8am-2pm.

**Police:** Tel. 60 08, in the same building as the post office. Open 24hr.

**Post Office:** Across the street from Arous el-Waha Hotel in the northwestern part of town. Open Sat.-Thurs. 8am-2pm.

**Telephone Code:** 03, but calling Siwa from elsewhere in Egypt is difficult.

## ACCOMMODATIONS

All but one of the crash pads in Siwa are in or near the town center. During summer months, there isn't much business and you'll have your pick of the line-up. In winter months, however, especially around Christmas and New Year's, the entire town is filled to the gills. If you know the dates you are heading to Siwa well in advance, consider writing a letter to the tourist office to reserve a spot.

**Palm Tree Hotel** (tel 63 04), 20m down a side road from the market square. Clean, comfortable doubles with fans and balconies, some with private bath, although the common baths are large and spotless. Shady garden in back with wicker furniture and split date palm benches. Rooms overlooking the garden are choicest. Laundry service. Bike rental. E£5.50 per bed, E£6.50 with bath.

**Yousef Hotel,** a clean option smack dab in the center of town. Balconies have a view of Siwa and beyond. The roof is great for kicking back or sleeping during summer. E£5 per bed.

**Cleopatra Hotel** (tel. 148), south of the town square on the main road past the Shali fortress. A new and comfortable establishment, though somewhat pricier, with spacious balconies, great views, and immaculate bathrooms. Fans available in summer. Dorm beds (3 to a room, no fan or balcony) E£5. Back view doubles E£10-12.50, with bath E£18. Front-view doubles E£22.50. Breakfast E£4.50, lunch E£12.50, dinner E£13.50.

**Badwi Hotel,** south of town on the same road to Cleopatra Hotel, take a right at the first large four-story building. The sign says "Badawi." The management is adding a slew of new rooms, all with firm beds, thick mattresses, and hot water. Their only request: "Women and men in separated rooms." E£3 per bed.

**El Medina Hotel,** next to Yousef Hotel in the town center. As one traveler wrote in the comment book, "Medina serves its purpose." Squatter toilets and well-slept-in rooms without fans set you back only E£3 per night.

**Amun Hotel,** (tel. 26) at Dakrur Mountain, 4km east of town (take a *caretta* for 20min. or ride a bike until your butt is sore). If Siwa isn't off the beaten track enough, consider staying here. Dorm rooms are small, stuffy, and fanless, but have unbelievable views across the sea of palm tops to the salt lakes. Bring food and supplies. Doubles E£8.

Free **camping** in shelters is available on Dakrur Mountain, 4km south of town, and at **Well #1,** 12km south (see Av.). Bring your sleeping bag and insect repellent. Also Check with Mr. Hweity at the tourist office before pitching your tent.

## FOOD

Several restaurants line the two market squares and are generally open from 8 or 10am to midnight or 1am. In summertime the menus shrink. Standard offerings include macaroni, chicken, couscous, omelettes, and *shakshuka* (a mixture of meat, eggs, and sauce) for E£1-5. For breakfast try pancakes with banana, honey, and yogurt (E£2.50). Siwan eateries are pretty much indistinguishable from one another, but a couple tried and true places are **Lekany,** on the northeastern corner of town, and **Abdou's Restaurant** further west. The latter serves excellent couscous and mint tea. Local **stores** are well stocked with canned goods, cold soda, mineral water, and (in season) fresh and dried dates and figs.

Because Siwans tend to be more reserved than residents of most Egyptian towns, the traveler will be lucky to receive an **invitation** to eat or stay with a local family. Invitations are usually offered by children, but sometimes by men. At dinner, your hosts may want to sell you homemade handicrafts, or they may simply want to engage in conversation. Women will be allowed to enter a home much more readily than men. As always, exercise caution before accepting hospitality. Solo women should generally decline invitations from single Siwan men.

## SIGHTS

Surrounded by gashes of black rock, waves of sand, and piercing blue desert sky, Siwa is Egypt's most beautiful oasis. From atop the ruins of the crumbling medieval fortress-town of **Shali** (which simply means "town" in Siwi), the quiet streets of Siwa town wind through a cluster of mud houses and luxuriant palm gardens. Shali's encircling wall once protected the Siwans from marauding Berbers and Bedouin. Houses within the walls were cramped, and the stagnant, sweltering air did little to facilitate breathing. To make matters worse, twice a century, apocalyptic rains wash away all buildings on the acropolis. It's not surprising that Siwans gradually moved from their mountaintop abodes to the more spacious homes at the base. The flight began when Muhammad Ali conquered Siwa in 1820. By 1900 the ancient city had become a virtual ghost town. Wandering among the haunting skeletons of these ancient abodes, you will find inhabitants in random dwellings and old men turning corners on their way to unknown business. The most recent rains, in 1985, washed away much of Shali and most of the Siwan mud-dwellings, but due to the increased number of concrete buildings, the devastation was not total. The rains were enough to scare the Canadian ambassador, however. Fearing the washing away of history, he raised funds to construct the permanent **Traditional Siwan House,** opposite the tourist office. The house serves as a museum of traditional Siwan garb, silver jewelry, and children's toys. Abou Bakr, the knowledgable English-speaking guide, will gladly show you around and chat about soccer. (Open Sat.-Thurs. 10am-noon; ask at the tourist office if you'd like to see the museum at another time. Admission E£1.50.)

A second acropolis, **Gabal el-Mawta** (Hill of the Dead) rises 1km to the northeast of ancient Siwa (free). The hill is home to several Ptolemaic-era tombs that were robbed and reused by Romans. Many of these tombs were discovered during World War II when Siwan families crammed into caves seeking shelter from Italian bombs. The scattered human bones and mummy wrappings that litter the sight belonged to the Romans, as do the niches damaging the ancient frescoes. A custodian is on hand to unlock the tombs daily 9am-1pm but it is best to confirm the custodian's whereabouts with Mr. Hweity at the tourist office. Bring a flashlight (available at a store on the road from the town square to the mountain for E£2.50-3). The steep ascent to the top of the hill is rewarded with an exhilarating Kodak moment, although one needn't climb to the summit to enter the tombs. The **Tomb of Si-Amun** boasts a beautifully painted ceiling depicting the six stages of the sun's journey across the sky. Marred murals on the walls show the Hellenized portrayal of the bearded nobleman Si-Amun and his sons worshiping Egyptian deities. The **Tomb of Niperpathot,** the oldest tomb in Siwa, housed the body of a nobleman of the 26th Dynasty. The **Tomb of Mesu-Isis** is 5m to the east of Si-Amun and has ancient frescoes depicting the gods Isis and Osiris. E£2 *bakhsheesh* is appropriate but not necessary.

Like Siwa town, the village of **Aghurmi,** 3km to the east, rests peacefully at the foot of a formerly inhabited acropolis. To get there, rent a bike from town or hail a *caretta* (E£4-5 per load) and rattle off through the palm groves. A 13th-century gate made of palm logs graces the entrance to the acropolis. Pass a sturdy old mud **mosque** and you'll see, perched dramatically atop a cliff, the well-preserved **Oracle of Amun,** where Alexander came to consult the renowned priests of Amun. You'll have to go through the same steps that he did to reach the oracle: pass through the stone temple's simple gateway into the outer court, then cross the inner court to reach the center. Greek and Roman historians recall the mystical rituals to invoke an answer from the oracle. Priests carried a sacred boat containing the image of Amun as women sang and danced in procession. The oracle is said to have confirmed suspicion that Alexander was a god-king, proclaiming him the "son of Amun." Alexander also asked the oracle a question in private, but what that was we'll never know. The secret died with him, fewer than ten years after his visit. The Oracle of Amun is thought to date from the 26th Dynasty (c. 660 BCE). It became widely celebrated in later dynasties and was well known to the ancient Greeks, who constructed many shrines to Amun in their own country. Twentieth-century visitors enjoy unrestricted access to the entire Aghurmi acropolis—no guards, no fees, but alas, no answer-spewing oracle. Unless…

One km southeast of Aghurmi lie the emaciated remains of the **Temple of Amun.** Beyond the temple, about 2km south on the same road, lies the cool and mossy **Pool of Cleopatra.** Like many of the approximately 200 natural springs in Siwa, it has been encircled with a stone basin, with an irrigation duct running out one end. Although the pool is mostly frequented by men, fully clothed women should also feel comfortable swimming here (as comfortable as swimming fully clothed can possibly be) and may enter the enclosure next to the spring. If you visit these sights at sunrise or in the late evening, you may be the only person there. Continue another 1km east to **Dakrur Mountain,** where nearly 1000 rheumatics congregate each summer for ten-day stints in the **hammam ramel** (sand baths). These sand saunas have been popular for 300 years. In 1975, a Danish man, looking for a cure for his ailing daughter, came to Siwa. After a two-week treatment, his young child was able to walk again. You can try the bath for E£15, but be forewarned that you'll sweat like a demon, and your pores will dilate to the size of donuts.

Behind Dakrur Mt., perfectly rounded sand dunes make for an interesting walk. Every October at the full moon, Siwans gather for a huge feast at the rocks of **Dakrur.** A "chief of the feast" oversees the distribution of food to small groups spread over the plain. Each family contributes money for the purchase of meat and all donate 10 pieces of bread. Community problems are arbitrated by the head honchos. No one may begin to eat until the chief climbs to the top of the rock and hollers *"Bismallah!"* (in the name of God). Tourists are invited to attend. Contact the tourist office for the exact date of this and other harvest time (fall) festivities.

All of Siwa is idyllic, but the best place to watch the late afternoon sun dip into the endless sands is the breathtaking **Pool of Fatnas,** 4km west of town. Accessible by a small causeway, the Fatnas Pool is slightly smaller than the Cleopatra Pool but not as frequented by the locals. From the far western point of the adjoining garden, you can see across a glistening salt lake to a limitless sea of sand. The road west to **El Maraqi,** which traverses a low desert pass, is lined with craggy yellow buttes honeycombed with caves and Roman tombs. The assemblage of villages which make up El Maraqi lie in their own lush oasis, virtually severed from the rest of Siwa by the clenching fingers of the desert. The gruesome awaits you 9km from Siwa at the recently discovered tombs of **Deheyba.** Human skulls, thigh bones, and feet are strewn amidst the sand and sea fossils after a rather careless excavation a year and a half ago. A full mummy lies unprotected from the elements in tomb #18. Further west is the **White Mountain** and the village of **El Jari** at its base. On the southern side of the mountain are over 110 tombs and a fabulous view of Fatnas, the Sea of Sands, and Siwa. You can take a refreshing dip in the salt lake here before you peddle back to town. If you are on a tour sponsored by Mr. Hweity at the tourist office, you'll continue west to some of the springs, the other villages of El Maraqi, and the supposed **Tomb of Alexander** (closed to the public in the summer of 1996). A half-day trip for four people is a bargain at E£60. If you rent a bike, Deheyba and the White Mountain make for a fabulous day trip, but be sure to bring ample water and sunscreen. **Campers** can ask for special permission to sleep overnight in these parts and then take the bus back to Siwa the next morning.

**Bir Wahed** (Well #1), 12km south of Siwa, surrounded by lush vegetation, sports hot water clean enough to bathe in. Ahmad, at the Alexander Restaurant, will drive you across the sand dunes in a 4x4 to Bir Wahed for E£40 per person (E£50 if you camp out overnight). If you spend the night, bring a blanket from your hotel—it gets cold at night in the desert, even in mid-July. About 6km from Siwa and only 1km off the main road, a fabulous stretch of water erupts amidst sand dunes (locally called the **fish farm**). It's accessible by bike, although you'll have to walk the 1km from the road into the rolling dunes.

While in Siwa, you can shop for exquisite **handicrafts,** including intricately embroidered clothing, veils, and *margunahs* (large decorated baskets that weave elegance into every Siwan household). Several stores have sprung up around the town square: **Siwa Original Handicraft,** to the left of Abdou Restaurant, and **Hassan's Handicrafts,** next to the phone office. Don't try to bargain in craft shops because the women set the prices and aren't around to haggle. Many crafts are changing to accommodate tourist demands—the baskets and shawls are most authentic. It's also quite likely that precocious children will drag you into a private home to view their family's selection of handiwork.

## ■ Moving On: The Siwa-Bahariyya Road

The eight-hour crossing from Siwa to Bahariyya is easiest in winter, when truckloads leave every few days to make the long, bumpy journey east. You'll be lucky to find the 7-10 people that make it affordable during the summer months. **Abdullah Addas** runs safe, tent-covered Toyota trucks to Bahariyya for E£450. If you leave in the evening, you can camp out in the middle of the desert. Abdullah will cook up a storm with food you bought at the market in Siwa. Overnight trips get you to Bahariyya no later than noon if all goes well. **Ahmad** (of Alexander Restaurant) runs 4x4's to Bahariyya for E£600. He is reliable, safe, and knows the road well. Ahmad actually trained Abdullah before the two went their separate ways. On any trans-desert journey, make sure to bring plenty of potable water (5 bottles per person). Flat tires are inevitable—make sure your driver has spares. Be sure your driver knows he's supposed to collect firewood. The trip to Bahariyya is long and isolated, and a stranded vehicle may sit for days or longer before someone else comes down the road. If you can manage to

---

### Smooth Cruisin'

Not long ago, Siwans ran a smuggling operation, secretly carrying goods from Libya into Egypt on donkeys. The nighttime treks would proceed perfectly until the beast, unaware of the clandestine nature of the mission, would bray, alerting the Border patrol officials and spoiling the whole kit 'n caboodle. Siwans wracked their brains to figure out a way to pacify the carriers. An ingenious plan was developed: someone (somehow) discovered that if the asses' asses were greased, the brutes were unable to create the force needed to let air out of their mouths. A team of French scientists is currently conducting further research on this exciting discovery.

relax, you'll experience dark yellow sunsets and a burning white moon—scenes not visible from the oases.

**Abu Shrouf,** 40km east of Siwa towards Bahariyya, is cooler, deeper, and cleaner than any of Siwa's pools. Local legend has it that Abu Shrouf is the only place in the oasis with female donkeys. If a male donkey escapes from Siwa, the first place they look is Abu Shrouf. If a Siwan man has a pleasant night with his wife, he tells his buds "Last night I went to Abu Shrouf!" A round-trip carload from Siwa costs E£25.

# Nile Valley وادى النيل

> How doth the little crocodile
> Improve his shining tail
> And pour the waters of the Nile
> On every Golden Scale.
>
> —Lewis Carroll

Originating at the equatorial high water marks of Lake Victoria and Lake Taru, the Nile winds its way north through Uganda, Ethiopia, and the Sudan, pouring into Lake Nasser and Egypt, where its banks are home to 95% of the country's millions.

Before the construction of the Aswan High Dam in the late 60s, the Nile over-flowed its banks every year, depositing the rich silt that made the valley the most fertile region in the world. This yearly inundation was the most important time of the year for ancient Egyptians, and the reason that much of the Egyptian religion was centered around the river's cycles. More important for today's Egyptian tourists, it's the reason that the length of the Valley is chock full of temples and monuments.

The region between Cairo and Luxor is known as **Middle Egypt,** home to the majority of the country's Copts. Akhenaton built his capital at Tel el-Amarna; further south stand the quietly impressive temples at Abydos and Dendera. Travel in this area is dangerous (see **warning** below).

Luxor marks the northern boundary of **Upper Egypt,** stretching all the way upstream to Lake Nasser and the Sudanese border (formerly Lower Nubia). There are busloads of sights in Upper Egypt, and trainloads of tourists to see them. Highlights include the vast Theban necropolis, lonesome Kalabsha, and the large and in charge temples of Abu Simbel.

In the summertime, when the weather is hot, temperatures often average over 45°C, frequently breaking 50°C. This is rather warm, but the complete lack of humidity makes it possible to continue most essential biological processes even as the sand turns to glass.

Scalding heat makes summer the low season for tourism. Hoteliers, guides, and others of their ilk are desperate, so bargain hard. If you don't like the heat, plan to do most of your touring between 6 and 11am; if you don't like the crowds, shoot for high noon. November through May, prices increase as the temperature drops.

---

As of summer 1996, the Egyptian and U.S. governments strongly discourage any surface travel through Middle Egypt. Political instability and the rise in extremist activity have made the area unsafe for tourists. There is a massive police and military presence in the area, making visits unpleasant as well as ill-advised. *Let's Go* heeded the warnings of the U.S. State Department and Egyptian Ministry of Tourism and did not send a researcher to sights or cities between Beni Suef and Luxor this year. The temple at Abydos is closed to the public, as are many other sites.

## GETTING AROUND

### By Taxi, Bus, or Train

Traveling by **service taxi** is the most efficient, cheap, and convenient option for shuttling between the river towns at almost any time of day. You'll need nerves of steel, however, to cope with the insanity of the drivers. In Luxor, take them from behind the museum:

**Luxor to:** Esna (1hr., E£6), Edfu (1½hr., E£9), Kom Ombo (2-3hr., E£13), Aswan (3-4hr., E£14).
**Aswan to:** Kom Ombo (45min.-1hr., E£2), Edfu (2½hr., E£4), Esna (2-3hr., E£6).
**Kom Ombo to:** Edfu (1hr., E£2), Daraw (15min., 50pt).
**Esna to:** Edfu (1hr., E£2).

**Buses** are often cheaper than *service*, though not by much. They run more frequently, but are horribly slow, hot, and break down regularly. Most stop running at 6pm. Buses are best for transport out of Luxor or Aswan, where you can reserve the A/C buses by going to the station a day or two in advance. In the smaller towns in between, you may not find an empty seat, and schedule reliability plummets.

**Luxor to:** Esna (1½hr., E£5), Edfu (2hr., E£10), Kom Ombo (3hr., E£10), Aswan (5hr., E£14). Buses depart from behind the Luxor Temple.
**Aswan to:** Daraw (1hr., E£1), Kom Ombo (1hr., E£2), Edfu (2hr., E£3), Esna (3½hr., E£4), Luxor (4hr., E£6.50).

**Trains** are a hassle for short runs. For the entire Luxor-Aswan haul, however, the trains with first- or second-class air-conditioned compartments are great. (From Aswan to all points north at 5:30am and 6pm; 5hr. to Luxor, E£10-20. Southbound from Luxor at 6:30am and 4:30pm; 5hr. to Aswan, E£11-14). As of summer 1996, authorities were discouraging tourists from taking third-class trains.

### By Nile Cruiser

Tough times for tourism in Egypt have opened up an option for the budget traveler on a binge. You can book a cabin on triple-decker, pool-topped cruise ships and slip from Luxor to Aswan or back (2 nights) hobnobbing with French tourists. Travel agents can book for you at a mark-up (US$35 per night) or you can go to the dock yourself and chat with the boat receptionist about open cabins (as low as US$25 a night). The air-conditioned, two-room suites have TVs and showers, and all meals are included. Drinks are extra, and extra pricey. A *kalish* will cart you to the temple and back at each stop. Several travel agents dot the corniche south of the Winter Palace in Luxor (Eastmar, Misr Travel). In Aswan, agencies can be found near the corniche tourist office. If you find a bargain, you'll enjoy two days of pure bliss: sitting by the pool sunning yourself, watching the palms and desert float by, getting interrupted only to be fed three times a day.

### By Felucca

If you are on a tight budget but still want the semi-pharaonic experience of cruising from temple to temple on the Nile, a *felucca* cruise is a slow-paced way for you to absorb the Egyptian countryside and regain your sanity after days in overcrowded *service*. To ensure an enjoyable experience, you should be aware of the inherent **risks** in *felucca* travel. We don't want to sound like killjoys, but you must be on guard *at all times*, from the moment you start shopping for a captain until you reach your final destination. Police records and hotel comment books are filled with tales of watery woe: druggings, beatings, theft, rape, harassment, and even death.

First off, a definition. The word *felucca* simply means boat; the typical Nile-cruising variety sleeps up to eight people, has a single tall mast with a characteristically angled boom, and is piloted by an English-speaking Arab or Nubian Egyptian. To get a group

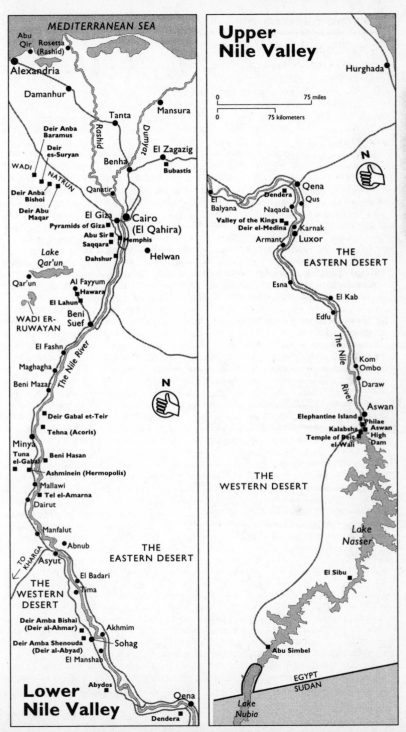

EGYPT

**MEDITERRANEAN SEA**

Abu Qir
Rosetta (Rashid)
Alexandria
Damanhur
Tanta
Mansura
Deir Anba Baramus
Deir es-Suryan
El Zagazig
Benha
Bubastis
WADI
NATRUN
Deir Anba Bishoi
Qanatir
Deir Abu Maqar
El Giza
Cairo (El Qahira)
Pyramids of Giza
Abu Sir
Memphis
Saqqara
Helwan
Dahshur
Lake Qar'un
Qar'un
Al Fayyum
Hawara
WADI ER-RUWAYAN
El Lahun
Beni Suef
El Fashn
The Nile River
Maghagha
Beni Mazar
Deir Gabal et-Teir
Tehna (Acoris)
Minya
Tuna el-Gabal
Beni Hasan
Ashminein (Hermopolis)
Mallawi
Tel el-Amarna
Dairut
Manfalut
Abnub
THE EASTERN DESERT
TO KHARGA
Asyut
El Badari
Tima
THE WESTERN DESERT
Deir Amba Bishai (Deir al-Ahmar)
Akhmim
Deir Amba Shenouda (Deir al-Abyad)
Sohag
El Manshah
Abydos
Qena
**Lower Nile Valley**
Dendera

**Upper Nile Valley**

Hurghada

0 — 75 miles
0 — 75 kilometers

N

Qena
El Balyana
Dendera
Qus
Naqada
Valley of the Kings
Deir el-Medina
Karnak
Armant
Luxor
THE EASTERN DESERT
Esna
El Kab
Edfu
The Nile River
Kom Ombo
Daraw
Aswan
Elephantine Island
Philae
Kalabsha
Aswan High Dam
Temple of Beit el-Wali
THE WESTERN DESERT
Lake Nasser
El Sibu
Abu Simbel
EGYPT
SUDAN
Lake Nubia

together when not traveling with friends, try to meet like-minded tourists (aim for a group of six) in hotel lobbies or the many restaurants along the Nile. You can also ask at the tourist office (a good resource throughout the *felucca* planning process). As a last resort, you can join a group already assembled by a captain. Be sure to meet these people beforehand, or you may find yourself in some horrifying Middle Eastern version of MTV's *Real World.*

Starting from the moment you step off the train in Aswan, you will be approached every 28 seconds by a *felucca* captain or, more often, a middleman sent out to round up suckers. Every hotel manager and every man in the local *ahwah* has his favorite *felucca* man (from whom he receives a commission) so the word on the street is almost useless. You should go down to the river yourself, meet and talk with several captains, inspect several boats, and take a list of potential candidates to the tourist office to make sure they aren't pirates or perverts. Ask to see comment books and talk to fellow travelers. Be skeptical of any cute **nicknames** the captain uses; an honest captain will tell you his real name if asked. Also be wary of captains who speak little English. These typically younger captains often lack the experience necessary to handle sailing emergencies. There have been several capsizings in recent years caused by high winds and inept sailors. You are better off with a gnarled, crusty old man who speaks English well (if a bit colorfully) than with some punk who is just learning the ropes. Don't book *felucca* trips through commission-charging hotels.

You'll probably embark from the *felucca* capital of Aswan. Most trips last two days and end in Edfu. If you'd like to spend more time on the river, be persistent and have a group to back you; captains would rather stay close to home (it takes them longer to return to Aswan against the current). Be sure you have arranged the final destination, and that it is clearly understood by the captain. Unscrupulous boatsmen have been known to drop their passengers off 40km from a town, claiming that it was "close enough."

Purveying provisions has become an opportunity for a scam (it's the sailor's loophole for making up the money he lost in giving you that "special price"). Many a traveler has arrived at his or her destination either sick from low-quality food or hungry from low rations. You have two options: shop with the captain and choose what you want to eat yourself (a time-consuming process), or review the planned menu carefully, insisting on adding whatever's on your wish list, and asking to see it all before you set out. For greater leisure, choosing a captain who takes care of the cooking himself is highly recommended. An extra-special captain who cooks Nubian dishes in the *felucca* or arranges to stop at his village for a home-cooked meal is a godsend. He should also bring at least two cartons of bottled water; make sure it is aboard before you depart and check that the tabs are sealed, lest it be tap water. In addition, bring at least three bottles of water per person per day for drinking, cooking, and brewing tea. You can also ask for a big jerry can of tap water to be brought along which can be used instead of the Nile for washing dishes and faces.

Your *felucca* journey could be one of the most relaxing and enjoyable parts of your trip to Egypt, but be vigilant: keep all belongings well-secured. Sleep with passports, money, airline tickets, and traveler's checks adhered to your flesh (theft of money-belts is common). Most *feluccas* have a compartment in front that locks, but their safety is suspect. Groups of women alone should not embark unless they see the trip as a singles cruise with their captain as the only eligible bachelor on board. The unfortunate fact is that most Egyptian men either respect or fear men far more than women. Let the captain think that nerd from Wyoming in Tevas is your boyfriend. The law prohibits any Egyptians, apart from the captain and his minimal crew (often just a young boy who helps him out) from traveling with foreigners. If someone attempts to hop on board, throw a fit and then throw him into the Nile, or you will be unable to relax all trip. Some *felucca* parties like to party; there is a growing drug scene on many Nile trips. Be careful: Egyptian law is harsh and entrapment is fairly common.

Officially, members of a six- to eight-person group leaving Aswan should pay E£25 each to Kom Ombo (1 day, 1 night), E£45 to Edfu (3 days, 2 nights), E£50 to Esna (4 days, 3 nights), and E£60 to Luxor (5 days, 4 nights). Most captains add to this E£5 per day for food and water, and a E£5 registration fee. Prices don't vary much from captain to captain; the most important variable is the vibe you get.

For registration in Aswan, your captain will ask for your passport and the E£5. Brush up on the relaxation skills you will need for the trip by letting him do the paperwork for you, but have an assembled group before you do, or the captain may keep your passports as collateral until he can corral other passengers.

Finally, although there are many dangers inherent in a *felucca* cruise, do not forget that there are also many honest, reputable captains out there and that a trip by *felucca* should ease your worries, not aggravate them. Have fun, but be careful.

# ■ Luxor الاقصر

*And so sepulch'red in such pomp dost lie,*
*That kings for such a tomb would wish to die.*

—John Milton

The glory of Luxor is timeless. This ancient capital of Upper and Lower Egypt still humbles visitors three millennia after it reached the height of its power. The city is built on the site of *Ta Ipet* (known by its Greek name, Thebes), and flexed its influential muscles during the five-century rule of the New Kingdom (18th-20th Dynasties, 1550-1070 BCE). It's incredible how little has changed: mammoth pylons tower over forests of sandstone columns, obelisks point skyward in the east bank temples, and tombs store kings and their treasures deep in the west bank necropolis.

Unfortunately, many elements of Luxor are 20th-century additions. The tourism industry has spawned a society of ruthless hoteliers, greedy guides, and conning cabdrivers. More than in any other "temple town," travelers must be careful where they place their trust. If somebody says the word "free," walk away—nothing is free in Luxor. If you act tough and stay smart, you may find an honest bargain. A few pounds a day can buy decent accommodations, tasty food, and access to unforgettable sights. In less troubled times, the sights of Middle Egypt were convenient day trips from Luxor, but travel to the north is currently discouraged by the government. Points south (Esna, Edfu) are perfectly safe and rewarding destinations.

## ORIENTATION AND PRACTICAL INFORMATION

Luxor is located on the eastern bank of the Nile, 670km upstream from Cairo and 220km downstream from Aswan. Surrounded by a heavily cultivated floodplain, Luxor is an agricultural center (with a *souq* on Tuesdays). Archaeologically, the city can be divided into three sectors: Luxor City, the village of Karnak a few kilometers north, and Thebes on the West Bank. Although there are only a few street signs, finding your way around Luxor is easy as long as you know the main thoroughfares. **El Mahatta Street** (Station St.) runs perpendicular to the Nile and connects the **bus stop** and **train station,** 750m inland on the eastern edge of Luxor. Exit the train station at a 45° angle to your left and you will eventually reach **Television Street,** where signs advertising the many budget hotels and pensions in town begin to appear. **En-Nil Street** (the corniche) runs along the river, turning into Khalid ibn al-Walid St. past the **Novotel.** The bus stop is on **El Karnak Street,** running parallel to En-Nil St. slightly inland. **Luxor Temple** is on the corniche at the center of town, and **Karnak Temple** is 3km further northeast one block inland from the corniche.

You can easily get around Luxor by foot, but if you'd rather ride, **kalishes** (carriages) line the Nile. A ride is good for easy transport of baggage, a pleasant trip out to Karnak Temple (E£5), or making that budding romance bloom (E£2 plus commitment). Luckless singles can rent a **bicycle** (E£5-7 for the whole day); El Mahatta St. and Television St. have several rental places, or ask at your hotel. Sherif Hotel on Television St. rents **motorbikes** (E£50-60 per day), but provides no helmets. The cheapest transportation in the city is by **minibus** (25pt). The most common route is El Karnak St. to El Mahatta St. to Television St.

**Tourist Office:** In the **tourist bazaar** next to the New Winter Palace Hotel (tel. 37 22 15 or 32 94). Open daily (including Ramadan) 8am-8pm. Branch at the **train station** (tel. 37 02 59) open 8am-8pm, perhaps later. Another branch in the **airport** (tel. 37 23 06). Staff can provide maps and an official price list of services and outings. Generally, not much that you couldn't get from your hotel lobby.

**Tourist Police:** In the **tourist bazaar** on En-Nil St. (tel. 37 66 20) and **train station** (tel. 37 65 42). Both open 24hr. It's best to deliver complaints in person.

**Passport Office:** Khalid Ibn Al-Walid St. (tel. 38 08 85), 1km south of the Novotel, by the Mandera Restaurant. Register passports and extend visas in the foreigners' office. Open Sat.-Thurs. 8:30am-2pm and 5-9pm, Fri. 10am-2pm. Visa business Sat.-Thurs. 10am-2pm. During Ramadan 10am-2pm and 8-10pm.

**Telephones: Central Telephone Office** off El Karnak St. to the left 1½ blocks past the Emilio Hotel. Open 24hr. Other offices are on En-Nil St. in front of the Old Winter Palace Hotel and in the train station (open 8am-10pm). Send **telegrams** from the main post office or telephone offices. **Directory assistance:** Tel. 16.

**Fax: IBA/Federal Express,** El Funun St. off Idris St.(tel. 37 56 04). Open 8am-5pm. Also provides **Western Union** money wiring service.

**Currency Exchange:** Most luxury hotels change money 8am-10pm for a commission. Smaller non-bank exchange places include the **Bank Exchange** on El Karnak St. across from the bus stop (open 8am-2pm and 5-8pm). **Bank of Alexandria,** El Karnak St., just north of intersection with Nefertiti St., is open daily 8:30am-2pm, additional currency exchange hours 6-9pm (winter 5-8pm). New branch on the corniche open Sun.-Thurs. 8:30am-2pm, Ramadan 10am-1:30pm. **National Bank of Egypt,** En-Nil St., 50m south of Old Winter Palace Hotel, is open daily 9am-10pm. There is an **ATM** machine outside **Banque Misr,** south of the *service*/bus stand; Visa, MC, Plus, AmEx, and Cirrus accepted.

**American Express:** Old Winter Palace Hotel on En-Nil St. (tel. 37 28 62), south of Luxor Temple. Holds mail. Sells traveler's cheques. Wire money or send mail through Cairo office. Exchanges money and checks. Open daily 8am-7pm.

**Thomas Cook:** Winter Palace Hotel (tel. 38 21 96; fax 38 65 02). Books cruises and tours, and changes money. Open daily 8am-8pm.

**Airport:** 5km northeast of town (no bus; taxi E£10). Served by **EgyptAir** (tel. 38 05 80), next to the Old Winter Palace. In summer, to: Cairo (4-5 per day, 1hr., E£361); Aswan (3 per day, E£163); Sharm esh-Sheikh (2 per week, E£412); and Hurghada (2 per week, E£163); in winter, 15 per day to Cairo (all fares one-way).

**Trains:** Station is at the head of El Mahatta St. (Station St.), 750m inland from Luxor Temple (tel. 37 20 18). Looks like a temple itself. **Lockers** 90pt per day. For security, tourists are often restricted to two express trains to Cairo (11:30am and 11:30pm, 8-12hr., A/C 2nd class E£24-34). Trains to Aswan (6:30am and 4:30pm, 4-5hr., A/C 2nd class E£14, students E£11) are less comfortable than *service* or *feluccas*. It's possible to pay a walk-on fee but safer to reserve a seat. Cairo trains are especially crowded. Sleeper cars should be reserved 3 days in advance.

**Buses:** Station at El Karnak and El Mahatta St., by the mosque behind the Luxor Temple. To Cairo: 6 and 10am, 11-12hr. (E£49). Seats may be available on the bus from Aswan to Cairo which passes through Luxor at 8:30pm (A/C). Service every hr. 6am-10pm to Esna (1hr., E£5); Edfu (1½hr., E£10); Kom Ombo (3hr., E£10); and Aswan (4½hr., E£14). To Hurghada: 3hr., 6:30am (E£8), 11:30am (E£10), 2:30 and 7:30pm (E£16). Hours and rates change frequently.

**Service Taxis:** Off El Karnak St., 1 block inland from the Luxor Museum. Early morning and late afternoon *service* leave whenever they fill up, about every 15min. The following are suggested prices; start the bidding a little lower: Qena (1hr., E£6); Esna (1hr., E£6); Edfu (2hr., E£9); Kom Ombo (2½hr., E£13); and Aswan (3-4hr., E£14). There is also a station on the west bank where the local ferry docks, but departures are less frequent.

**Laundromat:** Listed hotels have free self-serve laundry unless otherwise noted.

**Swimming Pools:** A small but pleasant pool at the **Luxor Wena Hotel** charges E£15. The dramatically situated soup at the **Novotel** is the same price. The smallish

EGYPT

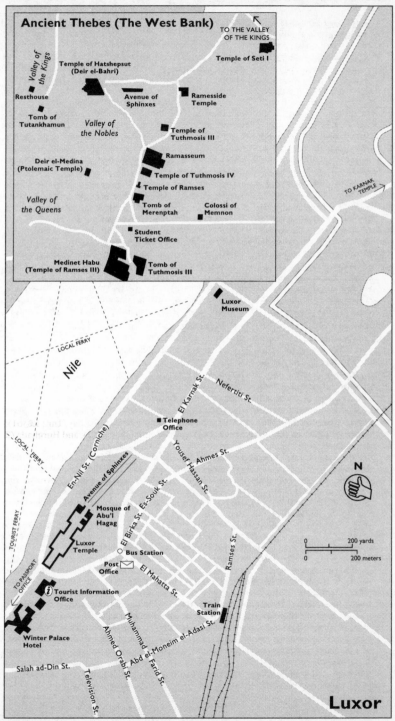

Ancient Thebes (The West Bank)

TO THE VALLEY
OF THE KINGS

Temple of Seti I

Valley of the Kings

Temple of Hatshepsut
(Deir el-Bahri)

Resthouse

Avenue of
Sphinxes

Ramesside
Temple

Tomb of
Tutankhamun

Valley of
the Nobles

Temple of
Tuthmosis III

Ramasseum

Deir el-Medina
(Ptolemaic Temple)

Temple of Tuthmosis IV

Temple of Ramses

Valley of
the Queens

Tomb of
Merenptah

Colossi of
Memnon

Student
Ticket Office

Medinet Habu
(Temple of Ramses III)

Tomb of
Tuthmosis III

TO KARNAK
TEMPLE

Luxor
Museum

Nile

LOCAL FERRY

LOCAL FERRY

El Karnak St.

Nefertiti St.

Telephone
Office

En-Nil St. (Corniche)

Avenue of Sphinxes

Youser Hassan St.

Ahmes St.

N

TOURIST FERRY

Mosque of
Abu'l
Hagag

El Birka St.

Es-Souk St.

Luxor
Temple

Bus Station

Ramses St.

TO PASSPORT OFFICE

Post
Office

El Mahatta St.

0        200 yards
0        200 meters

Tourist Information
Office

Train
Station

Winter Palace
Hotel

Muhammad
Ahmed Orabi St.

Abd el-Moneim el-Adasi St.

El Farid St.

Salah ad-Din St.

Television St.

Luxor

**Emilio** on Yousef Hassan, **Shady** on Television St., **Karnak** behind the Hilton, and **St. Joseph** on Khalid Ibn Walid are bargains at E£7-10. The distant **Rezeiky Camp and Motel** on El Karnak charges E£5 to *Let's Go* readers.

**English Bookstore: Aboudi Bookstore,** in the tourist bazaar on En-Nil St. Mainly French, but many English books about Egypt and sappy romances. Open Sat.-Thurs. 8am-10pm. A kiosk in front of the tourist office sells foreign periodicals.

**Supermarkets:** A couple at the end of Television St. are good. The **Mini Market** on Karnak St. across from St. Mark Hospital carries staple foods and Gilette Sensor razor blades (75pt each). Bottle of water E£1.25. Open 9am-midnight.

**Pharmacy:** 24-hr. pharmacy duty rotates—try asking a hotel employee. **St. George Pharmacy** (open 7am-2pm) and **El Rahman Pharmacy** (tel. 38 01 77; open 8am-noon) on Muthaf St. near the bus station are well-stocked.

**Hospital: Luxor General Hospital,** En-Nil St. (tel. 37 20 25), north of the museum. A newer hospital is at the eastern end of Television St. (tel. 37 26 98).

**Medical Emergency:** Tel. 123.

**Police:** Off El Karnak St., about 200m north of Luxor Temple (tel. 37 23 50).

**Post Office: Poste restante** and **Express Mail** (until noon) on El Mahatta St., 100m east of Luxor Temple. Other branches near the tourist office and in the train station. Open Sun.-Thurs. 8am-2pm. Train station branch open 8am-noon and 2-8pm. You can send packages via **Federal Express** (see **Fax,** above).

**Telephone code:** 095.

## ACCOMMODATIONS

If you come to Luxor by train, you will disembark into a writhing mass of arms waving hotel cards. Some agents are legit, some are not; be wise. Often people masquerade as employees of the popular hotels in town, then lead you elsewhere. The hotels are a short walk from the train station and easy to find. Be sure to bargain down initial price quotes. You'll be surprised at the high concentration of budget hotels, so shop around. Women traveling alone can bet on sexual advances from young employees of smaller hotels. If a refusal doesn't do the trick, complain to the manager or the Tourist Police. All travelers should carry anything of value on their persons at all times.

Most budget hotels cluster around Television St. and Salah ad-Din Sq. Competition is fierce, so you don't have to settle for their first offer. Extreme shoestringers can ask to sleep on a roof or terrace mattress for E£3-4. Listed accommodations all have 24-hr. hot water, fans, and free use of washers and kitchens, unless otherwise noted. Most provide information, maps, and organized tours (sometimes scams).

**Everest Hotel,** En-Nozha St. (tel. 37 00 17). Take the 2nd left off Television St. and follow the signs. This hotel and its helpful staff have established a good reputation in their first few years. All rooms have A/C and modern bathrooms with scaldingly hot water. Tiled floors and new paint exemplify the hotel's cleanliness. Coming soon: full restaurant, roof garden with ping pong, and an information/library room. Singles E£15, doubles E£25, triples E£30, quads E£40. Breakfast included.

**Fontana Hotel** (tel. 38 06 63), a left turn off Television St. after the bus garage (you can't miss the sign). Posted train and bus schedules and multinational guests make the lobby resemble a major transit hub. Customers praise the well-kept rooms (some with private baths and balconies) and shared bathrooms. Rooms are clustered around cozy living rooms, allowing for culture-sharing conversation. Doubles E£10, with breakfast E£15. Prices E£10 higher in winter.

**Pyramids Hotel,** Yousef Hassan St. (tel. 37 32 43); from the train station, take a right down Ramses St. and turn left at the end; it's 200m down on the right. Spacious, carpeted rooms, with baths and A/C that sometimes work. In the winter, the roof garden is a nice place to down a Stella (E£5). Manager Ziggy goes out of his way to please and entertain. After *Let's Go* discount: Singles E£15, doubles E£20, triples E£30. Breakfast included.

**Sherif Hotel,** Badr St. (tel. 37 07 57), first right off Television St. Bob Marley's image, music, and habits thrive in this new, friendly establishment. Some rooms have potted plants and balconies, although the vistas of downtown Luxor are hardly epiphanic. Relax on the aging couches in the small, dim lobby. Singles E£5, with A/C E£10. Doubles E£12, with A/C and private bath E£15.

**Oasis Hotel,** Muhammad Farid St. (tel. 38 16 99). From the train station, go left down Abd el-Moneim el-Adasi St., and take a 2nd left after 2 blocks (at the juice stand). Clean, spacious rooms, with a sitting room on every floor. VCR/TV and a library of travel guides and brochures in dining room make up for some soft porn hanging in the lobby. Small roof garden with a limited view. Doubles E£12, with A/C E£29. Triples E£21, in winter E£24. Breakfast included.

**New Sinai Hotel,** just off Television St. (tel. 37 47 52). The owner is proud of the new paintings on the walls—they give the place a rare bit of class. There is a caged pigeon and an international phone in the lobby. Singles E£9, with A/C E£13. Doubles E£14, with A/C E£16. Triples E£15, with A/C E£21. Quads E£20, with A/C E£28. Breakfast included.

**Happy Land,** on El Qamar St (tel. 37 18 28). Take the 2nd right before the bus station off Television St. onto El Madina St., go 100m, then take another right. Obsessively spotless rooms and bathrooms, but cheap for a reason. Free maps and tea. Doubles E£8, with private bath E£10, with bath and A/C E£12.

**Moon Valley Hotel,** Ash-Shams St. (tel. 37 57 10). Make first right off Television St., slanting onto Al Medina-Amanaw St. It's 6 blocks down on the right. Clean lobby with sumptuous sofas. The owner fancies himself a Michael Jackson look-alike, so images of the Great Gloved One are everywhere. Most rooms have A/C. Singles E£8, doubles E£15, triples E£20. Breakfast included.

**Arabesque Hotel,** Muhammad Farid St. (tel. 37 12 99), behind the Luxor Temple. A bit more than the rest, but classier. Name matches the design. Spotless rooms, some with a Nile view. Cool roof garden, restaurant, and swimming pool. Singles US$28. Doubles US$35. All rooms have A/C and TV. Bargain, especially in the summer. Breakfast E£6. Accepts Visa and MC with a 4% commission.

The **Rezeiky Camp and Motel** just before Karnak Temple on El Karnak St. has resort-like **camping** with a pool, deck, bar, and international phone and fax. (E£10 per person. Bungalows E£12 per person. A/C rooms E£25 per person. 10% *Let's Go* discount.) The **YMCA Day-Camp,** on El Karnak St. 180m north of the *service* stand (tel. 37 28 25) is often full of partying Egyptians. The campground has billiards, ping pong, and a cheap café (sandwiches E£1-4), hot water and a 24-hr. guard. Coptic weddings are held here on Sundays. (E£3 per person, E£2.80 for motorcycles, E£5 for cars, and E£25 for caravans. Gates close at midnight.)

## Accommodations on the West Bank (Ancient Thebes)

It is generally preferable to sleep on the East Bank in Luxor proper, but if you can stomach the inconvenience, the West Bank offers quiet surroundings and the chance to roll out of bed and into the Theban necropolis at the opening bell. Unfortunately, you don't get quite as much for your money. Call ahead before lugging your bags across the river. A taxi from the ferry docks (E£5) is the only practical way to get to hotels. For information on crossing the Nile, see **Getting There,** p. 186. The **Pharoah's Hotel** (tel. 31 02 02), behind the student ticket kiosk on an unpaved road, is the west bank's best hotel with carpeted, air conditioned rooms, and a flowery garden out back with ping pong. (Singles E£25, E£30 in winter. Doubles E£50, with bath E£60, E£10 more in winter. Breakfast included.)

## FOOD

Luxor may be an archaeologist's paradise, but it is purgatory for the frugal gourmet. Learn to love the three k's of Egyptian cuisine: *kofta, kabab,* and *kushari.* All three are sold in stands along El Mahatta St. or near Salah ad-Din Sq. Two *kushari* houses stand out from the pack: **Sayyida Zeinab** (on Television St.) and **Sayyida Nafisa** (on Yousef Hassan St.). *Ta'miyya* (falafel) and *fuul* stands are everywhere.

Fresh produce and bread are sold in the *souq* parallel to El Karnak St. beyond the tourist shops. Juice and fruit stands crowd Salah ad-Din Sq. You can always survive on a sugar high from **Twinky Pastries** opposite the train station, with candy, ice cream, and more combinations of honey, butter, and nuts than you ever knew existed. The **New Winter Palace Hotel** (supposedly always open) has a surprising bargain in the E£12 all-you-can-eat *buffet des salades*. Vegetarians, meativores, and sweetivores will enjoy the excellent Middle Eastern and Mediterranean concoctions, not to mention the jamming live band in the background. There are **liquor stores** on Ramses St. directly to the right if you're walking out of the train station and on El Mahatta St. Pension managers can procure beer for you (less than E£5.50).

A big drawback to staying on the **west bank** is its lack of decent, cheap restaurants. **Tutankhamun** and **Africa** next to the ferry landing offer the usual chicken and *kabab* dinners for E£15-20. Most hotels have restaurants, but they're often closed and the quality is inconsistent, especially when business is slow.

**El Houda,** Television St., 100m past the bus garage. Excellent, hearty pizza starts at E£4. Better than Mish Mish, which serves the same food at higher prices across the street. The *escalope* is enormous and well-prepared (E£9). *Shish tawouq* E£6 or ¼-chicken E£4.50. A/C. Open daily 10am-midnight.

**Restaurant Khased Khear** (tel. 38 45 80), on El Mahatta, 1 block from the train station. A/C and an outdoor kitchen (manned by 3 chefs, they'll have you know) keeps this tiny, 2-level restaurant cool. The specialty is *kabab* (beef or lamb, sandwich or platter, starting at E£4). Takeout available. Open daily 10am-2am.

**Abu-Haggar** (tel. 37 63 06), on the street linking the train station and Television St. An upper-crust Egyptian restaurant recommended by locals. Escape the dirt and grime of the outside world and dine surrounded by beautiful marble. *Kofta* E£6.50. Chicken E£7. Veggies E£2.50. Open daily noon-4am.

**Pyramids Hotel Restaurant,** Yousef Hassan St. (tel. 37 32 43). This place prides itself on its *kabab*-rice-salad-chips meal (E£10; same deal with chicken E£8). The lentil soup, which doesn't actually contain any lentils, still tastes good (E£1.75). 20% student discount (cancels out taxes). Open daily 11:30am-11:30pm.

**New Karnak Restaurant,** next to the New Karnak Hotel, opposite the train station. Omelette specialists (cheese, herb, African, or Spanish E£2.25-3.25). Tomato-rich chicken casserole can fill a stomach (E£5.50). Ice cream E£1.25. Cheeseburgers and fries may disappoint (E£6.25/1.50). Open daily 7:30am-10:30pm.

**Abu el-Hassan el-Shuzly Restaurant,** on Muhammad Farid St., across from the Everest Hotel. This new Egyptian restaurant serves up the usual Egyptian grub in a relatively nice atmosphere. Painted windows, ceiling fans, tiled walls, and clean floors. Club sandwich E£7, *kofta* E£6, and *sheesha*. Open daily 10am-11pm.

**The Classic Restaurant** (tel. 38 17 07), Khalid Ibn el-Walid St. A bit pricey, but a welcome break from Egyptian food (although that's also on the menu). Wide range of European dishes peaks at E£30 for steak with mushrooms. Fantastic free bread. Packed with foreigners, especially Aussies. Polished, professional service. Look for the blinking yellow sign near the passport office. Ask for a discount card. Accepts MC, Visa, AmEx. Open daily 6-10:45pm.

## SIGHTS IN LUXOR

Luxor has two big temples and a museum. Luxor Temple, the smaller of the two, stands in the heart of the city adjacent to the Nile. Going north along the corniche, the small but excellent Luxor Museum of Ancient Egyptian Art houses fantastic sculptures unearthed at Karnak and elsewhere. Karnak Temple, the Godzilla of pharaonic architecture, sprawls just a few km further north. All three could be visited in one day, but visiting them on separate afternoons after mornings of tomb hopping on the west bank will help preserve sanity.

### Luxor Temple

Most of Luxor Temple, built by Amenhotep III on top of a Middle Kingdom site, dates from around 1380 BCE. It was meant to serve as a Love Nest for the Gods. Once a year, during the Opet festival, the statues of Amun and his consort Mut would be taken from Karnak temple and loaded onto a ceremonial sacred boat. Amidst much

## Stealing Mummies in the Night

In the late 1870s, members of the Antiquities Service noticed a large number of New Kingdom funerary objects appearing on the European black market. Charles Wilbur, a wealthy American antiquer, was enlisted to go undercover and identify the source of the treasures. By making clear that he would pay high prices for authentic pieces, Wilbur was eventually led to Luxor. Across the river in the town of Qurna, he was shown a piece that had obviously come from a recently opened royal burial. Wilbur secretly telegraphed Gaston Maspero, the Director General of the Antiquities Service, who rushed to Luxor and began intense questioning of all involved. Several weeks later, Muhammad Abd er-Rasul, the head of the most prominent antiquities dealing family in Luxor, confessed that his family had found a tomb near the Mortuary Temple of Hatshepsut. Archaeologists were quickly summoned, and it was found that the deep shaft burial contained the mummies of the New Kingdom's greatest kings: Thutmosis III, Amosis (founder of the New Kingdom), and the legendary Ramses II, among many others. The Abd er-Rasul family had kept the shaft a secret for ten years, quietly selling the stash to Europeans. The Antiquities Service, aware of the security risk that a public disclosure would cause, employed hundreds of local men to load the hushed mummies onto ships. The bodies were hurried down the Nile at top speed and now reside in the Egyptian Museum.

rejoicing and drinking of beer, the happy couple was carried on the shoulders of priests to the Luxor Temple, where they spent 24 days and nights together in the sanctuary. During this time, the moon god Khonsu was conceived, completing the Theban triad.

Later work on the temple was done by Ramses II, who built the enormous **First Pylon,** nearly 24m tall and 65m wide. The pylon is inscribed with images of Ramses II smiting the Hittites. In front of the pylon stand three of the originally six **Colossi of Ramses II,** two seated and one standing. There is a solitary red granite obelisk flanking the doorway; its twin was given to France in 1819 and now graces the Place de la Concorde in Paris.

The granite statues of the **Court of Ramses II,** past the pylon, originally portrayed Amenhotep, but were altered when ancient Egypt's favorite egomaniac assumed the throne. Continue through the court's papyrus columns to the **Colonnade of Amenhotep III,** where the columns have open lotus crowns. The walls of the colonnade were inscribed with scenes from the festival of Opet by Tutankhamun. From here, proceed into the **Court of Amenhotep III.** Beyond this court rises the hypostyle hall, or antechamber, and its 32 gigantic columns. Latin inscriptions to Julius Caesar adorn an altar in a room to the left of the pillared hall. Alexander appears in pharaonic attire before Amun and other deities in some bas-reliefs in the **Sanctuary of Alexander the Great** at the end of the corridor. Overzealous fertility god Min receives disproportionate attention in the sanctuary. The Romans used the whole temple as a *castrum* (military camp) in the 4th century CE. The excavation of the temple remains incomplete, as the Mosque of Abul-Haggag, added by the Fatimids in 1077 CE, prevents the excavation of the left-hand gallery. The mosque, towering 20m overhead, is still in use today and serves as a startling reminder of the depth of sand and rubble that have been cleared by archaeologists.

The temple and its well-groomed lawns make for a comfortable retreat, especially at night. (Open daily 6am-10pm; in winter 6am-9pm; during Ramadan 6am-6:30pm and 8-11pm. The lights go on at 7:30pm year-round. Enter on En-Nil St., 400m north of the New Winter Palace. Admission E£10, students E£5; ½-price after 7pm.)

## Karnak Temple

**Karnak Temple** is overwhelming in its intricacy and proportions. Every major period in Egypt's ancient history since the collapse of the Middle Kingdom is represented in the additions to this complex of shrines dedicated to Amun and his family. Karnak represented the power of the Theban ruler and the importance of the cult of Amun. It was also the center of power for Amun's high priest, whose powers often exceeded those of the pharaoh.

The Karnak complex covers over five acres of land, and is difficult to cover in detail without spending many hours. If you seek more than a general impression of the place, a guided tour is useful (sneaky people can almost always latch onto one). The **sound and light show** is another way of exploring the temple (English shows Mon. 7:45pm, Tues. 10:15pm, Tues.-Sun. at 9pm during the summer. Winter performances Mon. 6pm, Tues. 9pm, Wed.-Sun. 7:30pm. Admission E£33.) The entire 3km route between the temples of Luxor and Karnak was once connected by the sacred **Avenue of the Sphinxes,** built by Queen Hatshepsut. Ramses II took the liberty of adding a small statuette of himself to each sphinx. The final stretch of the avenue remains complete with two rows of sphinxes at the northern end of El Karnak St. by the **Temple of Khonsu,** to the right of the main entry to Karnak Temple.

Enter Karnak Temple from the west with the Nile at your back and pass through the **Avenue of the Rams,** another double-rowed boulevard of creatures (lions' bodies with rams' heads) dedicated to Ramses II. The curly-horned ram was one of Amun's sacred animals. The temple is a hodge-podge of additions and alterations spanning millennia, but because of the traditionalism of pharaonic architecture, the different pieces comprise a harmonious whole. The Karnak complex expands outward from the center, where you will find most of the oldest treasures. The further you proceed from the entrance, the farther back in time you go. The temple is oriented along two axes; a primary east-west axis that follows the path of the sun god Amun and a secondary axis proceeding north-south to Luxor Temple.

The first and largest pylon was never completed and probably dates from the 25th dynasty. The **Great Court,** the single largest individual element of the temple complex, dates from around the same time. Chambers on the left are dedicated to the Theban triad of Amun, Mut, and Khonsu. They were built during the 29th dynasty. On the right is a temple built under Ramses III and lined with 20 7m-tall statues of himself. The three chapels behind the temple's inner court are also dedicated to the Theban Triad. An open papyrus column in the center of the Great Court is all that's left of the pavilion of the Ethiopian king Taharq of the 25th dynasty (689-664 BCE).

Pass through the recycled second pylon (Ramses II made it with blocks from one of Akhenaton's temples) into the **Great Hypostyle Hall.** With 12 central columns and 122 subsidiary columns, it's one of the pinnacles of pharaonic architecture. The central colonnade (1375 BCE) is the oldest part of the hall; other additions are by Ramses II. Emerging from the forest of sandstone, find the 30m-high pink granite **Obelisk of Queen Hatshepsut,** the tallest obelisk in Egypt, in front of the fourth pylon. Hatshepsut, who considered herself a female king, brought the stones from Aswan and inlaid them with bushels of gold. Every centimeter of the ceiling, walls, and columns is carved with inscriptions. Note the depictions of the fertility god Min doing what he does best. Passing through the rubble of the fifth pylon and the granite sixth pylon, enter the **Hall of Records,** containing two elegantly proportioned granite pillars, one decorated with carvings of the lotus of Upper Egypt, the other with the papyrus of Lower Egypt. The **Sanctuary of the Sacred Boats,** behind the hall, was added by Philip, Alexander the Great's brother, around 300 BCE.

Straight ahead, the **Festival Hall of Thutmosis III** dominates the eastern edge of the Karnak complex. Built to commemorate the pharaoh's victories in the mysterious north, it contains carvings of strange plants and animals brought back from his campaigns. The star-studded ceiling survives intact, supported by 52 tapering pillars. Some of the bases were actually whittled down to make room for large processions. In the 6th century CE, the hall was converted into a church; frescoes of haloed saints still adorn the interior walls and column shafts. Beyond a low wall to the east, the **Gate of Nectanebo** marks an early entrance to the complex. South of the Festival Hall, the limpid waters of the **Sacred Lake** sizzle in the heat. Every morning, priests purified themselves in the holy waters of this rectangular pool before performing ceremonies within the temple. Note the large scarab beetle on the southwestern corner

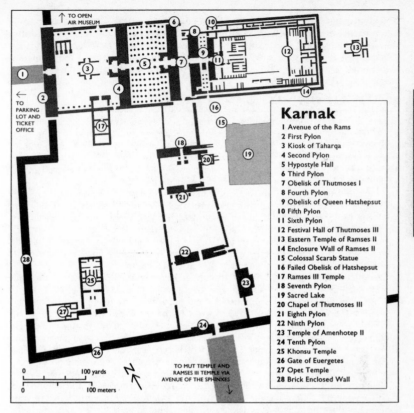

**Karnak**

1 Avenue of the Rams
2 First Pylon
3 Kiosk of Taharqa
4 Second Pylon
5 Hypostyle Hall
6 Third Pylon
7 Obelisk of Thutmoses I
8 Fourth Pylon
9 Obelisk of Queen Hatshepsut
10 Fifth Pylon
11 Sixth Pylon
12 Festival Hall of Thutmoses III
13 Eastern Temple of Ramses II
14 Enclosure Wall of Ramses II
15 Colossal Scarab Statue
16 Failed Obelisk of Hatshepsut
17 Ramses III Temple
18 Seventh Pylon
19 Sacred Lake
20 Chapel of Thutmoses III
21 Eighth Pylon
22 Ninth Pylon
23 Temple of Amenhotep II
24 Tenth Pylon
25 Khonsu Temple
26 Gate of Euergetes
27 Opet Temple
28 Brick Enclosed Wall

of the lake—it is said that if you run around the scarab in a clockwise direction three times, you will soon be pregnant.

You can also visit the **Karnak Open Air Museum,** to the north of the great court; look for a small sign and return toward the entrance. The museum is comprised of three excavated chapels and a motley collection of well-labeled wall fragments. The **Red Chapel** of Queen Hatshepsut is displayed in long rows of blocks, along with the Middle Kingdom **Alabaster Chapel.** The later has white walls streaked with brown, a welcome relief from the acres of sandstone.

It takes a long time to see the temple, so bring water and come early in the day. There are hideously overpriced refreshments available near the sacred lake. Jill Kamil's *Luxor* is an excellent guide to the complex (E£30-40). You can reach the temple by bike, foot or *kalish* (E£5-10). Local minibuses run between Karnak Temple and the train station (25pt). Ask first to make sure the driver is going as far as the temple. (Temple open daily 6am-5pm in summer; 6am-4pm in winter. Admission E£10, students E£5; includes open-air museum.)

### Luxor Museum

The Luxor Museum is a testament to the fact that less is sometimes more. Facing the Nile midway between Luxor and Karnak Temples, the museum has a small but stellar collection displayed with the help of the Brooklyn Museum of New York. Featured treasures from the neighboring temples and the Valley of the Kings include a relief of ancient gymnasts and acrobats, model funerary boats from the celebrated tomb of Tutankhamun, and two very well preserved statues of Akhenaton. Also worth seeing is the reconstructed Tulutat's wall containing hundreds of scenes of ancient Egypt and a colorful portrayal of Akhenaton and beautiful Nefertiti. The New Hall showcases 16 pieces of marble and granite statues, among which the giant cobra and the confident Amenhotep III are the most striking. The museum is within walking distance (2km) of both Luxor and Karnak Temples, a pleasant stroll along the corniche. (Open daily 9am-1pm, additional evening hours 4-9pm in summer; 4-8pm in winter. Admission E£15, students E£7.50.)

## SIGHTS ON THE WEST BANK (ANCIENT THEBES)

When they weren't preoccupied with empire-building and invader-expelling, the rulers of Thebes busied themselves by preparing for eternity. As followers of the sun god Amun, the elite of the New Kingdom aspired to tombs on the west bank, where the sun sets and the afterlife commences. Pharaonic obsession with the afterlife made the necropolis of Thebes into what is quite possibly the world's best-endowed graveyard. Over millennia, robbers and archaeologists have nabbed much of the treasure, but the site still features an unparalleled collection of Egyptian funerary art.

Security was key for the New Kingdom rulers. Earlier pharaohs had been too convinced of the inviolability of their sacred tombs. Thieves had mastered the delicate art of pyramid pilfering at Memphis, making off with many of the afterlife amenities thought to make the second go-round a little easier for expired royalty. A radical change in burial practices was in order. The pharaohs of Thebes would not have their treasure rest anywhere but beside their mummified remains.

To conceal the location, contents, and design of the tombs, the work was done in utmost secrecy by a team of laborers who dwelt within the necropolis itself. Perfecting techniques of tomb construction, decoration, and mummification, this community of 300 artisans devoted itself to the City of the Dead over the course of generations, passing its expertise down through its families. The remains of Deir el-Medina (the Workers' Walled City) have been thoroughly excavated and are among the most complete town remnants in Egypt. Tomb design reflected the new emphasis on secrecy. Instead of a single ostentatious pyramid, there were pairs of funerary monuments: an underground grave, lavishly outfitted with the articles demanded by the hectic afterlife and sequestered in an obscure recess of the desert, and a grandiose mortuary temple where the monarch could be worshiped for eternity. Architects incorporated dead-end passages, fake sarcophagi, hidden doorways, and deep shafts to foil the most cunning robbers. Once a stiff pharaoh was safely stowed, workers immediately began to construct the tomb destined for his successor.

One region in particular seemed ideal for entombment: a narrow, winding valley walled on three sides by jagged limestone cliffs and approachable by a single rocky footpath. This isolated canyon, known as the **Valley of the Kings,** became the burial place of New Kingdom pharaohs. Although it looked promising on papyrus, it failed to deter hoodlums, and few of the tombs escaped vandalism.

Queens, favored consorts, and select offspring were accorded ceremonial burial with full honors and security precautions in a separate corner of the west bank, the **Valley of the Queens** (which is constantly under renovation). Esteemed members of the Theban aristocracy also practiced elaborate burial customs, and several of the resulting **Tombs of the Nobles** rival royal burial chambers in craft and design. Last but not least, the **Valley of the Artisans** has two very impressive tombs of pharaonic artists. Over 400 tombs molder in the necropolis, but only a handful are accessible.

In addition to tombs, the west bank hosts massive mortuary temples. Most imposing are the **Temple of Hatshepsut** in Deir el-Bahri and **Madinet Habu** near the Valley of the Queens. The ruins of the **Ramasseum,** though shattered, still merit a visit.

### Getting There

The first step is admitting that you have to cross the river. The cheapest way across is to take a **local ferry.** One docks directly in front of Luxor Temple (E£1, bicycles 25pt extra), the other docks just north of the Novotel (E£1, bikes free). **Tourist ferries** are faster and more frequent (E£2, no bikes allowed). One docks about 300m north of Luxor Temple, the other in front of the Winter Palace Hotel, 200m south of the temple. Both tourist ferries shuttle you to the non-student ticket kiosk and operate daily 6am-5pm. Local ferries run later. **Private motorboats** can take you across, but charge E£5-10 per boat. From the local ferry landing, it's a 3km bike, taxi, or donkey ride down Memnon St. to the entrance and the student ticket kiosk.

There are several options for exploring the West Bank. **Bicycles** are cheap (E£3-5) and allow for individual freedom and a chance to view the surrounding scenery of green fields abutting sandy dunes. There are a few serious hills (nearly unbearable in summer). You can rent bikes in Luxor or by the local ferry landing.

Hiring a **taxi** is more expensive (E£30-40 for the morning after endless bargaining), but allows you to cover the most ground. Hordes of drivers wait at both ferry landings. You can hire a taxi in Luxor, but the car ferry is slow and erratic. When bargaining, ignore any nonsense about government rates and per person charges.

Mark Twain wrote that riding a **donkey** in Egypt "was a fresh, new, exhilarating sensation worth a hundred worn and threadbare pleasures." This was before Egyptian regulations required visitors to wear clothes while touring the ancient sites. The novelty of donkey travel (which has a way of wearing off quickly) and the fantastic views afforded by the trail as it climbs its way up and around to the Valley of the Kings has led to a burgeoning burro-borrow market. Through your pensione, you can arrange an excursion which includes donkey (with guide) and ferry (E£30-40). Or do away with middlemen and hire your own animal in the village of Gezira just inland from the ferry or at the local ferry dock. This allows you more leeway with your itinerary—the tours usually take you only to the Valley of the Kings, the Temple of Hatshepsut (Deir el-Bahri), the Ramasseum, and the Colossi of Memnon.

If you have time and stamina, the best way to see the sights on the west bank is to **walk** to them. All of the sights (except for the Valley of the Kings) are within a 3km radius of the student ticket kiosk, which is an easy 3km from the ferry landing. The Valley of the Kings is 8km by paved road, but the better route follows the donkey trail up and over the **Gabal al-Qurn** (Hill of the Horn). The peak was once sacred to the goddess Mirtseger, "she who loves silence." You don't have to go to the top of the hill to cross into the Valley of the Kings, but the view is well worth the extra effort. To conserve time and energy, a good strategy is to take a taxi from ferry to kiosk to first sight (the Valley of the Kings is a good candidate), then hike from sight to sight (taxis should be E£10-15 after bargaining, maybe less in summer). Walking in the middle of the day lets you have the sights to yourself, but you must be extremely cautious in the unforgiving sun and heat.

**Guided tours** in air-conditioned coaches with English-speaking guides can be arranged through the various corniche travel agents (E£70-100 per person, including admission; Isis Travel and Misr Travel on the corniche are good places to start). Most tours visit the Valley of the Kings, the Valley of the Queens, the Colossi of Memnon, and Temple of Hatshepsut. Ziggy at the Pyramids Hotel arranges discounted tours for E£50-60, and will lower the price just because you're using this yellow tomb tome. The larger your group, the better your bargaining leverage.

A final option is to rent a **motorbike.** Many hotels, the Everest and Sherif included, rent bikes for E£50 a day. Helmets and leather are nowhere to be found.

### Sight-seeing Strategy

Although most travelers get their fill of West Theban sights in two or three days, the wealth of ancient relics have occupied Egyptologists for lifetimes. Decide what you would like to see before you head out. Consider content, location, and mode of transport before purchasing tickets. (For example, those planning to ride donkeys one day might save the Valley of the Kings for the day of the ride.) One suggested donkey route includes the Valley of the Kings, around to the Temple of Hatshepsut and the Ramasseum. This same route can be done on foot if you first get a ride to the Valley of the Kings. For a chock-full two day itinerary, head north (Valley of Kings, Seti Temple, Hatshepsut, Ramasseum, and the Tombs of the Nobles) and then south (Valley of the Queens, Madinet Habu, and the Valley of the Artisans).

Early morning and late afternoon are the most pleasant (and crowded) times of day to visit. Winter afternoons are sometimes less crowded. Guards at the less-visited sights tend to lock up and head home a little early, especially in the summer. All sites open at 6am, offering about three hours of peace and pleasant temperatures. The sites officially close at 4pm in winter, 5pm in summer, but if you get in before closing time you won't be kicked out. Drinks are sold at some of the ruins, but play it safe by bringing plenty of water. Guards will demand *bakhsheesh* just for gracing you with their presence. Don't feel obligated to give them anything. You have already paid steep foreign prices to see the sights. Women should be aware that guards have been known to harass female visitors; a slap on the wrist and a shout for the tourist police will put it to rest. The tombs are illuminated, but a **flashlight** is useful for ceilings or side passages. Even though the "guards" will let you take pictures if you pay them, flash photography is prohibited as it damages the paintings.

### Tickets

There are two ticket kiosks. The regular **tourist kiosk** is on the western bank of the Nile next to the tourist ferry dock. The **student kiosk** is 3km farther inland on Memnon St., just beyond the Colossi of Memnon. Both kiosks are open daily 6am-5pm. Tickets are non-refundable and good on the day of purchase only. All sites are E£6 (E£3 with ISIC), with three exceptions. Admission to the Valley of the Kings costs E£10 (E£5 with ISIC) and includes access to three tombs. You must buy extra admission tickets for each three additional tombs you want to visit. The Tomb of Tutankhamun has a special admission fee of E£10 (no student discount).

The recently-opened Tomb of Nefertari costs an eye-popping E£100 (E£50 with ISIC). Only 150 tickets are sold per day, and each person may visit for only 10 minutes (open in summer 7:30am-noon and 1-5pm, in winter 8:30am-noon and 1-4pm).

### Valley of the Kings وادى الملوك

The Valley of the Kings lies 5km from the Nile but there's no direct path. There are two possible routes to the beginning of the Valley road: students should head 3km straight inland past the Colossi of Memnon to the student kiosk, then 3km northeast past the sites of the necropolis to the beginning of the Valley road. Non-students with tickets from the Nile-side office can turn right (northeast) at the canal (follow the signs) and go 2km along the canal, then turn west by the Abul Kasem Hotel and go 1.5km to the base of the Valley road. The well-paved, gently sloping road winds for 5km into desolate mountain valleys. The Valley of the Kings itself, no more than 400m long and 200m wide, can easily be toured on foot using the clearly marked, well-groomed gravel paths. Over 64 known and numbered tombs honeycomb the valley; the numbering is in the order of discovery. Most of them are not open to the public, but the best-known tombs are almost always accessible.

The west bank's most renowned tourist attraction, the **Tomb of Tutankhamun (#62),** stands directly in front of the Rest House in the middle of the valley. It requires a special ticket (E£10). The real treasures are at the museum in Cairo and the interior of this small tomb may not be worth the extra ticket. In any case, if you plan to see it, visit it first or you'll probably be disappointed after seeing the others; size may not count for much, but it does make an impression.

Tutankhamun's mummy was encased in the innermost of four snugly nested, superbly decorated cases, three of which can be seen in the Egyptian Museum. Fortunately, the raiding Egyptologists left behind the outermost case, a gilded wood extravagance luxuriating in rich jewels, along with Tut's exquisitely carved sarcophagus. The interior walls of the burial chamber, perfectly preserved, depict colorful scenes from the *Book of the Dead.* The only pharaonic tomb to evade grave robbers, Tut's treasure box was discovered in 1922 by archaeologist Howard Carter. The king's priceless belongings have toured the world several times and now reside permanently in the Egyptian Museum in Cairo. Egyptologists had expected that the tomb would contain little of interest because the pharaoh reigned only two years before he died. Carter ignored professional censure, toiling for six seasons in the Valley of the

Kings. After more than 200,000 tons of rubble had been moved, Carter's patron reluctantly decided to abort the project. Before admitting failure, Carter explored one more possibility: a site in front of the tomb of Ramses VI, in an area covered with workers' huts. Confounding the critics, he chanced upon an ancient doorway beneath the shanties. The tomb had been opened by robbers, but the luckless thieves had apparently been caught in the act by necropolis guards, because the treasures had been hastily stacked and the entrance resealed. Three mummies were found in the tomb, including that of the boy-king himself.

The 12th-century BCE **Tomb of Ramses IX (#6),** on your left once you enter the valley, features fantastic ceiling murals of gold figures manifesting their *joie de mourir* against a deep blue background. To the right of the entrance the pharaoh is shown offering a gazelle to Amun-Re. Farther on the right the reliefs show him making offerings to the God of Justice (the guy with the balance) and to Osiris, god of resurrection. Through 136 negative confessions (I never lied, I never spent time in a Turkish prison...), he is seeking to enter the heavens. Directly opposite these reliefs, Ramses is playing the same game with Horus to gain safe passage through the two lakes of fire. A long corridor descends to an anteroom covered with protective demons, serpents, and wild beasts. Beyond, a pit in the burial chamber once held Ramses IX's sarcophagus. The ceiling of the chamber was not smoothed and the text appears in a short band form because Ramses IX died before his tomb was ready. Most of the painting was done during the 70 days needed for mummification.

The tomb of his grandfather, **Ramses IV (#2),** the first one on the right was used as a Byzantine church. The well-preserved wall decorations contain excerpts from the *Book of the Dead* and *Book of Fates*. On both sides of the tomb, 365 small statues of the Pharaoh's guardian spirit were believed to facilitate his resurrection every night of the year when Amun-Re crossed to the west bank. A technicolor ceiling and huge, cartouche-shaped sarcophagus make this one of the best in the valley.

The most dramatically situated burial site in the necropolis is the cliffside **Tomb of Thutmosis III (#34),** reached by a long, steep staircase that ascends a precipitous ravine squeezed between towering limestone cliffs. This location provides the ultimate example of 18th dynasty pharaohs' attempts to hide their tombs. Thutmosis III's is built in a fault, where it became naturally concealed by debris left from flash floods. This strategy was short-lived because it, like so many others, failed to deceive grave robbers. Thutmosis III, Hatshepsut's stepson and rival, was a great military leader (although freakishly short). His conquests reached as far as the fourth cataract of the Nile to the south, Crete and Cyprus to the north, and the Euphrates to the east. His grave is decorated with unusual heiratic (short-hand hieroglyphic) text and strangely beautiful stick-figure representations of Khnum and other gods. The novel cartouche-shaped burial chamber still contains his red granite sarcophagus (don't tip the guard for showing you that it's empty). To get to the tomb, follow the dirt road that begins next to the Tomb of Ramses III leading southwest up the hill.

Named the "Tomb of the Harp Players" after two musicians depicted plucking away in one of its interior chambers, the **Tomb of Ramses III (#11)** boasts a vividly colorful portrayal of ancient races on the left side of the penultimate chamber. Luckless Ramses III was killed in a palace plot, burgled post-mortem, and as a final insult, kidnapped and shipped in his magnificent sarcophagus to the Louvre.

The steep entrance next to the Tomb of Seti I descends into the **Tomb of Ramses I (#16),** a single burial chamber dominated by Ramses' pink granite sarcophagus. The tomb walls, some of the most vivid in the valley, are painted with scenes of Ramses (founder of the 19th dynasty) hobnobbing with the gods. The first corridor is the shortest in the valley, a consequence of Ramses' brief rule (1320-1318 BCE).

The **Tomb of Meneptah-Siptah (#18)** includes some very nice ceilings painted with vultures and ram-headed falcons (19th dynasty, 13th century BCE). The rough-hewn burial chamber has suffered a good deal of damage, but the large red granite sarcophagus (carved with images of crocodiles and cobras) is still intact.

Three other tombs, closed at press time, are worth visits if they reopen. The **Tomb of Seti I (#17),** the valley's longest tomb, honors the great 19th-dynasty military

EGYPT

leader. The **Tomb of Ramses VI (#9)** is known for its ceiling depictions of headless bodies, people with elongated limbs and torsos, and naked men riding cobras. The **Tomb of Amenhotep II (#35)** is inscribed with the entire text of the Book of the Dead and still contains a beautiful red sarcophagus.

There is a **Rest House** near the entrance to the necropolis featuring overpriced water and warm juice. Public toilets are also available. (Open daily 6am-5pm in summer, 8am-4pm in winter.)

## Mortuary Temples

The pharaohs may have hid their tombs beneath a valley, but they didn't want the living world to forget about them. In addition to the spectacular rock-hewn tombs, the west bank is peppered with **mortuary temples,** mammoth structures honoring the royal stiffs. Though overshadowed by Luxor's Karnak Temple in scale and importance, the West Theban temples of Hatshepsut (Deir el-Bahri), Ramses III (Medinat Habu), Ramses II (Ramesseum), and Seti I are still stupefying.

The following temples, all accessible from a road that runs parallel to the Nile, are described from south to north. From the ferry docks, head inland 3km past the Colossi of Memnon until you come to an intersection. A road to the left leads to Medinet Habu, 500m to the southwest.

All that remains of the largest mortuary temple, that of Amenhotep III, are the **Colossi of Memnon,** a pair of towering statues seated in magnificent isolation on the northern side of the entrance road to the necropolis (free admission). Looking over the plain from a height of 20m, these figures of Amenhotep were Thebes' greatest tourist attraction during the Roman era. At night, an eerie whistling sound emanated from the statues, which the Romans interpreted as the voice of Memnon, mythical son of the goddess of dawn, Aurora, who wailed in anticipation of his mother's rays. The sound, according to scientists, was actually produced by grains of sand splitting off from the statues as the rocks contracted in the cool night air. Unfortunately, the Colossi ceased to sing after repairs during the reign of Antoninus Pius.

### Medinet Habu

To the left at the end of the road after the Colossi stands **Medinet Habu**, a series of well-preserved edifices constructed in several stages. The most impressive structure in the complex is the **Mortuary Temple of Ramses III,** decorated with reliefs of the pharaoh's numerous successful military campaigns, including his victories over the mysterious "Sea Peoples" and the Libyan tribes. The temple is warrior-themed throughout; the main pylon, also known as the Royal Pavilion, resembles a military fortress rather than a temple. A relief explains the importance of securing houses of worship so that peace and order could then spread elsewhere. Other reliefs show

---

### It's All Hieroglyphs to Me

Hieroglyphic writing was used in instances of special religious significance, such as inscriptions on a temple wall, or spells designed to speed a pharaoh to a happy afterlife. They also served an ornamental purpose and are frequently inscribed with remarkable artistic skill. Since the inscriptions are in part decorative, they are often written in mirror-image pairs; in such cases, the writings are read from different directions. To tell which direction is the beginning, look for a human character; the direction the person or god is facing is usually the beginning. Before the discovery of the Rosetta Stone, the most popular theory was that each glyph represented an idea. Elaborate, fanciful, and utterly incorrect translations were made from many papyri and inscriptions. The Rosetta Stone provided the revolutionary insight that each glyph stood for an individual sound, rather than a complex meaning. The hieroglyphic alphabet uses combinations of sounds to represent words, much like the English alphabet. To provide more exact syntax, the hieroglyphic alphabet also includes characters that impart the meaning to the sounds and resolve the problem of homonyms.

prisoners being put to death. Beyond the gate are two relief-rich courts. In the second court on the left side is a window opening supported by statues of human heads. This "window of appearances" was used for royal speeches and was meant to show the king standing on the heads of his vanquished enemies. Relatively few tourists visit the site; a tranquil hour is enough to take it in.

### The Ramesseum

Farther north, beyond the student ticket office, is the **Mortuary Temple of Ramses II**, or the **Ramesseum.** The same pharaoh who had Abu Simbel tailor-made to his specifications built the Ramesseum to house another mammoth exercise in narcissism. The 1000-ton, 17m **Colossus of Ramses II** (the forefingers alone are over 1m long) was transported in one piece from the pharaoh's granite quarries in Aswan to Thebes. Even shattered, the remnants (including head, upper arms, and one foot) are imposing. This colossus originally overlooked the passageway leading into the second court. A tour of the Ramesseum won't exceed half an hour.

### The Temple of Hatshepsut (Deir el-Bahri)

Just north of the Ramesseum, a paved road leaves the main north-south thoroughfare and heads northwest, winding around to the **Temple of Hatshepsut.** If you are on foot, you can save some time by cutting through the village on the left side of the road (before it splits). Located in the center of the necropolis, the temple is 500m north of the Tombs of the Nobles. Hatshepsut's masterpiece rises in three broad, columned terraces from the desert floor against a backdrop of sheer limestone cliffs. The Temple's ancient Egyptian name, Djeser Djesern, means "most splendid of all."

After the death of her husband Thutmosis II, Hatshepsut became the ruler of the kingdom, the only woman to assume the title of Pharaoh. Her temple, currently under excavation by a team of Polish archaeologists, has been skillfully restored with modern materials. No images of Hatshepsut remain intact; after her death, the great Thutmosis III, who had to wait 20 years in her shadow before coming into his own as Pharaoh (she refused to marry him), defaced virtually all of them. Men.

Walk from the lower court up a wide ramp to the central court. The colonnaded back wall contains, from left to right, the Shrine of Hathor, the Colonnade of the Expedition to Punt, the Birth Colonnade, and Shrine to Anubis. The Punt reliefs show Egyptian expeditions to that land (today's Somalia), and the exchange of goods (trees, animals, etc.) with the locals. The Birth Colonnade details Hatshepsut's birth and childhood. Another huge ramp leads to the upper court with a rock-cut sanctuary. Badly ruined, and sadly defaced by Christians who used the temple as a Coptic monastery in the 7th century, this court is closed to the public.

### Temple of Seti I

You'll have a fair amount of trouble getting here and there's not that much to see. From the Temple of Hatshepsut return to the main road, turn north, and follow it to the end. Turn right to visit what remains of the **Mortuary Temple of Seti I,** father of Ramses II, a warrior who enlarged the Egyptian empire to include the island of Cyprus and parts of Mesopotamia. Seti was also one of the first men to wear earrings—archaeologists could tell this from his well-preserved mummy-lobes. Although the booty from his successful campaigns has been stolen, the relief work, among the finest executed in ancient Egypt, remains.

### Valley of the Artisans (Deir el-Medina)

To reach the plentiful though visually uninspiring remains of the **Workers' Walled City,** start from the student ticket office and follow the small road west. About 60m down the road stands the small temple of **Deir el-Medina** (Monastery of the Town), an elegant shrine dating from the Ptolemaic era. Dedicated to Hathor, the goddess of love, and Maat, the representation of divine order (see **Religion in Ancient Egypt,** p. 57), the temple was named during Christian times when monks constructed a monastery next door. The Workers' Walled City was the only inhabited area on the west bank necropolis during the New Kingdom. Since the workers and artists knew the whereabouts of the tombs they were digging and were using precious, expensive materials, their movements were strictly controlled and observed and they lived in isolation (the entire walled city was roofed over). Many of the workers were killed when construction was completed. A typical house consisted of a kitchen, a living room, and one bedroom. Some had stairways for access to the rooftops, a welcome relief from the heat and smell below.

Several **Tombs of Artisans** can also be found here. The accessible ones are in such excellent condition that it is hard to believe they were painted so many centuries ago. Unlike the formal decorations dictated by priests on the walls of royal tombs, these tombs contain very creative drawings of the afterlife that can be considered a form of free-hand art. Perhaps it's the exceptionally long painting time that led to the imposing relief—some spent almost 30 years building their tombs. They could only work on their own tombs on the single rest day of the ancient ten-day week. Two amazing tombs are open to the public—the **Tomb of Sen-nedjen,** artist of Ramses III, and **Tomb of Inherku,** "deputy master of the two Egypts in Truth Square;" in short: head artist of Ramses IV. A single admission ticket includes the Temple of Deir el-Medina, the two tombs, and the Workers' Walled City.

## Tombs of the Nobles

A few hundred meters southeast of the Temple of Hatshepsut is the west bank's sardine-packed burial site, the more than 400 Tombs of the Nobles. The area is divided into four regions: the Tombs of Rekhmire and Sennofer; the Tombs of Ramose, Userhet the Scribe, and Khaemhut; the Tombs of Nakht and Mena; and the Asasif Tombs. You must buy a separate ticket for each. The first two groups provide the most punch for your tomb-going pound. A guide is unnecessary, but many villagers will volunteer their services. Maps are available in bookstores on the East Bank, and you can ask villagers to point the way.

Throughout the New Kingdom, Theban aristocrats had *de facto* control over much of the pharaoh's empire and served as advisors. The pharaoh often remained ignorant of the most crucial political developments while members of the elite fought amongst themselves for control of the kingdom. Some aristocrats affected pharaonic status by amply providing themselves with luxuries for the afterlife and devising well-hidden underground tombs. Unlike the divine pharaoh who would assuredly live among the gods after his death, Theban aristocrats needed more assurance that a comfortable existence awaited them in the afterlife. Accordingly, every facet of their earthly lives was carefully recorded on the walls of their tombs, leaving the decoration more naturalistic and mundane than the reliefs found in pharaonic tombs. Because the limestone in this portion of the necropolis was inferior, artisans could not carve in relief; instead they painted murals on a whitewashed stone surface. These tombs are architecturally simpler than those of the Pharaohs; they all start with a terrace leading to a decorated vestibule followed by a corridor.

### Tombs of Ramose, Userhet, and Khaemhut

The **Tomb of Ramose (#55)** was built during the reign of the heretic king Akhenaton (Amenhotep IV). Ramose was Governor of Thebes and Vizier under Amenhotep and Akhenaton, and was apparently one of the first converts to Akhenaton's new god, the Aton.

In the columned first chamber, all of Egypt pays obeisance to Aton, a blood-red disk emitting shafts of light which end in small hands holding *ankhs* and other religious symbols. On the wall through which you enter, the images carved in unpainted relief reflect the traditional, stylized tastes of the Old Kingdom, with scenes of Ramose and his family making offerings and Egyptians cheering Ramose's conversion to the Aton cult. In contrast, the wall to the left as you enter displays the strangely distorted figures and realistic composition typical of Akhenaton's reign. The tomb was never completed and a lot of the carvings were left unpainted since Ramose abandoned this tomb and chose to build a bigger one in the monotheistic necropolis of Tel el-Amarna, near Minya. An interesting theory about Akhenaton is supported in these images.

The sun-disc Aton looks startlingly like a flying saucer. The oblong heads and elongated arms resemble modern representations of space aliens. Hmmm. The guard will offer to show you the dull, dark burial chamber, perhaps not worth the *bakhsheesh* he will demand.

Continue up from the depression containing the Tomb of Ramose to the **Tomb of Userhet the Scribe (#56),** a few meters to the south. Although an early Christian monk who made his home within the chamber destroyed most of the female figures adorning the walls, the tomb's decor retains a certain blithe spirit because of the unusual pink tones of the interior frescos. Userhet, Amenhotep II's royal scribe (around 1408 BCE), had his resting place painted with every-day scenes: on the right-hand wall of the first chamber, men wait their turn in line for the local barber, while hunting and duck-offering scenes cover the wall of the entrance.

Next is the less-than-impressive **Tomb of Khaemhut (#57),** another of Amenhotep's scribes. The only thing worth seeing are the statues of the scribe and his wife.

### Tomb of Nakht

Slightly north of the Tomb of Ramose, a trail leads off the main road and winds east a short distance to the **Tomb of Nakht (#52).** The first chamber contains a reconstruction of an exquisite statue of Nakht, scribe of the royal granaries under Thutmosis IV (the original was lost at sea on its way to the U.S. during World War I). Also in the first chamber are photographs of some of the other removed contents and a series of well-labeled diagrams explaining the images within the second chamber. The most famous image from the Tombs of the Nobles, three musicians playing the flute, harp, and lute, is on the left wall; Nakht's wife was a singer.

### Tombs of Rekhmire and Sennofer

The westernmost tomb belongs to Rekhmire, a governor of Thebes who advised Thutmosis III and prided himself on his administrative genius. A historian's delight, the **Tomb of Rekhmire (#100)** is comprised of biographical narratives depicting the full range of activities Rekhmire oversaw. This tomb is perhaps the most absorbing of all the tombs in the Theban necropolis.

In the first chamber, tax evaders are tried by Rekhmire, who sits with a set of rolled papyrus texts strewn at the foot of his judgment throne; the presence of the papyrus suggests that written law existed as early as 1500 BCE. On the inner, left-hand wall, a procession of tribute-paying expeditions arrives from Crete (top), Syria (middle), and the African Kingdoms of Punt and Nubia (bottom). Making contributions to the pharaonic menagerie, Nubian representatives offer a giraffe, assorted monkeys, a tiger, and an elephant tusk. Other scenes show Egyptians getting hammered during what was known as the "Festival of the Valley." The niche at the top of the rear wall was intended to contain a statue of Rekhmire himself.

Trek 50m up the hill to the west of Rekhmire's tomb to reach the **Tomb of Sennofer (#96).** This impressively vivid tomb is known as "Tomb of the Vines," after the filigree grapevine crawling all over the ceiling. The delightful lattice of purple and green simulates a shady arbor for Sennofer, overseer of the royal gardens of Amun under Amenhotep II. The plan of the tomb is as unusual as its decor: a curving wall leads into the first room, which in turn leads straight back into the pillared burial chamber. The big, wet eyes of Hathor the love-cow follow you around the tomb from the tops of the columns. The superb condition and remarkable expressiveness of the paintings of this small tomb make it worth the detour.

### Asasif Tombs

Southwest of the Temple of Hatshepsut lies **Asasif,** a current archaeological hot spot. Asasif became the most popular aristocratic burial area during the 25th and 26th dynasties (about the 7th century BCE), though the **Tomb of Kheruef (#192),** the finest portion of the necropolis, was constructed 700 years earlier. Enter the burial site through an outer courtyard containing other tombs, where a series of well-wrought reliefs stands against a protecting wall. Note the provocative ceremonial dance featuring a chorus line of women, a jumping bird, a noisy monkey, flutists, and drummers to the left of the doorway. On the right, pharaonic heartthrob Amenhotep III is surrounded by 16 swooning princesses.

As you enter the **Tomb of Kiki (#409),** about 10m to the north of Kheruef, the gods Thoth and Anubis discuss the readings of a giant scale. The burial chamber remains unfinished, leaving a series of faceless figures outlined in red. To get to the **Tomb of Nefer-hotep (#48),** walk 100m east along the dirt path from Kiki, then turn right (south) and walk 20m to the tomb, immediately in front of a village house. Most of the seated stone figures within the tomb are fairly intact.

### Valley of the Queens وادى الملكات

During the later years of the New Kingdom, a special burial area was chosen for the wives and children of the pharaohs. Traditionally, the pharaoh's closest relatives were buried beside the monarch, but this arrangement changed during the reign of Ramses I (14th century BCE), when princes, consorts, and wives were buried in the Valley of the Queens. Directly west of the Colossi of Memnon at the end of the main road, the Valley of the Queens contains fewer than 30 royal tombs. Check at the ticket kiosks to find out which are currently open.

The **Tomb of Amonherkhepeshef (#55)** is richly bedecked with bas-relief carvings: Ramses III introduces his nine-year-old son to each of the major deities and Amonherkhepeshef wears the groomed topknot of a pharaonic prince. The colored scenes of deities and farmers fill entire walls—a rare sight in Theban tombs. The small sarcophagus that held the prince's mummy stands in the rear burial chamber. A desiccated fetus lies curled in a small glass display next to the sarcophagus. The extremely pricey **Tomb of Queen Nefertari (#66)** is open to the first 150 people who can afford a ticket (E£100, students E£50). The paintings and reliefs have been expertly restored, and are some of the best specimens of New Kingdom art. Unfortunately, the guards will rush you through the tomb's seven chambers, so stay alert.

## ENTERTAINMENT

This ain't no Cairo or Alexandria. For true Luxor-y diversion, fritter away afternoons aboard a **felucca** on the Nile. **Banana Island** is a popular destination; two miles upriver, it's a small peninsula studded with palms and fruit trees (small green bananas E£1). Overpriced souvenir stands detract from an otherwise rustic experience. *Feluccas* are prohibited from sailing after sunset. (Round-trip 2-3hr.; E£10 per person for groups over 4.)

You will probably be invited to a wedding party while in Luxor (or at least asked to get liquor at the duty free store "for my sister's wedding tomorrow"). Think twice before disrupting a wedding party—often "invitees" are expected to pay admission.

The **Mercure (a.k.a. ETAP) Hotel,** on the corniche, is the most happening **discothèque** in Luxor. There is a E£20 minimum charge, but nobody pays attention to it during the summer. Every night at 11:30pm, the music changes from Top 40 dance remixes to drum machine and synthesizer Arabic music and the belly dancing starts. An older crowd joins the youngsters for the nightly display of undulating flesh. The audience is encouraged to participate by the high-energy bartenders and managers, often by example. Stella costs E£8 and makes the place much better (open nightly 10pm-2am). Most popular with local swingers is **Disco on Le Lotus** at the Novotel (intersection of Salah ad-Din and the corniche), located on a boat docked behind the hotel (open 10pm-2am; E£20 minimum). Drinks hover around E£12 at the self-proclaimed **Ultimate Night Spot,** where American and European music reverberates late into the night. You can make requests or bring in your own music.

Quieter options are **billiards** at the **Mercure** (E£5 per game) or **backgammon** and **foosball** at the downstairs **Novopub** in the Novotel (drinks around E£12). The **New Winter Palace Hotel** has a breezy terrace and a live band (drinks E£15), and the **Pyramid Hotel** has a relaxing roof garden in winter (drinks and food around E£5).

**Ahwahs** are filled with Egyptians smoking *sheesha,* drinking coffee, and playing dominoes and backgammon until the wee hours. Foreigners are usually welcome, but solo women may attract unwanted comments. The **Tikkya,** on Television St., is comfortable and friendlier than the other shops. If you have money you don't need, you can lose it at the Hilton **casino** (open 8pm-1am, foreign currency only). Finally, you can check out the Luxor Museum or Temple by night, or witness the infotainment spectacular of the Karnak **sound and light show** (see **Karnak Temple,** p. 183).

## ■ Near Luxor: Dendera

The **Temple of Hathor** at Dendera is one of the few sights in Middle Egypt that has remained accessible throughout the fundamentalist uprising. A visit is only recommended for die-hard temple fans. Public transportation to the nearby town of Qena is strongly discouraged and hard to come by. The only mode of transport approved for tourists is a boat from Luxor, emptying wallets at E£150 per person for a day cruise including lunch (book with a travel agent on the corniche). Once there, you'll be surrounded by police who will rush you through your visit. For your trouble, you'll get to see a temple without the crowds of Karnak or Luxor. The temple is smaller and not as old, but still an impressive display of ancient devotion to the gods.

The **Temple of Hathor** only dates from the first century BCE, although worship of Hathor is much older. The late Ptolemies and the Romans found it politically expedient to associate themselves with the benevolent goddess. Hathor is depicted as cow-headed or with cow's ears, or shown wearing a crown of two horns cradling the sun disk. Because her specialty was love, Hathor, the "Golden One," was identified by the Greeks as Aphrodite. During an annual festival, a statue of Hathor was carried in a sacred procession down the Nile to meet Horus of Edfu.

Eighteen columns are topped by cow heads in the **Great Hypostyle Hall.** In the temple's inner sanctum, wall paintings portray the embalmer's art, while the ceiling is decorated with pictures of the goddess Nut. The second hypostyle hall, also called the **Hall of Appearances,** gives way to the **Hall of Offerings,** where the daily rites were performed. In the kiosk in the southwest corner of the roof, priests performed the ceremony of "touching the disk," in which the soul of the sun god Ra appeared in the form of light. If you look to the right you will notice a gently sloping staircase which leads up to the roof.

The **Hall of the Ennead** immediately precedes the inner sanctuary. The chamber on the left is the wardrobe; opposite it, a doorway leads through a small treasury into the **Court of the New Year** where sacrifices were performed during the New Year festival. On the ceiling of the colorful portico, Nut gives birth to the sun, whose rays shine upon the head of Hathor. The **Mysterious Corridor** surrounds the **Sanctuary** on three sides, and 11 chapels, each with a distinct religious function, open off of it. A small chamber known as the **Throne of Ra** sits behind the northernmost of the three doorways behind the sanctuary. A minuscule opening in its floor leads to the crypt, a subterranean hallway embellished with reliefs, some of inlaid alabaster. Many rooms on the upper floors carry ceiling paintings of Nut swallowing the sun at sundown and giving birth to it at dawn. On the roof of the temple, near the edge, is graffiti left by French soldiers in 1799. During the summer, bats inhabit the secluded portions of the temple; a flashlight comes in handy.

## ■ Between Luxor & Aswan

Along the 228km stretch of the Nile from Luxor to Aswan you'll pass the drowsy rural towns of Esna (58km south), Edfu (50km farther), and Kom Ombo (100km farther). Bright green corn and date palm fields line the riverbank and quickly give way to lifeless desert. The area is dotted with hamlets of mud-brick houses honeycombed together on the cliff face at the desert's edge. Going by river is the sweetest of joys. The area is an enchanting mixture of older Arab *fellaheen* communities and Nubian villages created by those whose homes are now submerged by Lake Nasser. Each of the major towns is graced by an outstanding Ptolemaic temple.

Whether you go by *service,* bus, train, or *felucca,* you'll have no difficulty stopping in Esna, Edfu, and Kom Ombo. These towns also make excellent daytrips: Esna and

Edfu from Luxor; Edfu, Kom Ombo, and the camel market at Daraw from Aswan. By boat, the entire Luxor-Aswan route takes three to five days, including Ptolemaic ports of call in Esna, Edfu, and Kom Ombo.

# ESNA اسنا

A quiet, provincial town 55km south of Luxor, Esna snoozes on the western bank of the Nile and boasts blue, blue waters, a turn-of-the-century British barrage, and the remains of a Roman-era temple sitting in a hole in the ground in the middle of town. From Esna, a small highway ambles along the western bank to West Thebes. As always, expect to be bombarded by *kalish* drivers and others wanting to be your "friend." For transportation information, see p. 174.

**Orientation and Practical Information** Esna has only a few main streets for tourists. The highway and rail lines are on the eastern side of the river, connected to the town by a bridge. Once you have crossed to the west bank of the Nile, you will, appropriately enough, be on **Nile Street.** Following it south, you will find the **telephone and telegraph office,** 50m to the right (tel. 40 07 77; open 24hr.; international calls). Nile St. then veers slightly west and crosses a canal to the **police station** (tel. 40 08 89; open 24hr.). From here it saunters 20m to **El Malak Pharmacy,** then cuts sharply left and then right to follow the river. From the river it's about 300m south to the **Bank of Alexandria** (tel. 40 05 26; open summer Sun.-Thurs. 8:30am-2pm, 6-9pm for exchange; winter 5-8pm; during Ramadan 10am-1:30pm). There is currently no post office in Esna, but there are several red postal boxes past the mosque on Nile St. Another 100m brings you to the temple ticket booth. (Open summer 6am-6:30pm, winter 6am-5:30pm. Admission E£4, students E£2. Don't buy tickets from hawkers in the bazaar.) At the ticket booth, Nile St. is met by **Souq Street,** a 200m stretch of tourist bazaars which runs up to the temple, passing the **tourist police** (tel. 40 06 86) on the left. Esna is delighted to have a **hospital** (tel. 40 07 09; for **ambulance** dial 502). The town's **telephone code** is 095.

There is little to keep you in Esna beyond a temple visit, but if you must stay, the worn out **Hotel El Haramen** (tel. 40 03 40) provides acceptable if lackluster housing at a decent price. (Singles E£6, with bath E£12. Doubles E£10, with bath E£15. Triples E£15, with bath E£20. Quads E£20.) The hotel is 1km south (through the *souq*) of the temple's eastern wall (pass to the right of the white wall enclosing a gray concrete building, and walk another 100m). The *souq* can provide *ta'miyya, fuul,* and produce.

The **train station** lies to the east of town on the other side of the Nile. The **bus** and **service stations** are at the town's western edge, down the street just south of the telephone office (E£1 to temple). You can take a **kalish** from either station to the temple (don't pay more than E£1.50-2 for a ride anywhere in town), or walk (2km).

**Sights** Khnum was a ram-headed creator god worshipped in the area of the first cataract before and after Egypt's unification. This local deity, who reputedly molded the first human being on a potter's wheel, had his sanctuary on Aswan's Elephantine Island. The cataract was an important regional center for the area south of Luxor, and the pharaohs of the 18th dynasty, seeking stronger popular support, dedicated this temple to the local deity. Although the **Temple of Khnum** was begun in the 18th dynasty, it is largely a Roman creation and was in many ways a feeble imitation of inherited technical and artistic achievements. Archaeologists discovered the elaborate hallway in excellent condition. Today the temple is an astounding spectacle lying in a pit, surrounded by the *souq* and the everyday bustle of modern life.

The Romans, attempting to decorate the temple in a pharaonic manner, carved a procession of stiff, oddly deformed figures marching solemnly across the walls. The ceiling designs are among the more interesting aspects in the temple. Faint blue and red hues on the tops of the 24 columns hint at the interior's former brilliance (open summer daily 6am-6:30pm; winter 6am-5:30pm; admission E£4, students E£2).

Just to the north of the turn off to the temple, a **barrage** (a series of gates that can be raised or lowered to control water flow) completed in 1908 stretches across the river. Upgraded and restored in the 1940s to meet increased demand, the old barrage has nevertheless been made obsolete by a new one (financed with Italian help) 1km to the north. The government hopes that the new barrage will help reclaim some 300,000 *feddans* of land.

## EL KAB AND GEBEL ES-SILSILAH الكاب و جبل السلسلة

If you have time and energy to spare while traveling between Esna and Edfu, either by the main highway or by *felucca*, consider a stop at **El Kab**, 20km north of Edfu and 3km south of the village of **El Mahamid**. The government has only recently developed El Kab for tourism, and the site has yet to become overrun. Many taxi drivers haven't heard of it, while others refuse to drive there. The upside is that if you manage to get to El Kab, you will probably have the site to yourself. The downside is that if you want to visit the temples, which lie at 2.5 and 4km from the roadside tombs and city wall, you'll have to walk; bring several bottles of water (there's not a leaf of shade). If you come by *felucca*, your captain might not know where El Kab is; give him the distances indicated here and be on the lookout for the Roman wall on the east bank of the Nile.

The religious center of El Kab was dedicated to the vulture-goddess Nekhbet, protector of the pharaohs and lady of the mouth of the desert. The remains are interesting, but not on the order of Edfu or Valley of the Kings. The escarpment by the road is pocked with a number of tombs. The four most important ones date from 1570-1320 BCE. They have locked gates and a stairway up to them; the guard will let you in. The most well-preserved is the **Tomb of the Paheri.** A multi-talented royal servant, Paheri was chief priest, royal tutor to Prince Wadjmose (son of Pharaoh Thutmosis I), and scribe of the accounts of corn. This tomb features brightly colored illustrations of long lines of seated lotus-sniffers, Egyptians cultivating crops, fishing, shipping, and making wine, as well as an impressive assortment of international 19th-century graffiti and a statue of happy Paheri flanked by two female figures. **The Tomb of Setau** belongs to the powerful high priest of Amun under Ramses III through IX (20th dynasty). The **Tomb of Aahmes** is the resting place of a warship captain who suppressed a rebellion in Upper Egypt and led 18th dynasty forces under Amenhotep I and Thutmosis I in Nubia and Syria. Both tombs are poorly preserved. The **Tomb of Renini,** superintendent of priests under Amenhotep I, contains a geometrically painted ceiling and two big eyes which look out from either side of a broken central statue.

Two and a half km along an unpaved but passable track brings you to the tiny **Chapel of Thoth** (1320-1200 BCE), built by the high priest of El Kab for Ramses II and dedicated to Nekhbet, Thoth (Wisdom), and Horus. The much larger **Ptolemaic Temple** built under Ptolemies IX through XI has an impressive ramped entryway leading to a forecourt with a few nice broken capitals and a chamber with ceiling paintings and inscriptions. Wake up the guard in the shack across the road to open the locked gates; he'll then ride with you another 1.5km to the small **Temple of Amenophis III** with well-preserved colored paintings and carvings of Nekhbet herself coiffed with a swinging 60s *That Girl* bob. Caravans going to and coming from gold mines deeper in the desert once stopped here for prayer.

The quarries at **Gebel es-Silsilah** are a fascinating bonus prize for *felucca* travelers who are charming enough to persuade their captain to stop here. Although a ramp and stairs have been built down to the water's edge in anticipation of Nile cruiser stops, the site is not yet officially open. *Bakhsheesh* to the guard and a promise to be quick about it should win you access. The sandstone quarries were in use from the New Kingdom (1500 BCE) up to the Ptolemaic (and possibly the Roman period). They are actually on both sides of the Nile, but you'll dock on the west bank, where a guard can unlock a well-preserved **temple** constructed under the anti-Aten Pharaoh Horemheb, a general under Tutankhamun who seized the throne during the power struggles after Tut's death. The forecourt has well-preserved relief scenes. From the temple, a 200m path leads south along a bluff 15m above the Nile, ending in the cavernous belly of the quarry. Here, huge blocks of sandstone were cut from the cliff, loaded onto boats, and transported along the Nile to construction sites. Notice the boat and ostrich graffiti etched into the wall's face. You can scramble to the top of the cliff for a fine Nile view.

## EDFU ادفو

Edfu is a tiny town with a *big* temple. Like many temple towns in the Valley, there is a good deal of hustling going on, but here the psychological warfare waged by *kalish* drivers and bazaar hawkers is a bit calmer. A few blocks beyond the town's central square, oblivious to 2000 years of change, stands a stunningly well-preserved Temple of Horus. The intricacy of this temple rivals the serenity of Kalabsha and even the awesome scale of Abu Simbel, making it one of Upper Egypt's most spectacular sights. If you can time your visit to avoid the periodic inundations of tourists, exploring the dark, eerie chambers and towering columns can be quite a thrill.

**Orientation and Practical Information** Edfu lies 50km south of Esna on the western bank of the Nile, roughly halfway between Luxor (112km south) and Aswan (121km north). The Edfu bridge, with the **train station** on its eastern end and the **service taxi station** near its western end, crosses the Nile at the northern edge of town. Local **pick-up trucks** (E£1) or **private taxis** (E£3-5) can take you from either station to the temple. Trains run north and south until 9 or 10pm, as do *service*. From the bridge, the riverfront road runs 100m south to the **telephone office** (tel. 70 17 77; open 24hr.) and another 200m to **El Maglis Street,** which links the Nile with Temple Sq. Another 200m down on your right is the **Bank of Cairo** (tel. 70 36 97; open summer Sun.-Thurs. 8:30am-2pm and 6-9pm; winter 8:30am-2pm and 5-8pm). Across the street from the bank is the **Ezzat Pharmacy** (tel. 70 38 60; open Mon.-Sat. 7:30am-11pm).

The cleanest budget hotel in town (admittedly not a bold claim) is the **El Madina Hotel,** located just off Temple Sq. (tel. 70 13 26; singles with bath and breakfast E£13, with shared bath E£10). The **SemiRamis Hotel,** near the bank, is, well, E£3 per bed—don't expect much. The **New Egypt Restaurant,** off Temple Sq., serves rice, vegetables, salad, and either meat or half a chicken for E£7. Edfu's produce *souq* (open Sat.-Thurs. 8am-9pm) is to the left on Goumhouriyya St. To the right is a *ta'miyya, fuul,* and tea stand market. The **bus station** is 50m north of Temple Sq. (a right turn off El Maglis St.). Buses run north and south hourly until 6pm (at the latest). The **post office** is on Tahrir St., on the right side 50m south of Temple Sq. (open Sat.-Thurs. 8am-2:30pm). One hundred meters from Temple Sq. is a tourist bazaar, the **tourist police** (tel. 70 01 34; open 7am-5pm), and the **temple.** Edfu's **phone code** is 089.

**Sights** The **Temple of Horus** took over 200 years to construct and was not completed until 57 BCE, making it one of the last great Egyptian monuments. The Ptolemies designed this temple and the one at Dendera, dedicated to Horus's wife Hathor, as a matched set. Like Dendera and many other locations in the Valley, Edfu has been the site of a temple since at least New Kingdom times, the current building being just the most recent incarnation. Several important religious festivals dealing with the life of Horus were celebrated at Edfu. During the annual "Union with the Solar Disk," Horus's earthly form was brought to the roof of the temple to be rejuvenated by the rays of the sun. Another important ritual was the "Festival of the Happy Reunion," in which the god's icon was removed from the temple in a ceremonial boat and taken to Dendera to bring Hathor home to Edfu for some postmortem cavorting. There is a polished black granite shrine in the inner sanctuary that once held the icon statue of Horus. In a chamber behind the sanctuary, there is a modern reconstruction of the ceremonial boat used to carry the statue during festivals.

Enter the temple through the 12 gigantic columns of the **Great Hypostyle Hall** and proceed to the second Hypostyle Hall, outfitted with a similar arrangement of smaller pillars. Doorways on either side lead to the **ambulatory,** a narrow exterior passage-way running between the temple and its protective wall. The temple is honey-combed with smaller passageways that enabled the priests to walk around the entire complex without crossing in front of the sanctuary or speaking to one another. The doorway on the right side of the second hall leads to a side chapel with an amazing ceiling depiction of the sky goddess Nut reaching around the Zodiac.

Outside the temple, directly in front of the main entrance pylon, is a well-preserved Roman *mammisis* (birthhouse), where the birth of Horus was reenacted annually with appropriate hoopla. Copts later defaced the images of the growing god on the columns of the *mammisis.* Note the images of pot-bellied pygmies, brought to court for the royalty's entertainment, atop of the exterior side columns (site open daily 6am-6pm; winter 7am-4pm; admission E£10, students E£5).

## KOM OMBO كوم أمبو

Forty-five km north of Aswan on the east bank of the Nile stands Kom Ombo, the site of an Egyptian temple as renowned for its location as for its unique construction and design. Unlike many of the temples in Upper Egypt, Kom Ombo is still situated in its original spot along the banks of the Nile, giving virtually the same visual impression today as it did during Ptolemaic ptimes. The temple is unique in that it was dedicated to two gods and is therefore rigorously symmetrical throughout. Double halls and double colonnades lead to double doorways to double chambers and sanctuaries. The two-fold temple was dedicated to the deity duo of Sobek, the crocodile god who was locally important due to the many crocs patrolling the Nile near Kom Ombo, and Horus the elder, avenger of Osiris and the source of the pharaohs' divine power.

**Orientation and Practical Information** The layout of Kom Ombo town is fairly symmetrical; everything you will need lies on a few main streets. The Cairo-Aswan highway runs north-south, paralleling the nearby train tracks. **Port Said Street** runs north-south and lies 150m east of the tracks (away from the Nile). Situated 300m west of the tracks is **26th July Street,** which runs north-south. **Goumhouriyya Street** runs east-west on a slight diagonal, intersecting all the others and heading down to the Nile. A footbridge crosses the railroad tracks 100m south of Goumhouriyya St. and lets you out onto the main **souq street,** also called Nabin Monsur St.

The **bus station** is on 26th July St., 150m south of Goumhouriyya St. The **service taxi station** awaits you on the northern edge of the intersection of 26th July and Goumhouriyya St. (Aswan E£2, Daraw 50pt, Silsilah 50pt). There is also a small *service* stand on the Cairo-Aswan highway 50m south of Goumhouriyya St. The **train station** is on the east side of the tracks between Goumhouriyya St. and the footbridge. Trains run north and south, usually twice daily, in the morning and in the evening. Ask at the station well in advance and be prepared to wait. If the ticket office is closed (it probably will be), don't fret—the conductor will sell you a ticket on the train.

The **police station** sits 200m south of Goumhouriyya St. on Port Said St. (tel. 50 00 23). The **Bank of Alexandria** is down a small alley behind the mosque on the Cairo-Aswan highway, on the left side coming from the highway (open daily 8am-2pm and 6-9pm). **El Fateh Pharmacy** is 100m south of Goumhouriyya St. on the Cairo-Aswan highway. The **post office** is on the corner of Port Said St. and Nabin Monsur St. at the Welcome Visitors sign (open Sun.-Thurs. 8am-2pm).

Covered **pick-up trucks** run between the center of town and the river, about 1km north of the temple (E£1). Private taxis cost E£3-5 each way. If you're coming from Aswan by *service* or bus, ask to be let off at the well-marked turn-off to the "tembel" 2km south of town. From the turn-off, walk 1.5km along the road to the temple site.

**Accommodations and Food** The **Cleopatra Hotel** (tel. 50 03 25), just off 26th July St. and the *service* stand, may be the best place to stay between Luxor and Aswan. Rooms come with towels and fans, and the bathrooms are impeccable (singles E£9.50, doubles E£16, triples E£21, quads E£22). The **Venus Cafeteria and Restaurant,** on the Nile halfway between the temple and the taxi stop, serves up *kofta* sandwiches with ruby red tomatoes, overpriced soda, and ice cream with raisins and coconut (all E£2), all in a shaded, breezy riverfront setting (open daily 24hr.). Produce, *fuul* vendors, and tea shops can be found in the *souq*.

**Sights**  Although a temple has stood here since the time of the Middle Kingdom, the current edifice dates back only to 150 BCE. The older portions of the **Temple of Kom Ombo** now rest at the Louvre and the Egyptian Museum in Cairo. After the decline of paganism and the Roman Empire, the rising waters of the river left the temple almost completely buried in silt. In later years the portion above ground was used as a quarry for neighboring edifices; as a result, the side walls have vanished.

The temple's dualism is evident throughout the site, but is especially clear in the columns of the hypostyle hall. Designs on the right columns feature razor-toothed Sobek, while those on the left depict bird-beaked Horus. The ceiling of the adjoining vestibule is strikingly well-preserved; bright blue and black images of Horus hover protectively over the chamber. The temple interior contains the less substantial remains of the Hall of Offerings and the inner sanctuary homes of Sobek and Horus.

Adjoining the northern edge of the temple are the Roman water supply tanks and, to the west, the remains of a Roman *mammisis*. The now-putrescent well is rumored to have crawled with crocodiles in days gone by. Of course, it is also claimed that Cleopatra's bubble bath is nearby, so believe what you will. The **Chapel of Hathor,** to your right as you enter the compound, houses a graphic collection of crocodile mummies unearthed near the road leading to the site (open daily 7am-6pm, winter until 4:30pm; admission E£4, students E£2).

### Near Kom Ombo: Daraw دراو

Sudanese merchants, Bishari tribespeople, and Egyptian *fellaheen* convene in Daraw (de-RAU) every Tuesday morning for a **camel market.** The Bishari, Saharan nomads with their own language and culture, purchase camels for the equivalent of E£200, march for one month through the desert to Daraw, and resell the be-humped beasts at a 500% profit. Look for the occasional businessman in full traditional dress: flowing pants, fighting sword and dagger, and a cloak draped over the shoulders. Typically, a Sudanese camel-owner will pay a Sudanese or Bishari shepherd to drive his camels north to Egypt. The owner then flies up to oversee the selling. If you think the slobbery creatures are cute, the going rate for a big male camel is E£1200-1500, a saving of E£1000 over prices in Cairo.

Tuesday is the only summer market day; in winter, camels are sometimes sold on Sundays and Mondays. The camel market is adjoined by a **fruit and vegetable market** and a **livestock market** where farmers sell cattle, water buffalo, sheep, and goats. The animals are hauled in by truck or occasionally toted on the merchants' shoulders. On market day, impromptu shaded *fuul* and tea stands offer refreshment to merchants, buyers, and gawkers. The market runs from 7am to 2pm but starts deteriorating after about 11am. A good strategy is to rise very early in Aswan, visit the camel market, and move on to see the temple at Kom Ombo.

**Service taxis** careen to Daraw from Kom Ombo, 8km to the north (10min.), and Aswan, 37km to the south (1hr.). Some trains and buses running between Luxor and Aswan stop in Daraw. The **taxi stand, bus station,** and **train station** all lie along the main highway. Thirty meters north of the main shopping street that runs down to the market is a **telephone office** (domestic calls only). To reach the market from the stations, walk 300m down the main street toward the Nile. You'll pass *ta'miyya* and juice shops on your left and the **hospital** on your right. When you reach a dead end, bear right for 20m, then left; just follow everyone else. You'll know you've arrived when you see 200 people smacking the heinies of bound, groaning camels to display their vigor. If you're gliding by on a *felucca*, have the captain stop at the Daraw ferry landing and a covered pick-up truck will take you to the market.

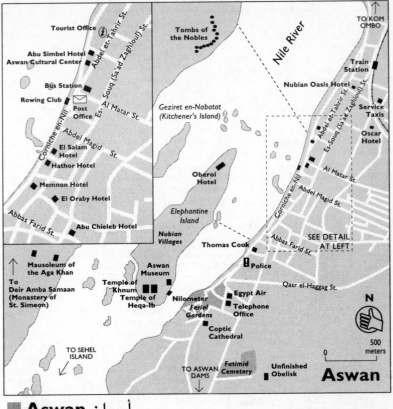

**EGYPT**

# ■ Aswan أسوان

Nine hundred km south of Cairo, Aswan is the southernmost city in Egypt, a trading center where the Middle East overlaps with Africa and Upper Egypt gives way to Lower Nubia. The Soviet-designed High Dam, an engineering miracle when it was completed in 1971, created nearby Lake Nasser (the world's largest reservoir) and boosted Egypt's agricultural and energy potential. Unfortunately, the dam also flooded most of Nubia, causing massive migrations to Egypt and Sudan.

The fertile corridor nourished by the Nile is very narrow this far south—so much so that the desert nearly reaches the banks themselves. Summer temperatures average over 40°C, though they dip to a chilly 35°C in winter. The river also harbors a thriving *felucca* industry, with nearly 400 Aswani boat captains preying on an ever-declining number of tourists. The otherwise pleasant corniche is the main hunting ground for these men and their young helpers.

Summer, when temperatures are high and tourists are few, may be the best time to experience the sun-smoke-sleep-swim *felucca* trip (yes, *swim*—Nile water here is cleaner here than anywhere else in Egypt, but *not* clean enough to drink). In the winter the city becomes a resort, and the restaurants along the elegant corniche buzz with activity. Foreigners are welcomed in any season, though; restaurants, hotels, and shops here are very accommodating when there's money to be made.

A large Nubian community gives the city an African flavor not found elsewhere in Egypt. The gentle charm of the Nubians and the cool breeze along the corniche mellow the heat and coax travelers into extending their visits.

## ORIENTATION

You're rarely more than two blocks from the river in Aswan. The northern half of the city lies along three long avenues parallel to the Nile. The riverfront **Corniche en-Nil** is the most picturesque, featuring several hotels, shops, banks, floating restaurants, and cruise ship and *felucca* docks. Two blocks inland, the market-lined **Sa'ad Zaghloul Street** features everything from watermelons to waterpipes. Also called Es-Souq St., this street begins at the train station at the northeast corner of town and runs south 2km to Abbas Farid St. In the southern half of town, the corniche continues for another 1km and ends at the **Ferial Gardens**. The northern grid pattern falls apart at the central market. South of the *souq*, inland streets form a labyrinth of alleys. Sandwiched between the corniche and the market street, **Abtal at-Tahrir Street** begins at the youth hostel in the north and culminates in a small cluster of tourist bazaars, resuming as a narrow lane farther south.

After haggling, a horse-drawn **kalish** should cost E£5 for a short ride, E£10 for a more extended tour. **Taxis,** everywhere along the corniche, shouldn't be more than E£5 for all city travel. Walking is a pleasant option, especially in the evenings.

Aswan is the obvious base for exploring the southernmost parts of Egypt; plan on four days if you want to see the sights in a sane fashion. You can also take *felucca* trips to Kom Ombo, Edfu, and even Luxor (see **Getting Around,** p. 174).

## PRACTICAL INFORMATION

**Tourist Office:** This beige box (tel. 31 28 11) on the right as you exit the train station, is a good first stop in Aswan. Hakeem Hussein or Shukri Sa'ad can give you info on everything, including reputable *felucca* captains. Open daily 9am-3pm and 6-8pm. Another office is next to the corniche; walking north along the corniche turn right at the Abu Simbel Hotel, make the first left, and go two blocks. Open daily 8:30am-2pm and 6-8pm, in Ramadan 10am-2pm and 7-9pm.

**Tourist Police:** Above the corniche tourist office, open daily 9am-3pm and 8pm-1am (tel. 31 43 93). 24-hr. branch on the south side of train station (tel. 30 31 63).

**Passport Office:** Corniche en-Nil (tel. 32 30 26), in the police building's 3rd floor. Will register passports and extend visas. Open Sat.-Thurs. 8am-3pm and 9pm-1am.

**Currency Exchange: Banque Misr,** 103 Corniche en-Nil (tel. 31 66 92, 93, or 95; fax 31 66 94), does Visa and Mastercard advances. Open Sun.-Thurs. 8:30am-2pm. There's an **ATM** next to Banque Misr on the corniche. **National Bank of Egypt,** on Corniche en-Nil (tel. 31 20 13), does Visa advances and accepts Eurocheques. Supposedly open daily 8am-2am.

**American Express:** At the southernmost end of the corniche (tel./fax 30 29 09), in the lobby of the Old Cataract Hotel. Offers exchange and banking services and will hold mail for anyone. Open daily 8am-7pm.

**Thomas Cook:** On the corniche just north of the police building (tel. 30 40 11 or 68 39; fax 30 62 09). Offers travel and financial services, open daily 8am-8pm.

**Telephones: Telephone office** (tel. 31 38 69), 2 doors south of EgyptAir. Open daily 24hr. **Fax** service available 8am-2pm and 6-9pm, E£30 for 3min. to the U.S. International lines are also available in most hotels and at the **Business Center** (tel. 30 39 15), open daily 8am-11pm. **Telephone information:** Tel. 16.

**Airport:** 23km south of town (tel. 48 03 20), near the High Dam. E£15-20 one-way by taxi. Served by **EgyptAir** (tel. 31 50 00; fax 31 50 05), Corniche en-Nil, at the southern end near the Ferial Gardens (open daily 8am-8pm). Another office at the airport (tel 48 03 07). 4 flights daily to Cairo, 7-8 in winter (E£497 one way). Also 3 per day to Abu Simbel (E£439 round-trip). **Airport Police:** Tel. 48 03 07.

**Train Station:** Northern end of Sa'ad Zaghloul St. (tel. 31 47 54). 1st and 2nd class A/C trains depart for points north at 5:30am and 6pm. Luxor is 5hr. away, Cairo 15hr. The tourist office can give the most current fares (roughly E£10-20 to Luxor, E£85 to Cairo). Also frequent trains south to the High Dam (9 daily, 30min., 25-55pt.). There are often student discounts on trains.

**Bus Station:** On Abtal at-Tahrir St. (tel. 30 32 25), behind the Abu Simbel Hotel. 10 buses per day to Kom Ombo (E£2, 1hr.); Daraw (E£1, 45min.); Edfu (2hr., E£3); and Luxor (4hr., E£6.50). Buses to Qena (5:30 and 11:30am, and 12:30pm, 5hr.,

E£8.50); Asyut (7am, 8hr., E£16); Hurghada (8am and 3:30pm, 7hr., E£18); Cairo (3:30pm, 10hr., E£50); Suez (7am, 3:30 and 5pm, 12hr., E£30); and Abu Simbel (8am and 3pm, 4hr., E£26 roundtrip; returns to Aswan at 6:30am and 2pm). Also service to the Old Dam; ask at the tourist office.

**Local Ferries:** Get to Elephantine Island from Esh-Shatii Restaurant on the southern end of the corniche, or across from the EgyptAir office even farther south (every 15-20min. 6am-6pm, E£1). Float to the western bank tombs and villages in a **Seti Tours** ferry, opposite the corniche tourist office (every 20min. 6am-6pm, E£1).

**Service Taxis:** Taxis leave from the covered station 1km south of the train station, east of the tracks and next to a large underpass. They run from roughly 4am-6pm, leaving every 15-30min. depending on demand. To: Daraw or Kom Ombo (40min., E£1.50); Edfu (1¼hr., E£3); Esna (2-3hr., E£6); Luxor (3hr., E£8); Qena (4hr., E£9); and Khazan/Old Dam (75pt). Taxis to Aswan environs and south wait in the square at the base of Et-Tabia Mosque (Aswan's main mosque, perched on a hill and illuminated at night).

**Bike Rental:** 3 locations: on Abtal at-Tahrir St. next to the *poste restante* office, near the train station on es-Souq St., and farther down es-Souq St. next to the Nubian Oasis Hotel. E£5 per day or E£1 per hr., though may double in winter. The youth hostel (on Abtal et-Tahrir St.) occasionally organizes winter bike tours.

**Photo Developing: Photo Sabry,** Corniche en-Nil (tel. 30 64 52), just north of EgyptAir, will print 36 color exposures (4x6 print) for E£35. Open Sat.-Thurs. 9am-2:30pm. There's a smaller one across from the Nubian Oasis Hotel.

**Bookstore:** On Corniche en-Nil, opposite and just past Salah ad-Din St. Paltry selection of used books in English and other languages. Open daily 8am-2pm. **Islamic Books,** next to the Abu Simbel Hotel, sells translations of Islamic works.

**Laundromat:** Most hotels do laundry for 50pt-E£1 per garment. Several also offer do-it-yourself laundry for free. There's a laundry service and dry-cleaning shop under the Nubian Oasis Hotel. Open Sat.-Thurs. 8am-2pm.

**Swimming Pools:** The nicest hotels have the nicest pools, including the **New Cataract Hotel** (E£35, including up to that amount in food and drink), and the **Oberoi Hotel** (E£25). The **Hathor Hotel** rooftop pool is cheap, but sometimes low on water (E£5).

**Pharmacy: El-Nile Pharmacy** (tel. 30 26 74), on the corniche across from the Isis gateway, is open daily 7am-midnight.

**Hospital: German Evangelical Mission Hospital,** on the southern end of the corniche (tel. 32 21 76), is open 24hr. The **Government Hospital** (tel. 32 28 55 or 24 19), a 2nd choice, is several km inland from EgyptAir on Qasr el-Hagga St.

**Medical Emergency:** Tel. 123.

**Police:** Tel. 122.

**Post Office:** Corniche en-Nil, toward the northern end of town. Open Sat.-Thurs. 8am-2pm. Offers **EMS** and **telegraph** services. For **poste restante,** walk south from the main post office and turn left down Salah ad-Din St. It's in the yellow and black building. Open Sun.-Thurs. 8am-2pm.

**Telephone Code:** 097. Some numbers beginning with 32 may soon switch to 30.

## ACCOMMODATIONS

All rates listed are approximate. Prices rise in winter and plummet in summer. All listed hotels have laundry service and breakfast; none dance that credit card tango.

**Memnon Hotel,** Corniche en-Nil (tel. 30 04 83), entrance behind the National Bank of Egypt sign. A homey 30-room, Nile-view throwback to the early 60s. TV lounge has American cowboy movies in the evening with Arabic subtitles. Rooms have A/C and private bath. Singles E£25. Doubles E£40, without view E£35. Triples E£60. Suites E£60. Lunch E£10, dinner E£12. Student discounts.

**New Abu Simbel Hotel,** near the train station on Atlas St. next to the Aswan stadium, in the large, modern stucco building (tel. 31 21 43; fax 30 20 10). Has a garden patio, a high-ceilinged lobby, and spacious, spotless A/C rooms. TV for E£3 extra. Singles E£20, doubles E£35, triples E£45. Lunch E£10.30, dinner E£12.

**El Salam Hotel,** 101 Corniche en-Nil (tel. 32 36 49). Beautiful, wrap-around balconies and gigantic, pristine tiled bathrooms distinguish El Salam from the competition. All rooms have bath and A/C. Singles E£27, doubles E£40-45, triples E£50-60.

**Nubian Oasis Hotel,** 234 Sa'ad Zaghloul St. (tel. 31 21 23 or 26; fax 31 21 24), in a white building with red letters. A big TV lounge, clean bathrooms, and more *felucca* paintings than you could shake an oar at. Singles E£10, with bath E£13, with bath and A/C E£15. Doubles with bath E£20, with A/C E£25. Triples with bath and A/C E£30. Lunch E£8, dinner E£8.50.

**Abu Simbel Hotel,** at the northern end of Corniche en-Nil near the tourist office (tel. 32 23 27, 28 88, or 24 53; fax 31 59 31). All rooms have private bath, most have an excellent river view. Student and off-season discounts. Singles E£29, doubles E£38. Extra bed E£15. Lunch E£10, dinner E£12.

**El Oraby Hotel,** El Mahkama el-Qadima St. (tel./fax 31 75 78); from the corniche walk up Salah ad-Din St. to Es-Souq St., turn right, go 300m and take a left at the Khan el-Khali Center. It's 75m up, with an outstretched ibis over the doorway. Wood-paneled interior, hammocks and ping-pong on the roof garden, and an informational library room. A/C everywhere! Singles with bath E£12. Doubles with bath E£20. Triples E£21, with bath E£30. 10% student discount during the high season. Lunch E£5, dinner E£7.

**Hathor Hotel,** Corniche en-Nil (tel. 31 45 80; fax 30 34 62), right in the middle. New ceramic floor and wood furniture give the Hathor a relatively sophisticated air. Sometimes there's water in the tiny rooftop pool. All rooms have bath, most have A/C. Singles E£25, with A/C E£30. Doubles E£35, with A/C E£40. Triples E£45, with A/C E£50. Rooms are 25% cheaper without a view. International phone line. Lunch E£10, dinner E£12.

**Aswan Youth Hostel (HI),** 96 Abtal et-Tahrir St., (tel. 32 22 35) 2 blocks from the train station. Reminiscent of a warehouse in both size and cleanliness. Caustic pink and green color scheme, worn-out mattresses, and loud, inefficient fans make for an unharmonious stay. Can't beat the price, though: E£8 with bath, E£5 without. Breakfast not included.

There is a **campground** 2km south of town adjacent to the unfinished obelisk, but it's currently in a sorry state. Contact the tourist office before planning a stay. The campground is inconvenient without motorized transport—expect to pay at least E£3-4 for a taxi into town.

## FOOD

Fruit, vegetables, bread, and pigeon, not to mention falafel, liver sandwiches, and *kushari,* are available in Aswan's **souq.** Beware of *ta'miyya* vendors, who will sometimes use the same oil for many days. The highest concentration of vendors is at the southern end of Es-Souq St. where it intersects Es-Sayyida Nafisa. The vegetable markets lie to the north. A large **vegetable souq** is tucked away near the train station, on the northeast edge of Es-Souq St. Shop here in the morning.

At the other extreme, you can swing out on huge buffets and gourmet Arab and continental cuisine at the luxury hotels. The Oberoi offers an elegant E£22 **breakfast buffet** (6-10:30am) in their stunning cupola-covered ballroom restaurant.

**Sayyida Nafisa,** just off Es-Souq St., 1.5km south of the train station. Better than average Egyptian food E£7-10. Refreshing juices E£1-2.

**Darwish Restaurant,** Sa'ad Zaghloul St., 2 blocks from the train station. Hospital white and hospital clean, Darwish's easily spotted flashing neon sign marks the spot for some of the best pigeon in Aswan (E£8 fried). All meals come with vegetables, soup, rice, and salad. Open daily 11am-1am.

**Hamam Restaurant,** Corniche en-Nil. Mirrors and *felucca* murals decorate this cafeteria. Rice with your choice of meats (E£8-15). Fear the frightening, recycled soda bottles filled with "spicy ketchup." Open daily 24hr.

**La Trattoria,** in the Isis Hotel on the corniche. Pleasantly cool and ivy-strewn, this small restaurant serves small portions from an even smaller menu. The vaguely Italian minestrone and assorted scallopini dishes provide much-needed relief from *fuul* and *ta'miyya,* even if entrees start around E£20.

## Floating Restaurants

This is the true heart of the Aswan restaurant scene. Popular with Egyptians as well as tourists, these aquatic eateries offer decent meals and the perfect setting for watching the sun set over the desert hills of the west bank. They all serve basically the same array of meat dishes (E£4-12) and salads, dips, drinks, and desserts (E£1-4), with slightly differing quality and atmosphere. They're listed from south to north; just look for the blinking lights.

**Aswan Panorama** (tel. 30 61 69), the best of its floating neighbors, looks more like a kitsch-museum than a restaurant. They do a non-greasy fish and chips. The service is impeccable; the food top-notch. No seating after 9pm.

**Monalisa,** where the deafening cacophony of frogs on the patio is preferable to the terrifying technicolor dance hall upstairs. A good place to find *felucca* captains (never *too* difficult) and decent vegetable *tajen.* The mango juice has chunks of cane sugar in it. The spaghetti is locally popular.

**EMY's.** Lonely neon letters top the only actual boat among the floating restaurants. Sit on the top level of the barge to sway gently as you chew (and chew and chew) your kabab. They even serve breakfast (E£3). 20% student discount.

**Aswan Moon Restaurant,** most popular of the floating restaurants, also wins the prize for most blinking lights. Arabian-themed platform hosts Nubian musicians and *felucca* chiefs chatting up tourists. Service can be slow, but what's the hurry?

## SIGHTS

On the west bank of the Nile, directly across from the city, the wind-swept sand piles into dunes with pronounced edges and sweeping contours, in sharp contrast to the lush palms by the water. Along the desert horizon, a mausoleum, a monastery, and cliffside tombs blend in with the blowing sands. In the middle of the river floats a cluster of islets where the remainder of the city's official attractions can be found. The largest of these, **Elephantine Island,** hosts the **Aswan Archaeological Museum,** admission to which covers the museum, adjacent ruins, and the Nilometer. The museum's collection is miniscule; highlights include a few gilt sarcophagi and a mutilated skull. (Open 8am-4pm; admission E£12, students E£6.)

Carved into a rock to the left of the museum's entrance is a **Nilometer.** Built during the Pharaonic era and renovated by the Romans, the long stairway-shaft was used to measure the depth of the Nile. In ancient times nothing was of greater practical significance than the Nilometer's oracle. Its reports could predict a bountiful harvest or hunger and misery. The ancient econometric device was also used to set pharaonic taxes based on projected agricultural output.

Aswan grew from Elephantine Island much as Paris grew from Île de la Cité. The remains of the ancient settlement have been excavated on the southeast corner of the island, directly behind the museum. You will find here the **Temple of Khnum** and the modest **Temple of Heqa-Ib** (particularly attractive when viewed from the Nile), in addition to a small Ptolemaic temple dedicated to Alexander II. The temple of Heqa-Ib is currently being excavated by German archaeologists. The central section of the island has several Nubian villages where you'll find friendly residents, adoring youngsters, and brightly-painted homes. Be modest in your dress and behavior. Less spoiled villages are found at the northern end of the west bank, reachable by local ferry (see Practical Information, p. 202). The Oberoi Hotel and adjacent construction sites dominate the northern half of the island. The hotel is surrounded by a tall *cordon sanitaire;* to reach the inner sanctum take one of their silly-looking ferries from the launching point at the center of the corniche.

Behind Elephantine Island and not visible from central Aswan, **Geziret en-Nabatat** ("Island of the Plants," or Kitchener's Island) is a lovely botanical garden where African and Asian tropical plants flourish and a variety of exotic and flamboyant birds congregate. Bilingual tree plaques provide the names of plant species. To reach the island, you can hire a *felucca* to combine an island visit with stops along the west bank and Elephantine Island (rent one for a full afternoon at E£10 per hr.). It is also possible to hire a rowboat from the west side of Elephantine Island (about E£3 for one or two passengers only). Make sure boats wait for you or come back to pick you up by withholding payment until the end of the trip. (Open daily 7am-6pm; admission E£5.)

The most placid attraction on the west bank of the Nile is the **Mausoleum of the Aga Khan,** a short climb from where the *felucca* docks. Aga Khans, the hereditary titles of the *imams* of the Isma'ili Muslims, are believed to be direct descendants of Muhammad and the inheritors of his spiritual responsibilities of guidance. They used to rule from Pakistan (where their followers were once known as the *Assassins*), but political shifts sent them westward. Aswan became the favorite winter retreat of Sultan Muhammad Shah Al-Husaini, Aga Khan III (1877-1957), the 48th *imam* of the Isma'ilis. Upon his death, the Begum (the Aga Khan's wife) oversaw the construction of the mausoleum. While the edifice sports an imposing fortress-like exterior, the interior, modeled after the Fatimid tombs of Cairo, has the quiet simplicity of a peace palace. Opposite the entrance stands a marble sarcophagus inscribed with passages from the Qur'an. A *bakhsheesh*-free zone with commanding views up and down the Nile, the mausoleum is a calm respite from the jostle of central Aswan. (Open Tues.-Sun. 9am-4pm. Free. Remember to take off your shoes.)

**Deir Amba Samaan** (Monastery of St. Simeon) stands isolated and majestic in the desert, 1km inland from the mausoleum. Built in the 6th and 7th centuries CE and abandoned in the 13th, the monastery is on a terrace carved into the steep hills visible from the mausoleum. With its 6m turreted walls, the monastery appears more like a fort than a religious sanctuary. The original walls of the complex stood 10m high and enclosed a community of 300 resident monks. Upstairs, the monks' cells and their stone beds (with Bible and *gallabiyya* wall slots) are currently occupied by bats. The monastery also had a church and accommodations sufficient for several hundred pilgrims and their camels. There are remnants of the baptismal fount and drain pipe, well preserved paintings of Mary and Joseph, and Communion wine-making facilities in St. Simeon's chamber (where there is a slot in the roof for a piece of rope he slipped around his neck to keep him awake and on his feet during all-night prayer vigils). (Open Tues.-Sun. 7am-4pm; admission E£12, students E£6.)

To reach the monastery, follow the paved path that starts in front of the Mausoleum of the Aga Khan (15-20min.) or hire a camel near the *felucca* stop. (E£10 per camel, good for 2 people.) Women should not need to cling tightly to the camel driver, despite his concerns for safety, nor should the driver need to grab his passengers' legs to ensure stability. If you feel at all uncomfortable, forget the beasts and their camels entirely.

The **Tombs of the Nobles** lie farther north along the west bank of the Nile, honeycombed into the face of desert cliffs and impressively illuminated at night. These tombs of governors and dignitaries date from the 23rd- to the 18th-centuries BCE. Four millennia of decay and pilfering have severely damaged most of the tombs. The bright color and detail of the reliefs in the **Tomb of Sarenput II,** however, merit the easy trip across the Nile. Note the sacrificial stone slab with a blood drainage spout. The mummy shuffled to Cairo, but there are plenty of bones in the corner. The interconnected 6th-dynasty **Tombs of Nikhu and Sabni,** father and son, have swell depictions of donkeys, water buffalo, fish, and birds. The cheapest way to visit the tombs is to take the ferry from the corniche (across the small park from the tourist office; E£1). Once across, walk uphill to the office on the left. (Open daily 7am-4pm. Admission E£12, students E£6. Photo permission E£10.)

For a taste of Egyptian flavor not found north of Aswan, visit a **Nubian village.** You may even be invited to join the celebrations and ululations of a wedding ceremony; the Nubians consider it a mark of honor to have guests from far-flung villages attend their nuptial festivities. Nubian weddings traditionally involve 15 days of partying, but the demands of modern life have trimmed the celebration down to three or four. Nubians may feel slighted if you reject their offers of hospitality, so be diplomatic if you decline. The large Nubian houses, made of Nile mud, consist of six rooms around a courtyard; each cluster of rooms has its own dome or cylindrical roof. The brightly-painted huts belong to families that have completed the *hajj*, or pilgrimage, to Mecca. When the High Dam threatened to destroy this traditional style, architect-genius Hasan Fathy stopped by and whipped up these reconstructed and relocated villages, vaulting Nubian architecture into the international limelight.

The ferry to the west bank tombs (E£1) can bring you to **Gharb Aswan,** a series of Nubian villages less frequented by tourists than those of Elephantine Island. From the ferry dock catch a pick-up truck north to the villages (about E£1). Whether or not you make it to a village, a E£6 tape of rhythmic Nubian music from the Aswan *souq* is sure to bring a smile to your face and a snap to your step.

To reach the sights on the west bank of the Nile, it's easiest to hire a *felucca*. The official rate for *felucca* transport in the vicinity of Aswan is E£10 per hour regardless of the number of passengers, but it'll take some negotiation. A complete tour of Elephantine Island, Geziret en-Nabatat, the Aga Khan's Mausoleum, St. Simeon's Monastery, and the northern tombs goes for E£30 per group. A cheap alternative is to hire a rowboat or motorboat to the west bank (E£2-3) then trek from sight to sight on foot. Transport back to the corniche or Elephantine Island, either by ferry (E£1) or rowboat (E£8) is easy, as long as you don't get stranded late in the day, when the boatmen have you at their mercy.

## SHOPPING AND ENTERTAINMENT

Trade heats up from 8 to 10pm. If you seek more than the ubiquitous alphabetical hieroglyphics t-shirt, peruse Es-Sayyida Nafisa St. for western-style garments made to order. Tailors will cut your garment with lightning speed while you watch. (Pants E£10-25, shorts and simple shirts E£10-15, shirts with collars and buttons E£25-35.) For Egyptian wear, there are numerous *gallabiyya* and *koftan* merchants in the *souq*. If you have the time, you can go to one of the government shops on the corniche (Benzion is a large one), buy high-quality government cloth at posted government prices, then have your garments made to order by one of the many tailors on Sa'ad Zaghloul St.

**Nightclub** here means a group of drummers and tambourinists with a loud organ player and a male singer/M.C./encourager, plus the miraculous gyrations of a sequin-clad belly dancer enticing the men into tossing bills. Beware the belly. Check one out at Salah ad-Din Restaurant on the water or at the Ramses Hotel in town. There are often cover charges or minimums for discos and nightclubs, but they change frequently (usually E£5-10 cover or 2-drink minimum). The Oberoi has a **piano bar** (you can even sit down and play; drinks E£10-35) and a little disco with a pounding rap/dance mix (no cover but drinking is encouraged). The New Cataract has a **pub** and disco (open 7pm-2am, E£15 minimum for disco), and then there's the comfortable, no minimum Pullman **bar** in the Old Cataract. For more subdued enjoyment, try the **pool and snooker** tables at the Basma Hotel (on the corniche, south past the Kalabsha Hotel, E£5-15 cover) next to EMY's restaurant.

In winter, the **Aswan Cultural Center** on Corniche en-Nil across from the Rowing Club features Nubian dancing and handicrafts (open Sat.-Thurs. 9-11pm; admission E£5). There are also many cafés where you can join locals for a cup of tea, a puff of *sheesha*, or a game of dominoes late into the night. And let's not forget the Philae Temple's **sound and light show** (see **Philae**, p. 210).

For a taste of the good life, walk south along the corniche and around the Ferial Gardens to the elegant **Pullman Cataract Hotel** (the Old and New Cataract Hotels are within a single compound). Walking through the gorgeous gardens, pool, and outdoor terrace café that overlooks the Nile, it's easy to see why Agatha Christie's *Death on the Nile* was filmed here (drinks E£15 and up, no shorts on the terrace after 3pm). For the athletically inclined, spontaneous *futbol* games spring up around the stadium in the northern part of town. For more structured exertion, report to the Oberoi's health spa (tel. 30 34 55) for a host of relaxing and rejuvenating treatments and exercises (priced individually from US$3-20).

# ■ South of Aswan

Aswan proper may lack spectacular antiquities, but the 15km stretch of the Nile upstream of Aswan will blow your mind. The region of the **first cataract** includes two dams, two temples, and most of an obelisk. The **Old Dam,** 5km south of Aswan, was built by the British in 1902, only to be dwarfed by the Soviet-designed **High Dam** 10km upstream. On an island in the lake between the two, the lovingly-preserved **Philae Temple** proclaims the glory of Isis. Beyond the west end of the High Dam, the desolate **Temple of Kalabsha** sinks peacefully into the desert on the banks of Lake Nasser. The red granite and alabaster that fed pharaonic monument building was taken from quarries just south of Aswan. Here you'll find the **Unfinished Obelisk** in all its almost-glory. All sights are easily reachable from Aswan.

### Getting Around

Public transportation doesn't completely cover the area south of Aswan, but private means are cheap and easy to arrange. An excellent road follows the Nile from Aswan to Khazan, a village near the Old Dam, providing access to both the Dam and the motorboat launch to Philae Temple. The route to Khazan is served by *service* (50pt-E£1, depart from *service* stand) and by public bus (25pt-E£1). Both run frequently until about 9:30pm. Frequent trains run to the High Dam, leaving you at the station on the eastern end of the dam. Vehicles and pedestrians are not allowed to cross the dam after 6pm.

Many hotels offer combination trips to Abu Simbel and the other antiquities in the area. The "short" trip that just visits Abu Simbel and the High Dam costs E£25. If you must see everything in one day, take the epic trip to Abu Simbel, both Dams, Philae, Kalabsha, and the Unfinished Obelisk (E£35). A more relaxed, enjoyable itinerary runs as follows: Abu Simbel and the quarries in one day, the High Dam and Kalabsha on another, then the Philae temple at night.

## THE DAMS AND QUARRIES

The best-known attraction in the area is modern Egypt's great monument, the **High Dam (Es-Sidd el-Ali),** completed in 1971. The dam is more interesting intellectually than visually; it may take a while to realize you're there. The High Dam lacks the aesthetic magnificence of ancient Egypt's colossi, but it could teach them a thing or two about size: 1km thick at the base, 3.6km long, and 111m high, the dam contains more than 17 times the material used in the Great Pyramid of Cheops. The construction of the dam created **Lake Nasser,** the world's largest artificial lake, and covered all of Lower Nubia in waters as deep as 200m. Thousands of Sudanese and Nubians were forced to relocate. Ancient Nubia's archaeological treasures were doomed; the Egyptian government sent out an international plea for help and many countries responded both individually and under an ambitious UNESCO plan. The long-term environmental effects of the massive project are unknown. A rise in the Sahara's water table has been noticed as far away as Algeria, and archaeologists suspect that this effect has damaged the necropolis at Luxor. Another danger of the dam is the possibility of sabotage. Should the dam be destroyed, the Noah-proportioned flood would wipe out all but 2% of Egypt's population.

On the brighter side, the dam's 12 turbines doubled Egypt's electrical output. Thanks to the dam, agricultural productivity has been greatly enhanced, and the acreage of Egypt's arable soil has been increased by 30%. The dam enabled Egypt to enjoy an undiminished water supply during the drought of the past decade, and in August 1988 it saved Egypt from the floods suffered by the Sudanese when the Nile overflowed after heavy rains.

The High Dam has had significant international repercussions as well. Plans for the construction were unveiled after World War II, when it became apparent that Egypt had achieved maximum agricultural output and could no longer feed its rapidly increasing population. When the United States reneged on offers to provide loans for the High Dam project in 1956, President Nasser ordered the nationalization of the

Suez Canal as a means of generating the necessary hard currency. This triggered the Suez Crisis, in which France, Britain, and Israel invaded Egypt. The Soviet Union decided to provide the necessary loans and technology, and work began on the dam in 1960. Despite over a decade of cooperation on the dam's construction, Egypt severed its Soviet relations and turned to the United States shortly after its completion, which accompanied Anwar Sadat's rise to power.

On the eastern bank (near the train station), just before the dam, the **Visitor's Pavilion** features plaques and sculptures blending Soviet socialist-realist motifs with Egyptian figures and symbols (open daily 7am-5pm; free). Plans for the construction of the dam—written in Russian and Arabic—include a map and some technical drawings. At the center of the pavilion is a dusty 15m model of the High Dam and its environs, minus the water. It also includes pictures and diagrams of Abu Simbel's relocation. The domed pavilion is well off the road from the dam and most taxis will not stop at it unless you insist; ask for the *mekat* (model).

To cross the dam you must pay E£3. The soldiers at the eastern end won't let you walk across the dam but will stop passing vehicles and make them give you a ride. At the other end is the towering Soviet-Egyptian friendship monument, perhaps premature given the alacrity with which the Egyptians spurned their Soviet benefactors once the dam was complete. A stylized lotus blossom, the monument looks eerily like an ICBM silo springing into action. Due to the rise in terrorist activity, you are supposed to secure police permission if you want to go to the top, either in Aswan or in the large yellow gift shop west of the monument (open 7am-2pm). Some have been known to illegally *bakhsheesh* their way to the top if the dam authorities are closed (E£1-2).

The **Old Dam** is 10km to the north. Built by the Brits between 1898 and 1902, the dam supplied most of Egypt's power for years. The Old Dam can be reached by taking *service* or a temperamental public bus from the Aswan corniche to Khazan (see **Getting Around**, p. 208). The fertile area known as the **First Cataract** is one of the most idyllic spots in the Aswan area. The view of what is left of these rapid waters, churning around rocky outcrops to the north from the Old Dam, gives some idea of the peril of early Nile expeditions, when ships were hauled past this dangerous spot with ropes. In the picturesque village of **Khazan,** 90-year-old British villas, now Britless, are nestled peacefully within walled gardens.

Just below the waters of the First Cataract, **Sehel Island,** boasting a hospitable Nubian village, scanty ruins, and a variety of inscriptions ranging from the 4th dynasty to the Ptolemaic period, attracts very few tourists. This island makes a nice destination for longer *felucca* rides out of Aswan (a 3-hr. tour...a 3-hr. tour).

If traveling by taxi back to Aswan after touring the High Dam or Philae, you might ask the driver to stop at the Fatimid Tombs, the adjacent Unfinished Obelisk, and the nearby granite quarries. These sites are all near the camping area, 300m east of the main road at a turn-off 1km south of Aswan and are all easily within walking or *kalish* (E£5-7) range. The **Fatimid Tombs** are typical early Islamic shrines: squat, square stone buildings with crescents on their roofs. They are easily spotted across the street from the Obelisk. The tombs have been more or less abandoned; it can be spooky wandering around the dark cemetery, empty except for ghosts. The **Unfinished Obelisk** was abandoned at its site because of a flaw in the granite; it was to have soared to a whopping 41.7m on a base 4.2m on each side. In its unadorned, supine state, the obelisk looks—well, it looks unfinished. But it gives you some sense of the mammoth effort that went into creating such a monument. Notice the channels along each side with curved indentations just big enough for a man to sit in and pound away with a diarite ball (diarite being harder than granite). The earthbound side of the massive shaft would have been cut free either with copper or bronze chisels, or by pounding passages with diarite balls, inserting wooden beams and flooding the channels so that the expanding wood would break the remaining stone. The adjacent, unarousing **granite quarries** supplied most of ancient Egypt with the hard pink or black granite and porphyry that was favored for temple and monument building. Alabaster quarries lie farther west. (Obelisk and quarries open daily 7am-6pm, but the guard often shoves off early. Admission E£10, students E£5.)

## PHILAE فيلة

Called by one of Napoleon's soldiers "the pearl of Egypt," the beautiful temple of Isis at Philae has attracted visitors since classical times, drawing both the pious and the curious. The completion of the Old Dam by the British in 1902 partially submerged the temples only a few years after their resurrection as a popular tourist destination. Victorian vandals floated around the pillars and chipped their names into the protruding columns. The graffiti now marks the earlier water level. Archaeologists feared the waters would eventually undermine the foundations of the temples and hasten their collapse. The construction of the High Dam would have utterly destroyed Philae were it not for the efforts of UNESCO and the Egyptian Antiquities Department. Between 1972 and 1980, the entire complex of temples was transferred from Philae Island to higher ground on nearby Agilkia Island. In 1980, the new site of the ancient temples reopened to tourism.

You can visit Philae most easily by **taxi** as part of an itinerary including other sights, or you can take a **bus** to the Old Dam from the Aswan corniche; get off when it stops at the checkpoint on the east end of the dam. A **service** to Khazan is faster (see **Practical Information,** p. 202). Tell the driver to let you off at the Old Dam (Es-Sidd el-Qadeem). From the checkpoint, walk south along the shore to the concrete boat dock (about 2km). After purchasing an admission ticket, you must hire a **motorboat** to reach the island at the official rate of E£20 per boat roundtrip. Wait until a few travelers show up to share the expense of the boat (it could be a long wait in the summer). The captain will try to con you into paying more, so be firm. If there are serious problems, complain at the tourist office back in town. The boat captain is obligated to wait for you as you tour the site, so there is no need to rush (open daily 7am-4pm; admission E£20, students E£10).

The well-preserved **Temple of Isis,** the last bastion of ancient Egyptian religion, dominates the island's northern edge. Isis was the mother of nature, protector of humans, goddess of purity and sexuality, and sister-wife of the legendary hero Osiris (see **Religion in Ancient Egypt,** p. 57). Her cult following continued long after the establishment of Christianity, fizzling out only in the 6th century during the reign of Justinian, who successfully replaced her with Mary. Nearly all the structures on Philae date from the Ptolemaic and Roman eras, when Egyptian artistic quality was in decline—hence the inferior quality of the decorative relief work. Nile waters may have damaged their intrinsic beauty, but the temple remains an impressive edifice.

From the landing at the southern tip of the island, climb the short slope up to the temple complex past Philae's oldest structure, the **Portico of Nectanebo.** The paved portico once formed the vestibule of a temple. The arrangement of Philae's courtyards corresponds to the status of the people allowed in each: the outermost courtyard was for commoners, while each successive inner courtyard was reserved for increasingly important people—the innermost for High Priests. The larger edifice has been washed away, but the eastern side of the colonnade remains. Ptolemy, Isis, and Horus are depicted on the **first pylon,** which rises 18m on either side of the temple's main entrance. Note the channels cut into the face of the pylon on either side of the doorway where brightly painted square-cut cedar flagpoles once stood. Through this entrance is the **central court,** on the western edge of which reclines a Roman *mammisis* (birthhouse) devoted to Horus, its elegant columns emblazoned with the head of the cow-goddess Hathor, his consort. The walls depict the falcon god in the marshes of his birth. On the temple wall opposite the *mammisis,* Horus is shown being transported in a boat on the shoulders of servants en route to visit another member of the divine family. To the north is the slightly off-center **second pylon,** marking the way to the temple's inner sanctum. The *pronaos* (vestibule) was converted into a church by early Christians, who inscribed Byzantine crosses on the chamber walls and added a small altar. Farther north is the *naos,* the temple's innermost sanctuary. With a little *bakhsheesh* you can climb to the roof of the temple, or enter a trap door on the interior right side leading to an inscribed crypt. Outside the temple, at left-rear, is a **Nilometer** with a stairwell and the grooves used to measure the depths of the water. The stairwell is directly across from a French inscription from Napoleon's expedition. Because Egyptian gods liked to make house calls, outside the temple (to the right) is **Trajan's Kiosk,** the beautiful columned open air garage (called **pharaoh's bed** by the Victorians), which housed the bark of whatever god (or its icon) came to visit Isis. In true Egyptian temple style, Philae has a **sound and light show.** (English performances in summer Wed., Fri.-Sat. at 8pm, Mon.-Tues. at 9:30pm; in winter Wed., Fri.-Sat. at 6pm, Mon.-Tues. at 7:30pm.)

## KALABSHA كلبشة

The enormous **Temple of Kalabsha,** dramatically situated above the placid waters of Lake Nasser, is one of the most striking pharaonic ruins in the Aswan area. Dedicated to the Nubian god Mandulis (who was renowned for his hundreds of wives and legions of children), the temple was begun by Amenhotep II, continued during the reign of Augustus, and used as a church during the Christian era. In 1962-63, the West German government paid to have the entire temple dismantled and transported in 13,000 pieces from its Nasser-flooded home to the present site, 50km north of the original. Many Egyptologists consider well-preserved Kalabsha to be second only to the treasures of Abu Simbel.

Somewhat difficult to reach and poorly publicized, the temple allows its visitors a chance to explore in relative peace and quiet. The temple is just south of the High Dam on the western bank, about 2km past the military checkpoint. The cheapest way to reach Kalabsha is to take the **train** to the eastern end of the dam, ride to the western end (you will have to pay the damn E£3 dam fee), then walk to the boat landing for the temple (from the western checkpoint, continue straight ahead for 100m, then veer left through the shipyard, following the curve of the water). Less of a hassle but more expensive is a **taxi** from Aswan. Try bargaining down to E£15-20, perhaps a bit more for large groups. Don't forget that the High Dam closes to traffic at 6pm. No matter what other forms of transport you take, you will have to walk the last 1km through all manner of decrepit ships and fishing boats. Bring lots of water, cover your head, and watch your step. To cross the water to the temple, you can get a rowboat (E£10 per load, which holds no more than 2-3 people) or a larger motorboat (E£20 for a load of 10 or so). The crossing is full of wrecked, sunk ships and other debris—instant tetanus even for Aquaman.

Pick your way through more nautical refuse to an immense causeway of dressed stone that leads from the water to the temple's main entrance. The first pylon is off-center from both the causeway and the inner gateways of the temple itself. A carving of St. George and Coptic inscriptions survive from early Christian times. The grand forecourt between the pylon and the vestibule is surrounded by 14 columns, each with a unique capital. This is one of the only temples in Egypt where you can legally get to the top: take the stairs to the roof from a small room just beyond the vestibule for a commanding view of the entire site.

Because the temple faces east, light flows into the **Holy of Holies** (innermost chamber) only in the early morning. Bring a flashlight at other times, and be prepared for bats. A passageway leads north through the vestibule to an inner encircling wall; around the wall to the south is a well-preserved **Nilometer.** Extraordinary carvings of Mandulis, Isis, Horus, and Osiris cover the outside walls.

Outside the huge fortress-like wall, the remains of a small **shrine** are visible to the southeast; the present structure is largely a reconstructed façade. The Nubian reliefs include pre-dynastic elephants, a large giraffe, and gazelles. The double-image technique, characteristic of Nubian art, is used to portray motion in some of the drawings. Carcasses of enormous desiccated fish are surrealistically scattered amongst the sand, as are lonesome disembodied stone heads. Slightly to the southwest of Kalabsha Temple are ruins of the **Temple of Kertassi.** Two Hathor columns remain, as well as four columns with elaborate floral capitals and a lone monolithic architrave.

A stone pathway leads up the hill behind and to the right of the Temple of Kertassi to the **Rock Temple, Beit el-Wali** (House of the Holy Man), rescued from the encroaching waters of Lake Nasser with the aid of the U.S. government. Ask the guard to let you in. One of many Nubian temples constructed by Ramses II, it features typically modest poses of Ramses conquering foreigners, Ramses receiving prisoners, and the particularly understated scene of Ramses storming a castle half his size. Like a miniature Abu Simbel, this cave-temple was hewn from solid rock. Examine the bas-relief scenes closely: political and social history are portrayed in everything from graphic chariot battles to household squabbles over whose turn it is to walk the camel.

## ABU SIMBEL أبو سمبل

The grandeur of the pharaonic monuments reaches its peak at Egypt's southernmost tip. Four 22m-tall statues of Ramses II, carved out of a single slab of rock, greet the sunrise over Lake Nasser from the Great Temple of Abu Simbel. Ramses II had this grand sanctuary and the nearby Temple of Hathor built more than 3200 years ago to impress the Nubians with the power and glory of Egyptian rule; Abu Simbel still serves its purpose, leaving no visitor unmoved. For a sneak preview of the site, look at the back of the Egyptian one pound note.

**Practical Information** Abu Simbel, 50km from the Sudanese border, is a long 297km south of Aswan (due to political tensions, the border between Egypt and Sudan is not passable and should not be approached by tourists for any reason). Two **buses** come here from Aswan (8am and 5pm, E£10, E£26 roundtrip); the morning bus gives you an ample 2½hr. to explore the temple. Buy your ticket at the Aswan bus station a day in advance; buy the return ticket on the way back. Neither bus has air conditioning.

The tourist office and most hotels in Aswan arrange minibus trips to Abu Simbel. The trips generally cost E£25-35, and sometimes include the other sights south of Aswan (entrance fees not included). You generally leave at 4am and return in Aswan by 2pm. You'll be miserable if your minibus doesn't have air conditioning, since blowing sands preclude opening the windows for much of the trip. A private taxi, arranged on your own, could save money if you have a group of seven. A Peugeot with air conditioning and desperate driver could be as little as E£20 per person.

For those who cannot make the moonscape roadtrip, several flights wing it between Aswan and Abu Simbel. Frequency depends on demand, but there are generally 2-3 daily. EgyptAir provides shuttle service from the airport to the temple; after a whirlwind tour, you'll be driven back for the return flight (normal price E£441, but watch for frequent special fares; 50% off for one way, but it's too far to walk back). The ritziest way to go is by **cruise ship,** which allows you to see sights otherwise inaccessible. The cost is prohibitive, however, at over US$100 per night. Contact **Belle Époque,** 17 Tunis St., New Maadi, Cairo (tel. (02) 352 47 75 or 87 54) for more information.

**Sights** When the rising waters of Lake Nasser threatened to inundate one of the planet's greatest treasures, Egypt sent out a call for help. Nations joined together and relocated the two great temples at Abu Simbel to higher ground as part of an effort that moved 23 temples and sanctuaries to nearby sites. The international effort was not entirely selfless, though—any country that assisted could claim half of the antiquities it helped to rescue and would receive special archaeological concessions for future research. As a result, the temple of Dendur is now sheltered in New York's Metropolitan Museum of Art, Debed temple is now in Madrid, and El Lessiya was claimed by Turin. At a cost of US$36 million, teams of engineers from five countries painstakingly wrested the temples from the solid rock, breaking them into 3000 pieces weighing between 10 and 40 tons each. The pieces were moved 200m, the temples reconstructed and carefully oriented in their original directions, and a hollow mountain was built around them. It's hard to say which achievement—the temple, its relocation, or mammoth Lake Nasser—most impresses in this arid frontier land.

The **Great Temple of Abu Simbel** is Ramses II's masterpiece. This temple is supposedly dedicated to the god Ra-Hurakhti, but as in all of Ramses' monuments, the focus is clearly on the great pharaoh himself. As you proceed through the temple, the artwork depicts Ramses first as a great king, then as a servant of the gods, next as a companion of the gods, and finally, in the inner sanctuary, as a card-carrying deity. The entrance is guarded by 3½ 20m-tall statues of the king wearing the Old and New Kingdom versions of the crowns of Upper and Lower Egypt. An earthquake in 27 BCE crumbled the upper portion of one of the Colossi. Modern engineers were unable to reconstruct the figure (and there were debates about whether they should—if it's been broken for 2000 years, don't fix it), so they left it in its faceless state. There are (much) smaller statues of mother Tuya, wife Nefertari, and some of the kids, along with rows of praying baboons. Ancient Egyptians admired the baboon's habit of warming themselves in the sun's morning rays; they thought the beasts quite pious to pray to the sun god every dawn.

Farther into the temple are antechambers that once stored objects of worship; the walls show Ramses making sacrifices to the gods. In the inner sanctum, four seated statues facing the entrance depict Ramses and the gods Ra-Hurakhti, Amun, and Ptah. Originally encased in gold, the statues now wait with divine patience for February 22 and October 22, when the first rays of the sun reach 100m into the temple to bathe all except Ptah in light. February 21 was Ramses's birthday and October 21 his coronation date, but when the temple was moved, the timing of these natural feats shifted by one day. They just don't build temples like they used to.

The smaller **Temple of Hathor** next door was built for Ramses II's favorite wife Nefertari, and dedicated to the young goddess Hathor. Six 10m statues of King Ramses and Queen Nefertari (as the goddess) adorn the façade. Along with the temple of Hatshepsut in West Thebes, this is one of the only temples in Egypt dedicated to a woman. Ramses is all over the place, of course; scenes on the walls depict his coronation with the god Horus placing the crowns of Egypt on his head. The temple was constructed in the typical three-room style; the first chamber was open to the public, the second chamber to nobles and priests, and the inner sanctuary only to the pharaoh and the high priest (site open 6am-5pm; admission E£42, students E£24).

# Western Desert Oases

Scattered across the expanses of the Western Desert, the oases dot the sea of sand and rock like a green archipelago. Fed by hot and cold springs, the oases are surprisingly lush amidst the imposing desert. Groves of dates, oranges, and mangoes, fields of watermelons, cucumbers, and corn, as well as rice paddies, flourish astonishingly in searing heat. Though the Bedouin and Egyptian *fellaheen* (peasants) who dwell beside the robust fields greet strangers with comforting hospitality, this is an adventure for the rugged. Getting around is more difficult than along the Nile. While there is at least (and sometimes only) one reasonably comfortable place to stay in each oasis, tourist facilities are basic, and diverse meals are few and far between. But for those of sound body and free spirit, the oasis circuit offers one of the most impressive journeys in Egypt.

Known as the Libyan Desert until World War II, the Western Desert is the largest in the world, covering two-thirds of the area of Egypt yet supporting only 1% of the country's population. The series of oases sprinkled throughout—**Bahariyya, Farafra, Dakhla,** and **Kharga**—marks the trail of a prehistoric branch of the Nile. It is one of the driest areas on earth and boasts some of the highest temperatures on record. Each oasis sits in a depression surrounded by an escarpment, or ridge, the top of which marks the usual level of the desert floor. Because the depressions are at or near sea level, subterranean water is more accessible. A flow of water originating with the rains of Equatorial Africa supposedly replenishes the wells and springs annually. This water takes thousands of years to journey north through underground fissures. Kharga, Dakhla, Farafra, and Bahariyya have sweeter and more plentiful water than their northerly cousin Siwa, where the water becomes highly saline before emptying into the Mediterranean.

The fortunes of the people of the oases have ebbed and flowed with the water supply. While dinosaurs romped at Bahariyya oasis during the Cretaceous period, by the end of the last Ice Age (around 8000 BCE), the depressions had taken their present form and the dry desert climate had set in. The hunter-gatherers and later farmers of the region, who had formerly enjoyed a milder climate with rain and lakes, high-tailed it to the depressions, where water was still available.

The Romans, with their waterwheels and aqueducts, were able to tap deeper water and push back the desert. Today, there are as many as 400 *Ain Romani*, the ancient wells drilled by the Egyptians and Romans in each oasis. The population burgeoned and prospered for approximately 300 years, but over-irrigation and abandonment of fallow farming eventually hindered productivity. The oases slipped into a slow decline that lasted until 1958, when the government released studies that showed considerable stores of water below the desert floor, accessible with new drilling techniques. The government's **New Valley Project** was designed to fully exploit this underground water for the promotion of agriculture and habitation in the desert, and a massive relocation of landless peasants from the Delta to the New Valley was begun. Unfortunately, experts now disagree as to whether the underground water is replenished by seepage or is just a finite supply left over from 6000 to 12,000 years ago, which may run out in a few hundred years. Government attention has meant radical change for those living in the oases, as new roads and other recently introduced conveniences usher in Western culture.

October through April is the best time to visit the oases, which are similar in clime to their latitudinal sisters on the Nile (Bahariyya is like Minya, Kharga like Luxor). It is not unusual for summer temperatures, especially at Dakhla or Kharga, to reach the 52°C mark. Even at night, summer temperatures persist into the upper 20s—and you won't find air conditioning *anywhere,* except Kharga (which makes it a good first or last stop, depending on whether you like your sweet dessert before or after your harsh desert). In any case, finding accommodations is a cinch in summer.

Dr. Ahmed "Oasis King" Fakhry's *Bahariyya and Farafra Oases* is an extremely readable introduction to the life and history of these areas. It and Fakhry's *Siwa Oasis* are available at several of Cairo's English-language bookstores. Cassandra Vivian's *Islands of the Blest: A Guide to the Oases and Western Desert of Egypt,* available at major English-language bookstores, is a treasure trove of history, geography, and culture covering the Western Desert oases as well as Fayyum and Wadi Natrun. It also has good, detachable, topographical maps of each oasis.

## GETTING AROUND

Daily **buses** run from the Al Azhar bus station in Cairo to the oases. Inexpensive buses also run from Asyut to Kharga and Dakhla (see **warning,** p. 173). Between the various oases, bus travel requires a little more flexibility than in the rest of Egypt. Published schedules are the roughest of guesstimates, and bus officials, townies, and passers-by all peddle wildly contradictory and inaccurate departure times. Ask as many people as possible, follow the consensus, arrive early, and bring your thumbs for twiddling. Your best information will come from the local tourist offices and bus officials. Kharga is served twice weekly by EgyptAir **flights** from Cairo and Luxor. Call 392 74 44 in Cairo for reservations and information. **Service taxis** travel to Bahariyya from Cairo, and to Kharga from Asyut, and can sometimes offer a faster and more comfortable journey—check out what the vehicle looks like and how many people will be stuffed in. (See the individual chapters on the oases, Cairo, and Asyut for detailed transportation information.) *Service* between all oases are affordable and often quicker than buses. Some people **hitchhike** from one oasis to the next, but they often have to wait a day or so for a ride, especially between Farafra and Dakhla. For those who hitch, the military checkpoints outside each oasis are the most promising spots to find a ride. **In the heat and isolation, hitchers run a real risk—Let's Go strongly discourages hitchhiking.**

**Car rental** is a convenient and comfortable, though expensive, option for desert travel. A giant loop along the Great Desert Road and the Lower Nile Valley in either direction beginning in Cairo is about 1700km (over 1000 miles). Any car must be in top condition and fully outfitted for intense desert travel in order to survive the long, hot, poorly maintained roads. Four-wheel-drive is highly recommended. The less wild at heart might look for a caravan (trailer); renting one can solve a lot of problems, including those of transporting food, water, and extra gas, and finding a comfortable place to sleep. If split among a few people, caravans can be economical.

A number of caveats are in order concerning **desert driving.** It is always a long way between gas stations. While every oasis has at least one fuel pump, it is essential to buy jerry cans and fill them with enough gas to cover the vast distances between towns. A caravan guzzles huge quantities of fuel; bring enough extra to fill an entire tank. Several containers of potable water are also vital in case you get stranded. Foreigners are (probably wisely) prohibited from leaving the main road. Try to drive in the cool of the morning or in late afternoon, but never drive at night—the chances of getting lost on unlit roads increases exponentially and hidden potholes are especially lethal. Don't pull a *Lawrence of Arabia:* never, ever drive in a **sandstorm.** If you do get caught in one, stop, turn the car's rear to the wind, and wait.

## SOME TIPS

The best alternative to staying in hotels in the oases is **camping.** Most fertile land belongs to farmers who will usually permit you to pitch your tent. The ideal spot is just outside the main town of an oasis, where you can usually find a small pool of water (ask the locals for the *bir,* or spring) and the sound of silence. The desert itself may be more comfortable, as cool temperatures and breezes carry away the mosquitoes, and sand makes for a soft mattress substitute, but sleeping on the dunes can be dangerous. You might be sharing the desert expanse with ticks, wasps, scorpions, cheetah, the fennec fox, mice, rats, and a tiny hedgehog that rolls into a spiky ball when frightened. There are also seven kinds of poisonous snakes in Egypt. They come out to drink at night and hibernate in winter. Common sense, secured food, and a first aid and snake bite kit are all recommended. If you prefer mosquito bites to reptile venom, each oasis has at least one bearable and cheap **hotel** or **rest house.**

Oasis groundwater tastes much better than that of the other Egyptian municipalities; if you want to risk the local grog-o-the-earth, this would be a safer place than the cities. Then again, is it really worth ruining the rest of your trip? The main towns of all the oases have restaurants and market places where you can fill up on **food,** but don't expect variety or refinement. The best meals are at people's homes—with a winning smile and a little luck you can taste for yourself.

**Women** should follow certain guidelines when swimming in oasis springs. In isolated springs unfrequented by locals, female travelers are not likely to be bothered. The same goes for pools cordoned off and connected to tourist rest houses. Women should not, however, enter pools where men are already bathing. Sometimes there is a separate pool where women may bathe, provided they wear a *gallabiyya* (loose-fitting robes). Local women bathe separately from men, often in the evening.

The requirement for foreigners to obtain permission to visit the oases was lifted in 1985-86. Despite what out-of-date sources may tell you, you need only flash a **passport** at the numerous military checkpoints. In Dakhla, Kharga, or Farafra, you will be asked to pay a E£4.50 **tourism development tax** by a tourist officer or by an employee of your hotel. Keep the receipt as proof or you may have to pay again.

The beauty of the Western Desert, with its traditional village lifestyle, stunning landscapes, and low prices, has been attracting increasing numbers of visitors. With them comes the slowly creeping disease that the smell of tourist money inevitably brings. In each oasis you will find those whose English is good, whose knowledge of the area is fair, and whose sense of capitalism is extraordinary. They are often friendly and helpful, but the assistance has a bloated price tag trailing behind. If you want the best information and fairest prices, head for the New Valley's **tourist officers.** In Kharga, the extraordinarily competent and friendly Ibrahim M. Hassan, in Dakhla, the punctilious and knowledgable Omar Ahmed, and in Farafra, the authoritative and entertaining Muhammad Ra'afat all speak excellent English and will answer your questions and arrange for guides and transportation at the fairest prices. Without them, you are at the mercy of the wolves. Bargain hard. A fair price is likely to be ¼ of that proposed. As always, any assistance you receive from a tourist officer should be *free* of charge. Women traveling without men should not embark on overnight desert excursions unless pre-arranged by a tourist officer. Even then, care and common sense are required. Lone women heading for the oases should be prepared to deal with harassment and might well find themselves in danger. For more information, see **Women and Travel** (p. 31).

## ■ Bahariyya الواحات البحرية

This small oasis is historically significant as a stopover for caravans traveling between the Nile Valley and the rest of North Africa. It lies about 330km south of Cairo and is linked by a decently paved road which leads past the Pyramids of Giza and southwest across the desert to Bawiti, a four- or five-hour car trip. Since pharaonic times, the arrival of merchants and their heavily laden camels was a major event in Bahariyya; for many centuries, pilgrims on their way to Mecca would join traders on the trans-desert trek and enjoy an enthusiastic welcome from Bahariyya's faithful. Nowadays, the only "pilgrims" in Bahariyya are the caravans of rip-roaring European adventurers gallivanting through the oasis in Land Rovers.

Because of its relative proximity to Cairo, Bahariyya attracts many foreign visitors who crave a couple of days in the desert but no more. The constant traveler traffic has created an atmosphere far more commercial and cutthroat than that of the other oases. Bahariyyan men badger tourists with spiels about safari trips and desert picnics, while kids mercilessly chant their *"mumkin pen, mumkin camera"* mantra.

Bahariyya's ancient ruins are scanty and largely inaccessible, and **Bawiti,** the main village, is downright oppressive. The nearby gardens, springs, and desert offer some relief, but not enough to convince the average traveler to stay any longer than they have to. The town's conveniences, including food stores, a market, four or five coffee shops, and three gas stations, serve to make the oasis a viable (and unavoidable) pitstop for those heading to Farafra.

### ORIENTATION AND PRACTICAL INFORMATION

All services in Bawiti are on or just off a 500m stretch of the main road.

**Tourist Office:** First floor of the government compound. The building, with a green and red sign on its façade, is on your right as you walk into town from the Cairo end. Staffed by city council member Muhammad Abd el-Qader. Open daily 8am-2pm. After 2pm, look for Mr. Abd el-Qader in the Paradise Hotel.

**Currency Exchange: Bank el-Watani** is next to the post office. Look for the massive **National Bank for Development** sign. No traveler's checks; cash only. Open Sun.-Thurs. 8am-2pm.

**Telephone Office:** In a driveway 10m off the main road, on the side of a building beside the government compound. No international calls; 3min. to Cairo E£1. Within town dial 1404; the operator will connect you. Open 8am-midnight.

**Buses:** The **bus ticket and reservation office** is on the 2nd floor of the telephone office building. Open 8-11am and roughly 9-11pm, and if someone happens to be around during the day. Cairo to Bahariyya: Buses leave from Al Azhar station Mon., Thurs., and Sat. 8am and 10am; Tues., Wed., and Sun. 10am, 5hr., E£10. All 8am buses continue to Farafra after taking a short break at the coffee shop in Bahariyya

(Mon., Thurs., and Sat. approx. 2pm, 3hr., E£10). Get on the bus early to secure a seat. Bahariyya to Cairo: Daily at 7am and Tues., Fri., and Sun. at 9am, 5hrs., E£10.

**Minibuses:** Minibuses run daily from Bahariyya to Cairo (4 per day, 5hr., E£11). The same service runs to Bahariyya from Sayyida Zeinab bus station in Cairo.

**Taxis:** Cairo to Bahariyya: *Service* taxis leave from the Qahwa el-Waha Café, on a corner of Qadry St., a few blocks south of Port Said St., west of the Citadel in the Sayyida district. Bahariyya to Cairo: *Service* leave from the front of Bayoumi's Popular Restaurant (a few per day, leaving at 8am and 2 or 3pm; E£10-15). You could also ask in the tea shops or the Popular Restaurant for a *service* to Farafra (once 7-10 people are assembled it will take off, E£15).

**Gas Stations:** One next to the police station, 2 more on the main road as you head out of town toward Cairo.

**Police:** Across the street from the telephone building. They speak no English and have no phone on which to speak no English. Stick with the tourist office.

**Post Office:** Two buildings down from the government compound, as you move toward Farafra. Limited services. Open Sat.-Thurs. 8:30am-3pm.

**Telephone Code:** 10.

## ACCOMMODATIONS AND FOOD

As a traveler in Bahariyya, you don't have many choices for where to lay your head. One of the better options is **Ahmad's Safari Camp**, 4km south from the center of town. The massive grapevine-covered veranda, clean common bathrooms, good food, and free rides to and from town sweeten the fanless rooms, lack of hot water, and isolated location. (Bare-bones hut E£5 per person. Concrete cabana with breakfast E£10 per person. Deluxe, white-domed gazebo with shower, fan, and breakfast E£40.) The **Paradise Hotel** is across from the telephone office on the main drag. This government hostel has a small but pleasant garden with patio furniture and basic rooms which are cleaner and nicer than the cabanas at Ahmad's. The shared bathrooms are rather grimy but at E£3.50 per person you can't complain. Standing with your back to the city council building and the tourist office, head down the street in front of you to the white-domed **Hotel Alpenblick,** 250m past the "cheapest shop in town" sign. Rooms here are luxurious compared to the other options in Bawiti: carpet, fan, turned-down sheets, a well-kept garden, and large, clean bathrooms. (Singles E£20. Doubles E£35, with bath E£46m. Triples E£53, with bath E£69. Breakfast included.) **Saleh's Campground** at Bir Ghaba spring is 18km from town. The folks at Alpenblick may give you a ride. A concrete slab in a straw hut runs you E£5 per person and gets you away from the hassles of Bahariyya. Bring food, water, plenty of insect repellent, and a flashlight.

There are but a few "restaurants" in Bawiti. Bayoumi's **Popular Restaurant** (full meal E£8) provides Stella (E£5), but ask in advance about prices. The restaurant is next to the government compound across from the police station, just off the main road to Cairo. You might also try the kitchen at the Alpenblick. Otherwise, the **Paradise** restaurant, **Kimo,** and **El Gahsh** all offer standard meals for about E£6. In the mornings, El Gahsh serves *fuul* and falafel. Despite these few places, food options are pretty grim.

## SIGHTS

As you leave metropolitan Cairo you'll pass just north of the Pyramids of Giza. Beyond lies **October 6th City,** one of Egypt's new planned cities designed to accommodate some of the country's burgeoning population. On the approach to Bahariyya, the entire landscape lurches into a deep shade of red: vast deposits of iron are quarried in an immense **iron mine** just off the highway 40km before Bawiti.

Nature is Bahariyya's real attraction, but two museums in Bawiti might also be worth a visit. Friendly and talented local artist Mahmoud Eed creates and stocks his **Oasis Heritage Museum** with curious clay figurines, creating dioramas that depict traditional oasis life. It's about 900m out of the town center on the left as you head towards Cairo (free but for the voluntary contribution box; some small figurines and jewelry for sale). About 400m back towards town, up a dirt drive on the opposite side of the road, is the government **antiquities museum.** Closed to the public, this is where they hoard all the great stuff from the surrounding ruins. You can ask at the tourist office to arrange a free visit.

**Bir el-Ramla** (2km out of Bawiti along a village track parallel to the road to Cairo) features a 45°C hot spring. The walk here passes apricot and date gardens. Men can bathe here in shorts, but women must be fully clothed and may swim only later at night. **Bir el-Mattar's** cold (25°C), slightly sulphurous water pours out of a viaduct into a small cement pool. The government operates a spartan camp here for E£5 per hut. Taxis to this popular site (8km southeast of Bawiti) cost E£10 round-trip. Men bathe here by day, women by night. The "road" (really a desert track—drivers beware) to Bir el-Mattar continues southeast through the desert to **Bir el-Ghaba,** 17km from Bawiti, with both a hot and cold spring in another sumptuous oasis landscape. Men and women can swim in this deserted spot, a E£25 round-trip taxi fare. Much less appealing, but closer, is **Bir el-Ghilis,** a steamy, pump-activated spring only 2.5km out of the town center. Nine km from town stands a large natural pyramid, sometimes called **Pyramid Mountain,** surrounded and topped by dunes. Closer to town (about 2.5km from Bawiti on the track heading to Bir el-Mattar) sits **Black Mountain** (called **Gabal El Engeliz,** or English Mountain, by the locals), a flat-topped hill with ruined fortifications from the British occupation.

Ruined chapels, tombs, and temples from the 26th dynasty cluster **El Qasr,** Bawiti's western sibling and the capital of Bahariyya in pharaonic times. Inquire at the tourist office to obtain permission to visit these locked sights.

All of the hotel managers run tours of the area. For *no more* than E£10 a head with six people (less if you are a larger group), you should be able to visit all the nearby springs, sights, and viewpoints. You can hire a taxi through the tourist office, or on your own (full day about E£40).

## THE ROAD TO FARAFRA

The paved road from Bawiti to Farafra oasis (183km) features spectacular canyons, wind-blown mesas, rugged desertscape, and the roughest, dustiest, and most pock-marked surface of any route ever graced with the title "road." The precipitous eastern and western escarpments of the Bahariyyan depression meet at a point about 60km south of Bawiti. The road winds through this pass and onto a brief plateau, then plummets into the Farafra depression.

The fabulous terrain between the oases is marred only by the outrageous prices demanded by the Bahariyyans who offer desert tours. All points except El Wadi Oasis can be reached by regular car, but dune-cruising in a 4x4 can be a fabulous rush. For overnight tours including food, a pick-up taxi should not exceed E£60-80, a more comfortable Peugeot E£70-90, and a 4x4 E£150-175. Summer is the cheapest time to go, but the hardest time to find riding partners. Jeep jockeys will probably start the bidding at E£800 for a trip to Farafra. Depending on the supply and demand curves of the week, they have been known to get at least that much. Bargain hard.

Leaving Bawiti, the scenery is stunning as you pass through the **Black Desert** with its dark mesas and crumbly flats peppered with tufts of dry desert grass. The idyllic oasis village of **El Hayiz** (E£50 per truckload as a daytrip from Bawiti) lies 5km off the main road to Farafra, 40km from Bawiti. Gardens, a spring, and simple village life-styles make this a nice spot to camp overnight, with fresh watermelon or apricots for breakfast. Between El Hayiz and Farafra lie dunes and flats, punctuated occasionally by mesas. **Crystal Mountain** (really just a rise by the roadside with some quartz deposits) rises about 100km from Bawiti. Further along is **Al Sillim Pass,** affording a fine view of the escarpment cascading off into the distance of the desert pan. The palm trees and small, desolate spring of deserted **El Wadi Oasis** (the only place you'll need a 4x4 to reach) lie about 140km from Bawiti. The oasis's resolute existence amidst towering dunes is striking, as are the grazing gazelles of the early morning. The most spectacular area is the **White Desert,** only 20km from Farafra, where spooky fungoid rock formations stand stark white in daytime and glow shades of blush and bashful fuchsia by dusk, orange by daybreak. Leaving the White Desert at the main road there is a cold spring—the final rinse before Farafra.

If you want to arrange a **tour** from Bahariyya, Muhammad Abd el-Qader (at the tourist office or Paradise Hotel), Yehi Kandil, or Badry Mahcpool (in the Popular Restaurant or at home, tel. 276) are all helpful. Ahmad's Safari Camp also offers tours. From Farafra, you can organize an overnight to the desert with Muhammad Ra'afat (p. 219). If you can't put together a posse, you can still see this interesting area from the window of the public bus (sit on the left side for the best views).

# ■ Farafra واحة الفرافرة

Among the 26 provinces in Egypt, Farafra claims an impressive 16% of the land, with its borders caressing Libya and Sudan. Two years ago, the area was home to a mere 5,000 people but the population has swelled to over 12,000 as migrants flock to the oasis's land. Province president Muhammad Ra'afat Amin has spearheaded the campaign to provide government funding for land reclamation through a massive irrigation effort—an effort that happily has done little to increase tourism in the area. The 3,000 people who live in the sleepy main city still use donkey carts and bicycles despite new roads and a brand new gas station. Farafra makes a great place to chill in the hot sands or to plan a trip to the nearby White Desert, 40km to the north.

**Orientation and Practical Information** The bus and all service taxis arrive and depart from the café on the Bahariyya-Dakhla road. Heading back toward Bahariyya, you'll pass the **police station** and the **post office and telephone service** (open Sun.-Thurs. 8am-2pm, telephone available daily 8am-midnight) before you arrive at the white arches marked with colorful murals at the **city hall.** (Open Sun.-Thurs. 8am-2pm.) This is where you can meet the knowledgeable Muhammad Ra'afat Amin who is helpful in organizing whatever excursions you may desire. If he's not in the office, you can ask someone to take you to his massive hilltop house 2km from town (E£2 is a fair price). During the summer of 1996, a new 60 bed **hospital** was being built farther up the road to Bahariyya.

Buses to Bahariyya depart in front of the café (Sun., Tues., and Fri. 6am, 3hr., E£10) and continue on to Cairo (8hr., E£25). There's also a daily private sector bus to Cairo (9pm, 8hr., E£25) which must be booked ahead of time with Muhammad Ra'afat Amin at City Hall. Buses from Cairo leave Al Azhar Station (Mon., Thurs., and Sat. 8am, 8hr., E£25) and stop in Bahariyya along the way. **Minibuses** and **service taxis** are the only way to get to Dakhla (early morning is best; ask around the night before to secure a seat, 5hr., E£15). If you're considering hitchhiking, reconsider; (see **Getting Around,** p. 214).

**Accommodations and Food** You can count the hotels in Farafra on one very small finger. The **Tourist Rest House,** 1.5km from the bus stop (or ask to be let off at the red and white tower outside of town), has reasonably clean rooms with temperamental showers (E£9.50 per person). In summer, the E£8 meal may migrate with the chef. **Camping** in the nearby desert or at **Bir Sitta** (6km from town) might make for a more organic experience but be sure to temper it with plenty of insect repellent and to check your shoes and pants before getting dressed—scorpions and huge biting ants thrive in these parts. Always let Muhammad Ra'afat Amin know your travel plans. Clustered around the bus station are several **restaurants** which do omelettes (E£1), macaroni (E£2), and full meals with meat (E£5).

**Sights** In town, the **Art Museum,** a unique project by local artist Badr, displays expressive sculptures and paintings, many of which depict life in Farafra. Mounted local wildlife and an exhibit of Farafran artifacts round out the collection. The museum, in the mud-brick building with the decorated façade, is near the city hall about 100m to the northwest behind a school (open capriciously). Many of Badr's murals also adorn the outside walls of local houses. The hot **Bir Sitta** (Well #6), 6km west of town, is an idyllic spot to swim and camp (transportation about E£5 per car-load). Sometime in the next two years a 150-person vacation village will spring up next to Bir Sitta, most likely squeezing this area out of the budget traveler's budget. The **White Desert** (40km from Farafra) offers overnight camping opportunities and breathtaking views. An average overnight trip in a 4x4 from Farafra should be about E£300 a carload and you'll visit both **Wadi Henis** and **Karaween**, whose springs and gazelles are marvelous. Once again, contact Muhammad Ra'afat to help you plan your trip. For more information on desert trips, see **The Road to Farafra,** p. 218.

## THE ROAD TO DAKHLA

The 310km road from Farafra to Dakhla was constructed in 1982 and is rapidly deteriorating. Much of its foundation is made of chalky rock, heaped up to prevent the road and the vehicles on it from slipping into the quicksand on either side. Be careful where you step and drive—shifting dunes have obscured the southern part of this road for years, making travel between Dakhla and Farafra an unpredictable undertaking. The road is now kept partially clear, yet sees little traffic. Buses and taxis make the journey without much ado, save for the occasional swerve to avoid a mischievous sand dune. If there is a good wind, sand will blow eerily across the road like fog in Yoda's living room.

Ten km south of Farafra is a tiny, uninhabited oasis officially considered part of the town. Although the villagers take care to cultivate the land there and an occasional farmer wanders across the road, the spot is deserted and quiet—the best place in the area to pitch a tent. Still farther down the road toward Dakhla, about 35km from Farafra, is the diminutive, sparsely inhabited **Oasis of Sheikh Merzuq,** where you'll find a sulphur spring with a viaduct carrying water into a coed concrete pool. The locals will show you the way to an ancient **Roman well,** where fresh water splurts from a deep spring. These watering holes can only be reached via private transport; the bus doesn't stop here.

## ■ Dakhla الواحات الداخلة

Dakhla's fields, rice paddies, and fruit orchards stubbornly hold out against the harsh, engulfing desert. At two junctures the desert does indeed consume the greenery, segmenting Dakhla into three separate oases. Regardless, 75,000 Dakhlans are the clear victors in the struggles of water versus stone and farmer versus dune. Basking in government attention, the people of Dakhla have reclaimed this recalcitrant wasteland, planting peanuts and rice before introducing more fragile crops which expand in variety each year. The New Valley Project may have rendered the urban center of Kharga unappealing to visitors, but in Dakhla—dubbed the "pink oasis" for the pink cliffs jabbing the horizon—something of the opposite has occurred. Here the oasians beam under broad-brimmed straw hats and share their infectious enthusiasm with visitors. In the villages around Mut, visitors will be closer to the traditional life of the oases than anywhere else in the New Valley.

## ORIENTATION AND PRACTICAL INFORMATION

Farthest from Cairo of all the oases, Dakhla bubbles 310km from Farafra and 200km from Kharga. The center and capital of the oasis is **Mut** (pronounced "moot"), named for the Egyptian goddess married to Amun. **West Mawhub,** 80km west of Mut, and **Tineida,** 45km east of Mut, are smaller repositories of green which mark the oasis's edges. Cultivated regions dot the main, well-paved highway. The three most appealing and historic towns are **El Qasr,** 32km west of Mut and **Balaat** and **Bashendi,** 35 and 40km east of Mut.

Life in Mut has two focal points: **Tahrir Sq.,** encompassing the intersection of New Valley St. and the Kharga-Farafra Highway (running southeast-northwest), and **New Mosque Sq.,** 1km south along New Valley Street.

**Tourist Information Office:** The new office (tel. 94 16 86 or 15 85) is 750m away from Tahrir Sq. on the road to Farafra, across the street from Abu Muhammad Restaurant, in a building it shares with the Egyptian Tourist Authority. The old office (tel. 94 04 07) is on the corner across from the mosque in New Mosque Sq. in the same building as the government's Tourist Rest House. The knowledgeable Omar Ahmed speaks English and will go the distance to assist you, including arranging transportation. If he's not in, feel free to reach him at home (tel. 94 07 82). Both offices open Sun.-Thurs. 8am-2pm and 8-11pm.

**Bank: Misr Bank,** Tahrir Sq. (tel. 94 00 63), near the police station. Changes traveler's checks and cash. Open Sun.-Thurs. 8am-2pm and 6-9pm, sporadically open Sat. 8am-2pm for changing money.

**Telephone Office:** El Ganeim St. From New Mosque Sq., walk east along 23 July St. to Anwar Restaurant, then veer left toward the red and white tower about 30m ahead on your left. Calls within Egypt, and potluck global service. Open 24hr.

**Buses and Service: Mut Station** (tel. 94 15 38) located in New Mosque Sq. To go **to Cairo** (6am and 7am (A/C), 13hr., E£28 and E£37 respectively) reservations should be made a day in advance. Buses depart at 8:30am and 4pm for Kharga (3hr., E£7) and Asyut (6hr., E£17), or you can take any Cairo-bound bus to either city. **Service taxis** and **minibuses** go to Kharga (E£7) and to Farafra (6am or whenever one fills up, 5hr., E£15).

**Local buses:** Buses go to Balaat and Bashendi (7:30, 8:30am, and 2pm, 50pt, return to Mut 1hr. later) and El Qasr (10:30am and 2pm, 50pt, return to Mut 2hr. later).

**Taxis:** Special sight-seeing tours E£40 for 1 day, E£8-10 for a trip to eastern or western Dakhla. Ask in New Mosque Sq. Covered pick-up trucks shuttle frequently between Tahrir Sq. and El Qasr and between the hospital stand and Balaat and Bashendi (75pt- E£1 one way). The early bird catches the truck.

**Bicycle Rental: Nasser's Hotel** (E£5 per day), **Abu Muhammad's Restaurant** (E£5), and the **Gardens Hotel** (E£7), less if you rent for a few hours or ½-day.

**Gas Station:** The outskirts of eastern Mut, on the Kharga Hwy. (on your left as you leave town). Open 24hr.

**Pharmacies:** There are 3 pharmacies on New Mosque St. Most are open daily 8am-2pm and occasionally at night.

**Hospitals:** The main hospital (tel. 94 15 55 or 13 32) is 1km from Tahrir Sq. towards Kharga. Smaller hospitals in each village.

**Ambulance:** Tel. 94 13 33.

**Police:** Tel. 94 15 00, in Tahrir Sq.

**Post Office:** One in New Mosque Sq., another on El Ganeim St., around the corner from the telephone office. Both open Sun.-Thurs. 8am-2pm.

**Telephone Code:** 092.

## ACCOMMODATIONS

If you're visiting during the winter months, consider staying in one of the hotels on the outskirts of town (listed below)—transport into town will be easier than during summer months and the quiet, retreat-like atmosphere is more relaxing than town. In summer, though, these fanless hotels are deathly.

**Gardens Hotel** (tel. 94 15 77), 20m down a dirt road from Anwar's Desert Paradise Restaurant, has patio furniture, a pleasant garden, and friendly management. Clean, breezy rooms with fans, or a desert-sky rooftop bed. Singles E£10, with bath E£12. Doubles E£12, with bath E£16. Good eats available.

**Tourist Rest House** (tel. 94 04 07), in the same building as the Tourist Office in New Mosque Sq. This marginally clean government establishment is a low-budget option in the town center. Crisp sheets but saggy mattresses. Cold showers only. E£4.35 per person.

**Mebarez** (tel. 94 15 24), on the edge of town, 800m from Tahrir Sq., on the road to Farafra; look for the 4-story mustard-yellow building. More upscale than the Gardens, the Mebarez handles large tour groups from Europe in the winter and can place international phone calls. Rooms are carpeted with balconies and fans. Breakfast included. Singles E£23, with bath E£28, with A/C E£38. Doubles E£34, with bath E£40, with A/C E£50.

**Hot Springs Rest House** (tel. 94 15 30), 3km out of town on the road to Farafra. Built between rice paddies and sand dunes, this is the government's Art Deco incarnation of a rejuvenating spa. Two large, circular pools are replenished with "curative," orange, 42°C water from the nearby hot spring. Swimming is free for non-residents who paid the tourism development tax. With no fans, the double rooms with bath (E£5 per bed, E£8 per room) may be too hot in the summer. Separate villa with garden and quiet back porch has 2 quads and 2 triples, 1 with bath and a fan (E£5 per bed).

**Nasser's Hotel,** 5km out of town on the road to Kharga on the edge of a traditional farming village, is surrounded by fields replete with waterwheels, water buffalo, and goats. Very isolated, with basic facilities, shared bathrooms, and a kitchen. E£5 per person, no singles. Nasser speaks English and will arrange day or overnight trips by car, camel, donkey, or motorcycle to out-of-the-way villages, springs, and dunes. To get to the hotel, find Nasser at Hamdy Restaurant (which he runs with his brother), 100m before the Mebarez Hotel on the road to Farafra.

## FOOD

While it's not saying much, Dakhla probably has the best food in the oases. **Hamdy Restaurant,** just before the Mebarez Hotel, serves chicken or meat meals for about E£10. The brothers worked in the kitchen of an American petroleum company in Saudi Arabia, so they can whip up pancakes and other tourist delights. Around the corner from the Garden Hotel is **Anwar's Desert Paradise Restaurant** (full meal E£7.50). Along the highway, **Shehaab,** just west of New Valley St., is a local favorite (full meal E£5). **Abu Muhammad's Restaurant,** across from the new Tourist Office, serves mountainous meals for E£8, and the comment book makes excellent reading. Be sure to confirm the price of any meal in town before you dig in.

## SIGHTS

Strolling near the New Mosque Sq., you'll stumble upon the future site of the **tourist village** designed by Hassan Fathy. The arched ceilings provide for natural air conditioning while the mud-brick walls contribute to both atmospheric and aesthetic coolness. Across the street you'll find one of the local **cemeteries.** From here you can meander into the dunes or rice paddies. For less agricultural excitement, the **Dakhla Ethnographic Museum** (tel. 94 13 11) has exhibits which explain traditional oasis culture through a reconstruction of a typical Dakhlan family dwelling. Expressive clay figurines, created by Mabruk, an artist from the Kharga oasis, recreate scenes of village life, including the preparation of a bride for marriage and the celebration of a pilgrim's return from the *hajj.* The museum is two blocks past Anwar's restaurant to the left of the fork. Arrange a visit through the tourist office or by calling Ibrahim Kamel Abdallah, the museum's curator, at the Ministry of Culture office on New Valley St. near the cinema, or call him at home at 94 17 69 (admission E£2).

Mut points you to the rewarding outlying villages. See Practical Information for transport options, p. 220. In the cooler months, you may want to bike to some spots. Be sure to rent one with strong tires and brakes, and bring camels of water.

### Western Dakhla

Traveling west from Mut for 6km will bring you to the small bedouin village of **El Douhous.** The road then splits for 25km before joining up again. The left fork takes you to the distinctly medieval village of **Kalamoun,** the capital of Dakhla in Mamluk times. In the Islamic era, Kalamoun was an administrative center; its inhabitants today claim Turkish and Mamluk ancestry. Two translations vie for the name's meaning—Amun's pens (*kalam* means pen), for the scribes who lived here, or Amun's citadel (*kala'a* means fortress). Like most oasis towns, Kalamoun's panoramic hilltop perch offered both military and climactic defense. Near the center lies an Ayyubid mosque which can be reached by winding through the maze of narrow passages and traditional mud brick houses. Leaving the town and continuing on the road for 5km you reach **El Gedida,** or "new town," so named because it's only 300 years old. The nascent village is well known for its **arabesque factory** which, in cooperation with Ain Shams University and the German Embassy, makes decorated woodwork with palm tree branches (open Sat.-Thurs. 8am-2pm; free). For more delicious handiwork, sample the town's sweet harvests: apricots (May), mangoes (July), and dates (Oct.). Three km further down the road is **Mushiya,** whose gardens boast old, broken water-wheels. Six km on brings you to the ruins of a yet-to-be-excavated Roman village, **Amheida.** You rejoin the main road 8km farther down.

Joining the main road and traveling west (to the left) for 3km will bring you to the turn-off for **Mousawaka Tombs,** Amheida's cemetery. The local bus to West Mawhub or a pick-up truck taxi can drop you off here. Head 1km south on the well-marked asphalt road to reach the guarded tombs, hewn into a rock outcropping. Souls were laid to rest in three levels, animals in the top two, humans at the bottom. The two-chambered **Tomb of Petosiris** features brightly painted funerary scenes with a half ancient Egyptian, half Greco-Roman cast of characters. The ceiling is ablaze with Hel-lenistic angels, portraits of folks passed on, and an overwrought zodiac. The adjacent **Tomb of Sadosiris** features unusual images of a two-faced man looking simulta-neously back at life and toward the afterlife, a mummy carrier with wooden wheels, another zodiac, and a bunch of grapes. These two are the most interesting of the hun-dreds of Greco-Roman tombs in the immediate vicinity. They were closed for repairs during the summer of 1996, but if you give Omar Ahmed of the tourist office one or two day's notice, he can arrange to get the key (admission E£8, students E£4). Two km farther along the main road from the Mousawaka turn-off is a dirt road which twists and turns around a small village passing three large Roman remains before lead-ing up to a ridge from which the Roman temple of **Deir el-Haggar** is within view. The temple is a 1.5km dirt track trek from here. Dedicated to the Theban triad of Mut, Amun, and Khonsu, it was built in the first century BCE during the reign of Nero and added to by his immediate successors. (Open daily with a 24hr. guard. Admission E£10.)

Heading back towards town about 3km past the junction with the loop road, or 32km from Mut on the northern fork, is the village of **El Qasr,** probably the most edi-fying daytrip from Dakhla. This charming contemporary town was built in and around the substantial remains of Dakhla's medieval Islamic capital. A model of com-fortable architecture, its mud buildings remain cool in summer and warm in winter. The **old village** of El Qasr lies 400m to the north of the main road through the new village. At the western edge of town on the main road is a large map of the village. Within the old village arrows direct you to the sights.

The **Minaret of Nasr ed-Din** is the only extant part of an 11th-century Ayyubid mosque. A 19th-century mosque surrounds the old tower. Down the gnarled alleys north of the minaret is **Qasr Madrasa,** an intact two-story mud-brick building that is thought to have been either an Ayyubid schoolhouse or the entertainment hall of an Ottoman palace; villagers later used the building as a courtroom. Many of the door-ways of the old village are adorned with ornate wooden lintels that reveal the name of the owner, builder, and carpenter as well as the date of construction. A pharaonic arch and a Roman doorway hint at El Qasr's pre-Islamic past. On the southern fringes of the old town you can see a waterwheel and functioning **pottery works,** where the villagers churn out everything from ashtrays to chamberpots. On the main road, at the turnoff to the old village, is the **El Qasr Tourist Rest House,** serving simple meals of cheese and omelettes in summer and a more complete menu in winter. Cold drinks and ice cream are also available (full meal E£6). There are four nice double rooms, two with balcony views of El Qasr, and a 24-hr. hot shower (E£5 per bed). Rounding out the small town are a small market, 30m from the hotel on the same side of the road, and a **telephone office** (open 24hr.) and **medical clinic** on the opposite side, 50m toward Mut.

Heading back to Mut, 4km east of El Qasr, is the turn-off for **Bir el-Gabal,** or "tour-ism wells." The hot spring is connected to the main highway by a 6km road which passes a little farming settlement. Travelers who are dropped off by a pick-up or pub-lic bus will have to walk or hitch a ride with some workers from the nearby quarry.

At the end of the asphalt road you'll see a small rise on the left with a dilapidated mud house; hang a left and follow the palm frond fence around. You'll arrive at a paradisiacal pool overhung by two palms (that frothy orange gunk around the edges is just oxidized iron). Another 12km along the main road (16km from Mut), you can stop for a back-pounding water massage at the spring just past **Budkhulu**. Lukewarm water pours forcefully out of a pipe into a large concrete pool. The spring lies 30m down a wide dirt track, by the side of the road between the village and a long row of eucalyptus trees.

You can do this entire loop by hiring a pickup for a day (E£40) or by leapfrogging on the pickup truck taxis which circle the sites daily.

### Eastern Dakhla

Two historic villages on the eastern side of Mut may restore your faith in rural living. In the crowded old section of Islamic **Balaat** (pop. 5000), long, dark passageways burst into a courtyard with palm fronds and grape vines. These ceilinged pathways were not built to make you feel claustrophobic—they were a defense tactic. During invasions, the camels and horses atop which the bad guys rode could not fit through the alleys. This village has the reputation of being the cleanest in the area, perhaps because its pathways are strewn with bright orange sand a few times each day. Ask to be shown the mayor's house with its assembly courtyard, speech balcony, and ornate wrought iron lamps and bedframes. Balaat was the capital of the ever-shifting Dakhla in pharaonic times.

The unguarded red-brick tombs of **Ed-Daba,** where Dakhla's pharaonic governors were buried during the 6th dynasty, are behind the village, just northeast of the main road. First walk 1km east from the official bus stop to a building with white stone columns; from there, walk 750m straight into the desert. The ongoing work of a team of French archaeologists has revealed several bizarre inverted step pyramids (open daily 8am-6pm. Admission E£10, E£5 with ISIC).

**Bashendi** is 5km farther east, 40km from Mut. Though less picturesque than Balaat, its ruins reward the trip. The village stands on top of a recently discovered temple and various Roman-era tombs. The large stone **Tomb of Ketenus** contains six rooms, including one decorated with scenes of its 2nd-century Roman owner mingling with the gods Min and Seth. (Arrows point the way, but the key is held by a villager whom locals will look for upon request. Admission E£8, students E£4.) Next door, the prominent **Tomb of Bashendi,** the base of which is a Roman foundation but whose domed roof is distinctly Islamic, commemorates the village's beloved namesake; you might join locals who decorate the inside of the holy man's tomb with *henna* in hopes of finding missing objects. If the guard isn't around to open the tombs, a villager may do the honors. There are also a number of hot and cold springs to which locals can direct you, though village leaders would rather lead you to the Bashendi **carpet works,** where local youths are trained to weave.

The **road to Kharga,** with views of sphinx-shaped mountains and natural pyramids, should only take about two hours. The rest house at the midway point has *sheesha,* tea, and *samsa* biscuits. Crescent-shaped sand dunes creep across the road just outside Kharga, necessitating occasional detours.

# ▓ Kharga الخارجة

Egypt's most effective attempt at a desert boomtown is the city of Kharga, capital of the New Valley Province (El Wadi El Gideed) and the most accessible and developed of all the Western Desert oases. Little is known about Kharga in early pharaonic times, although it must have been agriculturally sound for its hieroglyphic name is *hibis,* or "plow." It became prosperous during Roman times due to its proximity to trade routes, including **Darb El Arba'een** (the forty days road), the important slave trade route beginning in Sudan's Darfur Province and ending in Asyut, which thrived until 1884, when the rise of the Dervish empire closed the Egyptian-Sudanese border. Beginning in the 4th century, Kharga became a large Christian settlement and a cen-

ter for monasticism where major figures, including Bishop Nastorius, former Patriarch of Constantinople, were exiled by religious and political rivals. The oasis's
Australia-like function as a distant exile continued into the 20th century when Nasser
banished Mustafa Amin, founder of *Al-Akhbar*, Egypt's largest circulating daily, to
Kharga after the 1952 revolution. When the New Valley Project was begun in earnest
in the early 1980s, the town once again prospered. The greater Kharga population is
now in six figures. Modern Kharga, with its cookie-cutter apartments and wide,
empty streets, is a largely lifeless and boring town by Egyptian standards, but the
ruins on its periphery are astounding. Welcome (albeit temporary) relief from
Kharga's New Town can be found in the narrow alleyways of the Old Town. Locally-
made ceramics, carpets, and souvenir beef entrails are available in the *souq* which
begins at Showla Sq.

## ORIENTATION

Of all the oases in Egypt's Western Desert, Kharga lies closest to the Nile Valley,
240km from Asyut. The greenery begins about 20km north of the town of Kharga. A
newly paved road heads south from Kharga, skirting sand dunes and small oases on
the way to **Bulaq** (15km south), **Baris** (90km south), and numerous smaller settlements in between.

Sprawling Kharga's orientation is sponsored by the letter "L." The stalk of the "L,"
**Gamal Abdel Nasser St.**, runs north-south and is intersected in the middle by **En-
Nada St.** (which heads west to Dakhla) where you'll find the Misr Bank, the police
and fire stations, and the cinema. At the northernmost end of the stalk, you'll find the
tourist information office and rest house before the road heads off to the ruins and
then on to Asyut. The southern end of the "L" connects the stalk to the east-west
base, **En-Nabawi el-Mohandis St.** This street in turn curves slightly northeast to Esh-
Showla Sq., where you'll find the service taxi and minibus station, the *souq*, and the
old town. Convenient covered truck taxis scurry along Nabawi St. from Showla Sq.,
turn up Nasser St., and head for the tourist information office at the northern end
(10pt.). These taxis make getting around quick, cheap, and easy.

## PRACTICAL INFORMATION

**Tourist Information Office:** At the northern end of Nasser St. (tel. 90 12 05 or 06),
in the Modernist building with the off-white concrete canopy. Tourist officer Mr.
Ibrahim Hassan, well-versed in New Valley trivia, is committed to making your stay
in Kharga as pleasant as possible. Open Sun.-Thurs. 8:30am-2pm and daily 8pm-
midnight. Over 2km from the bus station, so grab a pick-up taxi (10pt).

**Tourist Police:** (tel. 90 13 67), next to the tourist office. Open 24hr.

**Currency Exchange: Misr Bank,** opposite Cinema Hibis, corner of Nasser St. and
En-Nada St. Changes traveler's checks and cash and will do Visa cash advances.
Open Sun.-Thurs. 8:30am-2pm, and 6-9pm in summer, 5-8pm in winter. **Cairo
Bank,** 100m east of the 1st traffic circle (tel. 90 15 51 or 35 55; fax 90 42 22).
Exchanges traveler's checks. Open Sun.-Thurs. 8:30am-2pm.

**Passport Office:** Faces tourist office (tel. 90 10 96). Open Sat.-Thurs. 8am-2pm.

**Telephone and Telegram Office:** Opposite the main post office. Open 24hr.
Dodgy international service. Branch in Shoqla Sq. open 8am-midnight.

**Planes: EgyptAir,** (tel. 90 16 95), 2 blocks north of Misr Bank intersection on
Nasser St. Airport turn-off is 3km north of town on Asyut Rd., then another 2km
southeast. On Sun. and Wed. from Cairo via Luxor (7:30am) and back to Cairo
(8:50am). Cairo-Kharga E£394, Luxor-Kharga E£311, no flights *from* Kharga *to*
Luxor. Minibus or shared taxi from Showla Sq. E£5.

**Buses: Intercity buses** arrive and depart from the main station on Muhammad Farid
St. 1 block south of el-Waha Hotel near Midan Besatin. They swing by Shoqla Sq.
before leaving town. To Cairo: 6am and 9am, 12hr., E£32. Buses from Dakhla
bound for Cairo also pick up passengers (8pm and 10pm, 12hr., E£32). To Asyut: 7
per day, 4hr., E£6. To Dakhla: 7am, 1 and 5pm, 3hr., E£7.

**Local buses:** To Baris: 7am, noon, and 2:30pm, 3hr., E£1.60. The 2:30pm bus goes
on to Dush, where the driver lives. From Baris: 6, 11am, and 3pm, 3hr., E£1.60.

**Service Taxis and Minibuses:** Catch them in Showla Sq. Fairly frequent service to Asyut (3½hr., E£8) where you can transfer to a Peugeot for Cairo (5½hr., E£15). Occasionally to Dakhla (E£8). "Special" (unshared) to Dakhla, E£56. Irregular service to Baris (E£1-2), or hire one for the day (E£50).

**Pharmacy: El Mhaba Pharmacy,** 1 block east of Showla Sq. on En-Nabawi St. Open daily 8am-2pm and occasionally in the late evenings.

**Hospital:** Tel. 122 or 90 15 02,. Main branch off Nasser St. north of En-Nabawy St. intersection. Open 24hr. **Ambulance:** Tel. 123.

**Police:** Tel. 122 or 90 10 44. Opposite Misr Bank.

**Fire:** Tel. 180, next to the police station.

**Post Office:** Main office off Nasser St., behind Cinema Hibis has **EMS.** A smaller branch is in Old Kharga's Showla Sq. Both open Sat.-Thurs. 8am-2pm.

**Telephone Code:** 092.

## ACCOMMODATIONS AND FOOD

In summer, splurge for a room with a fan or you'll drown in a pool of hot sweat.

**Waha Hotel,** towers over En-Nabawi St. just east of Nasser St. (tel. 90 03 93). Kharga's cheap spot. Floors and walls bear reminders of erstwhile clients, but the linen and bathrooms are clean. No hot water in common bathrooms, though plenty of hot air—get the pricier room if you want to survive during the summer. Singles E£6, with hot water, bath and fan E£15. Doubles E£15/E£20. Bare necessity triples E£15. Near groceries and restaurants, and a block from the bus station.

**El Goumhoureah Rest House,** 70m down the street directly across from the tourist office. Lounge, garden, and upstairs rooms with fan or A/C. Take the taxi to town for dinner and water. Singles E£12, with or without A/C. Doubles E£8 a bed.

**Tourist Office Rest House,** adjacent to the Tourist Information Office on Nasser St. Ideal for groups of 4 or more, these villas have living rooms with TV, kitchens with stoves and fridges, and bedrooms with A/C. Large chalets (E£97) can comfortably sleep 9, smaller versions for 4 are E£35. During the summer, depending on your timing and smile, you might coax them to rent you a single bed for E£20.

**Hamad Allah Hotel** (tel. 90 06 38), just off En-Nada St., 1 block from the telecom tower. The better value of the 2 upscale options (the other being the Kharga Hotel near the Tourist Office). Large sitting rooms on each floor give a VIP waiting room feel. Clean doubles with refrigerator, A/C, TV, bath, and towels. One person E£53, 2 people E£75; includes breakfast. Lunch E£15, dinner E£17.

Khargan cuisine is adequate at best, though fairly good rotisserie chicken seems to be a specialty—buy the whole or the half bird (E£8 or E£4). Plan to subsist on chicken, beans, and watermelon. The *souq* adjacent to Showla Sq. satisfies fresh produce cravings, and a **falafel** stand therein supplies tasty sandwiches (25-50pt). **Restaurant** (no other English name) in Showla Sq. offers the usual Egyptian favorites: chicken, *kabab,* and *kufta* (E£2-5), or try the hotels. A calm café beneath the Waha Hotel offers cheap, standard Egyptian lunches and dinners (E£1-7).

## SIGHTS

In addition to the antiquities, a few other Kharga spots are of interest. A little more than 500m south of Nawaby St. down Nasser St. is the **Pottery and Carpet Factory** where local handicrafts are made and sold (Sun.-Thurs. 8am-2pm). Another 300m down Nasser St. is the **date factory,** where 200 women at conveyor belts take plucked, washed, steamed, dried, and sorted dates and stuff them with peanuts and other goodies (Aug.-Feb., Sat.-Thurs. 8am-1:30pm, free). Yet 200m past the date factory is the **duck farm** where thousands of them quack placidly on a pond. The *pièce de resistance* of the New Valley's tourism drive is the sparkling new **Museum of Alwady el-Gadid,** housing a massive collection of artifacts collected from the New Valley oases (open daily 8am-3pm. Admission E£10, students E£5).

Kharga's important ruins cluster at the northern end of town. A shared covered taxi will take you as far as the tourist office (possibly farther if you give the driver

E£1), within walking distance of the sites. The **Temple of Hibis,** 2km north of the Hotel El Kharga and close to the road on the left, was begun in 588 BCE by Apnias of the 26th dynasty and completed by Darius I in 522 BCE, making it one of only two Persian-built Egyptian temples (the other was also in Kharga). While dedicated to the Theban triad of Amun, Mut, and Khonsu, the temple is distinguished by its depictions of Persians and the god of the Oases, Seth (blue body, falcon head). First-century Roman inscriptions discuss legal issues including women's rights. (Covered with wooden scaffolding during the summer of 1996, the site will soon be open daily 8am-6pm. Admission E£10, students E£5.) Across the road to the southeast, the **Temple of Nadura,** built in the 2nd century BCE during the reign of Roman Emperor Antonius, crowns a knoll. Little of it stands today, but the site provides an exemplary view of the oasis.

The spooky 263 above-ground tombs (also called chapels) of the Christian **Necropolis of El Bagawat** stand at the desert's edge, 500m past Temple of Hibis on the road to Asyut. From the 3rd to 8th centuries CE, a sizable Christian community, including many hermits and some of the religion's first monks, inhabited Kharga. Most fled or were exiled during the divisive 4th and 5th centuries, when Constantinople attempted to force the Melkite doctrine (stating that Jesus was not always of the same essence as the Father) on Egypt. Egypt's Christians resisted, and clung to their original Monophysite position. The Egyptian view had been put forth by Athanasios, a Khargan exile, at the first great Christian Council at Nicea in 325. The necropolis is visible from the road, and an asphalt road leads to the ticket booth. If you go up the hill along the marked path, you'll come to the **Chapel of Exodus.** Inside, the ceiling mural depicts the pharaoh's Roman-looking army chasing the Jews as they flee from Egypt. Other scenes show Adam and Eve and *ankh*-like crosses. In front of the Chapel of Exodus are the interconnected frescoed chapels #23-35, the resting place of members of a local wealthy family. The interior frescoes of biblical scenes in the **Chapel of Peace** (#80) exemplify Coptic painting of the early Alexandrian style. Greek inscriptions identify Adam and Eve, Noah's Ark, and the Virgin Mary. Atop the cemetery's central hill are the remains of a 4th-century mud-brick basilica. (Open Apr.-Sept. 8am-6pm, Oct.-Mar. 8am-5pm. Admission E£10, students E£5.)

## THE ROAD TO BARIS

If you've come all the way to Kharga, don't miss the road along the old 40-day camel trail south to Baris. This legendary caravan route extended from the western Sudan all the way to the Egyptian Nile Valley and trafficked more slaves than any other land route in the world, making the Kharga region strategically important ever since pharaonic times.

Vast sandscapes are all that thrive between Kharga and **Khwita Temple,** 17km to the south. The impressive 10m walls of the temple-*cum*-fortress command a hill 2km east of the road. Dedicated to Amun, Mut, and Khonsu, and built by Darius I with later Ptolemaic additions, the temple served as the center of a thriving community famous in pharaonic times for its grape production. This site was later used to garrison troops for guarding the caravan route; today, remnants of the fortress surround the temple itself. (Open 8am-6pm, 5pm in summer. Admission E£8, students E£4.) At the 25km mark you'll come across the shaded, dirty **Nasser Wells.** Farther on, the better-developed **Bulaq Wells** offer a simple government-run **rest house** (beds E£5, meals E£8-12) and hot springs that encourage participants to let off steam. **Zayan Temple,** dedicated to Amun, is 5km east of Nasser Wells near the village of Araf, on a road that loops around from the north of Khwita Temple to a point north of Bulaq. Originally built in the Ptolemaic era, it was restored by the Romans who used the site to build a fortress of which there are still remains (open 8am-6pm, until 5pm in summer. Admission E£8, students E£4).

The secluded village of **Baris** (the sign at the edge of the town ironically reads "Paris") is 90km south of Kharga and infernally hot in summer (over 50°C). Merchants make a 40-day camel trek from here to the border of Chad to purchase an ingredient used in local soap. It is estimated that each expedition brings the merchant

E£20,000 in profit. Think twice before going into business for yourself, however, since only one family in town is privy to the location of vital water wells along the way. There is a government **rest house** north of town, but no sign to mark it; look for the yellow, gray, and red buildings, in a row perpendicular to the highway, about 500m north of the "Paris" sign. You can arrange your stay through the tourist office in Kharga, or rouse the groundskeeper to let you in (beds E£5). Tourist officer Mr. Farkhat is available in Baris Thurs.-Sun.; during the rest of the week he can be found in Kharga. If you walk down the central street, perpendicular to the main road, old Baris will be on your right, the gardens straight ahead. Half a dozen small **kiosks** sell soda, mineral water, and canned goods. The blue structure resembling a doghouse sells *kabab, fuul,* and falafel every day except Friday.

A public housing complex designed by modern Egyptian architect Hassan Fathy (using cooling properties of traditional oasis architecture) stands 300m northwest of the rest house. Sponsored by the government, construction was halted during the 1967 war with Israel and never resumed; the government wisely decided that villagers would not want to live in buildings resembling tombs. Americans seem to mind less: Fathy built a similar complex in New Mexico. The Ministry of Culture has plans to open this complex as an Arts Center.

A recently paved road leads 23km southeast to the **Dush Temple.** The building has an overabundance of heat and isolation during the summer, but there's more to it than first meets the eye. Originally built for the worship of Serapis and Isis, the temple dates back to the Roman emperors Trajan and Hadrian. Only the temple is completely excavated, but around it the sand is slowly parting, revealing a church, pottery shards, and a well with clay pipes leading to an underground city. It seems that Dush, a prosperous settlement, was abandoned when the wells ran dry.

The easiest way to get to these sights is to hire a **pickup taxi** for a day from Kharga (E£50-60). Plenty of shared taxis go from Kharga as far as Bulaq (50pt). Catch them at the southern end of Nasser St. Each day, three **buses** go to Baris (7am, noon, and 2:30pm, 3hr., E£1.60) and three return (6am, 11am, and 3pm, 3hr., E£1.60). The 7:30pm Baris bus continues on to Dush, where the driver lives (3½hr. from Kharga; E£2) and doesn't return until the next morning (6am). Baris pickup taxi drivers will make a special round trip to Dush for E£20 (waiting included), but are sometimes hard to find. Instead of tackling Baris in a day (your road-time will total 7hr.), consider doing an overnight here, where the kind folk and the countryside will soothe your soul. For transportation to Zayan Temple, hop on a pickup or public bus headed for Baris and have the driver drop you off on the way. To return to Kharga or continue on to Baris, walk the 1km to Bulaq and catch a pickup taxi, or wait by the road (bring lots of water). Those who hitchhike find it difficult and dangerous—the road is sparsely traveled, especially beyond Baris.

You may want to take the **road from Baris to Luxor** to avoid going to Asyut—it's passable and paved all the way, but rough going in spots. No public transportation travels this road, and there are no towns, gas stations, or rest stops, but it is an impressive desert drive. During the winter you might be able to find the people it takes to make the E£200 "special" *service* taxi affordable; consult the tourist office and ask around Shoqla Sq. Don't hold your breath during summer, when tourism plummets. The road pulls its way up the escarpment to rejoin the normal level of the desert pan and winds through an old dry river valley before penetrating the lush green fields at the Nile's edge.

The 240km **road to Asyut** passes miles of monotonous desert, punctuated only by telephones lines. After several hours, you'll land in the rock quarries, and concrete factories that dot the armageddon-like, Mad Max world of Asyut. The **Al Obbur Rest House,** also called the **112km resthouse,** serving water and refreshments, is located halfway to Asyut. The Egyptian government and *Let's Go* strongly discourage tourists from passing through Asyut (see **warning,** p. 173). If you dare, you can use Asyut as a quick transfer before heading north to Cairo or south to Luxor.

# Suez Canal    قناة السويس

The strategically located Suez Canal is a miracle of 19th-century engineering, but based on an idea introduced much earlier. In the 18th century, Napoleon Bonaparte considered digging a canal between the Mediterranean and the Red Sea but feared that the waters of the Red Sea were higher than those of the Mediterranean. Another Frenchman, Ferdinand de Lesseps, came up with a similar plan and persuaded Said Pasha, the *khedive* of Egypt, to start digging on April 25, 1859. The canal was opened ten years later, on November 18, 1869.

If the Suez had been a root canal, the novocaine still wouldn't have worn off. Spanning 195km and reaching a maximum depth of 15m, the canal connects Port Said on the Mediterranean to Suez on the Red Sea. Because it allowed for rapid travel from Europe to the Indian Ocean, the canal became a crucial element of the infrastructure of the British Empire. Nasser nationalized the canal in 1956, precipitating a British-French-Israeli invasion (see The Suez Crisis, p. 50). During the 1967 War against Israel, Nasser blocked the canal with sunken ships. It remained closed through the 1973 War, and was reopened in 1975.

The Suez Canal's business has traditionally been business, not tourism. In a nation as rich with sights as Egypt, this region may rank low on the first-time traveler's itinerary. But Port Said is fast becoming an alternative to the crowded beaches of Alexandria, and Suez's proximity to 'Ain Sukhna lures a few (mainly Egyptian) tourists. Ismailiyya remains relatively unvisited. Get there before the hordes do.

## ■ Port Said    بور سعيد

Founded in 1860, Port Said (Bor Sa'id) became Africa's gateway to the Mediterranean with the building of the Suez Canal. Many Egyptians speak of the European flavor of Port Said. In fact, Port Said seems to be marked by a lack of any distinct flavor. Strolling down its clean, breezy, tree-lined streets you might be in Tel Aviv, Sorrento, Perth, or any pretty seaside city.

Since 1976, when it was declared a tax-free zone, Port Said has developed into a shopping resort chock-full of Egyptians flocking to cash in on duty-free deals. The town is saturated with clothing stores, most containing over-priced, unattractive fashions. At night, fluorescent signs advertising duty-free heaven, seafood restaurants, and pharmacies illuminate the streets, giving the town the feel of a giant amusement park. Even so, Port Said offers a fresh breath from the noise and pollution of Cairo. You can relax on the beach, stroll or bike through the pleasant streets, or simply revel in the friendly and hassle-free environment.

### ORIENTATION AND PRACTICAL INFORMATION

Port Said is 343km east of Alexandria and 220km northeast of Cairo. The Suez Canal and the Mediterranean beaches run at a 45° angle to each other, joining at the town's northeast edge. If you've spent any time in Egypt you've probably guessed that the street running along the sea is called the **corniche. Palestine Street** follows the canal. **Goumhouriyya Street** (spelled El Gamhoria on the tourist office map) runs parallel to Palestine St., two blocks inland. Another important thoroughfare, **July 23rd Street** runs east-west about 4 blocks south of the Corniche.

**Tourist office:** Two blocks from the southwest end of Palestine St. (tel. 23 52 89). Open Sat.-Thurs. 9am-1:30pm and 4-8pm. Provides a very good map of the city with a map of Suez on the back. Depending on the day, you might find someone who speaks English quite well or someone who can only mangle a few words. The **American Express Office** might help answer some basic questions.

**Tourist police:** Right near the tourist office on Hafiz Ibrahim St. (tel. 22 85 70), with a branch office in the train station (both open 24hr.). Most tourist police speak very little English. This is tempered by their inability to understand English.

**Currency exchange:** Small, reputable offices abound around town. The most convenient is **Thomas Cook,** 43 Goumhouriyya St. (tel. 22 75 59; fax 23 61 11). Open daily 9am-6pm. The **Bank of Alexandria** (tel. 22 28 81 or 23 60 94), also on Goumhouriyya St., is officially open 9am-2pm; sometimes also opens at night.

**American Express Office: Menatours,** 18 Goumhouriyya St. (tel. 22 57 42). Provides AmEx services to both card and non-card holders. Will hold mail. Open 9am-7pm.

**Telephone office:** (tel. 16; fax 325 705/ 325 706)) about halfway up Palestine St. Phone cards available for E£15 and E£30. Offers direct international dialing (to the U.S., E£24 every three minutes). Open 24hr. The 4-star **Sosnet Hotel** at the northwest end of Goumhouriyya St. will connect you to a long distance operator for an appalling E£2 for three minutes, not including the charge for the call.

**Trains:** Go to the southwest end of Goumhouriyya St. and turn right onto Mustafa Kamel St. The jam-packed station is 1km down, on your left; trains go to Cairo via Ismailiyya (6 per day, 2nd class E£6.30, with A/C E£14, 4½hr.); to Ismailiyya (7 per day, 2nd class E£1.75, with A/C E£4.30, 1¾hr.; to go on to Suez, add E£1).

**Buses:** The **West Delta Bus Company** (tel. 22 68 83) depot is located on Salah ad-Din St., on the western side of Ferial Gardens, two blocks west of Goumhouriyya St. Daily buses to Cairo (every hr. 6am-7pm, E£10-12), Alexandria (7, 10am, 1:30, and 4:30pm, E£11-15), Ismailiyya (every hr. 6am-6pm, E£4.25, 1½hr.), and Suez (6, 10am, 1, and 4pm, E£6.75). Not to be confused with the East Delta Bus company. The **Superjet** bus depot is next to the train station at the southwest end of Goumhouriyya St., with buses to Cairo (9 per day, E£13, 3hr.) and to Alexandria (1 per day, E£18, 4hr.).

**Service taxis** (ask for *taxi ugra*) also run to and from Port Said. The taxi stand is located near the train station and the Superjet depot. A microbus can be hired (driver included) for E£5 per hour.

**Bicycles** are a great way to get around the city. They can be rented on Hafiz Ibrahim St., just northwest of the tourist office for E£2 per hour.

**Hussein Pharmacy** (tel. 33 98 88; fax 33 97 77), almost directly across from Hotel de la Poste on Goumhouriyya St. Open 9am-1am. A number of other pharmacies line Goumhouriyya St.

**Al-Mabarrah Hospital:** Port Said's most modern hospital. At the western end of July 23rd St. (tel. 22 05 60). The **Et-Tadaman Hospital** also serves tourists (tel. 22 17 90).

**Medical emergencies:** tel. 123.

**Port Said Police:** tel. 122.

**Post office:** At the southeast corner of the Ferial Gardens. To get to Ferial Gardens, walk three blocks along the canal from the tourist office on Palestine St. Take a left on Muhammad Mahmoud St. and continue to its intersection with El Geish St. **Poste restante.** Open Sat.-Thurs. 9am-2pm.

**Telephone code:** 048.

## ACCOMMODATIONS

Most of the accommodations in town are either on or just off of Goumhouriyya St. Super cheap hotels are hard to come by, but attractive rooms for E£20-30 are easy to find.

**Akri Palace Hotel,** 24 Goumhouriyya St. (tel. 22 10 13), two blocks from the southern end of Goumhouriyya St. Owned by the friendly Greek Nicolandis brothers, the Akri has a well-worn charm. Rooms have old-fashioned iron bedsteads and (sometimes) a view. Ask for a balcony. Singles E£13. Doubles E£20. Triples E£25. Private bath E£4.

**Hotel de la Poste,** about halfway up Goumhouriyya St. (tel. 22 96 55 or 99 94). Cheerful red carpeting leads you into classy rooms with hardwood floors, and lots of amenities—TV, fan, fridge, balcony, and bath. The view of Goumhouriyya St. is

EGYPT

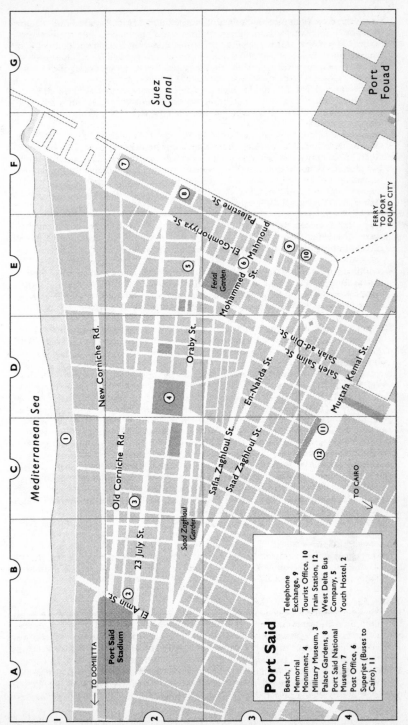

Mediterranean Sea

Suez Canal

Port Fouad

FERRY TO PORT FOUAD CITY

Palestine St.

El-Gomhoriyya St.

Mohammed Mahmoud St.

Ferial Garden

Oraby St.

New Corniche Rd.

Old Corniche Rd.

23 July St.

En-Nahda St.

Saleh Salim St.

Salah ad-Din St.

Mustafa Kemal St.

Safia Zaghloul St.

Saad Zaghloul St.

Saad Zaghloul Garden

TO CAIRO

El Amin St.

Port Said Stadium

← TO DOMIETTA

**Port Said**

Beach, 1
Memorial Monument, 4
Military Museum, 3
Palace Gardens, 8
Port Said National Museum, 7
Post Office, 6
Superjet (Buses to Cairo), 11

Telephone Exchange, 9
Tourist Office, 10
Train Station, 12
West Delta Bus Company, 5
Youth Hostel, 2

worth the extra pounds. Singles E£22, facing the street E£25. Doubles E£27, facing the street E£33. Triples E£36.

**El Ghazl Hotel,** July 23rd St. (tel. 22 35 86), across from the immense Abdel Rahman Mosque, 3 blocks east of Goumhouriyya. As always, ask for a balcony—only this time you may get a view of the Mediterranean itself. Rooms are simple but spacious. Singles E£21. Doubles E£29. Triples E£33.

**Qasr el-Baron Hotel,** 2 Deghla St. (tel. 23 23 00), two blocks east of the Akri Palace. Rooms are elegant, furnished with pseudo-Victorian furniture. Most have TV, fridge, phone, and fan; all have private bath. Singles E£30. Doubles E£40. Add E£3 for A/C. Triples E£50 (no A/C).

**Youth Hostel (HI),** on Muhammad el-Sayed Sirhan St. (tel. 22 87 02), opposite the stadium. A 20min. walk or E£1.5 taxi ride from the center of town. Modern and clean, but dark. Dorm beds E£8.10 (6 per room), triples E£14.10. Breakfast included. Right by the beach amidst a number of upscale yet reasonably priced restaurants.

## FOOD

It's no surprise that in this part of Egypt, seafood is the main fare. You'll have to search a little harder than usual for *fuul* and falafel. **4 Stars** (sign written only in Arabic) on Goumhouriyya St. just south of the Akri Palace should get you started.

**Galal Restaurant,** 60 El Goumhouriyya St. (tel. 22 96 68). Standard Egyptian food at reasonable prices. Have another Stella and a *kufta* sandwich (E£1). Seafood dishes for E£15, rice and lentils for E£4; make the most of your money by sitting outside, facing the street. Ignore or befriend the large plastic crustaceans above your table. Open daily 7am-2am; closed during Ramadan. Visa.

**Crystal Restaurant** (tel. 22 27 47), on Atef el-Sadat St. right near the Youth Hostel. Airy, air-conditioned, and elegant with a nice view of the beach. Excellent baba ghanoush and hummus. Make sure to ask if you don't see it on the menu. Seafood dishes between E£10-25. The aspiring writer Zarek will be happy to suggest Arabic writers to you and would love to hear literary recommendations from your native country. Open 9am-4am. Amex, Visa, Mastercard. 20% off with GO25 card.

**Grill Stube** (tel 23 97 11), at the northwest end of Goumhouriyya St., almost on the beach. This German-run restaurant is perfect for quick bites in between naps on the beach. Makes just about every kind of sandwich under the sun (all E£1.50).

**Haman,** on a side street just off Goumhouriyya. With Galal on your left, take a right on the small street by the gas station. Haman will be a few feet forward on your right. The yellow and red florescent sign is only in Arabic. See the people standing outside or sitting in their cars drinking mugs of cloudy beer with a small head? This isn't a drive-through Stella bar. The cloudy, heady beverage is fresh-pressed sugar cane juice. Sip the 50pt frothy mugsfull into the early morning.

**Reana,** across the street from the Akri Palace, next to Cecil's. For those who need a break from both *fuul* and seafood, Reana offers Asian fare. A bit overpriced (vegetarian dishes E£10, meat E£20-25). Popular with British tourists. Open noon-1am. Visa.

**Restaurant Soufer** (tel. 22 43 95), just past the Akri Hotel on Degla St. off Goumhouriyya St. Offers a tremendous variety of seafood. Try the shrimp platters (E£10-12), the *kusa bil laban* (E£9), or *kobeba bit tahina* (E£7). Open daily 8am-midnight; during Ramadan 8am-11pm.

## SIGHTS

The **Port Said National Museum,** at the north end of Palestine St., houses an impressive collection of Egyptian historical artifacts ranging from delicate bone needles from the Islamic period to Khedive Ismail's horse carriage, which paraded in the canal's inauguration. It's cool and usually empty, perfect for casual browsing. (Open Sat.-Thurs. 9am-4pm, Fri. 9am-noon and 2-4pm; Ramadan 8:30am-1pm. Admission E£6, students E£3, camera privileges E£5.) Port Said's **Military Museum** (tel. 22 46 57), west of the obelisk on July 23rd St., has dioramas of pharaonic and Islamic battles but concentrates on Egyptian victories in the 1973 Arab-Israeli War. (Open Sat.-Thurs. 9am-2pm, 7:30pm-8:30pm, and Fri. 10am-1pm. Admission E£2.) In front of the museum, the not-so-clean **beach** extends east to the canal. Beach chairs and umbrellas can be rented for E£5, and showers are located every 100m along the beach. If the words "duty-free" make your wallet tremble with anticipation, there's always the shopping *melee* on **El Togary, El Nahda,** and **El Goumhouriyya Streets.**

# ■ Ismailiyya الاسماعيلية

Once known as Timsah Village, Ismailiyya was named after Ismail, the last independent *khedive* of Egypt. Situated halfway between Port Said and Suez, Ismailiyya is considered the capital of the Suez Canal District. Surprisingly, this tiny, tranquil town of tree-lined boulevards is home to a tremendous canal trade and over 50,000 people. Heavily damaged during the Arab-Israeli Wars of 1967 and 1973, Ismailiyya has been completely rebuilt. During the construction of the canal, tremendous care was taken to retain the town's provincial charm. Whether wandering through quiet, shaded avenues, vegging in the sprawling gardens in the middle of town, or relaxing on the beaches at nearby **Lake Timsah** (Crocodile Lake—just a name, not a warning) or the **El-Morra** (Bitter) **Lakes,** this care is immediately obvious. Ismailiyya's charm is heightened by its lack of tourists: you won't be the only *khawaga* in town, but fielding a game of basketball might prove difficult.

## ORIENTATION AND PRACTICAL INFORMATION

Midway along the Suez Canal, Ismailiyya is linked by road and the Ismailiyya Canal to the Delta, and by highway and railroad to Cairo (140km) and Alexandria (280km). Ismailiyya's two main roads, **Sultan Hussein Street** and **Goumhouriyya Street,** flank **Orabi Square,** the city's center. On Sultan Hussein St., the quieter and prettier of the two, you'll find many restaurants and shops. The main bus station is on the busier Goumhouriyya St. **Mallaha Park** stretches along Salah Salem St., perpendicular to Sultan Hussein.

**Tourist Office:** In the back of the Governorate Building on Salah Salem St.; gives away the not very helpful *Ismailiyya Tourist Guide* for free.

**Currency Exchange:** The **Bank of Alexandria,** on the eastern side of Orabi Sq. next to Travel Misr (open Sat.-Thurs. 9am-2pm and 6-9pm), is your best bet. With the bank on your left, take the first street on your left. An **ATM** is one block up.

**American Express:** At **Menatours** on 12 Sultan Hussein St. (tel. 32 43 61), next to Groppi. Provides all AmEx services for members and plebes. Open daily 9am-2pm and 6-9pm; closed for renovations at press time, but should be open by 1997.

**Telephones:** A 24-hr. office is on Orabi Sq. (tel. 22 41 61). **Information:** 16.

**Buses:** The station in Orabi Sq. runs buses to Cairo (every hr. 5am-7pm, 2hr., E£5-6) and to Alexandria (2 per day, 4½hr., E£14). The **East Delta Bus Company,** in the main bus station on Goumhouriyya St., services El Arish (4 per day, 4hr., E£6.25-7) and has frequent departures to Port Said (until 6pm, 1½hr., E£4) and Suez (until 6pm, 1½hr., E£3).

**Service taxis:** Opposite the bus station, with frequent and fast service to Cairo (E£4.50), Port Said (E£3), and El Arish (E£6). *Service* are faster than the train but hotter and not as safe.

**Trains:** Another option to get to Cairo (6 per day; 2nd class E£3.40, with A/C E£9).

**Pharmacy:** The **Ismailiyya Pharmacy,** 24 Sultan Hussein St. (tel. 22 93 19), run by Dr. Kamel Sa'ad, is a good choice. Open daily 9am-3pm and 6-11:30pm.

**Hospital:** The **general hospital** is on Hospital St. in the El Arishayat Masr district (tel. 22 20 46 or 47; open 24hr.). Dial 123 or 22 31 03 for an **ambulance.**

**Police:** The station is one block west of the Governorate Building on Salah Salem St., along the canal (tel. 32 10 71, ext. 306).

**Post office:** In Orabi Sq. (tel. 22 41 13), open Sat.-Thurs. 8am-3pm; closed holidays.

**Telephone Code:** 064.

## ACCOMMODATIONS

**Ismailiyya Youth Hostel (HI),** Omhara Rd. (tel. 32 28 50; fax 33 14 29), is a little far from the center of town (a 1-km hike or a E£1.50-2 taxi ride), but otherwise a great choice. Lake Timsah provides a wonderful setting for this new, spotless 266-room youth hostel, while the large, bright sitting area, outdoor porch by the water, ping-pong table, makeshift volleyball court, and reasonably-priced restaurant and café give it a budget-resort feel. Singles E£27. Doubles E£18.10 per person. Triples E£15.10 per person. 6-person suites E£8.10 per person. Breakfast included. All but the singles have a private bath. Flexible 11:30pm curfew. Non-members E£1 extra.

**Nefertari Hotel,** 41 Sultan Hussein St. (tel. 32 28 22), three blocks north of Bank Misr, offers budget elegance with clean bathrooms and cool A/C. A live band entertains disco and bar guests nightly. First-floor restaurant has slow service but good meat. Singles E£28. Doubles E£30, E£25 without bath. Extra beds E£5 each. Add 12% for service and tax. Breakfast E£2.10, lunch E£4.85, dinner E£5.30.

**New Palace Hotel,** next to the Bank of Alexandria in Orabi Sq, offers small rooms with high ceilings. Some rooms have color TV and A/C at no extra charge and most have private bathrooms. Singles E£25, doubles E£50, triples E£75; breakfast E£5. Bargaining's worth a try.

**Isis Hotel** (tel. 22 78 21), the cheapest of the budget hotels, but the rooms are dark. Fans, possibly flies in each room. Clean bathrooms. Singles E£7-10, with bath E£13. Doubles E£12-15, with bath E£20. Breakfast in the cafeteria E£3.

## FOOD, SIGHTS, AND ENTERTAINMENT

Vendors line the streets with cheap offerings, but for excellent seafood, try Ismailiyya's sit-down venues. **Nefertiti's,** on Sultan Hussein St. south of the Nefertari Hotel (tel. 22 04 94), specializes in fish (E£12) but serves meat dishes (E£10) and delicious shrimp (E£25). Alcohol available (open noon-11pm). **George's Restaurant,** next door to Nefertiti's on Sultan Hussein St. is pricier, but most Ismailiyyans name this elegant, intimate Greek–owned restaurant the best in town. Good seafood with other options; if all else fails, make a meal out of the full bar. Meals go for E£20-30, and you can charge them. For a glimpse of baseball caps and sweatshirts, the **Pizza Inn** (tel. 33 39 90) at 41 Gomhoriya St. boasts of burgers (E£3.50) and pizza (E£6) made from "American ingredients" (open daily 10am-2am; free delivery). Signs throughout the city tout the **King Edward Restaurant** on 171 Tahrir St. just off Sultan Hussein St. (tel. 32 54 51). The food is more expensive than Nefertiti's (entrees E£15-20) and the decor is cheesier, but beer and billiards cast their spell. For dessert, **Groppi's Supermarket** (tel. 32 82 28), across from Nefertiti's, serves tempting pastries for E£1.25 (open Sat.-Thurs. 9:30am-9:30pm; closed Sundays and the first half of Ramadan).

The **Ismailiyya Regional Museum,** near the canal at the northern end of town on Salah Salem St., has pharaonic, Islamic, and Roman collections (open Wed.-Mon. 9am-3pm; admission E£3, students E£1.50). Near the museum, the **Garden of the Stelae** contains sphinxes from the age of Ramses II. Inquire at the museum entrance for permission to visit. If another little carving of Nefertiti's head doesn't make you tremble with excitement, you might want to skip the museum and frolic in **Mallaha Park's** 210 hectares of rare flowers, trees, and palms. For more virile entertainment, **Cinema Royal,** next to the Nefertari Hotel on Sultan Hussein St., shows American action films at about 5pm.

# ■ Suez السويس

Located at the junction of the Red Sea and the Suez Canal, Suez (Es-Suweis) counts as its main attractions the Gulf of Suez and, you guessed it, the canal. The city itself holds nothing of interest, although nearby areas attract a few tourists. It's a long-standing joke that the residents of Suez are touchy and mean, either because of their wealth or the city's historic role as a favorite target for foreign missiles. This is a myth. Be prepared for overly friendly greetings (you may even be slapped on the back of the neck and dragged into a shop for some conversation, tea, and *sheesha*). The only real unfriendliness you will encounter will come in response to calling the city ugly or boring, as most tourists and some inhabitants do. These same travelers simply hold (or thumb) their noses while passing through Suez en route from Cairo to the Sinai, by way of the Ahmed Hamoli Tunnel (running under the canal 30km north of town), or on their way south along the Red Sea Coast. They may have the right idea. Nearby **'Ain Sukhna**, however, is quite beautiful; its proximity to Cairo provides a viable sunswim-snorkel option for those either too lazy or too pressed for time to jaunt off to Hurghada. Suez serves as a base for trips to the Western Sinai.

**Orientation and Practical Information** Suez is centered on **El Geish Street**, running east-west from the **bus station** and across the canal to **Port Tawfik**, where the **tourist office** (tel. 22 35 89) is located. The **tourist police** (tel. 22 11 40) share the office (open daily 3-6pm). For transport within the city, exit the bus station and go behind the row of food stands. **Minibus** drivers will be yelling out their destinations. **Service taxis** gather one street over from the buses, while the **train station** is about 4km farther west at the end of El Geish. **American Express** services are available at **Menatours** (tel. 22 88 21) in Port Tawfik. The **Bank of Alexandria,** near the bus station, exchanges currency (summer daily 8am-2pm and 5-8pm, winter 8am-2pm and 6-9pm). The **post office** (with **poste restante**) is on Hoda Sharawi St., one block north of and parallel to El Geish (open Sat.-Thurs. 8am-3pm). Another branch is next door to the tourist office in Port Tawfik (same hours). The **telecommunications office** is about three blocks south of El Geish on the corner of Shohada'a and Sa'ad Zaghloul St. (open 24hr.). Alternatively, you can call Cairo from Hotel Sinai for E£2 per 3min. The **telephone code** is 062.

**Buses** shuttle from Suez to Cairo (every 30min. 6am-5pm, every hr. 5-8pm; 2hr.; E£7), Ismailiyya (every 15min. 6am-6pm, 1¼hr., E£3), and through Cairo to Alexandria (9 and 11am, 5hrs., E£11-12). There are also buses for Port Said (4 per day, last bus 3:30pm, 2½hr., E£9), Hurghada (over the Red Sea Highway, 5 per day, last bus 6pm, 6hrs., E£12-15), 'Ain Sukhna (6 and 10am, and 2pm; 1½hr., E£1.75), Uyoun Mussa, Ras Sudr, and Hammam Far'aun. Tickets to Hurghada and Alexandria should be reserved a couple of days in advance. **Service taxis** travel these routes (except for Alexandria) at similar prices (Cairo E£4.50, Port Said E£7, Ismailiyya E£3, Hurghada E£20). They usually depart more frequently than buses, but don't expect A/C. Six **trains** per day rattle along to Cairo (E£1-3) and Ismailiyya (90pt), but the coaches are hot and uncomfortable.

Suez is the main launching ground for forays into the **Sinai**. Buses run daily to Sharm esh-Sheikh (11am, 1, and 3pm, 6hr., E£16-18), St. Catherine's (2pm, 6hr., E£18), Dahab (11am, 7hr., E£22), Nuweiba' (11am and 3pm, 4hr., E£25), and Taba (3pm, 6hr., E£17-20). *Service* drivers charge by the trip, so the more people in the van the less you will pay (clowns ride for almost nothing). Taxis to the Sinai are generally prohibitively expensive—the bus is the best option.

**Accommodations and Food** The **Star Hotel,** 17 Bank Misr St. (tel. 22 87 37), has large, clean rooms, all equipped with fans. (Singles E£9, with bath E£12. Doubles E£12, with bath E£15. Triples E£18. Breakfast E£3.) The comfortable **Hotel Sina** is right next to the Star at 21 Bank Misr St. (tel. 22 03 94). Rooms have ceiling fans, TVs, and phones, but not much charm. (Singles E£13.30. Doubles E£18. Triples with bath E£23.30. Some have A/C for E£5 extra. Breakfast E£3. During high season, add about E£5 to the prices.) The **Misr Palace,** around the corner at two Sa'ad Zaghloul St. (tel. 22 30 31), six blocks east of the bus station, has cheap, dirt-free, furniture-free, and fan-free rooms. Don't get too excited about the sign for a Korean restaurant—it's been out of business since the transparent skirts of the 19th Dynasty went out of style. (Singles E£11.50, with bath E£18. Doubles E£24, with bath E£31.25. A/C E£8, fans E£1.50, TV E£2. Breakfast E£3. Prices may rise E£4-5 in the high season.) The **HI youth hostel** (tel. 22 19 45) is on Salah Naseem St. opposite the stadium. From El Geish, take a right off Sa'ad Zaghloul St., between the Misr Palace and Bel Air hotels, then take a right on El Galaa, which becomes Salah Naseem. You may want to take a private taxi (no more than E£3). This is not Egypt's cleanest hostel. (No sheets provided. One fan per room. Curfew 11pm. 12-bed dorms, E£3 per person, nonmembers E£3.50.)

On the culinary front, stick with fish, the one thing guaranteed to be somewhat fresh and tasty. There are some good seafood restaurants on El Geish St. **Abo Ali Seafood** (tel. 22 26 28) serves a full course meal for E£7, and you may get served by Ahmed Abu Ela, affectionately known around Suez as the "Eddie Murphy of Egypt." The *qahwa* of choice is the **El Tayib Coffee Shop** on Hoda Sha'rawi St. (tel. 22 59 88), four blocks west of the post office. This long, dome-shaped joint is a great place for *sheesha* and a cup of joe (open daily 7am-3pm and 4pm-midnight). A faded pink, yellow, and blue sign on El Geish before the Bel Air marks **Sweet Spot,** an astoundingly cheap sandwich, *shawerma*, and sweets shop which serves great baked macaroni in béchamel sauce. **Food stands** lurking near the bus stop may not be safe.

**Sights** The only monuments in town are three American-made tanks on the corniche, captured from Israel in 1973. However, the beach at **'Ain Sukhna** (Hot Spring), 55km south along the Red Sea, rivals those of the Sinai. **Buses** run there early in the day (6 and 10am, and 2pm; 1½hr., E£1.75) and return roughly 1½ hours later (thus the last bus back to Suez is at 3:30pm or so). **Service** also run down the coast from Suez to 'Ain Sukhna. The hot spring (35°C), originating in the Ataka Mountains, is an attractive place for snorkeling, diving, or just lying on the beach. 'Ain Sukhna offers many of the same things as Hurghada (except affordable accommodations) and remains relatively undiscovered. The **'Ain Sukhna Hotel** (tel. 77 23 67 or 18 10) provides cabins for two for E£80 and chalets and doubles for E£110, with minimal student discounts. Day-trippers can pay the E£15 day-use fee for chairs and umbrellas and enjoy the perfectly clear water from anywhere on the beach. The coral reefs and the small spring-fed waterfall are north of the beach. It's wise to bring your own food, as the few supermarkets and hotel restaurants will soak you quicker than the water.

# Red Sea Coast

## ■ Monasteries of St. Paul and St. Anthony

The isolated monasteries of St. Paul and St. Anthony lie 30km apart (82km by road) near the Red Sea. These centers of faith, dating from the early Christian monastic tradition, are inhabited by monks whose austere lifestyle differs remarkably little from that of 16 centuries ago. You'd better be serious if you want to reach the monasteries; the carless will have a tough time getting here. A group of seven can hire a taxi from Suez or Hurghada. In Suez, if you deal directly with a taxi driver you should pay E£110 for both sites. Travel agencies can arrange the trip starting at E£180.

Another way to reach the monasteries is to join a church expedition. For further information in Cairo, contact the monasteries' administration office (tel. (02) 90 60 25) or the YMCA, 27 El Goumhouriyya St. (tel. (02) 91 73 60). The former sends a car to the monasteries every week. Note that you must have a letter of recommendation from the administration office in Cairo if you plan to stay overnight at either of the two monasteries (tel. 90 02 18), although the monks may overlook this if their monastery doesn't already have many guests. Only men can stay at St. Anthony's; St. Paul's accommodates both men and women. The monks provide food and water. Both monasteries are open 9am-5pm.

St. Anthony's is the more interesting of the two monasteries and also the harder one to reach. If you attempt to get there by public transportation, the closest stop is **Ras Za'frana,** about 33km east of St. Anthony's (Deir Anba Anton). From there, you might be able to catch a ride with a Christian family. The closest stop to St. Paul's from a Hurghada-bound bus is by the St. Bola sign. The monastery lies a sweaty 12km walk from the road, but a pilgrim driving by might give you a lift. The best time to hitch is Sunday. Although pilgrims tend to be friendly and catching a ride relatively easy, hitchhiking, especially in the desert, is an inherently risky proposition.

## ST. ANTHONY'S MONASTERY

St. Anthony, raised in the Nile Valley, scorned worldly concerns and retreated into the Eastern Desert where he became the first famous ascetic of the Christian Church. Anthony's dramatic move reflected the restlessness that overtook some Christians in the 4th century CE when Constantine made Christianity the official religion of the Roman Empire. This was a disturbing development for many who felt that the church had gained worldly security and wealth at the expense of its spiritual focus. In Egypt, some of these Christians, mostly educated middle-class men, sought to escape the secular world by retreating to the desert where they could pray in solitude and render their lives unto God, not Caesar.

St. Anthony suffered paradoxically; his desert hermitages became popular pilgrimage sites, and crowds of the pious and the curious deprived the recluse of precious penitent isolation. Icons of Antonius adorn the walls of many Coptic churches in Egypt. Soon after the saint's death, his disciple St. Athanasius told the story of his choice of poverty and hardship, his wild battles with demons, and his wise counsel to monks and layfolk. Athanasius' *Life of Anthony* became the prototype for much of later Christian hagiography.

A few years after St. Anthony's death, his followers settled at the present site and established the first Christian monastery. The Monastery of St. Anthony served as a refuge for some of the monks of Wadi Natrun when their own sanctuaries were attacked by Bedouin in the 6th century. During the 7th and 8th centuries the monastery was occupied by Melkite monks, and in the 11th it was pillaged by the army of Nasr ed-Dawla. About 100 years after the sacking, it was restored and transferred to Coptic hands. The **Church of St. Anthony** and the southern walls are the only remains predating the 16th-century construction of the present monastery.

With ancient frescoes embellishing each of their sections, Anthony's church and its small chapel are the most impressive parts of the monastery. East of the Church of St. Anthony, the **Church of the Apostles** contains three haikals. During Lent, the monks cantellate the liturgy in the 18th-century Church of St. Mark. As in the Wadi Natrun monasteries, the Chapel of St. Michael is on the top floor of the keep. The impressive library contains more than 1700 manuscripts.

The major religious attraction in the vicinity of the church is the **Cave of St. Anthony,** where the ascetic himself is said to have lived. The vista from the cave, 276m above the Red Sea, rewards the 1½ hours of hoofing and huffing. The best time to climb the mountain is when the sun is relatively low, before 6am or after 4pm. Try to return before dark (or light) and remember to bring oceans of water. St. Anthony's has a small snack shop (soda and cookies) and a gift shop. It is good etiquette to make a donation.

## ST. PAUL'S MONASTERY

**St. Paul** (not the disciple) was born into an affluent Alexandrian family in the 3rd century CE. When his father died he left his estate to young Paul and his brother. This caused instantaneous squabbling between the two and, when the family had heard enough, they were sent off to see a judge. Not on speaking terms, the two young men took separate routes. Paul happened to pass the funeral service of a wealthy man and, for some unexplained reason, was profoundly affected (why he wasn't so moved at his father's funeral no one knows). Like St. Anthony, St. Paul cast off all worldly concerns and, guided by an angel, headed for the hills. He lived in a cave near Mt. Nemra and made his garments from palm leaves and branches. Legend has it his strict ascetic diet of one half loaf of bread per day was dropped to him by a crow; water came from a secret source high in the mountains (which still exists today). These divine provisions enabled St. Paul to live alone for over 80 years.

The original monastery was built on the cave site not too long after St. Paul's death—probably before 400 CE. St. Paul's has been attacked by Bedouin throughout its history, most notably in 1484 when the churches were burned, the library destroyed, and all of the monks killed. Bedouin occupied the monastery for 80 years. After they left, Coptic Patriarch Gabriel VII sent replacement monks to rebuild the churches, but the buildings were destroyed again a hundred years later.

Finally, at the end of the 16th century, Coptic Patriarch Ioannis had monks from St. Anthony's reconstruct and inhabit St. Paul's. These monks were the wisest yet: they built a five-story tower with a drawbridge leading to the fourth story. The first two floors of the tower were for food and water storage and allowed the monks to endure sieges of up to three months.

The monastery was most recently renovated in 1974 but, aside from the electrical generators and guesthouse, it is the same as it has been for centuries. The most impressive part of the monastery is the **Church of St. Paul**, built in the cave where the famed hermit dwelled. Many of the church's 4th and 7th century frescoes have somehow survived. Ostrich eggs symbolizing the Resurrection hang from the roof. You can fill your Baraka bottles with holy water coming from the same secret source St. Paul was believed to have lived on.

The monks at both monasteries live much the way they have for centuries, rising early and praying for four hours every morning. They warmly welcome visitors, most in excellent English, and are happy to answer questions. While it's possible to visit one of the monasteries in a few hours, spending the night would be much more enlightening.

# ■ Hurghada الغردقة

Since the early 1980s, when peace with Israel opened Egypt to foreign investors and tourists, scores of resorts and shopping complexes have sprung (and continue to spring) from the sands of Hurghada, making it the fastest-growing town in the country. Developers hope that within five years, the entire 500km between Hurghada and the Sudanese border will be littered with holiday villages. While Na'ama Bay can be enjoyed only by those with bottomless wallets, Hurghada (pronounced El Erdaha) offers aquatic splendors, along with a slew of budget accommodations and backpacker-friendly amenities. Luxury yachts and Rolex watches have been spotted on outlying beaches, but *Let's Goers* own the downtown area.

Unfortunately, the beauty of the coastline has been marred by overzealous developers without zoning restrictions. Some oil has been spotted on the public beaches (perhaps oozing from slick shop owners), and streets are lined with shops selling shiny conchs and marine life (dried out, stuffed with newspaper, and shellacked). Snorkelers and inexperienced divers alike have been quick to ravage the reefs. Since there are no land attractions to speak of, once the reefs go, so will Hurghada's appeal. "Save the Red Sea" posters are now ubiquitous and strict penalties are supposedly being enforced. Unless drastic changes occur, most experienced divers estimate that within 10-15 years, the tourist boom will move south. Buying shells or coral in the stores is not only a blow to the reefs, but a waste of money—your souvenirs may be confiscated at the airport.

Hurghada is oriented more towards getting you in the water than letting you lie beside it. The only clean beaches are private and costly, and dive shops aggressively recruit customers. Lazy loungers should steer clear of Hurghada. Better beaches lie farther south and in the Sinai.

## ORIENTATION

Paved highways link Hurghada with population centers, but the town itself is remote. From Qena, 70km north of Luxor in the Nile Valley, it's a barren, mountainous 160km to Port Safaga on the Red Sea coast, and another 50km of coastline north to

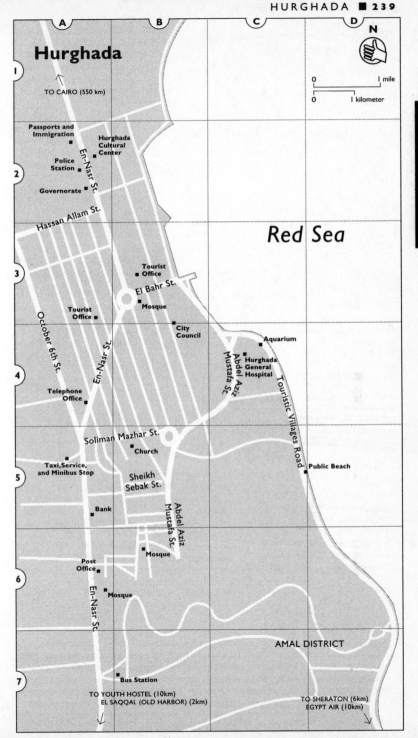

EGYPT

# Hurghada

TO CAIRO (550 km)

Passports and Immigration

Hurghada Cultural Center

Police Station

En-Nasr St.

Governorate

Hassan Allam St.

Red Sea

Tourist Office

El Bahr St.

Mosque

Tourist Office

October 6th St.

En-Nasr St.

City Council

Aquarium

Mustafa St.

Abdel Aziz

Hurghada General Hospital

Telephone Office

Touristic Villages Road

Soliman Mazhar St.

Church

Taxi, Service, and Minibus Stop

Sheikh Sebak St.

Public Beach

Bank

Abdel Aziz Mustafa St.

Mosque

Post Office

En-Nasr St.

Mosque

AMAL DISTRICT

Bus Station

TO YOUTH HOSTEL (10km)
EL SAQQAL (OLD HARBOR) (2km)

TO SHERATON (6km)
EGYPT AIR (10km)

N

0     1 mile
0     1 kilometer

### St. Anthony and St. Paul

St. Anthony and St. Paul actually met and became friends towards the end of St. Paul's life. God wanted to reveal the holiness of St. Paul and led St. Anthony to his cave. As the two conversed, St. Paul's crow dropped a *whole* loaf of bread for them. St. Paul, realizing that he was talking to another holy man, told St. Anthony that he was nearing death and asked, as one final request, to wear the robe of Pope Athanasius. St. Anthony immediately departed to fetch the garment. On his return he had a vision of angels carrying St. Paul's soul to heaven. He arrived at the cave to find St. Paul dead. While pondering what to do with the body, two lions descended from the mountain and dug a grave. St. Anthony wrapped St. Paul in the papal robe and buried him. He then carried St. Paul's palm leaf garment back to Athanasius, who sported it every Christmas, Epiphany, and Easter.

Hurghada. And that's the short way—Suez lies 410km north at the far end of the Gulf of Suez, with Cairo another 130km west.

Hurghada is a typical coastal town, growing long along the coast and not very wide inland. The **main town** of Hurghada, a cluster of hotels, restaurants, shops, and homes, lies 2km north of the **harbor** *(dahar)* of **Saqala,** the original fishing town out of which Hurghada grew. Buses and *service* arrive in the main town, where budget accommodations await. Heading south along the coastal road, things become progressively more remote and more expensive—Saqala has plenty of dive shops and cafés, but few budget hotels. Farther south are a string of resorts.

**En-Nasr Road,** the main thoroughfare, begins inland from the coastal road and connects the town and harbor. Everything you need, from the passport office in the north to the bus station in the south, lies along a 2km stretch of this street. Smaller streets to the east of En-Nasr Rd. contain budget hotels, restaurants, tourist bazaars, and the **souq,** all separated from the sea by a small mound posing as **El Afish "mountain."** Many hotels are on or just off **Abd el-Aziz Mustafa Street,** which leads from the center of town and En-Nasr to the beach.

## PRACTICAL INFORMATION

**Tourist Office:** Off En-Nasr Rd. (tel. 54 65 13), 800m north of the bus station in a dilapidated shack next to the Ritz Hotel. Other branches on El Bahr St. by the Reem Hotel, in the bus station, and in Saqala between the main square and the port. Provides mediocre maps and help with directions and phone numbers, but little else. Open Sat.-Thurs. 8am-2pm.

**Tourist Police:** In the first tourist office shack (tel. 54 67 65). Open 24hr.

**Currency Exchange: National Bank of Egypt,** open summer Sat.-Thurs. 8:30am-2pm and 6-9pm, Fri. 9-11:30am and 6-9pm; winter Sat.-Thurs. 8:30am-2pm and 5-8pm, Fri. 9-11:30am and 5-8pm. **Banque Misr,** open summer Sun.-Thurs. 8:30am-9pm, Fri. 8am-noon and 6-9pm, Sat. 10am-2pm and 6-9pm, both on En-Nasr Rd., 500m north of the bus station. Outside Banque Misr is an **ATM** (Visa, MC, Plus, Cirrus). **Thomas Cook,** on Sheraton St. Open daily 9am-2pm and 6-9:30pm.

**American Express:** En-Nasr Rd. (tel. 54 74 64), across from the bus station and slightly north; look for the large "Xerox" sign. Open Sat.-Thurs. 9am-2pm and 5-10pm, Sun. and Fri. 5-11pm. Only service seems to be replacing lost AmEx cards.

**Passport Office:** En-Nasr Rd. (tel. 44 67 27), to the left of the Red Sea Security Dept. building at the northern edge of town, 2km from the bus station. Open Sat.-Thurs. 8am-2pm and 7-9pm, Fri. 10am-noon.Visas handled in afternoons and Fri.

**Federal Express:** Sheraton St. (tel. 44 27 71; fax 44 27 72), 1km south of Saqala. Expensive but reliable worldwide express mail. Open daily 8am-5pm.

**Telephones:** En-Nasr Rd., on the left just after the road turns at the police station. Open 24hr. A few shops in the tourist bazaar offer prompt connections abroad for a small surcharge. **Fax** in a hut across from the phone office (tel./fax 44 38 45; open Sat.-Thurs. 8am-2pm and 8-10pm.)

**Airport:** 15km south of town, about 1.5km inland (tel. 44 28 31 or 37 94). Taxis are E£5-10. Served by **EgyptAir** (tel. 44 35 92 or 93), on the coastal road 9km south of Saqala, accessible by minibus. Daily to Cairo (E£329 one way).

**Buses:** En-Nasr Rd., 300m from the southern end of town. Book seats at least 1 day in advance. Standing room may be available at the last minute. Buses to Cairo (9 per day, 6hr., E£10-40), Suez (13 per day, 5hr., E£14-16); Alexandria (7pm, 10hr., E£37); and through Qena (E£6) to Luxor (noon, 11pm, 4hr., E£9). **Minibuses** run between town and harbor (E£1) and up and down En-Nasr (50pt). Catch them behind the post office and on the adjacent street or along their route.

**Service Taxis:** Off En-Nasr Rd., 800m north of bus station. Go left across from Omar el-Khayyam restaurant just before the bend in the road. To Qena (2hr., E£8). From there trains, buses, and trucks connect to points north and south. To Suez (4hr., E£15). Groups may try to arrange "special" *service* for the 550km ride to Cairo (5hr., E£25).

**Ferries:** Leave for Sharm esh-Sheikh. Reserve at least 1 day in advance. E£100, regardless of whether you book with **Sea Cruisers** (tel. 44 62 82), your hotel manager, or the harbor itself. There is only one ship, the *Capt. Al Masri,* and the trip should take 6-7hrs., though breakdowns are not uncommon (Sun., Tues., Thurs. 9:30am). Keep warm clothes accessible and Dramamine if you need it. Soda, tea, and cheese sandwiches sold on board, E£1 each. An elusive **hydrofoil** is supposed to make the trip (1½hr.), but rarely does.

**Bike Rental:** Between En-Nasr and the beach they go for E£10-15 per day. Shops in the harbor charge E£20 per day.

**English Books:** There is a small bookshop on En-Nasr Rd. across from the post office, and **Aboudi Books,** across from Peanuts Bar, has a large selection. Books and newspapers available in most five-star resorts and hotels. Open daily 10am-midnight, Visa and MC accepted. 15% discount with GO25 card.

**Laundry:** Most hotels will send your clothes out for about E£1-3 per piece. Quality varies. **Stop Shop** (tel. 44 75 28) at the southern edge of town. Outrageous prices (E£1-8, most pieces E£5-6), but does a good job. Open daily 7am-11pm.

**Pharmacy:** Dr. Montaser Rand on Abd el-Aziz Mustafa behind Sherry Hand Restaurant (tel. 54 48 90). Open daily 9am-1am.

**Hospital: Es-Safa Hospital** (tel. 54 69 65), on En-Nasr Rd. just south of bus station. **Public hospital** on Abd el-Aziz Moustafa St. near the aquarium.

**Police:** En-Nasr Rd. (tel. 122), at a bend in the road 900m north of the bus station.

**Post Office:** En-Nasr Rd., 300m north of the bus station on the right. **Poste Restante, EMS,** and orange international phones. Open Sat.-Thurs. 8am-2pm.

**Telephone code:** 065.

## ACCOMMODATIONS

Hurghada is a piaster-pincher's paradise. You may have to fight off hotel-hawkers insisting you come with them, but budget accommodations are plentiful and inviting. As always, see a room and fix a price before resting bags and body. Most convenient are the hotels on **Sheikh Sebak St.,** near both the beach and the *souq.* **Abd el-Aziz Mustafa St.** hosts a slew of hotels starting at the Shakespeare and ending at the California; these are often more visually appealing than those near the *souq.* Hurghada is still recovering from a few terrorist scares a couple of years ago, so you may find you have an entire hotel to yourself. Many of the cheaper hotels work with diving centers and get hefty commissions for the customers they bring. This can mean that you'll be strongly "encouraged" to dive or snorkel or it can mean that you cannot stay in the hotel *unless* you book a trip with them. If you plan to dive or snorkel, check the prices of the hotel before taking a room. You're better off booking through the same place in which you're staying. The **Sea Oasis** right by the public beach has large, cheap, and clean rooms, but will kick you out unless you are patronizing their pricey diving/snorkeling outfit. Their prices, especially for snorkeling, are swollen. Bargain for all hotels, especially if you plan to stay more than a few nights. All hotel rooms listed below have ceiling fans, unless otherwise noted.

### Closest to the beach

**Oscar Hotel** (tel. 44 84 13). Enormous, airy rooms with new furniture and futon beds. Doubles E£15, triples E£24. Generous breakfast included. If you take their 5-day diving course you can stay for free.

**Sea Waves,** across and up a hill from the public beach, behind Sea Oasis. Brand new hotel with large, spotless rooms and bathrooms. Likely to push diving and snorkeling on customers, but you should be allowed to stay even if you decide to stay dry. Singles E£10. Doubles E£20. Triples E£24. Quads E£28. Breakfast E£2.50. They work with the Sea Oasis Dive Center.

**Luxor Palace** (tel. 54 92 60), just before the California. Clean but plain. Doubles (shared baths) E£15. Breakfast included. Kitchen and washing machine available.

**Alaska Hotel,** in the block of hotels between Shakespeare and Hotel California, about 500m from the circle where Abd el-Aziz Mustafa St. turns seaward. Clean rooms, sparkling baths. Doubles E£15, plus 15% tax and service. Breakfast E£2.

**Hotel California,** where Abd el-Aziz Mustafa St. meets the sea. Fairly clean, close to the beach. Singles E£10. Doubles E£20, with bath E£25. "Preference" given to those booking snorkeling/diving at the Sea Ray Dive Center. Breakfast included.

### Downtown

**Sunshine House** (tel./fax 54 51 13), almost directly across from the bus station. Large dorms (3 beds per room) with ceiling fans and clean separate-sex bathrooms in the hall. The dining room becomes a hangout in the late afternoon. E£5 per person. Doubles E£15. E£2.50 for breakfast. Friendly and knowledgeable Hassan can arrange snorkeling trips (E£40, 10% student discount) and night parties on Geftun Island. By 1997, Hassan plans to have a new rooftop terrace.

**Happy House Hotel** (tel. 44 75 07), on Mosque St. behind the post office. Different from the Happy *Home* Hotel. Great location near both the downtown area and the beach. Helpful Ahmed welcomes guests into his "House" and organizes fishing trips (E£35). Clean doubles and triples E£5 per person. Breakfast E£1.50. Free use of fridge and kitchen.

**Shakespeare Hotel** (tel. 44 62 56), at the circle where Abd el-Aziz Mustafa St. turns to the beach. Family atmosphere. Comfortable lounges and fridges on every floor. Towels provided. Clean, inviting rooms, small garden, and roof restaurant. Doubles E£22.50, with bath E£28. Triples E£28, with bath E£34. Breakfast E£5.

**Gobal Hotel** (tel. 44 66 47), on the corner of Abd el-Aziz Mustafa and Sheikh Sebak St. Clean but stuffy rooms with portable fans and bidets. Classy rooftop cafeteria. Free use of beach and pool at Sand Beach. Singles E£15, doubles E£25, triples E£35. Breakfast included. Hallways look well-used.

**St. George's** (tel. 44 82 46), off En-Nasr, behind Banque Misr. Well-lit lobby with wood paneling. Comfortable, charming rooms. Doubles E£25. Triples E£35. E£5 extra for private bath. E£2.50 for breakfast.

**Camping** in Hurghada and on the Red Sea coast is more trouble than it's worth. It's heavily frowned upon (most people don't even know it's legal) and you'll have to hike north or south of the town or port to find a spot. You must first acquire a **permission request form** from the small security office behind the large mosque at the northern end of En-Nasr Rd. Then offer your passport, the form, a lock of hair, and E£1.30 in stamps at another office on En-Nasr Rd., across the street from the large mosque (offices open daily 8am-noon and 8-9pm). If you don't get permission, you'll face the wrath of an unforgiving military officer. In either case, campers brave theft and sometimes assault.

## FOOD

Hurghada's menus offer more than their counterparts in the Nile Valley, for slightly higher prices. You can feast on shrimp, calamari, fish, or lobster, or seek the *kushari* and falafel stands that ring the **bus station.** Traditional, inexpensive meals (E£4- 6) are served in the *souq* area between En-Nasr Rd. and Abd el-Aziz Mustafa St. There are juice stands around every corner serving up fresh-squeezed love for E£2 a mug and fruit salad for E£3 a mug. You can get cheap fillers at **Felfela's,** the ubiquitous Egyptian chain, near the port, or take-away fish sandwiches (E£2-2.50) at **Del Mare** on En-Nasr Rd. **Omar Khayyam,** on En-Nasr, has take-out **alcohol.**

In **Saqala,** *fuul* stands line the main square. Here the local flavor is much stronger than downtown, and eating is slightly cheaper. The **Omda Café** serves the usual cheapie meals (*fuul, kushari, ta'miyya*), and follows it up with a *sheesha.* Just north of the Federal Express office are two *fatir* (Egyptian pizza/pastry) places.

**Bella Riviera,** on Abd el-Aziz Mustafa St., south of the Shakespeare Hotel. Good pigging for the pound. Amuse yourself by watching the waiters scamper in and out of the secret door in the wall. Some Egyptian dishes aren't on the menu. Provides cheap drinks, lasagna (E£3), salads (E£1.25-2.50), and pizzas (E£5-8). A/C.

**Norhan Restaurant,** between Shakespeare and Alaska hotels. It doesn't look like much from the outside, but Norhan's grows its own fresh basil in flowerpots beside the tables and the pungent *spaghetti basilicum* (E£4.75) is delicious. Close your eyes, cover your ears, and taste—you could be in Italy (well, almost). Zesty *tzatziki* (E£2.75). Main dishes E£10-15. Pizza starting at E£4.

**Nefertiti Restaurant,** near the corner of Sheikh Sebak St. and Abd el-Aziz Mustafa St. (around the corner from the Gobal Hotel). Serves delicious, creative, and reasonably priced meals (try the chicken *kabab* with fried onions, tomatoes, and peppers), and prides itself on its selection of American music. Entrees E£5-10.

**Red Sea Restaurant,** just off En-Nasr Rd. and the main *midan* downtown. One of Hurghada's upper-echelon restaurants. Great open-air roof garden and Hurghada's best seafood and pizza. Entrees E£15-35. *Sheesha* E£4.

**Kanti's Indian Restaurant,** next to Three Corners Hotel, serves a few tasty curries (E£12.50) and sandwiches (E£3.50-4.50). Wonderfully thick milkshakes (try the coffee) E£2.25. Say no to the *pakoras.* A/C and MTV inside.

**Young Kang,** by the Gobal Hotel. U.S. Navy hangout. Huge menu, generous portions (noodles E£8-15.50, chicken E£11.50-15.50, seafood E£17.50-20). Visa, MC.

**Zeko's,** across from Happy House Hotel, a full meal (¼-chicken, macaroni in *béchamel* sauce, green salad, *tahina* salad, and bread) is E£4. Top-notch falafel sandwiches 25pt. Popular with locals.

**Geisum,** on the beach 300m south of Hotel California. Fancy-schmantzy but surprisingly affordable. Grilled fish E£10.

## SIGHTS AND ENTERTAINMENT

Hurghada's attractions are silent and submerged. Red Sea creatures flabbergast with their array of colors, shapes, and sizes. Buck-toothed trigger fish, iridescent parrot fish, rays with blue polka dots, sea cucumbers, giant clams, and a million others star in this briny show. The shimmering, variegated blues of Hurghada's waters have been spared the terrors of oil exploration (for the moment anyway), and the shifting colors will woo even the sternest terranean (see Sinai: Underwater Adventures, p. 247, for important information on snorkeling and scuba diving).

There are a few reefs you can reach without a boat, including one near the Sheraton, but to reach Hurghada's most brilliant scenery you must take a barge. Hotels offer an all-day trip to **Geftun Island,** usually including two one-hour snorkeling stops near the island and a fish meal prepared on board. Most hotels advertise the trip at E£40, though some charge E£30-35; you may be able to bargain as low as E£25. Some Geftun-bound boats are as crammed as cattle cars and stop only once for snorkeling. In addition, the reefs have been damaged by heavy tourist traffic. Snorkeling from a dive-boat might give you access to better underwater sights but is a little more expensive. The best (and least crowded) reefs are north of Hurghada. Unlike in the south, the northern waters aren't shielded by islands, so you'll have to wait for calm days to go there.

To save money, try getting a group together and making independent arrangements with a boat owner, perhaps a fisherman in Saqala, or with one of the sea-trip offices around town. You could go to Geftun and see different reefs, or organize an overnight (E£60 to E£90 per person, includes meals). Excursions to other locales can be less crowded and cheaper. For information, talk to Adel Shazly of **Nefertiti Sea**

**Trips,** near Nefertiti Restaurant, Muhammad Emad and Hassan of **Sunshine Sea Trips,** next to the Sunshine House, Muhammad Awad of **Red Sea Wonderland,** next to Happy House Hotel, Sally of **Sea Oasis Dive Center,** by the public beach, and Hosni Bakeet of **Hurghada Sea Trips,** at Three Corners Hotel. Independents can rent their own **equipment** (E£5-10 per day for mask, snorkel, and fins) at any office in town. GO25 cards might give you discounts; flash them everywhere.

**Scuba divers** should not expect bargains in Hurghada: prices correspond with the pocket depth of German vacationers, not the cost of *kushari*. Some less-desirable centers have unofficial instructors teaching courses and provide only a photo ID; for your own **safety** check for certification before committing. The running rate around town for one day (2 dives and lunch) is US$40-45. Beginners should expect to pay US$45-60 for an introductory lecture and two dives. The above-listed centers offer PADI open-water dive courses for about US$230.

The **beaches** lack high surf and are often mobbed and noisy, but compensate with gorgeous warm water. Public beaches next to the Geisum Hotel and the port in Saqala are the smelliest and most packed. Women will undoubtedly feel uncomfortable here if they choose to bare anything more than toes. Head to the hotels for more liberal bathing fashions; all of their beaches are nearly identical. Just north of the public beach downtown, the **Shedwan, Three Corners,** and **Sand Beach Hotel** all open their beaches to non-guests for E£15. (Shedwan and Sand Beach also have pools.) **Geisum** charges E£10. A skilled charmer may be able to bypass the fee. Another option is **Shellghada Beach** just before the Sheraton, where E£10 buys a day on their soft, clean sand, and use of showers. The **Sheraton** is considered one of the nicer beaches, but the harbor and boats encroach on the swimming area. Five-star resorts charge E£30 for use of their beaches and pools. A sandbar and bay make **Magawish** the nicest beach, but you can *buy* a beach for less (E£60). These beaches can be reached by minibus (E£1 from Saqala) or taxi (E£5-10).

Nightlife in Hurghada is mostly controlled by the big hotels, and is more active than any Nile Valley town. All the major resorts have pubs or bars and some have nightclubs. Rack up a game of **pool** or jive to "world famous" Daoud and his soft-rock cover band at **The Pub,** the Sonesta's hopping joint. For more ethnic flavor, the Sand Beach Hotel sponsors **"oriental evenings"** including dinner, and nights of **Russian dancing** (when three Slavic women change costumes faster than you can blink). The best party in town is on Tuesday nights, when people hang out at **Peanut's Bar** (grilled sandwiches E£7, beer E£7—try to ignore the Jim Crowish caricatures staring at you from various corners of the bar) until 11pm or midnight and then head to the **Cha Cha,** in the Shedwan. Belly-dancing starts at 11:30pm daily except Tuesdays, when the Belgian proprietor pipes in the latest music from Europe. Be forewarned: the E£30 minimum charge doesn't even cover the price of two drinks. The small **Arabia Disco** in the Sand Beach Hotel plays more Arabic music. **Scruples** pub and steak house, on En-Nasr Rd. near the center of town, buzzes and pops with neon lights, beer, and Germans. If you've got the money, visit the new **bowling** center across the street from the Sinbad Resort, just north of the Sonesta (E£25 per game). The Bedouin tent next door to the Sinbad has Egyptian music and belly dancers spanning the good, the bad, and the ugly.

# Sinai ‎سيناء

The desiccated Sinai is the collision point of two continents—an enormous tectonic summit where the only consistent agreement between the two land masses is to continue applying pressure to the steep peaks soaring above the Gulf of Aqaba coast. The sandy shelf where mountains meet sea is broad enough to accommodate a highway and a handful of small towns. The rest of the peninsula is an arena for survival of the fittest, and only the Bedouin succeed. The greatest profusion of life is in the warm

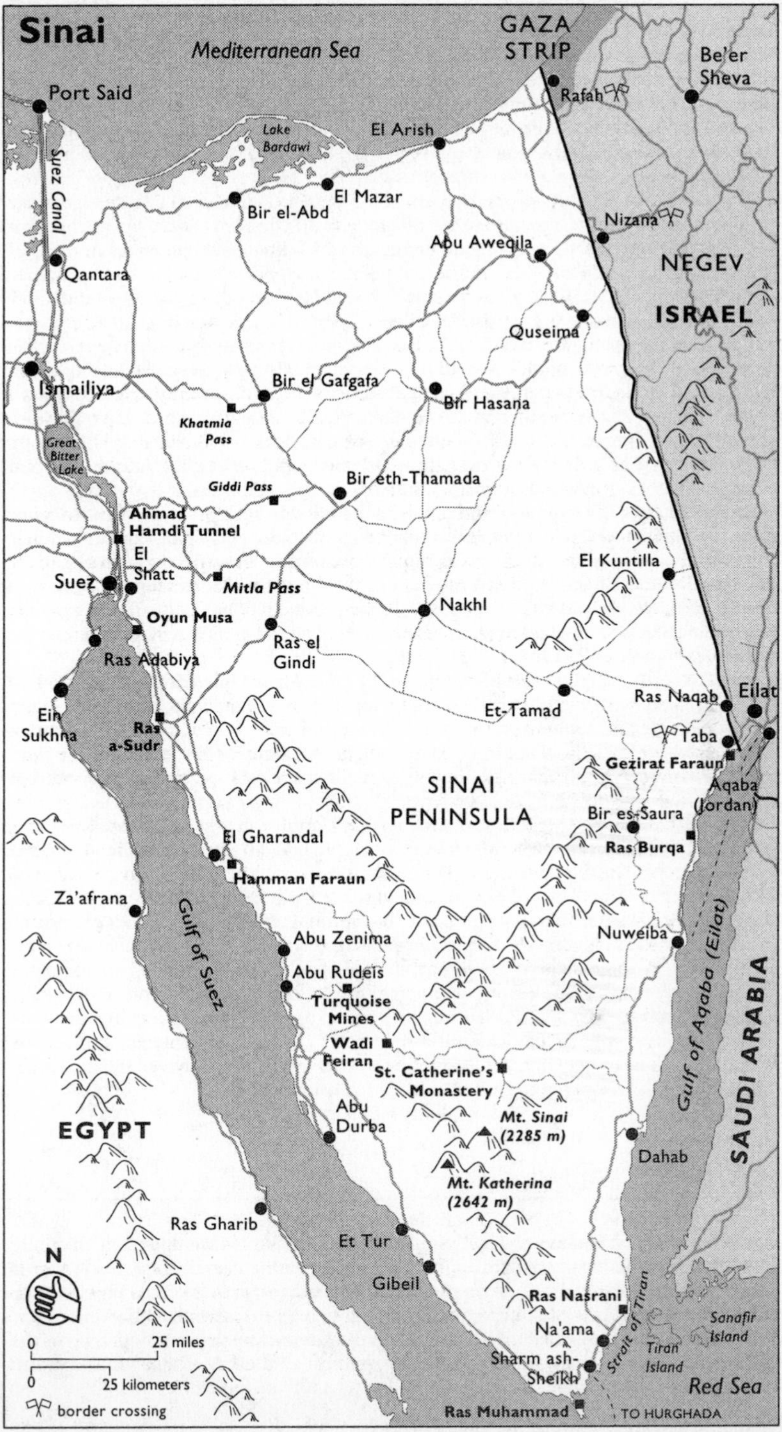
Sinai
Mediterranean Sea
GAZA STRIP
Be'er Sheva
Rafah
Port Said
Lake Bardawi
El Arish
Suez Canal
El Mazar
Bir el-Abd
Nizana
Abu Aweqila
NEGEV
Qantara
ISRAEL
Quseima
Ismailiya
Bir el Gafgafa
Bir Hasana
Khatmia Pass
Great Bitter Lake
Bir eth-Thamada
Giddi Pass
Ahmad Hamdi Tunnel
El Shatt
El Kuntilla
Suez
Mitla Pass
Nakhl
Oyun Musa
Ras el Gindi
Ras Adabiya
Ras Naqab
Eilat
Ein Sukhna
Ras a-Sudr
Et-Tamad
Taba
Gezirat Faraun
SINAI PENINSULA
Aqaba (Jordan)
Bir es-Saura
El Gharandal
Ras Burqa
Hamman Faraun
Za'afrana
Gulf of Suez
Nuweiba
Abu Zenima
Abu Rudeis
Turquoise Mines
Gulf of Aqaba (Eilat)
SAUDI ARABIA
Wadi Feiran
St. Catherine's Monastery
Abu Durba
Mt. Sinai (2285 m)
EGYPT
Dahab
Mt. Katherina (2642 m)
Ras Gharib
Et Tur
N
Gibeil
Ras Nasrani
Sanafir Island
Strait of Tiran
Na'ama
Tiran Island
0
25 miles
0
25 kilometers
Sharm ash-Sheikh
Red Sea
border crossing
Ras Muhammad
TO HURGHADA

waters of the upper Gulf of Aqaba, where a carnival of brilliant coral and fish thrive just offshore.

The Sinai, a major historical crossroads linking Africa and Asia, has had a surprisingly long history of war for a peninsula of lifeless rocks. Pharaohs' troops trampled the broad plains of the northern Sinai on the march to Syria and Canaan, and marauding, Egypt-bound Hyksos, Assyrians, Persians, Greeks, Arabs, and Turks all trod the same ground.

In 1903, the British drew the borders of the Sinai from Rafah to Eilat in an attempt to keep Turkey and Germany a safe distance from the Suez Canal. After the 1948 Arab-Israeli War, this border became the armistice line between Israel and Egypt. Israel captured all of the Sinai in the 1956 Suez War, but returned it due to intense American and Soviet pressure as well as a United Nations promise to keep the Straits of Tiran (formerly under Egyptian blockade) open to Israeli shipping. In 1967, Israel recaptured the Sinai four days into the Six-Day War. This time Israel refused to unilaterally return the Sinai and held on to the territory, building a defensive line along the Suez Canal, paving roads, and settling civilians in several places along the Red Sea and Mediterranean coasts. Suddenly, the Sinai was easily accessible to tourists. The new development altered the lives of many Bedouin, who began to give camel tours and help out in hotels. For the first time they had large amounts of cash, and some began to abandon their traditional nomadic lifestyle.

In the 1973 War, Egyptian forces crossed the canal in a surprise offensive to recapture the Sinai. The Egyptian army rapidly broke through the Israeli Bar-Lev defense, but later Israeli counterattacks recaptured most of the peninsula. Israel retained the Sinai until the land was returned to Egypt in two stages under the terms of the 1979 Camp David accords: the first half in 1979, the second in 1982. U.N. troops stationed in the Sinai monitor the treaty, most visibly at the MFO base in Sharm esh-Sheikh. (See **War and Peace: 1970-1981,** p. 52.)

Persians and Assyrians left no mark on the Sinai—their sandy footprints are long gone. Newer invaders now arrive by bus from Cairo or Eilat, by boat from Aqaba, or by jet from Scandinavia; they are armed not with spears but with traveler's checks and disposable cameras. One has only to look at Hurghada or Eilat to know how rampant tourism can hurt the fragile Red Sea coast; already garbage is piling up and coral reefs are wearing down.

Travel in the Sinai is unquestionably easier than in the rest of Egypt. Women in most places can comfortably wear shorts and sleeveless shirts, and professional conartists are rare. Those who hate sticking out are in luck—you'll never be the only *khawaga* in a restaurant or on a Sinai bus. Although many Bedouin have given up their camels for Camaros, there are still places in the Sinai where travelers can experience the ancient nomadic lifestyle of these masters of the desert.

If you're planning on going beyond the Sinai into the rest of Egypt, you should consider ending rather than beginning your journey in this splendid region. The lethargy that will undoubtedly set in at Dahab or other camps will be more enjoyable if you feel you've earned it by exploring the overwhelming temples in Luxor or surviving the craziness of Cairo. This way, you won't have to acknowledge that you're giving up some of the world's most ancient sites for one more day of sea, relaxation, and perhaps Bedouin tobacco. Leave plenty of time—you won't want to be torn away from this desert paradise too soon.

## GETTING AROUND

The major destination in the Sinai is the Gulf of Aqaba Coast. Towns are located on the single coastal highway, so all you really need to know about getting around is which side of the road to wait on (mountain-side cars go south, beach-side cars go north). The noble machines of the **East Delta Bus Company,** battered cruelly by the rocks, ruts, and dust of Sinai roads, heroically tread the scorched highway. With towns few and far between, separated by mountain passes, it's no surprise that schedules reflect an administrator's fantasy, seldom realized. (A philosophical attitude can ease your bus-tration: the bus station has a beauty all its own.)

A reasonably priced and convenient alternative to buses is the **service taxi.** Weathered old Peugeot 504s piloted by Bedouin cabbies are ubiquitous; you'll see them everywhere, circling relentlessly in search of prey. You can hop in with some other passengers, or negotiate first with a driver and wait while he recruits more travelers to your destination. Women should not take taxis alone. *Service* are comparable in price (under ideal circumstances) to the bus, but only with a full load of seven. You'll get to where you're going a lot faster, but this speed has its perils. Traffic laws do not apply; the laws of physics, however mutilated, are the bottom line here. Prices will drop immediately before the arrival of a bus, then rise like a nuclear phoenix after the bus has departed.

This just in: **Hitchhiking** is not recommended, though some find it handy. Keep in mind that you're in the desert, it's dry, and you're a fragile mammal with serious water requirements. Women should *never* hitch alone; all should be wary.

## PRACTICAL INFORMATION

A number of **regulations** govern travelers to the Sinai. Unguided travel is restricted to main roads and settlements, but you can visit parts of the desert interior with a Bedouin guide. Sleeping on the beach is prohibited in some areas (notably Na'ama Bay), and the police often harass sleeping backpackers. Since these areas are not always marked, ask around before settling down for the night. Nude sunbathing is illegal, as is the oft-hawked hash. You cannot bring a rented car or any four-wheel drive vehicle into the Sinai from Israel. If you hold a standard, one-month Egyptian visa, you must **register your passport** with the police in any town within seven days of your arrival in Egypt. Don't wait until Sharm esh-Sheikh to do this, since the passport office there is a long hike south of town.

Virtually none of the police in the Sinai speak English; even with someone translating, confusion looms. If they're uncertain whether you've registered (and they may overlook the rather obvious triangular stamp on your passport), they may insist that you register in every town you visit. Any Arabic you know goes a long way.

**Prices** are higher in the Sinai than elsewhere in Egypt. If you're coming from the Nile Valley, change money before arriving in the Sinai. Foreign currency is accepted by some storekeepers, but don't depend on it. Food is cheapest at Dahab, and most expensive around Na'ama Bay. Beware the **bottled water black market**—before you pay for Baraka (small 75pt, large E£1.50), be sure that the plastic seal is intact.

Budget **accommodations** are basic, but cheap and abundant. Sheets are not usually provided. In winter, warm clothes and a sleeping bag are advisable. Toilet paper and tampons are now widely obtainable, but it can't hurt to bring your own supply.

**Weather** in the Sinai can be as extreme and erratic as a monkey in a lingerie boutique. Cold nights melt into broiling afternoons, snowy winters are forgotten during infernal summers. In summer, the mercury bubbles up to 50°C (122°F). Nights are cool in the mountains, but on the coast it's always hot. Drink about a bathtub of bottled water every day. Winter is dramatically different—St. Catherine's may see snow or ice. Spring and early summer is **bug season** in the Sinai. Dahab is periodically clouded by mosquitoes and flies with the munchies. Cairo, Eilat, and Aqaba stores sell insect repellent. Some travelers rig mosquito nets; others claim that sleeping by the beach keeps the buggers away. (For more anti-insect tips, see p. 20.) In summer no one wears or carries very much, and it only takes a few days before most travelers begin to reexamine conventions of hygiene and appearance. "Washing" begins to mean nothing more than the first two syllables of a great democracy's capital city.

The **telephone code** for all of the Sinai is 062.

## UNDERWATER ADVENTURES

Without question, the Red Sea has some of the greatest coral reefs and marine life in the world. All coral reefs from Dahab south to Ras Muhammad are under the jurisdiction of the Ras Muhammad National Park; regulations forbid removing or damaging

### Ten million ways to die. Choose one.

Hidden among the crevices in the reef are creatures capable of inflicting serious injury or death. If you see something that looks like an aquatic pin cushion, it's probably a **sea urchin** or **blowfish,** both of which should be touched only as sushi. Avoid the feathery **lionfish** as well—its harmless-looking spines can deliver a paralyzing sting. The well named **fire coral** can bloat a leg to mammoth proportions, leaving welts the size of croquet balls. The **stonefish** is camouflaged flawlessly to resemble a mossy lump of coral or rock—step on one, then puff up and die in a few of hours. Reach into a hole and a 2m-long **moray eel** will lock its jaws onto your hand. The list is long—before plunging in, ask at any diving shop for a look at one of the cards that pictorially identifies these nautical nasties.

When snorkeling, try to enter the water in a sandy area to avoid damaging underwater plants and animals. If you have no choice but to enter where sea creatures and coral may be dwelling, be sure to wear foot protection. **Sharks** are attracted by blood, so never enter the water with an open wound or if menstruating. Panicking and thrashing tends to excite sharks—if you see one, calmly climb out of the water and casually share the news. Most sharks, however, are not aggressive and wouldn't (even if they could) give you the time of day. Marine animals are just like the U.S. Army: the only reason they get aggressive is because *you* have done something threatening or irritating. If you see an animal getting defensive, simply back away slowly, keeping an eye on it at all times. Last but not least, underwater wonders may make you forget ongoing solar action: the scorching sun can paint your back red—wear protective sunscreen or clothing.

any material, living or dead, animal, plant, or shell, from the sea. The park is fighting a difficult battle with developers hungry to exploit the region for tourism.

You can do your part to preserve the reefs by observing a simple rule: look but don't touch. Ras Muhammad, like most James Bond movies, has underwater police who will chase you out of the water if they see you breaking this rule. Even accidentally bumping the coral can damage it, so try to be graceful underwater. For more information, see **Ras Muhammad National Park,** p. 256.

### Equipment and Courses

**Snorkeling gear** can be rented all over, but it's convenient to buy a set in Na'ama Bay and sell it when you leave. **Dive shops** are concentrated mainly in Dahab and Sharm esh-Sheikh. You must be certified to rent equipment; most five-day courses provide certification and cost around US$300. Dahab and Na'ama Bay have decompression chambers, but the newest one is in Sharm esh-Sheikh. If you're certified but rusty, you can take a check-out dive for US$35.

Beginning divers should be certain their instructor speaks their language flawlessly (little misunderstandings can have big significance underwater: "Tanks!" "You're welcome."). Also be sure the instructor is certified to teach your particular course, whether it's PADI, CMAS, or NAUII—ask to see his or her card. Some clubs are active in protecting the reefs, participating in annual clean-up dives, and making sure their operations have minimal impact on the marine ecosystems. The size of the club is also an important factor: larger centers often have more scheduled dives and more extensive facilities, but smaller ones will give you personal treatment and will usually run a course for just one or two people rather than wait for six to sign up Reputation, quality of equipment, and safety records are important. Ask lots of people, preferably divers.

## ■ Western Sinai

The Sinai Peninsula's west coast doesn't compare in beauty to the Aqaba Gulf side. The Gulf of Suez is a much shallower body of water with neither reefs nor rugged peaks hugging the beaches. It's therefore less of a tragedy that the Suez coast is dotted with oil rigs and flame-belching smokestacks. If you see this area out the window of the Cairo-Sharm esh-Sheikh bus, you've seen enough. Then again, if you don't like hanging out with truck loads of western tourists, then seek out your adventures on this side of the peninsula.

Moses buffs everywhere will be enthralled by **Uyoun Mussa,** 15km south of Suez. This is where Moses impressed the heck out of his people by dipping a tree in some bitter water. Presto—sweet as Kool-Aid! Today there are several circular wells, some of which you can swim in, but it's pretty boring unless you're a migratory bird or over 60 and have bad rheumatism. For the advanced seeker of obscure places, **Ras el-Gundi** is a spot 50km inland from Ras el-Sudr that features the ruins of Salah ad-Din's 800-year-old fortress known as **Qal'at el-Gundi,** "the Fortress of the Soldier." If you take the bus to Sudr, you'll have to hire a taxi for E£60-80, so as usual, get a group together. The ruins stand impressively on top of a small mountain (about a 1hr. climb). Bring gallons of water, a camera, and a solid pair of hiking shoes. Be careful, as the path drops off considerably on either side: one misstep and you'll wind up next to your sleeping taxi driver below. Farther south on the coast you can steep in the **Far'aun Hot Springs** just off the main highway 80km south of Suez, where you'll also find a nice beach. Buses come by here very infrequently; it's best to rent a car or hire a taxi from Suez (E£100) or St. Catherine's (E£60).

If you're looking for a logistical challenge, try to get to **Sarabit el-Khadim.** You'll have to rent or hire a four wheel-drive vehicle. If you can't, a taxi driver will demand a hefty pound to push his Peugeot over the washed out *wadi* roads, which turn off the highway about 100km south of Suez. Sarabit el-Khadim is the site of an ancient temple, extending over 200m of desert. During the 12th dynasty (c.1900 BCE), a small chapel was dedicated to the goddesses Hathor, "Mistress of Turquoise," and Sodpu. Later, in the 18th dynasty, the temple was elongated and expanded. Ramses VI (c.1100 BCE) was the last pharaoh to visit the temple. The stones of the ruins are decorated with religious spells you can recite and accounts of mining expeditions you can go on. All around the temple are ancient turquoise mines waiting to be explored. This adventure, should you choose to undertake it, takes about three days (two for traveling, at least one for exploring).

Still farther down the coast is **Hammam Far'aun,** which means "the bath of the pharaoh." This is the alleged spot where the pharaoh who gave chase to Moses and the Israelites departed with the Red Sea. Boiling hot sulfuric water trickles along an otherwise nice beach. If you take a bus from Suez to Hammam Far'aun, you'll be dropped off about 10km from the spot. Catching a ride is possible but shouldn't be depended upon. You might also run into difficulty finding a bus back. Hammam Far'aun is attractive but not spectacular and probably not worth the effort.

## ▓ Mount Sinai

*And Mount Sinai was wrapped in smoke, because the Lord descended
upon it in fire; and the smoke of it went up like the smoke of a kiln, and
the whole mountain quaked greatly.*

—Exodus 19:18

*By the Fig, and by the Olive!
By Mount Sinai, and this inviolate land!
We moulded man into a most noble image and in
the end We shall reduce him to the lowest of the low.*

—Qur'an (Surah 95)

The Holy Peak of Mt. Sinai (Gabal Mussa) stands 2285m above sea level. The Bible describes a fiery, thundery mountain that Moses ascended to receive the Ten Commandments while the Israelites built a golden calf at its base. Mt. Sinai is one of only two places in the Old Testament where God revealed himself to the people, making the desolate peak sacred for both Christians and Muslims (Jews have not universally identified the modern Mt. Sinai with the promontory made famous in the Bible). In the Book of Exodus, God warned the people, "Take heed that you do not go up into the mountain or touch the border of it; whoever touches the mountain shall be put to death" (Exodus 19:12). This prohibition has long been forgotten—busloads of tourists climb the peak each day. The thousands who flock to Mt. Sinai have also forgotten another golden rule: they have not done unto the mountain as they'd have it do unto them—a trail of trash leads to the top. The summit can be crowded, and the Turkish toilets make the aroma anything but spiritual. Still, sunset over the craggy peaks of the desert can be as divinely inspired as it must have been ages ago.

The climb to the top is challenging but certainly not grueling. You should leave all but the bare essentials behind. (The monks of St. Catherine's will allow you to leave your bags in a room for E£2 per piece, or you can leave your luggage with the tourist police at the bottom of the hill before the monastery for the same price.) The **Steps of Repentance,** the shorter of the two paths up (about 2hr.), is actually the more difficult route. It is said that the 3000 steps were built by a single monk in order to fulfill his pledge of penitence. The monk cut corners here and there (who could blame him?) and made many of the steps the height of two or three mortal ones. Just think of the climb as a Stairmaster set on random. The steps are treacherous by night; if you arrive after dark they will be difficult to follow even with a flashlight. Save them for the descent in the morning.

The other route, a **camel path** carved in the 19th century (about 2½hr. by toed foot, 1½hr. by cloven), begins directly behind the monastery. Camel rides up the mountain usually cost E£30 during peak hours, but if you can stand the sun and the heat, you can get a ride up in the middle of the day for the low low price of E£10. Unfortunately, the camels are not always available when you need them—you may arrive at the dispatch area and find only dung.

To find either path, walk up the hill to the monastery, bear left at the fork, and continue to the back of the monastery structure. The path continues for 100m or so, until you reach a graphic sign at a fork in the path indicating "camel" or "steps." One juncture that usually confuses hikers is the point at which the camel path intersects with the steps, soon after you pass through the camel trail's narrow, steeply walled stone corridor. Turn left to reach the summit. The camel path stops here. Riders will have to get off their high humps and huff up the rest of the way.

If you turn right at the juncture about two-thirds of the way up, you'll arrive at a 500-year-old cypress tree dominating the depressional plain known as **Elijah's Hollow.** Here the prophet Elijah is said to have heard the voice of God after fleeing the wrath of Jezebel (I Kings 19:8-18; see also **Muhraqa,** p. 366). Two small chapels now occupy the site, one dedicated to Elijah and the other to his successor Elisha. Moses supposedly hid in the cave below when he first came face to face with God: "while my glory passes by, I will put you in a cleft of the rock, and I will cover you with my hand until I have passed by" (Exodus 33:22). The chapel is almost always unattended and closed in the afternoons, but is usually open immediately after sunrise for one to two hours. You can still see the watering hole used by the prophet.

Most people choose to begin their climb (via the camel path) at around 2am. You can enjoy the cool night and catch the sunrise at the top. The modern invention of the flashlight takes on a mystical quality here. Pilgrims, tourist-trap vultures, and grungy travelers are briefly united as the separate beams of lights form a trail slowly zigzagging up the mountain. Unfortunately, the unity and charm is lost once the anonymous lights become dreaded crowds at the top.

Some people opt to hike when it's still light, watch the sunset, and sleep on the summit. Socialites can stake out a spot directly on the summit platform by the tea and refreshment stands; this becomes a zoo station in the early morning hours. You can find a secluded spot by carefully picking your way through boulders and human feces down the sloping shoulder to the west. Walk about 40m until you cross a ravine; the small summit ahead has several campsites protected by stone windbreaks. Don't try this at night—**cliffs** loom on every side. Sleeping in Elijah's Hollow or climbing at midday are good ways to beat the crowds. Mt. Sinai at night is a religious experience. The canopy of stars in the inky skies will make you a believer.

Overnighters should bring ample food and everyone should bring enough water for the ascent (2-3 bottles). The cheapest place to buy water is in the supermarkets in St. Catherine's town. The monastery rest house also sells snacks and water at reasonable prices. There are refreshment stands on the way up, but prices increase with altitude. If you plan to spend the night on the mountain, bring a **sleeping bag** and warm clothes. Even in the summer, it's often 8-10°C at night and the breeze makes it feel much colder. A stand at the summit sells candles (50pt apiece) and rents blankets (E£2.50 per night) for people who haven't followed the Boy Scout motto. There are also "toilets" at the summit (holes in the ground with little privacy and many flies). Hikers should bring a warm change of clothing—sweaty shirts quickly turns to frozen shirts. You don't need a guide.

# ■ Saint Catherine's

The region's rich history of monasticism started in the 2nd century CE when Christian hermits, attracted by the tradition designating the valley below as the site of the Burning Bush, migrated here in a quest for holiness and freedom from Roman persecution. Living in complete poverty and isolation (except on holy days, when they gathered at the Burning Bush), these hermits often fell victim to harsh weather and raiding nomads. In 330 CE they sought and received the patronage of St. Eleni, the mother of Emperor Constantine. Around 530 CE, Emperor Justinian ordered a splendid basilica within a walled fortress to be constructed on the top of Mt. Sinai. When Stephanos, Justinian's trusted architect, found the mountain's peak too narrow, he built the Church of the Transformation next to St. Eleni's chapel instead. The peeved emperor ordered Stephanos's execution, but the builder lived out his days in the safety of the monastery and achieved sainthood. His bones are in the ossuary. The monastery has thrived for the ensuing 1400 years, continually protected by the rulers of the day (including Muhammad and Napoleon). As a tribute to the monks' tradition of hospitality to Christians and Muslims alike, it has never been conquered.

Today pilgrims and curious tourists of all persuasions frequent St. Catherine's throughout the year. They are attracted to the Burning Bush and Mt. Sinai, as well as to the private library which cloisters the oldest (5th century) translation of the Gospels and a collection of over 3000 ancient manuscripts and 5000 books. The Monastery is closed on Fridays, Sundays, and frequent holidays.

## PRACTICAL INFORMATION AND FOOD

St. Catherine's monastery is hidden away, at an elevation of about 1600m, in the mountainous interior of the southern Sinai. Excellent roads run west to the Gulf of Suez and east to the Gulf of Aqaba, both about 100km away. St. Catherine's town (also referred to as the tourist village) lies about 5km east of the monastery.

If you're going straight to St. Catherine's, ask the driver to let you off on the road to the monastery. Otherwise you'll be deposited in the town, which boasts a few modern conveniences. The **bus station** is at the main square (it's not a "station" *per se*, but a point in space where the bus is assumed to stop). On one side of the square is an arcade with a **Bank Misr** which exchanges money or traveler's checks (open Sun.-Thurs. 8:30am-2pm and 6-9pm, Fri. 9am-noon and 6-9pm, Sat. 10am-1:30pm and 6-9pm), **gift shops, supermarkets,** and **restaurants** serving spaghetti or rice and chicken (E£5-8; open 6am-10pm). The restaurants are virtually identical, offering hearty food and laid-back service (you may have to fetch your food from the kitchen yourself). Some of them will even cook food you've purchased from a supermarket. On the other side are the **tourist police** and a **hospital** (tel. 47 03 68; 24hr.). Opposite the mosque is a traditional brick-oven **bakery** (5 fresh pitas E£1). Nearby are the **post office** (open 8am-2pm) and the 24-hr. **telecommunications office** with **telegraph** and **international phone** service. The **police station** is farther up the hill.

**Buses** leave daily for Cairo (1:30pm, 9hr., E£35), Suez (6am, 6hr., E£19), Sharm esh-Sheikh (1pm, 2hr., E£12) via Dahab (1hr., E£10), and Taba (3:30pm, 3hr., E£18) via Nuweiba' (2hr., E£10). **Taxis** occasionally fill up for runs to Dahab (E£15-20 per person, E£90 per car), Na'ama Bay (varies, but definitely more expensive than Dahab), and Cairo (E£40). Lone women should generally avoid them. Taxis hover around the central square during daylight hours; ask at the market if you don't see any. Intimidate the driver by growling or hissing while you bargain.

## ACCOMMODATIONS

The cheapest and most popular choice in the area is **camping** on Mt. Sinai's cool peak. The nearest budget alternative is the monastery's **youth hostel** (tel. 77 09 45) on the left-hand side of the monastery complex; reception is through the door marked "manager" across from the gift shop. The hostel offers clean but cramped rooms. (Gates close 10pm. 7-8 person dorm room bed E£35. Beds in 3-4 person rooms with private bath E£40. All meals included.)

A cheaper option at the bottom is the **Alfairoz Hotel** (tel. 77 02 21), behind the tourist village and to the left, where you can bring your own tent or sleeping bag and camp in the huge courtyard (E£3.50) or use one of the hotel's tents (E£6.50). If you want a roof over your head and don't mind spending the night nearly on top of other fragrant travelers, try the Alfairoz **hostel** rooms (mattress on a concrete slab E£15, 4-person room with single beds and private bath E£60). Five km east of the entrance road to the monastery is **Zeituna Camping** (stone hut E£10, tents E£5), a E£5 taxi ride for each group of three. Another option is the **Green Lodge Camp,** 10km east of the monastery (huts E£10, dorm rooms E£20). They'll drive you there for free from their office, next to the Milga post office.

## SIGHTS

**Saint Catherine's Monastery** is believed to be the oldest example of unrestored Byzantine architecture in the world. Once the hoppin' home of hundreds of monks, the monastery's population has dwindled to a handful. The remaining monks, members of one of the strictest orders, never eat meat or drink wine, and wake up at some ungodly hour each morning when the bell of the **Church of the Transfiguration** is rung 33 times. If you hear one of the monks chatting about the Sox with a perfect American accent, it's probably the new member of the order—an American from a Greek Orthodox monastery in Boston. He is the first monk of non-Greek origin ever to be admitted and will be happy to talk to an inquisitive visitor.

Both St. Eleni and Justinian dedicated their structures to the Virgin Mary, since Christian tradition asserts that the Burning Bush foreshadowed the Annunciation. The main church became known as the "Church of the Transfiguration," owing to its spectacular almond-shaped mosaic depiction of this event in Jesus' life. The complex was named St. Catherine's Monastery after the body of the martyred Alexandrian evangelist was miraculously found on top of Gabal Katerina, to the south. About to be tortured on a wheel of knives for converting members of the Roman emperor's family, Catherine was miraculously saved by a malfunction in the wheel. They slit her throat anyway. Her body showed up centuries later on top of the isolated mountain. In the 7th century, Muhammad dictated a long document granting protection to the monastery and exempting it from taxes; a copy of this document still hangs in the icon gallery, near a similar letter penned by Napoleon in 1798.

The monastery possesses many treasures, including over 2000 exquisite 5th-century icons. The icons with brushed gold halos have a near holographic effect—an artistic style unique to the Sinai. The monastery is currently working on copying their world-renowned collection of ancient, sacred manuscripts onto microfiche so they can be accessible to scholars everywhere. It's an expensive and time-consuming project, but they're receiving Princely support from Charles.

Unfortunately, only the central nave of the Church of the Transfiguration is open to the public. On tiptoe you can see mosaics of a barefoot Moses in the **Chapel of the**

### The Mystery of Manna

"The quails came up and covered the camp: and in the morning...when the dew that lay was gone up, behold upon the face of the wilderness there lay a small round thing, as small as the hoar frost on the ground. And when the children of Israel saw it, they said one to another, it is manna..." (Exodus 16:13-15).

The quails and manna mentioned in the Bible have mystified people for years. In *The Bible as History*, Werner Keller recounts the findings of botanists and environmentalists who discovered that Biblical quails are the same birds that Bedouin eat today. The birds migrate from Africa to Europe and often stop in the Sinai to gather energy for their next flight. Worn out from their journey, they can be caught by hand. The curious manna, a sweet seed-like food which gave the children of Israel vital fuel, is actually a secretion from an insect that invades the Tamarind trees. The Bedouin still collect manna today—a sweet, welcome addition to their diet.

**Burning Bush** behind the altar. Should you manage to visit the icons back there, you'll have to remove your shoes, as the roots of the sacred shrub extend under the floor. Such privileges are only accorded to true pilgrims, who are traditionally allowed to ask God for one favor. The monks themselves, with the help of the local Gabaliyya Bedouin (descended from Byzantine slaves), built a **mosque** within the fortress walls to convince advancing Ottoman armies that the complex was partly Muslim. The gruesome **ossuary,** a separate building outside the walls, houses ossume heaps belonging to former monks (bishops have special niches in the wall—the skeleton in black vestments is Stephanos). A **gift shop** sells books on the monastery's history for E£8 (modest dress required to tour the complex; free).

Entering the monastery may pose a challenge (open Mon.-Thurs. and Sat. 9am-noon; closed on all Orthodox holidays—in 1997: Jan. 6, 7, 14, 18, Feb. 15, March 10-12, April 7, 24, 26, 28, June 5, 16, July 12; Aug. 19, 28, Sept. 11, 27, Nov. 14, 18, 25, and Dec. 4, 8). People have been known to travel six hours from Cairo only to find that the monks have closed the doors early. A good plan is to spend the night on the mountaintop, watch the sunrise, then hike down at 7am and reach the monastery just as the doors are opened (by doing this you'll also avoid the crowds). To get to the monastery from the access road, continue straight past the tourist police for about five minutes until you get to a fork in the road, then bear right and go through the gate. The left side of the fork leads behind the monastery to the mountain trails—use it at night after the monastery gate has been closed.

## ■ Exploring the High Sinai

If the climb up Mt. Sinai is too tame, the path too littered with Baraka bottles, and the top too crowded and touristy—there is an escape. You are, after all, in the heart of a desert that extends for 60,000 sq. km and surrounded by a natural world vastly different from the tour bus pasture known as St. Catherine's. *Wadis,* shrouded in misty heat, lead in every direction, snaking their way through and around mountain ranges, lush oases, and Bedouin homesteads. Many of the more appealing sites, such as the oases, are as yet untouched by the wear and tear of tourism.

These hikes are not for the faint of heart, but you can tell your guide what pace you wish to go and he will accommodate you. You should also consider the weather. Spring and fall are nicest. In the blistering summer you may spend a lot of the day resting in the shade with the Bedouin until the sun calms down, and in winter you'll freeze. The nights are more constant: they're very cold year-round. You may be able to rent blankets from the Bedouin, but don't count on it; bring warm **sleeping bags.** The area has yet to be declared a National Park, but it should be treated as such anyway.

To venture into of any of the mountains besides Gabal Katerina (St. Catherine's mountain) and Gabal Mussa (Mt. Sinai), you must be accompanied by a Bedouin guide and you must have a regular **Egyptian tourist visa**—the Sinai only visa won't do. **Sheikh Mussa,** the hiking chief in the area, has a monopoly on all the mountains and every trip must be arranged through him. You are required by law to leave your passport with Mr. Mussa; he will notify the army of your whereabouts. To get to his office in St. Catherine's town (tel. 47 04 57 or 01 84), walk uphill from the town square, away from the mosque and toward the Bedouin huts on the town periphery. Go past a blue "City Council" sign and turn right on the second dirt road. This leads to Sheikh Mussa's base, where you may see a few camels parked outside.

The Sheikh will procure both a guide and a permit for you. The price is E£70 per day, regardless of the number of people. The ideal group is 3-5 people—larger ones are slow and unwieldy. Extra camels can be rented to haul your gear around (E£35 per day), and surplus gear can be stored in Sheikh Mussa's house. You'll leave for your hike within an hour of arriving at Sheikh Mussa's, making just one stop at the supermarket in town to buy food (E£25 per day). Buying food with your guide guarantees extra cheap prices. There's a wide range of desert landscapes to choose from: mountain springs, pools, secret gardens, or apricot and berry trees. You and your guide will camp with the Bedouin, so be prepared for long nights by the fire, smoking "Bedouin Tobacco," drinking tea, and learning a great deal about a highly neglected culture. If the little sparrow-like birds the Bedouin boys kill, clean, and eat over the fire don't seem appetizing, your guide will bake fresh bread for you.

Tell Sheikh Mussa what you want to see and at what pace you'd like to travel, and he'll come up with a tailor-made itinerary. The following are some possibilities.

**Gabal Banat:** A mountain north of the town of St. Catherine overlooking a vast desert landscape. 2 days.

**Gabal Bab:** From this peak you can see west all the way to the Gulf of Suez. 2 days.

**Gabal Katherina:** The highest mountain in Egypt (2642m). The path to the top is more difficult, secluded, and beautiful than Mt. Sinai's highway. A chapel replenishes you with shade at the summit. 6km south of Mt. Sinai. 11hr. roundtrip.

**Gabal Abbas Pasha:** A rock with a ruined palace and excellent views. 2 days.

**Gulat el-Agrod:** A deep, crystal clear mountain pool for swimming in the shade of overhanging trees. You can dive off of the surrounding rocks. 3 days.

**Wadi Talla:** There are two, a big one and a small one. Go to the big one for some swimming in spring-fed pools. 3 days.

**Wadi Nogra:** A rocky valley with a natural dam (Nogra Dam). The water trickles off moss-covered boulders to form a natural shower. By the time you get there you'll need it. 3 days.

**Sheikh Owat:** A picturesque oasis with a few tall palm trees, a deep well, and a lot of goats. 3 days.

**Farsh Romana:** A good campground equipped with showers! On the way to Gabal Banat. 2 days.

**Wadi Feiran:** An amazingly lush oasis 50km west of St. Catherine's Monastery; Islamic tradition holds that Hagar fled there when banished from Abraham and Sarah's camp. Today there is a nunnery in the center of the valley. The best way to get here is by taxi from St. Catherine's (E£70 roundtrip). Although buses to and from Cairo pass by, the schedules are unpredictable, and you might get stranded.

You'll feel like an ancient Israelite who has been wandering for 40 years as you climb mountains and see for miles, like a Bedouin as you descend into walled gardens and sleep outside stone huts, and like a pack animal as your bag turns your legs into noodles. Your trip will be a lot more enjoyable if you remember to bring a few **necessities:** a solid pair of hiking shoes or sneakers (no sandals), a warm sleeping bag, lip balm, sunscreen, bug spray, a flashlight, a good pair of socks, a basic first aid kit, toilet paper, matches, plastic bags (to take your trash out of the desert), a swimsuit, a hat, a cooking pot (if you already have one—Sheikh Mussa will provide plates, glasses, and utensils), water purification tablets (many tourists drink from the mountain springs every year with no problem, but considering the number of goats, camels, and donkeys in the area, you may wish to purify), and a few pounds for the Bedouin who will offer you their undying hospitality.

**Organized tours** can be arranged in Israel through **SPNI**. For more information, see **Useful Addresses,** p. 269. **Neot Ha-Kikar,** an Israeli travel outfit, specializes in Sinai tours (offices in Tel Aviv, Jerusalem, and Eilat; see those cities for specifics), with trips beginning in Eilat and Cairo (6-day high range circuit US$360). No matter where in Israel you book your tour, you'll eventually end up at Sheikh Mussa's office. You'll save a lot of money by starting there, too. If you're lucky, Bedouin working at the monastery hostel might take you on informal hikes for free.

## ■ Sharm esh-Sheikh شرم الشيخ

You won't come to Sharm esh-Sheikh for the sights, though with the dozens of wrecking balls, cranes, and half-built buildings, you'll have ample opportunity to see ruins. Sharm esh-Sheikh and Na'ama Bay are often called twin resorts, but they are far from identical. Na'ama got the good looks and good-looking travelers, Sharm got the big boats and big buildings. Many Italian and German vacationers fill the four- and five-star hotels, but most backpackers head elsewhere. There is no beach to speak of (the water drops steeply off the shore) and no nightlife. The tiny bay is crammed with private yachts whose owners are attracted by the calmness of the water (due to the naturally narrow opening of the bay). This means that the water doesn't circulate very much, leaving the surface slick with yacht oil, and making swimming a slimy experience.

**Practical Information** Sharm esh-Sheikh attracts many visitors due to its function as a **transportation hub.** The **ferry** to Hurghada leaves here three times weekly (Mon., Wed., and Sat. 11am; one-way E£100) from the far side of the bay. You probably won't need reservations, but to be on the safe side double check at the harbor the night before you leave. (For more information, see Hurghada's ferry listing, p. 241.) By **bus,** there are daily connections to Cairo (7, 8, and 10am, 1, 4:30, and 11:30pm; 7hr.; first and last buses E£35; all others E£30); Taba (9am, 3hr., E£15); St. Catherine's (7:30am, 2½hr., E£15); Dahab (7:30 and 9am, 3 and 5pm; 1½hr.; E£8); and Nuweiba' (9am and 5pm, 2hr., E£10).

On top of the hill, near the Hilton, there's a row of banks for **currency exchange** (all open 8:30am-2pm and 6-9pm). The **Banque de Cairo** allows money withdrawal with MC/Visa. The **National Bank of Egypt** next to Safetyland has an **ATM.** The **tourist police** (tel. 60 03 11; open 24hr.) and a **telephone office** (tel. 60 06 02 or 08 00; open 24hr.) are at the top of the hill. There are also several **pharmacies** open until 1am. For a **taxi,** call 60 03 57; for an **ambulance,** call 60 04 25. Contact the **police** at 60 04 15. The **post office** (tel. 60 05 18), with **poste restante** and **EMS,** is at the top of the hill (open 8am-2pm). There are two **dive clubs: Diving World** (tel. 60 01 67), across from the yacht jetty, and **Tentoria** (tel. 60 03 50), next to Safetyland. Sharm esh-Sheikh's **telephone code** is 062.

**Accommodations** If places in Na'ama Bay are full, it's possible to stay in Sharm. The cheapest place is the **Youth Hostel (HI)** (tel. 60 06 44), on the hill before the banks and the post office (from the bus station, follow the signs for the Cliff Top Hotel). Clean dorm beds cost E£15.50 (add E£1 for non-members; breakfast included). Another quasi-budget option is **Safetyland** (tel. 60 03 59; fax 60 03 73), located at the bottom of the hill, at the intersection of the road leading to Na'ama Bay and the road leading to the Sharm bus station. They have stuffy thatched bungalows with locking doors. Ask for a fan. (Singles E£43, doubles E£66, extra mattress on floor E£25, 3-person tents E£22 per person, open tent sites E£9 per person; breakfast included; reception open 24hr.) Lastly, you can settle down at the **El Kheima Hotel** (tel./fax 60 01 66) next to the Diving World Dive Club. (Bungalow singles E£45, doubles E£60. With portable fans. Breakfast included; be sure to tell them that you *only* want bed and breakfast, or they'll charge double and include dinner.)

## ■ Near Sharm esh-Sheikh: Ras Muhammad

Sticking out into the Red Sea at the tip of the Sinai peninsula, **Ras Muhammad National Park** is the most famous dive site in Egypt and arguably the most spectacular in the world. The tiny neck of land is bordered on the west by the Gulf of Suez and on the east by the Gulf of Aqaba (park open daily 8am-5pm, strict closing time; admission US$5 per person, US$5 per car).

Above sea level, the park is brown, rocky, and apparently lifeless, but below the surface, life flourishes in vivid splendor. Deep red and purple fans gently wave in the current, while brilliant yellow, turquoise and orange fish wander in the warm, clear water. The waters of Ras Muhammad contain over 1000 species of fish. Many species are unique to the Red Sea, and one species of shrimp is found only within the boundaries of the park. In the 1980s, it became clear that tourist and fishing traffic was destroying the underwater treasures of Ras Muhammad; the Egyptian government established this park in 1989. As the underwater habitat is very fragile, most of it is closed to the public. In a good year, coral may grow only 1cm. It is against Egyptian law to remove any material, living or dead, from the park. Picking up coral doesn't merely hurt the environment; it may hurt you—the creatures are surprisingly sharp (for other underwater warnings, see **10 Million,** p. 248). Diving, snorkeling, and swimming are only permitted in specified areas, mostly around the very tip of the peninsula.

The park is accessible by boat and taxi (E£100), although you'll have a lengthy surface swim to get to the wall reef. On rough days, snorkeling at Ras Muhammad can be difficult. The park is beyond the jurisdiction of a Sinai-only visa, so you need your **passport** and a full **Egyptian tourist visa** to go there. Dive shops run trips to the park, and you may not need a full visa if you stick to their boats. A good resource for Ras Muhammad activities is Michael Pearson, the park director (tel. 60 05 59).

## ■ Na'ama Bay

This hamlet of five-star resorts is the center of Egypt's anti-backpacker sentiment. If you look nice and clean (and act like you own the place) you can freely roam the waterfront shops and hotels. But as soon as you don your most recently purchased apparel from Dahab or strap on your backpack, you invite interrogations along the promenade and bar yourself from certain areas. The diving mecca of the world, this resort town revolves around underwater attractions and therefore caters its landbound parts to the fantastically wealthy clientele that such a sport lures. Most of the beach is owned by five-star hotels. As you stroll along the promenade, you'll cross from Hilton land to Marriott country. Nevertheless, undaunted by the inevitable discrimination they will experience, many budget travelers flock here each year. It's quite easy to get a **job** at a hotel or dive center. The pay is not very high, but it's enough for food and entertainment (if you work for a hotel, you usually get free accommodations; if you work at a dive club, you get free diving lessons or courses). Arabic is not necessary but French and Italian are helpful.

### PRACTICAL INFORMATION

Na'ama Bay is basically a long strip of hotels on the water side of the highway (the town's only street) with a second row of hotels being hastily constructed on the desert side of the road. The **bus stop** is officially in front of the Marina Sharm Hotel, but the bus will drop you off at any hotel along the road. To nearby Sharm esh-Sheikh, take the open-sided *tuf tuf* bus (50pt) or any taxi (E£1-2 for shared cabs).

The **tourist police** (tel. 60 05 54) are located past the Aquamarine. The **National Bank of Egypt** has branches in the Marina Sharm, Gazala, Mövenpick, and Hilton Hotels, and will exchange money (open 8:30am-2pm and 6-9pm). In the central shopping center there is an **ATM** outside the **Bank Misr.** Much of the town shuts down between 3-7pm. **Public showers** are available in the Aquamarine and Hilton hotels, and the **public beach** is just south of Gafy Land Hotel. The **post office** is in

Sharm esh-Sheikh, but most hotels will deliver mail for you. Call 60 04 25 for an **ambulance.**

## ACCOMMODATIONS AND FOOD

**Pigeonhouse,** at the northern end of the bay (tel. 60 09 96; fax 60 09 95), is the only relatively cheap place to roost in Na'ama itself. Thatched huts are equipped with fans (singles E£38, doubles E£48). Otherwise, your dive shop may be able to arrange cheap dormitory-style accommodations. **Camping** on the beach is outlawed, but there's lots of unclaimed sand to the north of town. **Ras Nasrani,** near the southern end of the airstrip, has pristine camping and prime diving. Another popular option is **Shark's Bay** (tel. 60 09 42; fax 60 09 44), a quiet development 4km north of town, right on the beach, with its own dive club, nightly bonfires, and Bedouin-style food (camping E£10, tents E£15, huts E£35). Taxis back to town, however, cost E£20.

Food in Na'ama Bay is of high quality, at least along the main hotel strip, so you can relax the dietary caution that applies to the rest of the Sinai and satiate that carnivorous urge. Of course, quality costs a pretty piaster here. Beware the price-less menu. **Tam Tam Oriental Corner,** on Ghazala Hotel beach (bordering Hilton Beach), is the cheapest place in town (open 9am-12:30pm), serving *kushari* (E£3.75), *fuul* (E£3), and falafel (E£3). **Viva Pizza,** opposite the Red Sea Diving College in Kanabesh beach serves a variety of tasty pizzas for E£12 (open noon-midnight; not to be confused with the pricey Viva Restaurant). There's a good **Chinese restaurant** in the mall at the south end of the beach, but it's expensive (entrees E£20-30; open 11am-midnight; Visa, MC).

## SIGHTS AND ENTERTAINMENT

Na'ama Bay itself has no spectacular reefs, but just outside the bay, to the north and south, lie veritable coral cities. Dive centers have maps of the reefscape; pick one up and put on your flippers. The closest sites are **Near Gardens** to the north and **Sodfa** to the south; both are moderate walks down the beach. Wild ones can venture farther along to **Tower, Turtle Bay, Paradise,** and **Fiasco.**

Those in the know swear that boat-based snorkeling is the best. For US$15-25 you can spend a day on a boat and dive in spectacular water. Arrange trips through the dive clubs. The legendary reefs of **Tiran Island** are distant and accessible by boat only. **Ras Nasrani** and **Ras Umm Sidd** are also good sites, and a little closer to town.

You can probably find two dozen **diving centers** in Na'ama Bay. A magazine called *The Sharmer,* available for free at most hotels and dive centers, publishes listings and phone numbers of most of them. Prices are fairly standard, with a five-day PADI course US$280-300, not including certification (US$30). Introductory dives are US$40-45, full gear rental US$20, and five-day diving packages around US$200. **Camel Dive Club** (tel. 60 07 00; fax 60 06 01), across from Cataract Resort, has a friendly staff, and has been around since 1986. Owner Hisham Gabor, one of the top divers in the world and the first to open a dive shop in South Sinai, has just established his dive school as the headquarters for SSI scuba schools in Egypt. The restaurant, rooms, and pool (with windows and video cameras so divers can see their mistakes) should be finished by January 1997. **Red Sea Diving College** (tel. 60 01 45; fax 60 01 44), next to Kanabesh Hotel, specializes in PADI instruction and has clean rooms available at the diving center for US$26 per diver, dorm beds for US$10 (breakfast included). **Red Sea Diving Club** (tel. 60 03 43; fax 60 03 42) has its own jetty and decompression chamber, and affiliates with **Aquamarine** (tel. 60 02 67; fax 60 01 76) for dorm lodging packages (about US$10 per night). **Oonas Dive Club** (tel. 60 05 81; fax 60 05 82), next to Wings 'n' Things, has party-style night dives, including dinner. You can arrange snorkeling trips through these centers as well. There are many other safe and reputable diving clubs, with new ones emerging all the time. All centers accept major credit cards, even when wet.

Water activities are not restricted to diving. **Sun-n-Fun** booths at the Hilton and Aquamarine beaches have **windsurfing** (E£40 per hr., lessons E£55 per hr.), **water-**

skiing (E£40 per hr.), **jet skiing** (1-person jet E£50 per 15min., 2-person E£70), and **catamarans** (E£120 per hr.). There are even **glass bottom boats** for passive water fans (every hr. 10am-4pm, E£25 per person, E£55 for the big *Discovery*).

Landlubbers should stay out of Na'ama, but if your seafaring friends have dragged you here, don't despair—you can play **minigolf** at the Hilton (E£10 per game), and **horseback and camel riding** (US$15 for 1hr., US$20 for 2hr.) are available at the Hilton reception. Or, you can bike away from the madness to **Nabq,** a gorgeous, untouristed wildlife reserve on the coast 20km north of Na'ama Bay (rent bikes along the beach for E£5-10 per hr.). The region of Nabq is over 500 sq. km, but the most notable site is a strip of coastline where the largest mangrove forest in the Sinai flourishes, attracting herons, ospreys, foxes, and hard-to-spot gazelles. The mangroves sprout in a few feet of warm clear water with a sandy bottom, making Nabq an ideal swim and relaxation spot. The problem of maintaining traditional Bedouin lifestyles in the modern world is being actively addressed in Nabq: a Bedouin "reservation" attempts to preserve the culture, and openly welcomes visitors.

More popular (and touristed) than Nabq is **Wadi Kid,** a deep, fertile canyon 40km north of Na'ama Bay, where you can hike among rock formations and fruit trees. The **Tourist Services Center** (tel. 60 02 08), at the Sanaqir Hotel (a travel agency with a fancy name), arranges trips and **sunset desert tours** by jeep (US$30) or camel (US$35), including a Bedouin dinner (full-day trips US$55). Alawy, a famous tour leader at the Pigeonhouse, arranges trips for similar prices (tel. 60 09 66).

Nightlife in Na'ama Bay follows a set pattern: in the late afternoon, divers come back from the sea, take a shower, change clothes, and lounge around the Pigeonhouse Hotel's bedouin-tent courtyard. Slowly, they cross the street and head to **Wings 'n' Things,** adjacent to the Oonas Dive Club—an American-style bar with bumper stickers, football pennants, and posters of Cindy Crawford and Elvis. Bring your dive card to get an excellent, cheap daily special. (Happy Hour and a Half 5:30-7pm; 2 large beers E£7, plenty of wings and burgers E£12.95.) Eventually, people walk along the paved beachfront promenade to the **Sanafir Hotel,** *the* night spot in Na'ama Bay; the *sheesha*-smoke-filled **disco** opens at 10pm (no cover). The Sanafir has a domed white entrance on the desert side of the road, at the northern end of the bay, across from the Kanabesh Hotel. The **Billiards Club** at Gafy Land (E£10 per hr.) and the **Cactus Disco** at the Mövenpick (opens nightly 10pm, E£15 cover) attract a wealthier, more reserved clientele.

# ■ Dahab دهب

Here the word "Jamaica" is uttered with the same reverence as "Mecca" in the rest of the Arab world. The collective inertia of dope-anaesthetized bohemians, young and old, tends to focus at select points around the world and has a way of sucking in the weary traveler. Those who plan on spending one day stay five, others find a week-long visit stretching into a month, or six. The simple daily routine involves combinations of smoking, eating, playing backgammon, and sleeping, with sporadic episodes of swimming, smoking, sleeping, camel-riding, or safari. The beauty of such a schedule is that it can be repeated endlessly with no complications—save, perhaps, the nagging awareness that one's pocketbook is being eroded at the rate of US$10 per day, not to mention one's brain cells. Sweet scents permeate everything, so if you find yourself fidgeting or worrying about worldly concerns, just sit back, relax, and breathe deeply. Here the only real worry is when you'll get the munchies, and what you'll eat to satisfy that hunger. Then there's the other school of thought, educated at less popular Sinai spots, which sees Dahab as a once-peaceful haven gone bad. When the smoke clears, what appears before your eyes is a dirty, overcrowded tourist trap where Bedouin girls hound you to buy bracelets, predatory camel owners pounce at every turn, and crowds of tie-dyed travelers become one inky blur. Most fall somewhere between these views: they scorn the inauthenticity of Dahab while settling in for a week of lethargy and hedonism.

## ORIENTATION AND PRACTICAL INFORMATION

Dahab city is of almost no significance to the budget traveler, who only glimpses it between climbing off the bus and getting into a taxi headed for the Bedouin Village—the "real" Dahab as far as tourists are concerned. Use the city for exchanging money at the **National Bank of Egypt** (open summer daily 8:30am-2pm and 6-9pm; winter 9am-1pm and 5-8pm). There is also a **post office** with **poste restante** (open Sat.-Thurs. 8am-3pm), **supermarket** (open daily 8am-10pm), **police station,** and **telephone office** where you can make calls within Egypt or through Cairo to an international operator (open 24hr.). In the Bedouin village there are a few supermarkets which have phones connecting to Cairo and a **Banque de Cairo** where you can draw money with a credit card. There is also a **clinic** at the village's southern end.

There are two **bus** stops in Dahab. The first is at the "Bus Stop Cafeteria" off the Pullman Hotel resort, where you will face crowds of anxious taxi drivers. A taxi to the village costs E£1 per person, E£3 if traveling alone, so go for the driver that's already attracted some customers. You don't need a specific destination in the village: nothing is more than a five-minute walk away from the taxi drop-off, and the driver will try to double the fare if he drives you an extra minute along the village's single dirt road.

The second bus stop is next to the East Delta Bus Company office in the town proper. Taxis from the village drop you off here. **Buses** go to Cairo (8am E£45, 11pm E£60, 7hr.); Suez (8am, E£21, 5hr.); Taba (10:30am, E£12, 3hr.); Nuweiba' (10:30am, 6:30pm, and sometimes 1am; 1½hr.; E£10); Sharm esh-Sheikh (8, 8:30, 10am, 5:30, and 9:30pm; E£8, 1hr.); and St. Catherine's (9:30am, E£10, 1hr.). There are usually *service* to Mt. Sinai at 11pm (E£15-20). The buses here, especially at night, are unreliable. Always double check times and expect to be stood up.

## ACCOMMODATIONS AND FOOD

There are over 50 **camps** in the Bedouin village, and the number grows by the week. Dahab camps are an unfortunate bastardization of the thatched beach hut; someone came up with the brilliant idea of casting the huts in concrete, and connecting them in rows wrapped around a central courtyard—creating what amounts to bare cells with minimal ventilation. To their credit, mattresses here run cheap (room with mattress E£4, raised concrete "bed" E£5-7, wooden bed E£10, room with private bath E£15-20). The huts mostly serve as a storage space for your stuff while you're lounging outside in one of the restaurants. The camps are many, and an untrained observer might say they all look the same; one can, however, detect subtle variations in color, smell, and taste that distinguish the atrocious from the truly sublime. **Santana Camp,** next to the bank at the north end, has clean, if stuffy rooms and warm owners. **Muhammad Ali Camp** is clean, cheap, and right in the middle of the action. **Four Seasons** has colorful frescoes, table tennis in the courtyard, and relatively clean rooms. For those looking to get away from the scene and willing to pay for it, the **Jasmine Pension and Restaurant** at the southern end offers quiet, clean, luxurious rooms (8 in total) and snorkeling right out the back door. Rabia, the owner/chef, will whip up delicious, gourmet meals to order (E£7-10) while you watch the day pass from the comfortable lounge (doubles E£30-50, all with bath, some with sea views and balcony).

The combination of intense heat during the day and non-existent ventilation at night has a funny effect: the rooms get hot. Travelers have been known to approach this problem in three ways: (1) take all their clothes off, throw the covers on the floor, and still sweat profusely in bed; (2) put all their clothes on and walk with the sheets into the shower, drench everything thoroughly, then go to sleep wet; or (3) take the room key and a sheet and go sleep in the "million-star hotel" outside, braving mosquitoes. Don't be too concerned about losing sleep at night—you'll make it up during the day.

Food, like sleep, is an important part of the ritual of Dahab living, and is actually intermingled with it: dishes take about one hour to prepare, so most travelers order, take a nap, and then eat. Bedouin village restaurants are notorious for serving up a little dysentery or food poisoning along with the meals, so be careful. Avoid those deadly little lettuce leaves. Standards are reputedly on the rise, however, and sickness is less common. Most of the restaurants face the sea, have cushions to lie on in place of chairs, and feature a standard menu of pizza, pasta, meat, and salads with few deviations and similar prices. Pancakes (E£4), served with bananas, apples, ice cream, or honey/chocolate are a Dahab specialty available in most restaurants. You can eat quite well in Dahab for E£10-15 per meal (complete with drinks and dessert). Ask other travelers where they've eaten—everybody has a favorite place. **The Fighting Kangaroo** has a 5-course dinner special with a lot of variety for E£8. **Al Capone's** attracts mobs and serves tasty lasagna for E£6. The **Crazy House** (look for the sign featuring the demented chef with a menu on his apron) is one of Dahab's only restaurants with tables and chairs, a liquor license, and good, clean food (a tad expensive: entrees E£15-20, 3 for the price of 2 beer special from 8-10pm). **Tota,** in the green and white beached ship, has excellent food (lasagna E£8, damn good chocolate cake E£4), very clean premises, and serves alcohol. **Pizzeria Trattoria** serves guess what, starting at E£8. **Green Valley** is known for big helpings and good food. There are numerous **"supermarkets"** that stock some staples. Children run through the village selling fresh pita that contains only a few stones and insects and is otherwise quite tasty. The sweet pita is good too, but too much is generally a ticket to diarrheadom.

## SIGHTS AND ENTERTAINMENT

The **Bedouin village** is no longer really that. It's so loaded with tourists that the Bedouin themselves have moved north to 'Aslah. These days, the bay is lined with restaurants, camps, and gift shops that peddle the famous "Dahab pants" (E£15) and the kind of colorful backpack (large E£10, small E£7) that is now commonly sighted in places like Nepal or Thailand. Meanwhile, camels and horses trot up and down the beach road carrying Dutch women or pink-hued Brits (per 30min.: camels E£5, horses E£10). Bedouin tent-like arrangements hug the beach; it's quite a sight at night when cheerfully illuminated by electric lights and floating water-bottle-borne candles (an innovative use for these pesky petroleum products which will someday bury the entire town). Dahab has a style different from any other Sinai town.

Dahab sports two well-known dive sites: **Canyon** and **Blue Hole.** The latter is an 80m deep hole about 15m out from the shore that swallows several divers each year. The dive involves a traverse through a passage at a depth of 60m; experienced divers say this is just plain nuts, and they're right. There's plenty of excellent diving that's less death-defying, and several dive clubs to help you get started. The Blue Hole is great for snorkeling. **Canyon Dive Club** (tel. 64 00 43; fax 640 30 15) is a few km north of the village near the dive site (taxi E£8-10). It's a beautiful spot and you have the option of staying in the nearby hotel. In the village are **Fantasea** (tel. 64 00 43), a two-story white house at the north end, **Nesima Diving Center** (tel. 64 03 20 or 03 21) at the south end, with nice facilities and rooms for divers, and **Inmo Diving Center,** the oldest established club in Dahab. **Sinai Dive Club** is at the Holiday Village Inn (often referred to as the Pullman). Prices are comparable to Na'ama Bay (5-day PADI certification course US$280-300, 2 guided dives with full gear US$50-55, introductory dive US$40-45, credit cards accepted). Fantasea has the lowest prices for individual dives. The **snorkeling** is excellent as well; enter the blue at either end of the bay where you see waves breaking on the reefs (just be sure to enter the water via one of the sandy areas, or you'll be stuck with coral needles in your feet). Trips to Blue Hole and Canyon are arranged every morning by most camps, and you can rent snorkel gear at camps or on the beach (E£5). Make sure the gear fits, the mask doesn't leak, and the snorkel works before paying. For double the price, it may be worth it to rent new gear. Paddleboats are available for rental near the northern part of the village (E£15 per hr.; use them to truck to some of the more secluded spots).

Other popular excursions are by jeep to the **Colored Canyon** (E£50 per person for a group of 6), by camel or truck to the brackish oasis of **Wadi Gnay** (E£25 per person), or a one-day camel trip to **Nabq** (E£35-50). Hammad the Lobster Man runs **Crazy Camel Camp** and takes people on night **lobster-hunting** trips that culminate in lobster feasts on the beach. If you want to go anywhere, ask at your camp. The Bedouin know these hills better than anyone, including those fancy Egyptian safari outfits. It's also a tight-knit community and they'll usually have no trouble finding out about others who want to go to your destination. Traditional Bedouin believe that in photographing someone, you take a part of their soul. The women are especially resistant to pictures. Ask before snapping a shot.

In order to get an alcohol license in the Sinai, an establishment must first possess a building license (obliging the owner to keep his building above certain standards) and pay a property tax. Thus, there are only five sources of booze in Dahab: the restaurant at the Nesima Dive Club, the bar at Green Valley Village, Tota, Crazy House in the Bedouin village, and the Black Prince Disco (see below). It's not surprising, then, that Dahab **entertainment** is characterized by an absence of alcohol and an abundance of cheap pot. Restaurants play a lot of Pink Floyd and reggae. The click of backgammon pieces is often the only noise emerging from slow-moving groups of loungers in tents. Note that despite the ubiquitousness of pot here, possession of drugs is illegal in Egypt, and Egyptian jails rate low on the Michelin system, and dealers may win an all-expenses-paid trip to the hereafter via firing squad. Still, travelers smoke openly in the restaurants before, during, and after meals—police who gather up a few tourists on periodic raids seem to have little effect on consumption.

The **Black Prince Disco** is an experience in itself, singlehandedly embodying the entire scope of Dahab nightlife. A free truck shuttle gets you from the town square (in front of the *faux* Hard Rock Café) to the disco 1km south (of course, it costs E£1 to get back to town). The disco opens nightly at midnight, but Dahabitants don't begin to trickle down until around 12:45am, ready to dance madly until dawn. With the crazy mix of Egyptians, Israelis, Ethiopians, and Europeans, anything could happen, and probably will (no cover charge; warm Stella E£6.50). Try a nice quiet game of pool at **Napoleon's** in the center of town instead (E£10 per game).

# ■ Nuweiba' نويبع

One of Sinai's natural oases, Nuweiba' lies at the mouth of an enormous *wadi*. For about 10 months of the year the *wadi* is filled with drifting sand, but in winter, a sudden, rampaging wall of water 3m high may charge down its banks to the sea. Nuweiba' resembles a younger version of Dahab: a town with no inherent appeal or style, fortunate enough to have a cheap, carefree Bedouin camp and a magnificent beach. Although large-scale resorts are under construction, there are still a couple affordable places to stay in the town itself.

## PRACTICAL INFORMATION

Nuweiba', named after the Bedouin tribe whose territory reaches to Taba, is divided into **Nuweiba' Port** and **Nuweiba' City,** 10km to the north. **Ferries** leave for Aqaba from the port (for more information, see **From and To Jordan,** p. 246). Supposedly, there exists a bus station in Nuweiba' City, but whoever put it there must have forgotten to tell the East Delta Bus Company because the bus only stops at the big parking lot in front of the Helnan Hotel. Daily **buses** to Cairo (10:30am, 9hr., E£40; 2:30pm, 5hr., E£50); Sharm esh-Sheikh (2hr., E£10) via Dahab (7am and 3:30pm, 1½hr., E£6); Taba (5:30am E£15, 11:30am E£6, 1hr.); and St. Catherine's (10:30am, 2hr., E£15) leave from this same parking lot. Next to the Helnan, there is a **National Bank** (open 8:30am-noon and 6-8pm) and **tourist police** (tel. 50 02 31). To get to **Tarabin,** either walk north along the beach (30min.), or take a taxi (E£8 per load).

Nuweiba' City has one road, and it's not even that big. Most stores are in one of two **commercial centers,** aptly named the new one and the old one. Both centers have supermarkets and food stores, but the old center keeps longer hours. A **newsstand** in the old center has English Egyptian newspapers, international telephone service, and bus schedule info. The old center also houses the **pharmacy** (open 8am-11pm). Farther north, past a communications antenna is a **telephone office** (open 24hr.), a **post**

---

### Betrayal of the Bedouin

The recent explosion of resorts and dive centers along the Red Sea has introduced a sticky issue: whose land is the Sinai? Political control of the desert peninsula has been juggled back and forth between Egypt and Israel, but the only group with a history of habitation in the Sinai identifies with neither. Generations of Bedouin have lived in the Sinai long before any hotels were built here. According to Egyptian law, developers need only pay money to the Egyptian government before beginning to build. In reality, companies must also cut a deal with the local Bedouin tribe. A hotel in bad standing with the Bedouin faces serious trouble. Although the hotels and tourist services provide jobs and increase the standard of living for many Bedouin, the development has irreversibly altered their nomadic lifestyle. Some Bedouin now live on government land reserves, reminiscent of the Native American reservations in the United States.

---

**office** with **EMS** (open 8am-2pm), the **hospital** (tel. 50 03 02; open 24hr.), and the **police station** (tel. 50 03 04; open 24hr.).

## ACCOMMODATIONS AND FOOD

Budget accommodations are available near the white sand beaches toward the southern end of town. Sleeping on the beach can be cheap, provided nobody steals your unguarded valuables. **El Waha Village** (tel. 50 04 20; fax 50 01 40), adjacent to the holiday village camp on the southern side, has solid new bungalows (singles E£25, doubles E£35, triples E£45; breakfast E£8.50), large tents with mattresses (E£8), and an immaculate beach (E£4 per person for sleeping bags). Just north of El Waha is **Morgana Beach and Cafe** where you can sleep on the beach for E£5.

**Dr. Shishkabab** and **Ali Baba,** in the old commercial center, offer sandwiches (E£3-4), meat entrees (E£8-10), and vegetarian dishes (E£6). In the garden of the center is the newly built **Shagrh Coffee Shop,** where you can drink your beverage next to a dried-out pond. All three restaurants have virtually the same, simple menu and similar prices (all open 7am-1am). If it's not summer, you might be able to catch a play or concert in the amphitheater next door.

## SIGHTS AND SAFARIS

Like all Sinai coast towns, Nuweiba' is surrounded by beautiful coral reefs, but unlike the reefs in Dahab, Na'ama Bay, or Sharm esh-Sheikh, these Nuweiba' spots are not teeming with schools of divers from a dozen dive clubs. There are only two dive clubs in town. **Diving Camp Nuweiba'** (tel. 50 04 03; fax 50 02 25), in the Helnan Hotel, combines a professional staff with a laid-back atmosphere and "lots of love" (5-day open water course including SSI certification US$300, 2-day diving safari US$130, introductory dive US$45, night dive US$25). The **Hilton Dive Club** (tel. 52 03 20; fax 52 03 27) opened in 1996 and has newer equipment and somewhat lower prices (5-day open water course including SSI certification US$280, introductory dive US$40, 2 dives US$65).

The attractions in Nuweiba' are not limited to the waters. The town is an excellent starting point for **camel or jeep safaris** to remarkable desert terrain. There are several safari "offices" in the area: **Explore Sinai** (tel. 50 01 41; tel./fax 50 01 40), in the new commercial center (open 9am-4pm and 7:30-11pm), **Sinai Adventures** (tel. 50 03 28), across the street from the tourist police (open 8am-11pm), and **Tarabin Survival Safari** (tel. 50 02 99) next to the Moonland camp in Tarabin (open 9am-11pm). All charge E£65 per person per day for camel safaris and E£50 per person per day for jeep safaris. Neg the seedy-looking offices and save E£10-15 per day by dealing directly with a guide. Look for one at Tarabin if none approach you. Bedouin guides here are generally trustworthy and safe.

Some of the more popular trips are as follows: the **Colored Canyon,** a *wadi* with cliffs of beautifully patterned sandstone, is the best-known destination, 30km from

## The dolphin and the deaf boy

The most popular sight in Nuweiba' is **dolphin beach.** The animals that give the beach its name saved a Bedouin boy and sustain his community. The boy, who was deaf and mute, befriended two dolphins and swam with them every day. One day, one of his companions was caught in a fishing net, mistaken for a shark, and killed. In horror, the boy and the remaining dolphin embraced. Afterwards, whenever the boy entered the water, the surviving dolphin would rush to his side. Tourists, lured by the chance to swim with wild dolphins, flocked to the beach. The money they brought in allowed the boy to go to Israel, where he is now receiving therapy, learning to speak, and studying dolphin behavior.

Nuweiba' (4-hr. jeep tour); **Ain Umm Ahmed** is a frequently-visited desert oasis which can be reached by jeep (2 days); **Ain Furtuga,** only 10km out of town (camel range!) is another popular oasis; **Ain Khoudra** and **Bayar al-Sabreyer** are both oases in the spectacular **Wadi Khoudra,** (1-day jeep trip) on the road to St. Catherine's (within 2-day camel range of Nuweiba').

Technically, you need permission just to step off the highway in the Sinai. Desert trips require a permit, achieved by some mysterious passport fermentation process at your friendly neighborhood police station. Your guide will take care of it for you (permit costs E£2 per person per day for camel safaris and E£10 per person per day for jeep tours, but these fees are normally included in the cost of the trip). The price always includes food, but often excludes water. The price of bottled water rises dramatically during the safari, so be sure to start off with a large supply.

### GOING TO JORDAN

To go to Aqaba from Nuweiba' you can take a ferry from the port. The regular ferry supposedly leaves daily at 10am and 4pm and theoretically takes 3½hr. One way passage on deck costs US$32. Show up an hour before scheduled departure to deal with customs, ticketing, Egyptian hassles, and quagmirean queues. Two-week or one-month Jordanian visas can be obtained on board (Australia free, Canada JD31, Ireland JD5, New Zealand JD4, S. Africa free, UK JD23, US JD15). There is also a speed boat which leaves daily from Nuweiba' at 2pm and costs US$42. The extra US$10 may be well worth it. The speed boat tends to leave closer to schedule and sometimes actually takes an hour as it is supposed to. It is also less crowded. There is no Egyptian departure tax. Nuweiba' buses will drop you off at the port. Taxis from Nuweiba' city or Tarabin to the port cost between E£10-15. Buses from Cairo to the ferry can be overcrowded with Egyptians bound for jobs in Jordan, Saudi Arabia, and the Gulf states.

# ■ Northern Aqaba Coast

The 70km stretch between Nuweiba' and Taba is undoubtedly the most magnificent part of the Sinai: the beaches are almost untouched by hotels, the mountains are free of litter, and the only sign of human beings is the gracefully winding highway making its way along the shore. Shutterbugs will kick themselves if they stow their cameras on the bus; this is one of the most beautiful coastlines in the world.

From Nuweiba', you can either walk or take a *service* north to the **camps** just off the highway. The bus heading south from Taba will stop anywhere; ask the driver rather than the ticket collector for your stop. Huts may not have electricity; a **flashlight** is useful. Most camps have restaurants; **food** is more expensive than in Nuweiba' but of higher quality. It's quiet out here—backgammon, stargazing, and hanky-panky are the main components of nightlife.

## TARABIN طربين

In Tarabin, unlike Dahab, there's actually a beach and most of the camps are right on it. The sand is clean and the water warm and clear. Dahab-bashing is popular since Tarabin is quieter and less-developed (but if you venture farther north, you'll find serenity-seekers disdaining Tarabin's overdevelopment). Pot is scarce and officials are determined to keep Tarabin drug-free, having arrived in Dahab too late.

There is little difference in the quality of the huts at most of the camps. Most charge E£5-10 and have their own Bedouin-style restaurant. Gabriel and Muhammad, who run the Carmina Camp at the southern end of town, will treat you like family and fill you with delicious food. You might have to reverse-haggle with them to ensure that they don't *under*charge you. The **Moon Land Camp**, run by Mossallam Farrag, offers guided **camel, jeep, and trekking tours.** For reasonably-priced **taxis** to Taba or points south and great company, ask at the taxi stand for Jackson.

## FARTHER NORTH

Still more cheapie camps lie 16km north of Nuweiba'. **Maagana Beach,** a Bedouin camp near colorful rock formations, has reefs and a restaurant nearby (huts E£7, but they'll reduce it to E£5 if you stay a week). **Devil's Head** (Ras Shaytan), is its mirror image 5km north on the other side of the rocky point (huts for one E£10, for two E£12). Nearby **Bawaki** is only for the wealthy, but does have a few non-A/C sheds for E£40, and you'll be able to use their pool. The brand new **Dolphin Camp** (tel. 77 19 32) has a disco, bar, and restaurant (huts E£13).

Farther north is a remote and beautiful spot called **The Fjord,** where a small inlet cuts into the steep hills. The **Salima Restaurant and Camp** (tel. 53 01 30 or 37) is right off the highway on a small ledge overlooking the sleepy bay. There are a few rooms crammed between the restaurant and the rock slope behind it (E£25 per person), or you can camp on the beach (E£6).

## Basata بساطة

"Basata" means "simplicity" in Arabic. Indeed, this super-environmentally-conscious place (about 23km north of Nuweiba', 43km south of Taba) outlaws loud music and television, has a trash-free beach, and is a world apart from other camps along the Red Sea coast. It is also three times more expensive. The camp is run by German-educated Sherif Ghamrawy (tel. 50 04 81).

Garbage is recycled when possible, and organic trash is either used as fertilizer or livestock feed. A vegetarian (E£14) or fish (E£20) meal is cooked every evening. Water is desalinated and electricity generated on site. The fully-stocked kitchen functions on trust: take what you want and write down what you took, but beware the prices. The atmosphere at Basata is family-oriented, with nightly communal dinners, a comfy common area with games and books, and rules, rules, rules: no public displays of affection, no drugs or alcohol, no sleeping in the common area, and no dirty dishes (camping E£12, bamboo hut singles E£20, doubles E£30).

Sherif organizes **camel and jeep tours.** (Camel tours E£70 per day. Jeep tours E£55-60.) **Snorkeling** equipment (E£20) is also available. Due to recent publicity, Basata has gotten quite popular.

## Pharaoh's Island جزيرة فرعون

**Pharaoh's Island** (Gazirat Faraun; Israelis call it Coral Island), 8km south of Taba, is a rocky outcrop just offshore which holds the extensively renovated ruins of a Crusader castle built around 1115. Salah ad-Din took the fortress in 1171 but abandoned it in 1183 after European counterattacks. The ruins have a few neat towers and passageways and a large water cistern. A boat ferries visitors to the island (E£14 or JD20 from Aqaba), where you must then buy another ticket to tour the castle (E£10, student E£5). Unless you're going to dive or snorkel, you're better off staying on shore (the view of Sinai from the castle is shamefully ruined by the 5-star Salah ad-Din Hotel, and the view of the castle is best from the mainland). Pharaoh's Island is a popular excursion from Eilat, Aqaba, and Taba. The complex coral reef formations off the northeastern tip of the island are great for diving, though snorkeling equipment rents for E£15. Bring your own food, as food on the island is overpriced and often unavailable.

## GOING TO ISRAEL

To go to Israel from Egypt you must cross from **Taba** to **Eilat.** You'll need a valid standard Israeli **visa** (unnecessary for U.S. citizens), available at the border in two flavors: two weeks or one month. (At all other border crossings into Israel you will obtain a 3-month visa. Many travelers stay in Israel for much longer than the 3-month limit by crossing to Aqaba or Cypress and coming back, automatically obtaining another free 3-month visa.) You will have to pay a E£2 exit tax if you have travelled beyond the Sinai. The uneventful walk through the stations shouldn't take more than an hour. You will automatically get an Israeli stamp in your passport unless you request to get it on a separate sheet. You can get rid of your extra Egyptian pounds at the Israeli snack bar. The border is open 24 hours.

See specific Sinai towns for information on transportation to Taba. Bus #15 runs every 15 minutes from the border checkpoint to Eilat daily until about 11pm (NIS3.20). Visitors in private cars must present a valid driving license and *carnet de passage;* rented cars are not allowed to cross in either direction.

EGYPT

# ISRAEL ישראל

US$1=3.13 shekels (NIS)
CDN$1=NIS2.27
UK£1=NIS5
IR£1=NIS5
AUS$1=NIS2.44
NZ$1=NIS2.17
SAR1=NIS0.70

NIS1=US$0.32
NIS1=CDN$0.44
NIS1=UK£0.20
NIS1=IR£0.20
NIS1=AUS$0.41
NIS1=NZ$0.46
NIS1=SAR1.43

> For important information on travel in Israel, see the Essentials section of this book. Israel's **international phone code** is 972.

At age 49, a fractious Israel (Yisrael) still doesn't know what it wants to be when it grows up. The Jewish state is variously "a light unto the nations," a pariah among some of its neighbors, and an increasingly Westernized country. Even its origins are controversial: from persecution culminating in the Holocaust, Jews came together, mingling diverse cultures and backgrounds to make a brand new kind of state and to remaking themselves in the process—sometimes at the expense of indigenous Palestinian Arabs. With the country's identity in constant flux, all Israelis have their own vision of what Israel should be. To give one eloquent example, Amos Oz, Israel's leading novelist, sees his fellow Israelis not as "the 'Maccabeans reborn' that Herzl talked of," but as "a warm-hearted, hot-tempered Mediterranean people that is gradually learning, through great suffering and in a tumult of sound and fury, to find release both from the bloodcurdling nightmares of the past and from delusions of grandeur, both ancient and modern." Of course, many Israelis see Oz as a stuck-up intellectual, and will tell you at length about how *they* see their country. As the saying goes, if you have two Israelis in a room, you have three opinions. But talk with Israelis about their bewildering country for long enough, and they will eventually smile or shrug and say, *"Yihiyeh tov"* (It'll be OK).

# ONCE THERE

## ■ Entry

Security upon arrival in Israel is fairly relaxed (less so for visitors of Arab origin), especially compared to the scrutiny your luggage will receive at Ben-Gurion Airport upon your departure. Normally you can take the "Green Channel" to exit the airport. Most items can be brought in duty-free as long as you intend to carry them out when you depart. Take the "Red Channel" if you need to declare articles. Duty must be paid on large quantities of perfume, alcohol, and cigarettes.

There is a **Government Tourist Information Office (GTIO)** in the arrival hall at Ben-Gurion (tel. (03) 971 14 85). **Egged buses** run regularly to major cities (#475 to Tel Aviv). **Sherut (shared) taxis** run regularly from the airport to Jerusalem (NIS30).

## ■ Getting Around

**Buses** Buses are the most popular and convenient means of travel. Except for the **Dan Company** (tel. (03) 639 44 44) in Tel Aviv and the **Arab buses** serving the West Bank, Galilee, and Gaza, the **Egged Bus Cooperative** (tel. (03) 537 55 55) has a monopoly on intercity and most intracity buses in Israel. The modern, air-conditioned buses are either direct *(yashar)*, express, or local *(me'asef)*. Students with ISIC

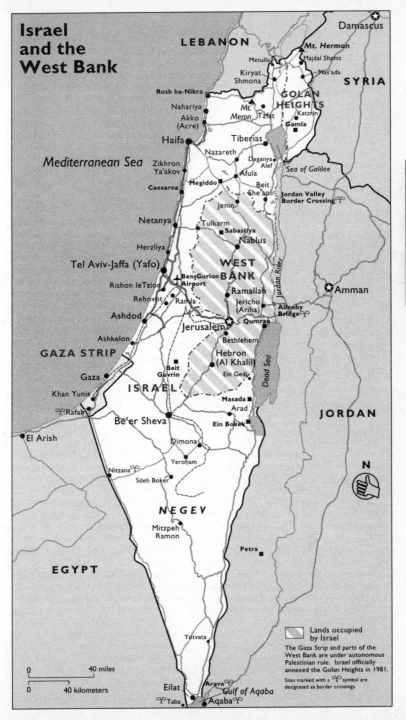

# Israel and the West Bank

LEBANON

Damascus

Mt. Hermon

Metulla

Majdal Shams

Kiryat Shmona

Mas'ada

SYRIA

Rosh ha-Nikra

GOLAN HEIGHTS

Nahariya

Akko (Acre)

Mt. Meron

Tzfat

Katzrin

Gamla

Haifa

Tiberias

Mediterranean Sea

Nazareth

Zikhron Ya'akov

Deganya Alef

Sea of Galilee

Caesarea

Megiddo

Afula

Beit She'an

Jordan Valley Border Crossing

Jenin

Netanya

Tulkarm

Sabastiya

Herzliya

Nablus

Tel Aviv-Jaffa (Yafo)

WEST BANK

Rishon leTzion

Ben Gurion Airport

Ramallah

Amman

Rehovot

Ramla

Jericho (Ariha)

Allenby Bridge

Ashdod

Jerusalem

Qumran

Ashkelon

Bethlehem

GAZA STRIP

Hebron (Al Khalil)

Ein Gedi

Dead Sea

Gaza

Beit Guvrin

ISRAEL

Khan Yunis

Masada

Rafah

Arad

JORDAN

El Arish

Be'er Sheva

Ein Bokek

Dimona

Yeroham

Nitzana

Sdeh Boker

N

EGYPT

NEGEV

Mitzpeh Ramon

Petra

Lands occupied by Israel

The Gaza Strip and parts of the West Bank are under autonomous Palestinian rule. Israel officially annexed the Golan Heights in 1981.

Sites marked with a symbol are designated as border crossings.

0    40 miles

0    40 kilometers

Yotvata

Eilat

Arava

Gulf of Aqaba

Taba

Aqaba

ISRAEL

receive a 10% discount on all fares; be sure to show your ID first to the ticket seller, then to the driver, then to the ticket inspector. Buses are sometimes crowded, especially on Saturday nights after *Shabbat* and during morning and afternoon rush hours. You can shove your way into and out of the bus, as long as you preface each push with the word *sliḥa*, as Israelis do.

Egged sells *ḥofshi ḥodshi* monthly **bus passes,** good for unlimited travel in a specified city during a calendar month (*not* any four weeks in a row); an NIS132 pass works for Egged buses in Jerusalem and Haifa. In Tel Aviv most buses are operated by Dan; they have their own Tel Aviv passes for NIS122. These are well worth the price if you will be staying in one area for a longish time. Egged also offers **Israbus,** an unlimited bus pass valid all over the country; buy it at any Egged Tours office (must be bought with shekels; 7 days NIS219, 14 days NIS349, 21 days NIS425, 30 days NIS480; call (177) 022 55 55 for the office nearest you). Otherwise, you can buy a *kartis* from any bus driver (NIS32); this gives you 11 rides for the price of ten. Most local routes cost NIS3.30.

Most bus stations have printed schedules, often in English. Egged has intercity **information lines** in the major cities (tel. (03) 537 55 55 in Tel Aviv, (04) 854 95 55 in Haifa, (02) 530 45 55 in Jerusalem). For information on local lines, call the local central bus station. Signs in stations direct you to buy your ticket at the ticket window. This is only really necessary for highly-traveled long-distance routes; otherwise, buy the ticket from the driver. Buses between cities usually leave from the central bus station *(taḥanat merkazit)*. If you buy roundtrip tickets rather than one-way, you will usually get a 10% discount.

**Taxis**  Israeli companies offer both private and less expensive **sherut** (shared) taxis. Regular private taxi rides are called special (pronounced "spatial"). City taxis operating as special must have meters *(moneh);* make the driver turn it on. Offers of special but unspecified "discount" rates (translation: no meter and an exorbitant fare) should be adamantly refused. If you know the route and can estimate a decent price, you can get a better rate by setting the price before you enter the taxi.

Sherut taxis hold up to seven people. Certain companies operate sherut taxis seven days a week from offices in each city. Intercity sherut operate on loose schedules, departing when they fill up; on Saturdays, they often whiz along the streets in search of passengers. Intracity sherut never follow a schedule and cruise the streets daily. Most routes have set fares comparable to bus prices; ask for quotes at tourist offices or from the nearest Israeli. Always settle on a price before you depart.

**Cars**  The leading cause of death in Israel is unrelated to the fact that every other person carries a gun. More Israelis die in **automobile accidents** than from any other cause. A popular bumper sticker during the Gulf War read, "I'm not a Scud and you're not a Patriot, so back off." Widespread public transportation makes cars generally unnecessary; but some places (especially the Golan) are most easily reached by a little coupe of your own. The legal driving age is 17, but most agencies will only rent to credit-card holders aged 21 years or older (a few will rent to 18-year-olds). An American license works just as well as an International Driver's License. Roads are usually well-marked, and maps are available at all tourist offices. Israelis drive on the right. Rentals usually run about US$55-70 per day with a 250km daily limit. There is often a discount for rentals of three days or more. Prices in shekels are considerably higher in some cases, and deals arranged beforehand from overseas are often *much* cheaper. See Practical Information in each city for agency addresses.

**Trains**  Rail service in Israel is useful only for travel along the northern coast. The circuitous Tel Aviv-Jerusalem line is slower than highway travel but considerably more scenic. Like buses, trains screech to a halt during *Shabbat*. Avoid traveling on Friday afternoons when the trains are most crowded. Train fares are slightly cheaper than bus fares. Students with an ISIC receive a 50% discount.

**Hitchhiking** The incidence of sexual harassment and assault has increased dramatically in recent years. License plates carry meaning here; yellow are Israeli, black with a ש are army, red are police, blue or gray are occupied territories, and white are diplomatic. Those who hitch in the Negev or Golan (where sometimes the only option is a military vehicle) run the risk of getting a ride that doesn't go all the way to their destination, in which case you are stranded and fried. Hitchers flag cars by pointing to the far side of the road with the index finger. Those who stick out their thumb will get nothing but rude looks—the thumbs up sign means something very different in the Middle East.

> *Let's Go* does *not* recommend hitchhiking. *Tremping*, as it's called, is not what it used to be in Israel. **Women are strongly advised not to hitchhike alone.**

**Off the Beaten Path** Israel's most splendid scenery is often accessible only by foot. The **Society for the Protection of Nature in Israel (SPNI)** is an invaluable source of information, maps, and advice. They have offices in the big cities and field schools *(beit sefer sadeh)* everywhere. Their excellent **hiking map** (1:50,000 topo), though in Hebrew, is color-coded to match the marked trail system (NIS48, members NIS43). SPNI people will be happy to mark English names on the map for you. They will also be happy to book you one of their many excellent English or Hebrew guided tours; a large group can hire a field school-based guide (as little as NIS90 per person or NIS400 per day; arrange in advance) for expert instruction. The SPNI also know a lot about the Sinai and lead treks there as well. SPNI stores carry key **publications** for nature explorers; look for *A Guide to Hiking in Israel* (NIS39) by Joel Roskin. The *Guide* tells all and covers the Golan, Galilee, West Bank, Judean Desert, and Eilat Mountains. It also gives car and bus directions to hike starting-points, plus spiels on **Jeep tours, mountain biking, horseback riding,** and **kayaking.**

A fun (though expensive) way to explore Israel's scenic rock faces is by **rapelling** (mysteriously termed *snappling*); **Itamar** guides trips in the Judean Desert, Rosh Ha-Nikra, and the Golan (tel. (02) 996 19 39 or (050) 301 297; US$60 per person per day, prices slightly higher for small groups).

# ■ Useful Addresses

## TOURIST AND TRAVEL SERVICES

**Israel Ministry of Tourism:** 24 King George St., Jerusalem 94262 (tel. (02) 675 48 11). Maps, transportation schedules, and information on current events. The ministry arranges for foreigners to spend an evening with Israeli families (the *Meet the Israelis* program). They also have a complaint department for troubled tourists. Jerusalem-specific queries are handled by the GTIO (see **Practical Information,** p. 286).

**Israel Youth Hostels Association (A.N.A.):** 1 Shazar St., P.O. Box 6001, Jerusalem 91009 (tel. (02) 655 84 00; fax 655 84 30). Operates 31 hostels. Organizes tours for groups and individual packages to Israel, Sinai, Jordan, and Egypt.

**National Parks Authority:** 4 Rav Aluf M. Makleff St., P.O. Box 7028, Tel Aviv 61070 (tel. (03) 576 68 88; fax 691 02 62). Material on parks and historical sites. Also sells an NIS49 ticket for admission to all sites, good for 14 days.

**Society for the Protection of Nature in Israel (Ha-Ḥevra LeHaganat Ha-Teva, SPNI): Tel Aviv** (main office), 4 Ha-Shfela St. (tel. (03) 638 86 77); other offices in major cities. In the **U.S.,** ASPNI, 28 Arrandale Ave., Great Neck, NY 11024 (tel. (212) 398-6750; fax (212) 398-1665). Call (800) 323-0035 for reservations and nature trails brochure. Organizes hikes, sight-seeing tours in English, and camping trips. Dues US$25 per year (tax deductible; includes discounts on trips).

**Israel Student Travel Association (ISSTA): Jerusalem,** 31 Ha-Nevi'im St. (tel. (02) 625 72 57); **Tel Aviv,** 109 Ben-Yehuda St. (tel. (03) 521 05 55); **Haifa,** 2 Balfour St. (tel. (04) 867 02 22 or 832 67 39). Information on tours, flights, student IDs.

# ■ Emergency Information

Emergency assistance is available throughout Israel, and most doctors speak English. **Magen David Adom** (Red Star of David) provides first aid and other emergency help. Emergency hospitals are open 24 hours, including *Shabbat* and holidays; emergency pharmacies can handle after-hours calls. There are also universal emergency numbers. For **Fire,** dial 102. For **Medical emergencies,** dial 101. For the **Police,** dial 100.

# ■ Money Matters

**Currency and Exchange**  The primary unit of currency is the **new Israeli shekel (NIS).** Notes come in denominations of NIS200, NIS100, NIS50, NIS20, and NIS10; coins come in NIS10, NIS5, NIS1, NIS0.50, 10 agorot, and 5 agorot.

Money can be exchanged at any bank or authorized hotel; always bring your passport. Hotel rates of exchange are usually slightly worse than those in banks. A maximum of US$500 worth of shekels can be reconverted at banks. To change more than US$500 (up to US$5000), show a receipt verifying your original conversion into shekels. Banks are generally open Sun., Tues., and Thurs. 8:30am-12:30pm and 4-5:30pm, Mon. and Wed. 8:30am-12:30pm, Fri. and holidays 8:30am-noon.

**ATMs** are abundant in Israel; **Bank Ha-Poalim** ATMs take **bank cards** affiliated with *Cirrus* and often *Plus* networks for free, but your home bank may charge you. Inquire before you go. See **Essentials,** p. 14, for important money information. **Credit cards** are widely accepted, but only at relatively upscale places.

**Use of Foreign Currency**  Many services and shops accept Australian, Canadian, and U.S. dollars and British pounds in addition to shekels. If you pay in foreign currency, your change will come back in shekels and you will be exempt from the domestic **Value Added Tax (VAT)** on goods and services (17%). Many shops include VAT in listed prices in shekels, so you may have to insist that 17% be removed from your charge if you pay in foreign currency. VAT refunds can also be obtained if you present receipts from your purchases at any export bank upon your departure. There are limitations to this refund; purchases must be made at stores bearing the proper logos, must be worth at least US$50, must be wrapped in a plastic bag that will remain closed for the duration of your trip, must be on your person and not packed in a suitcase, and must have been manufactured in Israel. And you thought you were getting something for nothing. The *Customs Guide for the Reimbursement of VAT to Tourists* is available at the airport when you arrive. The refund will be in the currency you used; if the bank cannot scrape together enough, it will be mailed to your home address. A new policy allows Eurocheques to be written in shekels and counted as foreign currency for discounts.

You may bring an unlimited amount of currency, foreign or shekels, into the country. Upon departure you are permitted to take up to US$100 cash. Anything over this must be accompanied by receipts to prove that it was brought into the country. Unless you want to wallpaper your kitchen, exchange all your shekels before leaving Israel.

**Tipping**  A 10% tip is expected in restaurants, bars, and hotels, unless a service charge is already included in the bill. Taxi drivers will happily accept tips, but they are not expected.

**Business Hours**  Business hours in Israel are difficult to pinpoint. Because of the variety of religions, different shops close on different days. Most Jewish shops and offices are closed for *Shabbat* from early Friday afternoon until Sunday; some stores reopen after sundown on Saturday. Typical shopping hours are Sunday through Thursday from 8am to 7pm and Friday from 8am to 2pm. Some establishments close for a *siesta* (around 1-4pm), though this practice is on the wane. Shopping malls are open until 9-10pm. Muslim-owned establishments close on Fridays, while Christian businesses close on Sundays. **Entertainment** spots are usually open every day, with extended hours on weekends. Bars begin to fill up around midnight. **Public transportation,** including Egged and Dan bus lines, also shuts down for *Shabbat* throughout the country, though some lines still run in Haifa. Don't expect to catch a bus after 2pm on Friday. Arab buses and taxis, however, do continue to run (at increased prices) on *Shabbat.*

Businesses close down on major Jewish holidays, keeping Friday hours the day before. During *Sukkot* and *Pesaḥ,* shops close entirely for the first and last days and are open until early afternoon during intermediate days. In Arab areas, some restaurants close for the entire month of Ramadan; many others close during the day. For more information, see When To Go (p. 2).

# ■ Accommodations

**Hostels**   Although often crowded in summer, Israel's **Hostelling International (HI)** youth hostels are usually clean and close to historic sites and scenic areas. You can obtain a list of hostels from the **Israel Youth Hostel Association** (see **Tourist and Travel Services,** p. 269). Hostel locations are also listed on the back of the GTIO's survey map. Most HI hostels accept reservations and have no age limit; a few have a maximum stay of three nights. HI hostels are generally more expensive than privately owned ones. Hostels usually offer lunch and dinner for an additional fee. While some have 24-hour reception, many follow a strict schedule: they are open 5-9pm for check-in, 7am-noon for check-out, and are closed the rest of the day (check specific listings). There are many excellent unofficial hostels and pensions in Israel. **Most dorm rooms and bathrooms in Israeli hostels are coed.**

Guard your valuables. All accommodations are required by law to have safes for use free of charge; many also have lockers, for a minimal fee.

The Israel Youth Hostel Association offers package tours for individuals and groups, and HI members get discounted admission to some national parks. Write to the Hostel Association for "Israel on the Youth Hostel Trail" deals.

**Hotels**   Hotel accommodations are usually too costly for the budget traveler. There are some reasonably priced one- and two-star hotels in the larger cities; a few have singles for approximately US$25-30 and doubles for US$35-40. Prices can often be bargained down substantially when business is slow. Ask at the tourist office for booklets *Israel: A Youth and Student Adventure* and *Israel Tourist Hotels.*

**Camping**   Israel's campsites usually provide electricity, sanitary facilities, public telephones, first aid, a restaurant and/or store, a night guard, and on-site or nearby swimming areas. During July and August most sites charge NIS10-20 per night for adults. For information, contact the **Israel Camping Organization** (see **Useful Addresses: Tourist and Travel Services,** p. 269.

Think twice before crashing in areas not officially designated for camping. Certain stretches of beach are off-limits for security reasons, and others are dens o' thieves (Haifa, Tel Aviv, and Eilat). **Women should not camp alone.** Finally, heed mine field warning signs, unless you fancy yourself immortal.

**Alternative Accommodations**   If you plan to sleep in Nazareth or Jerusalem, consider staying in a **Christian hospice,** also on Mount Tabor, in Tiberias, and in Jaffa. They are officially designed to provide reasonably-priced room and board for Christian pilgrims, but all those listed in this book welcome tourists as well. Bed and breakfast costs US$18-25 per person at most places. Though austere, the hospices are conveniently located in important religious centers and are usually quiet, comfortable, and impeccable; most also serve cheap, filling meals. But accommodations are limited, and sometimes difficult to obtain in the tourist season. For a list of hospices write to the Ministry of Tourism, c/o Nancy Shelaz, Pilgrimage Promotion Committee, 23 Hillel St., Jerusalem P.O. Box 1018 91009 (tel. (02) 623 73 11 or 79 62; fax 625 86 70).

In some cities it is possible to rent a room in a **private home.** The GTIO and some private travel agencies can arrange accommodations. Consider finding a place on your own; prices should be no more than what you would pay at a hostel. But exercise caution, as quality varies greatly. Hometours International, Inc., P.O. Box 11503, Knoxville, TN 37939 (tel. (800) 367-4668 or (423) 588-8722), helps travelers find short-term **apartment rentals** in Jerusalem, Tel Aviv, and Netanya from the United States. They also have **bed-and-breakfast, kibbutz,** and moshav locations throughout Israel (US$50 fee; US$25 goes towards rent).

Some kibbutzim offer accommodations at **Kibbutz Hotels.** Most are resort-like and expensive, and have three-star ratings from the Ministry of Tourism. For information, contact them at 90 Ben-Yehuda St., Tel Aviv 63437 (tel. (03) 524 6161). Finally, try **ISSTA** (see **Tourist and Travel Services,** p. 269) for cheap package deals on accommodations.

## ■ Keeping in Touch

Post offices are usually open Sunday through Tuesday and Thursday 8am-12:30pm and 3:30-6pm, Wednesday 8am-2pm, Friday 8am-1pm, and are closed Saturdays and holidays. In the larger cities some offices may keep longer hours. Mail from North America to Israel can take up to two weeks; mail sent from Israel to North America is considerably faster. On the street, yellow mailboxes are for mail within the same city, red mailboxes are for all other mail. Most post offices offer international **Express Mail Service (EMS),** which supposedly takes three days (reality: 4 at least).

Travelers have two means of receiving mail: *poste restante (doar shamur)* and American Express Client Letter Service. See Essentials: **Keeping in Touch,** p. 41, for information on these services.

You can send a **telegram** from a post office or hotel. **Fax** is available in many post offices around the country.

**Telephone**   **Public telephones** are everywhere. Older telephones devour *asimonim* (tokens) for local calls (NIS0.50; avoid calling long distance direct from an old pay phone—making a connection may take hours and bucketfuls of *asimonim*). Far more common are the beige-colored telephones (marked with yellow signs) that operate with **Telecards** (10 units of calling time NIS5, 20 units NIS10, 50 units NIS23.50—buy them at the post office). Telecards are good for long distance and

---

### Yakity Yak

The Israeli love affair with talking—already a major reason for the Levant's hot air—has reached new heights. They're now gabbing everywhere and anywhere using shiny black cellular phones (known in Israel by the trademark Pelephone which means "wonderphone"). Bedouin on camel, soldiers at line-up, and kids heading to school all carry little flip-phones. Over 600,000 cellular phones are currently in use, and two million are expected to be operational in three years (that's more than one for every three people). Due to cheaper rates and the break-up of the Pelephone monopoly, Israel now leads the world in per capita customer calling time. On average, Israelis spend 500 minutes per month chatting via satellite. As these phones penetrate the country at warp speed, the need for cellphone etiquette lessons prompt many to doubt whether the cellular revolution is really a leap forward. Calls can be "mistakenly" received at weddings and funerals, and no classroom is without an intrusive beep. Many theaters, restaurants, and hospitals are now affixing "no cellular phones" signs adjacent to their "no smoking" signs. The Pelephone is in no danger of going out of vogue, however. Ask any Israeli—all the chest hair in the world doesn't make a man seem as cool as when a little beep emanates from his back pocket.

international calls (roughly NIS5.90 per min. to the U.S.). International rates drop by up to 50% late at night and on Saturday and Sunday.

**Bezek,** Israel's phone company, has offices with metered phones for international calls in Tel Aviv and Jerusalem. It may be more economical to call overseas from there, because they charge only for the time you were on the phone; phone cards must be purchased with a fixed set of units and you may be left with extra units at the end of the call. Nonetheless, there's nothing you can do at a telephone office that you can't do from a pay phone. English telephone directories are available at hotels and main post offices, or dial 144 for the **operator** or **information.**

**Toll-free direct-dial** numbers (toll-free numbers begin with 177) are the easiest way to make overseas calls; you dial an overseas operator who places your collect or calling-card call. The following toll-free numbers (preceded by 177) are for **AT&T:** (177) 100 27 27 (USADirect, WorldConnect, or collect calls), 440 27 27 (BT Direct, for the U.K.), 105 27 27 (Canada Direct), 353 27 27 (Ireland Direct), 640 27 27 (New Zealand), and 270 27 27 (South Africa). For **MCI** World Phone, dial (177) 150 27 27.

For **direct international calling,** dial 00, then the country code, area code, and telephone number. For collect, person-to-person, and credit card calls dial 188 for an **overseas operator.** The same number works for **international directory assistance.** Israel's **international phone code** is 972.

# LIFE AND TIMES

## ■ Government & Politics

Israel is a parliamentary democracy. There is no written constitution; instead, a series of Basic Laws form the constitutional framework for legislation. The Israeli parliament is called the Knesset. Israelis do not directly elect individual candidates for seats in the Knesset; instead they vote for political parties, eleven of which are represented in the present Knesset. The percentage of the popular vote received by a given party is then converted to a proportion of the 120 seats of the Knesset, provided that the party receives at least 1.5% of the national vote. In the past, the head of the party receiving a plurality of votes would form a government, over which he or she would preside as Prime Minister. Under this system, it was generally necessary for the Prime Minister's party to form a coalition with one or more smaller parties, so that at least 61 Knesset members supported the government and could thus defeat a vote of no confidence by the parliamentary opposition. This political necessity tended to give small parties political power beyond their numbers, an oft-criticized aspect of the electoral system.

Public dissatisfaction with the system prompted legislative revision in 1992. As of the 1996 election, Israelis now elect their prime minister directly, in addition to voting for a parliamentary party. Intended to bolster the stability of the government by reducing the leverage of smaller parties, the current system enables the directly elected prime minister to claim a national mandate irrespective of party politics in the Knesset. A vote of no confidence in the prime minister by a majority of the Knesset must be immediately followed by new elections for both the premiership and the entire Knesset.

The two major parties are **Labor** (*Avoda,* sometimes still referred to as *Ma'arakh,* or Alignment) and **Likud.** Labor's roots are in old-style Labor Zionism, while the Likud still carries the banner of Revisionist Zionism. The critical issue separating left and right in Israeli politics is the question of territorial compromise in exchange for peace (see **The Gulf War and the Peace Process,** p. 55). The 1984 and 1988 elections ended in virtual ties, with the two big parties forming National Unity Governments largely paralyzed by internal dissent. In 1990, hard-liner Yitzhak Shamir formed a Likud-led government supported by religious and far-right parties. A general election in June 1992 decisively ousted Shamir and replaced him with a coalition dominated by the left-of-center Labor Party. The government was headed by Prime Minister Yitzhak Rabin. After Rabin's assassination in 1995, Foreign Minister Shimon Peres took the reigns. In May 1996, Likud's Benjamin Netanyahu squeaked by Peres in the first ever direct prime ministerial election (50.4% to 49.6%). The new Likud government has vowed to continue the peace process, but will undoubtedly slow the pace of the negotiations considerably.

After the big two, Israeli parties run the political gamut, from right-wing to left-wing Zionist parties and from Orthodox Jewish parties to Arab parties. The big winners in the 1996 election were the **religious parties.** Under their influence, the government has tried to close some streets on *Shabbat,* leading to angry protests in Jerusalem. **Shas** is the biggest minor party in the Knesset with 11 seats, and the **National Religious Party** is a close second with 10. **United Torah Judaism,** the other religious party, controls four seats. Three left-wing Zionist parties (Ratz, Shinui, and Mapam) recently combined on a platform of territorial concessions, civil rights and separation of religion and state to form **Meretz,** which now controls nine seats. The newest force on the political scene is Russian immigrant Natan Scharansky's **Yisra'el Ba-Aliyah** party, which controls seven seats and pushes for more housing jobs and immigrant rights. The ultra-right wing **Moledet** won two seats in the recent election, and the liberal **United Arab List** controls four seats. The centrist **Third Way** party, which favors increasing PA autonomy but opposes pulling out of the Golan, controls four seats. **Ḥadash** (the Commies) has five seats.

# ▓ Economy

Poor in natural resources, stymied by socialist inefficiencies, and carrying the burdens of large defense expenditures and Jewish refugee absorption, Israel for years relied upon substantial financial assistance from diaspora Jewish communities and foreign governments (especially the U.S.). Throughout the last few years, however, the country has begun to reap the fruits of extensive privatization, free trade with the U.S. and the European Community, and the development of a high-tech export-oriented economy. Israel is currently in the midst of an unprecedented economic boom, with steady growth of about 5% per year and a GNP of US$70 billion. The country's main industries are chemicals, diamond cutting and polishing, textiles, high-tech (especially bio-medical and computer) products, and military hardware. Israel is also a leader in desert agriculture and plant genetics. The high inflation rates of the past have given way to a new stability of currency; the new Israeli shekel (NIS) has held steady against the dollar for the past four years.

The peace process has led to further economic optimism. Increased international confidence in the stability of the area has led to a surge of foreign investment and an upgrading of Israel's international credit rating. Israeli businesses are also developing profitable relationships with foreign companies that previously feared the Arab boycott. Finally, trade between Israel and its Arab neighbors is growing and the possibilities for large-scale regional economic cooperation, should real peace ensue, are enormous. Plans are already in the works for major economic projects such as integrated power-grids, road networks, and shared ports to be undertaken jointly by Israel and neighboring Arab states.

In addition, the immigration over the past few years of approximately 500,000 Jews from the former USSR has flooded Israel with highly educated workers and professionals. While it took time for the economy to accommodate so many skilled individuals (horror stories abound of scientists forced to sweep streets), the net result has been a tremendous economic boom. With Israeli incomes rising and Palestinians increasingly prevented from entering Israel to work, Israel has begun importing tens of thousands of workers from Asia and Eastern Europe to work the menial jobs Israelis no longer want. Israel's newfound prosperity and the current trends of the U.S. government to concentrate on domestic issues have led many to predict that the large American foreign aid traditionally received (US$3 billion per year plus loan guarantees) will be significantly reduced in coming years.

# ■ Kibbutzim & Moshavim

Three percent of the Israeli population lives on **kibbutzim** (plural of kibbutz), some-what socialist rural societies where production is controlled by members. Kibbutzim are responsible for much of Israel's agricultural production and political leadership. The kibbutzim of today hardly resemble the fiercely ideological pioneer agricultural settlements that began 80 years ago. These days, most rely more on industry than on agriculture. In addition, the passion for austerity is subsiding; kibbutzniks now demand the same luxuries enjoyed by other Israelis (i.e. larger living quarters, TVs and VCRs, Bart Simpson rhinestone jackets). Many kibbutz children now live with their parents in nuclear family homes, whereas just a decade or two ago nearly all lived in separate dormitories and saw their parents only at certain times.

Today's kibbutzim face mounting problems. Labor shortages are on the rise as two-thirds of younger members leave the settlements to test their skills elsewhere. In addi-tion, debt is becoming a daunting threat; kibbutzim collectively owe over US$4 bil-lion, more than US$31,000 per kibbutznik.

**Moshavim** (plural of *moshav*), another type of rural settlement, provide roughly 40% of Israel's food. Members of a *moshav* typically harvest their own piece of land, though marketing is often done collectively; some have a crop that all members help cultivate. Recently, many *moshavim* near big cities have gone suburban—their mem-bers commute to the city.

# ■ The Army

Israel is unusually proud of its army, known as Tzahal (the Hebrew acronym for Tz'va Hagana LeYisrael.) In English, the army is called the Israel Defense Forces (IDF). All 18-year-olds are drafted—men for three years, women for two—with certain excep-tions, most notably non-Druze Arabs (who may enlist if they choose but are not con-scripted) and *yeshiva* students. The result is an informal, highly motivated, and highly visible citizen's army. The IDF is a fact of life for Israeli men aged 18 to 55, when reserve duty *(miluim)* ceases. Women are not called for reserve service.

# ■ Religion & Ethnicity

Freedom of religion has been safeguarded by the state; in 1967, the Law for the Pro-tection of Holy Places was passed after Israel annexed Jerusalem's sacred sites. **Jews** make up 88% of the population (4,400,000), **Muslims** 10% (500,000); the remaining 2% (100,000) includes Christians and Druze. Each community operates its own reli-gious courts, funded by the Ministry of Religion, and controls its own holy sites. Every religion's days of rest are guaranteed by law.

The vast majority of Israeli **Jews** are secular; only about 15% are Orthodox or Ultra-Orthodox (though in Jerusalem it might appear otherwise). The religious establish-ment is quite powerful; the electoral system has helped Jewish religious parties to wield disproportionate power. Much to the aggravation of many secular Israelis, Rab-binical courts have a state monopoly on matrimonial issues.

Israeli Jews are divided along ethnic lines: **Sephardi** Jews (many of pre-1492 Span-ish origins) come from Arab or other Mediterranean countries; **Ashkenazi** Jews have northern or eastern European origins. The rift in Israeli society is deep and wide, and goes back to the 1950s, when Sephardi Jews from Morocco and Iraq were brought to an already established, Ashkenazi-dominated state. While Sephardim compose more than 50% of the Jewish population in Israel, Ashkenazim still fill most of the power positions in government, economy, the military, and academia, while Sephardim are the vast majority among the poor.

After Mecca and Medina, the most important **Muslim** holy site is in Jerusalem—the Al Aqsa Mosque. Muslim *hadith* tells of Muhammad's journey from Mecca to Al Aqsa (The Farthest) and up through the Seven Heavens to meet with God.

ISRAEL

Many **Christian** sects are represented in Israel, including the Armenian Orthodox, Abyssinian, Anglican, Coptic, Greek Orthodox, Roman Catholic, and Syrian Orthodox. Most are Arab by language and origin.

Israel's **Druze** population is divided between the Galilee and the Golan Heights. Those in the Galilee remain loyal to Israel and serve in the army, while those in the Golan long to return to Syria. Druze generally live in separate villages and have their own communal institutions. See **Introduction to the Region: Religion,** p. 57 for a more detailed discussion of religion.

## ■ Language

The contemporary Hebrew language was created from biblical Hebrew by **Eliezer Ben-Yehuda,** who compiled the first modern dictionary in the 1920s. In a surprisingly short period, the revived biblical dialect matured into a full-fledged language, spanning from colloquial speech to poetry. While a Semitic language (like Arabic) in structure, modern Hebrew contains elements of European languages; many words for which no equivalent biblical concept exists have been lifted almost as-is.

Most Israelis speak English, and signs are usually written in English (and sometimes Russian) as well as Hebrew and Arabic, the official languages of Israel. You may want to learn a few Hebrew phrases; one of the best phrasebooks is the Dover publication *Say It in Modern Hebrew* (US$3.50).

The **appendix** of this book contains a list of useful Hebrew words and phrases.

## ■ The Arts

### LITERATURE

The compilation of the biblical narrative was followed by the age of the *Mishnah* (200 BCE-700 CE), when *halakha* (laws derived from the Bible) and *agada* (elaboration on the Bible) were compiled. This age also saw the growth of the *piyyut* (liturgical poem). In the Middle Ages, Jewish poetry included *Megillat Antiohus* and *Megillat Ḥanuka,* while narrative prose focused on demonological legends.

The revival of Hebrew as a secular language in the 18th century brought a drastic shift in Hebrew literature. Josef Perl and Isaac Erter parodied Ḥasidic works in their writings. In Czarist Russia, Abraham Mapu wrote *The Hypocrite,* the first novel to portray modern Jewish social life in a fictional context. The generations that followed moved toward realism, often employing Yiddish, a more versatile language.

At the turn of the 20th century, Hebrew was revived for literature by Joseph Brenner, whose hallmark character was the tragic, uprooted settler. His works are remarkable not only for their influence on subsequent generations of Israeli writers, but also for their pessimistic depictions of social interaction between Jews and Arabs. In the 1920s and 1930s Nobel Laureate Shmuel Yosef (Shai) Agnon confronted the breakdown of cultural cohesion among modern Jews in *A Guest for the Night, The Bridal Canopy,* and *Twenty-One Stories.*

Just before the creation of the State of Israel, a group of native Hebrew authors rose to prominence. Their style, characterized by concern for the landscape and the moment, is exemplified in S. Yizhar's *Efrayim Returns to Alfalfa.* Beginning in the late 1950s, writers such as Amos Oz and A. B. Yehoshua began to experiment with psychological realism, allegory, and symbolism. In the 1960s, new skepticism surfaced in Israeli literature. David Shahar has been called the Proust of Hebrew literature for his *The Palace of Shattered Vessels,* set in Jerusalem in the 1930s and 40s. Ya'akov Shabtai's *Past Continuous,* about Tel Aviv in the 1970s, is perhaps the best Israeli novel of the decade. A stunning, though initially confusing, must-read is *Arabesques,* by Anton Shammas, an Arab Israeli writing in Hebrew. On the poetry front, a read through the gripping work of Yehuda Amichai will ensure that you never look at Jerusalem stone in the same way again. Most major Israeli works have been translated into English.

An increasingly prominent genre of Israeli literature focuses on the Israeli-Palestinian conflict by way of fiction, nonfiction, or some combination thereof. Oz's *In the Land of Israel* is a series of interviews with native Israelis and West Bank Palestinians that documents the wide range of political sentiment; his *A Perfect Peace* is a semi-allegorical account of kibbutz life just before the Six-Day War. David Grossman's *Yellow Wind* tells of one Israeli Jew's journey to the West Bank just prior to the *intifada*, while his *Sleeping on a Wire* explores the precarious predicament of Israeli Arabs. For informative accounts written from the Palestinian perspective, check out *The West Bank Story* by Rafik Halabi, an Israeli Druze television reporter, and Fawaz Turki's autobiographical *The Disinherited*. To wipe your tears, pick up Ze'ev Chafetz's *Heroes and Hustlers, Hard Hats and Holy Men*, a hilarious satire of Israeli society and politics.

Israel's short but tumultuous history has inspired a number of historical novels. Consider trying Ḥayim Potok's *Wanderings*, James Michener's *The Source*, and Leon Uris' *Exodus*. For a more sober textbook history of the land read Barbara Tuchman's *Bible and Sword*, which chronicles Palestine from the Bronze Age to the Balfour Declaration of 1917. The elegant works of Solomon Grayzel also give historical background. The dense but provocative *The Arabs in Israel*, by Sabri Jiryis, describes just that. Serious academic types should pick up Nadav Safran's hefty *Israel: The Embattled Ally* or Conor Cruise O'Brien's lighter *The Siege*.

The Israeli **press** is far livelier than the Western norm; politics are taken seriously and opinions expressed vociferously. The liberal *Ha'Aretz* is the most respected daily; *Ma'ariv* leans just right of center. *Yediot Aḥronot* is more tabloid-esque and therefore more widely read. *The Jerusalem Post*, the only English-language daily, tilts to the right, while the bi-weekly English-language *Jerusalem Report* has high-quality reporting and analysis and dovish editors. The *Post* reprints *The New York Times* "Week in Review" section each Monday.

## MUSIC

Music became organized after World War I, when Jews in Palestine assembled chamber groups, a symphony orchestra, an opera company, and a choral society. During the 1930s, with the rise of Nazism in Europe, Jewish musicians fled to Israel. This influx spurred the formation of several music groups. Today seasonal music activities from October into July are held in such varied settings as the historic Crusader Castle at Akko and the modern, 3000-seat Mann Auditorium in Tel Aviv.

Israeli **popular music** started emerging from its folk-chant origins (often echoing Russian folk melodies) in the late 1960s. Since the 70s, Israel has been catching up with international music fashions; local bands momentarily lingered on punk, reggae, heavy metal, grunge, and even rap. MTV now keeps Israeli youth abreast of the goings-on in London and Seattle, and they expect nothing less of their own local acts. Tel Aviv is the unequivocal hub of the cutting-edge music scene in Israel, though performances occur throughout the country. If faced with the opportunity to see a concert atop Masada, grab it.

The most popular performers in Israel play music that's somewhere in between kick-butt rock and a more mellow, acoustic sound. Some native classics still on the performance circuit are David Broza, Shlomo Artzi, Achinoam Nini, Yehudit Ravitz, and Gidi Gov. In many places you can hear simple Middle Eastern-style music, heavy on synthesizers and drum machines, blasting from car stereos and boomboxes: this is *muzika mizraḥit* ("oriental music"), very popular with Sephardic Jews (if you're interested, pick up a recording of Avihu Medina's *mizraḥi* tunes).

# ■ Food

Some Israelis' diets are affected by *kashrut* (meaning proper or properly prepared), the Jewish dietary laws. Observant Jews will not eat or shop in a place that carries non-kosher goods; consequently, to keep kosher clientele coming, the big supermarket chains in Israel carry only kosher products, and many restaurants (and most hotels) serve only kosher food. Still, observance of *kashrut* is hardly the norm in Israel—many restaurants, particularly in Haifa and Tel Aviv, are avidly *non*-kosher.

The typical Israeli eats a large breakfast, returns home for a big mid-day dinner, and has a light, late supper. Because of the poor quality and high cost of beef and lamb, Israelis rely largely on chicken, dairy, and vegetable products. Popular items in the Israeli diet include hummus (mashed chick-peas, garlic, lemon, and *tahina*); the Israeli salad, a finely chopped mix of tomatoes and cucumbers, garnished with oil and vinegar; *gvina levana*, soft white cheese; *schnitzel*, breaded and fried chicken breast; *chips* (french fries); and a variety of sweet dairy snacks.

Israel's most popular **street food** is a Mid-Eastern staple: falafel are deep-fried ground chick-pea balls served in pita bread with vegetables and *tahina* sauce. Other common pita-fillers are hummus and *shawerma* (chunks of roast turkey, sometimes posing as lamb). Falafel, hummus, and *shawerma* stands always have a colorful selection of salads and toppings such as *harif,* a red-hot sauce. *Burekas* (filo dough folded over a cheese, potato, spinach, or meat filling) come in different shapes and are available at pastry and some fast-food shops. Pizza also abounds. On hot summer days, street vendors sell what look like hand grenades. Not to worry—these are *sabras* (a prickly cactus fruit), and the inside is edible, although the seeds give some indigestion. (*Sabra* is also a term for a native-born Israeli; both the fruit and the people are said to be thorny on the outside, sweet on the inside.)

The variety of ethnic cuisines in Israel is impressive; **restaurants** run the gamut from Chinese to French to Moroccan to American to Yemenite. Many restaurants serve typical Middle Eastern food. In Yemenite restaurants, *malawah,* thin fried dough usually dipped in a watery tomato sauce, is a cheap specialty. Restaurants serving Eastern European Jewish food are few and very expensive; go to New York.

**Preparing your own food** is cheap, especially in summer, when fresh fruits and vegetables are available in every outdoor *shuk* (market). You can buy groceries inexpensively at local *shuks,* at the neighborhood *makolet* (small grocery store), or in supermarkets. Israeli bread is tasty and cheap; on Thursdays and Fridays, stores sell fresh loaves of *hallah,* egg bread sprinkled with sesame or poppy seeds. Supermarket refrigerators sport a huge selection of dairy products, from low-fat yogurts (try Prikef)

---

### Ofer's Guide to Falafel

Falafel in Israel is not so much eaten as *experienced.* Street-corner stands foster a communal, raucous, even violent ritual in which sustenance is secondary.

The daunting task begins when you are handed an empty pita and faced with the challenging prospect of constructing a meal. It's best to box out the other customers so that you can proceed with the task undisturbed. When you've squeezed in the Israeli salad, carrot salad, potato salad, sauerkraut, pickled vegetables, and other, unidentifiable mixtures, and spread tahini over the entire mess, you'll notice that the strain of excessive packing has taken its toll on the pita itself. Weak and burgeoning, it begins to leak and crack at vital points.

The exercise now becomes one of precision biting. Survey the pita from all angles, eyeing the most vulnerable parts. Quickly and efficiently, take large bites while trying to inhale as much of the contents of the pita as possible. As the later rounds at the salad bar cause further pita breakdown, you may be forced to adopt the straddle position to prevent spillage. For reassurance, look to your slobbering, already straddling companions. Within time, you'll be holding falafel balls and salad, the pita having schmutzed into nothingness.

**Note:** similar rules apply to *shawerma.*

to cream-topped chocolate snacks (try Milki). In the deli section you can get food-to-go by the gram, including cookies, miniature *burekas,* and other pastries, as well as an assortment of salads, pickles, and olives.

Two Israeli **beers** are the decent, deep-amber Goldstar and the lesser Maccabee lager. Goldstar is a common draft beer; Maccabee comes in bottles only. Other brews commonly available on tap are Carlsberg, Tuborg, and Heineken. Supermarkets carry a small selection of liquor; note that Nesher "black beer" is a sweet, non-alcoholic malt brew. The official drinking age (not strictly enforced) is 18.

In Arab restaurants, if you ask for **coffee** with no specifications, you'll get a small cup of strong, sweet, Arabic coffee, sometimes referred to as *turki* (Turkish). If you want something resembling American coffee, ask in Hebrew for *hafukh* (mixed with milk) or *filter.* Instant coffee *(nes)* is also popular. "Black" *(shahor)* or "mud" *(botz)* coffee is Turkish coffee brewed in a cup; watch out for the sediment.

# Jerusalem ירושלים القدس

When the sun sets over the Judean hills, Jerusalem's white stone turns gold and peace seems to be within the city's grasp. The domes, spires, and minarets of three faiths' places of worship rise over crenelated walls in quiet harmony. But Jerusalem is not always as serene as its evening breeze and rooftop view. The blindingly white stone, a requirement on all of Jerusalem's buildings, is indelibly, if invisibly, stained with the blood of centuries.

In this city where religion and the freedom to practice it are inextricably tied to daily life, the magnificent spirituality that defines Jerusalem can itself become a burden. As Israeli poet Yehuda Amiḥai commented, the "air over Jerusalem is saturated with prayers and dreams, like the air over industrial cities. It's hard to breathe."

Spiritual over-saturation doesn't hinder Jerusalem's magnetic attraction; it heightens it. Jews, from ultra-Orthodox to secular, Palestinians, both Christian and Muslim, Armenians, Mormon missionaries, pilgrims and tourists from every continent, fanatics, mystics, and raving lunatics all come and bring their spiritual baggage with them. Jerusalem is timeless and on the verge of history. It is the modern capital for ancient peoples and a headline grabber for age-old disputes. The time warp is most evident on a city bus, where black robes, habits, and *kafias* mingle with halter-tops and baseball caps. All go about their daily business along the city's eternal streets.

## ■ History

During Jerusalem's 5000 years, 18 conquerors have presided over the city. Archaeological findings indicate that Jerusalem (Jebus, then) was a Canaanite settlement for 2000-3000 years before King David's conquest around 1000 BCE (II Samuel 5). David established Jerusalem as the capital of the Israelite kingdom; his son Solomon extended the city's boundaries northward to include the present-day Temple Mount. Solomon built the First Temple on the Mount, where sacrificial observances were to be centralized and the Ark of the Covenant was kept.

The Israelite kingdom split shortly after Solomon's death in 933 BCE. The tribes of the northern Kingdom of Israel created their own capital, while those of the south retained Jerusalem as the center of the Kingdom of Judah. Over three prosperous centuries, Judah's citizens developed Judaism and the Jewish identity. Then, in 596 BCE, a Babylonian army led by King Nebuchadnezzar besieged the city and forced its capitulation. The Babylonians kidnapped the aristocracy and kept Jerusalem disarmed and powerless. When Zedekiah instigated a rebellion ten years later, a wrathful King Nebuchadnezzar ordered the exile of the Jews to Babylon and the burning of Jerusalem's finest buildings, including the Temple. In 539 BCE, though, the Babylonians succumbed to Cyrus of Persia who permitted the Jews to return from exile (2

ISRAEL

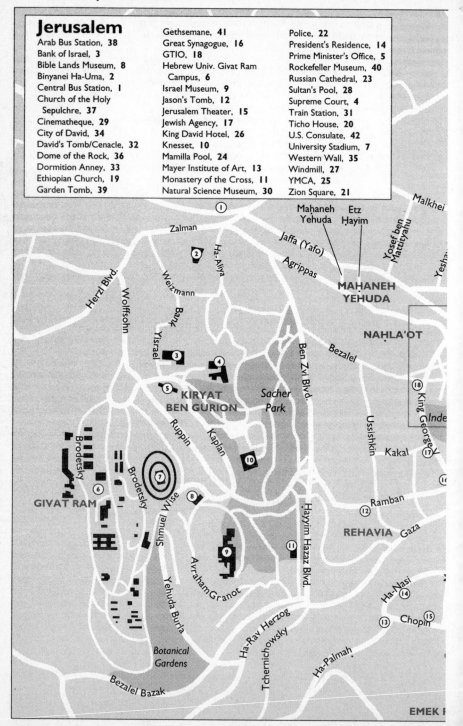

# Jerusalem

Arab Bus Station, 38
Bank of Israel, 3
Bible Lands Museum, 8
Binyanei Ha-Uma, 2
Central Bus Station, 1
Church of the Holy
  Sepulchre, 37
Cinematheque, 29
City of David, 34
David's Tomb/Cenacle, 32
Dome of the Rock, 36
Dormition Anney, 33
Ethiopian Church, 19
Garden Tomb, 39

Gethsemane, 41
Great Synagogue, 16
GTIO, 18
Hebrew Univ. Givat Ram
  Campus, 6
Israel Museum, 9
Jason's Tomb, 12
Jerusalem Theater, 15
Jewish Agency, 17
King David Hotel, 26
Knesset, 10
Mamilla Pool, 24
Mayer Institute of Art, 13
Monastery of the Cross, 11
Natural Science Museum, 30

Police, 22
President's Residence, 14
Prime Minister's Office, 5
Rockefeller Museum, 40
Russian Cathedral, 23
Sultan's Pool, 28
Supreme Court, 4
Train Station, 31
Ticho House, 20
U.S. Consulate, 42
University Stadium, 7
Western Wall, 35
Windmill, 27
YMCA, 25
Zion Square, 21

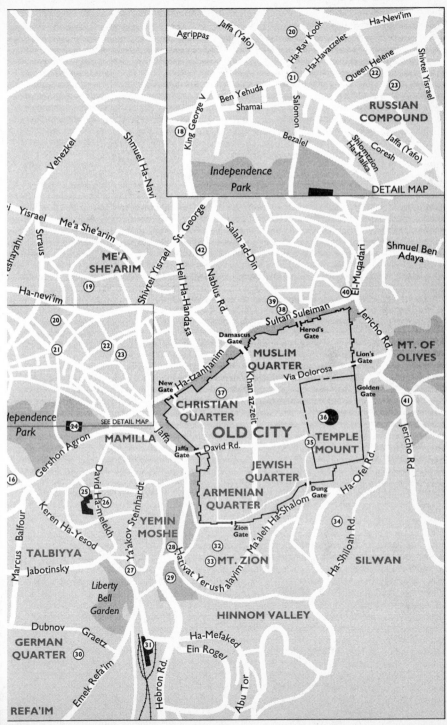

DETAIL MAP

Jaffa (Yafo)
Agrippas
Ha-Rav Kook
Ha-Nevi'im
20
Ha-Havatzelet
21
Queen Helene
22
Shivtei Yisrael
23
Ben Yehuda
Shamai
Salomon
RUSSIAN
COMPOUND
18
King George V
Bezalel
Shlomzion
Ha-Malka
Coresh
Jaffa (Yafo)
Independence
Park

Vehezkel
Shmuel Ha-Navi
St. George
Salah ad-Din
El-Muqadari
Shmuel Ben
Adaya
Yisrael
Me'a She'arim
42
shayahu
Strauss
ME'A
SHE'ARIM
Shivtei Yisrael
Heil Ha-Handasa
Nablus Rd.
19
39
38
40
Ha-nevi'im
Sultan Suleiman
MT. OF
OLIVES
20
Damascus
Gate
Herod's
Gate
Lion's
Gate
Jericho Rd.
21
22
23
Ha-tzanhanim
MUSLIM
QUARTER
Via Dolorosa
New Gate
Khan az-zeit
Golden
Gate
41
dependence
Park
24
SEE DETAIL MAP
CHRISTIAN
QUARTER
37
36
Jericho Rd.
MAMILLA
Jaffa
OLD CITY
35
TEMPLE
MOUNT
16
Gershon Agron
Jaffa
Gate
David Rd.
JEWISH
QUARTER
Ha-Ofel Rd.
David Ha-melekh
25
26
Keren Ha-Yesod
ARMENIAN
QUARTER
Dung
Gate
34
Ma'aleh Ha-Shalom
Ha-Shiloah Rd.
Balfour
Marcus
Ya'akov Steinhardt
YEMIN
MOSHE
Zion Gate
SILWAN
TALBIYYA
28
32
Jabotinsky
27
33
MT. ZION
Hativat Yerushalayim
Liberty
Bell
Garden
29
HINNOM VALLEY
Dubnov
Graetz
31
Ha-Mefaked
Ein Rogel
GERMAN
QUARTER
30
Emek Refa'im
Hebron Rd.
Abu Tor
REFA'IM

Chronicles 36). Reconstruction commenced soon thereafter, and in 515 BCE the Second Temple was rededicated (Ezra 6:15).

Jerusalem enjoyed more than a century of undisturbed revival under the Persians until Alexander the Great swept through the city in 332 BCE. Hellenization was soon embraced by much of the educated population. After a century and a half of Hellenic rule and a brief spell of Egyptian Ptolemaic control, the Seleucid Empire took Jerusalem (198 BCE). King Antiochus IV forbade all Jewish practices, including *Shabbat* observance, circumcision, and the reading of the Torah. When he installed the cult of Zeus in the Temple, non-Hellenized Jews revolted. The rebels, led by Judas Maccabeus, were successful. In 164 BCE, the temple was resanctified and the priestly hierarchy assumed control of the city. The resulting Hasmonean dynasty zealously ruled the area's Jews for the next century.

Roman general Pompey seized control of Jerusalem in 64 BCE, ushering in six and a half centuries of Roman rule. The Romans installed Herod the Great, child of a Jewish father and Samaritan mother, to reign over what they called the Kingdom of Judea. While occupying the throne (37-4 BCE), Herod commanded the reconstruction of the temple and the creation of the well-known and partially extant Western Wall to better support the enlarged Temple Mount. In 6 CE the Romans bequeathed the governance of the province to a series of procurators, the most famous of whom was Pontius Pilate. Sixty years later, the Jews revolted against Rome. The Roman commander Titus crushed the revolt after four years, destroying the temple, razing the city, and casting many Jews into slavery or exile; life in the Diaspora had begun. After the Bar Kokhba Revolt (a second Jewish revolt named for its leader) ended in 135 CE, the city was destroyed once again by Emperor Hadrian and Jerusalem was declared off limits to the Jews.

That very year Hadrian built a new city over Jerusalem, Aelia Capitolina, to serve as a Roman colony. The pattern of the present-day Old City corresponds to the plan of Hadrian's city: divided into quarters by two major roads (the Cardo and Decumanus) and oriented north to south. You can see the remains of the Cardo in the Old City's Jewish Quarter. When Roman Emperor Constantine adopted and legalized Christianity in 331 CE, his mother Eleni visited the Holy Land in order to identify and consecrate Christian sites. Subsequent Byzantine rulers devoted their energies to the construction of basilicas and churches for the glorification and celebration of the city's Christian heritage.

Following a brief period of Persian rule in the early 7th century, Muslim caliph Omar, one of the *Rashidun* (Rightly Guided Caliphs), conquered Aelia in 638. The Temple Mount was cleansed and hallowed anew as a center of Muslim worship. In 691 his successors completed the Dome of the Rock (see p. 300). Under the tolerant Muslim rule, Jews were allowed to return to the city.

In the 10th century Jerusalem fell into Egyptian hands. The Fatimid despots destroyed all synagogues and churches (the "mad caliph" Al Hakim sacked the Holy Sepulchre), and passed on their policy of persecuting non-Muslims to their successors, the Seljuk Turks. Their rumored closing of pilgrimage routes enraged Western Christians and added fuel to the fire of the Crusades, culminating in the Christian capture of Jerusalem in 1099. With cries of *"Deus vult"* (God wills it), the Crusaders mercilessly slaughtered Jerusalem's Muslim and Jewish inhabitants. The Crusader Kingdom of Jerusalem lasted almost 90 years. During this time, churches were built or rebuilt; hospices, hospitals, and monastic orders were founded; and non-Christian sites of worship were desecrated. In 1187 Salah ad-Din expelled the Crusaders, and both Muslims and Jews once again began to resettle the city. Jerusalem became a thriving center for Muslim scholarship from the 13th to the 15th century under the Mamluks.

In 1516 Jerusalem capitulated to the Ottoman Turks, the city's rulers for the next 400 years. In 1537 Ottoman emperor Suleiman the Magnificent set out to rebuild the city walls, a task that took four years. The planners deviated from the older design, leaving Mount Zion and King David's tomb beyond the walls (see **The Walls and the Citadel**, p. 298). This negligence infuriated Suleiman, who had the architects' heads put beyond the walls, too. In later centuries, many foreign countries began demanding extra-territorial rights for their citizens living under Turkish rule. The world political climate forced the Ottoman sultan to issue the 1856 "Edict of Toleration" for all religions. The small, deeply religious Jewish and Christian communities in Jerusalem still needed charity from abroad to make ends meet, but the trickle of immigrants coming from Europe and Russia increased to a steady flow.

Sir Moses Montefiore, a British Jew, took several trips to Palestine between 1827 and 1874, sponsoring Jewish settlements outside the city walls. These areas soon expanded into bustling neighborhoods, the foundations of West Jerusalem. Heavier Western influence and the increasing influx of European immigrants led to the designation of Jerusalem as an independent *sanjak* (Ottoman province) in 1889, with its own *pasha* (governor) appointed directly from Istanbul.

Ottoman rule over Jerusalem ended in 1917, when the city fell without resistance to the British army. Both Jews and Arabs came to resent the increasing influence of the British in Jerusalem. During World War I, Britain made separate declarations to both Zionists and Arab nationalists, implying that each would eventually gain sole sovereignty over the city. In the end, though, the British kept Palestine for themselves as a League of Nations Mandate. Under British rule, tension between the Jewish and Arab communities heightened, bursting into violent confrontations in 1929 and 1933, and virtual civil war between 1936 and 1939.

The uneasy World War II truce between Arabs and Jews quickly dissolved when the war ended, and violence ravaged Palestine for the next three years. The British announced that they were no longer capable of governing the country. They solicited a settlement from the newly formed United Nations, which resolved to split Palestine into separate Jewish and Arab states, leaving Jerusalem an international city.

In the war that followed the 1948 British evacuation, West Jerusalem and the Jewish Quarter were besieged by the Arabs, who blocked the single road out of the city. West Jerusalem held out until the first cease-fire, but the Jewish Quarter of the Old City capitulated to the Jordanian Arab Legion after extensive and exhaustive house-to-house fighting. Jordan demolished the ancient Quarter and dynamited synagogues. The Jordanian-ruled and Israeli sectors of the city were separated by a buffer zone. This division lasted nearly two decades.

When the 1967 (Six-Day) War broke out, Israel requested that Jordan not get involved; King Hussein attacked West Jerusalem nonetheless. In the course of the Six-Day War Israel captured East Jerusalem, the Old City, and the West Bank from the Jordanians; on June 29 that year Israel declared the newly unified Jerusalem its "eternal capital." The walls separating the Israeli and Arab sectors were torn down, and life under Israeli rule began for Jerusalem's Arabs.

The 25 years following the Six-Day War saw large scale construction outside the Old City. Land owned by Palestinians who had fled during the war was taken over by Israel. Vast new Israeli housing developments were built north and south of the city, assuring a Jewish presence in areas previously under Jordanian rule. The old campus of the Hebrew University on Mt. Scopus, maintained as a military post since 1948, was expanded. Intensive gardening projects blossomed throughout the city including verdant parks that now encircle the Old City.

The 1987 outbreak of the *intifada* (uprising) of Palestinians protesting Israeli occupation had some effect on Jerusalem, though demonstrations were more common in West Bank towns. The Palestinians made it clear that they still regarded East Jerusalem as a part of the West Bank and the future capital of their desired Palestinian State. Meanwhile, violent clashes between the Israeli army and stone-throwing Palestinians, as well as occasional stabbings of Jews in the Old City, turned East Jerusalem and the Old City into alien territory for most residents of West Jerusalem and other Israelis visiting town. Matters were made worse in October 1990 when fighting broke out between Jews and Palestinians at the Western Wall. Israeli police killed 17 Palestinians and wounded almost 150 others during the ensuing crackdown. In February 1996, the militant Palestinian group Hamas brought bloodshed to West Jerusalem in two bus bombings killing dozens of commuters.

The future of Jerusalem is perhaps the most sensitive issue of the current Israeli-Palestinian negotiations. Israel adamantly refuses to discuss withdrawing from its capital, while Palestinians fervently oppose abandoning claims to their most important city. Despite the recent terrorism, Jerusalem continues to draw tourists from across the world, including Jordan, whose citizens are now permitted to visit their ancient neighbor following the peace treaty.

# ■ Orientation

Known as **Yerushalayim** in Hebrew and **Al Quds** (the holy) in Arabic, the Israeli capital is a sprawling city, most of which was only developed in the last 50 years of Jerusalem's three-millennia history.

**West Jerusalem** denotes the Jewish parts of Jerusalem, from French Hill in the northeast and East Talpiyot in the southeast, to Kiryat Menahem in the southwest and Ramot in the northwest. West Jerusalem's main street is **Jaffa Road** (Derekh Yafo), running from the end of the Jerusalem-Tel Aviv highway (where the bus station is located) to the Old City's Jaffa Gate. Midway between the two, Jerusalem's triangular downtown area prospers. With Jaffa Rd. as one of the sides, **King George Street** (Ha-Melekh George) and **Ben-Yehuda Street** enclose the area. At the corner of Ben-Yehuda and Jaffa is **Zion Square** (Kikkar Tzion), and on Ben-Yehuda between Jaffa and King George is the popular *midrahov*. In the direction of the bus station between Jaffa Rd. and Agrippas St. you'll find West Jerusalem's chaotic open-air market, **Mahaneh Yehuda**.

Jerusalem's most important historical and religious sites are concentrated within the walls of the **Old City,** still divided into the four quadrants laid out by the Romans in 135 CE. To get from the city center to the Old City, take Jaffa Rd. past the post office to **Jaffa Gate.** Here you can follow the promenade along the ancient walls to most of the seven other gates. The main road in the Old City is the roof-covered **David Street,** an extension of which, **Baab as-Silsilah Street** (Gate of the Chain), runs just up to the Western Wall. The **Armenian Quarter** is to the right as you enter through Jaffa Gate and is directly accessible via **Zion Gate.** Left of Jaffa Gate is the **Christian Quarter,** which can also be reached directly from the **New Gate.** Damascus Gate provides direct entry into the heavily populated **Muslim Quarter.** To get there from Jaffa Gate, turn left onto **Khan az-Zeit** from David Rd. and it will be on the right. A right turn off David Rd. onto **Ha-Yehudim Street** leads to the **Jewish Quarter,** which is directly accessible via **Dung Gate.**

The old Green Line separating Jordan from Israel pre-1967 runs along Derekh Ha-Shalom (Peace Rd.), and is still a good general demarcation between Palestinian and Jewish areas of Jerusalem. **East Jerusalem** is the name normally given to the Palestinian parts of Jerusalem, and sometimes includes the Old City. East Jerusalem stretches in the areas immediately to the north and east of the Old City. **Suleiman Street,** in front of **Damascus Gate,** and **Salah ad-Din Street,** which runs out from Herod's Gate, are the main roads in central East Jerusalem. The latter is a haven for offices and stores. Two Arab bus stations serve the area, the larger of which is located on Suleiman St. between Nablus Rd. (Derekh Shekhem) and Salah ad-Din St. The other station, located on Nablus Rd., serves routes northward. **Ha-Nevi'im Street** (Musrada in Arabic), which converges with Nablus Rd. at Damascus Gate, has many dry goods stores and hostels. Central East Jerusalem is the financial and cultural hub for the Arab community.

---

Tensions sometimes make East Jerusalem and parts of the Old City unfriendly to Israelis and Jewish foreigners. When you visit, make your tourist status as pronounced as possible. *Kippot* are a particularly bad idea in the Arab parts of town.

---

# ■ Transportation

## GETTING AROUND TOWN

Most distances in Jerusalem make for reasonable, pleasant walks, as long as you can take the heat and the hills. You can reach any section of the city by bus from the **central bus station** on Jaffa Rd. (tel. 530 45 55), west of city center (NIS3.30; a NIS33 *kartisiya* buys 11 rides for adults, 20 for people under 18). For more information, see Getting Around (p. 266). Egged buses stop along the road outside the station entrance, and in front of **Binyanei Ha-Umma Convention Center** (across the street from the station through the underpass). Arab buses run every day; Egged service stops at about 4:30pm on Fridays, resuming after sunset on Saturday.

**#1** (from Binyanei Ha'Umma): To Mea She'arim, Jaffa Gate, Western Wall.
**#4A:** To Emek Refa'im, Liberty Bell Park, Ramat Eshkol, Mt. Scopus.
**#5, 6, 8, 13, 18, 20, 21:** To West Jerusalem center; get off at the intersection of Jaffa Rd. and King George St. #5, 8, and 21 go to the train station.
**#9:** To the Knesset and the Israel Museum, Mt. Scopus, West Jerusalem center, and Hebrew University at Givat Ram.
**#13, 20, 23:** Down Jaffa Rd., to Jaffa Gate by the Old City.
**#27:** To West Jerusalem center, Damascus Gate, and East Jerusalem.
**#99, the Jerusalem Circular Line:** From Jaffa Gate or central bus station, passes 34 major tourist sights. In summer, Sun.-Thurs. (every hr. 10am-4pm except 3pm; Fri. every hr. 10am-1pm. Runs less frequently in winter. One loop NIS15. For information, call 624 81 44 or 77 83, or 530 48 68. With a knack of figuring out bus routes, you can visit the sights quicker and more cheaply on the regular lines.

All Egged routes are marked on the detailed English bus route map; this map is also a good street map of Jerusalem (but not the Old City). Get it free from the Egged Public Relations office in the Beit Egged office building, 208 Jaffa Rd. #307 (open Sun.-Thurs. 7:30am-noon and 1-3:30pm).

If you want a taxi, check out **Jerusalem Taxi,** 4 Ha-Histadrut St. (tel. 625 52 33), near the junction of King George and Ben-Yehuda St. (open Thurs.-Sun. 6am-11:30pm, Fri. 6am-1hr. before *Shabbat,* Sat. sunset-11:30pm); and **Taxi Israel,** 11 Ha-Histadrut (tel. 562 52 33-36).

## GETTING OUT OF TOWN

### By Train

Trains depart from Remez Sq. (tel. 673 37 64), southwest of the Old City, just south of Liberty Bell park. To get to the station from downtown, take bus #21 or 48. Trains to Tel Aviv (2:55pm, 2hr., NIS13, students NIS10) and Haifa (2:55pm, 3hr., NIS26, students NIS20) are slower than buses but a bit cheaper and more scenic.

### By Bus

**Egged Central Bus Station** has information, posted destinations and fares, and ticket windows, but they don't speak much English. Flash your ISIC for a 10% discount, and keep your passport handy for stickler drivers to inspect. Buses run to:

**Tel Aviv Central Station,** #405 direct (every 5-20min., Sun.-Thurs. 5:50am-midnight, Fri. 5:50am-5pm, Sat. sundown-midnight; NIS14, students NIS12.50); Tel Aviv Arlozorov terminal, #480 direct (every 15-20min., 6am-10pm).
**Haifa,** #940 direct (Sun.-Thurs. roughly every 30min. 6:30am-7:15pm, Fri. 7:30am-3½hrs. before sundown, Sat. sundown-10:35pm; NIS28.50, students NIS25.50).
**Ben-Gurion Airport,** #945 or 947 (Sun.-Thurs. every 15-40min. 6am-8:30pm, Fri. 7:30am-4pm, Sat. sundown-11pm; NIS15.50, students NIS14).

**Eilat,** #444 (Sun.-Thurs. every 2-3hrs., 7am-5pm and 12:30am; Fri. every 2-2½hrs., 7am-3:30pm, less frequently in winter; NIS44, students NIS40; round-trip NIS79.20, book in advance).
**Be'er Sheva,** #446 direct (every 30-60min. 6am-8:30pm, Fri. 6am-4:30pm, Sat. sundown-10:30pm) or #470 (irregular—check schedule; 6:20am-6:15pm, Fri. 10am-3:15pm); both buses NIS24, students NIS21.

Two bus stations serve the **West Bank. Suleiman St. Station,** in East Jerusalem between Herod's and Damascus Gates, serves routes south while **Nablus Rd. Station** serves points north. See West Bank: **Getting Around** (p. 444) for routes and prices and **West Bank: Coming and Going** (p. 442) for information on travel to the West Bank from Israel.

**By Taxi**

Jerusalem is served by two main **Intercity Sherut Taxi** companies. **Ha Bira** (tel. 628 99 99), at the corner of Ha-Ravkook St. and Jaffa Rd. (near Zion Sq.) goes to Tel Aviv. It boasts a central location, fixed rates, and service on *Shabbat* while the rest of the city slumbers. (Daily 6am-11pm. NIS14, students NIS12. *Shabbat* NIS20.) *Sherut* taxis also leave from the Central Bus Station to points through Israel. Split four ways, they can be as cheap as buses. **Nesher,** 21 King George St. (tel. 625 72 27 or 623 12 31), can hook you up with door-to-door service to the airport (NIS29), but you must reserve 1 day ahead (available 24hr.).

# ■ Practical Information

**Municipal Tourist Information Office (MTIO):** 17 Jaffa Rd. at Tzahal Sq. (tel. 625 88 44; open Sun.-Thurs. 9am-3:30pm, Fri. 9am-noon) and inside Jaffa Gate in the Old City (tel. 628 04 57 or 03 82; open Sun.-Thurs. 8:30am-5:45pm, Fri. 8:30am-1:45pm). Both offices offer pamphlets, maps, and minimal advice. Free Sat. **walking tours** from Tzahal Sq. (10am).
**Government Tourist Information Office Golden Screen Computer:** 24 King George St., at the corner of Schatz St., outside the old Knesset building. Provides a wealth of info and data, but stick with the MTIO for human contact. Open 24hr.
**Tours:** Every Saturday at 10am the municipality sponsors a free **Shabbat Walking Tour** in Hebrew and English (info tel. 625 88 44). Meet at 32 Jaffa Rd. at the entrance to the Russian Compound, near Zion Sq. *This Week in Jerusalem* lists itineraries (also posted at the MTIO office at 17 Jaffa Rd.). **Zion Walking Tours** (tel. 628 78 66 or 671 35 43) offers 3-hr. tours of the Old City. Buy tickets inside Jaffa Gate, across from the Citadel (US$10, students US$9). Zion's 3½-hr. tour includes rooftops and the Western Wall tunnel (US$14, students US$13). Other routes (Mt. of Olives, the Southern Wall excavations) are US$15-18, students US$14-17. **Archaeological Seminars Ltd.** (tel. 627 35 15) offers guided tunnel and ramparts walks as well as tours of the Jewish Quarter, the City of David, Mt. Zion, and other areas. 3-hr. tour at 9:30am is US$15. 2-hr. tour at 2pm is US$12. Reserve in advance. Meet at 34 Ḥabad St. above the Cardo 15min. beforehand. Guided walking tours are available through the **King George, Ben Yehuda,** and other hostels in the area for NIS15 or US$5. **Society for the Protection of Nature in Israel (SPNI),** 13 Helena Ha-Malka St. (tel. 625 76 82), organizes tours throughout Israel and the Sinai. Tours range from 1-day explorations of Jerusalem (US$44) to 7-day Grand Sinai tours (US$380). In July and Aug. they give 3-hr. Jerusalem tours along unusual routes (NIS25-37). Some *Shabbat* tours are free. Reserve in advance. Open Sun.-Tues. 9am-3:45pm, Wed. 9am-4:45pm, Thurs. 9am-5:45pm, Fri. 9am-12:30pm.
**Budget Travel: Mazada Tours,** 9 Koresh St., corner of Shlomo Ha-Melekh (tel. 623 57 77), runs guided trips to Jordan (2-4 days, US$234-400) and Egypt (3-8 days, US$179-333), and transportation service to Amman and Cairo. Open Sun.-Thurs. 9am-7pm, Fri. 8am-2pm. **Budget Travel Consultants,** 3 Ben Sira St., just off Hillel St. (tel. 623 39 90) offers 1-4 day trips to Jordan (US$149-459) and 4-10 day jaunts to Egypt (US$150-600). Open Sun.-Thurs. 9am-6pm, Fri. 9am-1pm. **Neot Ha-Kikar,** 5 Shlomzion Ha-Malka St. (tel. 623 62 62), has similar trips and prices, and

specializes in Sinai tours (US$55 for 1 day). Open Sun.-Thurs. 9am-6pm, Fri. 9am-12:30pm. **ISSTA,** 31 Ha-Nevi'im St. (tel. 625 27 99). ISIC costs NIS30; bring proof of student status and a photo. Student discounts on flights to Europe and Cairo, car rentals, and Eurail Passes. Lines can be long. Not always the best deal in town. Open Sun.-Tues. and Thurs. 9am-6pm, Wed. and Fri. 9am-1pm. Also on Mt. Scopus Hebrew U. campus in the Goldsmith Building (tel. 582 61 16) and at Givat Ram campus (tel. 651 87 80). Both open Sun.-Thurs. 8:30am-4pm. Call toll free for flight info and ticketing (tel. (177) 022 66 65).

**Consulates:** You must go to the East Jerusalem branch of the **U.S.** consulate, 27 Nablus Rd., East Jerusalem (tel. 628 24 52). Open Mon.-Fri. 8am-noon; answers phone calls 2-4pm. Closes for Israeli and U.S. holidays. Visas, passports. **U.K.,** 19 Nashashibi St., East Jerusalem (tel. 582 82 81), near Sheikh Jarrah. Visas, passports. Open Mon.-Fri. 8am-noon, Wed. also 1-3pm. Most other countries have consulates in Tel Aviv only.

**Currency Exchange: Changepoint,** 33 Jaffa Rd. (tel. 625 24 55) and 2 Ben Yehuda, generally has better rates than banks and charges no commission. Zion Sq. has a couple money-changing options: Savvy travelers frequent a popular kiosk while by-the-book law-abiders go to **Bank Ha-Poalim** (tel. 620 70 70), open Sun., Tues., and Thurs. 8:30am-12:30pm and 4-6pm, Mon. and Wed. 8:30am-12:30pm, Fri. 8:30am-noon. **Bank Leumi,** 21 Jaffa Rd. (tel. 629 16 11), next to the main post office, is open Sun.-Thurs. 8:30am-1:30pm, Fri. 8:30am-noon. They also have a **Foreign Resident and Tourist Center** on 16 King George St. (tel. 620 76 76), with the same hours.

**American Express:** 40 Jaffa Rd. (tel. 623 17 10; fax 623 15 20). Full service office with traveler's check cashing, purchasing, and replacement for cardholders. Mail held, but not packages. If you lose your traveler's checks, call toll-free (177) 440 86 94, 24hr. Open Sun.-Thurs. 9am-5pm, Fri. 9am-1pm.

**Telephones: Solan Communications,** 2 Luntz St. (tel. 625 89 08; fax 625 88 79), off Ben-Yehuda St., on the *midraḥov*. Fax and telegram services, private booths for reduced-price local and international calls (cheaper than with telecard), and cellular phone rentals. **Information:** Tel. 144.

**Flight information:** For arrivals and departures in English, call (03) 973 1122. **El Al** has advance check-in in Jerusalem: bags for morning flights can be checked in and inspected the night before at Center 1, 49 Yirmeyahu St., on the corner of Jaffa Rd. near the central bus station (tel. 624 67 25 or 26). Buses to **Ben-Gurion Airport** leave from the central bus station; for early morning flights you may have to pay extra for *sherut* (see Intercity Sherut Taxis, below).

**Car Rental: Superdrive,** 10 King David St. (tel. 625 08 43), will rent to drivers 18 and older. US$65 per day, US$60 for two days. Jul.-Aug. US$75 per day, US$70 for two days. Complete insurance coverage. Credit card required. Open Sun.-Thurs. 8am-5 or 6pm, Fri. 8am-1:30pm. **Thrifty,** 8 King David St. (tel. 625 08 33); open Sun.-Thurs. 8am-6pm, Fri. 8am-2pm. Minimum age 21. High season US$69 per day. Low season US$57 per day.

**English Bookstores: Sefer va-Sefel,** 2 Ya'avetz St. (tel. 624 82 37), near the corner of 49 Jaffa Rd.; 3rd door on the right and up the stairs. By far, Jerusalem's best place for books and browsing. Huge inventory. Read your purchase in the pleasant balcony café. Open Sun.-Thurs. 8am-8pm, Fri. 8am-2:30pm, Sat. sunset-11:30pm. **Yalkut Books—New and Used,** 8 Aliash St. (tel. 625 70 58), in Kikkar Rejwan, upstairs from the Lev Yerushalayim Hotel. Good selection of fiction paperbacks. Open Sun.-Thurs. 8am-7pm, Fri. 8am-1:30pm. **Steimatzky,** 7 Ben-Yehuda St. (tel. 625 54 87), on the *midraḥov;* other locations as well. Great for maps, magazines, travel and gift books. Open Sun.-Thurs. 8:30am-9pm, Fri. 8:30am-2pm, Sat. sunset-11pm. **Gur Arieh Books,** 8 Yoel Solomon St. (tel. 625 74 86). Decent selection. Open Sun.-Thurs. 9am-midnight, Fri. 9am-3pm, Sat. sunset-midnight. The **SPNI Bookstore** (see **Tours,** p. 286) often has the lowest prices on guidebooks and maps.

**Christian Information Center:** P.O. Box 14308 (tel. 627 26 92; fax 628 64 17), inside Jaffa Gate and to the right, just past the Citadel. Genuinely friendly staff sells books and provides maps and detailed lists of Christian services, hospices, and sites in Jerusalem. Open Mon.-Sat. 8:30am-1pm.

ISRAEL

**Franciscan Pilgrims Office:** P.O. Box 186 (tel. 627 26 97), same building as the Christian Information Center. Makes reservations for mass at all Franciscan sanctuaries. Talk to the priest here about going to Christmas midnight mass in Bethlehem. Want to prove you've been to the Holy Land? Pilgrimage certificates available (US$3). Open Mon.-Fri. 9am-noon and 3:30-5:30pm, Sat. 9am-noon.

**Jewish Student Information Center:** 5 Beit El, Jewish Quarter (tel. 628 26 34, after-hours (050) 344 341; fax 288 338), across from the Ḥurva Arch. The roving info center is known as Jeff Seidel. If he doesn't find you first, he's often at Mt. Scopus, the Wall, or Ben Yehuda. Offers *Shabbat* hospitality, Jewish classes, and Old City tours. Primarily geared for those just beginning to explore their Jewish roots. Free *Shabbat* meals with religious families (ask Jeff when to meet at the Wall). While some travelers have wonderful experiences here, others find the JSIC to proselytize. Open Sun.-Thurs. 9am-7pm, Fri. 9am-*Shabbat.*

**Lesbian Organization:** KLAF (tel. 625 12 71) has info on community activities.

**Ticket Agencies: Bimot,** 8 Shammai St. (tel. 624 08 96), and **Kla'im,** 12 Shammai St. (tel. 625 68 69), often have discount tickets for students and tourists for concerts, shows, and sporting events throughout Israel. Both open Sun.-Thurs. 9am-7pm, Fri. 9am-1pm. **Ben Na'im,** 38 Jaffa Rd. (tel. 625 40 08) is primarily for sporting events. Open Sun.-Thurs. 8:30am-2pm and 3-7pm, Fri. 8:30am-1pm.

**Laundry: Tzipor Ha-Nefesh,** 10 Rivlin St. (tel. 624 98 90). Awesome café/laundromat/e-mail center. Do your wash (5kg wash and dry NIS14) and eat mouth-watering cuisine. Open Sun.-Thurs. 8am-1pm., Fri. 8am-5pm., Sat. after *Shabbat*-1am. **Baka Washmatic,** 35 Emek Refa'im St. (tel. 563 18 78). Take bus #4, 14, 18, or 24, get off at Emek Refa'im post office, cross the street, and continue for ½ block. Open Sun.-Thurs. 8am-7pm, Fri. 8am-2pm. 10kg wash, dry, and fold NIS41; 7kg NIS37. 20% *Let's Go* discount. **Ha-Merkaz Laundry,** 11 Kakal St. (tel. 566 42 46), just off Usishkin St. Open Sun.-Thurs. 8am-1pm and 3-7pm, Fri. 8am-1pm. 5kg wash and dry NIS30. **Laundry Place,** 12 Shammai St. (tel. 25 77 14). Do your own laundry (NIS8 for 7kg; dry NIS13 per 10min.) while watching MTV. Drinks and video games available. Detergent NIS3. Open Sun.-Thurs. 8am-midnight. Fri. 8am-5pm.

**Swimming Pools: Jerusalem Swimming Pool,** Emek Refa'im St. (tel. 563 20 92), open daily 7am-7pm (NIS30, students NIS25). Bus #4 or 18. Get *Shabbat* tickets in advance. **Beit Zayit** (tel. 534 67 09), take bus #151 (10 per day) from central station to the last stop. NIS22, children NIS17; Fri. and Sat. NIS27. Open daily 9am-7pm and some evenings.

**Camping Supplies:** The most extensive stock of camping gear is at **Orcha Camping,** 12 Yoel Solomon (tel. 624 06 55). Affiliated with SPNI. Open Sun.-Thurs. 8:30am-7pm, Fri. 8:30am-3pm. To be like the cool Israelis, buy a backpack from **Steve's Packs** at two locations—in the *kenyon* (tel. 679 34 34),or on the *midraḥov,* 11 Ben Hillel (tel. 534 83 02). **Jerusalem Camping,** 14 Ben Hillel, off the *midraḥov* (tel. 625 11 40), has a decent selection. Open Sun.-Thurs. 8:30am-8:30pm, Fri. 8:30am-3:30pm, Sat. after *shabbat*-midnight.

**Film Developing: Photo Yeḥezkel,** 47 Jaffa Rd. (tel. 625 55 90), in alley opposite Lotto booth. NIS30 for 36 prints. 1 free enlargement per roll. 1-hr. processing available. Open Sun.-Thurs. 8am-7pm, Fri. 9am-2pm. **Focus,** 6 King George St. (tel. 23 34 40). 36 prints for NIS40.70 in 1hr. Great quality. 2-hr. black and white processing. On-site developing. Open Sun.-Thurs. 9am-7:30pm, Fri. 9am-2:30pm.

**Help Lines: Rape Crisis Center** (tel. 625 55 58). Open 24hr., will accompany you to the police and explain procedures. **Mental Health Hotline** (tel. 561 03 03), also called **Eran,** assists tourists. Open 8am-11pm. **Alcoholics Anonymous** (tel. 563 05 24 or 50 62). **Na'an** offers advice to mentally disturbed teens (tel. (177) 022-3011). Open Sun.-Thurs 5-8pm.

**Services for the Disabled: Yad Sarah Organization,** 43 Ha-Nevi'im St. (tel. 624 42 42). Free loans of medical equipment. Look for a big blue ex-train. They can meet you at the airport. Open Sun.-Thurs. 9am-7pm, Fri. 9am-noon.

**Pharmacy: Superpharm,** 5 Burla St. (tel. 678 41 39 or 679 59 33), near Hebrew Univ. Givat Ram campus; bus #17. Open Sun.-Thurs. 8:30am-midnight, Fri. 8:30am-3pm, Sat. 9pm-midnight. Also at 3 Ha-Histadrut (tel. 624 62 44 or 45), between Ben-Yehuda and King George St. Open Sun.-Thurs. 8:30am-11pm, Fri. 8:30am-3pm, Sat. sundown-11pm. **Alba Pharmacy,** 7 Ben-Yehuda St. (tel. 625 77 85). Open Sun.-

---

Dorm beds, roof mats, private rooms and studio apts. are available. Reasonable prices.

## Special offer to LET'S GO readers :

If you arrive from the airport, your bus fare to the hostel will be fully refunded !

If you arrive from another city, you get a 10 NIS. discount !

### Directions

Take bus No. 46 from floor 1 in Tel-Aviv central bus station and get off after the clock tower.

8 Olei Tzion St. Jaffa - Tel-Aviv

Tel. 03 - 6822316, 6822370 Fax: 972-3-6822316

E.mail: ojhostel @ shani.net

Thurs. 8am-7pm, Fri. 8am-2pm. There are no 24-hr. pharmacies. Two are on duty nightly and on *Shabbat* on a rotating schedule. Schedules and phone numbers available on any pharmacy door and in newspapers.

**Medical Emergency:** Tel. 101. **Magen David Adom** (first aid; tel. 652 31 33), next to the central bus station. Open 24hr. Will see any medical problem (NIS160); treatment may cost more. Hospital emergency rooms are much more expensive— it's better to have the hospital recommend a doctor to see during office hours. Newspapers list hospitals on duty for emergencies. **Blue Cross-Blue Shield** members may be eligible for medical coverage at Hadassah Ein Kerem and Mt. Scopus hospitals (call tel. 677 60 29 for information).

**Police:** Tel. 100 for emergencies. Located in the Russian Compound (tel. 539 11 11), off Jaffa Rd. in West Jerusalem. Has a tourist desk (tel. 539 12 54 or 63). There is also an Old City branch, inside Jaffa Gate to your right (tel. 622 62 22).

**Central Post Office:** 23 Jaffa Rd. (tel. 629 08 98). Open Sun.-Thurs. 7am-7pm, Fri. 7am-noon. **Poste restante, Western Union, telegram,** and **fax** services available. For telegrams, you can also dial 171 (24hr.). Open Sun.-Thurs. 7am-7pm, Fri. 7am-noon. **Branch post offices** exist throughout the city.

**Telephone code:** 02.

## MAPS AND BOOKS

A good **map** is essential for navigating the streets and alleyways in Jerusalem. The Old City and Jaffa Rd. tourist offices give out free ones, but are often out of stock. The pamphlet-guide *This Week in Jerusalem* (free in hotels and MTIOs) has a good map. The best map of the city is **Carta's Map** (NIS26), sold at Steimatzky's and other fine stores. The Christian Information Center inside Jaffa Gate sells old city maps for a mere NIS3, as well as several maps of biblical interest.

Jerusalem may be the most written-about city in the world. A comprehensive **book** can greatly enrich your visit. *Marty's Walking Tours of Biblical Jerusalem* (NIS15 used), by Marty Isaacs, provides a humorous look at the City of Gold. It's out of print, but used bookstores may have it. Nitza Rosovsky's *Jerusalemwalks,* also out of print but easy to find in used bookstores (NIS35), is by far the most thoughtful guide to the city's lesser known avenues and well worth the price. *Quartertour Walking Tour of the Jewish Quarter* (NIS5) is cheap, interesting, and comprehensive. *Guide to the Holy Land* (US\$11 at the Christian Information Center), written by a Franciscan monk, describes sites of Catholic significance in exhaustive detail. Roadrunners should pick up *Carta's Jogger's Guide to Jerusalem* (NIS27), with detailed routes through historic areas and sights. *The Walls of Jerusalem* (NIS35), by Roni Ellenblum and Amnon Ramon, will make your walk along the Old City ramparts a degree-worthy learning experience. **Hebrew Union College,** 13 King David St. (tel. 620 33 33), has an air-conditioned library with an extensive collection on Jerusalem lore (open Sun.-Thurs. 8:30am-5pm).

---

### Tour of Duty

One of the most competitive professions in Israel is the tour guide. All tour guides must complete a two-year course and receive a government license. Each year, over 500 (and some years as many as 1000) applicants hope to get into tour guide school, but the ruthless admissions committee takes only a lucky 45. After two years of intense training in religion, archaeology, geology, botany, zoology, folklore, and history, about half of the admitted class receives the coveted license. To even be considered for tour guide school, applicants must speak at least two foreign languages fluently, but many candidates speak three or four. Once licensed, guides must complete annual recertification courses, where they are kept up to date on new sights and archaeological discoveries. Israel's licensed tour guides are respected throughout the country, and regarded as walking encyclopedias.

# ■ Accommodations

## WEST JERUSALEM

Accommodations in West Jerusalem are generally roomier, cleaner, safer, comfier, and more conveniently located than their old city counterparts. They are correspondingly more expensive, and what they boast by way of amenities they lack in rustic charm. Hostels here are better for club-goers; many have no curfew, and some are located directly above the action. You may not have to pay the 17%VAT if you pay in your home currency. Accommodations in private houses are a second choice. Locals may approach you at the bus station, but be aware that their places may not be licensed and therefore not subject to government inspection. Women should be especially cautious, even if approached by a female.

**Jerusalem Inn Youth Hostel,** 6 Ha-Histadrut St. (tel. 625 12 94; fax 625 12 97). From Zion Sq., Ben-Yehuda St. is intersected by Ha-Histadrut St. 1 block before King George St. Take bus #14, 17, 31, or 32 from the central station. Friendly, clean place in the middle of town. A lounge/reception area outfitted with cable TV is a relaxing spot for a drink (NIS2-4). Mostly young, English-speaking guests. Strict no visitors policy and locked front door. Communal refrigerator and small, shared baths. Crowded, clean rooms have ceiling fans and 24-hr. heating in winter. No smoking. Check-in before 11:30pm. Check-out 10:30am. Midnight curfew, but keys given for NIS20 deposit. Dorm beds US$12. Singles US$32-36, doubles US$40-48, triples US$51-57. Significantly cheaper in winter.

**Hotel Noga,** 4 Bezalel St. (tel. 625 45 90 until 1pm, 566 18 88 after; ask for Mr. or Mrs. Kristal). Near corner of Shmuel Ha-Nagid St. Like having a private apartment. Managers leave at night and give you a key to the front door. 10 bright, airy rooms on 3 floors, each with a kitchen (free tea and coffee). 2 spotless balconies overlook the Bezalel Art Institute. Free luggage storage; heated in winter. Mr. Kristal loans tennis rackets and balls for free and might be coaxed into giving free lessons. Parking in back. Min. 2-night stay, special price for extended stays. Singles US$28, doubles US$35, triples US$45, quads US$55. The porch room (bathroom attached) is US$12 per night. Reserve in advance.

**Ben Yehuda Hostel,** 23 Ben Yehuda St. (tel. 624 80 21 or 625 71 25; fax 625 30 32). Cable TV lounge with photos of smiling ex-hostelers. Nestled quietly up on the 3rd floor. Drinks NIS2-4. Lockers NIS5. Laundry NIS20, wash and dry. 24-hr. check-in. Check-out 10am. No lock-out. No curfew. Dorm beds (6-8 per spacious room) NIS30 or US$8. Doubles NIS109 or US$32. Triples NIS132 or US$39. Quads NIS163 or US$48. Sat. checkout can be extended until after *Shabbat* for small fee.

**Jerusalem Inn Guest House,** 7 Horkanos St., just off Heleni Ha-Malka (tel. 625 27 57). Bus #6, 18, or 21 from the central bus station. Undeniably beautiful accommodations with myriad amenities—cable TV, phones, ceiling fans, balconies, and full bath in every room. Quiet, classy atmosphere. Singles US$40, doubles US$54-68, triples US$66-69, 6-person rooms US$133. Cheaper in off-season. Reception 8am-midnight. Checkout 10:30am. No curfew. Reservations by credit card.

**Beit Shmuel Guest House (HI),** 6 Shammai St. (tel. 620 34 73 until 5pm), near the King David Hotel. Part of the Beit Shmuel Center for Progressive Judaism complex; enter through the Safdie-designed Hebrew Union College. Clean, safe, remarkably hotel-like. Lounges, courtyard, gardens, coffee shop, Fri. night concerts (guests receive 10% discount), all on the premises. Wheelchair accessible. Elevator, A/C, heat in winter. 24-hr. reception. Check-in 3-11pm. Check-out 10am. No curfew. Dorm beds (6 per room) US$19.50. Singles US$38.50. Doubles US$53. (Non-members US$29, US$70, and US$76.) Breakfast included.Prices drop during low season (Oct.-April).

**Davidka Hostel (HI),** 67 Ha-Nevi'im St. (tel. 638 45 55). Take bus #27, 35, 36, or 39 from central bus station. New, safe, clean, A/C rooms, all with private baths, in huge 250-bed complex. No curfew or lockout. Free lockers and safe. 24-hr. reception. Checkout 10am. Cafeteria serves munchies from 8am-midnight. Dorm beds US$18. Singles US$37, doubles US$50. Nonmembers add US$1.50 per person.

NIS20 surcharge for checkout after *Shabbat*. Breakfast included. Reservations recommended. Visa, MC.

**Beit Bernstein Youth Hostel (HI),** 1 Keren Ha-Yesod St. (tel. 625 82 86), at the corner of Agron St., tucked behind a synagogue. Take bus #7, 8, 9, 14, 31, or 32 from the central bus station. Clean, fan-cooled rooms, a sparse TV lounge, and a great garden in the back await those who can keep the midnight curfew. Reception open 9am-noon and 2pm-midnight. Check-in 2pm. Check-out 9am. Dorm beds (single-sex floors, 4-7 per room, heated in winter) US$14. Breakfast included. Often filled with teen tour groups during the summer.

**Capital Hostel,** 1 Yoel Solomon St. (tel. 622 14 18). Basic, no-frills beds. Don't plan on sleeping before 3 or 4am—this place is right above the Underground Disco. The reception desk sells earplugs. Hostel guests get a 20-min. all-you-can-chug free beer deal at the Underground. Laundry NIS16. Luggage storage NIS1 per hr. Free safe for valuables. Check-out 10am. No curfew. Dorm beds NIS25. Private rooms NIS80. Reservations recommended in summer.

## OLD CITY

Many of Jerusalem's cheapest hostels—from quiet sanctuaries to hang-from-the-rafters hangouts—are located in the Old City. You get great views from rooftops and balconies, proximity to major sights, and a free wake-up call provided by *muezzins*. Conditions vary within a given hostel; a fellow traveler may be sleeping on a piece of foam while you land a Sealy Posturpedic. Bargain if you sense you're getting shafted or if business seems slow. Lodgings cluster near Jaffa and Damascus Gates. Most have "flexible curfews" (managers will let you in late if you inform them ahead of time and if the night guard stays awake). Reservations are recommended.

Don't leave luggage unattended in hotel rooms if you can avoid it. All hostels have safes for your valuables. In most places, you can pay in either U.S. dollars or shekels.

> Be extremely cautious in the empty streets of the Old City after dark. Those staying in the Muslim Quarter should avoid walking alone and should make their tourist status pronounced. Only the busiest streets in the Old City are lit at night, so you should learn your way back to your hostel during the day.

### Near Jaffa Gate

Walk down Jaffa Rd. or Agron St. to the end, or take bus #13, 19, 20, 21, 23, 30, or 99.

**Citadel Youth Hostel,** 20 St. Mark's Rd. (tel. 627 43 75). Take the first alleyway on the right off David St. and go up the stairs that curve left; the hostel is on your right. Super tidy rooms have high, stone walls and vaulted ceilings. Rooftop solarium has beds and a classic view, but gets hot on breezeless days. Atrium sitting area, TV room, and common kitchen. 24-hr. check-in. Check-out 11am. Flexible midnight curfew. Eye-popping low prices: Dorm beds NIS20; students NIS15. Singles NIS50, doubles NIS60. Maximum stay 2 weeks.

**Lutheran Youth Hostel,** 7 St. Mark's Rd. (tel. 628 21 20), after the Citadel Hostel on your right. Luxuriously calm, with a courtyard, lush gardens, and a kitchen and dining hall worthy of the Last Supper. Women's dungeon-like dorm room has 40 beds and medieval appeal. Men's room (above ground) has 20 beds (NIS23). Check-out 10am. Lockout 9am-noon. 10:30pm curfew. Free lockers. Singles NIS118, doubles NIS200. Prices may fluctuate with the season. Check-in noon.

**Lark Hotel,** 4 Latin Patriarchate Rd. (tel. 628 36 20), the first left from Jaffa Gate. Spotless rooms with showers. Small 2nd-floor balcony and sitting space overlooks quiet street. 1st-floor Armenian restaurant run by same friendly people. Open 6:30am-11pm, but keys available. Check-out anytime. Singles, doubles, and triples about US$22 per person; prices very flexible. Continental breakfast included.

**Jaffa Gate Youth Hostel,** off the Jaffa Gate square area, across from the entrance to the Tower of David; look for the sign (tel. 627 64 02). Long dorm rooms walls are painted to look like stone, but to ill effect. Homey TV lounge, common kitchen and outdoor eating area. Young guests have schlepped their packs all over the world

ISRAEL

and have the smell to prove it. Check-out noon. Curfew midnight. Dorm beds NIS25. Private rooms with bath NIS125-150.

**New Swedish Hostel,** 29 David St. (tel. 589 41 24 or 627 78 55), straight into the *souq.* Hopping with travelers, but conditions not stereotypically Scandinavian, aside from the spotless modern bathrooms and showers, and occasional flying fish. Kitchen, TV lounge, and free tea and coffee. Check-in until 3am. Check-out 11am. Curfew 3am. Dorm beds NIS13. Private rooms NIS 40-45. Lockers NIS3 for as long as you stay. Co-ed and single-sex accommodations.

**Petra Hostel** (tel. 628 23 56), the first hostel on your left on David St. just before you enter the *souq.* Petra's ad campaign will find you. Adequate, Spartan accommodations host grungy travelers. Hot water available at selected times. 24-hr. check-in. Check-out 11am. No curfew; knock after midnight. Loft mattress NIS12, loft beds NIS15. Dorm beds NIS20. Singles NIS60, doubles NIS60-80.

## Near Damascus Gate

Reach Damascus Gate by walking to the end of Ha-Nevi'im St. or by taking a left from Jaffa St. onto Ha-Tzanḥanim St. from the city center. Buses #1, 13, 23, and 37 go here. Hostels here are cheaper and livelier, but the area is less safe after dark.

**Armenian Hospice,** 36 Via Dolorosa (tel. 626 08 80). Lavish wood furnishings, gleaming tile floors, and possibly the thickest mattresses in town. Gold linens make the place feel like a palace. New TVs and phones in every room. Sparkling bathrooms have hair dryers. 24-hr. reception. No curfew or lockout. Check-out noon. Central heating in winter. Dorm beds US$10. Singles US$40, doubles US$50, triples US$66. The old section is not as palatial or expensive: clean, sunny, building has dorm beds (US$6) and private rooms (US$25). Visa, MC.

**Austrian Hospice,** 37 Via Dolorosa, P.O. Box 19600 (tel. 627 46 36), just on the corner of Al Wad Rd. Embassy-like building has lush grounds and spotless tiled rooms. Wheelchair accessible. German library, private chapel, and glorious roof view. Dark, tightly packed basement dorms. *Wiener Kaffeehaus* inside (open daily 9am-10pm) serves Austrian cakes (NIS7) and drinks (NIS4-7). Check-in 10pm. Check-out 10am. Strict 10pm curfew. Dorm beds US$10. Singles US$42, doubles US$64, triples US$90. Breakfast included. 3-course meals US$9 for guests. Reservations recommended.

**El Hashimi Hotel and Hostel,** 73 Khan az-Zeit (tel. 628 44 10), a right turn from Damascus Gate. Brand new, sunny 3-story hostel has glowing white walls and floors, and incredible views of the Dome of the Rock. Squeaky clean bathrooms, sturdy beds. Kitchen facilities, with free tea and coffee, and TV room. Laundry NIS20 per load. Heat in winter. 24-hr. reception. Check-out 10:30am. Curfew 3am. Roof beds NIS10. Dorm beds NIS15. Singles NIS80, doubles NIS90. Accepts and exchanges traveler's checks.

**Ecce Homo Convent,** Eastern Via Dolorosa, P.O. Box 19056 (tel. 627 72 92). Turn left onto Via Dolorosa from Al Wad Rd. Look for the "Notre Dame de Sion" sign down the road on a door on the left. The sisters provide blissful refuge and a transcendental view of Jerusalem. Kitchen and study areas. Curfew 11pm. Check-out 10am. Reception open daily 6:30am-11pm. Dorm beds (women only) US$8. Dorms in coed guest house (10-12 beds per room) US$16. Singles US$31. Breakfast included. Lunch or dinner US$10.

**Tabasco Hostel,** 8 Akabat Tekreh (tel. 628 34 61), just off Khan az-Zeit Rd. A huge, clean, dirt cheap hostel with rows of beds. Dorm beds NIS14, with ISIC NIS12. Roof mattress NIS6. Private rooms NIS40-50. Hot showers. Soon to be completed outdoor café will overlook the 9th station of Via Dolorosa. No lockout or curfew. Checkout noon. Check-in 24hr. Management runs cheap daytrips to Masada, Jericho, refugee camps, and Gaza.

**Al-Arab,** Khan az-Zeit (tel. 628 35 37), just before El Hashimi. Not as renovated as some of its neighbors. Kitchen, TV, free tea and coffee, free use of safe; heated in winter. Free accommodation for a week if you can beat manager Abu Hasan at ping pong (50 public push-ups if you lose). Tiny bathrooms. Kitchen and dining area. 24-hr. check-in. Check-out 10am. Curfew 1:30am. Roof beds NIS10. Dorm beds

(10-13 per room) NIS15. Reservations recommended in summer and during Christmas. Manager leads trips to West Bank Refugee camps and Gaza.

**Al-Ahram Hostel,** 64 Al Wad Rd. (tel. 628 09 26). Enter Damascus Gate and bear left onto Al Wad at the fork. Opposite 3rd station of Via Dolorosa, and some parts of the building seem to have been around since His time. Midnight curfew, but keys may be procured. Check-out 10am. Free safe. Roof beds NIS10. Dorm beds (4-7 per room, co-ed and single sex) NIS15. Doubles with shower NIS60. Triples NIS70-90. Higher prices in winter. Free luggage storage.

**Black Horse Hostel,** 28 Aqabat Darwish St. (tel. 628 03 28), off Via Dolorosa. Crowded, cavernous hostel. Bedouin tent-style sitting room/bar. Heated in winter. Happy hour 8-9:30pm. Phone and fax service, kitchen, TV, and video. Check-in 7:30am-1:30am. Check-out 11am. Curfew 1:30am. No lockout. The alley can be dark and isolated at night. Dorm beds NIS15, with ISIC NIS13. Singles/doubles NIS50-70. Breakfast NIS12; courtyard barbecues NIS15 on Sat. nights.

### Jewish Quarter

**Jewish Quarter Youth Hostel (HI),** 2 Ararat St. (tel. 628 86 11). Walk down David St. into the market and follow the signs: a right onto St. Mark's Rd., a right again across from the Lutheran Hostel, and up the narrow street with half-arches. Behind the iron gate is a renovated hospital with high ceilings, sparkling-clean rooms, and common bathrooms. No smoking, TV, or radio on *Shabbat*. Lockout 10am-5pm. Check-out 9am. Flexible 11pm curfew. Dorm rooms US$10, non-members US$11. Singles US$20, doubles US$30-40, triples US$45-60. Kosher breakfast included.

**Heritage House:** Office: 90 Ḥabad St. #14 (tel. 627 19 16; fax 628 83 02). Men's hostel: 2 Or Ḥayim St. (tel. 627 22 24). Women's hostel: 7 Ha-Malaḥ St. (tel. 628 18 20). Rabbi Meir Schuster and gang welcome non-observant Jews into their hostels and their Jewish-education classes. Perfect for the curious, but Jewish travelers merely looking for a free place to crash stay here, as well. Non-Jews may stay only when traveling in primarily Jewish groups. Generally friendly, though some guests have experienced uncomfortable proselytizing. Hostels open Sun.-Thurs. 7-9am and 5pm-midnight, Fri. 7-9am and 4pm-*Shabbat* (winter 3pm-*Shabbat*), Sat. night-fall-1am. Office open Sun.-Thurs. 9-5pm; you can leave your bags here. Check-in 5pm-midnight. Curfew Sun.-Thurs. midnight, Fri. and Sat. 1am. Free Sat.-Thurs.; Fri. night stays cost NIS20, including Fri. night dinner, Sat. lunch with a family, and obligatory educational program.

## EAST JERUSALEM

East Jerusalem, radically different from the Western part of the city, can be a hotbed of tension. Feel out the situation before you decide to stay here. In quiet times, this can be a great place to experience the Palestinian lifestyle. Travelers, especially women, should not walk alone at night here. Visibly Jewish travelers (particularly men in *kippot*) should probably stay away. Several hostels line Ha-Nevi'im St., which intersects Suleiman St. and Nablus Rd. across from Damascus Gate.

**Cairo Youth Hostel,** 21 Nablus Rd. (tel. 627 72 16). Laid-back hostel on East Jerusalem's major street (the last stop on bus #27). Clean, with large sitting area, never-ending roof, high ceilings, and a sunny kitchen and balcony. Heat in winter. Free luggage storage. Check-in and curfew 1:30am. Check-out 11am. Dorm beds NIS15. Private rooms (for 1-4 guests) NIS60.

**Palm Hostel,** 6 Ha-Nevi'im St. (tel. 627 31 89). "Run by backpackers for the back-packers" is their motto. You can play checkers, smoke, or catch several videos a day in the upper common room. Lee, the British backpacker manager, is the life of the hostel. Solar heating system brings you 24-hr. hot water. Heated in winter. Check-out 10am. Roof beds under awning NIS10. Dorm beds NIS16. Doubles NIS60, triples NIS69, quads NIS76. Storage NIS3.

**Faisal Youth Hostel,** 4 Ha-Nevi'im St. (tel. 627 24 92). Pleasant, if slightly dirty atmosphere with crowded bunks, TV, a large kitchen, several cats, and manager Ali's Bedouin hospitality. Gorgeous balcony view of Damascus Gate. Heated in winter. Check-out 11am. Curfew 1am. 24-hr. guard. Washing machine use NIS10. Beds on covered porch NIS13. Single-sex dorm beds NIS15. Private rooms NIS60.

## LONGER STAYS

If you'll be in Jerusalem for over two months, consider renting an **apartment.** During July and August college students go on vacation and many rent out their flats. A single room in a shared apartment will cost at least US$200 per month. The best source of information is the classified section of the local weekly *Kol Ha-Ir.* If you find someone to translate, you can submit a free ad of your own requesting an apartment. A more thorough but expensive option is the **She'al Service,** 21 King George St. (tel. 625 69 19), which grants one month's access to its voluminous listings in English for NIS95 (open Sun.-Thurs. 8:30am-7pm, Fri. 8:30am-1pm). The **Ma'agar Meida,** 5 Dorot Rishonim, on the *midraḥov* (tel. 625 37 28), offers an identical service (open Sun.-Thurs. 8am-8pm, Fri. 9am-1:30pm). The bulletin boards at Hebrew University and upstairs at the Israel Center on the corner of Strauss and Ha-Nevi'im St. may also be helpful. The "Bed and Breakfast" listings at the GTIO are a reliable source for monthly rentals. Also check out the bulletin board at Tmol Shilshom restaurant off Naḥalat Shiva Rd.

# ■ Food

The *Jerusalem Post* "Good Food Guide" and *Jerusalem Menus* magazine are distributed at hotels and tourist offices, and include an array of cuisine options from every continent.

## OLD CITY

Cheap Middle Eastern food stands and restaurants lurk behind the unsavory aroma of the Old City markets. Most places are deep within the bustling markets and narrow alleys, but a few huddle close to the gates. The iron-stomached can try the popular chicken restaurants on **Khan az-Zeit** (look for the huge rotisseries and follow the smell). The market also drips with sugary shops selling honey-drenched Arab pastries for NIS8-12 per 0.5kg. You'll find loads of fresh veggies in and around Damascus Gate. Street vendors sell fresh, large, soft sesame *ka'ak* throughout the *souq;* ask for *za'tar* to go with it and dip away. It should cost NIS1.5-2, but you'll see clueless camera carriers paying thrice that. For a genuine *Old* City experience, try Jerusalem's only Roman restaurant, the **Culinaria** (tel. 589 41 55) in the Jewish Quarter Cardo. The waiters will wrap you in togas and bring you plate after plate of chicken, fish, salad, and pita and olive oil. Unfortunately, inflation has been a killer over the last 2000 years—meals are now NIS85 per person (open Sun.-Fri. noon-2pm, dinner by reservation only).

**Abu Shukri,** 63 Al Wad Rd. (tel. 627 15 38), 200m from Damascus Gate. Don't mind the grandmother's-bathroom-pink-tile walls. Given thumbs up by the Israeli press, and frequented by tourists and locals alike. Falafel platters NIS8. Open daily 8am-4 or 5pm.

**The Coffee Shop** (tel. 626 40 90), near Jaffa Gate, next to the Christ Church Hospice. Ivy stenciling, Jerusalem-tiled tables, and a no smoking rule make this A/C hall the most pristine restaurant in the Old City. All-you-can-eat soup and salad NIS21. Sandwiches NIS9-10. Open Tues.-Sun. 11am-6:30pm.

**The Armenian Tavern,** 79 Armenian Orthodox Patriarchate Rd. (tel. 627 38 54), through Jaffa Gate and to your right. Armenian music echoes in the mosaic-floored underground room that serves up all sorts of tasty Armenian edibles. Sandwiches NIS8-10. Salads NIS5-20. Meat dishes NIS25-35. Special Armenian Fri. night dinners. Open daily 11am-11pm. Visa, MC.

**Bakery Muhammad Ali** (a.k.a. **The Green Door**), 5 Aqabat Sheikh Rihan, left off Damascus Gate Rd. The room has few tables and is often empty, but Abu and son bake good, inexpensive pizza (NIS4) in their stone oven. Open daily 7am-10pm.

**Abu Seif and Sons,** just inside Jaffa Gate, beyond the tourist office (tel. 628 68 12). Good quality grub, but you pay a premium for the location. Omelettes and juices NIS5-7, Turkish and Lebanese salads NIS8, falafel NIS10. Open 8am-8pm.

**Quarter Café** (tel. 626 41 55), above the corner of Tiferet Yisrael and Ha-Sho'arim St., Jewish Quarter (look for the sign). Epic view from roof and balcony tables warrant a cake or salad stop (NIS8-15). Full lunches are overpriced (NIS35-45). Open Sun.-Thurs. 9am-6:30pm, Fri. 9am-4pm. Kosher.

## EAST JERUSALEM

East Jerusalem is crawling with vendors selling falafel, spicy *kabab,* rolls, and ears of corn, all for less than NIS4. Follow the smoke, smells, and solicitations to the corner of Suleiman and Nablus St. **Nasser Eddin Bros.** on Suleiman St. across from Damascus Gate and to the right, just past the bus station, stocks Arabic delights (open daily 8am-7pm). Boxes along Suleiman St. overflow with the cheapest produce in the city (1kg zucchini NIS1-2). Salah ad-Din, Az-Zahra, and Suleiman St. have run the restaurant gamut, from bustling rotisserie and falafel places to quieter haunts with extensive and expensive menus. **Al Amin** (tel. 628 83 34), at 14 Ha-Nevi'im, is a sweet-smelling 24-hour bakery with delicious egg pizza *(ras el bed)* for NIS4.

**Kan Zaman,** patio of the Jerusalem Hotel, on Nablus Rd. (tel. 628 32 82). The height of East Jerusalem chic. Delicate tables shaded by vines. Vegetarian dishes NIS14-15, meat and fish meals NIS20-29, sandwiches NIS10-15, and salads NIS6-15. Saturday night Lebanese buffet NIS50. Live classical Arabic music Thurs. and Sat. nights. Open daily 11am-11pm.

**Al Quds Restaurant,** 23 Suleiman St. (tel. 627 20 52). The semicircle English sign is hard to see, so keep your eyes peeled. You might feel like a roasted chicken as you walk through the hot smoky aisle past the rows of rotisseries, but there is a light at the end of the tunnel: clean white tables and a delicious feast for a mere NIS12-14. *Shawerma, shish kabab,* or chicken platter (includes salad, fries, and pita) NIS15. Open daily 8am-midnight.

**Al Ayed,** 4 Ha-Nevi'im St., across from Damascus Gate. Delicious falafel in pita NIS2.50 or *shawerma* NIS6. Open Sun.-Fri. 8am-6pm.

## WEST JERUSALEM

West Jerusalem's restaurant scene reflects the cosmopolitan, international makeup of its growing population. Dining here spans a full spectrum of price ranges, from fancy French to fried falafel and from sushi to *shawerma.* Restaurant goers have the choice of cool stone terraces or crowded tables on the *midraḥov.*

For the cheapest of the fresh and the freshest of the cheap head for **Maḥaneh Yehuda,** the raucous open-air market between Jaffa Rd. and Agrippas St., to the west of the city center. Elbow your way past bag-laden fellow shoppers to the fruit and vegetable stands, pita bakeries, and sumptuous displays of pastries that line the alleys. There's a small grocery store *(makolet)* with rock-bottom prices at almost every corner. You can get 10 loaves of pita here for NIS2 or less; 1kg tomatoes goes for the same price. The Yemenite section (follow the alleys east from Maḥaneh Yehuda St.) is the cheapest for produce, and the stands along Etz Ha-Ḥayim St. sell the best *halva* at NIS5 per 0.5kg. **Mispar Eḥad** (Number One) sells excellent hummus and salads for NIS3.5-4.5 per ¼kg; from Agrippas St., take your first right into the *shuk,* climb some stairs, and look to your right. **Marzipan** (tel. 623 26 18), at 44 Agrippas St., sells *rugelaḥ* to die for—eat a kilo (NIS12) and you just might. *Me'orav* ("assortment"), a mix of inner parts grilled with onions and packed in pita pockets, is an area specialty. The choicest innards are on **Agrippas Street.** A small portion *(mana ketana)* is plenty, but sharing a large one is a better deal. *Shishlik* (cubes of grilled meat) and *kabab* are never far behind. On the corner of Agrippas and the uncovered *shuk* street, falafel is good and cheap (NIS5, *esh tanoor* NIS6).

The best hours to visit are at closing time (Sat.-Thurs. 7-8pm, Fri. 1-2hr. before sundown) when merchants lower their prices shekel by shekel to sell off the day's goods. Friday morning prices are the highest, but they plummet in the afternoon, when thousands scramble through the alleys in a frantic effort to stock up for *Shabbat*. If you don't want to spend any money, head to the meat market in the alleys west of Mahaneh Yehuda St., where a stroll among the skinned and dangling carcasses may keep you fasting for days. **Supermarkets** include **Co-Op,** in the basement of Ha-Mashbir department store at the intersection of King George and Ben-Yehuda St. (tel. 625 78 30; open Sun.-Thurs. 8am-7:30pm and Fri. 8am-2:30pm), and **Supersol** on the corner of Agron and Keren Ha-Yesod St. (tel. 625 06 57; open Sun.-Thurs. 7am-midnight, Fri. 7am-3pm, Sat. sundown-midnight).

**Tzipor Ha-Nefesh,** 10 Rivlin St. (tel. 624 98 90). Decked in flowers and perched on the third floor, this café means bird of the soul, and strives to create a free-flowing atmosphere. Dirty, homesick travelers can do laundry (NIS14 for a wash and dry) and check e-mail (NIS10 per 30min.). The restaurant serves food, too. Huge menu has curries, baked potatoes drenched with toppings, pastas, salads, and pizzas at great prices (NIS16-30). Juices are divine (NIS 8-10). Open Sun.-Thurs. 8am-11pm, Fri. 8am-sundown, Sat. sundown-1am. Visa accepted. Kosher.

**Village Green,** 10 Ben Yehuda St. (tel. 625 20 07 or 14 64), and 1 Bezalel St. Scrumptious made-from-scratch vegetarian food served up cafeteria style. Soups (NIS13) and pastas (NIS16-22) served with all the whole wheat bread, tahini, and dressings you can eat. A hungry budget traveler's dream. Open Sun.-Thurs. 11am-10pm, Fri. 11am-3pm. Visa, MC, AmEx accepted. Kosher.

**Pepperoni's,** 4 Rabbi Akiva St. (tel. 625 78 29). By far the best Italian restaurant in Jerusalem. A full lunch (fresh baked bread, 12 types of salads and antipasti, sausage, drink, and main course) is NIS33. The shebang minus the main course is NIS24. Prices go up for dinner (NIS45-60). Open daily noon-midnight. Visa, MC, AmEx accepted.

**Steakiat Hatzot,** 123 Agrippas St. (tel. 624 40 14). Uniquely spiced meats lure athletes, politicians, and actors to the "Midnight Steakhouse," an Israeli legend past the *shuk*. *Me'orav* (mixed grill), liver, *kabab, shishlik,* or chicken grilled to your liking in a pita (NIS20-26), or on a plate with salad, fries, pita, and dip (NIS33-45). Hummus NIS10. Huge portions. Open Sun.-Thurs. 10am-1am, Sat. sundown-1am.

**Bali-Baguette,** 31 Jaffa Rd. (tel. 625 67 15), near Rivlin St. Scrumptious foot-long baguettes stuffed with meats and salads (NIS9) prove that it's possible for both your stomach and your wallet to be full. Friendly owner takes photos of travelers and pastes them on the walls. Open Sun.-Thurs. 9am-4am, Fri. 9am-5pm. Kosher.

**Bonkers,** 41 Jaffa St. (tel. 624 41 15) in Zion Sq., and King George St. near Agrippas St. The end of an era of kvetching over the dearth of real American bagels in the Jewish state. Little space to sit. Bagels NIS2.50, topped with cream cheese NIS6, with tuna and cheese NIS7. Open 24hr., but closed on *Shabbat*. Kosher.

**Fat Danny's Diner,** 3 Yoel Solomon (tel. 625 11 98). American 50s style food stop with a juke box and Norman Rockwell prints. Fried chicken with French fries NIS21-19. Eggs, hash browns, veggies, and coffee (free refills) NIS19-23. An order of pancakes or waffles NIS15. Open daily 24hr. Visa, MC, AmEx accepted.

**Me Ta'amei Ha-Muhan,** 119 Jaffa Rd. (tel. 623 29 59), in the heart of the Mahaneh Yehuda market district. This small restaurant's appropriate appellation means "tasty and ready." Well-balanced cafeteria-style meals that would make your mom proud. For NIS25, get a main dish with two sides. Choose from lovingly-made goulash, chicken, veggies, mashed potatoes, or *kugel*. Side dishes NIS5. Open Sun.-Thurs. 10am-10pm, Fri. 10am-4:30pm. Eat in or take-out. Glatt Kosher.

**The Yemenite Step,** 10 Yoel Salomon St. (tel. 624 04 77). Grand stone building with high ceilings and outdoor seating. Try the heavenly *malawah*, their specialty (NIS11, with filling NIS32 and up). Open Sun.-Thurs. noon-12:30am, Fri. noon-4pm, Sat. after *Shabbat*-12:30am. Kosher.

**The Seventh Place,** 37 Hillel St. (the Beit Agron building), 2nd floor (tel. 625 44 95). Excellent Indian food. Main dishes NIS17-29, appetizers NIS10-12. Free live music most nights: Sat.-Sun. American folk; Tues. gypsy; Wed. jazz; Thurs. Israeli folk. Open Sun.-Thurs. 9am-1am, Fri. 8am-4pm, Sat. sundown-2am. Visa, MC, AmEx. Kosher.

**Alumah,** 8 Ya'avetz St. (tel. 625 50 14), off Jaffa Rd. between King George St. and Zion Sq. Quiet, spacious stone veranda; botanical interior. Everything is made from scratch. Specializes in stone-ground, yeast-less whole wheat, sourdough, and rye bread. The quiche here is as organic and delicious as they come (NIS23). Main dishes NIS18-29, all served with bread and raw vegetables. Open Sun.-Thurs. 10am-11pm, Fri. 10am-2pm. Visa, MC. Glatt kosher.

**Mama Mia's,** 38 King George St. (tel. 248 080), behind parking lot. Perhaps the best place to splurge, if you feel like a treat. Crisp, white interior with stucco ceilings and green trim. Peaceful patio, romantic table for two on a small balcony, and a separate non-smoking room. Delicious fettuccine NIS25-36, pizza NIS32-40, and great homemade ravioli NIS27-36. Open Sun.-Thurs. noon-11pm, Fri. noon-3pm, Sat. sundown-11pm. Visa, MC, AmEx. Kosher.

### Cheap Quickies

There is nothing like the quest for cheap falafel to unite natives and tourists in common pursuit. The West Jerusalem center teems with small, crowded stands and sit-downs for pizza, *shawerma,* ice cream, and fruit juice. Creating the ultimate **falafel** or **shawerma** is an art all its own, and many stops on King George St. between Jaffa Rd. and Ben-Yehuda or in Maḥaneh Yehuda come close to perfecting it.

**Shalom Falafel** (tel. 623 14 36), at 19 Bezalel, on the corner of Even Sapir St., a few blocks behind the Mashbir Department Store. Israelis cluster around a hole in the wall that pours forth savory falafel (NIS5) and *esh tanoor* (in *lafa* bread, NIS6).

**Melekh Ha-Falafel ve Ha-Shawerma** (tel. 625 85 16), on the same corner as Shalom Falafel, serving the same food for the same prices.

**Ta'ami,** 3 Shammai St. (tel. 625 36 44). Favorite hummus den, notorious for urging folks to finish up and get out. Open Sun.-Thurs. 9:30am-6pm, Fri. 9:30am-noon.

**Apple Pizza,** 13 Dorot Rishonim St. (tel. 625 04 67), off Ben-Yehuda. Serves thin-crust "Big Apple" pizza baked to the tune of rock classics. Open Sun.-Thurs. 10:30am-midnight, Fri. 10:30am-4pm, Sat. 8:30pm-midnight. Kosher.

**Mystic Pizza,** 1 Agron St. (tel. 623 63 33), at the corner of King George. Good and crispy, with tiny pine tables. Cheese pizza NIS6, with toppings NIS6.50.

The **Merkaz Ha-Pa'amon** shopping center, on King George and the *midraḥov,* has an **Angel's Pizza** (tel. 623 31 05; NIS5-5.50 per slice). The long-awaited, much-debated, non-kosher **McDonald's** (tel. 624 93 52), on 4 Shammai St., near the *midraḥov,* doles out Big Macs for NIS10.30. This may signal the decline of Israel's own **Burger Ranch,** 18 King George St. (tel. 623 37 66), near Hamashbir department store, where a Ranchburger goes for NIS10.70.

The best place for **ice cream** is **Katzefet** (tel. 625 37 22), on the *midraḥov* at the corner of Ben-Yehuda and Luntz St. (ice cream NIS4). Their specialty is frozen yogurt (pronounced *frrrozen*) blended with your choice of fresh fruits, nuts, or chocolates (small with 3 flavors NIS7). **Ben and Jerry's,** at 5 Hillel St. (tel. 624 27 67), just off King George St., scoops its signature stuff for NIS7.90 for an order of two scoops. Several stands near the Ben Yehuda-King George intersection concoct fresh **juice** on the spot. Choose among mango, fig, peach, watermelon, and many others (regular size NIS2.50-3.50, medium NIS4.50-6; orange juice NIS5.50).

# ■ Sights

## OLD CITY

If you take a shovel, pick any spot in the Old City and dig, you'll probably be face to face with ancient marvels in no time. Excavations under the Old City have uncovered over 20 distinct layers of civilization. There's something about this tiny plot of land that makes it holy, not only for Jews, Christians, and Muslims, but to dozens of ancient religious groups as well. Before beginning a tour, it's helpful to get an idea of what the city looked like in ages past. The **Holyland Hotel** in West Jerusalem (tel.

ISRAEL

643 77 77) has an excellent knee-high model of Jerusalem circa 66 CE, towards the end of the Second Temple Period. Take bus #21 from downtown (open daily 8am-10pm; admission NIS15, NIS12 with ISIC). The entire Old City is only about one square km; a walking tour is a great way to get to know it (see **Tours,** p. 286).

## The Walls and the Citadel

The present walls of the Old City were built by Suleiman the Magnificent in 1542. The city had been without walls since 1219, when Al Muazzan tore them down to prevent the Crusaders from seizing a fortified city. There are eight gates, some of which have three names: Christian/Latin, Jewish/Hebrew, and Muslim/Arabic (the most commonly used names are listed here). **Golden Gate,** blocked by Muslim graves, has been sealed since the 1600s. It is thought to lie over the Closed Gate of the First Temple, the entrance through which the Messiah will purportedly pass (Ezekiel 44:1-3). Of the other seven gates, **Jaffa Gate** is the most convenient from West Jerusalem and is the traditional entrance for pilgrims; there has been a gate here since 135 CE. (Some people don't give Jaffa Gate the respect it deserves. Gustave Flaubert recalled: "We enter through Jaffa Gate and I let a fart escape as I cross the threshold very involuntarily. I was even annoyed at bottom by this Voltaireanism of my anus." No doubt his companions were, too.) Going clockwise from Jaffa Gate is **New Gate,** opened in 1889 to facilitate access to the Christian Quarter. **Damascus Gate** serves East Jerusalem. **Herod's Gate** stands to the east of Damascus Gate. **St. Stephen's Gate** (or Lion's Gate), is the beginning of the Via Dolorosa. **Dung Gate,** first mentioned in 445 BCE by Neḥemiah, opens near the Western Wall and was given its name in medieval times because dumping dung here was considered an especially worthy act. **Zion Gate** connects the Armenian Quarter with Mt. Zion.

The walls embrace a circumference of 4km. You can walk the entire circuit except the parts by the Temple Mount and the Citadel. This **ramparts walk** provides an unsurpassed view of the Old City and an idea of the wall's military importance through the centuries. Tickets to the ramparts are sold at the Citadel and Damascus and Jaffa Gates (tel. 625 44 03). They are good for unlimited admission for two days after the purchase, three days if purchased on a Friday (walls open Sat.-Thurs. 9am-4pm, Fri. 9am-2pm; admission NIS8, students NIS4). The Citadel divides the walk into two sections; from Jaffa Gate, you can walk in either direction. To go to the Christian and Muslim Quarters, ascend the rampart on the left as you enter the gate. For the Armenian and Jewish Quarters, enter the Citadel parking lot and follow the building around to the left.

To ascend the ramparts from **Damascus Gate,** you must go down the steps to the right before you cross the bridge, walk under the gate, and continue through the ancient carriageway to the left of the plaza. The level of the carriageways on either side corresponds to the middle Roman period in the 2nd century CE. At the rampart entrance you can visit the **Roman Square Museum,** set among the excavations from Aelia Capitolina (as the city was known in 200 CE). The museum displays a copy of the 6th-century **Madaba map** from Madaba, Jordan; the map is the earliest known blueprint of the city's layout. The huge centipede that seems to crawl from Damascus Gate at the northern tip to Dung Gate at the southern is actually a two-dimensional rendition of the **Cardo,** the main thoroughfare; its "feet" are the Roman columns lining the street. The map has aided archaeologists in concluding that the Cardo recently unearthed in the Jewish Quarter is not part of the Roman original, but a Byzantine addition. Scholars have also discovered a plaza at the gate's entrance with a statue of Hadrian mounted on a huge column. This explains the Arabic name for Damascus Gate: *Baab al-Amud* (Gate of the Column). The plaza has been partially uncovered, but the black column is missing; you'll have to settle for the hologram on display. (Museum open Sat.-Thurs. 9am-4pm, Fri. 9am-2pm. Admission NIS2.50, students NIS1.80.)

Another place to dig the history of the Old City is the **Citadel** complex just inside Jaffa Gate and to the right. The Citadel, sometimes called the **Tower of David** (*Migdal David* in Hebrew), resembles a Lego caricature of overlapping Hasmonean,

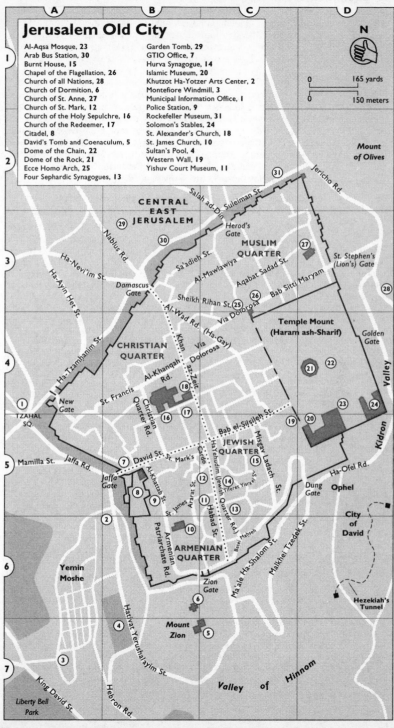

# Jerusalem Old City

Al-Aqsa Mosque, 23
Arab Bus Station, 30
Burnt House, 15
Chapel of the Flagellation, 26
Church of all Nations, 28
Church of Dormition, 6
Church of St. Anne, 27
Church of St. Mark, 12
Church of the Holy Sepulchre, 16
Church of the Redeemer, 17
Citadel, 8
David's Tomb and Coenaculum, 5
Dome of the Chain, 22
Dome of the Rock, 21
Ecce Homo Arch, 25
Four Sephardic Synagogues, 13

Garden Tomb, 29
GTIO Office, 7
Hurva Synagogue, 14
Islamic Museum, 20
Khutzot Ha-Yotzer Arts Center, 2
Montefiore Windmill, 3
Municipal Information Office, 1
Police Station, 9
Rockefeller Museum, 31
Solomon's Stables, 24
St. Alexander's Church, 18
St. James Church, 10
Sultan's Pool, 4
Western Wall, 19
Yishuv Court Museum, 11

**N**

0          165 yards

0          150 meters

ISRAEL

*Mount of Olives*

CENTRAL EAST JERUSALEM

*Herod's Gate*

MUSLIM QUARTER

*St. Stephen's (Lion's) Gate*

*Salah ad-Din*

*Suleiman St.*

*Nablus Rd.*

*Ha-Nevi'im St.*

*Ha-Ayin Het St.*

*Sa'adieh St.*

*Al-Mawlawiya*

*Aqabat Sadad St.*

*Bab Sitti Maryam*

*Damascus Gate*

*Sheikh Rihan St.*

*Via Dolorosa*

**Temple Mount (Haram ash-Sharif)**

*Golden Gate*

*Al-Wad Rd. (Ha-Gay)*

CHRISTIAN QUARTER

*Ha-Tzamhanim St.*

*St. Francis*

*Al-Khanqah Rd.*

*Via Dolorosa*

*az-Zeit*

*Khan*

*Christian Quarter Rd.*

*New Gate*

*TZAHAL SQ.*

*Kidron Valley*

*Mamilla St.*

*Jaffa Rd.*

*David St.*

*Bab el-Silsileh St.*

JEWISH QUARTER

*Misgav Ladach St.*

*Ha-Ofel Rd.*

*Jaffa Gate*

*Al-Khatib St.*

*St. Mark's*

*St. James*

*Ararat St.*

*Ha-Yehudim (Jewish Quarter) Rd.*

*Tiferet Yisrael St.*

*Habad St.*

*Dung Gate*

*Ophel*

*City of David*

**Yemin Moshe**

*Armenian Patriarchate Rd.*

ARMENIAN QUARTER

*Beit Mahseh*

*Ma'ale Ha-Shalom St.*

*Malkhei Tzedek St.*

*Hezekiah's Tunnel*

*Zion Gate*

**Mount Zion**

*Hatzvat Yerushalayim St.*

*Hebron Rd.*

*King David St.*

*Liberty Bell Park*

**Valley of Hinnom**

Herodian, Roman, Byzantine, Muslim, Mamluk, and Ottoman ruins, but nothing from David's era (during his reign, this was outside the city and unsettled). The tower provides a superb vantage point for surveying the Holy City. Winding through the rooms of the fortress, the high-tech, information-packed **Museum of the History of Jerusalem** tells the story of the city in Hebrew, Arabic, and English through videos, holograms, and talking models. (Open in summer Sun.-Thurs. 9am-5pm, Fri.-Sat. 9am-2pm, winter Sun.-Thurs. 10am-4pm, Fri.-Sat. 10am-2pm. Admission NIS20, students NIS15, children NIS10; price includes guided tour in English Sun.-Fri. 11am.) At night, there's a 45-minute English **sound and lightshow.** Booming voices tell the history of Jerusalem as splotches of light are tossed around a few stone walls (April-Oct. Mon. and Wed. 9:30pm, Sat. 10:30pm. Admission NIS20, students NIS14, children NIS10; combined tickets with museum entrance NIS35, students NIS25, children NIS18.) In spring and summer, you can play the Citadel's game of **Murder Mystery**—a full costumed cast helps you find the culprit Saturday evenings at 9pm.

### Temple Mount/Dome of the Rock Area and Western Wall

The **Temple Mount** (Al Haram ash-Sharif in Arabic, Har Ha-Bayit in Hebrew), a 35-acre area in the southeastern corner of the Old City, is one of the most venerated religious sites in the world. A seeming spiritual magnet, the hill is central today to Judaism and Islam and served as a holy site for at least 10 ancient religions. The Temple Mount is traditionally identified with the biblical Mt. Moriah, where God asked Abraham to sacrifice his son Isaac (Genesis 22:2). The First Temple was built here by King Solomon in the middle of the 10th century BCE (2 Chronicles 3:1), and destroyed by Nebuchadnezzar in 587 BCE, when the Jews were led into captivity (I Kings 5-8; II Kings 24-25). The Second Temple was built in 516 BCE, after the Jews' return from exile (Ezra 3-7). In 20 BCE, King Herod rebuilt the temple and enlarged the Mount, reinforcing it with four retaining walls. Parts of the southern, eastern, and western retaining walls still stand. Religious scholars believe that the Holy of Holies, the most sacred and important spot on the Temple where only the High Priest was allowed to enter once a year, was closest to what is now the **Western Wall,** making this wall the holiest approachable site in Judaism. Observant Jews will not ascend the Mount because of the possibility that they will walk on the Holy of Holies, off limits until the Messiah arrives.

The Second Temple is remembered by Christians as the backdrop to the Passion of Christ. Like the First Temple, it lasted only a few hundred years. In the fourth year of the Jewish Revolt (70 CE), Roman legions sacked Jerusalem and razed the second Temple. Hadrian built a temple to Jupiter over the site, but the Byzantines destroyed it and used the platform as a municipal sewage facility (giving nearby Dung Gate its name). After Caliph Omar conquered Jerusalem in 638 (just six years after Muhammad's death) he ascended the Mount and began the clean-up himself, personally removing an armful of brown gook. The Umayyad Caliphs built the two Arab shrines that still dominate the Temple Mount: the silver-domed **Al Aqsa Mosque** (built in 715 and rebuilt several times after earthquakes), and the magnificent **Dome of the Rock** (built in 691). A stunning display of mosaics and metallic domes, the complex is the third-holiest Muslim site, after the Ka'ba in Mecca and the Mosque of the Prophet in Medina. According to Muslim tradition, this is the point to which God took Muhammad on his mystical Night Journey *(miraj)* from the Holy Mosque at Mecca to the outer Mosque *(al aqsa* means "the farthest") and then on to heaven (17:17). The Dome of the Rock surrounds what Muslims believe was Abraham's makeshift altar where he almost sacrificed Ishmael, his son by Sarah's maid Hagar (not Isaac, as Christians and Jews believe).

Although the dome was once of solid gold, it was eventually melted down to pay the caliphs' debts. The domes of the mosques and shrines were plated with lusterless lead until the structures received aluminum caps during the restoration work done from 1958 to 1964. The golden hue of the Dome of the Rock was previously achieved with an aluminum-bronze alloy, but in 1993 it was re-coated with new metal plates faced with a thin coating of 24-karat gold, leaving it more brilliant than ever. Many of the tiles covering the walls of the Dome of the Rock were affixed during the reign of Suleiman the Magnificent, who had the city walls built in the 16th century. Scrutiny will distinguish these from the ceramic tiles added in the 1950s and 60s and paid for with Jordanian King Hussein's private funds.

Next to the Dome of the Rock is the much smaller **Dome of the Chain,** the exact center of Al Haram ash-Sharif, where Muslims believe a chain which could be grasped only by the righteous hung from heaven. Between the two shrines flows a *sabil* (fountain) called **Al Kas,** where Muslims perform ablutions before prayer. Built in 709 CE, the fountain is connected to underground cisterns capable of holding 10 million gallons. The arches on the Temple Mount, according to Muslim legend, will be used to hang scales to weigh people's good and bad deeds. The **Islamic Museum,** by the ramp entrance beside the Western Wall, is filled with fantastic relics such as crescent-topped spires that once crowned older domes, and elaborately decorated Qur'ans.

Al Haram ash-Sharif and the museum are open Saturday through Thursday 8am-12:30pm and 1:30pm-3:30pm. All hours are subject to change during Ramadan and other Islamic holidays, although the Mount is usually open 8am-10:30am. The entrance to the mount is just right of the Western Wall, up the ramp. (Tickets sold at a booth between Al Aqsa and the museum. Admission NIS22, students NIS12. Ticket booth closes at 3pm.) The Mount is sometimes closed without notice, and you might inexplicably be denied entrance. Remember that the area is highly sensitive—incidents in the past have resulted in violence. Any conspicuous action, no matter how innocent, may get you ejected. Bring modest dress, although hare krishna-like gowns are provided for those who need them. Also be aware that many sections considered off-limits by the police are not marked as such. These include the walls around Al Aqsa, the area through the door to the south between Al Aqsa and the museum, and the Muslim cemetery.

The 18m tall **Western Wall** (Ha-Kotel Ha-Ma'aravi in Hebrew) is part of the retaining wall of the Temple Mount, built about 20 BCE, and was the largest section of the Temple area that remained standing after its destruction in 70 CE. The Wailing Wall, a dated moniker, refers to Jewish worshipers who visited the wall in centuries past to mourn the destruction of the Temple. Today's visitors, Jewish or otherwise, often see the Wall as a direct connection with God, and tuck written prayers into its crannies. Don't expect your scribble to wait there for the Messiah: all notes are periodically removed from the overburdened wall and buried, in accordance with Jewish Law. An innovative service from Bezek (the telephone company) lets you fax in urgent messages to be deposited in the crevices (fax 561 22 22). The Wall can be reached by foot from Dung Gate, the Jewish Quarter, Baab as-Silsilah St., or Al Wad Rd. About 3m off the ground, a gray line indicates the surface level before 1967. Nearly 20m of Herodian wall still lies underground. You can identify the Herodian stones by their carved frames, or dressing; the smaller stones that lie above were added by Byzantines, Arabs, and Turks.

Pre-1948 photos show Orthodox Jews praying at the wall in a crowded alley; after the 1967 War, the present plaza was built, and Israeli paratroopers are sworn here to recall the Wall's capture. The Ministry of Religion has decreed that all rules applying to Orthodox synagogues also apply to the Wall. Men must cover their heads (paper *kippot* are in a box by the entrance) and women must cover their legs (wraps can be borrowed from the Holy Sites Authority). The prayer areas for men and women are separated by a screen with the Torah scrolls kept on the men's side, along with recently excavated sections of the Wall. **Wilson's Arch** (named for the English archaeologist who discovered it), located inside a large, arched room to the left of the Wall, was once part of a bridge that spanned Cheesemakers' Valley, allowing Jewish priests to cross from their Upper City homes to the Temple. A peek down the two illuminated shafts in the floor of this room gives a sense of the wall's original height (women may not enter). The wall continues from here through closed tunnels for over 500m. Women and groups can enter the passageways through an archway to the south, near the telephones. Underneath the Western Wall is an underground pas-

ISRAEL

sage where Jewish radicals hid explosives in the early 1980s in a plot to destroy the Dome of the Rock. To get into the passage, call the **Western Wall Heritage Foundation** (tel. 627 13 33). English tours are held irregularly (NIS10). **Archaeological Seminars** and **Zion Walking Tours** both visit the tunnels as part of their walking tours (see **Tours,** p. 286).

At the far end of the Wall plaza (near the bathrooms), halfway up the stairs, is the **Holocaust Memorial Hall.** The sculpture and room inside are designed by Agam, designer of the Dizengoff fountain in Tel Aviv. His steel tree contains 1200 brilliant lights, and the ceiling and floor tiles are in triangles that can be arranged into stars of David (open Sun.-Thurs. 11am-4pm; free).

On Fridays, Yeshivat Ha-Kotel organizes dancing to usher in *Shabbat.* The festivities start before sundown and go until late. Half a dozen Bar Mitzvahs occur at the Wall simultaneously on Monday and Thursday mornings. These ceremonies mark the coming of age of Jewish boys (see **The Synagogue and Jewish Life,** p. 59). Photography is appropriate at these occasions, unlike on *Shabbat* or holidays. At night, the Wall is brightly lit, the air cool, and the atmosphere reflective and quiet.

The excavations at the southern wall of the Temple Mount are known as the **Ophel** (tel. 625 44 03), though "Ophel" technically refers to the hill just outside the southern wall, where the City of David is located. (Open Sun.-Fri. 7am-6pm. Admission NIS8, students NIS4. English tours daily 9am NIS25, children NIS15.) Scholars have uncovered 22 layers from 12 periods of the city's history. A tunnel brings you outside the city walls to the foot of the steps leading to the Temple Mount. **Archaeological Seminars** runs an excellent walking tour of the area (see **Tours,** p. 286).

### Jewish Quarter

The Jewish Quarter is in the southeast quadrant of the Old City, the site of the posh Upper City during the Second Temple era. The quarter extends from Ha-Shalshelet St. (Baab as-Silsilah) in the north to the city's southern wall, and from Ararat St. in the west to the Western Wall in the east. Reach the quarter by climbing the stairs diagonally across from the Western Wall. From Jaffa Gate, either head down David St. and turn right at the sign for the Cardo Maximus or turn right past the Citadel onto Armenian Orthodox Patriarch Rd. and make the first left onto St. James Rd. Jews settled here when they returned to Jerusalem in the 15th century. The Jewish community grew from 2000 in 1800 to 11,000 in 1865, when settlement began outside the walls. Today, about 650 families live in the Jewish Quarter.

Much of the Jewish Quarter was damaged in the 1948 War and after two decades of Jordanian rule the Quarter lay in ruins. The Israelis annexed the Old City after the 1967 War and immediately began extensive restoration of the neighborhood. City planners made archaeological discoveries with every lift of the shovel, and have managed to gracefully integrate the ancient remains into the new neighborhood. Today the gentrified Jewish Quarter is an upper-middle-class neighborhood, with an almost exclusively Orthodox Jewish (and largely American) population.

If you follow St. James Rd. from the Jaffa Gate until it becomes Or Ḥayim Rd., you'll see the **Yishuv Court Museum** at 6 Or Ḥayim St. (tel. 284 636), on your right. The small exhibition depicts life in the Jewish Quarter before 1948. Sephardic and Ashkenazi-style guest rooms are furnished with period artifacts. A highlight of the collection is a display of wooden Torah cases (open Sun.-Thurs. 9am-2pm; admission NIS6, students NIS5).

If you continue down Or Ḥayim St. pass Ḥabad St. and descend a staircase, you'll see remains of the **Cardo,** Jerusalem's main thoroughfare during Roman and Byzantine times. A large part of the Cardo has been excavated alongside Jewish Quarter Rd. (make a left at the bottom of the stairs). The uncovered section is built over a Byzantine extension of Emperor Hadrian's Cardo Maximus, which ran from Damascus Gate to about as far south as David St. Archaeologists suspect that Justinian constructed the addition so that the Cardo would extend as far as the Nea Church (beneath Yeshivat Ha-Kotel). Sheltered by the Cardo's vaulted roof are expensive gift shops and art galleries. Near the entrance to the Cardo, you can climb down to an excavated section of the Hasmonean city walls and remains of buildings from the First Temple period. Farther along the Cardo is an enlarged mosaic reproduction of the Madaba map, the 6th-century plan of Jerusalem discovered in Jordan. The Cardo is open and illuminated until 11pm. The enormous remaining pillars denote its original monumental proportions. Between the expensive Cardo shops is the **One Last Day Museum** (in the same building as the Cardo Culinaria), which recounts with photographs the fall of the Jewish Quarter in 1948 (open Sun.-Thurs. 9am-5pm, Fri. 9am-1pm; admission NIS5, students NIS4).

The **Broad Wall,** near the post office on Plugat Ha-Kotel Rd. off Jewish Quarter Rd., is the remains of the Israelite wall that encircled the City of David, the Temple Mount, and the Upper City. The wall was built by King Hezekiah in the 7th century BCE and, along with his famous tunnel, formed part of the city's defenses (see **City of David,** p. 309). The small chunk of wall is over 4m thick—much broader than the current Ottoman fortifications. Continue left on Plugat Ha-Kotel and turn right onto Shonei Ha-Laḥot St. to find the **Israelite Tower,** part of the same defense system as the broad wall. You can descend beneath the tower to see the remains of two older defensive towers which were important bastions for the first wall built in the north of the city. Maps indicate how the city walls have changed over the centuries (open Sun.-Thurs. 9am-5pm., Fri. 9am-1pm; admission NIS4, students NIS3). Across the street is the **First Temple Period Model** (tel. 628 62 88). Admission includes a 30-minute film presentation which explains the history in detail. Call for a schedule of presentations in English (open Sun.-Thurs. 9am-4pm, Fri. 9am-1pm; admission NIS8, students NIS6).

Across Jewish Quarter Rd. and on the left from the southern end of the Cardo, a single stone arch soars above the ruins of the **Ḥurva Synagogue.** Built in 1700 by followers of Rabbi Yehuda the Ḥasid, the synagogue was destroyed by Muslims when the Ashkenazi community could no longer afford to uphold its place of worship. It was then that the synagogue earned its name (*ḥurva* means "ruin"). This proved an ominous title; in 1856 the building was restored as the National Ashkenazic Synagogue, only to be destroyed once again during the 1948 War. In 1967, renovators opted to rebuild only the single arch as a reminder of the destruction. The **Ramban Synagogue** next door was named for Rabbi Moshe Ben-Naḥman, also known as Naḥmanides ("Ramban" is an acronym for his name). Inside is a letter written by the rabbi describing Jerusalem's Jewish community in 1267, the year he arrived from Spain. During a period of nearly four centuries (1599-1967), Jews were forbidden to worship here, and the building had stints as a store, butter factory, and mosque. Today it is open for morning and evening prayers.

From the main plaza area near the Ḥurva Synagogue, Ha-Kara'im St. (heading east from the telephones) leads to the **Herodian Quarter** (tel. 628 34 48), an excavation of three mansions built for the Second Temple's high priests (*kohanim*). The posh houses contain mosaics, several ritual baths (*mikvaot*), and fine pottery (Open Sun.-Thurs. 9am-5pm, Fri. 9am-1pm. Admission NIS10, students NIS9; combined ticket to Burnt House and Herodian Quarter NIS12, students NIS11.)

Ha-Karaim St. leads directly to the **Tiferet Yisrael Synagogue.** From the plaza, you can reach the synagogue by walking down Tiferet Yisrael St. and taking the stairs on the right. The synagogue showcases old photographs that depict the house of worship's heyday. Built by Ḥasidic Jews during the 19th century, the synagogue was captured and destroyed by Jordan in 1948. The **Karaite Synagogue** next door was established by this divergent sect of Judaism, and is now the center of the Karaite community in Jerusalem (see **Other Sects,** p. 65).

Farther east on Tiferet Yisrael Rd. smolders the **Burnt House** (tel. 628 72 11), the remains of the dwelling of a priest's family from the Second Temple era. In 70 CE, the fourth year of the Jewish Revolt, the Romans destroyed the Second Temple and broke into Jerusalem's Upper City, burning its buildings and killing its inhabitants. The excavation of the Burnt House provided direct evidence of the destruction of the Upper City. Near a stairwell the grisly bones of a severed arm reach for a carbonized spear. Sound and light shows are set inside the Burnt House, re-creating the events of its destruction (virtual fire, of course). Reservations are recommended for English presentations (open Sun.-Thurs. 9am-5pm; admission NIS6, students NIS5).

In the shadow of the Burnt House is the **Third Temple Museum,** on Ladakh St. off Tiferet Yisrael Rd. The folks here are actively hoping to rebuild the Jewish High Temple, and plan to relocate the Dome of the Rock (Muslim worshipers are not amused). The museum is filled with modern-built instruments to be used in the anticipated Third Temple. As much as possible, the objects are built to the ancient specifications as written in the Talmud.

From the main plaza near the Ḥurva Synagogue, the **Four Sephardic Synagogues** are down Mishmerot Ha-Kehuna St., near the parking lot. The synagogue of Rabbi Yoḥanan Ben-Zakkai, the Prophet Elijah Synagogue, the Central Synagogue, and the Istanbuli Synagogue (tel. 628 05 92) were built by Mediterranean Jews starting in the 16th century in accordance with a local law that prohibited the construction of synagogues taller than the surrounding houses. To attain a semblance of loftiness, these synagogues were built in large chambers deep underground. The current renovated structures date from 1835. The synagogues remain the spiritual center of Jerusalem's Sephardic community, with religious services held here twice a day. A Portuguese *minyan* gathers in the Istanbuli room. A small exhibition features photographs of the synagogues pre-destruction and pre-renovation. Cantor Aryen Grayewsky, who sells tickets, is a great source for history and stories. (Open Sun.-Mon. and Wed.-Thurs. 9:30am-4pm, Tues. and Fri. 9:30am-12:30pm. Admission NIS6, students NIS3.)

## Armenian Quarter

The Armenian Quarter, in the southwestern part of the Old City near Mt. Zion, is home to Jerusalem's small Armenian Christian population. Aramaic, the ancient language of the Levant, is spoken both during services and in casual conversation at the **Syrian Orthodox Convent** on Ararat St. The Syrian Church believes this to be the site of St. Mark's house and the Last Supper, while most other Christians recognize the Cenacle on Mt. Zion as that hallowed place. To reach the convent, enter Jaffa Gate and walk beside the Citadel onto Armenian Patriarchate Rd. Turn left onto St. James Rd. and left again onto Ararat St. A vivid mosaic marks the door to the convent. Visit during the afternoon, and ring the bell if the door is closed. The **Armenian Compound,** down Armenian Patriarchate Rd. past St. James Rd., is a city within a city, home to about 1000 Armenians and a slew of sites closed to tourists.

Farther down Armenian Patriarchate Rd. on the left is the entrance to the **Mardigian Museum,** chronicling the history of Armenia from the beginnings of its Christianization in 46 CE to the Turkish genocide of one and a half million Armenians in 1915. The ornate religious artifacts and grand courtyard are worth the NIS5 (students NIS3) admission fee (open Mon.-Sat. 9:30am-5pm).

The **St. James Cathedral** opposite the museum is open for services for a half-hour each day. The original structure was built during the 5th century CE, Armenia's golden age, to honor two St. Jameses. The first martyr, St. James the Greater, was beheaded in 44 CE by Herod Agrippas. His head, supposedly delivered to Mary on the wings of angels, rests under the gilded altar. St. James the Lesser, entombed in a northern chapel, served as the first bishop of Jerusalem, but was run out of town by Jews who disliked his version of Judaism. Persians destroyed the cathedral in the 7th century, Armenians rebuilt it in the 11th century, and Crusaders enlarged it in the 12th. Armenians make the tiled street signs for the entire Old City and cover the church with beautifully decorated tiles. Chandeliers, hanging lamps, and censers lighten the colorful space. Pilgrims left votive crosses in the courtyard before the entrance; the oldest cross dates from the 12th century. Enter the cathedral from Armenian Patriarchate Rd., just past St. James St. (open for services daily 3-3:30pm).

## Christian Quarter and Via Dolorosa

In the northwest corner of the Old City, the Christian Quarter surrounds the Church of the Holy Sepulchre, the site traditionally believed to be the place of Jesus' crucifixion, burial, and resurrection. The alleyways of the Quarter pass small churches and chapels of various denominations, and the streets bustle with pilgrims, nuns, monks, and merchants peddling rosaries and holy water.

The **Via Dolorosa** (Path of Sorrow) is the route that a cross-bearing Jesus followed from the site of his condemnation (the Praetorium) to the site of his crucifixion and grave (the Calvary). Each event on His walk now has a chapel commemorating it; together these chapels comprise the 14 Stations of the Cross. The present route was mapped out during the Crusader period and spans the Muslim and Christian Quarters. Modern New Testament scholars have suggested alternate routes based on more recent archaeological and historical reconstructions.

One bone of contention involves the beginning point of Jesus' final walk as a mortal. It is generally agreed that Jesus was brought before Pontius Pilate, the Roman procurator, for judgment. Normally, Roman governors resided and fulfilled their duties in the palace of Herod the Great, south of Jaffa Gate and the Citadel area. But on feast days such as Passover, the day of Jesus' condemnation, the governor and his soldiers presumably based themselves at Antonia's fortress (also built by Herod) to be closer to the Temple Mount. Reflecting this holiday relocation, the **Tower of Antonia,** near St. Stephen's (Lion's) Gate, is considered by most to be the First Station. Nevertheless, you may see small groups, notably the Catholic Dominican Order, setting out from Jaffa Gate. The placement of the last five stations inside the Church of the Holy Sepulchre contradicts an alternative hypothesis that the crucifixion took place at the skull-shaped Garden Tomb.

To begin the walk that Jesus and millions of tourists and pilgrims have taken, start at **St. Stephen's Gate.** If you are coming from Damascus or Jaffa Gates, you'll have to walk along part of the Via Dolorosa to get to your starting point and may be tempted to see the stations out of order. Waiting and following the traditional sequence will provide you with a more fulfilling and rewarding experience. On Fridays at 3pm (July-Aug. 4pm), you can walk the Via Dolorosa with a procession of pilgrims lead by Franciscan monks starting at Al Omariyyeh College.

Starting at St. Stephen's Gate, you will first see the **Church of St. Anne** on your right. Commemorating the birthplace of Jesus' mother Mary, the church is one of the best preserved pieces of Crusader architecture in Israel. The church survived the Islamic period intact because Salah ad-Din used it as a Muslim theological school, hence the Arabic inscription on the tympanum above the doors. Tradition is layers deep here: the simple, solemn, citadel-like structure stands over the ruins of a 5th-century basilica that is itself believed to cover a 2nd- or 3rd-century chapel. The church is tilted to one side, symbolizing the crucifixion.

Within the grounds of the church is the **Pool of Bethesda.** Crowds of the infirm used to wait beside the pool for an angel to disturb its waters; the first person in after the angel would supposedly be cured. Jesus also healed a sick man here (John 5:2-9). Also worth noting are the remains of a Byzantine cistern and a Crusader chapel façade. (Church and grounds open summer Mon.-Sat. 8am-noon and 2-6pm, winter Mon.-Sat. 8am-noon and 2-5pm. Admission NIS3.)

Two hundred meters west of St. Stephen's Gate, a blue ramp leads to the courtyard of the **Al Omariyyeh College,** one site identified as the **first station,** where Jesus was condemned. Opposite the school from the Via Dolorosa, enter the Franciscan monastery; to your left is the **Condemnation Chapel,** the **second station,** where Jesus was sentenced to crucifixion. On the right is the **Chapel of Flagellation,** where he was first flogged by Roman soldiers. A crown of thorns adorns the dome (open daily 8am-11:45am and 2-6pm; winter 8am-11:45am and 1-5pm).

Continuing along the Via Dolorosa, pass beneath the **Ecce Homo Arch,** where Pilate looked down upon a scourged Jesus and cried, "Behold the Man." The arch is actually part of the triumphal arch that commemorates Emperor Hadrian's suppression of the Bar Kokhba revolt in the 2nd century (open Mon.-Sat. 8:30am-12:30pm and 2-4pm). Adjacent lies the **Convent of the Sisters of Zion,** beneath which excavations have cleared a large chamber thought by some to be the judgment hall, making it an alternative first station. The convent is closed to the public, but the excavations are not. To get to them, walk down the Via Dolorosa from the second station and turn right on Aqabat ar-Rahbat St. Knock on the brown door on your left (open Mon.-Sat. 8:30am-12:30pm and 2-4:30pm; admission NIS3.50).

Although the following stations—the destinations of countless pilgrims—are all marked, they are nonetheless difficult to spot. At the **third station,** to the left on Al Wad Rd., Jesus fell to his knees for the first time. A small Polish chapel inside a blue gate marks the spot; a small relief above the entrance depicts Jesus kneeling beneath the cross. At the **fourth station,** a few meters farther on the left, just beyond the Armenian Orthodox Patriarchate, a small chapel commemorates the spot where Jesus saw his mother (look for the light blue iron doors). Turn right on Via Dolorosa to reach the **fifth station,** where Simon the Cyrene volunteered to carry Jesus' cross (look for the nearby brown door with the Roman numeral V). Fifty meters farther, the remains of a small column designate the **sixth station** (marked with a "VI"), where Veronica wiped Jesus' face with her handkerchief. The mark of his face was left on the cloth, now on display at the Greek Orthodox Patriarchate on the street of the same name.

The **seventh station,** at the intersection with Khan az-Zeit, marks Jesus' second fall—precipitated by the sudden steepness of the road. In the first century, a gate to the countryside opened here, and tradition holds that notices of Jesus' condemnation were posted on it. Crossing Khan az-Zeit, ascend Aqabat al-Khanqa and look beyond the Greek Orthodox Convent for the stone and Latin cross that mark the **eighth station.** Here Jesus turned to the women who mourned him, saying "Daughters of Jerusalem, do not weep for me, weep rather for yourselves and for your children" (Luke 23:28). Backtrack to Khan az-Zeit, ascend the wide stone stairway on the right, and continue through a winding passageway to the Coptic church. The remains of a column in its door mark the **ninth station,** where Jesus fell a third time. Again retrace your steps to the main street and work your way through the market to the entrance of the Church of the Holy Sepulchre, where the Via Dolorosa ends.

The **Church of the Holy Sepulchre** marks Golgotha, also called Calvary, the site of the Crucifixion. The location was first determined by Eleni, mother of the Emperor Constantine, during her pilgrimage in 326 CE. Eleni thought that Hadrian had erected a pagan temple to Venus and Jupiter on the site in order to divert Christians from their faith. As Jerusalem's first archaeologist, she sponsored excavations and uncovered the tomb of Joseph of Arimathea and three crosses, which she surmised had been hastily left there after the crucifixion as the Sabbath approached. Constantine built a small church over the site in 335, which was later destroyed by the Persians in 614, rebuilt, and destroyed again (this time by the Turks) in 1009. Part of the original church's foundations buttress the present Crusader structure, built in 1149. When the present building was erected, its architects decided to unite all the oratories, chapels, and other sanctuaries that had cropped up around the site under one monumental cross. By 1852, tremendous religious conflicts had developed within the Holy Sepulchre over such issues as who had the right to clean the doorstep. The uninterested Ottoman rulers divided the church among the Franciscan order, the Greek Orthodox, Armenian Orthodox, Coptic, Syrian, and Ethiopian churches. The first three are the major shareholders, entitled to hold Masses and processions and to burn incense in their shrines and chapels.

One of the most revered buildings on earth, the church is also somewhat decrepit. The bickering among the various denominations lends the structure some of its interest, but has also kept the building in shambles, marred by perpetual construction. The effects of major fires in 1808 and 1949 and an earthquake in 1927 demanded a level of cooperation and a pooling of resources that could not be mustered. Restoration work in any part of the basilica implies ownership, making each sect hesitant to assist and eager to hinder the others. The result is that little, if anything, is ever accomplished. In 1935 the church was in such a precarious state that the colonialists desperately propped it up with girders and wooden reinforcement. Since 1960, partial cooperation has allowed the supportive scaffolding to be gradually removed. To this day, however, the question of who gets to change a given light bulb can rage into a month-long controversy.

The church's entrance faces the slab on which Jesus was supposedly anointed before he was buried. To continue along the stations, go up the stairs to the right just after the entrance. The chapel at the top is divided into two naves: the right one belongs to the Franciscans, the left to the Greek Orthodox. At the entrance to the Franciscan Chapel is the **tenth station,** where Jesus was stripped of his clothes, and at the far end is the **eleventh,** where he was nailed to the cross. The **twelfth station,** to the left in the Greek chapel, is the unmistakable site of the Crucifixion: a life-size Jesus, clad in a metal loincloth, hangs among oil lamps, flowers, and enormous candles. Between the eleventh and twelfth stations is the **thirteenth,** where Mary received Jesus' body. The station is marked by an odd statue of Mary adorned with jewels, a silver dagger stuck into her breast.

Jesus' tomb on the ground floor is the **fourteenth** (and final) **station.** The **Holy Sepulchre,** in the center of the rotunda, is a large marble structure flanked by huge candles. The first chamber in the tomb, the Chapel of the Angel, is dedicated to the angel who announced Jesus' resurrection to Mary Magdalene. A tiny entrance leads from the chapel into the sepulchre itself, an equally tiny chamber lit by scores of candles and guarded by priests. The walls of the tomb have been covered, but if you're lucky, the priest in charge will show you a small section of the original wall hidden behind a picture of the Virgin Mary. The raised marble slab in the sepulchre covers the rock on which Jesus' body was laid. Nudging the back of the Holy Sepulchre is the tiny Coptic Chapel. To the right of the Sepulchre, the **Chapel of Mary Magdalene** recalls the place where Jesus appeared to her after his resurrection.

The rest of the church is a dark labyrinth of small chapels through which priests, pilgrims, and chatty tourists wander. Because a denomination's ability to hang anything on the church's walls also indicates ownership, the building houses only religious paintings and spindly oil lamps. Near the eastern end, steps lead down to two cavernous chapels commemorating the discovery of the true cross. In a small chapel on the ground floor just below Calvary, a fissure runs through the rock, supposedly caused by the earthquake following Jesus' death. According to legend, Adam (of Adam and Eve fame) was buried beneath Calvary, allowing Jesus' blood to drip through this cleft and anoint him. (Church open daily 5am-8pm; winter 4am-7pm. Men and women must cover their knees.)

**St. Alexander's Church,** a block east of the Church of the Holy Sepulchre on Via Dolorosa, houses the Russian mission-in-exile. Prayers for Czar Alexander III are held Thursdays at 7am (open Mon.-Sat. 9am-1pm and 3-5pm; admission NIS1.50; ring bell). Across the street is the **Lutheran Church of the Redeemer** (tel. 627 61 11); enter on Muristan St. and climb a seemingly endless narrow spiral staircase to the bell tower to see an amazing view along with your vertigo. (Open Mon.-Sat. 9am-1pm and 1:30-5pm. English service Sun. 9am. Admission NIS2, students NIS1.50.) The **Greek Orthodox Patriarchate Museum** (tel. 627 11 96), on the street of the same name, is a more recent addition to the Christian Quarter. Under the Patriarch Benedictos Papadopoulos, the scattered liturgical riches, gifts of pilgrims, and early printings of the Patriarchate's 19th-century press are arranged in a spacious, reconstructed Crusader building (open Tues.-Fri. 9am-1pm and 3-5pm, Sat. 9am-1pm; admission NIS3).

Take a left from the Russian mission, another onto Khan az-Zeit St., and walk up the stairs to the left to reach the **Ethiopian Monastery** (near the 9th station), over part of the Church of the Holy Sepulchre and open all day. The Ethiopians possess no part of the church itself, so they have become squatters on the roof. The modest compound is comprised of white buildings with green doors. Walk around and follow the "Please Watch Up Your Head" signs to the small but amazing church.

## Muslim Quarter (Excluding Via Dolorosa)

The Muslim Quarter, with architecture from the Ayyubid and Mamluk periods, is the largest and most heavily populated quarter in the Old City, but also the least known. Inquire at the GTIO or with individual tour groups about tours in the area. Self-appointed tour guides of varying quality linger around Jaffa Gate; agree on a price before setting out.

ISRAEL

During the day, the main streets are crowded with tourists and merchants. At night, the quarter becomes dark, isolated, and possibly dangerous. The stretch of **Baab as-Silsilah Street** extending to the Temple Mount is partly founded on the ancient Mamluk causeway which crossed the Tyropoeon Valley, linking the upper city to the temple platform. Mamluk architecture lines the street, but blends into the bustle. There are sites to see here, but not to enter. At the beginning of the street stands the **Khan as-Sultan** (or Al Wakala), a remarkably preserved Crusader-period caravanserai which provided lodging for merchants and their donkeys. Just past Misgav Ladakh St. (farther down the street on the right) is the **Tashtamuriya Building,** formerly an Islamic college, housing the tomb of its namesake (d. 1384). The multitude of Mamluk public institutions can be attributed to their system of succession, which prevented them from passing their wealth on to their children; constructing public institutions was the best way to preserve their legacy.

Continuing down Baab as-Silsilah to its intersection with Western Wall St. (Ha-Kotel), you'll arrive at the **Kilaniya Mausoleum,** with its characteristic Mamluk stalactite half-dome; the **Turba Turkan Khatun** (Tomb of Lady Turkan) is at #149. At the end of Baab as-Silsilah, on your right and often surrounded by tour guides in training, is the **Tankiziya Building,** built by a Mamluk slave who worked his way up to become governor of Damascus in 1312, and then back down to imprisonment and execution in Alexandria 30 years later. This venerated structure, on the site of the original seat of the Sanhedrin, is currently controlled by Israelis due to its proximity to the Western Wall and Temple Mount.

## EAST JERUSALEM (NEAR THE OLD CITY)

### Mount Zion

Rising outside the city walls opposite Zion Gate and the Armenian Quarter, Mt. Zion (Har Tzion) has long been considered the site of the Tomb of David, the Last Supper, and the descent of the Holy Spirit at Pentecost. The name Zion, which is also applied to Israel as a whole, is derived from the Jebusite fortress called Zion, first seized by King David when he conquered the eastern territory. During the siege of the Jewish Quarter in 1948, the area around **Zion Gate** was the scene of some of the fiercest fighting in Jerusalem; bombshell pock marks remain. To reach the mount, you can take Egged buses #1 or 38, which run between Jaffa Gate and Mt. Zion (#1 goes through Me'a She'arim to the central bus station, #38 goes to the center of town). On foot, you should exit the Old City through Zion Gate, turn left, and follow the wall around, forking right at the convent. At the next fork, take a left.

A stairway through the grey door on your left leads to the bare **Coenaculum (Cenacle),** identified by most as the site of the Last Supper. Its no-frills appearance is due in part to a law from the British Mandate forbidding any changes, including decorations, to be made to the church. This attempt to avoid sectarian disputes came into effect three centuries after the building was used as a mosque. As a result, the mosque's *mihrab* is still visible in the southern wall (open 8:30am-4pm).

To enter **David's Tomb,** exit the grey door and turn right. Above the turquoise, velvet-draped cave tomb, silver crowns mark the years since the creation of the State of Israel. Archaeologists doubt the authenticity of the site, because it is written that kings and only kings were buried within the city, and Mt. Zion was never encompassed by David's walls. (Tomb open summer Sat.-Thurs. 8am-6pm, Fri. 8am-2pm; winter Sat.-Thurs. 8am-5pm, Fri. 8am-1pm. Free.)

The **Palombo Museum** (Beit Palombo, tel. 673 66 40), across the street and to the left, displays works by the sculptor who crafted the gate to the Knesset and contributed works to Yad Va-Shem (open by appointment; free).

The huge, fortress-like **Basilica of the Dormition Abbey** (tel. 671 99 27) lies off the right fork of the road leading to the Cenacle, on a site that has harbored many memorials. The present edifice, commemorating the death of the Virgin Mary, was completed in 1910. Parts of the precariously situated basilica were damaged during battles in 1948 and 1967 and never repaired. The ground floor is inlaid with zodiac symbols, and the crypt contains a figurine of the Virgin (open Mon.-Sat. 8am-noon and 12:30-6pm, Sun. 9:30am-noon and 12:30-6pm; free).

## The City of David and the Kidron Valley

The quest for the origins of Biblical Jerusalem has been an ongoing progress since 1850. The **City of David** stands on the spot where the Israelite capital reputedly began, though only recently have the pieces of the puzzle begun to fit together. Archaeologists have confirmed that the ridge of Ophel—south of the Temple Mount and outside the city walls—is the site of Jebus, the original Canaanite city captured by King David.

Excavations of the earliest Canaanite walls indicate that the Jebusites were confined to an area of about eight acres. The size and location of the city, above the Kidron Valley, were chosen so that the inhabitants would have access to the nearby water source (the Gihon Spring) and at the same time remain high enough on the ridge to ensure adequate defense. In times of peace, townspeople passed through a "water gate" to bring water into the city. For continued supply during times of siege, a shaft enabled them to have access to water without leaving the walls. This shaft played an important part in David's strategy for taking Jebus (II Samuel 5:8): his soldier Joab simply climbed its walls. In 1867, Warren confirmed this biblical account when he discovered the long, sleek shaft that now bears his name. In the 1960s, Kathleen Kenyon located the Jebusite city walls which date from 1800 BCE and lie just above the Gihon Spring.

Later, King Hezekiah devised a system to prevent David's strategy from being turned against the Israelites: he built a 500m-long tunnel to bring the Gihon waters into the city walls and store them in a pool, hiding the entrance of the spring and keeping invaders such as the Assyrians from finding water when they camped outside the wall. In 1880, a few years after the tunnel was excavated, a local boy discovered an inscription carved by Hezekiah's engineers describing the jubilant moment when the north and south construction crews met underground. The original inscription is in Istanbul, but a copy is on display at the Israel Museum (see p. 313).

You can slosh through **Hezekiah's Tunnel** with a flashlight or a candle, but you probably shouldn't do it alone. The water is about 0.75m high, and wading through it takes about 30 minutes. There are two ways to tackle the tunnel; both will get you wet. You can start at the Gihon Spring source on Shiloah Way, which branches to the right from Jericho Rd. as you approach the Kidron Valley from the bottom of the Mount of Olives. The tunnel ends at the Pool of Shiloah (Silwan in Arabic, Silo'am in Hebrew). Alternatively, you can start from the Pool of Shiloah, only a short walk from Dung Gate. Walk left from the gate and make a right onto Ma'alot Ir David St. After the small playground on your left, turn left into the alleyway; the entrance is on your left. (Open 8:30am-4:30pm. Free, although several little boys will try to convince you otherwise.)

Several organizations offer tours; check at the tourist office for schedules. Recent years have witnessed increasing tension in this much-disputed area. Orthodox Jewish nationalists have attempted to establish a Jewish presence in the midst of Arab **Silwan;** Arab homes were quietly purchased and their residents evicted in a dramatic, middle-of-the-night maneuver. A Jewish bastion, guarded by barbed wire, is perched precariously and conspicuously in the center of this Arab neighborhood; unaware tourists may find themselves walking into a potentially dangerous situation. As always, read newspapers and consult tourist offices before exploring.

About 100m past the entrance to the City of David is a small museum with photos of the most recent excavations. A spiral staircase leads down to **Warren's Shaft** (tel. 628 81 41). With a flashlight, you'll be able to see the entire length of the walls that Joab scaled (open Sun.-Thurs. 9am-5pm, Fri. 9am-1pm; admission NIS5).

To see excavations in progress, walk out of Dung Gate, turn left, and walk downhill to the City of David entrance, on your right just past the UNRWA office. The excavations in this part of the Ophel, called **Section G,** were halted in 1981 when a group of Orthodox Jews protested that the area might have once been the Jewish cemetery mentioned in the diaries of several medieval pilgrims. After considerable political and sometimes violent ballyhoo, the Supreme Court of Israel ruled that the site should be closed. As a compromise the Israeli government promised that digging would continue only under rabbinic supervision. No bones have been found.

Four tombs are located down Shiloah Way, in the **Kidron Valley.** The first is **Absalom's Pillar,** allegedly the tomb of David's favored but feisty son (II Samuel 15-18). Behind it and to the left is the **Tomb of Jehosaphat.** A dirt path on the left leads to the impressive rock-hewn **Tomb of B'nei Hezir** and the **Tomb of Zechariah.**

## The Mount of Olives

The bone-dry slopes of the **Mount of Olives** (Har Ha-Zeitim in Hebrew) to the east of the Old City are dotted with churches marking the sites of Jesus' triumphant entry into Jerusalem, his teaching, his agony and betrayal in Gethsemane, and his ascension to heaven. That the Mount of Olives has three gardens of Gethsemane and two points of Ascension may cast doubt on the precision of the locations, but nothing can detract from the splendor. Jews believe that the Messiah will arrive in Jerusalem from the Mount of Olives. Tradition holds that the thousands of people buried here will be the first to be resurrected upon his arrival.

The best way to visit all the important churches, tombs, gardens, and observation points is to take a cab to the top (NIS15-20) and walk down on the winding road that passes through the hill's sights. This is most enjoyable in the morning, when the sun shines at your back and permits sparkling views of the Old City. Most churches are closed on Sundays and from about noon to 3pm.

The **Chapel of Christ's Ascension** is the geographical apex of noteworthy sites, if not the aesthetic peak. Built in 392, this was the first church erected to commemorate the event. Towards the end of the 11th century, the Crusaders adorned the Chapel with columns and arches, and in the late 12th century Salah ad-Din fortified the chapel with walls and added a domed roof. Inside there's a sacred footprint, unidentifiable after generations of non-sacred treadings of relic-happy pilgrims. (Open 8am-5pm; ask for a guard in the mosque courtyard if it's closed. Admission NIS2).

Descending from the chapel and turning left, the next important stop is the **Church of the Pater Noster** (Latin for "Our Father"). When St. Eleni founded the church in the 4th century she named it the Church of the Disciples; it is also referred to as the **Church of the Eleona** (Greek for "olive grove"). This was the site of the grotto where Jesus revealed the "inscrutable mysteries" to his disciples—foretelling the destruction of Jerusalem and his Second Coming. The church commemorates the first recitation of the Lord's Prayer. Polyglots can read the prayer in 77 languages (including Old Frisian) on the tiled walls. In the midst of the translations is the tomb of the Princesse de la Tour d'Auvergne, the woman who worked here for 17 years (1857-74) and financed the excavations and renovations. The Lord's Prayer was her favorite, and she was determined to uncover the long-lost grotto where it was originally taught (tel. 689 49 04; open Mon.-Sat. 8:30-11:45am and 3-4:45pm).

For a monumental view of the Old City, stop by the observation promenade outside the nearby **Seven Arches Hotel.** To the north, the bell tower of the **Augusta Victoria** hospital on Mt. Scopus marks the highest point in Jerusalem (903m above sea level). It, too, provides a great view, but the staff will not look kindly upon hordes of traipsing backpackers.

Down from the Seven Arches, a gate on the left leads to two tunnels, traditionally identified as the **Tombs of the Prophets** Malachi, Haggai, and the wily Zechariah. Archaeological evidence, however, suggests that the graves are far too recent—probably dating from the 4th century CE (open daily 8am-3pm). The orange sign with black Hebrew lettering marks the **Common Grave** of those who died defending the Jewish Quarter in 1948. Next to the Common Grave lies the **National Cemetery,** and farther down the path sprawls the immense **Jewish Graveyard,** the largest Jewish cemetery in the world.

Continuing on the path you'll reach the **Sanctuary of Dominus Flevit** ("the Lord wept"), erected in 1955 to mark the spot where Jesus wept for Jerusalem. During the construction, supervised by the renowned Italian architect Antonio Barluzzi, several unrelated ruins were unearthed (open daily 8am-noon and 2:30-5pm). Farther down the road on the right stands the **Russian Church of Mary Magdalene,** with seven golden onion domes (tel. 628 43 71). Czar Alexander III built the church in 1885 in the lavish 17th-century Muscovite style and dedicated it to his mother, the Empress Maria Alexandrovna. The crypt houses the body of a Russian grand duchess, smuggled to Jerusalem via Beijing after her death in the Russian Revolution. Now a convent, the church basks in the aura of the sacred shrines that surround it, and even claims a part of the Garden of Gethsemane (ordinarily open Tues. and Thurs. 10-11:30am, but call to make sure; free).

Near the bottom of the path, deep in the valley, the **Church of All Nations** (Basilica of the Agony) faces west toward the Old City. Enter through the gate to the Garden of Gethsemane, just below the Church of Mary Magdalene. The garden is the place where Jesus purportedly spent his last night in prayer and was betrayed by Judas (Mark 14:32-42). Although the site has been venerated since the 4th century, the present building, also designed by Barluzzi, was built with international contributions after World War I. Inside, mosaics depict Jesus' last days, including the proverbial kiss of death. The building's façade portrays Jesus bringing peace to all nations (open Apr.-Oct. 8am-noon and 2:30-6pm, Nov.-March 2:30-5pm). The nearby **Tomb of the Virgin Mary** and **Cave of Gethsemane** are the last stops on the path (both open 8am-noon and 2:30-5pm).

### North of the Old City

Midway between Damascus and Herod's Gates, **Solomon's Quarries** plunge into the city's bowels and provide refuge from the midday heat. Many believe that it was in these cool caves, extending about 250m beneath the Old City, that workers quarried limestone for the building of ancient Jerusalem in the time of the First Temple. They used an Ancient Egyptian technique to remove blocks of stone from the cave walls: wooden planks were set in crevices and soaked with water, and the expanding planks wedged the stone apart. Legend has it that Zedekiah, Judah's last king, fled the city through a passage to Solomon's quarries when King Nebuchadnezzar of Babylonia invaded in 587 BCE. The sign for the quarries reads "Zedekiah's Cave" (open Sat.-Thurs. 9am-4pm, Fri. 9am-2pm; admission NIS5, students NIS2.50).

Farther east on Suleiman St., near the northeastern corner of the city walls, a driveway leads to the **Rockefeller Archaeological Museum** (tel. 628 22 51), one of the best in the country. The museum records the region's history, beginning with the remains of the 100,000-year-old Mt. Carmel Man, and chronicles the cultural impact of imperialism. Check out the impressive, intricately carved wood panels from the 9th-century Al Aqsa Mosque. The museum was designed in the 1920s by British architect Austin S.B. Harrison in his inimitable Orientalist-Gothic style. (Open Sun.-Thurs. 10am-5pm, Fri.-Sat. 10am-2pm. Admission NIS17, students NIS11. Take Egged bus #1, 27, or 23.)

A short distance up Nablus Rd. on Schick St., a sign points toward the **Garden Tomb,** noticed first by Otto Thenius in 1860. The garden is a candidate for Golgotha, the site of Christ's crucifixion. The hill does indeed resemble a skull, and some claim that a nearby tomb is that of Joseph of Arimathea, who placed Jesus' body in his own tomb after the crucifixion (open Mon.-Sat. 8am-12:15pm and 2:30-5:15pm. English service Sun. 9am). As you continue along Nablus Rd., stop at the lovely, seldom-visited **St. George's Cathedral.** The cathedral houses modest collections of Palestinian embroidery and pottery.

Following Salah ad-Din St. up to Nablus Rd., you'll find a Tombeau des Rois **(Tomb of the Kings)** sign on your right just before the intersection. Judean kings were thought to be buried here, but evidence shows that the tomb was in fact built in 45 CE by the Mesopotamian Queen Helena for her family. Bring a candle or flashlight (open Mon.-Sat. 8am-12:30pm and 2-5pm; admission NIS10, students NIS5). A little farther north up Nablus Rd. on the right is the elegant **American Colony Hotel,** a

**ISRAEL**

legendary hang-out of the foreign press. Built in 1881 in a late Ottoman style, the hotel serves expensive drinks to those in the know.

## WEST JERUSALEM

The fact that certain segments of the traveler population identify West Jerusalem solely with the eateries, dance clubs, and sandal stores of the Ben Yehuda *midraḥov* (pedestrian mall) is nothing short of a crime. The ever-popular *midraḥov* certainly provides many staples for the tourist, but explorations of West Jerusalem's subtler side, its dotted hills of elegant neighborhoods, well-kept parks, and impressive museums, are often much more rewarding. Since the first Jews moved outside the protective walls of the Old City in the 1860s, West Jerusalem has flourished, though often at the expense of other communities. By municipal law, all new buildings must be cased with the soft, off-white Jerusalem stone, creating a harmony between uninspired developments, ritzy architectural innovations, and the ancient buildings of the Old City.

### Near Zion Square (City Center)

**Zion Square** (Kikkar Tzion), at the eastern end of the *midraḥov*, is the center of West Jerusalem and one of the few places in the city that is lively at all hours. **Ticho House,** 7 Ha-Rav Kook St. (tel. 624 50 68), near Zion Sq. about two blocks up the hill, displays watercolors and drawings, including many Jerusalem scenes, by artist Anna Ticho. She lived here with her husband, whose collection of menorahs is also on display. The well-groomed building, gardens, and restaurant make for a relaxing mid-city respite (see **Food,** p. 294). (Museum open Sun. 10am-5pm, Tues. 10am-10pm, Fri. 10am-2pm; free. A small library shows a videotape of Anna Ticho's life and work upon request; open Sun.-Thurs. 11am-6pm, Fri. 10am-noon.)

The northern end of Ha-Rav Kook St. spills out onto Ha-Nevi'im St., across from which opens the quiet, stone-wall-lined Ethiopia St. Houses here are arranged in a checkerboard pattern, with alternating front and back walled-in gardens. At the end of the street on the right is the handsome **Ethiopian Church,** built at the turn of the century. Directly across from the entrance to the Church, at #11, is the one-time home of Hebrew language founder **Ben Yehuda,** but the building is now closed.

**Me'a She'arim** ("Hundredfold," an invocation of plenty), just north of Ethiopia St., is one of the few remaining examples of the Jewish *shtetl* communities that flourished in pre-Holocaust Eastern Europe. Several thousand Ultra-Orthodox Jews live here, preserving traditional habits, dress, customs, and beliefs with painstaking (and somewhat frightening) diligence. Me'a She'arim's relatively few extremists are vocal and receive a good deal of publicity. The Neturei Karta (City Keepers), the most extreme sect of the Satmar Ḥasidim, oppose the Israeli state, arguing that Jewish law prohibits the legitimate existence of a Jewish country until the coming of the Messiah. While many other Ultra-Orthodox Jews hold similar views, Neturei Karta once went so far as to ask Yassir Arafat to accept them as a minority in the future Palestinian state. If your Hebrew eavesdropping skills let you down here, it may because you're hearing Yiddish, spoken by some residents who consider Hebrew too holy for daily use.

Signs throughout the area read, "Daughters of Israel! The Torah requires you to dress modestly," and then proceed to explain exactly what this means. Whether you're Jewish or not, take this warning seriously if you don't wish to offend (and face the wrath and saliva of angry ḥasidim). Women should wear below-the-knee skirts and past-the-elbow shirts, men below-the-knee pants. Always ask before taking photographs.

Me'a She'arim is probably the cheapest place in the world for Jewish books and religious items. Bargaining is the rule; try stores on the eastern end of Me'a She'arim St. The neighborhood also has some of the city's best **bakeries,** most of which are open all night on Thursdays, baking *ḥallah* and cake for the Sabbath. The one at 15 Rabbenu Gershom St. (off Yeḥezkil St.) has great *burekas* and chocolate rolls.

**Naḥla'ot** and **Zikhron Yosef,** neighborhoods just south of the Maḥaneh Yehuda market, are also crowded and predominantly religious. Residents are mostly Jews from Yemen, Iran, Turkey, and Morocco, and, increasingly, artists and students in search of cheap housing. The narrow, winding alleys and tiny courtyards are festooned with laundry and lined with barber shops, blacksmiths, and sandal-makers.

The modern **Great Synagogue of Jerusalem,** 56 King George St. (tel. 624 71 12), across from the Sheraton Plaza, is enormous and ornate, but not terribly inspiring (open Sun.-Fri. 9am-1pm). Consider a stop at the **Wolfson Museum** next door, on the fourth floor of the Hekhal Shlomo building. The museum exhibits Jewish religious and ceremonial objects. Note the texts painted on eggshells and the Algerian Torah decorations (museum open Sun.-Thurs. 9am-1pm; admission NIS2). Also close to the city center is the **Italian Synagogue** and its **Nahon Museum of Italian Art,** 27 Hillel St. (tel. 624 16 10). Browse at the impressive collection of items including pieces from the Conegliano Veneto Synagogue dating from 1701 (open Sun.-Thurs. 10am-1pm, Wed. also 4-7pm; admission NIS4).

The **Underground Prisoners Museum** inside the Russian Compound off Jaffa Rd. (tel. 623 31 66) commemorates the work of Israel's underground movement in the pre-1948 struggle against British rule. Originally erected by Russian pilgrims, the hall was converted during the British Mandate into Jerusalem's main prison and now serves as a small but powerful exhibit. Enter through Heshin St., just off Jaffa Rd. where it splits with Shlomzion Ha-Malka St. Follow the green Museum signs (open Sun.-Thurs. 8am-4pm; admission NIS5, students NIS2).

## Giv'at Ram

The **Israel Museum** (tel. 670 88 11 or 73) is the largest and most comprehensive museum in Israel. With extensive collections of antiquities, sculptures, ancient and modern art, books, the legendary Dead Sea Scrolls, and a even children's section, the museum has nearly as many facets as the country itself.

Rock and rust enthusiasts should go straight to the **archaeology** section—30,000 years of human habitation in the Fertile Crescent are summarized with an extensive collection of tools and weapons. Guided English tours are given on Monday and Thursday at 2pm. Straight ahead from the bottom of the steps is the **ethnography** exhibit, tracing the important events of the Jewish life cycle. Guided tours of the Judaica and ethnography galleries are given on Sunday and Wednesday at 2pm.

The museum boasts a fabulous collection of **art,** including the largest display of Israeli art in the world. There is a fairly large Impressionist and Post-Impressionist collection, and even a few period rooms (including a spectacular French Rococo *salon* donated by the Rothschilds). The **Weisbord Pavilion,** directly across from the ticket building, houses a few Rodin sculptures and early modern paintings, and rotates contemporary art exhibitions. The **Billy Rose Sculpture Garden** displays some incredibly stationary masterworks by Henry Moore and Picasso. Pick up a schedule of evening outdoor concerts at the museum, and try to visit on a Tuesday night when the garden is illuminated.

The museum's biggest attraction is the **Shrine of the Book,** which displays the Dead Sea Scrolls. The building's white dome and black walls are supposed to symbolize the struggle between the Sons of Light and Dark, an important theme to the Qumran sect. Others suggest the structure pays homage to the Hershey Kiss. Yet another theory posits that the building resembles the covers of the pots in which the scrolls lay hidden for 2000 years in the Caves of Qumran near the Dead Sea. Dating from the 2nd century BCE to 70 CE and belonging to an apocalyptic, monastic sect called the Essenes, some of the scrolls contain versions of the Hebrew Bible almost identical to the books that passed through the hands of countless Jewish scribes. On the bottom level of the museum is a collection of letters and relics that pre-date the destruction of the Second Temple and have been crucial to scholars studying that period (late 1st- to early 2nd-century CE; guided tours in English Sun.-Mon. and Wed.-Thurs. 1:30pm, Tues. 3pm, and Fri. 12:45pm).

ISRAEL

To get to the museum, take bus #9, 17, or 24. From the ticket building, walk along a shrub-lined walkway and up the steps to the main building. There is also a free bus for disabled or elderly visitors and their escorts running every 10 minutes all day, except from 1-1:30pm. At the booth in the lobby you'll find museum maps, information on current exhibits, and schedules for special events, lectures, and tours; specific pamphlets are NIS1 each. (Open Sun.-Mon. and Wed.-Thurs. 10am-5pm, Tues. 4-10pm. The Shrine is open the same hours but Tues. 10am-10pm. Admission to museum and Shrine NIS22, students NIS17. Annual student membership is NIS95 and allows unlimited entrance to the Israel and Rockefeller Museums. English museum highlights tours Sun.-Mon. and Wed.-Fri. 11am, Tues. 4:30pm.)

While the Israel Museum overwhelms with its sheer magnitude, the new **Bible Lands Museum** (tel. 561 10 66) across the street is artfully arranged and much more manageable. The ancient pottery, jewelry, seals, and figurines comprise the private collection of Dr. Elie Borowski, an eager Canadian antiquities collector. An interactive computer program beckons you in with great graphics and catchy music, and teaches you everything you could possibly want to know about cylindrical stamps and seals. (Open Sun.-Tues. and Thurs. 9:30am-5:30pm, Wed. 9:30am-9:30pm, Fri. 9:30am-2pm, and Sat. 11am-3pm. English tour Sun.-Fri. 10am, Wed. also 5:30pm. Admission NIS20, students and children NIS12.)

At the **Knesset,** discover why Israeli schoolteachers insult excessively rowdy pupils by likening them to parliament members. Israel's Parliament is located on Eliezer Kaplan St. It's directly across the street from the Israel Museum, but you'll have to walk around the block to the entrance. You must have your **passport,** and you may be subjected to a body search. (Open sessions Mon. or Thurs. after 4pm and Wed. after 11am; call to see if the Knesset is in session.) Free tours (Sun. and Thurs. every ½hr. in 1 of 10 languages, 8:30am-2:30pm) include an explanation of the structure of the Israeli government and a look at the Chagall tapestry and mosaics that adorn the building. Take bus #9 or 24 (tel. 675 34 20 or 16 for information).

The **Wohl Rose Garden** is next to the Knesset and is a sublime picnic spot. A path leads from here to the gorgeous new seat of the **Israeli Supreme Court,** completed in late 1992. The designers (Karmi & Assoc.) combine Modernist architecture with themes from ancient Jerusalem building traditions. Sit in on a trial—it's like court TV, only live and in Hebrew (open Sun.-Thurs. 8:30am-2:30pm; movie in English at noon).

Across Rupin Rd. from the government center is the Giv'at Ram campus of **Hebrew University.** At the engaging **Bloomfield Science Museum** (tel. 561 81 28) kids will leap at the chance to interact with live phenomena like gravity. (Open Mon. and Wed.-Thurs. 10am-6pm, Tues. 10am-8pm, Fri. 10am-1pm, Sat. 10am-3pm; admission NIS15, students and children NIS12.) Another Giv'at Ram sight worth looking into is the fabulous **Ardon Window** in the **National Library** (tel. 658 50 27). One of the largest stained-glass windows in the world, it depicts Kabbalistic (Jewish mystical) symbols in rich, dark colors (open summer Sun.-Thurs. 9am-6pm, winter until 7pm, Fri. 9am-1pm; free).

## South of Zion Square

South of Independence Park lie some of Israel's most elegant and affluent residential areas. **Reḥavia,** the area trisected by Azza Rd. and Ramban St., was founded in the 1920s and became the refuge for the many German Jews fleeing Nazi persecution in the 30s. For years, it was famous as a *Deutsch* high-culture enclave, where dark wood libraries were lined with Goethe and Schiller, and Mozart grooved on the gramophone. Little of the German flavor remains today, but the legacy lives on in the many International Style houses, designed in the best tradition of German Modernism. Flowery hedges fill the spaces between the well-kept stone-dressed buildings, making a walk around the neighborhood's lush streets a verdant pleasure.

In the middle of Reḥavia on Alfassi St. is **Jason's Tomb** (near #12, the sign says "Rock Cut Tomb"), built around 100 BCE as the burial site of a wealthy Hasmonean-era Jewish family. Pottery found at the site indicates that three generations were buried there, while charcoal drawings on the plastered porch wall depict ships, suggesting that one of the deceased was involved in naval excursions. The pyramid topping the tomb is a reconstruction. Further east past Azza Rd. is the **Prime Minister's official residence,** in the guarded house at the corner of Balfour and Smolenskin St. Next door on Balfour St. is the **Schocken Library,** designed by renowned architect Erich Mendelssohn who resided in Jerusalem in the late 1930s (he lived in the windmill on Ramban St. near Kikkar Tzarfat, now a ritzy shopping complex).

Farther south are the neighborhoods of **Talbiyya** (Komemiyut) and **Qatamon** (Gonen), still known by the names they had before their Arab inhabitants were dispossessed in 1948. The ornate villas (one of which was the home of renowned cultural theorist Edward Said) have become favorites of Hebrew University faculty and, more recently, well-to-do professionals. The official residence of the Israeli President is on Ha-Nassi (President) St., and the plush **Jerusalem Theater** is on the other side of the block, on the corner of Chopin and Marcus Rds.

Around the corner from Ha-Nassi St. is the lizerific **Mayer Institute for Islamic Art,** 2 Ha-Palmaḥ St. (tel. 566 12 91), displaying a significant collection of miniatures, paintings, and artifacts from the Islamic world. Take bus #15 from the center of town. (Open Sun.-Mon. and Wed.-Thurs. 10am-5pm, Tues. 4-8pm, Fri.-Sat. 10am-2pm. Admission NIS12, students NIS8, under 18 NIS6; free on Sat.)

On the other end of Jabotinsky St. is **King David Street.** The Holy Land's most phormidable phallus is 300m up the street toward the city center: the **YMCA,** built in 1933, has an imposing bell tower offering fine views of the whole city (open Mon.-Sat. 8:30am-6pm, admission NIS2). Directly across the street, the historic **King David Hotel** retains an aura of old-world luxury, making it a favorite accommodation for international celebrities. The King David served as the British Headquarters and was bombed by Jewish underground forces during the 1948 War. Heading along King David St. towards the center of town you'll find **Hebrew Union College,** the American Reform Movement's outpost in Israel. Check out their **Skirball Museum,** 13 King David St. (tel. 620 33 33), showcasing an excellent exhibit of relics from three ancient cities: Laish, Gezer, and Aroer (open Sun.-Thurs. 10am-4pm, Sat. 10am-2pm; free). Down the other side of King David St., at the intersection with Keren Hayesod and Jabotinsky St., is the sprawling, green haven of **Liberty Bell Park** (Gan Ha-Pa'amon), where lawns intermingle with an amphitheater, basketball courts, climbable sculptures, and a Liberty Bell replica. On Saturday nights, the park hip-hops with folk-dancing festivities (take bus #14, 18, or 21 from the center).

Cross the street to get to the restored neighborhood of **Yemin Moshe.** It was here that Sir Moses Montefiore, a British Jew, first managed to convince a handful of residents from the Old City's overcrowded Jewish Quarter to spend occasional nights outside the city walls, thus founding West Jerusalem. To strengthen the settlers' confidence, Montefiore built **Mishkenot Sha'ananim** (Tranquil Settlement), a small compound with crenelated walls resembling those of the Old City. The original buildings, now housing an exclusive municipal guest house and a pricey French restaurant, are located at the bottom of the hill. Montefiore also erected a his famous stone windmill, now containing a tiny museum (open Sun.-Thurs. 9am-4pm, Fri. 9am-1pm; free). Yemin Moshe is now an artists' colony with galleries crammed between picturesque alleyways. The now-dry **Sultan's Pool** sits in the valley below. Named after Suleiman the Magnificent, renovator of this Second-Temple reservoir in the 16th century, the pool figures prominently in Palestinian novelist Jabra Ibrahim Jabra's *The Ship.* Today the Sultan's Pool is most famous for its open-air concerts.

If you walk farther south on King David St., turn right at the gas station, and bear right onto Emek Refa'im St., you'll reach the **German Colony,** a leafy neighborhood of somber European houses and spacious Arab villas. To the southeast, the **Haas Promenade,** on the road to Armon Ha-Natziv, is a hillside park and promenade with great views of the Old City and the Dead Sea, perfect for gazing, grazing, or blazing. The dusk experience alone is worth the trip (take bus #8, 44, 48, or 99).

## North of Zion Square

Bus #2 from the city center to Ha-Sanhedrin St. (off Yam Suf St.) takes you to a park carpeted with pebbles and pine needles and the **Tombs of the Sanhedrin.** Composed of esteemed male sages and leaders, the Sanhedrin was the high court of ancient times; it ruled on legal matters and even reviewed Jesus' case. Separate burial areas were designated for the members (open Sun.-Fri. 9am-sunset; free).

The **Tourjeman Post,** 4 Heil Ha-Handasa St. (tel. 628 12 78), recounts Jerusalem's history from its division in 1948 to its reunification in 1967. Although closed for extensive renovations in summer 1996, the museum is expected to reopen in 1997. The building withstood severe shelling during the 1948 War and became an Israeli command post from 1948 to 1967, when the Jordanian border was just across the street. To reach the building, walk northwest up the wide new road springing from Ha-Zanhanim St.; the museum will be on your left, just before the intersection with Shivtei Yisrael St. (Take bus #11 or 27. Expected hours Sun.-Thurs. 9am-5pm, Fri. 9am-1pm.)

Before the Six-Day War, **Ammunition Hill** (Giv'at Ha-Tahmoshet; tel. 582 84 42) was Jordan's most fortified position in the city and commanded much of northern Jerusalem. Taken by Israeli troops in a bloody battle, the hill now serves as a memorial to the Israeli soldiers who died in the Six-Day War. The somber, architecturally striking museum is housed in a reconstructed bunker and gives an account of the 1967 battle. Buses #4, 9, 25, 28, and 45 let you off at the foot of the hill. (Open summer Sun.-Thurs. 8am-6pm, Fri. 8am-2pm; winter Sun.-Thurs. 9am-5pm, Fri. 9am-1pm. Admission NIS8, students and children NIS4.)

After 1948, the **Hebrew University of Jerusalem** had to relocate from **Mt. Scopus** (Har Ha-Tzofim), where it was founded in 1925, to the new campus in **Giv'at Ram.** From 1948 to 1967, Mt. Scopus was a garrisoned Israeli enclave in Jordanian territory. After 1967, all but the natural and physical sciences departments moved back to the original campus. Massive reconstruction was funded largely by international donors, whose names emblazon the libraries, promenades, and pebbles that comprise modern Mt. Scopus. Free guided tours depart from the Bronfman Reception Center in the Sherman Administration Building (Sun.-Thurs. 11am). Pick up a map from the Reception Center to stroll around Israel's top university on your own. You can browse through the bookstore, library, computer labs, and botanical gardens. For a fabulous view of Jerusalem, head to the overlook point, outside the university gates along the south side of the campus. The **Hecht Synagogue** in the Humanities building, overlooking the Old City, is also worth a visit; enter via the Sherman Building. The university's gorgeous **amphitheater** faces the West Bank.

## Southwest of Zion Square

**Yad Va-Shem,** meaning "a memorial and a name" (tel. 675 16 11), is the largest and most moving of Israel's Holocaust museums. Don't plan to do too much right after your visit; the museum's several buildings deserve some time and take an emotional toll. It's best to start at the **historical museum,** which traces the origins and horrors of the Holocaust through photographs, documents, and relics. The exhibit ends with a simple, powerful memorial: symbolic tombs showing the number of Jews who were killed in each country, and a tiny shoe that belonged to one of the Holocaust's younger victims. **The Hall of Names** (closes 15min. before museum) contains an agonizingly long list of all known Holocaust victims. Visitors may fill out a Page of Testimony, recording the name and circumstances of death of family members killed by the Nazis. **The Hall Of Remembrance** houses a *ner tamid* (eternal fire) to memorialize the Holocaust's victims, with the name of each concentration camp engraved into the floor. The nearby **art museum** displays drawings and paintings composed by Jews in the ghettos and concentration camps; in the museum and on its grounds are a number of evocative works by sculptor Elsa Pollock. By far the most haunting part of Yad Va-Shem is the stirring **Children's Memorial,** where mirrors are positioned to create the illusion of an infinite sea of candles, while a recorded voice recites the names and ages of young victims. The **Valley of the Communities** is an enormous labyrinthine memorial dedicated to the destroyed villages of Europe. Carved in stone are the names of *shtetls* that are no more; surviving family members wander around in search of their former towns. To get to Yad Va-Shem, take bus #13, 17, 18, 20, 23, or 27 and get off at the huge, orange arch just past Mt. Herzl. Turn around and take a left on Ein Kerem St., then follow the signs down Ha-Zikaron St., for about ten minutes (open Sun.-Thurs. 9am-5pm, Fri. 9am-2pm; free guided English tour of Yad Va-shem Sun.-Fri. 11:30am and 2pm).

You'll see signs near the bus stop for **Mount Herzl** (Har Herzl), where the founder of modern political Zionism is buried. The **Herzl Museum** (tel. 651 11 08) encapsulates the energy of the man, a newspaper correspondent who made the most prominent modern articulations of Zionism and lobbied for the creation of a Jewish state until his death in 1904 (open Sun.-Thurs. 9am-6:30pm, Fri. 9am-1pm; admission NIS2, students NIS1). Ze'ev Jabotinsky, Levi Eshkol, Golda Meir, and Yitzhak Rabin are also buried here. Nearby is the **Israeli Military Cemetery,** the resting place of fallen soldiers. The Military Cemetery is two bus stops before Mount Herzl, but you should go to the Herzl Museum first to get a walking map.

The scenic **Jerusalem Forest** and the pastoral village of **Ein Kerem,** just west of Mt. Herzl, are perfect for picnics and short hikes. You can get to the village by taking city bus #17 or 17a from the central bus station or Zion Square (runs every 20-30min.). Formerly an Arab village, tiny Ein Kerem (fountain of vines) is the traditionally professed birthplace of John the Baptist. His mother certainly chose the spot well: the slow-paced village's tranquil streets pass olive groves, gazelles, hummingbirds, and flocks of sheep.

The **Church of St. John** (tel. 641 36 39), with its soaring clock tower, marks the spot where John was born. The church displays several paintings, including the *Decapitation of Saint John.* (Open March-Sept. daily 6am-noon and 2:30-6pm; Oct.-Feb. 6am-noon and 2:30-5pm. Italian Mass celebrated at Sun. 8:15am. Dress modestly. Free.) In the church's **Grotto of the Nativity** there is a lovely Byzantine mosaic of pheasants—the symbol of the Eucharist. Ask the guardian for a key.

Across the valley, down Ma'ayan St. from St. John's gate, the **Church of the Visitation** (tel. 641 72 91) recalls Mary's visit to Elizabeth and contains a rock behind which the infant St. John supposedly hid when the Romans came to kill babies. The newer Upper Chapel depicts the glorification of Mary. (Open March-Sept. daily 8-11:45am and 2:30-6pm, Oct.-Feb. 8-11:45am and 2:30-5pm.) The pink tower belongs to the **Russian Monastery** (tel. 625 25 65 or 641 28 87), which you can visit by appointment only.

The synagogue at the **Hadassah Medical Center** near Ein Kerem (tel. 677 62 71; not to be confused with Hadassah Hospital on Mt. Scopus) houses the **Chagall Windows,** depicting the 12 tribes of Israel in abstract stained-glass designs based on Genesis 49 and Deuteronomy 33. Chagall donated the windows to the hospital in 1962. When four of the windows were damaged in the 1967 War, Chagall was sent an urgent cable. He replied, "You worry about the war, I'll worry about my windows." Two years later he installed four replacements. Three of the windows still contain bullet holes. (Free tours Sun.-Thurs. every hr. on the half-hr. 8:30am-12:30pm and 2:30pm, Fri. every hr. 9:30-11:30am. Synagogue open Sun.-Thurs. 8am-1:15pm and 2-3:45pm, until 5pm in summer, Fri. 8am-12:45pm. Admission NIS9, students with ID NIS4.50.)

In the hospital's Tannenbaum Center, you can get a ride to the **Jerusalem Forest** (ask for Pinchas), and participate in the **Jewish National Fund's tree-planting program** (trees US$10 each, call 670 74 33 or 563 96 50 for information).

# ■ Entertainment

Tel-Avivians hate to admit it, but Jerusalem nightlife is no longer joke-worthy. After years of Jerusalemites having to descend on Tel Aviv for some action, Jerusalem in the 90s has seen a spurt of nocturnal additions. Once the city's conservative majority is safely tucked into bed, the bar and club scene comes to life, peaking Thursday to Saturday nights. Cultural events, from lunchtime chamber music to the early summer **Israel Festival,** long a source of Jerusalem pride, add to Jerusalem's blossoming arts scene. The best info is in *Kol Ha-Ir,* a Hebrew weekly. The entertainment section of Friday's *Jerusalem Post* and the MTIO will also help.

In June, look out for **Student Day** at Hebrew University, with trips during the day and fireworks at night—a barrel of monkeys open to all students.

## BARS

In the **Russian Compound** (Migrash Ha-Russim), two blocks east of Zion Sq., neon beer signs glow through the crisp night air. After midnight, stylish bars in old stone buildings fill to capacity (and overflow into the street) with a young, oh-so-hip crowd. It's not hard to choose a haunt that suits your mood: they're all concentrated around one block. Other bars tap the Yoel Solomon region.

**Shanty,** 4 Naḥalat Shiva St. (tel. 624 34 34), between Yoel Solomon and Rivlin St. Take the first left on Yoel Solomon from Zion Sq., turn left, and it's on your right. An Israeli enclave in a tourist domain; ensures an absence of teens by carding harder. Beer NIS10-15, toasts NIS22, salads NIS24. Open Sun.-Thurs. 7:30pm-3 or 4am, Fri. 9pm-3 or 4am, Sat. 8:30pm-3 or 4pm. Kitchen closes at 11pm.

**Glasnost,** 15 Heleni Ha-Malka St. (tel. 625 69 54), off Zion Sq., in the Russian Compound. Plays jazz, funk, and rock; live bands play salsa (Sun. 9pm) and reggae (Mon. 9pm). Sit indoors or outside on an airy, music-filled patio. Beer NIS10-18, daiquiris NIS20, hard liquor NIS15-30. Also serves spaghetti, chicken wings, burgers, and cakes (NIS12-35). Open 7pm-whenever.

**Sergey,** Heleni Ha-Malka St. (tel. 625 85 11), at the corner of Mounbaz St., next to Glasnost. Intellectual twenty-something crowd; packed with angst-ridden Bezalel Art Institute students so hip they don't even wear black. Italian food. Beer NIS10-16, mixed drinks NIS14 and up. Open 8pm-3 or 4am. Sun. is blues night.

**Strudel Internet Café and Wine Bar,** 11 Manbaz St. (tel. 623 21 01). Kick back and check e-mail, or just work on a puzzle. Good house wine NIS11. A cozy joint with 21st-century "fun." Open daily noon-2am or later. Visa, MC, AmEx.

**Mike's Place,** 14 Harkness St. Leave your neuroses at the door. Israeli and ex-pat crowd digs live blues and rock nightly, Tues.-Sat. No cover. Goldstar NIS10, whiskey NIS14. Open daily 7pm- until you hear the "mooo's" at your door.

**The Rock,** 11 Yoel Salomon (tel. 625 91 70), features good, loud music and sidewalk seating with unsurpassed population density on Thurs. and Sat. nights. Beer NIS8-14. Happy hour Sun.-Thurs. 5-9pm. Young tourists network here. Open Sun.-Thurs. 5pm-2 or 3am, Sat. nightfall-3 or 4am. Kosher.

**Gizmo,** 9 Heleni Ha-Malka St. (tel. 624 15 95). Candle-lit pub is relatively spacious, increasing discursive possibilities even on live music nights. Blues and jazz concerts Fri. (5pm), Sun., and Mon. (9:30-10pm). Beer NIS9-16, mixed drinks NIS14 and up. Open Sat.-Thurs. 6pm-3 or 4am, Fri. 6pm-4am.

## CAFÉS

**Tmol Shilshom,** 5 Yoel Solomon St. (tel. 623 27 58). Tucked behind the street up a staircase. This gay-owned bookstore-café is poet Yehuda Amiḥai's favorite. He and other local greats give readings here while aspiring writers scrawl over coffee and tea (NIS5.50-14). Open-mike poetry and live music jams. Curries, baked potatoes and salads NIS19-25. All-you-can-eat breakfast buffet Fri. morning NIS25. Open Sun.-Thurs. 8:30am-1:30am, Fri. 8:30am-3pm, Sat. 8:30pm-1:30am. Kosher.

**Café Ta'amon,** 27 King George St. (tel. 625 49 77), corner of Hillel St. A legendary hole in the wall, where older Israeli writers and intellectuals mingle with vodka lovers. Owner Mordekhai Kop's IOUs book is a veritable *Who's Who in Israel.* Coffee, tea, sandwiches, pastries NIS5. Beer NIS8-10. Fri. (1-5pm) is *cholent* day, when regulars come for the traditional Jewish meat and potato stew (NIS15). Open Sun.-Thurs. 6:30am-2am, Fri. 6:30am-5pm, Sat. sundown-2am.

**Caffit,** 35 Emek Refaim St. (tel. 635 284). Draws the post 20-something crowd to green umbrellas on a large patio. Usually a wait to get in. Generous cakes and pies (NIS14.50-20), large selection of coffee drinks (NIS7-10); ornately garnished veggie meals, including salads (NIS25) and corn soup (NIS15). Open Sun.-Thurs. 7:30am-2am, Fri. 7:30-sundown, Sat. after *Shabbat*-2am. Visa, MC, AmEx.

**Aroma,** 18 Hillel St. (tel. 625 53 65), corner of Rav Akiva. Hip 24-hr. espresso bar with good coffee and light meals. Coffee and croissant combo NIS8. Coffee drinks NIS 4.50-7.50; cheaper to take out. Closed Fri. 5-10pm, Sat. 5am-11am.

**Ha-Mizraka Tea House,** 12 Yoel Salomon St. (tel. 625 52 22). Serves 24 kinds of tea (NIS10 per pot, NIS4 more with rum) and assorted snacks in a candle-lit, cushion-clad cave. Open Sun.-Thurs. 7pm-2am, Fri. 9pm-3pm, Sat. sundown-2am.

**Café Atara,** 7 Ben-Yehuda St. (tel. 625 01 41). The meeting place of the Hagana and Jewish *Jerusalem Post* writers when it was still the *Palestine Post.* Visit this legend before it turns into a Pizza Hut. Sandwiches NIS17.50-29. Open Sun.-Thurs. 6am-midnight, Fri. 6am-4pm, Sat. sundown-1am. Kosher.

**Moment,** 30 Azza St. (tel. 566 67 56). From the *midraḥov,* turn left on King George, walk to the end, and turn right on Ben Maimon; fork left onto Azza. Bus #9. Chi-chi bar with small tables perfect for a beer (NIS8-10) or espresso (coffee drinks NIS5-12). For the young urban pre-professional. Great sandwiches NIS14-20, salads NIS18-20, and pastries NIS5-10. Open Sun.-Thurs. 8am-3am, Fri. 8am-5pm, Sat. sundown-2 or 3am.

## DANCING

The city center dance scene has been whittled down to two perennially packed, shamelessly cheesy clubs, plus one new and much cooler addition. The **Underground,** 8 Yoel Salomon St. (tel. 625 19 18), is the most popular, with a bar and a Batcave-like disco downstairs. It's musty with funky fluorescent graffiti and wall-to-wall sweaty, semi-trashed dancers bent on shedding burdensome layers of clothing as the hours turn wee. This is the dance club everyone hates but goes to anyway. From 7:50 to 8:10pm, get all the beer you can drink for NIS5. It's free to enter the rock music bar room, but to get into the techno dance lair you'll have to buy a drink (starting from NIS9). The **Arizona,** 37 Jaffa Rd., has a similar policy. This dance inferno is a mite smaller and cheesier, and features a Western-theme bar. The disco is a twin of the Underground's; in fact, they are separated by one (all too thin) wall. Both feature unduly confident clientele who grind atop picnic tables, and both are disproportionately testosterone-heavy. (Both open 7:30pm-4am, depending on crowds.) The **Q bar** (tel. 623 45 82), above the Underground, welcomes both gay and straight drinkers and dancers. Wednesday and Friday nights are the most popular, but it's open daily, 11:30pm-3 or 4am (beer NIS12, cokes NIS5).

Larger clubs are in Jerusalem's southern industrial neighborhood, **Talpiot,** down Hebron Rd., and include **Pythagoras, Decadance,** and **Opera.** The cover charges range from NIS15 to 25 for Friday and Saturday nights (open about 9pm-5am).

For a night of bacchanalian revelry, visit **Mo'adon Canaan** at 8 Ta'asiya St. (tel. 673 56 33 or 57 21; a NIS15 cab ride). NIS30 buys carafe after carafe of all the red and white wine you can drink as you jive to Israeli folk music-turned-rock. Don't be surprised if you start banging a tambourine and dancing on tables with a wild horde of Israelis and tourists. For NIS66, you also get a multi-course meat dinner (open Tues., Thurs., and Sat. 9:30pm-1:30am; reservations strongly recommended).

There are many options for folk dancing in Jerusalem. The **International Cultural Center for Youth** (ICCY), 12a Emek Refa'im St. (tel. 566 41 44), has dancing on Tuesdays at 8pm (take bus #4 or 18; NIS12). The **House for Hebrew Youth** (Beit Ha-No'ar), 105 Ha-Rav Herzog St. (tel. 678 86 42), holds folk-dancing classes (Wed.-Thurs. 8pm; bus #19, NIS12). For a freer setting for your gyrations, head to the **Liberty Bell Gardens** for a bit of post-*Shabbat* hopping. Dances from folk to modern jazz are taught to aspiring Astaires of all ages.

## PERFORMING ARTS

The **Jerusalem Symphony** performs frequently at the Jerusalem Theater on David Marcus and Chopin St. (tel. 561 14 98 after 4pm; ask about student discounts), while the **Israel Philharmonic Orchestra** plays at Binyanei Ha-Umma (tel. 625 24 81).

**ISRAEL**

Plays, dances, and concerts are held at the Israel Museum (tel. 563 62 31). **Asaf's Cave,** in the Mount Zion Cultural Center (tel. 671 68 41) near David's Tomb, stars the Diaspora Yeshiva Band; bid *Shabbat* good-bye here weekly at 9pm (in winter 8pm) with Hasidic dancing and English, Hebrew, and Yiddish music—a unique Jerusalem experience (cover NIS10; call to make sure there is a performance). Friday nights at 10:30pm, popular Israeli singers perform at **Beit Shmuel,** 6 Shammai St. (tel. 620 34 56; NIS30-60; reservations recommended). Seize any opportunity to attend a performance at **Sultan's Pool** (Brekhat Ha-Sultan), open in summer only (see p. 315). Tickets for American or British rock stars start at NIS80.

The **Palestinian National Theater** (Al Hakawati), on Nablus St. (tel. 628 09 57), near the American Colony Hotel, has survived through years of Israeli occupation and IDF raids. They stage plays and musicals, many of which are unabashedly political; English synopses are provided. Walk up Nablus Rd. and take the first right after the intersection with Salah ad-Din St. The theater is 100m farther on the right, at the end of a short driveway; look for the black door. Locals greet visitors cordially. (Admission NIS10. Call to inquire about performances.)

Built by Ottoman Turks in the 1880s as a caravan stop, the **Khan** (tel. 671 82 81), across from the railway station in Remez Sq., contains an intimate theater, restaurant, art gallery, and a café featuring Hebrew stand-up comedy, jazz (Tues. 10:30pm) and classical music concerts (NIS10-30). It's rarely frequented by tourists, but the concerts and plays, mostly in Hebrew, are critically acclaimed. (Egged buses #7, 8, 21, 30, and 48, and Arab buses #21 and 22 pass by the railway station.)

## FILM

At the **Jerusalem Cinemathèque** on Hebron Rd. in the Hinnom Valley (tel. 672 41 31), southwest of the Old City walls (bus #4, 4a, 7, 8, 14, 18, 21, or 48), two screens show several films every evening (Sun.-Thurs. 5-9:30pm, Fri. 2, 10pm, and midnight, Sat. 11am, 4, 8, and 10pm. Tickets NIS20; call to find out about Fri. night "movie marathons"). The annual **Israeli Film Festival** brings international films to Jerusalem and introduces local creations in the first part of July. Pick up a free book of listings (also in English) at the Cinematheque, or read the Friday supplement of the *Post*. For some films you'll need to buy tickets well in advance.

## SHOPPING

Budget shopping in Jerusalem can be fun if you keep your wits about you. Often the deal of the century is found after relentless comparison shopping or by bargaining until you're blue in the face. It's best to pay in foreign currency to avoid the VAT. Otherwise, be sure to get a refund form to be redeemed at the airport.

### Jewelry

You can buy jewelry anywhere you turn in Jerusalem—in Arab *souqs,* on the *midraḥov* Ben Yehuda, from street vendors, or from fine shops in hotels. **Eilat stone,** a green or turquoise semi-precious stone from the hills around Eilat, is a common element in rings, necklaces, earrings, and pendants. **Baltinester,** 40 Jaffa Rd. (tel. 625 66 46 or 624 40 28) has caseloads of jewelry in all price and quality ranges. Jewelry can be inscribed in 2-6 days (14K gold nameplate US$30-90). (Open Sun.-Thurs. 9am-7pm, Fri. 9am-2pm, Sat. after *Shabbat* until 10pm. Credit cards accepted). Booths of cheap jewelry abound at **The Pit,** an open-air market at the end of Yoel Solomon St. Merchants set up shop in the afternoons and evenings. On Friday, they start at 10am and end before *Shabbat.* On Saturday, they hawk from nightfall until late.

### Ceramics and Woodwork

Israel is home to many accomplished and impressive artisans. Often pieces are made from pine, olive wood, Jerusalem stone, and other native materials. **Jerusalem Pottery,** along Via Dolorosa between Al Wad St. and Khan az-Zeit St., has beautiful hand-painted ceramic tiles, cups, and containers. The Armenian owners paint the tiles that mark Old City streets. Their work appears throughout the souq, but the biggest selection is at their own store. Custom ceramic nameplates take ten days to make and are worth the wait (start at NIS15). At **Kakadu,** 12 Rivlin St. (tel. 623 30 73), Reut and Aaron Shaher hand-design beautiful pinewood trays, notebook covers, and other gift items using rich colors (open Sun.-Thurs. 10am-10pm, Fri. 10am-4pm; credit cards accepted). Owner Neḥemiah hand-carves all the wood himself at **Almaz Olive Wood Shop,** 26 Me'a She'arim (tel. 682 47 15). Boxes (NIS20), clocks (NIS50), bookstands (NIS35), and other items can be personally engraved (open Sun.-Thurs. 10am-8pm, Fri. 10am-3pm).

## Judaica

If you're looking for *menorot, mezuzot, kippot,* or other ritual items, you've come to the right city. The *Talmud* says that it is not enough to fulfill the commandments; one must beautify the ritual with pieces of art. As a result, ceremonial objects have been outlets for the most talented Jewish artists. Often items are crafted in precious metal and sold in jewelry stores. Rows of inexpensive Judaica shops crowd the streets of **Me'a She'arim. Yermiyahu's,** 3 Yanai St. (tel. 661 00 58), off Shlomzion Ha-Malka just before it intersects with Shlomo Ha-Melekh, sells very nice *kippot* and *tallitot* at bargain prices (open Sun.-Thurs. 8am-7pm, Fri. 8am-1pm). **Chen Eilat,** 11 Me'a She'arim (tel. 637 01 28), has a huge selection of *ḥallah* covers (NIS20-100), candles (NIS20-40), and all things Jewish (open Sun.-Thurs. 9:30am-7:30pm, Fri. 9:30am-2:30pm; credit cards accepted).

## Music

Pop songs in Israel can tackle subjects as heady as life in the army, the religious-secular conflict, and coping with terrorism. Lyrical folk songs by Naomi Shemmer and others have become second anthems to the young state, and capture the worries, and hopes of Israel better than a thousand pictures. **Derekh Ha-Ozen Music,** 23 Ben Yehuda (tel. 625 50 77), at the corner of King George (other location at 4 Luntz St. near the *midraḥov*) is the best and cheapest place to listen to and shop for Israeli music. The knowledgeable staff can help you find any type of Israeli, Jewish, or Ḥasidic music. Feel free to listen to any recording in the store. Ask a clerk and they'll gladly unwrap the cellophane and set you up at a listening station, without pressuring you to buy a thing (open Sun.-Thurs. 9am-9:45pm, Fri. 9am-4pm, Sat. after *Shabbat*-midnight).

## Old City Markets

The minute you cross the threshold of Jaffa Gate, marketeers begin shoving their wares in your face. **David Street** plunges into the heart of the Old City, and, along with **Baab as-Silsilah Street,** is the central artery of the bustling *souq.* Some of the Palestinian craftwork is quite beautiful, such as Hebron-style wine glasses, mother-of-pearl inlaid boxes, ceramic tiles, and spherical Jerusalem candles. Other items (cheap t-shirts and plastic-mold Domes of the Rock) aren't. Popular tourist purchases include the *tableh* (drum) and the decorative *argeileh* (water pipe). If you cannot throw out enough t-shirts to fit an *argeileh* into your pack, settle for a short but powerful smoke (NIS1-2) at a *qahwah.* Women should make sure the *qahwah* is not exclusively male before sitting down. The apple tobacco is especially delicious. At several local haunts inside Damascus Gate, you can rent an *argeileh* for NIS5, and they'll keep refilling the coals until your lungs say stop.

Do not buy from the first air-conditioned wonderland you enter. Often, the exact same wares are sold from closet-like alcoves for a lot less. There's a lot of supply in this market—remember the rules of economics and use them to your advantage.

Halfway down David St. on the left, two cavernous rooms house a **produce market** called *Souq Aftimos.* **Al Wad Road** connects the Western Wall area to Damascus Gate. A right off Al Wad onto **Via Dolorosa** leads to an array of small ceramics shops. Shops between **Christian Quarter Road** and the Church of the Holy Sepulchre have the largest selection of rosaries, crosses, and other Christian items. The **Khan az-Zeit** market extends north from David St. to Damascus Gate. Actual Old City-folk shop here and along Al Wad. There aren't many gifts, but cartloads of cheap shoes, clothing, sewing products, jewelry, lingerie, spices, and kitchenwares.

As you wind your way through the *souq,* notice the buildings. Much of the decorative masonry—stone set within stone over entries and passageways—is characteristic of Mamluk architecture. Paintings of the Dome of the Rock and the Ka'ba shrine of Mecca adorn doorways. A painting of the latter signifies that a member of the family has been on the *hajj,* the Islamic pilgrimage to Mecca and Medina. Women should dress modestly for a more heckling-free shopping excursion.

# BETWEEN JERUSALEM AND TEL AVIV

## ■ Abu Ghosh אבו גוש أبو غوش

Thirteen kilometers west of Jerusalem lies the Arab village of **Abu Ghosh.** One of many shared sacred sites in the region, Christians and Jews alike revere Abu Ghosh as an early site of the Ark of the Covenant, which King David later moved to Jerusalem. In the 18th century, Sheikh Abu Ghosh required pilgrims to pay a toll here as they traveled to the Holy City; the town was the last of a series of caravan stops en route to Jerusalem. Historically, the Arabs of the village have always had good relations with neighboring Jewish settlements, even during the 1948 War. The town now has a Jewish mayor. To get to Abu Ghosh, take Egged bus #185 or 186 (every 30 min., 20min., NIS7), which leaves from the central bus station. *Sherut* traveling between Jerusalem and Tel Aviv will stop at the exit, 2km from Abu Ghosh.

**Notre Dame de l'Arche d'Alliance** (Our Lady of the Ark of the Covenant; tel. (02) 342 818) at the top of the hill, was built on the site of the Ark's ancient holding place. The current church was built in the 1920s on the ruins of a demolished Byzantine church; fragments of the old mosaic floors remain. (Open daily 8:30-11:30am and 2:30-6pm, but you can usually enter at any reasonable hour.)

Below the sacred hill, in a beautiful garden, stands the magnificently preserved **Crusader Church of the Resurection,** built in 1142 and acquired by the French government in 1873. Excavations beneath the church have uncovered remains dating back to Neolithic times. The church lies below the main road; head for the minaret of the attached mosque and look for a door in the wall on your right. (Open Mon.-Wed. and Fri.-Sat. 8:30-11am and 2:30-5:30pm. Free.)

There are many restaurants to curb your midday **hunger** along the road connecting the two churches. Join the lunch-break hordes from Jerusalem at the **Caravan Inn Restaurant** (tel. (02) 342 744 or 333 573). While the meat dishes are a little pricey (*shishlik* for NIS27), you can get a plate of hummus for NIS8 and enjoy the breezy terrace with amazing views of Abu Gosh and the hills of Jerusalem (credit cards accepted).

The stalagmite and stalactite cave of **Avshalom** (the **Soreq Cave**) contains spectacular speleological splendors. Discovered less than thirty years ago when a routine blast at a nearby quarry exposed a view into the cave, this site has been transformed into a major tourist attraction. The artificial lighting and paved pathways may disappoint adventurous spelunking fantasies, but can't overshadow the natural majesty. The cave lies 19km southwest of Jerusalem, 7km from the village of Nes Harim. Stalwart hikers can take bus #184 (every 1-2hrs., NIS8.80) to Nes Harim and walk from there. Otherwise try hiring a taxi from Nes Harim or joining an organized tour such as Egged. (Open Sat.-Thurs. 8:30am-3:45pm, Fri. 8:30am-12:45pm.) Admission (NIS13, children NIS7) includes a slide show and guided tour (tel. 991 11 17). Photography and solo wanderings are permitted on Fridays only.

The **Bet Meir Youth Hostel (HI)** (tel. (02) 534 26 92; fax 534 20 98) is situated within a religious community about 20km west of Jerusalem. On bus #186 from

Jerusalem (NIS9.80, 40min.), continue past Abu Gosh to arrive at Bet Meir. Enter the *moshav*, take the first left and after about 200m, go down the road on your right. Follow the signs for Ramot Shapira. At the bottom of the hill lies a large complex housing 40 guest rooms and behind it a number of "cottages" containing dorm rooms. The cozy guest rooms have up to four beds, wall-to-wall carpeting, and A/C (US$22, US$21 for students with a three-person minimum). Those staying in the dorms must be contented with fans (US$18.50, US$17.50 for students). Both alternatives have attached shower and toilet, and breakfast is included. (Reception open 8am-4pm. No lockout or curfew. HI members receive 10% discount.)

## ■ Latrun לטרון

**Latrun** lies about halfway between Jerusalem and Tel Aviv and sports three varied attractions. The **Latrun Monastery** (tel. (08) 922 00 65; 925 51 80; fax 925 50 84) was founded by the French Trappist Order (belonging to the great monastic family of St. Benedict) as a center for contemplation and reflection. Famous for its wine, the monastery is built on a hillside granting it beautiful views of the surrounding area (particularly the biblical sites of Emmaus, Agalon, Bethoron, and others). An inspiring church and peaceful gardens sit beside the monastery (both are open Mon.-Sat. 8am-noon and 3:30pm-5pm). On Saturdays, a short film explaining the life of a monk is screened at 11am (and occasionally at 3pm). The shop near the main gate offers a wide selection of wines and spirits (Mon.-Sat. 9am-1pm, 2pm-6pm). To get to the monastery take the paved road opposite the PAZ filling station and continue for 600m until you see an uphill road on your left (avoid the first left turn which circles the monastery on the outside).

Opposite the Monastery (right next to the filling station) is the **Armored Corps Museum** (tel. (08) 925 52 68), a heaven on earth for those who are enchanted by the sight of tanks, containing over 120 armored battle vehicles. There is also an exhibit of stamps on the subject of armed forces from all over the world and a complete reconstruction of the tank planned by Leonardo da Vinci over 500 years ago. (Open Sun.-Thurs. 8:30am-4:30pm, Fri. 8:30am-12:30pm; Sat. 9am-4pm. Admission NIS10, NIS8 for students.)

On the other side of the Tel-Aviv-Jerusalem highway is the **Emmaus** (Nicopolis) **Church.** Now the site of the French Prehistorical Research Center, this is where Jesus was said to have appeared to two of his disciples after his resurrection (Mark 16:12-13, Luke 24:13-31). Another 100m along the road is the entrance to the **Canada Park**—a beautifully forested area which contains various water holes and the remains of an amphitheater.

Latrun can be reached by bus #404, 425, or 433, from either Jerusalem (30min., NIS12.70) or Ramla (20min., NIS10.70). Service is every 30min. Make sure you tell the driver in advance that you want to stop in Latrun (and remind him a few more times along the way).

# Tel Aviv-Jaffa תל אביב-יפו

Tel Aviv, with its cafés, clubs, and overly tanned youth, does its best to imitate a European way of life. Only 45 minutes away from Jerusalem, the bustling metropolis of Tel Aviv stands as its antithesis. Where Jerusalem thrives on the past, Tel Aviv lives for the moment; Jerusalem is sacred, Tel Aviv has no god; Jerusalem is built of stone, Tel Aviv was founded on shifting sands. Indeed, Tel Aviv invariably inspires emotion among travelers—some fall in love, others catch the first bus to Jerusalem.

Today an integral part of Tel Aviv, Jaffa (Yafo, or "beautiful," in Hebrew; Yafa in Arabic) has one of the oldest functioning harbors in the world. At one point the busiest port in the region, the modern shipping centers in Haifa and Ashdod have relegated Jaffa to harboring mainly small fishing boats. Starting in the 1960s, Israel undertook a massive renovation project, restoring and cleaning many of Jaffa's convents, mosques, alleyways, and crusader walls. The result may be a little too sterile, with restaurants and galleries catering mostly to tourists and generally avoided by locals. Still, the winding alleys of Old Jaffa are beautiful, and many parts retain a Middle Eastern quality that the Modernist city of Tel Aviv lacks.

Two-thirds of Israel's population resides along the 150km of muggy coastline centered on Tel Aviv. Here the moisture that hangs in the air soaks out orthodoxy: most Tel Aviv establishments stay open Friday night. This region includes the country's wealthiest, most commercialized city as well as some of its most fertile farmland.

# ■ History

Tel Aviv's history spans the time from Jonah and the whale to the murder of Prime Minister Yitzḥak Rabin. For a city that shuns history, Tel Aviv has a lot to remember.

According to the Bible, the recalcitrant prophet Jonah shirked his divine calling and fled to Jaffa to catch a boat to Tarshish. When a tempest threatened to destroy his ship, Jonah, knowing the Lord had created the storm, asked the crew to hurl him overboard. The sea calmed, but an enormous serpent-fish swallowed the prophet. After three days and nights, Jonah repented and the fish spewed him onto dry land.

The earliest archaeological finds in Jaffa date from the 18th century BCE. In 1468 BCE, the Egyptians conquered Jaffa by hiding soldiers in human-sized clay jars that were brought into the city market. King David conquered the city in about 1000 BCE, and under Solomon it became the main port of Judea, a position it maintained until the development of Caesarea under King Herod. During the 12th century, Jaffa was captured by the First Crusaders, Salah ad-Din, Richard the Lionheart, the Muslims, and then Louis IX, who built magnificent walls and towers, parts of which remain today. In 1267 the Mamluks overpowered the city, and Jaffa remained an important Arab stronghold until 1948.

Jewish immigrants began to settle in Jaffa as early as 1820; at that time the Palestinian town of Yafa served as the area's major port. Later in the century there were enough Jews to create the first two exclusively Jewish neighborhoods just to the north, **Neveh Tzedek** in 1887 and **Neveh Shalom** in 1891. As the Jewish population in Jaffa continued to increase, settlers decided to found a new suburb in this area. On April 11, 1909, they parceled out the land they had acquired north of Jaffa, naming the area, with sober Zionist practicality, **Aḥuzat Bayit** (Housing Estate). One year later, the suburb was renamed **Tel Aviv** (Spring Hill), after the imaginary town Theodore Herzl had envisioned in his turn-of-the-century utopian novel *Altneuland* (Old-New-Land). Appealing to more bourgeois Jewish immigrants from Eastern Europe, the new town quickly developed in the 1920s and 1930s, becoming the largest Jewish town in Palestine.

Newly arrived Tel-Avivians received a less-than warm welcome from their neighbors to the south. In 1929, 1936, and 1939, Jaffa was the scene of anti-Zionist riots. In the 1948 war, many of the Palestinians in Jaffa and its surrounding villages were displaced, some forcibly. Some of the villages were then razed; no trace of them remains beyond the memories of their former inhabitants. Jaffa was officially incorporated into the Tel Aviv municipality in 1949 and remains a mixed Jewish-Arab neighborhood today.

Tel Aviv acts as the home of Israel's foreign embassies and financial institutions. For a brief period in the winter of 1991, Tel Aviv got world attention (via CNN) as a favorite target for Saddam Hussein's SCUD missiles. For the first time in its short history, the city became a front line; but contrary to fears that the city would never be the same again, the very first night after cease-fire was declared, Tel Avivians went out partying as usual. That party was short-lived, as the events of the past year cast an even greater pall over the city. Hamas bombings have claimed a number of lives and inflicted further pain, and it was in this city that Yigal Amir unleashed the fatal bullet which killed Prime Minister Yitzḥak Rabin. The assassination was a loss of innocence for all Israelis, but no place felt it more acutely than Tel Aviv.

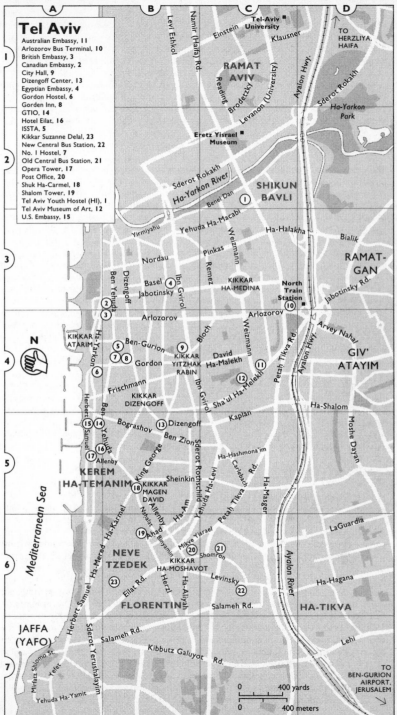

# Tel Aviv

Australian Embassy, 11
Arlozorov Bus Terminal, 10
British Embassy, 3
Canadian Embassy, 2
City Hall, 9
Dizengoff Center, 13
Egyptian Embassy, 4
Gordon Hostel, 6
Gorden Inn, 8
GTIO, 14
Hotel Eilat, 16
ISSTA, 5
Kikkar Suzanne Delal, 23
New Central Bus Station, 22
No. 1 Hostel, 7
Old Central Bus Station, 21
Opera Tower, 17
Post Office, 20
Shuk Ha-Carmel, 18
Shalom Tower, 19
Tel Aviv Youth Hostel (HI), 1
Tel Aviv Museum of Art, 12
U.S. Embassy, 15

## ■ Orientation

Located in the center of Israel's Mediterranean coastline, Tel Aviv is 63km (50min. bus ride) northwest of Jerusalem and 95km (1¼hr.) south of Haifa.

The two main points of entry into Tel Aviv are Ben-Gurion Airport (at Lod) and the new bus terminal. Frequent bus service from the airport is supplemented by vans sent by warring hostel establishments to lure potential customers.

Much of Tel Aviv's seemingly haphazard street layout was actually carefully planned, following the 19th-century English "garden suburb" scheme. Nothing like Hampstead in appearance, Tel Aviv is as difficult to navigate as London. House numbers generally increase from the sea eastward and from the more modest southern part of the city up to the wealthier north. The street signs are in English as well as Hebrew and announce the range of building numbers for that block.

Almost all hotels, restaurants, and places of interest are in the rectangle marked by the beach to the west, the **Ayalon Highway** to the east, the **Yarkon River** to the north, and **Salameh Rd.** to the south. Running along the beach beginning around Gordon St. and extending south to the Charles Clore Park is the **Tayelet** (Promenade), lined with chairs, gazebos, and inviting cafés. **Ha-Yarkon St.** runs parallel to the beach behind the first row of buildings facing the sea. The next major north-south artery, **Ben-Yehuda St.,** runs one block east of Ha-Yarkon and is lined with travel agencies and more affordable restaurants. Parallel to Ben-Yehuda, **Dizengoff St.** is loaded with Tel Aviv's trendy cafés, chic bars, and haute couture. **Ibn Gvirol Street,** with its shaded arcades, runs from the Yarkon river in the north until it turns into Yehuda Ha-Levi St. in the center; half-way is the vast **Kikkar Yitzḥak Rabin** (formerly Kikkar Malkhei Yisrael), in front of City Hall. **Namir Rd.** (which also still goes by its old name, **Haifa Rd.**) is a major thoroughfare farther east; the **central train station,** which has service to all major cities, is located at the intersection of Haifa Rd. and **Arlozorov St.,** which runs east-west all the way to Ha-Yarkon St.

**Kikkar Magen David** (at the corners of Allenby, King George, and Sheinkin) is the starting point of **Shuk Ha-Carmel** to the southwest, the *midraḥov* (pedestrian mall) of **Naḥalat Binyamin** to the south, and the hip **Sheinkin St.** to the east. Northwest of the *shuk* are the winding alleyways of **Kerem Ha-Temanim** (the Yemenite Quarter). The crumbling (but gradually gentrifying) neighborhood of **Neveh Tzedek,** with the beautiful **Kikkar Suzanne Delal,** lies just south of Shuk Ha-Carmel and Naḥalat Binyamin. **Jaffa** and its waterfront lie further south, outside the downtown area, gazing at Tel Aviv's bustling coast.

## ■ Transportation

### GETTING AROUND TOWN

For the most part, Tel Aviv is manageable by foot. On a hot August afternoon, though, a NIS3.30 bus ride may seem like the deal of the century. Buses in Tel Aviv are frequent, air-conditioned, and comfortable. The bus is a must for sights north of the Yarkon, in the Ramat Aviv area, or in Jaffa, which are beyond walking distance from the city center.

Opened in August 1993, the **New Central Bus Station** on Livinsky St. stands next to its grungy, now minimally used, predecessor. The new station transcends being a mere transportation hub. The six (soon to be seven) stories of its air-conditioned interior house music stores, banks, a McDonald's, and even buses. Over 3000 entrances, exits, and ramps in every direction make this the most convoluted bus station in the world. Information booths on the 3rd, 4th, and 6th floors are supplemented by scores of electronic bulletin boards which list intercity bus schedules in both English and Hebrew. Telephones and pay-to-pee restrooms (NIS1) abound, and **baggage check** rooms let you shed your load for NIS5 per item per day (bag check open Sun.-Thurs. 7am-11pm, Fri. and holiday eves 7am-3pm).

The majority of buses within Tel Aviv are operated by **Dan** (tel. 639 44 44). Generally, **city buses** run Sun.-Thurs. 5am-12:15am, Fri. 5am-5pm, and Sat. 8:15pm-12:15am, but some stop running earlier. Buses do not run on *Shabbat.* On extended stays, consider buying Dan's **monthly bus pass** (NIS122). Dan's central office is located at 39 Sha'ul Ha-Melekh (tel. 695 55 55). These six routes are the most important for tourists:

**#4:** From the New Central bus station (4th floor), runs parallel to the coastline up Allenby and Ben-Yehuda St. and back. Every 5min.

**#5:** From the New Central bus station (4th floor), runs north along Rothschild Blvd. and Dizengoff St. to Dizengoff Ctr., then turns around at Nordau and Yehuda Ha-Maccabee. Every 5min.

**#10:** Runs from city hall to Jaffa along Ben-Yehuda St. Every 15-20min.

**#25:** Runs between Tel Aviv University and Bat Yam via Haifa Rd., Yehuda Ha-Maccabee, Ibn Gvirol, King Solomon, King George, Allenby, Shuk Ha-Carmel, and Jaffa. Every 15-20min.

**#27:** From the New Central bus station (1st floor), runs along Petah Tikva Rd. and to Haifa Rd., the train station, Tel Aviv University, the *kenyon* (shopping mall) in Ramat Gan, and back. Every 10-15min.

**#46:** From the New Central bus station (1st floor) to Jaffa and back. Every 8-10min., every 15min. at night.

**Minibuses** operating as **sherut taxis** run along the routes of buses #4 and 5, and are numbered accordingly. At NIS3, they're cheaper than the bus and will stop for you anywhere along the route. Late at night and on *Shabbat* minibuses operate with less frequency and at a 25% higher fare. There's a **private taxi** stand at Allenby St. and Simhat Beit Ha-Shoeva, but you can hail a cab anywhere. Taxis also queue up by Migdal Shalom. You can call a taxi anytime (tel. 524 90 90 or 527 19 99).

## GETTING OUT OF TOWN

Most buses are operated by Egged (intercity info. tel. 537 55 55). The **Arlozorov terminal,** on Arlozorov St. across from Haifa Rd., has connections to major cities:

**Jerusalem:** #480 direct; every 15min., Sun.-Thurs. 6am-10pm, Fri. 6am-4pm, Sat. 8:30pm-11pm, 50 min., NIS14, students NIS12.50.

**Haifa:** #980 direct; every 20min., Sun.-Thurs., 6am-8:30pm, Fri. 6am-4pm, Sat. 8:30pm-10pm, 1¼hr., NIS14, students NIS12.50.

**Be'er Sheva:** #380 direct; on the half hr. Sun.-Thurs., 6am-8pm, Fri. 6am-4pm, Sat. 8:30pm-10:30pm, 1¾hr., NIS14, students NIS12.50.

The **new central bus station** has intercity departures on the sixth floor:

**Jerusalem:** #405 direct; every 10-15min. Sun.-Thurs. 5:40am-11:30pm, Fri. 5:40am-5:30pm, Sat. sundown-midnight; NIS16, students NIS14.40

**Haifa:** #900 direct; every 10-20min. Sun.-Thurs. 5:45am-9pm, Fri. 5:45am-4pm, Sat. sundown-10pm; NIS19.50, students 17.50. Late-night #901 express; every 20min. Sun.-Thurs. 9-11pm, NIS19.50, students 17.50.

**Be'er Sheva:** #370 direct; every 15-20min. Sun.-Thurs. 5:45am-9pm, Fri. 5:45am-4:40pm, Sat. sundown-11pm; NIS20, students NIS18.

The central **train station** is on Arlozorov St. across from Haifa Rd. (information tel. 693 75 15; open 6am-9pm). Several air-conditioned trains go to Haifa, Netanya, and Nahariya. Trains to Jerusalem leave at 10am (NIS13.50, students 25% off; 1¾hr.). Trains to Haifa leave every hour from 5:50am-10pm (NIS 15, students NIS11.50, 1hr. 20min.). Take bus #10, 18, 20, 32, 61, or 62 from the city center. There's an **intercity taxi** stand on Allenby Rd. at Ha-Moshavot Sq. Cars to most major cities are only slightly more expensive than buses.

ISRAEL

# ■ Practical Information

**Tourist Information Office:** Located in the New Central Bus Station on the 6th floor, near platform 630 (tel. 639 56 60). From the city center, take bus #4 or 5 heading south. Provides maps of Tel Aviv and other cities and information on accommodations, food, shopping, tours, and cultural events. Will book hotel and tour reservations. Open Sun.-Thurs. 9am-5pm, Fri. 9am-1pm.

**Tours: SPNI,** 3 Ha-Shfela St. (tel. 638 86 37), between Petaḥ Tikva Rd. and Ha-Sharon St. Open Sun.-Thurs. 8am-5pm, Fri. 8-noon. Their highly qualified English-speaking guides lead the best 1-12 day tours year round. Day tours are US$45-50. Not as uniformly spectacular as SPNI is **Egged Tours,** 59 Ben-Yehuda St. (tel. 527 12 12). Offers guided tours around Israel and to the Sinai (half-day tours of Jerusalem or Tel Aviv US$23, full-day US$51-61).

**Budget Travel: ISSTA,** 128 Ben-Yehuda St. (tel. 521 05 55), corner of Ben-Gurion St. For ISICs bring a photo, current student ID, and NIS30; for Youth Hostel cards bring a photo and NIS25. Open Sun.-Thurs. 9am-6pm, Fri. 9am-1pm. **Mona Tours,** 45 Ben-Yehuda St. (tel. 523 09 20), specializes in student and charter rates. ISIC not always required if you are under age 28. Open Sun.-Thurs. 9am-6pm, Fri. 9am-1pm. Both take credit cards.

**Consulates: U.S.,** 71 Ha-Yarkon St. (tel. 517 00 10). Separate lines for American citizens and Israelis—look for the signs. Open Mon.-Fri. 8am-11am and Wed. 2pm-3:30pm for passports; Mon.-Thurs. 8am-10am for visas. **Canada,** 7 Ḥavakuk St., north of Nordau St. (tel. 546 58 10). Open Mon.-Fri. 8am-noon. **U.K.** (also serves **New Zealanders**), 1 Ben-Yehuda St., Migdalor Building, 6th fl. (tel. 510 01 66 for passports, 510 04 97 for visas). Open Mon.-Fri. 8-11:30am for visas, 8am-1pm for passports. **Australia,** 37 Sha'ul Ha-Melekh Blvd., Europe House, 4th fl. (tel. 695 04 51). Open Mon.-Thurs. 8am-noon. **South Africa,** Top Tower, Dizengoff Ctr., 16th floor (tel. 525 25 66). Open Mon.-Fri. 9-11am, and Wed. 2-3pm. **Egypt,** 54 Basel St. (tel. 546 41 51 or 52), just off Ibn Gvirol. Open Sun.-Thurs. 9-11am. For a visa, bring your passport, photo, and NIS60 (U.S. citizens NIS40)—be sure to tell them if you are going beyond the Sinai, or you'll automatically get a "Sinai Only" visa. **Jordan,** 14 Aba Hillel in Ramat Gan (tel. 751 77 22). If crossing to Jordan through Allenby Bridge, you must get your visa beforehand. Open Mon.-Fri. 9am-1pm.

**Currency Exchange:** The best rates (no commission) are at **Change Point** at 94 Ha-Yarkon St. (tel. 524 55 05) or 70 Ben-Yehuda St. (tel. 527 28 58). **Change Spot,** at 140 Dizengoff St. (tel. 524 33 93), also offers no-commission exchange. Most **banks** are open Sun., Tues., and Thurs. 8:30am-12:30pm and 4-5:30pm, Mon., Wed., Fri., and holiday eves. 8:30am-12:30pm. Main bank offices: **Bank Ha-Poalim,** 104 Ha-Yarkon St. (tel. 520 06 12); **Israel Discount,** 27 Yehuda Ha-Levi St. (tel. 514 55 55); **Bank Leumi,** 130 Ben-Yehuda St. (tel. 520 37 37). Branches throughout the city and suburbs. Bank Ha-Poalim **ATMs** are compatible with most cards from abroad.

**American Express:** 112 Ha-Yarkon St. (tel. 524 22 11), near the Sheraton. Mail held for cardholders, but no packages. If you've lost your AmEx Traveler's Cheques, call their toll-free 24hr. line (177 440 86 94). Changes traveler's checks at bank rates, but without commission. Cardholders can buy traveler's checks with personal checks (1% service charge; bring your passport). 3% charge to buy traveler's checks with cash. Open Sun.-Thurs. 9am-5pm, Fri. 9am-1pm.

**Telephones: Solan Communications,** 13 Frishman St. (tel. 522 94 24; fax 522 94 49). Private booths for international calls. Local calls 10% cheaper than a regular telecard. Offers telecards, international calling cards, fax services. Open daily 24hr. **Change Spot,** 140 Dizengoff St. (tel. 524 33 93; fax 524 36 66), provides discounted international calls. Open Sun.-Thurs. 9am-11pm, Fri. 9am-2pm.

**Airport: Ben-Gurion Airport,** 22km southeast of Tel Aviv in Lod. For recorded information in English about flights on all airlines, call 973 11 22. Egged bus #475 to the airport leaves from the 6th floor of the New Central Bus Station (every 20min., Sun.-Thurs. 5:20am-11:35pm, Fri. 5:20am-5:30pm; NIS7). United Tours shuttle #222 (tel. 693 34 04) stops near several hotels on Ha-Yarkon St. (buses every hr. Sun.-Fri. 4am-midnight, Sat. 1pm-midnight; NIS8). Taxis from the airport to Tel Aviv run at a fixed tariff (about NIS48, each piece of luggage NIS2; 25% surcharge on evenings and *Shabbat*).

**Ferries: Caspi,** 1 Ben-Yehuda St. (tel. 517 57 49), Migdalor Bldg., facing the street. Boats to Cyprus leave Sun., Thurs. 8pm, arrive next morning 7am (US$58, winter $47); to Rhodes, Sun., Thurs. 8pm, 2 days travel (US$101, winter $81); to Piraeus, 3 days travel (US$106, return US$85; summer US$96.) Port tax additional US$22. **Mano Passenger Lines, Ltd.,** 97 Ben-Yehuda St. (tel. 522 46 11), books tickets on ships to Cyprus. Boats leave from Haifa Sun. at 8pm. Cabins only, US$65; return US$110. Lower in winter. Port tax additional US$25 each way. Open Sun.-Thurs. 9am-7pm, Fri. 9am-2pm; winter Sun.-Thurs. 9am-5pm, Fri. 9am-1pm. Both ferry lines take credit cards.

**Car Rental: You Car** (tel. 522 61 50), 134 Ya-Yarkon, US$55 per day; automatic US$60. 3-day rental US$44 per day. Young drivers welcome with US$1000 deposit on credit card. **I. Gindy Ltd. Rent-a-Car** (tel. 527 83 44), US$50 (in summer US$60) per day. Big discounts on weekly rental. Min. age 21. **Sharet Rent-a-Car** (tel. 522 20 55), US$50-60 per day depending on the season. Weekly discounts. Jeep rental. Min. age 21. **Avis** (tel. 527 17 52), min. age 23. **Budget** (tel. 523 15 51), min. age 23. **Rent-a-Reliable-Car** (tel. 524 97 94), min. age 24.

**Shopping Hours:** In general, 8:30am-1pm and 3-7pm, but many places stay open until 10pm, especially those in shopping malls. Most stores stay open late on Thurs. night, and almost all close Fri. by 2pm.

**English Bookstores:** A fabulous selection of magazines, comics, and cheap used books awaits you at **Katzman Gallery Books,** 152 Dizengoff (tel. 523 52 43). After you've finished reading your book, they'll buy it back. Open Sun.-Thurs. 10am-2pm and usually 5pm-8pm, Fri. 8am-3pm. **Modan Prosa Bookstore,** 162 Dizengoff St., (tel. 523 54 77), has a small but good selection of English fiction and non-fiction. Open Sun.-Thurs. 9am-8pm, Fri. 9am-3pm. Visa, MC. **Steimatzky** has many locations including 107 Allenby Rd., and 109 Dizengoff St., the Opera Tower at 1 Allenby Rd., Kikkar Ha-Medina, and the new Central Bus Station.

**Library: British Council Library,** 140 Ha-Yarkon St. (tel. 522 21 94). Offers English-language books, newspapers, videocassettes, and magazines to the public, as well as peaceful air-conditioned havens. Open Mon.-Thurs. 10am-1pm and 4-7pm, Fri. 10am-1pm.

**Camping Supplies: LaMetayel,** Dizengoff Center, Gate 3 or 5 (tel. 528 68 94), near the Lev Cinema. The largest camping store in the area; they carry books, maps, information, and a full range of equipment. The place to meet young Israelis gearing up for their post-military grand tour. Open Sun.-Thurs. 9:30am-8pm, Fri. 9:30am-2pm. **Maslool Travelers' Equipment and Information Center,** 36 Ben-Yehuda St. (tel. 528 84 18). Gives discounts for those who show a *Let's Go* guide; buys used equipment. Open Mon.-Thurs. 10am-4pm, Fri. 10am-2pm.

**Film Developing: Fotofilm,** 84 Allenby St. (tel. 517 12 41). 1-hr. developing, lenses, film, video supplies—anything you and your camera might possibly want. Open Sun.-Thurs. 9am-7pm, Fri. 9am-2pm. **Clarni,** (tel. 523 09 90) 154 Dizengoff St. 1-hr. developing, film supplies. Open Sun.-Thurs. 8am-7pm, Fri. 8am-2pm.

**Ticket Agencies: Rococo,** 93 Dizengoff St. (tel. 524 88 24 or 522 36 63). Open Sun.-Thurs. 9am-7pm, Fri. 9am-2pm. **Hadran,** 90 Ibn Gvirol St. (tel. 524 87 87), north of Kikkar Yitzhak Rabin. **Castel,** 150 Ibn Gvirol St. (tel. 604 76 78 or 47 25). **Le'an,** 101 Dizengoff St. (tel. 524 73 73). All sell tickets for concerts, plays, sporting events, and other performances. Discount student tickets available.

**Laundry:** Self-service laundromats abound on most streets, and hostels and hotels often have their own laundry services. **Nikita,** 98 Ben-Yehuda St., has coin-operated machines. NIS8 washes 7kg. NIS1 dries clothes for 4min. Detergent NIS2. **Bu'ot,** 49 Sheinkin St. (tel. 524 26 54 and 629 20 94) will pick up, clean, and drop off up to 6kg of laundry for NIS 26.

**Help Lines: Rape Crisis** (tel. 685 00 41), 24hr. **Drug Counseling** (tel. 546 35 87), Sun.-Thurs. 8am-8pm. Both speak English.

**Pharmacy: Ben-Yehuda Pharmacy,** 142 Ben-Yehuda St. (tel. 522 35 35). Open Sun.-Thurs. 8am-3am, Fri. 8am-4pm. **Superpharm** (tel. 620 37 98 or 07 95) in Dizengoff Center (and other locations) is more drugstore-like. There are no 24-hr. pharmacies in Tel Aviv, but two pharmacies are always on duty for night and *Shabbat* calls. Schedules and phone numbers available on pharmacy doors and in newspapers.

**Emergency: Fire:** Tel. 102. **First Aid:** Tel. 101.

ISRAEL

**Police:** Tel. 100.
**Post Office:** 7 Mikveh Yisrael St. (tel. 564 36 51), 2 blocks east of the south end of Allenby St. Open Sun.-Thurs. 7am-6pm, Fri. 7am-noon; **Post Restante** open Sun.-Thurs. 7am-10pm (tel. 564 36 60); office with **fax, telegram,** and **telex** services open Sun.-Thurs. 8am-6pm, Fri. 8am-noon, with many other branches throughout the city.
**Telephone code:** 03.

# ■ Accommodations

Most hostels are on or around Ben-Yehuda St. and Ha-Yarkon St., with some just off Allenby Rd. or Dizengoff St. When choosing, keep in mind that drunken revelry and honking horns downtown may continue late into the night. Hostels fill quickly, especially in summer, so make reservations and arrive on the early side. If all beds are taken, a rooftop mattress works, especially on summer nights. Prices drop by about 10% in the off-season, paying in foreign currency will generally save you the 17% VAT (see **Money Matters,** p. 270), and most places offer cheaper weekly rates. All places listed take credit cards unless otherwise noted. Sleeping on the beach is illegal and a bad idea—there have been cases of theft and sexual assault, especially against women traveling alone.

**Gordon Inn Guest House,** 17 Gordon St. (tel. 523 82 39), just off Ben Yehuda, 5min. from the beach and Dizengoff Ctr. Our pick for the best place to stay in Tel Aviv. The inn is spotless and recently renovated with a trendy bar/café. Dorm beds US$15, NIS53. Singles US$40, NIS140, doubles $US51, NIS180; private bath. A/C at night, fans during the day. Breakfast included. Single-sex and coed rooms. No curfew or lockout. Lockers NIS5. Credit card reservation requested.

**Tel Aviv Youth Hostel/Guest House (HI),** 36 B'nei Dan St. (tel. 544 17 48 or 546 07 19; fax 544 10 30), near Ha-Yarkon St. Out of the ordinary cleanliness, organization, and security, though quite far from the city center—take bus #5, 24, or 25 to Weizmann or Ha-Yarkon. Hostel beds (5-6 per room) NIS58. Roomier guest house beds NIS69 (4 per room). All rooms have A/C and private bath. Full Israeli breakfast included, dinner available with reservations (NIS28). Check-out 9am, Sat. noon. No lockout or curfew. Singles NIS117, doubles NIS166. Nonmembers add NIS3. Lockers NIS4 per day. Free safe for valuables.

**Hotel Eilat,** 59 Ha-Yarkon St. (tel. 510 24 53, 517 53 68). Incredible location coupled with full-amenities private rooms make this place one-of-a-kind. All rooms have A/C and private bath, some have gorgeous ocean views. Clean, small singles US$48, NIS150. Doubles (with phone and cable TV) US$60, NIS200. Triples US$80, NIS225. Quad US$80, NIS250. 24-hr. reception. No curfew or lockout.

**Hotel Nes Tziona,** 10 Nes Tziona St. (tel. 510 34 04; fax 510 60 84), just off Ben-Yehuda St. Sedate, with tidy linens and privacy to spare. Older clientele appreciates the 70s decor. All rooms have private bath; 5 have A/C. 24-hr. reception. Check-out noon. No lockout or curfew. Singles US$35, NIS130. Doubles US$40, NIS150. Cheaper rooms without bath sometimes available. Some rooms have balconies. Call ahead, reservations requested.

**Beit Immanuel Hostel,** 8 Auerbach St. (tel. 682 14 59; fax 682 98 17), corner of 10 Eilat St. In the newly renovated part of Old Yafo, this Christian hospice is immaculate. 11pm curfew ensures that guests are as pristine as the hostel's interior. Psalms adorn the walls. Secluded garden has tables and a small playground. Reception 7am-11pm. Check-out 10am. No lockout. No smoking. Single-sex dorm beds (10-13 per room) NIS39. Singles NIS95-115. Doubles NIS165-195. Dinner NIS27 (*Shabbat* NIS39). Laundry NIS15. Great for families. Cash only.

**Gordon Hostel,** 2 Gordon St. (tel. 522 98 70; fax 523 74 19), corner of Ha-Yarkon St. Great location near the beach, with several rooms overlooking the sea. For better or worse, late-night partyers fill the rooftop bar, downstairs bar, and bustling Ha-Yarkon St. Arranges cheap flights and tours. Arrive early. 24-hr. reception Check-out 11am. Lockout 11am-2pm, some rooms 10am-2pm. No curfew. Coed and single-sex dorm beds (6-8 per room) NIS28. Free safe. Laundry service NIS10.

**No. 1 Hostel,** 84 Ben-Yehuda St., 4th floor (tel. 523 78 07). Two blocks away from the beach. Bright blue and yellow haven with sunny reception lounge, cable TV, wicker chairs, and foosball table. 24-hr. reception. Check-out by 10:30am. Lockout 11am-2pm. No curfew. Kitchen closes at 11pm. Co-ed and single-sex dorm beds (4-8 per room) NIS31. Private single/double NIS105. Breakfast included. Free safe deposit for documents. Lockers NIS3 per day. Wash and dry NIS8.

**Old Yafo Hostel,** 8 Olei Tzion St. (tel. 682 23 70; fax 682 23 16), 3 blocks south of the clock tower, entrance in the back. Located in the middle of Jaffa's *Shuk Ha-Pishpeshim* (flea market), this hostel is famed for converting day-trippers into semi-permanent residents. Hippie crowd drinks Dutch beer (NIS3) and sleeps on the roof (NIS19) or in bungalows (NIS25). Co-ed and single-sex dorm beds (10 per room) NIS23. Singles NIS60. Doubles NIS80. The "royal room" for NIS150 gets you a spacious suite with A/C, kitchenette, shower, and a big-screen TV with cable. Computer system lets you eat and sleep on credit and gives an itemized bill. Free airport pickup with advance reservation. Check-out noon. No lockout or curfew, but lights go off at 11pm. Free use of kitchen and safe. Storage NIS1.

**Dizengoff Square Hostel,** 11 Dizengoff Sq. (tel. 522 51 84; fax 522 51 81), next to Chen movie theater. Newly renovated, with rugs, TV room, and art-deco walls. Personable staff knows residents' names and the night manager is the patron saint of travelers. Popular with the long-term crowd. 24-hr. reception. Check-out 10:30am. Lockout 10:30am-2:30pm. No curfew. Coed and single-sex dorm beds (6-11 per room) NIS31. Private rooms US$39-49, NIS115-145. Private doubles NIS89. Beds in a rooftop bungalow are NIS27 each. Free safe. Lockers NIS8. Wash and dry NIS6 each.

**Hotel Joseph,** 15 Bugrashov St. (tel. 525 70 70), right off Ben-Yehuda St. Cable TV, kitchen, and a lively hardwood bar with an array of beers. Travel agency on premises. Coed and single-sex dorm beds (4 per room) NIS27, NIS25 with higher person-to-bathroom ratios. Single or double NIS95. All with fan. Cash only.

**Sea & Sun Hostel,** 62 Ha-Yarkon St. (tel./fax 517 33 13 or 73), corner of Nes Tziona. A stumble away from the beach and nighttime hotspots. Spacious balcony with TV room. Large rooms (with 4-18 beds), all co-ed (NIS30). Doubles NIS 140. 24-hr. reception. Check-out 11am. Lockout 11am-2pm. No curfew.

# ■ Food

Tel Aviv is at its most cosmopolitan come mealtime. Restaurants range from southwest Tex-Mex to southeast Asian, from falafel and hummus to French *haute-cuisine.* After a brain-melting day at the beach, however, fast food and frozen yogurt might sound just as good. You'll have plenty of time to make up your mind—almost all restaurants stay open until midnight or later, on weeknights and weekends alike.

For quick, cheap belly-fillers, head for the self-service eateries on Ben-Yehuda St. Sandwiches and burgers with a side of chips go for under NIS8, and most places let you "customize" your falafel with various toppings. The trick for monk-on-a-budget freaks is to find a place selling falafel by the pita; you can keep refilling it until your

---

### New York Bagels Invade Israel

In the U.S., Jewish culture is closely tied to food, and one of the strongest ties is the bagel. Few American Jewish breakfasts lack the crusty outside and soft inside of this round treat, often smeared with cream cheese and lox. In Israel, however, if your bread has a hole in it, it's usually a bad sign (it means one of your falafel balls is about to fall out). Recently, like so many things from the home of the brave, bagels have been making inroads into the Jewish state. Not surprisingly, the first bagel bakery in Israel sprung up in the country's most westernized, America-mimicking city: Tel Aviv. Just two years ago, Rafi Fidler brought the breakfast staple to Israel at his stars and stripes eatery "Bagel America" on Carlebach St. Eager to jump on the bandwagon, Bonker's Bagels sprung up all over—their flagship is in the heart of Jerusalem in Zion Sq.

stomach hits the ground. The eateries near Shuk Ha-Carmel and along Bezalel St. off Allenby and Ha-Melekh George stay open the latest (usually until 1:30am).

**Kerem Ha-Temanim** (the Yemenite Quarter), between Shuk Ha-Carmel and the beach, boasts moderately priced Yemeni spicy fried-dough foods, often stuffed with meat, among its small red-roofed houses and narrow streets.

**Shechunat Ha-Tikva,** in Tel Aviv's southeastern-most quarter, is renowned for its lamb, chicken, and beef skewers, often accompanied by cheap beer. Israelis flock from nearby cities to have kabab or *la'afa* here. Take bus #15, 16, or 41 to Ha-Tikva—it's too far (and not safe) to walk.

The maze of narrow streets surrounding the **Jaffa Clock Tower** is peppered with cheap falafel stands, *al-ha'esh* (barbecued) meat establishments, and sweets vendors. More romantic is the beautifully renovated **Old Jaffa,** where you can eat among gardens overlooking the Mediterranean, but beware of unlisted prices. In **Jaffa Port,** just south of the renovated old city off Pasteur St., picturesque waterfront restaurants offer seafood so fresh you can almost see the gills moving (daily catch entrees are around NIS30).

Back in town, **Dizengoff Square** and the stretch of **Dizengoff Street** just north of the Square are lined with pizza parlors, blintz joints, and hot dog stands, where crowds of tourists and throngs of young Israelis gorge themselves amidst exhaust-spitting vehicles. The northern end of the street, around Yirmeyahu Street, which runs between Dizengoff and Ben-Yehuda just before they intersect, has another agglomeration of restaurants. They tend to be better (and pricier) than those around the Square, and you're less likely to choke on bus fumes while dining *al fresco*.

Fast-food yearnings can be quelled at **McDavid's** (43 Frischmann St., off Dizengoff) or **Subway** (130 Dizengoff St.), where a cheap and delicious 6-inch sub goes for NIS6-8 (open daily until midnight). **Domino's** delivers medium-sized pizzas for NIS22 (NIS4 per topping; call 527 23 30 for northern locations, 562 77 70 for southern locations and after midnight).

Reluctant spenders should shop at the large, outdoor **Shuk Ha-Carmel.** Most of the produce stands are at the southwestern end of the market, on and near Ha-Carmel St. To catch prices at their lowest (and crowds at their loudest), shop an hour or two before the beginning of *Shabbat*. **Supermarkets** can be found throughout town. **Supersol,** 79 Ben-Yehuda St. near Gordon St., may be the most convenient (open Sun.-Tues. 7am-midnight, Wed.-Thurs. 24hr., Sat. after sundown); other Supersol branches are on the corner of Arlozorov and Yehoshua Ben-Nun and on Ibn Gvirol and Nordau. **Co-op** has branches right in Dizengoff Sq. (open daily 7am-8pm), in the basement of the Ha-Mashbir department store in Dizengoff Center, and on Ibn Gvirol St. near the junction of Sha'ul Ha-Melekh.

Keep hydrated while about-towning, but be sure to watch prices: a Kinley mango drink on Dizengoff costs NIS5-6, while the same money at a supermarket nets you a 1.5L bottle of mineral water or cola. The following restaurants take credit cards unless otherwise noted.

**Dr. Shakshuka,** 3 Beit Eshel, corner of Yefet St., Jaffa (tel. 682 28 42). Scrumptious Libyan food in the heart of Old Jaffa. Eponymous dish is the *shakshuka*—a mouth-watering tomato and egg concoction (NIS13). Couscous (real, authentic stuff) with meat or veggies NIS35, so big you'll want to share it with a friend. Open Sun.-Thurs. 9am-1am, Fri. 9am-sundown, Sat. sundown-2am.

**Eternity,** 60 Ben-Yehuda St. (tel. 620 31 51). Run by members of the Black Hebrew community, a group whose dietary laws prohibit both milk and meat. Creative (and nutritious) alternatives. Veggie hot dogs (NIS10), steaks (NIS14), burgers (NIS9), and *shawerma* (NIS9) are all quite tasty. Non-dairy ice cream (NIS4) and other non-dairy, no-egg desserts sold as well. Open Sun.-Thurs. 9am-11pm, Fri. 9am-3pm, Sat. after sundown-midnight. Kosher. No credit cards.

**Alexander's,** 81 Yehuda HaMaccabee St. (tel. 605 89 10). Take bus #5 to the end. *The* restaurant, according to the overly stylish. Free lemonade in summer, cider in winter, sweetens the wait. Gourmet salads NIS30, main courses NIS40-60, vegetarian stuffed baked potato jackets NIS28 and famous warm chocolate cake (NIS24). Open Sun.-Thurs. 7am-1am, Fri.-Sat. 7:30am-3am.

**Ilana Goor Museum Café,** 4 Mazal Dagim St. (tel. 683 76 76), is the trendiest place to grab a bite in Jaffa. Situated in the heart of the artists' colony, the rooftop café overlooks Jaffa Port. Feast on delicious salads (NIS6) and quiche (NIS24) or simply take in the artsy ambience with a frothy cappuccino (NIS6.50-8). Don't miss the great museum downstairs (see **Jaffa,** p. 339). Open Sun.-Mon., Wed., Sat. 10am-10pm, Tues., Thurs. 10am-2pm, Fri. 10am-4pm.

**Café Nordau,** 145 Ben-Yehuda St. (tel. 524 01 34), corner of Arlozorov. Good food, generous portions, lively setting. Largely, but not exclusively, gay clientele; sells *Maga'im* (the gay newspaper) and provides current info on gay life and hot spots. Full meals NIS25-40. Open Sun.-Fri. 8am-2am, Sat. 10am-2am.

**Said Abou Elafia and Sons,** 1 block behind the Jaffa Clock Tower. Popularly known as "Aboulafia," this bakery is so famous that its name is used by Israelis to denote all stuffed-pita foods. Wade through the crowds to taste fresh sesame-covered *bagelah, samuza* stuffed with thyme and potatoes, and pizza-like products, all for NIS4-6. Take-out only. Open 24hr. Cash only.

**Souss Etz,** 20 Sheinkin St. (tel. 528 79 55). One of many popular, hip cafés on this street. Salads and pasta NIS22-32, stuffed bagel toasts NIS22, desserts NIS12. Open Sun.-Fri. 9am-1am, Sat. noon-midnight.

**Café Kazze,** 19 Sheinkin St. (tel. 629 37 56). Israeli stars sometimes dine at this trendy café. Eat in sunny, airy rooms or on the garden patio in back. Fast, friendly service, large portions. Vegetarian *couscous* (NIS26) and shepherd's salad with goat cheese (NIS28) are popular. Open Sun.-Thurs. 8:30am-12:30am, Fri. 8:30am-4:30pm, Sat. 8:30am-8pm. Kosher.

**Dizengoff 99,** address same (tel. 527 48 08), close to the heart of the city, this trendy, blue and yellow bedecked Italian bistro serves up *gnocchi* and ravioli galore (NIS22-30), as well as pizza (NIS20-28). Lengthy, luscious dessert menu. Open Sun.-Thurs. 8am-2am, Fri.-Sat. 8am-4am.

**Cactus,** 66 Ha-Yarkon St. corner of Trumpeldor St. (tel. 510 59 69). Mexican to the bone—real cacti, tequila, and sombreros surround customers as they gorge on *chimichangas* (NIS28), chicken and beef enchiladas (NIS32), and other great Mexican faves. Great vegetarian selection. Open Sun.-Thurs. 11am-12:30am, and until customers leave on Fri. and Sat.

**Yotvata B'Ir,** 78 Herbert Samuel St. (tel. 510 79 84), off the *tayelet*. Kibbutz Yotvata, renowned producers of dairy goods, ventures into the city with this well-lit oasis of fresh veggies, cheeses, and fruits. Dauntingly diverse menu features gargantuan salads (NIS35), toasts (NIS30-40), and pasta dishes (NIS35-45). Open daily 7:30am-4am.

**Mon Jardin,** 186 Ben-Yehuda St. (tel. 523 1792). Recently remodeled Romanian grill. Stuffed vine leaves NIS9, *mousaka* or *tzorba* soup NIS15, and Romanian kebabs and chicken; full meals NIS25-50. Schmancy, upscale atmosphere. Open daily noon-midnight.

**Chin Chin,** 42 Frischmann St. (tel. 524 58 02), off Dizengoff St. Tasty Chinese food served up in a jiffy. Lunch specials from NIS15, entrees NIS20.50-21.50. Special vegetarian dishes. Delivery (charge varies with order and destination) and take-out. Open daily noon-midnight.

**Dalas Restaurant,** 68 Etzel St. (tel. 687 43 49), in the southeastern Ha-Tikva neighborhood. The combination of wall-paintings of Southfork Ranch and outstanding Yemenite food is positively surreal. In one of Tel Aviv's poorer sections, accessible by bus #7a, 15, 16, or 41. Hummus (NIS7), delicious Iraqi pita (thick, fluffy, pocketless, NIS1.50), and *kabab* (NIS9-15 per skewer) attract many locals. Every cow part is served including bone marrow, testicles, spleen, and udder (Trust us, it all tastes like chicken). Open Sun.-Thurs. 11:30am-3am, Fri. 11am-1 hr. before sundown, Sat. 8:30pm-2am. Kosher.

There are several good ice cream places in Tel Aviv. **Dr. Lek,** in the Opera Tower and just up from the Jaffa clock tower on the main road heading north to the Promenade, has excellent ice cream, but sorbets are their specialty (try the cinnamon cheesecake). **Ben and Jerry's** sell their usual rich concoctions all over Tel Aviv, including creameries at the northern end of the promenade, below the Ramada Continental Hotel and at 93 and 284 Dizengoff St. The superb **Glida Be'er Sheva,** on the corner of

Dizengoff and Nordau, has the biggest and most inventive ice cream selection in town. Most ice cream places scoop until 1am. Prices run NIS6.50-8.70 for two scoops.

# ■ Sights

There's more to *do* in Tel Aviv than there is to simply see. Tel Aviv is all about activity, no matter how debilitating the humid summer heat may feel. Sight-seeing here is anything but a spectator sport.

The best-known attraction in Tel Aviv is its graceful **Promenade** along the beach, where lovers stroll, vendors sell, and folk dancers strut their stuff. Nearby, at the intersection of Allenby and Ha-Yarkon, stands the Miami Vice-esque **Opera Tower.** The interior features a magnificent atrium, with statues overlooking both a fountain and Israel's first **Tower Records** store. For a more down-and-dirty shopping experience, famed **Shuk Ha-Carmel** (Carmel Market) is located at the intersection of Allenby Rd. and Ha-Melekh George St. The chaos here will entertain even the most jaded of tourists. Waving polyester undergarments and red plastic sandals, vendors bellow their products' virtues. Farther south, toward the parking lot, you can buy fresh fruit and vegetables at the lowest prices in the city. Huge mounds of plucked chickens make for a fowl sight. One block south of the shuk lies Naḥalat Binyamin and Ramban Street *midraḥov,* which transforms into a street fair on Tuesdays and Fridays. From 10am-4pm (weather permitting) local artists and craftspeople sell jewelry, pottery, original paintings, Judaica, and bizarre candelabras. The winding cobblestone street is full of musicians, mimes, and pushy passers-by. Sip a beverage from the sidelines, or shove your way through with the best of them.

If too much shoving makes you lose your sanity, rise above it. You can look down on the chaos of the market and the entire city from the tranquil rooftop observatory (tel. 517 73 04) in nearby **Migdal Shalom.** Standing at 1 Herzl St. and Aḥad Ha-Am St., this 40-story tower was the tallest structure in the Middle East until its recent eclipse by the slightly taller communication tower in the military base near the Tel Aviv Museum (*if* you count antennae). The observatory offers an unmatched view of Tel Aviv and environs. (Open Sun.-Thurs. 10am-5:30pm, Fri. 10am-2pm. Admission NIS7, students NIS5; combination Israeli Wax Museum/observatory tickets NIS14, students NIS11.)

The **Great Synagogue** at 110 Allenby St. (tel. 560 49 05 or 560 40 66) stands just east of the Shalom Tower. Completed in 1926 and renovated in 1970, this huge, domed building showcases arches and stained glass windows from synagogues around the world. Ancient musical instruments are also on display. (Open Sun.-Fri. 8am-9pm, Sat. 8-11am. Saturday prayer open to the public; head coverings and modest dress are required.)

---

### Goodbye, Friend שלום חבר

On November 4, 1995, Kikkar Malkhei Yisrael (Kings of Israel Square) was alive with songs, banners, and hope. The enormous swath of land in the middle of Tel Aviv was the site of a mammoth peace rally. Israelis of all ages came to pray for an end to war, and to encourage their leader, Prime Minister Yitzḥak Rabin, to go forward with negotiations with the Palestinians and neighboring Arab countries. Rabin was standing before his people, and all were singing about peace, when a bullet pierced the Prime Minister's lung and devastated the country. The square has since been renamed Kikkar Yitzḥak Rabin in memory of the slain leader. While a formal monument has yet to be erected, the makeshift shrine of photos, candles, flowers, and graffiti is a poignant display of a country in mourning. Some scrawlings on the concrete platform where Rabin was killed are heart-wrenching poems of lost hope. Many people simply wrote two heartfelt words: *Shalom ḥaver,* goodbye friend.

More architecturally inspiring are Tel Aviv's **historic neighborhoods. Neveh Tzedek,** just west of the intersection of Herzl and Aḥad Ha-Am streets, is the oldest Jewish neighborhood outside of Jaffa and one of the few Tel Aviv neighborhoods with a 100-year-old-history. The area is being gradually renovated to accommodate local yuppies attracted to the Mediterranean-village charm of its narrow streets and humble stone architecture. The **Suzanne Delal Center,** in the heart of Neveh Tzedek at 5 Yekhieli St., near Amzalag and Ḥeloukhe St. (tel. 510 56 56) is the hot spot for theater and dance. The newly renovated buildings and courtyard amphitheater of this performing arts center are worth a peek, even if you skip the performances. Happily unrenovated is **Kerem Ha-Temanim** (the Yemenite Quarter), northwest of Allenby and Ha-Melekh George, near Shuk Ha-Carmel. This area maintains its village-like appearance despite the relentless sky-scraping all around it.

**Tel Aviv University** remains Ramat Aviv's star attraction, and is home of the superb Beit Ha-Tfutzot (see **Museums,** p. 335). Take bus #25, 24, 6, 13 or 27 to get there. Directly behind Beit Ha-Tfutzot from Gate 2 is the vast central lawn, flanked by pleasant Modernist buildings. Facing the sea, the first building on your right is the Central Library. From here you can go straight down the gently sloping path to the glitzy new main gate complex on Levanon St. The **University Gallery** is in the pink pavilion right next to the gate. The grim concrete building across the street houses the university dorms—most students prefer to live off-campus. There is life, however, on campus, at least in the daylight hours during the school year. Ask people to direct you to the Gilman or Law cafeterias for a peek at the chic student scene, or stop by the **Einstein Café,** the on-campus version of the set of *Friends.*

West of Namir (Haifa) Rd. (bus #25) is the **Sportek,** a collection of sports fields, and a miniature-golf course. Tel Avivians crowd the park just across the river from Sportek as well as the nearby Gan Ha-Yehoshua. To arrive at Gan Ha-Yehoshua from the city center, take bus #47 or 48 from King George, or 21 from Dizengoff St. Barbecue some *kebab* and play some *matkot;* you'll fit right in.

Baby rhinos frolic (really, they do) at the **Zoological Center** in Ramat Gan (tel. 631 21 81). This combination drive-through safari park and zoo features 250 acres of African game in a natural habitat. You can walk within one meter of tigers, or stare over a *wadi* at Syrian bears and intelligent-looking gorillas. Bring a picnic, or have lunch at the moderately priced restaurant. For the carless, the park runs its own vehicles through the habitat. Pedestrian tours offered as well. Take bus #30, 35, or 43 to Ramat Gan. (Open Sun.-Thurs. 9am-4pm, Fri. 9am-1pm. Admission NIS38, children NIS33.) Continue beastwatching across the street at the massive **Ramat Gan National Park** (open dawn-dusk; free).

# ▓ Museums

The **Eretz Yisrael Museum,** 2 Lebanon St. (tel. 641 52 44) in Ramat Aviv (the northernmost part of the city) is a large complex composed of eight pavilion museums built around an archaeological site. One admission ticket (NIS154, students NIS12) gives access to all eight pavilions and the Eretz Yisrael Library, containing over 30,000 books and periodicals. The most famous attraction in the complex is the **Glass Museum,** with one of the finest collections of glassware in the world. Across the patio, the **Kadman Numismatic Museum** traces the history of the region through ancient coins. The **Ceramics Pavilion** has an extensive collection of Arabic pottery, especially the Gaza and Acre styles. The **Nehushtan Pavilion** houses the discoveries of the excavations of the ancient copper industries at Timna, better known as King Solomon's Mines. Across the entrance area past the grassy amphitheater is the **Man and His Work Center,** an exhibition of Arab and other folk crafts and techniques. To the southeast, still in the museum complex, are the **Tel Qasila Excavations,** which have revealed a 12th-century BCE Philistine port city and ruins dating from around 1000 BCE. The area at the top of the hill contains the remains of three separate Philistine temples built one on top of another. Down the hill to the south are scattered remains of the residential and industrial quarter of the Philistine town. A useful free guide to the *tel* is available in the small **Tel Qasila Pavilion** (open Sun.-Thurs. 9am-2pm) to the east, which displays artifacts found at the site. Past the Philistine town is the **Folklore Pavilion,** with Jewish religious art, ceremonial objects, and ethnic clothing. The Eretz Yisrael complex also houses the **Alphabet Museum,** the **Lasky Planetarium** (shows in Hebrew only), and the **Museum of Science and Technology.** Take any bus (#24, 29, 45, 74, or 86) to the Ramat Aviv Hotel from the central bus station. (Complex open Sun.-Tues., Thurs. 9am-2pm, Wed. 9am-7pm, Sat. 10am-2pm.)

Also in Ramat Aviv is **Beit Ha-Tfutzot (The Diaspora Museum)** on the Tel Aviv University Campus (tel. 646 20 20). This outstanding museum chronicles the history of Jewish life outside the land of Israel from the Babylonian exile (596 BCE) to present-day diaspora communities. A display of synagogue models shows how Jews incorporated local architectural ideas in building their houses of worship: one synagogue resembles an Italian villa, another an American ranch, and another a Chinese pagoda. Short films and multi-media displays throughout the museum recount the stories of Judaism's far-flung communities in both Hebrew and English. The museum also has a **Genealogy Department** that can trace Jewish family trees back dozens of generations. (Museum open Sun.-Tues. and Thurs. 10am-4pm, Wed. 10am-6pm, Fri. 9am-1pm. Admission NIS22, students and seniors citizens NIS16.)

Uptown, the **Tel Aviv Museum of Art,** 27 Sha'ul Ha-Melekh Blvd. (tel. 695 73 61), has split-level galleries and a sizable collection of Israeli and international modern art. The handsome lobby boasts a Lichtenstein (look back as you enter). There's also Impressionist art, including canvases by Corot, Renoir, Pissaro, Monet, and Dufy, with a Degas sculpture and some works by Utrillo. Post-Impressionist masters such as Picasso, Juan Gris, and Matisse have a section as well, and a permanent exhibition of contemporary Israeli art rounds out the collection. Rotating exhibits, however, are often the most rewarding. An English program, listing exhibits and events, is available in the ticket booth, or check the Friday *Jerusalem Post.* Take bus #7a, 9, 18, 28, or 70. (Open Sun.-Mon. and Wed. 10am-6pm, Tues. 10am-10pm, Fri.-Sat. 10am-2pm. Admission NIS20, seniors and students NIS14.)

Just north of the *shuk,* off Allenby St., lies Bialik St., named after Ḥayim Naḥman Bialik, Israel's national poet. His recently restored home, now the **Beit Bialik Museum,** 22 Bialik St. (tel. 525 45 30) is maintained exactly as it was when he died; it is a fine example of 1920s eclectic Tel Aviv architecture. Bialik's manuscripts, photographs, articles, letters, and 94 books (with translations in 28 languages) are on display. An English brochure is available, but the dearth of English translations on the display cases makes this museum difficult for non-Hebrew speakers. (Open Sun.-Thurs. 9am-4:45pm, Sat. 11am-1:45pm. Closed on Sat. in July and Aug. Free.) At 38 Ha-Melekh George St., the Likud party headquarters, is the new **Etzel Irgun Tzva'i Le'umi Museum** (National Military Organization) (tel. 528 40 01 or 525 13 87), which traces the pre-1948 history of late Israeli prime minister Menaḥem Begin's military movement. (Open Sun.-Thurs. 8:30am-4pm. Admission NIS5, students NIS2.) A second Etzel Museum with large models depicting the 1947-48 history is found in a half-stone, half-glass building along the Promenade, between Tel Aviv and Jaffa, on the #25 bus line. (Open Sun.-Thurs. 8:30am-4pm. Admission NIS5, students NIS2.) The **Jabotinsky Institute** (tel. 528 73 20), in the same building, houses works written by and about Ze'ev Jabotinsky, father of right-wing Zionism. (Open Sun.-Thurs. 8am-4pm. Free.)

The building at 23 Rothschild Blvd., one block south of the Great Synagogue, is the **Hagana Museum** (tel. 560 86 24), which traces the history of the IDF. Movies glorify the Yom Kippur War and the Hagana's efforts to break the British blockade of ships carrying World War II refugees to Palestine. (Open Sun.-Thurs. 8am-4pm, Fri. 8am-2pm. Admission NIS5, students and children NIS2.)

Nearer to the shore, you can visit the **David Ben-Gurion House,** at 17 Ben-Gurion Ave. (tel. 522 10 10). Ogle an exciting exhibition of books, pictures, and momentos of Israel's first prime minister, including letters from Ben-Gurion to John F. Kennedy, Winston Churchill, Charles de Gaulle, and other world leaders. In the **Hillel Cohen Lecture Hall** next door you can invade the poor man's privacy even further, as you examine Ben-Gurion's passports and one of his salary slips. (Both house and lecture hall open Sun. and Tues.-Thurs. 8am-3pm, Mon. 8am-5pm, Fri. 8am-1pm. Free.)

What tourist boardwalk would be complete without a wax museum? Although it's no Madame Tussaud's, the **Israeli Wax Museum** in the Shalom Tower (tel. 517 73 04) was recently updated. Modern scenes, like the Madrid Peace Conference, join old ones, like the 1492 expulsion of Jews from Spain. (Open Sun.-Thurs. 10am-5:30pm, Fri. 10am-2pm. Museum admission NIS11, students NIS9; combination museum/observatory ticket NIS14, students NIS11.)

# ■ Entertainment

Though frying themselves by day and sucking down Goldstar by night seems to be the preferred activity for most travelers, Tel Aviv is the capital of the Israeli jet set, and activities range much farther than mere beaches and brew. The Promenade and Sheinken St. are lined with jazzy cafés, and elsewhere one can find sweaty discothèques, highbrow concert halls, and world-class theater.

## BEACHES

The Hebrew word for beach is *hof*. Familiarize yourself with the flag language of the beach as well: black means swimming is forbidden, red means swimming is dangerous, white means swim on. Most beaches have lifeguards on duty until 4pm.

The beaches within the city are sandy, clean, and free, and all have relatively clean showers, toilets, and changing rooms. The beaches are (from north to south) Sheraton, Hilton (behind those hotels), Gordon, Frischmann (at the ends of those streets), and the Jerusalem beach at the end of Allenby Rd.—the last three are almost one continuous beach. The southern coastline, with fewer amenities and no luxury hotels, tends to be quieter during the day. The **Sheraton beach** is also quite peaceful, populated by children and their grandparents. **Gordon** is packed with tourists and people trying to pick them up, while the **Hilton beach** swarms with surfers and those trying to pick *them* up. If you want to get picked up, a marina near Kikkar Atarim rents sailboats, surfboards, and windsurfers. Beware the spastic *matkot* (paddleball) players who'll trample you to continue a volley. Skip past the over-priced refreshment stands. Ben-Yehuda St., with cheap food and drink, is never more than a two-minute walk from the beach. All of Tel Aviv's beaches are rife with theft—if possible, lock your valuables away before you hit the sands.

## CAFÉS AND PROMENADES

The Mediterranean art of laid-back people-watching can be perfected in Tel Aviv's streets and cafés. The wide sidewalks of **Dizengoff Street** are the most crowded showcase in town. The northern parts of the street, lined with many high-concept, high-priced boutiques, are great for a relaxed early evening stroll. **Dizengoff Square** is the site of an ever-changing human scene, from retirees basking in the midday sun to late-night punks cluttering the overpass stairs. The revolving, multi-level, multi-colored, water-spurting, fire-spitting **fountain,** designed by the illustrious Israeli artist Agam (yes, he did the Dan Hotel coloring, too), crowns the square with an unsurpassed celebration of municipal kitsch. The tunes come from the fountain itself, orchestrating its own hourly multi-media show to music ranging from Ravel's *Bolero* to Israeli folk songs.

**Sheinken Street** is also designed for crowd-gazing, if the kind of crowd you want to watch wears silver platform shoes and sheer half-shirts revealing multiple belly-button rings. For the quintessential Sheinken experience, park yourself in the **Tamar Café,** 57 Sheinken St. (tel. 685 23 76), immortalized in a song by the Israeli pop trio Mango ("Living on Sheinken/drinking coffee at the Tamar Café/my dream is to make a short film"). The Tamar is open Sun.-Thurs. 7am-8pm and Fri. 7am-7pm. Hipper-than-thou former Sheinken devotees have recently relocated to **Basel Street** (just south of Nordau, between Dizengoff St. and Ibn Guirol St.), which has sprouted its own crop of chi-chi cafés.

There's always the **Promenade,** where cafés stretch below the end of Gordon St. **Ha-Ḥof Ha-Ma'aravi** (the Western Beach), at the northern end of the Charles Clore Park, rocks every Thursday night with Brazilian music and swarms of Israeli youth.

## DISCOS AND LIVE MUSIC

Tel Aviv's dance scene changes as quickly as political alliances. The *only* club one year may be empty the next and a hardware store after that. Patron demographics are no more stable—current bastions of the pubescent may have been collegiate havens in their prime. Most of Tel Aviv's discos open at 10pm, but it's considered lame to arrive before midnight. The best nights for clubbing are Thursday, Friday, and Saturday when Israeli soldiers get time off and are looking to blow off steam. Expect to pay at least NIS15 cover at most places.

**Allenby 58** (at that very address, coincidentally enough) is famous for its theme nights. Past themes have included zoo night, when dancers dress like animals, and banana night, when everyone goes Chiquita. Thursday nights are a house party, while Friday and Saturday nights play a range of danceable, jammable rock (opens after midnight). To groove under the stars with Israelis and tourists alike, shimmy at **Shanbo,** 33 Lillienblum St. (tel. 517 44 08; cover NIS15-25). **KU,** 117 Salameh Rd., not far from Herzl St., say they're specialists in "Happy House" soul and funk (cover NIS25; beer NIS8; open Tues. and Fri.-Sat. midnight-6am). For deafening reggae of all varieties, slide over to **Soweto,** 6 Frischmann St. (tel. 524 08 25), at the corner of Ha-Yarkon (cover Mon.-Wed. NIS10, Thurs.-Sat. NIS15). The **Colosseum,** at Atarim Sq. (tel. 527 11 77), attracts a huge tourist crowd and plenty Israelis making unabashed attempts to pick them up. The cover is NIS15-20 for men, nothing for women. Drinks are cheap and the first three are free. On Saturdays, men pay NIS25 to enter, and women still get in free. Get the picture?

Tel Aviv is the headquarters for young Israeli rock bands. **Cat Blue** (pronounced "Baloo"), 10 Ben Avigdor St. (tel. 562 03 10), features live performances. When the music is good (which is the norm) the crowd takes to dancing on the tables. Nearby, **Echoes,** 14 Twersky St., another big hangout, features alternative rock bands (open Thurs.-Sat. nights only). The basement of **Camelot,** 16 Shalom Aleichem St. (tel. 528 53 33), echoes with blues and R&B (cover NIS10-25), while the upstairs pub stays mellower. Reserve tickets before going to **Logos,** off Naḥalat Binyamin St. on Shefer St. (tel. 516 11 76), which features rock and blues performances nightly at 11pm; cover varies with the band's fame. An upstairs café shows the downstairs concerts on TV screens and occasionally hosts milder acts of its own. Two amphitheaters at **Ha-Yarkon Park** also have concerts. *Ha-Ir*, a weekly Hebrew magazine, has a section called "Akhbar Ha-Ir," with comprehensive listings.

## BARS

Bars in Tel Aviv are as varied as the tortures in Dante's *Inferno*, but start later. Most get crowded around midnight, and seats are scarce after 1am (especially Thursday through Saturday). Bars abound on **Ha-Yarkon St.** and around hostel-heavy **Allenby Rd.** The **Hard Rock Café** in Dizengoff Ctr. (tel. 525 13 36; open Sun.-Thurs. noon-12:30am, Fri. noon-3am, Sat. noon-1am) features a young crowd, Israeli rock paraphernalia, and a suit worn by Elvis. Israelis frequent **Ha-Arba'a St.,** off Carlebach and Ibn Gvirol, near the Tel Aviv Cinemathèque, where about six pubs compete for hotspot status. Pick your poison:

> **Lola,** 54 Allenby St. (tel. 517 37 88), is a favorite Israeli student hangout with old German newspapers on the walls and faux marble tables. 11 kinds of tequila (NIS17-24), fresh-baked baguettes, and Addams Family pinball. Goldstar NIS9.
>
> **Leprechaun's,** corner of Ha-Yarkon and Ha-Yarden. Hardly a native in sight. Packed with sweaty, sunburnt English speakers drinking cheap beer.

**The Church,** 58 Ha-Yarkon St., has heavy tables, loud music, and a boisterous crowd that spills onto the bar's church steps and sidewalk. Carlsberg NIS7.

**M.A.S.H. (More Alcohol Served Here),** 275 Dizengoff (tel. 605 10 07). A trek to the north; take bus #4. Tourists and Israelis alike slam drinks to music from the 60s to the 90s. Good burgers NIS19. Open daily 10pm-5am. Local beer NIS7, imported NIS9-11. During 5-8pm happy hour, drinks are 25% off.

**Ha-Shoftim,** 39 Ibn Gvirol St., corner of Ha-Shoftim, attracts 30-somethings with its outdoor seating, dark interior, and blues/jazz. Open nightly 7pm-3am.

**Ha-Misba'a,** 344 Dizengoff St. (tel. 604 23 60). Wilder and more expensive. Live music (often Israeli folk) every night at midnight; arrive at 11 to get a seat. When all are sufficiently ripped, people might dance on chairs and sing along. The crowd stays until the musicians collapse. Open daily 10pm-5am. Cover NIS40-50.

## CULTURE

There are plenty of things to do in Tel Aviv that won't get you sunburnt or smashed: nightly opera, ballet, jazz, classical music, and dance performances. There are also more than 40 **movie theaters** showing American and Israeli flicks. Check the *Jerusalem Post* for English listings for the **Tel Aviv Cinemathèque,** 2 Sprinzak St., at the corner of Carlebach St.

The **Suzanne Delal Center,** 5 Yeḥiely St., in Neveh Tzedek has indoor and outdoor dance, theater, and musical performances, to name a few. Call 510 56 56 for a schedule. Take bus #8, 10, 25, or 61 from downtown or 40 or 46 from the central bus station. The center is best known as the home of the Inbal (tel. 517 37 11) and Bat Sheva (tel. 517 14 71) dance companies, both of which perform contemporary ethnic dances. Inbal's performances are less expensive at NIS35; tickets to the Bat Sheva shows are NIS45-60. Your passport will get you a 20% tourist discount (box office open Sun.-Thurs. 10am-5pm, Fri. 10am-1pm; Visa and Diners Club accepted). **Beit Lessin,** 34 Weizmann St. (tel. 694 11 11), has live jazz acts (NIS25). The **Tel Aviv Cameri Theater,** 101 Dizengoff St. (tel. 523 33 35), at the corner of Frischmann St., offers simultaneous-translation earphones during performances for NIS5 (tickets NIS65-90).

For the most detailed information on performance schedules and other activities in the Tel Aviv area, see *Tel Aviv Today, Events in Tel Aviv,* and *This Week in Tel Aviv,* all free at the tourist information office and major hotels.

# ■ Jaffa (Yafo) יפו يافا

An Israeli folk song describes Jaffa as possessing a "mysterious and unknown" element which allows its atmosphere "to seep like wine into the blood." Jaffa's stone houses and winding streets do, indeed, intoxicate. Next to Tel Aviv's skyscraper hotels and glass storefronts, historical Jaffa is a breath of fresh Mediterranean air.

The **Jaffa Clock Tower,** completed in 1906, stands by the entrance to Jaffa from Tel Aviv and is a useful marker for all other destinations in the city. A free **tour** of Old Jaffa by the Tourism Association begins here (Wed. 9:30am, line up at 9). Bus #46 from the new central bus station will plunk you right in front of the clock tower. To get to the **Old City** of Jaffa, make a right bit south of the clock tower, and head towards the sea. The main road becomes the **Mifratz Shlomo Promenade,** with unbelievable views of Tel Aviv's action-packed coast and skyline. Along the promenade, you'll find the **Museum of Antiquities of Tel Aviv-Jaffa** (tel. 682 53 75), containing artifacts from nearby sites in the old city and a comprehensive collection of Jaffan coins. (Admission NIS5, students NIS3. Open Sun., Mon., Thurs. 9am-2pm; Tues., Wed., 9am-7pm, Sat. 10am-2pm.) Up the Promenade sits **Kikkar Kedumim,** Jaffa's commercial, historical, and tourist center, and site of outdoor summer concerts. Following signs to the Visitors' Center, head down the stairs to take a peek at archaeological excavations from 2300-year-old Tel Yafo featuring Hellenistic, Roman, Byzantine, and early Arab remains. (Open Sun.-Thurs. 9am-11pm, Fri. 9am-2pm, Sat. 10am-11pm. Free.)

Near Kikkar Kedumim, the colorful Greek Orthodox **Church of St. Michael** and the Catholic **Monastery of St. Peter** (visiting hours March-Sept. daily 8-11:45am, 3-6pm; Oct.-Feb. 8-11:45am, 3-5pm) are worth a brief tour. **Andromeda's Rock,** site of Perseus's rescue of the Greek princess, is visible from the lighthouse to the south.

Down the stairs from Kikkar Kedumim is the cluster of museums, restaurants and galleries that make up Jaffa's touristy artists' colony. The hippest spot in the neighborhood is the new **Ilana Goor Museum,** on Mazal Dagim St. (tel. 683 76 76), established in September 1995. This artist's home-turned-museum, once an Ottoman soap factory, then a shelter for pilgrims, and later the city's first Jewish hostel, now houses Goor's art. Her work, casually displayed, includes furniture, jewelry, and sculpture made mostly of metal and leather. The museum encourages visitors to "please touch" the artist's creations. (Admission NIS15, students NIS12. Open Sun., Mon., Wed., Sat. 10am-10pm, Tues., Thurs. 10am-2pm, Fri. 10am-4pm.) On the top floor is an absolutely incredible café overlooking Jaffa port (see **Food,** p. 278). Another spot worth a browse is the **Frank Meisler Gallery,** 25 Mazal Arie St. (tel. 681 35 02), home of kitschy, interactive sculptures made of gold, silver, bronze, and pewter. His pieces come with hefty price tags, but are fun to look at. Check out the human figurines whose stomachs open up to expose what "they're really made of"—usually sexy women and other interesting lascivious goodies. His work is often commissioned by Israeli heads of state to be presented on official visits.

A wooden footbridge from Kikkar Kedumim leads to the grassy **Ha-Pisga Gardens,** containing a small, modern amphitheater as well as a tiny excavation of an 18th-century BCE Hyksos town and a later Egyptian city. A white, ladder-like sculpture dominates one hill in the gardens; its three sections depict the fall of Jericho, the sacrifice of Isaac, and Jacob's dream. Down Mifratz Shlomo, towards the clock tower, is the minaret of the **Al Mahmudiyya Mosque,** an enormous structure erected in 1812 into which only Muslims can enter.

Jaffa's large **Shuk Ha-Pishpeshim** (Flea Market) is one of the more lively markets in Israel, with covered rows of overflowing stalls offering dust-covered Middle Eastern knick-knacks, cheap, modern hand-dyed clothing, Persian carpets, leather goods, and brassware. A vast selection of enormous *narghilas* (waterpipes) is also available. Bargaining is a given—you should begin by offering no more than half the asking price (and usually much less). To reach the flea market from the clock tower, continue one block south on Yefet St. and turn left. The market is squeezed between Olei Tzion and Beit Eshel St. and is closed on Saturdays.

The **Jaffa Port,** just south of Ha-Aliya Ha-Shuiya St., is still an active fishermen's wharf. The fishermen usually mend their nets in the afternoon, leave for sea at nightfall, and return in the early morning with their fresh catch.

# NEAR TEL AVIV

## ■ Rishon LeTzion ראשון לציון

**Rishon leTzion** (First to Zion) was the first modern Jewish settlement in Palestine. The world's first national Hebrew school opened in "Rishon," as the city is nicknamed, and it was here that the Jewish National Fund was created. But you wouldn't know all of this at first glance. Like many Israeli towns, Rishon has exploded in recent

---

### Bargaining in Jaffa

Don't be guilt-tripped into a sale. In fact, feel free to be rude—the salespeople certainly do. A firm but complimentary stance will yield the most for your shekels. ("It's very beautiful. I'll give you—insert abominably low number—shekels for it.") If you go too far and lose, chances are that duplicates of those "one-of-a-kind" goodies can be found crowding the racks of the next booth over.

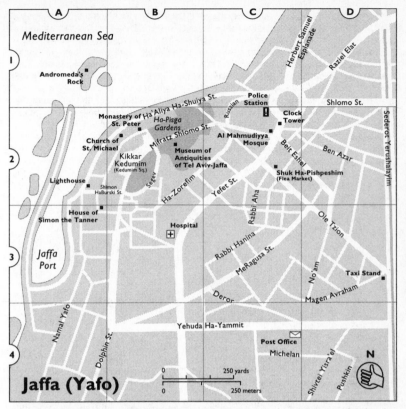

Jaffa (Yafo)

years with immigrants. Speedily built concrete apartment buildings claw for the sky, leaving Rishon looking anything but old.

The **Rishon leTzion Museum,** 2-4 Aḥad Ha'Am St. (tel. (03) 964 16 21 or 968 24 35), at Rothschild St. across from the Great Synagogue, traces the history of the town from the early pioneers to the present. This small museum displays the tools of the early settlers and various memorabilia and photographs. Admission to the museum (with an English-speaking tour guide) costs NIS8 and includes a sound and light show in the old **Village Well,** further down Rothschild St. (Museum open Sun. and Tues.-Thurs. 9am-2pm, Mon. 9am-1pm and 4-8pm, Fri. groups only, with advance reservations, 9am-1pm. Free tours and admission 10am-2pm on the first Sat. of every month.)

A yellow line path painted along Rishon's pavement marks the **Pioneer's Way,** which directs you to 18 of the town's historic sites, each marked with a plaque. Walk south two blocks on Herzl St., turn left onto Rothschild, a pedestrian thoroughfare, and walk uphill until the pedestrian mall ends. The yellow streak leads down Ha-Carmel St., where you will pass the **Winery,** 25 Ha-Carmel St. (tel. (03) 964 20 21), built by Baron Edmond de Rothschild in 1887 and still used today to produce Carmel Mizraḥi wine. One-hour tours of the winery feature an audio-visual presentation, an explication of a remarkable life-size mural by German painter Gershom Schwarze, a tasting, and a souvenir bottle. (Open Sun.-Thurs. 9am-4pm. Admission NIS12, seniors and students NIS10; tours usually begin at 9am, 11am, 1pm, and 3pm.) At night, the audio-visual room turns into a rollicking pub. Across the street from the winery, you can buy booze at wholesale prices at **Sokolik** (tel. (03) 964 13 43; open Sun.-Wed. 6am-2:30pm, Thurs. 6am-5pm, Fri. 6am-3pm).

For an inexpensive bite, join Rishonians at the **Madari Kiosk**, the only hole-in-the-wall **falafel** joint that switches locations during the day. The owners can't bear to part with either spot, so they begin their day at the corner of Rothschild St. and Mohliever St., where the street begins after the *midraḥov*. After 1pm, they move further up Rothschild, behind a bus stop on the left. Both locations are unmarked, but come lunchtime you can't miss the line (falafel NIS7). You can also sit down at **The Well**, 19 Rothschild St. (tel. 966 81 03), which offers an extremely varied menu (at least compared to the falafel joints outside). Most main courses go for NIS25-35, including fish, pasta, and meat dishes. During the day the restaurant is usually empty, but by night you'll need some luck to snag a table. Open daily 10am-2am.

The Rishon leTzion **bus station** is on Herzl St. Buses #200, #201, #371, #301 from Tel Aviv stop in Rishon and continue on to Reḥovot (every 15-30min., NIS5.20); you can also come here from Reḥovot (NIS5.20).

# ■ Reḥovot רחובות

Reḥovot, a quiet and somewhat secluded town, is known primarily for its world-famous **Weizmann Institute of Science,** a fun afternoon jaunt from Tel Aviv. The institute is named for Israel's first president, Dr. Ḥayim Weizmann, a research chemist who, during World War I, discovered an innovative way to produce acetone, the smelly liquid that proved essential to England's military effort (as well as nail polish removal). Weizmann's discovery, combined with his formidable character and convictions, helped persuade Lord Balfour to issue the 1917 Balfour Declaration favoring the establishment of a Jewish national homeland.

In the southeast corner of the institute stands the **Weizmann House** (tel. (08) 934 33 84), an elegant example of early International Style and Israel's first presidential residence (house open Sun.-Thurs. 9am-3pm, and the first Sat. of each month, 10am-2pm; admission NIS10). On the way to the house, you'll pass the **Weizmann Archives,** holding the scientist-statesman's letters and papers, and affording the overheated traveler some forested relief. The main gate to the Weizmann Institute is at the north end of Herzl St., a 20-minute walk from Bilou St., Manchester Sq., and the central **bus station.** Many inter-city buses also have stops near the Institute's white stone entrance.

The institute's scientific staff conducts research in all of the natural sciences. Projects include research on cancer, immunology, aging, and the environment. Pick up maps and brochures at the **Visitors Section** (tel. (08) 934 37 49), in the Wix Library Building, the first building on the right from the main gate (enter through the second door; open Sun.-Thurs. 9:30am-12:30pm, 1pm-3:30pm).

Back on Bilou St., you'll find Reḥovot's central fruit and vegetable **market**. The city's main avenue, Herzl St., is lined with falafel shops and self-service restaurants (falafel NIS7-8). For authentic, spicy Yemeni dishes, head south along Herzl St. several blocks from the bus station to the **Sha'arayim** neighborhood and its wealth of restaurants. Buses #200 (express) and #201 make the 20km trip from Tel Aviv every 15 min. (NIS8).

# ■ Ramla רמלה

Founded in 716 by the formidable Umayyad Caliph Suleiman ibn Abd el-Malik, Ramla is the only town in Israel that was founded and developed by Arabs. At one time, Ramla was the capital of Palestine with magnificent palaces and mosques. Today the community is predominantly composed of Jewish immigrants and a minority of Christian Arabs. On Thursdays, Ramla springs to life with a hopping market. On other days, the dusty town deserves a brief visit when traveling from Tel Aviv to Jerusalem for those who, somehow, haven't seen enough places of worship.

Among the main sites are the **Great Mosque** (formerly the crusader Cathedral of St. John) and the **Church and Hospice of St. Nicodemus and St. Joseph Arimathea.** The former is hard to miss because of the white minaret which rises majestically above the mosque. For NIS2, the guard will let you into the mosque to get a peek at the medieval vaulted arches. (Open Sun.-Thurs. 8am-1pm.) The Church, on the corner of Bialik and Herzl, is a large stone complex built in the 1500s but renovated in 1902. Ask the monk (by ringing the bell) to show you around. Further north along Danny Moss St. is the majestic **Tower of Forty Martyrs** (a.k.a. the **White Tower**).

Ramla's *shuk* thrives on Thursdays. Israelis from neighboring towns come here to wander among endless stalls of clothing, toys, and cheap food. The *shuk* is on Ze'ev Z'abutinski, which is closed to traffic until 7pm.

The *shuk's* alimentary offerings should satisfy most appetites and budgets. For a more ordered culinary experience, head to the **Chalil Restaurant**, 6 Kehilat Detroit (tel. (08) 922 22 84). With hummus for NIS9 and kebab for NIS17, this is a simple but tasty Middle Eastern restaurant. Open daily 8am-8pm; all credit cards accepted.

To get to Ramla from Tel Aviv, take bus #450, #451, or #475 (NIS7, 30min.).

# SOUTH OF TEL AVIV

## ■ Ashkelon אשקלון

Ashkelon could be Anytown, Israel. Its streets, its shuk, and its *midraḥov* (pedestrian mall) are typically Israeli. Since Ashkelon is not the recipient of flocks of tourists, it's easy to get a good feel for the local culture. An independent city and important center of trade and agriculture for centuries, today Ashkelon's historical significance is its greatest attraction. While the modern city's growing collection of shopping malls, cineplexes, and housing projects could be found in any part of the industrialized world, a seaside national park enclosing eras of ruins makes Ashkelon a worthwhile daytrip from Tel Aviv.

One of the oldest inhabited cities in the world, Ashkelon was first settled in the third millennium BCE. In biblical times, Ashkelon was one of the Philistines' five great cities. The Bible records its all-to-common conflicts with the Hebrews: Samson, as a young man, "went down to Ashkelon, and slew thirty men" (Judges 14:19). And later when King Saul was killed, David ordered, "Publish it not in the streets of Ashkelon, lest the daughters of the Philistines rejoice" (2 Samuel 1:20). By the Byzantine period, the city was far more receptive, allowing Jews to maintain a synagogue there. In 1948, the state of Israel declared its independence here.

### ORIENTATION AND PRACTICAL INFORMATION

Ashkelon lies 56 km down the coast from Tel Aviv. **Afridar** is the new commercial neighborhood and contains the bus station, the museum and **Zephania Square.** To the east, **Migdal** is a much older part of town. The narrower streets, *midraḥov*, and *shuk* give the neighborhood a more familiar Israeli feel. Afridar fronts **Bar Kokhba Beach.** To the south is the more popular **Delila Beach,** and further south, along the sea, is the **National Park.**

**Tourist Office:** Located in the City Hall behind the bus station (tel. 677 01 73 or 174). To find it, walk down the alleyway between the concrete block wall and the Giron Mall to Ha-Gvurah St., make a left, and continue halfway down to the shopping center. The sign is only in Hebrew so look for the flags flying by the entrance. Get your standard supply of maps and schedules here (open Sun., Tues. 7:30am-1pm and 4-6pm; Mon., Wed.-Thurs. 7:30am-2pm).

**Currency Exchange: Bank Ha-Poalim,** located a few stores past the tourist office, is your best bet. They have **ATMs** which accept NYCE and Cirrus cards.

**Buses**: Ashkelon's **central bus station** (info. tel. 675 02 21) is located on Ben-Gurion St., about a 25-min. walk from the beach. The information booth is supplemented by an electronic bulletin board that flashes in Hebrew and English. Buses to: Tel Aviv (#300 or 301 until 9pm, every 15-30min., NIS15.50, students NIS14); Jerusalem (#437 until 7:15pm, every 30min.-hr., NIS17.50, students NIS16); Be'er Sheva (#363 or 364 until 10pm, every 40-60min., NIS17, students NIS15.50).

**Public Transportation:** Local bus #5 goes to Zephaniah Sq. in the heart of the Afridar neighborhood and to the *midraḥov* in the old Migdal area, stopping in between at the central bus station. Bus #6 (as well as bus #13 in July-Aug.) will take you near the National Park, to the beaches, and then to Migdal. It only runs once an hour, so plan carefully or be prepared to hoof it.

**Sherut taxis:** To Tel Aviv (NIS13) try **Moniot Ha-Merkaz,** across from the central bus station; also call them for a cab around town (tel. 673 30 77).

**Pharmacy:** Next to the bus station is the Kenyon Giron, a shopping mall with a **Super-Pharm** (tel. 671 14 31; open Sun.-Thurs. 9am-11pm, Fri. 9am-3pm, Sat. 10am-midnight)

**Emergency:** For first aid call 101 or 672 33 33; for fire call 102.

**Police:** At the corner of Ha-Nassi and Eli Cohen St. (tel. 100 or 677 14 44).

**Post Office:** Central branch at 18 Herzl St. offers **Poste Restante.** Open Sun.-Tues. and Thurs. 8am-12:30pm and 4-6:30pm, Wed. 8am-1pm, Fri. 8am-12:30pm; Poste Restante open Sun.-Thurs. 7am-7pm, Fri. 7am-2pm.

**Telephone code:** 07.

## CAMPING AND FOOD

There are no youth hostels or pensions in Ashkelon; if you're keen on staying indoors, you should probably stay in Tel Aviv (45- to 60-min. bus ride) and make this a daytrip. If you are interested in roughing it for a night, **camping** is available at **Park Leumi Ashkelon** (Ashkelon National Park). Those who have their own tents can settle on one of the grassy areas for free, though there are no toilets or showers. Entrance to the park is free if you go on foot (NIS10 by car). The snack bar and two beach-side restaurants in the park itself are convenient and relatively inexpensive (steak, *shishlik,* or hamburger on a pita NIS8-12). Camping on the beach adjacent to the city is dangerous and not recommended.

The highest concentration of affordable eateries is on and off the Herzl St. *midraḥov* in Migdal. Air-conditioned **Nitzaḥon,** 30 Herzl St. (tel. 675 12 00), on the last block of the *midraḥov,* has the town's best selection of steaks, *me'orav* (mixed grill), kabab, and stuffed cabbage for NIS14-20 per plate. A few doors down, at **Sandwich Tunisien** (the sign in Hebrew goes by a different title: Shawerma Shel Ha-Ḥakham—the wise man's *shawerma*) on 31 Herzl, Tunisian Amos Sidbon serves traditional sandwiches outside on the *midraḥov.* For NIS8, you'll get a baguette stuffed with tuna, capers, salads, potatoes, hot peppers, spicy *harisa,* lemon, and olives. Delicious, well-endowed falafel is NIS5. A cheap and lively **outdoor shuk** sells everything from fruit to spices; from the *midraḥov* take Ha-Karem St. towards David Remez St. The *shuk* is between the *midraḥov* and Remez St. (open Mon. 6am-1pm, Wed. 6am-9pm, Thurs. 5:30am-9pm).

In Afridar, there are a number of outdoor, locally frequented, inexpensive restaurants on the corner of Ha-Nasi St. and Zephania at the Afridar Center (*schnitzel,* hamburger, *kebab* NIS12-15). **Delila Beach** showcases the city's collection of fish restaurants (meals NIS22-58). Dinners are served under the stars in a quasi-romantic Mediterranean setting. You can pick up supplies for your own romantic beachside meal at the **Hypercol Supermarket,** in the Kenyon Giron shopping mall right next to the bus station (tel. 671 14 22; open Sun.-Tues. 8am-10pm, Wed.-Thurs. 8am-midnight, Fri. 8am-3pm, Sat. after *Shabbat*-midnight).

## SIGHTS AND ENTERTAINMENT

Along the waterfront lies Ashkelon's **National Park** (tel. 673 64 44), its crown jewel. Buses #6 (year round) or 13 (July and Aug. only) take you to a path leading to the park's entrance, but they run infrequently. The walk from the central bus station takes about 35min. and offers enticing peeks at the sea. From the station, take a right onto Ben-Gurion Blvd. and follow it around the curve to the end, where you turn left onto the path to the park. The park was built on the site of 4000-year-old Canaanite remains buried beneath ruins of Philistine, Greek, Roman, Byzantine, Crusader, and Muslim cities. Free maps are available at the main entrance. (Park open Mon.-Thurs. 7am-7:30pm, Fri. 7am-9pm, Sat. 7am-7pm. Closed during the rainy winter months except on Sat. if it's not pouring. Admission free, NIS 10 with car.)

In between the well-maintained lawns tower the remains of a once-thriving Philistine city. A Roman colonnade and a series of Hellenistic and Roman columns, capitals, and statues, including two magnificent statues of Nike, the winged goddess of victory, grace the park's center. Coming through the main gate, you will see the **Bouleuterion,** the Council House Square when Ashkelon was an autonomous city-state under Severius in the 3rd century CE. The sunken courtyard-like area on the right is actually the inside of a Herodian assembly hall. There is also an Italian marble statue of the goddess Isis with her god-child Horus, sculpted between 200 BCE and 100 CE. Behind the Bouleuterion lies a fine **amphitheater.**

Along the southern edge of the park are segments of wall from the 12th-century Crusader city. The most peculiar feature of the site is the assembly of Roman columns sticking out of the ancient Byzantine sea wall on the beach. Originally these columns were used to support the walls, which were destroyed in 1191 by Salah ad-Din. Richard Lionheart partly restored them in 1192, as did Richard Cornwall in 1240, only to have them finally demolished by the Sultan Baybars in 1270.

Ashkelon's coast hosts four beaches where swimming is permitted—**Delila Beach** being the best of the bunch. While other beaches often fly the daunting black flag, the undertow-stopping breakers at Delila permit you to swim without fear of being whisked away to Italy. Shady canopies and snack bars give relief to sun-scorched bathers. For fun in the water—*sans* sand—there's the **Ashkeluna water park** (tel. 673 99 70) near Delila Beach and the road to the National Park. Israelis from Be'er Sheva to Yavneh flock to Ashkelon's cheesiest attraction, which boasts water slides, aerobics sessions, and games with prizes. (Open daily 9am-5pm; closes an hour early on Saturdays in May and June; NIS25-35, depending on the month.)

Of relative interest in Ashkelon is **Kikkar Ha-Atzma'ut** (Independence Sq.), one block behind the Migdal stop on buses #4, 5, 6, or 7. Once a caravan rest stop, this dilapidated intersection was the site of the first reading of Israel's Declaration of Independence in 1948. The **Ashkelon Museum,** in the square, traces the history of Ashkelon from Roman times to the present. A few minutes is adequate for both sights (open Sun.-Thurs. 9am-1pm and 4-6pm, Fri. 9am-1pm, Sat. 10am-1pm; free).

Far more appealing is Afridar's **Signon Pub,** a favorite local pub, with live music played by local artists on Tuesday and Thursday nights and karaoke on Wednesdays (open nightly 7:30pm-2am). Other popular watering holes are the **Bangi,** perched above the sand, and the **Harley** discotheque.

# ■ Near Ashkelon

## YAD MORDEKHAI יד מרדכי

From May 19th to 24th, 1948, the 165 members of Kibbutz Yad Mordekhai withstood an attack by an Egyptian battalion of 2500. The kibbutz has built a model of the battle, complete with soldiers, tanks, weapons, and a recorded explanation. The famous **museum** (tel. (07) 672 05 29) also illustrates the story of the Warsaw ghetto resistance movement. (Museum and battlefield open daily 8am-4pm. Admission NIS7, students NIS5, senior citizens NIS3.50.) Buses #19 and 37 run from Ashkelon to Yad Mordekhai (Sun.-Thurs. noon and 6:05pm, Fri. noon; last bus (#379) returns to Tel Aviv at 2:10pm, Fri. 2:30pm; NIS 17). Other buses will take you to the Mordekhai junction, but not directly to the kibbutz. If you get stuck in the late afternoon, go back to the bus stop on the highway and try flagging a passing bus from Rafah.

## KIRYAT GAT AND BEIT GUVRIN קרית גת ובית גוברין

About 22km east of Ashkelon, **Kiryat Gat** is easily accessible by bus from Tel Aviv (#369, every 30-45min., NIS14.50), Jerusalem (#446, every 30-45min., NIS17), and

Ashkelon (#25, every 30min., NIS8). This small industrial town is the capital of the **Lakhish** region—a network of 30 villages established in 1954—and the launching pad for exploration of several sites.

**Beit Guvrin National Park,** encompassing the ruins of Maresha and Beit Guvrin, is one of Israel's hidden gems. Its complex caves and magnificent views make this site unforgettable. The biblical city Maresha was one of the cities of Judah fortified by Rehoboam (Joshua 16:44). The area was settled by Edomites after the destruction of the First Temple, Sidonians during the 4th century BCE, and eventually Greeks, who converted the area into a bustling economic center. Before the turn of the first century BCE, the Hasmonean king John Hyrcanus I perpetrated one of the relatively few historical instances in which Jews forced conversion upon others. Many angry Hellenes left the city, and in the year 40 BCE, the Parthian army destroyed it.

Nearby **Beit Guvrin** was a flourishing Jewish metropolis in the fourth and third centuries BCE and in the years between the destruction of the Second Temple and the Bar Kokhba Revolt (132-135 CE). The Arab village of Beit Jibrin stood nearby until the 1948 War, when its inhabitants were evacuated; since 1949, the modern kibbutz of **Beit Guvrin** has stood on its ruins.

The park is located just off Rte. 35, near Kibbutz Beit Guvrin, across from the gas station. It's best to go by car or taxi from Kiryat Gat. Getting to and from Beit Guvrin by bus requires advance planning. Bus #11 from Kiryat Gat goes directly to the kibbutz (Sun.-Thurs. 8:05am and 5:10pm, Fri. 8:05am and 2:15pm, NIS 6; return from Beit Guvrin at 8:25am and 5:30pm, Fri. 8:25am and 2:30pm. You'll have to catch one of the morning buses if you don't want to spend the night.) Some of the Kiryat Gat-Hebron buses pass by Beit Guvrin; ask the driver to let you off here since there is no regular stop. Taxis run from Tel Aviv's central bus station to Beit Guvrin, Tel Maresha, and Tel Lakhish. (Open Sun.-Thurs. 8am-5pm, Fri. 8am-4pm; winter Sun.-Thurs. 8am-4pm, Fri. 8am-3pm; admission NIS14, students NIS10.50.)

Even if you ache at the sight of ruins, the unbelievable 360° view from **Tel Maresha,** makes the trip worth your time. On a clear day, you can see Tel Aviv and the Mediterranean to the west, and the Jordanian hills and the Dead Sea to the east. The ruins in the lower city, near the *tel,* are also worth the hot and hefty walk. Most impressive are the Hellenistic houses with maze-like series of cisterns underneath them. There are also two spooky Sidonian burial caves.

The Beit Guvrin region is characterized by some 800 **bell-shaped caves,** hidden among the cacti and fig trees. Most of the caves were carved by Greeks, Byzantines, and others as they quarried for limestone. The shape of the caves is a product of the quarrying technique, in which a narrow hole dug in the crust of the earth was widened at greater depths. Once dug, the caves were used for storage, penning animals, water collection, and later became sanctuaries for hermits and monks. St. John and others came here seeking solitude, and often carved crosses and altars into the walls. The saintly Sylvester Stallone was here for the filming of *Rambo III.* The site is well-tended with marked trails and some facilities (free).

At nearby **Tel Sandahanna,** excavations uncovered vivid, beautifully-preserved Byzantine mosaics of birds and flowers. These served as floors in 5th- and 6th-century churches, but not much is left. More recently, excavations have uncovered a Roman mosaic floor in better condition. Two of the caves were used for burials and have niches for the appropriate urns. Since the sites are unmarked and the *tel* is large, kibbutzniks from Beit Guvrin, 20 minutes down the hill, can help. (Most get off work about 12:30-1:30pm and will show interested travelers around. Ask to see the site of the house of King Abdallah, grandfather of King Hussein of Jordan.)

# Ha-Sharon

This stretch of coast between Tel Aviv and Haifa is home to most of Israel's population and agricultural output. Beaches along the shore are crowded with Israeli vacationers and dotted with Roman ruins. Ha-Sharon is, in many ways, the meat of Israel. When pioneers arrived in the beginning of the 20th century, they drained the swamps of the coastal plain, clearing the path for the modern, industrial state.

## ■ Herzliya הרצליה

Named after Theodore Herzl, Herzliya and its affluent western suburb Herzliya Pituah are located only 15km outside of Tel Aviv. The latter is home to beautiful beaches, luxury hotels, and foreigners who tan and schmooze for a living. Neither, however, have any cheap accommodations and are best visited as a day trip or afternoon jaunt from Tel Aviv. Bus #501 or #502 from Tel Aviv (every 20min., 15min., NIS5.20) will get you here. From the Herzliya bus station, two blocks south on Ben-Gurion St. on the corner of Ha-Bouim St. is the diminutive **Herzliya Museum of Art** (tel. (09) 850 42 70; open Sun.-Thurs. 4pm-8pm, Fri.-Sat. 10am-2pm; free). The museum is in the **Yad Labanim Memorial Center,** which also houses the **Israeli Center for Propaganda Research,** where tourists are generously encouraged to sample the wares (call (09) 855 10 11 for lecture schedules). An amphitheater in the same building is the setting for concerts by the **Herzliya Chamber Orchestra** (call (09) 854 71 75 for concert schedules). Surrounding the building is an extensive modern **Sculpture Garden.**

A few blocks north of the Herzliya central bus station is the **Beit Rishonim** (First Settlers' House) **Founders Museum,** at 8 Ha-Nadiv St. off Sokolov St. The museum, located in a pleasant garden, has a life-like statue of Herzl leaning against the second-floor balcony. The museum reconstructs the story of Herzliya from its days as a colony in 1924 via computerized presentations as well as furnishings and tools from the early settlement period. (Open Sun. and Thurs.-Fri. 8:30am-12:30pm, Mon. 8:30am-12:30pm and 4:30pm-6:30pm. Admission NIS7, NIS3.50 for students.)

The attractions in **Herzliya Pituah** are centered around the beach, and accordingly most of the large beaches charge admission (NIS5-15). From Herzliya central bus station, take bus #29 to **Nof Yam** and **Sidna Ali Beaches** which are happily both free of tourists and admission fees. Get off the bus, follow the dirt road up the hill and go through the gate in the fence. You will pass the prominent **Sidna Ali Mosque** which you will not be able to enter if you've dressed for a day at the beach.

Once at the beach, you may notice Herzliya Pituah's most notable attraction, an inhabited sand castle known as the **Hermit's House.** Built into the face of the cliff, this private home is probably the most unique residence in Israel. Resembling a boat over which a peacock has spread its fan in some places and a gargoyle in others, this structure is like nothing you've ever seen. Nissim Kakhalon has been building his fantastic home for the past 25 years with natural sea materials as well as tires, bottles, broken plates, and other debris that washed ashore. Plenty of greenery covers the walls, and graceful panther statues are strewn all over. Peevish Israeli authorities have so far been unable to oust Mr. Kakhalon. Look for his latest inspired addition, the "sand bar" snack stand, sporadically serving cold drinks (NIS4) and hummus on homemade pita (NIS6) under a covered veranda. Ask for a tour of his architectural creations and the network of tunnels that he has dug to connect them. Plans for a school to teach people "how to make things" are being hatched. On the cliffs above the beach, a few hundred meters farther north, are the barely discernible ruins of Apollonia, a Roman port fortified by medieval Crusaders.

# ■ Netanya נתניה

Founded in the 1920s as an agricultural center, Netanya has grown into a popular beach resort full of affluent retirees who don't know a plow from a hoe. This Miami-on-the-Med's bridge club, orchestra, and singles mixers cater to wealthy tourists, whether they're from Amarillo, Texas, or Amman, Jordan. Even so, a growing variety of activities and businesses indicate an effort to attract young people and budgeteers. There are even a few Israelis here (someone has to run the information office). Located roughly between Haifa and Tel Aviv, although tending towards Tel Aviv in both location and ethos, Netanya serves as an excellent base for exploring the sites between these two cities.

## ORIENTATION AND PRACTICAL INFORMATION

To get to the center of the action from the central bus station (tel. 833 70 52), push your way through neon-lit snack stands to Binyamin Blvd. (which turns into Weizmann Blvd. farther north) and walk one block north to **Herzl St.,** the town's main shopping area. Turning left on Herzl, you'll get to Dizengoff St. and arrive at the **midraḥov** (pedestrian zone), lined with expensive outdoor cafés, *shawerma* stands, and dairy restaurants. On the other side of the *midraḥov,* (past King David St.) is **Ha-Atzma'ut Sq.** (Independence Sq.). Behind the square is **Ha-Melech Park,** where palm trees provide welcome shade for a picnic or a game of chess. The park also has an outdoor amphitheater where you can sit and watch the waves' well-practiced performance. From the park, stairs lead down to the beach and the well-kept promenade continues to the north.

**Tourist Information Office:** Located in a small, strangely-shaped brick building in the southwest corner of Ha-Atzma'ut Sq. (tel. 882 72 86), next to the stairs to the beach. City maps, bus schedules, and events schedules available. Open Sun.-Thurs. 8:30am-7pm, Fri. 9am-noon.

**Currency Exchange: Change Point** (tel. 884 49 66; fax 884 49 04), at the north side of Ha-Atzma'ut Sq., changes money with no commission. Open Sun.-Thurs. 9am-7pm, Fri. 9am-1pm. **Bank Hapoalim** and **Bank Leumi** also flank the square Both open Sun.-Fri. 8:30am-12:30pm, Sun., Tue., and Thurs. 4pm-5:30pm.

**Telephones: Solan** (tel. 862 21 31) at 8 Ha-Atzma'ut Sq. offers private booths for discount international phone, fax, and telegram services. Open daily 24hr.

**Buses:** The central bus station is at 3 Binyamin Blvd (tel. 833 70 52). Buses #600, #605, and #602 run to Tel Aviv (approx. every 10min., 30min., NIS8.80). Bus #945 runs to Haifa (every 30min., 45min., NIS15.50). From Jerusalem take bus #947 (every 30min., 1½hr., NIS23.50). Schedules are displayed on the electronic timetable board facing the information booth.

**Taxis:** The main services include **Ha-Shahar** (tel. 861 44 44), **Ha-Sheron** (tel. 882 23 23), **Hen** (tel. 833 33 33), and **Netanya** (tel. 834 44 43).

**Car rental: Hertz** (tel. 882 88 90), **Tamir-Rent-A-Car** (tel. 833 18 31), and **Eldan** (tel. 861 69 82) have offices at Ha'Atzma'ut Sq.

**Pharmacies:** Massive, air-conditioned **Centerpharm,** 1 King David St. (tel. 884 15 31), stays open the latest (Sun.-Thurs. 8am-midnight, Fri. 8am-5pm). At least one pharmacy is always open for emergencies; the roster is posted on each door.

**Hospital:** The main hospital is **Laniado Hospital** (tel. 860 46 66).

**Emergency:** For **first aid** dial **Magen David Adom** at 101 or 862 33 33 or 35; for **police,** dial 100 or 860 44 44; for **fire** dial 102.

**Post office:** The branch at 59 Herzl St. (tel. 862 15 77) offers **Poste Restante.** Another branch is located at 2 Herzl St. (tel. 862 77 97). Open Sun.-Tues. and Thurs. 8am-12:30pm and 3:30-6pm, Wed. 8am-1:30pm, Fri. 8am-noon.

**Phone code:** 09.

## ACCOMMODATIONS AND FOOD

The **Atzma'uth Hostel** (tel. 882 25 62 or 862 13 15), at the corner of Ha-Atzma'ut Sq. and Usishkin St., is the only youth hostel in town. Occupying the third and fourth floors of an elevator-equipped building, this two-year-old hostel still sparkles. Each room has A/C, fridge, and private bath. The friendly, multilingual staff will let you leave your bags during day trips. There's a TV lounge and free safe for valuables. (No lockout. No curfew. Check-out 11am. Dorm beds US$10, singles US$20, doubles US$30.) The **Orit Hotel,** 21 Ḥen Blvd. (tel./fax. 861 68 18), off Jabotinsky St. south of Ha-Atzma'ut Sq., is the next-cheapest option. The Swedish management keeps scrupulously clean rooms, a pleasant common room, a small library (in a variety of languages), and a communal fridge. Rooms have private baths, fans, and balconies. (Quiet after 11:30pm. No smoking. Reception open 7am-9pm, till 11pm in summer. Check-out 10am. No curfew—you'll get a key. Singles US$30, doubles US$45; winter dorm rooms US$15; reduced rates for kibbutzniks; children ages 2-6 are 50% off, ages 7-12 25% off; includes breakfast.)

Almost all hotels in Netanya are expensive, but many lower their prices by 10-15% from November to February. The most popular areas for **beach-sleeping** are near the 24-hr. cafés. As always, camping on the beach is especially unsafe for solo women and unguarded valuables.

Cheap food *is* available in Netanya. In **Ha-Atzma'ut Square,** pizza goes for about NIS7 and *malawah* for NIS10. Closer to the Central bus station, the prices go down. **Sha'ar Ha-Gai Street** is lined with falafel stands and self-service restaurants which will stuff just about anything permitted by law into a pita (falafel NIS6, *shawerma* NIS9, *schnitzel* NIS10). **Binyamin Blvd.,** at the end of Sha'ar Ha-Gai, has two 24-hr. bakeries, where *burekas* go for NIS3-4 and sweet pastries for NIS1-3: **Hatachana** bakery at 11 Benyamin Blvd., and **Bel-Vil** bakery, at 4 Benyamin Blvd. (tel. 862 59 33), the latter specializing in hearty pizza bagels (NIS5). Before picnicking on the grass or sand, stock up at the **Nitza supermarket** (tel. 862 82 16), 8 Nitza Blvd. (off King David St.). For fresh fruits and vegetables, shop at the **open market** on Zangwill St., 2 blocks east of Weizmann Blvd. near the center of town (open Sun.-Thurs. 7am-6:30pm, Fri. 7am-2pm). From Ha'Atzma'ut Sq., take King David St. past King Solomon's Hotel to Nitza Blvd. The **Kenion Ha-Sharon mall,** located at the intersection of Petach Tikva Rd. and Herzl, has a **CoOp** supermarket.

For a more satisfying (and expensive) experience, consider some of Netanya's midrange restaurants. The **Mini Golf Restaurant and Pub,** 21 Nitza Blvd. (tel. 861 77 35), is perched on the edge of a cliff overlooking the sea. The atmosphere is relaxing and romantic, with separate milk and meat areas. The grilled dishes (NIS20-26) are excellent, while the blintzes (NIS24) will make even the most bloodthirsty carnivore into a dairy believer (open Sun.-Thurs. 11am-3am, Fri. 11am-7pm, Sat. 8:30pm-3am). **Apropo** (tel. 862 44 82) is conveniently located between the amphitheater and the stairs to the beach. Sample from the new Thai menu (NIS35-45) while sea-gazing through the restaurant's glass walls. Pastas (NIS26-31) and toasts (NIS27-34) are served in large portions (open Sun.-Thurs. 9am-midnight, Fri. 9am-5pm, Sat. 6pm-midnight). **Patisserie Antverpia,** 1 Eliyahu Krause St. (tel. 833 53 90), one block south of Herzl St. off Smilansky St., serves fresh *ḥallah* and luscious cream pastries at slightly lower prices than its tourist-district counterparts. Sandwiches at NIS7-9, hearty breakfasts for NIS16. (Open Sun.-Thurs. 7:30am-9pm, Fri. 7:30am-3pm.) Credit cards accepted at all three restaurants.

## SIGHTS AND ENTERTAINMENT

Netanya's **beaches**—11km of them—are all free; the northernmost are least crowded. You can go **horseback riding** along the beach and reenact scenes from *Planet of the Apes.* At NIS30 per ½hr, though, your wallet may tire before your thighs. For information, call Cactus Ranch Horseback Riding (tel. 865 12 39) or take bus #7 to the intersection of Itamar Ben-Avi St. and Jabotinsky St. and ask them in person (open daily 11am-7pm).

The Netanya municipality organizes various forms of free entertainment practically every night during the summer and often during the winter. The tourist information office has complete listings of concerts, movies, and a host of other activities. During the summer, you can watch the sun set over the Mediterranean while listening to classical music in the **Ha-Melekh Park** amphitheater (Sun.-Thurs. 6-8pm). There is a performance of Israeli songs and songs of the 60s in the lobby of the Park Hotel every Friday (info. tel. 862 33 44). Talented Russian musicians play classical music at 11 Ha-Atzama'ut Sq. (Mon. noon-1pm). If you'd rather see karats than hear clarinets, there are a number of diamond centers which give free guided tours of their premises: **National Diamond Center** (90 Herzl St., tel. 862 47 70), **Inbar Diamond Center** (1 Usishkin, tel. 882 22 33), and **Orco Jewelry** (11 Raziel St., tel. 882 90 70). Most are open Sun.-Thurs. 8am-7pm, but call ahead to be sure.)

The favorite spot come pub time is **Uri's Pub,** also known as Uri's Garden, on 26 Dizengoff St. (tel. 882 87 31). Coming from Ha-Atzma'ut Sq., take a right at the eastern end of the *midraḥov*. A concrete path leads to a small room, empty in summer when everyone is gathered in the garden. Goldstar (NIS8) and watermelon with Bulgarian cheese (NIS13) will keep you happy.

## ■ Near Netanya

The beautiful **Poleg Nature Reserve,** about 8km south of Netanya, begins where the Poleg River meets the sea. The walk upstream leads past flowering plants and eucalyptus trees planted during the last century to dry up the swamps that once covered the Plain of Sharon. A few kilometers south, near **Kibbutz Ga'ash,** seaside cliffs reach 60m, forming a beautiful backdrop for one of Israel's loveliest and least crowded beaches. Take Egged bus #601 or #604 (every 30min. 5:30am-10:30pm, from Netanya NIS5.20, from Tel Aviv NIS8); ask to be let off at Ga'ash or Naḥal Poleg. Just before the main kibbutz gate turn left and continue south for about 200m along the unpaved road. Head west along the field until you reach a small dirt "parking lot" (about 1½km). A path that begins at the southwest corner of the parking lot leads to the beach, or you can follow the jeeps that continue along the unpaved roads several km north to one of Israel's favorite **nude beaches.**

Bus #1A goes to the **Jewish Legion Museum** (tel. 882 22 12), less than 5km north of Netanya, in Aviḥa'il. The tiny museum documents the story of Britain's Jewish units in World War I. Although photographs, personal and official statements, and dioramas abound, they are probably of little interest except to the knowledgeable visitor. (Open Sun.-Thurs. 8am-4pm; admission NIS5, students NIS2.)

The tranquil **Emek Ḥefer Youth Hostel (HI)** (tel. (09) 866 60 32) is in its own grove 6km north of Netanya, only a short walk from gorgeous, free **beaches.** Take bus #857, 872, or 901 from Tel Aviv (NIS12), #29 or 706 from Netanya (NIS6.20), or #901 or 921 from Haifa (NIS15.50), get off at Tzomet Ben Yanai at Kfar Vitkin, then walk north on the eastern side of the highway until you see the open gate. The reception building is through the parking lot (closed 2-5pm). Rooms are in a central building, a collection of stucco huts, and double bungalows. Most have private baths, fridges, and fans, and all have access to the basketball court. The hostel may have A/C by summer 1997. (No lockout or curfew. 4-8 bed dorm rooms US$18 per person, members US$16.50. Doubles US$20 per person, members US$18.50. Breakfast included, lunch US$8, dinner US$6. All credit cards accepted.) **Ḥanout Shohar Supermarket** (open daily 8am-8pm, Fri. 8am-4pm, summer until 5pm; Sat. 9am-8pm) and the **Original Israeli Pancake House** (open 24hr.; pancakes NIS14-29, Mexican menu NIS25-28; alcohol served) supplement the hostel food.

In addition to the beautiful beaches on the other side of the highway, you can explore the **Naḥal Alexander Nature Reserve** along the banks of the Alexander River, only 1km north of the hostel.

## ■ Caesarea קיסריה

At the end of the first century BCE, Herod the Great built this city (Kay-SAHR-ya in Hebrew) on the site of a small Phoenician anchorage. Caesarea was a planned city, with a network of crisscrossing streets, a temple, a theater, an amphitheater, markets, and residential quarters. Built in only 12 years, this city transformed rapidly into a great commercial center and became the headquarters of the Roman government in Palestine. Excavations began in 1873 by the Palestine Exploration Fund and have unearthed the Roman theater and amphitheater, Byzantine mosaics, aqueducts, a Crusader city, and an extremely sophisticated 2000-year-old harbor. Caesarea's multi-layered ruins already constitute one of Israel's finest archaeological sites, and archaeologists continue to dig.

Not far from the ancient ruins, a growing residential community boasts some of the most beautiful villas in Israel. Add to this the Dan Caesarea (a five-star hotel) and the country's only golf course and it's not hard to see why Caesarea has become a popular choice for Israel's *nouveau riche*. Although the town's Roman townhouses are set apart from the modern ones, touristy cafés and gift shops have managed to nestle themselves among the antique buildings. Bus service to Caesarea is infrequent. Have faith in the old saying that the best things come to those who wait—they just might.

## HISTORY

Phoenician travelers of the 4th century BCE established a small town and harbor called Strato's Tower on the main trading route between Phoenicia (present-day Lebanon and coastal Syria) and Egypt. The town and surrounding coastal strip were soon captured by Greeks and later fell into the hands of Augustus Caesar, who granted it to Herod the Great, vassal king of Judea. Because of its strategic location and access to the harbor, Herod transformed Strato's Tower into one of the eastern Roman Empire's great cities, renaming it "Caesarea" in honor of the emperor. Construction began in 22 BCE and within 12 years the city boasted a theater, a hippodrome for chariot racing, aqueducts carrying fresh water from the north, and a harbor capable of accommodating 300 ships. In 6 CE, Caesarea became the capital of the Roman province of Judea, and it remained the seat of Roman power in the area until the fall of the Empire. It was Pontius Pilate, the Roman prefect of Caesarea from 26 to 36 CE, who ordered the crucifixion of Jesus. The first evidence of Pilate's existence outside the accounts of the Gospels and the historian Josephus was uncovered here in 1961.

In 66 CE, fighting between Jews and Romans in Caesarea sparked the six-year Jewish Rebellion (the Great Revolt), which resulted in the destruction of Jerusalem's Second Temple in 70 CE. The Romans celebrated Jerusalem's fall by slaughtering thousands of Jews in Caesarea's amphitheater. Sixty years later, ten Jewish sages, among them the famous Rabbi Akiva, were tortured to death in the arena as punishment for their participation in the Bar Kokhba revolt, a second Jewish uprising against Rome. Ironically, Caesarea later became a center of Jewish and Christian scholarship.

During the Crusades, Caesarea changed hands four times before finally falling to King Louis IX of France. Saint Louis strengthened and expanded the city's fortifications in 1254, building the massive ramparts, battlements, and moat, all of which are still in excellent condition. Despite Louis' efforts, Caesarea was conquered and destroyed in 1275 by the Sultan Baybars. The city remained uninhabited until 1878 when the Muslim Boshnaqs (Bosnians) resettled it in 1878. Caesarea's population was driven out a final time in the 1948 War, but within decades Caesarea began to thrive once again—this time as a tourist site and resort for wealthy Israelis.

## PRACTICAL INFORMATION

Getting to Caesarea is by no means simple—the only practical way is via **Hadera,** the nearest town. Be warned that while buses to Hadera are plentiful (#852 or 872 from Tel Aviv, NIS12, 40 min.; #706 from Netanya, NIS8, 20 min.; #921 (1 hr.) or 941 (30 min.) from Haifa, NIS12, and #945 from Jerusalem, NIS23, 1½ hr., the only bus to or from the ruins is #76 from Hadera, NIS6.20, 30 min.), which travels several times per day in each direction. Call ahead to avoid a two-hour wait in Hadera's boring central bus station or in the heat outside the Caesarea ruins. While it is possible to get a taxi from the station in Hadera for NIS25, you won't find one for the ride back from the ruins unless you arrange in advance, which will cost NIS30 each way. Those who don't mind sweating can take an intercity Egged bus to the Caesarea exit along the old Ḥadera-Haifa road, an unrewarding 3km west of the ruins (ask the driver for Tzomet Or Akiva and watch carefully). Caesaria's **telephone code** is 06.

## ACCOMMODATIONS AND FOOD

There are only two options for budget accommodations around Caesarea. Just south of the Roman theater is **Kibbutz Sdot Yam,** which maintains 16 private apartments (all have A/C, private baths, refrigerators, TVs, and telephones), ideal for families or for three to four person groups (singles US$57, doubles US$84, additional people US$36 each; winter singles US$31, doubles US$62.50, additional people US$23.50 each). For independent travellers, there are two types of hostel-style rooms: 6-7 bed dorm rooms with showers and toilets in the hall cost US$16 per person. For an additional US$4, you can be in a five-bed dorm room with a private shower and toilet. All rooms are equipped with A/C, and washing machines are available. Call in advance (tel. 636 44 70 or 44; fax 636 22 11. Open daily 7am-7pm, winter 7am-4pm.) To get to the reception office, enter the kibbutz's main gate near the Roman theater (the last stop on bus #76), pass the tile factory and bus stop, and bear right at the fork in the road. Look for the small white building with the colorful "Kef Yam" sign on it.

Next to the southern end of the kibbutz, near the beach, is the **Caesarea Sports Center,** which maintains two buildings with guest rooms. The Beit Gil Building has 40 rooms with A/C and private baths. (Dorm beds (4-5 per room) range from NIS155-205). The Hostel Building has no A/C and baths are shared by five rooms, but the prices are a bit lower. (Dorm beds (4-5 per room) range from NIS110-140). August is the most expensive time to stay, and rates jump NIS10-20 for Saturday stays. Full board is included in all dorm prices. To get to the Center, go through Kibbutz Sdot Yam, head toward the beach, turn left at the "T," and walk past the Hannah Senesh House; the center is just beyond the big brown building. Call in advance (tel. 636 43 94, or 13 73, or 41 29; fax 636 15 79) to make reservations.

Many visitors to Caesarea simply unroll their sleeping bags on the beach, but camping in some places, such as Hofshonit Beach, is forbidden. Restaurant prices in Caesarea are as high as the Crusader walls, though places like **Charly's Café Restaurant** and the **Citadel Restaurant** have great views. The **Sdot Yam Cafeteria** in the kibbutz offers all-you-can-eat breakfasts (NIS21), lunch (NIS30), and dinner (NIS21). They serve pretty standard, yet tasty kibbutz food—*litsitsot*, salads, mashed potatoes, etc.

## SIGHTS

Caesarea's sights include a Roman city and an ancient port. Though the Roman city is not fully excavated, most of the site is well marked; relics include the main road and several statues. The granaries and residences are Arab remains, and the walls and churches date from the Crusader period. Don't be surprised to find pieces of a marble column used as street pavement—medieval contractors frequently re-used Roman remains when erecting cities. The harbor and beaches of Caesarea are also of major archaeological significance. Extending along the ancient city is Herod's now-submerged port which included the first breakwater in the Eastern Mediterranean. A constant stream of international archaeologists and volunteers continue to excavate both the dry ground and underwater areas of Caesarea

The enormous, restored **Roman Theater** is a 500m stroll south of the Crusader city (tel. 636 13 58). Reopened in 1961, this 3500-seat structure has hosted Eric Clapton, the Bolshoi Ballet, and the New Israeli Opera. Admission (NIS14, seniors and students NIS10.50) covers both the city and the Roman Theater; the other sites are free. You can purchase tickets and get a free map at either site (both open daily 8am-6pm, winter 8am-4pm, Fri. and holidays eves until 5pm). By visiting the Roman city after hours, you can avoid the entrance fee *and* get a Mediterranean sunset thrown in as a bonus. The catch is that you won't be able to get into the theater.

Although most of the ruins are within the Crusader walls, a number of interesting Roman remnants lie outside the site proper. Behind the café, across from the entrance to the Crusader city, is an excavated **Byzantine street** and Caesarea's most famous find: colossal **Roman statues** from the 2nd century CE. The two headless figures, one of red porphyry, the other of white marble, were discovered accidentally by kibbutzniks ploughing fields. A one-km walk north along either the water or the road that runs along the Crusader walls leads to Caesarea's beach and the excellently preserved **Roman aqueduct.** The most recent excavations have uncovered another Herodian amphitheater (at press time it was inaccessible to the public).

The intensely blue cool water is inviting, but swimming within the walls of the city costs NIS20. Unless you wish to go snorkeling in the ancient harbor, you are better off heading to the free public beach behind the aqueduct. Diving in the harbor is an expensive but rewarding experience at the **Caesarea Diving Center** (tel. 636 17 87; fax 636 03 11). Full equipment is NIS150 per day.

About one km along the main road running east from the theater stands an archway leading to the ruins of the **Roman Hippodrome,** now overgrown with banana and orange groves cultivated by nearby Kibbutz Sdot Yam. In its heyday, the 352m by 68m racetrack could hold 20,000 spectators. Most of the relics unearthed, including coins and inscriptions, have been put on display at the **Sdot Yam Museum of Caesarea Antiquities** (tel. 636 43 67), located within the kibbutz. Next to the museum is the **Beit Hannah Senesh,** built in honor of a Sdot Yam parachutist who died while trying to save Jews from the Nazis during World War II. (Both open Sat.-Thurs. 10am-4pm; Fri. and holiday eves 10am-2pm. Admission to the memorial's museum and film is NIS7 each.) The **Kef Yam Office** in the kibbutz offers glass-bottomed boat tours of the ancient harbor (NIS27 per person). You *must* call ahead for reservations (tel. 636 44 44).

# ■ Near Caesarea

Just outside Moshav Beit Ḥananya, on the old coastal road between Caesarea and Ma'agan Mikha'el, are two well-preserved **Roman aqueducts,** believed to have carried water from the Shuni springs northeast of present-day Binyamina down to the ancient city of Caesarea. North of the *moshav,* excavations are in progress at **Tel Mevoraḥ,** where several important Roman artifacts have been unearthed. Two of the marble sarcophagi discovered in the ruins of a Roman mausoleum are on display in the Rockefeller Museum in Jerusalem.

**Kibbutz Ma'agan Mikha'el** is one of the largest and loveliest kibbutzim in Israel. Take the #921 from Haifa (NIS12, 1hr.) or Tel-Aviv (NIS15½, 1½hr.) and get off at the Ma'agan Mikha'el intersection. The huge industrial plant at the entrance belies the cultivated fields and acres of neat, rectangular fish ponds set between the coastal road and the sea. Part of the kibbutz is a wildlife preserve with an aviary and a small museum displaying archaeological finds from the fields.

The gorgeous **beach** at **Dor** is protected by four small, rocky islands, each a bird sanctuary, explorable at low tide (NIS10 entrance fee, open 7am-6pm, tel. 634 09 22). To get here, take bus #921 from either Haifa (NIS8, 30min.) or Tel Aviv (NIS16, 2hr.), and get off at the Kibbutz Dor intersection; it's a 3km walk to the beach. The **Tel Dor** archaeological site is on the hill at the far northern end of the beach; you'll need shoes to traverse the rusty-wire-and-sand road. Though the site was probably founded in the 15th century BCE and was part of King David's empire, most of the important remains at Dor date from the Greek and Roman periods. The site includes temples dedicated to Zeus and Astarte, as well as the ruins of a Byzantine church.

Next to the beach, within the boundaries of **Kibbutz Nachsholim,** is the Center of Nautical and Regional Archaeology (CONRAD), also known as **Hamizgaga Museum.** The unique stone edifice was formerly a glass factory built by Baron Edmond de Rothschild. Today it serves as a repository and display for objects found at Tel Dor and for underwater archaeological finds retrieved by the center's diving team. There is also a special exhibition which traces the history of the building (tel. 639 09 50; NIS8, NIS6 for students and seniors; Sun.-Fri. 8:30am-2pm, Sat. and holidays 10:30am-3pm).

Nearby, next to **Kibbutz Ein Karmel,** is the **Naḥal Me'arot Nature Reserve** with prehistoric caves inhabited some two hundred thousand years ago. Experienced guides explain the significance of the nearby caves and can suggest or lead longer hikes in the surrounding area. The admission price of NIS13 (under 18 pay NIS7) includes a film inside one of the caves which recreates the life of prehistoric man (tel. (04) 984 17 50 or 22, 8am-4pm). To get to the site, take bus #421 (from Haifa: NIS8, 20min.; from Tel Aviv: NIS17, 2 hr.) and get off at Ein Carmel Junction. Walk a few minutes south along the road until you see a sign indicating the Nature Reserve. A few hundred meters east of the main road is the entrance to the caves.

# ■ Zikhron Ya'akov זיכרון יעקב

Zikhron Ya'akov (shortened to Zikhron by locals) was established in 1882 on swamplands drained with the generous financial assistance of Baron Edmond de Rothschild. The town's name means "Jacob's Memorial" (for the Baron's father) and is known today for the nectar produced from surrounding vineyards.

Bus #872 from Tel Aviv (NIS16, 1½hr.) and #202 from Haifa (NIS12, 30min.) will take you to the small **central bus station.** The white building behind the station is the **tourist office** (tel. 639 88 92; tel./fax 639 88 11), which is well-equipped with maps, brochures, and information about city events (open Sun.-Thurs. 8:30am-1pm, Fri. 8:30am-noon). Zikhron's **telephone code** is 06. To the right of the central bus station, two blocks past the concrete arches, is the newly-renovated, cobblestone **Ha-Meyasdim St.,** with old-fashioned decorative lamp posts on both sides. Along this picturesque strip are a number of pricey restaurants. The only real budget food option is a packed lunch.

Just outside the city limits lies **Ramat Ha-Nadiv,** the Rothschild Family Tomb and Gardens. *Sherut* taxis on their way to Binyamina will drop you off at the side road leading to the estate for a mere NIS2.50. The remaining 15 to 20 minute walk features inspiring views of the valley below. The rock-hewn crypt containing the remains of Edmond de Rothschild and his wife is modest relative to the Baron's wealth. More impressive is the greenery. The rose garden, palm garden, cascade garden, fragrance garden, and small amphitheater are all separated by masterfully landscaped meadows. (Open Sun.-Thurs. 6:30am-4pm, Fri. 6:30am-2pm, Sat. 8am-4pm, though the crypt itself is closed on Sat. and holidays. Free.)

Zikhron Ya'akov is best known for the **Carmel-Mizraḥi Winery** (tel. 634 12 41), founded 100 years ago by the Baron himself. The winery now produces a significant share of Israel's domestic wine as well as a large stock for export. The one-hour tour of the winery includes a look at the old wine cellars, an audio-visual presentation, wine tasting, and a souvenir bottle. It's best to visit during the harvest season (Aug.-Oct.). From the central bus station turn right onto Ha-Meyasdim St. Continue downhill for a few blocks and turn right onto Ha-Nadiv St. where the cobblestone ends. The winery is at the bottom of the hill. (Open Sun.-Thurs. 9am-3pm., Fri. 9am-noon. Admission NIS12, students NIS10. Call ahead for tours in English.) The winery also hosts wild wine and cheese parties, usually accompanied by an Israeli singer (you *must* call in advance, tel. 639 78 83; NIS60-65).

Other sites of interest in Zikhron Ya'akov include the beautiful **Ohel Ya'akov Synagogue** which was erected in 1886 (situated on the junction of Ha-Meyasdim St. and Ha-Nadiv St.) and the **Beit Daniel** music center which hosts a chamber music festival every year on *Pesakh* and *Sukkot* (tel. 639 90 01). If you're hungry for more cork sniffing and bouquet evaluating, you can head down to the **Baron's Winery** (tel. 638 04 34) which is located down the hill from the entrance to the Baron's Tomb in Ramat Ha-Nadiv. The smaller winery also gives tours which include wine tasting for NIS10 (Open Sun.-Thurs. 8am-4pm, Fri. 8am-3pm), but Carmel-Mizraḥi is worth the extra two shekels.

# Northern Coast

## ■ Haifa חיפה جيفا

A prosperous city built on the steep, forested slopes of Mt. Carmel, Haifa is Israel's capital of the North. Though it boasts the country's largest port, two of Israel's eleven universities, and the most diverse topography in the state, Haifa does not compete with Tel Aviv or Jerusalem for tourists. Budget accommodations are sparse, the seafront distant, and the museums less than spectacular; however, the city has recently embarked on the "Haifa 2000" project to transform its coastal beaches into a tourist-trapping, Riviera-esque strip. Regardless of the ebb and flow of its sandy future, Haifa's real gems, its thickly forested neighborhoods and striking vistas, will likely remain the city's most powerful and memorable points of attraction.

Since the prophet Elijah fled from the wrath of King Ahab to the caves of Mt. Carmel (I Kings 18-19), Haifa has maintained a tradition for harboring religious minorities. Crusaders built the first of several monasteries above Elijah's cave, which eventually gave shelter to the wandering (but now settled) Carmelite Order of monks (see Sights, Walks, Parks, p. 362). German Templars, who established Haifa's German colony, and Baha'is, whose world headquarters are in Haifa, have also found homes here. Throughout the 1930's, waves of European Jews seeking refuge from Nazism poured onto the beaches of Haifa. In the 1948 War, Haifa was the first territory secured by Jewish forces.

While Haifa contains a small Orthodox Jewish community, the prevailing tenor of the city is decidedly (and proudly) secular. Haifa's population of a quarter million includes a sizable Arab minority, but there is little tension; in fact, supporters of the Israel-Palestinian peace accords often cite Haifa as the paradigm for peaceful Jewish-Arab co-existence. As such, Haifa was one of the few strongholds for Shimon Peres in the 1996 election.

### ORIENTATION

Haifa, Israel's principal port and a hub for ferry transport, lies on a small peninsula on the Mediterranean coast, about 100km south of Lebanon and due west of the Sea of Galilee. Built into the northern slopes of the Carmel mountain, the city is unofficially divided into three terraces. In this vertically-oriented town, social stratification is more than just a metaphor. The rich really do live on the top, the poor at the bottom. The **Ha-Ir** area, aptly named "downtown," is at the foot of the mountain. The **central bus station** is adjoined to the **train station** on this level, at the intersection of **Derekh Yafo** (Jaffa Rd.) and **Rothschild Blvd.** If you follow Jaffa Rd., you'll find yourself in the Old City area, across from the **Haifa Port.** Haifa's **beaches** lie along the peninsula's northern coast, near the bus and train stations. Perpendicular to Jaffa Rd. and running straight up to the Baha'i Shrine is **Ben-Gurion Blvd.,** which ends at **Ha-Geffen St.** further up the mountain.

The middle terrace is the **Hadar** district, home to businesses, cafés, bakeries, and bazaar stands. Its main street is **Herzl St.,** along which several staircases make for easy climbing up and down the mountain. **Ha-Ḥalutz St.,** parallel to Herzl but one street down (i.e., north, or toward the port), contains the lion's share of falafel stands. Buses from this street go to the central bus station rather than up the mountain. The street parallel to and above Herzl is the **Nordan Midraḥov** (pedestrian zone), bordered on the west by **Balfour St.** and on the east by **Arlozorov St.**

The highest area is known as **Carmel Center,** characterized by posh homes, five-star hotels, restaurants, and discos. This district is traversed by **Ha-Nassi Blvd.** and **Yefeh Nof St.,** both of which run west to east past all the major hotels. Follow either of these streets to the Dan Panorama Hotel and go one block up to reach **Gan Ha-Eim** (Mother's Park), which has a peaceful **promenade** and a panoramic view of the lower city and the port area. From Carmel Center, Moriya St. takes you to **Ahuza**—a previously bare intersection, now graced with stylish cafes, restaurants, and a large shopping center, Merkaz Horev.

## TRANSPORTATION

The decentralization of the transportation system in Haifa can be explained by the city's topography, most obviously by the 300m elevation drop between Carmel Center and the port. The **central bus station,** like the city itself, has three tiers. Buses bound for other cities leave from the first floor, Haifa city buses do their business on the second, and the third floor welcomes both inter- and intra-city arrivals. Take these second-floor buses to the city's neighborhoods: Ha-Ir (#17, 41), Hadar (#21, 24, 28, 37), and Carmel Center (#21, 28, 37). All urban rides are NIS3.30. If you're going to be in Haifa for a few days, a *cartisiya* (NIS33 for 20 trips) is cheaper and more convenient.

On weekdays, buses run from around 5:30am to midnight. On Fridays, they stop at 5:30pm; on Saturdays, they begin running at 9:30am and run less frequently than their weekday counterparts. Saturday buses do *not* run from the central bus station but from the Hadar area, many from Daniel St. A final confusing detail about the bus system in Haifa is that the *only* place from which you can catch buses heading back to the central bus station is **Ha-Ḥalutz Street;** all other streets lead up toward Carmel Center.

Haifa's main mode of transportation is the **Carmelit subway** system, running from the downtown area to Carmel Center. Though this subway has only one line, its six stops are great for conquering the distance between **Kikkar Paris** and **Gan Ha-Eim** in less than six minutes. Ascending the hill, the subway stops at Solel Boneh, Ha-Nevi'im (Hadar), Masada, and Golomb. Yellow pavilions indicate entrances. Trains run every 6-7 min. (Open Sun.-Thurs. 6am-10pm, Fri. 6:30am-3pm, Sat. 15min. after sundown-midnight; NIS3.30 per ride, 10-ride pass NIS 29.70.)

A more scenic alternative for getting from bottom to top and back is to take the **Rakbal cable cars** (tel. 833 59 70 or 00 09). Colloquially known as "the Carmel's Eggs" for their spherical shape, the cable cars run down the Carmel's northwestern slope, shuttling between the **Bat Galim Promenade** at the beach and the **Stella Maris monastery** area at the mountain's peak. To reach the bottom station, walk west on Ha-Hagana Blvd. from the central bus station for five minutes. There is a small walkway underneath the elevated train tracks on the right. From the tracks, walk one block down Raḥaf St. and turn left onto Ha-Aliya Ha-Shniya St. The station is several blocks down. You can also take bus #42 to its last stop. While the view from the car is striking, the trip is short, and the pre-recorded explanation (your choice of English or Hebrew) is rushed and uninformative (open Sun.-Thurs., Sat. 10am-5:45pm, Fri. 9am-1:45pm, NIS11, round-trip NIS17).

## PRACTICAL INFORMATION

**Tourist Information Office (TIO):** 18 Herzl St. (tel. 866 65 21 or 22, or 864 36 16; fax 862 20 75) in Hadar. Take bus #10 or 12 from the port area or #21 or 28 from the central bus station to **Beit Ha-Kranot.** Maps, train schedules, and an incredible CD-ROM computer that provides and prints information in Hebrew or English. Ask for the bimonthly *Events in Haifa* booklet. Open Sun.-Thurs. 8:30am-5pm, Fri. 8:30am-1pm. A smaller office is conveniently located on the lowest level of the **Egged Central Bus Station** (tel. 851 22 08), open Sun.-Thurs. 9:30am-5pm, Fri. 9:30am-2pm. Two other offices: at **City Hall** in Hadar, 14 Hassan Shuki St. (tel. 835 62 00; open Sun.-Thurs. 8am-1pm), and in **Carmel,** 106 Ha-Nassi Blvd. (tel. 837 40 10; open Sun.-Thurs. 8am-7pm, Fri. 8am-1pm; winter Sun.-Thurs. 8am-6pm, Fri. 8am-1pm). But wait, there's more: **Passenger Hall** at the Port (tel. 851 82 45), open when ships arrive (Sun. and Thurs. 6-9:30am).

**Tours: Society for the Protection of Nature in Israel (SPNI):** 18 Hillel St. (tel. 866 41 35, 36, or 59; fax 866 58 25). Ask about hiking trips into the Carmel Mountains. Most day tours (with a tour bus) cost between NIS80-150 (with English tours lean-

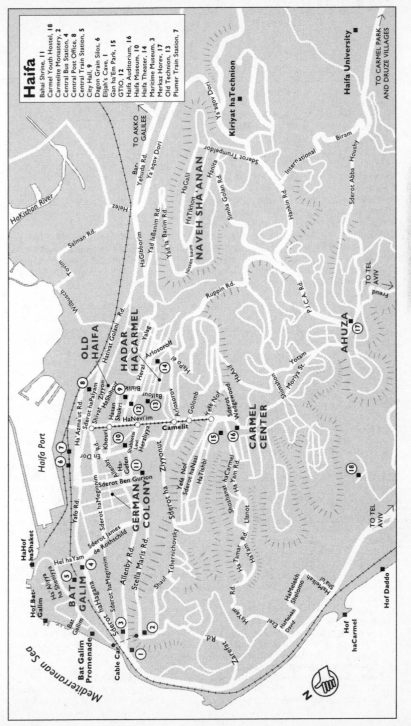

**ISRAEL**

## Haifa

Bahai Shrine, 11
Carmel Youth Hostel, 18
Carmelite Monastery, 2
Central Bus Station, 4
Central Post Office, 8
Central Train Station, 5
City Hall, 9
Dagon Grain Silos, 6
Elijah's Cave, 1
Gan ha'Em Park, 15
GTIO, 12
Haifa Auditorium, 16
Haifa Museum, 10
Haifa Theater, 14
Maritime Museum, 3
Merkaz Horev, 17
Old Technion, 13
Plumer Train Station, 7

TO AKKO
GALILEE

Haifa University

TO CARMEL PARK
AND DRUZE VILLAGES

Kiriyat haTechnion

NAVEH SHA'ANAN

OLD
HAIFA

HADAR
HACARMEL

AHUZA

TO TEL
AVIV

CARMEL
CENTER

GERMAN
COLONY

Haifa Port

BAT
GALIM

HaHof
haShaket

Bat Galim Promenade

Mediterranean Sea

HaKishon River

TO TEL
AVIV

Hof
haCarmel

Hof Daddo

Cable Car

N

ing towards the higher end). Open Mon., Wed. 9am-3:45pm, Tue., Fri. 9am-12:30pm, Sun. 9am-5pm.

**Budget Travel (ISSTA):** 2 Balfour St. (tel. 866 91 39 or 867 02 22). ISICs and HI memberships NIS30. Offers student rates on plane and ferry tickets. Open Sun.-Tue., Thurs. 9am-6pm, Wed., Fri. 8:30am-1pm. Another location at **Technion** (tel. 832 67 39; fax 832 67 41), in the Student Building. Open Sun.-Thurs. 9am-3:30pm, Fri. (summer only) 9-11:30am.

**American Consulate:** 12 Yerushalayim St. (tel. 867 06 15; fax 867 57 57), in Hadar. Call Sun.-Thurs. 9am-1pm (consular services by appointment only).

**Currency Exchange: Barclays Discount,** 65 Ha-Atzma'ut St. (tel. 852 22 91); **Ha-Poalim,** 5 Ha-Palyam Blvd. (tel. 868 15 74); **Israel Discount,** 47 Ha-Atzma'ut St. (tel. 854 61 11); **Leumi,** in the new Ha-Meginim Tower at 21 Yafo St. (tel. 854 71 11), and branches throughout the city. General hours Sun., Tues., and Thurs. 8:30am-12:30pm and 4-6pm; Mon., Wed., and Fri. 8:30am-noon. It's easy to exchange money in Haifa's **black market,** but it's also easy to get ripped off.

**American Express: Meditrad Ltd.,** 2 Khayat Sq., P.O. Box 1266 (tel. 864 22 66 or 58 35; fax 864 22 67). Entrance in alleyway next to Steimatzky off Ha-Atzma'ut St., opposite Sha'ar Palmer St. **Client Letter Service** available. Open Sun.-Thurs. 8:30am-5pm, Fri. 8:30am-1pm.

**Trains:** Station is in Bat Galim (tel. 865 45 64 or 830 31 33 for Hebrew-only updated schedule and prices), connected by tunnels to the central bus station. Trains to Tel Aviv (NIS15), Netanya (NIS14), Nahariya (NIS9), and Akko (NIS7.5). To get to Jerusalem you'll have to change stations, so you're better off taking the bus. 20% discount with ISIC. The TIO has schedules. Trains are generally the best choice when travelling north.

**Buses:** Central Bus Station is on Jaffa Rd. (tel. 854 95 55 for intercity lines, 854 91 31 for city lines) at the corner of Rothschild Blvd. **Baggage storage** on the lower level (up the small concrete ramp, around the corner, and through 2 doors). Open Sun.-Thurs. 8am-4:30pm, Fri. 8am-12:30pm. NIS7 per item. **Lost and Found** also operates from here. Buses #251, 270, 271, and 272 go to Akko and Nahariya (every 15-20min., Sun.-Thurs. 5:15am-11:30pm, Fri. 5:15am-5:20pm, Sat. 4:25pm-midnight; Akko NIS8, 30min.; Nahariya NIS9.80, 40min.). #900 and 980 (direct) and 901 (express) go to Tel Aviv's central bus station (every 20min., Sun.-Thurs. 5:30am-11pm, Fri. 5:30am-5pm, Sat. 8:10-11pm; NIS17, 1½hr.). #940, 945, and 947 go to Jerusalem (every 30-45min., Sun.-Thurs. 6:15am-8pm, Fri. 7:30am-3:20pm, Sat. after 8:30pm; NIS28.50, 2½hr.). #331, 332, 341, and 431 go to Nazareth (every 30min., 5:30am-8:40pm, NIS12.70, 40min.). #430 and 431 go to Tiberias (every 30-40min., 5:30am-8pm, NIS17, 1½hr.). To Ben-Gurion airport, take either #945 or #947 (NIS21, 2 hr.) There are also buses to Tzfat and Eilat.

**Ferries:** Terminal next to the train station. Ferries to Cyprus, Crete, and mainland Greece leave Sun. and Thurs. 8pm (but you need to be there 3:30-6pm for security check) and Fri. 7pm for Cyprus only (be there by 1pm for security check; the port closes by 1pm, so you won't be able to enter later). South Africans need visas to enter both countries. All people need *Let's Go: Greece & Turkey.* Buy tickets at **Caspi Travel,** 76 Ha-Atzma'ut St. (tel. 867 44 44), **Mano,** 2 Sha'ar Palmer St. (tel. 866 77 22; open Sun.-Thurs. 8am-6pm, Fri. 8am-1pm), and **Dolphin,** 104 Ha-Atzma'ut St. (tel. 852 39 53; open Sun.-Thurs. 8am-6pm, Fri. 8am-1pm). Ferry tickets also available through ISSTA, which may be more convenient

**Taxis:** Most taxis leave from Eliyahu St. in Paris Sq. near the Carmelit stop. For "special" taxis call **Kavei Ha-Galil** (tel. 866 44 44 or 45; home pick-up). To Akko (NIS70), Nahariya (NIS80), or Lod (NIS190). **Amal's** Sherut service (tel. 866 23 24) will take you from 6 Ha-Ḥalutz St. in Hadar to Tel Aviv for NIS17 and to Ben-Gurion airport for NIS40. Other taxi services include **Carmel Ahuza** (tel. 838 27 27) and **Merkaz Mitzye** (tel. 866 25 25).

**Car Rental: Avis,** 7 Ben-Gurion Blvd. (tel. 851 30 50); **Budget,** 46 Ha-Histadrut Blvd. (tel. 842 28 32); **Hertz,** 90 Ha-Atzma'ut St. (tel. 853 12 34); **Reliable,** 33 Ha-Histadrut Blvd. (tel. 842 40 04); **Eldan,** 12 Ha-Histadrut Blvd. (tel. 842 11 14). All open Sun.-Thurs. 8am-6pm, Fri. 8am-2pm. Most require minimum age of 23; Hertz and Eldan rent to 21-year-olds with double insurance payments

**Shopping Hours:** Most shops are open Sun.-Thurs. 8:30am-1:30pm and 4-7pm, Fri. 8:30am-2pm, Sat. 8-11pm. Department stores and malls are usually open all day, 8:30am-7pm.

**English Bookstores: Beverly's Books,** 18 Herzl St. (tel. 866 48 10), Beit Ha-Kranot on second floor. Buys and exchanges used books. Open Sun.-Tues. and Thurs.-Fri. 9am-1pm, call to see if open Wed. 4-6pm. **Shmilovitz Book Center,** 31 Ha-Ḥalutz St. (tel. 864 53 84). **Studio 5,** 5 Ha-Yam St., in Merkaz Ha-Carmel district, sells used English books. Open Sun.-Mon. and Wed.-Thurs. 9am-1pm and 4-7pm, Tues. and Fri. 9am-1pm. **Steimatzky** has branches downtown, in Hadar, in Carmel Center, and 2 in the bus station. All open Sun.-Thurs. 8:30am-7pm, Fri. 8:30am-2pm.

**Ticket Offices:** As Israel's third largest city, Haifa boasts an array of plays, musicals and concerts. **Haifa,** 11 Baerwald St. (tel. 866 22 44), open Sun.-Thurs. 9am-1pm and 4-7pm, Fri 9am-2pm; **Garber,** 129 Ha-Nassi Blvd. (tel. 838 47 77), open Sun.-Thurs. 9am-1pm and 4-7pm, Fri. 9am-2pm; and **Nova,** 15 Nordau St. (tel. 866 52 72), open Sun.-Mon. and Wed.-Thurs. 10am-1pm and 4-6:30pm, Tues. 10am-1pm, Fri. 10am-1:30pm.

**Swimming Pools: Maccabee Pool,** 19 Bikurim St. (tel. 838 83 41), in central Carmel. Outdoor in summer, heated and covered in winter. Open Sun., Tues., and Thurs. 6am-2pm and 4-10pm, Mon. and Wed. 6am-2pm and 6:30-10pm, Fri. 6am-2pm and 4-6pm. Admission NIS30. The **Dan Panorama Hotel,** 207 Ha-Nassi Blvd., has a pool open to the public daily 8am-5pm. Admission weekdays NIS25, Sat. NIS33. The **Technion Pool** (tel. 823 59 44, 829 33 00) has a 50m pool and a sauna in addition to a few smaller pools. However, the cheapest way to swim is with a NIS180 six-visit pass. Open Sun.-Thurs. 6am-8pm, Fri. 6am-6pm.

**Crisis Lines: Rape Crisis Center** (tel. 866 01 11) and **Emotional First Aid** (tel. 867 22 22) are both open 24 hrs. English spoken on both.

**Hospitals: Rambam,** Bat Galin (tel. 854 31 11); **Benei Zion (Rothschild),** 47 Golomb St. (tel. 835 93 59); **Carmel,** 7 Michal St. (tel. 825 02 11); **Haifa Medical Center (HMC),** 15 Horev St. (tel. 830 52 22).

**Pharmacies: Shomron,** 44 Yafo St. (tel. 852 41 71), downtown; open Sun.-Thurs. 7am-4pm, Fri. 7am-2pm. **Ha-Ḥalutz,** 12 Ha-Ḥalutz St. (tel. 866 29 62) in Hadar; open Sun.-Thurs. 8am-1pm and 4-7pm, Fri. 8am-1pm. **Merkaz,** 130 Ha-Nassi Blvd. (tel. 838 19 79) in Carmel Center; open Sun.-Thurs. 8am-7pm, Fri. 8am-2pm.

**Emergency: First Aid:** 6 Yitzḥak Sadeh St. (tel. 101). **Fire:** Tel. 102.

**Police:** 28 Yafo Rd. (tel. 100).

**Post Office:** At Shabtai Levi and Ha-Nevi'im St. (tel. 864 09 17) in Hadar. Open Sun.-Thurs. 8am-7pm, Fri. 8am-1:30pm. Other branches at 152 Jaffa Rd. on corner of Sha'ar Palmer; 19 Ha-Palyam Blvd. in port area; 63 Herzl St. in Hadar; and 7 Wedge-wood Blvd. in Carmel. Most branches open Sun.-Thurs. 7am-7pm, Fri. 7am-noon. **Poste Restante** at Ha-Palyam branch only (tel. 830 41 58 or 59).

**Telephone Code:** 04.

## ACCOMMODATIONS

Slim pickings. Haifa is short on budget hotels, and its youth hostels and campsites, while close to the sea, are far from the city center. The Hadar district is your best bet if you want to stay in town, but it's not terribly cheap. Cheaper accommodations lurk near the port, where you may have to sacrifice safety for shekels. Christian hospices offer better quality and prices, but their strictly enforced curfews may take you back to those elementary school days (without the milk and cookies).

**Carmel Youth Hostel (HI)** (tel. 853 19 44; fax 853 25 16), 4km south of the city at Ḥof Ha-Carmel (Carmel beach). Beautiful view of the Mediterranean, but far from the center of town. Bus #30 *alef* goes past the hostel; ask the driver to stop. Buses #45 and 47 run more frequently but drop you off on the main road; ask to be dropped off at the Sports and Recreation Center. Cross Ha-Hagana St. toward the gas station on Flieman St. and turn left just past it. Follow the road as it curves uphill and to the right. Dorm beds (6 per room, no A/C) US$16.50/NIS58. Beds in a room with A/C, toilet, and showers US$18/NIS67. Under 18, US$15 and US$16.

10% discount for HI members. Breakfast included, lunch and dinner each US$8/NIS29 (US$7 for under 18). Lockers NIS4 per day. If you are planning to arrive before 7am or after 11pm, call ahead so that a key will be left at the reception.

**Saint Charles Hospice,** 105 Jaffa Rd. (tel. 855 37 05), 2 blocks off Ben-Gurion St.; look for the green gate. Primarily a convent, but welcomes tourists. Newly renovated, large rooms with high ceilings and single beds. Terrace overlooking pretty garden with a view of the slopes of the Carmel; kitchen facilities. Dorm beds (3-4 per room) US$18. Singles US$22. Doubles US$40. Breakfast included. 10pm lockout and curfew (strictly enforced). 9am check-out.

**Bethel Hostel,** 40 Ha-Geffen St. (tel. 852 11 10), west of Ben-Gurion St. Take bus #22 from central bus station to Ben-Gurion St. close to Ha-Geffen, or walk 15-20min. up De Rothschild Blvd., following the curve to the left onto Ha-Baron Hirsch, which becomes Ha-Geffen. The pamphlets lining the walls (*My Heart, Christ's Home, Becoming a Christian,* etc.) make their point, but the staff is friendly. All rooms have fans, men's rooms have 3-level bunks. Free barbecues on Mon., soup and dessert on Fri. No smoking. Check-in Sat.-Thurs. 5-10pm, Fri. 4-9pm. Lockout 9am-5pm, but charming lounge and garden open all day. New arrivals can leave bags in locked storage and return to register. Strict 11pm curfew. Single-sex only dorm beds (8-12 per room) US$10/NIS30. Under 35 only; those under 18 must be accompanied by an adult.

**Nesher Hotel,** 53 Herzl St. (tel. 862 06 44; fax 862 73 05), near Hayim St. intersection, above Mercantile Discount Bank. Simple hotel in the heart of Hadar, with 15 rooms, a small roof balcony, and a TV lounge. Reception open 8am-midnight. Check-out noon. Midnight curfew. Singles US$27. Doubles US$40. Triples US$55. Quads US$65. Some rooms have A/C, others have fans. Most rooms have private showers (no toilets) but all rooms cost the same. Breakfast included.

**Eden Hotel,** 8 Shmaryahu-Levin St. (tel. 866 48 16 or 85 93) on the corner of Ha-Halutz. Basic hotel with a TV lounge. Most of the 20 rooms have A/C, toilet, and showers. 24 hr. reception. Singles US$30, doubles US$40 (as a double bed), triples US$50. Check-out by 1pm. Ask for a room with a view of the Carmel.

**Talpiyot,** 61 Herzl St. (tel. 867 37 53), where Arlozorov branches off Herzl. A no-frills hotel on a busy street. Nice sea breeze, helpful owner. TV lounge with balcony. Fans in all rooms; some have private bath for the same price. 24-hr. reception. Check-out 11am. No lockout. No curfew. Singles US$32. Doubles US$42. Triples US$62.

**Aliya Hotel,** Ha-Halutz St. (tel. 862 39 18), up the side steps. Plain, but located in the heart of Hadar, near the open-air market. 24-hr. reception. Noon check-out No lockout or curfew. Singles NIS80. Doubles NIS120. Triples NIS150. Quads NIS160. Quints NIS200.

## FOOD

In downtown, follow **Yafo St.** from the central bus station toward the port and you'll walk past a dozen different *shawerma* and falafel shops. **Allenby St.,** between Ha-Tzionut St. and Ben-Gurion Blvd., is crammed with incredibly cheap restaurants specializing in Arabic food. In Hadar, the quantity of Middle Eastern fast food along **Ha-Halutz St.** has prompted locals to call it "Falafel St." **Nevi'im St.,** a few blocks away, is progressing along the same trend, but the **Nordau Midrahov** (pedestrian section) gives a welcome break from such fare with slightly more expensive open-air cafés, and even pricier restaurants serving anything from Arabic to Tex-Mex dishes. In Carmel Center you'll find plenty of cafés along **Ha-Nassi Blvd.** and **Yefeh Nof St.** The area around the **Gan Ha-Eim** Carmelit stop is especially packed, with a McDonald's and several popular cafés.

There is an inexpensive **fruit and vegetable market** just west of the Kikkar Paris station between Nahum and Nathan St. Walking east on Nathan, the shop at #777 sells cow spleen at NIS13; you'll go nuts over the ox testicles at a mere NIS7. Another **shuk** lies one block down from Ha-Halutz St. Haifans come here for clothes, groceries, and wine. The best deals are toward the center of the market.

## Downtown

**Iraqi Shishkabab,** 59 Ben-Gurion St. (tel. 852 75 76), corner of Ha-Geffen St. A local favorite for *shishlik, kabab, sambusa,* and other Middle Eastern specialties. Two skewers and salad in pita NIS13, meat pastries NIS4. Open Sun.-Thurs. 12:30-11:30pm.

**Avraham, King of Falafel,** 34 Allenby St. at Ha-Tzionut St. (tel. 852 50 29). Sign in Hebrew only, but look for the yellow crowns and Pepsi cans next to the name. Haifans crowd around this falafel stand, a local favorite and, at 52 years, probably the oldest in the Holy Land. Falafel NIS7, NIS6 for students. Has everything you could want in a salad bar. Open daily 7am-midnight, Sat. after sundown-midnight.

**Jacko,** 12 Ha-Dekalim St. (tel. 866 88 13), near Kikkar Paris Carmelit station and past the *shuk.* Owner is a former fisherman who still gets fresh seafood daily. Excellent calamari, sea bass, and sesame-seed shrimp. Entrees NIS20-40. Open Sun.-Fri. noon-11pm, Sat. noon-6pm.

**Taiwan,** 59 Ben-Gurion St. (tel. 852 00 88 or 853 20 82). Next to the Iraqi Shishkabab. This intimate Chinese restaurant provides a break from eating everything out of pita bread. With chopsticks in hand, you might forget you're in Israel. Meat dishes, NIS35-45. Open daily noon-3pm, 7pm-midnight. Credit cards accepted

**Ma'ayan Ha-Bira,** 4 Nathanson St. (tel. 862 31 93). The "Beer Fountain" (as the name reads in Hebrew) serves its namesake on tap (NIS8 for 0.5L), but this unpretentious diner's claim to fame is its excellent home-smoked meats. Spareribs NIS19, hot pastrami NIS20. Open Sun.-Fri. 9am-5pm. Credit cards accepted. Frequented more often by Tel-Avivians than Haifans.

## Hadar

**Tzimzḥonit Ḥayim,** 30 Herzl St. (tel. 867 46 67). A vegetarian restaurant founded in the 1930s. Primarily elderly clientele. Offers *kreplach* at NIS6, blintzes at NIS9, salad from NIS7 and fish from NIS8. Open Sun.-Thurs. 9am-8pm, Fri. 9am-1pm.

**Kosher Veta'im,** 40 Herzl St., near Ḥayim St. (tel. 864 59 76). Look for a bespectacled mannequin beckoning above this self-service kosher restaurant. Large portions of *schnitzel* or beef with sides for NIS14. Soups, salads, and desserts for NIS4. Comfy and clean dining area. Open Sun.-Thurs. 10am-6pm, Fri. 10am-3pm.

**Voilà,** 21 Nordau St. (tel. 866 45 29). Tucked away along the *midraḥov,* this romantic and secluded restaurant has excellent French cuisine and a peaceful terrace for outdoor dining. A little pricey (entrees from NIS40, salads from NIS30) but it may be worth getting away from the surrounding bustle of falafel stands. Open Sat.-Thurs. noon-midnight, Fri. noon-3:30pm, 7:30-midnight. Credit cards accepted.

**Hamber,** 61 Herzl St. (tel. 866 67 39), on the corner of Arlozorov St. Popular with French tourists. Offers kosher meat with salads at NIS18. Ooh-la-la. (Open Sun.-Thurs. 8am-7pm, Fri. 8am-3:30pm.)

## Carmel Center

**Casa Ristorante Italiano,** at 119 Ha-Nassi Blvd. (tel. 838 13 36), next to McDonald's. Homey place run by the same family for 30 years. A favorite among Knesset members and celebrities—just ask to see the guest books. Try the comfy brown chairs outside. Spaghetti and other pasta from NIS22.90, homemade minestrone NIS11.90, pizza NIS19.90. Open Sun.-Thurs. noon-3pm and 6-11pm, Sat. noon-11pm. Credit cards accepted.

**Middle East Food Restaurant,** 115 Ha-Nassi Blvd. (tel. 838 76 47), next to the Dan Panorama Hotel. This popular tourist spot with music and outdoor tables has Hadar food and prices at a Carmel Center address: *shishlik* and *shawerma* NIS10, steak NIS12. Open Sun.-Thurs. 10am-1am, Fri. 10am-5pm, Sat. 6pm-1am. Kosher.

**Jackie's Place,** 1 Wedgewood Blvd. (tel. 838 26 86). Homemade kosher cuisine with self-service and friendly staff. Nothing special, but good, cheap food (No small find for Carmel Center). Meat sandwiches NIS9, hot meals with two side dishes NIS15. Also soups and salads; take-away if you wish. Open Sun.-Thurs. 7am-7pm, Fri. 7am-4pm. Kosher. Credit cards accepted.

## SIGHTS, WALKS, PARKS

The best way to see all of Haifa is to take a bus to the top and then work your way down. The various tourist offices all provide maps of the heart of Haifa criss-crossed with four-colored **walking tours.** On Saturdays, the Haifa Municipal Tourist Office offers free, guided versions of the same tour (2½hr., meet at 10am at corner of Yefeh Nof and Sha'ar Ha-Levanon St., dress modestly for stops at Baha'i holy places).

The top level is the best place to watch the "beautiful people." **Carmel Center,** with its pine-shaded, quiet side streets, is perfect for strolling. Ha-Yam Rd. and the area just south of it, behind the Haifa Auditorium, are the best spots to catch a glimpse of Haifa's appeal as a residential town. The breezy **Louis Promenade,** on Yefeh Nof St., commands stunning views of Haifa below. On clear days, you can see the Upper Galilee, Lebanon, and even snowy Mt. Ḥermon far to the northeast.

**Gan Ha-Eim** (Mother's Park), with its shrub-lined walkways, serves as the locus for Haifa's natural attractions. The **Municipal Zoo** in Gan Ha-Eim (tel. 837 23 90 or 28 86), across from the Carmelit steps, might surprise even Noah with its variety of Levant-indigenous beasts. (Open Sun.-Thurs. 8am-6pm, Fri. 8am-1pm, Sat. 9am-4pm; in July and August the zoo is open until 6pm; admission NIS20, students NIS17.) The zoo also contains three museums (see **Museums,** p. 363). The **Mount Carmel National Park,** the biggest park in Israel, is 15 minutes by bus from Gan Ha-Eim (#24, 37, or 192). For a brush with nature in the middle of the city, a **SPNI nature trail** begins in Gan Ha-Eim to the right of the shell-shaped stage. Follow the blue signs; the trail (2km, 1hr.) will lead you around the zoo and through tangled greenery into a *wadi* in the lower Carmel. (Bus #3 or 5 will get you back uptown.)

Those who prefer concrete to tree bark can visit Haifa's two institutes of higher learning. To reach **Haifa University,** boasting a larger percentage of Arab students than any of Israel's other universities, take bus #24 or 37 from the central bus station, Herzl St., or the Carmel Center and ask to be let off at the next to last stop. The university's landmark is the elegant 30-story **Eshkol Tower,** crowning the vast flat main building which serves as the center of student activities. Designed by renowned Brazilian architect Oscar Niemeier, the original bold scheme (see the model in the main lobby) was never completed. The tower's **observatory** offers spectacular panoramic views. (Info. tel. 824 00 97. Open Sun.-Thurs. 8am-4pm. Free student-guided tours of the campus Sun.-Thurs. 10am-noon, starting from the main building.) After hours, go all the way to the edge of the huge slab at the foot of the tower (above the bus stops) for less commanding views of the city below. You can also visit the Reuben and Edith Hecht Museum (see **Museums,** p. 363).

The **Technion,** on the slope directly below the university, is Israel's internationally acclaimed institute of technology, founded in 1913 in Hadar. In the mid-1980s, the last department (architecture) moved out of the old Technion building off Balfour St. to the forested, ever-expanding new campus near Neve Sha'anan. At the **Coler Visitors Center** (tel. 832 06 68 or 64), displays and a video describe the history and achievements of the institution. (Open Sun.-Thurs. 8am-3:30pm. Free.) Take bus #17 from downtown, #31 from Carmel Center, or #19 from the central bus station or Herzl St. to Kiryat Ha-Technion.

Haifa's allure goes far beyond the modern parks, buildings, and neighborhoods that cut across its slopes. In the heart of the city are several important religious sites whose significance long predates the establishment of the State of Israel. Haifa's main attraction is the golden-domed **Baha'i Temple** (tel. 835 83 58), halfway up Mt. Carmel on Ha-Tzionut Ave. Until recently, a magnificent garden of cypress, palm, and pine trees surrounded the Temple; new landscaping scheduled for completion in a few years has left a bald patch on the slope. A large section remains intact, however, and is open to visitors. The shrine commemorates the Persian Sayyid Ali Muhammad (the "Bab"), the first Baha'i prophet, and was built on the exact spot where Baháʼulláh, the sect's founder, pitched his tent following his exile from Persia to Akko (see Religion, p. 57). The Bab's bones, brought to Haifa in 1809, now rest next to the shrine. Modest dress is required for the shrine, but not necessarily for the gardens. To reach the temple, take bus #22 from the central bus station or bus #23, 25, 26, or 32 from Ha-Nevi'im and Herzl St. For a stunning view of the entire grounds, stand at the intersection of Ben Gurion and Ha-Geffen St. and look up. Unfortunately, the stairs are closed until the landscaping is completed. (Open 9am-noon, but call in advance to make sure; gardens open daily 8am-5pm. Free.) Other Baha'i buildings are scattered around the grounds, but are not open to the public; the marble **Universal House of Justice** (visible from the Golomb-Arlozorov St. curve) is the center of international Baha'i operations. Near the shrine, but unrelated to anything Baha'i, is a **sculpture garden** (opposite 135 Ha-Tzion St.) with striking bronzes by Ursula Malbin. (Open 24hr. Free.)

Buses #25, 26, and 31 climb Mt. Carmel to the monastery of the **Carmelite Order,** which stands on a promontory over Haifa Bay (get off at the Seminar Gordon stop). A more expensive and scenic way to get to the monastery is via the Rakbal cable car (see **Transportation,** p. 356). A Latin monk named Berthold founded the order in 1150. Napoleon's siege of Akko in 1799 forced the Discalced ("barefoot") Carmelite Order to move to their current location. The monks currently live in a relatively new church and monastery complex called **Stella Maris** (Star of the Sea, tel. 833 77 58), built in 1836 on the ruins of an ancient Byzantine chapel and a medieval Greek church. The church's dome is crowned by paintings of Elijah flying in his chariot of fire, King David plucking his harp, and scenes of the Holy Family. An exquisite statuette of the Virgin Mary (with whom the order is associated) cradling the baby Jesus stands inside. Knees and shoulders must be covered. (Open daily 8:30am-1:30pm and 3-6pm.) Inside the Carmelite monastery is a small museum containing fragments of former Mt. Carmel cloisters dating from the Byzantine and Crusader periods, a fascinating display for those who enjoy looking at pint-sized pieces of stone. (Hours same as the monastery. Free.) Because of the Carmelites' affinity for Elijah (a.k.a. St. Elias), the Feast of St. Elias (July 20) is a great time to visit. In the days preceding the Feast, Christian Arabs set up booths with food and games, and a carnival atmosphere takes over the complex.

Just across from the monastery entrance lies an inconspicuous trail leading down to the shrine at **Elijah's Cave,** 230 Allenby St. (tel. 852 74 30). Three of the world's major faiths revere these sacred grounds. According to the Bible, the caves at the base of Mount Carmel sheltered Elijah from the wrath of King Ahab and Queen Jezebel, who were more than a bit peeved at the prophet's drastic attempt to win the hearts of northern Israelites from Ba'al in the 9th century BCE (I Kings 18). Muslims revere Elijah as Al-Khadar, the "green prophet" of the same-colored mountains; Jews believe he will return as the harbinger of the Messiah; and Christians hold that the caves safeguarded the Holy Family upon their return from Egypt. Adherants of each religion now pray quietly in the dim light. Modest dress is required. If you don't want to part with your pocket change, decline offers to be blessed by religious (and not so religious) worshipers. On *Shabbat*, Bus #45 runs to Edmund Fley St. near the Carmelite Monastery above the cave. Approaching from below, the stairs leading to the cave's entrance are just across the street from the naval museum. (Cave open daily 8am-5:45pm. Free.)

## MUSEUMS

While Haifa cannot compete with Tel Aviv on the museum front, there are a few that are definitely worth visiting. The **Haifa Museum** is in fact composed of three different museums located in different venues (about as far away from each other as possible, with each on a different level of the city). All three museums are open Sun.-Mon. and Wed.-Thurs. 10am-5pm, Tues. 4pm-8pm, Fri. and holidays 10am-1pm, Sat. 10am-2pm. Admission (good for all three) NIS12, students NIS10.

**Museum of Art,** in the Hadar district, 26 Shabtai Levi St. (tel. 852 32 55), reachable by bus #10, 12, 21, or 28. Exhibiting works from all over the world, this branch of the Haifa museum prides itself on its collection of 20th century graphics and contemporary Israeli paintings, sculptures, crafts, and photography. The museum was recently renovated and reopened in mid-1996.

**Tikotin Museum of Japanese Art** in Carmel Center, 89 Ha-Nassi Blvd (tel. 838 35 54, 837 44 97), between the Nof Hotel and the Dan Carmel Hotel. Bus #21-23, 27, 30 or 31 will get you there. In keeping with the Japanese tradition of displaying beautiful objects in harmony with the season, this branch of the Haifa Museum changes exhibits frequently. *Shoji*, sliding partitions made of wood and paper, soften the sunlight and make for delightful browsing.

**National Maritime Museum,** 198 Allenby Rd. (tel. 853 66 22), right opposite Elijah's Cave. The lowest branch of the Haifa Museum, reachable by bus #3, 5, or 43-45, chronicles over 5000 years of maritime history emphasizing the Eastern Mediterranean as the cradle of shipping in the Western world. Detailed legends and explanations can occupy you for hours. Those lacking patience can still gawk at the intricate model ships.

**Clandestine Immigration and Naval Museum,** 204 Allenby Rd. (tel. 853 62 49), next to the National Maritime Museum and opposite the lower cable car station. Accessible via bus #43 or 44. This well-presented museum, one of the most interesting in Haifa, is devoted to *Ha-Apala*, the dangerous smuggling of immigrants into Palestine during the British Mandate. This defining period in the formation of the State of Israel is explained with clarity and poignancy. Look for the *Af-Al-Pi-Khen* (In Spite Of Everything), an old immigrant ship now perched atop the museum. Open Sun.-Thurs. 9am-4pm, Fri. 9am-1pm. Admission NIS6, NIS3 for students or children under 18.

**Mané Katz Art Museum,** 89 Yefeh Nof St. (tel. 838 34 82), in the heart of Carmel Center just behind Panorama Center. Displays sculptures and canvases by Mané Katz, a member of the Paris group of Jewish Expressionists that included Modigliani, Chagall, and Cremegne. Open Sun.-Mon. and Wed.-Thurs. 10am-4pm, Tues. 2-6pm, Fri. 10am-1pm, Sat. 10am-2pm. Free.

**Reuben and Edith Hecht Museum** (tel. 825 77 73 or 824 05 77) in the main building of Haifa University. Houses an exhibit called *The People of Israel in the Land of Israel,* displaying a magnificent collection of archaeological finds from the university excavations. The small art wing contains some Impressionist paintings and a few others from the Jewish School of Paris. Tours available, call ahead. Open Sun.-Thurs. 10am-4pm, Fri. 10am-1pm, Sat. 10am-2pm. Free.

**National Museum of Science, Planning, and Technology,** on Balfour St. (uphill from Herzl St.), marked by a red-and-white sign. Reachable by bus #12, 21, 28, or 37. Housed in the old Technion building, this small museum touts the latest technological advances in Israeli industry. Open Mon. and Wed.-Thurs. 9am-5pm, Tues. 9am-7pm, Fri. 9am-1pm, Sat. 10am-2pm; in July, also open Sun. 9am-5pm. Admission NIS12, students NIS8.

Three mediocre museums within the municipal zoo, the **Biological Museum,** the **Natural History Museum,** and the **M. Stekelis Museum of Prehistory** merit a quick look only if you're already in the zoo. All open Sun.-Thurs. 8am-3pm, Fri. 8am-1pm, Sat. 10am-2pm. Admission to zoo includes Biological Museum. Other museums NIS3 each.

## ENTERTAINMENT

Free **beaches** sprawl along the northern coast past the Dagon Silo. **Ha-Ḥof Ha-Shaket,** the only religious beach, has separate bathing days for men and women (Sun., Tue., Thurs. women only; Mon., Wed., Fri. men only); take bus #41 from the Hadar district or the central bus station, or walk (10min. from the central bus station). **Ḥof Bat Galim,** also near the central bus station, is small and frequently crowded. On Saturdays, head south to beaches where you can see sand between bathers. Take bus #44 or 45 to **Ḥof Ha-Carmel** or **Ḥof Dado,** farther south. Between here and Atlit, it's basically one long, free, beautiful beach; privacy increases with distance from the city, while the average age decreases. **Shehafit Windsurfing Center,** in the small white building next to the cable car station, rents sailboards (NIS30 per hr.) and snorkeling (NIS8 per day) or scuba gear (NIS100 per day).

When asked about the city's sparse entertainment, Haifa's first mayor pointed to the city's factories and said, "There is our nightlife." This is no longer the case. The TIO give out *Events in Haifa and the Northern Region.* Or call the **What's Hot in Haifa Hotline** (tel. 837 42 53). Nightlife gets livelier at higher altitudes—must be the oxygen. The **Bat Galim Promenade,** along the shore behind the central bus station, has ice cream and frozen yogurt places and fish restaurants. The **Panas Boded Pub** blasts music videos from near the center of the Promenade and encourages sloshed-ness with a large variety of beers (NIS8-10) served until morning light. The outdoor tables overlooking the waves absolutely thunder with tourists and their idle talk (open nightly at 5pm). Also check out **Ha-Sandak** at 30 Kdoshei Bagdad St. near Kikkar Paris, a popular pub for Israelis in their mid-twenties.

The center of nightlife in Hadar is the Nordau *midrahov,* where free concerts and dances rock the amphitheater (check with TIO for a schedule). Here you'll find **Ha-Olam Hazeh** (by Hayim St.), which caters to both locals and tourists from 7pm-2am nightly. Four blocks "up" from Nordau you'll find the **Rodeo Pub** at 23 Balfour St., across from Masada St. (open nightly 9pm-2am).

Real ragers go to Carmel Center. The pub with the best view (and music) is **Mitz-por,** at 115 Yefeh Nof. It's built on the Carmel slope itself; go down the ramp marked "Allenby Garden." Happy customers bring their cheap beers and excellent fruit twister-shakes to the picnic tables outside. The **Jazz Café,** in an alley on the left side of Ha-Yam St. (near the corner of Ha-Nassi Blvd.), has a classy atmosphere and sizzling jazz. **Little Haifa,** at 4 Sha'ar Ha-Levanon St. between Ha-Nassi and Yefeh Nof Streets (look up for the Carlsburg Beer signs), is the oldest pub in the area (29 years and still going strong). What it lacks in a view it more than makes up for with loud music and the rocking atmosphere you've been looking for (open nightly from 8:30pm until the last customer passes out or leaves). The **Red Bar** next to the auditorium (opposite the PAZ filling station) and down some steps, has a color scheme to match its name. The trance music keeps a packed crowd swaying and busy barhopping even mid-week. About 200m further down Moriah St. is **Cenzano,** a small, intimate pub with outdoor seating in summer—perfect for a quiet drink. Other pubs in the area include the **Bear Pub** at 135 Ha-Nassi Blvd. and the neighboring **Paradise Pub** and **B-52** (both in Gan Ha'Eim, across from the stage; open weekends starting at 8:30pm). Less accessible, but far more hip, are the new bars that have sprung up around **Kikkar Kiryat Sefer** on Moriah Blvd., the main road on top of the ridge south of Carmel Center. Ahuza, further down the road, is host to two popular hot-spots: **Ha-Shmura** (near the Horev Center shopping mall, make a right at the light; it's at the entrance to the grove), and, on the western side of the square, **Rizzling,** with a classy wooden interior and weekly strip-tease shows. The popular new **Camel Café** on the Hof Ha-Carmel beach fea-tures outdoor tables, food, and exotic drinks and is crowded nightly with young Israe-lis and U.S. naval officers. Buses #37, 28, and 23 only run along Moriah and Horev St. until 11:30pm, so you'll need other arrangements to get back.

Many **dance clubs** have the unfortunate tendency of being inaccessible to car-less visitors. Most convenient is **City Hall,** on Shabtai Levi just past the post office. Occu-pying two floors, the converted cinema plays staple 90s music until dawn (Thurs. 18+, Fri. guys are 24+, dolls 22+). Find **Fever** in Gan Ha'Eim, next to the zoo (open after 11pm, 25+ on Thurs. nights). **Valentine's,** 120 Yefeh Nof, is also centrally located and has a dance floor surrounded by mirrors and an aquarium. Friday and Sat-urday are 18+; go on a weeknight to avoid the pampers parade (opens at 11:30pm). **Indigo,** 2 Liberia St. (tel. 341 521), is high up in the posh Dania neighborhood. Ask locals to direct you to **Hai Bar, Klafte,** and **Ha-Muza** in the dilapidated Wadi Salib neighborhood downtown. Most dance clubs charge around NIS25.

You can take a break from the dance clubs by hopping across the road from the Klafte to **Jack and the Bears,** a popular bar that resembles a cave with high ceilings and walls of stone (mostly frequented by soldiers and students).

Nightlife in Haifa doesn't get going until at least 11pm. Because what's hot tonight might be passé tomorrow (especially in Haifa), the best recommendations come from

Haifans themselves. Tourist offices will also provide you with a list of popular bars and discos.

Events at the **Technion** and at **Haifa University** offer opportunities to meet young Israelis, particularly during the school year. The Technion has nightly dances in the student building in July and August (8pm-1am). For more information, call 832 06 64; you may have to bring student ID and passport. **Ha-Bustan,** near the entrance to Haifa University campus, is a popular student hangout.

Those staying in Haifa from June 27-30 in '97 should check out the **Haifa Blues Festival** down at the port. Ray Charles once performed at this annual mob scene, but the main events are more often pop than blues (tickets NIS150 per night).

# ■ Near Haifa

## ISFIYA & DALIYAT AL KARMEL עוספיה ודלית אל-כרמל

Isfiya and Daliyat Al Karmel are all that remain of 14 Druze villages that once prospered on the Carmel. In 1830, a rebellion against the Egyptian *pasha* was crushed and the villages were destroyed. Thirty years later, the Turks welcomed Druze back to Isfiya and Daliyat, hoping that the towns would serve as buffers against Bedouin marauders and convert-seeking Christians. Today some 17,000 Druze make their homes here. Religious Druze elders are recognizable by their thick mustaches, baggy pants, and flowing white headdresses, while observant Druze women wear traditional dark robes and white shawls despite the sweltering sun (see Religion, p. 57). A large portion of the population, however, is secular. Unlike those residing in the Golan Heights, the Druze of the Carmel are proud to be Israeli citizens and send their sons to the army. The Druze are also known for being extremely congenial, even while hawking their wares.

Once picturesque mountain villages, Isfiya and Daliyat are today afflicted with unattractive concrete houses. Tourists flock to **Daliyat al-Karmel** to shop in the small bazaar on the main road. The bazaar is busiest on Saturdays, but come on a weekday if you want lower prices and a better opportunity to converse with locals. This is an excellent place to hone your bargaining skills. There is plenty of jewelry, pottery, embroidery, and other hand-made crafts for sale, but the Levis and Power Rangers detract from that authentic *shuk* feel. Be aware that most of the clothes and jewelry are imported from India, while the furniture comes from Gaza. Wheat stalk baskets, embroidery, and tapestry work are mainly local goods. In a back room of the bazaar's Mifqash Ha-Akhim restaurant is the **Druze Heritage House** (tel. (04) 839 32 42 or 31 69; admission NIS7), filled with artifacts and explanations of all things Druze. Ask the restaurant owner to let you take a peek. The house will also host a group of 30 or more for a lecture about the Druze people followed by tea and baklava (NIS15). Call ahead and ask Sheikh Fadel Nasser ad-Din if you can join.

The Zionist and Christian mystic Sir Lawrence Oliphant was one of few outsiders close to the Druze sect. In the late 19th century, he and his wife lived in Daliyat for five years, helping the Druze build their homes. Since 1980, the Israeli Defense Ministry has been restoring Oliphant's house on the outskirts of town. It is now a memorial to the scores of Druze soldiers killed in Israel's wars. Although street names are not used, anyone can direct you to **Beit Oliphant,** the stone building next to the dome. Sir Lawrence sheltered Arab and Jewish insurgents against the British in the cave between the sculpture garden in the rear and the main house. Oliphant's secretary, the Hebrew poet Naftali Hertz Imber, later wrote the words to "Ha-Tikva" (The Hope), Israel's national anthem, at this site. The memorial is less than spectacular, but it is dear to Daliyat's Druze.

Four kilometers from Daliyat Al Karmel is the site where Elijah massacred 450 priests of Ba'al (1 Kings 18:40). **Muhraqa,** the Arabic name, refers to the burnt sacrifice that the prophet offered God on an altar here. Pleased with the Israelites' renewed faith, God sent rain clouds that relieved the land's drought (the drought was the reason for Ba'al's renewed popularity). The Carmelites later interpreted the clouds as symbols of the Virgin Mary, to whom their order is devoted. In 1886 they built a small **monastery** here. A short flight of stairs leads to the roof, where a magnificent view of the surrounding area awaits; on a clear day you may even catch sight of snow-capped Mt. Ḥermon. (Monastery open Mon.-Sat. 8am-1:30pm and 2:30-5pm, Sun. 8am-1:30pm. Admission to the rooftop viewing area NIS1.) There is no bus service to the monastery; you'll have to call a taxi (NIS10-12). If you're walking from Daliyat (not advisable), bear left at the only fork along the way or you'll head toward Elyakim.

Although Daliyat is by far the more touristed (and interesting) of the Druze villages, a visit to **Isfiya** might provide a more authentic glimpse of Druze life. Isfiya's only accommodation/attraction is the excellent **Stella Carmel Hospice** (tel. (04) 839 16 92; fax 839 02 33), run by the Anglican Church and open to all. A converted Arab villa, the hospice has a small, quiet library and a lounge filled with antique Persian rugs. Ask the bus driver to let you off on the main road just outside Isfiya. The hospice is marked by a small, tree-shaded sign and is located up the hill on the right side of the road opposite the PAZ gas station. There's an annex where double rooms come with private baths, but unmarried couples may not share the same room. The hospice fills up, so call ahead. (Flexible 10:30pm curfew, check-out 10:30am. Dorm rooms outside main house US$12. Beds in main house US$22.50, 2 per room. Annex beds US$28.) The hospice organizes occasional **walking tours** to the site for pilgrims. The most eventful day at Muhraqa is the Feast of St. Elias (Elijah) on July 20, when Christian Arabs celebrate in the park surrounding the monastery.

The Druze villages can be visited as a day trip from Haifa. Bus #192 (NIS9.80; 30min.) leaves infrequently from the central bus station, stopping first in Isfiya and then continuing along the main road to Daliyat. You can also catch a *sherut* on Eliyahu Ha-Navi St. off Ha-Atzma'ut St. (NIS7 to Isfiya, NIS10 to Daliyat) and wait by the Egged bus stop to get one back. The last bus leaves Daliyat at 2:10pm, but *sherut* taxis run and stores stay open until about 8pm.

Riding along the mountain road to the Druze villages might get your hiking hormones flowing, and rightfully so: the ridges and forests of the **Carmel mountains** spread dramatically into the Yizre'el valley to the southeast and the Mediterranean to the west. SPNI carries detailed trail maps, but ideal picnic spots are often just a few steps from the main road (see **Practical Information,** p. 356).

## BEIT SHE'ARIM בית שערים

Nineteen centuries ago, Beit She'arim became the center of Jewish life, and the subterranean graveyard housing the rich and famous of ancient Israel remains to prove it. Following the Romans' destruction of Jerusalem in 70 CE, Judaism's hub shifted to the Galilee, and Beit She'arim became a prominent Jewish city. Once it served as the gathering place for the Sanhedrin, recognized by the Roman Empire in the 2nd century CE as the Supreme Rabbinical Council and judicial authority over all of world Jewry. Two hundred years later, when Jews were barred from Jerusalem's Mount of Olives cemetery, Beit She'arim became the site of a sacred Jewish burial ground. Since 1936, archaeologists have unearthed a labyrinth of some 20 caves whose walls are lined with dozens of intricately adorned sarcophagi. According to inscriptions found on the sarcophagi, many of the buried were brought from as far away as Sidon, Tyre, Babylon, or southern Arabia to rest peacefully beneath the Carmel soil. Rabbi Yehuda Ha-Nassi, patriarch of the Sanhedrin, compiled the *Mishnah* in Beit She'arim and is among those buried in the catacombs (p. 276). Two of these fascinating caves are usually open to the public, but Rabbi Yehuda's tomb has been closed due to the proliferation of graffiti. Bring your Indiana Jones bullwhip and a cool hat as you explore the dark passages and half-opened sarcophagi. One of the caves has a small museum with a display of artifacts found at Beit She'arim.

Buses don't run directly to the park; the closest you can get is the access road. Many buses from Haifa go near Beit She'arim, but bus #301 (every 20min., 20min., NIS8) is the most convenient. Ask the driver to let you off at the Beit She'arim archaeological site, not the *moshav.* From the bus stop, turn right and head down Izrael St.

Turn right at the fork after a 20-minute walk and pass the unimpressive ruins of an ancient synagogue and olive press. The steep road uphill on the left leads to a statue of Alexander Zaid, an early Jewish settler, and the foundations of an ancient basilica. Continue down the road to reach the entrance to the catacombs. (Site tel. (04) 983 16 43. Open Sat.-Thurs. 8am-5pm, Fri. 8am-4pm. Closes 1hr. earlier in winter. Admission NIS10, students NIS7.50.)

## EIN HOD עין הוד

Located 14km south of Haifa on the western slopes of Mt. Carmel, Ein Hod ("Spring of Grandeur" or "Spring of Garden Rows") is a must-see for all art enthusiasts. Within this tiny, scenic village of private homes and studios, artists create everything from needle crafts to abstract paintings. Bronze statues grace backyards, mobiles swing between trees, and stone figures recline lazily against fences.

Ein Hod has been a place to escape the drudgery of the work world ever since its establishment as a resort town for weary Crusaders stationed in nearby Atlit. Ein Hod's subsequent Arab inhabitants fled their homes in the face of Israeli military threats during the war of 1948. In 1953, the deserted village was transformed into an artist colony by Marcel Janco, one of the founding fathers of the Dadaist cultural movement.

**Workshops** in glass blowing, pottery, and other crafts are offered on Saturdays, but no buses run at that time, and only residents can park their cars in the village (visitors can park in the lot up the hill). Only groups can call to arrange workshops (tel. (04) 984 27 02; ask for Mara), but solo travelers can easily find one by following the multitude of signs around town. The **Main Artists' Gallery** (free), the largest gallery in Israel, displays the work of many resident artists (currently numbering 150). Exhibits change every three months, and the pieces, in a variety of media, are magnificent. The **Janco-Dada Museum** (tel. (04) 984 23 50; admission NIS8, students NIS6) features shows by contemporary Israeli Dadaist artists, a permanent display of Janco's work, and a film explaining the Dada movement's origins. The Main Gallery, the museum, and the **Art and Wear Gallery** (free) form the nucleus of town (all three open Sat.-Thurs. 9:30am-5pm, Fri. 9:30am-4pm). In summer, Friday evening concerts ranging from rock to classical music are held at the small amphitheater (tel. (04) 984 20 29 or check local newspapers for listings). No transportation is available after the shows. For some grub, stop by at the **Ein Hod Restaurant** (tel. (04) 984 20 16), where a classy interior and a breezy terrace make for pleasant dining. Most main courses are around NIS20-30 (open 10am-midnight Sat.-Thurs., 10am-2am on Fri.).

To get to Ein Hod, take bus #921or 202 from Haifa heading south along the old Haifa-Ḥadera road (20 min.From the Ein Hod junction where the bus lets you off, the town is a 2km walk (20 min. uphill, excellent view). To get to the center of town, turn right at the colorful sign and then right again at the fork.

## ▓ Akko (Acre) עכו عكا

The Old City of Akko, surrounded on three sides by the Mediterranean, gazes toward the timeless sea, seeming to relate more to the ancient waters than to the ever-encroaching modern city behind it. At the opposite end of the bay from Haifa, Akko ('Akka in Arabic, historically written "Acre" in English) is a medieval fortress town with crenelated walls, stone embattlements, winding alleyways, and a vast underground Crusader city. Soaring above the maze of cobblestone streets is the emerald-domed 18th-century Mosque of Al-Jazzar. During the hot summer months, tourists and locals dine at charming restaurants along the coast, watching small fishing boats shuttle around the piers and breakwaters.

Each contending army that washed over Akko left behind tell-tale architectural jetsam. The Canaanite city-state of Akko is first mentioned in Egyptian documents dating as early as the 19th century BCE. It was conquered repeatedly, by Egyptians, Persians, Greeks, Romans, Umayyads, and finally Crusaders, who came to the city in 1104 on

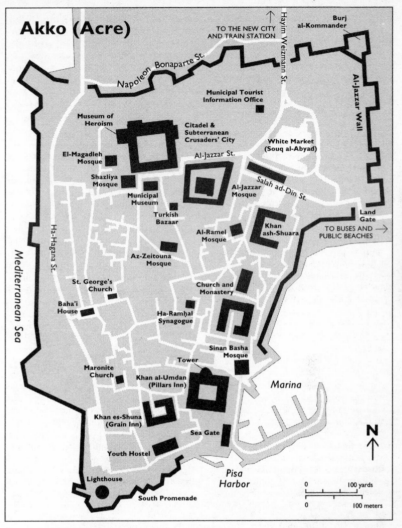

# Akko (Acre)

Burj
al-Kommander

Hayim Weizmann St.

Napoleon Bonaparte St.

Al-Jazzar Wall

Municipal Tourist
Information Office

Museum of
Heroism

Citadel &
Subterranean
Crusaders' City

White Market
(Souq al-Abyad)

El-Magadleh
Mosque

Al-Jazzar St.

Shazliya
Mosque

Salah ad-Din St.

Al-Jazzar
Mosque

Municipal
Museum

Land
Gate

Turkish
Bazaar

Al-Ramel
Mosque

Khan
ash-Shuara

TO BUSES AND →
PUBLIC BEACHES

Ha-Hagana St.

Az-Zeitouna
Mosque

St. George's
Church

Mediterranean Sea

Church and
Monastery

Baha'i
House

Ha-Ramhal
Synagogue

Sinan Basha
Mosque

Maronite
Church

Tower

Khan al-Umdan
(Pillars Inn)

Marina

Khan es-Shuna
(Grain Inn)

Sea Gate

N
↑

Youth Hostel

Lighthouse

Pisa
Harbor

South Promenade

0          100 yards

0          100 meters

their campaign to recapture the Holy Land for Christianity. After losing control of Jerusalem in 1187, they retreated to peaceful Akko, transforming it into the greatest port of their empire and a world-class showpiece of culture and architecture. The Mamluks ended Crusader rule in 1291, and almost 500 years later the Druze prince Fakhr ad-Din rebuilt the city. The Muslims couldn't disassemble the Crusader network of tunnels and basements, and opted to leave the subterranean labyrinth for wide-eyed tourists, building their city directly over it. Fakhr ad-Din's work was continued by Tahir al-Omar, who was murdered and succeeded in 1775 by Ahmed Jazzar, an Ottoman *pasha* of Bosnian extraction. Napoleon later claimed that had Akko fallen to him, "the world would have been mine." Unfortunately for him, his 1799 siege failed. After a stint under the Egyptian Ibrahim Pasha (1833-1840), control of Akko returned to the Ottomans. When the British captured the port in 1918, it had a predominantly Arab population of 8000. Members of Zionist groups employing terrorist tactics against the British were held captive in the Citadel during World War II.

Akko was designed for the pedestrian, so allow time to amble and explore. During school vacations, you may find yourself awarded an informative, if somewhat tiresome, self-appointed guide in the Arab town. The young men who so boldly approach you are often only interested in practicing their English, picking up young women, and impressing their friends, so offering a tip may be taken as an insult. Steer clear of any drugs offered on the streets; the police keep a close watch on dealers and usually confine foreign offenders to the local prison for several nightmarish days before expelling them from the country. It's best not to prowl the alleys of the Old City after dark, but the waterfront boardwalk is crowded and well-lit at night.

## ORIENTATION AND PRACTICAL INFORMATION

New and old Akko are connected by **Ḥayim Weizmann Street.** From the central bus station, Ben-Ami and Herzl St. run to Weizmann. **Ha-Hagana Street** borders the sea from the new city to the lighthouse at Akko's southern tip. At the northern end, **Al-Jazzar** and **Salah ad-Din Streets** extend in opposite directions from the end of Weizmann. On Al-Jazzar St. are the mosque, Crusader City, and information office. The Old City bus stops are opposite the parking lot. The central post office, Wolfson Auditorium, and City Hall are on **Ha-Atzma'ut,** the major street in the new city. The passages of the peninsular Old City are poorly marked: locals and monuments make good navigational tools. **Khan al-Umdan** (Inn of Pillars) is an important landmark, located near the Isnan Pasha Mosque and the fishing port. The market winds its way through the middle of the peninsula. The **Southern Promenade,** at the end of Ha-Hagana St., has been developed as a tourist area, with several restaurants and sitting areas built into the old Pisan Harbor walls and towers.

**Municipal Tourist Information Office (MTIO),** at the Crusader City entrance (inside) on Al-Jazzar St. across from the mosque (tel. 991 17 64). Sells a great map (NIS3), but Akko is small enough wandering and relying on others' directions is seldom disastrous. Open summer Sun.-Thurs. 8am-6pm, winter 8am-4pm.

**Currency exchange: Mercantile Discount Bank,** corner of Al-Jazzar and Weizmann St. Open Sun., Tues., and Thurs. 8:30am-1pm and 4-5:30pm, Mon. and Wed. 8:30am-1pm, Fri. 8:30am-noon. **Bank Leumi,** on Ben-Ami St. near Weizmann St. Open Sun., Tues., and Thurs. 8:30am-12:30pm and 4-6pm, Mon. and Wed. 8:30am-12:30pm, Fri. 8:30am-noon. Banks outside the Old City have **ATMs.**

**Trains:** Often the best way to get to Haifa, especially during rush hour. The station is on David Remez St. (tel. 991 23 50) across from the central bus station. To Haifa (25min., NIS7.50), Nahariya (10min., NIS4.50), and Tel Aviv (2hr., NIS22). Trains run 6am-7pm every 1-2hr.

**Buses:** The **central bus station** is on Ha-Arba'a Rd. in the new city (tel. 854 95 55 for information). To Haifa: #262 and 272 (express), 45min., NIS8; #251 is local. To Nahariya: #272, 20min., NIS5.20; #271 is local. Buses from platform #16, near the Egged restaurant, take weary travelers the short distance to the old city (stops running at 3:30pm).

**Sherut Taxis:** Off Ha-Arba'a St., across from the bus station (to Haifa NIS8).

**Taxis: Akko Tzafon** (tel. 991 66 66) or **Ariyeh** (tel. 991 33 69).

**Luggage storage:** Knights Parking Lot on Weizzman St. in the old city, just north of Al-Jazzar. NIS4 per item. Open daily 7am-6pm.

**Library: Canada-Akko Library,** 13 Weizmann St. (tel. 991 08 60), near the old city. Delightful A/C reading room with multilingual collection, including many English books. Open Sun.-Thurs. 9-12am and 3-7pm.

**First aid: Magen David Adom** (tel. 101 or 991 23 33).

**Pharmacy:** On Ben-Ami St.: **Akko** (tel. 991 20 21) and **Merkaz** (tel. 991 47 02).

**Police:** 16 Ha-Hagana St. (tel. 100 or 991 98 88).

**Post Office:** Central branch at 11 Ha-Atzma'ut St. **Poste restante.** Open Mon.-Tues. and Thurs. 8am-12:30pm and 4-6pm, Wed. and Fri. 8am-12:30pm. Another branch in the entrance to the Crusader city next to the MTIO (same hours).

**Telephone Code:** 04.

## ACCOMMODATIONS

All of the following accommodations have heating for Akko's chilly winter. The **Akko Youth Hostel (HI)** is across from the lighthouse within the old city walls (tel./fax 991 19 82). The airy lounge and several of the commodious rooms have a fabulous view of the sea over the ramparts. The place fills up, especially in summer. The lighthouse is at the tip of the peninsula; walk through the market or follow Ha-Hagana St. along the coast. (Check-out 9am. Curfew 10:30pm. 6-8 bed dorm rooms NIS41 per person, nonmembers NIS45. Breakfast included. Lockers NIS4. Reception open 6:30am-10:30pm. Cash only.) **Walied's Gate Hostel,** on Salah ad-Din St. (tel. 991 04 10; fax 981 55 30), next to Land Gate, is simple and family-run, with a kitchen available. (24-hr. reception. Midnight curfew during winter. Coed and single-sex dorm beds. NIS20. Dorm beds on patio NIS15. Doubles NIS80, with showers, A/C, and toilet NIS120. Breakfast NIS10 in the new adjoining pub/restaurant. Laundry NIS20 per load.) Walied leads tours to the Golan Heights in his van (one day NIS100). **Paul's Hostel and Souvenir Shop** just across the road from the lighthouse at the southern end of Ha-Hagana St. under a large blue awning (tel. 991 28 57 or 981 76 86) is a cozy alternative. Paul Elias and his family own the 35-bed domed Crusader building behind his shop. Rooms are large and clean with an adjacent bath and kitchen. Each guest gets a key. (Dorm NIS20. Doubles NIS75. Laundry NIS4 per load. Free pick-up from bus station. 24-hr. check-in. Check-out anytime. No curfew. Cash only. Shop open daily 9am-8pm.) There are additional unofficial and unregulated hostels or rooms for rent in the old city, but you should get the tourist office's opinion of the place before making a decision you might regret. Beach camping is forbidden.

## FOOD

**The Lighthouse Restaurant** (tel. 991 76 40), under its namesake near the HI hostel, has tables overlooking the water and invites evening idling. Hostel patrons receive a 10% discount (*kabab* or *shishlik* NIS25, hummus NIS10, *ba'laweh* NIS3; credit cards accepted; open daily 1pm-2am). For cheap food away from the tourist scene, try **Peace Meeting** (tel. 981 18 37), opened by an Arab family three days before the famous Arafat-Rabin handshake. The restaurant is at the *souq* entrance near Salah ad-Din St.; look for the pink sign. (Falafel with drink NIS5 Half grilled chicken with salad and chips NIS20, *shawerma* NIS9; open Wed.-Mon. 8am-6pm, Tues. 8am-noon). Diagonally across from the lighthouse, next to the souvenir shop, is the tiny **Pita Bakery,** source of piping hot, cheap bread. **Café Tuscana** (tel. 981 60 27), up the stairs in the Pisan Harbor, serves ice cream and drinks with a postcard-quality view of the sea and old Akko (open daily 8:30am-midnight). Past the lighthouse on Ha-Hagana St. is **Al Nawrus Restaurant** (tel. 991 55 57), also with a great view, although a bit pricey (fish entrees from NIS30, breakfast NIS15; open daily 7am-1pm). *Argeileh* smokers hang out at **Shami's House of Coffee** (tel. 991 14 29) in the *Souq Ha-Lavan.* You can buy food at the outdoor **market** next to the central bus station and at the *souq* in the old city. Farther away are the food stands and small **supermarkets** on Yehoshafat St. off Ben-Ami St.

## SIGHTS AND ENTERTAINMENT

The battlements and dungeons of Old Akko leave no doubt that this city was wrought with ancient conflicts. To reach the **old city** from the bus station by foot, walk down Ben-Ami St. to Weizmann St. and turn left. The entrance to the old city is just past Eli Cohen Park on the left. As you pass the Al-Jazzar wall, look for horses grazing in the moat beneath Burj al-Kommander to the left. The entrance to the **Mosque of Al-Jazzar** is a short walk to your right, on Al-Jazzar St. The third-largest mosque in Israel, it dominates this city of monuments with its green dome and sleek minaret. Ahmed al-Jazzar ordered its construction in 1781 on what is believed to have been the site of San Croce, the original Christian cathedral of Akko. Inside is an attractive courtyard with Roman columns taken from Caesarea. The western end of the courtyard rests upon the cellar of a Crusader fortress. The surrounding structures are lodgings for students of the Qur'an and the personnel of the mosque. The tower was destroyed by an earthquake in 1927, but promptly restored; the rest of the complex is in magnificent condition.

In front of the mosque sits an octagonal *sabil* (fountain) where the faithful perform *wudhu,* the ritual washing of their heads, hands, and feet before praying. Inside, in the green cage on the marble stand, is a shrine containing a hair from the beard of the prophet Muhammad. As in all mosques, prayers are conducted five times per day, and you will be asked to wait or return in 20 minutes if you arrive during a prayer session. Modest dress is required; scarves are available for those not already covered. To the right of the mosque is a small building containing the sarcophagi of Al-Jazzar and son; you can peek through the barred windows at the marble boxes, now covered with soil and green plants. Al-Jazzar turned the buried Crusader cathedral into an underground water reservoir, filled by rainfall. The recently renovated reservoir is accessible through a door and underground stairway at the left end of the mosque. Look for the small green sign and red arrows. Guides offer tours of varying quality (open daily 8am-12:30pm, 1:15-4:15pm, and 4:45-6:30pm; admission NIS2).

A restored white stone gate, the entrance to the subterranean **Crusader City** (tel. 991 17 64) stands across from the mosque on Al-Jazzar St. When first discovered, the rooms were thought to have been built underground, but archaeologists have since determined that Al-Jazzar simply built his city on top of once above-land buildings. Because excavations were halted for fear that the Arab town above might collapse, most of the Crusader City remains buried; only the area originally known as the "Hospitaller's Quarter" is open. Keep your ticket, as it allows access to all Crusader sights. Detailed explanations at every stop of the way are provided by the so-called "Easy Guide"—a hand held tape recorder. In the entrance halls, three enormous pillars stand amidst a variety of architectural styles. Decorations with images of flowers or human forms are Crusader work, while the more abstract embellishments and the Arabic calligraphy are from the Ottomans. The 12th-century halls were probably part of a medical complex where the Hospitaller Order treated pilgrims. The arches project directly from the floor, indicating that the current floor is some 4m above the original level. The barrels and girders are modern additions used to support the original walls.

From the courtyard beyond the entrance hall, you can see fortifications built by Fakhr ad-Din and Tahir al-Omar. The Ottoman gate on the left (above an earlier Crusader gate) is the entrance to the Hospitaller's fort. Turning right from here will bring you to the center of the original Crusader complex. The now-buried halls have great acoustics, and are used for concerts by the **Haifa Symphony Orchestra** in July and the acclaimed **Israel Fringe Theater Festival** each fall. The four-day extravaganza occurs during the Jewish festival of *Sukkot* (Oct. 16-22 in 1997), and attracts small theater groups from all over Israel. Only a few of the performances are in English (check with the tourist office). During *Sukkot,* there are also prolific street performances for those who lack the money to pay for the seated shows.

The passageway from the Hospitaller's fort to the **Refectory** or **Crypt of St. John** has been closed since 1990 for fear that the roof will collapse. To reach the crypt, leave the Crusader City the way you came in, turn right, and follow the signs to the crypt entrance; look for the black-and-white "crypte" sign on a metal door. The most magnificent and famous of the buried rooms, it once housed Crusader feasts.

Next to the third column in the crypt is a staircase connected to a long underground passageway which in turn leads to six adjacent rooms and a central courtyard. The passageway may have been dug by the Crusaders as a hiding place in case of attack, or possibly as an elaborate sewage system. It was restored by Al-Jazzar to serve as a means of escape if Napoleon gained entrance to the city walls. The complex of arched rooms at the other end of the tunnel was used as a hospital for wounded knights. The Turks turned the rooms into a post office. (Crusader City open Sun.-Thurs. 8:30am-6:30pm, Fri. 8:30am-3:30pm, Sat. 9am-6pm; winter, Sun.-Thurs.

8:30am-5pm, Fri. 8:30am-2pm, Sat. 9am-5pm. Admission NIS11, students NIS10, ticket for both Okashi Museum and Crusader City NIS15, students NIS14.)

The adjacent **Municipal Museum** (really a Turkish bath, operating until 1947) is accessible through the metal door opposite the crypt entrance or the one opposite the main entrance around the corner. Its rooms are appropriately named "hot," "cold," and "lukewarm."

From the entrance to the Municipal Museum, a right turn will bring you to the *souq,* a tumultuous avenue of butchers, grocers, bakers, and copper, brass, and leather vendors. Food stands along the *souq* offer *kabab,* falafel, and sandwiches (market active 7am-7pm). Near the market crouch several caravanserais (*khanat* in Arabic). The most impressive is **Khan al-Umdan** (Inn of Pillars), just past the Isnan Pasha Mosque and the fishing port. Al-Jazzar built this *khan* for Ottoman merchants at the end of the 18th century. The lower stories of the courts served as rented store-rooms for merchants, while the upper galleries served as boarding rooms. The *khan's* slender, square clock tower, erected in 1906 to celebrate the jubilee of the Ottoman Sultan Abdulhamit, is marked with the Turkish half-moon and star.

Near Khan al-Umdan is the **Akko Marina.** You can rent diving equipment from **Ramy's Diving Center** (tel. 991 89 90; fax 343 006), located inside Khan al-Umdan on the left (PADI, NAVI, and CMAS affiliated). Diving tours (US$75) explore a 30m-deep Italian submarine from WWII. The *Princess of Akko* (tel. 050 50 37 48) gives fun 25-minute boat rides from the marina to the sea walls (NIS10, students NIS8), but will not depart until filled with enough tourists.

Around the corner from the Crusader City is the **Okashi Museum,** named after late Akko resident Avshalom Okashi, a painter known for richly textured (often 3-D) abstract paintings. The museum houses many of his great works. (Open Sun.-Thurs. 8:30am-4:30pm, Fri. 8:30am-2pm, Sat. 9am-4:30pm. Admission NIS5, students NIS4; combination ticket with the Crusader City NIS15, student NIS14.)

In the northern part of the Old City, the commanding **Citadel** adjoins the Crusader City on Ha-Hagana St., opposite the sea wall. This stronghold, used by the British as their central prison, now houses the **Museum of Heroism** (tel. 991 82 64, 82 65, or 82 66), a monument to Zionist guerilla organizations. The citadel was built in the late 1700s on 13th-century Crusader foundations and was used as an Ottoman prison. The most famous inmate during Ottoman rule was Baha'u'llah, founder of the Baha'i faith, who was imprisoned on the second floor in 1868. During the British Mandate, the prison housed about 560 inmates under the guard of about half as many British soldiers. Members of the Palmaḥ, Hagana, and Irgun, including Ze'ev Jabotinsky, were imprisoned here for violent anti-British activities. After losing eight members to the citadel's gallows between 1938 and 1947, the Irgun retaliated by hanging a British officer. The Gallows Room displays the noose in place along with photographs of the eight Irgun members. On May 4, 1947, the Irgun staged a prison break that freed 11 of its members and 255 other inmates (later depicted in the movie *Exodus,* shot on location). To reach the museum, follow the stone stairs down to the lower garden, then the metal stairs up and around the side of the prison (open Sun.-Thurs. 9am-5pm, Fri. 9am-1pm; admission NIS6, students NIS3). Across the street from the museum looms **Burj al-Kuraim** (Fortress of the Vineyards), often referred to as the British Fortress despite its Crusader and Ottoman construction.

Renowned throughout history as the most secure port in the Eastern Mediterranean, Akko remains a city of battlements and bastions. Akko's defense in recent centuries has relied upon the **Al-Jazzar Wall,** running along the northern and eastern sides of the city and surrounded by a sea water moat. The best place from which to view the wall, which originally ran the length of the harbor, is **Burj al-Kommander** (Commander's Fortress), an enormous Crusader bastion at the northeastern corner. To enter the watchtower, climb the steps beginning where Weizmann St. meets the wall. The **Tower of the Flies,** the site of the original lighthouse and at one time connected to the walls, solemnly broods in the middle of the bay. Its fortifications were toppled by a devastating earthquake in 1837. At the eastern corner near the shoreline yawns the so-called **Land Gate,** once the only entrance to the city.

## ■ Near Akko

Loḥamei Ha-Geta'ot ("Fighters of the Ghettos"), a kibbutz founded by survivors of concentration camps and the Warsaw Ghetto uprising, lies outside Akko toward Nahariya. The **Ghetto Fighters' House** (tel. 995 80 80; fax 995 80 07) examines the Warsaw Ghetto uprising, Nazi atrocities, and the cultural life of the Warsaw Ghetto (in particular the poetry of Yitzḥak Katzenelson), and artwork by prisoners and survivors. The recently constructed **Yad La-Yeled** in an adjoining building is a memorial to the million and a half children who perished in the Holocaust. The exhibition (winding up an inscribed 4-story tower) recounts the lost lives with audio-visual displays and stories collected from diaries, letters, and testimonies. To reach the kibbutz, take bus #271 (runs daily from Akko and Nahariya, 20min., NIS4.80). Make sure that the bus is local *(me'asef)*. (Museum and Yad La-Yeled open summer Sun.-Thurs. 9am-6pm, Fri. 9am-1pm, Sat. 10am-5pm; winter Sun.-Thurs. 9am-4pm, Fri. 9am-1pm, Sat. 10am-5pm. Free, but donation requested.)

The **Roman aqueduct** just outside the museum to the south is remarkably well preserved, largely because it's not Roman. Al-Jazzar had it built in 1780 to carry water 15km from the Kabri springs to Akko. You'll have great views of the aqueduct from the bus between Akko and Nahariya.

The **Baha'i Gardens** (tel. 981 15 69), 2km south of the kibbutz, bloom in a riveting mix of Occidental and Oriental styles. The gardens, planted from 1952 to 1956, hold the villa and shrine of Baha'u'llah, the prophet and founder of the Baha'i faith (shrine open Mon. and Fri.-Sun. 9am-noon; gardens open daily 9am-4pm; free). The gate on the main road is for Baha'is; all others should get off the bus just north of the gate at the yellow "traffic signal ahead" sign. Walk east 500m past the military base and enter at the small gate on the right. The gardens are on the main Akko-Nahariya road, via bus #271 (10min. from Akko). For a challenging daytrip, consider the 1km hike through **Naḥal Shagur** (also called **Naḥal Beit Ha-Kerem**), a tributary of the Ḥilazon River east of Akko, which divides the Upper and Lower Galilee.

## ■ Nahariya נהריה

Nahariya is the definitive one-street resort town: bus and train station on one end, ocean on the other, and pleasant commercial strip in between. In recent years, Katyusha rockets from *Hizballah* guerillas have interrupted the sun-soaked bacchanalia (but attacks are very few and far between). Russian immigrants have given the town a new "Siberia by the sea" feel. The beaches are packed by day, but the dim colored lights along the promenade reflect the subdued atmosphere of Nahariyan evenings. In 1934, German Jews settled the area as a farming village on the Ga'aton River, which, dwindled by upstream pumps, now trickles unimpressively in a concrete channel down the center of the main thoroughfare. The many buses leaving Nahariya make it a convenient base for sights on the northern coast and in the Western Galilee, but accommodations are more expensive than those in nearby Akko.

### ORIENTATION AND PRACTICAL INFORMATION

Nahariya is the northernmost town on Israel's coast, situated 10km north of Akko and south of Rosh Ha-Nikra. The town is minuscule; nearly everything you'll need is on **Ha-Ga'aton Blvd.** To reach the beaches, walk a few blocks west and stop when you get wet.

**Municipal Tourist Information Office (MTIO):** Ha-Ga'aton Blvd. (tel. 987 98 00), on the ground floor of the Municipality Building. From the bus station, walk west on Ha-Ga'aton; the MTIO is in the large white building at the end of the plaza past Herzl St. Open Sun.-Thurs. 8am-1pm and 4-7pm, Fri. 8am-1pm.

**Currency Exchange: Mercantile Discount Bank** (tel. 992 46 11) and **Bank Leumi** (tel. 992 56 31). Both on Ha-Ga'aton Blvd. and open Sun., Tues., and Thurs. 8:30am-12:30pm and 4-6pm, Mon. and Wed. 8:30am-12:30pm, Fri. 8:30am-noon.

**Trains:** Trains think they can at the 1 Ha-Ga'aton Blvd. station (tel. 856 44 46). Single line to: Akko (15min., NIS4.50), Haifa (40min, NIS9), Tel Aviv (2¼hr., NIS23.50). Connections to Jerusalem and elsewhere. Trains depart Sun.-Fri. at 5:50, 7:40, 9:40, 11:35am, 3:10, 4:40, 5:50, and 6:30pm.

**Buses:** Station is at 3 Ha-Ga'aton Blvd. (tel. 854 95 55). Buses #272 (express), 270, and 271 depart for Nahariya from both Haifa (45min., NIS9.80) and Akko (20min., NIS5.20). Buses #20 (2:30pm) and 22 (9:10 and 11:30am) go to Rosh Ha-Nikra (15min., NIS6.30). Buses from platform #5 run often to Akhziv (6:30am-9:15pm, 10min., NIS5.20). Bus #44 to Peki'in (45min., NIS12).

**English Bookstore: Doron Books,** 32 Ha-Ga'aton Blvd. (tel. 992 10 79) Open Sun.-Mon. and Wed.-Thurs. 8:30am-1pm and 4-7:30pm, Tues. 8am-1pm, Fri. 8am-2pm.

**First aid:** tel. 101 or 982 33 33.

**Pharmacy: Szabo Pharmacy,** 3 Ha-Ga'aton Blvd. (tel. 992 04 54 or 11 97), in front of the bus station. Open Sun.-Thurs. 8am-1:30pm and 4-7:30pm, Fri. 8am-2:30pm.

**Hospital:** Ben-Tzvi St., tel. 985 05 05.

**Police:** 5 Ben-Tzvi St., tel. 100 or 992 03 44.

**Post Office:** 40 Ha-Ga'aton Blvd. (tel. 992 01 80), has **poste restante** and **international calls.** Open Sun.-Tues. and Thurs. 8am-12:30pm and 3:30-6pm, Wed. 8am-1:30pm, Fri. 8am-noon.

**Telephone code:** 04.

## ACCOMMODATIONS AND FOOD

For cheap beds, head south to Akko. In summer, rooms are available in private homes. "Rooms to Rent" signs are common on Jabotinsky St.; head west on Ha-Ga'aton to the post office and turn right (NIS60 or more; polite bargaining may help). The MTIO keeps a list of rooms, but not a list of prices. **Motel Arieli,** 1 Jabotinsky St. (tel. 992 10 76), next to Ha-Ga'aton and the beach, offers neat, air-conditioned rooms in either bungalows or a main building. (Check-out 10am. 24-hr. reception 2-bed bungalows NIS80. Doubles NIS120). The **Kalman Hotel (HI),** 27 Jabotinsky St. (tel. 992 03 55; fax 992 65 39), one block from the beach, is spotless and spacious, with air conditioning, TVs, and private baths. Owner Miron Teichner gives out coupons for the beach and restaurants, and shows off the signatures of big-shots who've stayed here, including Ezer Weizmann, Shimon Peres, and Sophia Loren. (No curfew. Rates for *Let's Go* holders: singles US$30, doubles US$55, triples US$75. Buffet breakfast included.) **Beit Gabiazda,** 12 Jabotinsky St. (tel. 992 10 49), has air conditioning and private baths, a TV lounge, and a kitchen. (Doubles NIS100; prices go up in July-Aug. and down when you bargain.) **Sirtash House,** 22 Jabotinsky St. (tel. 992 25 86), has a few lean, cozy doubles with air conditioning, TVs, private baths, and some kitchenettes (Check-out 10am. July-Aug. NIS120, Sept.-June NIS90). As Nahariya is only a few km from Lebanon, camping on the beach is strictly forbidden.

The restaurant-cafés and falafel stands lining Ha-Ga'aton Blvd. peddle familiar Middle Eastern food. Nahariya's beaches and gardens make beautiful, lush picnic grounds; shop at the **Co-op Tzafon supermarket** (tel. 992 72 10) on the corner of Ha-Ga'aton and Herzl St., or fruit and vegetable stores on Herzl between Ha-Ga'aton and Ha-Meyasdim. A Moroccan bakery across from the Hod theater on Herzl (side entry, no sign) sells several dozen varieties of cookies (NIS10-15 per kg). Established when Nahariya was a six-year-old farm town, **Penguin Café,** on Ha-Ga'aton Blvd. near Jabotinsky St., attracts a hip, young crowd (Italian dishes NIS23-30, omelettes NIS16-21, *blintzes* NIS22).

## ENTERTAINMENT AND SIGHTS

Nahariya's *raison d'être* is to slowly roast visitors along its sandy strip. The main beach, **Galei Galil,** has a breakwater, a lifeguard, and lots of sand. You'll be hard pressed to see any sand on Saturdays, though. The beach is a right turn off the end of Ha-Ga'aton Blvd. (open July-Aug. 8am-6pm; Sept.-June 8am-5pm; free. Admission to the nearby indoor pool NIS16, NIS8 for students. Pool open Sun.-Thurs. 6am-3pm and 7-10pm, Fri. 6am-3pm, Sat. 6am-4pm and 6-10pm.) A free **beach,** south of Galei Galil, has neither a lifeguard nor a breakwater. Local youth surf here and learn to develop the nerves they'll need to become functioning Israeli drivers.

The **Hod Cinema** (tel. 992 05 02), on Herzl across from the market, often shows movies in English, as does the **Hekhal Ha-Tarbout** (tel. 992 79 35) on Ha'Atzma'ut Rd., but the latest movies play closer to Haifa.

Nahariyan nightlife is quiet, although some revelers manage to make noise late into the weekend. A local favorite is **BK Pub,** across from the bus station on Ha-Ga'aton (enter from the side at the intersection with Ha'Atzma'ut St.). To pace your drinking with the tides, head to oceanside pub **Makom Batayelet** and its neighbor **Mull Hayam** (turn left where Ha-Ga'aton meets the sand). For those with lots of money or local buddies (they all seem to get in free), there's dancing at the **Carlton Hotel disco,** also on Ha-Ga'aton (opens Fri. 10pm and various other weekdays; admission normally NIS50). There's fun **folk dancing** at the amphitheater on the corner of Balfour St. and Ha-Ga'aton Blvd. All ages participate (late May-early Oct. Tues. and Sat. nights 7:30-9:30pm).

The unimpressive but important remains of a 4000-year-old **Canaanite Temple** dedicated to Asherah (the goddess of fertility) were discovered in 1947 on a hill next to the shore (a 20-min. walk south on the beach). The **Nahariya Municipal Museum,** in the Municipality Building near the bus terminal, has exhibits on art, archaeology, malacology (seashells), history, and Central European Jewry (open Sun. and Wed. 10am-noon and 4-6pm, Mon.-Tues. and Thurs.-Sat. 10am-noon; free). An ornate mosaic floor is all that remains of a 4th-century **Byzantine church** (tel. 982 30 70) on Bielefeld St. near the Katzenelson School. Call ahead for a free visit.

# ■ Near Nahariya

## AKHZIV אכזיב

Like Nahariya, Akhziv's claim to fame is its sunny shoreline. The **Akhziv beach,** which begins 4km north of Nahariya, is popular (and populated, though quiet spots can be found) and has a full range of amenities (open 8am-7pm; admission NIS10). Two roads lead to the beach: the paved one along the coast and the unpaved, non-coastal road along which buses stop. Every July a **Reggae Festival** is held at the beach. Call for details (beach tel. (04) 982 39 88 or 82 01).

The heart of the area is the **Akhziv National Park** (tel. (04) 982 32 63), with sprawling lawns, a sheltered beach forming two beautiful lagoons, showers and changing rooms all built on the site of an 8th-century BCE Phoenician port town. (Open April-Sept. Mon.-Thurs. 8am-4pm, July-Aug. until 6pm, Fri. and Sun. 8am-7pm, Sat. 7am-7pm. Admission NIS14, NIS12 for students.) Bordering the park on its southern side is a **Club Med;** to the north is **Akhzibland,** a self-proclaimed independent state founded in 1952 by the eccentric Eli Avivi, who leased the land from an unamused Israeli government. An eye-catching figure in flowing robes, Avivi is unforgettable—especially when kvetchy customs officials try to figure out the "Akhzibland" stamp on your passport. Eli is currently busying himself building a Parliament building where visitors will be able to take part in debates (expected to be completed by 1997). **Eli's Museum** (tel. (04) 982 32 50), housed in a deteriorated but striking Arab mansion, exhibits the benevolent dictator's extensive and esoteric collection of mostly Phoenician implements, statue fragments, and maps (open 24hr.; admission NIS10, students NIS7, includes coffee). Sleeping in the run-down **camping area** costs NIS25, and beds in the dorms or in one of Eli's newly constructed guest rooms NIS50 (beach and museum admission included). Eli might waive the fee if you help him with menial chores (such as passing legislation).

Across the road is the **Akhziv Diving Center** (tel. (04) 982 36 71), where you can rent snorkeling equipment for NIS30. Diving classes are a hefty NIS900; groups of 6 or more can request English instruction. Introductory dives hurt slightly less at NIS150 (English available). The center runs jeep and sailing excursions as well.

About 300m north, the **SPNI Field School** (tel. 982 37 62; fax 982 30 15) leads walks around the area (mostly for children; open 8am-4pm). Their facility, often filled with youth groups, also rents private rooms. (Dorms for students only NIS29, US$9.60. Singles NIS155, doubles NIS185; extra adult NIS63, extra child NIS32. Meat meals NIS24.50, students NIS16; dairy meals and packed lunches NIS19, students NIS13.) All **buses** from platform #5 in Nahariya (buses #22-25, 28) go to the field school, hostel, beach, and campground (2 per hr., 10min., NIS5.20). *Sherut* run between Akhziv and Nahariya as well.

## ROSH HA-NIKRA ראש הנקרה

The spectacular white chalk cliffs and grottos of Rosh Ha-Nikra make up the northernmost point on Israel's coastline. The tour buses and cable car shift focus away from the mountain of barbed wire and soldiers with Uzis guarding the tense Lebanese border only a few steps from the parking lot. Rosh Ha-Nikra's caves were sculpted by millennia of lashing waves. The British enlarged these natural grottos when they dug a tunnel through the cliffs during WWII (originally designed as a train route between Haifa and Beirut). The nearby kibbutz, smelling the chance for a new tourist trap, blasted additional tunnels through the rock to improve access to the sea caves, topped the cliffs with an observation point and cafeteria, and connected the highway to the caves with a cable car. Don't expect any arduous spelunking here; a pleasant walk through the grottos is at most a half-hour event.

Down by the grottos you'll also find the "Peace Train," an audio-visual presentation featuring a mellifluous voice and 3-D glasses (in English on the half-hour). Arrive early or be caught in a throng of tour and youth groups in the afternoon. (Tel. 985 71 08 or 09. Cable car runs April-June and Sept. Sat.-Thurs. 8:30am-6pm, Fri. 8:30am-4pm; July-Aug. Sat.-Thurs. 8:30am-11pm, Fri. 8:30am-4pm; Oct.-March Sat.-Fri. 8:30am-4pm. Peace Train runs every 30min. Admission NIS25, students NIS22.)

The worse the weather, the better the show at Rosh Ha-Nikra—waves pound the caverns, forming powerful cross-currents and whirlpools and echoing thunderously through the tunnels. Bathing at Rosh Ha-Nikra is illegal—if a crashing wave doesn't get you, a soldier's bullet will. The desolate beach south of Rosh Ha-Nikra is rumored to be a favorite of some nudists.

Five minutes from the grottos, just off the main road, is the **Rosh Ha-Nikra Youth Hostel (HI)** (tel. (04) 982 51 69 or 13 30; fax 982 13 30), with lush grounds, a large recreation room, a pool, air conditioning, and private baths. (Reception open Sun.-Fri. 8am-7pm. Check-in 1pm. Check-out 9am. No curfew or lockout. Singles US$28.50, doubles US$37. Add US$1.50 per person for non-members. Breakfast included. Wheelchair accessible. Reservations a must. Credit cards accepted.)

Near Rosh Ha-Nikra is the new, spotless **Shlomi Youth Hostel and Guest House (HI)** (tel. (04) 980 89 75 or 91 61; fax 980 91 63), with air-conditioned rooms and private baths. (Reception open 8am-9pm. Check-in 2pm. Check-out 10am. No curfew or lockout. Doubles US$40.50, US$12.50 for extra people (up to 2). Non-members pay US$1.50 more per person. Breakfast included. Dinner US$8, weekend US$9.50. Packed lunch US$5. Wheelchair accessible.)

All buses from platform #5 in Nahariya (#20, 22, 24, 28, 32, 33) leave for Rosh Ha-Nikra (roughly every 40min., 35min., NIS6.30). Buses #22 and 23 leave from the Rosh Ha-Nikra junction (9:20 and 11:40am, 6:15pm). Bus #25 (8:15pm) runs from Goren Park on the hill opposite Montfort. A *sherut* taxi from Nahariya may be willing to take you to the junction (NIS5).

## MONTFORT AND NAHAL KEZIV מונטפורת ונחל כזיב

The Crusader castle of Montfort rewards a challenging hike with splendid scenery and ruins. Windswept and solitary, the fortification dramatically overlooks the western Galilee's steep **Keziv Valley.** The main structure was built by the Knights Templar early in the 12th century and partially destroyed by Salah ad-Din in 1187. Enlarged by the Hospitaller Knights in 1230, the fortress was called Starkenburg or Montfort ("strong mountain" in German or French). Among the remains of the fortress complex are the impressive 18m tower and 20m main hall.

Frequent buses (#40, 41, 44, and 45) leave Nahariya for the Christian Arab village of **Mi'ilya** (20min., NIS6.80). From the stop, turn left onto the steep road toward Mi'ilya, climbing it for about 30 minutes. At the wooden sign for Montfort, the road veers right to Hilla. Continue straight and follow the red-and-white markers down the rocky path to the castle (another 30 min.). The set of stone steps on the right is an alternate path to the ruins. The original trail turns to the right shortly, then travels across a small bridge and up the rocks to the castle. The site is currently under renovation and officially closed, but visitors can still prowl around.

The most rewarding (and challenging) way to visit is to take a longer hike, saving the castle for last. The 4-hour hiking loop with spectacular views begins at the lookout point on the road to Hilla (coming from Mi'ilya, turn right at the wooden sign), descends into the Naḥal Keziv valley, then circles back up to Montfort. Follow black-and-white or blue-and-white markers down into the valley, green-and-white while along the river, and red-and-white up to the castle and back to Mi'ilya.

Several other trails branch off the loop. Following the river away from Montfort, green-and-white markers lead you to the **Ein Tamir** and **Ein Ziv** springs. Ascending the slope opposite Montfort lands you in **Goren Park** (red-and-white markers), from which you can enjoy a perfect view of the castle complex (spectacular at sunset). Bus #25 (8:15pm only) leaves from the park to the Shlomi Youth Hostel (p. 377).

Just north of Montfort is the **Naḥal Betzet nature reserve,** another fabulous stomping ground for hikers. The blue-and-white trail follows the river upstream. To get to the enormous **Bow Cave**, a natural arch whose top affords dramatic views of the forested Galilean hills, take the red-and-white-marked trail which begins 2km from Montfort, along the road to Kibbutz Adamit.

The Keziv River extends to the Akhziv coastline (near the SPNI field school) from deep into the Galilee. Serious hikers use the trail as the first or last leg of a 3-day **Yam Le-Yam** (Mediterranean Sea to Sea of Galilee) trek. SPNI, with a field school in Akhziv, is an invaluable resource for planning any hike.

## YEḤI'AM (JUDIN) FORTRESS מבצר יחיעם

Built in the 12th century by the Templars, **Judin Fortress** (tel. (04) 985 60 04) was inherited by the Teutonic Knights and destroyed by Sultan Baybars in 1265. Tahir al-Omar's restoration efforts, made 500 years later, draw tourists today. Kibbutz Yeḥi'am was established in 1946 by a group that settled in the deserted castle; the fortress is still within the kibbutz grounds, the source of its new Hebrew name. Views of the western Galilee are amazing from the well-preserved tower (open Sun.-Thurs. 8am-5pm, Fri. and holidays 8am-4pm. Admission NIS7, students NIS5.25). Buses #39 and 42 run from Nahariya and stop by the fortress (3-4 buses per day, 20min., NIS6.30). Surrounding the fort are several defense posts left over from the War of Independence when the kibbutz was an important Galilee holdout.

At the far right-hand side of the castle's parking lot, a wooden post marks the entrance to the **Naḥal Yeḥi'am nature reserve,** home of a beautiful, easy, 1½-hour hike. Enter through the green door, follow the green-and-white markers, and descend into the brilliantly verdant Yeḥi'am Forest. When the trail turns into a road, follow it straight for about 30 minutes. The beautiful houses built into the surrounding hills are part of **Klil**, a village founded by Israeli environmentalists. Turn right at the first fork and, a short distance later, turn right again onto the two-way road. From here on, it's all paved walking (3km), but the road passes through a pleasant landscape of lush orchards and pastures. When you reach the Jatt Junction (on the main Tzfat-Kabri road), stay on the same side of the street to catch a *sherut* back to Nahariya (NIS5).

## PEKI'IN (BKE'AH) بقيعة פקיעין

Peki'in (Bke'ah in Arabic) is where Rabbi Shimon Bar-Yoḥai and his son, Eliezer, fled to after a Roman decree banned the study of Torah. For 12 years, the erudite duo hid in a small hillside cave, and, sustained by a nearby spring and a generous carob tree, delved into the most heavenly of secrets. It was during this period, some Jews say, that Bar-Yoḥai composed the *Zohar,* the central text of Kabbala (Jewish mysticism). According to popular legend, his years of mystical immersion elevated Bar-Yoḥai to such a high level of holiness that when he emerged from hiding, his gaze consumed the fields of those less worthy with angry fire. God was less than pleased with this visual outburst and sent Bar-Yoḥai back into the cave to chill out for another year.

In its present state, the cave does not live up to the colorful legend surrounding it. Bus #44 (7-8 times per day, 50min., NIS12) makes the round trip to Peki'in from Nahariya and will let you off just above the cave if you ask the driver. Be sure to be let off at Peki'in Ha'Atika (Old Peki'in), not Peki'in Ha-Ḥadasha (New Peki'in). At the blue and white sign, turn right and descend the stairs. When you reach a large bush with houses behind it, turn right and walk between two large rocks. The cave is the tiny hole about 3m away.

Peki'in is the only city in Israel claiming continuous Jewish occupation since the Second Temple period. The Jewish presence currently perpetuates itself in the form of an old lady and an 18th-century synagogue with Temple-era stones built into the wall. To visit the synagogue, continue down the staircase near the cave. Veer right until you reach Kikkar Ha-Ma'ayan ("Spring Square") with its oddly-shaped pool. Follow the street at the far right of the square, turn left at the first intersection, and follow this curving road down to the white synagogue gate to your right. If the gate is closed, knock on the white door with a blue star, located around the corner and upstairs. A small donation is requested.

# Galilee הגליל الجليل

When the ancient Israelites described their country as flowing with milk and honey, they must have been thinking about the Galilee. This lush region, bordering the West Bank to the south, the Golan to the east, Lebanon to the north, and the Mediterranean coast to the west, is sluiced by rivers and carpeted with rolling, green hills. Called *Ha-Galil* (the district) in Hebrew, the Galilee is an ancient province of the Israelite kingdom. Jesus grew up in Nazareth, he performed his first miracle at Cana, his apostles lived in Capernaum, and he gave his famous sermon atop the Mount of Beatitudes. Ever since Israel captured the Golan in 1967, putting the Galilee out of range of Syrian rockets, the region has blossomed into a tourist mecca. Busloads of pilgrims descend a massive metal staircase into the Jordan River at the site where John is believed to have baptized Jesus, banana boats and booze cruises skim over the Sea of Galilee to deposit passengers upon the bustling Tiberias promenade, and hikers crowd the trails of the Upper Galilee where Crusader fortresses keep their tired watch over forested valleys. Meanwhile, the ancient synagogues of Tzfat and back-alley churches of Nazareth continue to attract the devoted.

## ▓ Nazareth נצרת الناصرة

A vibrant center of Arab life in the Galilee, Nazareth (An-Nassra in Arabic, Natzrat in Hebrew) is a far cry from the Christmas card picture of pastoral churches, quiet convents, and grazing sheep. Nazareth is indeed dear to Christian pilgrims as the setting of Jesus's younger years and the traditional home of Mary and Joseph, but it is also an engrossingly gritty town. While the faithful worship in dimly lit back-alley churches, drivers are swerving maniacally to avoid running down pedestrians on the main road and crowds are clamoring in the business district. Nazareth's population is about half Christian and half Muslim. For the most part, Nazarean Arabs are content as Israeli citizens, but life here is worlds away from the beaches of Haifa and Tel Aviv. Visitors here (especially women) should dress modestly, or you may be harassed on the street and denied entrance to churches.

## ORIENTATION AND PRACTICAL INFORMATION

Nazareth is 40km southeast of Haifa and 30km southwest of Tiberias, on a hill north of the Jezreel Valley. All the Christian sights are located in the old **Arab Town; Natzrat Illit** (Upper Nazareth), the new, Jewish section of town, is of no interest to tourists. The Arab town's main road, **Paul VI St.**, crosses the town east of most of the places of interest. Its intersection with **Casa Nova St.** is the busiest part of town. Up the hill from Casa Nova St., interspersed with churches, is the town's market area. Continue up the hill towards Salesian St. to reach the higher quality accommodations and the panoramic views.

Obtain a map of the city from the GTIO before braving it. Most of the winding streets have only numbers for names, and there are few signs anyway. Navigational aids include towers, domes, and locals. Nazareth's Christian community rolls up the sidewalks on Sundays, but most establishments are open on *Shabbat.*

**Government Tourist Information Office (GTIO):** Casa Nova St. (tel. 657 30 03 or 05 55; fax 657 30 78), near intersection with Paul VI St. Knowledgeable staff distributes brochures and map. Open Mon.-Fri. 8:30am-5pm, Sat. 8:30am-2pm.

**Currency Exchange:** The **Change Spot Nazareth,** in a jewelry store on Paul VI St., south of the Casa Nova St., charges no commission and avoids bank hassles (open Mon.-Sat. 8:30am-8:15pm). **Bank Ha-Poalim,** Paul VI St. (tel. 657 09 23), to the right of the Mashbir department store. Open Mon.-Tues. and Thurs. 8:30am-12:30pm and 4-6pm, Sun. and Wed. 8:30am-12:30pm, Fri. 8:30am-noon.

**Telephones:** International calls available at the post office.

**Buses:** The central "bus station" consists of a few stops on Paul VI St., near Bank Ha-Poalim, a gas station, and the Basilica. Egged info. (tel. (04) 854 95 55) on Paul VI St. across from the bank (open daily 6am-6:30pm). Bus #431 from Haifa (every 20-60min., 30-35min., NIS12.70) continues to Tiberias (30min., NIS12.70). Lines #355, 357, 823, and 824 run to Afula (about every 20min., 20min., NIS6.20). Buses #823, 824, and 826 go to Megiddo (NIS8.50, watch for the hill, as drivers fly by it) and then continue to Tel Aviv (1½hrs., NIS22).

**Baggage storage:** Try the taxi stand north of the GTIO, near the Mazzawi souvenir stand; they'll usually store your bags for NIS5 each. Open Mon.-Sat. 6am-10pm.

**Taxis: Ma'ayan,** Paul VI St. (tel. 655 51 05), **Abu Elassel** (tel. 655 47 45), **Galil** (tel. 655 55 36), and **Saiegh** (tel. 657 11 76). **Sherut** (tel. 657 11 40) on side street off Paul VI St. near bus station. Haifa NIS9, Tiberias NIS15, Tel Aviv NIS24.

**Car Rental: Europcar** (tel. 655 41 29) and **Hertz** (tel. 657 53 13). Minimum age 23.

**First Aid: Magen David Adom** (tel. 101).

**Pharmacy: Farah Pharmacy** (tel. 655 40 18), next to Egged info. Open Mon.-Tues. and Thurs.-Fri. 9am-1pm and 4-6:30pm, Wed. and Sat. 8am-2pm.

**Hospitals: Nazareth Hospital** (tel. 657 15 01 or 02), **Holy Family Hospital** (tel. 657 45 35), **French Hospital** (tel. 657 45 30-33).

**Police:** Tel. 100 or 657 44 44. **Fire:** Tel. 102.

**Post Office** (tel. 655 40 19 or 51 88): Central branch on Paul VI St. two blocks west of Mary's Well. **Poste restante** at far right window. Open Mon.-Tues. and Thurs.-Fri. 8am-12:30pm and 3:30-6pm, Wed. 8am-1:30pm, Sat. 8am-noon.

**Telephone code:** 06.

## ACCOMMODATIONS

During Christian holidays, you'll need divine intervention to find a free room here. At other times, hospices are crowded, but often have a bed or two to spare.

**Sisters of Nazareth,** P.O. Box 274 (tel. 655 43 04 or 65 09; fax 646 07 41), near the Basilica, is a pristine dormitory with a beautiful courtyard and superb facilities. Walking uphill, take a left off Casa Nova St. after the Casa Nova Hospice; it will be on the right. Kitchen, dining room, and living room. Check-in 4pm, but you can

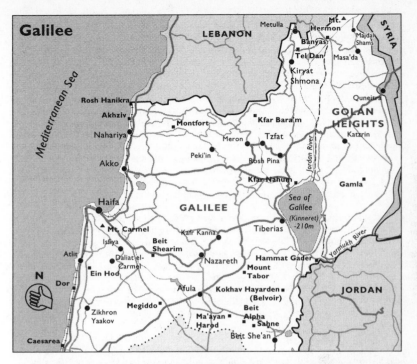

Galilee

LEBANON
Mediterranean Sea
Metulla
Mt. Hermon
Banyas
Tel Dan
Kiryat Shmona
Masa'da
Majdal Shams
SYRIA
Rosh Hanikra
Akhziv
Montfort
Kfar Bara'm
GOLAN HEIGHTS
Quneitra
Nahariya
Meron
Tzfat
Katzrin
Akko
Peki'in
Rosh Pina
Jordan River
Kfar Nahum
Gamla
Haifa
GALILEE
Sea of Galilee (Kinneret) -210m
Mt. Carmel
Kafr Kanna
Tiberias
Isfiya
Beit Shearim
Daliat el-Carmel
Nazareth
Hammat Gader
Yarmukh River
Atlit
Ein Hod
Mount Tabor
JORDAN
N
Dor
Afula
Kokhav Hayarden (Belvoir)
Zikhron Yaakov
Megiddo
Ma'ayan Harod
Beit Alpha
Sahne
Caesarea
Beit She'an

ISRAEL

leave your pack if you arrive earlier. Flexible 10am check-out and 9pm curfew. Dorm beds NIS22. Private rooms from US$18 per person, US$21 with breakfast. Beneath the convent are impressive excavations from the first century CE, including a tomb sealed by a rolling stone; ask one of the sisters to take you down.

**Casa Nova Pilgrim's House** (tel. 657 13 67; fax 657 96 30), across from the Basilica. More expensive and often full of Italian pilgrims. Check-in 2pm, check-out 9am; curfew 11pm. Doubles and triples US$25 per person. Private singles US$35. Breakfast and one meal included, US$5 more for full board. 5% service charge.

**St. Gabriel Monastery Hotel,** P.O. Box 2448, Salesian St. (tel. 656 73 49, 657 21 33; fax 655 40 71). This brand new hotel with a panoramic view of the city is housed in a white stone, red roofed monastery with its own church and bell tower. Rooms have TV, telephone, and bathroom. Singles US$42, doubles US$60. Breakfast US$5 per person. Student discount 20% (you may have to fight for it).

## FOOD

Nazareth's cuisine is not known for diversity. Falafel stands and Middle Eastern sweet shops freckle downtown. Try the crowded **Mahroum's Café** on Casa Nova St. for fresh pastries (NIS33 per kg or NIS3-5 per piece). **Grocery and produce** markets line Paul VI St. where the buses stop. The center of town is littered with identical "Oriental" restaurants. NIS11-12 gets you hummus or *shawerma*. Chicken dishes go for twice that much. Hours are generally 7am-9pm, but many places close early on Sunday. For excellent (if unoriginal) cuisine try the **El Genina Restaurant** (tel. 655 40 22 or 02 92), near Mary's Well, further north along Paul VI St. For NIS55 you get a main course, a plate of hummus or *tahini*, salad, and a soft drink. (Open Mon.-Sat. 8am-8pm. Credit cards accepted.)

## SIGHTS

Nazareth is synonymous with churches, and none is more prominent than the **Basilica of the Annunciation,** dominating downtown with its great faceted lantern tower. Completed in 1969, the basilica sits over the site believed to be Mary's home, where the archangel Gabriel heralded the birth of Jesus. Beyond the huge, bronze doors depicting the life of Jesus, the modern basilica harmonizes with ancient ruins. On the ground floor, services take place before the **Grotto of the Annunciation,** on the remains of churches dating back to 356 CE. A gallery overlooking the Biblical site is lined with a series of international artistic interpretations of the Annunciation. Excavations of ancient Nazareth lie in a garden underneath the plaza, accessible from the upper floor of the church. Ask one of the Franciscan monks to show you around. To get to the Basilica, walk north from the GTIO; it's on your right. (Open Mon.-Sat. 8:30-11:45am and 2-5:30pm, Sun. and feasts 2-5:30pm; winter, Mon.-Sat. 9-11:45am and 2-4:30pm, Sun. and feasts 2-4:30pm. Exposed knees not allowed.)

Across the plaza stands **St. Joseph's Church,** built over the cave thought to be Joseph's house. The present structure, built in 1914, incorporates remnants of a Byzantine church. Inside, stairs descend to caves that once stored grain and oil. Although this is usually referred to as **Joseph's workshop,** evidence suggests that these caves have been used since the late Stone Age. The **Greek-Catholic Synagogue Church** in the center of the Arab market is the site of the synagogue where young Jesus is believed to have preached. To get there, enter the *souq* from Casa Nova St., bear left at the first fork, then take the first right. The entrance will be on your right, at the yellow gate. An 18th century **Maronite Church** (Lebanese Christian), is up the street past the Synagogue Church. Take the first left, and continue up the alleyway with the (thankfully) former sewage channel running down the middle (it's officially closed, but you might get lucky on Sunday morning).

For an extraordinary view of Nazareth's rooftops and the Galilean hills, take bus #13 to the **Salesian Church** (or scale the 250-plus stairs to the top). The 20-minute ascent through Nazareth's old stone alleyways allows you to see a side of the village that is far more endearing than the chaos of Paul VI St. below. Hopefully, the cool, majestic sanctuary will be open, but the view merits the climb even if it's not.

Paul VI St. goes uphill from the buses to a circle-shaped building with a water faucet at an ugly traffic intersection-park. Welcome to Mary's Well! Many believe that the well's water miraculously heals; pity it can't heal its surroundings. Left and uphill from the well is the **Orthodox Church of the Archangel Gabriel,** standing over the town's ancient water source. The original church was erected in 356 CE over the spring where Mary drew water and where the Greek Orthodox believe Gabriel appeared. The present church, built in 1750, has elaborate Byzantine-style paintings and decorations. Ancient tiles adorn the entrance in the well area. (All churches in Nazareth claim to be open 8:30-11:45am and 2-5:45pm; winter 9-11:45am and 2-4:45pm; but many close in the afternoon. Sun. mornings are reserved for services. Modest dress required at all times.)

Nazareth's lively **souq** (open Mon.-Tues. and Thurs.-Fri. 9am-5pm, Wed. and Sat. 9am-2pm), best reached via Casa Nova St., is the place to go for olive wood camels and Bart Simpson underwear. The market area is best avoided at night, when drug addicts lurk in its dark alleyways.

## ■ Near Nazareth

### MOUNT TABOR הר תבור

Mt. Tabor (Har Tavor in Hebrew), the traditional site of Christ's Transfiguration, has become a standard stop on pilgrimage tours. The 588m-high hilltop is shared by Franciscan and Greek Orthodox monks. The **Basilica of the Transfiguration,** built in 1924, sits atop a 6th-century CE Byzantine church and marks the spot where Jesus

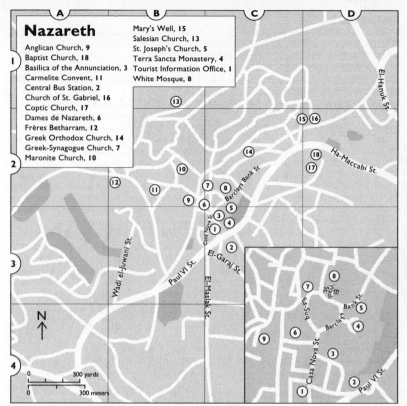

# Nazareth

Anglican Church, 9
Baptist Church, 18
Basilica of the Annunciation, 3
Carmelite Convent, 11
Central Bus Station, 2
Church of St. Gabriel, 16
Coptic Church, 17
Dames de Nazareth, 6
Frères Betharram, 12
Greek Orthodox Church, 14
Greek-Synagogue Church, 7
Maronite Church, 10

Mary's Well, 15
Salesian Church, 13
St. Joseph's Church, 5
Terra Sancta Monastery, 4
Tourist Information Office, 1
White Mosque, 8

ISRAEL

spoke with Elijah and Moses and was transfigured in the presence of apostles Peter, James, and John (Luke 9:28-36). The **Church of Elijah** nearby, built atop the **Cave of Melkhizedek,** can be entered from the outside through a small iron door. The limestone fortification, once an Arab fortress called **Al Adil,** dates from 1211. Mt. Tabor is also the site where the prophetess Deborah led the Israelites to victory over Sisera's army (Judges 4-5). (Churches open April-Sept. 8am-noon and 2:30-6pm; Oct.-March 8am-noon and 2-5pm. Modest dress required.) Take bus #357 from the Egged information office in Nazareth (4 per day, returns 45min. later, 40min., NIS9.80). Finding a *sherut* to Nazareth from the mountain is difficult if not impossible; a driver might agree to take you to Afula for NIS7. Buses #823 and 824 leave Afula for Nazareth Illit (every 45-60min., 20min., NIS6.20). From the base of Mt. Tabor, it's a steep 3km walk up a long and winding road. If there's space, taxis taking Nazareth-based tour groups may drive an individual traveler up for US$6 round-trip. To join a tour, inquire at the GTIO.

At the foot of the mountain, in the village of Shibli, is the **Galilee Bedouin Heritage Center** (tel. (06) 676 78 75). The center has a museum honoring traditional Bedouin lifestyle. Those without a passion for things Bedouin may soon regret the NIS10 entrance fee (open Sat.-Thurs. 9am-5pm, NIS8 for students).

## ZIPPORI צפורי

About 6.5km northwest of Nazareth, excavations at Zippori (Sepphoris) are uncovering a rich legacy from the Judeo-Christian, Roman, and Byzantine periods. The town was the seat of the Sanhedrin in the 3rd century CE as well as one of the places where Rabbi Yehuda Ha-Nassi gathered the most learned rabbinic scholars to compile the *Mishnah*. Extensive finds include the remains of a 4000-seat Roman amphitheater, exquisite mosaics, a crusader fortress, and a synagogue. Within the crusader citadel are a variety of multimedia programs that present the history of the city and an exhibit of archaeological finds. One km east of the main excavations is an ancient reservoir, once part of the area's water supply system, now a vast dry shell that's fun to explore. (Site tel. (06) 656 82 72 or 646 60 30. Open Sat.-Thurs. 8am-5pm, Fri. 8am-4pm; closes 1hr. earlier in winter. Admission NIS14, students NIS10.50.) Direct buses pose a scheduling problem: #16 leaves Nazareth daily at 1:10pm with no return (NIS5.20). Frequent buses (#343) pass the junction about 3km south of the site (NIS4.70). Inquire at the GTIO about *sherut* taxis to the site.

## TEL MEGIDDO (ARMAGEDDON) תל מגידו

From Bible fans to heavy metal gurus, everyone's heard of Armageddon, but few realize that this demonic battleground for the End of Days (Revelations 16:16) is actually "Har Megiddo" (Mt. Megiddo), an ancient *tel* located just southeast of Haifa. Excavations of the site have uncovered an astounding 20 layers of ruins, ranging in time from the late Chalcolithic Age (c. 3500 BCE) to the 5th century BCE.

The vision of Megiddo as an apocalyptic gathering place is derived from the city's central location. Commanding the crossroads between several ancient trading routes that linked Egypt to Syria and Mesopotamia, the fortress town was the site of many fierce battles. Megiddo was razed and rebuilt by numerous civilizations, including Canaanites, Hyksos, Egyptians, Assyrians, and Israelites. The most impressive remains include a Canaanite temple dedicated to Astarte (20th century BCE), chariot stables and a palace from Solomon's time (10th century BCE), a public grain silo built during the reign of the Israelite king Jeroboam II (8th century BCE), and a man-made tunnel engineered to allow access to water during a siege. Some of the ruins have been reconstructed, and excavations are still underway.

Before negotiating the *tel*, check out the **museum** at the site's entrance. It explains some of Megiddo's layers, displays a model of Solomon's chariot city, and shows a video in Hebrew and English. Three gift shops surround the site. Groups of American volunteers scatter themselves among the ruins, digging enthusiastically under the midday sun.

From the observation point atop the *tel*, you can look out over the **Jezreel Valley** *(Emek Yizre'el)*, mostly swamp until 1920 when it was drained by Jewish immigrants. The lone mountain in the distance is Mt. Tabor; also visible are the Gilboa range and the hills of Nazareth.

The water tunnel terminates outside the ruins, so make sure it's your last stop at the site. When you exit, turn right and walk 500m back to the museum entrance and main road. (Site and museum tel. (06) 652 68 15; open Sat.-Thurs. 8am-5pm, Fri. 8am-4pm; closes 1hr. earlier in winter. Admission NIS14, students NIS10.50.) Bus #823 runs between Nazareth and Tel Aviv, and stops at Megiddo (approx. 1 per hr.; NIS17 to Tel Aviv, NIS12 to Nazareth). Stay alert; drivers sometimes whiz by the *tel* and may charge you in advance for the return trip.

# ■ Tiberias טבריה طبرية

Tiberias has become a splashing ground rivaling the waterfront hot spots of Netanya and Eilat. On summer evenings, fish restaurants along the leafy promenade provide an expansive view of the lake. Later, music pours out of the pubs and young crowds drink and dance until the sun comes up. Tiberias (T'verya in Hebrew) is an ideal tour-

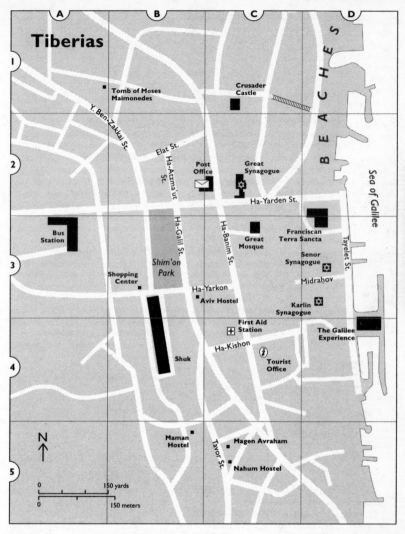

Tiberias

A · B · C · D

1

Tomb of Moses
Maimonedes

Crusader
Castle

B
E
A
C
H
E
S

Y. Ben-Zakkai St.

Elat St.

Ha-Atzma'ut St.

2

Post
Office

Great
Synagogue

Ha-Yarden St.

Sea of Galilee

ISRAEL

Bus
Station

Ha-Galil St.

Great
Mosque

Franciscan
Terra Sancta

Ha-Banim St.

Tayelet St.

3

Shim'on
Park

Shopping
Center

Senor
Synagogue

Midraḥov

Ha-Yarkon

Aviv Hostel

Karlin
Synagogue

First Aid
Station

The Galilee
Experience

Ha-Kishon

Shuk

Tourist
Office

4

N
↑

Maman
Hostel

Tavor St.

Magen Avraham

Nahum Hostel

5

0        150 yards

0        150 meters

ing base for the Galilee and the Golan Heights, but its position 200m below sea level
guarantees a hot and humid July and August.

Though its main attraction is fun and sun, Tiberias's history spans two millennia.
Built in 18 CE by Herod Antipas, puppet King of Judea and tetrarch of Galilee, the city
was named for the Roman Emperor Tiberius. Despite the Romans' attempt to bring in
settlers, most Jews, including Jesus, refused to enter the town because it was built on
the site of older Jewish graves. In the 2nd century CE, Rabbi Shimon Bar-Yoḥai
declared the town ritually pure, and it soon became the seat of the Sanhedrin and the
religious center of the Jews. The *Talmud* was edited here, and its editors now rest in
hillside tombs above the city.

During subsequent conquests by the Persians (614) and Arabs (636), Jews from
Tiberias packed up and moved to Babylon and Jerusalem. In 1247 Tiberias was
destroyed by Baybars the Mamluk and remained deserted until the beginning of Otto-

man rule in 1517. Fifty-four years later, Sultan Suleiman the Magnificent handed the town over to a Jewish refugee from Spain who set up a Jewish state under the sovereignty of the Ottomans and his mother-in-law. Their unsuccessful city fell into decay until Bedouin sheikh Taher al-Omar rebuilt the city and its citadel in 1738 and settled Jews there. In 1837 Tiberias was devastated by an earthquake that rocked all of northern Palestine, but it was soon rebuilt. The city's 1940 population of 12,000 was evenly divided between Jews and Arabs. Since the 1948 war, Tiberias has remained more or less entirely Jewish.

## ORIENTATION AND PRACTICAL INFORMATION

Tiberias has three tiers: the **old city** by the water, the **new city** (Kiryat Shmuel) up the hill (bus #5), and **uptown** at the top of the hill (bus #7, 8, or 9). Although there aren't many ruins, most tourists never leave the old city. Boozing, boating, and beaching all take place in this area. **Ha-Galil Street** (the main thoroughfare in Tiberias) and **Ha-Banim Street** run parallel to the water; **Ha-Yarden Street** runs perpendicular to them to the north. The smaller **Ha-Yarkon** and **Ha-Kishon** streets intersect Ha-Galil and Ha-Banim to the south. The *midraḥov* (pedestrian mall) runs from Ha-Galil to the promenade.

**Tourist Office: Government Tourist Information Office (GTIO)** (tel. 672 56 66; fax 672 52 62), Ha-Banim St., in the Archaeological Park, next to the Jordan River and Moriah Plaza hotels. Open Sun.-Thurs. 8:30am-3:30pm, Fri. 8:30am-noon.

**Currency Exchange: Money Net Ltd.** (tel. 672 40 48) changes foreign currency with no commission at the *midraḥov* on the second floor, close to Ha-Banim St. (open daily 9am-9pm). **Bank Ha-Poalim,** Ha-Banim St. (tel. 679 84 11), between Ha-Yarden and Ha-Yarkon, has a 24-hr. **ATM. Bank Leumi** (tel. 672 71 11), on the corner of Ha-Yarden and Ha-Banim, has a 24-hr. **money-changing machine.**

**Telephones: Solan Express** (tel. 672 64 70), on the *midraḥov*, has fax and A/C phone booths, and charges 10% less per unit than public phones. Open 24hr.

**Buses:** Ha-Yarden St. (tel. 679 10 80 or 81; info. (04) 854 95 55). To Jerusalem: bus #961, 963, or 964 (every 30-45min., 6am-6pm, last Fri. bus around 3pm, 2½hr., NIS30). To Tel Aviv: bus #836 (direct), 840 (express), 830, 832, or 841 (at least every hr., 5:30am-8:30pm, last direct bus on Fri. around 3pm, 2hr., NIS25). To Haifa: bus #430, 431 or 434 (every 20-45min., about 5:30am-8pm, last direct on Fri. around 4:30pm, 1hr., NIS17).

**Taxis:** *Sherut* and private cabs wait in front of the bus station (last Fri. car 3:30pm). **Tiberias Taxi** (tel. 672 04 44). **Aviv** (tel. 672 00 98), on Al Hadef St. next to the gas station around the corner from the Ha-Yarden post office, has regular service to Tel Aviv only (NIS23.30). No *Shabbat* service. Call the night before.

**Rental Cars:** All of the following are on Ha-Banim St.: **Reliable** (tel. 672 34 64 or 41 12), **City Car** (tel. 674 27 66, sometimes waives the age requirement), **Autorent** (tel. 672 56 88), **Eldan** (tel. 672 03 85 or 679 18 22), **Hertz** (tel. 672 39 39), and **Budget** (tel. 672 08 64 or 34 96). Get cars here for trips to the Golan.

**Bicycles:** Hostel Aviv and Maman Hostel are well-stocked. 18-speed mountain bike for NIS40, return on night of rental. See **accommodations** for addresses.

**English Bookstore: Steimatzky,** 3 Ha-Galil St. (tel. 679 12 88). Open Sun.-Thurs. 8am-1pm and 4:30-7:30pm (winter 4-7pm), Tues. 8am-1pm, Fri. 8am-2pm.

**Laundromat: Panorama** (tel. 672 43 24), on Ha-Galil, south of Ha-Kishon St. and across from the city wall remnants. Wash, dry, and fold 7kg for NIS35. Open Sun.-Mon. and Wed.-Thurs. 8am-6pm, Tues. and Fri. 8am-2pm.

**Pharmacy: Schwartz Pharmacy** (tel. 672 09 94), on Ha-Galil St. opposite the park. Open Sun.-Thurs. 8am-8pm. **Netanel Pharmacy** (tel. 679 06 13), corner of Bibas and Ha-Galil. Open Sun.-Thurs. 8am-8pm, Fri. 8am-3pm.

**Emergencies:** Tel. 101. **First Aid (Magen David Adom):** Tel. 679 01 11, corner of Ha-Banim and Ha-Kishon St. Open 24hr. **Fire:** Tel. 102.

**Police:** Tel. 100 or 679 24 44.

**Post Office:** Central office with **poste restante** on Ha-Yarden St. (tel. 672 00 19). Take a right onto Ha-Yarden St. as you exit the bus station; the office is on the left

ISRAEL

just before Al Hadef St. Open Sun.-Tues. and Thurs. 8am-12:30pm and 3:30-6pm, Wed. 8am-1:30pm, Fri. 8am-12:30pm. Branch office in **Kiryat Shmuel** (tel. 672 08 94), on the corner of Bialik and Ehrlich St.

**Telephone Code:** 06.

## ACCOMMODATIONS

For its size, Tiberias has more possibilities than Macgyver in a hardware store. Competition is fierce; hoteliers rush to woo you the second you step off the bus. Prices rise between July and September, and reservations are recommended. The Jewish holidays of Pesaḥ, Rosh Ha-Shana, and Sukkot are mob scenes. Some hostels will arrange Golan tours. None of the hostels have lockouts. Accommodations take credit cards unless otherwise noted.

**Meyouhas Hostel (HI),** Ha-Yarden St. (tel. 672 17 75 or 679 03 50; fax 672 03 72), at the corner of Ha-Banim and Ha-Yarden, in a beautiful 1862 building made of local black basalt rock. Clean and airy, with TV room, balcony, A/C, and 24-hr. reception. Check-in 2pm, check-out 10am. No curfew. Dorm beds (4-6 per room) US$16, nonmembers US$17.50. Singles US$34, doubles US$48, triples US$61.50, quads US$80, quints US$95. Breakfast included. Lockers NIS4. Reservations recommended; members have priority.

**Maman Hostel,** Atzmon St. (tel. 679 29 86). From Ha-Yarden St., turn south on Ha-Galil, then bear right on Tavor St. and turn right at the first intersection, where a red-and-white sign directs you to the hostel. Easygoing atmosphere, clean baths, pool, kitchen, and A/C. Reception open 7am-midnight. No curfew (key given). Dorm beds (4-8 per room) July-Aug. US$12, Sept.-June US$8. Private rooms July-Aug. US$40, Sept.-June US$30.

**Hostel Aviv,** Ha-Galil St. (tel./fax 672 35 10), 1 block south of intersection of Ha-Galil and Ha-Banim St. All rooms have fridge and A/C, many have balconies. Kitchen, TV room, and bar. Clean, lively backpacker atmosphere with super owners. Golan tours are US$32 for a day in a 14-person truck. 24-hr. reception. Check-out 10am. Dorm beds (4-7 per room) US$8, low season US$7. Doubles US$28, low season US$21; with private bath US$35, low season US$28. Lockers NIS5.

**Minilon Hostel,** 8 Achiva (tel. 679 04 34), turn right at the Panorama Hotel. Run by the same friendly folk as the Hostel Aviv. Large rooms have fridge, A/C, shower, toilet, and cable TV. Peaceful atmosphere. Dorm bed US$8, doubles July-Aug. US$40, Sept.-June US$37. 24-hr reception. Some rooms have kitchen facilities.

**Naḥum Hostel,** Tavor St. (tel. 672 15 05). From Ha-Yarden St. turn south on Ha-Galil, then right on Tavor St. Relaxed, with clean rooms, most with private bath and A/C. Downstairs rooms are dim, but have kitchenette and private bath. Lively rooftop bar with MTV and breezy Galilee views. Reception open 8am-11pm. Dorm beds (6-7 per room) NIS20, doubles NIS80. Cash only.

**Hostel Adler,** Ha-Galil (tel. 672 00 31). Central location, with A/C, TV room, bar, and kitchen. 24-hr. reception. Check-out 11am. Dorm beds (3-4 per room) NIS20, doubles with bath NIS70. Breakfast NIS11. Cash only.

**Adina's Hostel,** 15 Ha-Shiloaḥ St. (tel. 672 25 07 and 60 65). Head south from the bus station. This pleasant and quiet converted house caters to religious Jews. A/C, kosher kitchen, private baths, TV lounge. 24-hr. reception. Check-out 10am. Dorm beds NIS40. Private rooms (2-4 beds) July-Aug. NIS100, Sept.-June NIS70, Sat. in summer NIS150. Sat. check-out only at 8pm. Cash only.

**Camping** is a good way to escape the city heat. Before you throw down your sleeping bag, check out the MTIO/SPNI information booth (tel. 675 20 56) at Tzemaḥ on the southern tip of the lake (open summer 9am-5pm; take bus #18, 21, 22, 24, 26, or 28). Their free map shows the 25 lakeside campgrounds interspersed among the private beaches (NIS35 per car; free for car-less campers). You provide the food, water, and insect repellent and the government kicks in with jiffy johns and trash bins. Take the Ein Gev bus from Tiberias and get off when you see a site, or walk south along the coast. Be wary of theft. Women should never camp alone.

## FOOD

The **shuk,** in a square block starting at Bibas St. and going south, sells cheap, high-quality produce every day except *Shabbat.* For some variety, pick up a light meal at one of Tiberias's many falafel stands on Ha-Yarden St., running from Ha-Banim St. toward the bus station. Grilleries near the *midraḥov* serve *shishlik* with salad and pita for about NIS10, and waterfront seafood restaurants offer idyllic settings if you can block out the jet skiers and flotillas of plastic bottles. A dinner of St. Peter's fish, a Sea of Galilee specialty, costs about NIS35-40. Ha-Galil and Ha-Banim and the squares in between burgeon with culinary possibility. Two inexpensive Ha-Galil establishments are **Stekiat Aḥim Elfassi,** near Ha-Kishon St., where a barbecued feast goes for NIS8, and kosher **Weizmann's Pizza,** where a slice is NIS4. There is a **Co-op supermarket** in the Great Mosque Plaza across from Meyouhas Hostel (open Sun.-Fri. 7am-8pm).

**Maman Restaurant,** Ha-Galil St. (tel. 672 11 26), corner of Bibas St. Crammed with Israeli regulars. Hummus or *tahina* NIS8, *shishlik*, chips, and salad NIS18. A/C. Kosher. Open Sun.-Thurs. 11am-11pm, Fri. 11am-sundown.

**Little Tiberias,** Ha-Kishon St. (tel. 679 21 48 or 28 06). Excellent French and Italian cuisine and seafood in a cozy retreat from *midraḥov* mayhem. Filet steak NIS55, lasagna NIS23, salads NIS10. Open daily noon-2am. Credit cards accepted.

**Guy Restaurant,** Ha-Galil St. (tel. 672 30 36 or 19 73), south of Ha-Kishon. Cool, quiet, kosher Moroccan kitchen. Stuffed vegetables (NIS7-9) and various salads. Specialties include assorted eggplant (7 types) and fried, meat-filled "cigars" (NIS3). Open Sun.-Thurs. noon-11pm, Fri noon-sundown, Sat. after dark.

**Karamba Vegetarian Restaurant** (tel. 679 15 46), on the promenade. Take the alley leading to the waterfront from the Meyouhas hostel. Exotic, with a tree growing through the roof. Pizza margherita NIS20, house-style artichoke NIS15, salads NIS24. Open daily 11:30am-midnight. Credit cards accepted.

**Kohinoor** (tel./fax 672 49 39), at the old wharf; go south on the promenade. Scrumptious kosher Indian food, in purple A/C splendor. Dinners NIS55-60, appetizers and desserts NIS15. Specialty tandoor plates with date, mango, or mint sauce. Nightly Indian dancing show. Open Sun.-Thurs. 12:30-3:30pm and 6:30pm-12:30am, Sat. sundown-12:30am. Credit cards accepted.

**El Gaucho,** 19 Ha-Banim (tel. 672 41 71), next to the *midraḥov.* Sumptuous Argentinian grill. Between noon and 5pm, get a meal for NIS39. Large chef's salad for NIS18. Open Sun.-Thurs. noon-midnight, Fri. noon-6pm, Sat. 7pm-midnight.

## SIGHTS

The **old city,** shaken by earthquakes and conquerors, is now merely a few wall fragments littering the modern town. To get a sense of its former glory, join a free walking tour with archaeologist Edna Amos (tel. 679 22 33; Sat. 10am; 1½hr.; leaves from Moriah Plaza lobby). The **Tomb of Moses Maimonides,** on Ben-Zakkai St., commemorates the controversial but hugely influential 13th-century rabbi and philosopher whose works synthesized neo-Aristotelian-Arab philosophy with Judaism. According to legend, an unguided camel carried his coffin to Tiberias. To reach the tomb, take Ha-Yarden St. east (toward the water) and turn left on Ben-Zakkai St. The tomb is two blocks up on the right. You'll see a red fence and black pillars; the white half-cylinder with Hebrew writing is the actual tomb. Ask for the tomb of "Rambam," the rabbi's Hebrew acronym (Rabbi Moshe Ben-Maimon). Tomb junkies can also visit the **Tomb of Rabbi Akiva,** on the hillside above the Galilee (take bus #4 and ask for directions). Believers gather to have their illnesses cured at the hillside tomb of Akiva's student, **Rabbi Meir Ba'al Ha-Nes,** above the hot springs. (Tombs open Sun.-Thurs. 8am-7pm, Fri. 8am-2pm. Modest dress required.)

On the promenade next to the Caesar Hotel stands the **Franciscan Terra Sancta Church** (known as St. Peter's), built in the 12th century to commemorate St. Peter's role in the growth of Christianity (tel. 672 05 16). The apse behind the altar is arched like the bow of a boat, in honor of his pre-apostolic fishing career. In the courtyard is a statue of the Virgin Mary created by Polish troops quartered in the church from 1942 to 1945. (Open daily 8-11:45am and 2-5pm.)

Farther south is a blue-and-red marina, home to shops and the **Galilee Experience** (tel. 672 36 20), a 36-minute must-see film on the past 4000 years in the Galilee emphasizing the life of Jesus and the formation of Israel. Composed of almost 2000 slides and 27 slide projectors, this is an informative way to escape the midday heat. (Shown every hr. 8am-10pm except during *Shabbat.* Admission US$6, students US$5. Screenings in 10 languages.)

Kick back in the slimy waters of the world's earliest known **hot mineral springs.** One legend maintains that the springs were formed in the Great Flood when the earth's insides boiled. Another holds that demons heat the water under standing orders from King Solomon. Cleanse body and wallet (NIS40, Sat. NIS45). Admission includes pools, sauna, jacuzzi, and beach. A massage is NIS92 (Sat. NIS102) and a private mineral bath NIS68 (Sat. NIS78). The older building, **Tiberias Hot Springs** (tel. 679 19 67) has single-sex baths with very hot water (open Sun.-Fri. July-Aug 7am-4pm, Sept.-June. 7am-2pm). The newer building, **Tiberias Hot Springs Spa** (tel. 679 19 67), serves those seeking less scalding rejuvenation (open Sun.-Mon. and Wed. 8am-8pm, Tues. and Thurs. 8am-11pm, Fri. 8am-6pm, Sat. 8:30am-8pm). The springs are 3km south of town on the coastal road; bus #5 (every 20min.) runs from the central bus station and Ha-Galil St.

The small **Lehmann museum** (tel. 672 52 87) displays Tiberias's hot spring history. Walk out the museum's back door to reach the ruins of the **Ḥammat Synagogues,** six ancient buildings constructed on top of one another. The four upper synagogues were used from the 6th to the 8th centuries CE. Below these ruins are the remains of Roman spas, still releasing scalding water. The jewel of the exhibit is a mosaic floor that was once part of three separate synagogues. (Museum and synagogues open Sun.-Thurs. 8am-5pm, Fri. 8am-4pm. NIS7, students NIS5.25.)

**Karnei Ḥittim** (the Horns of Ḥittim) is where Salah ad-Din gave the Crusaders their comeuppance in 1187. From this mountain peak, you can see Jordan to the east, the Mediterranean to the west, and Tzfat to the north. Take bus #42 and ask the driver where to get off. The walk to the top of the hill takes about 50 minutes, but the view will leave you more breathless than the climb (open 8am-5pm).

## ENTERTAINMENT

For many **beaches** on the Galilee, you'll have to bring your own sand. Otherwise, bring sandals for walking over the sizzling black rocks. Beaches in the city and the immediate vicinity are owned by hotels that charge hefty fees in exchange for changing rooms, showers, boat rentals, and food. The beaches farther north are located along Gedud Barak Rd., off Ha-Yarden.

**Lido Kinneret** (tel. 672 15 38), just off Ha-Yarden St., charges a finger for admission (NIS15) and two arms and a leg for waterskiing (NIS100 for 15min.; open daily 10am-5pm). Just north, the somewhat dilapidated **Nelson Beach** (NIS15; open 24hr.) has 2-person kayaks or 4- to 5-person paddle boats (NIS50 per hr.), water skiing (NIS90 for 15min., discount for group of four), and the only speed-boat-drawn **inflatable banana** on the Galilee (NIS30 for 15min.). In the summertime, these beaches have rock concerts and camping (NIS10). Further north are the meticulously tended **Quiet Beach** (tel. 679 01 25; NIS15; open 8am-6pm) and **Blue Beach** (tel. 672 01 05; NIS17, Sat. NIS20; open 8:30am-6pm). A 15-minute walk or a short ride on bus #5 south of Tiberias brings you to the **Municipal Beach** (tel. 672 07 09; NIS10; open 9am-5:45pm, Fri. 9am-4:45pm). Next to it is the **Holiday Inn Beach** (tel. 679 28 90; NIS15; open 8:30am-5pm). A **religious beach** on Gedud Barak Rd. (entrance opposite the Church of Scotland Guest House) is open to women Sunday, Tuesday, and Thursday, and men Monday, Wednesday, and Friday 8am-5pm. To avoid the hefty admission prices of most beaches, you can circle the old city walls at the southern end of the promenade and walk 200m along the dirt path through the field to a small **free beach.**

Nightlife in Tiberias centers on the *midraḥov* and promenade area. In summer, street musicians, popcorn vendors, and the occasional palm-reader set up shop here. Israelis dance on outdoor tables to live rock (Tues.-Wed. and Sat. 10 or 11pm) at **La Pirate Pub,** at the corner of the *midraḥov* and the promenade (0.5L beer NIS16; open daily 5pm-4am). **Big Ben,** toward the promenade end of the *midraḥov,* is less rowdy, despite being filled with young, drunk Brits seeking a clock away from home (0.25L of beer NIS11). At the northern end of the promenade is a bar known locally as **The Coconut,** with occasional live music (open Thurs.-Sat. 10pm-4am). Nearby **Papaya,** with its long bar and excellent music, was the hippest spot in summer 1996. **Amstel,** at the northern end of the marina, is chock full of Israeli youth (you can't miss the crowds). If you'd rather nurse your hangover than start another one, head to **Makom Baḥutz** (tel. 672 26 68), around the corner from the north end of the promenade. Their frozen yogurt with fresh fruit mix-ins (NIS9 for 3 toppings) and outdoor screenings of Israeli comedies or music videos make for a relaxed evening on the town.

Get out your white polyester duds and thigh highs for Lido Kinneret Beach and Kinneret Sailing's nightly **disco cruises** (departing nightly 8-11pm depending on the number of people amassed; NIS15). Overindulgence on powerboats may lead to powerboots—landlubbers should stick to La Pirate.

A tangle of waterslides swishes 1km south of Tiberias at **Luna Gai Beach** (tel. 679 07 90; open daily 9am-5pm; admission NIS40). Walk or take bus #5 from the central bus station or Ha-Galil St. The mother of all water parks is **Luna Gal,** operated by Moshav Ramot on the eastern shore. This **aquataganza** has bumper boats! slides! pools! waterfalls! an inner tube ride! all that AND an excellent beach! (Tel. 673 17 50; open daily 9:30am-6pm; admission NIS50.)

The **Sea of Galilee Festival** brings international folk troupes to Tiberias during the second week of July. Check at the GTIO for information on this and other area fests, including Ein Gev's **Passover Music Festival** (Apr. 22-28 in '97) and Tzemaḥ's **Tu be'Av Love Fest** (Aug. 18 in '97), where thousands of young Israelis gather for some love, sweat, and rock 'n' roll.

# ■ Near Tiberias: Beit She'an בית שאן

**Beit She'an** is a Sephardi development town containing a vast complex of mostly Roman and Byzantine ruins, one of the finest archaeological sites in the country. Excavations on **Tel al-Husn,** the main archaeological mound, have already revealed some 20 layers of settlements dating back as far as the 5th millennium BCE. Of particular interest is the **Roman theater,** one of the largest extant Roman constructions in Israel. Built in 200 CE by Emperor Septimius Severus, the theater accommodated 7000 riotous spectators in its three tiers of semi-circular seating.

The remains of other grand structures branching off from the theater include colonnaded Roman streets, a Byzantine bathhouse, and a Roman temple to Dionysus. Climb to the top of the *tel* to get your bearings. To the southeast are the remnants of a 2nd-century CE **Roman amphitheater,** used for gladiatorial spectacles, and a 4th-century CE Byzantine residential quarter. North of the *tel* is the **Monastery of the Noble Lady Maria,** founded in 567 CE and abandoned after the Persian invasion of 614. The monastery has a mosaic depicting the months of the year. A much earlier period of Egyptian control left the ruins of the **Ashtaroth Temple,** built by Ramses III for his Canaanite allies. Beit She'an can be fully explored in about an hour. To get to the site from the Beit She'an bus stop, turn left at the main street, right after Bank Leumi, and then follow the paved road. (Site tel. (06) 658 71 89. Open Sat.-Thurs. 8am-5pm, Fri. 8am-4pm; closes 1hr. earlier in winter. Admission NIS14, students NIS10.50. Tours available Sat. at 10am.) Buses #412 and 415 leave Afula for Beit She'an (every 20min., 35min., NIS8.80). From Tiberias, take bus #434, 961, 963, or 964 (50min., NIS14.50). Beit She'an's newest attraction is the **border crossing facility** into Jordan (take bus #16 from town, 8:15 and 9:20am and 2:15pm). This tiny bridge, built by Ottomans, is one of Israel's busiest crossings. Allow a half day to cross, especially on Thursday and Sunday, as the border closes on weekends.

### Near Beit She'an: The Road to Afula

Along the road from Beit She'an to Afula (buses #412 and 415 travel there) are several sights of natural and historical interest. To get to Afula from Nazareth take bus #355, 357, 823, or 824 (every hr., 20min., NIS6.20).

Within Kibbutz Hefziba is the 6th-century CE **Beit Alpha Synagogue** (tel. (06) 653 20 04), whose highlight is a magnificently preserved mosaic of a zodiac wheel surrounding the sun god Helios (identified with the prophet Elijah), reflecting the Hellenic influence on the area. Take bus #412, 415, or 417 from either Afula (30min., NIS8) or Beit She'an (20min., NIS5.20). (Open Sat.-Thurs. 8am-5pm, Fri. 8am-4pm; closes 1hr. earlier in winter. Admission NIS7, students NIS5.25.) Don't be misled by the sign for Kibbutz Beit Alpha (1km closer to Beit She'an).

**Gan Ha-Shlosha** (tel. (06) 658 62 19), also known as **Saḥne**, 1km west of Beit Alpha, is worth an afternoon excursion. Its waterfalls and crystal-clear swimming holes are refreshing in both summer and winter (at a constant 28°C). The springs have been popular since Roman times; the covered pool and waterslides haven't. Brave souls leap into the pools from the rocky ridges above. Watch out for theft on overcrowded weekends. Bus #412 and 415 from Afula (NIS8) or Beit She'an (NIS4.70) go to Saḥne (open Sat.-Thurs. 8am-6pm, Fri. 8am-5pm. Admission NIS19, students NIS14.25). A 10-minute walk along the road behind the park leads to the **Museum of Regional and Mediterranean Archaeology** (tel. (06) 644 80 45), a collection of Hellenistic and Islamic art and pottery gathered from a local Canaanite temple, an Israelite community, and a Roman colony. You can't miss the Greek columns scattered around the entrance. (Open Sun.-Thurs. 9am-2pm, Sat. and holidays 10am-2pm. Park admission required to see the museum. Opposite the museum, across the bridge, is the recently opened **Tel-Amal Stockade and Tower.** Critical in defending Israel in her formative years, the first stockade and tower settlement was set up here in 1936. The reconstructed tower offers wonderful views of the surrounding area. There is also an English and Hebrew audio-visual presentation (open Sun.-Thurs. 10am-2pm, Fri. 9am-12:30pm).

Three km from Afula is the **Ma'ayan Ḥarod National Park,** named after the Ḥarod spring which flows out of Mt. Gilboa. This is the site where Gideon's men were chosen to fight the Midionites. Above the spring are the graves of Yehoshua Hankin (who purchased the land for the JNF) and his wife Olga. Close by is a brass monument commemorating those who gave their lives in the struggle for independence. The hordes of Israeli schoolchildren who visit the park are not interested in any of this; they come for the large, icy **swimming pool.** After a perusal of the yawn-inspiring sights, you may understand why (park open daily 8am-4pm, admission NIS20).

An even better reason to visit the park is the **Ma'ayan Ḥarod Youth Hostel (HI)** next door (tel/fax (06) 653 16 60). Bus #35 from Afula (11:45am and 6:15pm) will take you directly to the hostel; bus #415 (express), 402, 405, and 412 bring you to the access road, 1km away. Just before the entrance to the national park, take a left (the green sign for the hostel is obscured by tree branches). All cabins have air conditioning and attached bathrooms. The reception has maps of the area, and the hostel is a great base to start hikes to surrounding sights. Guests get a 50% discount at the national park. You can pay in foreign currency, which saves you the tax. (Dorm beds US$16.50, July-Aug. US$18.50. Singles US$34, July-Aug. US$38.50. Doubles US$48, July-Aug. US$53. Breakfast included. Reception open 8am-noon, 4-7pm, Fri. till 2pm. Check–out 10am. US$1.50 HI discount. Call ahead July-Aug.)

You can walk the 10km from the Ma'ayan Ḥarod hostel (ask for a map) to **Belvoir** (Kokhav Ha-Yarden, or Star of the Jordan; tel. (06) 658 17 66) or take a Tiberias-Beit She'an bus (#434, 961, 963, 964; NIS8 from Tiberias, NIS7 from Beit She'an), which will let you off at the turn-off to this 12th-century Crusader fort. From there, it's a very steep 7km uphill walk—definitely a hat-and-water hike. The fort affords marvelous views of the entire Jordan Valley and, on a clear day, the Galilee. Six hundred meters above the Jordan River, it overlooks the medieval trade route from Egypt to Damascus. The area was the scene of several skirmishes between Crusaders and Muslims until, after the Battle of Hattin in 1187, the Muslims besieged the castle. After 18 months, the knights finally surrendered. In acknowledgment of their bravery they were permitted to depart unharmed. During the early 13th century, the castle was partially destroyed by the Sultan of Damascus to preempt Crusader re-occupation of the stronghold. The edifice, built with 3m-thick blocks of black stone and surrounded by a deep moat, is still imposing. (Open Sat.-Thurs. 8am-5pm, Fri. 8am-4pm; closes 1hr. earlier in winter. Admission NIS10, students NIS7.50.)

## ■ Near Tiberias: The Sea of Galilee (Lake Kinneret)

### GETTING AROUND

All the sights on the Sea of Galilee are in some way, shape, or form accessible by **bus** from Tiberias, but renting a **mountain bike** is the more convenient and scenic way to go (try Hostel Aviv, p. 387). A complete circuit of the lake takes four to five hours, plus the time you spend at the sights. As you peddle along, there are two creatures to watch out for: the furry, little, road-crossing hyrax (a close relative of the elephant) and the screeching, careening Israeli driver (a close relative of the Tasmanian Devil). Spring is the best time for biking; the hills are unbearable in summer. The **Lido Kinneret Sailing Co.** (tel. 672 15 38) operates a **ferry** between Lido Beach and Ginnosar (US$10 one way, US$15 roundtrip; no extra charge for bikes).

An excellent, albeit expensive, way to explore the northern coast of the Galilee is on **horseback.** Take bus #459, 541, 841, or 963 from Tiberias and get off at Korazim junction, in front of **Vered Ha-Galil.** A half-day guided ride through the Galilean hills, down to the sea, and then up to the Mount of Beatitudes costs US$60 per person. There's a bunkhouse where bed and American breakfast cost US$41-53 for one, US$54-69 for two. They also offer horse rentals (1hr. US$20, 2hr. US$36, full day with lunch US$120) and lessons (½hr. US$19, 1hr. US$32). For reservations, write to Vered Ha-Galil, Korazim, or call (06) 693 57 85. Several kibbutzim and *moshavim* also offer horseback riding; check at the Tiberias GTIO.

The region's **telephone code** is 06.

### SIGHTS ON THE SHORE

Thirty minutes southeast of Tiberias, the hot baths of **Ḥammat Gader** (Al Himma in Arabic, tel. 675 10 39) lie in former Syrian territory. In Roman times the town, combined with its other (Jordanian) half on the western side of the Yarmuk River, formed part of the Decapolis (see The Ancient Levant, p. 44). Though the more interesting remains are in Jordan, Roman ruins here, including large bathing areas and a smaller pool that was reserved for lepers, have been partially reconstructed. At the southwest corner of the complex is the hottest spring in the area, so hot (51°C) that the Jews call it *Ma'ayan Ha-Gehinom* (Hell's Pool) and the Arabs *Ain Maqla* (Frying Pool). The hot pool is crowded with families; the leper pool isn't. There is also an area for slathering on black mud that purportedly cures skin ailments. Just west of the Roman baths are the ruins of a 5th-century **synagogue.**

Ḥammat Gader boasts an **alligator park,** where hundreds of large, somnolent gators sun themselves or slog through murky water. Yes, indeed, the first generation was imported (or slithered) from Florida. The reserve now raises its young in a hothouse at the entrance to the ponds. There are also kitschy alligator and parrot shows at 11am, 1, and 3pm. (Open Mon.-Sat. 7am-midnight, Sun. 7am-5pm. Admission NIS33, students and children NIS30; Sat. NIS33 and 31.) Bus #24 leaves from Tiberias at 8:45 and 10:30am, returning at noon and 3pm (Fri. returns at noon and 1pm).

Near the spot where the Jordan River flows out of the Sea of Galilee, about 8km south of Tiberias and west of Ḥammat Gader, is **Deganya Alef,** Israel's first kibbutz and the birthplace of Moshe Dayan. Founded by Russians in 1909, the kibbutz now manufactures diamond tools. At the entrance to the kibbutz is a Syrian tank, a testimony to the War of Independence, when the Syrians were repelled from the lawns of Deganya Alef.

Did you ever wonder why every kibbutz and podunk town in Israel must have at least two museums? Ponder some more at nearby **Beit Gordon** (tel. 675 00 40). One is on Galilee archaeology, the other on natural history. Stuffed animal carcasses abound. (Open Sun.-Thurs. 9am-3:30pm, Fri. 9am-noon, Sat. 9:30am-noon. Admission NIS8.) Deganya's frightening uniformity leads easily to misdirection. Take a right after the tennis courts and ambulances and ask for directions. Next to Beit Gordon is the **SPNI Kinorot Field School** (tel. 675 23 40; fax 675 10 88; open Sun.-Thurs. 8am-3:30pm., Fri. 9am-1pm) with guides for hire and maps for sale. The best **hikes** in the area are the trails at **Mt. Arbel** and **Naḥal Amud,** both to the northwest of the Sea of Galilee. Naḥal Amud flows from the lake far out into the Galilee. Serious backpackers use the trail as either the first or last leg of a three-day **Yam L'Yam** (Sea of Galilee to Mediterranean Sea) trek (Naḥal Keziv is the other part; see Montfort and Naḥal Keziv, p. 377). Hiring a guide is strongly recommended, and consulting maps, compasses, and the SPNI are a must. The Naḥal Amud trail is also a small component of the **Israel Trail,** which stretches all the way from Metulla to Eilat. From Tiberias, bus #23, 24, 26, and 29 pass through town.

The low water level of the Galilee in 1985-86 had one serendipitous benefit—the discovery of an **ancient boat** under a segment of newly exposed lake bed off the beach of Kibbutz Ginnosar. Its wooden frame, turned to mush after centuries of marinating in mud, was encased in a fiberglass brace and hauled to shore. The boat, dating from 100 BCE to 100 CE, has been restored to near-pristine condition. Noting its age, some Christians have dubbed it "the Jesus boat." While it *is* a fishing boat, even of the sort the apostles might have used, archaeologists say it has as much to do with Jesus as RuPaul and suspect it was sunk in a great sea battle (described by Josephus) between the Romans and Jews (boat and 20min. film NIS9, students NIS6). It rests right next to the new **Yigal Allon Center** in an airtight glass tank, where it will undergo nine more years of cosmetic repair. The center is named after a central figure in the establishment of the state of Israel. It contains several exhibitions within its four floors: models and photographs of different settlements, a chance to reenact several military engagements (ranging from the Bar Kochba Revolt to the six-day war), and a multitude of audio-visual presentations. (tel. 672 29 05. Open Sat.-Thurs. 9am-5pm, Fri. 9am-1pm, Sat. 8:30am-4pm. Admission NIS13, students NIS11.)

Next door is shady green **Ginnosar Beach** (tel. 679 21 61; open 9am-6pm; NIS20, students NIS15; paddle boats NIS40 per hr., kayaks NIS30). To get here, take bus #459, 541, 841, or 963 from Tiberias to the Yigal Allon Center.

## NEW TESTAMENT SIGHTS

According to the New Testament, Jesus walked on the waters of the Sea of Galilee. Four of the most significant stories in Christian history are set in the steep hills of its northern coast.

**Migdal,** the birthplace of Mary Magdalene, lies north of Tiberias, halfway to Capernaum. Though an important town when the Crusaders built a church here in the 12th century, today it is an agricultural community (founded in 1910) with a tiny, white-domed shrine. Buses #459, 541, 841, and 963 run to Migdal from Tiberias.

In **Tabgha,** 2km southwest of Capernaum along the coastal road, the **Church of the Primacy of St. Peter** marks the site of the miracle of the loaves and fishes, and the spot where Jesus made Peter "Shepherd of his People." According to the Book of John, Peter led the apostles on a fishing expedition 100m offshore from Tabgha after the Resurrection. A man on shore called to them to throw their nets over the starboard side and assured them of a catch. When the nets hit the water, a swarm of fish swam in. Peter jumped off the boat and swam to shore, where he found the man, whom he now realized was Jesus, preparing a meal for the Twelve. When the others sailed in, Jesus told Peter to "Feed my lambs. Tend my sheep. Feed my sheep." (John

21:15-17). The Church of the Primacy is built around a rock said to be the table of this feast. The first church at this spot was built in the 4th century, destroyed in 614 CE, and rebuilt with black basalt by the Franciscans in 1933. On the seaward side of the church are the steps from which Jesus called out his instructions; on the shoreline is a series of six double or heart-shaped column bases built by early Christians and called the "thrones of the Apostles" (tel. 672 47 67; open Sun. 9:45am-5pm, Mon.-Thurs. 8:30am-5pm. Modest dress is required.)

Just west of the Church of the Primacy along the northern coast of the sea lies the **Church of the Multiplication of the Loaves and Fishes.** A mosaic inside relates how Jesus fed 5000 pilgrims with five loaves and two small fish (Matthew 15:29-39). A section of the mosaic has been removed, revealing the original 4th-century foundations (open Mon.-Sat. 8:30am-5pm, Sun. 10am-5pm, modest dress required). Around the right side of the church past the "private" sign and up the stairs is a small **hospice** (tel. 672 10 61; doubles with A/C (some have shower and toilet) NIS50 per person). Take bus #459, 541, 841, or 963, and get off at the Tabgha Junction.

On the **Mount of Beatitudes,** overlooking sea, field, and town, Jesus gave his Sermon on the Mount (Matthew 5). A church (funded by *Il Duce* himself, Benito Mussolini) stands on the Mount, its octagonal shape recalling Jesus' eight beatitudes. To reach the Mount, take bus #459, 541, or 963 from Tiberias; get off at the second stop after the bus turns uphill away from the lake. From here, a sign points the way to the church, 1km along a side road (open daily 8am-noon and 2:30-5pm, no shorts or bare shoulders).

From the Mount, the ancient town of **Capernaum** (Kfar Naḥum in Hebrew, Tel Num in Arabic) is 3km down to the coastal road, marked by a white signpost. This is where Jesus healed Simon's mother-in-law and the Roman Centurion's servant (Luke 4:31-37 and 7:1-10) and where Peter was born. A modern church arches over the ruins of a 5th-century octagonal church, marking the site believed to have held Peter's house. Nearby, the ruins of a synagogue, perched in the middle of the old town, contain Corinthian columns and friezes dating from the 4th century CE. Since Capernaum did not participate in the Jewish revolts against the Romans of the first and 2nd centuries CE, it survived unscathed. (Open daily 8:30am-4:15pm. Admission NIS2. Dress modestly.) Buses #459, 541, 841, and 963 from Tiberias pass the Capernaum junction about once an hour on the way north to Kiryat Shmona and Tzfat. Get off before the bus turns up the Mount and walk 3km along the shore.

Four km north of the Sea of Galilee and 2km east of the road from Tiberias to Rosh Pina, you will find the ruins of the Jewish town of **Korazim** (tel. 693 49 82), one of the unrepentant towns chastised by Jesus (Matthew 11:21). Don't be misled by the white sign to the modern town—follow the orange sign to the site. There is a synagogue dating from the Talmudic period (3rd-4th centuries CE). The bare, rolling landscape is strewn with the dark basalt rubble of what were once streets and dwellings. The remains display a basic village layout of the time: housing quarters centered around a paved courtyard, and a synagogue with some detailed ornamental pediments and a reconstructed interior cornice. (Open Sun.-Thurs. 8am-5pm, Fri. 8am-4pm; closes 1hr. earlier in winter. Admission NIS10, students NIS7.50.)

On the eastern side of the lake, 7km north of Ein Gev, lie the ruins of **Kursi** (tel. 673 19 83), a Christian settlement dating from Byzantine times (5th-6th centuries CE). According to the New Testament, it was at Kursi (Gergessa or Gerasa) that Jesus exorcised several demons from a man's body and caused the demons to possess a grazing herd of pigs; the pigs raced into the sea and drowned. Jesus' feat came to be known as the "Miracle of the Swine" (Luke 8:26-31, Matthew 8:23-34). The site, with impressive remains of a large monastery and a small chapel (both reconstructed, both with mosaic floors), is popular among Christian pilgrims. (Open Sat.-Thurs. 8am-5pm, Fri. 8am-4pm; closes 1 hr. earlier in winter; admission NIS7, students NIS5.25.) Buses #15, 17-19, 21, and 22 run from Tiberias to Kursi (30min., NIS9.70).

Perched above the Sea of Galilee is the **Poriya Youth Hostel (HI),** (tel. (06) 675 00 50; fax 675 16 28), on Rte. 7677, opposite Barniki Beach. The hostel has a great view, but only iron-leg hikers will make it up the 3km hike from the main road. (Dorm beds with A/C and private shower US$24. Dorms without either US$18. Wooden cabins US$26. Reception open 8am-11pm. Check-out 2pm. US$2 discount for HI members. Credit cards accepted.)

# ■ Tzfat (Safed) צפת صفد

You needn't be Jewish or religious to be enraptured by the mystical city of Tzfat; anyone who's ever had a profound thought (or faked one) will love it. Built upon Mt. Kenaan, Tzfat is a city of mesmerizing beauty and delightful tranquility. It's a rare place where the difference between history and myth is slight, and in which each street corner and alleyway has its own odd set of legends.

For the most part, Jewish traditions are taken seriously in Tzfat. While the Talmud translates the town's name as "vantage point" because of the city's panoramic view of the Galilean hills, others claim that the name derives from the root for "anticipation." Indeed, many in Tzfat await the arrival of the Messiah, whom they believe will pass through on His way from Mt. Meron to Jerusalem; some even sport buttons proclaiming "We want the Messiah now!" The modern-day mystics of Tzfat may dress in uniformly black garb, but they come from diverse backgrounds: some descend from a line of *shtetl* rabbis, others are born-again backpackers, and many are simply frozen-in-time flower children.

The city's contemporary security and religious homogeneity belie its history. The Crusader-built castle was captured by Salah ad-Din in 1188, then lost in 1240 to the Mamluk Sultan Baybars, who turned Tzfat into the major administrative center for the region. Persecuted European Jews arrived throughout the Middle Ages seeking refuge in the relatively tolerant Ottoman Empire. In 1578, the first printed Hebrew book was produced here.

Tzfat has been a holy town for Jews since Rabbi Isaac Luria (Ha'Ari) helped make it the center of Kabbalistic mysticism in the 16th century. The sages say that each holy city represents an "element," and that Tzfat's is the crisp, soul-searching air. Of course, it is possible to get too much of Tzfat's atmosphere: in 1777, a rabbi who had trekked to Tzfat all the way from Europe ultimately packed up and left for Tiberias, complaining that the angels here kept him up at night (hostels don't provide refunds for angel-heavy accommodations).

Despite an influx of Ḥasidic Jews from Poland in 1778, the population of Tzfat generally dwindled in the 19th century. In 1834 the town was pillaged by the Druze, and 1837 saw a horrendous earthquake. New settlements began in the second half of the 19th century. In 1929, Hajj Amin al-Husseini led Tzfat's Arabs in violent protests of the Jewish influx. By 1948 there were 12,000 Arabs and 1700 Jews. In May 1948, Israeli Palmaḥ troops managed to defeat the Iraqi and Syrian troops dug in atop the mountain. Tzfat's native Arab population fled with the armies; their evacuated homes now house a popular artists' colony.

## ORIENTATION AND PRACTICAL INFORMATION

Tzfat is arranged in circular terraces of streets descending from the castle ruins at the town center. **Jerusalem** (Yerushalayim) **Street,** behind the central bus station, follows the lines of what was once the castle's moat and makes a complete circle around **Gan Ha-Metzuda** (Park of the Citadel). **Ha-Palmaḥ Street** begins off Jerusalem St. near the central bus station and crosses the main street via a stone bridge.

The city could be divided into three districts: the **Park Area,** at the top of the mountain (ringed by Jerusalem St.), the **Artists' Quarter,** southwest and down the hill, and the **Synagogue Quarter** (Old City), immediately to the north of the Artists' Quarter on the other side of Ma'alot Oleh Ha-Gardom. The **Midraḥov** (pedestrian mall) is the strip of Jerusalem St. running southwest of the Park Area, up the hill from the Artists' and Synagogue Quarters.

ISRAEL

**Government Tourist Information Office (GTIO):** The ground floor of the Municipality Building, 50 Jerusalem St. (tel. 692 09 61-4; fax 697 47 03), a 7-min. uphill walk to the right as you leave the central bus station. Friendly staff gives a helpful, free map. Open Sun.-Mon., Wed.-Thurs. 8am-4pm, Tues. 8am-1pm and 4-6pm.

**Currency Exchange:** Several **banks** line Jerusalem St. Most open Sun., Tues., and Thurs. 8:30am-12:30pm and 4-6pm, Mon. and Wed. 8:30am-12:30pm, and Fri. 8:30am-noon.

**Buses: Central Bus Station,** Ha-Atzma'ut Sq. (tel. 692 11 22). #459 runs between Tiberias and Tzfat (every hr. until 7pm, NIS12). #361 and 362 go to and from Haifa through Akko (every 20min.; last bus Sun.-Thurs. 8:45pm, Fri. 5pm, first Sat. bus 9:10pm., 45min., NIS21). To Tel Aviv: #846 (5:15am and 5:35pm, 2½hr., NIS34). To Kiryat Shemona: #501 and 511 (every hr. until 7pm, 45min., NIS12.70). Bus #964 direct to Jerusalem on Fri. (12:30pm, 2½hr., NIS34).

**Taxis: Kenaan Taxis** (tel. 697 07 07), near bus station. No *sherut* or intercity.

**Laundry: Dry Cleaning** (tel. 697 38 77), a large sign on 38 Jerusalem St. NIS8 per kg. Open Sun.-Mon., Wed.-Thurs. 8:30am-2pm, 4-7pm; Tues., Fri. 8:30am-2pm.

**Pharmacy: Golan Pharmacy** (tel. 692 04 72), just opposite the Municipality building on Jerusalem St. **Canaan Pharmacy** (tel. 697 24 40), under the Ha-Palmach Bridge. Both open Sun.-Thurs. 8:30am-1pm and 4-7pm, Fri. 8:30am-1pm.

**First Aid (Magen David Adom):** Tel. 101 in emergencies, otherwise 692 03 33; next to the central bus station.

**Police:** Tel. 100 in emergencies, otherwise 692 04 44 or 697 24 44.

**Central Post Office:** Ha-Palmah St. (tel. 692 04 05), next to a radar dish visible from the corner with Aliya Bet. **Poste restante.** Open Sun.-Tues. and Thurs. 8am-12:30pm and 3:30-6pm, Wed. 8am-1:30pm, Fri. 8am-noon. A more convenient branch on Jerusalem St. near the GTIO has similar hours.

**Telephone Code:** 06.

## ACCOMMODATIONS

Tzfat's **youth hostel** is well equipped and only a short ride or 20-minute walk from the bus station. Other options, primarily in high season, are the inexpensive **guest rooms** and flats provided by town residents. The best way to find a rental is to let it find you: walk around the central bus station pathetically holding your luggage and wait. Don't pay until you see the quarters. You can also walk up Jerusalem St. and choose one of the places with a "rooms to let" *("haderim l'haskir")* sign (often in Hebrew only), or ask at the tourist office for a list of phone numbers. The official summertime prices are NIS60 for singles and NIS120 for doubles, but bargaining often helps, especially during low season. Ask the GTIO about any place you're considering. Check for heating or blankets—even Tzfat's summer nights can be chilly.

**Beit Binyamin (HI),** near the Amal Trade School in South Tzfat (tel. 692 10 86; fax 697 35 14). Take bus #6 or 7. Recently renovated, with private baths, a TV lounge, and a good mix of Israelis and tourists. Reception open 8am-2pm and 4-8pm. Dorm beds (4-6 per room) NIS58. Singles NIS117, doubles NIS164, triples NIS207. Members get NIS4 discount. Wheelchair accessible. Takes credit cards.

**Beit Lifshitz,** on Ha-Palmah bridge, in the alley around the corner from the yellow "Rimon Inn" sign and through the green door (tel. 697 47 10). Simple furnishings, but large airy rooms cluster around a pleasant central garden. Friendly staff. Fridge in each room, communal kitchen. 24-hr. check-in. No curfew or set check-out (NIS35 or US$12 per person, but prices flexible).

**Hadar Hotel,** Ridbaz St. (tel. 692 00 68). Take a right from the bus station; it's on an alley off Jerusalem St. Ridbaz is an alley off Jerusalem. Look for the yellow sign with an arrow. Cozy atmosphere. Spacious roof with view of the city. Rooms have bath and some are A/C. No smoking on *Shabbat.* Ring the bell after midnight. Check-out 11am. July-Aug. singles NIS80, doubles NIS160. Sept.-June NIS60; NIS120.

**Ascent Institute of Tzfat,** 2 Ha-Ari St. (tel. 692 13 64 or 697 14 07; fax 692 19 42; e-mail ascent@act.com.co.il). The first right off Jerusalem St. from the bus station. Jews only. Breakfast and walking tour or nature hike included (summer only). Free new-age mysticism, and access to a library and multimedia center. NIS5 rebate for each of two optional classes you attend while there. Secular Jews report feeling

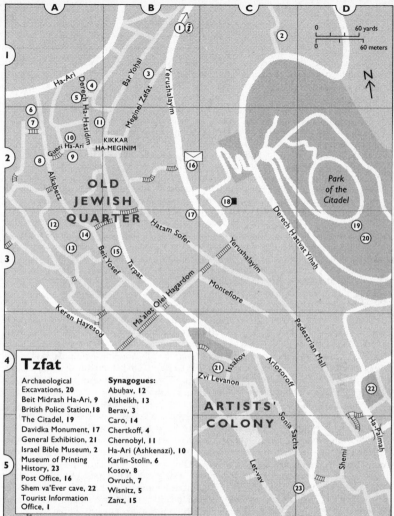

## Tzfat

Archaeological
Excavations, 20
Beit Midrash Ha-Ari, 9
British Police Station, 18
The Citadel, 19
Davidka Monument, 17
General Exhibition, 21
Israel Bible Museum, 2
Museum of Printing
History, 23
Post Office, 16
Shem va'Ever cave, 22
Tourist Information
Office, 1

**Synagogues:**
Abuḥav, 12
Alsheikh, 13
Berav, 3
Caro, 14
Chertkoff, 4
Chernobyl, 11
Ha-Ari (Ashkenazi), 10
Karlin-Stolin, 6
Kosov, 8
Ovruch, 7
Wisnitz, 5
Zanz, 15

comfortable. Reservations recommended. Reception open Sun.-Thurs. 9am-9pm, Fri. 9am-6pm; winter Sun.-Thurs. 9am-1pm and 5-8pm, Fri. 9am-4pm; you can always leave your bags. Check-in 4-9pm. Check-out 11am. Midnight curfew. Dorm beds (4-6 per room) NIS40, Sat. night NIS30. Takes credit cards.

**Shoshana's Hostel,** across the alley from Beit Lifshitz (tel. 697 39 39). Simple but clean, with kitchen facilities. Run by elderly, friendly Shoshana, who may or may not be there—call ahead. Dorm beds US$8, singles US$25. Check-out 9:30am.

**Ha-Galil Hotel,** 3 Ridbaz St. (tel. 692 12 47), near Ascent Institute. Tidy rooms, some with attached toilets and showers. Check-out 11am. Midnight curfew. Caters primarily to religious Jews (modest dress, no smoking on *Shabbat*). Doubles and triples NIS60 per bed, NIS100 in July and August. Often closed in winter.

**Bet Maman,** 59 Ha-Palmaḥ St. (tel. 697 04 73), before the bridge. Rooms have kitchen facilities. Singles July-Aug. NIS60, Sept.-June NIS40-50. Doubles NIS90; NIS70-80, triples NIS120;NIS90. Run by an elderly man who is usually asleep.

## FOOD

The stretch of Jerusalem St. north of the bridge to #48 is lined with falafel joints and fairly expensive restaurants. Many places close on *Shabbat;* if you don't shop before Friday afternoon you may starve. A fruit and vegetable **market** is held Wednesdays 6am-2pm next to the bus station. There are **supermarkets** throughout town, including a **HyperKol** on the *midraḥov* (open Sun.-Thurs. 9am-8pm, Fri. 7am-2pm).

**California Falafel,** 92 Jerusalem St., next to Ha-Palmaḥ bridge. Fries great falafel despite its dubious name, and is consistently filled with American tourists. Falafel NIS7. Open Mon.-Thurs. 9am-11pm, Fri. 9am-3pm. Kosher.

**Ha-Mifgash Restaurant,** 75 Jerusalem St. (tel. 692 05 10 or 697 47 34), opposite the small observation point and park, serves great kosher food in a homey cavern. *Shishlik, kabab,* or burgers with fries for NIS27; NIS10 pita sandwiches and a large salad selection. Open Sun.-Fri. 9am-midnight. Credit cards accepted.

**Rafi's Laffa,** 88 Jerusalem St. (no English sign; tel. 692 14 96). This tiny grill 2 doors west of the bridge serves up delicious *me'orav* (mixed grill) in pita (NIS10) or as a large *laffa* sandwich (NIS12). Falafel and omelettes NIS7.

**Café Baghdad** (tel. 697 40 65), halfway up the *midraḥov.* Spy a great view of Tzfat with your kosher vegetarian meal. Salads NIS20-30, pizza NIS20, pancakes NIS16-20. Open Sun.-Thurs. 8am-2am, Sat. from sundown. Credit cards accepted.

**Pizza Phone** (tel. 692 27 27), at the top of the *midraḥov* shopping center. Spectacular views; often more packed than your El-Al flight. Omelettes NIS15-19, spaghetti NIS18-20, excellent pizza NIS22. Open daily 8am-1am. Takes credit cards.

## SIGHTS

The tangled streets of Tzfat are sparsely labeled, but you'll be happy just to wander around. Tzfat is all about legends, and these are best told by the city's own **tour guides. Aviva Minoff** (tel. 692 09 01; mobile tel. (050) 640 91 87) gives entertaining tours starting from the Municipal building or the Rimon Inn Hotel (Mon.-Thurs. 10am, Fri. 10:30am, 2½hr.). **Yisrael Shalem** (tel. 697 18 70) leads tours on demand (2hr., call ahead, dress modestly), and his helpful book *Six Self-Guided Tours to Tzfat* (NIS15) is available at Greenbaum's Books on the *midraḥov.*

The meager ruins of the 12th-century Crusader fortress that once controlled the main route to Damascus grace **Gan Ha-Metzuda,** a wooded park good for picnics. There's also a monument to the Israelis who died here during the 1948 War. The **Davidka Monument** near the GTIO memorializes the weapon responsible for the Palmaḥ's victory in Tzfat—the duds it launched made a noise so frightening that the Arab forces feared an atomic attack and fled town.

The **Israel Bible Museum** (tel. 699 99 72), just north of the park and up the steep stone stairway, displays the work of Phillip Ratner, a modern American artist whose work depicting biblical scenes and personalities is also in permanent collections at the Statue of Liberty, the White House, and the U.S. Supreme Court. (Open June-Sept. Sun.-Thurs. 10am-4pm, Fri. 10am-1pm; Oct.-May Sun.-Thurs. 10am-2pm. Closed Jan. Free.) The **Shem va'Ever Cave** is believed to be where Noah's son Shem and grandson Ever were buried. If the shrine around the cave is locked, knock at the small, domed synagogue nearby. The cave is near the top of Ha-Palmaḥ bridge at the intersection of Jerusalem and Arlozorov St. A forest of English signs will direct you down the hill to the **General Exhibition** (tel. 692 00 87) displaying works by local artists and housed in the town's mosque, empty of worshippers since the 1948 War (open Sun.-Thurs. 9am-6pm, Fri. 9am-2pm, Sat. 10am-2pm). On the way, you can take a detour off Arlozorov St. into the **Artists' Quarter** and wander through the alleys and galleries just south of the Jerusalem-Arlozorov intersection. The quality of the art varies, but a keen eye might lead you to a few real jewels. A few artists to look for: Mike Leaf crafts hilarious, irreverent scenes in paper-maché, Arik Amir forges wrought-iron statuettes of fish, roosters, and other creatures, and Naomi Spiers paints water-color scenes of Tzfat. The galleries also sell tons of **micrography,** traditional Jewish texts written in picture form. (Most open 10am-1pm and 4-7pm.)

Navigating the gnarled **Synagogue Quarter** *(kiryat batei ha-knesset),* also called the Old City *(ha-ir ha-atika),* is a matter of luck. Note landmarks carefully, but when you get lost (and you will get lost) enjoy it: it's a nice place in which to lose your bearings. Each of the tiny synagogues described below are still used. The **Chernobyl Synagogue** was founded by Jews from that tragic Ukrainian town. Some believe the reactor was built over Jewish graves and that it melted down on the anniversary of the death of the chief rabbi buried beneath it. The **Chertkoff Synagogue's** chief rabbi predicted in 1840 that the messianic redemption would begin when 600,000 Jews inhabited the Land of Israel. It's almost 50 years late.

The **Caro** and **Ha-Ari (Ashkenazi) Synagogues** are the most famous in Tzfat. To reach the Caro Synagogue, take Ma'alot Oleh Ha-Gardom St. off Jerusalem St. and turn right onto Beit Yosef St. Ask to see the old books and Torah scrolls. It was here that Yosef Caro, chief rabbi of Tzfat and author of the vast *Shulḥan Arukh* ("The Set Table," a standard guide to daily life according to Jewish law), studied and taught in the 16th century. In the basement is the angel with whom he used to confer (Rabbi Alkabetz purportedly witnessed their talks). To reach Ha-Ari Synagogue, follow Beit Yosef until it becomes Alkabetz St., take a right up a stairway marked with stained glass Stars of David, and continue under the stone arch. The synagogue will be to your right on Najara St. Rabbi Isaac Luria, the famous mystic and founder of Lurianic *Kabbalah,* led congregants outside to welcome the Sabbath bride at this site. He is most famous for penning the *Kabbalah Shabbat,* an arrangement of prayers in preparation for the Sabbath; Alkabetz, his student, wrote the now-standard liturgical hymn *Lekha Dodi.* The lion at the top of the ornately decorated Ark was originally painted with the face of Moses, but some of the features have been rubbed off by those who deemed the hybrid beast blasphemous. Around the corner from Ha-Ari Synagogue is **Safed Candles** (tel. 692 10 93), a Ḥasidic factory producing intricate, colorful beeswax candles (starting at NIS9) and figurines. A Sephardic Ha-Ari Synagogue lies farther down the hill near the cemetery. Just downhill from the Caro Synagogue, off Abuhav St., stand the **Abuhav** and **Alsheih Synagogues.** Take a left off Beit Yosef St. onto Alsheiḥ St. and make a sharp right; both buildings will be to your right. Abuhav's ark contains a Torah written by the its namesake, Rabbi Issac Abuhav (1433-1493). Only Caro, Ha-Ari, and Abuhav are open to the public; dress modestly and don't take pictures on *Shabbat.*

Stenciled onto many of the Old City's buildings is a funny-looking Hebrew sentence that reads נ נח נחמ נחמן מאומן, or "Na-Naḥ-Naḥma-Naḥman from Uman." The words refer to the late Naḥman of Breslev, leader of the Breslever Ḥasidic sect, whose followers chant his name in this fashion to bring good fortune. The lucky charm is omnipresent in Tzfat, and can be spotted throughout the Galilee.

Three adjoining **cemeteries** sprawl on the western outskirts of the Old City off Ha-Ari St. Follow the steps all the way down, past the new stone buildings on the left. The small building on the left when the path turns into the cemetery is Ha-Ari men's *mikveh,* or ritual bath (women should not enter). This *mikveh* was the bathing place of Ha-Ari himself, and its vibes have attracted the interest of mystics the world over, including the Dalai Lama. Taking a dip in the ice-cold water is strictly a no-clothes affair; serious shock and shrinkage have been reported.

The oldest cemetery contains the 17th-century graves of the most famous Tzfat Kabbalists as well as a domed tomb built by the Karaites of Damascus to mark the grave of the prophet Hosea. Legend has it that hidden under this same hill lie Hannah and her seven sons, whose martyrdom at the hands of the Syrians is recorded in the Book of Maccabees. This cemetery is the domain of an eighth-generation Tzfat resident named Mordekhai Shebabo, who left his position as a pedicurist to single-handedly restore the graves. Every visible grave is the result of this man's prowess.

At the very bottom of the Oleh Ha-Gardom steps, **Beit Hameiri** (tel. 697 13 07) contains a museum of old tools and furniture and an institute for the study of the history of Jews in Tzfat. Mango-colored signs point the way here from anywhere in town. (Open Sun.-Thurs. 9am-2pm; Fri. 9am-1pm; Aug. Sun.-Thurs. 9am-2pm and possibly 4-6pm. Admission NIS6, students NIS5.)

## ENTERTAINMENT

*Shabbat* in Tzfat brings tranquility, introspection, and not much else. For those in need, there are two pools in which to chlorinate any mysticism away. To get to the **Blue Valley Swimming Pool and Leisure Center** (tel. 692 02 17), walk down Ha-Atzma'ut Rd. from the bus station and turn left. The turn-off will be 100m farther on the left. (Open July-Aug. Sat.-Thurs. 8am-7pm, Fri. 8am-6pm. Women only Tues. and Thurs. 1-5pm; men only Sun. and Fri. 1-5pm. Admission NIS17, students NIS10.) The other pool (tel. 697 42 94), in the industrial district of south Tzfat (take bus #6 or 7), is heated, has a sauna and ping-pong, and is open year-round. (Open Sun.-Thurs. noon-9pm, Fri. 11am-5pm, and Sat. 10am-5pm. Women only Mon. 6-8:30pm; men only Wed. 6-8:30pm. Admission NIS17, students NIS10.)

Tzfat's nightlife is as quiet as the cemetery down the hill. The only decent pub in town is **Rafi's Bar** (0.5L beer for NIS11) on the third floor of the *midrahov's* underground mall. Thursday night features live music, Friday has jazz and rock. A well-equipped kitchen serves steaks (NIS40) and frozen treats. Open daily 8pm-sunrise. The Yigal Allon Cultural Center on Ha-Halutz St. (tel. 697 19 80) occasionally shows recently released English **movies** on Saturday nights (NIS19).

For three days each summer the town draws huge crowds for its wild **klezmer festival** (Eastern European Jewish soul music) that has to be seen to be believed (outdoor concerts free, indoor concerts NIS30-50). Only Tzfat residents are permitted to park on the streets during the festival.

# ■ Near Tzfat

## MERON AND MT. MERON הר מירון

For two days every spring, the tranquil hillside surrounding Rabbi Shimon Bar-Yohai's tomb at Meron is transformed into the scene of a frenzied religious carnival. The 2nd-century Talmudic scholar Bar-Yohai is believed by some to have authored the *Zohar,* the central work of the Kabbala (Jewish mysticism). To commemorate the date of his death (the holiday of Lag Ba'Omer, May 25 in 1997), thousands of Jews converge upon the town and revel in his greatness. The square outside the tomb becomes a Hasidic mosh-pit as crowds dance, shove, and chant Bar-Yohai's name. Tzfat's Hasidim make their way to the tomb carrying an ancient Torah scroll from the Bana'a Synagogue in the Spanish Quarter, and makeshift shops lining the hill sell a wide assortment of rabbinic and messianic paraphernalia. Contact Tzfat's GTIO for details on the festival.

Near the tomb are the ruins of an aesthetically unimpressive but historically noteworthy synagogue dating from the 3rd century CE, a time when Meron was important in the booming olive oil trade. From Bar-Yohai's grave, go past the *yeshiva* and follow the uphill path to your left. The lintel, an engraved stone slab that once decorated the entrance of the synagogue, is virtually all that's left of the edifice. Legend has it that this lintel's fall will herald the coming of the Messiah. The Israeli Department of Antiquities has nervously buttressed the artifact with reinforced concrete, but every Lag Ba'Omer pious Jews from Tzfat enthusiastically dance and stomp in an effort to accelerate their salvation.

Just west of the village is **Har Meron** (Mount Meron), the highest mountain in the Galilee at 1208m. A superb trail affords tremendous vistas of Tzfat and the surrounding countryside; on clear days you can see Lebanon and Syria to the north, the Mediterranean to the west, and the Galilee to the southeast. It's possible to ascend the mountain from the village of Meron, but a more convenient option is to take bus #43 from Tzfat to Kibbutz Sasa, northwest of the mountain (departs 6:45am, 12:30 and 5pm; returns 7:50am, 1:50, and 6:05pm; NIS8). In summer, catch the early bus to avoid the midday heat. From the kibbutz, continue 1km to the turn-off on the left, then walk 1km and turn right for the SPNI field school. Their **information office** (tel. (06) 698 00 23) offers a trail map (NIS44) and some advice. To reach the trail, walk down the road from the field school turn-off until you pass an army base on the right and a small parking lot on the left. The **trail** begins in the back of the lot and is indicated by stone and striped black-and-white trail markers. A one-hour walk brings you to the summit, peppered with red-and-white markers. Stay on the trail skirting the summit, as the very top of the mountain is the site of an army radar installation. Twenty minutes farther along the path you'll approach a picnic site and a traffic circle on a road; make a left and follow it for 20m to where the trail begins again. A long, easy descent, again marked with the black-and-white-and-red-all-over blazes, ends on a dirt road just above the village of Meron. Return to Tzfat either by retracing your steps to the kibbutz or by catching bus #361, 362, or 501 from the village of Meron (every 20min., first bus around 6am, last bus around 8pm, NIS6.20).

A final option is a thickly-wooded 4-hr. **hike** beginning at the *wadi* near the Tzfat cemeteries and ending at Bar-Yoḥai's tomb in Meron, marked by a wooden sign. Follow the green-and-white and then black-and-white markers. There is a free camp ground with running water and bathrooms on the right side of the road from Tzfat just before the Meron junction.

## ALMA CAVE מערת עלמה

Legend has it that the maze-like tunnels of Alma Cave form an underground bridge between the holy cities of Tzfat and Jerusalem and contain the corpses of 900,000 "righteous men." *Let's Go* does not guarantee that a day-trip to the Alma Cave will land you at the Dome of the Rock or yield encounters with long-deceased rabbis, but if you would like to try your hand at the fine art of spelunking and are not daunted by mud, sweat, and claustrophobic conditions, the Alma Cave is a tailor-made adventure.

Do not bring large packs into the cave; they will not fit through some of the tighter spots. Bring one strong, reliable flashlight per person, and keep in mind that your clothes, hair, and skin will become saturated with mud. Alma Cave should only be tried by those who feel they can remain up to 108m beneath the earth for several hours without freaking out. It is safest to go during daylight hours with a group of at least three people.

The cave is situated between the Circassian-Muslim village, Reḥania, and the Tripolian-Jewish Alma. Bus #45 leaves Tzfat for Alma and Reḥania (NIS8) at 1:15, 4, and 6:30pm, and departs for Tzfat at 6:15, 9:15am, 1:45, 4:30, and 7pm. By car, drive north along the Tzfat-Meron highway, and continue past the Zeition Junction to Reḥania. Across the street from Reḥania village's entrance are several dirt paths heading in the direction of the cave. Some of them are fenced off, but don't despair. Stay close to Alma (to your left), and steer away from the hilly, tree-lined area to your right. The walk is about 1.5km and runs through fields of thorny shrubs (wear shoes and pants). The cave itself looks like a large boulder with a crack in the middle. Climb (or slide) down the hole, keeping to the right. At a depth of approximately 60m (one half to three-quarters of the way down) you should see two phallic rocks near the right-hand wall. Behind that lies a small hole leading to the "inner chambers" of the cave. There are markers indicating the correct path: white for the way in, red for the way out. When you reach a large room with a ridge and a steep slope, be sure to veer to your far right along the ridge instead of continuing down the slope. Near the end of the trail, the rocks become slippery and the caverns become filled with technicolor, dripping stalagmites and stalagtites. Getting out of the cave is a true physical challenge, involving steep climbs and tricky maneuvers.

## TEL ḤAZOR

The *tel* at Ḥazor is the largest archaeological mound in northern Israel. Excavations (still underway) have revealed 21 layers of settlements at the site, the oldest dating from the third millennium BCE. Like Megiddo overlooking the Jezreel Valley, Ḥazor was once a fortified city situated on the main trading route linking Egypt to Syria and Mesopotamia. In the Bible, Ḥazor is termed "the head of all those (northern Canaanite) kingdoms" (Joshua 11:10). The ferocious and brave Joshua, after winning a battle against a north Canaanite alliance at the Merom River, sacked Ḥazor and, following God's command, slaughtered the entire population. Ḥazor was rebuilt and expanded by Kings Solomon (10th century BCE) and Ahab (9th century BCE) and was finally laid to waste by Assyria's Tiglath-Pileser III during his army's march through the Galilee (732 BCE). At the *tel's* northern foot lies a vast lower city, still underground and currently closed to the public. The most impressive of the *tel's* ruins is the 38m-deep tunnel, engineered during Ahab's reign to bring water into the city in case of a siege; a spiral staircase lets you descend into the gaping pit.

Buses #501 or 511 from Tzfat (35min., NIS8.40) and all buses that run between Rosh Pina and Kiryat Shmona stop near the site. Don't get off at the sleepy town of Ḥazor Ha-Gelilit; rather, continue north to **Kibbutz Ayelet Ha-Shaḥor.** The kibbutz houses a small museum (tel. (06) 693 48 55) displaying Canaanite and Israelite artifacts and explaining some of the *tel's* layers. From there, the site's entrance is a 250m walk back up the road (tel. (06) 693 72 90; museum and site open Sat.-Thurs. 8am-5pm, Fri. and holidays 8am-4pm; admission for both NIS10, students NIS7.50).

### ROSH PINA ראש פינה

There is nothing to do in Rosh Pina but leave Rosh Pina. Located on the slopes of Mt. Kenaan, Rosh Pina ("cornerstone" in Hebrew) was the Galilee's first *moshav*. Because many buses heading north pass through, the town serves as a gateway to the Upper Galilee and Golan. From Tel Aviv, bus #842 goes to Rosh Pina (NIS27) and continues up to Kiryat Shmona. Bus #500 travels to Rosh Pina from Haifa (NIS21) and also continues to Kiryat Shmona. Take buses: #401, 459, 461, 501, or 511 to Tzfat (NIS7); #55, 56, or 57 to Katzrin (NIS8.80); and #480, 500, 842, 845, or 969 to Kiryat Shmona (NIS8.80). The **Nature Friends Youth Hostel** (tel. (06) 693 70 86; fax 693 43 12) is quiet and comfortable, with a fridge and fan in each room. Tent camping in the grassy area is NIS40 including breakfast, toilet, and shower. (Check-in 4-8pm. Checkout 10am. No curfew. Dorm beds NIS58, singles NIS117, doubles NIS166. Breakfast included.) Some travelers take the two-hour hike up the steep scenic road to Tzfat. Others wonder why they're here.

## ■ Kiryat Shmona קרית שמונה

**Kiryat Shmona** ("Town of Eight") commemorates Yosef Trumpeldor and seven others who were murdered in nearby Tel Ḥai in 1920. Situated on top of the ruins of the Arab village Al Khalsa (destroyed in the 1948 War), the city was given its new name in 1949. By virtue of its location on the Ḥula plain near the Lebanese border, Kiryat Shmona was the target of numerous bombings and terrorist attacks until Israel invaded Lebanon in 1982, and it has been subject to shelling by Iranian-backed *Hizballah* as recently as June 1996. The town thus graduated from its grim name to an even grimmer nickname: Kiryat Katyusha ("Town of Katyusha rockets").

Although it is the transportation and administrative center of the Upper Galilee, the city is little more than a pit-stop for most tourists. The **central bus station** (tel. 694 07 40 or 41, info. (04) 854 95 55) is on Tel Ḥai Blvd. (the main road). Buses #840, 841, or 963 run frequently between Tiberias and Kiryat Shmona (NIS15.40). To reach Tel Aviv, take bus #840, 841, 842, or 845 (NIS34). Buses #55 or 58 leave for Katzrin (Sat.-Thurs. 1:10 and 4:40pm, Fri. 12:45pm; return at 11:05am.) Rosh Pina is serviced by buses #480, 500, 842, 845, or 969 (30min., NIS8.80). Buses #501 or 511 go to Tzfat (every hr. until 7pm, 45min., NIS12.70). For a **taxi,** call Moniot Ha-Tzafon (tel. 699 23 33). For **first aid (Magen David Adom),** dial 101 or 694 43 34; for **police,** dial 100 or 694 34 44. The **post office** is south of the bus station and has **international telephone** and **poste restante** services (tel. 694 02 20; open Sun., Tues., and Thurs. 8am-12:30pm and 3:30-6pm, Wed. 8am-1:30pm, Fri. 8am-noon). Kiryat Shmona's **telephone code** is 06.

The nearest cheap accommodations are at the youth hostel in **Rosh Pina.** Falafel and *shawerma* stands sizzle around the intersection of Tel Ḥai Blvd. and Tch-

erniḥovsky St. Cafés and small restaurants can be found one block to the north and
south of the bus station. There is a **Co-op Tzafon supermarket** in the shopping complex just south of the bus station. On Thursday mornings there's an open-air *shuk* at
Tel Ḥai St., just north of the bus station.

# ■ Near Kiryat Shmona

## TEL ḤAI תל חי

Three km north of Kiryat Shmona, Tel Ḥai sits on a promontory overlooking the Ḥula
valley. Established in 1918 as a military outpost after the withdrawal of British forces
from the Upper Galilee, the town has become a symbol for Israel's early pioneer
movement and the struggle for the narrow mountain range west of the Ḥula Valley
region, known as "the finger of the Galilee."

Tel Ḥai has the dubious distinction of being the site of the first armed conflict
between Jews and Arabs within the current borders of the State of Israel. In 1920, a
group of Arabs gathered around the settlements of Tel Ḥai, Kfar Giladi, and Metulla
(then part of French-administered Syria and Lebanon) and accused the Jewish settlers
of protecting French soldiers who had been charged with encroachment on Arab
lands. Yosef Trumpeldor, the leader of Tel Ḥai, allowed four Arabs inside the settlement to search for the French agents. Once inside, the Arabs killed Trumpeldor and
seven others. The six men and two women were buried in nearby Kfar Giladi.
Trumpeldor's alleged last words, "No matter, it is good to die for our country," for
years epitomized Zionist convictions. The site offers a spectacular view of the Galilee
and the Golan Heights, and an audio-visual program tells the story in seven languages.

A monument to Trumpeldor stands on the compound's outskirts. The original
watchtower and stockade settlement has been reconstructed as a small **museum** (tel.
(06) 695 13 33) tastefully displaying farming tools (open Sun.-Thurs. 8am-4pm, Fri.
8am-1pm, Sat. 8:30am-2pm; admission NIS12, students NIS8). The recently opened
**Museum of Photography** (tel. (06) 695 07 69), in the industrial park on the right side
of the road, has a small display of modern Israeli photographs (open Sun.-Thurs. 9am-
4pm, Sat. 10am-5pm; admission to the park NIS8, students NIS4). There is a collection of antique cars in the building next to the photography exhibit.

Up a hill to the left of the main road is the **military cemetery** containing the graves
of the eight of Tel Ḥai. A statue of a roaring lion faces the mountains to the east. Fifty
meters farther, inside the gates of Kibbutz Kfar Giladi, is **Beit Ha-Shomer** (House of
the Guardian, tel. (06) 694 15 65), an IDF museum documenting the history of early
defense organizations in the Upper Galilee and the exploits of Jewish regiments in
the British Army during World War I (open Sun.-Thurs. 8am-3pm, Fri.-Sat. 8am-noon;
admission NIS5, students NIS2). **Buses** #20 or 21 from Kiryat Shmona go to Tel Ḥai (8
per day, NIS3.40). The hostel in Tel Ḥai is no longer open.

## KFAR BLUM כפר בלום

This kibbutz, southeast of Kiryat Shmona, has two unrelated attractions: classical
music and kayaking. The **Upper Galilee Chamber Music Days** feature a week-long
series of concerts in July. Tickets (NIS20-30 per concert) sell out rapidly, but you can
listen in on daytime rehearsals (call (06) 694 85 28 for details). On a different note, a
6km **kayaking** trip (tel. (06) 694 87 55) on the Jordan River costs NIS75 for two people and lasts about an hour. Inner tube rides (NIS25) are tamer but get your *tuchas*
wetter. Consult the *Galilee Guide,* available at the GTIO, for information on adventures in the region's gushing streams. Unfortunately, the streams tend to gush less
during summer, rendering some water adventures less than thrilling. Buses #29 or 30
run five times a day from Kiryat Shmona (NIS4.30).

## NATURE RESERVES OF THE ḤULA VALLEY

The five reserves of the Ḥula Valley showcase Israel's lush, forested, extreme north. Hikers in the reserve chance upon ice-cold streams and migrating birds. A **combined ticket** gets you Ḥula, Ḥorshat Tal, Tel Dan, Gamla, and Naḥal Ḥermon reserves for NIS26, and is available at all five areas.

In between Rosh Pina and Kiryat Shmona, the **Ḥula Nature Reserve** (tel. (06) 693 70 69) harbors what is left of the wildlife that once flourished in the swamplands of the Ḥula Valley before it was drained by Israel in the 1950s for agricultural use. The 775-acre reserve has dense cypress groves and open fields; a 1.5km trail circles through papyrus thickets, swamps, and reeds, the creeping ground of turtles, mongeese, waterbuffalo, and other critters. The **visitor's center** rents binoculars for bird enthusiasts (NIS7), and has a display and a 15-minute film about the area. Arrive early to see the most wildlife and to avoid crowded family-time in the forest. (Reserve open Sat.-Thurs. 8am-4pm, Fri. and holiday eves 8am-3pm. Admission NIS13.) Buses #501, 511, 840, or 841 (NIS8.80) leave Kiryat Shmona frequently and will take you to a junction 2.5km from the entrance to the reserve.

Huge hundred-year-old oak trees stand in the **Ḥorshat Tal Nature Reserve** (tel. (06) 694 23 60). According to a Muslim legend, the trees, which grow nowhere else in Israel, sprang into being thanks to the 10 warriors of Muhammad who once rested here. Finding a dearth of shade and not a single hitching post for their horses, they pounded their staffs into the earth to fasten their mounts. Overnight the sticks sprouted, and the holy men found themselves in a thick forest. The trees now tower over a grassy park which is crammed with picnicking families on Saturdays. The large, ice-cold **swimming pool** (actually the Dan River ingeniously diverted) is especially enticing. (Park open Sat.-Thurs. 8am-5pm, Fri. 8am-4pm; closes 1hr. earlier in winter; admission NIS19.) Next to the park is the **Ḥorshat Tal Camping Ground** (tel. (06) 694 23 60), on the banks of the Dan River. Sites next to the stream come with the soothing sound of gushing water (tent sites NIS25 per person, 4-person bungalows NIS140, prices rise 50% on *Shabbat* and holidays). From Kiryat Shmona, buses #26, 27, or 36 travel to Ḥorshat Tal (infrequently, NIS5.20).

Near Kibbutz Dan to the northeast of Ḥorshat Tal is the Ḥula Valley's most thickly forested nature reserve, **Tel Dan** (tel. (06) 695 15 79). Several short, easy walking loops follow the fast-flowing Dan River, a tributary of the Jordan. One of the trails is partially paved for wheelchair accessibility. Swimming is forbidden, but tired feet will find plenty of opportunities to wade in cool springs. Ongoing excavations at the *tel* have revealed the ancient Canaanite city of Laish, conquered and settled by the Israelite tribe of Dan around 1200BCE. The most interesting remains lie in the Cultic site, where King Jeroboam Ben-Nebat of the breakaway Kingdom of Israel placed a golden calf to rival Judah's seraphim-equipped religious center in Jerusalem (I Kings 12:28-29). Stick your head into one of the metal columns near the cultic site and feast your eyes on a miniature hologram of the ancient sacrificial scene. (Reserve open Sat.-Thurs. 8am-5pm, Fri. 8am-4pm. Admission NIS13. Ticket gives you a 25% discount at the Beit Usishkin Museum.)

In 1983 a remarkable find was made at Tel Dan: a broken stele, inscribed with the words "House of David" in 9th-century BCE Aramaic. To some, shattered earth; to Biblical history scholars, earth-shattering—the first known reference to the biblical King David outside the Good Book itself. A replica of the stele as well as other finds from the *tel* are on display in the **Beit Usishkin Museum,** a gray stone building on the way to Tel Dan. (Take a left at the wooden sign. Open Sun.-Thurs. 8:30am-4:30pm, Fri. 8:30am-3:30pm, Sat. 9:30am-4:30pm. Admission NIS9, students NIS7.50. Ticket gives you a 25% discount at the Tel Dan Reserve.) To reach the reserve, take bus #26 or 36 (NIS5) from Kiryat Shmona to Kibbutz Dan, continue up the main road, and turn left at the sign.

The Golan's **Naḥal Ḥermon Nature Reserve,** with its hugely popular **Banyas Waterfall,** is just a few kilometers east (see p. 409). The SPNI's **Ḥermon Field School** (tel. (06) 694 10 91) is in Kibbutz Senir, off the Banyas -Tel Dan road.

## METULLA מטולה

Nine km north of Kiryat Shmona, Metulla is Israel's largest village on the Lebanese border. The city's main attraction is **Ha-Gader Ha-Tova (The Good Fence)**, an opening in the border barrier between Lebanon and Israel through which Lebanese Christians and Druze are allowed to pass through to obtain free medical services, visit relatives, and work in Israel. Israel began passing aid and supplies through this point to Lebanese Christians in 1971, and in June 1976 the Good Fence was officially opened, remaining open even during the war in Lebanon. From the observation point you can see several Maronite Christian villages; on the farthest hill to the right (northwest) is the Crusader fortress of Beaufort, which was fortified by the PLO and used as a base for shelling Israel. A shop to the left of the fence sells Lebanese money. UN forces get a discount at the snack bar (careful—they card hard).

Israelis head to Metulla's new **Canada Centre** (tel. (06) 695 03 70 or 71), one of the top sports facilities in Israel and home to its only genuine ice-skating rink. The hefty admission fee (NIS30, students NIS22) includes skate rental, plus use of an enormous indoor pool with slides, a basketball court, jacuzzi, and sauna. Squash courts (NIS10 per hr.) and ping-pong tables (NIS5 per 45min.) are also available. Lockers are NIS3. (Open daily 10am-10pm).

**Bus #20** runs between Kiryat Shmona and Metulla (8 per day, NIS4.80). There are two pensions in Metulla, both along Ha-Rishonim, the main road. Metulla has spawned a handful of charming **pensions,** but there are no budget accommodations. If you stay in town, expect to pay at least NIS90 per person.

South of Metulla, the cool mountain air is moistened with mist from the 18m **Tanur Waterfall** in the **Iyun Nature Reserve.** The dense mist creates the illusion of billowing smoke and gives the waterfall its name: *tanur* means "oven." The torrent, magnificent in the snow-melting season, slows to a trickle after June. There are two other falls deeper in the reserve: Mill Falls cascades 21m down a broad wall to the widening cauldron at its foot, and Cascade Falls is topped by a small dam used by the British during World War II to draw water for their camps in the district. The Iyun reserve is accessible directly by bus #20 or 21 from Kiryat Shmona; ask for the turn-off to the waterfall *(mapal).* From there, it's a three-minute walk to the park (open Sat.-Thurs. 8am-5pm, Fri. 8am-4pm; admission NIS6, children NIS3.50).

# Golan Heights רמת הגולן

The Golan Heights offer visitors a relatively cool climate, breathtaking views, noteworthy archaeological sites, and dozens of streams and waterfalls bedecked with greenery. Best of all, this formerly volcanic plateau overlooking the Jordan Valley is sparsely-traveled—except in the springs, when busloads of loud Israeli teenagers on school-sponsored outings jam-pack the normally serene trails.

The first recorded mention of the Golan is the Biblical "Golan in Basham," a city established by Moses as a refuge for Israelites guilty of manslaughter (Deut. 4:43). An important holdout in the Jewish Revolt of 66-73 CE, one of the Golan's promontories sheltered the city of Gamla, called the Masada of the north (see Gamla, p. 407). In the next two centuries, the Golan became a center of Jewish population, as evidenced by excavations of ancient synagogues. As time passed, the Golan was little more than a backwater Syrian province until Turkish officials planted Circassian settlers there to block the activity of Bedouin highwaymen in the 1880s.

Recent history has again cast the Golan Heights into the jaws of political controversy. Throughout the 50s and 60s, Israeli towns in the Galilee were assailed by artillery fire from Syrian gunposts atop the Heights. Israel captured the Golan in the 1967 Six-Day War, but was pushed back by Syria's surprise attack in the 1973 war. Israeli forces quickly recovered and launched a counter-attack, capturing even more territory. As part of the 1974 disengagement accord, Israel returned both the newly conquered territory and part of the land captured in 1967. Israel officially annexed the remaining 768 square-km territory in 1981, arousing international protest. Today, Jewish settlements are scattered among Druze villages, rusting tanks, live minefields, and destroyed bunkers.

The future status of the Golan is currently under negotiation. Syria claims that the land was seized illegally and demands its return. Israeli officials had always invoked the issue of security in their refusal to budge from the Heights until the Rabin and Peres administrations announced their willingness to cede all or part of the Golan in exchange for peace and Syrian recognition of Israel. The reality is that whoever commands the elevated plateau enjoys strategic views of Damascus on one side and of all northern Israel on the other. The 1996 election was viewed by many as an indication of the Israeli public's opposition to a withdrawal from the Golan. Bitter anti-government protests and the popular bumper-sticker "the nation is with the Golan" attest to many Israelis' unwillingness to compromise with the same Syrian regime that fought Israel in two successive wars. Many of the Golan's 15,000 Druze, on the other hand, strongly identify with Syria and long to see their relatives across the border. Politics aside, the Golan is dear to Israelis as a major source of their water and as the home of ski slopes, apple orchards, wineries, and lush cattle pastures.

## GETTING AROUND

> The Golan Heights still contain active **land mine fields.** Stay on paved roads, and avoid fenced-off areas whether or not you see the yellow-and-red warning signs.

When wandering the Golan in the summer, you'll need a hat and buckets of water. Winter is cold, damp, foggy, and often snowy. The best time to visit the Golan is spring, when the heat is bearable and when cellophane flowers of yellow and green tower over your head.

The best way to see the Golan is to **rent a car** in Tiberias. If you don't plan on hiking, you can hit the major sights in two days. Don't be afraid to lean on your horn; in the Golan, two-way roads mean one of you pulls over to let the other one by.

Some sights in the Golan are accessible by **Egged bus,** but infrequent service along remote roads necessitates careful planning. Double-check all schedules and anticipate walking. Buses to sights near the Galilee generally leave from Tiberias. The Upper Galilee, Ḥula Valley, and northern Golan are served by buses from Kiryat Shmona and occasionally from Tzfat. Traveling by bus almost definitely writes off Gamla and many hiking trails.

Relatively few cars traverse the Golan, and reports of incidents in past years make hitchhiking inadvisable. If you decide to set out on your own, take a good map, several bottles of water, and at least a day's worth of food.

Organized **tours** are faster, more convenient, and can be less expensive, but may be rushed. **Egged** offers professionally guided full-day tours of the region from Tiberias (tel. (06) 679 10 80; March-Oct. Tues., Thurs., and Sat.; Nov.-Feb. Thurs.; US$35), Tel Aviv (tel. (03) 527 12 12; April-Oct. Sun. and Thurs.; Oct.-May, Thurs.; US$57), and Haifa (tel. (04) 854 94 86; April-Oct., Thurs.; US$53); there's a 10% discount for ISIC members. There are also private guides based in Tiberias. **Igal** (tel. (06) 672 45 74) attracts a young backpacker crowd and gives tours that combine sight-seeing with light hiking (NIS90). **Moshe Cohen** (tel. (06) 672 16 08) makes military history-oriented rounds in a taxi (NIS90). **Max Ballhorn** (tel. (06) 679 35 88) gives Egged-style tours (NIS90). Three-day **SPNI** hiking and camping trips visit some hard-to-reach spots and, in summer, could include kayaking down the Jordan River. All give tours in English.

**Moshav Ramot** (tel. (06) 673 23 17) on the eastern bank of the Sea of Galilee runs guided **jeep trips** (2-hr. trip NIS450 for 7 people; NIS85 for each additional hr.) and will take you exploring in incredibly rugged, one-person **tractoronim** (all-terrain vehicles; NIS100 for 1hr., NIS170 for 2hr.). **Shevil-Golan** (tel. (06) 679 76 71) at Zeelon Beach near Moshav Ramot has jeep and *tractoronim* trips for similar prices.

The Golan's **telephone code** is 06.

# ■ Katzrin קצרין

The town of Katzrin is the administrative and municipal center of the Golan Heights and the ideal base from which to explore the area. Katzrin enjoys a high standard of living for a young settlement, but its economic growth has slowed with the possibility of an Israeli withdrawal from the Golan.

**Practical Information** Bus #55 from Kiryat Shmona approaches Katzrin from the north, passing the towns at the base of Mt. Ḥermon along the way (2 per day, 45min., NIS19.10). Buses #55-57 go to Katzrin from Rosh Pina (25min., NIS8.80). From Tiberias, reach Katzrin by bus #15, 16, or 19 (45min., 4 per day, first bus around noon, NIS17).

Those who wish to hike in the Golan should visit the **SPNI Golan Field School** (tel. 696 12 34) on Zavitan St., off Daliyot St. (the main road). They sell maps (NIS44) and patiently explain the region's trail options (open Sun.-Thurs. 8am-7pm, Fri. 8am-2pm). Five hundred meters east along Zavitan is a **campground** (tel. 696 16 57 or 37 53). Pleasant bungalows (4-6 beds) cost NIS140 each and tent sites are NIS15 per person. Registration is purportedly open 24hr.; ask for the manager at the Field School if no one is there. The Field School will also give suggestions for **housing** with families in the region.

There's a **public pool** next to the Archaeological Museum (tel. 696 16 55; open daily 9am-5:45pm; admission NIS20, students NIS15). The town center has a **Bank Leumi** (open Sun., Tues., and Thurs. 8:30am-12:30pm and 4-6pm, Mon. and Wed. 8:30am-12:30pm, Fri. 8:30am-noon), and a **mall** with a **CoOp-Tzafon Supermarket** (open Sun.-Thurs. 8am-6pm, Fri. 8am-3pm) and a **post office** (open Sun.-Tues. and Thurs. 8am-12:30pm and 3:30-6pm, Wed. 8am-1:30pm, Fri. 8am-noon). **Moniot Ha-Golan** (tel. 696 11 11) has a special NIS60 **taxi** fare to Rosh Pina.

**Sights** The tiny **Golan Archaeological Museum** (tel. 696 24 12 or 13 50), in the north end of town, at the opposite end of Daliyot St. from the field school, has an excellent, bilingual exhibit displaying artifacts from ancient synagogues and houses, including 6200 coins, some dating back to the New Stone Age. They show a 20-min. film on the Great Revolt battle in Gamla. (Open Sun.-Thurs. 8am-5pm, Fri. 8am-3pm, Sat. 10am-4pm. Admission NIS11, students NIS6.50.) The ticket includes admission to **Ancient Katzrin Park,** located just outside modern Katzrin (2km southeast along the road heading for Gamla), where excavations have unearthed a richly ornamented synagogue dating from the 4th to 8th centuries CE. Two reconstructed houses with furnishings based on finds from the excavations give a sense of daily life in the Talmudic village.

## ■ Near Katzrin: Gamla גמלא

For years the lost city of Gamla was nothing more than a legend from the pages of *The Jewish War* by first-century Jewish historian Josephus Flavius (Book IV, Ch. 1). After the Six-Day War, archaeologists scoured the region for a spot corresponding to ancient descriptions. Shmaryahu Gutman, who worked with a copy of *The Jewish War* in hand, finally uncovered the site. The film at Katzrin's museum is a great introduction before your visit.

In 67 CE, the Romans laid siege to the religious hilltop fortress packed with 9000 Jewish refugees. After many months, Romans on the nearby hills stormed down the corridor of land leading to the town. When the legion penetrated Gamla's walls, hordes of Jews fled up the ridge. The Romans followed, and on the steep trails beyond the town's confines, the Jews turned and massacred their pursuers. Weeks later, a second attack proved too much for the Jews, who hurled themselves over the ridge's steep rock face (some archaeologists take issue with Josephus's proclivity for over-dramatization and claim that Gamla's inhabitants were pushed over the cliff in the mayhem of battle). Only two women survived to tell the tale.

Getting to Gamla is tricky without a car. Bus #22 will drop you a half-hour away from the site. Otherwise, get a ride from Katzrin and walk 1km to the ridge overlooking the ruins; the descent to the ruins along the Roman route takes about 20min.; you'll need about two hours at the site. (Site tel. 676 20 40. Open Sat.-Thurs. 8am-5pm, Fri. 8am-4pm; closes 1hr. earlier in the winter. Admission NIS12, combo ticket including Gamla and four nearby nature reserves NIS 26.)

If you continue along the red and white trail past the ruins, you'll reach a lookout point over the magnificent **Mapal Gamla,** the Golan's highest waterfall. As you hike, look in the sky for soaring, rare, black **Egyptian eagles** who frequent this area.

## GOLAN HIKES

Those who wish to hike in the Golan should purchase the 1:50,000 trail map on sale at SPNI offices (NIS44). It is also advisable to consult the field school in Katzrin for up-to-date advice and information. Beware of **land mines** (see **warning**, p. 406). For more detailed directions and alternative trail options in the Golan, check out a copy of Joel Roskin's *A Guide to Hiking in Israel*, on sale at Steimatzky bookstores (NIS39). It's not safe to drink water from the streams. Bus service to the trails, when it exists, is very irregular; call Egged and plan ahead carefully.

For the most exciting and challenging hiking in the Golan, head to the **Ya'ar Yehudiya Nature Reserve** southeast of Katzrin. Most trails begin in **Ḥenion Yehudiya,** accessible by Bus #15 from Tiberias (leaves Tiberias around 1:30 and 6:30pm, returns in the morning; NIS12.60). To get to the Ḥenion by car, drive north along the lake from Tiberias, head east towards Katzrin, pass the Yehudiya Junction, and continue along Rte. 87 until you see the orange sign marking the site. The Ḥenion (tel. 696 28 17) is equipped with a parking lot, bathroom facilities, a kiosk, telephones, and a SPNI information desk. Bags can be stored for NIS7 per locker and **camping** is NIS6 per person. (Reserve open Sat.-Thurs. 7am-5pm, Fri. and holidays 7am-4pm; leave no later than 1hr. after closing time. Admission NIS12 per car, free for those without a car—you've suffered enough.)

The most popular part of the reserve is the action-packed **Naḥal Yehudiya** trail, consisting of an upper and a lower half. To reach both sections, follow the red and white markers past the old Syrian houses and into the Yehudiya Valley. Upon completion of the **upper trail** (3hr.), ascend the green and white trail to return to the Ḥenion; to complete the **lower trail** (4hr.), continue along the red and white trail, which finishes with an extremely difficult climb and a 1.5km walk back along the road. Both sections are full of enticing waterfalls and pools, some of which you must swim across to complete your hike; bring a bathing suit and plastic bags to protect your food and valuables. Jumping off the 9m cliff at the second waterfall is possibly dangerous, definitely forbidden, and almost universally executed by trail trekkers.

The reserve is also home to the slightly drier but equally beautiful **Naḥal Zavitan,** with a number of trail options: one begins near the field school in Katzrin and several start at Ḥenion Yehudiya. The **Upper Zavitan** is good for all seasons; the more difficult **Lower Zavitan** should be avoided in the winter due to occasional flash floods; the **Black Canyon** can only be negotiated by rapelling. The spring at **Ein Netef** contains the only drinkable water in the reserve; from here follow the red-and-white blazes to the spectacular **Brekhat Ha-Meshushim** (Hexagon Pool), where hundreds of hexagonal rock columns skirt the water's edge. The trail ends 7km down the road from the Ḥenion.

Southeast of the Zavitan and Yehudiya Rivers is **Naḥal El-Al** (no relation to Israel's major airline). In winter and spring, there is enough water here to swim beneath the falls. Bus #18 leaves Tiberias for El-Al (3 per day), and buses #18 or 19 return to Tiberias from Avnei-Eitan (4 per day). Start at Kibbutz El-Al, follow the red and white trail to **Mapal Ha-Lavan** (white waterfall), continue on to **Mapal Ha-Shaḥor** (black waterfall), and finish outside of Kibbutz Avnei Eitan (total hiking time about 5hr.).

Head to **Zaki** for a view-less but extremely refreshing hike just south of the Yehudiya Junction. Zaki is best visited between August and September, when sweltering heat makes cool water a godsend and when overhanging grapes are ripe. Hike in the stream following the green and white trail 3km; when you reach a pipe, get out of the water on the left side and return by way of a dirt path.

# ■ Northern Golan

## BANYAS AND NIMROD'S FORTRESS בניס וקלעת נמרוד

The Banyas springs in the Naḥal Ḥermon nature reserve form the site of an odd religious mix: Jesus chose his first disciple here, Muslims built a shrine to the prophet Elijah (Nabi Khadar) in the adjacent hill, and an ancient sanctuary dedicated to Pan, Greek God of nature and shepherds, remains carved into the cliffside. Because of its ancient association with Pan, the area became known as *Paneas* (Pan's Place), which was rendered in 'P'-less Arabic as Banyas. The town of Banyas itself was settled by the Arabs in the 7th century and ruled by Crusaders until 1165. It remained an Arab village until the 1967 War. Families and other visitors now flock to the reserve for an afternoon of light hiking and swimming.

Banyas (tel. 695 02 72) lies only a few minutes down the road from Dan and Horshat Tal in the Upper Galilee. Although Banyas is the most popular site in the Upper Galilee-Golan area, public transportation here is woefully inadequate. During the winter, bus #14 from Kiryat Shmona to Neveh Ativ passes by (NIS7.90), leaving and returning once a day. Bus #55 travels from Kiryat Shmona through the Golan by way of Banyas twice per day, but the last bus back to Kiryat Shmona is at noon. If you want to spend the afternoon at the park, walk 5km west to Kibbutz Dan; the last bus (#35 or 36) leaves the kibbutz around 7:30pm. (Park open Sat.-Thurs. 8am-6pm, Fri. 8am-5pm. Admission NIS13. Combo ticket to 5 area reserves NIS26.)

An easy 45- to 60-min. hike from the park entrance leads to the **Banyas waterfall** *(Mapal Banyas)*, the largest falls in the region. Just across the stream running through the park is a wooden sign marking the beginning of a path to the waterfall. All subsequent signs are in Hebrew, but there are only two forks. Go right at the flour mill/Druze pita bakery. Farther along the path is a clearing by an ice-cold pool, where three paths intersect; the middle and right-hand paths lead to the waterfall.

**Nimrod's Fortress** *(Qal'at Nemrud)* stands 1.5km northeast of Banyas on an isolated hill. According to the biblical table of Noah's descendants, Nimrod was "the first on earth to be a mighty man" (Genesis 10:8). Legend holds that, besides fashioning sandals and building the Tower of Babel, he erected this gigantic fortress high enough to shoot arrows up to God. A plaque above one gate reads in Arabic: "God gave him the power to build this castle with his own strength," which must have been phenomenal, judging from the size of the stones he schlepped up the steep cliffs. Historians, who just love putting holes in myths, say the fortress was actually built by the Muslims and originally named Qal'at Subeiba. The view from the top of the fortress is unrivaled anywhere in the Upper Galilee or Golan. The one-hour, uphill approach to the castle, from which there is a clear view into the tiny Druze village of Ein Qinya, is just off bus route #55 between Kiryat Shmona and Katzrin; the road leading to the castle is directly across from the bus stop. Bus #14 from Kiryat Shmona to Neveh Ativ also passes by here. Alternatively, the castle is accessible by a footpath from Banyas, beginning directly above the springs. This shadeless walk takes about 45 minutes each way.

## MAS'ADA AND MAJDAL SHAMS مسعدة و مجدل شمس

The Druze of these two villages at the foot of Mt. Ḥermon differ from the Galilee's Druze in one major respect: most have remained loyal to Syria and many refuse to accept Israeli citizenship. In 1982 they staged a protest against Israeli rule and the IDF was sent in to restore control. Since then, the villages have been quiet.

Mas'ada and Majdal Shams are far less primed for tourists than their counterparts in Carmel—there's absolutely nothing to do. The emphasis here is more on tradition than on commercialism. Women walk around swathed in black and men wear black *shirwal* (low-hanging baggy pants), which date from Ottoman times.

**Mas'ada** is located at the foot of Mt. Hermon, at the intersection of the roads leading south to Katzrin and west to Kiryat Shmona. Mas'ada's farmers cultivate the valley and terrace the low-lying ridges around the mountain. Two km down the road is the locally famous lake, **Birket Ram.** The perfectly round body of water is something of a geological peculiarity formed by underground water-bearing strata. You'll know you've reached the lake when you see the parking lot of the excellent two-story **Birket Ram Restaurant** (tel. 698 16 38). Their specialty is "Lamb in the Oven" (NIS40), while standard *shishlik* (NIS38) and liver (NIS30) are also available (open daily 8:30am-6:30pm). From the restaurant's roof you'll see a postcard-worthy view of a Druze mosque beneath (seasonally) snowy Mt. Hermon. A small hut in the parking lot sells delicious Druze pita with *labaneh* and *za'tar* (NIS8). A lakefront swimming and picnic area costs NIS5 to enter (free for restaurant patrons).

**Majdal Shams** ("tower of the sun" in Arabic), the largest town in the Golan (pop. 8000), is a 5km walk along a quiet road through a lush valley. The town abuts the border with Syria; an Israeli lookout tower looming above the village sees eye-to-eye with its Syrian counterpart on the opposite peak, while a white UN base spans the neutral valley in between. Because the electric-fence border is closed and pocked with land mines, the lookout area on the outskirts of town has become the site of a sad but fascinating daily ritual. Majdal's Druze line up on the hillside (aptly dubbed *Givat Ha-Tza'akot* or "Shouting Mountain") and, armed with bullhorns, make small-talk with their relatives on the Syrian side. The best time to witness this is on Friday and Saturday afternoons.

Two km past Majdal Shams is **Moshav Neveh Ativ** (tel. 698 13 33), founded after the Golan was captured by Israel. The *moshav* has developed a horridly expensive resort village to take advantage of the ski slopes on the southern face of **Mount Hermon,** 10km away. Bus #55 travels from the *moshav* to the villages (2 per day, NIS8.80). It's also possible to take a *sherut* taxi from Mas'ada to Kiryat Shmona in the late afternoon for the same price. The road from Mas'ada to Kiryat Shmona is scenic, running west along a gorge and past the hilltop village of Ein Qinya and the silhouette of Nimrod's Fortress.

About 5km before the border with Syria are two kibbutzim, **Merom Golan** and **Ein Zivan.** These were the first Israeli settlements in the Golan, founded a few months after the Six-Day War. From the observation point you can see the destroyed Syrian city of **Quneitreh,** a border town-turned tourist attraction (see p. 536).

---

### Kosher Hot Dogs

Israel may not have Colorado's reputation as a skier's mecca, but its sole ski resort, Mt. Hermon, offers slopes that even frequenters of Vail will find enticing. The snow-capped peak rarely gets bitter cold, and in good seasons the trails are blanketed with meters of white stuff. The mountain straddles the Syrian border, and towers over 2800m (although the top of the cable car is actually much lower). Skiing on the Hermon can be challenging; there are no trees, and steep dips in the wide expanses are easy to miss. Beginners, however, should not fret—gentle runs descend from the top of each lift. On clear days, skiers can see the Galilee stretch out beneath them. On cloudy days, the mountain seems to jut out of a sea of vapor. Lift tickets are NIS110 and rentals are NIS90. Call (06) 698 13 37 or (03) 565 60 40 (year-round) for ski conditions and lodging information.

# The Negev הנגב

Pocked with craters and *wadis*, the Negev Desert covers just over half of Israel's territory. Long the domain of Bedouin, archaeologists, and visionaries like David Ben-Gurion, the Negev is entering mainstream Israeli life as towns and kibbutzim fulfill the Biblical prophecy of making the desert bloom. New technologies like drip irrigation and hydroponics are turning scorched red earth into banana and citrus groves, and new waves of immigrants are turning backwater desert settlements into boom towns. Be'er Sheva, the capital of the region, is the fastest growing city in Israel. As highrises and McDonald's spring up in Israel's cities, however, purists escape to the Negev's less populated parts: the craters and valleys of the desert are lined with miles of marked trails, and remote villages are becoming a haven for meditators.

Tourism in the Negev once revolved around two areas: the colorful beaches of Eilat and the mineral-rich waters of the Dead Sea. In recent years, the Negev Tourism Development Administration has sought to introduce travelers to the beauty of the harsh desert landscape. Their free pamphlet, *Sculpted Wilderness*, is available at tourist offices and offers a comprehensive introduction to the various regions of the Negev. Although tourism has skyrocketed, these 12,000 sq. km of desert have become no less forgiving. Temperatures soar at midday—those caught without a hat and water will see vultures circling overhead in a matter of minutes. Desert outfitters recommend that hikers bring one liter of water for every hour in the sun.

It's possible for hardy heat-lovers to tour the desert on vinyl Egged seats, but buses in the Negev are steamy and infrequent. Organized **tours** are a cooler option for carless sorts. The bus tour organized by the **Ben Yehuda Hostel** (tel. (02) 624 80 21) in Jerusalem gives a one-day overview of the desert and hits all the major sights, including sunrise on Masada and lunch in Jericho (12hr., NIS50). Hostel-run tours don't include sites admission. **SPNI** arranges excellent hiking tours around the Dead Sea. All-day Thursday tours are US$59, and two-day Friday-Saturday tours are US$177, including transportation, food, and lodging when applicable (Jerusalem office tel. (02) 625 23 57, Ein Gedi field school tel. (07) 658 42 88). A more exciting (though expensive) option to see the Negev is on a **jeep tour** (see **Desert Shade**, p. 429).

# THE DEAD SEA ים המלח

How low can you go? At almost 394m below sea level, this is about it—the Dead Sea is the lowest point on the surface of the planet. If that doesn't sound momentous, wait until you drive in from Be'er Sheva or Jerusalem, pass a "sea level" signpost, and then round a bend to see entire mountain ranges whose peaks are below you. The morbid moniker was coined by Christian pilgrims astonished by the apparent absence of any form of life in the sea's waters. Kill-joy scientists have recently discovered microorganisms in the lake. Its Hebrew name, Yam Ha-Melaḥ ("The Sea of Salt"), is more to the point: the lake has a salt concentration eight times that of ocean water. It is this high concentration of minerals that attracts tourists to the bitter, oily waters—the dissolved minerals make the water so dense that even fish would have to walk.

The Dead Sea is really a large lake, 65km long, up to 18km wide, and up to 400m deep. It's part of the Great Rift Valley that extends from southern Africa to Turkey and is filled with water from floods and underground streams in the surrounding desert. Although there is no outlet for the lake's water, the intense sun beating down on the valley used to evaporate just enough water to keep the water level constant. Recent Israeli and Jordanian water diversion projects have caused the Dead Sea to shrink—so much so that a sand bar has emerged, cutting off the southern tip of the lake

For many visitors, the Dead Sea is good for a quick dip, get the famous reading-a-magazine picture, and a much-needed shower. For others, the Dead Sea is **therapy.** According to a few scientists and all resort owners, concentrations of bromine, magnesium, and iodine 10 to 20 times higher than in the ocean can reduce skin allergies, stimulate glandular functions, and soothe the nervous system. Dead Sea mud is supposed to do wonders for the skin—those terrifying dark brown creatures by the shore are actually people caked in mud.

## ■ Practical Information

Caution: this water is powerful stuff. When it's good, it cures arthritis, but when it's bad, it's very bad. If Dead Sea water gets into your eyes, you're in for several minutes of painful blindness. Rinse your eyes immediately in the fresh-water showers found on all beaches. Don't shave the morning before you go swimming; the water will sear minor scrapes you didn't even know you had. Free public beaches are at **Ein Gedi** (located in the central Dead Sea area), **Ein Bokek** (about 40km south of Ein Gedi), and at **Ḥamei Zohar** (4km south of Ein Bokek, near the Moriah Hotel). Since you'll probably want to wash off as soon as you get out of the water, stick to these beaches, all with public showers. Ḥamei Zohar has a section of beach where men and women are separated—making both the religious and shy nudists quite happy. All are accessible by bus. Thermal baths, spas, and mud-baths are run out of hotels in and around Ein Bokek and have separate bus stops.

The Dead Sea does not have an ordinary desert climate—instead of being harsh and dry, it's harsh and humid. The sticky air, especially in the summer, makes high temperatures barely tolerable. Athletes may enjoy the clean air and 10% increase in oxygen concentration, but exertion is sane only in the early morning. The steamroom-like weather has been known to dehydrate people simply waiting at a shaded bus stop. Standard desert rules apply: keep your head covered and take a water bottle wherever you go. Don't assume that all shower and faucet water is safe to drink—most Dead Sea locations have special faucets marked "Drinking Water."

Only a few Egged lines travel the Dead Sea coast. Waits often last 45 to 90 minutes, so check schedules (under Practical Information for each site) and plan ahead. Take bus #444, 486, or 966 from Jerusalem to Eilat stop at Qumran, Ein Feshka, Ein Gedi, Masada, and Neveh Zohar. Bus #487, also from Jerusalem, runs only to Qumran, Ein Feshka, and Ein Gedi. Bus #385 makes about four trips per day (Sun.-Fri.) between Ein Gedi and Be'er Sheva via Arad, Ein Bokek, and Masada. Note that reservations for seats on the Eilat bus from Jerusalem cannot be made at Ein Gedi or Masada. Your chances of getting an unreserved seat are better at the height of the tourist season, since Egged often runs two buses at a time to accommodate the crowds.

Each of the region's attractions can be seen in a few hours or a half-day at most. Infrequent bus connections, the isolation of the sights, and the fact that some attractions can only be reached via long hikes from the main road make **renting a car** an excellent idea. Most companies offer a daily rental rate of about US$50-60. Driving in the Dead Sea region provides spectacular vistas, but be careful—steep, windy roads mean nothing to speed-demon Israeli drivers. The best place to rent is Jerusalem, since cutthroat competition drives prices down (see Practical Information, p. 286). If you are set on renting a car in the Dead Sea area, Rent-A-Reliable-Car (tel. 658 44 52) or Hertz (tel. 658 44 33), located in Ein Bokek, can get you rolling.

There are two **telephone codes** for the Dead Sea region: 02 for the northern part (Qumran and Ein Feshka), and 07 for Ein Gedi and points south.

## QUMRAN קומרן قمران

In 1947, a young Bedouin looking for a wayward sheep threw a rock into a cliffside cave and heard something break. Upon further inspection, he found a collection of earthenware jars containing 2000-year-old parchment manuscripts. These famed **Dead Sea Scrolls** are an important source for understanding the development of the Hebrew Bible. The largest, now displayed in the Shrine of the Book at the Israel

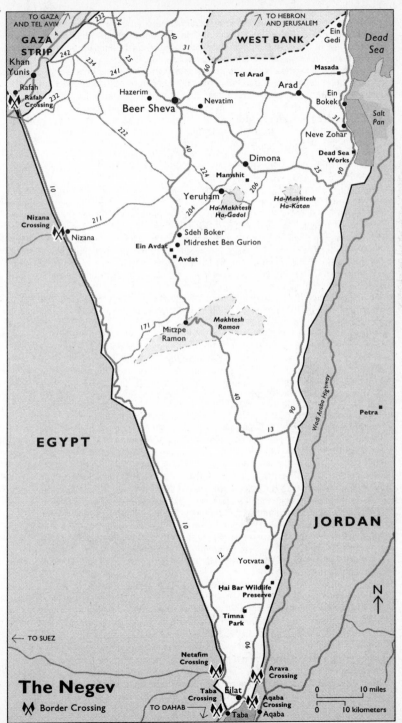

TO GAZA
AND TEL AVIV

TO HEBRON
AND JERUSALEM

**GAZA
STRIP**

WEST BANK

Ein
Gedi

*Dead
Sea*

Khan
Yunis

Rafah
Rafah
Crossing

Masada

Hazerim

Tel Arad

Arad

**Beer Sheva**

Nevatim

Ein
Bokek

Nizana
Crossing

Nizana

Dimona

Neve Zohar

*Salt
Pan*

**Dead Sea
Works**

Mamshit

Yeruham

*Ha-Makhtesh
Ha-Gadol*

*Ha-Makhtesh
Ha-Katan*

Sdeh Boker
Midreshet Ben Gurion

Ein Avdat

Avdat

*Makhtesh
Ramon*

Mitzpe
Ramon

Petra

**EGYPT**

**JORDAN**

TO SUEZ

Yotvata

Ḥai Bar Wildlife
Preserve

Timna
Park

Netafim
Crossing

Arava
Crossing

**The Negev**

Taba
Crossing

Eilat

Aqaba
Crossing

TO DAHAB

Taba

Aqaba

▼ **Border Crossing**

0        10 miles

0      10 kilometers

Museum in Jerusalem, was a 7m-long ancient Hebrew text of the Book of Isaiah. Encouraged by the discovery, French archaeologists searched the caves and excavated the foot of the cliffs. By 1956 they had found the village of the sect that wrote the Dead Sea Scrolls, as well as additional scrolls.

Archaeological evidence suggests that the site was settled as long ago as the 8th century BCE, re-inhabited in the 2nd century BCE, temporarily abandoned during the reign of Herod following an earthquake, and completely deserted after the Roman defeat of the Jewish revolt in 70 CE. Historians conclude that the authors of the scrolls were the **Essenes,** a Jewish sect whose members, disillusioned by the corruption and Hellenization of fellow Jerusalemites, sought refuge in the sands. The strict and devout Essenes believed that a great struggle would ensue between the Sons of Light (themselves and the angels) and the Sons of Darkness (everyone else). Excavations at Masada suggest that the members of the Qumran sect joined with the Jews there in the struggle against the Romans.

The main archaeological site is small. Look for the cisterns and channels that were used for storage and transport of water in the arid climate. The **watchtower** gives you a panoramic view of the site. Proceed to the **scriptorium,** the chamber in which the scrolls were probably written, still equipped with desks and inkstands. In the newly-excavated **honey press,** dates (rather than bees) were used to produce the sticky substance. The ruins are clearly marked, and a map of the site is posted just past the entrance. A short climb brings you to the **caves** themselves which are now empty and uninteresting. If you have a backpack, the staff at the reception booth will usually stare at it for no charge.

To see the ruins, take bus #421, 444, 486, or 487 from either Ein Gedi (NIS15) or Jerusalem (NIS16.50). When you get off the bus, cross the road to a steep hill with a road winding around its top. Don't panic—it's only a 100m hike, and the ruins are right around the bend. Make your way past the **boutique** selling the usual tourist crap (open daily 8am-5pm), then pass the adjoining clean, air-conditioned, self-service **cafeteria** (sandwiches NIS9, salad bar NIS16, hot lunch NIS26). To your right are **public bathrooms,** and across from them is the entrance to the site. The ticket counter (tel. 994 22 35) has brochures describing the history and layout of the ruins. (Admission NIS10, students NIS7.50, children NIS5. Open summer Sat.-Thurs. 8am-6pm; winter 8am-4pm.)

### Near Qumran: Ein Feshka فشكى عين עין פשקה

Relief from the heat is nearby: take any southbound bus (i.e. towards Masada, Ein Gedi, and Eilat) 3km to the salt- and fresh-water bathing spot at **Ein Feshka** (also called Enot Zukim; tel. 994 23 55), where springs wind through the *wadi's* tangled reeds and tumble into small pools. Ein Feshka is the only Dead Sea resort with fresh-water ponds adjacent to the swimming area. Ninety-five percent of the bathers here are West Bank residents; until several years ago, the place was popular with Jewish Israelis, who are now uncomfortable traveling via Jericho. There are many more men than women here, and the females who do show do not show much. Still, the welcoming management notes that travelers may dress as they like (admission NIS25, students NIS15). There are showers, changing rooms, bathrooms, and drinking water. The beach has a lifeguard (in case you don't float?) and plenty of gray **Dead Sea Mud** (open daily 8am-4pm).

Seven kilometers north of Qumran is **Attraction Water Park** (tel. 994 23 91) in Kalya Beach (bus #421, 444, 486, or 487 will take you, but be sure to cross the road from the ruins or you'll end up in Eilat). There are water slides, games, outdoor aerobics, and Saturday performances for anyone willing to spring the admission cost (NIS45; open daily March-Oct. 9am-5pm).

## ■ Ein Gedi עין גדי

Today, Ein Gedi's lush **nature reserve,** endowed with cascading waterfalls, wildlife, and shade, offers refuge from the desert sun. Hyenas, wolves, and the elusive leopard all call the reserve home; also keep your eyes open for the camouflaged ibex, the shy fox, and the insidious hyrax. Ein Gedi has a long history of providing shelter. David fled to this oasis to escape the wrath of King Saul (1 Samuel 24), and it was here that he forsook the choice opportunity to slay his pursuing father-in-law, who was easy prey while relieving himself in a cave. During the second Jewish revolt (132-5 CE), rebel leader Simon Bar-Kokhba sought refuge here. His hiding place, the Letter Cave, can be visited about 6km southwest of the main settlement.

## PRACTICAL INFORMATION

Bus connections to Ein Gedi are rare and require advance planning. From Ein Gedi, bus #421 or 444 (7 per day) will take you to Jerusalem (NIS22, students NIS19). Get bus schedules from the Central Bus Station in Jerusalem. Bus #384 or 385 (5 per day) goes to Be'er Sheva (NIS25, students NIS22) via Arad (NIS18, students NIS16). Bus #486 (4 per day) runs to Masada (NIS9.80) and to the hotels at Ein Bokek (NIS13, students NIS11.50). Bus #444 goes to Eilat (6 per day; NIS40, students NIS35.50). There are three bus stops in Ein Gedi: the northernmost one is where you get off for the nature reserve, the youth hostel, and the SPNI field school. Farther south is the Ein Gedi Beach stop, where you'll find the beach, campgrounds, a mini-market, a restaurant, a gas station, and a first-aid station. Get off at the southernmost stop for the thermal baths and spas.

## ACCOMMODATIONS AND FOOD

Nights in Ein Gedi can be as hot as the days—think twice about sleeping without air-conditioning. Rooms in the **Beit Sara Youth Hostel (HI)** (tel. 658 41 65), just uphill from the Naḥal David entrance to the reserve, are nicely decorated, clean, well air-conditioned, and have private baths. The outdoor **bar** (open nightly 6-11pm) and terrace overlook the Dead Sea. There's no rigid lockout, but they don't want you hanging out in the rooms between 9am and 4pm. (Office open 7am-9pm. Check-in 4-7pm. Check-out 9am. No curfew. Dorm beds (8 per room) US$15, NIS60. Singles US$32.50, NIS125. Doubles US$46.50, NIS178. Each additional person US$17.50, NIS60. Nonmembers add US$1.50 or NIS4.) A 10-minute walk from the hostel along the winding, uphill road will bring you to the **SPNI Field School** (tel. 658 42 88; take bus #384 or 385 from Be'er Sheva or #486 or 487 from Jerusalem). The staff gives advice on hiking, distributes trail maps, and runs its own air-conditioned hostel. The dorms are often crowded with Israeli school field trips, so reservations are a good idea. (Office open Sun.-Thurs. 8am-4pm, Fri. 8am-1pm. Check-in 4-8:30pm during the week, 4-7pm on weekends. Check-out 9am. Gates locked at 10pm. No lockout. Dorm beds NIS63. Singles NIS174. Doubles NIS215. Dinner NIS35 during the week, NIS40 on weekends. Breakfast included.) The hostel also has a public kitchen, a tiny museum, a snake collection, a fantastic observation point, and a 15-minute audiovisual show about desert flora and fauna (NIS6). Farther south, at the Ein Gedi Beach bus stop, **Ein Gedi Holiday Resort** (tel. 658 43 42 or 44 44; fax 658 44 55) is just behind and to the right of the gas station. Bring your own sleeping bag or tent and they'll give you a lovely spot of dirt and bathroom facilities for NIS24. Lockers NIS6 (every time you open it). The campground also offers slightly cramped, air-conditioned **caravans** with kitchenettes, private baths, and cushioned benches. (Singles US$64, NIS202. Doubles US$71, NIS223. Each additional adult US$19, NIS65. 4-adult and 2-child max. Visa, MC accepted.)

Quick snacks are available at kiosks near the entrances to the nature reserve. **Kiosk Ein Gedi** has beer (NIS8) and lots of other goodies (open 7:45am-8pm). Next door, **Pundak Ein Gedi** (tel. 659 47 61) might be worth the steeper prices. This kosher restaurant switches from milk to meat between breakfast and lunch. Yogurt and omelettes available until about 11am; meat lunches NIS25 (open daily 8am-6pm, last hot meal must be ordered by 5pm).

ISRAEL

## SIGHTS

Of the two entrances to the **Ein Gedi Nature Reserve** (tel. 658 42 85 or 45 17), only the Naḥal David entrance, just inland from the youth hostel, is accessible by bus. Trail maps, information and lockers (NIS4) are available here. Well-placed railings provide support in steep areas, so hiking is not too difficult—aside from the heat. Dead Sea temperatures can make even inhaling strenuous, so get going when they open the gates (8am). Always bring at least two 1.5L bottles of water (you can fill up at the faucets just outside the gate).

An enjoyable 15-minute hike takes you up to **Naḥal David** (David's Stream), a slender pillar of water dropping into a shallow pool. The best part of the hike is an invigorating swim in the delightfully cold water. Twenty meters below the waterfall, another trail climbs up the cliffside to **Shulamit Spring.** From the spring, continue up the cliff to **Dodim Cave** (Lover's Cave), a splendidly cool, mossy niche at the top of the fall (30-min. walk). Proceeding left from the spring will lead you to the fenced-in remains of what was once a **Chalcolithic Temple,** used 3000 years ago as a regional sanctuary. From the Temple, either retrace your steps or take the steeply descending path to **Ein Gedi Spring** (25min.). From Ein Gedi Spring a roundabout path runs to Shulamit Spring, near the base of the waterfall at Naḥal David.

A fairly difficult climb along **Naḥal Arugot,** which begins in the parking lot of the Naḥal Arugot Rd. about 2km in from Rte. 90, leads to a hidden waterfall. Don't forget your swimsuit for this one. It's a good 40-minute walk from the road (look for the sign), but if you follow the stream you can't get lost. A beautiful deep blue pool rewards the exertion. The reserve is open 8am-3pm, but you can exit until 4pm (in summer 8am-4pm, last exit 5pm); you may not start hikes to Dodim Cave and beyond after 1:30pm (in summer 2:30pm). There is no eating or smoking in the reserve (admission NIS11, under 18 NIS6).

Ein Gedi has a free **public beach,** where oversized umbrellas and occasional picnic tables speckle the rocky sand. You can store your stuff here for a small fee. The water is more reminiscent of the nearby Mediterranean than the fluorescent green shores of Ein Bokek. Take a left from the entrance and walk north for ten minutes to find vats of the famous **Dead Sea mud** as well as more freshwater springs.

# ■ Masada מצדה

"Masada shall not fall again," swear members of the armored division of the Israel Defense Forces each year at this site. The Jewish Zealots' tenacious defense of Masada has been fashioned into a symbol of modern Israel, with some controversy about the metaphor's implications. As one of the major pilgrimage sites in Israel, every *kova temple*-wearing tourist comes here, and with good reason: the view of the Dead Sea is spectacular, the ruins are impressive, and the tales of martyrdom forever invoke conflicting emotions of tragedy and triumph.

The huge fortress *(Metzada)* was built as a refuge from marauding Greeks and Syrians by the Jewish High Priest Jonathan Maccabeus around 150 BCE, and was expanded to 610m by 220m a few decades later by John Hyrcanus I. In 40 CE, King Herod fled to Masada to avoid being massacred by Parthian-backed Hasmoneans. Masada was used once again in 66 CE, when the Judeans rebelled against Roman occupation; a small band of rebels, the original Zealots, captured the outpost. When the Romans gradually crushed the revolt, taking Jerusalem in 70 CE and destroying the Second Temple, Masada was the last holdout in all of Israel. With years' worth of food, water, and military supplies stashed behind its two defensive walls, Masada was ideally suited for resistance. The 967 men, women, and children held off thousands of Roman legionnaires through a five-month siege. The Romans, frustrated at first, called in their best engineers and constructed a wall and camps in a ring around the mount. They ultimately built an enormous stone and gravel ramp up the side of the cliff, using Jewish slaves as laborers in order to prevent the Zealots from shooting them down as the ramp was built.

When the defenders realized that the Romans would break through the wall the next morning, the community leaders decided that it would be better to die than to live as slaves. Each family burned its possessions and joined in the communal suicide plan. The Jews placed stores of wheat and water in the citadel's courtyard to prove to the Romans that they did not perish from hunger. The following morning, when the Romans burst in, they encountered a deathly silence. The only survivors, two women and five children, told the story of the martyrs of Masada. The story was recorded by Josephus Flavius, a Jewish-Roman general and chronicler.

## PRACTICAL INFORMATION

Masada lies 20km south of Ein Gedi, a few km inland from the Arad-Be'er Sheva road. **Bus** #421, 444, or 486 will take you to Jerusalem (11 per day; NIS28, students NIS24.50); #444 will take you to Eilat (6 per day, last bus on Fri. 3:15pm; NIS36, students NIS32.50); and #384 or 385 will take you to Be'er Sheva (5 per day; NIS25, students NIS22.50) via Arad (NIS15.50, students NIS14). Jerusalem-bound buses stop at Ein Gedi, and buses to Be'er Sheva and Eilat travel via Ein Bokek (NIS7.70).

## ACCOMMODATIONS AND FOOD

The **Taylor Youth Hostel (HI)** (tel. 658 43 49; fax 658 46 50), in front of you and to the left as you get off the bus, is surrounded by grass and shady trees. Each impeccable room has air-conditioning and a private bath. A TV lounge and barbecue area are available for guests. (Office open Sun.-Fri. 8am-1pm and 3-7pm, Sat. 4-7pm. Check-in 4-7pm. Check-out 9am, Sat. 10am. Dorm beds (6-8 per room) US$15, NIS60. Singles US$32.50, NIS125. Doubles US$46.50, NIS178. Extra person US$17.50, NIS60. Non-members add US$1.50 or NIS4 per person. Breakfast included.) A newly-renovated dining room serves tasty kosher meat dinners (NIS32). Limited lockers are NIS4. A concrete pavilion in front of the hostel accommodates **campers** for free. Nearby restrooms are fine.

Until renovations on the **restaurant** between the hostel and the cable car are complete, hungry climbers will be faced with an agonizing choice between two **snack bars.** The one next to the restaurant-in-progress sells citrus products galore (open daily 6am-11pm). Fresh-squeezed OJ (NIS10) and oranges (7 for NIS5) are perfect for pre- or post-hike refreshment. The snack bar farther up the slope (open daily 8am-4pm) sells sandwiches (NIS8), cold drinks (NIS5), and ice cream (NIS5-7).

## SIGHTS

There are three ways to climb the mountain: by cable car or by either of two foot paths. The more popular, more scenic, most convenient for the carless, and more difficult of the two is the original **Snake Path,** named for its tortuous bends. The hike takes about 45 minutes, and if you start early enough (gates open at 4:30am), you'll see the sun slowly rising over the Dead Sea 450m below—one of the most dramatic experiences in Israel. The **Roman Ramp** is the easier of the two paths and starts on Arad Rd. on the west side of the mountain. The starting point of this 30-minute hike is not accessible by public transportation, and the walk around the base to the Roman Ramp is extremely arduous and time-consuming. If you hike down the Ramp and walk around the city to the east side, stick to the SPNI trail; *don't* descend on the incline with the water pipe. Admission of NIS14, NIS10.50 for students is paid at the top of the summit. It's best to start hiking *well* before the afternoon, both to avoid the heat and to leave enough time for exploring. Drinking water is available only at the summit, so begin your ascent loaded with liquid.

The hiking-averse may prefer the **cable car** that stops near the top of Snake Path. It runs 8am-4pm (summer until 5pm), on Friday 8am-2pm (summer until 3pm), leaving every half-hour or when 40 passengers have assembled for the three-minute ascent. (Round-trip cable car fare including admission is NIS40, students NIS22.50. One-way including admission is NIS29, students NIS18.50.) Popular options are to hike up in the early morning and then take the cable car down when it gets hot, or to take the cable car up in the afternoon and hike down when the sun is less strong. The site officially closes at 5pm.

The ruins at Masada were unearthed in 1963 by a team of archaeologists headed by Yigael Yadin. About one-third of the ruins you see are actually reconstructed—a black line indicates the extent of the original findings. Directly in front of the entrance to the site stands a large sign with a map of the ruins outlining several walking tours. From the entrance, the Northern Palace, Herod's own private pad, is up and to the right. Across the site is the Western Palace, and the Southern Citadel is down to the left at the far end of the mountaintop.

The centerpiece of the **Northern Palace,** the **central public bath,** is well preserved. The palace's lower terrace has painted frescoes and intact capitals on fluted columns, suggesting the splendor Herod enjoyed even on a remote desert butte. In the bathhouse of the lowest section, the skeletons of a man, woman, and child were found, along with a *tallit* (prayer shawl).

From the top of the Herodian palace stairs, you can skirt your way around the western edge of the mountain. You'll soon come across the **Zealots' synagogue,** one of the oldest synagogues in Israel. Scrolls were found here containing texts from several books of the Torah (most are now on display at the Israel Museum in Jerusalem; see p. 313). The scrolls and discoveries such as a *mikveh* (ritual bath) indicate that the community followed Jewish strictures despite mountainous isolation and the siege. Continuing along the edge, the **Western Palace** houses a bakery and more splendid Herodian wall decorations. Next to the palace you'll find the **Byzantine Chapel,** built by Christian monks who once occupied Masada.

Farther south are stone stairs descending into a hole. Go down into the large cistern: it's part of the reservoir system that allowed the defenders to store an eight-year supply of water. Drinking water pours out of several taps on the mountain.

The Masada **sound and light show** lights up the fortress like a Las Vegas marquee. Shows are in Hebrew, but simultaneous-translation earphones (NIS12) are available (shows March-Oct., Tues. and Thurs. 9pm; tickets NIS27, students NIS23). Arrange round-trip transportation from Arad MTIO (tel. 695 81 44 or 59 33) before 1pm the day of the show (NIS25). You can't see the show from the Masada hostel, because it's on the wrong side of the mountain. You can, however, watch the show from a campsite for NIS12 (show ticket, campground, and summit admission package NIS38, students NIS33).

## ■ Near Masada: Ein Bokek עין בוקק

**Ein Bokek** is home to hordes of luxury hotels, two shopping centers, and racks upon racks of postcards. In summer, the beach is tourist-infested, a bright, aquamarine, spectacle. All buses passing through Masada (5km away) also stop here. For a Dead Sea challenge, try lifting *both* your legs at least 5 inches out of the briny waters at the same time.

There is no longer a tourist information office here; if you feel the need for one, call the **Jamar Region Tourist Information Office** (tel. 659 44 08). Menus in Ein Bokek are both uninspired and expensive, but two restaurants give discounts for flashing your *Let's Go:* **Hordus Beach Restaurant** (tel. 658 46 36) has a salad bar for NIS15 (main dishes NIS25-30, desserts NIS7; open Sun.-Fri. 8am-4pm, Sat. 8am-7pm). **Kapulsky** (tel. 658 43 82) is the other option (main dishes NIS35-60, open daily 8am-midnight). You're probably better off sticking to the **mini-market** in the white mall, to your left as you get off the bus. The grassy **Tamar Garden,** opposite Hotel Lot, is a prime picnic spot. **Tamar Taxi** (tel. 658 43 92 or 93; open daily 7:30am-9pm) can get you to Masada (NIS50) or Ein Gedi (NIS75).

# CENTRAL NEGEV

## ■ Be'er Sheva באר שבע

Tell any traveler or Israeli that you're going to Be'er Sheva, and he or she will probably raise a confused eyebrow. Though the city is important as an administrative and commercial center, the capital of the Negev isn't as popular with tourists as, say, Jerusalem. Unless you're a Russian immigration buff or a volunteer, Be'er Sheva's greatest and most infamous attraction is its lively Thursday morning **Bedouin market.** The other parts of Israel's fastest growing city offer a look at development moving so fast, you can see the pre-fab apartments rise before your eyes.

Be'er Sheva means both "well of the oath" and "well of seven" in Hebrew, and the Bible (Genesis 21:25-31) offers both etymologies. The Arabic name, Bir As-Sabe', also means "well of seven." As the story goes, Abimelekh's servants seized a well that Abraham claimed to have dug. The dispute ended with a covenant in which Abraham offered seven ewes to Abimelekh in exchange for recognition as the well's rightful owner. You can still see what many claim is **Abraham's well** today.

The Ottomans proclaimed modern Be'er Sheva a city in 1906 upon establishing a seat of government, a mosque, a school, and the governor's residence. They hoped that the city would function as a political, commercial, and administrative center for Negev Bedouin. Since Israel inherited the city in 1948, it has absorbed Jewish immigrants at a startling pace. Its mushrooming housing projects are home to immigrants from Morocco, Syria, Russia, Argentina, and Ethiopia, as well as the largest Albanian Jewish community in the world. Today, Be'er Sheva's 150,000 residents are doing their best to make tens of thousands of newly-arrived, frost-bitten Russians feel at home in the middle of the desert, and to welcome streams of Ethiopian newcomers into its sand and concrete grasp. The city, though not big on affordable accommodations, serves well as a transit point for short forays into the Negev.

### ORIENTATION AND PRACTICAL INFORMATION

The city's **central bus station** is located on **Eilat Street,** across the road from **Kenyon Ha-Negev** (a shopping mall), a good landmark from which to orient yourself. The bus station is divided into two sections: one for the red, inter-city Egged buses, and the other for the blue, independently-run municipal lines.

West of the central bus station, across Eilat St., lies the **Muslim Cemetery,** and just west of that is the **old city** area, a neat grid designed by Ottoman-commissioned German engineers. Most attractions are concentrated here, and major renovations are making the area less grimy. The main east-west streets start with the northernmost **Herzl Street.** Parallel to it is **Ha-Histadrut Street,** followed by **He-Halutz Street, Mordei Ha-Geta'ot Street,** and **Trumpeldor Street** farther south. The main north-south avenues begin with **Keren Kayemet LeYisrael Street** (Kakal or KKL to those in the know), which is the town's newly fountained pedestrian section. One block west is **Ha-Atzma'ut Street** (on which you can see the tower of the Negev Museum), and then **Hadassa Street.** The old city streets are reassuringly close together, so miscounting blocks or making a wrong turn isn't disastrous. **Ha-Nesi'im Boulevard,** which meets Eilat St. at Kenyon Ha-Negev, will take you north to **Ben Gurion University,** and ultimately to Tel Aviv and Jerusalem.

**Municipal Tourist Information Office (MTIO):** 6 Ben-Tzvi St. (tel. 623 60 01 or 02; fax 623 60 02), opposite the main entrance to the bus station, 2 doors right of the Hertz sign. Free brochures. Maps NIS5. Open Sun.-Thurs. 8am-4pm.

**Currency Exchange: Bank Ha-Poalim,** 40 Ha-Atzma'ut St. (tel. 629 26 62), corner of He-Halutz St. Open Mon. and Wed. 8:30am-1pm, Sun., Tues., and Thurs. 8:30am-12:30pm and 4-6pm, Fri. 8:30am-noon. **ATM** serves all major banking services. **Bank Leumi,** just past the post office on Ha-Nesi'im (tel. 623 92 22). Open Sun.,

Tues., and Thurs. 8:30am-12:30pm and 4-5:30pm, Mon. 8:30am-2pm, Wed. 8:30am-12:30pm, Fri. 8:30am-noon. **ATM** serves only Visa and Diner's Club.

**Local Buses:** Leave from Central Bus Station between Ha-Nesi'im and Eilat St. (tel. 627 73 81 or 82). Buses #2, 3, 7-9, 11, 12, 18, 21, or 22 all go to the *shuk* and the old city (5:20am-11pm), and #13 follows Ha-Atzma'ut St. to the Negev Museum and the Youth Hostel (every 20min., 5:20am-11pm). All local rides NIS2.10.

**Intercity Buses:** Connections from Central Bus Station on red Egged buses (tel. 629 43 11). To Tel Aviv: #370 direct to new central bus station or #380 direct to Arloz-orov Terminal (both every 20-30min. 5:30am-8pm; 1¼hr.; NIS17.50, students NIS16). To Jerusalem: #470 direct (every hr., 7-9am and 3-5pm, 1½hr.) or #446 express (every 30min.-1hr., 6am-8pm) NIS23.50, students NIS21. To Eilat: #394 express (every 1-1½hr., 7:50am-1:45pm, 3hr.), and #392, 393, 395, and 397 (all local with irregular schedules), NIS38, students NIS34.

**Sherut Taxis: Moniot Ayal** (tel. 623 30 33 or 53 33), in a booth next to the central bus station. *Sherut* to Jerusalem, Eilat, and Tel Aviv; 10% cheaper than buses, but you may have to wait for them to fill up.

**Car Rental: Hertz,** 5a Ben-Tzvi St. (tel. 627 27 68), across from bus station. Open Sun.-Thurs. 8am-6pm, Fri. 8am-3pm; minimum age is 23. **AutoRent Full Car,** 3 Hebron Rd. (tel. 627 99 34), has a minimum age of 21.

**English Bookstore:** Extensive selection of used books at **Mini Book**. (tel. 644 33 69) in the passageway between Hadassah and Ha-Histadrut St., opposite Israel Dis-count Bank. Open Sun.-Thurs. 8:30am-1pm and 4-7pm, Fri. 8:30am-1:30pm. The *kenyon* across from the bus station has a **Steimatzky.**

**Camping Supplies: Reta,** in the *kenyon*, (tel. 623 35 77), open Sun.-Thurs. 9:30am-9pm, Fri. 9:30am-2pm, Sat. 8-10pm; another branch across the street in the central bus station (same tel.), open Sun.-Thurs. 8am-6pm, Fri. 8am-2pm.

**Pharmacies: Pharmline,** 34 Herzl St. (tel. 627 70 34), across from the police station, open Sun.-Thurs. 8am-8:30pm, Fri. 8am-2pm. **Super Pharm,** in the *kenyon* (tel. 628 13 71), open Sun.-Thurs. 9am-midnight, Fri. 8:30am-5pm, Sat. 10am-midnight. Phone numbers of emergency night workers posted on Super Pharm door.

**Hospital: Soroka Hospital,** Ha-Nesi'im Blvd. (tel. 640 01 11). Take bus #4 or 7 and tell the driver to let you off at the new emergency room.

**First Aid: Magen David Adom,** 40 Bialik St. (tel. 627 83 33; **emergencies** tel. 101).

**Police:** 30 Herzl St. (tel. 646 27 44; **emergencies** tel. 100), corner of KKL St.

**Post Office:** Corner of Ha-Nesi'im Blvd. and Ben-Tzvi St., diagonally across from the bus station (tel. 629 58 32). This modern main branch has **Poste Restante, West-ern Union,** and **EMS** services, and international calling. Smaller branches on **Hadassa Street** and in the **City Hall** building. All branches open Sun.-Tues. and Thurs. 8am-12:30pm and 4-6:30pm, Wed. 8am-1pm, Fri. 8am-12:30pm.

**Telephone Code:** 07.

## ACCOMMODATIONS

Be'er Sheva has a slim selection of budget accommodations. If you arrive early, you can see everything of interest in the city before moving on to more wallet-friendly hostels elsewhere. If you can afford to stay here, Be'er Sheva is an excellent base for exploring the Negev. Numerous bus connections will save you tons of time, not to mention *tzuris* (trouble).

**Beit Yatziv Youth Hostel (HI),** 79 Ha-Atzma'ut St. (tel. 627 74 44), 4 blocks from the old city (take bus #13). This well-kept, no-bunks hostel has its own pool (NIS12 for guests). Clean rooms have private bath, closet, A/C, and table. Check-in after 3pm. Check-out 9am. No lockout or curfew. Dorms (4 beds per room) NIS69. Next-door **Guest House** has singles (NIS112), doubles (NIS158), and triples (NIS222). Nonmembers add NIS4-6 each. Full Israeli breakfast included. Dinner NIS30-37. Credit cards accepted.

**Aviv Hotel,** 40 Mordei Ha-Geta'ot St. (tel. 627 80 59 or 82 58), off KKL St. Bulgarian owners Berta and Shlomo run a tidy 22-roomer with embroidered wall hangings and sofas in the common room. Not only are the floors carpeted, but so are half the walls. Rooms have ancient but functioning private baths, A/C, and TVs, and some have balconies. Singles NIS90, doubles NIS120. Croissant-and-coffee breakfast included. 24hr. reception. Credit cards accepted.

**Hotel Ha-Negev,** 26 Ha-Atzma'ut, (tel. 627 70 26 or 627 87 44). Old but usable rooms. US$20, NIS77 will get you a bed; for US$25, NIS82 they'll throw in A/C and a shower. Check-in after noon. After midnight, ring bell at the outside gate. Checkout 11am. Breakfast US$7, NIS23. No credit cards.

## FOOD

Lined with falafel, *shawerma,* pizza, and sandwich stands, the pedestrian section on **Keren Kayemet LeYisrael Street** is the best place for affordable eats. For an American food fix, head to the food court on the lower floor of Kenyon Ha-Negev across from the bus station. **Kenny Rogers Roasters** serves chicken sandwiches for NIS16, and **Subway** subs are NIS6-16. For fast food diversity, get a full meal at **China Town** for NIS20-22. There's also a **Pizza Hut, Burger Ranch,** a **Kapulsky,** and a **Burger King** on the ground floor. (Most restaurants in the *kenyon* open Sun.-Thurs. 9am-midnight, Fri. 9am-1am, Sat. 10am-10pm.) The mall also features a **Hypershuk supermarket.** The cheapest place to buy drinks and fresh produce is the *shuk,* located just south of the central bus station and easily identifiable by its arched metal rooftops. The Thursday **Bedouin market** also has cheap foodstuffs. This is the city that spawned **Glida Be'er Sheva,** the ice cream sensation that's sweeping the nation. A waffle cone with five luscious scoops is NIS9.90. (50 Hadassah St., open Sun.-Thurs. 9am-1am, Fri. 9am-9pm, Sat. 10am-2am.) Two additional branches are in the *kenyon.* The following restaurants are all in the old city area:

**Bulgarian Restaurant,** 112 KKL St. (tel. 623 85 04). Claims to have been the first restaurant in Be'er Sheva. *Kabab, schnitzel,* and goulash (NIS25-40 each) have been served here since 1949. Bavarian custard or chocolate mousse only NIS8; calf's foot jelly NIS9. Mmmm. Open Sun.-Thurs. 9am-11pm, Sat. 10:30am-7:30pm.

**Beit Ha-Ful,** 15 Ha-Histadrut St. (tel. 623 42 53). The Egyptian bean concoction in a pita with salads NIS9; in a bowl, with classy garnishings, it's NIS15. *Shawerma* in pita is NIS9. Outdoor eating and a foosball table. Open Sun.-Thurs. 8:30am-12:30am, Fri. 8:30am-3pm, Sat. 9:30pm-12:30am. Visa, MC.

**Bis Lekal Kis,** 98 Mordei Ha-Geta'ot St. (tel. 627 81 89) dishes out generous kosher meat or fish portions in an A/C room (NIS15-25). While dining, help the owner think of a catchy translation of the restaurant moniker, literally "a bite for every pocket." Hummus NIS4. Open Sun.-Thurs 11am-4pm, Fri. 11am-2:30pm.

**Apropo,** corner of Herzl St. and KKL St. (tel. 623 67 11). Standard, reliable food in this A/C, pricey chain. Thai dishes NIS30-40, omelettes NIS23-28, pasta NIS28-31, and salads NIS24-31. Open Sun.-Fri. 8am-1am, Sat. noon-1am. Credit cards.

## SIGHTS

Be'er Sheva's most exciting attraction is its Thursday **Bedouin Market,** established in 1905. The market is nirvana for *chatchke* lovers and bargain hunters. Amidst the clamor of screaming vendors you'll find cheap Bedouin food and excellent garments. Years ago, the Bedouin hawked camels and sheep—now they've added snow globes and t-shirts to the much-ballyhooed wares. The market recently moved to the north side of the city, at the final stop of bus #6. Trading begins early in the morning and goes all day. Many Bedouin here speak English and may compliment your beautiful eyes while charging six times the going rate for olive-wood camels. Many Israelis and other non-Bedouins try their hand at peddling as well. Pick up a snow-globe and give it a try.

The scope of this market puts even Jaffa's *shuk ha-pishpeshim* to shame. Hundreds of Bedouin, both the semi-settled from around Be'er Sheva and the nomads from deep in the desert, gather in the area to sell sheep, goats, clothes, cloth, jewelry, ceramics, spices, and digital watches. The northern part of the market features heaps of clothing. Most is junk—sift and ye shall find. As you head farther south, the quantity of rusty cans, scraps of paper and dust increases, the smell of goat dung becomes stronger, and you can buy live rabbits, chickens, doves, or even parakeets. Brave the kitsch and stench, for the southernmost part of the market houses the real gems: beaten copperware, Bedouin robes, fabrics, rugs, and ceramic items—all at prices too low to mention in this guide. Unfortunately, Gazans can no longer partake in the chaos, removing a once vibrant part of the colorful scene.

At the corner of Hebron St. and Keren Kayemet LeYisrael St., you'll find the disputed site of **Abraham's Well.** The well dates back to at least the 12th century CE, and many believe that it was the original well of Abraham. One such firm believer is the notoriously friendly Shosh, who has taken it upon herself to spruce up the site. Ask her about the history of the well and the donkey-powered wooden cogwheel system for bringing up water, a design which dates back to biblical times (open Sun.-Thurs. 8:30am-4pm, Fri. 8:30am-1pm, free).

The last of Be'er Sheva's showpieces, the **Negev Museum,** 60 Ha-Atzma'ut St., is housed in an old Turkish mosque and chronicles 5000 years of the region's history (currently closed for structural renovations but expected to reopen sometime in 1998). The square building adjacent to the museum with the graceful front arches is the **Governor's House** (tel. 628 02 56 or 07). Built by the Turks in 1906, it has served a variety of purposes throughout its existence. During World War I, it was used as a Red Crescent hospital. During the British Mandate, the building served as a boarding school for Bedouin children. After a brief stint as the Israel Defense Force's Southern Command Headquarters, the building was named Be'er Sheva's City Hall in 1949. It's now part of the Negev Museum, housing changing exhibitions, Israeli art, and artifacts from various periods of Negev history (open Sun.-Thurs. 10am-5pm, Fri.-Sat. 10am-1pm; admission NIS5, students NIS3).

The modern campus of **Ben-Gurion University,** founded in 1969, lies in the far northeastern corner of the city (bus #4 leaves from the central bus station every 15min.). Near the dorms at 50 Arlozorov St. is the Taubel Community Center, which houses the **Ethiopian Jewish Handicrafts Workshop** (tel. 623 05 20 or 649 22 88). Here, you can watch demonstrations of traditional methods of creating pottery, figurines, embroidery, and gourd decorations. The crafts are for sale, but not at budget prices (open Mon.-Tues. and Thurs. 8:30am-12:30pm; free).

Five km northeast of the city are the impressive ruins at **Tel Be'er Sheva,** recently upgraded to a national park. Signs will tell you one pile of unearthed rubble is a 2nd-century Roman fortress, another an 8th-century BCE house, and a third one a 12th-century BCE well. Detailed brochures and site maps are available at an information booth facing the entrance to the park. Take Rte. 60 out of the city, then make a right at the set of lights just past the gas stations. Buses # 51, 52, 55, and 57 run by the site (open Sun.-Thurs. 8am-5pm, Fri. 8am-4pm; admission NIS7). Solo women should not accept offers of personal tours of the site. Next to the ruins is a visitor's center with a cafeteria and an expensive restaurant.

Several km north of the *tel* is the fascinating **Joe Alon Bedouin Museum** (tel. 991 33 22), on the outskirts of Kibbutz Lahav (bus #42 and NIS9 will take you from the Be'er Sheva bus station to an intersection 500m from the museum). Head north on Rte. 40 to Tel Aviv; make a right at Beit Kama junction heading towards Lahav, then make a right at the Lahav Forest. The museum showcases all facets of the nomads' lives, including traditional tools, embroidery, and customary desert garb. There's also an audiovisual presentation describing their culture and famous hospitality. (Open Sun.-Thurs. 9am-4pm, Fri. 10am-2pm; admission NIS12, students NIS10.)

## ENTERTAINMENT

Be'er Sheva is surprisingly lively at night, especially around **Trumpeldor Street.** Most of the bars open at 8 or 9pm, but remain quiet until about 11pm, when an almost exclusively Israeli crowd starts pouring in. **Trombone,** 18 Ha-Avot St. (tel. 623 76 98), at the corner of Trumpeldor, is an informal restaurant/pub with an intimate atmosphere. Beer is NIS8 and entree-sized dishes NIS17 (open nightly 8pm-4am). The hottest hot spot is the **Forum,** in an industrial neighborhood (Kiryat Yehudit 232; tel. 627 76 72 or 78). Thursday and Friday are disco and rock nights (11pm-4am, NIS20-

30), and live bands jam on Saturdays (NIS50). Soldiers and Negev locals flock here. A cab from the old city costs NIS12-15. **Ha-Simta** (The Alley), at 16 Trumpeldor St. (tel. 627 36 53) spins a deafening mix of Israeli, American, and Euro tunes. (open nightly 8pm-3am, must be 18 or over). You can nurse your hangover at one of the mellow **coffeehouses** on Herzl St.

For fun that won't leave your ears ringing, try one of Be'er Sheva's **movie theaters,** four of which are in Kenyon Ha-Negev, or dive into the **swimming pool** at the Beit Yatziv Youth Hostel, 79 Ha-Atzma'ut St. (Open Mon.-Sat. 8:30am-5pm, Sun. 10:30am-5pm. Admission NIS16, *Shabbat* NIS17, NIS12 for hostel guests.)

# ■ Near Be'er Sheva

## ARAD ערד

Arad's biggest tourist draw is its cool, dry, pollen-free air. That says a lot about this desert outpost. If you're not an asthmatic, you may be happier at the hostels on the Dead Sea or in Be'er Sheva. The lack of tourists has both positive and negative effects. In its favor, Arad is a peaceful settlement, exemplifying the new Negev boom town—only 40 years ago, Arad was nothing but a barren plateau. Unfortunately, there isn't much more for tourists to do here than when it *was* a desert plateau. Arad's quiet streets used to rumble with the rhythmic foot tapping of thousands of Israeli teenagers during the four-day **Hebrew Music Festival.** Recent deaths at the festival, however, leave the future of the event in doubt.

**Practical Information** To get to the **Municipal Tourist Information Office** (tel. 995 81 44 or 89 33; fax 995 50 52), located across from the bus station and a little to the left, make a right after the grocery store, walk all the way up, and it's on your left. The office serves as a reservations center for organized tours and other attractions in the area, since there are no sights in Arad proper (open Sun.-Tues. 8am-7pm, Wed. 8am-4pm, Fri. 8:30am-noon).

Buses leave from the **central bus station** (4 plastic-encased benches and a parking lot) on Yehuda St., but are few and far between. Bus #389 goes to Tel Aviv (Sun.-Thurs. 6, 8:30am, and 2pm, last bus Fri. 1:30pm, Sat. 5 and 9pm; NIS27, students NIS24). To Be'er Sheva, take bus #388 (every 30-60min., 5:40am-9:30pm) or #384 (9:30, 11:30am, 2, and 5pm, both NIS12.70). Buses #384 and 385 (express) depart to Ein Bokek (NIS12.70), Masada (NIS16, students NIS14.50), and Ein Gedi (NIS17.50, students NIS16). The express leaves at 8, 11:15am, 12:30, 3:30, and 6pm, last Fri. bus 3:30pm). There is no direct service to Eilat or Jerusalem.

Everything you'll ever need in Arad is either next to the bus station or near the **Kenyon Arad,** a mall behind the *midrahov.* There are several ATM-equipped **banks** in the pedestrian mall (all open Sun., Tues., and Thurs. 8:30am-12:30pm and 4-6pm, Mon. and Wed. 8:30am-12:30pm, Fri. 8:30am-noon). There's a **SuperPharm pharmacy** (tel. 997 16 21) in the Kenyon Arad (open Sun.-Thurs. 9am-10pm, Fri. 9am-3pm, Sat. 11am-11pm; call here for emergencies). The **police station** (tel. 995 70 44 or 081; dial 100 for emergencies) is right next to the bus station. Its neighbor on the other side is **Magen David Adom First Aid** (tel. 995 72 22; dial 101 for emergencies). The main **post office** branch (tel. 995 70 88) is in the commercial center across from the bus station. Here you can make **international phone calls,** use **EMS,** and receive **poste restante** (open Sun.-Tues. and Thurs. 8am-12:30pm and 4-6:30pm, Wed. 8am-1pm, Fri. 8am-12:30pm). Arad's **telephone code** is 07.

**Accommodations and Food** The **Blau-Weiss Youth Hostel (HI)** on Arad St. (tel. 995 71 50) is a four-minute walk from the bus station. Turn right on Yehuda St., take the first right onto Palmah St., pass the soccer field on your left, then take the first left onto Atad St. and follow the signs. Named after the Zionist youth movement in Germany from which the Israeli youth hostels originated, this 200-bed complex has duplex and individual huts among small gardens and paths. Rooms are whistle-clean with private baths and killer air conditioning. The hostel has a kosher dining room and a sometimes-open cable TV room and kiosk. Relaxing, and often not crowded. (Check-in 4:30-7pm. Check-out 10am. Reception open 7:30am-1pm, 4-7:30pm. Dorm beds US$16.50, NIS70. Singles US$34, NIS129. Doubles US$48, NIS182. Triples US$63, NIS243. Members subtract NIS4 each. Prices 12% higher on Fri. and Sat. Breakfast included. MC, Visa accepted.)

The outdoor cafés in the *midraḥov* and the food court in the disconcertingly slick mall offer cheap, fast food (most places open daily until midnight). Those dining in **Apropo** (in the Kenyon Arad) often swoon at live piano accompaniment (pastas, salads, and great Thai cuisine NIS26-35). The **Burger Ranch** in the mall sells the usual for the usual (Ranchburgers NIS10.70). There's a **Supersol supermarket** (tel. 995 80 40) next to the visitor's center (open Sun.-Thurs. 7am-8pm, Fri. 7am-2pm) and a **CoOp** (tel. 995 51 03) across from the bus station (open Sun.-Wed. 7:30am-7:30pm, Thurs. 7:30am-8pm, Fri. 7:30am-2pm).

**Entertainment and Sights** The **MTIO** will arrange transportation for the **Masada Sound and Light Show** (see **Masada,** p. 416) or **Sussiya,** a 1400-year-old Hebrew city, with an impressive synagogue and a system of escape caves and tunnels. For **jeep tours,** contact Allan Levine (tel. 997 12 35; mobile phone (050) 284 301; fax 995 07 81). These wind-in-your-hair tours will truly make you love the desert (half-day NIS105, full-day NIS165 including food). The Judean desert tours are a great way to see hard-to-reach areas while avoiding waits for infrequent buses. Allan also offers enchanting night tours, with wine and music (5hr., NIS105), and a jeep tour/ Masada Sound and Light Show combo (NIS195). Journey possibilities include swimming in desert springs, getting acquainted with unique foliage, and collecting colored sand. Tell Allen *Let's Go* sent you and you'll get a 15% discount.

**The Arad Visitor's Center,** on Ben Yair St. (tel. 995 44 09; fax 995 58 66), is across from the tourist office. The **GTIO computer** inside gives you detailed lists and pictures of the entire country (monthly-updated entries on accommodations, food, and tours). **Nature Reserve Authority** staffers can give advice on hiking. The detailed topographical trail maps for hiking in the Negev or Dead Sea area are all in Hebrew, but you can ask them to pen in the English names. The center includes a small museum and offers two audio-visual presentations about the desert region complete with a mock flood (open Sat.-Thurs. 9am-5pm and Fri. 9am-2:30pm).

The most exciting thing in Arad is the explosive **Hebrew Music Festival** ("Festival Arad") in mid-July. In the summer of 1995, three teenagers were killed at the festival when a stampede broke out in the dangerously overcrowded arena. In response, the parents of the killed teens have begun a campaign to cancel the event. In 1996, a scaled-down festival was held in August, and many musicians refused to perform. At press time, organizers were unsure about the date or content of the 1997 festival. It is doubtful, however, that the festival will return to the days when venues were staged at the swimming pool and Masada to accommodate the crowds. Once the festival is over, not a tie-dyed trace remains. Head out of town to ancient Arad **(Tel Arad),** situated about 10km west of the modern town. Arad was an early Bronze Age Canaanite city, destroyed about 2700 BCE and never rebuilt. This makes Arad the only complete, undisturbed Bronze Age city in existence today. Later, in King Solomon's era, an **Israelite fortress** was built on a nearby hill; the fortress includes a cult sanctuary whose design is unique to the southern (Judahite) kingdom. (Open Sun.-Thurs. 8am-5pm, Fri. 8am-2pm; Oct.-March Sun.-Thurs. 8am-4pm, Fri. 8am-2pm. Admission NIS7, students NIS4. Take bus #388, tell the bus driver to let you off at Tel Arad, then walk 1.5km to the site.)

# DIMONA דימונה

In this tiny desert town near the Dead Sea, you'll find the unlikeliest of communities—Chicagoans. The **Hebrew Israelite Community,** referred to as the Black Hebrews' Village by non-members, is a unique sect of English-speaking immigrants who believe that their historical roots can be traced to ancient Israel. The community believes that the ancestors of black slaves in antebellum America lived in Israel until they were forced to migrate to Western Africa after the Roman onslaught in 70 CE. The group's vanguard returned to the Holy Land in 1969 under the leadership of spiritual guide Ben-Ami Ben Israel (formerly Ben-Ami Carter). The journey was prompted, says Ben Israel, by a vision he received, and was preceded by a brief stint in Liberia. The Israeli government at first refused to grant them citizenship unless they converted to Judaism, but the Black Hebrews insisted that they were already Jews. The government and the sect came to an agreement in 1990 on a multi-step process for normalizing the community's legal status.

To get to the Hebrew Israelites from Dimona's central bus station, turn left on Herzl St., pass the tall red monument to the right and continue straight for about 10 minutes. The village is on the left, through the green hedges. You'll feel like one of the popular kids in junior high as villagers stop to greet you with *"Shalom, boker tov."* The community of 37 settlers who came in 1969, plus 47 who arrived in 1970, has blossomed into an 1100-person village with its own school, musical groups, and an Academy for the Performing and Fine Arts. About 600 other members of the group live in smaller communities elsewhere in Israel. The community makes its own magnificent clothes, jewelry, and food (their religious beliefs require them to wear only pure natural fabrics and prohibit them from eating any animal parts or products, white sugar, or white flour). Though you're welcome to wander through the village on your own, community leaders prefer that you call ahead (tel. (07) 655 54 00) so that they will be able to arrange a tour and take you to their **Toflé** clothing store and **Boutique Africa,** where US$35 will buy you a pair of their woven Eco-shoes. Their **restaurant** is a godsend for protein-starved vegans, who should take the opportunity to stock up on scrambled tofu sandwiches (NIS6). The boutiques and restaurant keep irregular hours—drop by and they will probably magically open up. If you'd like to stay, the village has a three-room **guest house** (rooms US$20, breakfast and dinner included, call ahead). Around the second week of August, the Hebrew Israelites host the two-day **Naisik Ha-Shalom Music Festival** which highlights community entertainment and hosts Israeli bands. Daytime carnival activities are free, and nighttime concerts are almost so (tickets NIS10 and under—most way under). Singing groups from Dimona tour the country when they're not performing at home. Their music is unique—traditional Jewish texts set to a black gospel beat.

Dimona's other claim to fame lies in the mysterious factory a few km to the east. As any tour guide will tell you, the two ominous barbed wire fences and signs forbidding photography are covering a not-so-secret nuclear power plant. Officially, the place produces film, but officially, the U.S. military isn't hiding alien ships in New Mexico.

**Buses** #48 and 56 go to Be'er Sheva (every 15-20min., 35min., NIS10); #375, 393, and 394 go to Tel Aviv (NIS26, students NIS23); #395 and 397 go to Eilat (every hr., 6am-8pm; NIS40, students NIS35).

## MAMSHIT ממשית

The Nabateans have proven that people can conquer all, even in simmering desert heat. The city of Mamshit (tel. (07) 657 05 07), just outside modern-day Dimona, can attest to their ability to prosper in the least forgiving of environments. At this ancient site, archaeologists discovered regal villas with courts and balconies underneath the dirt and rubble. The Nabateans, like Leona Helmsley, settled for nothing but the best—they used only the finest dressed stone and built elaborate archways and columns. Even the view was majestic—the city is perched above Ha-Makhtesh Ha-Gadol (the big crater). Romans and later Byzantines inhabited the city. When Muslims conquered the area in 636 CE, the city was abandoned (site open 8am-5pm; admission NIS7, youth NIS4).

**Buses** running between Be'er Sheva and the Dead Sea will stop 1km outside Mamshit, along the main highway. By car, the drive through **Ha-Makhtesh Ha-Gadol** is smashingly beautiful. Head south on the road just east of Mamshit (Rte. 206). After driving roughly 15km, hang a right onto Rte. 225 heading toward Yeroḥam. If you're a risk taker, you can try to flag down tourists driving by in rental cars.

# ■ Sdeh Boker שדה בוקר

Settled amidst endless desert, verdant Sdeh Boker is named for the mountain behind it. Arabs call this mountain "Jabal Baqara" (Mt. Cow), which changed to the Hebrew "Har Boker" (Cowboy Mt.). The **kibbutz**, established in 1952, produces olives, kiwis, and other fruit, as well as wheat, corn, and livestock, though few cars.

**David Ben-Gurion,** Israel's first prime minister, considered settlement in the Negev a top priority. When experts advised that developing the Negev was a waste of time and money, Ben-Gurion insisted on searching for unconventional methods of "making the desert bloom," asking, "If the Nabateans could do it, why can't we?" He was so moved by the young pioneers building fledgling Sdeh Boker on a 1953 visit that he decided, at the age of 67, to resign from office and settle here. Now the area is steeped in Ben-Gurion tributes, sights, and memorabilia. Those less enamored by B.G. will find Sdeh Boker a base for some awesome desert exploration in the nearby **Ein Avdat Natural Reserve.** There are a tremendous number of hikes in this area traversing jagged desert cliffs, natural springs, canyons, and monk caves.

## PRACTICAL INFORMATION

The only public transportation to or from Sdeh Boker is Egged **bus #60,** running between Be'er Sheva and Mitzpeh Ramon (every 1-1½hr. until 9-10pm, NIS15.50, students NIS14). The bus makes three stops: at the gate of Kibbutz Sdeh Boker, at Ben-Gurion's Hut, and at the Ben-Gurion Institute for Desert Research. The stops are several km from each other, so plan carefully. Stop at the kibbutz gate to reach the center of the settlement. Make a left at the end of the main entry road, then the first right, and in a little plaza you'll find a **post office** (open Sun.-Mon., Wed.-Thurs. 8:30am-noon, 1-2pm; Tues. 8:30am-noon; Fri. 8:30-10:30am), **supermarket** (open Sun.-Thurs. 8am-7pm, Fri. 8am-2pm; Visa accepted), and **cafeteria** (open Sun.-Thurs. 8am-11pm, Fri. 8am-2pm; also accepts Visa). The **Ein Avdat Nature Reserve** and Ben Gurion's grave are best reached from the Institute stop. The **telephone code** for Sdeh Boker is 07.

To find the **SPNI Field School** (tel. 656 58 28 or 50 16; fax 656 57 21), make a right at the end of the main entry road and then a left at the large parking lot. The incredibly knowledgeable and helpful staff answers questions about hiking routes and desert flora and fauna and offers free maps of nearby trails. You can leave your bags here during day hikes (open Sun.-Thurs. 8am-5:30pm, Fri 8am-1pm and 5-7pm). The school has a sound and light show on Ben-Gurion's life, but only shows it to large tour groups. If a group shows up, they'll let lone travelers tag along.

## ACCOMMODATIONS AND FOOD

The **SPNI Hostel,** on the canyon's edge, has spotless, modern rooms with air-conditioning, private baths, and incredible views of the Zin Canyon. The six-bed dorm rooms, Sdeh Boker's only true budget lodgings, are reserved for students (NIS32 per person with free use of common kitchen). The field school also runs the **Hamburg Guest House** next door; rooms here are clean, spacious, and bank-breaking (singles NIS110, doubles NIS165; on weekends, singles NIS143, doubles NIS187). Both accommodations include free use of the community swimming pool and library. Food pickings are slim out here. The **Sdeh Boker Inn** (tel. 656 03 79), next door to Ben-Gurion's Hut, serves cafeteria-style meals (NIS15-25; open daily 8am-3pm).

---

### Don't Seize the Trees, Please

Many trees in the Negev and Sinai have cloth sacks tied to the branches. As the nomadic Bedouin wander around the desert, they often tie their non-essential belongings to trees rather than schlep them around in the heat. Sometimes they'll even leave valuables tied high in the branches, but theft is extremely rare. It's an unspoken rule of desert life never to touch a tree-bound bundle.

## SIGHTS AND HIKES

Although many tourists are attracted to Sdeh Boker because of its Ben-Gurion memorials, B.G. himself was attracted to the kibbutz because of its majestic setting. The best way to appreciate this setting is to try some of the blow-your-mind hikes in the area. The **Ein Avdat Nature Reserve** (tel. 655 56 84) in the Zin Canyon showcases the Negev at its most spectacular. Although the reserve has two entrances, the upper one, with no trailheads, is primarily a look-out point. You can get brochures and rough maps at either gate, but you're best off picking up a detailed map at the SPNI office. To get to the lower entrance, go to the Ben-Gurion Institute gate (Midreshet Ben-Gurion) and follow the road to your right (45-50 sweaty min.). From the lower entrance, you can hike to **Ein Avdat** (the lower pools) in 15 minutes. To do the full hike to the upper gate, plan for 45-60 minutes. If you don't have a car waiting for you at the end of the hike, you'll either need to make a big U-turn (turn around before climbing the ladders since it's not permitted to descend them) or extend your hike a few hours by walking along the rim of the canyon once you reach the top. Among the highlights of the various trails are a waterfall, fresh water pools, hermit caves, and the remains of a Byzantine fortress. Feel free to wander off the trail and explore oasis plant and animal life. (Reserve open daily May-Sept. 8am-4pm, Oct.-April 8am-3pm; admission NIS10, students NIS7.50).

There are other gorgeous, secluded hikes in the area that don't require an entrance fee, but be sure to have good maps and plenty of water as these off-the-beaten-track adventures are much less trafficked. The **Havarim/Karakash Wadi** is a magnificent three-hour hike which passes an inviting pond and waterfall. The trailhead is off the main road between Be'er Sheva and Eilat about 1km south of Midreshet Ben Gurion. An orange sign says "Havarim Water Cistern." Follow the blue trail signs, which will take you down to Ein Avdat. At night, when there's a full moon, this hike is spectacular. Other fun hikes lead to **Ein Zik** (5-6hr.), where there's great swimming at an oasis surrounded by palm trees, and **Ein Akev** (3-4hr., camping permitted). Maps for all area hikes are free at the SPNI office.

Back at the Ben-Gurion Institute, a walk along the canyon rim leads to the beautifully-landscaped **Ben-Gurion Tombs** overlooking the big chief's beloved Negev. In 1992, former Soviet premier Mikhail Gorbachev lay a wreath at Ben-Gurion's grave and praised the success of his style of socialism. Behind the tombs, there is a sound and light show about Ben-Gurion's life (tel. 656 57 17). The show is only offered to large tour groups, but individuals are sometimes allowed to crash; call ahead.

The **Ben-Gurion Institute** itself is worth a visit. Scientists and university students work year-round at the busy institute; their findings on desert irrigation and development are applied not only to the Negev, but to Africa and much of the world. The nearby **Research Center for Solar Energy** is a pioneer in the field. Those black panels and metal contraptions you see on every Israeli rooftop are solar-powered water heaters, required for households by Israeli law. The center gives tours by appointment (tel. 655 50 57; admission NIS5; open daily 9am-5pm). The institute's **Desert Sculpture Museum** displays art created from natural desert materials.

Two and a half km down the road and one bus stop in the direction of Be'er Sheva, you can see **Ben-Gurion's Hut** (tel. 656 03 20 or 655 84 44), only slightly larger than the residences of his kibbutz neighbors, furnished as he left it. Family pictures, lists of medications, and copied-down Biblical passages the secular leader found meaningful give the visitor an insight into the man behind the legend (open Sun.-Thurs. 8:30am-3:30pm, Fri. 8:30am-2pm, Sat. and holidays 9am-2:30pm; free).

# ■ Near Sdeh Boker

## AVDAT עבדת

The magnificently preserved ruins of a 4th-century BCE **Nabatean city** are perched upon a hill 11km south of Sdeh Boker. Avdat once thrived as a pit stop for caravans along the spice route from the Far East (via Petra) to Gaza that continued on to Europe. Nabateans used their strategic perch at Avdat to spy on caravans as far away as present-day Mitzpeh Ramon or Sdeh Boker. The Romans captured the city in 106 CE and it continued to flourish, reaching its economic peak during the Byzantine period. Most of the visible ruins date from this time. 7th-century Islamic marauders renovated the Roman baths but not much else. The most important Nabatean remains are a handsome esplanade on top of the hill, a winding staircase that led to a Nabatean temple, and a potter's workshop, all dating from the first century CE. When the Nabateans converted to Christianity around 300 CE, the temple became a church. The best of the 6th-century Byzantine remains include a 20-ft. high wall, a street, a monastery, two churches, and a baptistry. In this century, the site was resurrected on celluloid in the movie version of *Jesus Christ Superstar.*

Drinking water and bathrooms are across from the ticket booth. **Bus** #60 (12 per day Sun.-Thurs., 9 on Fri.; 35min.) runs from Be'er Sheva to Sdeh Boker, stopping in Avdat. Make it clear to the driver that you want to go to the archaeological site and *not* Ein Avdat (the oasis). Near the bus stop is a **gas station** and **restaurant.** Bring water for the 20-minute uphill hike to the ruins (tel. 655 09 54; open daily 8am-5pm; admission NIS12, students NIS9). The small grove just below the ruins is irrigated using ancient Nabatean water techniques and is staffed by rotating volunteers.

## YEROHAM ירוחם

Between Be'er Sheva and Sdeh Boker lies the industrial town of Yeroham. This pint-sized town typifies Negev settlements: exploding with immigrants and buzzing with activity. Just outside of town are two of the Negev's most startling natural anomalies. A few km southwest on Rte. 204 is **Yeroham Park,** home to the Negev's only lake, the result of a nearby dam built in the 1950s. Even in summer locals can fish for carp and paddle around in small boats. In winter, when the lake swells to a deep blue oval, residents from surrounding towns converge to enjoy the cool waters. A few km farther south are Yeroham's famous **iris fields.** In spring, the flowers turn the dry desert landscape into a deep purple carpet. Look for the signs for the Yeroham Nature Reserve. The park and reserve are only accessible by car.

# ■ Mitzpeh Ramon מצפה רמון

Mitzpeh Ramon sits on the rim of **Makhtesh Ramon** (Ramon Crater), the most gargantuan and impressive of the Negev's four craters. Weighing in at 400m deep, 9km wide, and 40km long, Ramon is the largest natural crater in the world. In the 1920s and 30s, Makhtesh Ramon was not on any British map. The young Israeli government came upon the crater while exploring the potential of the Negev. Until a direct route to Eilat was built from the Dead Sea in the 1970s, what is now known as "Mitzpeh Ramon" (Ramon Observation Point) was the central stop-off for those heading south. Today, the crater is a national park, with well-marked trails leading through mazes of stunning geological phenomena and breathtaking cliff views.

The fascinating rock formations in the *makhtesh* are millions of years old, the vegetation spans four distinct climatic zones, and evidence of human life in the area predates written history. Uphill treks wind towards phenomenal views of the desert expanse, passing bizarre insects and wildlife along the way. Around each curve of the sandy paths lie unexpected shapes and colors not normally associated with nature. Remember that the crater sinks in the middle of a desert. Bring one liter of **water** per person per hour. Afterwards, an evening on the rim comes with a free, all-natural, spectacular light show.

**Practical Information** From Mitzpeh Ramon, bus #60 runs to Be'er Sheva (every 1-1½hr., 6am-9:30pm, NIS17.50, students NIS16). Bus #391 runs to Tel Aviv (one per week, Sun. 6:30am, NIS33). Bus #392 comes through on its way from Be'er Sheva to Eilat and back; you can take it either way if there's room (8:20 and 10am, noon, 4:45 and 7:30pm; NIS33, students NIS28). Drivers are instructed to take 10-minute breaks if they feel drowsy on long desert treks, so don't panic if your bus is 10 to 40 minutes late. Mitzpeh Ramon has several bus stops. The first stop is the commercial center on Ben-Gurion St. (look for the strange fountain), near a **Bank Ha-Poalim** branch which lacks an ATM (tel. 658 80 86; open Sun., Tues., and Thurs. 8:30am-noon and 4-6pm, Mon. 8:30am-12:30pm, Fri. 8:30am-noon). In an adjoining building is a **post office** with **Western Union, fax** and **telegram** services, **EMS,** and **poste restante** (tel. 658 84 16; open Sun.-Tues. and Thurs. 8am-12:30pm and 4-6:30pm, Wed. 8am-1pm, Fri. 8am-12:30pm). To the left is the **municipal pool,** with a sauna and water slide (open Sun.-Thurs. 10am-6pm, Sat. 9am-5pm; admission NIS32). The second bus stop, at the **youth hostel,** also serves the **visitor's center,** Bio-Ramon, and the cliffside promenade. Nearby is the **Mitzpeh Pharmacy** (open Sun.-Thurs. 8am-1pm, 3-6:30pm, Fri. 8am-1pm). Mitzpeh's **telephone code** is 07.

There are two hiking resources in Mitzpeh Ramon: the first is the **Park Ramon Visitor's Center** (tel. 658 86 91; fax 658 86 20), housed in the round building with the flat top. Nature Reserve Authority staffers will help you plan your hike, give tips on potentially misleading spots, and provide a fabulous English map of the Negev and the crater. The audio-visual museum and the rooftop observatory will add to your appreciation of what you're about to see (or what you just saw). (Open Sun.-Thurs. 9am-5pm, Fri. 9am-4pm, Sat. 9am-5pm. Admission NIS13, children NIS8.80.) The gift shop across the plaza sells detailed topographical maps (NIS12), and other books and pamphlets about the crater and the Negev. The second resource is the **SPNI Field School** (tel. 658 61 01, 86 15, or 86 16), near the edge of the crater 500m southwest of Camel Observation Point (for directions see Accommodations, below). They too are equipped with reams of maps and literature about hiking in the region, and occasionally offer organized tours; call ahead to find out if one will be happening when you're in town. If you're planning an unguided expedition, leave your route description and estimated trip duration at the field school before you leave—they have an on-site rescue team and direct communication with army units in the area (open Sun.-Thurs. 8am-6pm, Fri. 8am-noon).

**Desert Shade** (tel. 658 62 29 or (03) 575 68 85; fax 658 62 08) leads excellent tours by jeep, foot, bike, and camel. (2hr. morning jeep tour NIS88. 3hr. sunset tour NIS118. 1½hr. camel ride NIS60. Full-day walking tours US$148. Daily bike rental NIS48. 2-day camel ride/hike along the Nabatean Spice Route US$154.) To get to Desert Shade, take bus #60 or 392 towards Be'er Sheva. It's a 15-minute walk past the gas station on the main road just outside town.

**Accommodations** The loveliest place to stay in Mitzpeh Ramon is **Chez Alexis,** a villa turned guest house at 7 Ein Saharonim St. (tel. 658 82 58 or 61 22, or 655 43 41). Beds are an absolute bargain at US$10-12 per person (doubles US$30). Adorable Mr. and Mrs. Ben Said own and run the place, which has a huge, fully equipped kitchen, a TV living room, and a fireplace. Walk one block down Ben-Gurion St. from its intersection with Eilat St., take the first right, then make a left after the minimarket (you can also take the bus). At the end of the street, turn right. The Ben Saids appreciate reservations, although they aren't absolutely necessary. Call them when you arrive. On the canyon's rim, across from the visitor's center, you'll find the **Mitzpeh Ramon Youth Hostel (HI)** (tel. 658 84 43; fax 658 80 74). There's no air conditioning in the spacious rooms, but you don't really need it. Rooms are crisp and clean, with private baths. There's a huge lounge with foosball, a TV room, an occasional disco in the basement, and a snack bar. (Reception open 7am-11pm. Checkout 9:30am. No lockout or curfew. Dorm beds (6 per room) NIS60. Singles NIS125, doubles NIS178. Each additional person NIS60. Nonmembers add NIS4. Breakfast included. Visa, MC.) The **SPNI Field School** (tel. 658 86 15) is a bit isolated but charges less than the hostel and has a trail leading down into the crater. Take bus #60 to Camel Observation Point and walk 10 minutes to the right along the cliffside trail until you see the tall antennas. All rooms have air conditioning and private baths, and guests may use the full kitchen. (Check-in Sun.-Thurs. 4-8pm, Fri. 8-11:30am, Sat.

ISRAEL

arrange in advance. Check-out 8am. Dorm beds (6 per room) NIS48 for students only. Singles NIS154. Doubles NIS200, each additional adult NIS75. Call ahead. Breakfast included. Lunch and dinner available NIS25-35. Kiosk open 8-10am and 5-10pm for snacks and drinks. Visa, MC.)

Staking out a campsite in the middle of the crater is forbidden. Though campers have been known to do it, they run the risk of being awakened by an angry ranger or an even angrier Asiatic wild ass. The only campground within the *makhtesh* is the **Be'erot Camping Site,** 16km from Mitzpeh. Shade, toilets (no showers), and picnic tables are free, and a night on a mattress in a Bedouin tent costs NIS14.50. The kiosk has cold drinks, ice cream (NIS3-4), and firewood. Head down the main road until you see two orange signs pointing toward the campsite—it's a one-hour walk from the road. The other official campground is along the main road in Mitzpeh, by the gas station north of the visitors center. Follow the path towards the crater and you'll come upon a series of Bedouin-inspired, traveler-adapted tents, run by Desert Shade. The place has a relaxed atmosphere conducive to music and yoga interludes. (Beds with sheets in tiny cabins NIS48. Toilets and showers on site. Breakfast included; vegetarian and Bedouin meals NIS30-40.)

For a new age desert experience there's **Succah in the Desert** (tel. 658 62 80), 7km outside town (accessible by foot or car only). The premises, a haven for artists and hard-core meditators, consist of seven *sukkot,* beautiful structures made of stones and dried palm leaves. The interiors, rich with tapestries and rugs, incorporate desert features like rock platforms for sleeping or sitting. (*Sukkot* NIS75-100 per night. Tent with carpets and pillows NIS20. Vegetarian dinners NIS25.)

**Food and Entertainment** The talented Esther cooks up a storm at **Hama-khtesh Restaurant,** 2 Naḥal Tzihor St. (tel. 658 84 90), one block down from the Youth Hostel. *Kabab, shishlik,* steak, and *schnitzel* (regular and veggie) go for NIS22 and come with pita, six salads, and rice or fries (open Sun.-Thurs. 9am-10pm, Sat. sundown-11pm, kosher). **Ha-Tzukit Restaurant,** near the visitor's center, has air conditioning, a stunning view, and often a family of ibex lazing outside. (Sandwiches NIS7, vegetarian meals NIS18, hot meat lunch NIS24. Open Sun.-Fri. 9am-5pm). **Hanna's Restaurant** (tel. 658 81 58) is connected to the Eilat St. gas station, between the commercial and visitor's centers. Sandwiches (NIS7-9) and meals (NIS25-30) are better than the unsavory location might indicate (open Sun.-Thurs. 5:30am-8pm, Fri. 5:30am-4pm, kosher). Before hiking, stock up on granola and tuna at the **Shekem supermarket** next to the post office (open Sun.-Thurs. 8:30am-1pm and 4-7:30pm, Fri. 8am-2:30pm).

**Pub Ha-Ḥaveet,** Mitzpeh Ramon's happening night spot, is in the commercial center next door to Bank Ha-Poalim. Dim lights, American rock, Iron Maiden posters, and great salads (NIS22; try the Mitzpai) attract soldiers, backpackers, and local youth (18 or older; beer NIS8; open daily noon-late).

For an evening cool-down, walk along one of two **promenades** on the rim of the crater, one behind the campgrounds near the gas station and the other behind the youth hostel. **Desert Sculpture gardens** in both areas display esoteric statuary inspired by the terrain. The **Matnas Culture Center** on 73 Ben-Gurion St. (tel. 658 84 42 or 88 65), two blocks left of the municipal swimming pool, hosts Israeli folk dancing (Sun. 8pm; admission NIS6). **Desert Archery** (tel. 658 72 74), a golf-based bow and arrow game (*sans* grass), sprawls on a 50-acre course 500m west of the city center. Individuals are welcome, but it's more fun in pairs or groups. (Equipment, explanation, and nearly limitless playing time NIS22, students NIS17. Call ahead.) **Bio-Ramon** (tel. 658 87 55), just downhill from the visitors center, houses desert insects, scorpions, spiders, snakes, and lovable rodents. (Open Sun.-Thurs. 8am-3pm, Fri. 8am-1pm., and Sat. 9am-4pm. Admission NIS5, children NIS4.)

**Hikes** The *makhtesh* (erosion crater) is a geological phenomenon unique to Israel. With colorful rock formations and unusual wildlife, Ramon has some of the best hiking in the country. Trailheads for the most interesting hikes are outside of town, but there are two beautiful trails originating from Mitzpeh. Although the trails are well marked, a pre-hike stop at the visitors center for maps and terrain info is a prudent idea. You may also want to leave your planned route and expected length of trip with the field school, youth hostel, or visitor's center. While hiking, keep a fix on the Eilat road; it's the place to go if you get caught in the dark. To get to far-flung trailheads, take bus #392 to Eilat, which follows the main highway through the crater. Hitchers say that thumbing it is easiest. Southbound drivers take off from the visitors center parking lot.

### Short Hikes from Mitzpeh

An excellent three-hour hike begins from the end of the promenade, near the mini amphitheater. Green trail markers lead to **Ha-Minsarah** (the Carpentry), where piles of prism-like rock, configured and baked by volcanic heat, resemble carpenter's supplies. A turn-off point marked in red will lead you on a five-hour day-hike through the crater. The fossil-happy **Ammonite Wall** lies along this trail. Another short hike follows the blue trail markers from the SPNI school, and eventually joins the green trail loop (3-5hr.). It's a short jaunt up the green trail to the rim, or you can extend your hike and complete the green loop's tour of the Carpentry.

### Har Ardon/Ein Saharonim Hike

This hike is long (6-7hr. from the campsite and back); you may want to split it into two day-trips, especially during the summer. From the campsite and back, each of the two parts takes about four to five hours.

To climb **Har Ardon** (Mt. Ardon), take a left out of the Be'erot campsite and follow the signs. A steep climb up the mountain ends with an incredible view and a tricky descent. Along the trail, you'll pass through the crimson sand and hills of the **Red Valley.** When you pass the black hill of **Givat Harut,** either take a right back to the campsite, or turn left and follow the blue markings into Wadi Ardon.

Along the colorful borders of **Wadi Ardon** jut several **dikes,** or intrusions of volcanic material. You'll first pass a pair of chunky intrusions, one big and one small, known as the father and son dikes. To continue on, take the right (red) path at the next fork. Soon you'll arrive at a three-way crossroad. The blue path points towards **Parsat Nekarot** (the Nekarot Horseshoe) which includes **Sha'ar Ramon** (the Ramon Gate), where water exits the crater. The rocky river bed is flanked by soaring cliffs and cave-like enclaves which make excellent shady stops.

From Parsat Nekarot, follow the blue markings to **Ein Saharonim.** The vegetation lasts all year, but the water evanesces to mere puddles during the summer. The remains of a Nabatean caravanserai stand at the end of the spring on the right. To return to the campsite or main road, take a left here, in the direction of Naḥal Gevanim and the Oil Road, and ascend the hill. Upon reaching the Oil Road, a left turn and a right turn soon thereafter will take you back to the main road (ignore the *Primeval Paradise* map, which would have you turn right and then left). A right turn at the Oil Road will return you to the campsite.

### Har Saharonim

Along the southern edge of the crater rises Har Saharonim (literally, Mountain of the Crescent-Shaped Ornaments). From the summit, you can see the Govai Mountains and the desert expanse to the southeast and the crater to the northwest.

Start the climb from the western side, closest to the main road. From the campsite, walk south on the Oil Road. Shortly after the Naḥal Gevanim turn-off, you'll see a steep incline. When you reach the top, turn left at the green markers.

The descent from Har Saharonim leads you by Ein Saharonim, from where you can follow the blue path through Parsat Nekarot or head back to the road, as in the previous route.

ISRAEL

# ■ Eilat אילת

Women, paint on the lip liner and slap on the tanning oil! Men, polish the gold chains and massage your pick-up lines! Eilat thinks it's pretty darn hip. We won't tell them if you don't.

Israel's number-one vacation spot is soaked with the sweat of rowdy Israelis, international backpackers, and European tourists. The air is abuzz with jet skis and cell phones. Some swear by Eilat's sun, coral, and nightlife, while others see the city as a huge tourist trap attached to a nice beach. Eilat has two goals—to get you tan and to make you poor. In between the cocktails and Coppertone, however, you may notice some of the most spectacular underwater life the world's seas have to offer.

The Israelites lost the port of Eloth at what is now Eilat in the 8th century BCE. It then saw the Egyptian Ptolemies, the Nabateans, the Romans, the Crusaders, Salah ad-Din, more Crusaders, the Mamluks, the Ottomans, the British, and finally the Israelis. Nobody comes here for history, however. The oldest thing you can hope to see is an unbuttoned polyester shirt in one of the discos. Israel's southernmost town is the country's biggest swimming and snorkeling resort, a major port for Japanese imports, and a starting point for excursions into the Sinai and the rest of Egypt.

The busiest times of the year are Passover (April 22-28 in 1997) and *Sukkot* (Oct. 16-22 in 1997), when nearly 100,000 Israelis descend upon the city. Don't fool yourself into thinking that this is a good time to visit. True, there are more parties and crowds at pubs, but hostels and restaurants charge double their normal rates, petty theft runs rampant, and every last inch of beach crawls with human flesh.

Eilat is a popular place to earn a little extra money. Proprietors at resorts, hostels, cafés, discos, and the Lunar Mini Park are often looking for newcomers because of the high turnover rate. Jobs with hotels and hostels often include lodging, and should offer a pittance as well. Unfortunately, most work is under-the-table (illegal), with long, hard hours and miserable wages (usually about US$400 per month). In the marina on the gate leading to the boats there are lists of yachts looking for workers. The pay is low but you get free room, board, and social life.

## ORIENTATION

Eilat is a 5km strip of coastline on the Negev's sandy bottom, the precarious intersection of Israel, Jordan, Egypt, and Saudi Arabia; at night you can see the lights of all four. The city is divided into three sections: the town itself on the hills above the sea, the hotel area and Lagoon Beach to the east, and the port to the south. About 10km farther south is **Taba,** just over the border in Egypt.

The first thing to realize about Eilat is that it was designed by aliens. The bizarre numbering system is completely different from the one familiar to Earthlings. Travelers will find that #60 can be followed by #4000; all sorts of slashes and dashes are also involved. These same planners put the airport in the exact center of town.

As you leave the central bus station via the main entrance, you'll find yourself on **Ha-Tmarim Boulevard,** which crosses the center of the city from southeast (downhill) to northwest (uphill). Across the street is the **commercial center,** with restaurants and cafés. If you stay on the bus station side of Ha-Tmarim and head downhill, you'll immediately pass the **Red Canyon Center,** resembling a futuristic Bedouin tent and housing the **post office, supermarket,** Burger Ranch, and **cinema.** Farther downhill the square spaceship on the tiered landing pad is the **Shalom Center.** Ha-Tmarim Blvd. ends here, perpendicular to **Ha-Arava Road.** If you follow Ha-Arava to the right, you'll pass the main entrance to the Eilat **airport.** A block later, at the intersection of **Yotam Road,** a three-level conglomeration of cheap restaurants and shops calls itself the **New Tourist Center.** Ha-Arava leads to Dolphin Reef, the Coral Beach reserve, the Underwater Observatory, and finally Taba Beach and the **Egyptian Border** (30min. walk). Bus #15 runs this route (every 15-20min., NIS2.10-3.20). Turning left at the intersection of Ha-Arava Rd. and Yotam St. will lead you to **Durban Street** and the **beach.**

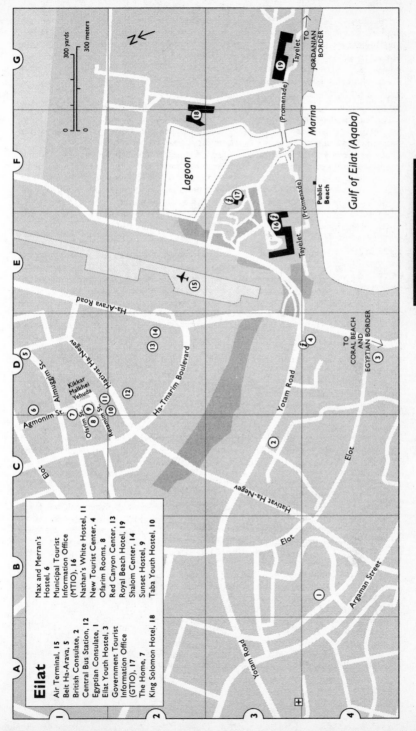

## Eilat

Air Terminal, 15
Beit Ha-Arava, 5
British Consulate, 2
Central Bus Station, 12
Egyptian Consulate, 1
Eilat Youth Hostel, 3
Government Tourist
Information Office
(GTIO), 17
The Home, 7
King Solomon Hotel, 18

Max and Merran's
Hostel, 6
Municipal Tourist
Information Office
(MTIO), 16
Nathan's White Hostel, 11
New Tourist Center, 4
Ofarim Rooms, 8
Red Canyon Center, 13
Royal Beach Hotel, 19
Shalom Center, 14
Sunset Center, 9
Taba Youth Hostel, 10

Numerous hostels cluster near the bus station off Ha-Tmarim St., reachable by turning right at the main exit of the station. The first intersection you'll cross is **Hativat Ha-Negev Street;** the next right-hand turn (unmarked) is **Retamim Street,** and the one after that is **Almogim Street** (U-shaped, with 2 entrances). The farthest north you'll need to go is **Eilat Street,** a wide boulevard separating the touristy part from the residential neighborhoods farther north.

## PRACTICAL INFORMATION

**Tourist Information Center:** corner of Yotam Rd. and Ha-Arava Rd. (tel. 637 21 11). Friendly center is an excellent source for info. Maps, brochures, coupons, and "infotour" computer. Open Sun.-Thurs. 9am-9pm, Fri.-Sat. 8am-3pm.

**Government Tourist Information Office (GTIO):** Bridge House (tel. 633 43 53), in the heart of the marina, near King Solomon's Wharf. Offers maps, brochures, transportation schedules, and border information. Will help find accommodations—crucial in high season. Infotour available. Open Sun.-Thurs. 8am-6pm, Fri. 8am-1pm. Take bus #15 from the station.

**Municipal Tourist Information Office (MTIO):** Rekhter Center (tel. 637 42 33). Good for maps. Open Sun.-Thurs. 8am-6pm, Fri. 8am-1pm.

**Nature Reserves Authority:** Coral Beach (tel. 637 68 29). Maps and information about hiking and diving. Open daily 9am-5pm.

**Consulates: U.K.** (tel. 637 23 44), above the New Tourist Center (next to the Adi Hotel). Call for services. **Egypt,** 68 Ha-Efroni St. (tel. 637 68 82). From the bus station, turn right on Ha-Tmarim Blvd. Make a left on Eilat St., go right at the Moore Center onto Anafa St., take the 3rd left onto Ha-Efroni and look for the flag at the end of the street. Visa services Sun.-Thurs. 9-11am and 1-1:30pm, Fri. 9-10am and 11am-noon. Morning hours for picking up and submitting applications, afternoon for receiving your visa. Visas must be paid for in Israeli currency (free for South Africans, NIS40 for US citizens, NIS65 for most others); bring a passport photo.

**Currency Exchange: Bank Leumi** (tel. 637 41 91) and **Bank Ha-Poalim** (tel. 637 51 84), across from the central bus station. Both open Sun.-Fri. 8:30am-noon. Bank Ha-Poalim also open Sun., Tues., and Thurs. 4:30-6pm; Bank Leumi open Sun., Tues., and Thurs. 5-6:30pm. There are 24-hr. **ATMs** outside Bank Ha-Poalim, next to the post office, and in the marina.

**Telephones: Starcom Gold,** New Tourist Center, main floor (tel. 637 22 37 or toll-free (177) 022 22 37; fax 637 19 20). Cheaper than the post office or public phones. With a credit card, you can call at their low rates from anywhere—even a hotel room. Open Sun.-Thurs. 9am-midnight, Fri. 9am-5pm, Sat. 8pm-1am.

**Airport:** Intersection of Ha-Tmarim Blvd. and Ha-Arava Rd., (info tel. 637 18 28). **Arkia Airlines** (tel. 637 61 02) flies to and from Tel Aviv (every 40min., Sun. and Thurs. every 20min.; one-way NIS206, NIS240 in high season), Jerusalem (3 per day; one-way NIS206, NIS240 in high season), and Haifa (2-3 per day; one-way NIS240, NIS280 in high season).

**Buses:** Central bus station on Ha-Tmarim Blvd. (tel. 637 51 61). Reserve tickets at station 2 days ahead (4 days in high season). Bus #444 takes you to Jerusalem via the Dead Sea (Sun.-Thurs. 4 per day low season, 6 per day high season, Fri. 2 per day low season, 4 per day high season, last Fri. bus 1pm, Sat. 1 bus at 4pm, 4½hr., NIS50); #394 to Tel Aviv (Sun.-Thurs. 10-12 per day, 4am-8pm, Fri. 5-7 per day 5am-2pm, Sat. 5-7 per day, 1-8pm, 5hr., NIS52); #991 to Haifa (Sun., Thurs. 8:30am, 2:30, and 11:30pm, Mon.-Wed. 2:30 and 11:30pm, Fri. 8:30am, Sat. 2:30 and 11:30pm, 6hr., NIS59). ISIC discounts. If full, take bus #392 or 394 to Be'er Sheva (every 1-1½hr. 4am-5pm, until 2pm on Fri., 3½hr., NIS43) and transfer.

**City Buses:** #15 runs down Ha-Tmarim Blvd. and Ha-Arava Rd., through the hotel area, and past the HI hostel and Coral Beach to Egypt (every 20-30min., Sun.-Thurs. 7am-9pm, Fri. 7am-4:30pm, Sat. 9am-9pm, NIS2.10-3.50). #1 and 2 shuttle between the town and hotel area (every 20-30min. Sun.-Thurs. 7am-9pm. No service Fri. 5pm-Sat. 9am., NIS3). #16 runs to the Jordanian border (every 20min. Sun.-Thurs. 7:30am-7:30pm, Fri. 7:30am-4:30pm, Sat. 8:30am-5:30pm, NIS4).

**Taxis: Arava** (tel. 637 41 41), **Taba** (tel. 637 22 12), and **Ha-Melekh Shlomo** (tel. 633 24 74). City rides NIS5, to underwater observatory NIS7, to border NIS10. Taxi sharing is common. In winter *sherut* run along #1, 2, and 15 bus routes.

**Car Rental: Hertz** (tel. 637 66 82), in Red Canyon Center; **Budget** (tel. 637 10 63), **Reliable** (tel. 637 41 26), and **Thrifty** (tel. 637 25 11), all in Shalom Center. 21 min. age. Prices start at US$12 per day plus 27¢ per km or US$50 per day for 250km and 27¢ per km thereafter (3-day minimum). Insurance is about US$15 per day. You can't take rentals into Egypt.

**Bike Rental: Eilat Sports** (tel. 631 57 20), in the Marina. US$15 per day. Open daily 9:30am-7pm. You can bike to Aqaba, into the Sinai, or around Eilat.

**Laundromat: Kuiskal,** Razin Center (tel. 637 48 38), on Ha-Tmarim St. Open Sun.-Thurs. 8am-9pm, Fri. 8am-2pm. **Fast Laundry** (name in Hebrew only) on the corner of Ha-Tmarim and Edom St. Open Sat.-Thurs. 9am-9pm, Fri. 9am-2pm. Both charge NIS25 for wash and dry. **Nikita laundry,** 23 Moore Center, charges about NIS18 for wash and dry but it's a long hike. Hostel laundry services are cheaper.

**Pharmacy: Avigdor,** New Tourist Center, ground floor (tel. 637 23 74). Open Sun.-Thurs. 10am-1pm and 5-10pm, Fri. 10am-1pm and 7-8pm, Sat. 11am-1pm and 8-10pm. **Eilat Pharmacy,** 25 Eilat St. (tel. 637 50 02). Open Sun.-Thurs. 8:15am-1:30pm and 4:45-8pm, Fri. 8:15am-2pm. **Super-Pharm** (tel. 637 68 70), in Sha'ar Ha-ir Mall. Open Sun.-Thurs. 9am-10pm, Fri. 9am-3pm and Sat. 11am-midnight.

**Hospital: Yoseftal Hospital,** Yotam Rd. (tel. 635 80 11 or 637 31 51).

**First Aid:** Ha-Tmarim Blvd. (tel. 101 for emergencies, otherwise 637 23 33). Magen David Adom first aid stations are located on some beaches.

**Fire:** Tel. 102 for emergencies; otherwise 637 22 22.

**Police:** Tel. 100 for emergencies, 633 24 44 to chat; on Avdat Blvd. at the eastern end of Ḥativat Ha-Negev. "Lost and found" for packs stolen from the beach.

**Post Office:** Red Canyon Center (tel. 637 23 02). **Western Union, poste restante.** Open Sun.-Tues., Thurs. 8am-12:30pm and 4-6pm, Wed. 8am-1pm, Fri. 8am-noon.

**Telephone Code:** 07.

## ACCOMMODATIONS

Finding a cheap room in Eilat is easy. Finding a safe, comfortable, and convenient cheap room is another story. As soon as you arrive at the bus station you'll be harassed by a gaggle of apartment hawkers. Yell *"Lo,"* give them the look of death, and walk away. Don't get into a cab with a random stranger, and don't make any commitments before you see the room and know how far from the center it is. Most travelers' hostels are located less than three blocks from the bus station—walk up the hill on Ha-Tmarim and take a right on Retamim. The atmosphere of a smaller hostel can add tremendously to your enjoyment of Eilat. Some of the bigger hostels are unfriendly and have been known to put out backpackers in favor of large groups or have you switch rooms in the middle of the night. The tourist office can assist if hostels are full. Prices below are for the off season; expect to pay double at some hostels in July, August, and the holidays.

**Max and Merran's Hostel,** 111/1 Agmonim St. (tel. 637 13 33). Welshwoman Pamela and her cats Wookie Monster and Cock-eyed Sneezer and dogs Lady and Buffalo Bill are gracious and welcoming hosts. Videos daily at 2 and 8pm in the pleasant kitchen/living room area. A/C. Caters to backpackers, not Israeli vacationers. Lockout 10am-noon. No curfew, visitors, or alcohol. Check-out 10am. Bunk beds NIS30 year round, or put up your own tent in the yard for NIS18. Free and safe luggage storage. Snorkeling gear rental is cheaper than at any beach.

**Beit Ha-Arava,** 106 Almogim St. (tel. 637 10 52 or 46 87), corner of Ḥativat Golani. From the bus station, take a right onto Ḥativat Ha-Negev, walk 2 blocks to the end, and turn left. Veranda, kitchen, a jukebox-foosball diner, and a beautiful view. Clean rooms with A/C and 6 beds max. 24-hr. guard. A home for travelers working in Eilat. Mixture of young Israelis and backpackers. No curfew or lockout. Outdoor tent mattress NIS15. Dorm beds NIS25. Doubles with bath NIS90-100. Breakfast NIS7-10. Lockers NIS4. Laundry NIS10.

**The Home,** 108/2 Almogim St. (tel. 637 24 03); gate is on Ofarim St. right before Ha-Tmarim. Really *is* a home for people hanging out long-term. Manager Aubrey and his champion Persian cats go out of their way to hook travelers up with **jobs,** and you might receive free board until the first paycheck kicks in. Free tea, coffee, bread, jam, and camaraderie all day, videos at night. Slightly cramped quarters but nice kitchen and storage. Warm company is a priority, cleanliness is not. Dorm beds (10-12 per room) NIS22, dorms in newly-renovated annex NIS20. Hot breakfast included. Laundry NIS12.

**Nathan's White House Hostel,** 131/1 Retamim St. (tel. 637 65 72 or 48 29). Go all the way down to the corner. A mural of 1600 Pennsylvania Ave. beautifies the veranda. A converted house with simple, clean rooms. Friendly staff sells and consumes beer. Kitchen, TV, and video. Many Israeli soldiers vacation here. Check-out 9am. No curfew. Dorm beds (4-8 per room) NIS25. Doubles NIS180.

**Corinne Hostel** (tel. 637 14 72), on Retamin just off Ha-Tmarim. Large, clean, A/C dorm rooms. Billiards/game room. No curfew or lock-out. Dorm beds NIS30.

**Eilat Youth Hostel (HI),** Ha-Arava Rd. (tel. 637 23 58 or 00 88; fax 637 58 35), 1 block from the New Tourist Center. Sports over 400 beds, a hotel-like lounge, balconies, and a discothèque (open for groups). Sterile atmosphere. A/C dorms (8 per room) NIS54. Quads NIS298. Nonmembers add NIS4. Breakfast included. Lockers NIS4. Refrigerators NIS15, TV rental NIS20, laundry NIS20 for 6kg.

**Ofarim Rooms,** 116/2 Ofarim St. (tel. 637 04 92; fax 637 62 89). Spotless dorms (4-8 beds) with attached baths. Quiet, boarding-house atmosphere, with an outdoor TV lounge. Kitchen facilities until midnight. No lockout or curfew. Dorm beds NIS35. Singles NIS80, doubles NIS100. Safe NIS5 per day. 5kg laundry NIS15.

**Villa Kibel** (tel./fax 637 69 11, cell phone (050) 634 53 66). Russell and Michelle offer fully furnished apartment-style rooms all with TV, mini-fridge, fresh linen, and cooking facilities. Doubles US$50, triples US$63, quads US$70. Groups of five looking for a quiet pad can rent a suite for US$15 per person. Prices negotiable, especially for longer stays. The complexes are in a few different places. Russell will pick you up from the bus station.

There are two **camping** options in Eilat: legal and expensive, or illegal and free. During July and August, hundreds of people happen not to see the "No Camping" signs on the public beach or in the park; year after year, many are victims of theft. Aside from burglars and sexual harrassers, there are also **rats** at these camps, who love biting ears and other appendages. Camping in sanctioned areas by Coral Beach avoids these hassles. Sleeping and tent-pitching on these farther beaches is legal, and there are toilets near most of them.

**Caroline Camping** (tel. 637 19 11 or 50 63), at the municipal campground opposite Coral Beach. Take bus #15. Clean institutional bathrooms and a compact cafeteria. NIS12 with your own tent. Unbearable shadelessness in July and August. 1- or 2-person bungalows with electricity NIS70. 5-person bungalow NIS160. Refrigerators NIS10. Free linens. 24-hr. office.

**Mamshit Camping** (tel. 637 44 11; fax 637 52 06), next to SPNI field school, across from Coral Beach Reserve. Take bus #15. Excellent snorkeling and skin-frying. Huge, well-kept grounds with friendly management. NIS14 with your own tent. Bungalow beds (8 per room) NIS24. 1- or 2-person bungalows NIS98.

## FOOD

Many falafel stands, pizzerias, and sandwich vendors are on Ha-Tmarim St. near the bus station and by the hostels near Retamim St. Americana-seekers rejoice: **Burger Ranch** in the Red Canyon Center and **McDavid's** on the Durban beachfront (where the Promenade ends) court lawsuits until about 11pm. Bars and pubs have the cheapest meals. A mixed bag of bars on **Almogim** serve cheap food and beer.

Since many accommodations in Eilat provide cooking facilities, backpackers can eat well and inexpensively by purchasing food at the **supermarket** at Eilat St. and Ha-Tmarim Blvd. (look for the blue and white squares on the building; open Sun.-Thurs. 7:30am-7:30pm, Fri. 7:30am-2pm). Closer to the center of town is **SuperKolbo**

**Supermarket** in the Rekhter Commercial Center (open Sat.-Thurs. 7am-11pm, Fri. 7am-9pm) and the **Shekem Supermarket** in the Red Canyon Center (open Sun.-Thurs. 8:30am-8:30pm, Fri. 8:30am-2:30pm). There are three bakeries on Ha-Tmarim north of the bus station with fresh pita and other pocketable treats.

**Country Road,** on the corner of Almogim St. and Agmonim St. is a bit of a dive but the Nigerian owner is extremely welcoming and serves good, cheap food. Generous portions of vegetarian chili, spaghetti *bolognese,* curried chicken, or egg and beans NIS8-10. Serves food daily 11am-11pm.

**Buston Margalis Vegetarian Dairy Restaurant,** on the Durban beach next to McDavid's and Pizza Hut. Inexpensive, tasty food providing an alternative to falafel. Economy bagels filled with cheese, sauce, and choice of toppings NIS8-10, veggie *schnitzel* NIS8, soup or pasta NIS9-12. Open daily 24hr. Kosher.

**Jackness** (tel. 637 65 34), a little far from the center of town but convenient if you're taking a trip to the Egyptian consulate next door. In the Moore center. Family-run place serving large, meaty home-cooked meals. Open daily 9am-4pm.

**Mandy's** (tel. 637 22 38; fax 637 66 96), in the Coral Reef next to Aqua Sports. The oldest and most say the best Chinese restaurant in town. Simple bamboo interior. Large selection of meat and vegetarian dishes. Entrees NIS20-30. Open Sun.-Fri. noon-3pm and 6:30pm-midnight, Sat. noon-midnight. Visa, MC accepted.

**Fisherman House** (tel. 637 98 30), adjacent to Coral Beach. Cheap and belly-busting cafeteria-style restaurant serving all-you-can-eat buffet of fish and meat, salads, rice, and hummus for NIS20.

**Pancake Eilat,** Shalom Center ground floor. Excellent steaks (NIS23); a menu-full of pancakes (NIS7-9). Hostels have 15%-off coupons. Open daily 10am-midnight.

**Tandoori Restaurant** (tel. 633 38 79), by King Solomon's Wharf near the Yacht pub. Offers an extensive range of high-quality Indian food. Curries and tender tandoor-cooked meat NIS34. *Saag paneer,* and other vegetarian delights NIS16-22. Mediocre Indian dancing and singing often accompanies the meal.

## SUNKEN SIGHTS

Eilat's brilliant underwater world of coral, emperor fish, blubberfish, and other creatures is the most spectacular sight the city has to offer. For important information on snorkeling and diving see **Underwater Adventures,** p. 247.

Snorkeling and diving are easiest and cheapest near **Coral Beach Nature Reserve** (tel. 637 68 29). Five "water trails" (marked by buoys) meander through the reef, and a bridge into the water protects the coral from human feet and vice versa (mask NIS6, snorkel NIS5, fins NIS7). Take bus #15 from the central bus station toward the sea. (Beach open 9am-6pm. Admission NIS13, children NIS7, seniors NIS6.50, 5-day pass NIS39. Coin-operated lockers NIS3.) A **SNUBA** lesson (tel. 637 27 22) will get you up close and personal with the sea creatures (NIS101 for 1½hr. of diving and instruction; office open 9am-6pm).

**Aqua Sport** next to Coral Beach also rents equipment (mask US$3.50, fins US$3.50, snorkel US$2, all 3 US$8; complete diving equipment US$45, introductory dive US$40), and sailboards (US$14 per hr.). A five-day diving course costs US$275; five qualification dives for two-star certification cost US$220. Sinai **camping and diving safaris** run by Aqua Sport leave for one to five days of fun south of the border if they have enough people (1 day snorkeling US$65, 5 days US$390, meals and equipment included). **Underwater scooters** cost US$30 for a few hours. **Classes** can be arranged in advance; call or write Aqua Sport (P.O. Box 300, Eilat 88102; tel. 634 44 04). **Eilat Sports,** at Bridge House #6 in the Marina (tel. 631 57 20 or 634 09 20; fax 631 57 21), runs cruises to Coral Island in Egypt (Gaziret Faraun or Pharaoh's Island) for US$45. Trips leave at 10am and return at 4pm and passports must be given at least one day in advance. (Snorkelling equipment and open buffet included in price. 10% discount for *Let's Go* users. See **Pharaoh's Island,** p.264.)

**Red Sea Sports Club** (tel. 637 65 69), across the street from Aqua Sport, at the King Solomon Hotel, offers night dives for US$45. Their office on North Beach near the lagoon offers windsurfing, sailing, water-skiing (NIS50), and parasailing (NIS85).

They also arrange **horseback riding** lessons at Texas Ranch (tel. 637 37 25; fax 638 22 00) across the street (1hr. US$25, 2hr. US$30, 3hr. US$29-55), and **camel** or **jeep tours** of the desert (2½hr. US$19, 4hr. US$28). Upstairs, the **Photo Shop** (tel. 637 31 45, ext. 272) rents **underwater cameras** (US$20-30 per day) and video cameras (US$110 per day). For those joining late in the paragraph, Coral Beach is the most trafficked reef territory in the Red Sea. Head to the Sinai for privacy.

The **Eilat Glass Bottom Boat** (tel. 637 55 28; 2hr., NIS40) is one of the city's many see-through ships. The **Jules Verne Explorer** (tel. 637 77 02 or 633 46 68) may not venture 20,000 leagues down, but with full glass walls, it's a true underwater observatory (2-hr. cruise to the Japanese Gardens NIS50). On Monday, Wednesday, and Friday at 9pm, there's a **Deep Water Laser Show** aquataganza (NIS50).

The **Coral World Underwater Observatory and Aquarium** (tel. 637 66 66) allows you to see the fishies without getting wet (NIS49, children NIS37; open Sun.-Thurs. 8:30am-5pm, Fri. 8:30am-3pm). The **Yellow Submarine** (tel. 637 63 37) goes deeper than divers are allowed to (60m) and arrives at an octopus's garden in the shade (NIS194, NIS113 for children). The lack of light results in different breeds of reef-life. **Dolphin Reef** (tel. 637 18 46), beyond the port on the #15 bus, features dolphin and sea lion shows (every 2hr., 10am-4pm), and nature films. For NIS100, you can swim alongside fenced-in Flipper and friends (open daily 9am-5pm; admission NIS20). Go to Nuweiba' if you want to swim with the real, wild thing (see p. 261).

Some say that the best Eilat wildlife is in the air. Avid **birdwatchers** flock to the salt ponds north of the lagoon mid-February through May and mid-September through November, when over 30 species fly by on their way to or from Africa. The **International Birdwatching Center (IBC)** (P.O. Box 774, Eilat 88106; tel. 637 42 76) in the Commercial Center runs walking tours (US$5) and jeep tours (US$50). There's a bird-watching festival in March. Call or write the IBC for more information (open Sun.-Thurs. 9am-1pm and 5-7pm, Fri. 9am-1pm). Pretend you're a bird at the **Airodium** (tel. 637 27 45), behind the Riviera Hotel. A special-suit/air-vent contraption suspends you for an expensive, but possibly fun 10 minutes (US$25).

## DRUNKEN SIGHTS

Eilat's inspired nightlife rivals its underwater circus; both teem with a wide diversity of life. At night, though, instead of clowning around with friendly fish, you get to be up close and sweaty with skanks, grease monkeys, and hyper-sexuals. Most pubs and nightclubs open at 10:30 or 11pm, get going at midnight or so, and don't close until 5 or 6am. The discos are expensive (covers around NIS25-30) and centered in the lagoon area. At discos in big hotels (sometimes open only to guests), shorts and sandals are a bad idea. The **Promenade** along the waterfront is free and mellow. Street vendors sell cheap jewelry and five-minute portraits, and Israeli studs try in vain to pick up female tourists with identical pick-up lines. People start arriving at about 9:30pm and stay until it's time to go to a pub.

### Bars

**Yacht Pub** (tel. 633 41 11), on the marina by King Solomon's Wharf. Huge place, with sailor-knots on the carpets and indoor and outdoor bars. Live entertainment at 11pm changes every few nights. Popular Israeli folk singers, or relaxing funk/soul bands. 0.5L Carlsberg NIS9. Open daily 10pm-3am (or later).

**The Underground** (tel. 637 02 39), in the New Tourist Center. Up-and-coming, with deals on meals: spaghetti or eggs and beans NIS9. Large draft beers NIS6, mixed drink of the day NIS4. Video-bar and live bands on Fri. make it popular with travelers. First 50 customers after 6pm get a free pasta or rice meal with the purchase of a NIS6 beer. Open daily 9am-5am.

**Peace Café,** 13 Almogim St. (tel. 637 16 29). A mix of backpackers, locals, and travelers turned jobless and drunk swaps messages on the Peace Board and competes in dart-throwing. Music videos by day, movies by night. Luggage storage NIS5 per night. Job placement. Goldstar NIS4, 2 for 1 special 8-9pm. Open daily 9am-2am.

**Hard Luck Café,** 15 Almogim St. (tel. 637 27 88), next to the Peace Café. Album covers and coasters decorate the walls, music plays loudly, and the TV shows soccer games (pray that England wins). Fish and chips, chicken, spaghetti, burgers, and *schnitzel* all NIS7. Goldstar NIS3, drinks NIS12. Open daily 3pm-whenever.

**Piccadilly Pub,** in the New Tourist Center. Tries its right hardest to be a spot-on olde English pub. Draft beer NIS6. Open daily 3pm-3am.

**Dolphin Reef** (tel. 637 42 92). The hottest spot east of Havana. Dance in the sand Mon. and Thurs. night, and Fri. afternoon. Packed in summer, but you can take a break on the beach. Cover NIS20 (less in low season) Microbrews (meaning the cups are small) NIS7. Open Mon.-Thurs. 10pm-late, Fri. 10am-late.

**Tropicana** (tel. 637 46 16), in the Shalom Center. Videos, cartoons, and Charlie Chaplin. 0.5L beer NIS5. Bottle of ¡tequila! NIS100. Happy 20min. for women 7-7:20pm (free booze). Draft beers NIS4 6-8pm. Open daily 4:30pm-late.

**Yaeni Pub,** in the Ostrich Farm across from Coral Beach. Take bus #15 or a cab. Light show 9pm. Desert feel. Goldstar NIS5. Open Mon.-Sat. 7pm-dawn.

## Clubs

**Sheba's,** at the King Solomon Hotel (tel. 637 41 11). Ultra-modern, maximum-reflection atmosphere with laser show. Mixes disco, pop, and new wave. Energetic bartenders and strong drinks; beware the stuffed panther. NIS30 cover includes 1 drink. Maccabee NIS8. Open Mon.-Sat. 11:30pm until empty.

**Ha-Nesiha,** at the Princess Hotel right before Taba Beach (take a cab). Hefty NIS40 cover, but you'll thrill to sophisticated sound and light systems and a rotating dance floor. For those who really want to dance.

**Royal Beach Hotel Disco** in the marina. Israelis dude up and show off on the shiny dance floor. NIS30 cover. Open daily 11pm-late.

The tourist office has information on events at the **Phillip Murray Cultural Center** (tel. 633 22 57) on Ḥativat Ha-Negev near the bus station. The jazz, classical, rock, film, and theater seasons run September-June. The center also has a television, a reading room, and rotating art exhibits (open daily 8am-8pm). The kids like **Luna Park** (tel. 637 60 95), in front of the Queen of Sheba Hotel. Rides like bumper cars and "Super-X Simulator" cost NIS8; kiddie thrills are NIS4 (open Mon.-Sat. 6pm-midnight). The week-long **Hebrew Rock Music Festival,** one week prior to Passover on Eilat Beach, and the end-of-August **Red Sea Jazz festival,** with 10 daily performances on four stages, are both popular annual events. Ask the GTIO for more information.

## GOING TO EGYPT

Crossing from Eilat to Taba takes a while and costs a couple of pounds. Before trying it, be sure that your passport is valid for at least another three months, and that your Israeli visa is valid (at least for the day on which you'll be traveling). If you want to go places other than the Sinai, you'll need to get a **visa** at the Egyptian consulate (see Practical Information, p. 434).

The border-crossing process unfolds in an orderly way, but involves a surprisingly long hike. Allow about two hours for the entire process, though it can take longer on a busy day. Keep your passport on hand after you disembark from the bus (#15 from Eilat); you'll have to show it frequently as you go through the 2km obstacle course to the bus depot on the other side. The 14 exciting steps: (1) Bus drop-off; (2) Little Taba snack bar ("last beer before Sinai" NIS5); (3) Passport pre-check; (4) Passport control booth (pay NIS47 exit tax); (5) Israeli last passport check (they automatically stamp your passport at this point unless you ask them not to); (6) Stroll through no-man's-land; (7) Egyptian passport control (fill out entry form, get stamp); (8) Intermission: dancing girls and silly monkeys; (9) Egyptian security (X-ray machine); (10) Post-border passport check; (11) 1-km hike; (12) Customs, hidden on the left-hand side of the street. Don't pass it by without declaring *everything* that's of any importance that you're bringing with you into the Sinai, or the strict Egyptian border authorities won't let you leave with it; (13) Show passport and pay E£18 Egyptian border tax. The Taba Hilton is the best place to **change money.** It's open 24 hours and charges no commission for foreign currency converted to Egyptian pounds; (14) Bus station. Welcome to Egypt!

If you plan on staying in the Sinai for 14 days or fewer and don't plan on going to other parts of Egypt, you can get a **Sinai-only visa** stamped into your passport on the Egyptian side of the border. This visa limits travel to the Gulf of Aqaba coast as far south as Sharm esh-Sheikh (but not the area around Sharm esh-Sheikh, including Ras Muhammad; see **Sharm esh-Sheikh**, p. 255) and to St. Catherine's monastery and Mt. Sinai (but not sites in the vicinity of St. Catherine's). Unlike ordinary one-month Egyptian visas, the Sinai-only visa has no grace period; you'll pay a hefty fine if you overextend your stay.

There is a 10am bus to Nuweiba' (1hr., E£10), a 3pm to Dahab (3hr., E£15), and a 2pm to Cairo (7hr., E£50). St. Catherine's can't be reached in a single day via public transportation; you have to transfer buses in Dahab. Only the 3pm "crazy bus" goes as far as Sharm esh-Sheikh (E£12). It's unclear whether the moniker comes from the driver who has blown a few fuses after too much shuttling up and down the scorching Aqaba Coast, or the passengers, who are demented enough to actually ride this tired heap. What's important is that the bus will go where it wants, when it wants; this could be all the way to Sharm or no farther than you could throw it. The one-way trip to Sharm esh-Sheikh takes six hours by bus or three by taxi. There are always taxis hanging out waiting to take people to Dahab, Cairo, or Nuweiba'. You could have a long wait until they fill up, but you shouldn't pay too much more than the bus fare—after the last bus, however, they have you at their mercy.

### GOING TO JORDAN

To cross from Eilat to Aqaba, everyone must pay a NIS51.70 exit tax. Jordanian visas can be obtained at the border and prices vary greatly according to nationality (US JD15, Canada JD31, UK JD23, Australia free, Ireland JD5, New Zealand JD4, South Africa free). Visas are valid up to one month. The process is easy and should take less than an hour. Changing money at the border is expensive. Take bus #16 to the border (NIS4). Taxis from the border to Aqaba cost JD4—there are no buses.

## ■ Near Eilat

The beauty of the red granite mountains towering over Eilat matches that of the coral reefs thriving beneath. Few guided tours are available for non-Hebrew speakers, but the **SPNI field school,** across from Coral Beach (take bus #15), will help you strike out on your own. They sell Hebrew trail maps (NIS30), and will help translate. Many of the sites are accessible by northbound bus #393, 394, or 397. Buses fill up fast during high season and on Sundays and Fridays; make reservations at the central bus station two days in advance or get stuck in the boonies.

The hike to **Mt. Tzfaḥot** is convenient and provides great views. The green-and-white trail begins at the left end of the fence separating the highway from the field school complex. The climb to the summit takes 45 minutes. From here, the blue trail heads north, ending at the Club Inn Hotel near Aqua Sport beach. The round trip takes about two hours and makes a great evening outing in summer. If you wander too far on paths leading south, you may end up in Egypt.

The most exciting terrain accessible from Eilat is to the north. Take bus #392 in the morning for **Ein Netafim, Mt. Shlomo** (through Mapalim Valley), or **Ha-Kanyon Ha-Adom** (Red Canyon). The bus driver will know when to let you off. These hikes are not advisable in summer unless you're impervious to boiling-point temperatures. From Red Canyon, you can hike to the lookout above **Moon Valley,** a pocked canyon in Egypt, and to the unusual **Amram's Pillars.** A half-day guided tour is US$19 (winter only) with **Egged Tours** (tel. 637 31 48; depart from the central bus station). **Avi Desert Safari** (tel. 637 88 71) offers similar half- and full-day tours. A Jeep trip is available for half (US$32) and full days (US$44) through **Johnny Desert Tours** (tel. 632 52 65) in the Shalom Center. **Camel Riders** (tel. 637 32 18) offer two-day caravans along old smugglers' routes (US$120) or Mt. Ḥorev (US$140). **Metzokei Gishron** (tel. 637 65 78) offers cliff climbing tours.

## Seeing Spots

The graceful and majestic leopard, mentioned eight times in the Bible, disappeared from the Negev about 100 years ago. In an effort to replenish desert wildlife, the Israeli government has designated three quarters of the Negev as nature reserves, and the ferocious spotted cat has returned to its home of old. The Hai Bar Preserve is the best place for leopard sightings. Wildlife experts say that the leopard's presence at the top of nature's hierarchy, proves that a full desert food chain is alive and kicking.

The **National Park** (tel. 635 62 15) at **Timna** is another hiking destination. The Timna copper mines, remarkably well preserved in the southeast corner of the park, were in mint condition 6000 years ago. Some people believe the Israelites passed through here on their way out of Egypt. Today you can find remains of workers' camps and cisterns dating from the 11th century BCE scattered amidst the whir of modern mining. The sandstone **King Solomon's Pillars** dominate the desert at a height of 50m near the 14th-century BCE Egyptian Temple of Hathor. The park's lake offers **camping** facilities (including showers) and a restaurant on its artificially created shores. **United Tours,** in the Shalom Center (tel. 637 17 29), runs tours to Timna Valley for about NIS65 per half-day. Alternately, most buses that go to Tel Aviv or Jerusalem will let you off at the sign for Alipaz (don't get off at the Timna Mines signpost). The entrance is 2km away (park open daily 7:30am-6:45pm; admission NIS10, ages 5-18 NIS4.50).

Most northbound buses will take you to the **Hai Bar Biblical Nature Reserve,** a wildlife park designed to repopulate animals indigenous in Biblical times, many of which have become rare in the region. Ask to get off at Yotvata. The reserve is home to roaming gazelles, Somali wild asses, ostriches, and 11 species of predators mentioned in the Bible, including leopards, wolves, and striped hyenas. (Open summer daily 9am-1pm, winter 9am-2pm; animal feeding 8-11am. Admission NIS16, children NIS10, includes coach tour.) The leopards are hungry—only closed vehicles may enter. Pedestrians can either wait for a vehicle with space or take one of the hourly tours in **Hai Bar Coaches** on Sunday, Tuesday, Thursday, and Saturday.

The entrance to Hai Bar is opposite the entrance to Kibbutz Samir, 5km south of Yotvata. At Kibbutz Yotvata, **Ye'elim Desert Holiday Village** (tel. 637 43 62) has tent space for NIS24. (Check-in 2pm. Caravan singles NIS82. Doubles NIS116. July-Aug. NIS140 and NIS195.) A **swimming pool** is free for guests, NIS10 for visitors. The **visitor's center** (tel. 637 60 18) opposite the kibbutz provides information and a film about Negev ecology (open daily 8am-3pm; NIS5 for the film, free with ticket to Hai Bar). You can munch on Yotvata's famous cheese and yogurt at the **cafeteria.**

ISRAEL

# WEST BANK الضفةالغربية

In summer 1996, the West Bank was anticipating dramatic political transformation. At press time, negotiations were still in progress. Imminent political changes, most significantly a redeployment of the IDF and transfer of authority to the PA (Palestinian Authority) in most West Bank towns, may alter everything from bus schedules to attitudes to the safety of travel in the area. The West Bank and Gaza have seen considerable conflict between Palestinian residents and Israeli settlers and security forces in the not-too-distant past. Be aware of the current situation in each town you plan to visit before you go, but also remember that the West Bank is safer in many ways than New York, Los Angeles, or Washington, D.C. Carry your passport at all times.

The rugged towns of the West Bank combine the historic splendor of the past, the impassioned politics of the present, and the psychological tax of an uncertain future. For the first time in history, the Palestinian flag flies over many towns ruled by the Palestinians themselves. The process by which self-rule was established has been a long and arduous one, the trials of which are easily read in the faces of West Bank residents. They know, too, that their struggle has not ended. At the same time, travel in the West Bank provides a physical immediacy to the events and characters of the Bible and the Qur'an. Jacob built a chapel in Beitin, Joshua leveled Jericho, and Jesus was born in Bethlehem.

While extremists on both sides struggle to destabilize daily life in an effort to derail the peace process, the very controversy makes the territory fascinating to explore. Well informed travelers will have no problem visiting the area and befriending locals. Tourists may be invited to Palestinian homes, where hot spiced tea, muddily delicious coffee, and an endless supply of cigarettes are accompanied by discussions of the *intifada* and occupation. The Israeli settlements are generally less accessible to tourists than the Palestinian towns, but visits can be arranged through the Jerusalem MTIO (see p. 419). Modest dress will make both men's and women's experiences here more enjoyable.

## ONCE THERE

### ■ Coming and Going

The Palestinians, Jordanians, and Israelis are still trying to figure this one out for themselves. We cannot guarantee much of the information here, although in summer 1996 the procedure was smooth for many travelers of different nationalities. It could change the first time Arafat, Hussein, or Netanyahu sneezes.

With a private car, you can visit the West Bank from Israel; expect numerous Israeli checkpoints and bring your passport along. Most public transportation connections are from Jerusalem. If you check with the Israeli GTIO before going, you'll probably get a standard governmental fright warning, which you should consider but also take with a grain of salt.

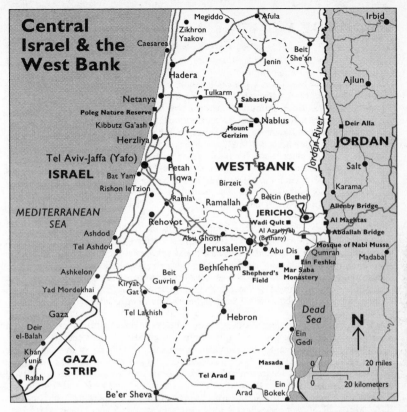

**Central Israel & the West Bank**

Megiddo
Afula
Irbid
Zikhron Yaakov
Caesarea
Beit She'an
Jenin
Ajlun
Hadera
Tulkarm
Sabastiya
Netanya
Nablus
Poleg Nature Reserve
Kibbutz Ga'ash
Mount Gerizim
Deir Alla
Herzliya
**JORDAN**
Tel Aviv-Jaffa (Yafo)
**WEST BANK**
Salt
**ISRAEL**
Petah Tiqwa
Bat Yam
Rishon leTzion
Birzeit
Karama
Ramla
Ramallah
Beitin (Bethel)
Allenby Bridge
*MEDITERRANEAN SEA*
Rehovot
JERICHO
Wadi Qult
Al Maghtas
Ashdod
Abu Ghosh
Al Azariyyah (Bethany)
Abdallah Bridge
Tel Ashdod
Jerusalem
Abu Dis
Mosque of Nabi Mussa
Qumran
Madaba
Ashkelon
Beit Guvrin
Bethlehem
Mar Saba Monastery
Ein Feshka
Yad Mordekhai
Kiryat Gat
Shepherd's Field
Gaza
Tel Lakhish
Hebron
*Dead Sea*
Deir el-Balah
**N**
Khan Yunis
**GAZA STRIP**
Ein Gedi
Rafah
Masada
0        20 miles
Tel Arad
0        20 kilometers
Be'er Sheva
Arad
Ein Bokek

The King Hussein/Allenby Bridge, open from 8am to 5pm every day except Saturday, is the only direct crossing point between Jordan and the West Bank. Everything remains unpredictable; get thorough, up-to-date information from your embassy or consulate before trying to cross. At press time, buses and *service* frequently left Amman's Abdali Station for the bridge. Public transportation goes to the first checkpoint. Shuttle buses take travelers to the next (see **Amman: Practical Information,** p. 476). Be prepared to pay JD5 to Jordanian customs officers upon leaving and reentering Jordan; for groups, the fee is usually waived. Another JD1.500 is collected on a special bus traversing the bridge. The Israeli side does not collect money. You may pay for transportation on the West Bank with Jordanian dinars. See **Border Crossings,** p. 38, for more information.

To get to Jordan from the West Bank, you'll need a Jordanian visa, obtainable in Tel Aviv, at the border crossings between Eilat and Aqaba, or at the Sheikh Hussein Bridge near Beit She'an (see **Tel Aviv: Practical Information,** p. 328) and **Eilat: Practical Information,** p. 434). You can also get the visa before leaving your home country from a Jordanian embassy or consulate (see p. 9). Start early in the morning. Board a *service* taxi bound for the Bridge. Make sure your *service* goes all the way to the border—some are authorized to go only as far as a checkpoint on the outskirts of town. No private vehicles are permitted to cross the bridge (this might change at the end of 1996). At the bridge, your passport and belongings will be inspected. Once on the Jordanian side, you can catch a *service* to Amman.

# ■ Getting Around

The West Bank is crisscrossed by a relatively reliable and cheap network of buses and shared taxis *(service)*. Private taxis, usually air-conditioned, are readily available, but are substantially more expensive.

A system of colored license plates differentiates vehicles and their drivers. Those registered in Israel, West Jerusalem, and Jewish settlements sport yellow plates. Blue plates signify Arabs' cars from the Territories, and green plates belong to Arab taxis and buses. Other hues are white (UN or diplomatic), red (police), and black (army). It's probably safer to travel with blue plates, but many Arab-owned cars that are registered in Israel proper (thus with yellow plates) travel hassle-free throughout the West Bank.

East Jerusalem is the transportation hub for the West Bank, but a 1992 closure made it impossible for local Palestinians to use Jerusalem as a transit terminal; as a result, some lines were re-routed to Ramallah, and *service* from Jerusalem to places such as Nablus became less frequent.

**Taxis** *Service* taxis are the most convenient mode of West Bank transportation. Although slightly more expensive than Arab buses, they are faster, more reliable, and more frequent. Use your time in a *service* to get to know some of your fellow passengers. If you get lost or disoriented, consult the drivers; they are knowledgeable in matters ranging from politics to the location of obscure ruins. Private taxis are more expensive but more practical for remote areas. Drivers will take you to the site, and (for a few extra shekels) wait while you admire your favorite landmark.

**Buses** Both Arab and Egged buses service the West Bank. Arab buses leave from two bus stations in East Jerusalem: the Suleiman St. Station between Herod's and Damascus Gates, for points south; and the Nablus Rd. Station, for points north. You can catch Egged buses at the West Jerusalem central bus station on Jaffa Rd. Egged buses should be a last resort in the West Bank. They cost more and often take you only to the outskirts of Palestinian towns. Take Egged to the Jewish settlements.

Arab bus schedules to the West Bank are, well, flexible; the intervals listed here are approximate. Transportation to Nablus is especially erratic. Buses may also pick people up from the side of the road. Arab buses have light blue stripes on the sides (except for the Ramallah bus, which is red), while Egged buses are red and white.

### From the Suleiman St. Station

**#22:** To Bethlehem (every 15min., NIS1.50).
**#23:** To Hebron (every 15min., NIS5).
**#28:** To Jericho (every 1½hr., NIS3.50).
**#36:** To Bethany (every hr., NIS1.50).
**#36:** To Abu Dees and Bethany (every hr., NIS1.50).

### From the Nablus Rd. Station

**#18:** To Ramallah (every 15min., NIS1.50).
**#23:** To Nablus (Tamini Bus Co., every 45min., NIS6).

# ■ Money Matters

The **new Israeli shekel (NIS)** is prevalent, although **Jordanian dinars (JD)** and **U.S. dollars (US$)** are also in use. Expect prices to increase by a significant margin if you offer to pay for your purchase in anything other than shekels. Although Palestinians take Israeli currency, they often don't like to speak Hebrew. English, Arabic, or Klingon are better options.

## ■ Keeping in Touch

The postal service in the West Bank is, for now at least, a part of the Israeli mail system; refer to **Israel: Keeping in Touch,** p. 272. All major towns in the West Bank have at least one post office with *poste restante*. Letters should be addressed: main post office, town, West Bank, via Israel. The Palestinian Authority in Jericho has its own postal system, with Palestinian stamps that are currently only good for sending letters between Jericho and Gaza, but their range may soon extend.

The telephone system is also part of the Israeli telephone network. All services, including collect and calling card calls, are available from any private or public telephone. Beige public telephones, operated by **telecards,** are conveniently located in most post offices, where you can also purchase the cards. Relevant area codes are (02) for Bethlehem, Ramallah, and the South, and (09) for Nablus and the North.

For now, direct calls to some Arab countries from Israel or the West Bank or vice-versa are officially impossible. Exceptions to this rule are Jordan, Egypt, and Morocco; more countries should soon become accessible. The international phone code for the West Bank is the same as that of Israel (972).

# LIFE AND TIMES

## ■ Political History

If it's the truth you seek, talking about West Bank politics will most probably leave you disappointed and confused. The problem is that around here no one wants to talk about anything else, and it's usually difficult to remove personal ideologies and emotional attachments from such a controversial discussion.

Historically, the West Bank represents the most complex facet of the Arab-Israeli conflict because of its relevance to three major groups: Israelis, Palestinian Arabs, and Jordanians. Jews have lived in the West Bank since long before the 1967 and even the 1948 wars. For the most part Jews were drawn to the holy city of Hebron, but in 1829 they fled town after Arab riots claimed 80 Jewish lives. Palestinian Arabs form the region's largest indigenous group and have resided throughout Israel and the West Bank for hundreds of years. Over 70% of the Jordanian population is of Palestinian origin, though the country is ruled by a Hashemite Bedouin family.

The political division now called the West Bank was created in the 1948 Arab-Israeli War, when Jordan conquered the territory to its west (the "western bank" of the Jordan River). King Abdallah angered most Palestinians by annexing the region rather than creating a separate state as the U.N. Partition Plan had stipulated. The Jordanian government subsequently did little to develop the West Bank and discriminated against its Palestinian residents. Their situation, however, was better than that of the Egyptian-occupied Gaza Strip's Palestinians, as the fertile West Bank was economically vital to Jordan.

In the 1967 Six Day War, the West Bank was one of several territories captured by Israeli forces. Rather than officially annex the area (excluding East Jerusalem, which was annexed), Israel placed it under military administration. Arab mayors and police kept their offices, Jordanian school curriculums continued to be taught, public welfare programs and National Social Security payments were instituted, and Israeli medical treatment was provided.

But Israeli occupation was much more complicated than this. Palestinians suffered curfews, mass arrests, and demolition of homes in retaliation for the alleged actions of one family member. There was no freedom of assembly—Palestinians could not have weddings, gatherings, or meetings without a permit from the Israeli authorities, which could be denied for a variety of reasons. Flying the Palestinian flag was illegal. In addition, the infrastructure, schools, and public works of the West Bank were neglected in comparison with those of towns in Israel proper. The Palestinians' own attempts at establishing institutions or some form of economic independence were likewise thwarted. Birzeit University was denied a building permit for years and shut down frequently. Cottage industries such as pickling, baking, and embroidery attained some success, but were often unceremoniously closed.

Israeli settlements in the West Bank were and continue to be a source of constant controversy. Some 130,000 Israeli Jews have settled in the West Bank since its seizure in 1967. Launched by Labor governments eager to establish an Israeli presence in areas of strategic importance such as the Jordan Valley, the settlement project has been an ideological cornerstone of right-wing Likud governments since 1977. They are motivated not only by strategic considerations, but also by *Eretz Yisrael* (the land of Israel), an area including Israel, the West Bank, the Gaza Strip, and a bit beyond. Often strategically situated on hilltops overlooking Palestinian towns, many settlements resemble military installations more than housing developments. They are surrounded by barbed wire and guarded by Israeli soldiers around the clock; most settlers conspicuously carry guns, while Palestinians may not bear arms.

In December 1987, the Palestinians of the occupied territories began the *intifada*. A traffic accident in the Gaza Strip provided the spark; two decades of occupation, economic stagnation, and increasing Israeli settlement activity erupted in stone-throwing, chanting, unfurling of the Palestinian flag, and expression of nationalistic pride. Forms of resistance included nonpayment of taxes, general strikes, and resignations from government service. The young Palestinians of the West Bank (many leaders of the *intifada* were not past their teenage years) set up underground "popular committees" that organized strikes, demonstrations, and funerals, and made sure that everyone had enough to eat. Many did time in Israeli jails; they used this time for educational and planning purposes. A new generation of Palestinians—those who knew nothing but Israeli occupation—had abruptly upstaged their elders, including the PLO, with a widespread resistance movement.

The *intifada* led to major changes in the nature of the Palestinian-Israeli conflict. The popular nature of the uprising and its televised brutal suppression by the Israeli army managed to draw far more international attention and sympathy than decades of PLO tactics; the Palestinian problem was reinstated as the focal point of the Arab-Israeli dispute. American Jewish groups and Israeli liberals expressed dismay at the sometimes brutal tactics of the Israeli army, and indicated to Israeli politicians that continued occupation of the territories would make them reconsider their financial and political support. After about six years of continued struggle, many Palestinians were worn out. Palestinians suspected of collaboration were dragged from their homes in the middle of the night, sometimes assaulted and even killed. The *intifada* had stopped making headlines by the time the Gulf Crisis began in 1991. In contrast to most Arab governments in the region, who joined a U.S.-led coalition opposing Saddam Hussein, the PLO, along with most Palestinians, supported Iraq. Some Palestinians cheered from rooftops when Iraq's SCUD missiles landed on Tel Aviv. Saudi Arabia and other oil-rich Gulf states, whose financial support had been trickling through the PLO into the territories, suspended their aid.

In the aftermath of the Gulf War, several factors convinced Middle Eastern governments that it was high time for a regional peace conference. After the historic Madrid conference in October 1991, negotiations between the Palestinians (in a joint Jordanian-Palestinian delegation) and the Israelis took place from 1991 to 1994 in Washington, D.C. The first Israeli delegation to the peace talks, headed by hard-line Likud prime minister Yitzhak Shamir, offered little with which to bargain. But the following center-left government, formed following the June 1992 elections, brought a significant change to Israeli policy toward Palestinians and the occupied territories. Late Prime Minister Yitzhak Rabin moved almost immediately to freeze all settlement activity, and pushed to promote the peace process with a special emphasis on the Israeli-Palestinian negotiations. The effect of the Israeli political swing back to Likud remains to be seen.

The talks raised a polarizing debate on both sides. In Israel, many feel that to turn the West Bank over to the Palestinians (and thereby expose the narrow coastal strip that houses three-fourths of Israel's population to hostile neighbors) would be tantamount to guiding a knife to their own throats. Others argue that until Israel makes peace with its neighbors, terrorism and war will continue to claim countless young lives. On the Palestinian side, moderates favoring a compromise with Israel (such as negotiators Faisal al-Husseini and Hanan Ashrawi) are challenged by Islamist Hamas, which was gaining popularity when the talks began. Hamas advocates continue armed struggle and cannot envision a Palestinian state peacefully existing alongside Israel, forever the enemy in the eyes of Hamas. See p. 55 for more on the peace process.

At the peace talks in Washington, the different delegations took turns in not showing up, storming out in protest, showing up late, and storming out in a huff when the other party showed up late. It took secret negotiations in Oslo (baby-sat by the Norwegian Foreign Minister) between representatives of the PLO and the Israeli government to rescue the ailing Washington talks and to lay the groundwork for Palestinian self-rule. The Oslo negotiations resulted in the drafting of the Declaration of Principles on Interim Self-Rule Arrangements (the DOP or Oslo Accord). The Oslo Accord provided for mutual recognition of Israel and the PLO, commitment by the parties to seek a non-violent settlement of their disputes, and successive stages of negotiations which would gradually transfer power to an autonomous Palestinian government over a five-year transitional period. This period is to be followed by an agreement on final status issues such as Jerusalem, refugees, settlements, security arrangements, borders, and foreign relations.

The Oslo agreement and the more detailed Cairo agreement, signed in May 1994 and calling for Israeli withdrawal from the Gaza strip and the Jericho area of the West Bank, were implemented in mid-1994. Much of the PLO leadership relocated from Tunisia to Gaza, where they established the Palestinian National Authority (PNA), more commonly referred to as the Palestinian Authority, (PA). In subsequent negotiations with Israel, some control over the remainder of the West Bank, excluding Israeli settlements and military outposts, was transferred to the PA. By the summer of 1995, the PA had complete control in Jericho and Gaza (except for a small number of settlements in Gaza), with Israeli powers essentially limited to foreign affairs and external security. The PA also had powers over taxation, education, social welfare, health, and tourism in the rest of the West Bank, excluding settlements and military outposts. A new round of intense negotiations during the summer led to the drafting of an interim agreement for the re-deployment of Israeli Defense Force units from Palestinian towns, the transfer of direct control over those areas to the PA, and the establishment of an elected Palestinian parliament. All IDF personnel in Arab cities—with the exception of Hebron, whose status is still under negotiation as of summer 1996—will be moved to four army bases in unpopulated areas. Palestinian security forces will then be responsible for policing the territory.

## ■ Economy

The economy of the West Bank has been controlled by the Israeli economy since the 1967 occupation. Throughout the occupation, crises in Israel's economy were felt even more sharply in the West Bank because Palestinians were the first to be laid off from jobs in times of hardship. Many West Bank Palestinians continue to work in Israel with no health insurance, job security, or workers' rights.

The West Bank economy was a major battleground of the *intifada*. Palestinians boycotted Israeli products in an attempt to rid themselves of their crippling economic dependence, and the Israeli government imposed economic sanctions on the Palestinian community as a form of punishment and as a way of extending domination. The Palestinian Authority has inherited this devastated economy, with an undeveloped infrastructure a quarter of a century old.

**WEST BANK**

## ■ Literature

Much Palestinian literature is concerned with the agony of foreign occupation and exile. Ghassan Kanafani, perhaps the greatest contemporary Palestinian fiction writer, recreates the desperation and aimlessness of the refugee in his short stories *All That Remains: Palestine's Children. Men in the Sun and Other Palestinian Stories* portrays the struggle through adult eyes. Palestinians' attachment to the land is portrayed in the wonderful poetry of Mahmoud Darwish, and the longing for a homeland in the poems of Fouzi al-Asmar, collected in *The Wind-Driven Reed and Other Poems.* Jabra Ibrahim Jabra's novel *The Ship* is engrossing. Israeli Arab Anton Shammas' *Arabesques* describes Palestinian identity crises; Fawaz Turki's autobiographical tomes discuss life in exile. The works of Sahar Khalifeh, Liyana Badr, Raymonda Tawil, and Samih al-Qassem are all noteworthy; most of these authors and many others are translated in Salma Khadra Jayyusi's behemoth *Modern Palestinian Literature.*

# WEST BANK SIGHTS

## ■ Jericho أريحا

Like many West Bank towns, Jericho (Ariha in Arabic, Yeriho in Hebrew) exudes a sense of magnanimous history. The first city to fly the Palestinian flag and the headquarters of the nascent Palestinian Authority, Jericho bustles with new, ground-breaking activity. Banners, flags, and portraits of Yassir Arafat strewn across the streets convey a feeling of pride and optimism.

Settled 10,000 years ago, Jericho is believed to be the world's oldest city. Excavations are extensive, but the ruins themselves aren't that spectacular (after all, the walls are famous for tumbling down). After the fierce warrior Joshua destroyed the city with a blow of his trumpet (Joshua 2-6), Jericho remained in shambles for centuries. The oasis town made a reluctant comeback under the Romans, Crusaders, and Mamluks, but it never became anything more than a sleepy palm grove village in the desert. The population skyrocketed after 1967, when thousands of Palestinian refugees fled here from Israel. Today, developers are busy turning the refugee tents into apartment buildings, and proudly creating a new autonomous Palestinian city.

### ORIENTATION AND PRACTICAL INFORMATION

Forty km east of Jerusalem, Jericho is on the road to Amman, at the junction of the highway to the Galilee. For information on crossing **to Jordan,** see p. 442.

The quickest and most reliable way to get to Jericho is by *service* taxi (NIS8). They leave from East Jerusalem, at the parking lot across from Damascus Gate, and drop you off at the central square in front of Jericho's municipality building. There is no schedule: they leave when full. Inquire at East Jerusalem's Arab bus station about bus #28. It used to run to Jericho and, depending on demand and the border crossing situation, may do so in the future. To return to Jerusalem, catch a taxi heading to Abu Dees (NIS5). From there switch into a taxi with a yellow license plate and go to Damascus Gate (NIS2). (See **West Bank: Coming and Going,** p. 442.)

**Tourist Information Office:** Run by the PA and located in the old city (tel. 992 29 35). As of the summer of 1996, the office still provided maps left over from its days as an Israeli GTIO; officials are currently working on a new map, and possibly other free goodies. All services also available in the Municipality building in the town center. Open Sat.-Thurs. 7:30am-2:30pm.

**Currency Exchange: Cairo Amman Bank** (tel. 992 36 29; fax 992 35 80), in the main square. Open Sat.-Thurs. 8:30am-12:30pm and 4-6pm.

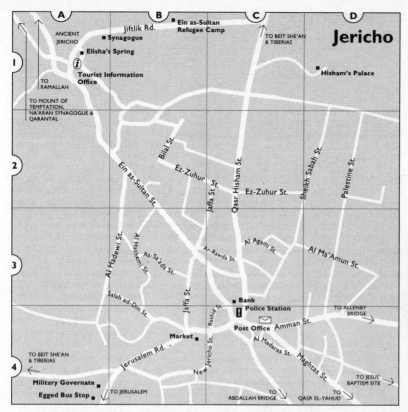

**Jericho**

Taxi: Will take you on a loop of the sights for about NIS30-50; agree in advance. One-way fare to the Old City is NIS4-5.

**Car Rental: Orabi Rent-a-car's** Jericho office is on Jerusalem Rd. (tel. 992 32 30), across from the Pension. Starts at US$30 per day—but the blue license plates might not be the best thing to have while touring the country.

**Bike Rental:** A great way to see the sights in Jericho. **Muhammad Tawili's Bicycle Shop** (tel. 992 36 25), in the central square, east of the municipality building, rents functional, balloon-tire bombers (NIS3 per hr.). Open Sat.-Thurs. 7am-8pm, Fri. 7am-1pm. Bring lots of water and bike on the left side of the road.

**Pharmacy: Al Marjah Pharmacy,** on Ein Sultan St., past Hisham's Palace Hotel.

**Red Cross:** On Ein es-Sultan St., (tel. 992 28 48), across from Hisham's Palace Hotel. Open Mon.-Tues. and Thurs. 8am-2pm.

**Hospital: Jericho Government Hospital** (tel. 992 24 06 or 25 73), off the square.

**Police:** Next to the bank (tel. 992 25 21).

**Post office:** Down Amman St. from the police station (tel. 992 13 00, fax 992 36 09). You can buy Palestinian National Authority (PNA) stamps starting at 5ag. For the time being, they're only good for Gaza-bound mail but they make great souvenirs. Open Sat.-Thurs. 8am-2pm.

**Telephone:** 02.

## ACCOMMODATIONS AND FOOD

As of now, travelers have three accommodating options, and budget travelers two. True to its name, the **New Jericho Pension** (tel. 992 22 15) opened in July 1995. Located across from the New Jericho mosque on Jerusalem Rd., the pension is close to the city center and across the street from a supermarket. Run by the kind Ibrahim, rooms have carved wooden beds with spring mattresses; the roomy common area has a TV and a radio (flexible check-out and prices: singles US$13-15, doubles US$20, triples US$30). **Hisham's Palace Hotel** (tel. 992 21 56), close to the city center on Ein as-Sultan St., doesn't have the newest facilities in town. Despite a nice outdoor porch, this is the definite second choice. The rooms have balconies, fans, and blindingly bright lights. (Noon check-out. Midnight curfew. Singles NIS40, with bath NIS100. Doubles NIS120.)

There is such a thing as a free lunch here; locals who befriend you may well bring you home to dine on chicken while groups of kids look on curiously. If not, many tasty, cheap restaurants cluster around the city center—the usual falafel, *shawerma, kabab, shishlik,* and chicken variety. Most places have Arabic signs with a simple English translation of "restaurant." Falafel should be about NIS2, *shawerma* NIS5. For a pricier, all-you-can-eat experience, head to the **Maxim Restaurant,** down Ein as-Sultan St. They offer great selection of salads (NIS14) and meats (NIS22), and let you eat until you *are* the hummus (open daily 7am-midnight).

## SIGHTS

Jericho's most popular sights, Hisham's Palace and ancient Jericho, lie on the outskirts of town. It's best to visit **Hisham's Palace** (tel. 992 25 22) first, since a cluster of restaurants and a cooling spring near the ancient city can provide a pleasant rest stop after your tour. To reach the palace, follow the signs along Qasr Hisham St. and head north 3km from the eastern side of Jericho's main square. Coming from ancient Jericho, head east on Jiftlik Rd., past the Synagogue and the **Ein as-Sultan refugee camp.** After 1.5km, turn right on the road back to Jericho town; the turn-off to Hisham's Palace appears almost immediately on your left.

Begun in 724 CE and completed in 743, Hisham's Palace was ravaged only four years later by an earthquake. Known as Khirbet al-Mafjar in Arabic, the palace was designed for the Umayyad Caliph Hisham as a winter retreat from Damascus. The extensive ruins here are a jaw-dropping sample of early Islamic architecture. The window in the courtyard, the site's most renowned feature, is in the shape of the six-pointed Umayyad star. A beautifully preserved mosaic depicts a sinister tableau in which foxes lick their chops as they watch naive gazelles frolic in the shade of the Tree of Life (open daily 8am-5pm; admission NIS8, students NIS6).

To get to ancient Jericho from the city center, follow Ein as-Sultan St. to its end. From Hisham's Palace 2km away, turn right onto the road that runs past the Palace, then take a left at the end. Follow the "Tel Jericho" signs. On the way is the **6th-century synagogue,** featuring an expansive mosaic floor, a *menorah,* a *shofar* (ram's horn), a *lulav* (palm branch), and the inscription *Shalom al Yisrael:* peace be upon Israel. As part of extensive preliminary agreements, the PA promised to watch over this synagogue, still a functioning *yeshiva.* A little past the synagogue towards Ancient Jericho, on the left is **Elisha's Spring** on the left. Papayas, grapes, oranges, bananas, and mint thrive behind the spring. The old city is across the street.

**Ancient Jericho,** thought to be the oldest city in the world (as opposed to Damascus, the oldest continually inhabited city), is now a heap of ruined walls. Called **Tel as-Sultan,** the mound contains layer upon layer of garbage from ancient (and modern) cities. The oldest fortifications, 12m down, are 7000 years old. Some of the finds date from the early Neolithic period, leading archaeologists to suspect that Jericho was inhabited as early as the eighth millennium BCE. A limited amount of excavation has exposed many levels of ancient walls, some of them 3.5m thick and 5.5m high. Your imagination will have to substitute for visible splendor at this site, which is distinctly unphotogenic save for its great view (tel. 992 29 09; open daily 8am-5pm; admission NIS8, students NIS6).

An imposing Greek Orthodox **monastery** stands on the edge of a cliff among the mountains west of Jericho; the peak is believed to be the New Testament's Mount of Temptation. The complex of buildings stands before a grotto, said to be the spot where Jesus fasted for 40 days and 40 nights after his baptism (Matthew 4:1-11). Six

Greek monks now live in the monastery, built in 1895. They can point out the rock where Jesus was tempted by the devil and served by angels. The summit of the mountain, named **Qarantal** after the Latin word for "forty," is also a pedestal for the Maccabean **Castle of Dok,** beside which lie the remains of a 4th-century Christian chapel (monastery open daily 9am-2pm and 3-5pm; modest dress required).

# ■ Near Jericho

The road from Jerusalem to Jericho slices through harsh desert landscape. About 8km from Jericho, the 13th-century **Mosque of Nabi Mussa** stands on a hill in a sea of sand, a short distance from the road. This spot is revered throughout the Muslim world as the grave of the prophet Moses, and many Muslims yearn to be buried by his side. Islamic tradition holds that God carried the bones of the prophet here for the faithful to come and pay their respects. The tomb is said to have special powers—run your hands over the velvet cloth of Mussa's Tomb while making a wish and see for yourself. Across from the tomb, stairs lead upwards into a minaret with incredible views of the surrounding Judean desert. Ask the souvenir-selling boys to let you in if the door is wired shut. The only way to visit is by car or taxi (a cab from Jericho shouldn't cost more than NIS40).

## WADI QELT

Threading 28km between imperious limestone cliffs and undulating ridges of bone-white chalk, the three fresh-water springs of Wadi Qelt nourish wildlife and lush greenery. Hiking through the *wadi,* where the arid desert cracks open 395m below sea level and reveals an oasis, is like carving into a pocked cantaloupe and arriving at luscious fruit. Unfortunately, the whole melon may be out of your reach. A string of murders, presumably political, have taken place here in the past several years, most recently in July 1995. Inquire at the MTIO or SPNI to determine the relative safety of hiking in the area. The SPNI offers one-day tours focusing on both natural and artificial attractions in the *wadi* (US$48). The pace may be slower than you'd like, but hiking with a group is much safer.

The most interesting and accessible section of the *wadi* extends from the spring of **Ein Qelt,** past the 6th-century St. George's Monastery, and down into Jericho, 10km east. The trek takes about four hours, adventures in dawdledom excluded. The best place to start is at the turn-off from the Jerusalem-Jericho highway about 9km west of Jericho, marked by the orange sign for "St. George's Monastery." Egged bus #173 (6 per day, 7am-10pm, NIS9.50) from the bus stop across from the central bus station in Jerusalem goes to the Mitzpeh Jericho turn-off. Another possibility is to take a *service* from East Jerusalem to Jericho (NIS5) and catch a cab from there. The trip from Jerusalem takes about an hour. If you're driving, it's possible to skip the hike and follow signs most of the way to St. George's.

**St. George's Monastery** dates from the 5th or 6th century CE. The floor of St. George's Church is decorated with Byzantine mosaics; look for the likeness of a two-headed eagle, the Byzantine symbol of power. The neighboring St. John's Church houses a spooky collection of skulls and bones of monks who were slaughtered when the Persians swept through the valley in 614 CE. The Greek Orthodox monks who maintain the monastery can refill your canteen for the rest of the journey into Jericho. (Open summer Mon.-Sat. 8am-1pm and 3-5pm; winter 8am-1pm and 3-4pm. Modest dress required, modest donation desired.)

On the way to Jericho from St. George's, the ruins of **Tel Abu Alayia** are on your right. The palaces here, used by the Hasmoneans and later by King Herod, have decorated walls, nearby bath houses, and pools.

# ▓ Bethlehem   בيت لحم בית לחם

Bethlehem (Beit Lahm in Arabic, Beit Leḥem in Hebrew) was the Biblical setting for Rachel's death, the love of Ruth and Boaz, and the discovery of the lyrical shepherd

David, future king of Israel. But what really put Bethlehem on the pilgrimage map was the pastoral birth of Jesus. Today, Biblical charm is hidden behind fleets of tour buses unloading believers in front of souvenir stands. Even as you try to peel off the layers of commercialism in your mind's eye, you will be suffocated by exhaust, blinded by flash bulbs, and drowned in floods of postcard-buying devout.

In 1995, Bethlehem celebrated Christmas for the first time under Palestinian rule. The changing of the guard has breathed new life into this small town; the mood is generally upbeat and optimistic, and the people are usually friendly and talkative. Townsfolk whose business involves tourism generally speak English. The best time to visit is during a holiday—Christmas in Bethlehem is unforgettable.

## PRACTICAL INFORMATION

Life for the religiously inquisitive revolves around **Manger Square,** across from the Basilica of the Nativity. **Najajreh** and **Star Street** are home to the town's shopping district and open-air **market** and lead into the Square. Bethlehem is 8km south of Jerusalem.

**PNA Ministry of Tourism:** Manger Sq. (tel. 674 15 81), above the Al Andalus Hotel. Get the new, free PNA town map, details about special events during Christmas and Easter, and transportation information. They also provide a list of accommodations. Open Mon.-Fri. 8am-3pm, Sat. 8am-1pm.

**Currency Exchange: Bank Leumi** (tel. 674 33 30 or 11 470; open Sun.-Thurs. 8am-1pm, Fri. 8am-noon) and **Cairo Amman Bank** (tel. 674 49 71; open Sun.-Thurs. 8:30am-12:30pm, closed Fri.), both in Manger Sq.

**Buses:** Bus station on Manger St., 50m northwest of Manger Sq., down the hill towards Jerusalem. Check with Bethlehem's tourist office to see if buses are running. Quite often they are not, due to border closings. To Jerusalem: #22 and 23 (from Hebron), #47 (from Beit Sahur), and #60 (from Obediyya), 30min., NIS1.50, last bus back at about 5-6pm. From Jerusalem, buses depart at Damascus or Jaffa Gate. The Hebron bus stops only at Rachel's Tomb and at the intersection with Paul VI St., 3km west of Manger Sq.

**Minibuses:** Deheisheh (#1) from Manger St. behind the police station, heads north to Rachel's Tomb, then south to the Deheisheh refugee camp via the road to Hebron (every 15-20min. 6am-6pm, NIS1). Another goes to Beit Sahur (NIS1).

**Taxis: Service taxis** run from Jaffa or Damascus Gate in Jerusalem to the Bethlehem city center until about 7pm (NIS2). To get to Manger Sq., take another local taxi (NIS1). To get back, get in a local cab (all rides NIS1) and either tell him you want to go to Jerusalem, whereby he'll drop you off at the appropriate spot to pick up a Jerusalem-going taxi, or ask to go to Rachel's Tomb (Dareekh Raha'il). From there it's easy to flag down Jerusalem-bound taxis. **Private (special) taxis** will take you to surrounding areas; negotiate a price before the journey.

**Police Station:** Manger Sq. (tel. 674 82 22).

**Post Office:** Manger Sq. (tel. 674 26 68), beside the tourist office. Open Mon., Wed., Fri., and Sat. 8am-2:30pm, Thurs. 8am-12:30pm. **Poste restante** available.

**Telephone Code:** 02.

## ACCOMMODATIONS

While Bethlehem's accommodations are expensive, the few extra shekels will let you sleep in a serene comfort foreign to Jerusalem's packed hostels.

**Franciscan Convent Pension,** Milk Grotto St. (tel. 674 24 41), on your left past the Milk Grotto. Rooms are Bible-equipped, and we're not talking Gideon's. Welcoming nuns rent sparkling, flower-bedecked rooms. Curfew 9pm, 8:30pm in winter. Private rooms US$11 per person, student types US$8. Breakfast US$4. Room with shower and included breakfast US$20.

**Casa Nova** (tel. 674 39 80 or 81; fax 674 35 40), off Manger Sq., tucked in a corner to the left of the Basilica's entrance. Marble floor and stained-glass lobby windows greet the serious pilgrim. Caters primarily to the seminary students or groups in which at least 3 members can recite the Synoptic Gospels, but even agnostics are welcome. Modern rooms and plenty of hot water; heated in winter. Check-out 9am. Bed and breakfast US$19. Half board US$22. Full board US$28. US$9 extra to convert your double room into a single. Reservations recommended. To stay during Christmas, reserve up to 6 months in advance.

**Al-Andalus Hotel** (tel. 674 13 48; fax 674 22 80), in Manger Sq., upstairs next to the Bank Leumi. If the door is bolted, just knock or ask for the owner at one of the shops downstairs or at Al-Andalus Restaurant around the corner to the right (10% discount if you stay at the hotel). Clean, adequate rooms with 70s motif. TV lounge. Check-out 11am. Singles with bath US$25. Doubles with bath US$46. Breakfast included in the dining room upstairs. Prices subject to change, depending on the season and mood of the owner. Bargain down winter price hikes.

**Palace Hotel,** Manger Sq. (tel. 674 27 98 or 41 00), to the left as you face the Basilica door. Extensive renovations should be finished by 1997; call for prices.

## FOOD

There's fuel for your church-hopping excursion in the form of falafel and *shawerma* at cheap stands in Manger Sq. and on Manger St. Tourists are charged slightly higher prices than locals, but bargaining helps. Many places offer student discounts.

**Al Quds Restaurant,** off Manger St., on the right up the tiny street next to the post office (tel. 674 10 58). Draws in locals with heavenly hummus (NIS5) and *shawerma* (NIS7 in pita). *Kabab* or half-chicken with hummus and salads (NIS17), or cheap sheep's liver (NIS15 for two 250g portions). Open daily 7am-8 or 9pm.

**Al Andalus Restaurant** (tel./fax 674 35 19). Caters to large tour groups. Affordable meals are cleverly disguised as "snacks." Hot dogs, hamburgers, and cheeseburgers (NIS12-20) come with salad and fries. Open daily 8am-midnight.

**Al-Atlal Restaurant** (tel. 674 11 04), one block from Manger Sq. on Milk Grotto St. Provides neo-Crusader arches and needed respite from the hordes. *Shishlik* or *kabab* NIS22, hummus or *labaneh* NIS5.

**Granada Bar and Restaurant** (tel. 674 43 00), on the same side of Manger Sq. as Bank Leumi. Shaded outdoor tables with an unobstructed view of the square. *Shawerma* platter NIS8, falafel NIS5.

**Quick, Lunch, Sandwiches,** next door to Granada (quick lunch sandwiches NIS7).

## SIGHTS

A church masquerading as a fortress, the massive **Basilica of the Nativity** on Manger Sq. is the oldest continuously used church in the world. It's come a long way in the past 16 centuries. A far cry from any previous incarnation as a reflective, quiet sanctuary, today's church bursts with pilgrims and tourists. Under the supervision of his mother Helena, Constantine the Great erected the first basilica in 326 over the site of Jesus' birth. It was destroyed in the Samaritan uprising of 525, then rebuilt by Justinian. During the 614 Persian invasion, virtually every Christian shrine in the Holy Land was demolished, with the exception of this basilica, reputedly spared because it contained a mosaic of the three (Persian) wise men which had special anti-artillery powers. Tancred, the brat of the First Crusade, claimed Bethlehem as a fief and extensively renovated the church. After the Crusaders kingdom fell, the church again lapsed into disrepair. By the 15th century it had become undeniably decrepit, but its importance as a holy shrine never waned. For this reason, during the ensuing centuries, struggle for its control among Roman Catholic, Greek, and Armenian Christians repeatedly led to bloodshed. In the 1840s the church was restored to its former dignity, but squabbles between the various sects over the division of the edifice continue. Established in 1751 and finalized 100 years later, an elaborate system of worship schedules has harmonized the competing claims of the different groups, but the confusion resulting from the Greek Orthodox Church's rejection of summer daylight savings time demonstrates the teetering balance of this arrangement.

Though it has an impressive history, the Basilica of the Nativity is not particularly attractive. The main entrance and windows were blocked up as a safety precaution

WEST BANK

during medieval times, rendering the façade markedly awkward. To enter you must assume the position and step through the narrow **Door of Humility**—a remnant of the days when Christians wanted to prevent Muslims from entering on horseback.

Fragments of beautiful mosaic floors are all that remain of Constantine's original church. View them beneath the huge wooden trap doors in the center of the marble Crusader floor. The four rows of reddish limestone Corinthian columns and the mosaic atoms along the walls date from Justinian's reconstruction. The oak ceiling was a gift from England's King Edward IV, while the handsome icons adorning the altar were bequeathed in 1764 by the Russian royal family.

The **Grotto of the Nativity** is in an underground sanctuary beneath the church. As you enter the womb-like space, notice the crosses etched into the columns on both sides of the doorway—religious graffiti from centuries of pilgrims. A star bearing the Latin inscription: *Hic De Virgine Maria Jesus Christus Natus Est* ("Here, of the Virgin Mary, Jesus Christ was born") marks the spot. The star, added by Catholics in 1717, was removed by Greeks in 1847 and restored by the Turkish government in 1853. Quarrels over the star supposedly contributed to the outbreak of the Crimean War. (Basilica complex open in summer daily 5:30am-7:30pm; in winter 7am-6pm. Free, although donations are encouraged. Modest dress required. For further information call 674 24 25 or 40.)

Simple and airy, the adjoining **St. Catherine's Church** (tel. 674 24 25), built by the Franciscans in 1881, is a welcome contrast to the grim interior of the basilica. Use the separate entrance to the north of the basilica, or face the altar in the basilica and pass through one of the doorways in the wall on your left. St. Catherine's broadcasts a Midnight Mass to a worldwide audience every Christmas Eve. Superbly detailed wood carvings of the 14 Stations of the Cross line the walls. The first room, the **Chapel of St. Joseph,** commemorates the carpenter's vision of an angel who advised him to flee with his family to Egypt to avoid Herod's wrath. The burial cave of children slaughtered by King Herod (Matthew 2:6) lies below the altar and through the grille in the **Chapel of the Innocents.** Beyond the altar, a narrow hallway leads to the Grotto of the Nativity. The way is blocked by a thick wood door pierced by a peephole. During times of greater hostility between Christian sects, this glimpse was as close as Catholics could get to the Greek Orthodox shrine. To the right of the altar, a series of rooms contain the tombs of St. Jerome, St. Paula, and St. Paula's daughter Eustochia. These lead to the spartan cell where St. Jerome produced the Vulgate, the 4th-century translation of the Hebrew Bible into Latin.

The Franciscan Fathers conduct a solemn procession to the basilica and underground chapels every day. To join in the 20 minutes of Gregorian cantillation and Latin prayer, arrive at St. Catherine's by noon (St. Catherine's and the tomb of St. Jerome both open daily 5:30am-noon and 2-8pm).

A five-minute walk from the Basilica of the Nativity down Milk Grotto St. leads to the **Milk Grotto Church** (tel. 674 24 25). The cellar here is thought to be the cave in which the Holy Family hid, and more importantly a spot where Mary breast-fed baby Jesus, when fleeing from Herod into Egypt. The cave and church take their names

---

### O Little Town of Bethlehem

Christmas in Bethlehem explodes with pilgrims and tourists. Nobody would say "how still we see thee lie." On Christmas, the town becomes a huge rollicking festival. Now that Palestinians have autonomy in the village, Yuletide has become a period of national celebration. Pilgrims won't find solitude, but they will find joy. Falafel stands play tapes of *Jingle Bells* and *White Christmas,* redrobed Santa Clauses smile in the streets, and strings of colored lights adorn storefronts and church façades. Getting a ticket to midnight Mass isn't easy, but the service is broadcast on TVs throughout Manger Sq. The tourist office has a list of Christmas activities. For Mass tickets, consult the the Franciscan Pilgrims Office in Jerusalem (p. 288).

WEST BANK

from the original milky white color of the rocks, which have now either been blackened by candle smoke or been painted blue. According to legend, some of Mary's milk fell while she was nursing the infant Jesus, whitewashing the rocks forever (well, almost forever). Male visitors may be slightly discomfited amid the women who come here to pray for fertility. (Open daily 8-11:30am and 2-5pm.) If it's locked, ring the bell and wait for a monk to admit you.

About 500m north of Manger Sq. along Star St., the three unremarkable **Wells of David** (tel. 674 24 77; open daily 8am-noon and 2-5pm) squat in the parking lot of the King David Cinema. The thirsty, swashbuckling David, while battling the Philistines, was brought water from the enemy's well. He in turn offered it as a sacrifice to God (2 Samuel 23:13-17). From Star St., turn right onto King David St.

The **Tomb of Rachel** (Kever Raḥel; tel. 674 20 20) is a sacred site for Jews, a spot where synagogues have been built and destroyed throughout history. On one side are fervently praying Hasidic men, and on the other weeping Yemeni women. The illustrious Rachel died in Bethlehem while giving birth to Benjamin (Genesis 35:19-20), and she became a timeless symbol of maternal devotion and suffering. Despite Rachel's misfortune, the tomb is revered as the place to pray for a child or a safe delivery. Men should don a paper *kippah* (head covering), available at the entrance.

While the IDF has left Bethlehem, the Israeli government has announced that it plans to retain control over the Tomb of Rachel, and that a special access road will link the tomb to Jerusalem, bypassing Bethlehem. The PA insists that the tomb is the property of the Islamic *Waqf*, though it intends to allow free access for Jewish worshipers. The tomb is on the northern edge of town on the road to Jerusalem, at the intersection of Manger St. and Hebron Rd. (open Sun.-Thurs. 8am-5pm, Fri. 8am-1pm). All buses between Jerusalem and Bethlehem or Hebron pass the tomb; minibus #1 also swings by. It's a 20-minute walk from the Basilica.

Bethlehem means "House of Meat" in Arabic *(Beit Lahm)* and "House of Bread" in Hebrew *(Beit Leḥem)*. The sprawling **market** which clings to the town's steep streets lives up to both names; it's up the stairs from Paul VI St. across from the Syrian Church, about two blocks west of Manger Sq. A few blocks down Paul VI from the market and toward the basilica is the **Bethlehem Museum** (tel. 674 25 89), exhibiting Palestinian crafts, traditional costumes, and a 19th-century Palestinian home (open Mon.-Sat. 9am-noon and 3-5pm; NIS3).

# ■ Near Bethlehem

## AL AZARIYYEH (BETHANY) العزرية

A relatively prosperous Palestinian village, Bethany was the home of Lazarus and his sisters Mary and Martha. A **Franciscan Church** (tel. 674 92 91) built in 1954 marks a spot where Jesus supposedly slept. The church features several impressive mosaics, including one of the resurrection of Lazarus and another of the Last Supper. Three earlier shrines, the earliest from the 4th century CE, have been excavated nearby. South of the church lie the remains of a vast abbey built in 1143 by Queen Melisende of Jerusalem (open daily March-Oct. 8-11:30am and 2-6pm, Nov.-Feb. 8-11:30am and 2-5pm; small donations appreciated).

Bethany is home to the first-century **Tomb of Lazarus.** When the Crusaders arrived, they built a church over Lazarus's tomb, a monastery over Mary and Martha's house, and a tower over Simon the Leper's abode (Simon was another resident of Bethany cured by Jesus). In the 16th century, Muslims erected a mosque over the shrine, and in the following century Christians dug another entrance to the tomb so they too could worship there. Head for the red domes of the **Greek Orthodox Church** above the tomb (the Franciscan Church is just downhill). As you approach the tomb, a person will come from across the street to show you the light switch (on the right as you enter) and ask for a donation (NIS2 is appropriate; tomb open daily 8am-7pm). Ten minutes farther along the main road, the **Greek Orthodox Convent** (silver dome) shelters the boulder upon which Jesus sat while awaiting Martha (ring the bell to see the rock).

To reach Bethany from Jerusalem (4km), take Arab bus #36 from Damascus Gate or a *service* from Herod's Gate (both NIS1.50), and get off in the town (look for the silver-domed church on your left). There are two #36 buses, one of which stops at Abu Dees first. Women should dress modestly and travel in groups.

## SHEPHERD'S FIELD

Beyond the Arab village of Beit Sahur on the eastern edge of Bethlehem is the **Field of Ruth,** believed to be the setting for the biblical Book of Ruth. The name of the village in Hebrew is "House of the Shepherds," and Christian tradition holds that this is **Shepherd's Field,** where those tending their flocks were greeted by the angel who pronounced the birth of Jesus (Luke 2:9-11). Take bus #47 (NIS1) from the stop behind the police station in Manger Sq., get off at Beit Sahur, and walk 20 minutes to the site. Otherwise, you can follow the signs and walk the 1.5km from Bethlehem. A cab should cost NIS15. A sign encouraging you to turn left leads to an alternate **Franciscan Shepherd's Field,** which includes a little chapel, a monastery, and an excavated Byzantine church (open daily 8am-11:30pm and 2-5pm). Across the street, you will see a building with a red dome. Take a right and walk in the direction of the site claimed by the Greek Patriarchate (tel. 647 31 35). Here you'll find the remains of a Byzantine **basilica,** thrice destroyed and repaired in the 5th, 6th, and 7th centuries. The **Holy Cave** (325 CE) features mosaic crosses on the floor. In the **baptistry** you can view 1300-year-old bones belonging to victims of the Persian invasion. The newest addition to the field is the red-dome-topped Byzantine-style church, opened in 1989 but still under construction. Inside are colorful frescoes of starving local saints and a Greek imported marble floor. Six monks affiliated with Mar Saba live in Saint Sawa's Monastery (open daily 8am-12:30pm and 2-5pm).

## MAR SABA MONASTERY

The remarkable Mar Saba Monastery stands isolated from nearby traffic. Carved into the walls of a remote canyon, the extensive monastery complex stands above the sewer-esque Kidron River. The monastery was built opposite the cave, marked by a cross, where St. Saba began his ascetic life in 478 CE. The attractive bones of St. Saba are on display in the main church. Women are strictly forbidden to enter and can only view the chapels and buildings from a nearby tower; men must wear long pants and sleeves. To get inside, pull the chain on the large blue door. Once inside, you'll be given a five-minute tour in English by one of the monks (ask for Father Lucas— he's from California). The monks occasionally ignore the doorbell on Sundays and late afternoons; try to arrive early. (Open daily 7-11am and 1:30-6pm, in winter until 5pm. Free, but a donation is expected.) You need to hire a private taxi from Bethlehem to get here (16km; about NIS60 round-trip, including waiting time).

# ▓ Ramallah رام الله

Perched 900m above sea level, Ramallah is famous for its cool, pleasant mountain air and its quietude. Before 1967, the then-prosperous town was known as the "Bride of Palestine," a summer haven for Arabs from Jordan, Lebanon, and the Gulf region. With vacationers long gone, Ramallah assumed a leading role in the *intifada.* When expansion of Palestinian self-rule finally comes about, Ramallah will replace Gaza as the administrative hub of the Palestinian Authority during the interim period. Indeed, it already houses several important PA offices, including the Ministries of Transportation and Education. Ramallah's PA prominence has also led to the building of new roads, the cleaning up of *intifada* graffiti, and the restoration of the town's traditional character. While definitely calm compared to Nablus or Hebron, Ramallah is still in the West Bank, where tranquility is measured in relative terms.

Palestinians in Ramallah live up to the old cliché about Arab hospitality. Visibly confused tourists are often surrounded by people offering countless solutions; the absence of street signs will put you in this position faster than you think. Use the opportunity to strike up a conversation, improve your Arabic, and gain insight into the Palestinian perspective on the latest events. The town is among the least conservative in the West Bank; women can go in pants and a T-shirt.

There are a few noteworthy tourist sites in Ramallah. The ebullient **market** (open Sat.-Thurs. until 3pm, Fri. until noon) bubbles by the bus station, and leafy neighborhoods away from the city center are great strolling zones. The **Silvana Chocolate Company** (tel. 995 64 58), 1.5km down Jaffa Blvd. from Manara Sq., offers tours and countless free samples (open Mon.-Sat. 7:30am-4pm; call to arrange a tour). Consider hiring a private taxi to drive you outside the city, where the terraced hills are lined with fruit trees, beautiful old homes, and shepherds tending their flocks.

Due to periodical closures of the West Bank, Ramallah has become a transportation hub for Arabs unable to get into East Jerusalem 16km to the south. You can go from here to most West Bank towns by direct *service.* From Jerusalem, take a **service taxi** (20min., NIS2.50) from outside Damascus Gate, or **Arab bus** #18 from the station on Nablus Rd., just north of Damascus Gate (40min., NIS1.50). Buses to Jerusalem leave from Jaffa Rd. in Ramallah, just off Manara Sq., the main traffic circle. The last bus leaves around 5pm, the last *service* around 6pm. Food, lodging, and most services are accessible from **Manara Square,** where the *service* stop.

Basem, a native of Ramallah, spent 10 years in Orange County, California learning the art of cooking real American cuisine; try the hella-fine fruits of his experience at the **Dome Restaurant** (tel. (050) 361 218), in the Surda Center on Radio St. Juicy Dome Burgers and grilled chicken platters are NIS12, pizza NIS10-37, milk shakes NIS5 (open Sat.-Thurs. 9am-10pm). Classier and more traditional is the **Al Bardouni Bar and Restaurant** on Jaffa St. (tel. 995 14 10), a garden affair where the food, flowers, and fountains attract PA officials and their guests. Their specialty is *musakhkhan,* a mouth-watering bread, onion, *summaq,* and chicken concoction (NIS30, half-portion NIS20); other specialties include *kabab* (NIS25), *shishlik* (NIS28), and salads (NIS6) (open daily 9am-roughly midnight). You can find good falafel (NIS2) and *shawerma* (NIS5) and an excellent variety of Arabic sweets throughout the town. The oval-shaped goods at **Badiya Falafel** are fresh and the salads plentiful. Take Maydan al-Moughtaribin St. from Manara to Oklok Sq.; it's on a corner on the right (open Sat.-Thurs. 7am-midnight). For a real treat, stop by **Rukab's Ice Cream,** 22 Main St., which is to ice cream (NIS5) what *Let's Go* is to global happiness; also try their cold lemonade (NIS2.50; open daily 8am-midnight).

# ■ Near Ramallah

## BEITIN (BETHEL)   بيتين

Beitin (Bethel), 5km northeast of Ramallah on the road to Nablus, is thought to be the place where Jacob lay down to sleep and dreamed of a ladder ascending to heaven traversed by angels. Upon awakening, Jacob built an altar and named the spot Beit-El, "House of God" (Genesis 28:12-19).

Until the agreement on Palestinian self-rule, Beitin was the headquarters of the Israeli civilian administration that governed the West Bank. The administration center itself is of no interest to tourists, but a visit to the nearby Jewish settlement of Beit-El may be worthwhile. Surrounded by barbed wire and guarded by army patrols, the settlement provides a glimpse of life in a West Bank Jewish settlement. Most of the working population commutes to Jerusalem, but there are also a few cottage industries, including a workshop that manufactures *tefillin* (phylacteries). To get here from Ramallah you can walk, take a taxi, or ride the bus going to Nablus.

## BIRZEIT بيرزيت

Twelve km northwest of Ramallah is the largest and most important university on the West Bank. **Birzeit University**'s 2500 students have a history of vocal opposition to the Israeli occupation; throughout the occupation, the university was often shut down by the Israeli army. In the first years of the *intifada*, Israeli authorities closed it altogether; it wasn't reopened until April 1992. No buses reach Birzeit. To get here from outside Ramallah, take a **service** and ask the driver to let you off at Birzeit taxi in Ramallah (on Radio Blvd., just off Manara Sq.); the taxi ride from there to Birzeit is NIS2. The old campus is next to the taxi office; the new campus lies 2km out of town on the road back to Ramallah.

# ■ Nablus نابلس

Beautiful, serene mountains surround the town of Nablus, founded by Titus near the site of Biblical Shekhem in 72 CE as the "New City" of Flavia Neapolis. Enjoy the serenity if you can; the city is not called *Jabal an-Nar* (Hill of Fire) in Arabic for nothing. Home to some of Palestine's oldest and wealthiest families, Nablus has a tradition of impassioned resistance to foreign occupation. Its citizens fought the Turks, the British, and the Jordanians, and were wholly consumed by the *intifada*. Now that the city is at last under Palestinian rule, its residents are zealously proud. Nablus is the largest city in the West Bank (not counting East Jerusalem), an industrial center, and home to the West Bank's second-largest university, An-Najah. Besides its predominantly Muslim population, Nablus is home to 500 Samaritans, about two-thirds of the world's total Samaritan population (see **Other Sects,** p. 65).

Nablus is a very conservative town; dress modestly. After introductions, it is not uncommon for Palestinians to invite you to their homes. Perhaps the most rewarding way to spend your time in this industrial hub is to accept the residents' hospitality and learn something of the life of West Bank Palestinians.

Nablus lies 63km north of Jerusalem, 46km north of Ramallah, and 50km south of Nazareth. Take one of the **Tamini Co. buses** from Nablus Rd. in Jerusalem (irregular schedule, 1½-2hrs., NIS7). **Service taxis** to and from Jerusalem are a safer bet; you will be dropped off in the center of town, after changing cars in Ramallah.

## SIGHTS

From the center of Nablus, wander south past a pleasant fresh fruit market (next to Nablus circle) and into the crowded streets and passageways of the **market,** overflowing with Nablus merchants, Palestinian customers, and tea-sipping onlookers. Try a piece of the famous, extraordinarily-rich *kinafeh nablusiyya*. Nablus churns out countless tray-fulls of this cheese concoction, which is topped with sweet orange flakes and syrup. Although you'll feel more comfortable if you're with a guide, stopping to chat and swap stories often dissipates any awkwardness.

Throughout the market you'll continue to see the smiling image of Zafer Masri, Nablus's Palestinian former mayor. A wreathed monument next to the municipality building marks the spot where he was slain in the winter of 1986. Many hold that his assassins were Palestinians who resented his alleged chumminess with Israeli leadership; the killing still haunts Nablusians.

To the east, 3km from the town center, lie two famous but unspectacular pilgrimage sites. **Jacob's Well,** now enclosed within a subterranean Greek Orthodox shrine, is believed to date from the time when Jacob bought the surrounding land to pitch his tents (Genesis 33:18-19). A few hundred meters north of the well lies the **Tomb of Joseph.** According to the Book of Joshua, the bones of Joseph were carried out of Egypt and buried in Shekhem (Joshua 24:32). The tomb was a Muslim site until 10 years ago, when it was taken over by Jewish authorities. Israeli soldiers guard the velvet-shrouded grave and the adjacent *yeshiva* (no shorts or bare shoulders permitted). *Service* run to both sites regularly from the town center.

## ■ Near Nablus

### MOUNT GERIZIM

This tree-covered slope southeast of Nablus features a terrific view of the Shomron Valley. Since the 4th century BCE, it has been the holy mountain of the Samaritans, who revere it as the spot where Abraham prepared to sacrifice his son Isaac and where the original Ten Commandments are buried. The Samaritans, an Israelite sect who were excommunicated in Biblical times, are distinguished by their literal interpretation of certain scriptures (see **Other Sects**, p. 65). The highlight of the Samaritan observance of Passover is the sacrifice of sheep atop Mt. Gerizim. Tourist buses from Jerusalem and Tel Aviv bring visitors to witness the bloody rite. The hike up the mountain is arduous but taxis make the climb for about NIS20.

### SABASTIYA سبسطية

An array of Israelite, Hellenistic, and Roman ruins crowd an unassuming hill 11km northwest of Nablus. The strategic peak on which the ruins lie was first settled by Omri, King of Israel, in the 9th century BCE as the city of **Shomron** (Samaria), and served as the capital of the Israelite kingdom until the Assyrian invasion of the 8th century BCE. Under Herod, the city was made into the showpiece of the Holy Land to win the favor of the Roman Emperor.

The ruins are just above the present-day Arab village of **Sabastiya.** Unfortunately, most of the ancient splendor is long gone. At the top of the hill lie the remnants of Israelite and Hellenistic walls, a Roman acropolis, and the bases of columns built for the **Temple of Augustus.** Watch your step: the narrow 1.5km path encircling the ruins is treacherous. *Service* taxis to Sabastiya are available from Nablus.

## ■ The Gaza Strip غزة

At the western edge of the Negev Desert, the city of **Gaza** (Ghazzeh in Arabic, Azza in Hebrew) is governed by the Palestinian National Authority. It is the capital of the **Gaza Strip,** a small stretch of coastline that was occupied by the advancing Egyptian army in 1948 and then by the Israeli military from 1967 to 1993. In December 1987, the *intifada* began here when a traffic accident resulting in Palestinian deaths sparked angry demonstrations which spread into a widespread protest movement (see **The Intifada,** p. 54).

With a population of 840,000 Palestinians, three-fourths of whom live in refugee camps, crammed into a mere 46 sq. km, the conditions are appalling. Twenty-seven years of Israeli occupation and 19 years under the Egyptians before that have left few jobs, little industry, and decrepit infrastructure. Most of Gaza's income came from Gazans working in Israel, but after terrorist attacks emanating from the strip prompted the Israeli government to close the border, opportunities for such labor have been cut short. Since autonomy, however, the PA has invested heavily in restoring livable conditions. Although the Gazans are far from prosperous, several accomplishments are symbolic of the growth achieved thus far. The new **Gaza International Airport** is scheduled to open by 1997, and may soon offer flights to Europe and even North America.

Gaza, and particularly the refugee camps here, have been the site of the angriest demonstrations, the harshest Israeli crackdowns, and the most brutal intra-Palestinian clashes. Four thousand Jewish settlers live in the Strip, and are greatly resented by local Arabs. About one-third of Gaza's residents claim loyalty to Hamas, the rejectionist, Islamist wing of Palestinian politics. Whether due to frustration with Arafat's regime or appreciation of the Hamas social services, Gazan allegiance to the militant organization is strong here. A string of Hamas terrorist bombings in 1996 prompted a PA crackdown on the organization, but Hamas still wields considerable influence on the Strip.

WEST BANK

Visiting Gaza on your own is difficult and dangerous. If you wish to go, seek out a humanitarian agency to take you around, or ask in Palestinian tourist offices about potential guides. Tours are offered through Arab-owned hostels in Old City for nothing more than bus fare (see **Old City hostels,** p. 291). Your embassy or consulate might also be able to help you. While on the Gaza strip, dress modestly. Both men and women should cover their entire arms and legs. Women should also wear skirts instead of pants and cover their hair with a large scarf.

WEST BANK

# JORDAN الاردن

US$1=0.709 Jordanian dinar (JD)
CDN$1=JD0.517
UK£1=JD1.102
IR£1=JD1.143
AUS$1=JD0.549
NZ$1=JD0.490
SAR1=JD0.160

JD1=US$1.410
JD1=CDN$1.937
JD1=UK£0.908
JD1=IR£0.875
JD1=AUS$1.822
JD1=NZ$2.061
JD1=SAR6.315

> For important information on travel in general and some specifics on Jordan, see the Essentials section of this book. Jordan's **international phone code** is 962.

Take it from King Hussein: "Jordan itself is a beautiful country. It is wild, with limitless deserts where the Bedouin roam, but the mountains of the north are clothed in green forests, and where the Jordan River flows it is fertile and warm in winter. Jordan has a strange, haunting beauty and a sense of timelessness. Dotted with the ruins of empires once great, it is the last resort of yesterday in the world of tomorrow. I love every inch of it." Of course that's what he would say—he's king of every inch of it. But the smiling monarch has a point. It *is* a beautiful country, one whose geographical diversity is appealing, and at times fascinating.

The Hashemite Kingdom of Jordan is where John the Baptist baptized Jesus in the Jordan River, and where desert trade routes flourished during the Roman Empire. Later a neglected chunk of the Ottoman *vilayet* of Syria, modern Jordan (Al Urdun) was created by the stroke of a British pen ("Now a giant mixing machine called the West has thrown us together," wrote former Prime Minister Kamel Abu Jaber, "and here we are loving it and hating it, constantly adjusting and readjusting..."). The kingdom today finds itself sandwiched between some of the rougher players in a rough neighborhood: Saudi Arabia, Israel, Syria, and Iraq. There are internal troubles too; the memory of 1970's Black September, a harsh suppression by Jordanian authorities of Palestinian political activity, has not disappeared. The more recent trauma of the Gulf Crisis brought a slew of immigrants from the Gulf and Iraq, but the 1994 peace treaty with Israel, signed by King Hussein and Israeli Prime Minister Yitzhak Rabin, has placed the Jordanians in a more favorable light in the West.

In addition to engrossing, hospitable people, Jordan has another bonus for the plucky budget traveler. Until recently, even the most awe-inspiring sight was relatively undiscovered. Despite growth in tourism over the past few years, most of the country and its sites of interest are uncommercialized (with the exception of Petra); Jordan is not a land of shrink-wrapped, for-tourists'-eyes-only sights and experiences. The Bedouin at Wadi Rum are the genuine article; close your eyes there or at Petra and you could be in any century. Conquer caves and remote desert castles as a bona fide explorer, and prowl the modern capital of Amman unjostled by throngs of tourists. But hurry up—hordes of Israelis are close on your heels.

# ONCE THERE

## ■ Entry

Upon arrival at **Queen Alia International Airport,** you will be welcomed with open arms by passport control, where procrastinators can purchase visas on the spot. Visas for American citizens, valid for one month but renewable at any police station, cost JD15. A **Housing Bank** and a **Jordan Bank** (ask the friendly customs officials to point them out) in the airport lobby will satisfy your every pecuniary desire. Purchase **JETT** bus tickets (850fils for the ½-hr. ride to Amman) next to the information booth, then join the jett-set at the bus stop right outside the airport's main entrance. Do not feel shy asking for help in the airport. The Jordanians, winners of the *Let's Go* award for hospitality for the fifth year running, will point, gesture, or grab you by the elbow and guide you to your destination.

# ■ Getting Around

Most visitors to Jordan stay long enough to see the major sites at Petra and Jerash, which is not long enough to master the chaotic transportation system. Organized **bus tours** and private **taxis** can cost JD4 to JD50 per day. The country has a fine train system, but only for freight, and the only reliable long-distance bus company, **JETT**, has a limited number of routes. Fleets of **shared taxis** (called *service* and pronounced "ser-VEES") and **minibuses** shuttle between all cities, towns, and villages. Hitchhiking is a common practice among Jordanians, though more so in the north than in the south, where a wagging thumb gesture is often mistaken for a friendly wave. *Let's Go*, however, does not recommend hitchhiking.

**Taxis** **Private taxis,** useful mainly in Amman (where you may have to wait a long time for an empty one), are yellow and conveniently have "taxi" written on them. Jordanian taxi drivers take their horns seriously, their fares a little less so, and the law not in the least. Insist that the driver use the meter. A few specialize in ripping off newly arrived tourists; be wary of those driving souped-up, chrome-encrusted Mercedes. Some cab drivers will even drive ridiculously round-about routes in order to increase your fare. If you think you've passed by the same hotel four times, speak up. The starting fare is 150fils. Drivers may also charge extra (illegally) for large amounts of baggage. Women should always sit in the back seat, whether or not there are other passengers. It's considered rude to give exact change; drivers expect you to round up from the meter fare.

**Service** are shared taxis, usually white or gray Mercedes with a white sign written in Arabic on their roofs (أ . جرة). The front doors have the route and number on them (again in Arabic numbers only). *Service* can be hailed en route. Payment takes place whenever the rider feels like it, traditionally just as the cab is negotiating an insanely sharp curve on two wheels. With drivers sneering at speed limits and holding their cars together with tin foil, *service* rides range from exhilarating to traumatic. Travel within downtown Amman is generally easier on foot (except when you have to go uphill, which somehow appears to be the case most of the time), but *service* are invaluable for interdistrict travel. There are specific *service* routes in Amman and between the central transport terminals in the larger cities. Within Amman, *service* cost 70 to 120fils; a ride from Amman to Aqaba goes for JD3.500. *Service* rarely run in the evenings and the long-distance ones may make only two or three trips per day. Schedules are (predictably) unpredictable—*service* leave when the car fills up. If you get into a *service* alone and want to leave before it's full, you'll have to pay for the empty seats. (For routes and rates, see individual towns.)

**Buses** **Public buses** supplement the *service* taxis in Amman. The crown prince has a government-granted monopoly on intercity bus service, so the **Jordan Express Tourist Transport (JETT)** is your only bus option. However sparse, these buses cover the most popular routes, and private minibuses travel to more remote areas. Regular service on JETT buses includes daily trips from Amman to Aqaba, Petra, Ma'an, the King Hussein/Allenby Bridge, Damascus, and Cairo via Aqaba and the Sinai. (For details about schedules and the station, see **Practical Information,** p.475) JETT also sponsors tours to Jerash, Madaba, Petra, Ajlun, and the Desert Castles. For information, call (06) 664 146. The **Arabella** and **Hijazi** bus companies travel to Jerash and Irbid. **Minibuses** are also used for intercity transport.

Bus fares are slightly lower than *service* rates, but buses are slow. The JETT luxury coaches cost more than regular buses but are air-conditioned, and those running

Haifa

To
Damascus

**SYRIA**

**Al Himma**
**Umm Qeis**

Irbid

■ Pella

Mafraq ●

■ Umm al-Jimal

Ajlun

Jerash

Tel Aviv-
Yafo

**Dibbin**
**Natl.**
**Park**

**Deir Alla**

Zarqa R.

**Zai Natl.**
**Park**

Qasr Hallabat ■

Salt ●

Zarqa ●

**King**
**Hussein Br.**
**(Allenby Br.)**

Jordan R.

Jericho ●

Wadi
Seer ●

Amman

Qasr
Azraq ■

Qasr
Amra ■

Jerusalem

Mt. ▲
Nebo

■ Qasr
Mushatta
Queen Alia
Intl. Airport

Azraq ●

Br.

**Madaba**
●

**Shaumari**
**Wildlife**
**Reserve**

Dead Sea

**Hammam**
**ez-Zarqa**

■ Qasr
Kharaneh

Be'er Sheva ●

■ Dhiban

■ **Al Lejjun**

Ba'ir ●

Karak ●

**ISRAEL**

Hasa ●

King's Hwy.

Shobak ●

Wadi Araba Hwy.

Petra ■

Desert Hwy.

Al Jafr ●

al Jafr
Depression

Ma'an ●

**Jordan**

**N**

Aqaba
Airport

Eilat

Aqaba

Wadi Rum

Jabal Rum ▲

**SAUDI**
**ARABI**

JORDAN

from Amman to Aqaba come with hosts, professional wrestling videos, and highly dramatic Egyptian movies. Do note, however, that you will be charged for each and every "in-flight" bottle of Pepsi you drink, regardless of how generous the attendant seems when handing you one. They ensure that you will drink at least one by forbidding carry-on food and drink—your bags *will* be searched. The buses depart more or less on schedule, and booking ahead is often necessary. Most towns have one main terminal shared by intercity buses and *service;* Amman and Irbid have several. In Amman, most buses follow the pattern of *service,* with traffic to the north leaving from Abdali Station and buses to the south leaving from Wahadat Station.

**Cars**  Some of Jordan's greatest attractions are not served by the public transportation system. For groups of four to six, renting a car can be an affordable and efficient way to reach less accessible sights. With a car, for example, the round-trip to Azraq via four or five desert castles can be done in eight to twelve hours. The unsurpassed Kings' Highway route, barely served by other modes of transportation, can be seen from a private car in another full day. Some rental agencies will even let you pick a car up in one city and drop it off in another; ask around.

If you can't split the costs, car rental in Jordan will break your budget. Most rental agencies charge JD22-36 per day, including insurance, plus 45-55fils per km. Unlimited mileage deals are cheaper (JD17-20 per day), but you must rent the car for at least a week. (For details, see **Amman** and **Aqaba: Practical Information,** p. 475 and p. 503.) Always ask whether the car has a fire extinguisher—no joke. Desert heat and police regulations require them. The four-wheel drive cars that companies push are unnecessary except to reach Qasr at-Touba, south of Azraq, and Wadi Rum, where a light four-wheeler is absolutely necessary to get off the beaten path. Ordinary cars will do everywhere else.

Gas costs about 230fils per liter. The law requires seatbelts to be worn (JD5 fine for naughtiness), and speeding tickets can reach an exorbitant JD50. Many rental companies require an International Driver's License but many do not, so call ahead to ask (see **Driving Permits** and **Insurance,** p.13). **Road accidents** should be reported to the traffic police (tel. (06) 896 390); for an **ambulance** call 193.

**Hitchhiking**  *Service* and minibuses are cheap enough to make hitching unnecessary. In remote areas such as along the King's Highway, *service* and minibuses are less frequent. For those feckless die-hards who insist on hitching, rides between small towns (Jordan Valley, Amman environs, Irbid area) are easy to come by. Even short waits in the sun can be dangerous, so if you want to hitch, bring lots of water and cover your head.

Those who try hitchhiking within a city (Amman, Irbid, Jerash, Ajlun) will be pestered by empty taxis' horns as they careen by. The steady stream of trucks serving the port facilities compensates, with many drivers eager for company on their long trans-Jordan hauls. To flag down an approaching vehicle, travelers stick their arms out with their palms facing the ground.

---

*Let's Go* does not recommend hitchhiking. **Women** especially should never hitchhike alone. Hitching along the Wadi Araba highway is prohibited for all.

---

# ■ Money Matters

**Currency and Exchange**  The **Jordanian dinar (JD)** is a decimal currency, divided into 1000fils. Prices are always labeled in fils, but the usual spoken practice is to call 10fils a piaster (pt). Thus, 500fils will be written as 500fils, but referred to as 50pt. A piaster is called a *qirsh* (plural *quroush*). Clear? Bills come in denominations of JD20, 10, 5, 1, and ½ (500fils). Coins are silver for 250fils, 100, 50, and 25, and copper for 10 and 5. (Two separate, nonidentical mints are currently in circulation; remember that the 100fils piece is equal to the 10*qirsh* piece.) Since confusion enriches life, the numerals Westerners call "Arabic" are not used in Jordan, so it's a good idea to learn the Arab forms (see the handy-dandy **Language Glossary,** p. 557). The currency itself is marked with Western-friendly numbers as well.

**Currency exchange** is easy to find in the larger cities, but more difficult elsewhere. Bank exchange hours are regularly 8:30am to 12:30pm, with some banks opening from 4 to 5:45pm as well. Branches of the national **Housing Bank** (Bank al-Iskan) are the best bets outside Amman; there are also exchange offices located in many of the *souqs*. Queen Alia Airport has exchange facilities for incoming passengers. A passport is *always* required to change traveler's checks. Credit cards are only accepted in expensive hotels. There are ATMs in Jordan, but they don't take anything but the cards of the particular bank.

**Tipping** A tip of 10% is expected in restaurants, unless "service included" appears on the menu. Taxi drivers do not expect tips, but will round off fares to their advantage. Members of large sight-seeing groups tip the bus driver about 500fils. A small tip (500fils) to the room cleaners and porters in hotels is appropriate.

**Business Hours** Jordan's business timetable has been shaped by various natural, religious, and economic forces. The desert sun converts the lunchtime hours into a siesta. Most stores and offices open around 8 to 9:30am, close from 1 to 3 or 4pm, and open again in the late afternoon; in the larger cities, the stores may remain open all afternoon. On an especially hot summer day anywhere in Jordan, stores may be closed extra-early. In Amman, retail stores usually close around 8 or 9pm, when the transportation system also falters. In some areas, such as Jabal Hussein, stores close as late as 11pm. Banks and government offices retain only a skeleton crew in the afternoon; if you care about getting something done, do it in the morning. Government offices are open Sat.-Thurs. 8am-2pm (in practice, usually 1:30); during Ramadan 9:30am-2:30pm.

Friday is a holiday throughout the Muslim world, although it is less scrupulously observed in Amman and Aqaba. Government offices, institutions, and sometimes even restaurants close, but some shops are open in the morning (until about noon). Foreign banks and offices generally observe both Friday and Saturday as holidays, though they may keep longer hours during the rest of the week. Schools and universities are closed on Thursdays and Fridays. Museums are closed on Tuesdays. The most reliable schedule for the last few centuries has been the Islamic call to prayer: five times per day, the faithful kneel facing the holy city of Mecca.

# ▓ Accommodations

Though the Jordanian government has gone to great lengths to establish adequate, regulated accommodations for some tourists, budget travelers have been left out for the most part. Regulated tourist hotels charge prices as high as Jordan's mid-summer temperatures. Jordan has no Hostelling International hostels.

**Hotels** Hotels in Jordan are inspected annually and rated by the government according to a five-star system. Bargaining is difficult, but hotel owners may be more flexible in the off-season winter months. Fall and spring are the busiest times throughout Jordan, though sunny Aqaba sees the most activity during the winter and spring seasons. Single women may feel uncomfortable at some of the cheaper hotels, and may on occasion not be admitted. Jordanian law bars unmarried couples from sharing a room. For foreign travelers, the rule seems to be that the more you pay, the less you are hassled, but if you're asked to split up, console yourself by remembering that in cheap hotels, the price is usually per bed rather than per room.

The Ministry of Tourism provides a comprehensive list of classified hotels and their prices (available at the Ministry's Public Relations Office in Amman). No matter how hard the government tries, however, chaos still prevails; many hotels have the official prices listed in Arabic (for instance, JD14 for singles in one-star hotels, JD18 for doubles), and cheaper prices listed in English.

Most hotels add a 10% service charge; ask whether it's included in the quoted price. If business is slow, use this surcharge as a bargaining chip. Some of the cheaper places charge an extra 500fils for a hot shower; many have modern toilets, though several still use the uncomfortable hole-in-the-ground system. The unclassified places usually have clean beds, but toilets and showers can be heinous. Hotel owners may ask to hold your passport for the length of your stay.

**Alternative Accommodations** Hotels are rare outside Amman, Aqaba, Irbid, and Petra. The primary alternatives are government **Rest Houses,** with rates hovering around JD15 per person per night. Not all Rest Houses have overnight facilities. To stay at one, especially in spring or fall, try to reserve in advance with the central office of the **Government Rest Houses** in Amman (tel. (06) 647 611).

**Camping** Camping is an option nearly everywhere in the country, although facilities are virtually nonexistent. Favorite sites include the beach north of Aqaba, Dibbin National Park, and the Dana Wildlands Campsite. Contact the Royal Society for the Conservation of Nature, P.O. Box 6354, Amman 11183 (tel. (06) 837 931 or 932; fax 847 411). Camping is allowed next to most of the government Rest Houses (free or JD1-2 per person per night, plus 10% tax); some hotels have been known to let guests (illegally) camp out on the roof for a small fee. You'll need a sleeping bag for the cool summer nights and winter evenings can bring freezing temperatures.

You can spend a night with the Bedouin, whom you'll find on the outskirts of most towns and scattered around the desert. Tea, Arabic coffee, and meals always accompany an invitation, although showers and toilets are rare. While the Bedouin won't accept money, a pack of Marlboros is always appreciated.

## ▓ Keeping in Touch

**Postage stamps** may be purchased from 7:30am to 7:30pm at the downtown post office in Amman and during regular business hours at other post offices. An **air mail letter** to North America costs 350fils, an aerogramme or postcard is 270fils; the cost to Europe is 270fils and 190fils, respectively. Mail from Jordan to North America and Europe takes one to two weeks if you're lucky; some letters never make it. International **Express Mail Service (EMS)** is available in major post offices. **Packages** may be sent from any post office. **Poste Restante** operates at the downtown post office in Amman and in the larger cities. Beware of sending and receiving many packages; the parcels will be opened and customs duties (sometimes quite hefty) will be assessed. **American Express** offices, located in Amman and Aqaba (look for International Traders offices), also hold mail.

Although the **telephone system** was revamped several years ago, international lines are often overloaded, especially around holidays. The rare pay phones are particularly erratic and require 50fils whether or not your call goes through. If you ask shop owners where to find a pay phone, they will probably invite you to use theirs as long as the call is local. Many businesses now have pseudo-pay phones, where coin guzzlers are hooked up to regular phones. Insert the coin in a slot and press the button on top when the person on the other end of the line answers; you lose the coin only if the call goes through. Another option is to use a hotel phone, but be sure to inquire about surcharges before doing so. Telephone offices are usually next door to post offices, and their hours are often limited and their lines long.

**International calls** can be made in Amman from the telephone center near the downtown post office(see **Practical Information,** p.475). Three minutes to North America will cost about JD6.600. In other parts of Jordan, international calls can be made at luxury hotels, where service will be faster, clearer, and even more expensive. Late night and early morning are the best times to dial overseas. An easier option is to use a private phone and reimburse the owner. You can dial directly to the U.S.,

Europe, and Australia (JD1.830-2.200 per min.; 30% cheaper 10pm-8am; for all international calls, dial 00 and international code). For an international operator, dial 0132. Dial 121 for information on local codes. For other **information,** dial 121. No **collect calls** can be made from Jordan. U.S. **calling cards** will connect you to the U.S., but generally not to anywhere else in the world.

**Telegrams** can be sent to North America (220fils per word) from larger post offices, the telephone office, and some hotels.

## ■ Dress & Etiquette

Jordan is predominantly Muslim and socially conservative, making modest dress a necessity. Though you will not be arrested, inappropriate dress will not only alienate you from the very people you have come to meet, but also encourage stares, comments, and even groping from strangers. The same modesty is required of both men and women. The code is simple: do not wear shorts. Pants for both men and women should come down to at least mid-shin. Shirts should cover the shoulders and upper arms. Women should wear head scarves in mosques. Skirts should be long and comfortable, but remember that desert breezes lift up light fabrics—onlookers are quite appreciative when a wind blows a skirt around, exposing legs (and sometimes more). Feet can be exposed freely. The exception to these rules is hedonistic Aqaba, where both men and women can wear shorts. You're also allowed a little more freedom if you're going out at night or to the pool in Amman. Looking foreign gives you extra leeway in these two towns, but don't push it: women risk greater harassment (and higher prices from offended merchants) and even an "accidental" butt-pinching if they wear shorts in the crowded streets of downtown Amman. Non-Muslims should not enter mosques during prayers, which occur five times per day.

# LIFE AND TIMES

## ■ Government & Politics

After about ten minutes in Jordan, you'll notice pictures of a little bald man with a smooth smile everywhere you look. Refrain from jokes, because he's the king and you are in his kingdom. Jordan is the fiefdom of Hussein bin Talal. The kingdom was a 1921 gift from Britain to the Hashemite royal family, who proudly trace their lineage directly to the Prophet Muhammad (see **Introduction to the Region,** p.43).

King Hussein has ruled since 1953. He divorced his first two queens, the gracious Dina and Muna (a Briton who changed her name from Antoinette Gardiner); his third, Alia (a Palestinian), died in a plane crash. The current queen, Noor (née Lisa Halaby), is an Arab-American and a Princeton grad. Hussein's brother, Crown Prince Hassan, serves as advisor and heir to the throne. Educated in Britain, King Hussein is generally moderate; but, as Palestinians will tell you, remembering their 20,000 dead from Black September, he can be brutal if his throne is at stake (see **The PLO and Jordan,** p.52). Above all, he is a brilliant politician; these skills have kept him alive through several wars. (Luck has also been a factor; the same bullets that killed his grandfather, King Abdallah, bounced off a medal on the young Hussein's chest.)

A meeting between King Hussein and Yitzhak Rabin in August 1994 opened the border between Aqaba and Eilat and led to the end of Jordan's 46-year-old policy of non-recognition of Israel. Much of Jordan's population is of Palestinian descent. Some Palestinians have very successfully integrated themselves into Jordanian society; others live in refugee camps harboring the dream of returning home to Palestine. In the summer of 1988, King Hussein cut all ties with the West Bank, allowing the Jordanian government to focus its efforts on relieving economic ills.

468 ■ LIFE AND TIMES

King Hussein's rule is a constant balancing act in the face of such pressures. He has accommodated and integrated his Palestinian subjects over the years, opening his cabinet to them as well as to the Bedouin who are the bedrock of the monarchy's support. When refugees from the 1948 and 1967 Wars flooded out of Palestine, Jordan was the only Arab country that offered them full citizenship. This was true again after the Gulf War, when Kuwait expelled almost all of its Palestinian community as punishment for Arafat's support of Saddam Hussein. The King, with open arms, met the first plane-full at Amman's airport. The conservative Hashemites have faced opposition from pan-Arabists, Nasserists, Palestinian nationalists, and, most recently, the Muslim Brotherhood. An attempt at democratic reform didn't turn out as the monarchy had hoped; in Jordan's first general elections in 22 years, held in November 1989, Islamists won almost half the seats in parliament. Regardless, reform has continued. In September 1992, King Hussein approved a law permitting political parties, which had been banned in 1957. Jordan's first multi-party election since 1954 took place in November 1993. A new one-person, one-vote policy weakened the Islamists; and the first woman ever was elected to Parliament. Municipal elections in summer 1995 showed a further shift towards the center in Jordanian political attitudes, and five women were elected to various municipal councils, including the first female mayor. However, the King's sudden and quick signing of a peace treaty with Rabin and his over-eagerness to normalize fully relations with Israel have left him alienated even amongst some of his traditional supporters. On the international level, a tide of pan-Arabism and defiance in the face of Western power-mongering led many Jordanians, including King Hussein, to support Saddam Hussein in the Gulf War (1991). But the weakening of Iraq since the war and the peace treaty with Israel have allowed the ever-flexible monarchy to reingratiate with the West. Meanwhile, the King's surgery for cancer in 1992 has raised the issue of succession.

A flood of refugees into Jordan from Kuwait and Iraq following the Gulf War has unfortunately begun to disrupt the normally placid Jordanian lifestyle. Where driving used to be a pleasant excursion, Jordan's cities are now overcrowded.

## ■ Economy

Unlike its Arab neighbors, Jordan has neither oil reserves nor abundant natural resources. The country remains dependent upon Arab and American financial aid to augment income, one source of which is the export of phosphates and pre-season vegetables grown in the Jordan Valley. Remittances from Palestinian and Jordanian workers in the Gulf states traditionally constituted Jordan's main source of income; but after the Gulf War about 320,000 of them (mostly from Kuwait) returned to Jordan to scramble for jobs in Amman.

Back when the Iran-Iraq War broke out in 1980, Iraq became a major importer of Jordanian goods and services, and the Jordanian economy boomed. In the late 1980s, when Iraq began threatening not to pay its war debts, Jordanian exporters were left with a heap of worthless Iraqi IOUs. In April 1989, following steep government-imposed price hikes on gasoline and other goods, Jordanians took to the streets in protest until King Hussein fired then Prime Minister Zaid Rifa'i and, more importantly, instituted democratic reforms. Stability returned, and a 1991 growth rate of 1% was actually a step up from 1989 and 1990.

The aftermath of the 1990-91 Gulf War dealt a devastating blow to the economy, bringing a 1990 annual per capita income of US$2000 down to US$1400 today. Jordan's refusal to join the anti-Iraq coalition of states cost the country dearly, spurring the United States, along with Saudi Arabia and the other Gulf countries, to suspend most aid to Jordan. In addition, the Palestinian and Jordanian workers in the Gulf were largely replaced by Egyptians, whose government the Saudis found to be more politically correct. Among the returnees, unemployment is at 80%. Unemployment in the general population has hit an alarming 30%.

The August 1994 Washington Declaration signed by King Hussein and Yitzhak Rabin of Israel put an end to the state of war between the two countries and re-activated the ATM between Washington and Amman. US$220 million in Jordanian debt was wiped out, with an additional US$350 million expected. England followed suit, relieving Jordan of a smaller debt. Unfortunately, this has had no real effect on the current state of the economy. Jordan hadn't been paying its debts anyway; what the economy needs is income.

# ■ Festivals and Holidays

The most important festivals of the year are Islamic celebrations (see **When to Go,** p.2); the national holidays are **Arab Revolution and Army Day** (June 10, marking the 1916 Arab Revolt against Ottoman rule), **Labor Day** (May 1), **Independence Day** (May 25), and, of course, King Hussein's **Accession Day** (Aug. 11) and **Birthday** (Nov. 14). Government offices and banks close on national holidays.

For the Christian community, the **Easter Celebrations** (all congregations follow the Eastern Calendar for Palm and Easter Sundays) are the most spectacular of the year. **Christmas** is a smaller feast, especially for the Coptic and Abyssinian Churches, which celebrate the holiday during the second week of January rather than on December 25.

The two-week **Jerash Festival** is held every year during July or August. Amid brilliantly illuminated Roman ruins and inside ancient amphitheaters, visitors witness performances by international artists. For more information, contact the **Jerash Festival Office,** P.O. Box 910 582, Amman (tel. (06) 675 199 or 686 197).

# ■ Language

The official language of the Hashemite Kingdom of Jordan is Arabic. However, the spoken Arabic dialect differs from classical Arabic and varies from that used in Egypt, the Gulf States, and North Africa. Very minor differences in pronunciation separate the dialects of Jordanians, Palestinians, Lebanese, and Syrians; see the **Language Glossary** for more on Arabic (p. 557).

Due to decades of British colonial rule, English is Jordan's second language, taught at both public and private schools. Almost all Jordanians have a knowledge of the language; many speak it quite well. Most signs are written in both Arabic and English, and Jordan Television's second channel broadcasts subtitled British and American programs after 8:30pm. French is taught as a third language by private schools and occasionally spoken badly by upper class Lebanese hopefuls.

# ■ The Arts

## LITERATURE

The Arabic language is shared by 21 nations, and Arabic literature from these countries is the proud heritage of the whole of the Arab world. The Jordanian region itself has a long tradition of prose: the oldest example of a Semitic script, the Mesha Stele, was found in Karak. Unfortunately, few Jordanian works are translated into other languages and thus remain inaccessible to most foreigners.

Among English travel accounts, C.M. Doughty's *Arabia Deserta* and Wilfred Thesiger's more recent *Arabian Sands* are powerful adventure stories inspired by a romanticized version of Bedouin lifestyle. T.E. Lawrence's *Seven Pillars of Wisdom* contains vivid descriptions of the battles fought and the territory explored during the Arab Revolt of 1916; even if you don't reach Wadi Rum in the Jordanian desert, see David Lean's magnificent *Lawrence of Arabia* on the big screen. King Abdallah's two-volume *Memoirs* and King Hussein's *Uneasy Lies the Head* are self-serving but dispel once and for all the myth that it's good to be king. The Arab Legion chief of the 1940s and 50s, John Bagot Glubb (Glubb Pasha), wrote *A Soldier With the Arabs* and several books based on his life. A little less adventurous but more erudite is Jonathan

Raban's *Arabia: A Journey through the Labyrinth*. Gertrude Bell, one of the first female Western travelers in the region, writes of her journeys through Jordan and Syria in *The Desert and the Sown*.

For the archaeologically and historically inclined there are G.L. Harding's *Antiquities of Jordan* and Julian Huxley's *From an Antique Land*. Ian Browning's *Petra* is wonderfully comprehensive. Finally, Agatha Christie's *Argument with Death* is a light introduction to the mesmerizing power of Petra.

## VISUAL ARTS

Both the Jordanian government and private groups are taking measures to promote and foster the arts. Like that of other countries of the Arab world, Jordanian art is an expression of Arab and often Muslim identity. But Jordanians are not sticklers for the traditional; contemporary artists have many more Western tendencies and use visual art as an outlet for personal as well as cultural expression. Modernity is eroding the traditional Islamic reluctance to portray human beings. Jordan's architecture, painting, and sculpture have all developed substantially in this century.

When it comes to folk art, Jordanians do abide by tradition. Techniques developed over centuries make for skillful weavers of wool and goat-hair rugs and tapestries. Leather handicrafts, pottery, ceramics, and coral curios also belong to the family of mastered Jordanian folk art. Painters often display their work in galleries in Amman. Nature, Bedouin life, and longing for Palestine are all common subjects. It is woodcarving, though, that is the Jordanian specialty. Artists can do beautiful carvings of your name right on the street, for an appropriate fee, naturally. You will find most of these crafts sold proudly on the streets of Jordan.

## POPULAR AND FOLK CULTURE

Homesick Yankees who aren't sticklers for highbrow culture can look for Bart Simpson to brighten their day or *The Bold and the Beautiful* to remind them of those weekday afternoons in front of the TV. These and other popular American and British shows appear on Jordanian television with Arabic subtitles. More authentic Jordanian programming includes music videos and disco dance extravaganzas. Much of the pop music in Jordan is Egyptian; listen for traditional Arabic themes under the cacophony of not-quite-Western sounds. Jordanians do, however, have their own traditional expressions of pop culture, most notably a strong oral tradition of stories, songs, and ballads. Villages often have their own individualized songs commemorating births, circumcisions, weddings, funerals, and planting. Several Cossack dances, including a sword dance that has to be seen to be believed, are popular in Jordan, as is *dabkeh*, a dance performed to the resonating rhythm of feet pounding on the floor. Eavesdrop on weddings in poorer neighborhoods for a taste of traditional folk music and for the women's salutatory shouts followed by ululation (*ha-WEEE-ha*).

# ■ Food

Jordanian cuisine has evolved through centuries of Bedouin cooking. The national dish, *mensaf,* ideally consists of eight to ten kilograms of rice on a large tray, topped with pine nuts, an entire lamb or goat, and a yogurt-based sauce. The Bedouin serve the head of the lamb on top, reserving the prize delicacies—eyes and tongue—for speechless and visually jaded guests. The right hand is used to ball the rice, and the flat bread to pull off chunks of meat and dip them into the warm *jamid* sauce.

Most other dishes include the main ingredients of *mensaf*. Traditional dinners are served between 2-3pm. Popular dinners include *musakhkhan*—chicken baked with olive oil and onions and a delicious spice called *summaq,* served on bread—and *mahshi,* a tray of vine leaves, squash, or eggplant stuffed with mincemeat, rice, and onions. *Mezze,* loosely translated as "hors d'oeuvres," encompasses a wide range of dishes including hummus with olive oil, *mutabbal* (an eggplant dip also known as baba ghanoush), *labneh* (thickened yogurt), cucumbers, tomatoes (*bandoorah*), and pickles. Supper is usually smaller. A combination of hummus, cheese, honey, butter, jam, bread, and sometimes *fuul* form a standard breakfast. A staple is *za'tar,* thyme mixed with sesame seeds and various spices and eaten either with little pieces of bread dipped first into olive oil and then into the mix, or pizza-style.

At restaurants, if the menu is in English, you can't afford the food. *Kabab* is skewered lamb, *shish tawouq* chicken, and *kofta* grilled ground beef with parsley (rather spicy). Hummus and falafel are cheap, as is *shawerma,* delicious sandwiches made of lamb (or chicken, a more recent innovation) sliced into Arabic bread with *summaq,* tahini sauce, vegetables, and sometimes pickles. Many deli-like places sell *mu'ajjanat,* dough wrapped around or topped with spinach *(sabanekh),* lamb (in which case it's called *sfeeha),* cheese, or *za'tar* and olive oil and then baked. Fresh *ka'ik,* a bread ring with sesame seeds, is a street favorite, as is corn-on-the-cob. With *ka'ik* you will be given *za'tar* in a piece of newspaper for dipping

As in the rest of the region, desserts are heavenly but overwhelmingly sweet—take them in small doses. Desserts include *ba'laweh, kinafeh* (made of soft cheese and shredded wheat, baked, soaked in syrup, and garnished with pistachios), *basbouseh* (wheat and syrup baked to moist goodness), pistachio nougat from candy stores, and ice cream *(booza).* Don't get chocolate. Mango, pistachio, and *mastika* are the best flavors. Some places advertise milk shakes, which are nearly always simply flavored milk. The exception is the Beefy Café in Amman, which is the only place in the entire country to get a good, thick milk shake. Some new *gelato* stores have opened up as well, especially in the Shmeisani area of Amman and in Aqaba. For relief on a hot day, their *gelato* can't be beat.

Water in Amman is piped in from Azraq oasis and the Euphrates River in Iraq. Although certainly potable, it is hardly pure. Toting bottled water (350fils, more at restaurants and tourist haunts) or iodine tablets, like extra molars, is a sign of wisdom. Jordan is a clean country; even salads should be safe to eat.

Jordanians drink tremendous amounts of tea *(shay),* almost always made with mint *(na'na').* You may never take milk in your tea again. Stereotypes hold that hicks *(fellaheen,* farmers) drink theirs syrupy sweet; restaurants will assume you are one unless you prove your gentility by asking for *sukkar aleel* (not too much sugar). A cup of Arabic coffee *(qahwa),* a thick, black, bittersweet brew, is espresso-strength. Avoid the silt in the bottom of the cup. American coffee and instant coffee (Nescafé), both way inferior and for wimps only, are also available at restaurants; for those who truly need iced coffee, Mr. Brown's is available in cans in upscale supermarkets and tourist spots.

Because most Muslims agree that drinking **alcohol** is prohibited by Islam, imbibing in Jordan is subject to some restrictions and conventions. It is illegal to possess alcohol in public unless at a place licensed for liquor. Drinking and driving, or even having alcohol in the car, would be a big mistake. Nonetheless, many Jordanians drink, and with no enforced drinking age, anyone who looks older than 16 may buy at a liquor store (usually owned by Christians; bottles of vodka run JD10). Amstel, locally-brewed under license, is the most popular alcoholic drink (900fils). Imports are also available. *'Araq* is a popular anise-seed hard alcohol that is mixed with water until a cloudy white suspension results. Liquor is very expensive, especially at bars and restaurants, where a drink may cost JD3.500-6.

# Amman عمان

The artistically dangerous dance of Amman's automobiles along the city's seven hills leaves visitors agape in Jordan's capital. Horns honk incessantly, but are overwhelmed five times a day by the beautiful call to prayer echoing from the minarets which grace the skyline. The din of the traffic will soon take second place in the visitor's mind to greetings of "Welcome to Jordan" coming from the smiling faces of

JORDAN

Amman's shopkeepers, bus drivers, and others who insist that the "Jordanian ethic" is, above all else, hospitality. When the sun goes down and the lights go up, Amman offers its jasmine-scented streets as the perfect setting for lazy summertime strolls.

The Ammonite capital in biblical times and later the Greco-Roman city of Philadelphia, modern Amman was a mere village in the decades preceding 1948. Following the Arab-Israeli wars of 1948 and 1967, many Palestinian refugees ended up in Amman, which soon boomed. Palestinians now form about 70% of Jordan's population, but sometimes experience discrimination at the hands of the Jordanian ruling minority. Some of these Palestinians are highly successful doctors, businesspeople, bankers, and politicians, while others still live in Amman's huge refugee camps and dream about returning to Palestine. Egyptian and Southeast Asian workers also form a segment of the city's population. Amman's nearly bursting seams were further expanded by the arrival of immigrants from Iraq and Kuwait following the 1991 Gulf War. The pre-1948 population of 6000 has exploded to well over a million inhabitants today, roughly one third of Jordan's total population.

Amman's central location makes it the country's principal transportation hub and the base for exploration of Jordan's other sights. Reasonable hotel prices combine with government services, embassies, and consulates to make a stay in the capital city a painless experience. Don't feel disdain for those other travelers returning to suburban five-star hotels. Pity them—it is the people of downtown Amman that are the city's most valuable treasure. The "welcomes" you hear are quite sincere, and should be responded to with a big smile. Chances are, it will lead to a cup of tea, a conversation, and an experience you will never forget.

# ▓ Orientation

Take advantage of Amman's summits to get a perspective on this roller-coaster city. Rocky **Jabal al-Qala'a** (Citadel Hill), where the Archaeological Museum sits amidst unearthed remains of Roman and Umayyad palaces, temples, and hilltop fortifications, provides a panoramic view of winding streets, tall buildings, mosques, and ruins, all of which will serve as useful landmarks.

Any round object dropped to the ground will roll into Amman's downtown district, **Al Balad,** which is neatly framed by the seven hills. This is the best location from which to orient yourself in Jordan's biggest city.

Downtown Amman has three major landmarks: the **Al Husseini Mosque,** the **Roman Amphitheater,** and (believe it or not) the **post office,** because everyone knows where it is. With your back to the mosque, the city's focal point, you will be facing up **King Faisal St.,** which leads northwest to the post office and numerous budget hotels. Turn to your right, and you will be looking up **Hashemi St.,** which leads to the Roman Amphitheater. To your left will be the city's **main market.** If you walk up King Faisal St. towards the post office, the **gold market** will be on your right-hand side. If you walk up Hashemi St. past the Roman Amphitheater, you will reach the **clock tower** and the recently built piazza.

Amman's eight **numbered traffic circles** follow a line leading westward out of town and through **Jabal Amman.** Beyond Third Circle, Amman's diplomatic center, where most foreign embassies are located, traffic circles have been replaced by busy intersections. Although the city is earnestly attempting to rename these intersections "squares," each is still fondly called a "circle," or *duwwar.* From Seventh Circle, traffic heads south to Queen Alia International Airport and the Desert Highway (Aqaba 335km), to the Kings' Highway via Madaba (35km; Karak 125km; Petra 260km), and via Na'ur to the Dead Sea and the border of Israel (90km). From Eighth Circle, you can continue west to Wadi Seer, or head north to Jerash (50km).

Following King Hussein St. northwest from the city center brings you to **Jabal al-Weibdeh,** a quiet middle-class residential district. Once in this neighborhood, the **JETT** and **Abdali Bus Stations** are the third right turn off King Hussein St.—the first right after the road flattens out. The blue dome and octagonal minaret of the jabal's enormous **King Abdallah Mosque** are visible from all surrounding heights.

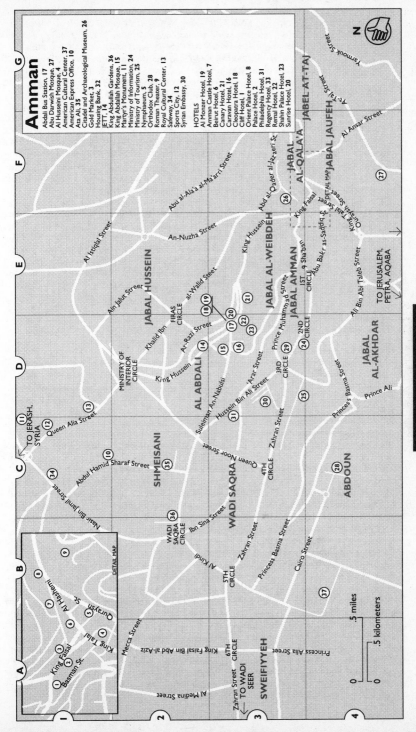

# Amman

Abdali Bus Station, 17
Abu Darwish Mosque, 27
Al Hussein Mosque, 4
American Cultural Center, 37
American Express Office, 10
Ata Ali, 35
Citadel and Archaeological Museum, 26
Gold Market, 3
Housing Bank, 32
JETT, 14
King Abdallah Gardens, 36
King Abdallah Mosque, 15
Martyr's Monument, 11
Ministry of Information, 24
Ministry of Tourism, 25
Nymphaeum, 5
Orthodox Club, 28
Roman Theater, 9
Royal Cultural Center, 13
Safeway, 34
Sports City, 12
Syrian Embassy, 30

**HOTELS**
Al Monzer Hotel, 19
Amman Castle Hotel, 7
Beirut Hotel, 6
Canary Hotel, 21
Caravan Hotel, 16
Cleopatra Hotel, 18
Cliff Hotel, 1
Orient Palace Hotel, 8
Palace Hotel, 2
Philadelphia Hotel, 31
Regency Hotel, 33
Remal Hotel, 22
Shahin Palace Hotel, 23
Sunrise Hotel, 20

**JORDAN**

To the north of the city lies **Jabal Hussein,** a largely residential district dominated by the Housing Bank complex (*mujamma' bank al-iskan*), an overgrown Love Boat next to the Forte Grand Hotel. This area is bordered to the northwest by the Ministry of Interior Circle (*duwwar ad-Dakhiliyyeh*) and the modern suburb of **Shmeisani,** complete with luxury hotels and American-style fast food restaurants. To the south of the city, in the direction of the airport, rises **Jabal al-Ashrafiyyeh.** Its ornate **Abu Darwish Mosque** can be seen above the **Wahdat Bus Station** and the Wahdat Palestinian refugee camp. While the Jordan Valley fertilizes the land to the north and west of Amman, the city recedes into desert in the south and east.

The government has installed some street signs in downtown Amman—some have English translations, some don't. Although most people know King Faisal and Hashemi St., other inquiries on street names are likely to produce blank stares. Directions usually run something like: "to the right of the third falafel stand; stop and say hello to Nabiyeh for me, he owns the place; then take a left in front of the mosque with the green dome." (Allah forbid anyone should, on a whim, repaint the green dome blue.) Many street signs are in English and street names are listed on maps, but in general, successful navigation of Amman depends on knowing Amman's landmarks. In addition to remembering the Al Husseini Mosque, the Roman Amphitheater, and the Wahdat and Abdali bus stations, try to find out what number circle your destination is near, and you'll have an easier time finding your way. Lastly, don't hesitate to ask a local for assistance—they will be happy to help you out. There are times when an entire neighborhood will start contacting their information network systems to get you where you're going—before you know it, Omar's uncle's sister's friend who owes him a favor is driving you around the city.

# ■ Transportation

## WITHIN AMMAN

To reach locations within the city or to find the departure point for buses and *service*, ask a downtown shopkeeper. At a minimum, you'll be pointed in the right direction; quite possibly you'll be escorted there, invited to dinner, and offered permanent lodging. You can flag buses and *service* anywhere along their routes, but *service* are often full (they take five passengers) from the beginning to the end of their prescribed courses. Public transportation stops at 8 or 9pm, a couple of hours earlier on Fridays; after that, walking in Amman is a great alternative for those with strong legs. Yellow **taxis,** at 150fils plus 100fils per day, are cheaper than buses in the U.S. or Europe and a good idea if you're pressed for time. Metered cabs prowl the streets in search of fares until 11pm, and sometimes later. Pay around 500fils to go from downtown to Third Circle or from Third to Sixth Circle, 350fils from downtown to Abdali. A taxi between the two bus/*service* stations should cost 800fils. The trip along Jabal Amman from First to Eighth Circle should cost no more than 800fils; check to make sure the meter is running. (See **Getting Around,** p.462.)

**Buses** traveling within Amman cost about 100fils; it's a little more if you're heading for the suburbs. Flag any bus traveling in your direction and ask the driver if it stops where you want to go, or find out at any bus station. Pay your fare after the ride has begun. Drivers and their assistants don't like making change, so carry 100fils pieces with you. Most buses have the name of their destination written in Arabic on the front, sides, or both. Some have numbers, but since buses going on different routes may display the same number, what worked one time may not the next. Asking around is the best way to find a bus.

Although it may cost a few hundred more fils, transportation by **service** or yellow taxi is much easier on the nerves. Perhaps the best thing about traveling by *service* is the opportunity they provide to meet Jordanians. *Service* are numbered and the names of their routes are listed on the doors in Arabic. All routes within the city originate downtown, where you can ask for help finding stops. You would do best to mention major destinations or well-known landmarks. Stopping a *service* en route may be difficult—many drive at breakneck speed, so try to make yourself visible without stepping in front of it. To stop the *service*, stick out your arm, palm down. Below are some popular *service* routes.

**#1** (١): Travels on Jabal Amman between Center City and Third Circle, passing First and Second Circles (70fils).

**#2** (٢): Starts on Basman St. (look for the Basman Theater) and travels on Jabal Amman to Malik Abd Ribiya St. between Second and Third Circles (70fils).

**#3** (٣): Starts on Kureisha St. and travels on Jabal Amman to Fourth Circle (90fils).

**#4** (٤): Runs from Basman St. to Al Amaneh Circle and gardens, passing near all points of interest on Jabal al-Weibdeh (70fils).

**(Not numbered):** Leaves from bottom of Omar al-Khayyam St. (opposite Cliff Hotel), travels up Jabal al-Weibdeh to Queen Alia Institute, just uphill from Abdali Station (70fils).

**#6** (٦): Starts on Malik Ghazi St. (better known as Cinema al-Hussein St.), then travels along King Faisal and King Hussein St. to Jamal Abd an-Nasser Circle, passing Abdali and JETT Stations (80fils).

**#7** (٧): Starts by Cinema al-Hussein St. and runs past Abdali Station to Shmeisani near the Ambassador Hotel and the Gallery Alia (70fils).

*Service* and minibuses to Wahdat Station start at Kureisha St. (also called Sakfi Seil) near Petra Bank and pass near Abu Darwish Mosque on Jabal Ashrafiyyeh. *Service* directly to Wahdat Station from Abdali costs 120fils. Another route starts at Shabsough St. near the gold market downtown, passing Abdali Station and Jabal Hussein to the Ministry of Interior Circle (80fils). Some prices will be slightly more or less than those listed, but *service* drivers rarely cheat you—prices are generally standard.

## INTERCITY

**Buses** to the north central and northwestern parts of the country, including the Jordan Valley, leave from **Abdali Bus Station** on King Hussein St. on Jabal al-Weibdeh. Destinations include Jerash, Ajlun, Irbid, Salt, and the King Hussein/Allenby Bridge, as well as Damascus. **Hashemi Street Station,** near the Roman amphitheater, launches traffic to the northeast, including Zarqa, Mafraq, and points east of Irbid. Traffic to and from the south is based at **Wahdat Station,** several km from downtown Amman between the Abu Darwish Mosque and the Wahdat Refugee Camp. Buses from here go to Madaba, Karak, Ma'an, Wadi Musa, and Aqaba. The **JETT** bus station, serving major towns in Jordan, Syria, and Iraq, is on King Hussein St., up the road from Abdali Bus Station (see Practical Information, below). It is wise to book bus tickets at least one day in advance. Intercity *service* leave from the same stations as buses, and go to the same regions. Fares tend to be 40-50% more expensive than comparable bus fares. All prices, bus and *service* alike, are government-regulated.

To go to Syria from Jordan you will need a **Syrian visa;** don't rely on the Syrian Embassy in Amman to issue visas, as they almost certainly won't. You should apply for a Syrian visa from the embassy nearest you *well* in advance of leaving your home country. Buses run often between Amman and Damascus. Unfortunately, you can't make round-trip reservations from either city. Definitely make reservations for the return trip to Jordan as soon as you arrive in Damascus, or vice versa. The road between the two capitals is heavily traveled on weekends (Thurs.-Sat.)—border-crossing on these days has been known to take as long as three hours. Luckily, the process at the border is not difficult as long as you have a visa.

# ■ Practical Information

**Ministry of Tourism:** P.O. Box 224 (tel. 642 311; fax 648 465). From 3rd Circle on Jabal Amman, walk down Zahran St., to the left of the Ministry of Information. Distributes free maps, hotel price lists, and lovely color brochures. Open Sat.-Thurs. 8am-2pm.

**Embassies: U.S.:** In Abdoun (tel. 820 163; fax 820 101). From 5th Circle take the third right on the street that goes toward the Orthodox Club. The fortress-like complex is 500m down that road and can't be missed. Consular division open Sun.-Thurs. 9am-4pm, for visas 9am-noon. **Canada:** In Shmeisani near the Petra Bank (tel. 666 124; fax 689 227). Open Sun.-Thurs. 9am-4:30pm, until 11am for visas. **U.K.:** Near the Orthodox Club in Abdoun (tel. 823 100; fax 813 759). Consular division open Sun.-Thurs. 8:30am-noon. **Australia:** 4th Circle on Jabal Amman (tel. 673 246; fax 673 263). Helpful with foreign visas. Open Sun.-Thurs. 7:30am-2:40pm. **Egypt:** Jabal Amman, between 4th and 5th Circles (tel. 605 203; fax 604 082). Take a right by the Japanese embassy and continue about 100m down the road. Embassy is on the left. Bring a photo and JD12 before noon, pick up visa on the same afternoon. Open Sat.-Thurs. 9:30am-2:30pm, until noon for visas. **Syria:** Jabal Amman, up from 3rd Circle toward the reflecting building (tel. 641 076; fax 655 651). Take a left at the intersection and head up the hill. Look for the Syrian flag (red, white, and black stripes with two green stars). In theory, a visa costs JD10 for Americans and JD38 for British nationals, but virtually nobody gets to the privileged paying stage. You must have a Jordanian entry stamp on your passport and no evidence of visits to the West Bank or Israel for any hope of a chance. Embassy open (for visa info) Sun.-Thurs. 9-11am.

**Currency Exchange:** Banking hours are ordinarily Sat.-Wed. 8:30am-12:30pm and 4-5:45pm, Thurs. 8:30am-12:30pm, some are closed on Friday. Many authorized **money changers,** found downtown between the Al Husseini Mosque and the post office, are open daily, usually late into the evening. They offer roughly the same exchange rates as banks, but will not leech the commission that banks demand. Bring your passport. The **British Bank of the Middle East** (tel. 660 471), opposite the post office, can give you a **cash advance** on your MC/Visa.

**American Express: International Traders,** P.O. Box 408 (tel. 607 014; fax 669 905), Abdul Hamid Sharaf St. in Shmeisani, opposite the Ambassador Hotel. Holds mail and can obtain visas when cardholders purchase plane tickets. Open Sat.-Thurs. 8am-6pm.

**Telephone Office:** Exit to your left from the post office on Prince Muhammad St. and take the very first left onto frighteningly steep Omar al-Khayyam St. The telephone office is a pulse-quickening, sweat-inspiring 200m on the left. The sign is in Arabic, but you'll see the phones through 30m of windows. Open daily 7:30am-11pm. Rate for 3min. to the U.S. JD6.600, Great Britain JD5.500, 30% cheaper after 10pm. Pay at the desk after your call. Overseas calls can be made from any post office, from most hotels at any time for a surcharge, or from private homes. Note that you cannot call collect or with a calling card in Jordan. All overseas calls can be paid in cash only. For more polite service and a better connection than at the telephone office, go to **Ziad Khalifeh's private telephone office** (tel. 688 063), located just downhill from the government one (look for the phone picture on the sign). Fax and photocopy services available. Open Sun.-Thurs. 9am-8pm. **Directory assistance** (in Arabic): Tel. 121 or 640 444.

**Airport: Queen Alia International Airport** (tel. (08) 530 70), is 35km south of Amman. Buses connect Abdali Bus Station and the airport every 30min. (7am-9pm, 40min., 750fils). A private taxi to the airport will cost JD6-7 during the day, JD12 after midnight. There is no *service* to the airport. Bank (open 24hr.) and tourist office (open 9am-2pm) are in the airport. Jordanian visas, good for one month, available at the airport upon arrival (JD15). There is a JD10 exit fee when leaving Jordan by air (JD4 if by land, JD6 if by sea).

**Intercity Buses: JETT** (tel. 664 146; fax 605 005) runs A/C buses to King Hussein/Allenby Bridge (daily 6:30am, 1hr., JD6); Petra (daily 6:30am, 3hr., JD11, round-trip tour including guide, horse, and lunch JD32.500); Aqaba (5 per day, 4hr., JD4; Damascus (4 per day, 4-5hr. depending on border crossing, visa req., JD4.500); Cairo (Sat., Mon., Tue., Thurs., 7:30am, 20-24hr., JD48 includes luggage); and Baghdad (daily 2pm, 15hr., JD12 plus JD4 departure tax, visa req.). Reserve two days in advance. Office open daily 6am-8pm. Other buses depart from either the Abdali or Wahdat bus stations, depending on direction. Fares to: Jerash 270fils, Ajlun 450fils,

Irbid 820fils, Salt 200fils, King Hussein/Allenby Bridge JD1.500. For more information, see **Transportation** (p. 474).

**Intercity Service Taxis:** From **Abdali Station,** fares to: Jerash 470fils, Ajlun 750fils, Irbid 880fils, Salt 350fils, and King Hussein/Allenby Bridge JD1.500. From **Wahdat Station,** fares to: Madaba 350fils, Karak down the King's Highway JD1.500, and Ma'an via the newer Desert Highway JD3.500; at Ma'an you can transfer for service to Wadi Musa (Petra) and Aqaba (500fils and JD1.500, respectively). Prices are government-regulated, but the naive tourist may get charged a higher price.

**Car Rental:** Local agencies have better deals and fewer restrictions, although a growing market has attracted big names like **EuroDollar** (tel. 693 399; fax 687 233) and the not-so-**Thrifty** (tel. 617 241). **International Rent A Car** at 3rd Circle rents cars for min. 3 days, unlimited mileage (JD60 per day). You need to be 18, with a valid driver's license and passport. **Reliable** (tel. 819 676) in Abdoun has brand new cars for JD20-30 per day, and boasts a 24hr. breakdown service.

**English Bookstores: Al 'Ulama Bookshop** (tel. 636 192), 50m uphill from the Amman Post Office, offers history books, travel guides, dictionaries, and a couple of American news magazines. Fax services available. **University Bookstore** (tel. 636 339), on Jabal al-Weibdeh near Khalaf Circle, sells fiction as well as books about Jordan. Open 8:30am-7:30pm. **Istiqlal Library** is located around the corner from the Turino Hotel in Sweyfiyyeh. A giant air-conditioned department store for books and supplies, the staff speaks excellent English and will point you to the diverse selection of reading material. Credit cards accepted. Open Sat.-Thurs. 8:30am-1:30pm and 3:30-7:30pm. The **Habib Bookshop** across the street from Citibank at 3rd Circle sells English newspapers, magazines, and trashy novels, and stocks random necessities like razors, batteries, and glue sticks. It has the cheapest photocopier in town at 50fils per copy. Open Sun.-Thurs. 7am-7pm. Most supermarkets also sell English newspapers and magazines.

**Local Press:** *Your Guide to Amman,* published monthly and available free at larger hotels, bookstores, and travel agencies, is full of helpful info. *The Jordan Times* (150fils), a daily newspaper with excellent coverage of the Middle East and Africa, also lists useful telephone numbers, all-night pharmacies, current government prices for fruits and vegetables (helpful for bargaining in the market), and cultural events in Amman. *Jordan Today,* published monthly and available at larger hotels, has invaluable information on tourism, culture, and entertainment. The *International Herald Tribune* arrives after 3pm one day late at newsstands. The weekly *Jerusalem Star* (350fils) lists cultural events and all the piddling details from the lives of the royals.

**Radio:** Those who crave an English-speaking voice and have access to a radio can tune in to the **BBC** on 1323AM and the **Voice of America** at night on 1260AM. 96.3FM plays familiar Top 40 from 6am-2am. For the sleepless jetlagged, 88.0 and 99.0FM have 24hr. Arabic-speaking DJs spinning records from Israeli pop to classical Arabic music.

**Department of Antiquities:** From 3rd Circle walk down Hussein Bin Ali St. to the mirrored-glass Ailco building, then up the street diagonally on the left (tel. 644 482). This is the national headquarters for research on digs. They have a library and distribute books and detailed maps highlighting archaeological sites. Open Sat.-Thurs. 8am-2pm.

**Friends of Archaeology:** P.O. Box 2440 (tel. 696 683), Jabal Amman. Facing west, take a left at 4th Circle. Turn right, left, and left again, and the FoA center will be on your right. This private local organization sponsors weekly field trips to sites. Most are for members only, but it may be possible to join a trip for a fee.

**American Cultural Center:** Abdoun, inside the American Embassy Complex (tel. 820 101; fax 813 759). Free American films every Sun. and Thurs., cable TV, and lectures by scholars and politicians visiting Jordan. Topics include Arab/American relations and Middle Eastern studies. The library has American magazines and newspapers, comfy couches, a video library, and a good selection of books, mostly non-fiction. Center and library open Sun.-Thurs. 9am-5pm.

**British Council:** Rainbow St. (tel. 636 147). Facing uphill at 1st Circle, go left. The BC is past the Saudi Arabian Embassy on the right hand side. Sponsors films, lectures, and various other stimulating activities. Library (with A/C) open Sat.-Wed. 10am-6pm, Thurs. 10am-2pm.

**Laundry: Sun Laundry and Dry Cleaners** (tel. 822 538), Umm Uthaina, does your shirts (800fils) and pants (JD1.200). One-hour service. Visa accepted. **Dry Clean** (tel. 641 955), Jabal Amman, across the street from the Ministry of Tourism charges 500fils for shirts and 750fils for pants. **Al-Jami'a Laundry** (tel. 847 857), on your first right heading away from the city past the main gate of Jordan University, is a do-it-yourself joint (wash and dry JD1.7). If you don't mind getting wet, washing by hand is a great option. The air in summer is so dry that clothes will be ready in several hours. Some hotels will provide you with soap and a bucket.

**Pharmacies:** The *Jordan Times* and *Your Guide to Amman* list all-night pharmacies and doctors, both rotating weekly. There is a pharmacy almost every block downtown. The **Rawhi Pharmacy** near the Intercontinental Hotel is known to have an excellent English-speaking staff (tel. 644 454). For daily 24-hr. (including holidays) service and wonderful conversation, try **Jacob's Pharmacy** in 3rd Circle (tel. 644 945). Others usually open Sat.-Thurs. 8am-7pm. For non-prescription medicine, try the **Safeway**, open daily 24hr., on the edge of Shmeisani.

**Emergency:** Anywhere in Jordan, call 192 for **police,** 193 for an **ambulance.** The *Jordan Times, Star,* and *Your Guide to Amman* list doctors and hospitals. Some good ones include: **Hussein Medical Center,** Mecca St. (tel. 813 832), and **Shmeisani Hospital,** Shmeisani (tel. 607 431). In case of **traffic accidents** in Amman, call 896 390.

**Post Office:** At the base of Prince Muhammad St., where it joins King Faisal St. downtown (tel. 121 for inquiries). Stamps and **Poste Restante** open Sat.-Thurs. 8am-7pm, Fri. 8am-1pm. Cables and faxes can be sent from this office. **EMS** (tel. 688 190) is on Lifta St., a dead-end behind Qawar Arthroscopy Center. From downtown, go up King Hussein St. past the Abdali and JETT bus stations. Take a right on Bir al-Sab'a St. and look left. Daily 8am-6pm, holidays 8am-2pm.

**Telephone Code:** 06.

# ■ Accommodations

Many clean and reputable hotels are located near the **Abdali Bus Station** in Jabal al-Weibdeh. This area is close to the city center and convenient for transport out of Amman. Just beyond Jabal al-Weibdeh lies the opulent **Shmeisani** district, with a few reasonably priced accommodations worth the hunt.

The **city center,** on the other hand, is overgrown with small, seedy hotels. Since every block has three or four cheapies and every alley at least one, look carefully and be sure to see a room before committing to staying somewhere.

Official hotel prices are set by the government. In the off-season (during non-summer months) and for longer stays, most hotel owners will give you a deal—don't be afraid to bargain with a smile. All rooms have private baths unless otherwise noted, and rooms near Abdali Station have phones. The hotels near Abdali Station also take credit cards (unless noted) while other hotels accept cash only.

Be aware that sometimes hotel managers pay cab drivers to bring tourists to their hotels (and many times hotel managers are related to cab drivers). These drivers may go so far as to say that the hotel you ask for is bad, full, or shut down; they may even pretend that they don't know where it is. Be insistent, or, if you feel that you can easily find another cab, simply ask the driver to let you out.

### Near Abdali Station

**Canary Hotel,** Karmaly St., P.O. Box 9062 (tel. 638 353; tel./fax 654 353), on Jabal al-Weibdeh near Terra Sancta College. Facing downhill from Abdali Station, walk 1½ blocks along the right side of King Hussein St. When the main road forks downhill to the left, continue straight on Al Ba'oniyah St. Take your first right on Karamaly St. and try and survive the final 1½-block climb. Khaleel Twal, a member of the friendliest family in Amman, will welcome you into his vine-entwined courtyard and comfy pastel-hued TV room. Reserve a few days in advance in summer.

Breakfast, lunch, and dinner available. Singles JD15-17. Doubles JD20-22. Triples and quads JD26 and up.

**Caravan Hotel,** Sa'id bin al-Harith St., P.O. Box 9062 (tel. 661 195 or 197; tel./fax 661 196), on Jabal al-Weibdeh. Looking downhill, head up Sa'id bin al-Harith St. which begins just before the big police station on the right. The hotel is 2 blocks up on the right, only 100m from Abdali Station next to the King Abdullah Mosque and two churches. Ihsan Twal will nourish your stay with Arabic food custom-cooked to fit your budget. 20% *Let's Go* discount. Singles JD18. Doubles JD24. Triples JD27. If you use your Visa card, the discount shrinks to 16%.

**Shahin Palace Hotel,** Muhammad Tash St., P.O. Box 921575 (tel. 648 138 or 139), Jabal al-Weibdeh. Take your first left off Sa'id bin al-Harith St. onto Beit Nouba St. Follow the circle around the park, and take a right on Muhammad Tash St. The hotel is 1½ blocks on the right. This quiet place offers serenity and plush, red-carpeted rooms with refrigerators, TVs, and clean bathrooms, all within a few blocks of a lush park. Singles JD14. Doubles JD18. Triples JD20.

**Remal Hotel,** 4 Sa'id Bin al-Harith St., P.O. Box 910477 (tel. 630 670; fax 655 751). Look downhill from the Abdali bus station for the police station on the right; the hotel is a good olive-seed-spit up the small street next to the station. Fresh paint and clean bathrooms make the rooms look great, but the street noise sometimes rivals that of a space shuttle launch. Restaurant attached on the right offers traditional Arabic fare. Singles JD14. Doubles JD18, plus a 10% service charge.

**Al Monzer Hotel,** King Hussein St., P.O. Box 926595 (tel. 639 469; fax 657 328). From the bus station, it's on the left when looking downhill. Upstairs waiting area has enormous lounge chairs. Clean rooms come with ceiling fans and balconies, and although the mattresses are thin, the rooms facing away from the bus station are quiet enough to ensure a good night's sleep. Singles JD12-14, doubles JD16, triples JD18, quads JD20. Cash only.

**Sunrise Hotel,** King Hussein St. (tel. 621 841 or 428). To the left of Abdali as you face downhill. Cool marble halls and complimentary flip-flops may entice late arrivers to Amman. Rooms are clean and quiet and come equipped with a fan. Singles JD9. Doubles JD12. Triples JD15, plus a 10% service charge. Cash only.

**Merryland Hotel,** King Hussein St., P.O. Box 9122 (tel. 615 441, 654 052, or 657 393; fax 657 392). Look downhill from the Abdali bus station and you will see the black walls and large yellow sign on the right. This hotel, with an adjoining restaurant, is a bit more expensive, but the place to go if you want to splurge. Rooms feature overstuffed mattresses, refrigerators, and sparkling new bathrooms. Singles JD20, doubles JD25, triples JD30. You can't charge the bill if it's under JD50.

## Downtown/Al Husseini Mosque Area

**Cliff Hotel,** King Faisal St. (tel. 624 273), at the top of the street across from the post office at the base of King Hussein St., on the third floor. The most popular traveler's spot in Amman, the Cliff is known from Hong Kong to Hanover. Manager Abu Suleiman calls it "the United Nations headquarters of the Middle East." Better than the Ministry of Tourism for honest information and directions and unbeatable for Arabic lessons and a little TLC. Abu Suleiman is so good, people staying at nearby hotels come for his travel advice. Offers tours at cheap rates to nearby sights—a great option for single travelers. Beds are sometimes left in poor condition. Singles JD5. Doubles JD8. "Terrace" mattress JD2. Hot showers 500fils. Reception sells bottled water and other conveniences. Reserve in advance.

**Farah Hotel** (tel. 651 443, -438; fax 651 437) on King Hussein St. just uphill from where King Hussein St. meets King Faisal St., marked by red signs with yellow writing. A worthy competitor of the Cliff, the newly-painted rooms have lockers, and each floor has a shared fridge and 2 immaculate bathrooms with free showers. Singles JD6. Shared rooms JD3.300 per person (negotiable for larger groups).

**Palace Hotel,** King Faisal St. (tel. 624 327; fax 650 602), 1½ blocks from Al Husseini Mosque. Look up for the red and blue "HOTEL" signs. Entrance in the alley on the left. The hotel features Roman pillar decor and a large dining/TV room with an indoor fountain and patio overlooking the city center. Rooms have telephones, but no fan. Common bathrooms are spic and span. Razors, chips, and other necessities for sale in the lobby. Singles JD8, doubles JD13, triples JD15.

**Amman Castle Hotel,** Shabsuq St. (tel./fax 642 766), 1½ blocks up an inclined avenue that runs directly into the Roman amphitheater. Look for "HOTEL" spelled out in red letters on a yellow background. Proprietors don't speak any English, but small rooms are comfortable and clean. Few foreigners. Not all rooms have bath. Third floor has a common kitchen. Singles JD5, doubles JD8, triples JD11.

**Beirut Hotel,** Al Hashemi St. (tel. 638 986; fax 650 916), between Al Husseini Mosque and the Roman amphitheater. Walking from the mosque, look for the blue sign with white English letters on the left side of the street. Small, cell-like yellow rooms with high windows are rather dark but adequate and clean. Private telephones and common bath. Can't beat the center-of-everything location. Singles JD5, doubles JD7, triples JD9.

**Orient Prince Hotel,** Al Hashemi St. (tel. 656 590; fax 656 472). On the left, a bit beyond the theater but before the piazza's clock tower. Look for a big green sign with yellow lettering. Entrance in an alley by the camera shop. Theater views are nice and make the dusty rooms, with their brown fur bedspreads, more appealing. Singles JD8, doubles JD12, triples JD18.

## Outlying Districts

**Nefertiti Hotel,** 26 Al Jahiz St. (tel. 603 865), in Shmeisani, in front of the Ambassador Hotel. Finding the Nefertiti will be a challenge, but well worth it. Uniformed attendants guide you down wide, well-lit corridors to rooms, many of which feature small terraces. Spacious accommodations and a relaxing, manicured courtyard. Restaurant attached to the hotel. Singles JD11.550. Doubles JD14.850. Triples JD18. Quads JD29.700.

**American Center for Oriental Research (ACOR)** (tel. 846 117 or 841 132; fax 844 181). Take a minibus from Abdali (100fils) and ask to get off at Jordan University. Look for the soccer field lights and the engineering building, an imposing five-story monstrosity. ACOR is on the opposite side of the street up the hill. Good luck finding it—there are no signs, only 4x4 vehicles parked out front. Home base for fieldworkers in Jordan (areas of interest include primarily archaeology, but also politics, history, economics, and international relations). Southwestern-style lobby and cozy library. Rooms US$22 per person, students US$18. Discounts for affiliates. Free private showers. Free Arabic-American lunch often features brownies and pecan pie; you can raid the fridge for breakfast and dinner. Laundry US$4 per load. Reservations recommended, in summer at least one month in advance. Monthly rates available.

# ■ Food

Amman's edibles combine the city's Bedouin and Palestinian heritages. The better sit-down restaurants cluster near Third Circle, in Shmeisani, and along Mecca St.; these places usually add a 10% service charge to the bill. The jewel of the city's offerings, however, are the various street foods, which are cheap, plentiful, and safe. If the listings are in Arabic, ask the vendor to translate.

**Shawerma** is always available for about 250fils; the most succulent stuff comes from the stands on Prince Muhammad St., on Second Circle, near the Lebanese

---

### Sugar and Spice and All Things Nice

Jordanians choose dessert much as you might choose a mate—the sweeter and stickier, the better. The most popular Jordanian sugary treats have roots in Syrian and Palestinian cuisines. Recipes for sweets like *burma* and *balorieh* were guarded secrets in immigrant kitchens until the **Jabri** and **Habiba** patisserie chains introduced them to mainstream Jordanian life around 1950. Jabri brought Damascene *ba'laweh* to happy mouths from Amman to Aqaba, while Habiba hooked the country on *kinafeh* from Nablus. Forty years later, the honey, nuts, sugar, and cavities are inseparable parts of Jordanian life.

© 1996 AT&T

# Someone back home *really* misses you.
# Please call.

With **AT&T Direct**<sup>SM</sup> Service it's easy to call back to the States from virtually anywhere your travels take you. Just dial the **AT&T Direct** Access Number for the country *you are in* from the chart below. You'll have English-language voice prompts or an AT&T Operator to guide your call. And our clearest,* fastest connections** will help you reach whoever it is that misses you most back home.

| | | |
|---|---|---|
| AUSTRIA● ............022-903-011 | GREECE● ...............00-800-1311 | NETHERLANDS● ...06-022-9111 |
| BELGIUM● ...........0-800-100-10 | INDIA✖ ...........................000-117 | RUSSIA●,▲,▶ (Moscow).755-5042 |
| CZECH REP▲ ......00-42-000-101 | IRELAND ............1-800-550-000 | SPAIN◇ .................900-99-00-11 |
| DENMARK.................8001-0010 | ISRAEL .................177-100-2727 | SWEDEN ...............020-795-611 |
| FRANCE...............0 800 99 0011 | ITALY● ........................172-1011 | SWITZERLAND● ..0-800-550011 |
| GERMANY.................0130-0010 | MEXICO▽ ........95-800-462-4240 | U.K.▲ ....................0800-89-0011 |

*Non-operator assisted calls to the U.S. only. **Based on customer preference testing. ●Public phones require coin or card deposit. Public phones require local coin payment through call duration. ◇From this country, AT&T Direct calls terminate to designated countries only. ▲May not be available from every phone/pay phone. ✖Not available from public phones. ▽When calling from public phones, use phones marked "Ladatel." ▶Additional charges apply when calling outside of Moscow.

Can't find the Access Number for the country you're calling from?
Just ask any operator for AT&T Direct Service.

Photo: R. Olken

# Greetings from LET'S GO

With pen and notebook in hand, a change of clothes in our backpack, and the tightest of budgets, we've spent our summer roaming the globe in search of travel bargains.

We've put the best of our research into the book that you're now holding. Our intrepid researcher-writers went on the road for months of exploration, from Anchorage to Angkor, Estonia to Ecuador, Iceland to India. Editors worked from spring to fall, massaging copy into witty and informative prose. A brand-new edition of each guide hits the shelves every fall, just months after it is researched, so you know you're getting the most reliable, up-to-date, and comprehensive information available.

We try to make this book an indispensable companion, but sometimes the best discoveries are the ones you make on your own. If you've got something to share, please drop us a line. We're Let's Go Publications, 67 Mount Auburn Street, Cambridge, MA 02138 USA (e-mail: fanmail@letsgo.com). Good luck and happy travels!

Embassy, but it has also been rumored that the **Al Faris Restaurant,** around the corner from the Turino Hotel and Restaurant in Shmeisani, has the best chicken *shawerma* in Jordan. **Falafel** and **corn on the cob** go for 110fils and 250fils respectively. Sides include **hummus** plates, *fuul,* and salads for 250-350fils.

Bread is a staple. *Khoubez* is your usual pita bread; rise at the crack of dawn to sample the freshest *ka'ik* (yummy, crunchy sesame rings). Both are available at stands for 100-200fils. Ask for *za'atar* (dried thyme, sesame seeds, and other spices) to sprinkle on top. Also try cheese or lamb *sfiebah* (Arabic pizzas) or *manaish* (bread baked with olive oil and *za'atar*), sold in many small restaurants and shops.

In the **downtown** area, rolled falafel sandwiches are 110fils. Two busy stands opposite Al Husseini Mosque are open until 11pm. Freshly squeezed **juices,** found in stands throughout the city, are too refreshing to miss (250-300fils). Options range from tomato and orange to banana, carrot, and a mysterious brown concoction that tastes like mangoes. Try them all, many times. Ask for a "cocktail," a blend of bananas, mangos, and strawberries with a pineapple wedge to boot.

If you're in **Sweiffiyeh,** check out the **Crema Creme** on Paris St. This popular spot is the place to go for ice cream, and is usually packed with people who triple-park their cars to get a taste of gelato and chat with friends. For the weight-conscious, **Frosti** down the street offers 60-calories-per-scoop ice cream. Unadventurous provincials should head to **Pizza Hut** or **Kentucky Fried Chicken** (can't miss the neon signs). Though prices are no higher than what you'd pay back home, a pizza will still cost more than your hotel room. For a real taste of Americana, forget Shmeisani's familiar fast-food joints and head to **Cheers Elite Café** in Sweifiyyeh's stylish Turino Hotel, instead. A relaxing atmosphere combines with affordable buffalo wings, pizzas, and gourmet burgers that will rival your favorites back home.

Anyone who is anyone mingles at the **Caffe Moka** in Abdoun. This brand new joint (opened in summer 1996) serves delectable strawberry tarts and frothing Italian cappuccino. Prices aren't rock bottom, but the people-watching elite aren't looking for a bargain.

The up-and-coming district of **Umm Uthaina,** by Sixth Circle, past Amra Hotel, offers a variety of appetizing, cheap foods. Grab some grilled *halloomi* (white cheese) wraps or stop in at **Al Baron** for tasty sandwiches. Purple neon signs and sidewalk cafés contribute to a festive atmosphere.

Westerners in Amman swear by the giant, air-conditioned **Safeway,** on the edge of Shmeisani (tel. 685 311). Any taxi driver will get you there in no time—everyone knows this place. This island of good old American abundance stocks all of your favorite brand name foods and offers dry cleaning, shoe repair, and a hardware store (open 24hr). The **Amman souq** is a huge vegetable market located by the Al Husseini Mosque (with your back to the mosque, turn left and look to your left for the huge stands overflowing with produce). Prices are listed in the *Jordan Times,* so read up and don't forget to bargain. Open Sun.-Thurs. 8:30am-sundown.

**Hashem Restaurant,** Prince Muhammad St., directly across from the Cliff Hotel. The Jordanian stop of choice for hummus since the 1950s, Hashem is a great place to see, hear, and feel Amman's pace. The hummus and *fuul* are served with an amazing pickled pepper concoction, the bread is freshly baked across the street, and everything is garnished with mint leaves and onions grown fresh in their garden. Tea, hummus, and an evening's conversation with a local will cost you well under 500fils. Open daily 24hr.

**Al Quds Restaurant,** King Hussein St. (tel. 630 168), around the corner from the post office and across from the Cliff Hotel. Though it looks like an American pancake house, Al Quds serves as a primary testing ground for Arabic cooking. Mounds of tempting, artistically-arranged sweets greet you upon entry. Its varied crowd includes families as well as the lonely budget traveler. Try their variation on *mensaf,* made with chicken instead of lamb (JD1.900). *Kabab* JD1.500, french fries 300fils, hummus 300fils. Open daily 7am-11pm.

**Unnamed food stand** on the left side of King Talal St., between Al Huseini Mosque and the Amphitheater, next to a used shoe stand. The greatest finds come in small packages. This tiny, no-name stand has delicious non-falafel vegetarian options, and you won't believe the prices: Spinach triangles (100fils), potato-stuffed bread (100fils), and mini-pizzas (250fils).

**Abu Saleh Restaurant,** King Faisal St. (tel. 622 782), a minute's walk downhill from the "SEIKO" sign, in the alley on the right. English translations opposite the Arabic dishes listed on the menu, but prices are conveniently left untranslated. ½-chicken and *kabab* go for JD1 each. Open daily 7:30am-10:30pm.

**Cairo Restaurant,** on a side street on the left two blocks away from the Al Husseini Mosque. With your back to the mosque, head left past the clothes booths, looking for the big red and white sign. You can eat your fill here inexpensively: roasted ½-chicken 900fils, *kabab* 800fils, *fasulya* (green beans cooked with lamb in tomato sauce) 500fils, breakfast *fuul* plates 250fils, and head of lamb (including eyes and tongue) JD1. Vegetarians beware—this place is a flesh orgy. Open daily 5am-10pm.

**Salaam Restaurant,** King Faisal St. (tel. 622 626), half a block away from the Al Husseini Mosque on the left-hand side of the street, next to the Bata shoe store. No English sign; look for spitted chickens in the window. The colorful crowd, tasty food, and A/C may lure you inside, but the pastries will make you stay. JD2.600 buys bread, bird, and fries. *Sfiehah* and *manaish* 200fils each. Menu is in Arabic but servers can describe the dishes in English. Open daily 7am-10pm.

**Abu Ahmad's New Orient Restaurant,** 10 Orient St. (tel. 641 879). Take the last right before 3rd Circle as you approach it from 2nd. The first left is Orient St. Visit Abu Ahmad's for a luxurious dining experience among vines, green checkered tablecloths, and a hyper-attentive and polite staff. Award-winning charcoal-grilled dishes JD2.300. An order of *mensaf* (JD2.300) is enough for two. Traveler's checks accepted. Open daily noon-midnight.

**Beefy Restaurant** (tel. 643 755), in the alley by Andalus Jewelry, downhill from Al Quds Restaurant. This American-style diner serves milkshakes (500fils), pizzas (JD1.650), and cheeseburgers topped with cucumbers and onions (520fils).

**Romero,** 3rd Circle, Jabal Amman (tel. 644 227).This romantic outdoor café with a sunny Mediterranean ambience serves the best Italian food in Amman. Try the *pizza pomodoro*. Entrees JD2-6. Open daily noon-midnight.

**Indian Restaurant,** 8th Circle (tel. 819 829). True to its name, this place serves great Indian food. There's no hummus or *mensaf* here: feast on vegetarian curry, basmati rice, and fresh-squeezed juice. The food is spicy and delicious. Entrees JD1.500-2.700. Open daily noon-4pm and 6:30pm-midnight. Visa, MC accepted.

**Al Saha al-Hashemieh,** directly in front of the Roman Amphitheater (tel. 612 330 or 331). Big red umbrellas, leafy terraces, and giant fans make this outdoor café a pleasant place to dine. A meal goes for JD4, complete with drink, salad, fries, and burger or *mensaf*. As an added bonus, there is an ice cream stand attached to the outside wall of this place, open until midnight, that serves up heavenly mango-apple swirl for 300fils. Open daily 8am-midnight.

**Pizza Italiano Alreef,** Al Madina Almunawra St., near University Hospital Bridge. With its polished wood interior and cool brick floors, this brand new authentic piz-zeria is a great place to escape your millionth falafel sandwich. The 10-min. taxi ride from downtown is a trek, but a family-size *pizza margherita* for a mere 800fils will reward your effort. Open Sun.-Fri. 11:30am-midnight.

# ■ Sights

The **Roman Amphitheater,** downtown on Jabal al-Qala'a, is the most renowned of Amman's historical sights. Built by Antonius Pius (138–161 CE), the amphitheater could accommodate 6000 spectators (open Wed.-Mon. 9am-5pm). It's free, but you'll be met by a line of eager "guides" who charge JD2 or your best price. Ignore them—you won't need help to find it.

Two museums are built into the foundations of the amphitheater on either side of the enclosed stage area. The **Folklore Museum** (tel. 651 742) displays histories of the diverse heritages of the Jordanian people, with Circassian military weaponry, Palestinian embroidery, and Bedouin encampments (open Wed.-Mon. 9am-5pm; admission JD1). The **Museum of Popular Traditions** (tel. 651 760) shows off attire and accessories from the country's past. The gallery to the right of the entrance displays 6th-century mosaics from Madaba and Jerash (open Wed.-Mon. 9am-5pm; admission JD1). Students can beg for free admission, which often works if there aren't many other visitors. Otherwise, JD1 is a bit much for either museum.

From the Roman Amphitheater, or any downtown locale, you can climb the steep steps and streets to the flat top of **Citadel Hill.** This is better done with a friend, especially for women traveling alone, in order to avoid harassment from locals who are a bit overzealous in their hospitality. On the southern slope of Jabal al-Qala'a, the citadel is the site of ancient Amman, called Rabbath-Ammon, or the "Great City of the Ammonites." The Ammonites make frequent guest appearances in the Bible. King David besieged Rabbath-Ammon twice, the second time improving his chances of marrying the already pregnant Bathsheba by putting her husband Uriah in the front line of battle. A few Byzantine and Umayyad ruins remain.

A trip to the top of Citadel Hill is a good idea for your first day in Amman. The view will give you the best perspective on the city's labyrinthine ups and downs. The **Archaeological Museum** (tel. 638 795), on Citadel Hill, contains a chronologically organized series of finds from ancient sites throughout Jordan. Displays range from 200,000-year-old dinner leftovers to Iron Age anthropomorphic sarcophagi, minimalist Nabatean portraits, and a Roman marble statuary (open Wed.-Mon. 9am-5pm; free). In front of the museum are the foundations of a 2nd-century CE Roman temple that housed a 10m statue of Hercules, to whom the temple was likely dedicated. Three of the statue's giant marble fingers hint at the shrine's former glory.

The best preserved and most intriguing of Amman's ruins lie behind the museum. Vaulted chambers tower 10m over a spacious courtyard where elaborate floral decorations can still be seen in the stonework. The 7th-century structure once supported a huge stone dome and was used as a mosque, audience hall, and residence. Below the Roman walls directly to the north, an open pit leads into the underground passageway that connected the fortified city to a hidden water supply. With a flashlight and fancy footwork you can enter the cavernous rock-hewn **cistern** by this route. The more conventional approach is from the gate on the street below.

The Citadel was the heart of ancient Amman; today the pulse emanates from downtown, in and around **Al Husseini Mosque.** The Ottoman-style structure was built in 1924 on the site of an ancient mosque, probably also the site of the Old Cathedral of Philadelphia. The nearby **Nymphaeum** was a sacred fountain and bathing ground for the ancient city.

The area around the Al Husseini Mosque is full of second-hand shoe shops. At the center of the triangle formed by the Citadel, the Mosque, and the post office is Amman's glittering **gold market,** featuring row upon row of gold jewelry. One or two shops vend antique Bedouin silver jewelry. Although bargaining is a way of life in much of Amman, prices in the gold market are fixed, as jewelry is priced strictly by weight (open Sat.-Thurs. 9am-9pm, Fri. 9am-1:30pm).

Barely out of a good muezzin's range from Al Husseini Mosque is Abdali's own **King Abdullah Mosque.** Constructed in seven years in memory of the late King, 3000 Muslims can kneel in prayer under its huge blue mosaic dome. Perched atop Jabal Ashrafiyyeh is the black-and-white checkered dome of the **Abu Darwish Mosque.** Built in the 1940s by Circassians, this is one of the most unusual religious structures in the Middle East. The mosque was constructed entirely from black basalt, brought from quarries in the northern part of the country, and white rock. The two colors were used not only for the structure of the building, but for its decoration and ornamentation as well.

The **Jordan Craft Center** (tel. 644 555), downhill from the Lebanese Embassy (Second Circle) and on the left, exhibits rugs, silver, glass, jewelry, embroidery, caftans, and pottery. (Open Sat.-Thurs. 9am-5pm; in winter Sun.-Thurs. 9am-1pm and 3-6pm. Free.) The **Jordan National Gallery,** on Jabal al-Weibdeh (tel. 630 128) at Muntazah Park, displays contemporary artwork from throughout the Islamic world. The range of art makes this place worth a visit. Modern Islamic pieces contain a surprising amount of criticism of daily life. The guy at the front desk may tell you to pay for a ticket, but donations are optional (open Wed.-Mon. 9am-5pm; free).

Amman's finest Byzantine artifact is the **Sweifiyyeh Mosaic,** found during construction at the western edge of the city in 1970. This 46 sq. m. mosaic floor illustrates the passing of the four seasons, and once belonged to a 6th-century church. Ask the caretaker to hose down the floor for a better look at the bizarre creatures, including leaf-bearded men, eagles with ears, and eely fish-men. Follow the signs from the first left west of Sixth Circle (open Sat.-Thurs. 9am-4pm, Fri. 9am-1:30pm; free). The **Martyr's Monument** and **Military Museum** (tel. 664 240) are in an odd square building overlooking the Hussein Sports City. The museum houses a chronological display of military memorabilia, dating from the Arab revolt in 1916 to the present (open Sun.-Fri. 9am-4pm; free). Both are closed to visitors when the Royal Family is entertaining, so call ahead.

# ■ Entertainment

Amman's nightlife thrives during summer. When the sweltering days give way to serene, cool evenings, nocturnal enthusiasts find fulfillment in bars or on dance floors. But Amman is not Cairo—even glamour boys and fly girls here bed down by 1 or 2am. Celebrating its fourth successful year, **Salute** remains the favorite amongst the younger members of Amman's privileged class, especially on Monday and Thursday nights, this city's "weekend nights." It is located between First and Second Circles (under the Villa d'Angelo Italian restaurant). If you can squeeze yourself onto their breezy patio, consider yourself a member of the "in" clique. (Unaccompanied men will not be admitted. No cover. Drinks around JD2-4.) Overflow from Salute and those who want to dance the night away in a more styling Euroclub atmosphere head to the **Roof Garden** in Sweifiyyeh. The view of the city is spectacular, but can only be enjoyed by those 21 and over with ID (cover JD3). **Coconut Grove,** near Abdoun Circle, caters to a chic Beverly Hills-type crowd, and features neon lights and sultry Algerian-beat rock, (no cover; drinks JD2-4.500). **Cavalier,** above the Olivier Restaurant down the street from Coconut Grove, is scheduled to reopen after renovations. Cavalier used to be a contender, and probably will continue to serve up some competition.

On the far side of Shmeisani (about twice as far as the Ambassador Hotel, on the same road) is the **Middle East Hotel,** which hosts the **Talk of the Town** disco on Monday and Thursday nights. The crowd is mostly made up of twenty-something Jordanians and foreigners; the tunes range from techno to reggae. **Scandel,** in the basement of the **San Rock Hotel** (Sixth Circle), has security people frisking club-goers at the door, mirrored walls, black upholstered booths, purple neon lights, and 40-year-old men trying to pick up airline stewardesses. Both are open until 3am, and people don't arrive until 10 or 11pm. A warning to younger readers: upholding Amman's newest custom, some bars and clubs (Salute is an exception) only admit those who are 21 years of age, or older.

**The Cellar,** in the basement of **Al Qasr Hotel** (Shmeisani, between the Ambassador and Nefertiti Hotels) is a mellower option. The American-style jazz bar features live music, mixed drinks (for around JD3), potato skins, and karaoke on Monday nights for a JD5 cover. Expats and beer drinkers cluster at the **Irish Pub** (downstairs in the **Dove Hotel,** between Fourth and Fifth circles). All the Guinness you can drink is here, but no singles are admitted (men or women). The **Caesar's Palace Restaurant** on Jabal al-Weibdeh offers more traditional Jordanian music and dancing, including belly dancing on Thurs. nights.

At first glance, the city center seems to lack the traditional Middle Eastern constellation of cafés and tea houses. Look up: they're mostly perched on second floors. The **Hilton Café** (across from the Cliff Hotel) overlooks the royal intersection of King Hussein and King Faisal St. (above the Seiko watch sign). There's a crowded and noisy *al fresco* hangout on the second floor, where you can learn local card games over a cup of Amman's sludgiest Arabic coffee (100fils and up) and entertain your recently acquired best friends by choking on the dense charcoal and tobacco smoke of an *argileh* (300fils). Jordanian society reserves such entertainments for members of the male gender; women probably will feel more comfortable elsewhere. **Babiche Café, Geneva,** and the new **Caffe Moka** in Shmeisani serve coffee, drinks, and pastries to a chi-chi crowd (including women, many of whom speak a strange offshoot of Esperanto made up of English, Arabic, and French). **Reem al-Bawady** (Tla' al-Ali, Al Ubeel circle) offers fruit-flavored tobacco for smoking *argileh* in traditional Bedouin camel-hair tents. Women, with male friends, are welcome.

During the late afternoon and early evening, Amman's central **souq** (market) becomes the city's most happening spot, swallowing several blocks southwest of Al Husseini Mosque. Most people rest between 2 and 4pm (*service* and buses become scarce), but cafés allow homeless budget travelers to linger over coffee in the shade. Try **Ma'atouk's,** outside the *souq,* on Third Circle (coffee 300fils).

There are three **cinemas** that show English-language films: the **Philadelphia,** Third Circle (tel. 634 149), **Concord,** Shmeisani, opposite the Forte Grande Hotel (tel. 677 420), and **Plaza,** at the Forte Grande in Shmeisani (tel. 699 238). The **Nabil & Hisham's Theater,** Rainbow St., First Circle (tel. 625 155) sometimes produces English-language plays. Call for more information.

The first **Euro-Arab Jazz Caravan** kicked off in the first three weeks of June 1996 and hopefully will become an annual tradition. Artists from Europe and the Arab world perform nightly at 9:30pm at the Roman Amphitheater for a JD2 entrance fee.

# NEAR AMMAN

## ■ Wadi Seer وادى السير

Burgeoning Amman has poked its urban tentacles westward into the quiet valley of Wadi Seer. Like much of the fertile hill country to the north and west of Amman, Wadi Seer was first settled by Circassians. These fair-skinned Muslims came from Russia during the Czarist persecutions of the 1870s and account for most blonde and red-headed Jordanians. Amman's Folklore Museum displays the traditional Circassian costume—a cylindrical fur cap and black waistcoat with red trim.

At Wadi Seer, the high desert plateau suddenly gives way to the Jordan Valley. Here, a little stream snakes through the countryside on its way to the Dead Sea. The narrow asphalt road that follows this valley out of town seems designed for daytripping motorists and tramping backpackers, but be prepared for scorching summer days. Verdant tobacco plants and olive trees, along with a bevy of children, line the 12km road which runs southwest to the remains of Qasr al-Abd.

Soon after leaving Wadi Seer you'll pass **Al Bassa Springs,** the source of the valley's fertility and a swimming pool for many of the area's children. Above the left bank of the *wadi,* **Ad-Deir** (the monastery) is carved into the face of the cliff. This extraordinary building merits the 20-minute climb, even if you don't find any of the Roman gold which villagers claim is buried under the floor. Each of the ossuary's thousands of triangular wall-niches once cradled a skull, the remnants of monks.

Local legend holds that **Qasr al-Abd** (Castle of the Slave), better known as **Qasr Iraq al-Emir** (Castle of the Prince) was built by a love-smitten slave named Tobiah. While his master was away on a journey, Tobiah built a palace and carved lions, panthers, and eagles into its walls in order to win the hand of the master's daughter. Unfortunately, the master returned before Tobiah could finish the work, and the slave's efforts went unrequited. This story is given credence by the Aramaic inscription "Tobiah" carved near the entrance of one of the eleven caves, 500 meters back up the valley road. These caves, **Iraq al-Emir,** are believed to have been dug by hand, and used to house horses.

Kill-joy historians explain the inscription and the castle remains with references to Tobiah the Ammonite Servant. This Tobiah was a rich priest in Jerusalem, and the name of the castle refers to his occupation as a servant of God. Ancient historian Josephus also records the wealth of a Tobiah family and the exploits of the young son Hyrcanus, who built a strong fortress constructed entirely of white marble and enclosed by a wide, deep moat.

The restoration of the ruins was completed in 1987. A French archaeologist spent three years assembling a cardboard model, then another seven years piecing together the actual castle. Several red stone lions remain intact, though there is no roof. The most impressive is the lioness on the northwest corner, but both lions have a unique twist: the male (with the flowing mane) is breast-feeding a baby with its female nipples—and the female lioness, prowling the corner alone, has male genitals. The guard or his son should let you in for free—a small donation of 100fils, however, is appreciated.

Much of the joy in visiting Iraq al-Emir is in the spectacular hilltop views and the dirt pathways lined with pomegranate and fig trees. The cool breezes and peaceful songs of goatherders set the scene for a memorable picnic lunch.

The easiest way to get to Wadi Seer begins at Al Husseini Mosque. As you face out of the mosque, turn left and walk past clucking chickens, spilled ice cream, and screeching taxis until you arrive at a fork in the road. This walk will take about 10 minutes. Head left at the fork and look for lines of minibuses; they'll drop you off at Wadi Seer for 100fils. From Wadi Seer, catch a minibus headed down the valley road (130fils). The whole trip can take between 45min. and 1½hr., depending on the wait between buses and the number of times they stop for stray chickens in the road. These buses leave when they are full, so bring water and plenty of patience—you may have a bit of a wait for the return trip.

# ■ Azraq and the Desert Castles

الازرق و القصور الصحراوية

Adjacent to sultry desert lava fields, Azraq's dusty green foliage comes as a welcome respite. The springs at Azraq are the only permanent bodies of water in an expanse of over 2500 sq. km of barren sand-and-scorpion desert. Unfortunately, because the water is being pumped to parched Amman throats, the area has dried up significantly. As recently as last year, the palm trees were green, the animals abundant, and the hundreds of species of exotic birds that rest at Azraq colored the sky. Sadly, what was once green is now a crunchy brown, and the only movement is of trucks and their drivers passing through.

The discovery of an enormous cache of flint hand-axes indicates that either Paleolithic settlers or extremely sophisticated camels hunted in the area 500,000 years ago. The most remarkable records of human habitation are the scattered Umayyad castles, a group of structures that originally formed a chain from the north of Damascus to Khirbet al-Mafjar, near Jericho. Built in the 7th and 8th centuries CE by the Umayyads, the castles were mysteriously abandoned a century later. The imposing stonework of **Qasr Kharaneh** and strategic location of **Qasr Azraq** and **Qasr Mushatta** support speculation that the castles sheltered caravans along the trade route between Syria, Arabia, and the Far East. The baths near **Qasr al-Hallabat** and the magnificent frescoes at **Qasr Amra** brought creature comforts to the desert.

## ORIENTATION AND PRACTICAL INFORMATION

A trip to Azraq oasis and the Desert Castles is fraught with uncertainty and annoyingly difficult to arrange, but the triumphant traveler will not regret it. Still relatively tourist-free, these quietly majestic ruins will awe you with the strength of their standing arches and the warmth of their Bedouin gatekeepers. There are only three easy options for transportation to the castles. First, you can hire a taxi from Amman for the official rate of JD24 (you may be able to bargain this down to under JD20). This will provide half a day's wheels and someone who knows the route. For a full day, the price will shoot to over JD30. Second, you can rent a car in Amman for JD20-30 or more for a day, with unlimited mileage and the option to return it in Aqaba or at the airport. **Reliable Rent a Car** (tel. 819 676) offers the best deals. Finally, **JETT buses** do full day tours of the desert castles; arrange this through a travel agent, who will set you up with a group.

As always, hitchhiking is discouraged and is potentially suicidal in this region. Before undertaking this risky fool's errand, you'll need an immense supply of food and water and an appetite for adventure. There are only a few hitchers and cars on the Damascus highway from Amman to Zarqa (30km). Alternatively, *service* from Abdali Station in Amman can take you to Zarqa quickly and cheaply (300fils). Be careful about accepting rides from military vehicles, since most will take you only as far as some lonely desert depot. The highway passes right by Qasr al-Hallabat (30km from Zarqa) before reaching Azraq (87km from Zarqa). From Azraq junction, you'll have to hitch 13km north to reach Qasr Azraq and then return to Azraq. If you take the southern highway back to Amman, you will pass near Qasr Amra (25km from Azraq), then Qasr Kharaneh (40km from Azraq), and Qasr Mushatta (about 90km from Azraq and 40km from Amman).

The following description of the castles and Azraq details a road trip that takes the northern route from Amman to Azraq and the southern highway on the return trip (a **clockwise tour**). Going the other way is deadly for hitchhikers, as cars come as frequently as snowstorms. If you have a car, you could go as easily in either direction. Drivers beware: the road from Amman to Zarqa passes through Jordan's most notorious speed trap, where gimlet-eyed cops dispense fines at a honking JD50, even if you're only going 1km over. Make sure you wear your seat belt; unprotected driving fines are hefty, too. The desert **telephone code** is 06.

## QASR AL-HALLABAT قصر الحلابات

Qasr al-Hallabat's ruined arches appear approximately 30km east into the desert from Zarqa. Angle off at the right, turn onto the paved road, and turn left up the track to the gate. The gatekeeper's tent is to the left of the crumbling castle; you're free to roam around whatever is left. Keep in mind that any gatekeeper who provides you with information will expect a few hundred fils in return. Originally built by Caracall (198-217 CE) as a Roman fort, it was re-used by the Byzantines as a monastery during the reign of Anastasius (491-518), and then rebuilt and used by Umayyads in the 8th century. The Umayyad conquerors added a mosque just meters away from the 2nd-century main defense structure. Look for the Byzantine carvings on what is left of the walls and fallen slabs of stone.

Back on the main highway, the sand and limestone desert to the south contrasts sharply with the gray volcanic desert to the north. Just off the road to the south is **Hammam Sarah,** the ruined bathhouse modeled after Amra (below). A 1000-year-old well lurks next to a shallow pool. *Let's Go* recommends admiring the well from above ground—be careful not to fall into the unmarked hole.

## AZRAQ الازرق

On the long and grinding road east of Hallabat, you'll hear nothing but the entreaties of your overheating engine. After years of drab desert, you'll suddenly come upon the formerly lush gardens of **Azraq Oasis,** Jordan's only permanent body of fresh water, which is quickly drying up. Relax and reassemble your bearings (both mental and mechanical) at Azraq Junction, where the highway to the northeast goes to Iraq and the southeastern road leads to the southern castles and on into Saudi Arabia.

About 13km north of Azraq Junction, on the highway to Iraq, squats **Qasr Azraq.** Most of the castle is in excellent condition thanks to extensive restoration. The kind Druze gatekeeper will muscle open the three-ton portal of the castle and show you his Lawrence of Arabia photograph collection (many of the photographs look suspiciously like the gatekeeper himself). The most interesting attractions lie within a few meters of the entrance. Looking up from the main door, you'll see the holes through which boiling oil and molten lead were poured on invaders' bald spots. Carved into the pavement behind the main gate is a Roman board game.

Just above the entrance is the room used by Lawrence himself during his short stay on the premises—it's no longer the fetid dungeon where he sought to punish himself for the failure of one of his missions. The castle, built by the Romans as a fort in 300 CE and later rebuilt by the Ayyubids in 1237, rose to three levels. Only parts of the second level survived the 1926 earthquake, including a ceiling that exposes a web of huge basalt beams.

Located on the north side of Azraq, down a tree-lined road, is the **Azraq Resthouse** (tel. 647 610, ext. 6). Rooms include bath, air-conditioning, color TV, minibar, and a view of the pool, which non-guests can use for JD2. (singles JD14, doubles JD19). The overpriced restaurant serves usual fare (complete meal JD5). There are many small markets and stands in town that provide cheaper nourishment for the weary wanderer. You'll also find a **post office** (open Sat.-Thurs. 7:30am-7pm, Fri. 7:30am-1pm) and a **Housing Bank** (open for exchange Sat.-Wed. 8:30am-1pm and 4-5pm, Thurs. 8:30am-1pm).

Throughout the trip, keep an eye out for desert wildlife, now making a comeback since Jordan started protecting the fragile habitat. In the **Shaumari Wildlife Preserve,** near Qasr Amra, the government is reintroducing armadillos, Himalayan dwarf hamsters (spelled to actual scale), ostriches, and Arabian oryxes. Cheetah and desert wolves roam in regions to the northeast and southwest of Azraq (park admission 500fils, students 300fils).

## QASR AMRA قصر عمرة

Despite the ill-fitting glass windows, the hunting lodge and bath complex of Qasr Amra impress visitors with the elegant simplicity of their designs. The interior is also the best preserved of the desert palaces; its vaulted ceilings are splashed with colorful frescos, and mosaics grace some of the floors. As you walk in, on the right, is a mural depicting the enemies of Islam, among them the emperors of Byzantium and of China. An early portrayal of the zodiac covers the domed ceiling of the *caldarium* (hot room). Since they ignore the Muslim tradition forbidding the pictorial representation of human beings, the frescoes are all the more riveting. Especially surprising are the many portrayals of nude women, which somehow escaped the decree of Umayyad Caliph Yazid II (720-724 CE) ordering all human images and likenesses destroyed. Some will even tell you he came here on the weekends to relax. You can reach Qasr Amra on the road heading southwest of Azraq Junction, about 28km from Qasr Azraq. The gatekeeper expects a small tip.

## QASR KHARANEH قصر الخرانة

One of the best preserved of the desert castles, Qasr Kharaneh is named for the small black stones that blanket the area. Some experts believe Kharaneh was a defensive fort, pointing to the four corner towers and the solid, square plan of a Roman fortress. Others note the lack of arrow slits and argue that it served as a retreat for Umayyad leaders to discuss matters of state. Most historians believe it was a *khan,* or inn—the first of the Islamic world. A painted dedication in a second-story room dates the building's construction to 711 CE. Greek inscriptions on the doorjambs imply that the Umayyads built upon an earlier structure. For a good view of the courtyard, climb the staircase on your left as you enter. You'll also see the neighboring military base and the maneuverings of Jordanian troops. When you've finished exploring, the gatekeeper will let you ride his camel for 500fils. As he leads you around the castle astride this gigantic animal, listen carefully; he insists that ghosts of horses, camels, and even people roam the ruins and get rowdy at night.

## QASR MUSHATTA قصر مشتا

To reach this final castle, take any turn-off to Queen Alia International Airport. Hitch-hikers often hire *service* from the village of **Muwaqaar** in the north to reach the castle. The castle is on the left as you approach the airport from the north, but the public access road turns off to the right and loops about 4km around the airport. If you're walking from the airport, don't take this marked turn-off. Instead, continue to the left of the airport, past the Alia cargo terminal, until Mushatta appears on the left (a ½-hr. walk). Soldiers and guards at checkpoints will ask to see your **passport.** The entrance to the 8th-century castle once beckoned travelers with wonderfully carved floral designs. Most of the carved stones, however, were delivered to Kaiser Wilhelm II as a gift from Ottoman Sultan Abdulhamid II, and only fragments remain. An entire piece of wall now resides in the Berlin Museum. Although the size of the ruins attest to the ambition of the construction, the castle, for unknown reasons, was never completed. Mushatta was constructed with smaller, weaker bricks than other castles. It's a testament to the architect's skill that his work still stands. From Qasr Mushatta and the airport, you can catch a taxi or bus to Amman. Hitchers reportedly find it an easy trip back into town.

# South of Amman

Three roads link Amman and Aqaba: the Wadi Araba (Jordan Valley) Highway, the Desert Highway, and the Kings' Highway. The **Wadi Araba Highway** hugs the Dead Sea Coast. Enormous trucks rumble impassively along the **Desert Highway,** the artery that ties the cities of the north to the port at Aqaba. Since the Iran-Iraq War, the Desert Highway has been the chief link between Europe and Turkey and the Persian (Arabian) Gulf. Major construction has made the highway smooth and swift, but even the King can do little about the scenery—three and a half hours of unchanging desert to Petra, an hour and a half more to Aqaba. Only the antics of bored drivers playfully bumping the narrow shoulders or squeezing between oncoming cars break the monotony. Gas and phones along the way are scarce.

Unless you are rushing from Amman to Aqaba or want to spend every one of your days in Jordan at Petra, the **Kings' Highway** (Wadi Mujib Road) is the ideal way to travel the length of Jordan. This ancient route journeys through spectacular canyons, passing Biblical sites, Crusader castles, and Byzantine churches and mosaics along the way. Known by the same name in Biblical times, this road was supposedly traveled by the Israelites during their exodus from Egypt. Caravans filled with cinnamon and myrrh crept from Arabia to Palestine and Syria on their way to Europe.

**Service** run most of the way from Amman to Petra, as do minibuses, but generally in the mornings only. Karak is a convenient overnight stop. **Hitchhiking** south of Amman is possible, but involves the risks inherent in hitching anywhere. Hitchers report that the Desert Highway is the easiest route. Hitching along the more deserted Kings' Highway is said to be difficult. It is illegal to hitchhike on the Wadi Araba Highway, which runs alongside the Israeli border. Since roadside bystanders often wave at passing cars in salutation, hitchers generally point at the curb beside their feet or stick their right arm out into the traffic—the gestures used to hail buses.

To get to the Desert Highway from downtown Amman, hitchikers head south on Jerusalem St. (in Jabal Nadhif across Wadi Abdoun), which metamorphoses into Rte. 15 (the Desert Highway). To get to the Kings' Highway, hitchers take a *service* from Amman's Wahdat Station to Madaba (330fils) and then try their luck on the road to Karak, which passes out of Madaba by the Apostles' Church. Small groups of hitchers stand by the mini-obelisk marking the intersection of the Kings' Highway and the Desert Highway, 18km south of Amman. People reach the intersection by taking a Madaba-bound *service* from Wahdat Station or by hitching south from Seventh Circle.

The distances are manageable: 33km from Amman to Madaba, 98km from Madaba to Karak, and 150km from Karak to Petra. The total distance from Amman to Petra is 282km along the Kings' Highway or 262km along the Desert Highway. Many people camp in the *wadis* north of Karak or in the desert regions between Karak and Petra. A rest house and a couple of hotels in Karak, in addition to one bed and breakfast in Madaba, provide the only indoor accommodations. The easiest route is to see Madaba, before heading to Karak for the night. Leaving early in the morning from Karak, the trip to Petra can be done comfortably in a day, stopping in Shobak and at the Dana nature reserve along the way.

# ■ The Dead Sea البحر الميت

The greatest obstacle in reaching the Dead Sea is getting to the highway that runs along its edge. Once there, hop on one of the many buses or *service* shuttling up and down the road. Buses from the Ras al-Ayn area in Amman go to the Dead Sea Rest House/Suweimeh (1-2hr., 600fils). To reach this area begin at Al Husseini Mosque. Exit the mosque, make a left, and walk for about ten minutes. When the road forks, go left and cross the busy intersection. Take a right on the big street and stay to the left. The buses are 20 minutes up the road. Don a panama, bring plenty of water, and don't forget your passport—you'll need it at several military roadblocks along the way. There are buses leaving every 30 minutes. Some go to Shouna, where you can catch a second bus to the Rest House.

After a minibus descent through rolling hills that will rival your 747's approach to Queen Alia airport, prepare to come as close to walking on water as is humanly possible. The Dead Sea's northeastern shore, 60 to 90 minutes from Amman or Deir Alla, hosts the only stretch of sand open to visitors on the Jordanian side. During the middle of the day, the sun reflects off the sea's still surface, creating the illusion that the entire body of water is about to spill into the Jordan Valley. The peculiar buoyancy of this briny water forces even the densest swimmer into a back float. The salt water causes a tiny paper cut to feel like an amputation without anaesthetic and it tastes awful. Don't get any in your eyes, or you'll have to beg to use one of the eye-flushing plastic water bottles that those in the know tote along to the beach. See **Israel: Dead Sea**, p. 411 for geographical information.

The **Dead Sea Rest House** (tel. (05) 572 901) offers showers to relieve you of Lot's wife's encrusted fate. Unless you swim around the barrier on the north, which closes off the nicest section of beach, you'll have to pay JD1 to enter the resort enclave. The complex contains showers, the air-conditioned Rest House, and an overpriced restaurant (buffet lunch JD7.200 per person, soft drinks a pocket-lightening 660fils). Those with calloused feet won't mind the walk into the water, but others may want to wear some form of foot protection. The beach also has shelters for those who prefer shade to the merciless sun. The last bus leaves at 6pm. If you miss it, the rest house will charge you JD33 for a new bungalow with A/C, bathroom, TV, and telephone. If you do get stranded, the sunset over the West Bank will almost make it worth it. (Rest House open daily 8am-10:30pm; swimming allowed until sundown.) About 5km past the Rest House, a natural swimming pool is nestled between the colorful cliffs.

Within 30km south on the highway to Aqaba (Rte. 35) is **Zarqa Ma'in**, a cascading hot spring. (See **Near Madaba**, p.492.) A road connecting the Dead Sea Rest House and Zarqa Ma'in is rumored to be in the works.

# ■ Madaba مادبا

Madaba is located on a plateau of orange groves overlooking the Jordan Valley. The scanty Roman columns next to the government Rest House hardly evoke visions of the flourishing trade center that was once the size of Jerash, but American archaeologists at work in the newly formed "Archaeological Park" in downtown Madaba are quickly revealing past glories. A Roman road, burnt palace, and several churches have been discovered only meters away from the Church of St. George, home of the famous mosaic map of the Holy Land. The several elaborate mosaics scattered throughout the town are a testament to Madaba's importance as a Byzantine ecclesiastical center; the town received its own bishop as early as the 5th century CE. Persians attacked Madaba in 614 CE, slaughtering the residents and damaging many Roman and Byzantine artifacts. Most of what still stood was leveled by an earthquake in the 8th century, leaving Madaba untouched for nearly 1100 years until Christian clans from Karak reinhabited the city in the late 1800s.

## PRACTICAL INFORMATION AND ACCOMMODATIONS

**Service** (350fils) and **buses** (220fils) shuttle between Madaba and Amman's Wahdat and Raghadan Stations regularly until 7pm in summer and 5pm in winter. To reach the city center from Madaba's bus station, take a *service* (70fils) or hike up the hill toward the ever-visible Church of St. George (20min.). The **tourist office** (tel. 545 527), around the corner from St. George's in a newly restored building, has colorful but unhelpful brochures (open Sat.-Thurs. 8am-2pm). The **Bank of Jordan** and **Housing Bank** (both open Sat.-Thurs. 8am-1pm and 4-5:30pm) are on King Abdallah St. around the corner from the tourist office. In a **medical emergency,** dial 193; dial 192 to reach the **police**. The nearest hospital, 1km from Madaba, is **Nadim Hospital** (tel. 541 700). The central **post office** (open Sat.-Thurs. 8am-7pm, Fri. 8am-1:30pm) is located on King Abdallah St., around the corner from the tourist office. Madaba's **telephone code** is 08.

The only hotel in the area is **Lulu's Pension** (tel. 543 678), a gorgeous home-turned bed and breakfast. Lulu's features full clean bathrooms and a cute kitchen with tablecloths, doilies, and fake flowers. The pre-bargaining price for a royal room with a king-sized bed is JD15 (JD10 for students). Ring the bell if the door is locked.

Join blonde, short-shorts-clad Germans at the **Rest House** (tel. 544 069), next to the tourist office. They cater mainly to groups, but individuals are welcome to join the party; their buffet lunch is for anyone who can pay the JD6 bill. A hummus and coke snack costs JD1.500, but prices are negotiable in the off-season. (Open daily 7:30am-approx. 10pm. Buffet lunch daily noon-4pm.)

## SIGHTS

Built in 1896 atop the foundation of a Byzantine church, the prominent, yellow-brick Greek Orthodox **Church of St. George** stands in the center of town, right off the square. Inside, parts of the 6th-century CE **Map of Palestine,** originally composed of 2.3 million tiles, remain intact. The map includes the Palestinian cities of Byzantium, most notably Nablus, Hebron, and Jericho. At one time the map depicted the entire Middle East, as shown by the few remaining tiles of Turkey, Lebanon, and Egypt. A map of Jerusalem, with representations of the buildings existing in the 6th century CE, including the Church of the Holy Sepulchre, is the most renowned section. Ask one of the postcard-selling faithful to point out some landmarks. The church is also known by some devout local Christians and Muslims for hosting the Virgin Mary in 1978. She made an appearance to heal the sick and give hope, according to faithful townsfolk. A small shrine in the crypt pictures Mary with a third arm and blue "healing hand" supernaturally imprinted on the icon during the Madonna's visit. Scientists have determined that there is no way the hand could have been painted on, except by divine magic. (Open Mon.-Thurs. and Sat. 8:30am-6pm, Fri. and Sun. 10:30am-6pm. Free, but a JD1 donation is requested.)

Madaba's modest **museum,** tucked in an alley down the hill from the Apostles' Church, features an extensive collection of mosaics, including a well-preserved depiction of the Garden of Eden, traditional dresses representative of the different regions in Jordan, and jewelry and pottery dating back to various ages. The museum was actually made from several adjoining houses, some of which had mosaic floors.

JORDAN

The complex is divided into three sections—the Old House of Madaba, a Folklore Museum, and an Archaeological Museum (open Wed.-Mon. 9am-5pm, holidays 10am-4pm; admission JD1).

Excavations and growing tourism have spawned new projects in Madaba. In the next few years, a school training technicians to restore mosaics and a recently uncovered **Roman street** will open. The **Apostles Church**, housing the town's largest intact mosaic, may open soon as well.

## ■ From Madaba to Karak: Mt. Nebo and environs

The Kings' Highway from Madaba to Karak chugs over plateaus and *wadis,* and the hills of the West Bank are visible across the Dead Sea. No wonder Moses' last request to God was for a view from **Mount Nebo.** The Bible says "no man knows the place of his [Moses'] burial to this day" (Deuteronomy 34:6), but Moses' grave is rumored to be in a secret cave somewhere along **Ain Musa.** On the **Siyagha Peak** of Nebo, the Christians of Madaba built a three-nave **Memorial Church,** next to which looms an imposing serpentine cross. Archaeological work has revealed a complete mosaic floor in the church dating from 531 CE, as well as foundations of monasteries from the 3rd century CE. In the 7th century, the chapel of the Theotokos, or Mary, mother of God, was added, with lavish decorations adorning the walls. The buildings (admission JD1 or your best price, depending on tourist traffic) close at 7pm. No buses go to Mt. Nebo; **taxis** are JD4 round-trip (including a 30min. stay at the site), or take a *service* from Madaba to Feisaliyyeh (100fils), and then bargain with the driver once the other passengers get off. For JD2.500, he should take you the extra 3km up, wait 30min., and bring you back to any point in Madaba. Without a pre-arranged ride, the only way off Mt. Nebo is to walk back to Feisaliyyeh.

Just beyond Feisaliyyeh, a marked turn-off leads to **Khirbet al-Mukheiyat,** the ancient village of Nebo on the southern base of the mountain. A one-hour hike (round-trip) will allow you to see the secular scenes of fishing, hunting, and wine-making that decorate another finely preserved Byzantine church floor. Cigarettes are the preferred *bakhsheesh* for the Bedouin gatekeeper who lives next on the hill at the end of the paved road (open till dusk, or whenever the gatekeeper leaves).

Herod the Great, Governor of Judea in 40 BCE, frequented the hot mineral springs at **Zarqa Ma'in** to relieve his rheumatism. As he lay dying, he was carried here from his breathtaking hilltop fortress at nearby **Mukawer**—where Salome later danced and John the Baptist lost his head (Matthew 14:1-12). Both men and women can swim in **Hammam az-Zarqa,** a hot indoor pool sunk in a cliff face, or bathe under the voluptuous torrents of hot waterfalls. Reach Zarqa Ma'in by **bus** from Madaba (100fils). The JETT Bus Company in Amman occasionally offers daytrips to the springs for JD8 with lunch (depart 8am, return 6pm; see **Getting Around,** p.462).

Further south lies the Biblical **Dhiban,** where Mesha, King of Moab, erected a stele celebrating his country's independence recently won from Omri, King of Israel, around the year 850 BCE. The basalt block now resides in the Louvre, but copies may be seen in both the Karak and Madaba Museums. An ancient **Roman mile marker** is on the road approaching the modern town of Dhiban. Shortly after town, the road descends into the vast **Wadi Mujib,** 4km wide and 1km deep. Cut from the rock by water and time, this is Jordan's version of the Grand Canyon. Although getting from Madaba to Karak along the Kings' Highway can be difficult, the breathtaking sights are worth the effort. Few buses run from Madaba to Karak along the highway. Some travelers say the easiest way to go is to hitch. Alternatively, you can catch a bus from Madaba to **Al Qasr,** which runs several times per day. After stepping off the bus in Al Qasr, you can see a very ruined Nabatean temple (c. 350 CE) before getting on a bus to Karak (200fils).

# ■ Karak الكرك

The ancient capital of Moab, Karak now humbles itself in the shadow of **Karak Castle,** the largest of the mountaintop Crusader castles which stretch from Turkey to the Sinai. The prosperous modern town of Karak extends away from the castle on its northern and eastern slopes and serves as an ideal resting place for travelers on the Kings' Highway.

## PRACTICAL INFORMATION

Karak's **tourist office** is on a side street, the first right turn downhill from the castle (sometimes open Sat.-Thurs. 8am-2pm). The **police station** is located down the street and on the right, next to the huge radio tower. For **medical emergencies,** dial 193. Karak's **Italian Hospital** (tel. 351 045 or 145), is downhill from the turn-off up to the castle, or in the direction of the elbow if you orient yourself via the manic horseman in the center circle of town. The **Housing Bank,** uphill from the Italian Hospital, will change traveler's checks and cash, but since they wait for the news from Amman about the day's rates, they may not open for exchange until as late as 10am (open Sat.-Thurs. 8am-12:30pm). The **post office** (open Sat.-Thurs. 7:30am-7pm, Fri. 8am-noon) is across the street from the Castle Hotel. The **telephone code** for Karak is 03.

Travel to Karak from Amman's Wahdat Station by **minibus** (1½hr., 750fils) or **service taxi** (JD1.500) along the desert highway. To reach Petra from Karak, take a minibus from the city center to Tafilah (30min., 500fils), and from Tafilah to Shobak (30min., 250fils). At times, no buses run to Shobak. Those who hitch say it's easy. Minibuses sometimes run from Shobak to Petra (Wadi Musa). A direct bus from Karak to Petra leaves at 9am, depending on the volume of tourist traffic. No *service* travel these routes, but a **private taxi** will take you directly from Karak to Petra for a vacation-ending JD40. **Buses** also run from Karak to Petra through Ma'an (JD1), although they may take longer than if you try your luck going through Shobak.

## ACCOMMODATIONS AND FOOD

The best room for your dinar is at the **Castle Hotel** (tel. 352 489; singles JD3.300, doubles JD8). The Castle offers smaller, more affordable rooms than the **Towers Hotel** (tel. 354 293) across the street which is owned by the same people and is cozy, spacious, spotless, and slightly more upscale. (Singles JD8. Doubles JD15. Private baths and shared baths available for correspondingly higher or lower prices.) The manager is more helpful than the tourist office and will make your stay worth more than you pay. Prices are negotiable during the off season. A couple of tiny hotels near the center of town offer less comfortable rooms for less.

For a tasty sit-down meal without inflated prices, try the **Tourist Peace Restaurant** (tel. 352 518), across the street, from the police station and the radio tower. *Mensaf* costs JD1.500 and the bidding for a tasty grill with salads and coffee or tea starts at JD2.500 (open daily 7am-10pm). Pocket change will get you falafel and fruit—stalls line the street to the left of the Tourist Peace Restaurant. True budgeteers picnic atop the sublime ruins. A lunch or dinner at the government **Rest House,** near the entrance to the castle, affords you a view of the Jordan Valley's descent to the Dead Sea, if you can afford the food (open until 10pm).

## SIGHTS

Steep mountain slopes turn into steeper jagged walls, making even a guided tour of the windblown remains of **Karak Castle** a challenge for the weak-stomached. In 1132, Baldwin I of Jerusalem built the castle midway between his capital and Shobak. Although the fortress wall has mostly collapsed, its building blocks remain large enough to inspire starry-eyed wonder. Inside, vaulted stone ceilings span only a few meters, resulting in a network of long, narrow halls and barracks. You can still see the bolt holes for mammoth stone doors that have since turned to dust. The castle is full of secret passageways and hidden rooms—bring a flashlight for easier exploration and allow at least two hours. To the west across the moat are battlements from which the charming Renauld de Chatillon cast prisoners 40m to their deaths (with wooden boxes fastened around their heads so that they would not lose consciousness too quickly). When Salah ad-Din took the castle after the 1187 Battle of Hittin, he personally saw to it that Chatillon's sick head was removed. Below, a 50m tunnel leads out of town through an arched gateway (castle open daily 9am-6pm). To the right of the castle entrance, a stone staircase descends to the **Archaeological Museum** with Nabatean, Roman, and Mamluk artifacts (open Wed.-Mon. 9am-5pm; admission to castle and museum JD1).

## ■ Near Karak

Highway 49/80 (for added confusion, maps may say 50) west from Karak drops 20m from the Kings' Highway to the Dead Sea "port" of **Mazra'a** and the Al Lisan (tongue) Peninsula. Five km before reaching Mazra'a and the Wadi Araba Highway to Aqaba, Highway 49/80 passes **Baab adh-Dhira.** The cemeteries here contain some 20,000 shaft tombs enshrining 500,000 bodies (an unfortunate 25-to-1 body-to-tomb ratio) and over three million pottery vessels. The length of the bones indicates that the average height in Baab adh-Dhira was a sturdy 2m.

Hitchers report that there is very little traffic between Mazra'a and Karak. Stop in at the **Mazra'a Police Post,** 5km north of the junction, if you need assistance. Heading out of Mazra'a the Wadi Araba highway runs alongside Israel and is sometimes closed to civilian travel; hitchhiking here is always prohibited.

Traveling east of Karak on Highway 49/80 toward Qatrana, you'll pass the turn-off for **Al Lejjun,** an excavated Roman frontier post. Streets, a tower, a church, and a *principium,* dating from 30 CE and destroyed by an earthquake in 551, have all been unearthed. Take a **service** (450fils) or **bus** (310fils) toward Qatrana and ask the driver to let you off at the "Lejjun" turn-off (the sign is in Arabic only). The site has been abandoned by the archaeological crew for now, and is inhabited by friendly Bedouin who may invite you to tea. If you have a free afternoon in Karak, the ruins make a pleasantly quiet and adventurous excursion into the un-touristed farmland surround the castle town.

In the towns surrounding Karak, tourist services are non-existent. If you're lost or need a ride or a place to stay, approach a friendly-looking store owner or businessperson and ask for help. They will usually offer a solution, and it's a good idea to offer a tip (500fils or JD1) in return. Although it may be refused, they will appreciate your gesture. Solo women should refuse hospitality from single men. The mosques at Mu'tah and at the nearby village of Mazar commemorate the Islamic generals who died in the first great battles between the forces of Islam and Byzantium in 632 CE. The green-domed mosque in Mazar houses a small **Islamic museum** on the first floor, open at the discretion of its keeper—usually 9am-4pm.

## SHOBAK شوبك

As he got older, he got better. Baldwin's first castle at Shobak pales in comparison to his later creation at Karak. **Shobak Castle,** 4km from the marked turn-off at the northern edge of Shobak town, could have used more men: the castle fell to Salah ad-Din in 1189, just 74 years after it was built. In 1260, the Mamluks gained possession of the castle, restored it, and inscribed records of their work on its main walls and towers. Although most of the castle is gone today, the view from the approach road across the natural moat is inspiring; colossal white stones silhouetted against desert brush and a cobalt sky. Villagers who lived inside the castle walls and depended upon the water from the rock-hewn well, 375 steps deep, have recently abandoned the area, leaving a secluded spot for free **camping.**

You might be able to reach Shobak in a shared **minibus** from Karak or Wadi Musa (near Petra), although most of the traffic between those towns takes the Desert Highway. If you hire a **taxi** (from Karak not more than JD2, from Wadi Musa not more than JD3), make sure the driver waits while you investigate.

# ■ Petra البتراء

*Match me such marvel save in Eastern clime,*
*a rose-red city 'half as old as Time'!*

—Dean Burgon

The once-lost city of Petra is now easy to find, but ease of access hardly lessens its magnificence. Nothing could. Peeking out from between the walls of a natural 3m-wide fissure are towering sculptures, raw mountains fashioned by human hands into impossibly delicate structures. Petra, meaning "stone" in ancient Greek, is perhaps the most astounding ancient city left to the modern world, and certainly a must-see for visitors to the Middle East.

For 700 years, Petra was lost to all but the few hundred members of a Bedouin tribe who guarded their treasure from outsiders. In the 19th century, Swiss explorer Johann Burkhardt heard Bedouin speaking of a "lost city," and he vowed to find it. Though Burkhardt was initially unable to find a guide, he guessed that the city he sought was the Petra of legend, the biblical Sela, which should have been near Mount Hor, the site of Aaron's tomb. Impersonating a Christian pilgrim, Burkhardt hired a guide and, on August 22, 1812, walked between the cliffs of Petra's *siq* (the mile-long rift which was the only entrance to Petra). Awed and driven to sketch the monuments and record his thoughts, the "pilgrim" aroused the suspicion of his Bedouin guide. The guide warned him of the spiritual significance of the ancient rocks, and a chastened Burkhardt left—to announce his discovery to the rest of the world. In the nearly two centuries since, Petra has become a feature tourist attraction. Admired by visitors from all over the world, including the film crew of *Indiana Jones and the Last Crusade,* Petra now has its own camel corps to protect the ruins from the many overzealous "pilgrims" who are following in Burkhardt's footsteps.

The area's principal water source, Ain Musa (Spring of Moses), is one of the many places where Moses supposedly struck a rock with his staff and extracted water (Exodus 17). Human history in the area dates back to the 8th millennium BCE. By the 6th century BCE, the Nabateans, a nomadic Arab tribe, had quietly moved onto land controlled by the Edomites and had begun to profit from the trade between lower Arabia and the Fertile Crescent. Over the next three centuries the Nabatean Kingdom, secure in its easily defended capital, flourished. The Nabateans carved their monumental temples out of the mountains, looking to Egyptian, Greek, and Roman styles for inspiration. Unique to the Nabateans are the crow-step (staircase) patterns that grace the crowns of many of the memorials. The crow-steps so decidedly resemble inverted stairways that the people of Meda'in Salih (a miniature Petra in Saudi Arabia) were able to sustain the claim that God threw Petra upside down and turned it to stone to punish its people's wickedness.

More historically verifiable evidence suggests that in 63 BCE the Nabatean King Aretas defeated Pompey's Roman Legions. The Romans controlled the entire area around Nabatea, however, prompting the later King Rabel III to strike a deal: as long as the Romans did not attack during his lifetime, they would be permitted to move in after he died. In 106 CE the Romans claimed the Nabatean Kingdom and inhabited the city of rosy Nubian sandstone.

In its heyday, Petra may have housed 20-30,000 people. But after an earthquake in 363 CE, a shift in the trade routes to Palmyra (Tadmor) in Syria, the expansion of the sea trade around Arabia, and another earthquake in 747 CE, much of Petra deteriorated to rubble. The city fell under Byzantine and then Arab control for a few centuries before the Crusaders tried to resurrect it by constructing a new fortress. But, shortly thereafter, it so declined that even its location was forgotten. A few explorers searched in vain for Petra, but not until Burkhardt schemed his way in was the city visited by anyone other than the Bedouin.

For decades, the Bedouin adapted to the influx of tourists by providing them with food and accommodations inside Petra. In 1984-85, however, the government outlawed this, out of concern for the monuments. While many of Petra's Bedouin have been relocated to a housing project near Wadi Musa, a large portion still make their homes in the more remote caves and hills of the city (which spans 50km, most of which the average tourist never sees). Many Bedouin sell souvenirs and drinks amidst the ruins; others tend goats—don't be surprised to hear a baaa emanating from inside an ancient tomb. If you venture on paths that go beyond the standard one-day itinerary, you will notice stones piled into neat columns. As long as these markers are in sight, you're near a trail, and Bedouin will pass by regularly.

## GETTING THERE

Petra is located in the rocky wilderness near the southern extreme of the Kings' Highway, about 282km from Amman, 262km via the Desert Highway. **JETT buses** leave Amman daily (6:30am, 3½hr., JD5; complete round-trip tour including lunch, guide, and horse, JD30). Reservations should be made at JETT stations well ahead of time, especially during the busy fall and spring seasons; these must be made in person, but questions can be handled by phone (tel. 664 146). You'll be dropped off at the Petra Visitor's Center. More than one day is needed to do longer hikes, but the JETT tour will cover the most impressive (and frequented) sights.

**Service** to Petra from Wahdat Station in Amman takes about five hours, plus a wait in Ma'an (JD2). Drivers will drop you off at either the Al-Anbat or the Wadi Musa Hotel; from Wadi Musa you could walk the 5km or take a **private taxi** (JD1) to Petra. From Aqaba, a two-hour **minibus** trip costs JD2. Start early in the morning to make any of these connections.

Leaving Petra, you can catch minibuses or *service* to Aqaba (JD1.500) or Amman (JD2) at the center of Wadi Musa, near the post office. The first bus leaves around 6am, with two to three later only leaving when full. A local bus to Ma'an leaves at 6am, returns at 2pm, and costs 400fils one way.

To reach Petra from the Kings' Highway, take the well-marked turn-off and head west into the colorful, steep-sided town of Wadi Musa. Halfway through Wadi Musa on the way to Petra, you'll pass the main traffic circle and travel through the main market area. A tortuous 5km from the traffic circle, the spur road leaves town and ends at the entrance to Petra. The cluster of buildings here includes the visitors center, the government Rest House, the lavish Forum Hotel, and the gatehouse to the valley that leads to the *siq* and Petra proper.

## PRACTICAL INFORMATION

The **tourist police** munch on cigar ends at the **Petra Visitor's Center** (tel. 336 060; open Sat.-Thurs. 7am-5pm), where you can hire an official guide for a "low tour" of the city center (JD7 per trip). More comprehensive guided tours go to Al Madbah (JD14), Ad-Deir (JD17), and Jabal Harun (JD25). Trips to more remote areas should be arranged with the guide directly; prices vary from JD25 to JD50 per guide. You can rent a horse (you're also responsible for renting the guide's horse), but it's more interesting to remain on foot. It's easy to tag along behind a group with a guide or to form a group of your own. The various guidebooks available at the visitor's center are helpful, but there's no substitute for the expertise of an official guide, especially for the more remote sites of Al Barid or Al Madras. On the other side of the visitor's center are the Rest House and the swinging gate marking the beginning of the trail down to the *siq*.

Wadi Musa has a **post office** with **poste restante** (tel. 336 224) next to the **Musa Spring Hotel** (open Sat.-Thurs. 7:30am-7pm, Fri. 7:30am-1:30pm). A second branch is located behind the visitor's center by the entrance to the *siq* (same hours).

Wadi Musa has no hospital, but the **government health center** (tel. 336 025), a 15-minute walk uphill from the main traffic circle, is open 24 hours. If you've fallen off your camel and can't get up, crawl over to the **Petra Polyclinic** (tel. 336 694) at the

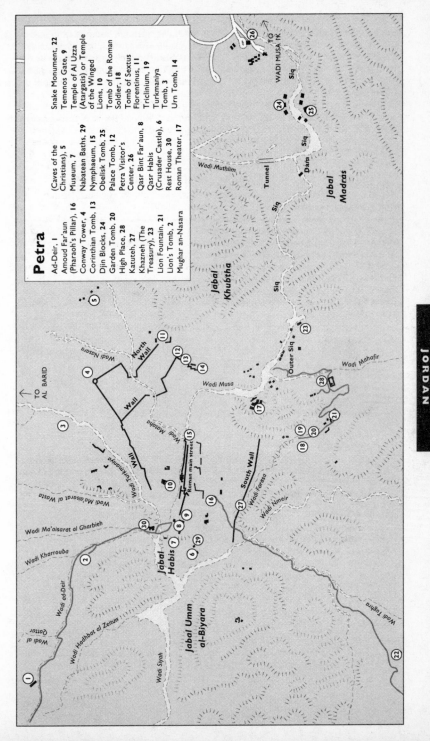

## Petra

Ad-Deir, 1
Amoud Far'aun
(Pharaoh's Pillar), 16
Conway Tower, 4
Corinthian Tomb, 13
Djin Blocks, 24
Garden Tomb, 20
High Place, 28
Katuteh, 27
Khazneh (The
Treasury), 23
Lion Fountain, 21
Lion's Tomb, 2
Mughar an-Nasara

(Caves of the
Christians), 5
Museum, 7
Nabatean Baths, 29
Nymphaeum, 15
Obelisk Tomb, 25
Palace Tomb, 12
Petra Visitor's
Center, 26
Qasr Bint Far'aun, 8
Qasr Habis
(Crusader Castle), 6
Rest House, 30
Roman Theater, 17

Snake Monument, 22
Temenos Gate, 9
Temple of Al Uzza
(Atargatis) or Temple
of the Winged
Lions, 10
Tomb of the Roman
Soldier, 18
Tomb of Sextus
Florentinus, 11
Triclinium, 19
Turkmaniya
Tomb, 3
Urn Tomb, 14

JORDAN

traffic circle. It's more expensive, but has modern equipment including an x-ray unit. The town **pharmacy** (tel. 383 444), on the main traffic circle, is open 24 hours.

There are three **banks** open for exchange Sat.-Thurs. 8:30am-12:30pm, and they all extract exorbitant commissions: the **Arab Bank** and the **Housing Bank** are in the town center, and the **Cairo Amman Bank** is in the Mövenpick Hotel just outside the entrance to Petra. You can also get a Visa **cash advance** from any bank. Petra's **telephone code** is 03.

**Admission** to the ancient city is JD20 for one day, JD25 for two days, and JD30 for three days. Children under 12 pay JD12.5 for one day, 50% off for two or three days. Those who can't afford a ticket have found ways in the back door. Beware, though, as scary guards in green robes and ammunition belts abound. Guides are expensive but recommended for four of the more remote hikes in Petra; the bureaucracy may fool you into thinking they're mandatory. Petra is open daily 6am-6pm, but these hours are only loosely enforced. If you choose to stay to see the sun set, you'll have no problem getting out.

## ACCOMMODATIONS

Ever since the peace treaty let visitors from Israel flood the Jordanian hillside, construction hasn't stopped in Wadi Musa. Most of the development revolves around luxury resorts, but there are enough cheapies to go around. Prices become extremely negotiable in the off season (May-July and Dec.-Feb.), and may be bargained down to as little as 50% of the original price.

**Musa Spring Hotel and Restaurant,** Wadi Musa Gate (tel. 336 310; fax 336 910). Next to Moses' Spring as you enter town from Amman, the Musa is renowned for evening showings of *Indiana Jones* and *Lawrence of Arabia*. Rooftop mattresses (JD2) with facilities (including hot showers) and plenty of budget traveler companionship. Free use of kitchen. Singles JD5. Doubles JD8, with bath JD10. Breakfast JD1.500; lunch or dinner all-you-can-eat buffet JD3. Free shuttle to Petra.

**Twaissi Hostel** (tel. 336 423), on an unmarked side street off the Wadi Musa's central circle. Facing downhill towards Petra, take a right. Continue up this street until you reach a house with a white flag. Turn right, and follow the road behind the first two houses to the Twaissi. Rooms are carpeted, with airy windows. Common kitchen and a homey TV room with free movies and board games. Breakfast and dinner available. Rooftop mattress at JD2 is among the cheapest in town. Bed in a shared room JD4.

**Al-Anbat Hotel** (tel. 336 265; fax 336 888). Follow the trough down from the spring until you see the hotel with the best view of the descent to Petra. Huge lounge chairs furnish TV rooms on each floor. Bathtubs, towels, and free soap come in handy after a sweaty day. Singles JD6. Doubles and triples JD5 per person. With breakfast and dinner, JD12 per person. Camping facilities (tents and showers) available for JD2. Free buses to Petra.

**Cleopetra Hotel** (tel./fax 337 090), 50m uphill from the main traffic circle, on the left. Genuinely friendly manager provides maps and info. Bargainers can get rooms with bath, soap, and towel for JD6 per person, JD8 with breakfast.

**Orient Hotel and Restaurant** (tel./fax 337 020), to the left of the traffic circle facing downhill. Small, cozy rooms have sparkling, white tiled baths. At only JD3 per person, the Orient would be perfect if it weren't for that dang street noise.

**Al-Rashid Hotel** (tel. 336 800; fax 336 801). Right on the main traffic circle, this seafoam-green palace has the most luxurious rooms in its price range. Gold chandeliers, high ceilings, and plush carpeted rooms are JD8 per person, JD10 with breakfast. MC, Visa, and Diner's Club.

**Sunset Hotel** (tel. 336 579; fax 336 950). About 200m uphill from the visitor's center. If your feet are sore and your bottom hurts from a Petra camel ride, this place is for you—the first inexpensive and clean option outside of the Mega Hotel complex. Doubles JD10, JD15 with private bath. Breakfast included.

**Camping** inside Petra is now illegal, but lingering explorers may receive invitations for overnight stays from hospitable Bedouin. It's also very possible to pick an off-the-beaten-path cave for a night, although explaining yourself to Jordanian police could turn you pinker than the ruins, or worse.

## FOOD

The farther you go from the ruins, the less you'll pay for falafel (within reason—prices start rising again around Paris). The best bargains are in Wadi Musa, especially in the streets to the right of its main circle as you approach from Petra. Many hotels have all-you-can-eat buffets at reasonable prices. The **Musa Springs Hotel** offers a filling meal with pasta, rice, chicken, salad, and bread for JD3 (daily 6-9pm). The **Star Supermarket** (on the left, uphill from the traffic circle) has the cheapest water at 300fils and the most reasonably-priced basics for bag lunches. If you want something non-Jordanian, you'll have to pay. **Papazzi,** uphill from the visitor's center, has great pizza, but a large one sauces you for JD10.

**Rose City Restaurant** (tel. 336 865), just outside the site. Energy for the hike uphill. ½-chicken JD2, hummus 500fils, soda 500fils. Open daily 6am-11:30pm.

**Petra Tourist Restaurant,** down the street from Petra Pearl. Modest, but the friendly Egyptian cooks will serve you rice, salad, bird, and bread for JD1.500, or a *shish* of *kabab* with salad for 450fils. Open daily 6am-midnight.

**The Treasury Restaurant,** around the corner from the Petra Tourist. Try their *mensaf* (JD3) or a tasty chicken *tourky* (JD2.500). Open daily 6am-1am.

**Khan Checken,** across from the Treasury Restaurant, has falafel sandwiches for 250fils and hummus for 500fils.

## SIGHTS

The Nabateans worshipped only two deities: Dushara, the god of strength, symbolized by sculpted rock, and Al Uzza (or Atargatis), the goddess of water and fertility. Still, the number of temples and tombs in Petra seems infinite. A little climbing will allow you to escape the tour groups crowding the inner valley. Many spectacular monuments are close enough to be viewed in a one-day junket, but a few require multi-day expeditions. Bedouin sell water throughout the park, but you'll need to empty the Treasury to pay for it—it's best to bring bottles from outside.

Even before you reach the narrow canyon-like *siq,* caves staring from distant mountain faces and large *djinn* monuments (ghost tombs) will draw you in. On the left, built high into the cliff, stands the **Obelisk Tomb.** Closer to the entrance of the *siq,* rock-cut channels once cradled ceramic pipes which brought Ain Musa's waters to the inner city and the surrounding farm country. A nearby dam burst in 1963, and the resulting flash flood killed 28 tourists in the *siq.* While designing a new dam, the Nabateans' ancient dam was uncovered and used as a model. Don't worry.

As you enter the *siq,* walls towering 200m on either side begin to block out the light, casting enormous shadows on the niches that once held icons of the gods meant to protect the entrance by hexing unwelcome visitors. The *siq* winds around for 1.5km, then slowly emits a faint pink glow at the first peek of the **Khazneh** (Treasury). At 90m wide and 130m tall, the Khazneh is the best preserved of Petra's monuments, although bullet holes are clearly visible on the upper urn. Believing the urn to be hollow and filled with ancient pharaonic treasures, Bedouin periodically fired at it, hoping to burst this petrified piñata. Actually, the treasury was a royal tomb and, like almost everything else at Petra, is quite solid. The rock melds from one color to the next like a geological mood ring: in the morning, the sun's rays give the monument a rich peach hue, in late afternoon it glistens rose, and by sunset, it drips blood red.

Down the road to the right as you face the Khazneh, Wadi Musa opens up to the 3000-seat **Roman Theater.** The long row of Royal Tombs on the face of Jabal Khubtha is on the right. The Romans built their theater under the red stone Nabatean necropolis, and the ancient carved caves still yawn above it. The theater has been restored to its 2nd-century appearance; audiences are returning after an almost unbearable 1500-year wait. A marble Hercules (now in the museum) was discovered just a few years ago in the curtained chambers beneath the stage.

Across the *wadi* are the **Royal Tombs.** The **Urn Tomb,** with its unmistakable recessed façade, commands a soul-scorching view of the still-widening valley. The two-tiered vault beneath the pillared façade is known as the prison, or *sijin.* A Greek inscription on an inner wall describes how the tomb, originally dedicated to the Nabatean King Malichus II in the first century CE, was converted to a church 400 years later. Nearby is the **Corinthian Tomb,** allegedly a replica of Nero's Golden Palace in Rome, and the **Palace Tomb** (or the Tomb in Two Stories), which literally juts out from the mountainside. The latter tomb had to be completed by attaching preassembled stones to its upper left-hand corner. Around the corner to the right is the **Tomb of Sextus Florentinus,** who was so enamored of these hewn heights that he asked his son to bury him in this ultimate outpost of the Roman Empire.

Around the bend to the left, a few restored columns dot either side of the paved Roman **main street.** Two thousand years ago, columns lined the full length of the street, shielding markets and residences. At the beginning of the street on the right, the **Nymphaeum** ruins outline the ancient public fountain near its base. On a rise to the right, before the triple-arched gate, recent excavations have uncovered the **Temple of Al Uzza (Atargatis),** also called the **Temple of the Winged Lions.** In the spring you can watch the progress of American-sponsored excavations which have already uncovered several workshops and some cracked Nabatean crocks.

Also recently excavated by a joint Jordanian-American team is an immense mosaic-rich **Byzantine church.** The site lies several hundred meters to the right of the Roman street, near the Temple of the Winged Lions, from which some of the church's column bases and capitals were probably lifted. Each of the church's side aisles is paved with 70 square meters of remarkably preserved mosaic, depicting native as well as exotic or mythological animals, humans of various professions, and representations of the four seasons. The church is thought to have been a major 5th- and 6th-century cathedral, likely the seat of the bishop of the Byzantine province of Palaestina Tertia, and challenges the belief that Petra was in decline by 600 CE.

Across the street, a team from Brown University is in the process of unearthing the **Southern Temple.** White hexagonal paving stones cover an extensive tunnel system marking the importance of this holy site. Farther along, the triple-arched **Temenos Gate** was once the front gate of the **Qasr Bint Far'aun** (Palace of the Pharaoh's Daughter), a Nabatean temple built to honor the god Dushara. On your left, just before the gate, are the **Nabatean Baths.** On the trail leading off behind the temple to the left, a single standing column gloats beside its two fallen comrades—**Amoud Far'aun** (Pharaoh's Pillar) marks the entrance to the ancient Roman city. To the right of the Nabatean temple, a rock-hewn staircase leads to a small **archaeological museum** which holds the spoils of the Winged Lions dig and carved stone figures from elsewhere in Petra. On the way to the monastery, the **Nabatean Museum** has nice artifacts, and air-conditioned **restrooms** with probably the world's best toilet seat view (both museums open daily 9am-4pm; free).

## Hikes to Remote Sights

Many people, content with daytrip dosage, will go home raving about Petra's first 10%. Few see the rest. You'll need two days to do the following seven treks, but you can easily spend a week wandering, especially if you venture beyond the ancient city limits. The Bedouin say that to appreciate Petra you must stay long enough to watch your nails grow long. Four places require a guide (JD25): **Sabra,** the **Snake Monument, Jabal Numair,** and **Jabal Haroun.** The requirement is not enforced, but it's not a good idea to hike the remote hills alone.

### Wadi Turkimaniya وادي تركمانية

The shortest and easiest of the hikes leads down the *wadi* to the left of and behind the Temple of the Winged Lions. Fifteen minutes of strolling down the road that runs through the rich green gardens of **Wadi Turkimaniya** guide you to the only tomb at Petra with a Nabatean inscription. The lengthy invocation above the entrance beseeches the god Dushara to safeguard the tomb and to protect its contents from violation. Unfortunately, Dushara took an interminable sabbatical and the chamber has been stripped bare.

### Qasr Habis قصر حابس

A second, more interesting climb begins at the end of the road that descends from the Pharaoh's Pillar to the cliff face, a few hundred meters left of the museum. The trail dribbles up to the **Qasr Habis** (Crusader Castle). The steps have been restored recently, but they don't lead up to much. A path winds all the way around the mountain, however, revealing gorgeous canyons and (you guessed it) more tombs on the western side. The climb to the top and back takes less than an hour.

### Jabal Harun جبل هارون

This climb begins just to the right of Jabal Habis, below the museum. A sign points to **Ad-Deir** (the Monastery) and leads northwest across Wadi Siyah, past the Forum Restaurant to Wadi Deir and its fragrant oleander. As you squeeze through the narrowing canyon you will confront a human-shaped hole in the façade of the **Lion's Tomb**. A hidden tomb awaits daredevils who try to climb the cleft to the right; less intrepid wanderers backtrack to the right and find the tomb a few minutes later. Back on the path, veer left to get to Petra's largest monument.

Ad-Deir, 50m wide and 45m tall, is larger, though less ornate, than the Khazneh. With a single inner chamber dating back to the first century CE, most scholars believe that Ad-Deir was originally either a Nabatean temple or an unfinished tomb dedicated to one of the later Nabatean kings. It picked up its orthodox appellation in the Byzantine period. On the left, a lone tree popping through a crack in the rock marks more ancient steps, which continue all the way up to the rim of the urn atop the monastery. Straight across the *wadi* looms the highest peak in the area, **Jabal Harun** (Aaron's Mountain or Mt. Hor). On top of the mountain, a white church reportedly houses the **Tomb of Aaron**. The whole trip takes a few hours, a few more if you detour into **Wadi Siyah** and visit its seasonal waterfall on the way back.

### Jabal Umm al-Biyara جبل أم البيارة

A grueling three-hour hike climbs **Jabal Umm al-Biyara** (Mother of Cisterns Mountain), which towers over the Crusader castle on Jabal Habis. Follow the trail from the left of the Nabatean temple past the Pharaoh's Pillar and down into the *wadi* to the right. If you scramble 50m up the rock chute to the left of the blue sign you'll reach the beginning of a stone ramp that leads to the top. It was here, at the site of Petra's

---

### Mountains Eternally Red

Many of the Bedouin in Petra's pink valleys speak a few words of Hebrew. They need to, as most visitors to the Nabatean city come from Jordan's western neighbor. After the Jordanian-Israeli peace treaty, Israelis have swarmed to the city of Rose by the thousands, drawn both by the beauty of the ancient monuments and by the thrill of visiting the once forbidden country. Before the peace treaty, a visit to Petra was more of a thrill. If an Israeli teen successfully crossed the border, peeked around the site, and returned home alive, he or she would achieve eternal hero status. Fueled by the thirst for adventure and discovery that so often are associated with Petra, hundreds of young Israelis were willing to sacrifice their lives for a glimpse of the famed hills. Many lives that were offered for sacrifice were, indeed, taken: an uncounted number of youths were shot by guards.

original acropolis and the biblical city of Sela, that a Judean king supposedly hurled thousands of Edomites over the cliff's edge. The gigantic piles of shards, over 8000 years old, are the only remnants of the mountains' first inhabitants.

If instead of climbing Umm al-Biyara you continue south along Wadi Tughra, which runs by its foot, you'll eventually reach the **Snake Monument,** one of the earliest Nabatean religious shrines. From here it's about two hours to Aaron's Tomb on Jabal Harun. The path meanders around Mount Hor before ascending it from the south. When it disappears on the rocks, follow the donkey droppings. As you start to climb Jabal Harun you'll see a lone tent. Inside, a Bedouin, the official holder of the keys, will escort you the rest of the way and open the building for you to explore. The entire trek takes five or six hours.

### The High Place الاماكن العليا

One of the most popular hikes is the circular route to the **High Place** on Jabal al-Madbah, a place of sacrifice with a full view of Petra. A staircase sliced in the rock leads to the left just as the Roman Theater comes into view. Follow the right prong when the trail levels and forks at the top of the stairs. On the left, **Obelisk Ridge** presents one obelisk to Dushara and another to Al Uzza. On the peak to the right, the Great High Place supports a string of grisly sights: two neatly cut altars, an ablution cistern, gutters for draining away sacrificial blood, and cliff-hewn bleachers for an unobstructed view of the animal sacrifices. Head downhill past the Pepsi stand, leaving the obelisks behind you, and backtrack under the western face of the Great High Place. If you hunt around you'll find a staircase leading down to a sculptured **Lion Fountain.** The first grotto complex beyond it is the **Garden Tomb.** Below it is the **Tomb of the Roman Soldier** (named for the tough guy carved in the façade) and across from it a rock **triclinium** (feast hall), which has the only decorated interior in Petra. The trail then leads into Wadi Farasa and ends near the Pillar. The circle, followed either way, takes about an hour and a half.

### Al Madras and Al Barid المدرس و البارد

Beyond Petra, tourist groups and commercialism disappears. Bedouin here have been unaltered by modernity, and the wildlife roam free. The isolated antiquities can only be reached by donkey or foot—all roads lead back to the Kings' Highway.

A trail branching to your left just past the Obelisk Tomb and just before the entrance to the *siq* leads to **Al Madras,** an ancient Petran suburb with almost as many monuments as Petra itself. On the way, watch for the short-eared desert hare and a full spectrum of long lanky lizards—purple, fuchsia, and iridescent blue. Come with water, a snack, and a guide. The round-trip takes four to eight hours.

Past the Tomb of Sextus Florentinus and the **Mughar an-Nasara** (Caves of the Christians), a trail chisels into the rock leading to the northern suburb of **Al Barid.** A road passing the new hotel in Wadi Musa also approaches this archaeological site. Al Barid is a curious miniature of Petra, complete with a short *siq,* several carved tombs, and caves. If you don't feel like hoofing it, a Wadi Musa taxi will take you there and wait for you at the entrance for an hour (JD7). Also off the new road past the hotel is **Al Beidha.** Excitement runs high among the members of the excavating expedition here; they've uncovered traces of a pre-pottery Neolithic village, a sedentary society dating to the 8th millennium BCE. This find would make Al Beidha, along with Jericho, one of the oldest known farming communities in the world. A Bedouin guide can lead you here via a painless trail (about 3hr. each way). Bring an extra JD2-3 or some of your own native trinkets to trade.

# ■ Aqaba العقبة

Set in a natural amphitheater beneath a crescent of rugged hills, Aqaba is land-locked Jordan's sole link to the high seas. Beneath the water, legions of brilliantly colored creatures flit through a surreal universe of coral. Above (and as a result of) the water, Aqaba is an important trade and military center; and has become the darling of the

Arab elite in need of a periodic escape from dry cityscapes. More liberal and relaxed than other parts of Jordan, Aqaba features bikini-clad Europeans drinking beer at the same bar with robed Saudis. Rumor has it that Aqaba has a thriving gay population, but you wouldn't know it—this is the Arab world, and everything takes place behind closed doors.

Situated at the tip of the gulf of the same name, Aqaba's strategic setting has been apparent since Biblical times, when King Solomon's copper-laden ships sailed from here. The Romans stationed their famous Tenth Legion at this point, and the Crusaders fortified the port and Pharaoh's Island 7km off the coast (now in Egyptian territory). During the 1917 Arab Revolt, Faisal ibn Hussein and T.E. Lawrence staged a desert raid on the Ottomans' fortifications and captured the port. In 1965 King Hussein shrewdly traded the Saudis 6000 square km of southeastern desert (before he knew there was black gold beneath the sand) for 13km of coastline, and started developing the city into a tourist paradise. After the reopening of the Suez Canal in 1957 and the increased traffic caused by the Iran-Iraq War, the harbor became packed with huge leviathans bulging with cargo. During the 1991 Gulf War, Aqaba was Iraq's chief illicit outlet, and a blockade slowed traffic considerably. Recent years has seen Aqaba bounce back—trade has resumed under international supervision, and the open border with Israel has brought a tsunami of tourists.

## ORIENTATION

Extending from King Hussein's villa on the Israeli border to the huge, fenced-in port facilities 4km down the arching corniche to the southeast, Aqaba is one elongated beach. Luxury hotels and military complexes have gobbled up a good part of the beach near town. Four countries come together in the small northern tip of the Gulf of Aqaba: Egypt meets Israel near the conspicuous resort hotels at Taba, Israel's Eilat faces Jordan's Aqaba across the border, and Saudi Arabia looms to the southeast. (For information on **border crossings,** see p. 263, p. 440, and p. 507).

Shops line the streets of central Aqaba branching from **Ailah Square.** South of the port and 10km from central Aqaba, the **ferry dock** handles the thousands of Egyptian workers and occasional foreign travelers who cross the Gulf of Aqaba to Nuweiba' in Egypt. One km past the ferry port you'll come to the **Marine Research Center** building, just past which you'll find Aqaba's finest coral reefs and a sandy beach that stretches south to the Saudi border.

Hitching around Aqaba is reportedly easy, as an army of trucks serves the port. Herds of six-wheeled beasts cover vast stretches along the highway 2km north of town. Truck stops make strategic starting points for hitching trips to the north. Taxi fare out to the truck stops is about 500fils; the road to the port, which bumps the eastern side of town, has closer hitching points. Hitching is inherently risky, especially for women, and is not recommended for anyone. Taxis to the port cost JD2.

## PRACTICAL INFORMATION

Aqaba's tree-lined streets and circles and the anchored ships offshore give a first impression of a sleepy seaside town. Don't be fooled; this city can be as hectic as the rest of Jordan. People don't change their driving habits just because they're in a warm municipality. There are road signs telling drivers to lay off their horns, which are as obeyed as the sign telling King Hussein to stop printing posters of himself.

**Visitors Center:** on the grounds of the new Islamic Museum, about halfway to the port from the town center (tel. 313 363 or 731). A long hike or a JD1 taxi ride. Maps, brochures, information on travel to nearby cities and Egypt, and a complaints box. Open daily 8am-1pm and 5-7pm.

**Tourist Police:** Tel. 313 513.

**Egyptian Consulate:** Al Istiqlal St. (tel. 316 171); turn right along the curve about 800m northwest of the Aquamarina II Hotel and look for an empty guard booth in front. Egyptian visas can be obtained in a day. Bring your passport, a photo, and JD12. Open daily 9am-2pm. Apply for visa 9-11am.

**Currency Exchange:** Bank hours are normally Sat.-Thurs. 8:30am-12:30pm, with some banks reopening Sat.-Wed. 4-6pm. Money exchanges are open in the morning and some stay open until midnight. Bring a passport to exchange traveler's checks. The **Jordan National Bank** in the Commercial Center on Al Yarmouk St., near the Jordan Flower Hotel, is the only bank in Aqaba that allows withdrawal with MasterCard. Minimum JD70. Open Sat.-Thurs. 8:30am-12:30pm and 5-6:30pm. Most banks accept Visa.

**American Express: International Traders Travel Agency Office,** P.O. Box 136 (tel. 313 757; fax 315 316), 1 block west of Ailah Sq., a few doors from the Ali Baba Restaurant. Will hold mail for anyone. Open Sat.-Thurs. 8am-1pm and 4-7pm, and occasionally a few hours Fri. mornings.

**Telephones:** Next to the post office. Open daily 7:30am-10:30pm. Cheap rates in evening and on Fridays.

**Flights: Royal Jordanian** (tel. 314 477) has 2 regular flights per day to and from Amman (45min., round-trip JD25, JD20 each way in high season). Some hotels run buses from Aqaba International Airport to the center of the city. The trip by taxi costs JD2 per person.

**Buses and Service:** Station is 2 blocks uphill from Ailah Sq. Minibuses to Petra usually begin to run at 6:30am and stop around 1pm, but won't leave until they're full (2½hr., JD2). Another way to Petra is to take a minibus from Aqaba to Ma'an (1½hr., JD1) and catch a Petra bus from there (1½hr., JD1). To Wadi Rum: 1 bus at 6:30am, return 3pm. It leaves when full and there are sometimes extras in high season (1½hr., JD1.500). The **JETT Bus station** (tel. 315 222) is 1km west of Ailah Sq., near the Miramar Hotel. Regular bus service to Amman (7 buses daily 7am-4:30pm, 4hr., JD4). Reserve in advance. JETT buses are luxury class, with stewardess service, A/C, and videos.

**Taxis:** Regular taxis offer groups (max. 4 people) quick transport to Petra (JD25), Wadi Rum (1hr.; round-trip JD20), and the Aqaba ferry terminal (10km, JD1.500).

**Car Rental:** Prices are controlled by the government and range from US$25-80 per day, plus 44-88¢ per km. Call around for specials and unlimited-mile options. Rental agencies include **Rum** (tel. 313 581), **Al-Cazar** (tel. 314 131), and **Avis** (tel. 312 111) at the airport.

**English Bookstore: Yamani Bookshop** (tel. 312 221) opposite the post office. Solid selection of magazines and tourist guides. Also sells film, snorkeling equipment, sunscreen, and Rx sundries. Open daily 10am-2:30pm and 6-10pm.

**Laundry:** Most hotels provide expensive laundry service. **Al Abbi Dry Cleaning,** 1 block down from the bus and *service* station on King Talal St. (tel. 315 722), is cheaper. Shirts 300fils, pants 400fils. Open Sat.-Thurs. 7-11am and 2-8pm.

**Pharmacies: Anteka Pharmacy** (tel. 315 050), next to the Jordan National Bank. Open 24hr. except on Friday, when it closes at 9:30pm. **Jerusalem Pharmacy** (tel. 314 747) on Al Hammamat al-Tunisich St. next to the Az-Zeitouna Hotel. Open Sat.-Thurs. 7am-midnight. Both pharmacies accept Visa, MC, and AmEx. There are many other pharmacies in the city.

**Medical Emergency: Princess Haya el-Hussein Hospital** (tel. 314 111 or 114), near the JETT Station on the way into town. One of Jordan's best hospitals, with decompression chambers and a staff capable of dealing with diving accidents.

**Police:** Tel. 312 411 or 412. Station down the steps and 100m to the right of the Palm Beach Hotel. Issues camping permits for JD1.

**Post Office:** 2 blocks uphill from Ailah Sq., next to the large radio tower (tel. 313 939). **Poste restante** and **EMS.** Open Sat.-Thurs. 7:30am-7pm, Fri. 7:30am-1pm.

**Telephone code:** 03.

## ACCOMMODATIONS

While Aqaba has some of the highest prices in Jordan (after Petra), there are several excellent values. The usual rules apply. Shop, bargain, walk out a few times, throw fish, and the prices will come down. In the summer, air conditioning is worth the extra dinar. The good budget hotels cluster around the downtown mosque.

**Nairoukh Hotel I** (tel. 319 284 or 285). Behind Ata Ali and Ali Baba restaurants, the Nairoukh Hotel is Aqaba's best, cleanest value. The employees whistle while they constantly clean, and may offer to rent videos for the beach-weary. Spacious rooms with A/C, TV, fridge, fluffy towels, and even complimentary soap. Mini-bus service for diving. Singles JD12. Doubles JD18.

**Red Sea Hotel** (tel./fax 312 156). Next door to Nairoukh 1. Basic, relatively clean rooms and bathrooms and friendly staff. Singles with bath JD5, doubles JD7. Singles with A/C, TV, and fridge JD10, doubles JD12.

**Amira Hotel** (tel. 318 840; fax 312 559). Next door to Nairoukh 1. Small rooms low on character but high on amenities: TV, small towel, private toilet, and A/C. Singles JD10, doubles JD12, triples JD15.

**Jordan Flower Hotel** (tel. 314 377; fax 314 378), in the commercial area near the Arab Bank. Rather dreary entrance but comfortable rooms, some with balcony view of the sea. Ceiling fans and outside bathrooms: singles JD5, doubles JD7, triples JD9. Rooms with A/C and fridge: singles JD9, doubles JD10, triples JD12.

**Al Khouli Hotel** (tel. 312 207), near the open food market and Ash-Shula Hotel. Relatively clean rooms with private bathrooms, A/C, and TV. Bargaining expected. Singles JD7, doubles JD12, triples JD15.

**Al-Shula Hotel,** Raghadan St. (tel. 315 206; fax 315 150), behind the Hussein Ibn Ali Mosque. Color TV, refrigerators, bidets, balconies, and a charming view of Eilat. Red curtains cast a gory pall over the rooms on sunny afternoons. Singles JD28. Doubles JD35. Breakfast included.

The only legal **camping** north of the port is in the lots beside some of the larger hotels. The **Aqaba Hotel** has a small site and the JD6 fee admits you to their private beach and showers. New, wonderfully scenic government camping facilities, 6km south of the port, have showers and bathrooms for only JD1. To get there, walk or take a taxi (no more than JD3).

## FOOD

Aqaba is filled with the usual restaurants and sandwich shops. Fresh fish, the obvious staple of a seaside town, is actually not all that abundant. Because of the low plankton content in the clear northern waters of the Gulf of Aqaba, there are few edible sea creatures afloat. Jordanians are not permitted to fish the richer Saudi waters and the Egyptian export tax is outlandish. There is a **market** (open daily 7am-11pm) just up from Ailah Sq. where you can fill up on fresh fruit, bread, and cheese, though your snout may be overwhelmed on windless summer days. Shops on the streets surrounding the square sell delicacies like ice cream and fried sloth, mostly at high prices. Lamb, beef, and falafel are everywhere around the Hussein Ibn Ali Mosque. The best restaurants stretch from the mosque to the area around the Aqaba Gulf Hotel. **Humam Supermarket,** 11 Petra St. (tel. 315 721), in the center of town near the post office, has a solid selection (open Sat.-Thurs. 10am-2pm and 4:30-10pm. Visa, MC accepted).

**Chicken Tikka,** An-Nahda St. (tel. 313 633), 100m west of the Aquamarina II Hotel on your right. Café tables outside, terrible music inside. Try the Tikka Special—two pieces of spicy chicken, fries, and *purri* (puffy fried bread)—for JD1.800. Open daily 11am-midnight, or later if you look desperately hungry.

**Chili House Restaurant** (tel. 312 435), next to the Aquamarina II hotel. Sterile chain atmosphere, but big dishes of flavorful veggie or meat chili with cheddar cheese and spaghetti or rice go for JD1.500-2. Burgers JD1-1.500. Open daily 9am-midnight. Visa accepted.

**Ata Ali Café** (tel. 315 200), to the north of the Hussein Ibn Ali Mosque. No trip to Aqaba is complete without daily trips to AA's sweetshop. Filling meals for JD3-3.500, hard or soft *kinafeh* 500fils, sugar cones 200fils, and mouth-watering 3-scoop sundaes 650fils. Open daily 7am-11:30pm or midnight.

**China Restaurant** (tel. 314 410), behind the post office. Fun, gaudy red interior and extensive menu of generally high quality food. Entrees JD2-4. Open daily 11:30am-3:30pm and 6:30-11:30pm.

**Captain's Restaurant,** An-Nahda St. (tel. 316 905), by the Aquamarina II Hotel, look for the blue-and-white veranda. Spaghetti JD1-2, fresh fish JD4, or omelettes 500fils. Excellent view of Pizza Hut across the street. Open daily 9am-midnight.

## SIGHTS

**Yemeniyyeh Reef,** just south of the Marine Research Center beyond the port, ranks among the world's best for scoping fish. The new **Royal Diving Center** (tel. 317 035) in the Yemeniyyeh area rents out snorkeling (JD2) and diving equipment (1 dive JD15, 2 dives JD24), and has a small pool. They run a bus between the center and all major hotels in Aqaba (to the center at 9am, back to Aqaba at 5pm) for 500fils. You can avoid the JD3 entrance fee and abuse from the staff by using the beach next to the center. Most luxury hotels also rent out equipment and organize outings. With a mask, snorkel, and pair of fins you can wander off on your own to some of the more isolated spots near the Saudi border, where the fish run on super-octane. See **Underwater Adventures,** p.247 for important information on snorkeling and scuba diving; for **emergency** medical help dial 193.

The **Seastar Watersports Center** (tel. 314 131 or 132; fax 314 133), in the Al-Cazar Hotel, conducts dives daily at 9am and 2pm (arrive 30min. early). Equipment rental for one dive is JD26, for two dives JD48, and JD7 for a half-day of snorkeling (prices include transportation). Beginners may take a free test dive. If you're serious about submerging, you can take the five-day American PCEI scuba diving training course (US$330 including equipment). Snorkeling fiends are best off investing in their own equipment and going solo. The **Yamani Bookstore** has the biggest selection of masks (JD8-12) and fins (JD12-20; see **Practical Information,** p. 504).

The **aquarium** is in the Marine Research Center (tel. 315 145), just beyond the port. There are a small number of bland, live fish, a few dead ones, and bits of information about the Red Sea (admission JD1; open daily 7:30am-5pm; taxis to the aquarium cost JD3). You'll see more in your first five minutes of snorkeling. A costly **glass-bottom boat ride** (about JD10), traveling up and down the coast, is good for those opposed to the whole wet thing.

In the early mornings and late afternoons the winds are strong enough to make **windsurfing** possible; the **Aquamarina Club** (tel. 314 333) charges JD3 per half-hour for a board. The Aquamarina also offers waterskiing (JD3) and, for the less adventurous, paddle-boating (JD1.500).

Near the Miramar Hotel is a free and relatively clean **public beach.** The majority of Aqaba's more scenic, clean, and empty free beaches are quite a distance away. The Aqaba Hotel has a gorgeous white sand beach, but will gouge you JD2.200 for the privilege of burning your feet—shade and lounge chairs are reserved for guests. Southeast of downtown, there's a free pebble beach behind a "Restricted Area—No Camping" sign. It's mostly an all-male scene, and women may become the focus of more attention than they want. The trek past the port on the 10km strip leading to Saudi Arabia is long, but it's your best bet for a sandy, dandy sun day.

Aqaba should thank its lucky starfish for its aquatic splendors, because the sights above sea level don't hold much water. The recently discovered ruins of **Aila** are the only exception, and they're not all that exceptional. In a seemingly plain beachside lot across from the Miramar Hotel, archaeologists have uncovered the original 120m by 160m city. In the 7th to 10th centuries CE, Aila ("god" in Aramaic) was an early Islamic port trading as far away as China. The sight is always open and visitors are free to wander amidst signs explaining the paltry ruins. Items recovered in the excavations, including Greek and Arabic inscriptions, pottery shards, and other small items are displayed in the recently completed **Aqaba Museum,** in the same building as the visitors center between the castle and the southern waterfront (open daily 8am-2pm; JD1). The **Medieval Castle,** built by the 16th-century CE Sultan Ganswa al-Ghouri, behind a dilapidated mosque and a palm grove, is gradually being restored by the Department of Antiquities.

An accord between Jordan and Egypt has recently opened up the Egyptian **Pharaoh's Island** (known in Jordanian Arabic as Jaziret Far'aun), 7km off shore, to tourists with Jordanian visas. Day-passes can be obtained in Aqaba and the boat ride takes about 45 minutes (JD20). Contact the Aqua Marina hotel for cruise details; see p. 264 for more on the island.

## GOING TO ISRAEL

To cross from Aqaba to Eilat, all nationalities must pay the JD4 exit fee. There is no entrance fee into Israel and free visas are given at the border. Bus #16 will take you to the center of Eilat for NIS4.

## GOING TO EGYPT

A ferry shuttles between Aqaba and Nuweiba'. You'll need an Egyptian Visa (2 week or 1 month), which can be obtained in one day at the Egyptian Consulate and costs JD12 (see **Practical Information,** p. 503). Visas can also be obtained on board the ferry for an extra charge or upon arrival in Nuweiba' if you're willing to wait in multi-hour lines. Taxis to the ferry terminal from Aqaba center cost JD2. There are two daily, overcrowded ferries at noon and 5pm which are supposed to take 3½hr. but often take much longer (US$19). A **speedboat** leaves daily at noon and costs US$27. The ride takes an hour and is less crowded and more punctual. Show up at least one hour before departure. Tickets can be purchased at any agency in Aqaba. There is a JD6 departure tax.

# ■ Near Aqaba: Wadi Rum وادي رام

In *Seven Pillars of Wisdom*, T.E. Lawrence wrote that when he passed between these rusty crags his "little caravan fell quiet, ashamed to flaunt itself in the presence of such stupendous hills." Those who most appreciate the majestic grandeur of Wadi Rum revel in its inaccessibility. Few buses and no *service* come here, and most Jordanians have never been to this area located nearly 300km south of Amman. Buses and *service* along the Desert Highway can drop you off 25km north of Aqaba at the turn-off marked "Rum 30km." From there many people hitch a ride east and south to the **Desert Police Headquarters** within Wadi Rum. Hitching, always dangerous, is not a feasible option in the summer due to the lack of traffic in the area. A far wiser option is to form a group and hire a taxi from Aqaba to transport you to and from Wadi Rum (JD15 per taxi). The taxi fare is one-way, but some drivers are willing to do a round-trip with a 2-3 hour stay for JD20. Hotel managers can usually help arrange a taxi ride. Another viable option is to rent a car. **Save Rent-a-Car,** in the Al-Cazar Hotel, rents 4-wheel drive vehicles for JD35 per day. The journey is 90 minutes from Aqaba. **Aquamarina** arranges ½-day trips to Wadi Rum for JD32 including food. Wadi Rum admission is JD1, which includes a complimentary cup of tea or coffee, plus JD4 if you bring in your own car.

> ### A Rockin' Good Time
>
> A fabulous but little known way to enjoy Wadi Rum is by rock climbing. Many Europeans (especially French) arrive each year with their gear for days of climbing in this spectacular region. Experienced climbers will take people with their own equipment on trips for very little money. Inquire at the Rest House for the rock climbing book, containing descriptions of a number of different climbing routes and visitors' accounts of their adventures. If you want to climb but don't have equipment, you can rent some from a Bedouin guide. One day of climbing, including equipment rental and a guide, will probably cost around JD35.

JORDAN

Two tectonic plates split to create the wide desert valley of Rum, and the sunset here is a wonder of darkness and light. At the southern end of the valley is the fort of the Desert Camel Corps, the descendants of the British-trained Arab Legion. The unabashed members of the Desert Patrol are proud to be photographed in their green robes and red *kafias*. When not posing for visitors, they chase smugglers and renegade Bedouin or offer nighttime desert jaunts to beautiful star-gazing areas.

Beyond the ruins of the Nabatean temple and behind the Bedouin tents, the great massif of Jabal Rum shoots up to 1754m. A jeep, or for those with calloused buttocks, a camel, can take you farther through the sheer rust-colored cliffs towering above the mud flats. These whopping slabs of granite and sandstone erupted through the desert floor millions of years ago; their striations in the bays and grottos point toward monumental vistas down the 30km-long *wadi*. The other-worldly lavender mountains cast against the empty sky have inspired the name **Valley of the Moon.** For JD5 a Bedouin will lead you on a camel to a crack in the rocks, the origin of the springs that support all the *wadi's* life. Dark stains point out the conduits carved by the ancient Nabateans to conserve the precious water. You may also be shown **Lawrence's Well,** where T.E. used to doze. The Bedouin can point to many mammoth boulders inscribed with millennia-old Thamudic graffiti.

Only jeeps or camels can continue through Wadi al-Umran to Khirbet Kithara back on the Desert Highway near Aqaba. Camel rides range from JD2 to JD24, depending on the destination. Jeep trips can cost anywhere from JD7 per car to Lawrence's Well to JD40 to the Rock Bridge. Arrange it with the tourism official in the camp in the middle of Wadi Rum when you arrive. You can often gather up a group to share a jeep at the Rest House. A full day jeep itinerary, with climbs through narrow *siqs* and hikes up sand dunes, can go for JD28. Try to plan your visit at dusk, when the *wadi* explodes with color.

As in Petra, the **Government Rest House** ruins the natural splendor with overpriced tourist trinkets, food, and drink (lunch JD5, water JD1). Visitors staying overnight can sleep on the rest house roof (JD2). A large tent beside the rest house is often the site of traditional Bedouin music and singing in the evenings. Bedouin may invite you to spend the night in more remote locations. Toys for the Bedouin kids make good barter items in exchange for lodging. There are some small Bedouin restaurants near the Rest House with cheaper prices.

# North of Amman

## ■ Salt السلط

Salt (pronounced like "sulk" but with a "t") was the thriving administrative center of the surrounding area during Ottoman rule. In the late 1920s, it seemed a likely choice for the capital of the new mandate of Transjordan; however, it was bypassed for the smaller but centrally located village of Amman. Because of that lost opportunity, Salt is better known today for its history than its present-day prowess—and its history is pretty impressive.

In the second half of the 19th century, Saltis built Jordan's first hospital and its first modern church. In 1925, Salt established Jordan's first secondary school, of which almost all of Jordan's ministers and prime ministers are alums.

A church destroyed during a war in Ottoman times was picked apart and used to construct local houses: look for whole sections of archways that are now cozily integrated into the yellow homes that date from that time. The Ottoman barracks, still intact, were built over a 13th-century fortress that was destroyed to prevent its capture by Crusaders. Salt is also known for its large Christian community, and church towers pepper the hillsides. If the adventurous spirit moves you, wander downhill from the bus station into **Wadi Sh'eib.** Look for the natural streams bubbling spontaneously out of the ground, both breaking through the pavement of the main road and off the beaten track. These can be refreshing to dip your hands into, but are unsafe to drink. Unexplored caves and abandoned stone houses dot the *wadi*, and numerous dirt paths lead you further down. Pink flowers and fruit trees line the narrow stream that winds through the bottom of the valley. Leave a trail of bread crumbs, or you might not find your way back.

The famous **Abu Jaber** house, located across from the Jordan Gulf bank, was constructed in 1894. Even if you can't get in to see the ceilings covered with Italian frescoes, a street-side perspective is enough to appreciate why this building is one of Jordan's finest architectural works. The focal point of Salt is the mosque on **Jabal Yushah,** which, according to Muslim legend, covers the site of the tomb of the prophet Hosea (Yushah), and it has been compared by locals to the famous Al Husseini mosque in downtown Amman.

To get to the **Salt Archaeological Museum** (tel. 555 653), go left where the road splits uphill from the bus station. On the right hand side, you'll see a white building with red stone around the outside, with a rather obscure blue sign on the second floor. It consists of two rooms with lots of coins, pottery, and jewelry dating from the Chalcolithic period (4000BCE) to the Islamic period (1516CE). Open Sat.-Thurs. 8am-4 or 5pm. Free. The **Salt Folklore Museum** (tel. 553 345) is off the main road. Walking uphill, you'll see the Islamic Bank on your left. At the end of the stone walkway to the right is the pink building housing the museum. A quick look reveals Saltis of old in traditional dress carrying out life's day to day tasks. Open Sat.-Thurs. 8am-5pm. Free.

Taking a **minibus** up Wadi Sh'eib is the most dramatic approach to Salt. Lush, terraced farmlands and eucalyptus groves tumble down the *wadi* to the southwest of town, descending to Shuneh Nimrin (South Shuneh) on the busy route from Amman to the King Hussein/Allenby Bridge (Jordan Valley Highway). From Amman, corner an Abdali bus driver to find the minibus going to Salt (30min., 175fils). A **service taxi** from Abdali costs 300fils. Salt has no hotels, and its tourist office across the hall from the Archaeological Museum is empty more often than not.

Delicious food is easy to find: for the best kebabs known to exist anywhere, eat at **Al Amad's,** established by Radi Al-Amad in 1927 and inherited by his son, who runs it today. If you ask (and even if you don't), he'll show you his guest book which has been signed by the head of the Central Bank and other dignitaries, all of whom ate there as students in Salt. There is also detailed documentation of what they ate. For good hummus, fuul, and the like, the **Canam Restaurant** (down past the Archaeological Museum) is a good bet, and cheap (hummus, mezze, and tea, 300fils). Finish up with some freshly-baked pastries at **Al Habiba,** up the road from Canam. Especially good is the *warbaht*. If you can only afford minimal food, go here. It may not be the healthiest dinner, but the sweets are too honey-fresh to pass up. The **post office** (tel. 553 475 or 556 276) is located uphill on the main road, a good 10min. walk from the circle at the bottom (open Sat.-Thurs. 7:30am-7pm). As in every town in Jordan, in case of **emergency,** dial 192. For a **medical emergency,** dial 193. Salt's **telephone code** is 05.

# ■ Jerash جرش

Stumbled upon by German traveler Ulrich Seetzen in 1806, Jerash is perhaps the most extensive provincial Roman city still in existence. Dubbed Gerasa in ancient times, this city was a member of the famed Decapolis, a loose association of trading cities allied with Rome (see **The Ancient Levant,** p.44). Because of Jerash's isolation in a remote valley, Jerash survived long after the other nine cities were destroyed.

Unlike the other great classical cities in this area, Jerash is typically Roman in design. The city's builders trampled over earlier settlements, so little evidence of pre-Roman days remains. Inscriptions calling the town Antioch reveal that the Seleucid king of that name had a prominent outpost here, but Jerash entered its golden age only after its conquest by the Roman general Pompey in 63 BCE. Over the following three centuries, Jerash experienced a period of prosperity rivaled only by the city's tourist boom of the 1990s. Granite was brought from as far away as Aswan and old temples were razed and rebuilt according to the latest architectural fads. The Emperor Trajan annexed the surrounding Nabatean lands in 106 CE and built a highway from Damascus to Aqaba that passed through Jerash. Hadrian visited the town in 129; the Triumphal Arch built for the occasion still stands. The town was converted to Christianity and had a bishop by the mid-4th century.

Following the destruction of the Syrian trading center at Palmyra and the decline of the Nabatean kingdom, trade routes shifted from the desert to the sea. Frantic construction continued through the 6th century, but without their former wealth, the citizens of Jerash could only replace the older monuments with flashy, inferior structures which were plundered by invading Persians in 635 CE. The great earthquake of 747 left few remnants for the Muslim Arabs, who by then controlled the city. The Crusaders described Jerash as uninhabited, and it remained abandoned until its rediscovery in the 19th century. After the invasion of the Ottoman Turks, Circassians built the modern town in what was once the main residential area.

## PRACTICAL INFORMATION

Jerash will dazzle you along the 1km walk from the South Gate down the Street of Columns to the North Gate. The tiny Chrysoras (Golden) River separates the ancient ruins on the western bank from the new town on the eastern bank. The **Visitors Information Center** (tel. 451 272; open daily 7:30 or 8am-6:30pm in summer, 8am-5pm in winter) is on the left of the main road entering the city from the south, about 400m north of the Triumphal Arch. Groups can hire guides for JD4 (plus a JD1 tip). Booklets including maps and explanations of the sights invite leisurely exploration and range in price from JD1 to JD6. There is a **post office** in town, behind the bus station (open daily 8am-7pm).

**Buses** and **service taxis** leave from the Jerash **bus station** on the western edge of the new city in front of the mosque. Buses to Amman's Abdali Station cost 300fils (350fils with A/C), and the ride takes about an hour (bus to Ajlun 250fils, to Irbid 320fils). *Service* generally cost 50% more than buses. Public transportation shuts down at around 7pm in summer and 5pm in winter. Hitchers to Amman, Dibbin, or Ajlun are known to walk south about 1km from the visitors center to the intersection with Highway 20. Turning right (west) leads to Ajlun and Dibbin National Park. Going straight takes you to Amman, and the main road continues through town, north to Irbid. Buses pass frequently towards Amman and are reportedly easy to flag. Hitchers stand back from the road as they signal the bus; drivers consider time and speed infinitely more important than toes.

## ACCOMMODATIONS AND FOOD

Because Jerash is such an easy daytrip from Amman, there are no accommodations in the town. You might consider either camping at Dibbin National Park, about 8km away, or taking a room at the Dibbin Rest House (see **Near Jerash,** p.512). At the **Jerash Rest House** (tel. 451 146), stomping ground for tour bus groups, soft drinks are a rip-off at 600fils and bottled water goes for a throat-drying JD1. At the **Al Khayyam Restaurant,** just past the visitor's center on the main road, JD3.500 buys bread, salad, and grilled meat (open daily 8am-10 or 11pm). Street stands surrounding the bus station sell cheap falafel and *fuul* (100-200fils). Houston-native Tony will be glad to chat with you over a burger, fries, and fresh-squeezed juice (all for JD3) at his newly opened **American Café,** across the street from the visitor's center.

## SIGHTS AND ENTERTAINMENT

Jerash's captivating claim to fame are its extensive ruins, even though the best parts are probably lying beneath your feet (over 90% of ancient Jerash awaits excavation).

The ruins are open daily 7am-7pm in summer, 7am-5pm in winter (admission JD2). The ruins are described from south to north.

Begin at the **Triumphal (Hadrianic) Arch,** 400m south of the ancient walls, built to honor the arrival of Emperor Hadrian in the winter of 129 CE. Examine the spare parts strewn about to get a feel for how big the structure once was. After your own majestic passage through the arch, you'll come upon the remaining stables and spectator seats of the **Hippodrome.** As the name implies, this arena hosted chariot races and other contests of skill for the amusement of up to 15,000 spectators. Continuing north, you'll see the **visitor's center** and enter the site proper.

Entering the **South Gate,** you arrive at the **Forum** or **Oval Plaza,** the most photographed part of the city. The Ionic Columns ringing the plaza have been reconstructed to first century CE form. The central podium was once topped with a statue. The Forum opens onto a main street intersected by two avenues.

A footpath to the left in the forum leads to the astounding **South Theater.** Greek doodles reveal that 4000 of Jerash's wealthiest citizens could once reserve seats here. The two-story backstage, furnished with curtains and marble statues, dominated the setting. Find "the spot," the groove in the floor of the stage where your voice will carry and magnify to several times its regular volume If you can't find it, look for the group of tourists belting out Barry Manilow—they're on top of it. The circular niches below the first row of seats are ancient telephones—speak into any one and your voice will be audible at any other "receiver." Stand in the top row of the theater's seats to get the best view of the ruined **Temple of Zeus,** which lies between the theater and the South Gate. Although only its outer walls remain, archaeologists swear that Zeus had himself a glorious temple in the late 2nd century CE and renovation efforts are currently underway.

The **Cardo** (Street of Columns) runs from the forum to the North Gate. Its 260 pairs of columns are Corinthian replacements for earlier Ionic columns and were once capped by aqueducts carrying water throughout the ancient city. The huge paving stones show grooves worn by chariots. The holes in the floor drained rainwater into a sophisticated sewer system. Massive sidewalk coverings protected pedestrians from the sun, but tragically only traces of these metropolitan parasols remain. The **Jerash Antiquities Museum** is on the right, halfway down the pillared promenade. Tall display cases mounted along the walls show neatly arranged artifacts from the Neolithic to the Ottoman periods. Coins, jewelry, theater "tickets" made of stone, and other household items highlight the museum's small collection (open Sat.-Thurs. 7:30am-5pm, closed on holidays; free). Opposite from the museum is the city's **Agora,** a newly restored meeting place with a central fountain. In its heyday, this small area served as the city's meat and fish market.

The main avenue's first intersection is named the **South Tetrapylon** after its four huge slabs of stone once accompanied by pillars and a large statue. Going west (left) at the cross street brings you to the remains of a 7th century Umayyad building. Back on the Cardo, look for frescoes depicting lizards, cats, and turtles on the floor of the 4th-century **Cathedral** to the left, unsanctimoniously built from, and on top of, the remains of a 2nd-century temple to Dionysus. Next along the street is the **Nymphaeum,** built in 191CE. Intricate stone carvings and the incorporation of marble and gypsum indicate that this two-story fountain was assembled at the height of Jerash's fortune, and was later used in an annual reenactment of the Miracle at Cana, where Jesus changed water into wine (John 2:1-11).

To the west, behind the Cathedral and Nymphaeum, lie a series of Byzantine churches built in the 6th century CE. One especially worth the walk is the **Church of St. Cosmos & St. Damius,** dedicated to a twin brother team of doctors who treated their patients for free. The church's mosaic floor, depicting the do-gooders surrounded by animals, is one of the few pieces of art to survive Umayyad Caliph Yazid II's attempt to destroy all "images and likenesses" of God's creations in 720CE.

The ominous columned structure at the top of the hill to the left of the Cardo is the **Temple of Artemis.** Dedicated to the patron Goddess of Jerash, the daughter of Zeus and the sister of Apollo, Artemis held special significance throughout the Decapolis,

JORDAN

once the stomping ground of similar goddesses Ishtar and Anat. Her temple consisted of a Great Gate, two flights of stairs leading up to a shrine-topped podium, and a courtyard surrounded by giant pillars. Opposite the Temple of Artemis are the **West Baths,** including a 2nd-century cold bath *(frigidarium),* warm bath *(tepidarium),* hot bath *(caldarium),* and changing rooms. The **East Baths,** across the *wadi* by the bus station, were built on an even larger, more majestic scale. Farther north along the Cardo, past the **North Tetrapylon** is the **North Theater** (under renovation) and what remains of the **North Gate.**

Occasionally, during the summer months (April-October), there is an hour-long **sound and light show** among the ruins, with special JETT buses to get you there. Check with the JETT office in Amman (tel. 664 146) for details.

Jerash is undergoing eternal restoration as the government attempts to raise the city's profile. The **Jerash Festival,** instituted in 1981, takes place under royal patronage every summer beginning in the second half of July. Check with the Jerash Festival office in Amman for details (tel. 675 199) or see *The Jordan Times* for complete coverage. The South Theater and Artemis Steps provide a dramatic setting for musical, theatrical, and dance groups from all over the world. Shows range from the Gary Burton Quintet to the Royal Jordan Orchestra to the Azerbaijan State Ballet to modern interpretations of *The Taming of the Shrew.* Recently, more Jordanian artists, such as renowned composer Yousef Khaso, are appearing on the schedule along with international performers. The famous Lebanese singer, Majdah ar-Roumi, has also delighted the crowds at the theater more than once. Ticket prices vary; if you arrive after 7:30pm you won't have to pay the JD2 entrance fee to the ruins.

**Transport** to and from Jerash during the festival is chaotic. The best option is to form a group and share a private taxi. *Service* are crowded. Hitchhikers have trouble finding rides, especially if they leave after 4pm. Coming home at about 10pm is less of a problem. Hithchhikers still report difficulty beacause most cars are full.

## ■ Near Jerash

The Aleppo pines and oaks of the fertile woodland are a remarkable sight in this desert country. Located in the hills 10km southwest of Jerash and 65km north of Amman, the **Dibbin National Park** encompasses some 20km of forest stretching south from the town of the same name.

On the old road to Jerash near Dibbin village is the **Dibbin Rest House** (tel. (04) 452 413; fax 813 246, Amman), offering semi-budget accommodations. The access road leaves the Amman-Jerash Highway about 2km south of Jerash; look for the signs. You'll have to take a car, as neither buses nor *service* access the park. Another option is the bus from Jerash to the nearby village of Dibbin; the hike from the village to the park is about 2km uphill. For nature-lovers, the park offers ideal campgrounds, free of charge and equally free of facilities.

## ■ Ajlun عجلون

Atop the highest peak overlooking Ajlun is **Qal'at ar-Rabadh,** a huge Arab castle built in 1184 by Azz ad-Din Ausama, nephew of and commander under Salah ad-Din. This is the castle you dreamed about visiting when you were young: the ultimate field trip that your lame 5th grade teacher could never plan. Built to contain the progress of the Latin kingdom in Transjordan, the original building was erected to outdo the Castle of Belvoir on Lake Tiberias. With its four corner towers and seven floors, Qal'at ar-Rabadh closely resembles the castle in Karak, south of Amman. Filled with secret passages, winding, crumbly staircases, and dark corridors, the castle begs visitors to let their imaginations run wild.

The castle controlled a long stretch of Jordan's northern valley, protecting communication lines between Jordan and Syria. Crusader knights spent decades unsuccessfully trying to capture the castle and nearby village. The name Kafranjah, a town in the area famous for its olive trees, suggests that the Franks *(Franjis* in Arabic) spent some time here—if only as prisoners. After the Crusader threat dissipated, Salah ad-Din used the castle as a base from which to work nearby iron mines and to transmit messages by beacon and pigeon; from Baghdad to Cairo, day or night, the relay could be made in 12 hours. During the Ottoman period, 50 soldiers were stationed in the castle at all times, and during the first quarter of the 17th century, Prince Fakhr ad-Din al-Ma'ni II, a relative of Salah ad-Din, used it during his fight against Ahmad ibn Tabay. The castle was mostly uninhabited after that time until the Swiss explorer Burkhardt (better known for discovering the lost city of Petra that same year) found the Barakat family living there in 1812. Two major earthquakes in 1837 and 1927 did the damage that the Crusades never could. While the castle is very good condition today, parts of it are still under restoration by the Department of Antiquities (open daily 8am-6 or 7pm, until 5pm in winter; admission JD1).

## ORIENTATION AND PRACTICAL INFORMATION

Ajlun lies a hilly 24km west of Jerash, and is also an easy hitch or bus ride from Amman (73km) or Irbid (88km). **Service** from Amman take 75 minutes (750fils); the **bus** is slower but cheaper (450fils). Both will drop you off a few streets down from the main circle. Simply follow the sounds of honking cars and the smells of roasting *shawerma* to the center of town. From the circle, the castle is four km up a gently sloping road. You can catch a taxi for JD1 round-trip or a minibus for 100fils. Especially on Fridays, public transportation can be slow—start walking uphill and flag the bus on the way. Generous passers-by may also give you a lift if you're looking tired (panting often helps). Ajlun's **post office** is located on Amman St., to your right as you enter the town, a few hundred yards from the circle (open Sat.-Thurs. 7:30am-7pm, closed Fri. and holidays). Exchange money at the **Arab Bank,** next door to the post office, the **Housing Bank,** on the center circle, or the **Bank of Jordan,** on Irbid St. uphill from the circle (all three open Sat.-Thurs. 8am-12:30pm, closed Fri. and holidays).

## ACCOMMODATIONS AND FOOD

There are two hotels in Ajlun, both within short walking distance of the castle along the road to town. The **Ar-Rabad Castle Hotel** (tel. 462 202) is the better deal for the dinar—singles are JD24, doubles JD32 including breakfast. The new, bright rooms come with a TV, a phone, a patio with chairs for watching spectacular sunsets, and immaculate bathrooms. The **Ajlun Hotel** (tel./fax 462 524), closer to the castle, offers dusty, simple singles and doubles with breakfast at identical prices to the Ar-Rabad Castle. The restaurants of both hotels offer a view with a side order of lunch for a whopping JD4-5, but the Ar-Rabad sports an outdoor café with a fountain and umbrellas, while the Ajlun Restaurant looks like a fully-enclosed ski chalet. The view's affordable if you stick to the 300-400fils *mezze* plates. Those who prefer to fill their bellies rather than their eyes should stop in at the **Green Mountain Restaurant** (open daily 6:30am-8:30pm) in Ajlun's center circle. A half-chicken clucks 800fils, *kabab* JD1.100, and hummus and *fuul* 220fils; 650fils buys a complete meal including rice, meat, and a vegetable. In front of the Green Mountain is a sprawling outdoor café with leafy trellises and red umbrellas: the **Abu al-Izz Restaurant** (tel. 462 625) offers the usual *kabab*, hummus, and fries for slightly higher prices than the Green Mountain, but with more ambience.

# ■ Irbid اربد

Much like Amman, Irbid (1hr. north of Jerash) is an industrial center which has overwhelmed the site of its ancient predecessor, in this case the Decapolis city Dion. But while expansion in Amman has left some areas uninhabited, Irbid's narrow streets are stuffed with merchants, kung fu theaters, and taxis. The fluorescent maze of shops and restaurants is also the home of Yarmouk University, one of the biggest in Jordan. The university gives parts of Irbid the feel of a college town, but despite its student-oriented charm, there is little to do here other than eat heartily and plan your trip to Umm Qeis, Al Himma, Umm al-Jimal, or Damascus.

## ORIENTATION AND PRACTICAL INFORMATION

Facing downhill from the **main circle** (next to the Al Ameen Hotel), the town **mosque** and **market** are located down the street to the right. The Hotel al-Wehdeh al-Arabiyyeh, Bank of Jordan, and Abu Bakr Hotel are up the street to the left. To get to the post office, walk downhill 10m and take the first left onto Baghdad St. after the Al Ameen Hotel. On your right you will see another big circle with a monument. Continue down Baghdad St. past the Omayed Hotel.

Irbid's **post office** is open Sat.-Thurs. 7:30am-7pm, Fri. and holidays 8am-1:30pm. The **telephone office,** with international phone and telex services, is open Sat.-Thurs. 7:30am-10pm; hours vary Fri. and holidays. **ANZ Grindlay's Bank,** across from the post office, exchanges cash and traveler's checks (open Sat.-Thurs. 8am-12:30pm). **DHL** services are available at the **Aramex International Courier** located on Baghdad St. downtown, across from the Omayed Hotel (open Sat.-Thurs. 8am-6pm, Fri. 9am-noon). Irbid's **telephone code** is 02.

Many travelers hitch to Irbid via Jerash, but the quickest and generally the safest way to the city from Amman is by the **Arabella** or **Hijazi** bus companies (1½hr., 600fils, with A/C 825fils). Taxis from the private bus station to the main circle downtown cost 500fils. **Minibuses** from Amman, Jerash, and Ajlun are cheaper but slower; they drop you off at Irbid's New South Station, from which you can take a service taxi downtown (60fils). Taxis to Yarmouk cost 700fils (JD1 at night).

To leave Irbid, head back to the New South Station (ask for *Bas ila Amman*). From here a minibus runs regularly to Ajlun (250fils) and to Amman's Abdali Station (500fils). The last buses depart for Amman at about 8pm (in winter sometimes as early as 5pm). *Service* also leave New South Station for Syria. The trip to Damascus costs JD4 and takes 4-5hr., depending on border crossings. You may have to pay as much as JD6 if the *service* isn't full. Bring your visa for the border crossing(see **Visas and Visa Extensions,** p.9).

For travel within the city, *service* run regularly from downtown to Yarmouk and to North Station. *Service* to Yarmouk (70fils) leave from Abu Bakr as-Siaddiqa St. Cross the street at the Omayed Hotel and take a left down one of the small streets off of Baghdad St. The *service* line up in front of the Chicken Palace Restaurant. For a *service* to North Station, take the first left after the Omayed Hotel facing toward the post office. Continue straight, across the street, until the road ends at a diagonal intersection. Turn right, walk for about 5min., then go right again when you see the big purple sign on your left. *Service* line up here and will drop you off one street up from the station. Buses to Al Himma and Umm Qeis leave often from North Station.

## ACCOMMODATIONS

**Al-Ameen al-Kabir Hotel** (tel. 242 384), on Midan Malek Abdallah St., one block from the city center and the Ministry of Antiquities building. Pleasant, breezy rooms with beautiful bedspreads and exceptionally courteous management; no fans. Singles JD5, doubles JD6. Try to bargain in off-season. Hot shower 500fils.

**Abu Bakr Hotel** (tel. 242 695), around the corner from the Al Ameen on Wasfi Et-Tal St. in the same building as the Bank of Jordan. Orange curtains, fans, and free flip-flops grace the quiet rooms upstairs. Downstairs, the lobby is a communal dorm room where you'll find snoozing locals. Earthy bathrooms. Singles JD5, doubles JD6. Bed in the communal room JD2. Free showers.

**Hotel Al-Wehdeh Al-Arabiah** (tel. 242 083), at the top of Al Jaish St., two blocks up from Abu Bakr. Dark but decent place (check out the disco ball in the foyer's tropical tree). Friendly management is very accommodating and willing to bargain. Singles JD4, doubles JD6.500. Extra bed JD2, hot shower 500fils.

**Omayed Hotel** (tel./fax 245 955) on Baghdad St., one block down from the post office. Luxury with a capital "L." All rooms have television, telephone, fan, and private bathroom. Receptionist Ahmad Mansour can tell you how to get anywhere you want to go. Single JD14. Doubles JD18 plus 10% tax.

## FOOD

The colorful streets around Yarmouk University are lined with wall-to-wall restaurants to tempt any palate. Around dinner time, everyone from students to local fortune-tellers crowd the outdoor cafés for a bit of food and a chance to argue about politics. If you've been unimpressed with falafel and *shawerma* so far, give the food stands on the main street a second chance. Fresh, hot, with no spice spared, the cheapest food in Irbid is some of Jordan's best (falafel sandwich 120fils, *shawerma* 200-250fils). The local market, held around the mosque visible from the main circle, is a great place to get lost while stocking up on fresh fruit (including the best peaches in the world), bread, and sweets. For a sit-down meal, the local favorite is the **Den of Happiness Restaurant** (*mat'am 'ush al-hana'a*). The big red and yellow sign is in Arabic only, but look for tables across from the mosque. The food is cheap and plentiful, and the menu includes hummus and cheese omelettes for 350fils.

**Assufara Restaurant,** on the main circle, offers reasonable local fare and drinks on sprawling patios. Entrees JD1.2-2. Open daily 8am-1am, 11pm in winter.
**Italian Café Amon,** next door, serves spaghetti for 750fils.
**Yarmouk University Cafeteria,** accessible at the North Gate. Go straight, then take a right just before the big sculpture. Look for a little round birdhouse chalet crammed with studious types inhaling huge meals for under JD1. Open 8am-8pm.
**Andalus Cafeteria,** by the post office. Good falafel and *shawerma* (120-220fils), and fresh juices for 500fils. A swell lunchtime hangout for local shopkeepers.
**Palestine Restaurant,** on Palestine St. past the main circle. The late-night hummus and *fuul* joint where mostly male customers play backgammon and dine.

## SIGHTS

The **Museum of Jordanian Heritage,** providing a narrative of Jordan's history, from prehistoric times to the present, is the best and biggest museum in Jordan and should not be missed. Appealing to a more select, Batesian crowd, the tiny **Natural History Museum** houses many stuffed birds and animals indigenous to Jordan. The area's moving wildlife is more interesting. Both museums are free and are open Wed.-Mon. 8am-5pm, 8am-3pm in June and July. To get to the Museum of Jordanian Heritage, enter the Yarmouk campus at the North Gate. Turn right at the second white monument and the museum will be on your left. The stationary birds and animals are to the left of the same white monument.

# ■ Near Irbid

## UMM QEIS أم قيس

Umm Qeis was the Biblical Gadara, where Jesus exorcised a sinner's demons into a herd of pigs which stampeded down the hill to drown in the Sea of Galilee. This thriving city was one of the ten cities of the Decapolis, founded by Pompey after his conquest of Syria and Palestine in 64 BCE. Once a resort for Romans vacationing at Al Himma's therapeutic hot springs, Umm Qeis was renowned for its theaters, writers, philosophers, and perhaps most of all, its legendary orgiastic extravagances. The epitaph on the grave of Germanus the Roman in the courtyard of the museum says it all: "To you I say, passerby, as you are now, I was. And as I am, you will soon be, so enjoy your mortal life."

The city was probably founded in the 4th century BCE. Its name comes from a Semitic word meaning "stronghold," reflecting the city's role as a fortified border town guarding the crucial land routes between southern Syria and northern Palestine. Earthquakes and plagues in the 7th and 8th centuries left Umm Qeis nothing more than a hamlet. Most of the standing structures date from the 2nd century CE.

Before paying the entrance fee (JD1), step inside the Roman tombs located just outside the guard's booth. The first one is **Germanus' Tomb,** the second **Modestos' Tomb.** The heavy stone doors with ornate carving are still very much intact, even though these tombs were used as barracks by the Jordanian army in the 1967 war.

After paying the entrance fee, follow the path past the **Eastern Necropolis,** a cemetery just outside the city walls where the Greco-Roman and later Arab residents of Umm Qeis were interred. On your left will be the entrance to the Roman **aqueduct,** which brought water from Ezra in Syria. Just before the aqueduct, the **Temple of Zeus** is being restored. The mass of Ottoman Buildings on the top of the hill covers what used to be an **acropolis** and the most important quarter of ancient Gadara.

Today, the two-story white limestone **museum** is the main building of interest. Check out **Tyche,** the Goddess of Gadara, who is missing a few important appendages but still holds onto her fruit-filled cornucopia, a symbol of fertility (open daily 8am-5pm; free). The white marble statue served as a sharp contrast to the black basalt **West Theater** in which it was once enshrined. In front of the museum, the shape of the **North Theater,** once accommodating 5000, is apparent. The Ottomans took the actual stones of the structure to build the village on the hill, but German archaeologists are attempting to reconstruct parts of it.

Before the west theater, to the left of the **Decumanus Maximus** (main road), lies the **Basilica Terrace.** Its black basalt Corinthian columns surround the octagonally arranged white limestone columns of what was a Byzantine church.

Farther along the main road, built into the perimeter of the Basilica Terrace, are fourteen barrel-vaulted rooms that used to be street-front shops. Recent reconstruction has the shops looking as they did in Roman times. A bit farther down the road lie the weed-embraced **East Baths** and **Nymphaeum.** At the end of the Decumanus sits a circular building of basalt rocks and, adjacent to that, an **underground mausoleum,** the only completely intact structure from Ancient Gadara. Holes in the ceiling of the mausoleum were used to drop food to the spirits of the interred, and now provide enough light to peek through the locked gate into the underground caverns. The main burial room, with six chambers on each of three walls, was expanded and reused by the Christian Byzantines.

The **Um-Qeis Hotel** (tel. 217 210, ext. 63) is about 100m up the hill from the ruins, on the left. Rooms (JD6 per person without bathroom, JD10 with bathroom) are new, freshly-painted, and sparsely furnished. Breakfast here will run you JD3, dinner JD4. The beautiful **Umm Qeis Rest House** (tel. 217 210, ext. 59), a joint project of the Department of Antiquities and the American Center for Oriental Research, serves overpriced refreshments to desperate travelers and overlooks the Golan Heights and the Sea of Galilee. For JD2-3 you can eat your fill of soup, salad, or pasta; an ice cream drips for 750fils. Traditional Middle Eastern food is available at a few cheap places along the main road before the ruins. There is a **post/phone office** along the main road through modern Umm Qeis (open 7:30am-7:30pm, call 217 210 for emergency access). If the door is locked, knock with aplomb. You can get stamps, post cards, and loads of invaluable historical information from Abd as-Salam at the reasonably-priced **Umm Qeis Gift Shop** (tel. 217 210, ext. 68). Start your tour of Umm Qeis here. Credit cards are accepted at the hotel, rest house, and gift shop.

## AL HIMMA الحمة

From Umm Qeis, you can catch a minibus from Irbid headed to Al Himma, 10km away. Just past Umm Qeis, a soldier will check your **passport** and may want to search your bags. Beyond the military roadblock gapes the valley of the Yarmouk River. Looming quietly across the wide green vale are the glorious Golan Heights.

After an exquisite descent, the bus will drop you at the entrance to the **mineral springs** complex. Swimming costs JD1, JD4.200 if you reserve a private bath with slightly cooler water (open daily 6am-8pm). Two-hour shifts alternate between the sexes (men first, 6-8am). After 8pm, you can reserve the mineral springs complex for JD7.5 per hour—if you don't mind the stench of sulphur. Women are not allowed to swim in the cool outdoor pool, and will be steered firmly towards the fully-enclosed baths, which can get uncomfortably steamy/smelly in summer. Groups of men and women may use a new, secluded outdoor pool for around JD8 per hour (price negotiable). The **Hotel al-Hamma al-Urdun** (tel. (02) 217 203), built like a staircase around the springs, has no-frills rooms, some of which are getting moldy from disuse (doubles JD8, triples JD10, "chalet triples" with unpredictable fridge and rusty gas cooker JD25). The **Jordanian Hammi Restaurant** (tel. (02) 217 203) on the east side of the complex serves *kabab* for an outlandish JD1.800 and juice for 500fils. Pack a lunch or head back to Umm Qeis for affordable snacks. **Buses** travel to Umm Qeis (200fils) and Al Himma (300fils) from Irbid's North Station. The last minibus to Umm Qeis/Al Himma leaves at 5:30 or 6pm.

JORDAN

# SYRIA سوريا

US$1=41.95 Syrian pounds (S£)      S£100=US$2.38
CDN$1=S£30.55                       S£100=CDN$3.27
UK£1=S£64.94                        S£100=UK£1.54
IR£1=S£67.35                        S£100=IR£1.48
AUS$1=S£32.83                       S£100=AUS$3.04
NZ$1=S£28.92                        S£100=NZ$3.45
SAR1=S£9.22                         S£100=SAR10.85

> For important information on travel in general and some specifics on Syria, see the Essentials section of this book. Syria's **international phone code** is 963.

"It can rightly be stated, then, that every cultured man belongs to two nations; his own, and Syria." So claims the Syrian Ministry of Tourism, and they're not entirely off the mark. Language, writing, art, architecture, crafts—all of them can be found in their earliest forms somewhere in the treasure chest of Syria's archaeological wealth. Though Syria may be known for ancient ruins and on-going disputes with Israel, recent peace negotiations and a loosening of the military regime indicate a bright future.

Traveling in Syria is not as difficult as you might think: public transportation is abundant, American Express has set foot in these parts, and the Syrians are very hospitable. Do your best, however, to avoid dealing with the government bureaucracy. Often staffed by recruits serving their 2½-year military commitment, officers tend to be inefficient and unhelpful. Be sure to get your visa from your home country. Trying to obtain one on foreign soil involves letters of recommendation from your embassy and as much luck as hassle.

# ONCE THERE

## ■ Getting Around

**Taxis**  Private **taxis** are yellow, easy to use, and relatively cheap. If they don't find you first, you can easily grab one in any city, although their ranks thin after 9pm. Most taxis have meters; drivers don't seem to be aware of this fact. This is not to say that you'll be cheated—negotiate beforehand for a fair price. For travelers with little knowledge of Syria or of Arabic, private taxis are the best option for local transportation. **Service taxis** are less expensive and come in the form of white minivans, but are more difficult to use. They run only within cities, are labeled in Arabic only, usually depart only when full, and drop you off at weird places.

**Buses**  **Karnak** (tel. (11) 222 14 92) is the government-run bus company. Routes go everywhere and fares are low. Buses tend to be ramshackle wrecks, but they sometimes even depart on schedule. Reservations are required and can be made at bus stations in the cities. **Pullman** buses are even worse than Karnak, though Karnak constantly strives to catch up. Over 50 **private bus companies** now operate in Syria; they have ship-shape coaches and competitive prices. Reservations are a good idea for these buses as well. Usually, Karnak, Pullman, and private buses leave from different stops in a city. Make sure you're at the right one. All tickets must be bought at the stations; drivers do not handle money. Gray minibuses, called **micros,** compete with buses, but they share the disadvantages of *service* travel for uninitiated visitors.

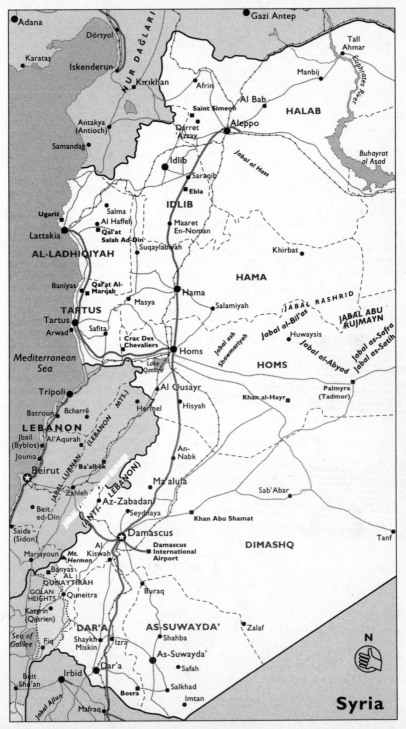

Syria

**Trains** Strictly speaking, trains connect cities in Syria. Frankly speaking, roller skates would serve you better. Trains are mind-numbingly slow, crowded, and dirty; and in most places they drop you off about 30km out of town. Use the buses.

**Cars** If for some reason buses and *micros* aren't good enough for you, you can rent a car at a few places in Damascus for US$37 per day plus mileage; unlimited mileage US$59 per day. Special weekly rates are only slightly cheaper. All the sights you could possibly want to see are easily accessible via cheap public transportation; the freedom of having a car is not worth the expense. In Syria, people drive on the right side of the road.

**Hitchhiking** Thumbing is neither possible nor necessary in Syria (if you stand by the side of a road, a *micro* will eventually pick you up and only cost you pocket change). Also, don't be too surprised if the friendly neighborhood police haul you in for questioning. *Let's Go* does not recommend hitchhiking—especially in Syria.

## ■ Useful Addresses

There are tourist information offices in all major Syrian cities. In Damascus, the office is at 29 Mai Ave. (tel. (11) 222 23 88). In Aleppo, there's a branch on Al Ma'ari St. (tel. (21) 221 220). The Ministry of Tour'sm, at the Hijaz rail station in Damascus, has free maps and information on almost any place in Syria. You might also contact the American Cultural Center in Damascus, 87 Rue Ata Ayoubi (tel. (11) 333 84 13). Travelers visiting Syria for more than two weeks must register with the police and apply for a visa extension (see **Damascus: Practical Information,** p. 530).

## ■ Health & Medicine

There are lots of hospitals and health-care professionals in Syria, especially in Damascus, and many doctors speak English; most received their training in Germany, England, or America, so the level of care is usually better than one would expect. However, hospitals expect immediate cash payment. It's unlikely that your health coverage extends to Syria. Contact your embassy or consulate for referral to an English-speaking doctor, a reputable hospital, or in-house assistance. A referral and appointment are a good idea. At least one pharmacy is open 24 hours in every Syrian city. Signs posted on pharmacy doors list (in Arabic) those pharmacies on duty.

Street food in Syria, especially in Damascus, should be approached with extreme caution. Carry diarrhea antidote with you. Toilet paper comes in handy too—only expensive hotels and restaurants provide it for you.

## ■ Money Matters

**Currency and Exchange** The basic unit of currency in Syria is the Syrian pound, also called the lira, abbreviated S£. Each pound is divided further into 100 piasters (*qirsh*, plural *qurush*), abbreviated pt. Paper currency comes in denominations of S£500, 100, 50, 25, 10, 5, and 1. Coins come in 100, 50, 25, 10, and 5pt values. There are as many exchange rates in Syria as bus companies: businesspeople get one rate, officials another, and light-haired tourists get a very special rate all their own. You can change money at the Commercial Bank of Syria, which has exchange desks in most of the major hotels, at the rates listed above. Hotels are supposed to exchange dollars at the rate of S£11.20 per US$1, so room prices listed in dollars may be up to four times as high as what you might expect. Try to pay in S£ whenever possible. Some hotels will unofficially change money for you at the black market rate, only marginally better than the bank rate. You should decide if the extra S£1-4 per US$1 are worth the risk of jail (entrapment is not uncommon).

Once in Syria, you can change money at any Commercial Bank branch. If you are in Cairo or Amman before coming to Syria, you can exchange money there for Syrian pounds at the free market rate, a bit higher than the official rate. In previous years, visitors were required to change US$100 into pounds (at the rip-off hotel rate) upon entering the country; this is no longer the case. You may bring as much foreign currency into the country as you like but may not leave with more than you bring in. Amounts up to US$5000 do not have to be declared.

It's a good idea to carry U.S. currency with you, both in cash (handy for some smaller transactions) and in traveler's checks, because many hotels only accept US$. However, transactions using US$ except to pay a hotel bill are illegal.

**Business Hours** In Syria, the work week begins on Saturday and ends on Thursday, with Friday being the official day off. Stores are generally open from 8am to 1:30pm, and then again from 4 to 8pm (7pm in winter). Some stores stay open all day in winter. Government offices are open from 8am to 2pm. It isn't unusual for some offices (telephone, post) to be open on Friday. Museums are generally open from 8am to 2pm every day but Tuesday. Restaurants open for lunch around 1pm and for dinner at 8pm. Hours are not always followed to the letter.

**Tipping and Bakhsheesh** It used to be the case that nothing would get done in Syria without a bit of palm-greasing. Nowadays, increased contact with the world market and a shift in general attitudes is changing all this. Still, some tipping is expected; specifically, taxi drivers, waiters, and movie theater employees should be given at least a 10% tip. If you stay multiple nights at a hotel that cleans its rooms daily, a small thank-you (S£20-40 per day) to the person responsible is appropriate. Be gracious; everything is inexpensive anyway.

# ■ Accommodations

There are no hostels in Syria. Instead, you have two options which vary wildly in price and quality: international chain-style (more expensive) hotels and basic hole-in-the-wall, bed-and-a-roof crash sites. The higher the quality of a room, the more likely it is that you'll have to pay in US$; all two-star or higher hotels carry this requirement. In most places there is an even split between hotels that charge US$ and S£, but in the more touristed places like Palmyra, prepare to part with the dead Presidents. Different employees of one establishment often quote contradictory rates; bargaining can save some money. Damascus and Aleppo hotels are less likely to haggle, but if they look empty, give it a shot. Even posted rates can sometimes be brought down, if only by a few pounds. Unmarried couples may have a difficult time getting a room together; generally this is less of a problem in the more expensive establishments.

Also be aware that electricity and hot water in Syria are sporadic. It is not uncommon for the electricity to go off and on randomly throughout the day. Keep this in mind, and remember that if a hotel does not have working electricity when you look into it, it probably will in a few hours. Grin and bear it.

# ■ Keeping in Touch

**Mail** Mail from Syria is inexpensive but slow (letters to the U.S. can take 3 weeks to arrive). It costs about S£20 to mail letters overseas, S£8 for postcards (rates vary—that's life). Take packages to a post office for inspection before wrapping them for delivery to another country. **Poste restante** service is available in Damascus's main post office. Bring your passport and your *Let's Go* to read while you wait in line. The American Express in Damascus has Client Letter Service.

**Telephone** Trials and tribulations abound. Damascus has a 24-hour telephone office, where you can place international calls, but you'll need your passport, lots of money, and patience (at least an hour's worth). Some other cities have offices as well. Most hotels have direct-dial international capabilities, but rates from Syria are exorbitant to begin with (US$12 for a 3-min. call to the U.S.), and hotels charge at least 200%

SYRIA

the phone office rates. It's much cheaper to have your party call you back or to call collect. The access code for **MCI's World Phone** program is 0800, for **AT&T's USA-Direct** it is 0801, and for **Sprint** 0888. You can now use phone cards to make local calls; they are available in denominations of S£200 and S£500.

## ■ Dress & Etiquette

Conservative dress is the norm in Syria; shorts, tank tops, and short skirts will invite stares, comments, and possibly unwanted sexual advances. Pants and skirts should fall to at least mid-calf and shirts should cover the shoulders and upper arms.

It is impolite in Syria to point directly at someone or to point the sole of your shoe at someone (as when sitting down and placing an ankle on one knee). When a Syrian tips his or her head up and makes a clucking noise, this means "no," although Westerners have been known to mistake it for a sign of acknowledgment or a "get in the back seat" gesture by a taxi driver. No means no.

# LIFE AND TIMES

## ■ Religion & Ethnicity

Islam is the dominant religion of Syria, with about 82% of the populace following the teachings of the Qur'an. 68% of the total population is Sunni, 14% Shi'a. The Shi'a branch is splintered into sects such as the Isma'ilis (1.5%), and the Alawites (11.5%), who include President Asad among their adherents. Another 13-14% of Syrians belong to the Catholic or Eastern Orthodox churches; 3% are Druze.

The statistics on Syria's ethnic composition vary, with different sources setting the percentage of Arabs in the country between 82% and 90%. The remainder of the population is Kurdish, Turkish, Armenian, or Circassian. Part of the Kurdish minority in Syria would like to create an independent Kurdish state, which would also include the Kurds in Turkey, Iran, and Iraq, but as of yet, their grievances have not been accompanied by positive action. Pamphlets distributed in 1992 advocating this proposal brought about the arrest of 200 Kurdish activists; some remain in prison today. Only about 5% of the world's Kurdish population lives within Syrian borders. Iraq's massacre of its own Kurdish population since the Gulf War brought the situation to the attention of the West, but efforts to create autonomy for the Kurds or to aid their independence struggles have not been forthcoming.

## ■ Government & Politics

Before Asad's ascent to power, the centralized Ba'th party system had no provisions for local governance, which meant that a complaint about the size of street signs in Ma'alula would end up on the desk of the prime minister. Asad mandated the election of local government councils and required them to be at least 51% workers or peasants. With representatives in every village, the government was decentralized, but the party still maintains a presence in local affairs. Asad has also stabilized government (mainly through elevating Alawites and his childhood friends to positions of authority throughout the nation) and continues to maintain a vaguely socialist infrastructure.

Today all political parties are associated with the National Progressive Front (NPF), a coalition dominated by the Ba'th party and run by Asad himself. The People's Council, a 250-member legislative body, has political power in theory, but is controlled by the NPF, meaning Ba'th policies are passed with a minimum of opposition. The cabinet advises Asad on policy, but they would probably have "Ba'th" tattooed on their foreheads if Asad asked them to. Syria has three vice-presidents (including Asad's brother, who attempted to take control of the country in 1984 and was exiled; he was later allowed to return to his post).

President Asad runs Syria with a personal touch, a nice way of saying that he is essentially a dictator. The man with the omnipresent face controls everything he can, from foreign policy to information flow to whose mug will be on taxicabs.

As with all dictatorships, Syria's future beyond Asad's reign is uncertain. If the Syrian election results are to be believed, however, this will not happen any time soon. In 1992, Asad was elected to his fourth seven-year term as president, with 99.9% of the vote. A generous person could attribute Asad's success to his policies, which have certainly improved the quality of life in Syria since the early 70s. Other explanations for his political longevity include his aggressive suppression of his enemies (some of whom were arrested in 1971 and remain incarcerated) and the always-around-the-corner internal security forces looking out for anti-Asad sentiment. The spy industry, combined with an abysmal human-rights record, has created an atmosphere of constant fear in Syria and invited the displeasure of foreign countries. Additionally, Syria has only recently begun to curb its nasty habit of harboring (some say training) terrorists.

Lately, Asad has been seeking Western aid in an attempt to revitalize his country's plodding economy. The government enthusiastically supported the allies during the Gulf War, and is even engaged in talks with Israel. These talks may lead to the establishment of diplomatic relations between the two countries, the return of part or all of the Golan Heights to Syria, and, eventually, economic benefits. The effect that Benjamin Netanyahu's election as Prime Minister of Israel will have on peace negotiations remains to be seen.

When traveling in Syria, **do not get involved in political discussions.** If you just can't avoid the topic, offer vaguely enthusiastic praise for Asad and quickly mention, say, new advancements in refrigeration.

# ▓ Economy

Syria is blessed with black gold or Texas tea (oil). The oil money of the early 1970s allowed Asad to go forward with a program of capital formation, including investments in agriculture, heavy industries, health services, and education. A drive toward speedy modernization shaped the mid-70s, aided by the double incentive of rebuilding after the destructive October War and taking advantage of the oil boom. Unfortunately, industries were haphazardly chosen and designed for development, leaving Syria with a legacy of wasteful, inefficient factories, like a paper mill that couldn't utilize Syrian wood pulp and an ammonium-urea facility that eventually proved so useless that converting to gas, at a cost of US$100 million, was more economical than continuing to operate it. A number of industries were profitable, including light crude oil, natural gas, phosphates, iron and steel, and light industries including rubber, glass, tobacco, and paper.

The Syrian per capita GDP is around US$5300. Although most of the population has access to health services, the infant mortality rate is moderate. Syria's illiteracy rate is 36%, and schooling is only required for 6 years. Those who choose to pursue higher education receive it free from the government.

The Syrian economy also suffers from the two-headed monster of rapid population growth and massive inflation. In Damascus, the population was growing at a 3.8% annual rate in 1994, leading to an extra 40,000 people to feed each year in that city alone. Inflation in 1987-88 reached 100%, and in November 1991, prices jumped 300% when the government relaxed price controls. Since then, inflation has dropped to a less stratospheric level (22%), but the Syrian pound is still far from a good investment option.

With such restraints on economic growth, Syria has had trouble improving the economy. Asad's uninspired attempt to reduce unemployment (which reached 35% in the 70s and 80s) created the situation today in which 1 of every 5 workers gets a paycheck signed by the government. Many of these government workers are unnecessary, unmotivated, and inefficient. Pity the poor traveler. The Syrian government no longer releases unemployment figures. In the 80s, government ministries encouraged private investors to support import substitution, tourism, and agricultural projects, but investors didn't share the state's enthusiasm for capital investment; instead, they put their money into real estate. Consequently, property prices rose dramatically, further worsening the Syrian economy.

As if that weren't enough, Syria often experiences power shortages, obviously not beneficial to any industry (except candle-making), due to Turkey's tendency to over-utilize the upstream portion of the Euphrates river for its own projects. The power equipment and network (as well as military material) are old, from Soviet-era Russia, and prone to mechanical failure. As a country in the midst of the politically unstable Middle East, Syria maintains a large standing army, accounting for about 60% of its total expenditures.

The result of these expenditures, Syria's past connections with terrorist groups, its support of Iran, and sporadic skirmishes with Jordan, have translated into low levels of foreign aid; but Asad has begun to change all this. In 1991, Syria's opposition to Iraq in the Gulf War garnered a great deal of aid from Saudi Arabia, Japan, and European nations, while talks with Israel and the loosening of travel restrictions for Syrian Jews (95% of whom had left the country by the end of 1994) curry favor with governments and private investors.

## ■ Festivals & Holidays

Muslim holidays (see **When to Go,** p. 2) are official days off in Syria; Christmas and Easter are celebrated by Christians but not legislated as holidays. Political holidays close everything down; they are **New Year's Day** (Jan. 15), **Revolution Day** (March 8), **Women's Day** (March 21), **Evacuation Day** (April 17), **Martyrs' Day** (May 6), **Security Force Day** (May 29), **October War Day** (Oct. 6), **Flight Day** (Oct. 16), **Correction Movement Day** (Nov. 16th), and **Peasant's Day** (Dec. 14).

## ■ Language

The oldest phonetic alphabet in the world, the Ugarit alphabet was discovered in Syrian ruins dating from the 14th century BCE. The find gives Syria a valid claim to the world's-earliest-civilization throne.

Although only 82-90% of Syrians claim Arab ancestry, all speak Arabic, which is the official language. French has long been a second language, and a fair amount of Syrian literature, if it has been translated into any Western tongue, will be in French. Recently, English has begun to replace French as the second language of record. The various minority groups in Syria maintain their own languages to a degree; Kurds in the east speak Kurdish, and the Armenian population, centered in Aleppo, continues to use their own language. In some villages you may encounter Turkish, or possibly even Aramaic, much to the delight of those who enjoy studying the Bible in its original language. Travelers with some knowledge of Arabic should not encounter communication problems anywhere in Syria. For some handy phrases, consult the **Language Glossary,** p. 557.

## ■ The Arts

Despite the wonders of Ugarit, Syria has not been a hotbed of modern literary activity. Most of Syria's illustrious *artistes* dictated to secretaries with quills, rather than slaving over word processors. In the late 7th century CE, Jacob of Edessa wrote many theological, historical, grammatical, and philosophical works. Early in his life he studied Greek and worked as a translator, which encouraged him to write studies of the Bible, as well as the books *Enchidron* and *The Book of Treasures.* He is best known, however, for codifying the Syrian language; his *Syriac Grammar* became the seminal work on the subject. In the middle of the 13th century, the philosopher Bar Hebraeus began writing philosophical treatises. His later work, *Book of the Pupils of the Eyes,* discussed logic; *Book of the Speech of Wisdom* explored physics and metaphysics. Mathematics and astronomy were also enriched by Hebraeus' research, as was hermitism: the *Book of the Dove* was a manual written by Hebraeus for the ascetically inclined. Other late-13th-century philosophers in Hebraeus's tradition were Abhd-Isho bar-Berikhou, Yabh-alaha III, and Timothy II.

While some works have been written in French or English, those written in Arabic have only recently begun to be translated for Western consumption. In *The Desert and the Sown,* Gertrude Bell writes about her travels through Syria and Jordan, and Ross Burn's *Monuments of Syria,* available in English-language bookstores, provides an excellent historical overview of the area.

Traditionally, Arab visual arts are works of abstract beauty, focusing on color and geometric design; Syrian art is no exception. Islamic law prohibits the depiction of human beings, though modern artists are beginning to discover the human body. In mosques and other buildings, you are most likely to encounter traditional art.

# ■ Food

With a few exceptions, Syrian food is pretty much the same as that of the rest of the Middle East. Foods that are considered snacks can be consumed morning, noon, or night without shame or funny looks from the native population. Two of the most popular snack foods, which have made massive inroads into Western culture, are hummus and falafel. Hummus is the Big Brother of Middle Eastern foods—it's everywhere. Chickpeas are ground into a paste seasoned with lemon, garlic, and salt, which is then scooped up with pieces of bread and consumed in mass quantities. Falafel is a similar paste, heavier on fava beans than chick peas, mixed with spices and fried, then rolled into a piece of bread with vegetables and *tahini* sauce. For the piasterless traveler, hummus plus falafel equals good eats indefinitely, but make sure you have a stomach of steel before you indulge in street food. If you want a little meat in your diet or a little lining on your arteries, try delicious *shawerma,* lamb (sometimes chicken) cooked beneath dripping fat, rolled in bread with vegetables and spices. There are other kinds of *shawerma,* as well, including liver, brains, etc.

If you get tired of eating food from roadside stands, or if a long-lost uncle unexpectedly leaves you a small fortune—say, US$4—why not blow it all on a main dish? You could start with *shish kabab,* lamb chunks on skewers, grilled, and served with bread. *Shish tawouq* is similarly-treated chicken. A dish uncommon in other Arab countries is *farooj,* roasted chicken served with chilis and onions. Also common at local restaurants and in homes are bean, spinach, and potato stews cooked with lamb in tomato sauce and ladled over rice. Beware of fish, except on the Mediterranean coast; it tends to be spiced to the hilt and saltier than a grumpy old sailor.

Don't leave Syria without trying one of its most unusual and delicious offerings. You'll find *bybil,* an exotic desert banana, in *souqs* and fancy restaurants. Its short growing season (culminating in a harvest around the first of October) and limited availability make it one of the most prized and beloved, though mysterious, fruits in the world. You'll recognize *bybil* by its soft, honey hue and elegant shape. One taste and you'll be hooked forever.

For dessert, Syrians favor pastries that are very, very sweet. Most of these *halawiyyat* have a fair amount of sugar and butter baked into them and are then drenched in syrup or honey. *Ba'laweh* is made of pistachios or almonds in fillo dough, *burma* of pistachios in shredded fried dough, and *basbouseh* of wheat and syrup. *Booza* is not alcohol but ice cream. Eat, drink, and be merry.

Speaking of drink, Syrians like their *qahwa* (coffee) like they like their *ba'laweh*—strong and sweet. Both *shay* (tea) and *qahwa* are consumed frequently, for caffeine highs rivaling a cocaine rush. (Espresso has a lot to learn from *qahwa.*) Stalls with bags of fruit hanging out front will be your oasis of cool liquid refreshment. Here you'll find *aseer* (juice) in abundance. One caveat: sometimes Syrians add milk to drinks. This will not make you a happy camper—stay away from the dairy additives.

*Mirinda* is the Syrian-brewed soft drink (it tastes like Orange Crush), and Pepsi *(beb-see)* is everywhere. These *gazooza* (fruity sodas) are very cheap. Finally, alcohol in Syria ranges from locally brewed beers and Amstel smuggled into Damascus from Lebanon to *'araq,* an anise-seed flavored liquor mixed with water and consumed slowly from shot glasses. Be careful with the *'araq*—it bites.

# Damascus دمشق

Damascus' monumental, centuries-long past wraps around an enigmatic present to create one of the most intriguing cities in the Middle East. Unchecked pollution and a frenetic city pace make Damascus look like any other urban jungle, but the city's *souqs,* the Umayyad Mosque, and the National Museum, not to mention the Qur'an and the Bible, uncover an overwhelmingly rich history.

Although Aleppans will try to convince you otherwise, the city of Damascus has been continuously inhabited longer than any other city in the world. Early historical references to the city include the Ebla tablets, written in 3000 BCE, as well as 15th-century BCE pharaonic inscriptions and records of the city as the capital of the Aramaic kingdom. Centuries later, Roman invaders left their mark, most notably in the form of the Temple of Jupiter, built by Apolodor the Damascene. During the Byzantine era, Christians converted the temple into a church and built other monuments that remain standing today. In 636 CE, Khaled Ibn al-Walid, the "sword of God," conquered Damascus in the name of Islam.

The city served as the capital of the Islamic Umayyad Empire for close to a century, at a time of enormous growth for the Islamic community. It was during the Umayyad period that Muslim rule spread as far as Transoxania in the East and Spain in the West. Damascus began to suffer when the Abbassids replaced the Umayyads and moved the capital of the Islamic empire to Baghdad.

In the ensuing centuries, Damascus fell under various Muslim dynasties and empires, including the Ottoman Turks, whose influence is quite visible in existing Damascene architecture. During World War One, German and Turkish armies used Damascus as a base. The League of Nations mandate gave France control of Syria in April of 1920. Resistance to French rule flamed until 1925, when the French crushed a popular revolt in Damascus. In 1946, Syria won its independence, and Damascus became the capital of a modern nation-state.

Today, the pulse, physical appearance, and odors of the city reflect contemporary realities rather than historical splendor. Damascus is a city of many faces: large fountains, parks, and wide avenues grace the newer parts of town, while the winding cobblestone streets of the Old City are home to Damascus' minority Christian population and a plethora of small craft shops and bakeries. A diverse population in class, race, and religion, Damascenes are bound together by a fierce pride in their country and history. While it is taboo to discuss politics openly, many locals are happy to tell you (in hushed voices) their thoughts on the Middle East peace process and the changes they feel it will bring.

## ■ Orientation

Damascus is a city of small, merchant-filled streets as well as wide avenues and spacious parks. With the help of a few landmarks, it is easy to navigate on foot. The **Hijaz Railway Station** is located at the intersection of **An-Nasr Street** and **Sa'ad al-Jabri Street,** and has an old railway car on display in front of its stone steps and crowded stone water fountain. Facing away from the station, Sa'ad al-Jabri St. is directly in front of you. Walking down this street, the **post office** and **exchange bank** are directly on your left-hand side. Before you reach the **footbridge** over **Quwatli Street,** you will pass by several two-star hotels and a good pharmacy. Across the well-traveled footbridge, Sa'ad al-Jabri St. becomes **Port Said Street.** Continuing on Port Said St. brings you to **Yousef al-Azmeh Square.** Just beyond this landmark are the **Tourist Information Center** and the five-star **Cham Palace Hotel.** Continuing past the Cham Palace brings you to **Abu Roumaneh Street,** one of the nicer residential areas of Damascus, and several embassies and cultural centers.

Another important area, especially for those seeking cheap eats and hotels, pistachio desserts, money changing, or Russian prostitutes, is **Al Marjeh Square** (also named, but never called, Ash-Shuhada' or Martyr's Square), two blocks off An-Nasr St. In the center of the square, the **Barada River** surfaces from its underground lair in the form of a big fountain. Continuing right on An-Nasr St. from the Hijaz Station takes you to the entrance of the **Souq al-Hamidiyyeh.** A walk through the covered *souq* brings you to the **Umayyad Mosque** (at the very end of the *souq*) and, behind the mosque, to the **Old City** entrance.

A left turn from the Hijaz Station onto **Al Baroudi Street** leads eventually to the **Foire Internationale de Damas,** where the Barada River flows and numerous fountains shoot high into the air. The **Takkiyeh as-Suleimaniyyeh Mosque** and the **Military Museum** are on the right as you walk away from the station. The **University of Damascus** and the **National Museum** border the river. Farther down, under Pres. Hafez al-Assad Bridge, lurks the huge **bus and service station** at the end of the street.

# ■ Transportation

**Private taxis** have meters; few use them. Negotiate prices before you get in. Even longer trips, like from the Hijaz Station to Abu Roumaneh, shouldn't cost more than S£40. Most drivers will give you an honest rate and appreciate a small tip (S£5-10).

**Service taxis** (white minivans) have predetermined routes and pick up passengers along the way. The routes are written in Arabic on the sides. If one is going your way, flag it down and jump in. For only S£2-5 per ride, even a short one may be worth the money. Rap on the window when you want out.

There is an extensive **city bus** system stationed with the service taxis past the National Museum, at the end of An-Nasr Ave. Crowded and dirty buses go everywhere for S£4 per ride, or you can buy tickets in packs of five for S£20. The ticket seller can help you find the right bus.

For **intercity transportation,** both of the private bus stations on An-Nasr Ave. have competitive rates. The **Damas Tour Co.** (tel. 235 300) at the larger station has a big, beautiful, blue fleet of buses and a wide variety of destinations. The government-run **Karnak Bus Company** (tel. 222 14 92) is located behind the Hijaz station, down the first street on the right. Smoky, run-down buses serve Aleppo (2 per day, 8am and 3pm, S£100); Bosra (7am, S£20); Homs (4 per day beginning at 7:30am, S£40); Lattakia (8am and 3pm, S£100); Palmyra (7am, S£100); Tartus (8am, S£65); Amman (7am and 3pm, S£150); and Beirut (7:30am, 3:30 and 4pm, S£125). Reservations are required. **Pullman buses, minibuses ("micros"),** and **service taxis** also have intercity service. The Pullmans are even less comfortable than Karnak, but have regular schedules. Minibuses and *service* are cheap and leave when full (*service* to Amman S£375; to Beirut S£350).

# ■ Practical Information

**Tourist Information Center:** 29 Mai Ave. (tel. 222 23 88). From Yousef al-Azmeh Sq., walk to the right of the white modern building. The poster-coated center will be on your right. Maps and information in English. Open Sat.-Thurs. 9am-7pm.

**Tourist Police:** Tel. 222 68 10.

**Embassies: U.S.,** 2 Al Mansour St. (tel. 333 32 32), in Abu Roumaneh. Take Al Jala'a Ave. away from Al Quwatli until Rawdat Abilalan Sq. You'll see the Stars and Stripes flying off to the left. Consular section open Sun.-Thurs. 8am-4pm. Observes all U.S. Federal holidays and most Syrian holidays. **U.K.,** Malki-Kurd Ali St. (tel. 371 25 61). **Australia,** 128 Al Farabi St., Mezze (tel. 664 317). **Egypt,** Al Jala'a Ave., Abu Rou-

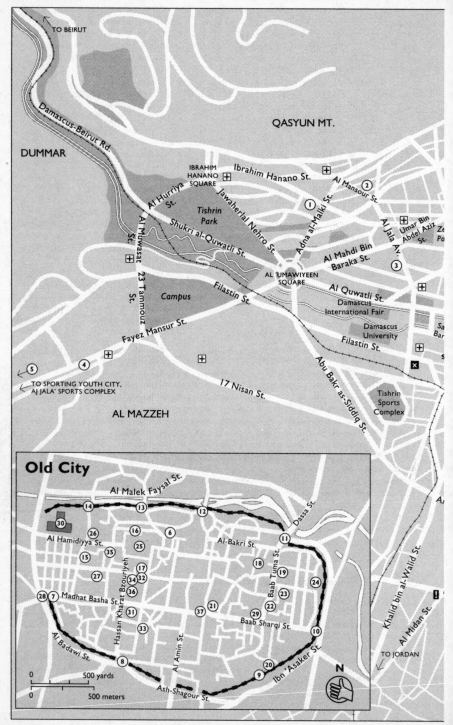

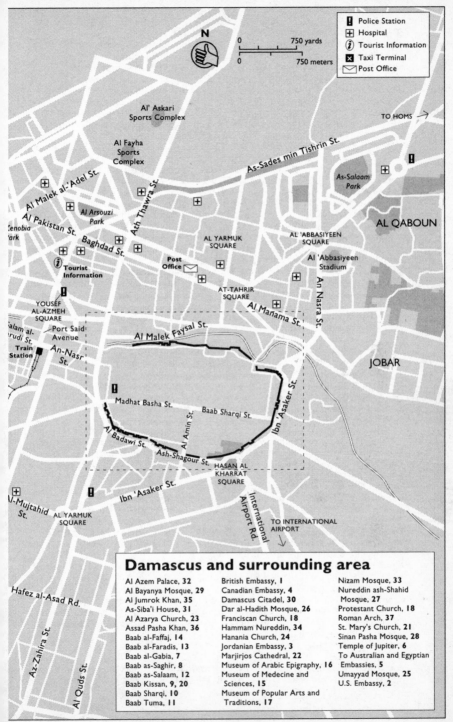

## Damascus and surrounding area

Al Azem Palace, 32
Al Bayanya Mosque, 29
Al Jumrok Khan, 35
As-Siba'i House, 31
Al Azarya Church, 23
Assad Pasha Khan, 36
Baab al-Faffaj, 14
Baab al-Faradis, 13
Baab al-Gabia, 7
Baab as-Saghir, 8
Baab as-Salaam, 12
Baab Kissan, 9, 20
Baab Sharqi, 10
Baab Tuma, 11

British Embassy, 1
Canadian Embassy, 4
Damascus Citadel, 30
Dar al-Hadith Mosque, 26
Franciscan Church, 18
Hammam Nureddin, 34
Hanania Church, 24
Jordanian Embassy, 3
Marjirjos Cathedral, 22
Museum of Arabic Epigraphy, 16
Museum of Medecine and
  Sciences, 15
Museum of Popular Arts and
  Traditions, 17

Nizam Mosque, 33
Nureddin ash-Shahid
  Mosque, 27
Protestant Church, 18
Roman Arch, 37
St. Mary's Church, 21
Sinan Pasha Mosque, 28
Temple of Jupiter, 6
To Australian and Egyptian
  Embassies, 5
Umayyad Mosque, 25
U.S. Embassy, 2

maneh (tel. 333 35 61). **Jordan,** Al Jala'a Ave., Abu Roumaneh (tel. 333 46 42). **Turkey,** 48 Ziad Ben Abi Sufian St. (tel. 333 14 11).

**Currency Exchange:** Always a chore. Even though it's illegal, many shop owners and travel agents in Damascus will offer to change foreign currency at higher rates than the banks. If you don't want to incur the risk of getting dragged to a Syrian detention center, stick with the banks. Banking hours are Sat.-Thurs. 9am-12:50pm. The **Commercial Bank of Syria,** at Yousef al-Azmeh Sq., has a foreign cash exchange window (open Sat.-Thurs. 8am-7pm). The branch in front of the Hijaz Station exchanges cash or traveler's checks (Sat.-Thurs. 10am-6pm and Fri. 10:30am-3pm). To change traveler's checks, bring your passport, your purchase record, and be prepared to pay S£25 for each check cashed.

**American Express:** Belkis St. (tel. 221 78 13 or 224 65 00; fax 222 37 07). From Hijaz St., take a left on Fardous St. and Belkis St. is the first left; AmEx is in the Sudan Airways office. They only hold mail and serve you tea. One lump or two? Open Sat.-Thurs. 8:30am-8pm and Fri. 9am-1:30pm and 5-8pm.

**Telephone Office:** An-Nasr Ave., 1 block down from the Hijaz Station. The office doesn't have a telephone number, but it's open 24hr. For international calls, bring your passport, lots of cash, and a good supply of patience—placing calls can take up to an hour.

**Visa Extension Office:** Off Sa'ad al-Jabri St. near the Barada Hotel. A near-flawless display of inefficiency. Travelers staying in Syria for longer than 2 weeks must register with the police and apply for a visa extension. You will be sent to various places, including a photocopy store (if they forget to use carbon paper) and possibly to a very special room downstairs where a uniformed man with your passport in his hand asks you for a tip. Just say no. Open 9am until sometime in early afternoon, usually whenever you show up. Go in the morning.

**Airport: Damascus International Airport,** southeast of Damascus. Buses to the airport leave from the Victoria Bridge on Al Quwatli St. (S£100) and *service* leave from the station near the Hijaz railway station (S£300). A taxi to the airport costs around US$10. Regular flights to European and Arab capitals; domestic one-way flights daily to Aleppo for only S£600! There is a S£100 exit fee if you leave Syria by air. The **SyrianAir** office (tel. 222 07 00) is in front of the post office.

**Car Rental:** There are a few places around the post office, but English is rare. For helpful driving information in English, try the agency at the Cham Palace Hotel. Rent for a day (US$37, unlimited mileage US$59) or a week (US$238/US$378).

**English Bookstores:** The **Librarie Universelle** (tel. 223 23 00), near the Cham Palace Hotel in Azmeh Sq., has 2 big shelves full of paperbacks, including Ludlum, Clancy, and Asimov. Yesterday's *International Herald Tribune* and last week's *Time* and *Newsweek* also available (open daily 9am-9pm). Ritzy hotels such as the **Cham Palace** and the **Meridien Hotels** offer less extensive selections. Most Arabic bookstores have simple **photocopiers** you can use for S£2 per copy.

**Cultural Centers: American Cultural Center,** 87 Rue Ata Ayoubi (tel. 333 84 13). **British Council,** Place Adnan al-Malki, open 9am-2pm. A/C reading room.

**Laundromat: Aous ash-Sharq** (tel. 222 45 76), off Salam al-Barudi St. Facing out from the Hijaz Station, the laundromat is on the second street on the left, across from the Sultan Hotel. Shirt S£25, pants S£40, socks/underwear S£20. Open Sat.-Thurs. 9am-7pm. A tiny laundry service near the Al Haramain Hotel will clean and press your clothes for the same prices.

**Pharmacies:** Hours are generally Sat.-Thurs. 9am-1:30pm and 5:30-9pm. Try **Kassar** (tel. 222 73 47), near the Hijaz Station on Sa'ad al-Jabri St., or **Al-Halabi** (tel. 221 55 50), closer to Azmeh Sq. Pharmacies rotate staying open at night; lists are posted in Arabic outside most pharmacies. Inquire at one of the larger hotels.

**Emergency:** U.S. citizens can call the embassy (tel. 333 32 32). The embassy nurse, Birgit Khatib (tel. 333 50 74, in emergencies 333 91 30), makes medical referrals, usually to Shami Hospital.

**Ambulance:** Tel. 110.

**Police:** Tel. 112.

**Post Office:** Sa'ad al-Jabri St. (tel. 119 000), in front of the Hijaz train station. Open Sat.-Thurs. 8am-7pm and Fri. 8am-1pm. **Poste restante** available. The **EMS** office

is directly behind the post office, in a little building in the parking lot. Open Sat.-Thurs. 8am-7pm.
**Telephone Code:** 11.

# ■ Accommodations

In two-star or better hotels, prices for foreigners are listed in US dollars. The Syrian government, eager to grab greenbacks, charges "wealthy" tourists two to three times what Syrians or those with residence permits pay in Syrian pounds. Most hotels accept traveler's checks and will give change in dollars, but it's a good idea to have small bills on hand to simplify exchange and avoid horrible hotel exchange rates. Although the best two-star hotels, located in the neighborhood of the Hijaz Station and the post office, are clean and safe, there are cheaper and just as comfortable options around Al Marjeh Sq. Many "hotels" in this area moonlight as brothels and may turn you away if you don't look like the type to pay extra for a bedmate. Don't let the sleazy places keep you from finding the jewels. Damascus does indeed have cheap hotels with high ceilings, clean bathrooms, and bug-free beds. Never forget to bargain, especially in the off-season or if a place looks empty.

## AL MARJEH SQUARE

**Al Haramain Hotel** (tel. 231 94 89), Bahsa St. From Al Marjeh Sq., head away from An-Nasr St., and go down the small street by the Omar al-Khayyam Hotel. Cross the big street and head to your right, looking for the signs. The hotel is down a small street on the left. By far the best place to stay in Damascus. Open courtyard with tiled floors and fountain. Cool, high-ceilinged rooms with fan, soft beds, and free hot showers. Laundry service and restaurant next door. Singles S£200, doubles S£325, triples S£425.

**Ar-Rabie Hotel** (tel. 221 83 73), next door to the Al Haramain and similar in style (although not as well maintained), with a green court and fountain. You can avoid the hectic telephone office by placing international calls here. Singles S£200, with bath S£250. Doubles S£375, triples S£475. Dorms (3 beds) S£150 per person.

**Hotel Negmit Sharq** (tel. 221 77 98), above the juice and *shawerma* stands. Shut the window and turn on the fan to avoid noise from the square below. Nice TV lounge, and you won't have to worry about prostitutes. Great rooftop, with fountain, plastic tables, and chairs. The few rooms on the roof have negotiable prices, but no windows—stick with the mattress. Singles with fan S£400, doubles with shower and toilet S£475. Rooftop room S£200, rooftop mattress S£150.

**Hotel Basman,** Rami St. (tel. 221 80 03; fax 224 66 89), up the street in front of the column in Marjeh Sq. Beautiful façade and lobby. Rooms are spacious and pleasant with fans and bath. Singles US$17, doubles US$34.

**Assia Hotel** (tel. 231 41 00 or 41 01). Head up Port Said St. from Marjeh Sq. in the direction of Al Azmeh Sq.; the Assia is on the right. It's pricey, but those looking for comfort should go no further. Quiet carpeted rooms have baths that look like they belong in a private home. Pink tubs, clean tiles, thick towels. Popular with Iranians. Singles US$30, doubles US$31, triples US$36. Breakfast US$4.

**Al-Tal Hotel** (tel. 221 90 10), Al Shuhada'a St., with an unmistakable yellow and green sign. Clean, A/C rooms are popular with Russian business people—so is the restaurant downstairs, which serves Russian dishes. Laundry service available. Singles US$24, doubles US$31.

## NEAR HIJAZ STATION

**Sultan Hotel,** Al Barudi St. (tel. 222 57 68 or 221 69 10). Turn left from the station, the Sultan is ½ block down across the street. Rooms are passably comfortable, with lamps, telephones, desks, and hard mattresses. Singles US$17. Doubles US$20, with bathroom US$23. Triples US$25, with bathroom US$28. Rooms with A/C US$1 extra. Breakfast US$3.

**Barada Hotel,** Sa'ad al-Jabri (tel. 221 25 46 or 224 14 45), down the street on the right. Relatively clean rooms with bath. Nice first floor lounge. Singles US$17, doubles US$23, triples US$28, quads US$32. Without bath US$3 cheaper.

**Al-Afamia Hotel** (tel. 222 91 52 or 89 63), off Furat St. Walk straight down al-Jabri past the post office and take the first left. Enormous, high beds, TV, and private bathrooms. Pleasant management. Doubles US$24, without bath US$20. TV US$1 extra. Breakfast US$2.

**Al-Hamra Hotel,** Furat St. (tel. 221 07 17), around the corner from Al Afamia. Rooms have TV and some have private bath. A good alternative if the Al Afamia is full. Doubles US$24, US$20 without bath.

# ▨ Food

Hummus, falafel, and *shawerma* comprise the Damascene staples. There are almost as many food stands around **Marjeh Square** as there are portraits of the crafty one around town. Fresh fruit stands serve juice drinks that are meals in themselves, although glasses are rarely cleaned (it's best to use the straws planted in the pulp). Prices are generally low (hummus S£30, falafel S£10, *shawerma* S£15, large juice S£40-50.) Be sure to sample the various honey-shellacked pistachio pastries. The best pastry shops are also around Marjeh Sq.

**Maysaloun St.,** just off Yousef al-Azmeh Sq. past the Cham Palace Hotel, is home to numerous sit-down restaurants and ice cream parlors. In the evenings, the street is crawling with cologne-scented sweets-lovers, strolling with a sundae or large juice in hand. The best ice cream in Damascus is at **Damer Patisserie** on Maysaloun St. (open Sat.-Thurs. 10am-1am). If you've had enough hummus, there are some good pizzerias on Abu Roumaneh St., one block down from Damer.

The Christian quarter in the Old City (Baab Touma Sq.) has great falafel, atmosphere, and a genuine fast-food pizza joint.

**Al Eez** (tel. 218 174), take the last left off Souq Al Hamidiyyeh before the ruins; the restaurant will be on your left. Modest, cramped entrance gives way to an Islamic palace, a built-in Bedouin tent, and the voice of Umm Kulthum. The food can entice you for several meals. Menu includes Eggs of Cheep (appetizer S£35) and Boiled Oily Meat (S£80), as well as the usual Middle Eastern fare (*shish tawouq* S£70). The best place in Damascus to soak up Syrian atmosphere and food. Open daily 8am-12:30am. After 3pm there's live music in the tent.

**Umayyad Palace Restaurant** (tel. 222 08 26 or 224 89 01), behind the mosque. Walk to the right of the mosque, turn right, and follow the many signs. The restaurant, once an antique shop, is downstairs. The owners have gone all-out to make this a truly amazing dining experience. The lunch buffet is S£350. Dinner S£600, S£700 on Tues., Thurs., and Sat. when Whirling Dervishes perform. There's live music on other nights. Open daily 12:30pm-midnight. Credit cards

**Al Arabi,** Marjeh Sq. (tel. 221 40 18), in a little alley as you head toward the Citadel from the Square. The café portion of the restaurant displays all sorts of meat and vegetable dishes, as well as Syria's own Double Cola. You can get an appetizer, meat, and drink for S£165. Get a full breakfast with eggs, cheese, toast, and tea for S£75 or an omelette for S£40. Open daily 24hr.

**Ali Baba,** Azmeh Sq. (tel. 221 98 81 or 222 54 34), in the basement of the shopping center on the corner of Fardous St. The lights get dimmer as you descend, and there's a waterfall in the corner. Excellent appetizers (S£20-60), meat, fish, and chicken dishes (S£100-200), and a tempting dessert menu that includes "milk budding." Open daily 8am-1am. Visa, MC.

**Abou Kamal,** Azmeh Sq. (tel. 221 11 59 or 224 48 80), upstairs in the same shopping center as Ali Baba. The dirt of Damascus' streets is nowhere to be found in this white, polished, tropical place. Appetizers from S£30, entrees from S£140 (*shish tawouq* S£175). Open daily 6am-3am.

**White Horse Restaurant** (tel. 333 81 28), on Abu Roumaneh St. Renowned since 1973 for its pizza and "lazanya," this brick and wood Italian bistro adds pizzazz to a

Middle Eastern diet. Pizzas S£125-185, with discounts for groups. Open daily 1-5pm and 7pm-1am.

**Station One** (tel. 333 45 75 or 62 24), Abu Roumaneh St. Hop aboard the "Luxury Wagon" (restaurant), the "Economy Train" (snack bar), or the "Express" (take away). For S£45-55, you get a burger and fries, chicken, or steak. The three "trains" are right next to each other, and those riding the Luxury Wagon or the Economy Train can sit at the beautiful outdoor café. Open daily 1pm-1am.

**Al Shamiat** (tel. 222 72 70), An-Nijma Sq. This local favorite is a standard Middle Eastern food joint with a twist—it has ambience. Beaded lamps, hanging woven baskets, and embroidered tablecloths make the hummus here an exquisite dining experience (appetizers S£25-50, meat entrees S£120-150). Open daily 24hr.

## ■ Sights

The **Citadel,** located next to the entrance to the Souq al-Hamidiyyeh, was built by the Seljuks in 1078 CE, and once housed elaborate baths, mosques, and schools. During the crusader invasions, it served as a headquarters for Egyptian and Syrian sultans, including Salah ad-Din. The Ayyubid Sultan Malek al-'Adel demolished and rebuilt the Citadel in 1202 because he felt it was no longer suitable for contemporary warfare. The new fortress has 300 arrow slits and was once surrounded by a deep moat. Now, the moat is filled in and serves as a *souq* floor. The Citadel itself is currently undergoing extensive renovation and will eventually open as a war museum and cultural center.

The **Souq al-Hamidiyyeh** begins next to the Citadel and stretches to the Temple of Jupiter and the Umayyad Mosque. Damascus *souqs* are some of the busiest and most diverse in the region. Children and store owners may bring you through the jumble of overcrowded stalls to have tea in their shops. Bargaining for one set of Bedouin knives or a backgammon board can become an entire afternoon's entertainment, and usually pays off.

Just before the Umayyad Mosque at the end of Souq Al Hamidiyyeh is the 3rd-century CE **Temple of Jupiter,** now a source of shade for magazine and Qur'an sellers. The few remaining pillars now blend into the chaos of the *souq*. To the left of the mosque on the way to the visitors' entrance is **Salah ad-Din's Tomb,** built in 1193 and restored by Kaiser Wilhelm II of Germany in the late 19th century. The famed fighter's body lies under a red dome in a peaceful garden mausoleum. Inside the building, both a wooden and a marble tomb occupy the place of honor. The marble was a gift from the Kaiser; Salah ad-Din chose to stay in his wooden abode (open daily 10am-4pm; free with paid entrance to the mosque).

The Caliph Walid Ibn Abd al-Malek supervised the building of the **Umayyad Mosque** in 705. Originally the site of an ancient temple dedicated to Hadad (an Aramaean god revered circa 1000 BCE), it was later the temple of Jupiter the Damascene. In the 4th century, a Byzantine church dedicated to St. John the Baptist was erected on this site. The church was destroyed to make room for the grand mosque; the only relic that survived was the head of St. John (known by Muslims as the prophet Yahia), now resting in its own shrine in the mosque's prayer hall. The shrine is a site of veneration for both Christians and Muslims. The mosque's three minarets were built in different styles and touched up by various empires since their original construction. The walls of the mosque are decorated with intricate mosaics; on the central dome are the names of some of the most significant figures in early Muslim history. In the courtyard stands the treasury, also covered with remarkable mosaics. (Mosque open daily 8am-8pm. Admission S£10. Keep the ticket, as you will need it to get into Salah ad-Din's Tomb.) Use the visitors' entrance to the left of the main entrance. All visitors will be provided with robes if necessary.

On the side of the mosque (to the right when approaching from the Souq al-Hamidiyyeh) is the **Azem Palace.** Built in 1749, the palace was the official home of As'ad Pasha al-Azem, the Ottoman governor of Damascus. Through the modest door, a courtyard with a fountain leads into the palace's specialized rooms: the bride's cham-

**SYRIA**

ber, mother-in-law's chamber, instrument room (with a phonograph imported from New York), king's room, room of the pilgrimage (featuring tiny Qur'ans), arms room, bath, and reception room. Above each room are painted and engraved wooden ceilings. A **Museum of Popular Traditions** is inside (palace and museum open Wed.-Mon. 9am-5:30pm; admission S£200, students S£25).

Behind the Umayyad Mosque, the narrow streets of the Old City begin their winding journey to the Christian quarter, centered around Baab Touma Sq. There you'll find the **Chapel of Ananias**, dedicated to the Christian disciple who restored sight to Saul of Tarsus (later St. Paul), and **St. Paul's Chapel,** from which that same saint was lowered out of a window in order to escape arrest by his Jewish enemies. Entrance to these buildings may involve knocking at the gate; the friendly multilingual staff will be happy to let you in and give you a religious history lesson. The Old City itself, crammed with craft shops, restaurants, and cafés, is a great place to get lost.

Modern Damascus holds many wonders as well. The **Taqiyyeh as-Suleimaniyyeh Mosque**, on Salam al-Barudi St., is a fascinating example of Ottoman architecture. Built in 1554 by the famed architect Sinan, its two lofty minarets frame a huge dome reflected in a courtyard fountain. Outdoor patios are crowned with archways where the faithful pray. The surrounding *madrasa* was converted into the **Artisanat**, an Ottoman market offering silver jewelry, oil paintings, and mother-of-pearl inlaid backgammon boards (most shops open daily 9am-9pm; Visa and MC accepted). Next door to the mosque and the market is the **Military Museum.** You can get a taste of the exhibits without going in: the area around the mosque is littered with old fighter planes. The museum is a memorial to Syria's military past, displaying both ancient and modern weapons and photos that pay homage to those who perished for their country (open Wed.-Mon. 9am-2pm; admission S£5).

One street over from the military museum, the **National Museum** has a shady green courtyard and an excellent collection of Ugaritic writings (the first alphabet, from the 14th century BCE). The museum contains Syrian sculpture, a Qur'an collection, Palmyran textiles from the first three centuries CE, and an entire reconstructed underground tomb from Palmyra. Beyond the door at the end of the last hall you will find the frescoed walls of a synagogue excavated from the 3rd-century CE town of Doura Europos. You may need to ask a guard to let you in. (Open Sat.-Thurs. 9am-6pm, Fri. 9am-12:30pm and 2-6pm; admission S£200, students S£25.)

# ▓ Entertainment

As the evenings cool, Damascenes take to the streets to nibble sweets, slurp juice, and relax at outdoor cafés. The area behind the Umayyad Mosque is peppered with cafés. By the end of the evening, the place grows into one big street party, as people pull up chairs to drink or smoke *argeileh* (also known as *hubbly bubblies* because of the water that bubbles as you inhale). **Maysaloun St.,** past the Cham Palace Hotel, hops until 1am, when the ice cream stores and juice stands close.

Most of the late-night and early-morning activity in Damascus takes place in the bars of the larger hotels. Women will not be received warmly at local bars unless they are there to sell their services. The **Piano Bar** (tel. 543 03 75) has live music and *karaoke* amidst classy Middle Eastern decor. There's no cover charge, but reservations are necessary and singles (men or women) are not admitted. The **Pig and Whistle Pub,** located near the British Embassy, is full of expats and some backpackers kicking back with pitchers of beer. Several embassies rotate hosting parties on Thursday nights; call the American or British embassies for details.

The high quality Cham Palace Theater has regular showings of American films at 3:30, 7:30, and 9:30pm (S£60). There are numerous **swimming pools** in Damascus, where you can take a dip for S£200. Maps of the city list their locations. For a steamier time, you might consider one of several **hammams** (Turkish baths) that gurgle around the *souq*. Look for smiling clean people. The Hammam Nour ed-Din (tel. 229 513), close to Azem Palace, is the most recently renovated establishment. Full massage, bath, soap, and sauna cost S£200. The baths here are for men only (open daily 9am-midnight).

# ■ Near Damascus

## BOSRA بصرة

Bosra, 20km from the Jordanian border, was the northern capital of the Nabatean kingdom 19 centuries ago. The Romans annexed the city in 106 CE, renamed it Neatrajana Bustra, and made it the capital of the Province of Arabia. They left the town with grand monuments, including a 15,000-seat theater. Muslim control began in 634, and over the next six centuries, the Roman theater was slowly converted into a citadel. Bosra remained an important crossroads and Muslim pilgrimage site until the 17th century, when increasing banditry made its trading routes unsafe.

The **Roman Theater-Arab Citadel** is today the most impressive structure in Bosra. The first walls of the Citadel were built during the Umayyad and 'Abbassid periods, with further fortification tacked on by the 11th-century Fatimids. The Roman theater inside the fortress walls is one of the best preserved in the world, with secret stairways and an undamaged stage (admission S£200, S£25 for students). Bosra is also home to the 8th- (some say 12th-) century **Mosque of Omar** and the 4th-century **Al Mabrak Mosque/Monastery,** where Muhammad met the Nestorian monk Boheira, who predicted the prophet's potential.

Although many people sleep in the theater for a night, the tiny town of Bosra is best seen as a daytrip. Karnak buses from Damascus leave for Bosra daily (7am, S£20), and the Damas Tour Co. has buses at 9:30am, noon, 3, 4:30, 5:30, and 6:30pm (2hr., S£45 one way). Microbuses from **Karaj Dar'a** on the southern edge of Damascus go to Dar'a for S£45 (it's then S£15 more to get to Bosra).

## MA'ALULA لا لولا

Forty-five km northeast of Damascus, the tiny town of Ma'alula lies hidden in the Al Qalamoun Mountains. Ancient churches and old mosques nestle among the blue

### Lebanon

Lebanon is an independent country. U.S. citizens are forbidden by their government from going to Lebanon, and will be fined and/or imprisoned if they show any evidence (exit and/or entry stamps) of having been there. Once considered the Riviera of the Middle East, the country only recently emerged from a ravaging spell of civil war. The southern parts of the country are still unsafe. Even so, Lebanon's long history, Mediterranean hospitality, stunning natural beauty, and delicious food make it a rewarding place to visit. As the political situation settles, more and more tourists are returning to enjoy the "jewel of the Middle East." From Damascus, Karnak buses run daily to Beirut at 7:30am and 3:30pm (S£125, 3½hr., depending on border crossing). Once in Lebanon, yellow taxis or white *service* can take you anywhere in the country. *Service* are cheaper, costing L£1000 per trip. Buses are also available to some destinations, and run frequently to Jbail and Tripoli for L£2000. Buses and *service* to points north of Beirut leave from Barbir Bridge (pronounced bar-*beer*); to go south and east, get a bus or *service* from the Cola Bridge. The tourist office at 550 Central Bank St. in Beirut (tel. (01) 34 09 40; open 8am-2pm) is the best in the Middle East, and will provide free maps, hotel listings, restaurant and nightclub information, and comprehensive pamphlets on every tourist site in the country. Budget travelers should be warned that prices in Lebanon are much higher than in neighboring countries (not to mention in Paris) for accommodations, food, and sights. For clean, cheap rooms, look for the many monasteries and convents, some of which also provide meals. If you have a problem, difficulty, or complaint, contact the Tourist Police (tel. (01) 35 09 01, 34 35 04, or 32 86).

houses that crowd the slopes. Ma'alula seems to linger in timeless stagnation. Townsfolk still speak Aramaic, the language in which Jesus preached and the Lord's Prayer was authored.

Carved into the face of a barren cliff, **St. Taqla's Monastery** is a destination for both Christian and Muslim pilgrims. Built in the 4th century, it now holds the remains of St. Taqla, daughter of a Seleucid prince and pupil of St. John. A convert to Christianity before such behavior became popular, the young Taqla was alerted by a servant that her father had plans to kill her. On the night that she was to be burned, Taqla escaped. While being pursued, an angel showed her towards safety: a mountain opened up for her and then quickly closed, crushing her father's soldiers. Luckily this same mountain path has opened up again, leading visitors another 4th-century monastery, the mountaintop one of **Mar Sakis.** Built on the remains of a pagan temple, it is named after St. Sarkis, a Syrian horseman during the reign of King Maximus in 297 CE. When you come to the end of the mountain path, turn right to get to the monastery. A left turn will take you to cliffs which provide spectacular views of the town below, marred only by the five-star Safir Hotel (the lone overnight option in Ma'alula). The town is an easy daytrip from Damascus, with frequent buses from **Karaj Ma'alula** on the east side of town (50min., S£20). To get to the *karaj*, take a *service* to Abasseyeen Sq.; it's down An-Nasra St., on the left.

## SEYDNAYA صيدنيا

Seydnaya, which means "Our Lady" in ancient Syriac, is located halfway between Damascus and Ma'alula, 20km and a 25-minute ride from either city. The hilltop convent in the center of town was built in 547 CE to honor the place where the Virgin Mary appeared before a wealthy hunter. Within a maze of stone stairways, a shrine to the Virgin contains an icon said to have been painted by St. Luke. Beside the church is the entrance to a small, underground sanctuary where Mary supposedly stood. It is adorned with Oriental rugs, gold-engraved icons, and portraits of the Virgin, all dimly lit by the glow of candles. The inscription outside the entrance echoes the commandment Moses was given before the burning bush: "Take off your shoes, for the ground you are treading on is sacred" (Exodus 3:5). To get to Seydnaya, pick up a Damascus-bound ride from Ma'alula or take a bus from Karaj Ma'alula (see **Ma'alula** above for directions). Those who have come to pray (or respectful passers-through) may spend one night in the clean, spacious rooms of the convent for free.

## QUNEITRA قنيطرة

The word Quneitra is a diminished form of *quantara,* meaning bridge. The war-ravaged town owes its misfortune to its strategic location beside the Golan heights, at an intersection of roads leading to four countries.

Quinetra was destroyed during the Syrian-Israeli conflict of 1967, and has recently been opened by the Syrian government as a "museum" and memorial to those who perished during the Israeli bombing. Your guide may be spewing out scripted Syrian propaganda, but the visit is nonetheless a moving insight into the effects of Middle East conflicts. Visitors are given a guided tour of the modern ruins, including a walk through the crumbled main street, now overgrown with weeds. From the blatantly out of place Quinetra Restaurant, a spacious new dining facility, binoculars are provided to gaze out over the U.N. Military Security zone and then to Israel, 500m away. Visitors must obtain **permission** from the Syrian Tourist Police before going to Quinetra. You can do this in ten minutes at the office behind Place Adnan al-Malki, up the stairs of the white monument, across the street to your left (look for two plainclothes men with rifles out front). Buses leave from **Baraki Station** for Khan Arnabeh (1½hr., S£12) and then from Khan Arnabeh to Quneitra (15min., S£5). You will pick up your mandatory guide/security officer between Khan Arnabeh and Quneitra. Bring your **passport**—it will be checked often along the way.

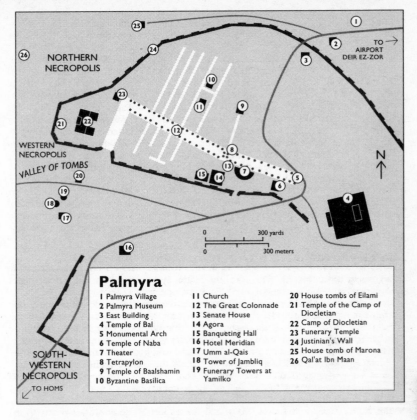

## Palmyra

| | | |
|---|---|---|
| **1** Palmyra Village | **11** Church | **20** House tombs of Eilami |
| **2** Palmyra Museum | **12** The Great Colonnade | **21** Temple of the Camp of |
| **3** East Building | **13** Senate House | Diocletian |
| **4** Temple of Bal | **14** Agora | **22** Camp of Diocletian |
| **5** Monumental Arch | **15** Banqueting Hall | **23** Funerary Temple |
| **6** Temple of Naba | **16** Hotel Meridian | **24** Justinian's Wall |
| **7** Theater | **17** Umm al-Qais | **25** House tomb of Marona |
| **8** Tetrapylon | **18** Tower of Jambliq | **26** Qal'at Ibn Maan |
| **9** Temple of Baalshamin | **19** Funerary Towers at | |
| **10** Byzantine Basilica | Yamilko | |

# Northwest Syria

## ■ Palmyra تدمـر

Once the capital of Queen Zenobia's renegade province of the Roman Empire, the city of Palmyra still maintains its former majesty. Standing proudly in a lush oasis surrounded by miles of uninhabited desert, Palmyra's grand column-lined avenues seem more monumental and glorious with every step. The ruins, weathered by centuries of war and sandstorms, remain among the most spectacular in the Middle East, and certainly a Syrian must-see. Despite its well-deserved fame, Palmyra (City of Palms) or Tadmor (City of Dates), as it is locally known, has managed to resist the claws of tourism. Visitors are coming in increasing numbers, and new hotels are going up every year, but sunsets over the castle are still sublime, and strolls among the spectacular ancient temples still awe with imperial silence.

Mentioned briefly in 19th century BCE tablets, Palmyra first flourished in the first century BCE as a stop for caravans passing from the Gulf to the Mediterranean. Its residents prospered on tax revenues collected from hot, thirsty traders taking advantage of Palmyra's green oasis. Palmyrans became even wealthier after their city was turned into a Roman colony in 129 CE. Most of the surviving remains date from this period of prosperity, when Palmyra was the keystone of the thriving trade between the Roman Empire, the Middle East, and India.

During the mid-2nd century CE, reduced trade and increasing Persian power inspired the Palmyran Odenathus to overthrow the city's senate and declare himself king. Odenathus and his son were assassinated in 267 after defeating the encroaching Persians, and his multi-lingual and strikingly beautiful second wife Zenobia took control of the city on behalf of her young son. Said by 18th-century historian Edward Gibbon to possess "manly understanding," this Greek-Arab woman achieved full independence from Rome, then actually attacked Roman territories, taking possession of lower Egypt and much of Asia Minor. Minting coins emblazoned with her image was the last straw; an infuriated Roman emperor Aurelian successfully attacked Palmyra and carted Zenobia to Rome—his most triumphant accomplishment. The rebellious spirit of Zenobia lived on among the residents of Palmyra long after her departure, but continued resistance only brought the city destruction. In succeeding years, Palmyra served as a Roman border fortress and, in the 7th century, was conquered by Muslims. Local emir Fakhr ad-Din built the castle overlooking the ancient site in the early 1600s, but the ruined city itself was only sporadically inhabited.

The modern lazy town was centered in the courtyard of the Temple of Bel, but between 1929 and 1932 was relocated northeast of the ruins. Clusters of hotels, restaurants, and antique shops have sprung up in the new town, catering to a growing number of travelers who stop to admire the famed site.

## ORIENTATION AND PRACTICAL INFORMATION

The **tourist office** (tel. 220 574) is on the highway, between the ruins and the new city (open daily 8am-1pm and 4-6pm). They give out one informative brochure and a few backgammon hints; more helpful books and guides are at the entrance to the Temple of Bel. The **post office** (tel. 229 947) is near the circle on the highway (open daily 8am-2pm). Two 24-hr. **telephones** are outside, but you must purchase your calling card during office hours. **Change money** before coming, though some hotels will change money if you're in a crunch. The **pharmacy** (tel. 220 455) is next to the Palmyra Hotel. For **medical emergencies,** call the **hospital** (tel. 551) or contact the police. The **police station** (tel. 112) is on the main street off the highway as you get to the first hotels in the new town. The **telephone code** is 31.

The **Karnak Station** (tel. 220 288) is near the circle by the post office. Karnak has daily 3pm service to Damascus (S£90) and Homs (S£50). The **Furat** bus company in the center of town makes three runs a day to Damascus (9:30, 11:30am, and 5:30pm, S£100); other private bus companies down the street (take a left at the little park) service Damascus, Homs, and several smaller towns. The **Pullman Station** will give you more options, but it's a lengthy walk out of town. Take a left on the big street before town, and don't turn right until you come to the next big street beyond the residential area.

## ACCOMMODATIONS

The town of Palmyra has been steadily encroaching upon the ruins for years; hotels are being renovated and prices are continually on the rise. There are still a good number of friendly cheapies, although they are slowly becoming an endangered species. Most hotels and good food options are on the main street starting at the highway. The hotels that charge in dollars are more comfortable and luxurious, but about six times more expensive. You can **camp** under one of the backyard olive trees at the luxury **Hotel Zenobia,** just yards away from the ruins, for S£200. Peak season is March-May; bargaining may work in the off-season, when simply walking away may be enough to lower a price by half.

**New Tourist Hotel,** on the main street (tel. 220 333). Decent rooms, unbeatable hospitality, and more free tea than you can pee. The rich guest comment book confirms this place as a backpackers' haven. Singles S£150, doubles S£325. Some rooms have private bath. Visa, MC.

**Afqa Hotel,** off the main street, before the Karnak station (tel. 910 386). Big fans and the thickest mattresses in Palmyra. Singles S£200 with private bath, doubles S£500 with bath and breakfast. Luxurious upstairs doubles S£600 with breakfast.

**Plaza Hotel,** a short right turn off the main street (tel./fax 911 707). Quiet cubicles are small, but fan, telephone, and clean private bathrooms with hot showers are included. Singles S£200, doubles S£400. Visa, MC, Diner's Club.

**Citadel Hotel,** across the street from the Karnak station and the museum (tel. 220 537). The first hotel you'll see when you get off the bus, but not the best. Clean and cramped upstairs rooms or dark, monastic, journey-to-the-center-of-the-earth, "student rooms." Doubles with bath S£700, without bath or window S£400. Student rooms S£100 per person, with free use of upstairs bathtubs and toilet.

**Tower Hotel,** on main street (tel. 910 01 16; fax 910 273). Grand entrance leads to cool, tiled lobby modeled after a Parisian café. Soft beds, high ceilings, views of ruins, and spacious blue bathrooms. Singles US$17, doubles US$23, triples US$28. TV, heat, A/C, and fridge extra. Breakfast US$2.

**Orient Hotel,** off the main street (tel. 220 131). Head toward the New Tourist Hotel and take a left. Luxury at appropriately higher prices. Immaculate mosaic floors, spacious, bright rooms, and a cool, comfy lobby. A rooftop restaurant with spectacular views is due to open in Sept. 1996. Singles US$22, doubles US$28, triples US$36. Breakfast included. Reservations are a good idea. Visa, MC.

## FOOD

Palmyra's main street is lined with restaurants whose sole purpose is to cater to tourists' every desire. Each has a special feature (student discounts, free tea, spaghetti), but value and quality don't differ greatly. Most places offer delicious meals—prices are not fixed, and bargaining is expected. Some of these serve beer for S£50 until 11pm, and almost all are open from 8am-midnight. Up the street, the local diners will be just as ready to feed you. They also may try to rip you off.

The **Palmyra Restaurant** (tel. 220 346) is the most refreshing oasis for a reasonably-priced sit-down meal. Surrounded by fountains, canopies, and an in-house boutique, you can get a *mezze* with chicken, mineral water, and salad for E£250 (enough for two). The **Tourist Oasis Restaurant** (tel. 221 439) and the **Al Khaiam Restaurant,** both next to the information office, offer *mezze* for S£100, S£150 with meat. Beer, wine, and *'araq* served (both open daily 8am-midnight).

## SIGHTS

Palmyra takes at least a full day to explore. The Ministry of Tourism would like you to begin at the **Temple of Bel,** the mammoth building enclosed by a largely reconstructed high wall. In the gate house, you'll find books on Syria and Palmyra as well as guides who may charge as much as S£1000 for one day. Bargaining can halve prices, and the guides are worthwhile for a more in-depth appreciation of the ruins, especially the Tombs and the Temple of Bel. (Gatehouse open daily 8am-1pm and 4-6pm; admission S£200, students S£15.)

The existing temple, begun in 32 CE, was built on the site of a Hellenistic site. Bel, identified with the Greek god Zeus and Roman god Jupiter, is a Babylonian pronunciation of the Semitic word "Ba'al," meaning master, and designated as the supreme god. In the middle of the temple, a **sacrificial altar** was used to slaughter animals. The blood ran into the drain in the floor, next to which are remnants of a large stone pipe that was part of a sophisticated plumbing system.

The **Great Colonnade** once led from the Temple of Bel to the monumental arch and the rest of the city, but is now cut by the highway. The **Ethnographic Museum** is an ill-fated attempt to make a "Museum of Popular Tradition" sound more interesting. It displays the usual wax statues and campfire scenes (admission S£100, students S£15). The oft-photographed **Monumental Arch,** constructed in 200CE, puts you back on the right track. The arches are richly decorated with rows of pearls, acorns, palm trunks, and acanthus, oak, and grape leaves.

SYRIA

Continuing on, you'll come to the **Temple of Nabo** on the left. Raised about two meters off the ground and dedicated to the Babylonian god of writing (later identified with Apollo), this first century CE construction, along with **Zenobia's Baths** to the right, is largely in ruins today. Up the colonnade and to the left is a newly (and overly) renovated **theater.** You can see the stage, the paved, semi-circular orchestra where the chorus performed, and the foundations of the actors' **dressing rooms** on either side of the stage. Adding a modern, personal touch, the Arabic script above the shiny new eastern door is a dedication to Hafez al-Asad.

Farther down the street to the left are the not-so-distinguishable remains of the **Agora,** a public forum, and the **Senate House.** Placement in the Agora was based on societal role: Palmyran or Roman officials in the northern portico, senators in the eastern portico, military persons in the western portico, and merchants and caravan leaders in the southern portico. Next door to the Agora is the **Banqueting Hall,** where religious fraternities congregated on holidays.

The prominent structure consisting of four groups of poorly rebuilt columns is the **Tetrapylon.** The pedestals in the center of each group of columns once supported statues, including the likenesses of the great Zenobia and her husband, Odenathus. To the right of the Tetrapylon, near the Zenobia Hotel, is the **Temple of Baalshamin,** dedicated to Zeus Baalshamin, Du-Rakhlun (the god of Rakhleh on the Hermon). Baalshamin, whose name means "Master of the Heavens," was the god of storms and fertilizing rains. The vestibule of the temple has six columns with platforms serving as bases for statues. Further to the right, in the ruins partially covered by the Zenobia Hotel, you can envision a **colonnaded courtyard** surrounded by rooms, one of them a **chapel.** This complex's role within the temple is unknown.

The imposing **Qal'at ibn Maan,** or Arab Castle, is attributed to Fakhr ed-Din the Ma'nite, once the ruler of the area between Mt. Lebanon and the Syrian desert. This fortress, built in the 12th or 13th century to protect Palmyra from eventual Crusader attacks, is *the* place to be at sunset. You can climb the 150m slope for free (about 30-45min.) or bargain for a ride from town (prices vary depending on the type of vehicle and presence of a guide).

To the left of the castle, are **funerary towers,** known as "eternal houses" in Palmyra. There are individual sepulchres, but each of the most important families had its own mausoleum. Guides may charge as much as S£500 for a trip out to the towers; cheaper rides without a guide can be found in front of the Citadel Hotel in town. From the main city, the tombs are a 30-minute walk, but the more interesting ones are locked—the keymaster hangs out at the Palmyra Museum. Once at the towers, most guides will let you latch on to their group for S£20. The Tomb of Elahbel and the Tomb of the Three Brothers are the most impressive. The **Tomb of Elahbel,** belonging to a rich Palmyran family, has stairs to the roof for a good view of the Valley of the Tombs. The **Tomb of the Three Brothers** is located southwest of the city (you'll need transportation to this one). The interior is painted with **colorful frescoes:** in the center panel, Achilles is depicted in feminine dress among the daughters of Lycomedes, king of Skyros, where he hid after the Delphic oracle foretold his death in the Trojan War. Upon seeing Ulysses, however, he suited up and fought until an arrow fatally pierced his now-famous left heel.

The **Palmyra Museum,** located at the entrance to the new town, displays statues taken from various family tombs, coins with godly depictions, a tacky model of an ancient Palmyran cave and its semi-naked inhabitants, and two very impressive mummies. An attendant with a key to the Tomb of the Three Brothers waits here at 8:30, 10:00, 11:30am, and 4:30pm, but you must arrange for transportation in town. (Open April-Oct. Wed.-Mon. 8am-1pm and 4-6pm, Nov.-March. Wed.-Mon. 8am-1pm and 2-4pm; admission S£200, students S£15.)

# ■ Homs حمص

Homs, Syria's third largest city, was built in 2400 BCE. Known in ancient times as Emesa, it was an important metropolis during the Roman era and a vital stop along the trade route that sprouted Palmyra. Unlike Palmyra, though, wars and earthquakes have destroyed most buildings of historical interest, leaving Homs an industrial waste-land strewn with bent telephone poles, hanging electrical wires, and rank streets. An oil refinery is now its claim to fame, processing the most sludge in Syria. As much as tourists may try to avoid the smoke-spewing city, Homs is often a mandatory transit point—roads from Hama, Palmyra, Damascus, and Tartus converge here, and Crac des Chevaliers is only a short bus ride away.

## ORIENTATION AND PRACTICAL INFORMATION

The **bus station** is located at the intersection of two large streets, **Al Corniche St.** and **Hama St.** A right turn out of the station brings you around the intersection to Hama St., where you'll find food vendors and small, cheap restaurants. Hama St. intersects **Quwatli St.** past the **Khalid ibn al-Walid Mosque,** at a bus stop and fountain. A right on Quwatli St. brings you to most of Homs' meager **accommodations.**

**Tourist information office:** A booth on Quwatli St. in a small park past the hotels, toward the clock tower. Open daily 8:30am-2pm and 4-10pm; erratic closings.

**Passport office:** On the right side of Ibn Khaldoun St., at the Quwatli St. intersec-tion. Open 9am-1pm for visa extensions. You'll need 4 passport-sized photos.

**Currency exchange:** Walking away from the small clock tower, take the first right at Quwatli St. It's at the end of the short block on the right. Ask in the neighboring shops if the booth is unstaffed.

**Buses:** To reach the bus station, follow Hama St. past the small clock tower circle and the Khalid Ibn al-Walid Mosque. **Minibuses** from the station go to Crac des Chevaliers (Qal'at al-Hosn) hourly until 5pm (1hr., S£25). **Microbuses** make daily runs to Damascus at 5:30pm (2hr., S£40), Aleppo at 1:30pm (2½hr., S£40), and Palmyra at 3pm (2hr., S£45). The **Karnak bus station** next door sends 4 buses daily to Damascus (2hr., S£50) and Hama (1hr., S£20), 3 to Lattakia (3hr., S£50) via Tartus (1½hr., S£30), and a 9am bus to Palmyra (2hr., S£50). Also daily buses to Cairo (S£2150), Istanbul (S£1500), Amman (S£2500), and Beirut (S£125).

**Late-Night Pharmacy:** Tel. 226 464. Across from the mosque on Hama St.

**Medical facilities:** Tel. 110. The government **hospital** is on Al Corniche St., a left turn out of the bus station; at the intersection with As-Salamiyeh St.

**Police:** Tel. 112. The headquarters are in the government building on Hashem al-Atasi St., a sharp left turn at the clock tower end of Quwatli St.

**Post office:** Quwatli St., past the tourist information office at the large clock tower circle. Open daily 8am-2:30pm. **Poste Restante** available.

**Telephone Code:** 31.

## ACCOMMODATIONS

Hotel options in Homs are not great, especially if you're traveling solo (there are two single rooms in the entire city, only one of which is a viable option). Most of these less-than-clean rooms are in large, old buildings on Quwatli St. in varying states of dis-repair. The Hotel Naser al-Jadid is your best bet.

**Hotel Naser al-Jadid** (tel. 227 243). In the middle of Quwatli St. Huge sitting room with high ceilings, comfy couches, and a breezy balcony. Rooms are relatively clean and sport supercool fans. Friendly management. The single Single S£200. Doubles S£300 for 1or 2 people. Cold showers S£25, hot showers S£50.

**Ghazi Hotel** (tel. 222 160), 1 block from the Naser al-Jadid (English sign says HOTEL). If you can't get a single at the Naser, the Ghazi has the only other one in town—a stuffy shoebox with no window or fan. Doubles are more pleasant, with windows and high ceilings. Singles S£200, doubles S£300. Shower included.

**Basman Grand Hotel** (tel. 225 009), on Abo Alaa St., parallel to Quwatli St. Take a left at the Hotel al-Khayam and the Basman will be on your right. Friendly manage-ment and clean private baths, but you pay a premium for the privacy: Singles US$15, doubles US$22, triples US$25.

**Hotel al-Khayam** (tel. 223 959), next door to the Ghazi. A last resort, with less than sparkling bathrooms. Free shower barely works. Doubles S£300.

## FOOD

Falafel, *shawerma,* and pastry shops, some open until midnight, line Hama St. between the bus station and Quwatli St. Roving merchants hawk fresh-roasted corn on the cob, fruits and vegetables, and sweets and nuts here. Several **juice and snack shops** squeeze on the street parallel to Quwatli St., behind the Hotel Naser al-Jadid. They're open late and offer affordable sandwiches and light fare. The diner-like restaurants between the park and the hotels are the stomping grounds of army officers from the Homs military headquarters. The **Nile Restaurant's** special is *fatteh,* a huge bowl of hummus, pieces of pita, lemon juice, and olive oil eaten with a spoon (S£17). For a sit-down meal try the **Toledo Restaurant,** behind the tourist office and park. Appetizers begin at S£40, entrees at S£150. Across the park from the Toledo, Syrians crowd into the semi-outdoor **Public Restaurant,** serving cheap, simple meat dishes for S£100. An enormous **café** across from the park showcases *argileh* smokers, tea sippers, and coffee addicts. Women are not welcome here after dark.

## SIGHTS

The **Khalid Ibn al-Walid Mosque** is on Hama Street between the city center and the bus station. The imposing mosque is dedicated to the Arab commander who brought Islam to Syria in the year 636 CE and was dubbed "the Sword of God" for his martial ability; his tomb lies inside. Built at the time of King adh-Dhaher Baybars and rebuilt in 1910 at the end of the Ottoman period, the mosque mixes Byzantine, Ottoman, and Arab styles. Its nine silver domes are surrounded by a pleasant park.

The **Great an-Nouri Mosque** is near the gate of the *souq* at the intersection of Hama St. and Quwatli St. Built in 1162 by Ayyubid commander Nour ad-Din Zanki (Nuraddin), the mosque is famous for its square minaret and wooden pulpit. The nearby **souqs** date back to the Ayyubid, Mamluk, and Ottoman periods, and are easy to get lost in.

In the old city, the fifth major right off of Al Hamidiyyeh St. brings you to the **Umm az-Zunnar Church,** built in 59 CE. Homs's earliest Christians worshipped here secretly, in fear of their pagan rulers' persecution. Expanded during the Christian era, it holds the so-called **Belt of the Virgin Mary,** found under the altar in 1953.

Homs's **museum,** located on Quwatli St. across from the hotel block, displays the usual pottery, jewelry, Ottoman swords, and handwritten Qur'ans. (Open Wed.-Thurs. 8am-4pm. Admission S£100, students S£15, but if you look interested they may turn on the lights and let you in for free.)

### Crac Des Chevaliers    قلعة الحصن

The Crusader castle **Crac des Chevaliers** (Qal'at al-Hosn in Arabic) is one of the best sights in Syria, and arguably the greatest castle in the world. A governor of Homs built it in 1031, leaving a Kurdish garrison in the castle for defense against enemy attacks on the Tripoli-Homs-Hama road. In 1110, Crusaders nearly destroyed the fortress while capturing it. They built a new castle on the ruins of the old and used it to control the "Homs Gap," a narrow pass linking the coast with the Orontes Valley. The Crusaders held the medieval fortress for 161 years. Even Salah ad-Din is rumored to have withdrawn his troops upon viewing the castle. It finally fell to the Mamluk army under the command of Sultan Baybars in 1271 after a month of intense fighting. The Crusaders were allowed to leave the country peacefully.

Perched on a hill 750m above sea level and spreading over 30,000 square meters, the castle's high towers afford you panoramic views of the Mediterranean, the Port of Tripoli, the Tower of Safita, and the Homs Lake. For extra security and architectural bragging rights, Crac is really a castle within a castle, with a moat separating the two and a larger moat surrounding the entire structure.

Upon entering through the main door, continue up the ramp past the **guard rooms** and **stables** on your left. You will come to a tower which leads to a **moat** and the outer wall if you go straight, or to the **main courtyard** if you take a sharp right turn. In front of the courtyard, the **seven-arched façade,** bearing two doors and five windows, is the castle's most aesthetically impressive feature. Behind it is the **main assembly room,** with Gothic, vaulted roofs, where Crusader kings were received by the knights of the castle. The **long room** against the castle's back wall contains a huge oven, five meters in diameter. To the right is a **cathedral** that was converted into a mosque in 1271. In another room, the bases of large clay oil jars still remain. The top floor of the Tower of the Daughter of the King is now a **café.**

Bring a flashlight to explore the secret passages and the dark corridors of the walls and castle (open daily 9am-5pm; admission S£200, students S£15).

Buses and *service* leave the Homs station for Qal'at al Hosn daily, about once an hour from 7am until 5pm (S£25). The last bus returns to the town at around 6pm. At the **Roundtable Restaurant and Hotel,** 100m to the right of the castle entrance, you can get a passable bed and bath for S£500 and a meal for about S£200. The **Restaurant Des Chevaliers,** in front of the main entrance, has similar prices and food.

# ▓ Hama حماة

The green Orontes River flows through the heart of Hama, and its slow-moving waters seem to dictate the town's pace. Hama has seen many empires rise and fall on the banks of its river, among them the Amorite, Babylonian, Hittite, Persian, Greek, Hellenistic, and Seleucid. It was not until 638 CE that the Muslim Arabs moved in. Although Hama has been inhabited since the 4th millennium BCE and was once an important trade center, few of its ancient monuments remain—except, of course, for the **norias** (Aramaic for "water wheels"). These impressive structures were built to raise water which was then shuttled to irrigate farmland. The low-pitched groaning sound is produced by wood rubbing wood; the same sound has been heard here since the *norias'* construction in the Middle Ages.

Today the constant groaning serves as a reminder of the painful events the town suffered in 1982. In February of that year, a small uprising by the Muslim Brotherhood was brutally quelled by the Syrian government. Unofficial reports say that President Hafez al-Assad sent in 8000 soldiers with air support and ordered the "round up" of men, women, and children for six bloody days. No one knows for sure how many people died by the end of this operation, but estimates range from 10,000 to 25,000. Up to 10,000 remain in a high-security prison in the desert near Palmyra. Nearly all residents were affected and the event is still of great sensitivity to both the townspeople and the secret police; the issue should not be addressed.

Nevertheless, life in Hama, like the beautiful *norias,* has gone on. The Orontes River and the numerous parks on its banks make the town an ideal place to spend a relaxing couple of days.

## ORIENTATION AND PRACTICAL INFORMATION

Getting around the small city of Hama is easy. The intersection of **Quwatli Street** and **Sadiq Avenue** marks the city center. Most budget hotels and restaurants are on Quwatli St., on the opposite side of the intersection from the bank and post office. This direction also leads to Al Murabet St. and the city's second major intersection. If you ever get lost, walking toward the grinding sound will bring you to the river.

**Tourist office:** On Sadiq Ave., across the river from the central intersection (tel. 511 033). Open daily 8am-2pm.

**Currency Exchange: Commercial Bank of Syria,** next to the post office. Cash and traveler's checks exchanged. Open daily 9am-2pm and 5-8pm.

**Federal Express:** Across from the post office. Open daily 9am-2pm and 4-6pm.

**Telephone office:** Around the corner from the post office; looks like a hot dog stand. Open daily 8am-9pm. Hama **directory assistance** is 142.

**Passport office:** Take a right at the intersection of Murabet and Quwatli.

**Minibuses:** A left turn (away from the river) at the intersection of Mubaret and Quwatli leads you to the depot. Conquer the hill by foot (20min.) or hop on a city bus headed in that direction (S£2). Minibuses to Damascus (4hr., S£32), Aleppo (3hr., S£25), and Homs (1hr., S£10) depart when full. **Service** leave from here.

**Buses: Al Aliah** bus station has service to all major Syrian cities in big, beautiful buses. Go past the Basman Grand Hotel, and take a left after the large, white government building—the station is on your left around the corner. The **Karnak** bus station is on the corniche in the middle of town, doubling as a pastry shop.

**Pharmacy:** A good one is on the small street behind the post office building. All pharmacies in Hama close at 9:30pm.

**Hospital: Medical Center Hospital** (tel. 222 012), just down the street from the Al Ahliah bus station.

**Emergency:** Tel. 11 (also for **police**).

**Post office:** A right on Quwatli St. when facing the river from the town center. Minimal services. Open daily 8am-2pm and sometimes 4-6:30pm.

**Telephone Code:** 33.

## ACCOMMODATIONS

Hotel prices in Hama vary drastically between summer and winter (high season and low season), and according to how well business has been going. Listed prices are only meant to give an idea of each hotel's range.

**Cairo Hotel,** on Quwatli St. near its intersection with Jamal abd en-Nasr St (tel. 222 280; fax 511 715). Manager Anas is a gracious host; rooms are spotless and some have A/C. Singles S£200. Doubles S£400, with bath S£450. Triples S£500, with bath S£600. Roof bed S£100.

**Riad Hotel,** right next door (tel. 239 512). Similar quality, but most of their single rooms are windowless. Singles S£300, with bath S£350. Doubles S£600. Triples S£750. Rooftop mattress and facilities S£100. Breakfast S£100.

**Noria Hotel,** on Quwatli St. towards Al Murabet St., across from the Riad and Cairo (tel. 512 414; fax 511 715). Luxurious and welcoming, the Noria is under the same impeccable management as the Cairo, but is much more upscale than its budget-conscious cousin. All rooms come with A/C and continental breakfast. Singles US$18, doubles US$28, triples US$36. Magnificent suites with kitchen, living room, and picture windows of the *norias* are US$60 for 3 people. Visa, MC.

## FOOD

Most of the restaurants in Hama are of the chicken, meat, and falafel variety. In those scattered among the hotels on Quwatli St., chickens are plump, portions are large, and a full meal, complete with salad, soda, and meat, won't cost more than S£100. The other dining options are the more expensive restaurants along the waterfront. The **Al Rawdah Restaurant** (tel. 239 890), along the pier in the center of town, offers *kabab* (S£155), *tabouli* (S£15), and ice cream (S£17). A 15-minute walk from the center of town with the river on your left takes you to **Four Norias,** an upscale riverfront restaurant (tel. 221 013). A complete Middle Eastern meal here costs S£200-250; *'araq* and Sharq beer are available (open daily 8am-2am). The **Sultan Restaurant** (tel. 235 104; behind the Hama Museum, on the river) provides a less commercialized riverside meal. Enjoy some fish (S£150) or just an Arabic coffee (S£15) and *argeileh* (S£35) in a quiet cabana (open daily 8am-8pm).

## SIGHTS

Most of Hama's sights can be seen by taking a stroll along the river. When facing the Orontes from the center of town, walk left along the bank and enter the cobblestone road of the **Old City.** These narrow, winding streets were built to afford protection from the sun at all hours of the day. A small Arabic sign above an old door on the left marks the entrance to **Hammam Othmania,** a Turkish bath from the Ottoman era. A bath with soap and a massage is only S£70 (open for women 7-11am, men 7pm-midnight).

The **Hama Museum,** located in the Old Azem Palace, is a bit farther on the right. As'ad Pasha al-Azem, governor of Hama from 1700 to 1742, built the palace as his residence. When he was promoted to a post in Damascus, he built an even grander structure of the same name. The palace had a men's section, the *Salamlek,* and a women's section, the *Haramlek,* which conveniently joined at the baths (open Wed.-Mon. 9am-6pm; admission S£125, students S£15).

After passing the Al Jabariyya water wheel (home of late-afternoon dare-devil diving kids), the road opens up at the **An-Nouri Mosque.** Built in 1162 by Ayyubid commander Nour ad-Din Zanki (Nuraddin), the mosque is famous for its square minaret and wooden pulpit. Unfortunately, the pulpit is housed in the Hama Museum while the mosque undergoes reconstruction.

A left turn at the mosque brings you to the **Citadel,** the center of the old city and a popular spot for evening strolls. Supposedly, relics from the 6th millennium BCE were unearthed from under this hill. Today, the only digging is done by kids playing in the huge park planted on top. You might be asked to pay a S£5 entrance fee.

Behind the Citadel, the **Grand Mosque** used to be one of Hama's biggest attractions, although you won't find it listed in the official literature anymore. This Umayyad structure, along with the tombs of Hama's 13th-century emirs, was destroyed during the 1982 uprising. Greek writing from a previous edifice still marks some of the fallen stones. The structure is currently being rebuilt.

# ■ Aleppo حلب

Aleppo (*Halab* in Arabic), the "second capital of Syria" 350km north of Damascus, has been a flourishing city since the 3rd millennium BCE. Abraham is said to have milked his grey cow on the acropolis here—hence the name *Halab ash-Shahba,* or "milk of the grey." The famous Citadel sits on the same *tel* today.

Situated at the crossroads of several vital trade routes, Aleppo has been of great commercial and military importance since the 2nd millennium BCE. The city controlled "The Great Syrian Passage" connecting Mesopotamia and Persia with the Mediterranean Sea. Such stellar positioning made Aleppo appealing to many kingdoms, and the Hittites, Egyptians, Assyrians, Persians, Greeks, and Romans all laid an occasional siege on the city. After the division of the Roman Empire, Aleppo became part of the Byzantine Empire; its early Christian atmosphere is still tangible today. The conflict between Byzantium and Persia resulted in Persia's occupation and plundering of the city in 440 CE.

Arab armies stormed the city in 636. Aleppo flourished under the Umayyads and Abbassids, but it was not until the days of the Hamadanis that Aleppo reached its peak. Sayf al-Dawla, who established the Hamadani state in 944, built the city's towering citadel and kept in his court the great poets Al Mutanabbi and Abu al-Firas. During this period, Aleppo was an architect's playground; splendid mosques, schools, and tombs sprang up like rabbits. The city's *khans* (or caravanserai) were built later to accommodate the many traders passing through; several still stand. Building continued during Ottoman rule, and expanded trade with Europe added a western tinge to Aleppo's style. The cafés and outdoor restaurants which crowd the city's wide, tree-lined streets continue this European tradition.

Aleppo today is a cosmopolitan metropolis. Expanded trade in textiles and glassware has brought this ancient city an air of sophistication and a freewheeling sense of fun not felt in the bigger, older capital to the south.

## ORIENTATION

Mastery of Aleppo's layout is simple. You'll find all budget **accommodations** and some **restaurants** in the area bounded by **Al Ma'ari** and **Quwatli Streets** (running east/west), and **Baron** and **Bab al-Faraj Streets** (running north/south). Late-night

SYRIA

walks in this area can be unpleasant, especially when the 70s American porno flicks let out. Men and women may be ogled or touched by panting passers-by. Starting from the **National Museum** and going up- (then down-) hill, you'll pass the **tourist information office, private bus services, travel agents,** the **Karnak bus station,** the **Commercial Bank of Syria,** and even a couple of expensive restaurants.

The city's wealthy residents strut their stuff in and around the restaurants and cafés of the **Christian Quarter.** Foot-propelled progress doesn't cost anything and is enjoyable in the cool evenings here, especially Aleppo's enormous **Public Garden.**

Several branches of the Commercial Bank of Syria remain closed most of the time on congested **Al Mutanabbi Street** between the hotel district, the **souqs,** and the **Citadel.** The easiest way to get a perspective on Syria's second-largest city is to hike up the Citadel's bridge and climb the western wall.

## PRACTICAL INFORMATION

**Tourist Information Office:** Al Ma'ari St. (tel. 221 200), at the intersection with Baron St., across from the National Museum. Get their map with bus and transportation information. Open Sat.-Thurs. 8:30am-2pm. The policemen who occupy the building in the afternoon may be able to help you.

**Tourist Police:** Tel. 119.

**Currency Exchange:** Changing anything but cash in Aleppo is a hassle. The **Commercial Bank of Syria** Branch #6, on Baron St. just past the Ugarit theater accepts traveler's checks for a small commission and a huge headache; bring your passport and your waiting-in-line shoes. Other branches on Al Mutanabbi St. only change cash. All branches open daily 8am-noon. An **exchange booth** at the intersection of Quwatli and Bab al-Faraj St. changes cash only. Open daily 8am-8pm, closed for an hour during Friday prayers.

**Telephone Office:** Inside the post office. Bring your calling card and pay at the desk after your call. Open daily 8am-9pm. 1min. to US S£125; to UK S£100.

**Flights: Syrian Air,** Baron St. (tel. 241 232), across from the Baron Hotel. Flights to Damascus (mornings daily, S£600), Istanbul (US$239), Cairo (US$182), and Paris (US$650). Prices vary seasonally. Open daily 8am-8pm. Lufthansa, Air France, British Airways, KLM, Saudi, and Turkish lines have offices on Baron St.

**Buses and service:** To ride a local bus, purchase a card valid for 4 rides (S£10). A bus leaves regularly during the day for the airport from a station across from the tourist office. **Service taxis** stop next to the **Pullman Station,** behind the palatial Amir Palace Hotel. Many **private bus companies** have offices on Ibrahim Hanano St. (a few minutes' walk to the right when facing the Amir Palace), and in the parking lot across the street from the Baron hotel. The **Pan bus company** (tel. 224 276) has daily services to just about any destination in **Turkey,** including Antakya (6am and 2pm, S£300); Iskenderun (6am and 2pm, S£550); and Istanbul (6am and 2pm, S£900). US$20 gets you a visa at the border. **Karnak** station (tel. 210 248) faces the Baron; daily buses to Lattakia (7am, 3hr., S£52) and Tartus (8am, 4hr., S£77), hourly runs to Homs (3½hr., S£62) and Hama (3hr., S£74), and two to Damascus (5am and noon, 5hr., S£100).

**English Bookstores:** Follow Baron St. away from the sleazy theaters toward the park. The **Omnia Bookshop,** on the left side of the street near the corner of Faris al-Khoury St., carries some international news magazines and a few English paperbacks. Take a right on Faris al-Khoury St. and look on the left for another **bookshop** with a better selection of English titles.

**Pharmacies: Al Mughrabi** (tel. 237 231), near Cham Palace Hotel, and **Al Mathaf** (tel. 246 419), across from the National Museum. Pharmacies in Aleppo are open 9:30am-1:30pm and 5-9pm. They rotate late-night duties.

**Doctor:** The English-speaking Dr. Faher (tel. 215 252), renowned for treating American Fulbright Scholars in Aleppo, is the best medical assistance option.

**Medical Emergencies:** Tel. 112.

**Post Office:** Al Jala'a St. (tel. 221 200), near Quwatli St. and the park; a green-shuttered building with postcard sellers blocking the entrance. Open daily 8am-8pm. **EMS** available Sat.-Thurs. 8am-5am. Bring your passport.

**Telephone Code:** 21.

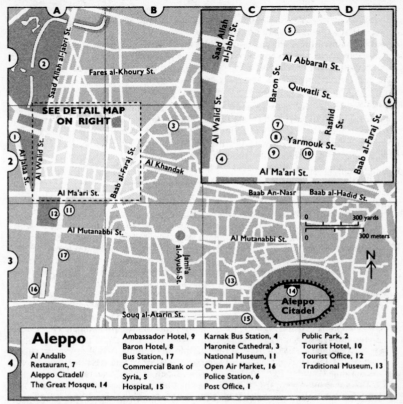

**Aleppo**

Al Andalib
Restaurant, 7
Aleppo Citadel/
The Great Mosque, 14

Ambassador Hotel, 9
Baron Hotel, 8
Bus Station, 17
Commercial Bank of
Syria, 5
Hospital, 15

Karnak Bus Station, 4
Maronite Cathedral, 3
National Museum, 11
Open Air Market, 16
Police Station, 6
Post Office, 1

Public Park, 2
Tourist Hotel, 10
Tourist Office, 12
Traditional Museum, 13

## ACCOMMODATIONS

Hotels in Aleppo range from the seat of sleaze to the lap of luxury, with enough in between to satisfy any budget. Higher-priced options cluster on Baron St. in the center of town; more affordable places are scattered among the spare car parts of the streets behind the Baron and Al Ma'ari St. Those searching for very cheap hotels should be warned that many are frequented by Russian prostitutes. Look carefully before letting go of your cash.

**Tourist Hotel** (tel. 216 583), off Yarmouk St. across from the museum. Head down Al Ma'ari St. and take a left at the Syria Hotel. Spotless rooms are cleaned and inspected by white-gloved Madame Olga, the distinguished owner who loves to stay up late chatting in French. Singles S£350. Doubles S£650 with shower.

**Hotel Najem Akhdar** (tel. 239 157). When facing the library from the clock tower, take a left and then a right around the mosque; the hotel is on your right. A basic bed in a basic room with a fan goes for S£150. Not as nice as the Tourist Hotel, but cheaper and also has friendly management.

**Hotel Yarmouk,** Al Ma'ari St. (tel. 217 510), across from the National Museum. An elevator on its last legs carries you high above street noise. Don't get your hopes up: quiet rooms are almost always reserved for Russian groups on trading sprees. Singles S£250, doubles S£400, triples S£550.

**Baron Hotel,** Baron St. (tel. 210 880 or 881). Aleppo was once the end of the line on the Orient Express, and the Baron Hotel was once a stopover for such illustrious guests as T.E. Lawrence, Agatha Christie, Kemal Ataturk, and Hafez al-Assad. The

Baron still exercises a certain majestic charm and romanticism, but oh, the prices: singles US$29, doubles US$39.

**Ambassador Hotel,** Baron St. (tel. 211 833), next to the Baron Hotel. Cool rooms are expansive. Singles US$14, with bath US$17. Doubles US$20, with bath US$23. Triples US$23, with bath US$29.

## FOOD

For great inexpensive restaurants and cafés, go around the corner from the exchange booth on Quwatli St. onto Bab al-Faraj St. Take a right at the fruit shake stands and you'll see six or seven places on your right. Baron St. has some nicer places with bird's-eye views of the crowds, but they're more expensive. All sorts of European- and American-style restaurants and cafés have sprung up in the Christian neighborhood near the park off Sa'adullah al-Jabri St., including Pizza House and a golden arch bedecked burger-and-pizza place that ain't no Mickey D's.

**Abu Nouwas** (tel. 210 388). From Al Ma'ari St., take the last left before Bab al-Faraj St. This clean, A/C diner is 2 blocks uphill on the left. *Kabab* served with warm pita, onions, tomatoes, and peppers. Outstanding lentil soup. Full meal (soup, salad, meat, and drink) under S£200; breakfast S£60. Open daily 8am-11:30pm.

**Al Andaleeb,** just to the left of the Baron Hotel when facing it from the street (tel. 224 030). This roof-top *mat'am* has a daily lunch or dinner special featuring *kabab* or 2 big *shishes* plus salad and hummus or *mutabbal* for S£150. *'Araq* and beer served. Open daily 10am-midnight.

**Ali Baba Restaurant** (tel. 215 024). From the clock tower, head up Bab al-Faraj St. and take a left at the "cocktail" stands. Another rooftop wonder, its cuisine was voted best in Aleppo (by the in-house chefs). Their specialty is the *kabab halab* (S£80). Sharq beer (S£40) and plenty of *'araq* (S£50) are sipped by the mostly male dinner guests.

**Sage,** Sa'adullah al-Jabri St. (tel. 215 870), in front of the park. Cakes, pizzas, cheese sandwiches, banana splits, and all the sugary incentive you need for a stroll away from the city center. Puff up for S£100-150. Open daily 8:30am-midnight.

**Patisserie Mousattat,** Quwatli St., next to the exchange booth. Can't stomach *shawerma* before noon? Bring your morning munchies here and ask for *ma'moniyya:* a yummy cream-of-wheat-like starch, drenched in warm syrup, topped with something in between butter and cheese, and eaten with pita bread. If you can't pronounce it, just point to what the locals at the next table are eating.

## SIGHTS AND ENTERTAINMENT

If you begin your sight-seeing tour of Aleppo at the intimidating **Citadel,** you'll get an outstanding view of the city. After crossing over the bridge, enter the enormous gate, fortified with three sets of steel doors. Built in the 10th century CE by Sayf ad-Dawla, the Citadel stands 50m above the city on a hill heightened by the remains of prior civilizations. In times of war, Aleppans took refuge in this fortress, equipped with numerous defense structures and plentiful provisions. The 12th-century moat is 20m deep and 30m wide, lined with smooth stones to make climbing difficult (some of these tiles are still in place today). The watery defense is now full of garbage, though not for the first time. Historical accounts gruesomely, if hyperbolically, recount how in 1400, Timor's Central Asian forces couldn't penetrate the Citadel until the moat was brimming with fallen soldiers' bodies.

To the immediate left of the inside main path lies a **bath** that was at one time used as a metal-working studio. Beyond that is the **small mosque,** with a well in the middle of its courtyard, the **great mosque** (only slightly bigger than the small mosque but with a fountain instead of a well), and a cafeteria. To the right of the main path are **storage rooms** for keeping food and water to be consumed during sieges, followed by stairs which lead to the **Royal Palace.** One of the most interesting sections of the Citadel, this area has its own baths and a courtyard paved with black and white marble. From the Palace, a passage leads to the opulent but overly restored **Throne Room,** which sits directly above the main entrance. In front of the main path and connected to the cafeteria are the **barracks,** now a museum displaying objects found during the Citadel's excavation. (Citadel open Wed.-Mon. 9am-6pm. Admission S£200, students S£25; museum admission S£100, students S£15.)

Outside the Citadel, the **Hammam Yalboagha An-Nasiri** waits to steam and wash the sweat and grime off dirty, sore bodies. This restored 14th-century bath is now heavily pushed by the Ministry of Tourism. (Open for women Sat., Mon., and Thurs. 10am-6pm; for men Sat., Mon., and Thurs. 7pm-midnight and every other day 9am-2am. S£365 gets you a soaping, massage, and cup of coffee or tea.)

Between the Hammam/Citadel area and the hotel district is perhaps the best **souq** in the Eastern Mediterranean. Bursting with leather goods, backgammon boards, carpets, tablecloths, Qur'ans, *argeilehs,* brass goodies, *kafiyyehs,* and gold and silver jewelry, the 9km of Aleppo's *souqs* provide several days of wide-eyed delight. Even if the mood to spend doesn't strike, merchants' invitations for a perusal of their goods and a glass of tea provide opportunities for conversation and insight into the lives of Aleppo's diverse population. Almost everything here is closed on Fridays. Several **khans** or caravanserais are scattered among the *souqs.* These beautifully designed inns housed worldly traders during the Mamluk and Ottoman periods.

Also in the *souq* area are several important mosques. **Al Jami' al-Kabir,** the Great Mosque of the Umayyads (also known as Zacharias's Mosque, after the Father of John the Baptist), was built on top of a Byzantine cathedral in the 8th century. Not far is the 600-year-old **insane asylum,** in surprisingly good condition (though empty). Wander through to see where the insane, the not-so-insane, and the very rich were kept locked up by their families. The clean smell emanates from two **soap factories** around the corner—Aleppo soap is known all over the Middle East for its excellent quality. Both factories have been in the same spotless families for generations.

The **National Museum,** across from the tourist office on Baron St., is second only to the Damascus museum in exhibit quality. Several 100,000-year-old flint axes from Ugarit, a basalt altar from the 3rd millennium BCE city of Ebla, and a stone guard lion from an 18th-century BCE temple will leave you reeling with wonder at the relative insignificance of your own temporal existence. The third floor includes a modern art wing; you may have to ask a guard to open it for you (open Wed.-Mon. 9am-6pm; admission S£200, students S£25).

On Sundays the shops in the **Christian Quarter** shops close, but the narrow streets lined with fabulous 17th and 18th century homes are alive with the faithful. Within a few blocks, churches from four different denominations attract worshippers. Walk down Quwatli St. past Baab al-Faraj St. and take a left at a weird-looking stone gate. Down a a narrow alley to the right is a 19th-century **Maronite Cathedral.** To the right is a gorgeous **Greek Catholic Church.** When you get to the store with underwear hanging in the window, take a right to visit the **Greek Orthodox Church** and the **Armenian Church of the Forty Martyrs.** These magnificent buildings feature 3rd-century artwork, engraved marble altars and sanctuaries, antique chandeliers, and gracefully constructed ceilings and supports. Throughout the neighborhood, you'll see fabulous 17th- and 18th-century homes. The tiny **Museum of Popular Traditions** shows clothes, tools, and furniture from these historic homes. (Museum open Wed.-Mon. 8am-2pm. Admission S£200, students S£25.)

# ■ Near Aleppo

## THE BASILICA OF SAINT SIMEON قلعة سمان

Born in a small mountain village in 386 CE, Saint Simeon of Stylites acquired the first and last parts of his name by spending decades preaching from atop a "stylite" (from the Greek *sylos,* meaning "pillar"). Simeon, a shepherd, had chained himself to a railing atop the pillar after receiving divine instruction in a dream. Local peasants heard about his actions and began coming to the chained man for advice. Before long, people came from all around to hear Simeon preach. With so many fans, Simeon had to find higher and higher pillars to sanctify, eventually ending up 15m in the air. Simple

Simeon would accept only two supplies of rations a week, and, while he would gladly answer male pilgrims' spiritual questions, he refused to talk to women—not even his beaming mom.

Simeon's death in 459 did not stop pilgrims from coming, and the emperor Zenon had a cathedral, now considered a masterpiece of pre-Islamic architecture, built around his home. A large dome covered the octagonal courtyard in which the pillar stood, surrounded by four basilicas which formed a giant cross. One basilica was a chapel, the other three housed pilgrims. The rear wall of the chapel was decorated with delicate acanthus leaves and Byzantine crosses, widespread decorations of the time. An earthquake destroyed the structure less than 50 years after its completion, causing pilgrims to question the site's holiness and deterring pious investors from rebuilding the cathedral. The 5th-century remains are impressive nonetheless. In the 10th century, the site was converted to a Byzantine fort with 27 towers along an enclosing wall. The fortifications are easily distinguishable from the cathedral ruins.

To reach St. Simeon from Aleppo, take a microbus to **Darret 'Azzay** (S£5). From this small town, you can negotiate with locals for the 15km ride to the cathedral. The *service* minivans will ask for S£100 for one way, but locals in brightly colored three-wheelers might do a round trip for only a bit more. Use a side-trip to **Qatura** as a bargaining chip. This Roman tomb is carved into rock about 1km off the road to St. Simeon. Above the entrance to the main tomb, an eagle with spread wings symbolizes the soul; it's identical to one in Palmyra's Temple of Bel, carved around the same time (open Wed.-Thurs. 9am-3pm; admission S£200).

## EBLA أبلا

This *tel* 60km south of Aleppo is the most significant archaeological site found in recent years (1964), and excavations are still in progress. Ebla is thought to have been the oldest city in Syria, dating back to the 3rd millennium BCE. Over 17,000 cuneiform tablets have been recovered in an ancient palace library, revealing much about Syria's early history. Apparently, Ebla was the center of an important north Syrian empire around 2000 BCE, but a 17th-century BCE Hittite invasion ended its important rule.

From the Aleppo station, take a microbus headed to **Maaret En-Noman** and ask to get off at the road to Ebla. It's a half-hour walk to the site and there is no food or water available (admission S£100, students S£15, when the guy is there to collect it). Back on the highway, it's easy to catch a bus back to Aleppo; they come often from both Maaret En-Noman and Hama.

# MEDITERRANEAN COAST

## ■ Lattakia اللاذقية

Lattakia is a decidedly practical city. Far from being the Mediterranean resort some Ministry of Tourism pamphlets would have you believe, Lattakia's tall buildings and crowded streets have a congested, big-city feel. Lattakia is Syria's largest seaport and serves as the country's major import-export center. It is equipped with plenty of cheap eats and budget accommodations, and serves as a base for exploring the ruins at Ugarit and the castle of Salah ad-Din. The only clean beach is at the 5-star Cham Palace Hotel (accessible by *service* from the station near the mosque), where for S£250, you can enjoy the white sands and shimmering sea seen in the brochures.

Constructed in the 2nd century BCE by the Seleucids, Lattakia was named after the mother of its architect (Laudetia). The only ancient remains are a few columns, a Roman arch from 200 CE, and some Ugarit artifacts. You can these at the museum, housed in the Ottoman Khan ad-Dukhan (open Wed.-Mon. 9am-6pm; admission S£200, students S£25).

## ORIENTATION AND PRACTICAL INFORMATION

The main street in Lattakia is 14 Ramadan Street, running northeast away from the water and ending at the tourist office (tel. 416 926; open daily 8am-2pm). At its intersection with Hanano St., the Place Hanano is home to an Asad statue and many budget accommodations. A little bit inland, running north and south from the beginning of 14 Ramadan St., is 8 Azar Street, which turns into Baghdad Avenue south at the Al Quds Street intersection. Continuing south, a right on the next street brings you to the surprisingly efficient post office (Sayf al-Dawla St., open daily 8am-7:30pm for stamps, telex, fax, and telegram service). The telephone office is housed in the same building. (Open daily 8am-10pm. Purchase a calling card at the booth; 1 minute to U.S. costs S£125, S£100 to the U.K., S£115 to Australia.) Across the street is a DHL international office (open Sat.-Thurs. 8:30am-7pm, Fri. 9am-2pm). Exchange money at the Commercial Bank of Syria on the right side of 8 Azar St. before reaching the traffic circle (open 8am-2pm and 5pm-8pm; traveler's checks not exchanged in evening). In case of emergencies, call the Basil Asad Hospital (tel. 238 825) or the police (tel. 112). The telephone code is 41.

The Karnak bus station (tel. 233 553) is on the corner of Baghdad Ave. and Sayf al-Dawla St. (turn left off Baghdad Ave. opposite the post office). Buses to Damascus (5hr., S£90) via Homs (3hr., S£45) leave at 7, 8am, 2:30, and 3:30pm (reserve a day ahead or get to the office by 7am). There's also daily service to Aleppo (3pm, 3hr., S£50) and Beirut (6pm, 4hr., S£175). Pullman offices on 14 Ramadan Street have hourly departures to Aleppo (S£100) and Damascus (S£140). The Bessma bus station (tel. 228 945), across from the Al-Nous Hotel on Ramadan St., has a daily 7:30am departure to Turkey (Antakya S£530, Adana S£550, Mersin S£550; call in advance). Bring your passport and US$20 to the border to get a visa.

Travel within the city by taxi (bargain *before* you get in the car) or by *service*, which take the form of white mini-vans. To get to the microbus station, with regular departures to neighboring areas, walk down Ramadan St. toward the tourist office, break left on Al Maghreb al-Arabi Street at the big traffic circle, then take your first right and continue for about 500m.

## ACCOMMODATIONS AND FOOD

The Hotel Lattakia (tel. 239 927) is to the right when facing the outdoor café from the Asad Statue. Walk down the right-hand street and take your first right; look for the yellow "Hotel" sign. Friendly management provides fan, balcony, a clean bath, and a welcoming cup of tea (doubles with bath S£300). The Dounia Hotel (tel. 421 296) is also a great value. Facing away from the Asad statue and outdoor café, take your second right; the small hotel is on your left. A bed in a clean room and a pair of slippers for the walk to the cold shower are yours for S£100. You get what you pay for at the blue Omaya Hotel, to the left when facing the outdoor café from the Asad statue. Rooms are livable and super-cheap (singles S£50, with bath S£55, doubles S£75, with bath S£90, triples S£105, with bath S£115).

Eating meals in Lattakia works the usual way—walk around enough and the raw meat and overcooked chicken in the windows start to look appetizing. Before seeking out their 317th falafel sandwich, vegivores should check out the Alexandria Restaurant on the corner of Ramadan St. near the Dounia Hotel, where a spicy plate of beans and rice goes for S£40. Next door, the Sindbad Restaurant makes a pizza-like dish with ground beef, onions, and green peppers for S£55. The Tea Room, near the Commercial Bank of Syria on Azar St., is a the perfect place for an after-dinner cup (tea or coffee S£20). They have honey-drenched sweets, a pleasant terrace, and the best lemonade in the known world.

## ■ Near Lattakia

### RAS SHAMRA AND UGARIT رأس الشمرة

This tiny town 16km north of Lattakia is the site of the historic Kingdom of Ugarit. In 1928, an unsuspecting peasant farmer unearthed a few slabs of stone marking a spot originally settled in the 7th millennium BCE. Ugarit's greatest gift to our time is its twenty-eight-letter **alphabet,** preserved in a stone tablet from the 14th century BCE. The oldest phonetic alphabet in the world, Ugaritic is the probable ancestor of both the Phoenician and Hebrew alphabets (though not the languages), and from there those of Latin and Greek. You can see the tablet in the National Museum in Damascus. The maze of ruins are mostly overgrown with weeds, and a professional guide is necessary to truly appreciate the structures. English and French-speaking guides hang out at the entrance; they'll take your best offer. As you enter, the **royal palace** (where the alphabet was found) is to the right; the **residential quarters** and **acropolis** are further down along the main path. To get to Ugarit, take a *service* (S£5 at the stop downhill from the Lattakia mosque) to Ras Shamra and ask the driver to drop you off at the ruins (open daily 9am-6pm; admission S£200, students S£25).

### QAL'AT SALAH AD-DIN قلعة صلاح الدين

Situated 35km east of Lattakia, this fortress is named for the exalted warrior who took the "impregnable" castle from the Crusaders in 1188. Perched on a plateau flanked by two deep gorges, the site's most impressive feature is the 156km long, 18m wide, and 28m deep trench that was cut by hand to completely isolate the fortress from the adjacent land. The lone column of rock in the gorge was used to support a lowering drawbridge. Inside the walls, you'll find the arched entry to a stable on your right, along with a dungeon in the drawbridge tower. Holes in the dungeon walls mark where prisoners' chains were drilled into the stone. Inside the next tower up the path, a hollow column conceals a secret staircase. Soldiers on the roof could descend to the moat and attack the enemy from behind. Across from the entrance is a huge cistern that collected rain water for 4000 soldiers' teas. To the left are remains of Byzantine and Crusader churches, and directly in front is the mosque (castle open daily 9am-5pm; admission S£200, S£25 with ISIC).

From Lattakia, take a microbus to Al Haffeh (S£10, 45min.). The easiest ride from here is to hire the services of one of the Honda mopeds across the street. For S£100 they take you to the castle, wait for an hour, and bring you back to the bus stop. Taxis will ask for S£100 for a one-way trip, and they know how few cars there are along the 7km road to the castle (hitchers should think twice).

## ■ Tartus طرطوس

Tartus is Syria's second major seaport, located 90km to the south of Lattakia and possessing more charm than its big sister to the north. This Mediterranean town was called Antardus by the Phoenicians and Tortusa by the Byzantines, and is referenced in cuneiform texts dating back to the 2nd millennium BCE. Tartus was one of the main supply ports for the Crusaders and an important military base until its capture by Salah ad-Din in 1188; the patchwork architecture of the medieval city underscores its diverse past. Modern-day Tartusians still inhabit the narrow lanes and arched buildings of the old town.

### ORIENTATION AND PRACTICAL INFORMATION

The downtown area of Tartus is bounded by three main streets, forming a rectangle along with the corniche. **First Street** and **Ibn al-Walid Street** run from the sea to **Ath-Thawra Avenue.** Most of Tartus's reasonably priced hotels and many restaurants line **First Street,** running east from the corniche at the **Arwad dock.** At the **clock tower circle,** a left on **Ath-Thawra Avenue** sends you in the direction of another circle near the **police station.** A block farther and to the right of Ath-Thawra are the **post** and **telephone offices** (post office open daily 8am-2pm, phone office open daily 8am-7pm). A right turn at the circle onto Ibn al-Walid St. takes you past the **Commercial Bank of Syria** and the **tourist information office,** and deposits you back on the corniche in front of the **Old City.**

The **Kadmous Transportation Co.** on Ibn al-Walid St. next to the information office has daily buses to Damascus (4hr., S£110), Aleppo (5hr., S£115), and Lattakia (1hr., S£30). The **microbus station,** a good 15-minute walk from the town center (take either of the two main streets away from the sea, pass Ath-Thawra Ave. and turn right on Tichrin Ave.), services nearby destinations.

## ACCOMMODATIONS AND FOOD

Tartus has enough budget hotel and restaurant options to make any brief stay a pleasant one. The **Daniel Hotel** (tel. 220 581), a block and a half up from the beach on First St., has spotless rooms with fans and private baths. (S£300 for a bed, S£400 with breakfast; S£400 for a double room, S£500 with breakfast.) Up the street on the right of the next intersection is the **Republic Hotel** (tel. 200 220). Clean rooms come with a fan and a sink; a hot shower costs S£30 extra (singles S£225, doubles S£300). Rooms are cheaper, though less inviting, farther up First St. at the **Hotel Tourism** (tel. 221 763). Rooms have telephones and either a balcony or a fan (singles S£100, doubles S£200). On the more expensive end, the **Blue Beach Hotel** (tel. 220 650), on the corner of the corniche and First St., will exchange a room with a few amenities and a balcony over the sea for a close-up view of more than a few greenbacks. (Singles US$13, doubles US$17, triples US$21.)

The **Venicia Restaurant,** near the Blue Beach Hotel, sells the usual meat, chicken, and *mezze* dishes for reasonable prices. Fresh fish is a catch at S£500-700. If you come after 7:30pm, the pizza (S£75 per slice) that the sign advertises may be ready. Tables for two on the balcony overlook the sea and Arwad dock. Just across First St., the **Al Nabil Restaurant** (tel. 220 959) offers similar cuisine at similar prices. Pleasant outdoor tables have their own mini-fountains (fresh fish S£500 per kg; meat, salad, and soda S£125-150). Up the street from Al Nabil and just past the pharmacy is a cheap, delicious den called **Nabil.** Gobble and gab with the local fishermen: a filling meal of hummus or *fuul* and *mezze* goes for S£20. For a more luxurious dining experience, treat yourself to **The Cave,** on the waterfront by the Old City. Chef Ahmed spent 18 years as a cook on a Greek ship and brews his own *araq.* Local fish with all the trimmings costs S£700-800 but serves two.

## SIGHTS

The medieval **Old City** bustles with modern life. Almost entirely unrenovated, the sturdy walls enclose a hive of activity and chronologically jumbled architecture. The fortified, 12th-century **cathedral** claims to be the location of the world's oldest altar dedicated to the Virgin Mary. Now a **museum,** the cathedral houses an eclectic collection of artifacts from all over coastal Syria (open Wed.-Mon. 9am-6pm; admission S£200, students S£25). For evening entertainment, nothing beats a sunset stroll along the corniche.

# ■ Near Tartus

## ARWAD ارواد

Syria's sole island, Arwad is positioned just 3km from the coast of Tartus. In ancient times Arwad served as a sanctuary for those seeking protection from foreign invaders. As such, it was the last Crusader stronghold to return to Muslim hands. More recently, its citadel was used by the French as a prison for Syrian nationalists. The Phoenician kingdom of Aradus was centered on the island, and though its renowned defensive walls no longer stand, two medieval forts remain, one of which now calls itself a museum (admission S£200, students S£25). Your time would be just as well spent wandering the narrow lanes or enjoying a sea-side cup of tea.

Ferries run every 15 minutes or so from Arwad port in Tartus. The round trip costs S£20, which you pay on the island before returning. The last boat leaves at 8:30pm and there are no formal lodgings available on the island.

## SAFITA سفيتة

Of the once majestic **Castle le Blanc,** only one remaining tower stands guard over the tiled roofed houses and olive trees of the small mountain town of Safita. The tower's entrance level is graced by a beautiful chapel that has never been deconsecrated and is still used for services today. Upstairs are the spacious living quarters, and above them the roof, offering panoramic views.

To get to Castle le Blanc, take a microbus from Tartus to Safita (S£7, 45min.). Round-trip *service* and minibuses leave every 15 minutes or so from the town center. Alternatively, you can hoof it from the town center: walk up the steepest street and look for the cobblestone side-road on the right leading up to the tower. Admission is free, but a tip (around S£10) may be expected on the way out. (Open daily summer 8am-1pm and 4pm-7:30pm; winter 8am-1pm and 3-6pm.)

## QAL'AT AL-MARQAB قلعة المرقب

Arabic for "control," al-Marqab Citadel holds a dominant position over the surrounding mountain range and sea. The enormous black basalt citadel has 14 imposing towers and was designed to house 1000 soldiers. Built by Muslims in 1062 CE, the castle was occupied by Crusaders in the 12th century before being retaken by the Mamluks in 1285. To reach the citadel, take a microbus to Baniyas (S£12, 30min.) and then catch a local *service* (S£5) to the castle's entrance. You can also hire a moped for a thrilling ride up to the castle and back (S£100, and the driver should wait an hour). Ask the guard to show you the Byzantine frescoes in the church—S£10 tip should suffice. (Open in summer 9am-6pm, 9am-4pm in winter; admission S£200, students S£25.)

# Appendix

## ■ Climate

| Temp in °C Rain in cm | January Temp | Rain | April Temp | Rain | July Temp | Rain | October Temp | Rain |
|---|---|---|---|---|---|---|---|---|
| Aleppo | 10/2 | 8.9 | 24/9 | 2.8 | 34/21 | 0 | 27/12 | 2.5 |
| Alexandria | 19/11 | 4.8 | 23/15 | .3 | 30/23 | 0 | 28/20 | .5 |
| Amman | 16/4 | 6.9 | 23/9 | 1.5 | 32/18 | 0 | 27/14 | .5 |
| Aqaba/Eilat | 21/10 | 0 | 31/18 | .5 | 40/25 | 0 | 33/21 | 0 |
| Aswan | 25/10 | 0 | 36/19 | 0 | 42/26 | 0 | 37/22 | 0 |
| Cairo | 18/8 | .5 | 28/14 | .3 | 36/21 | 0 | 30/18 | .3 |
| Damascus | 12/2 | 4.3 | 24/9 | 1.3 | 36/18 | 0 | 27/12 | 1.0 |
| Haifa | 17/8 | 17.5 | 25/14 | 2.5 | 30/20 | 0 | 29/20 | 2.5 |
| Jerusalem | 11/6 | 13.2 | 23/10 | 2.8 | 29/19 | 0 | 27/15 | 1.3 |

## ■ Area Codes

| EGYPT | 20 |
|---|---|
| Alexandria | 03 |
| Aswan | 097 |
| Bahariyya | 010 |
| Cairo | 02 |
| Dakhla | 092 |
| Dendera | 096 |
| Esna | 095 |
| Fayyum | 047 |
| Hurghada | 065 |
| Ismailiyya | 064 |
| Kharga | 092 |
| Luxor | 095 |
| Port Said | 048 |
| Qena | 096 |
| Sinai (all) | 062 |
| Suez | 062 |

| ISRAEL | 972 |
|---|---|
| Akko/Haifa | 04 |
| Ashkelon | 07 |
| Be'er Sheva | 07 |
| Caesarea | 06 |
| Eilat | 07 |
| Golan | 06 |
| Jerusalem | 02 |
| Nahariyya | 04 |
| Nazareth | 06 |
| Netanya | 099 |
| Qumran | 02 |
| Safad | 06 |
| Tel Aviv | 03 |
| Tiberias | 06 |
| Ramallah/ S. West Bank | 02 |
| Nablus/ N. West Bank | 09 |

| JORDAN | 962 |
|---|---|
| Ajloun | 04 |
| Amman | 06 |
| Aqaba | 03 |
| Dead Sea | 05 |
| The Desert | 06 |
| Irbid | 02 |
| Kerak | 03 |
| Madaba | 08 |
| Petra | 03 |
| Salt | 03 |

| SYRIA | 963 |
|---|---|
| Aleppo | 21 |
| Damascus | 11 |
| Hama | 21 |
| Homs | 31 |
| Lattakia | 31 |
| Palmyra | 34 |

## ■ Festivals

All festivals and holidays in Israel last from sundown the night before to nightfall the next day. For the holiday periods of Passover and Sukkot, businesses are closed for the first day (and in the case of Passover, the last day) but remain open for the rest of the time period. Be aware that Friday (Juma'a) is the holy day in the Muslim world and that Saturday (Shabbat) is the holy day in Israel; expect many businesses to be closed on these days. For a complete explanation of festivals and holidays, especially in Israel, see **When to Go,** p. 2, and individual country introductions.

| ISLAMIC | DATE IN 1997 | JEWISH/ISRAELI | DATE IN 1997 |
|---|---|---|---|
| **First Day of Ramadan** | Jan. 11 | **Purim** | Mar. 23 |
| **Nuzulul Qur'an** | Jan. 27 | **Passover** | Apr. 22-28 |
| **'Eid al-Fitr** | Feb.. 9 | **Yom Ha-Shoah** | May 4 |
| **'Eid al-Adha** | Apr. 18 | **Yom Ha-Zikaron** | May 11 |
| **Islamic New Year** | May 8 | **Yom Ha-Atzmaut** | May 12 |
| **Ashoora** | May 17 | **Yom Yerushalyim** | Jun. 4 |
| **Mawlid Nabi** | Jul. 17 | **Shavuot** | Jun. 11 |
| **Isra' and Miraj** | Nov. 28 | **Ninth of Av** | Aug. 12 |
| **First Day of Ramadan** | Dec. 31 | **Rosh Ha-Shanah** | Oct. 2-3 |
| | | **Yom Kippur** | Oct. 11 |
| **JORDANIAN** | | **Sukkot** | Oct. 16-22 |
| **Tree Day** | Jan. 15 | **Simhat Torah** | Oct. 23 |
| **Arab League Day** | Mar. 22 | **Hanukah** | Dec. 24-31 |
| **Labour Day** | May 25 | | |
| **Army Day and Anniversary of the Great Revolt** | Jun. 10 | **EGYPTIAN** | |
| **King Hussein's Accession** | Aug. 11 | **New Year's Day** | Jan. 1 |
| **King Hussein's Birthday** | Nov. 14 | **Union Day** | Feb. 28 |
| | | **Sinai Liberation Day** | Apr. 25 |
| **SYRIAN** | | **May Day** | May 1 |
| **New Year's Day** | Jan. 1 | **Evacuation Day** | Jun. 18 |
| **Revolution Day** | Mar. 8 | **Revolution Day** | Jul. 23 |
| **Women's Day** | Mar. 21 | **National Day** | Oct. 6 |
| **Arab League Day** | Mar. 22 | **Suez City & National Liberation Day** | Oct. 24 |
| **Evacuation Day** | Apr. 17 | **Victory Day** | Dec. 23 |
| **Martyr's Day** | May 6 | | |
| **Security Force Day** | May 29 | | |
| **October War Day** | Oct. 6 | | |
| **Flight Day** | Oct. 16 | | |
| **Correction Movement Day** | Nov. 16 | | |
| **Peasant's Day** | Dec. 14 | | |
| **Christmas** | Dec. 25 | | |

APPENDIX

# LANGUAGE GLOSSARY

## ■ Arabic (Al 'Arabi) العربى

Today's Arabic is actually two (some say three) distinct languages, and many, many dialects. **Classical Arabic, Fus-ha,** was the language of pre-Islamic Arabs and the Qur'an. Its complex rules of grammar were not derived until the Umayyad period, when the Islamic Empire rapidly expanded to include people of non-Arab origin (i.e., Turks and Persians). Today, the intricate grammar of the Classical, rigorously taught in schools and used for Qur'anic recitation, is every student's horror. A simplified version is used for writing, public speeches, and even cartoons on television. This less rigid form of classical Arabic has been packaged and sold to Westerners as "Modern Standard Arabic." With knowledge of Modern Standard, you can read newspapers and understand television broadcasts throughout the Arab world; but the language is really an invention, Classical Arabic taken down a notch and updated with terms like تكسى (*taksee,* taxi). The second (third if you count Modern Standard) brand is the **Colloquial ('Amiyya),** the language of daily life. Dialects are so diverse that an Iraqi and a Palestinian meeting for the first time would sound like a Monty Python sketch; and *no one* understands the North Africans. But educated Arabs can always fall back on the Classical, however stilted it may sound in conversation.

Arabic uses eight sounds not heard in English. *Kh* (خ) is like the Scottish or German *ch*; *gh* (غ) is like the French *r*. There are two "h" sounds; one (ه) sounds like an English "h" and the other (ح, in Muhammad) is somewhere between *kh* and plain *h*. The letter *'ayn* (ع) comes from the throat; it is indicated by an apostrophe in transliteration. Finally, *s, d, t, th,* and *k* have two sounds each, one heavier than the other.

The heavy *k* (ق), represented by a "q" in transliteration, is not commonly pronounced (one exception is in the word Qur'an). Instead, city people replace it with a glottal stop (the hard vowel sound heard in English when a vowel begins a word). Upper Egyptians and *fellaheen* ("peasants") use a "g" sound instead of the glottal stop. So a word like *qamar* (moon) is pronounced "gamar" by, say, Mubarak.

Vowels and consonants can be either long or short, often an important distinction. For example, *jamaal* is "beauty," *jamal* means "camel." A doubled consonant can mean the difference between *ham-mam* (bathroom) and *hamam* (pigeons).

*R* is pronounced as a trill, similar to Spanish. In Egypt, all *g*'s (ج) are pronounced hard (as in "giddy"); Palestinians, Jordanians, and Syrians say *j* (as in the French *"je"*). Thus "hill" is spelled *gabal* in Egypt, *jabal* elsewhere. The definite article is the prefix *al*, in Egypt pronounced more like *el*. When *al* comes before the sounds t, th, j, d, dh, r, z, s, sh, or n , the *l* is not pronounced. Never say *"ihna fee al-nar"* (we are in Hell); a more correct pronunciation is *"ihna fee an-nar."*

Although Arabic is read from right to left, numerals are read from left to right.

## NUMERALS

| ٠ | ١ | ٢ | ٣ | ٤ | ٥ | ٦ | ٧ | ٨ | ٩ | ١٠ | ٢٠ |
|---|---|---|---|---|---|---|---|---|---|----|----|
| 0 | 1 | 2 | 3 | 4 | 5 | 6 | 7 | 8 | 9 | 10 | 20 |
| sifr | waahid | tinein | talaata | arba'a | khamsa | sitta | sab'a | tamanya | tis'a | 'ashara | 'ishrin |

## USEFUL WORDS AND PHRASES

### Greetings and Courtesies

| | |
|---|---|
| hello (informal) | marhaba |
| hello (formal) | salaam aleikum |
| (response) | aleikum as-salaam |
| welcome | ahlan, ahlein, ahlan wa sahlan |
| (response) | shukran or ahlein feek (m)/feekee (f) |

| | |
|---|---|
| good morning | sabah al-kheir |
| (response) | sabah an-nour, sabah al-ishta if you're in a really cheesy mood. |
| good evening | masa' al-kheir |
| (response) | masa' an-nour |
| good-bye | ma' as-salaama |
| yes (formal) | na'am |
| yes | often aa in the Levant, aiwa in Egypt |
| no | la, la-a for emphasis |
| thank you | shukran |
| please | min fadlak (m), min fadlik (f) |
| I'm sorry | ana aasif (m), ana aasfa (f) |
| excuse me (to get attention) | 'an iznak (m), 'an iznik (f) |
| God willing | in sha allah, shortened to inshaala |
| Praise God | al hamdu lillah |
| what is your name? (Levant) | eish ismak (m), eish ismik (f) |
| what is your name? (Egypt) | ismak eh (m), ismik eh (f) |
| my name is... | ismi... |
| how are you? (in Levant only) | kifak? (m), kifik? (f) |
| how are you? (in Egypt only) | izzayyak (m), izzayyek (f) |
| I'm fine (in Levant only) | mabsuut (m), mabsuuta (f) (I'm happy) |
| I'm fine (in Egypt only) | kuwayyis (m), kuwayyisa (f) |
| I'm tired | ana ta'baan (m), ana ta'baana (f) |
| I feel like I'm about to die | rah a moot (Levant), ha moot (Egypt) |
| I'm not a dumb tourist (in Egypt) | ana mish khawaga |
| student (male) | talib |
| student (female) | taliba |

## Getting Around

| | |
|---|---|
| Let's Go! | Yalla! or Yalla beena! |
| Where? or Where is …? | fein?, wein?, or ayna? |
| when? | eimta |
| why? | leish in the Levant, leih in Egypt |
| I'm going to … | ana rayih (m)/rayha (f) ila... |
| There is … or Is there …? | Fee …/? |
| There is no … or Isn't there any …? | Mafeesh …/? |
| restaurant | mat'am |
| post office | maktab al-bareed (Levant), bosta (Egypt) |
| street | share' |
| market | souq or sou' |
| museum | mat-haf |
| mosque | masjed/jaame' (L), masgid/gaame' (E) |
| church | kineesa |
| university | jaam'a (Levant), gaam'a (Egypt) |
| hotel | funduq or (h)otel |
| room | oda or ghurfa |
| airport | mataar |
| station | mahatta |
| traffic circle, public square | midan |
| hour, time | saa'a |
| day | yoam |
| week | usbuu' |
| month | shaher (Levant), shahr (Egypt) |
| year | sana |

| today | al-yoam |
|---|---|
| yesterday | imbaareh, ams (formal) |
| tomorrow | bukra |
| Sunday | yoam al-ahad |
| Monday | yoam al-itnein |
| Tuesday | yoam at-talaat |
| Wednesday | yoam al-arba'a |
| Thursday | yoam al-khamees |
| Friday | yoam aj-jum'a (L), eg-goum'a (E) |
| Saturday | yoam as-sabt |
| what time is it? | addeish as-saa'a? (L), es-saa'a kaam? (E) |
| right (direction) | yameen |
| left | shmal or yasaar |
| straight | dughree |
| bus | baas (Levant), utubeese (Egypt) |
| automobile | sayyaara (Levant), 'arabiyya (Egypt) |
| tourist (s) | saa-ih (m), saa-iha (f), suwwaah (pl) |
| back off, dude | 'iff 'annee (m), 'iffee 'annee (f) (Levant), imshee! (L and E, pretty insulting) |
| none of your damn business | mish shughlak (m), mish shughlik (f) (Levant), eh dakh-khalak? (m) eh dakh-khalik? (f) (Egypt) |

## Shopping and Dining

Also see **Getting Around** (above) and **Food** in individual country introductions.

| how much? | addeish? (Levant) bikaam? (Egypt) |
|---|---|
| no way! | mish mumkin! |
| will you take half? | taakhud nuss? (m), taakhdee nuss? (f) |
| money | masaari (Levant), fulous (Egypt) |
| change | fraata (Levant), fakka (Egypt) |
| I want... | biddee (L), 'ayiz (m), 'ayza (f) (E) |
| water | mayya |

## Emergency

| Do you speak English? | bitihkee inglizi? (L), bititkallim inglizi (m), bititkallimee inglizi (f) (E) |
|---|---|
| I don't speak Arabic. | ana ma bahki 'arabi (Levant), ana mish batkallim 'arabi (Egypt) |
| tourist police (Egypt only) | bolees es-siyaaha |
| hospital | mustashfa |
| doctor | duktoor |
| passport | basbor, jawaz (L)/gawaz (E) safar |
| embassy | safaarah |
| never mind, no big deal | ma'lish |

# ■ Hebrew (Ivrit) עברית

See Israel: "Language" on page 276, for historical background. The transliterations $ḥ$ (ח) and $kh$ (כ) are both guttural, as in the German word *ach*. The Hebrew *r* is close to the French *r*, although an Arabic (or even English) *r* is also understood. Hebrew vowels are shorter than English ones, which leads to discrepancies in transliteration. The definite article is the prefix *ha*. Feminine adjectives add an "-ah" at the end.

Although Hebrew is read from right to left, numerals are read from left to right.

## USEFUL WORDS AND PHRASES

### Greetings and Courtesies

| | |
|---|---|
| hello or good-bye or peace | shalom |
| good morning | boker tov |
| good evening | erev tov |
| good-bye | l'hitra'ot |
| what's up? | ma nishma? |
| yes | ken |
| no | lo |
| thank you | toda |
| excuse me/I'm sorry | sliḥa |
| please/you're welcome | bevakasha |
| what is your name? (to male/to female) | eikh korim lekhah/lakh? |
| my name is... | shmi... |
| how are you? (to male/to female) | ma shlomkha/shlomekh? |
| fine, OK | b'seder |
| not good | lo tov |
| excellent | metzuyan |
| I'm tired (male/female) | ani ayef/ayefa |
| student (male/female) | student/studentit |

### Shopping and Dining

| | |
|---|---|
| do you have...? (to male/female) | yesh lekha/lakh...? |
| how much? | kama zeh oleh? |
| I want... (male/female) | ani rotzeh/rotzah... |
| I don't want... (male/female) | lo rotzeh/rotzah... |
| go away | tistalek |
| go to hell | lekh l'azazel |
| money | kesef |
| change (lit. "leftovers") | odef |
| waiter (male/female) | meltzar/meltzarit |
| water | mayim |
| coffee | kafeh |
| tea | teh |

### Emergencies

| | |
|---|---|
| do you speak English? (to female) | ata (aht) medaber (medaberet) Anglit? |
| I don't speak Hebrew (female) | ani lo medaber (m'daberet) Ivrit |
| police | mishtara |
| hospital | beit ḥolim |
| doctor | rofee |
| passport | darkon |
| airport | s'deh te'ufa |

## Getting Around

| | |
|---|---|
| where is....? | eifoh...? |
| when | matai |
| why | lama |
| I'm going to... | ani nose'a l'... |
| there is... | yesh... |
| there is no... | ain... |
| do you (you, a female) know where...is? | ata yodea (aht yoda'at) eifoh nimtza... |
| wait (for authenticity, bring fingertips together and gesture as you say this) | rega |
| restaurant | mis'adah |
| post office | do'ar |
| street | reḥov |
| boulevard | sderot |
| market | shuk |
| museum | muzaion |
| synagogue | beit knesset |
| church | knaissia |
| central bus station | taḥana merkazit |
| hotel | malon |
| hostel | akhsaniya |
| room | ḥeder |
| university | universita |
| beach | ḥof |
| grocery store | makolet |
| how much is it? | kama zeh? |
| what is this? | ma zeh? |
| food | okhel |
| hour, time | sha'a |
| day | yom |
| week | shavua |
| month | ḥodesh |
| year | shana |
| today | ha'yom |
| yesterday | etmol |
| tomorrow | maḥar |
| Sunday | yom rishon |
| Monday | yom shaini |
| Tuesday | yom shlishi |
| Wednesday | yom revi'i |
| Thursday | yom ḥamishi |
| Friday | yom shishi |
| sabbath, Saturday | shabbat |
| what time is it? | ma hasha'a? |
| right (direction) | yamin |
| left | smol |
| straight | yashar |
| taxi | monit, taxi |
| automobile | mekhonit |
| train | rakevet |
| bus | otoboos |

# Index